Formulas

1. *CPU time* = Instruction count × Clock cycles per instruction × Clock cycle time

2. *Amdahl's Law:* $\text{Speedup}_{\text{overall}} = \dfrac{\text{Execution time}_{\text{old}}}{\text{Execution time}_{\text{new}}} = \dfrac{1}{(1 - \text{Fraction}_{\text{enhanced}}) + \dfrac{\text{Fraction}_{\text{enhanced}}}{\text{Speedup}_{\text{enhanced}}}}$

3. *Average memory-access time* = Hit time + Miss rate × Miss penalty

4. *Means*—arithmetic (AM), weighted arithmetic (WAM), harmonic (HM), and weighted harmonic (WHM):

$$\text{AM} = \frac{1}{n}\sum_{i=1}^{n} \text{Time}_i \qquad \text{WAM} = \sum_{i=1}^{n} \text{Weight}_i \times \text{Time}_i \qquad \text{HM} = \frac{n}{\displaystyle\sum_{i=1}^{n} \frac{1}{\text{Rate}_i}} \qquad \text{WHM} = \frac{1}{\displaystyle\sum_{i=1}^{n} \frac{\text{Weight}_i}{\text{Rate}_i}}$$

where Time_i is the execution time for the *i*th program of a total of *n* in the workload, Weight_i is the weighting of the *i*th program in the workload, and Rate_i is a function of $1/\text{Time}_i$

5. *Cost of integrated circuit* $= \dfrac{\text{Cost of die} + \text{Cost of testing die} + \text{Cost of packaging and final test}}{\text{Final test yield}}$

6. *Die yield* $= \text{Wafer yield} \times \left(1 + \dfrac{\text{Defects per unit area} \times \text{Die area}}{\alpha}\right)^{-\alpha}$

   where Wafer yield accounts for wafers that are so bad they need not be tested and α corresponds to the number of masking levels critical to die yield (usually $\alpha = 3.0$)

7. *Speedup from pipelining* $= \dfrac{1}{1 + \text{Pipeline stall cycles per instruction}} \times \dfrac{\text{Clock cycle unpipelined}}{\text{Clock cycle pipelined}}$

   $= \dfrac{1}{1 + \text{Pipeline stall cycles per instruction}} \times \text{Pipeline depth}$

   where pipeline stall cycles account for clock cycles lost due to pipeline hazards

8. *Little's Law:* Mean number of tasks in system = Arrival rate × Mean response time assuming the system is in equilibrium

Rules of Thumb

1. *Amdahl/Case Rule:* A balanced computer system needs about 1 MB of main memory capacity and 1 megabit per second of I/O bandwidth per MIPS of CPU performance.

2. *90/10 Locality Rule:* A program executes about 90% of its instructions in 10% of its code.

3. *DRAM-Growth Rule:* Density increases by between 40% and 60% per year, quadrupling in three to four years.

4. *Disk-Growth Rule:* Density increases by about 50% per year, quadrupling in just over three years.

5. *85/60 Branch-Taken Rule:* About 85% of backward-going branches are taken while about 60% of forward-going branches are taken.

6. *2:1 Cache Rule:* The miss rate of a direct-mapped cache of size *N* is about the same as a two-way set-associative cache of size *N*/2.

Computer Architecture
A Quantitative Approach

Third Edition

John L. Hennessy is the president of Stanford University, where he has been a member of the faculty since 1977 in the departments of electrical engineering and computer science. Hennessy is a Fellow of the IEEE and ACM, a member of the National Academy of Engineering, and a Fellow of the American Academy of Arts and Sciences. He received the 2001 Eckert-Mauchly Award for his contributions to RISC technology, the 2001 Seymour Cray Computer Engineering Award, and shared the John von Neumann Award in 2000 with David Patterson. Hennessy's original research group at Stanford developed several of the techniques now in commercial use for optimizing compilers. In 1981, he started the MIPS project at Stanford with a handful of graduate students.

After completing the project in 1984, he took a one-year leave from the university to cofound MIPS Computer Systems, which developed one of the first commercial RISC microprocessors. After being acquired by Silicon Graphics in 1991, MIPS Technologies became an independent company in 1998, focusing on microprocessors for the embedded marketplace. As of 2001, over 200 million MIPS microprocessors have been shipped in devices ranging from video games and palmtop computers to laser printers and network switches.

Hennessy's more recent research at Stanford focuses on the area of designing and exploiting multiprocessors. He helped lead the design of the DASH multiprocessor architecture, the first distributed shared-memory multiprocessors supporting cache coherency and the basis for several commercial multiprocessor designs, including the Silicon Graphics Origin multiprocessors.

David A. Patterson has been teaching computer architecture at the University of California, Berkeley, since joining the faculty in 1977, and he holds the Pardee Chair of Computer Science. His teaching has been honored by the ACM and the University of California. In 2000 he won the James H. Mulligan, Jr. Education Medal from IEEE "for inspirational teaching through the development of creative curricula and teaching methodology, for important textbooks, and for effective integration of education and research missions." Patterson has also received the 1995 IEEE Technical Achievement Award for contributions to RISC and shared the 1999 IEEE Reynold B. Johnson Information Storage Award for contributions to RAID. In 2000 he shared the IEEE John von Neumann Medal with John Hennessy "for creating a revolution in computer architecture through their exploration, popularization, and commercialization of architectural innovations." Patterson is a member of the National Academy of Engineering and is a Fellow of both the ACM and the IEEE. In the past, he has been chair of the CS division in the EECS department at Berkeley, the ACM SIG in computer architecture, and the Computing Research Association.

At Berkeley, Patterson led the design and implementation of RISC I, likely the first VLSI reduced instruction set computer. This research became the foundation of the SPARC architecture, currently used by Sun Microsystems, Fujitsu, and others. He was a leader of the redundant arrays of inexpensive disks (RAID) project, which led to high-performance storage systems from many companies. He was also involved in the network of workstations (NOW) project, which led to cluster technology used by Internet companies. These projects earned three dissertation awards from the ACM. His current research project is called recovery oriented computing (ROC), which is developing techniques for building dependable, maintainable, and scalable Internet services.

Computer Architecture
A Quantitative Approach

Third Edition

John L. Hennessy
Stanford University

David A. Patterson
University of California at Berkeley

With Contributions by

David Goldberg
Xerox Palo Alto Research Center

Krste Asanovic
Department of Electrical Engineering and Computer Science
Massachusetts Institute of Technology

MORGAN KAUFMANN
An Imprint of Elsevier

Computer Architecture: A Quantitative Approach, 3/e
Hennessy and Patterson

Morgan Kaufmann Publishers
An Imprint of Elsevier
340 Pine Street, Sixth floor, San Francisco, CA 94194-3205, USA

© 1990, 1996, 2003 by Elsevier Science (USA)

Original ISBN: 1-55860-596-7

First Printed in India 2003
Reprinted 2004
Reprinted 2005
Reprinted 2006 (twice)

Indian Reprint ISBN-13: 978-81-8147-205-2
Indian Reprint ISBN-10: 81-8147-205-5

Published by Elsevier, a division of Reed Elsevier India Private Limited,
Shri Pratap Udyog, 274, Captain Gaur Marg, Sriniwaspuri, New Delhi-110 065 (India)

Printed and bound at Rajkamal Electric Press
B-35/9, G.T. Karnal Road, Delhi-110 033.

To Andrea, Linda, and our four sons

Foreword

by Bill Joy, Chief Scientist and Corporate Executive Officer
Sun Microsystems, Inc.

I am very lucky to have studied computer architecture under Prof. David Patterson at U.C. Berkeley more than 20 years ago. I enjoyed the courses I took from him, in the early days of RISC architecture. Since leaving Berkeley to help found Sun Microsystems, I have used the ideas from his courses and many more that are described in this important book.

The good news today is that this book covers incredibly important and contemporary material. The further good news is that much exciting and challenging work remains to be done, and that working from *Computer Architecture: A Quantitative Approach* is a great way to start.

The most successful architectural projects that I have been involved in have always started from simple ideas, with advantages explainable using simple numerical models derived from hunches and rules of thumb. The continuing rapid advances in computing technology and new applications ensure that we will need new similarly simple models to understand what is possible in the future, and that new classes of applications will stress systems in different and interesting ways. The quantitative approach introduced in Chapter 1 is essential to understanding these issues. In particular, we expect to see, in the near future, much more emphasis on minimizing power to meet the demands of a given application, across all sizes of systems; much remains to be learned in this area.

I have worked with many different instruction sets in my career. I first programmed a PDP-8, whose instruction set was so simple that a friend easily learned to disassemble programs just by glancing at the hole punches in paper tape! I wrote a lot of code in PDP-11 assembler, including an interpreter for the Pascal programming language and for the VAX (which was used as an example in the first edition of this book); the success of the VAX led to the widespread use of UNIX on the early Internet.

The PDP-11 and VAX were very conventional complex instruction set (CISC) computer architectures, with relatively compact instruction sets that proved nearly impossible to pipeline. For a number of years in public talks I used the performance of the VAX 11/780 as the baseline; its speed was extremely well known because faster implementations of the architecture were so long delayed. VAX performance stalled out just as the x86 and 680x0 CISC architectures were appearing in microprocessors; the strong economic advantages of microprocessors led to their overwhelming dominance. Then the simpler reduced instruction set (RISC) computer architectures—pioneered by John Cocke at IBM; promoted and named by Patterson and Hennessy; and commercialized in POWER PC, MIPS, and SPARC—were implemented as microprocessors and permitted high-performance pipeline implementations through the use of their simple register-oriented instruction sets. A downside of RISC was the larger code size of programs and resulting greater instruction fetch bandwidth, a cost that could be seen to be acceptable using the techniques of Chapter 1 and by believing in the future CMOS technology trends promoted in the now-classic views of Carver Mead. The kind of clear-thinking approach to the present problems and to the shape of future computing advances that led to RISC architecture is the focus of this book.

Chapter 2 (and various appendices) presents interesting examples of contemporary and important historical instruction set architecture. RISC architecture—the focus of so much work in the last twenty years—is by no means the final word here. I worked on the design of the SPARC architecture and several implementations for a decade, but more recently have worked on two different styles of processor: picoJava, which implemented most of the Java Virtual Machine instructions—a compact, high-level, bytecoded instruction set—and MAJC, a very simple and multithreaded VLIW for Java and media-intensive applications. These two architectures addressed different and new market needs: for low-power chips to run embedded devices where space and power are at a premium, and for high performance for a given amount of power and cost where parallel applications are possible. While neither has achieved widespread commercial success, I expect that the future will see many opportunities for different ISAs, and an in-depth knowledge of history here often gives great guidance—the relationships between key factors, such as the program size, execution speed, and power consumption, returning to previous balances that led to great designs in the past.

Chapters 3 and 4 describe instruction-level parallelism (ILP): the ability to execute more than one instruction at a time. This has been aided greatly, in the last 20 years, by techniques such as RISC and VLIW (very long instruction word) computing. But as later chapters here point out, both RISC and especially VLIW as practiced in the Intel itanium architecture are very power intensive. In our attempts to extract more instruction-level parallelism, we are running up against the fact that the complexity of a design that attempts to execute N instructions simultaneously grows like N^2: the number of transistors and number of watts to produce each result increases dramatically as we attempt to execute many instructions of arbitrary programs simultaneously. There is thus a clear countertrend emerging: using simpler pipelines with more realistic levels of ILP while exploiting other kinds of parallelism by running both multiple threads of execution per processor and, often, multiple processors on a single chip. The challenge for designers of high-performance systems of the future is to understand when simultaneous execution is possible, but then to use these techniques judiciously in combination with other, less granular techniques that are less power intensive and complex.

In graduate school I would often joke that cache memories were the only great idea in computer science. But truly, where you put things affects profoundly the design of computer systems. Chapter 5 describes the classical design of cache and main memory hierarchies and virtual memory. And now, new, higher-level programming languages like Java support much more reliable software because they insist on the use of garbage collection and array bounds checking, so that security breaches from "buffer overflow" and insidious bugs from false sharing of memory do not creep into large programs. It is only languages, such as Java, that insist on the use of automatic storage management that can implement true software components. But garbage collectors are notoriously hard on memory hierarchies, and the design of systems and language implementations to work well for such areas is an active area of research, where much good work has been done but much exciting work remains.

Java also strongly supports thread-level parallelism—a key to simple, power-efficient, and high-performance system implementations that avoids the N^2 problem discussed earlier but brings challenges of its own. A good foundational understanding of these issues can be had in Chapter 6. Traditionally, each processor was a separate chip, and keeping the various processors synchronized was expensive, both because of its impact on the memory hierarchy and because the synchronization operations themselves were very expensive. The Java language is also trying to address these issues: we tried, in the Java Language Specification, which I coauthored, to write a description of the memory model implied by the language. While this description turned out to have (fixable) technical problems, it is increasingly clear that we need to think about the memory hierarchy in the design of languages that are intended to work well on the newer system platforms. We view the Java specification as a first step in much good work to be done in the future.

As Chapter 7 describes, storage has evolved from being connected to individual computers to being a separate network resource. This is reminiscent of computer graphics, where graphics processing that was previously done in a host processor often became a separate function as the importance of graphics increased. All this is likely to change radically in the coming years—massively parallel host processors are likely to be able to do graphics better than dedicated outboard graphics units, and new breakthroughs in storage technologies, such as memories made from molecular electronics and other atomic-level nanotechnologies, should greatly reduce both the cost of storage and the access time. The resulting dramatic decreases in storage cost and access time will strongly encourage the use of multiple copies of data stored on individual computing nodes, rather than shared over a network. The "wheel of reincarnation," familiar from graphics, will appear in storage.

It is also critical that storage systems, and indeed all systems, become much more robust in the face of failures, not only of hardware, but also of software flaws and human error. This is an enormous challenge in the years ahead.

Chapter 8 provides a great foundational description of computer interconnects and networks. My model of these comes from Andy Bechtolsheim, another of the cofounders of Sun, who famously said, "Ethernet always wins." More modestly stated: given the need for a new networking interconnect, and despite its short-comings, adapted versions of the Ethernet protocols seem to have met with over-whelming success in the marketplace. Why? Factors such as the simplicity and familiarity of the protocols are obvious, but quite possibly the most likely reason is that the people who are adapting Ethernet can get on with the job at hand rather than arguing about details that, in the end, aren't dispositive. This lesson can be generalized to apply to all the areas of computer architecture discussed in this book.

One of the things I remember Dave Patterson saying many years ago is that for each new project you only get so many "cleverness beans." That is, you can be very clever in a few areas of your design, but if you try to be clever in all of them, the design will probably fail to achieve its goals—or even fail to work or to be finished at all. The overriding lesson that I have learned in 20 plus years of work-ing on these kinds of designs is that you must choose what is important and focus on that; true wisdom is to know what to leave out. A deep knowledge of what has gone before is key to this ability.

And you must also choose your assumptions carefully. Many years ago I attended a conference in Hawaii (yes, it was a boondoggle, but read on) where Maurice Wilkes, the legendary computer architect, gave a speech. What he said, paraphrased in my memory, is that good research often consists of assuming something that seems untrue or unlikely today will become true and investigating the consequences of that assumption. And if the unlikely assumption indeed then becomes true in the world, you will have done timely and sometimes, then, even great research! So, for example, the research group at Xerox PARC assumed that everyone would have access to a personal computer with a graphics display con-nected to others by an internetwork and the ability to print inexpensively using Xerography. How true all this became, and how seminally important their work was!

In our time, and in the field of computer architecture, I think there are a num-ber of assumptions that will become true. Some are not controversial, such as that Moore's Law is likely to continue for another decade or so and that the com-plexity of large chip designs is reaching practical limits, often beyond the point of positive returns for additional complexity. More controversially, perhaps, molecular electronics is likely to greatly reduce the cost of storage and probably logic elements as well, optical interconnects will greatly increase the bandwidth and reduce the error rates of interconnects, software will continue to be unreli-able because it is so difficult, and security will continue to be important because its absence is so debilitating.

Taking advantage of the strong positive trends detailed in this book and using them to mitigate the negative ones will challenge the next generation of computer architects, to design a range of systems of many shapes and sizes.

Computer architecture design problems are becoming more varied and inter-esting. Now is an exciting time to be starting out or reacquainting yourself with the latest in this field, and this book is the best place to start. See you in the chips!

Contents

Chapter 3   Instruction-Level Parallelism and Its Dynamic Exploitation

Chapter 4   Exploiting Instruction-Level Parallelism with Software Approaches

Appendix A   Pipelining: Basic and Intermediate Concepts

Appendix B   Solutions to Selected Exercises

Preface

Why We Wrote This Book

Through three editions of this book, our goal has been to describe the basic principles underlying what will be tomorrow's technological developments. Our excitement about the opportunities in computer architecture has not abated, and we echo what we said about the field in the first edition: "It is not a dreary science of paper machines that will never work. No! It's a discipline of keen intellectual interest, requiring the balance of marketplace forces to cost-performance-power, leading to glorious failures and some notable successes."

Our primary objective in writing our first book was to change the way people learn and think about computer architecture. We feel this goal is still valid and important. The field is changing daily and must be studied with real examples and measurements on real computers, rather than simply as a collection of definitions and designs that will never need to be realized. We offer an enthusiastic welcome to anyone who came along with us in the past, as well as to those who are joining us now. Either way, we can promise the same quantitative approach to, and analysis of, real systems.

As with earlier versions, we have strived to produce a new edition that will continue to be as relevant for professional engineers and architects as it is for those involved in advanced computer architecture and design courses. As much as its predecessors, this edition aims to demystify computer architecture through an emphasis on cost-performance-power trade-offs and good engineering design. We believe that the field has continued to mature and move toward the rigorous quantitative foundation of long-established scientific and engineering disciplines. Our greatest satisfaction derives from the fact that the principles described in our first edition in 1990 and the second edition in 1996 could be applied successfully to help predict the landscape of computing technology that exists today. We hope that this third edition will allow readers to apply the fundamentals for similar results as we look forward to the coming decades.

This Edition

The third edition of *Computer Architecture: A Quantitative Approach* should have been easy to write. After all, our quantitative approach hasn't changed, and we sought to continue our focus on the basic principles of computer design through two editions. The examples had to be updated, of course, just as we did for the second edition. The dramatic and ongoing advances in the field as well as the creation of new markets for computers and new approaches for those markets, however, led us to rewrite almost the entire book.

The pace of innovation in computer architecture continued unabated in the six years since the second edition. As when we wrote the second edition, we found that numerous new concepts needed to be introduced, and other material designated as more basic. Although this is officially the third edition of *Computer Architecture: A Quantitative Approach,* it is really our fifth book in a series that began with the first edition, continued with *Computer Organization and Design: The Hardware/Software Interface* (COD:HSI), and then the second edition of both books. Over time ideas that were once found here have moved to COD:HSI or to background tutorials in the appendices. This migration, combined with our goal to present concepts in the context of the most recent computers, meant there was remarkably little from the second edition that could be preserved intact, and practically nothing is left from the first edition.

Perhaps the biggest surprise for us was the realization that the computer architecture field had split into three related but different market segments, each with their own needs and somewhat different architectures to address them. The cost-performance theme of our first and second editions is currently best exemplified by desktop computers. The two new paths are embedded computers and server computers. This major shift in the field is reflected in this edition by two major changes. First, throughout the text we broaden the topics considered as well as the metrics of success. Second, a new section, called "Another View," supplements the more traditional examples in "Putting It All Together" with examples that include video games, digital cameras, and cell phones.

Embedded computers have much lower cost targets than do desktop computers. They are often employed in environments where they run a single application. Also, embedded computers often rely on batteries and cannot use active cooling mechanisms, and energy/power efficiency is thus critical. To illustrate the design trade-offs and approaches in embedded processors we made several additions: the EEMBC benchmarks are used to evaluate performance, media processor and DSP instruction set principles and measurements are examined, the most popular embedded instruction set architectures are surveyed in the appendices, and performance-power trade-offs are explored in several chapters. Power-sensitive examples include the Transmeta and low-power MIPS processors, and embedded systems examples include the PlayStation-2 video game, Sanyo digital camera, and Nokia cell phone.

Server computers place more emphasis on reliability, scalability, and on throughput rather than latency to measure performance. Thus, these systems typically include multiple processors and disks. This edition explains the concept of dependability and includes rarely found statistics on the frequency of component failures. In addition to the SPEC2000 benchmarks for processors, we examine the TPC database benchmarks and the SPEC benchmarks for file servers. Examples of server processors include the Intel IA-64 and the Sun UltraSPARC III, and examples of server systems include the Sun Fire 6800, the Sun Wildfire, EMC Symmetrix, EMC Celerra, the Google cluster, and an IBM cluster for transaction processing.

This edition continues the tradition of using real-world examples to demonstrate the ideas, and the "Putting It All Together" sections are essentially 100% new. The "Putting It All Together" sections of this book include the MIPS64 instruction set architecture, the Intel Pentium III and 4 pipeline organization, the Intel IA-64 architecture and microarchitecture, the Alpha 21264 memory hierarchy, the Sun Wildfire multiprocessor, the EMC Symmetrix storage array, the EMC Celerra file server, and the Google search engine. The "Another View" sections pick real-world examples from the embedded and server communities. This list has the Trimedia TMS media processor, a PowerPC multithreaded processor, the memory hierarchy of Emotion Engine in the Sony Playstation-2, Sun Fire 6800/UltraSPARC III memory hierarchy, EmpowerTel MXP embedded multiprocessor, Sanyo digital camera, and Nokia cell phone.

In response to numerous comments, considerable effort was focused on revising and enhancing the exercises. In particular, all the exercises were reviewed to try to reduce ambiguities and eliminate unproductive exercises, and many new exercises were developed. As many readers requested, Appendix B provides answers to selected exercises.

We also added some new features that should help readers. We replaced the synthetic 32-bit DLX architecture with the popular 64-bit MIPS architecture, as it just made more sense to use existing software rather than recreate and maintain compilers ourselves. We also added a large set of appendices that contains descriptions of a dozen instruction set architectures plus tutorials on basic pipelining, vector processors, and floating-point arithmetic.

Topic Selection and Organization

As before, we have taken a conservative approach to topic selection, for there are many more interesting ideas in the field than can reasonably be covered in a treatment of basic principles. We have steered away from a comprehensive survey of every architecture a reader might encounter. Instead, our presentation focuses on core concepts likely to be found in any new machine. The key criterion remains that of selecting ideas that have been examined and utilized successfully enough to permit their discussion in quantitative terms.

Our first dilemma in determining the new topic selections was that topics requiring only a few pages in the prior editions have since exploded in their importance. Second, topics that we excluded previously have matured to a point where they can be discussed based on our quantitative criteria and their success in the marketplace. To allow for this new material, we reduced the extent of introductory material, assuming the knowledge of the concepts in our introductory text *Computer Organization and Design: The Hardware/Software Interface.* Appendix A on pipelining was added as a valuable tutorial for readers not familiar with the basics of pipelining. (Readers interested strictly in a more basic introduction to computer architecture should read *Computer Organization and Design: The Hardware/Software Interface.*)

Our intent has always been to focus on material that is not available in equivalent form from other sources, so we continue to emphasize advanced content wherever possible. Indeed, there are several systems here whose descriptions cannot be found in the literature.

An Overview of the Content

Chapter 1 covers the basic quantitative principles of computer design and performance measurement. It also addresses the role of technology and the factors affecting the cost of computer systems. It concludes by examining performance and price-performance measurements of processors designed for the desktop, server, and embedded markets, as well as considering the power efficiency of embedded processors.

Chapter 2 covers instruction set design principles and examples. In addition to giving quantitative data on instruction set usage based on the SPEC2000 benchmarks, it describes the MIPS64 architecture used throughout the book. New to this edition are principles of digital signal processor architectures, including common features and measurements. It describes the structure of modern compilers and how that affects the utility of instruction sets for traditional computers, DSPs, and media extensions. It also gives the Trimedia TM5200 as a contrasting example of a media processor, offering instruction mixes for both it and MIPS. Appendices C to G extend this chapter by describing a dozen other popular instruction sets.

Chapters 3 and 4 cover the exploitation of instruction-level parallelism in high-performance processors, including superscalar execution, branch prediction, speculation, dynamic scheduling, and the relevant compiler technology. These topics have grown so much that, even with the creation of a 100-page appendix based on Chapter 3 of the second edition, we still needed two chapters to cover the advanced material. Chapter 3 of this edition focuses on hardware-based approaches to exploiting instruction-level parallelism, while Chapter 4 focuses on more static approaches that rely on more sophisticated compiler technology. The Intel Pentium series is used as the major example in Chapter 3, while Chapter 4 examines the IA-64 architecture and its first implementation in Itanium.

Chapter 5 starts with an introductory review of cache principles. It then reorganizes the optimizations in memory hierarchy design to what are the major challenges today. In addition to real-world examples from traditional computers such as the Alpha 21264, AMD Athlon, and Intel Pentium III and 4, it describes the memory hierarchy of the Emotion Engine in the Sony Playstation-2 video game and the Sun Fire 6800 server with its UltraSPARC III processor. This edition describes the techniques of the bandwidth-optimized DRAM chips such as RAMBUS, and comments on their cost-performance. It also includes cache performance of multimedia and server applications in addition to the SPEC2000 benchmarks for the desktop.

Chapter 6 discusses multiprocessor systems, focusing on shared-memory architectures. The chapter begins by examining the properties of different application domains with thread-level parallelism. It then explores symmetric and distributed memory architectures, examining both organizational principles and performance. Topics in synchronization, memory consistency models, and multithreading (including simultaneous multithreading) complete the foundational chapters. Sun's Wildfire design, which uses a distributed memory architecture to extend the reach of a symmetric approach, is discussed and analyzed.

Chapter 7, "Storage Systems," saw a surprising amount of revision. There is an expansion of reliability and availability, a tutorial on RAID, availability benchmarks, and rarely found failure statistics of real systems. It continues to provide an introduction to queuing theory and I/O performance benchmarks. It extends the description of traditional buses with embedded and server buses. The five design examples in later sections evolve an I/O system through increasingly realistic performance assumptions, plus an evaluation of the mean time to failure. EMC supplies the examples that put it all together, which is the first time these systems have been documented publicly. The anatomy of a digital camera offers an embedded perspective on storage systems, and the historical perspective includes a ringside view of the development and popularity of RAID.

A goal of Chapter 8 is to provide an introduction to networks from the computer architecture point of view. Since this field is vast and quickly moving, the emphasis here is on an introduction to the terminology and principles. It starts with providing a common framework for the design principles in local area networks, storage area networks, and wide area networks, concluding with a description of the technology of the Internet. The second part of Chapter 8 is an in-depth exploration of clusters and the pros and cons of the use of clusters in both scientific computing and database applications. There is a detailed evaluation of the cost-performance of clusters, including the cost of machine room space and network bandwidth. The first description of the cluster used to provide the popular Google search engine puts this chapter together.

This brings us to Appendices A through I. Appendix A is a tutorial on basic pipelining concepts. Readers relatively new to pipelining should read this appendix before Chapters 3 and 4. As mentioned earlier, Appendix B contains solutions to selected exercises. Given the ubiquity of the Web today, the remaining appendices are online, which allows us to add relevant information without increasing the weight or cost of the book. Appendix C updates the second edition RISC appendix, describing 64-bit versions of Alpha, MIPS, PowerPC, and SPARC and their multimedia extensions. Also included in this appendix are popular embedded instruction sets: ARM, Thumb, SuperH, MIPS16, and Mitsubishi M32R. Appendix D describes the 80x86 architecture. Since we have no page budget for the online appendices, we include two architectures of more historical interest: the VAX (Appendix E) and IBM 360/370 (Appendix F). Appendix G includes an updated description of vector processors. Finally, Appendix H describes computer arithmetic, and Appendix I describes implementing coherence protocols.

In summary, about 70% of the pages are new to this edition. The third edition is also about 10% longer than the first if we don't include the online appendices, and about 30% longer if we do.

Navigating the text

There is no single best order in which to approach these chapters. We wrote the text so that it can be covered in several ways, the only real restriction being that some chapters should be read in sequence, namely, Chapters 2, 3, and 4 (pipelining) and Chapters 7 and 8 (storage systems, interconnection networks, and clusters). Readers should start with Chapter 1 and should read Chapter 5 (memory hierarchy design) before Chapter 6 (multiprocessors). Appendices C, D, E, F, and H should be read after Chapter 2. If Appendix A is going to be read, it should be read before Chapters 3 and 4. Appendix G is an interesting contrast to the ideas in Chapters 3 and 4.

Despite the many ways to read this book, we expect two primary paths:

1. *Inside out:* The philosophy of this choice is that processor design is still the cornerstone of computer architecture, and the nonprocessor topics are covered as time permits. Start with Chapter 1, then inside the processor (Chapters 2, 3, 4), then memory hierarchy (5), followed by multiprocessors (6), storage (7), and finish with networks and clusters (8).

2. *Outside in:* The philosophy of this path is that the most interesting challenges in computer architecture today are outside the processor, and that processor internals are covered as time permits. Start again with Chapter 1, then memory hierarchy (5), followed by multiprocessors (6), storage (7), networks and clusters (8), and conclude with instruction sets and pipelining (Chapters 2, 3, 4).

Chapter Structure and Exercises

The material we have selected has been stretched upon a consistent framework that is followed in each chapter. We start by explaining the ideas of a chapter. These ideas are followed by a "Crosscutting Issues" section, a feature that shows how the ideas covered in one chapter interact with those given in other chapters. This is followed by a "Putting It All Together" section that ties these ideas together by showing how they are used in a real machine. This is followed by one or two sections titled "Another View," a new feature for the third edition that gives a real-world example from the embedded or server space.

Next in the sequence is "Fallacies and Pitfalls," which lets readers learn from the mistakes of others. We show examples of common misunderstandings and architectural traps that are difficult to avoid even when you know they are lying in wait for you. Each chapter ends with a "Concluding Remarks" section, followed by a "Historical Perspective and References" section that attempts to give proper credit for the ideas in the chapter and a sense of the history surrounding the inventions. We like to think of this as presenting the human drama of computer design. It also supplies references that the student of architecture may want to pursue. If you have time, we recommend reading some of the classic papers in the field that are mentioned in these sections. It is both enjoyable and educational to hear the ideas directly from the creators. The "Fallacies and Pitfalls" and "Historical Perspective" sections are two of the most popular sections of prior editions.

Each chapter ends with exercises, over 200 in total, which vary from one-minute reviews to term projects. Brackets for each exercise (<chapter.section>) indicate the text sections of primary relevance to answering the question. We hope this helps readers to avoid exercises for which they haven't read the corresponding section, in addition to providing the source for review. Note that we provide solutions to selected exercises in Appendix B, which we indicate with the ✪ symbol. We also rate the exercises, estimating the amount of time a problem might take:

[10] Less than 5 minutes (to read and understand)

[20] 15 to 20 minutes for a full answer

[25] 1 hour for a full written answer

[30] Short programming project: less than 1 full day of programming

[40] Significant programming project: 2 weeks of elapsed time

[50] Term project (2 to 4 weeks by a team)

[Discussion] Topic for discussion with others

Supplements

An instructor's manual with fully worked-out solutions to the exercises in the book is available from the publisher to official instructors teaching from this book.

The numerous appendices are available to readers at the Morgan Kaufmann home page on the Web at *www.mkp.com*. Since we are now using a standard instruction set architecture, we no longer need supply special software. The Web page includes pointers to simulators, compilers, assemblers, and so on for the MIPS architecture. This page also contains a list of errata, eps versions of the numbered figures in the book, and pointers to related material that readers may enjoy. In response to your continued support, the publisher will add new materials and establish links to other sites on a regular basis.

Helping Improve this Book

Finally, it is possible to make money while reading this book. (Talk about cost-performance!) If you read the Acknowledgments that follow, you will see that we went to great lengths to correct mistakes. Since a book goes through many printings, we have the opportunity to make even more corrections. If you uncover any remaining resilient bugs, please contact the publisher by electronic mail (*ca3bugs@mkp.com*). The first reader to report an error with a fix that we incorporate in a future printing will be rewarded with a $1.00 bounty. Please check the errata sheet on the home page (*www.mkp.com*) to see if the bug has already been reported. We process the bugs and send the checks about once a year or so, so please be patient.

We welcome general comments to the text and invite you to send them to a separate email address at *ca3comments@mkp.com*.

Concluding Remarks

Once again this book is a true co-authorship, with each of us writing half the chapters and an equal share of the appendices. We can't imagine how long it would have taken without someone else doing half the work, offering inspiration when the task seemed hopeless, providing the key insight to explain a difficult concept, supplying reviews over the weekend of 100-page chapters, and commiserating when the weight of our other obligations made it hard to pick up the pen. (These obligations have escalated exponentially with the number of editions, as one of us is now in charge of a university.) Thus, once again we share equally the blame for what you are about to read.

John Hennessy ■ *David Patterson*

Acknowledgments

Although this is only the third edition of this book, we have actually created seven different versions of the text: three versions of the first edition (alpha, beta, and final), two versions of this edition (beta and final), and two versions of the third edition (beta and final). Along the way, we have received help from hundreds of reviewers and users. Each of these people has helped make this book better. Thus, we have chosen to list all of the people who have made contributions to some version of this book, as well as those who have been the leading bug reporters.

Contributors to the Third Edition

As you can see from the preface, this edition had conceptual changes as well as updates to the material. The insight of those changes came from looking at the comments of people who evaluated an initial proposal in the summer of 1999: Mark D. Hill and Guri Sohi, University of Wisconsin at Madison; James R. Larus, Microsoft Research; Mateo Valero, Universidad Politécnica de Cataluña, Barcelona; and Maurice Wilkes, who needs no affiliation. Reflection on these comments led to a revised proposal the following winter, which led to a more enthusiastic response from George Adams, Purdue University; Mark D. Hill and Jim Smith, University of Wisconsin at Madison; Josh Fisher, Hewlett-Packard Labs, Cambridge; Kai Li, Princeton University; Kourosh Gharachorloo, Compaq Western Research Laboratory; and James R. Larus, Microsoft Research. Don Knuth provided us with a detailed review from his thorough reading of the second edition; he uncovered a number of bugs and ambiguities, a few of which had escaped detection since the first edition!

With an outline in place, we received help on the ideas within some chapters, new real-world examples to populate "Putting It All Together" and "Another View," and the numbers to drive scores of tables and figures in this book. Note to potential authors: the downside of a quantitative approach is that it takes CPU centuries to update the figures each edition, and real-world examples rely on friends and strangers to understand the anatomy of systems that have never been described publicly. Hence we thank each group by chapter.

Chapter 2 relied on measurements of SPEC2000 benchmarks on real machines to collect the instruction set statistics. Thanks go to Dave Albonesi, Alper Buyuk-tosunoglu, Lei Chen, Wael El-Essawy, and Greg Semeraro, all of the University of Rochester, for collecting this vast amount of data. They were aided by John Henning of Compaq, who helped them resolve compiler problems and interpret the results. Kees A. Vissers and Sebastian Mirolo of Trimedia Corporation supplied the instruction mix statistics on their media processor, and Sarita Adve and Chris Hughes of the University of Illinois at Urbana-Champaign supplied cache measurements on the media benchmarks. Finally, Jeff Bier of BDTI supplied the history of DSPs. Without the collective efforts of all these people, Chapter 2 would be antiquated.

The detailed examination of the Pentium III data path in Chapter 3 is based on work by Bhandarkar and Ding. Dileep Bhandarkar provided the original data, which greatly eased the creation of the plots in the chapter. Kees A. Vissers of Trimedia Corporation graciously updated the architectural description we had written of the Trimedia architecture in Chapter 4 so that it describes the latest version.

We expected Chapter 5 to be one of our easier chapters, but out-of-order CPUs meant we needed to move from miss rates and average memory access times to misses per instruction and performance to evaluate memory hierarchies. Susan Eggers of the University of Washington and Mark Hill of the University of Wisconsin at Madison helped us see the light. Mark Hill and Jason F. Cantin then proceeded to collect the vast information on SPEC2000 for these new efforts. Resources were made available and computing resources provided by Condor, Midship (NSF CDA-9623632), and Multifacet (NSF EIA-9971256) projects and by Compaq Computer Corp. through John Kowaleski. Richard Kessler and Zarka Cvetanovic supplied measurements and hitherto unknown details of the Alpha 21264, as did Gary Lauterbach of Sun Microsystems for the UltraSPARC III and the Sun Fire 6800.

The performance analysis data on commercial workloads in Chapter 6 came from the work of L. Barroso, K. Gharachorloo, and E. Bugnion at Compaq's Western Research Lab. They supplied the data in raw form, which made generation of the plots much easier. Advice and a review of the material on simultaneous multithreading (SMT) came from Susan Eggers of the University of Washington. The data on SMT performance came from the SMT research group at the University of Washington, and special simulations to obtain the data were performed by Steve Swanson and Luke McDowell. Finally, Lisa Noordergraaf of Sun Micro-systems provided the raw data on Wildfire performance from her paper on the Wildfire prototype.

Chapter 7 was shaped by discussions with Howard Alt, before he resigned as CTO of Sun Microsystems Storage Division to create a start-up company, and by Ric Wheeler of EMC. We are indebted to David Black, Dan Lambright, and Ric Wheeler of EMC, as well as to their employer, for supplying the description and measurements of the EMC Symmetrix and Celerra computers. Mike Dahlin of the University of Texas, Austin, supplied data on the history of cost and capacity of disks, and John Best of IBM explained some of the quirks of disk technology and reliability. Aaron Brown of U.C. Berkeley supplied the availability benchmark results, and Patty Enriquez of Mills supplied the update on FCC failure data. A final thanks goes to Alexander Thomasian of the New Jersey Institute of Technology for guidance on queuing theory.

Chapter 8 was shaped by discussions with Alan Mainwaring of Intel Berkeley Research Labs and Rich Martin of Rutgers. We are indebted to Urs Hoelzle of Google, and once again his employer, for allowing us to describe their cluster. Vern Paxson of the Center for Internet Research supplied Internet measurements and advice on reading material in networking.

The vector appendix (G) was revised by Krste Asanovic of the Massachusetts Institute of Technology, and the floating-point appendix (H) was written originally by David Goldberg of Xerox PARC.

In addition to updating the contents of the chapters, we needed to update the exercises. George Adams of Purdue University generously enhanced and revised the exercises and provided solutions for most of the chapters. Others who contributed exercises include Todd M. Bezenek of the University of Wisconsin at Madison (in remembrance of his grandmother Ethel Eshom); Ethan L. Miller, University of California, Santa Cruz; Brandon Schwartz, University of Wisconsin at Madison; and Parthasarathy Ranganathan, Compaq Western Research Laboratory.

For the third time we made substantial changes to the book as a result of class testing. The class test site institutions and instructors for Fall 2000 were

Sarita Adve, University of Illinois at Urbana-Champaign

Doug Burger, University of Texas at Austin

David Patterson, University of California at Berkeley

Arnold L. Rosenberg, University of Massachusetts at Amherst

For Spring 2001 the group included

George Adams, Purdue University

Sarita Adve, University of Illinois at Urbana-Champaign

Lori Liebrock, University of Alaska, Fairbanks

Mikko Lipasti, University of Wisconsin at Madison

Steve Reinhardt, University of Michigan

Hank Walker, Texas A&M

We thank the students and instructors for helping us improve this edition.

In addition to class testing, we had many reviewers give us feedback on the first manuscript, which also guided our revisions:

Krste Asanovic, Massachusetts Institute of Technology

James Goodman, University of Wisconsin at Madison

David Harris, Harvey Mudd College

Norm Jouppi, Compaq

Jim Larus, Microsoft Research

David Kaeli, Northeastern University

David Nagle, Carnegie Mellon University

Emilio Salgueiro, Unysis

Guri Sohi, University of Wisconsin at Madison

Shlomo Weiss, Tel Aviv University

Finally, a special thanks to Mark Smotherman of Clemson University, who gave a final technical reading of our revised manuscript just before it was sent to the publisher. Mark found numerous bugs and ambiguities, and the book is much cleaner as a result.

This book could not have been published without a publisher, of course. We selected Morgan Kaufmann Publishers when we wrote the first edition, and we have not regretted that decision. We are not aware of another publisher who could have kept pace with such a rigorous schedule and we thank all the Morgan Kaufmann staff for their efforts and support. For this third edition, we particularly want to thank Cheri Palmer, our production editor, who ran the show, and Alyson Day, who coordinated all the reviews. Courtney Garnaas also helped with early versions of the manuscript. Our warmest thanks to our editor, Denise Penrose, for her inspiration and perseverance in our continuing writing saga.

We must also thank our university staff, Margaret Rowland and Willa Walker, for countless express mailings, as well as for holding down the fort at Stanford and Berkeley while we worked on the book.

Our final thanks go to our families for their suffering through long nights and early mornings of reading, thinking, and typing.

Contributors to the Second Edition

The development process for this edition was equal in extent to that of the first edition, and we have many people to thank for their contributions.

Before we started extensive work on this edition, we received valuable comments on an outline of our ideas from a number of people: Jim Archibald of Brigham Young University, Jean-Loup Baer of the University of Washington, Paul Barr of Northeastern University, Barry Fagin of Dartmouth, Joel Ferguson of the University of California at Santa Cruz, David Goldberg of the Xerox Palo Alto Research Center, Mark Hill of the University of Wisconsin at Madison, Jim Larus of the University of Wisconsin, William Michalson of Worcester Polytechnic Institute, Richard Reid of Michigan State University, Jim Smith of the University of Wisconsin, Mark Smotherman of Clemson University, Arun Somani of the University of Washington, Thorsten von Eicken of Cornell University, and Shlomo Weiss of the University of Maryland and Tel Aviv.

Our manuscript went through several iterations during its development, and at each stage the chapters were carefully reviewed by contributors from both industry and academia. The following people reviewed one or more chapters of the beta or final manuscript: George Adams of Purdue University, Rajendra V. Boppana of the University of Texas at San Antonio, John Burger of SGI, Peter Chen of the University of Michigan, Tim Coe of Vitesse Semiconductor, Bob Colwell of Intel, Josh Fisher of Hewlett-Packard Laboratories, Rob Fowler of DIKU, Kourosh Gharachorloo of DEC, Mark Heinrich of Stanford, Mark Hill of the University of Wisconsin, Martin Hopkins of IBM, Jerry Huck of Hewlett-Packard Laboratories, Norm Jouppi of DEC, Jeff Kuskin of Stanford, Corinna Lee of the University of Toronto, Gyula Mago of the University of North Carolina, Trevor Mudge of the University of Michigan, Greg Papadapoulous of Sun, Steven Przybylski, Dan Siewiorek of Carnegie Mellon University, J. P. Singh of Princeton, Ashok Singhal, Mike Smith of Harvard University, Mark Smotherman of Clemson University, Guri Sohi of the University of Wisconsin, Evan Tick of the University of Oregon, Thorsten von Eicken of Cornell University, Roy Want of the Xerox Palo Alto Research Center, David Weaver of Sun, Mike Westall of Clemson University, and Larry Wittie of SUNY Stony Brook. Thanks also to Jorge Stolfi for inspiring the section on DIV and MOD for negative numbers in Appendix A.

As with both of our previous books, we enlisted the help of instructors, teaching assistants, and hundreds of students who used the beta in the 1994–95 academic year. And once again, we made substantial changes to the book as a result of the beta testing. The beta test site institutions and instructors were Clemson University—Gene Tagliarin; Cornell University—Anthony Reeves, Georgia Institute of Technology—Kishore Ramachandran and Ellen Witte Zegura, Purdue University—George Adams and Kaushik Roy, Stanford University—Kunle Olukotun, State University of New York at Stony Brook—Larry Wittie, University of California at Berkeley—David Patterson, University of California at Los Angeles—Dave Rennels, University of California at Santa Cruz Anujan Varma, University of North Carolina at Chapel Hill—Gyula A. Mago, University of Oregon—Evan Tick, University of Texas at San Antonio—Rajendra V. Boppana, University of Washington—Susan Eggers, University of Wisconsin at Madison—Mark Hill.

We would like to acknowledge everyone who participated for their efforts in hunting for numerous bugs in the beta. The following people reported the most bugs: Ravi Murthy, Yung-Hsiang Lu, Chen-Chung Chang, Ajay Sreekanth, Mark Callaghan, Lewis Jordan, Lawrence Prince, Darren Staples, Chao-Huang Lin, Biswadeep Nag, Peter Ashenden, and Ronald Greenberg. We would also like to thank those who have continued to submit bugs for the first edition of the book.

In pursuing our goal of publishing the cleanest book possible, we submitted our manuscript to a final technical review, which consisted of a detailed examination of the final version. This daunting task was undertaken by the following individuals: Nikolas Gloy of Harvard University, Evan Tick of the University of Oregon, and George Adams, Allan Knies, and Thomas Willis of Purdue University. Our thanks go to them for greatly improving the accuracy of this edition.

Contributors to the First Edition

The first edition had its roots in an alpha version developed in 1988 and used in the 1988–89 school year. We thank the instructors, teaching assistants, and reviewers of the earliest version of this book, including Thomas Casavant, David Douglas, Joel Emer, Jim Goodman, Truman Joe, Roger Kieckhafer, Earl Killian, Hank Levy, Bryan Martin, Norman Matloff, David Meyer, Trevor Mudge, Todd Narter, Victor Nelson, Richard Reid, Margo Seltzer, Jim Smith, Mark Smotherman, David Wells, and Eric Williams. We also extend a special thanks to the students at Stanford and Berkeley who endured our first attempts at creating this book.

Following the alpha, a beta version of the text was created and used in the 1989–90 school year. Many people reviewed portions of the beta version, including Paul Barr, Bill Dally, Susan Eggers, Jim Goodman, Mark Hill, Hank Levy, David Meyer, James Mooney, Joseph Pfeiffer, and Larry Wittie. Input and material for individual chapters was sought from a number of academic and industrial experts, including Tom Adams, Anant Agarwal, Mitch Alsup, Dave Anderson, David Bailey, Andy Bechtolsheim, Fred Berkowitz, Dileep Bhandarkar, Mark Birman, David Boggs, Jim Brady, Forrest Brewer, Paul Carrick, Pete Chen, Nhan Chu, Bob Cmelik, John Crawford, Merrick Darley, John DeRosa, Lloyd Dickman, Milos Ercegovac, Robert Garner, Garth Gibson, Ben Hao, Danny Hillis, David Hodges, David Hough, Ed Hudson, Mark Johnson, Norm Jouppi, William Kahan, Randy Katz, Ed Kelly, Les Kohn, Corinna Lee, Ruby Lee, Don Lewine, Ken Lutz, Al Marston, John Mashey, Steven Przybylski, Chris Rowen, Bill Shannon, Behrooz Shirazi, Robert Shomler, Jim Slager, Charles Stapper, Peter Stoll, Bob Supnik, Paul Taysom, Shreekant Thakkar, David Weaver, and Richard Zimmermann. We appreciate the willingness of our colleagues to lend their expertise and advice.

The beta test site institutions and instructors for the first edition were Carnegie Mellon University—Daniel Siewiorek, Clemson University—Mark Smotherman, Cornell University—Keshav Pingali, Pennsylvania State University—Mary Jane Irwin and Bob Owens, San Francisco State University—Vojin Oklobdzija, Southeast Missouri State University—Anthony Duben, Southern Methodist University—Behrooz Shirazi, Stanford University—John Hennessy, State University of New York at Stony Brook—Larry Wittie, University of California at Berkeley—Vojin Oklobdzija, University of California at Los Angeles—David Rennels, University of California at Santa Cruz—Daniel Helman, University of Nebraska—Roger Kieckhafer, University of North Carolina at Chapel Hill—Akhilesh Tyagi, University of Texas at Austin—Joseph Rameh, University of Waterloo—Bruno Preiss, University of Wisconsin at Madison—Mark Hill, Washington University (St. Louis)—Mark Franklin.

Special mention should be given to Daniel Helman, Mark Hill, Mark Smotherman, and Larry Wittie, who were especially generous with their feedback. The classes at SUNY Stony Brook, Carnegie Mellon, Stanford, Clemson, and Wisconsin supplied us with the greatest number of bug discoveries in the beta version of the first edition. A number of individuals were especially helpful in chasing down bugs in the first edition beta: Michael Butler, Rohit Chandra, David Cummings, David Filo, Carl Feynman, John Heinlein, Jim Quinlan, Andras Radics, Peter Schnorf, and Malcolm Wing. Finally, we thank the 750 students who used the beta version of the first edition.

In all three editions of this book, we have relied on the extensive firsthand knowledge of C. Gordon Bell and Maurice Wilkes in writing the historical sections.

Special Acknowledgments

When we decided to add a floating-point appendix featuring the IEEE standard, we asked many colleagues to recommend a person who understood that standard and who could write well and explain complex ideas simply. David Goldberg, of the Xerox Palo Alto Research Center, fulfilled all those tasks admirably. The second edition version of Appendix A, "Computer Arithmetic," has again improved the quality and scope of the book.

Among the over 300 people who have reviewed some portion of the first or second edition, one person's name deserves special mention: Doug Clark. Previously at DEC and currently of Princeton University, Doug has been a faithful reader and critic. He deserves special thanks for his valuable suggestions and his patience in helping us explain simply and clearly some of the most complex concepts in the book.

We also want to thank the Defense Advanced Research Projects Agency for supporting our research for many years. This research forms the basis of many of the ideas that we discuss in this book. In particular, we want to thank current and former program managers Duane Adams, Paul Losleben, Mark Pullen, Steve Squires, Bill Bandy, John Toole, Bob Parker, and Bob Lucas.

Thanks go to the staff of the DEC Western Research Laboratory for providing us a hideout for writing the alpha and beta versions of the first edition.

Contributors to Exercises and Solutions

We have found that developing high-quality exercises and informative solutions has been one of the biggest challenges in writing this book. We have attempted to create exercises that ask the reader to think, rather than simply inserting numbers into a formula, and that ask the reader to evaluate design decisions without prescribing exactly how to do the design. The difficulty lies in also making such exercises unambiguous. Earlier editions benefited from the contributions of numerous people, including Evan Tick, Susan Eggers, Anoop Gupta, Mark Smotherman, David Hayes, Michael Scott, Mike Smith, Mark Hill, Dan Siewiorek, George Adams, Allan Knies, and Thomas Willis.

John Hennessy ▪ *David Patterson*

1

Fundamentals of Computer Design

And now for something completely different.

Monty Python's Flying Circus

1.1   Introduction

Computer technology has made incredible progress in the roughly 55 years since the first general-purpose electronic computer was created. Today, less than a thousand dollars will purchase a personal computer that has more performance, more main memory, and more disk storage than a computer bought in 1980 for 1 million dollars. This rapid rate of improvement has come both from advances in the technology used to build computers and from innovation in computer design.

Although technological improvements have been fairly steady, progress arising from better computer architectures has been much less consistent. During the first 25 years of electronic computers, both forces made a major contribution; but beginning in about 1970, computer designers became largely dependent upon integrated circuit technology. During the 1970s, performance continued to improve at about 25% to 30% per year for the mainframes and minicomputers that dominated the industry.

The late 1970s saw the emergence of the microprocessor. The ability of the microprocessor to ride the improvements in integrated circuit technology more closely than the less integrated mainframes and minicomputers led to a higher rate of improvement—roughly 35% growth per year in performance.

This growth rate, combined with the cost advantages of a mass-produced microprocessor, led to an increasing fraction of the computer business being based on microprocessors. In addition, two significant changes in the computer marketplace made it easier than ever before to be commercially successful with a new architecture. First, the virtual elimination of assembly language programming reduced the need for object-code compatibility. Second, the creation of standardized, vendor-independent operating systems, such as UNIX and its clone, Linux, lowered the cost and risk of bringing out a new architecture.

These changes made it possible to successfully develop a new set of architectures, called RISC (Reduced Instruction Set Computer) architectures, in the early 1980s. The RISC-based machines focused the attention of designers on two critical performance techniques, the exploitation of instruction-level parallelism (initially through pipelining and later through multiple instruction issue) and the use of caches (initially in simple forms and later using more sophisticated organizations and optimizations). The combination of architectural and organizational enhancements has led to 20 years of sustained growth in performance at an annual rate of over 50%. Figure 1.1 shows the effect of this difference in performance growth rates.

The effect of this dramatic growth rate has been twofold. First, it has significantly enhanced the capability available to computer users. For many applications, the highest-performance microprocessors of today outperform the supercomputer of less than 10 years ago.

Second, this dramatic rate of improvement has led to the dominance of microprocessor-based computers across the entire range of the computer design. Workstations and PCs have emerged as major products in the computer industry. Minicomputers, which were traditionally made from off-the-shelf logic or from

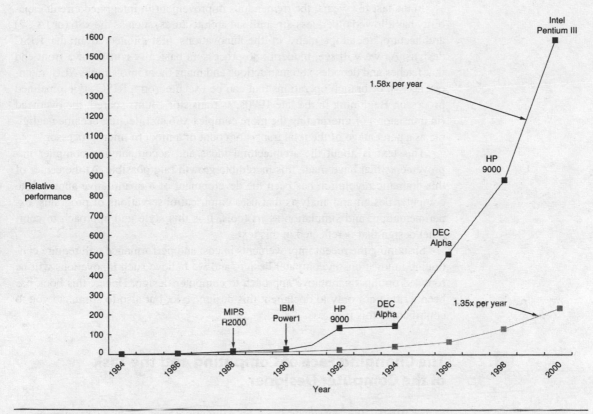

Figure 1.1 Growth in microprocessor performance since the mid-1980s has been substantially higher than in earlier years as shown by plotting SPECint performance. This chart plots relative performance as measured by the SPECint benchmarks with base of one being a VAX 11/780. Since SPEC has changed over the years, performance of newer machines is estimated by a scaling factor that relates the performance for two different versions of SPEC (e.g., SPEC92 and SPEC95). Prior to the mid-1980s, microprocessor performance growth was largely technology driven and averaged about 35% per year. The increase in growth since then is attributable to more advanced architectural and organizational ideas. By 2001 this growth led to a difference in performance of about a factor of 15. Performance for floating-point-oriented calculations has increased even faster.

gate arrays, have been replaced by servers made using microprocessors. Mainframes have been almost completely replaced with multiprocessors consisting of small numbers of off-the-shelf microprocessors. Even high-end supercomputers are being built with collections of microprocessors.

Freedom from compatibility with old designs and the use of microprocessor technology led to a renaissance in computer design, which emphasized both architectural innovation and efficient use of technology improvements. This renaissance is responsible for the higher performance growth shown in Figure 1.1—a rate that is unprecedented in the computer industry. This rate of growth has compounded so that by 2001, the difference between the highest-performance microprocessors and what would have been obtained by relying solely on technology, including improved circuit design, was about a factor of 15.

In the last few years, the tremendous improvement in integrated circuit capability has allowed older, less-streamlined architectures, such as the x86 (or IA-32) architecture, to adopt many of the innovations first pioneered in the RISC designs. As we will see, modern x86 processors basically consist of a front end that fetches and decodes x86 instructions and maps them into simple ALU, memory access, or branch operations that can be executed on a RISC-style pipelined processor. Beginning in the late 1990s, as transistor counts soared, the overhead (in transistors) of interpreting the more complex x86 architecture became negligible as a percentage of the total transistor count of a modern microprocessor.

This text is about the architectural ideas and accompanying compiler improvements that have made this incredible growth rate possible. At the center of this dramatic revolution has been the development of a quantitative approach to computer design and analysis that uses empirical observations of programs, experimentation, and simulation as its tools. It is this style and approach to computer design that is reflected in this text.

Sustaining the recent improvements in cost and performance will require continuing innovations in computer design, and we believe such innovations will be founded on this quantitative approach to computer design. Hence, this book has been written not only to document this design style, but also to stimulate you to contribute to this progress.

1.2 The Changing Face of Computing and the Task of the Computer Designer

In the 1960s, the dominant form of computing was on large mainframes—machines costing millions of dollars and stored in computer rooms with multiple operators overseeing their support. Typical applications included business data processing and large-scale scientific computing. The 1970s saw the birth of the minicomputer, a smaller-sized machine initially focused on applications in scientific laboratories, but rapidly branching out as the technology of time-sharing—multiple users sharing a computer interactively through independent terminals—became widespread. The 1980s saw the rise of the desktop computer based on microprocessors, in the form of both personal computers and workstations. The individually owned desktop computer replaced time-sharing and led to the rise of servers—computers that provided larger-scale services such as reliable, long-term file storage and access, larger memory, and more computing power. The 1990s saw the emergence of the Internet and the World Wide Web, the first successful handheld computing devices (personal digital assistants or PDAs), and the emergence of high-performance digital consumer electronics, from video games to set-top boxes.

These changes have set the stage for a dramatic change in how we view computing, computing applications, and the computer markets at the beginning of the millennium. Not since the creation of the personal computer more than 20 years ago have we seen such dramatic changes in the way computers appear and in how

they are used. These changes in computer use have led to three different computing markets, each characterized by different applications, requirements, and computing technologies.

Desktop Computing

The first, and still the largest market in dollar terms, is desktop computing. Desktop computing spans from low-end systems that sell for under $1000 to high-end,
heavily configured workstations that may sell for over $10,000. Throughout this
range in price and capability, the desktop market tends to be driven to optimize
price-performance. This combination of performance (measured primarily in
terms of compute performance and graphics performance) and price of a system
is what matters most to customers in this market, and hence to computer designers. As a result, desktop systems often are where the newest, highest-performance
microprocessors appear, as well as where recently cost-reduced microprocessors
and systems appear first (see Section 1.4 for a discussion of the issues affecting
the cost of computers).

Desktop computing also tends to be reasonably well characterized in terms of
applications and benchmarking, though the increasing use of Web-centric, interactive applications poses new challenges in performance evaluation. As we discuss in Section 1.9, the PC portion of the desktop space seems recently to have
become focused on clock rate as the direct measure of performance, and this
focus can lead to poor decisions by consumers as well as by designers who
respond to this predilection.

Servers

As the shift to desktop computing occurred, the role of servers to provide larger-
scale and more reliable file and computing services grew. The emergence of the
World Wide Web accelerated this trend because of the tremendous growth in
demand for Web servers and the growth in sophistication of Web-based services.
Such servers have become the backbone of large-scale enterprise computing,
replacing the traditional mainframe.

For servers, different characteristics are important. First, availability is critical. We use the term "availability," which means that the system can reliably and
effectively provide a service. This term is to be distinguished from "reliability,"
which says that the system never fails. Parts of large-scale systems unavoidably
fail; the challenge in a server is to maintain system availability in the face of component failures, usually through the use of redundancy. This topic is discussed in
detail in Chapter 7.

Why is availability crucial? Consider the servers running Yahoo!, taking
orders for Cisco, or running auctions on eBay. Obviously such systems must be
operating seven days a week, 24 hours a day. Failure of such a server system is far
more catastrophic than failure of a single desktop. Although it is hard to estimate
the cost of downtime, Figure 1.2 shows one analysis, assuming that downtime is

Application	Cost of downtime per hour (thousands of $)	Annual losses (millions of $) with downtime of		
		1% (87.6 hrs/yr)	0.5% (43.8 hrs/yr)	0.1% (8.8 hrs/yr)
Brokerage operations	$6450	$565	$283	$56.5
Credit card authorization	$2600	$228	$114	$22.8
Package shipping services	$150	$13	$6.6	$1.3
Home shopping channel	$113	$9.9	$4.9	$1.0
Catalog sales center	$90	$7.9	$3.9	$0.8
Airline reservation center	$89	$7.9	$3.9	$0.8
Cellular service activation	$41	$3.6	$1.8	$0.4
Online network fees	$25	$2.2	$1.1	$0.2
ATM service fees	$14	$1.2	$0.6	$0.1

Figure 1.2 The cost of an unavailable system is shown by analyzing the cost of downtime (in terms of immediately lost revenue), assuming three different levels of availability and that downtime is distributed uniformly. These data are from Kembel [2000] and were collected and analyzed by Contingency Planning Research.

distributed uniformly and does not occur solely during idle times. As we can see, the estimated costs of an unavailable system are high, and the estimated costs in Figure 1.2 are purely lost revenue and do not account for the cost of unhappy customers!

A second key feature of server systems is an emphasis on scalability. Server systems often grow over their lifetime in response to a growing demand for the services they support or an increase in functional requirements. Thus, the ability to scale up the computing capacity, the memory, the storage, and the I/O bandwidth of a server is crucial.

Lastly, servers are designed for efficient throughput. That is, the overall performance of the server—in terms of transactions per minute or Web pages served per second—is what is crucial. Responsiveness to an individual request remains important, but overall efficiency and cost-effectiveness, as determined by how many requests can be handled in a unit time, are the key metrics for most servers. (We return to the issue of performance and assessing performance for different types of computing environments in Section 1.5).

Embedded Computers

Embedded computers—computers lodged in other devices where the presence of the computers is not immediately obvious—are the fastest growing portion of the computer market. These devices range from everyday machines (most microwaves, most washing machines, most printers, most networking switches, and all cars contain simple embedded microprocessors) to handheld digital devices (such as palmtops, cell phones, and smart cards) to video games and digital set-top boxes. Although in some applications (such as palmtops) the computers are programmable, in many embedded applications the only programming occurs in connection with the initial loading of the application code or a later software upgrade of that application. Thus, the application can usually be carefully tuned for the processor and system. This process sometimes includes limited use of assembly language in key loops, although time-to-market pressures and good software engineering practice usually restrict such assembly language coding to a small fraction of the application. This use of assembly language, together with the presence of standardized operating systems, and a large code base has meant that instruction set compatibility has become an important concern in the embedded market. Simply put, like other computing applications, software costs are often a large part of the total cost of an embedded system.

Embedded computers have the widest range of processing power and cost—from low-end 8-bit and 16-bit processors that may cost less than a dollar, to full 32-bit microprocessors capable of executing 50 million instructions per second that cost under 10 dollars, to high-end embedded processors that cost hundreds of dollars and can execute a billion instructions per second for the newest video game or for a high-end network switch. Although the range of computing power in the embedded computing market is very large, price is a key factor in the design of computers for this space. Performance requirements do exist, of course, but the primary goal is often meeting the performance need at a minimum price, rather than achieving higher performance at a higher price.

Often, the performance requirement in an embedded application is a real-time requirement. A *real-time performance requirement* is one where a segment of the application has an absolute maximum execution time that is allowed. For example, in a digital set-top box the time to process each video frame is limited, since the processor must accept and process the next frame shortly. In some applications, a more sophisticated requirement exists: the average time for a particular task is constrained as well as the number of instances when some maximum time is exceeded. Such approaches (sometimes called *soft real-time*) arise when it is possible to occasionally miss the time constraint on an event, as long as not too many are missed. Real-time performance tends to be highly application dependent. It is usually measured using kernels either from the application or from a standardized benchmark (see the EEMBC benchmarks described in Section 1.5). With the growth in the use of embedded microprocessors, a wide range of benchmark requirements exist, from the ability to run small, limited code segments to the ability to perform well on applications involving tens to hundreds of thousands of lines of code.

Two other key characteristics exist in many embedded applications: the need to minimize memory and the need to minimize power. In many embedded applications, the memory can be a substantial portion of the system cost, and it is important to optimize memory size in such cases. Sometimes the application is expected to fit totally in the memory on the processor chip; other times the application needs to fit totally in a small off-chip memory. In any event, the importance of memory size translates to an emphasis on code size, since data size is dictated by the application. As we will see in the next chapter, some architectures have special instruction set capabilities to reduce code size. Larger memories also mean more power, and optimizing power is often critical in embedded applications. Although the emphasis on low power is frequently driven by the use of batteries, the need to use less expensive packaging (plastic versus ceramic) and the absence of a fan for cooling also limit total power consumption. We examine the issue of power in more detail later in the chapter.

Another important trend in embedded systems is the use of processor cores together with application-specific circuitry. Often an application's functional and performance requirements are met by combining a custom hardware solution together with software running on a standardized embedded processor core, which is designed to interface to such special-purpose hardware. In practice, embedded problems are usually solved by one of three approaches:

1. The designer uses a combined hardware/software solution that includes some custom hardware and an embedded processor core that is integrated with the custom hardware, often on the same chip.

2. The designer uses custom software running on an off-the-shelf embedded processor.

3. The designer uses a digital signal processor and custom software for the processor. *Digital signal processors* (DSPs) are processors specially tailored for signal-processing applications. We discuss some of the important differences between digital signal processors and general-purpose embedded processors in the next chapter.

Most of what we discuss in this book applies to the design, use, and performance of embedded processors, whether they are off-the-shelf microprocessors or microprocessor cores, which will be assembled with other special-purpose hardware. The design of special-purpose, application-specific hardware and architecture and the use of DSPs, however, are outside of the scope of this book. Figure 1.3 summarizes these three classes of computing environments and their important characteristics.

The Task of the Computer Designer

The task the computer designer faces is a complex one: Determine what attributes are important for a new machine, then design a machine to maximize performance while staying within cost and power constraints. This task has many aspects, including instruction set design, functional organization, logic design, and implementation. The implementation may encompass integrated circuit design, packaging, power, and cooling. Optimizing the design requires familiarity with a very wide range of technologies, from compilers and operating systems to logic design and packaging.

In the past, the term *computer architecture* often referred only to instruction set design. Other aspects of computer design were called *implementation,* often

Feature	Desktop	Server	Embedded
Price of system	$1000–$10,000	$10,000–$10,000,000	$10–$100,000 (including network routers at the high end)
Price of microprocessor module	$100–$1000	$200–$2000 (per processor)	$0.20–$200 (per processor)
Microprocessors sold per year (estimates for 2000)	150,000,000	4,000,000	300,000,000 (32-bit and 64-bit processors only)
Critical system design issues	Price-performance, graphics performance	Throughput, availability, scalability	Price, power consumption, application-specific performance

Figure 1.3 A summary of the three computing classes and their system characteristics. Note the wide range in system price for servers and embedded systems. For servers, this range arises from the need for very large-scale multiprocessor systems for high-end transaction processing and Web server applications. For embedded systems, one significant high-end application is a network router, which could include multiple processors as well as lots of memory and other electronics. The total number of embedded processors sold in 2000 is estimated to exceed 1 billion, if you include 8-bit and 16-bit microprocessors. In fact, the largest selling microprocessor of all time is an 8-bit microcontroller sold by Intel! It is difficult to separate the low end of the server market from the desktop market, since low-end servers—especially those costing less than $5000—are essentially no different from desktop PCs. Hence, up to a few million of the PC units may be effectively servers.

insinuating that implementation is uninteresting or less challenging. We believe this view is not only incorrect, but is even responsible for mistakes in the design of new instruction sets. The architect's or designer's job is much more than instruction set design, and the technical hurdles in the other aspects of the project are certainly as challenging as those encountered in instruction set design. This challenge is particularly acute at the present, when the differences among instruction sets are small and when there are three rather distinct application areas.

In this book the term *instruction set architecture* refers to the actual programmer-visible instruction set. The instruction set architecture serves as the boundary between the software and hardware, and that topic is the focus of Chapter 2. The implementation of a machine has two components: organization and hardware.

The term *organization* includes the high-level aspects of a computer's design, such as the memory system, the bus structure, and the design of the internal CPU (central processing unit—where arithmetic, logic, branching, and data transfer are implemented). For example, two embedded processors with identical instruction set architectures but very different organizations are the NEC VR 5432 and the NEC VR 4122. Both processors implement the MIPS64 instruction set, but they have very different pipeline and cache organizations. In addition, the 4122 implements the floating-point instructions in software rather than hardware!

Hardware is used to refer to the specifics of a machine, including the detailed logic design and the packaging technology of the machine. Often a line of machines contains machines with identical instruction set architectures and nearly identical organizations, but they differ in the detailed hardware implementation. For example, the Pentium II and Celeron are nearly identical, but offer different clock rates and different memory systems, making the Celeron more effective for low-end computers. In this book the word *architecture* is intended to cover all three aspects of computer design—instruction set architecture, organization, and hardware.

Computer architects must design a computer to meet functional requirements as well as price, power, and performance goals. Often, they also have to determine what the functional requirements are, which can be a major task. The requirements may be specific features inspired by the market. Application software often drives the choice of certain functional requirements by determining how the machine will be used. If a large body of software exists for a certain instruction set architecture, the architect may decide that a new machine should implement an existing instruction set. The presence of a large market for a particular class of applications might encourage the designers to incorporate requirements that would make the machine competitive in that market. Figure 1.4

Functional requirements	Typical features required or supported
Application area	*Target of computer*
General-purpose desktop	Balanced performance for a range of tasks, including interactive performance for graphics, video, and audio (Ch. 2, 3, 4, 5)
Scientific desktops and servers	High-performance floating point and graphics (App. G, H)
Commercial servers	Support for databases and transaction processing; enhancements for reliability and availability; support for scalability (Ch. 2, 6, 8)
Embedded computing	Often requires special support for graphics or video (or other application-specific extension); power limitations and power control may be required (Ch. 2, 3, 4, 5)
Level of software compatibility	*Determines amount of existing software for machine*
At programming language	Most flexible for designer; need new compiler (Ch. 2, 6)
Object code or binary compatible	Instruction set architecture is completely defined—little flexibility—but no investment needed in software or porting programs
Operating system requirements	*Necessary features to support chosen OS (Ch. 5, 8)*
Size of address space	Very important feature (Ch. 5); may limit applications
Memory management	Required for modern OS; may be paged or segmented (Ch. 5)
Protection	Different OS and application needs: page vs. segment protection (Ch. 5)
Standards	*Certain standards may be required by marketplace*
Floating point	Format and arithmetic: IEEE 754 standard (App. H), special arithmetic for graphics or signal processing
I/O bus	For I/O devices: Ultra ATA, Ultra SCSI, PCI (Ch. 7, 8)
Operating systems	UNIX, PalmOS, Windows, Windows NT, Windows CE, CISCO IOS
Networks	Support required for different networks: Ethernet, Infiniband (Ch. 8)
Programming languages	Languages (ANSI C, C++, Java, FORTRAN) affect instruction set (Ch. 2)

Figure 1.4 **Summary of some of the most important functional requirements an architect faces.** The left-hand column describes the class of requirement, while the right-hand column gives examples of specific features that might be needed. The right-hand column also contains references to chapters and appendices that deal with the specific issues.

summarizes some requirements that need to be considered in designing a new machine. Many of these requirements and features will be examined in depth in later chapters.

Once a set of functional requirements has been established, the architect must try to optimize the design. Which design choices are optimal depends, of course, on the choice of metrics. The changes in the computer applications space over the last decade have dramatically changed the metrics. Although desktop computers remain focused on optimizing cost-performance as measured by a single user, servers focus on availability, scalability, and throughput cost-performance, and embedded computers are driven by price and often power issues.

These differences and the diversity and size of these different markets lead to fundamentally different design efforts. For the desktop market, much of the effort goes into designing a leading-edge microprocessor and into the graphics and I/O system that integrate with the microprocessor. In the server area, the focus is on integrating state-of-the-art microprocessors, often in a multiprocessor architecture, and designing scalable and highly available I/O systems to accompany the processors. Finally, in the leading edge of the embedded processor market, the challenge lies in adopting the high-end microprocessor techniques to deliver most of the performance at a lower fraction of the price, while paying attention to demanding limits on power and sometimes a need for high-performance graphics or video processing.

In addition to performance and cost, designers must be aware of important trends in both the implementation technology and the use of computers. Such trends not only impact future cost, but also determine the longevity of an architecture. The next two sections discuss technology and cost trends.

1.3   Technology Trends

If an instruction set architecture is to be successful, it must be designed to survive rapid changes in computer technology. After all, a successful new instruction set architecture may last decades—the core of the IBM mainframe has been in use for more than 35 years. An architect must plan for technology changes that can increase the lifetime of a successful computer.

To plan for the evolution of a machine, the designer must be especially aware of rapidly occurring changes in implementation technology. Four implementation technologies, which change at a dramatic pace, are critical to modern implementations:

■ *Integrated circuit logic technology*—Transistor density increases by about 35% per year, quadrupling in somewhat over four years. Increases in die size are less predictable and slower, ranging from 10% to 20% per year. The combined effect is a growth rate in transistor count on a chip of about 55% per year. Device speed scales more slowly, as we discuss below.

- *Semiconductor DRAM* (dynamic random-access memory)—Density increases by between 40% and 60% per year, quadrupling in three to four years. Cycle time has improved very slowly, decreasing by about one-third in 10 years. Bandwidth per chip increases about twice as fast as latency decreases. In addition, changes to the DRAM interface have also improved the bandwidth; these are discussed in Chapter 5.

- *Magnetic disk technology*—Recently, disk density has been improving by more than 100% per year, quadrupling in two years. Prior to 1990, density increased by about 30% per year, doubling in three years. It appears that disk technology will continue the faster density growth rate for some time to come. Access time has improved by one-third in 10 years. This technology is central to Chapter 7, and we discuss the trends in greater detail there.

- *Network technology*—Network performance depends both on the performance of switches and on the performance of the transmission system. Both latency and bandwidth can be improved, though recently bandwidth has been the primary focus. For many years, networking technology appeared to improve slowly: for example, it took about 10 years for Ethernet technology to move from 10 Mb to 100 Mb. The increased importance of networking has led to a faster rate of progress, with 1 Gb Ethernet becoming available about five years after 100 Mb. The Internet infrastructure in the United States has seen even faster growth (roughly doubling in bandwidth every year), both through the use of optical media and through the deployment of much more switching hardware.

These rapidly changing technologies impact the design of a microprocessor that may, with speed and technology enhancements, have a lifetime of five or more years. Even within the span of a single product cycle for a computing system (two years of design and two to three years of production), key technologies, such as DRAM, change sufficiently that the designer must plan for these changes. Indeed, designers often design for the next technology, knowing that when a product begins shipping in volume that next technology may be the most cost-effective or may have performance advantages. Traditionally, cost has decreased at about the rate at which density increases.

Although technology improves fairly continuously, the impact of these improvements is sometimes seen in discrete leaps, as a threshold that allows a new capability is reached. For example, when MOS technology reached the point where it could put between 25,000 and 50,000 transistors on a single chip in the early 1980s, it became possible to build a 32-bit microprocessor on a single chip. By the late 1980s, first-level caches could go on chip. By eliminating chip crossings within the processor and between the processor and the cache, a dramatic increase in cost-performance and performance/power was possible. This design was simply infeasible until the technology reached a certain point. Such technology thresholds are not rare and have a significant impact on a wide variety of design decisions.

Scaling of Transistor Performance, Wires, and Power in Integrated Circuits

Integrated circuit processes are characterized by the *feature size,* which is the minimum size of a transistor or a wire in either the x or y dimension. Feature sizes have decreased from 10 microns in 1971 to 0.18 microns in 2001. Since the transistor count per square millimeter of silicon is determined by the surface area of a transistor, the density of transistors increases quadratically with a linear decrease in feature size. The increase in transistor performance, however, is more complex. As feature sizes shrink, devices shrink quadratically in the horizontal dimension and also shrink in the vertical dimension. The shrink in the vertical dimension requires a reduction in operating voltage to maintain correct operation and reliability of the transistors. This combination of scaling factors leads to a complex interrelationship between transistor performance and process feature size. To a first approximation, transistor performance improves linearly with decreasing feature size.

The fact that transistor count improves quadratically with a linear improvement in transistor performance is both the challenge and the opportunity that computer architects were created for! In the early days of microprocessors, the higher rate of improvement in density was used to quickly move from 4-bit, to 8-bit, to 16-bit, to 32-bit microprocessors. More recently, density improvements have supported the introduction of 64-bit microprocessors as well as many of the innovations in pipelining and caches, which we discuss in Chapters 3, 4, and 5.

Although transistors generally improve in performance with decreased feature size, wires in an integrated circuit do not. In particular, the signal delay for a wire increases in proportion to the product of its resistance and capacitance. Of course, as feature size shrinks, wires get shorter, but the resistance and capacitance per unit length get worse. This relationship is complex, since both resistance and capacitance depend on detailed aspects of the process, the geometry of a wire, the loading on a wire, and even the adjacency to other structures. There are occasional process enhancements, such as the introduction of copper, which provide one-time improvements in wire delay. In general, however, wire delay scales poorly compared to transistor performance, creating additional challenges for the designer. In the past few years, wire delay has become a major design limitation for large integrated circuits and is often more critical than transistor switching delay. Larger and larger fractions of the clock cycle have been consumed by the propagation delay of signals on wires. In 2001, the Pentium 4 broke new ground by allocating 2 stages of its 20+-stage pipeline just for propagating signals across the chip.

Power also provides challenges as devices are scaled. For modern CMOS microprocessors, the dominant energy consumption is in switching transistors. The energy required per transistor is proportional to the product of the load capacitance of the transistor, the frequency of switching, and the square of the voltage. As we move from one process to the next, the increase in the number of transistors switching, and the frequency with which they switch, dominates the decrease in load capacitance and voltage, leading to an overall growth in power consumption. The first microprocessors consumed tenths of a watt, while a 2 GHz Pentium 4 consumes close to 100 watts. The fastest workstation and server microprocessors in 2001 consumed between 100 and 150 watts. Distributing the power, removing the heat, and preventing hot spots have become increasingly difficult challenges, and it is likely that power rather than raw transistor count will become the major limitation in the near future.

1.4 Cost, Price, and Their Trends

Although there are computer designs where costs tend to be less important—specifically supercomputers—cost-sensitive designs are of growing significance: More than half the PCs sold in 1999 were priced at less than $1000, and the average price of a 32-bit microprocessor for an embedded application is in the tens of dollars. Indeed, in the past 15 years, the use of technology improvements to achieve lower cost, as well as increased performance, has been a major theme in the computer industry.

Textbooks often ignore the cost half of cost-performance because costs change, thereby dating books, and because the issues are subtle and differ across industry segments. Yet an understanding of cost and its factors is essential for designers to be able to make intelligent decisions about whether or not a new feature should be included in designs where cost is an issue. (Imagine architects designing skyscrapers without any information on costs of steel beams and concrete!)

This section focuses on cost and price, specifically on the relationship between price and cost: price is what you sell a finished good for, and cost is the amount spent to produce it, including overhead. We also discuss the major trends and factors that affect cost and how it changes over time. The exercises and examples use specific cost data that will change over time, though the basic determinants of cost are less time sensitive. This section will introduce you to these topics by discussing some of the major factors that influence the cost of a computer design and how these factors are changing over time.

The Impact of Time, Volume, and Commodification

The cost of a manufactured computer component decreases over time even without major improvements in the basic implementation technology. The underlying principle that drives costs down is the *learning curve*—manufacturing costs decrease over time. The learning curve itself is best measured by change in *yield*—the percentage of manufactured devices that survives the testing procedure. Whether it is a chip, a board, or a system, designs that have twice the yield will have basically half the cost.

Understanding how the learning curve will improve yield is key to projecting costs over the life of the product. As an example of the learning curve in action, the price per megabyte of DRAM drops over the long term by 40% per year.

Since DRAMs tend to be priced in close relationship to cost—with the exception of periods when there is a shortage—price and cost of DRAM track closely. In fact, there are some periods (for example, early 2001) in which it appears that price is less than cost; of course, the manufacturers hope that such periods are both infrequent and short!

Figure 1.5 plots the price of a new DRAM chip over its lifetime. Between the start of a project and the shipping of a product, say, two years, the cost of a new DRAM drops by a factor of between 5 and 10 in constant dollars. Since not all component costs change at the same rate, designs based on projected costs result in different cost-performance trade-offs than those using current costs. The caption of Figure 1.5 discusses some of the long-term trends in DRAM price.

Microprocessor prices also drop over time, but because they are less standardized than DRAMs, the relationship between price and cost is more complex. In a

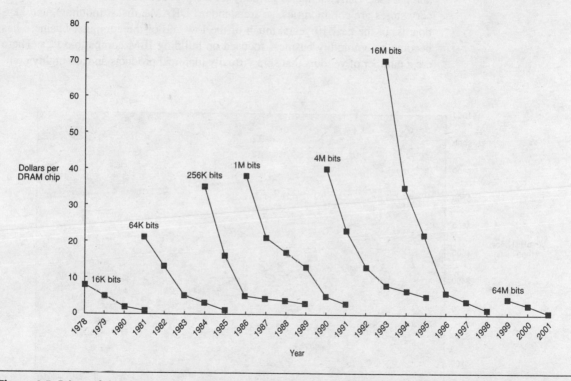

Figure 1.5 **Prices of six generations of DRAMs (from 16K bits to 64M bits) over time in 1977 dollars, showing the learning curve at work.** A 1977 dollar is worth about $2.95 in 2001; more than half of this inflation occurred in the five-year period of 1977–82, during which the value changed to $1.59. The cost of a megabyte of memory has dropped *incredibly* during this period, from over $5000 in 1977 to about $0.35 in 2000, and an amazing $0.08 in 2001 (in 1977 dollars)! Each generation drops in constant dollar price by a factor of 10 to 30 over its lifetime. Starting in about 1996, an explosion of manufacturers has dramatically reduced margins and increased the rate at which prices fall, as well as the eventual final price for a DRAM. Periods when demand exceeded supply, such as 1987–88 and 1992–93, have led to temporary higher pricing, which shows up as a slowing in the rate of price decrease; more dramatic short-term fluctuations have been smoothed out. In late 2000 and through 2001, there has been tremendous oversupply, leading to an accelerated price decrease, which is probably not sustainable.

period of significant competition, price tends to track cost closely, although microprocessor vendors probably rarely sell at a loss. Figure 1.6 shows processor price trends for the Pentium III.

Volume is a second key factor in determining cost. Increasing volumes affect cost in several ways. First, they decrease the time needed to get down the learning curve, which is partly proportional to the number of systems (or chips) manufactured. Second, volume decreases cost, since it increases purchasing and manufacturing efficiency. As a rule of thumb, some designers have estimated that cost decreases about 10% for each doubling of volume. Also, volume decreases the amount of development cost that must be amortized by each machine, thus allowing cost and selling price to be closer. We will return to the other factors influencing selling price shortly.

Commodities are products that are sold by multiple vendors in large volumes and are essentially identical. Virtually all the products sold on the shelves of grocery stores are commodities, as are standard DRAMs, disks, monitors, and keyboards. In the past 10 years, much of the low end of the computer business has become a commodity business focused on building IBM-compatible PCs. There are a number of vendors that ship virtually identical products and are highly com-

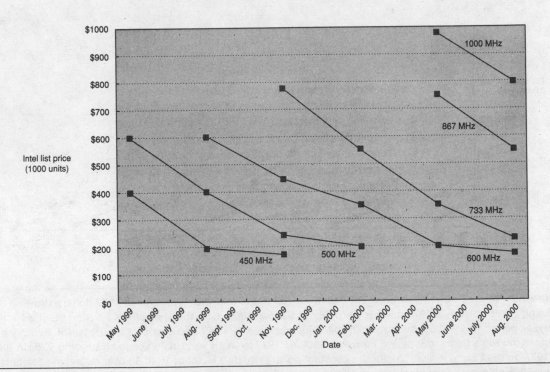

Figure 1.6 The price of an Intel Pentium III at a given frequency decreases over time as yield enhancements decrease the cost of a good die and competition forces price reductions. Data courtesy of *Microprocessor Report,* May 2000 issue. The most recent introductions will continue to decrease until they reach similar prices to the lowest-cost parts available today ($100–$200). Such price decreases assume a competitive environment where price decreases track cost decreases closely.

Figure 1.7 Photograph of an Intel Pentium 4 microprocessor die. (Courtesy Intel.)

petitive. Of course, this competition decreases the gap between cost and selling price, but it also decreases cost. Reductions occur because a commodity market has both volume and a clear product definition, which allows multiple suppliers to compete in building components for the commodity product. As a result, the overall product cost is lower because of the competition among the suppliers of the components and the volume efficiencies the suppliers can achieve. This has led to the low end of the computer business being able to achieve better price-performance than other sectors and yielded greater growth at the low end, although with very limited profits (as is typical in any commodity business).

Cost of an Integrated Circuit

Why would a computer architecture book have a section on integrated circuit costs? In an increasingly competitive computer marketplace where standard parts—disks, DRAMs, and so on—are becoming a significant portion of any system's cost, integrated circuit costs are becoming a greater portion of the cost that varies between machines, especially in the high-volume, cost-sensitive portion of the market. Thus computer designers must understand the costs of chips to understand the costs of current computers.

Although the costs of integrated circuits have dropped exponentially, the basic procedure of silicon manufacture is unchanged: A *wafer* is still tested and chopped into *dies* that are packaged (see Figures 1.7 and 1.8). Thus the cost of a packaged integrated circuit is

Figure 1.8 **This 8-inch wafer contains 564 MIPS64 R20K processors implemented in a 0.18μ process.** The R20K is an implementation of the MIPS64 architecture with instruction set extensions, called MIPS-3D, for use in three-dimensional graphics computations. The R20K is available at speeds from 500 to 750 MHz and is capable of executing two integer operations every clock cycle. Using the MIPS-3D instructions, the R20K can perform up to 3 billion floating-point operations per second. (Courtesy MIPS Technologies, Inc.)

$$\text{Cost of integrated circuit} = \frac{\text{Cost of die} + \text{Cost of testing die} + \text{Cost of packaging and final test}}{\text{Final test yield}}$$

In this section, we focus on the cost of dies, summarizing the key issues in testing and packaging at the end. A longer discussion of the testing costs and packaging costs appears in the exercises.

Learning how to predict the number of good chips per wafer requires first learning how many dies fit on a wafer and then learning how to predict the percentage of those that will work. From there it is simple to predict cost:

$$\text{Cost of die} = \frac{\text{Cost of wafer}}{\text{Dies per wafer} \times \text{Die yield}}$$

The most interesting feature of this first term of the chip cost equation is its sensitivity to die size, shown below.

The number of dies per wafer is basically the area of the wafer divided by the area of the die. It can be more accurately estimated by

$$\text{Dies per wafer} = \frac{\pi \times (\text{Wafer diameter}/2)^2}{\text{Die area}} - \frac{\pi \times \text{Wafer diameter}}{\sqrt{2} \times \text{Die area}}$$

The first term is the ratio of wafer area (πr^2) to die area. The second compensates for the "square peg in a round hole" problem—rectangular dies near the periphery of round wafers. Dividing the circumference (πd) by the diagonal of a square die is approximately the number of dies along the edge. For example, a wafer 30 cm ($\approx$ 12 inches) in diameter produces $\pi \times 225 - (\pi \times 30/1.41) = 640$ 1-cm dies.

Example   Find the number of dies per 30 cm wafer for a die that is 0.7 cm on a side.

Answer   The total die area is 0.49 cm^2. Thus

$$\text{Dies per wafer} = \frac{\pi \times (30/2)^2}{0.49} - \frac{\pi \times 30}{\sqrt{2 \times 0.49}} = \frac{706.5}{0.49} - \frac{94.2}{0.99} = 1347$$

But this only gives the maximum number of dies per wafer. The critical question is, What is the fraction or percentage of good dies on a wafer number, or the *die yield*? A simple empirical model of integrated circuit yield, which assumes that defects are randomly distributed over the wafer and that yield is inversely proportional to the complexity of the fabrication process, leads to the following:

$$\text{Die yield} = \text{Wafer yield} \times \left(1 + \frac{\text{Defects per unit area} \times \text{Die area}}{\alpha}\right)^{-\alpha}$$

where *wafer yield* accounts for wafers that are completely bad and so need not be tested. For simplicity, we'll just assume the wafer yield is 100%. Defects per unit area is a measure of the random manufacturing defects that occur. In 2001, these values typically range between 0.4 and 0.8 per square centimeter, depending on the maturity of the process (recall the learning curve, mentioned earlier). Lastly, α is a parameter that corresponds inversely to the number of masking levels, a measure of manufacturing complexity, critical to die yield. For today's multilevel metal CMOS processes, a good estimate is $\alpha = 4.0$.

Example   Find the die yield for dies that are 1 cm on a side and 0.7 cm on a side, assuming a defect density of 0.6 per cm^2.

Answer   The total die areas are 1 cm^2 and 0.49 cm^2. For the larger die the yield is

$$\text{Die yield} = \left(1 + \frac{0.6 \times 1}{4.0}\right)^{-4} = 0.57$$

For the smaller die, it is

$$\text{Die yield} = \left(1 + \frac{0.6 \times 0.49}{4.0}\right)^{-4} = 0.75$$

The bottom line is the number of good dies per wafer, which comes from multiplying dies per wafer by die yield (which incorporates the effects of defects). The examples above predict 366 good 1 cm^2 dies from the 30 cm wafer and 1014 good 0.49 cm^2 dies. Most 32-bit and 64-bit microprocessors in a modern 0.25μ technology fall between these two sizes, with some processors being as large as 2 cm^2 in the prototype process before a shrink. Low-end embedded 32-bit processors are sometimes as small as 0.25 cm^2, while processors used for embedded control (in printers, automobiles, etc.) are often less than 0.1 cm^2. Figure 1.34 for Exercise 1.8 shows the die size and technology for several current microprocessors.

Given the tremendous price pressures on commodity products such as DRAM and SRAM, designers have included redundancy as a way to raise yield. For a number of years, DRAMs have regularly included some redundant memory cells, so that a certain number of flaws can be accommodated. Designers have used similar techniques in both standard SRAMs and in large SRAM arrays used for caches within microprocessors. Obviously, the presence of redundant entries can be used to significantly boost the yield.

Processing a 30 cm diameter wafer in a leading-edge technology with four to six metal layers costs between $5000 and $6000 in 2001. Assuming a processed wafer cost of $5500, the cost of the 0.49 cm^2 die would be around $5.42, while the cost per die of the 1 cm^2 die would be about $15.03, or almost three times the cost for a die that is two times larger.

What should a computer designer remember about chip costs? The manufacturing process dictates the wafer cost, wafer yield, and defects per unit area, so the sole control of the designer is die area. Since α is around 4 for the advanced processes in use today, it would appear that the cost of a die would grow with the fourth power of the die size. In practice, however, because the number of defects per unit area is small, the number of good dies per wafer, and hence the cost per die, grows roughly as the square of the die area. The computer designer affects die size, and hence cost, both by what functions are included on or excluded from the die and by the number of I/O pins.

Before we have a part that is ready for use in a computer, the die must be tested (to separate the good dies from the bad), packaged, and tested again after packaging. These steps all add significant costs. These processes and their contribution to cost are discussed and evaluated in Exercise 1.8.

The above analysis has focused on the variable costs of producing a functional die, which is appropriate for high-volume integrated circuits. There is, however, one very important part of the fixed cost that can significantly impact the cost of an integrated circuit for low volumes (less than 1 million parts), namely, the cost of a mask set. Each step in the integrated circuit process requires a separate mask. Thus, for modern high-density fabrication processes with four to six metal layers, mask costs often exceed $1 million. Obviously, this large fixed cost affects the cost of prototyping and debugging runs and, for small-volume production, can be a significant part of the production cost. Since mask costs are likely to continue to increase, designers may incorporate reconfigurable logic to enhance the flexibility of a part, or choose to use gate arrays (which have fewer custom mask levels) and thus reduce the cost implications of masks.

Distribution of Cost in a System: An Example

To put the costs of silicon in perspective, Figure 1.9 shows the approximate cost breakdown for a $1000 PC in 2001. Although the costs of some parts of this machine can be expected to drop over time, other components, such as the packaging and power supply, have little room for improvement. Furthermore, we can expect that future machines will have larger memories and disks, meaning that prices drop more slowly than the technology improvement.

System	Subsystem	Fraction of total
Cabinet	Sheet metal, plastic	2%
	Power supply, fans	2%
	Cables, nuts, bolts	1%
	Shipping box, manuals	1%
	Subtotal	**6%**
Processor board	Processor	22%
	DRAM (128 MB)	5%
	Video card	5%
	Motherboard with basic I/O support, networking	5%
	Subtotal	**37%**
I/O devices	Keyboard and mouse	3%
	Monitor	19%
	Hard disk (20 GB)	9%
	DVD drive	6%
	Subtotal	**37%**
Software	OS + Basic Office Suite	20%

Figure 1.9 Estimated distribution of costs of the components in a $1000 PC in 2001. Notice that the largest single item is the CPU, closely followed by the monitor. (Interestingly, in 1995, the DRAM memory at about 1/3 of the total cost was the most expensive component! Since then, cost per MB has dropped by about a factor of 15!) Touma [1993] discusses computer system costs and pricing in more detail. These numbers are based on estimates of volume pricing for the various components.

Cost versus Price—Why They Differ and By How Much

Costs of components may confine a designer's desires, but they are still far from representing what the customer must pay. But why should a computer architecture book contain pricing information? Cost goes through a number of changes before it becomes price, and the computer designer should understand how a design decision will affect the potential selling price. For example, changing cost by $1000 may change price by $3000 to $4000. Without understanding the relationship of cost to price the computer designer may not understand the impact on price of adding, deleting, or replacing components.

The relationship between price and volume can increase the impact of changes in cost, especially at the low end of the market. Typically, fewer computers are sold as the price increases. Furthermore, as volume decreases, costs rise, leading to further increases in price. Thus, small changes in cost can have a larger than obvious impact. The relationship between cost and price is a complex one, and entire books have been written on the subject. The purpose of this section is to give you a simple introduction to what factors determine price, and to typical ranges for these factors.

The categories that make up price can be shown either as a tax on cost or as a percentage of the price. We will look at the information both ways. These differences between price and cost also depend on where in the computer marketplace a company is selling. To show these differences, Figure 1.10 shows how the difference between cost of materials and list price is decomposed, with the price increasing from left to right as we add each type of overhead.

Direct costs refer to the costs directly related to making a product. These include labor costs, purchasing components, scrap (the leftover from yield), and warranty, which covers the costs of systems that fail at the customer's site during the warranty period. Direct cost typically adds 10% to 30% to component cost. Service or maintenance costs are not included because the customer typically pays those costs, although a warranty allowance may be included here or in gross margin, discussed next.

The next addition is called the *gross margin,* the company's overhead that cannot be billed directly to one product. This can be thought of as indirect cost. It includes the company's research and development (R&D), marketing, sales, manufacturing equipment maintenance, building rental, cost of financing, pretax profits, and taxes. When the component costs are added to the direct cost and gross margin, we reach the *average selling price*—ASP in the language of MBAs—the money that comes directly to the company for each product sold. The gross margin is typically 10% to 45% of the average selling price, depending on the uniqueness of the product. Manufacturers of low-end PCs have lower gross margins for several reasons. First, their R&D expenses are lower. Second, their cost of sales is lower, since they use indirect distribution (by mail, the Internet, phone order, or retail store) rather than salespeople. Third, because their products are less distinctive, competition is more intense, thus forcing lower prices and often lower profits, which in turn lead to a lower gross margin.

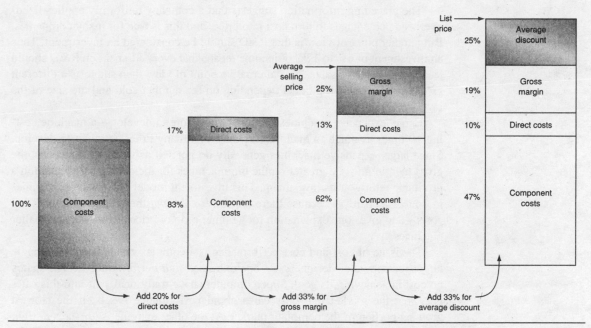

Figure 1.10 The components of price for a $1000 PC. Each increase is shown along the bottom as a tax on the prior price. The percentages of the new price for all elements are shown on the left of each column.

List price and average selling price are not the same, since companies typically offer volume discounts, lowering the average selling price. As personal computers became commodity products, the retail markups have dropped significantly, so list price and average selling price have closed.

As we said, pricing is sensitive to competition: A company may not be able to sell its product at a price that includes the desired gross margin. In the worst case, the price must be significantly reduced, lowering gross margin until profit becomes negative! A company striving for market share can reduce price and profit to increase the attractiveness of its products. If the volume grows sufficiently, costs can be reduced. Remember that these relationships are extremely complex and to understand them in depth would require an entire book, as opposed to one section in one chapter. For example, if a company cuts prices, but does not obtain a sufficient growth in product volume, the chief impact would be lower profits.

Many engineers are surprised to find that most companies spend only 4% (in the commodity PC business) to 12% (in the high-end server business) of their income on R&D, which includes all engineering (except for manufacturing and field engineering). This well-established percentage is reported in companies' annual reports and tabulated in national magazines, so this percentage is unlikely to change over time. In fact, experience has shown that computer companies with R&D percentages of 15–20% rarely prosper over the long term.

The preceding information suggests that a company uniformly applies fixed-overhead percentages to turn cost into price, and this is true for many companies. But another point of view is that R&D should be considered an investment. Thus an investment of 4% to 12% of income means that every $1 spent on R&D should lead to $8 to $25 in sales. This alternative point of view then suggests a different gross margin for each product depending on the number sold and the size of the investment.

Large, expensive machines generally cost more to develop—a machine costing 10 times as much to manufacture may cost many times as much to develop. Since large, expensive machines generally do not sell as well as small ones, the gross margin must be greater on the big machines for the company to maintain a profitable return on its investment. This investment model places large machines in double jeopardy—because there are fewer sold *and* they require larger R&D costs—and gives one explanation for a higher ratio of price to cost versus smaller machines.

The issue of cost and cost-performance is a complex one. There is no single target for computer designers. At one extreme, *high-performance design* spares no cost in achieving its goal. Supercomputers have traditionally fit into this category, but the market that only cares about performance has been the slowest growing portion of the computer market. At the other extreme is *low-cost design,* where performance is sacrificed to achieve lowest cost; some portions of the embedded market—for example, the market for cell phone microprocessors—behave exactly like this. Between these extremes is *cost-performance design,* where the designer balances cost versus performance. Most of the PC market, the workstation market, and most of the server market (at least including both low-end and midrange servers) operate in this region. In the past 10 years, as computers have downsized, both low-cost design and cost-performance design have become increasingly important. This section has introduced some of the most important factors in determining cost; the next section deals with performance.

1.5 Measuring and Reporting Performance

When we say one computer is faster than another, what do we mean? The user of a desktop machine may say a computer is faster when a program runs in less time, while the computer center manager running a large server system may say a computer is faster when it completes more jobs in an hour. The computer user is interested in reducing *response time*—the time between the start and the completion of an event—also referred to as *execution time*. The manager of a large data processing center may be interested in increasing *throughput*—the total amount of work done in a given time.

In comparing design alternatives, we often want to relate the performance of two different machines, say, X and Y. The phrase "X is faster than Y" is used here to mean that the response time or execution time is lower on X than on Y for the given task. In particular, "X is *n* times faster than Y" will mean

$$\frac{\text{Execution time}_Y}{\text{Execution time}_X} = n$$

Since execution time is the reciprocal of performance, the following relationship holds:

$$n = \frac{\text{Execution time}_Y}{\text{Execution time}_X} = \frac{\dfrac{1}{\text{Performance}_Y}}{\dfrac{1}{\text{Performance}_X}} = \frac{\text{Performance}_X}{\text{Performance}_Y}$$

The phrase "the throughput of X is 1.3 times higher than Y" signifies here that the number of tasks completed per unit time on machine X is 1.3 times the number completed on Y.

Because performance and execution time are reciprocals, increasing performance decreases execution time. To help avoid confusion between the terms *increasing* and *decreasing,* we usually say "improve performance" or "improve execution time" when we mean *increase* performance and *decrease* execution time.

Whether we are interested in throughput or response time, the key measurement is time: The computer that performs the same amount of work in the least time is the fastest. The difference is whether we measure one task (response time) or many tasks (throughput). Unfortunately, time is not always the metric quoted in comparing the performance of computers. A number of popular measures have been adopted in the quest for an easily understood, universal measure of computer performance, with the result that a few innocent terms have been abducted from their well-defined environment and forced into a service for which they were never intended. Our position is that the only consistent and reliable measure of performance is the execution time of real programs, and that all proposed alternatives to time as the metric or to real programs as the items measured have eventually led to misleading claims or even mistakes in computer design. The dangers of a few popular alternatives are shown in Section 1.9.

Measuring Performance

Even execution time can be defined in different ways depending on what we count. The most straightforward definition of time is called *wall-clock time, response time,* or *elapsed time,* which is the latency to complete a task, including disk accesses, memory accesses, input/output activities, operating system overhead—everything. With multiprogramming the CPU works on another program while waiting for I/O and may not necessarily minimize the elapsed time of one program. Hence we need a term to take this activity into account. *CPU time* recognizes this distinction and means the time the CPU is computing, *not* including the time waiting for I/O or running other programs. (Clearly the response time seen by the user is the elapsed time of the program, not the CPU time.) CPU time can be further divided into the CPU time spent in the program, called *user CPU time,* and the CPU time spent in the operating system performing tasks requested by the program, called *system CPU time.*

These distinctions are reflected in the UNIX time command, which returns four measurements when applied to an executing program:

```
90.7u 12.9s 2:39 65%
```

User CPU time is 90.7 seconds, system CPU time is 12.9 seconds, elapsed time is 2 minutes and 39 seconds (159 seconds), and the percentage of elapsed time that is CPU time is (90.7 + 12.9)/159 or 65%. More than a third of the elapsed time in this example was spent waiting for I/O or running other programs or both. Many measurements ignore system CPU time because of the inaccuracy of operating systems' self-measurement (the above inaccurate measurement came from UNIX) and the inequity of including system CPU time when comparing performance between machines with differing system codes. On the other hand, system code on some machines is user code on others, and no program runs without some operating system running on the hardware, so a case can be made for using the sum of user CPU time and system CPU time.

In the present discussion, a distinction is maintained between performance based on elapsed time and that based on CPU time. The term *system performance* is used to refer to elapsed time on an *unloaded* system, while *CPU performance* refers to *user* CPU time on an unloaded system. We will focus on CPU performance in this chapter, though we do consider performance measurements based on elapsed time.

Choosing Programs to Evaluate Performance

Dhrystone does not use floating point. Typical programs don't ...

Rick Richardson
Clarification of Dhrystone (1988)

This program is the result of extensive research to determine the instruction mix of a typical Fortran program. The results of this program on different machines should give a good indication of which machine performs better under a typical load of Fortran programs. The statements are purposely arranged to defeat optimizations by the compiler.

H. J. Curnow and B. A. Wichmann
Comments on the Whetstone benchmark (1976)

A computer user who runs the same programs day in and day out would be the perfect candidate to evaluate a new computer. To evaluate a new system the user would simply compare the execution time of her *workload*—the mixture of programs and operating system commands that users run on a machine. Few are in this happy situation, however. Most must rely on other methods to evaluate machines and often other evaluators, hoping that these methods will predict performance for their usage of the new machine. There are five levels of programs used in such circumstances, listed below in decreasing order of accuracy of prediction.

1. *Real applications*—Although the buyer may not know what fraction of time is spent on these programs, she knows that some users will run them to solve real problems. Examples are compilers for C, text-processing software like Word, and other applications like Photoshop. Real applications have input, output, and options that a user can select when running the program. There is one major downside to using real applications as benchmarks: Real applications often encounter portability problems arising from dependences on the operating system or compiler. Enhancing portability often means modifying the source and sometimes eliminating some important activity, such as interactive graphics, which tends to be more system dependent.

2. *Modified (or scripted) applications*—In many cases, real applications are used as the building blocks for a benchmark, either with modifications to the application or with a script that acts as stimulus to the application. Applications are modified for one of two primary reasons: to enhance portability or to focus on one particular aspect of system performance. For example, to create a CPU-oriented benchmark, I/O may be removed or restructured to minimize its impact on execution time. Scripts are used to simulate application programs so as to reproduce interactive behavior, which might occur on a desktop system, or to simulate complex multiuser interaction, which occurs in a server system.

3. *Kernels*—Several attempts have been made to extract small, key pieces from real programs and use them to evaluate performance. "Livermore Loops" and Linpack are the best known examples. Unlike real programs, no user would run kernel programs; they exist solely to evaluate performance. Kernels are best used to isolate performance of individual features of a machine to explain the reasons for differences in performance of real programs.

4. *Toy benchmarks*—Toy benchmarks are typically between 10 and 100 lines of code and produce a result the user already knows before running the toy program. Programs like Sieve of Eratosthenes, Puzzle, and Quicksort are popular because they are small, easy to type, and run on almost any computer. The best use of such programs is beginning programming assignments.

5. *Synthetic benchmarks*—Similar in philosophy to kernels, synthetic benchmarks try to match the average frequency of operations and operands of a large set of programs. Whetstone and Dhrystone are the most popular synthetic benchmarks. A description of these benchmarks and some of their flaws appears in Section 1.9. No user runs synthetic benchmarks because they don't compute anything a user could want. Synthetic benchmarks are, in fact, even further removed from reality than kernels because kernel code is extracted from real programs, while synthetic code is created artificially to match an average execution profile. Synthetic benchmarks are not even *pieces* of real programs, although kernels might be.

Because computer companies thrive or go bust depending on price-performance of their products relative to others in the marketplace, tremendous resources are available to improve performance of programs widely used in evaluating machines. Such pressures can skew hardware and software engineering efforts to add optimizations that improve performance of synthetic programs, toy programs, kernels, and even real programs. The advantage of the last of these is that adding such optimizations is more difficult in real programs, though not impossible. This fact has caused some benchmark providers to specify the rules under which compilers must operate, as we will see shortly.

Benchmark Suites

Recently, it has become popular to put together collections of benchmarks to try to measure the performance of processors with a variety of applications. Of course, such suites are only as good as the constituent individual benchmarks. Nonetheless, a key advantage of such suites is that the weakness of any one benchmark is lessened by the presence of the other benchmarks. This advantage is especially true if the methods used for summarizing the performance of the benchmark suite reflect the time to run the entire suite, as opposed to rewarding performance increases on programs that may be defeated by targeted optimizations. Later in this section, we discuss the strengths and weaknesses of different methods for summarizing performance.

One of the most successful attempts to create standardized benchmark application suites has been the SPEC (Standard Performance Evaluation Corporation), which had its roots in the late 1980s efforts to deliver better benchmarks for workstations. Just as the computer industry has evolved over time, so has the need for different benchmark suites, and there are now SPEC benchmarks to cover different application classes, as well as other suites based on the SPEC model. All the SPEC benchmark suites are documented, together with reported results, at *www.spec.org*.

Although we focus our discussion on the SPEC benchmarks in many of the following sections, there is also a large set of benchmarks that have been developed for PCs running the Windows operating system, covering a variety of different application environments, as Figure 1.11 shows.

Desktop Benchmarks

Desktop benchmarks divide into two broad classes: CPU-intensive benchmarks and graphics-intensive benchmarks (although many graphics benchmarks include intensive CPU activity). SPEC originally created a benchmark set focusing on CPU performance (initially called SPEC89), which has evolved into its fourth generation: SPEC CPU2000, which follows SPEC95 and SPEC92. (Figure 1.30 in Section 1.9 discusses the evolution of the benchmarks.) SPEC CPU2000, summarized in Figure 1.12, consists of a set of 11 integer benchmarks (CINT2000)

Benchmark name	Benchmark description
Business Winstone	Runs a script consisting of Netscape Navigator and several office suite products (Microsoft, Corel, WordPerfect). The script simulates a user switching among and running different applications.
CC Winstone	Simulates multiple applications focused on content creation, such as Photoshop, Premiere, Navigator, and various audio-editing programs.
Winbench	Runs a variety of scripts that test CPU performance, video system performance, and disk performance using kernels focused on each subsystem.

Figure 1.11 A sample of some of the many PC benchmarks. The first two are scripts using real applications, and the last is a mixture of kernels and synthetic benchmarks. These are all now maintained by Ziff Davis, a publisher of much of the literature in the PC space. Ziff Davis also provides independent testing services. For more information on these benchmarks, see *www.etestinglabs.com/benchmarks/*.

and 14 floating-point benchmarks (CFP2000). The SPEC benchmarks are real programs, modified for portability and to minimize the role of I/O in overall benchmark performance. The integer benchmarks vary from part of a C compiler to a VLSI place-and-route tool to a graphics application. The floating-point benchmarks include code for quantum chromodynamics, finite element modeling, and fluid dynamics. The SPEC CPU suite is useful for CPU benchmarking for both desktop systems and single-processor servers. We will see data on many of these programs throughout this text.

In the next subsection, we show how a SPEC2000 report describes the machine, compiler, and OS configuration. In Section 1.9 we describe some of the pitfalls that have occurred in attempting to develop the SPEC benchmark suite, as well as the challenges in maintaining a useful and predictive benchmark suite.

Although SPEC CPU2000 is aimed at CPU performance, two different types of graphics benchmarks were created by SPEC: SPECviewperf (see *www.spec.org*) is used for benchmarking systems supporting the OpenGL graphics library, while SPECapc consists of applications that make extensive use of graphics. SPECviewperf measures the 3D rendering performance of systems running under OpenGL using a 3D model and a series of OpenGL calls that transform the model. SPECapc consists of runs of several large applications, including

1. *Pro/Engineer*—A solid modeling application that does extensive 3D rendering. The input script is a model of a photocopying machine consisting of 370,000 triangles.

2. *SolidWorks 2001*—A 3D CAD/CAM design tool running a series of five tests varying from I/O intensive to CPU intensive. The largest input is a model of an assembly line consisting of 276,000 triangles.

Benchmark	Type	Source	Description
gzip	Integer	C	Compression using the Lempel-Ziv algorithm
vpr	Integer	C	FPGA circuit placement and routing
gcc	Integer	C	Consists of the GNU C compiler generating optimized machine code
mcf	Integer	C	Combinatorial optimization of public transit scheduling
crafty	Integer	C	Chess-playing program
parser	Integer	C	Syntactic English language parser
eon	Integer	C++	Graphics visualization using probabilistic ray tracing
perlmbk	Integer	C	Perl (an interpreted string-processing language) with four input scripts
gap	Integer	C	A group theory application package
vortex	Integer	C	An object-oriented database system
bzip2	Integer	C	A block-sorting compression algorithm
twolf	Integer	C	Timberwolf: a simulated annealing algorithm for VLSI place and route
wupwise	FP	F77	Lattice gauge theory model of quantum chromodynamics
swim	FP	F77	Solves shallow water equations using finite difference equations
mgrid	FP	F77	Multigrid solver over three-dimensional field
apply	FP	F77	Parabolic and elliptic partial differential equation solver
mesa	FP	C	Three-dimensional graphics library
galgel	FP	F90	Computational fluid dynamics
art	FP	C	Image recognition of a thermal image using neural networks
equake	FP	C	Simulation of seismic wave propagation
facerec	FP	C	Face recognition using wavelets and graph matching
ammp	FP	C	Molecular dynamics simulation of a protein in water
lucas	FP	F90	Performs primality testing for Mersenne primes
fma3d	FP	F90	Finite element modeling of crash simulation
sixtrack	FP	F77	High-energy physics accelerator design simulation
apsi	FP	F77	A meteorological simulation of pollution distribution

Figure 1.12 The programs in the SPEC CPU2000 benchmark suites. The 11 integer programs (all in C, except one in C++) are used for the CINT2000 measurement, while the 14 floating-point programs (6 in FORTRAN-77, 5 in C, and 3 in FORTRAN-90) are used for the CFP2000 measurement. See *www.spec.org* for more on these benchmarks.

3. *Unigraphics V15*—Based on an aircraft model and covering a wide spectrum of Unigraphics functionality, including assembly, drafting, numeric control machining, solid modeling, and optimization. The inputs are all part of an aircraft design.

Server Benchmarks

Just as servers have multiple functions, so there are multiple types of benchmarks. The simplest benchmark is perhaps a CPU throughput-oriented benchmark. SPEC CPU2000 uses the SPEC CPU benchmarks to construct a simple throughput benchmark where the processing rate of a multiprocessor can be measured by running multiple copies (usually as many as there are CPUs) of each SPEC CPU benchmark and converting the CPU time into a rate. This leads to a measurement called the SPECrate.

Other than SPECrate, most server applications and benchmarks have significant I/O activity arising from either disk or network traffic, including benchmarks for file server systems, for Web servers, and for database and transaction-processing systems. SPEC offers both a file server benchmark (SPECSFS) and a Web server benchmark (SPECWeb). SPECSFS is a benchmark for measuring NFS (Network File System) performance using a script of file server requests; it tests the performance of the I/O system (both disk and network I/O) as well as the CPU. SPECSFS is a throughput-oriented benchmark but with important response time requirements. (Chapter 7 discusses some file and I/O system benchmarks in detail.) SPECWeb is a Web server benchmark that simulates multiple clients requesting both static and dynamic pages from a server, as well as clients posting data to the server.

Transaction-processing (TP) benchmarks measure the ability of a system to handle transactions, which consist of database accesses and updates. An airline reservation system or a bank ATM system are typical simple TP systems; more complex TP systems involve complex databases and decision making. In the mid-1980s, a group of concerned engineers formed the vendor-independent Transaction Processing Council (TPC) to try to create a set of realistic and fair benchmarks for transaction processing. The first TPC benchmark, TPC-A, was published in 1985 and has since been replaced and enhanced by four different benchmarks. TPC-C, initially created in 1992, simulates a complex query environment. TPC-H models ad hoc decision support—the queries are unrelated and knowledge of past queries cannot be used to optimize future queries; the result is that query execution times can be very long. TPC-R simulates a business decision support system where users run a standard set of queries. In TPC-R, preknowledge of the queries is taken for granted, and the DBMS system can be optimized to run these queries. TPC-W is a Web-based transaction benchmark that simulates the activities of a business-oriented transactional Web server. It exercises the database system as well as the underlying Web server software. The TPC benchmarks are described at *www.tpc.org/*.

All the TPC benchmarks measure performance in transactions per second. In addition, they include a response time requirement, so that throughput performance is measured only when the response time limit is met. To model real-world systems, higher transaction rates are also associated with larger systems, both in terms of users and the database that the transactions are applied to. Finally, the system cost for a benchmark system must also be included, allowing accurate comparisons of cost-performance.

Embedded Benchmarks

Benchmarks for embedded computing systems are in a far more nascent state than those for either desktop or server environments. In fact, many manufacturers quote Dhrystone performance, a benchmark that was criticized and given up by desktop systems more than 10 years ago! As mentioned earlier, the enormous variety in embedded applications, as well as differences in performance requirements (hard real time, soft real time, and overall cost-performance), make the use of a single set of benchmarks unrealistic. In practice, many designers of embedded systems devise benchmarks that reflect their application, either as kernels or as stand-alone versions of the entire application.

For those embedded applications that can be characterized well by kernel performance, the best standardized set of benchmarks appears to be a new benchmark set: the EDN Embedded Microprocessor Benchmark Consortium (or EEMBC, pronounced "embassy"). The EEMBC benchmarks fall into five classes: automotive/industrial, consumer, networking, office automation, and telecommunications. Figure 1.13 shows the five different application classes, which include 34 benchmarks.

Although many embedded applications are sensitive to the performance of small kernels, remember that often the overall performance of the entire application (which may be thousands of lines) is also critical. Thus, for many embedded systems, the EMBCC benchmarks can only be used to partially assess performance.

Reporting Performance Results

The guiding principle of reporting performance measurements should be *reproducibility*—list everything another experimenter would need to duplicate the results. A SPEC benchmark report requires a fairly complete description of the

Benchmark type	Number of kernels	Example benchmarks
Automotive/industrial	16	6 microbenchmarks (arithmetic operations, pointer chasing, memory performance, matrix arithmetic, table lookup, bit manipulation), 5 automobile control benchmarks, and 5 filter or FFT benchmarks
Consumer	5	5 multimedia benchmarks (JPEG compress/decompress, filtering, and RGB conversions)
Networking	3	Shortest-path calculation, IP routing, and packet flow operations
Office automation	4	Graphics and text benchmarks (Bézier curve calculation, dithering, image rotation, text processing)
Telecommunications	6	Filtering and DSP benchmarks (autocorrelation, FFT, decoder, encoder)

Figure 1.13 The EEMBC benchmark suite, consisting of 34 kernels in five different classes. See *www.eembc.org* for more information on the benchmarks and for scores.

machine and the compiler flags, as well as the publication of both the baseline and optimized results. As an example, Figure 1.14 shows portions of the SPEC CINT2000 report for a Dell Precision Workstation 410. In addition to hardware, software, and baseline tuning parameter descriptions, a SPEC report contains the actual performance times, shown both in tabular form and as a graph. A TPC benchmark report is even more complete, since it must include results of a benchmarking audit and must also include cost information.

A system's software configuration can significantly affect the performance results for a benchmark. For example, operating systems performance and support can be very important in server benchmarks. For this reason, these benchmarks are sometimes run in single-user mode to reduce overhead. Additionally, operating system enhancements are sometimes made to increase performance on the TPC benchmarks. Likewise, compiler technology can play a big role in the performance of compute-oriented benchmarks. The impact of compiler technology can be especially large when modification of the source is allowed (see the example with the EEMBC benchmarks in Figure 1.31 in Section 1.9) or when a benchmark is particularly susceptible to an optimization (see the example from SPEC described on page 58). For these reasons it is important to describe exactly the software system being measured as well as whether any special nonstandard modifications have been made.

Another way to customize the software to improve the performance of a benchmark has been through the use of benchmark-specific flags; these flags often caused transformations that would be illegal on many programs or would slow down performance on others. To restrict this process and increase the significance of the SPEC results, the SPEC organization created a *baseline performance* measurement in addition to the optimized performance measurement. Baseline performance restricts the vendor to one compiler and one set of flags for all the programs in the same language (C or FORTRAN). Figure 1.14 shows the parameters for the baseline performance; in Section 1.9, we'll see the tuning parameters for the optimized performance runs on this machine.

In addition to the question of flags and optimization, another key question is whether source code modifications or hand-generated assembly language are allowed. There are four different approaches to addressing this question:

1. No source code modifications are allowed. The SPEC benchmarks fall into this class, as do most of the standard PC benchmarks.

2. Source code modifications are allowed, but are essentially difficult or impossible. Benchmarks like TPC-C rely on standard databases, such as Oracle or Microsoft's SQL server. Although these third-party vendors are interested in the overall performance of their systems on important industry-standard benchmarks, they are highly unlikely to make vendor-specific changes to enhance the performance for one particular customer. TPC-C also relies heavily on the operating system, which can be changed, provided those changes become part of the production version.

Hardware		Software	
Model number	Precision WorkStation 410	O/S and version	Windows NT 4.0
CPU	700 MHz, Pentium III	Compilers and version	Intel C/C++ Compiler 4.5
Number of CPUs	1	Other software	See below
Primary cache	16KBI+16KBD on chip	File system type	NTFS
Secondary cache	256KB(I+D) on chip	System state	Default
Other cache	None		
Memory	256 MB ECC PC100 SDRAM		
Disk subsystem	SCSI		
Other hardware	None		

SPEC CINT2000 base tuning parameters/notes/summary of changes:

+FDO: PASS1=-Qprof_gen PASS2=-Qprof_use

    Base tuning: -QxK -Qipo_wp shlW32M.lib +FDO

    shlW32M.lib is the SmartHeap library V5.0 from MicroQuill www.microquill.com

    Portability flags:

    176.gcc: -Dalloca=_alloca /F10000000 -Op

    186.crafy: -DNT_i386

    253.perlbmk: -DSPEC_CPU2000_NTOS -DPERLDLL /MT

    254.gap: -DSYS_HAS_CALLOC_PROTO -DSYS_HAS_MALLOC_PROTO

Figure 1.14 The machine, software, and baseline tuning parameters for the CINT2000 base report on a Dell Precision WorkStation 410. These data are for the base CINT2000 report. The data are available online at *www.spec.org /osg/cpu2000/results/cpu2000.html.*

3. Source modifications are allowed. Several supercomputer benchmark suites allow modification of the source code. For example, the NAS supercomputer benchmarks specify the input and output and supply a version of the source, but vendors are allowed to rewrite the source, including changing the algorithms, as long as the modified version produces the same output. EEMBC also allows source-level changes to its benchmarks and reports these as "optimized" measurements, versus "out-of-the-box" measurements, which allow no changes.

4. Hand-coding is allowed. EEMBC allows assembly language coding of its benchmarks. The small size of its kernels makes this approach attractive, although in practice with larger embedded applications it is unlikely to be used, except for small loops. Figure 1.31 in Section 1.9 shows the significant benefits from hand-coding on several different embedded processors.

The key issue that benchmark designers face in deciding to allow modification of the source is whether such modifications will reflect real practice and provide useful insight to users, or whether such modifications simply reduce the accuracy of the benchmarks as predictors of real performance.

Comparing and Summarizing Performance

Comparing performance of computers is rarely a dull event, especially when the designers are involved. Charges and countercharges fly across the Internet; one is accused of underhanded tactics, and another of misleading statements. Since careers sometimes depend on the results of such performance comparisons, it is understandable that the truth is occasionally stretched. But more frequently discrepancies can be explained by differing assumptions or lack of information.

We would like to think that if we could just agree on the programs, the experimental environments, and the definition of *faster,* then misunderstandings would be avoided, leaving the networks free for scholarly discourse. Unfortunately, that's not the reality. Once we agree on the basics, battles are then fought over what is the fair way to summarize relative performance of a collection of programs. For example, two articles on summarizing performance in the same journal took opposing points of view. Figure 1.15, taken from one of the articles, is an example of the confusion that can arise.

Using our definition of *faster than,* the following statements hold:

A is 10 times faster than B for program P1.

B is 10 times faster than A for program P2.

A is 20 times faster than C for program P1.

C is 50 times faster than A for program P2.

B is 2 times faster than C for program P1.

C is 5 times faster than B for program P2.

Taken individually, any one of these statements may be of use. Collectively, however, they present a confusing picture—the relative performance of computers A, B, and C is unclear.

	Computer A	Computer B	Computer C
Program P1 (secs)	1	10	20
Program P2 (secs)	1000	100	20
Total time (secs)	1001	110	40

Figure 1.15 Execution times of two programs on three machines. Data from Figure I of Smith [1988].

Total Execution Time: A Consistent Summary Measure

The simplest approach to summarizing relative performance is to use total execution time of the two programs. Thus

B is 9.1 times faster than A for programs P1 and P2.

C is 25 times faster than A for programs P1 and P2.

C is 2.75 times faster than B for programs P1 and P2.

This summary tracks execution time, our final measure of performance. If the workload consisted of running programs P1 and P2 an equal number of times, the statements above would predict the relative execution times for the workload on each machine.

An average of the execution times that tracks total execution time is the *arithmetic mean:*

$$\frac{1}{n} \sum_{i=1}^{n} \text{Time}_i$$

where Time_i is the execution time for the ith program of a total of n in the workload.

Weighted Execution Time

The question arises: What is the proper mixture of programs for the workload? Are programs P1 and P2 in fact run equally in the workload, as assumed by the arithmetic mean? If not, then there are two approaches that have been tried for summarizing performance. The first approach when given an unequal mix of programs in the workload is to assign a weighting factor w_i to each program to indicate the relative frequency of the program in that workload. If, for example, 20% of the tasks in the workload were program P1 and 80% of the tasks in the workload were program P2, then the weighting factors would be 0.2 and 0.8. (Weighting factors add up to 1.) By summing the products of weighting factors and execution times, a clear picture of performance of the workload is obtained. This is called the *weighted arithmetic mean:*

$$\sum_{i=1}^{n} \text{Weight}_i \times \text{Time}_i$$

where Weight_i is the frequency of the ith program in the workload and Time_i is the execution time of that program. Figure 1.16 shows the data from Figure 1.15 with three different weightings, each proportional to the execution time of a workload with a given mix.

	Programs			Weightings		
	A	B	C	W(1)	W(2)	W(3)
Program P1 (secs)	1.00	10.00	20.00	0.50	0.909	0.999
Program P2 (secs)	1000.00	100.00	20.00	0.50	0.091	0.001
Arithmetic mean: W(1)	500.50	55.00	20.00			
Arithmetic mean: W(2)	91.91	18.19	20.00			
Arithmetic mean: W(3)	2.00	10.09	20.00			

Figure 1.16 Weighted arithmetic mean execution times for three machines (A, B, C) and two programs (P1 and P2) using three weightings (W1, W2, W3). The top table contains the original execution time measurements and the weighting factors, while the bottom table shows the resulting weighted arithmetic means for each weighting. W(1) equally weights the programs, resulting in a mean (row 3) that is the same as the unweighted arithmetic mean. W(2) makes the mix of programs inversely proportional to the execution times on machine B; row 4 shows the arithmetic mean for that weighting. W(3) weights the programs in inverse proportion to the execution times of the two programs on machine A; the arithmetic mean with this weighting is given in the last row. The net effect of the second and third weightings is to "normalize" the weightings to the execution times of programs running on that machine, so that the running time will be spent evenly between each program for that machine. For a set of n programs each taking $Time_i$ on one machine, the equal-time weightings on that machine are $$w_i = \frac{1}{Time_i \times \sum_{i=1}^{n} \left(\frac{1}{Time_j}\right)}.$$

Normalized Execution Time and the Pros and Cons of Geometric Means

A second approach to unequal mixture of programs in the workload is to normalize execution times to a reference machine and then take the average of the normalized execution times. This is the approach used by the SPEC benchmarks, where a base time on a SPARCstation is used for reference. This measurement gives a warm fuzzy feeling because it suggests that performance of new programs can be predicted by simply multiplying this number times its performance on the reference machine.

Average normalized execution time can be expressed as either an arithmetic or *geometric* mean. The formula for the geometric mean is

$$\sqrt[n]{\prod_{i=1}^{n} \text{Execution time ratio}_i}$$

where Execution time ratio$_i$ is the execution time, normalized to the reference machine, for the ith program of a total of n in the workload. Geometric means also have a nice property for two samples X_i and Y_i:

$$\frac{\text{Geometric mean}(X_i)}{\text{Geometric mean}(Y_i)} = \text{Geometric mean}\left(\frac{X_i}{Y_i}\right)$$

As a result, taking either the ratio of the means or the mean of the ratios yields the same result. In contrast to arithmetic means, geometric means of normalized execution times are consistent no matter which machine is the reference. Hence, the arithmetic mean should *not* be used to average normalized execution times. Figure 1.17 shows some variations using both arithmetic and geometric means of normalized times.

Because the weightings in weighted arithmetic means are set proportionate to execution times on a given machine, as in Figure 1.16, they are influenced not only by frequency of use in the workload, but also by the peculiarities of a particular machine and the size of program input. The geometric mean of normalized execution times, on the other hand, is independent of the running times of the individual programs, and it doesn't matter which machine is used to normalize. If a situation arose in comparative performance evaluation where the programs were fixed but the inputs were not, then competitors could rig the results of weighted arithmetic means by making their best performing benchmark have the largest input and therefore dominate execution time. In such a situation the geometric mean would be less misleading than the arithmetic mean.

The strong drawback to geometric means of normalized execution times is that they violate our fundamental principle of performance measurement—they do not predict execution time. The geometric means from Figure 1.17 suggest that for programs P1 and P2 the performance of machines A and B is the same, yet this would only be true for a workload that ran program P1 100 times for every occurrence of program P2 (Figure 1.16). The total execution time for such a workload suggests that machines A and B are about 50% faster than machine C, in contrast to the geometric mean, which says machine C is faster than A and B! In general there is *no workload* for three or more machines that will match the performance predicted by the geometric means of normalized execution times. Our original reason for examining geometric means of normalized performance

	Normalized to A			Normalized to B			Normalized to C		
	A	B	C	A	B	C	A	B	C
Program P1	1.0	10.0	20.0	0.1	1.0	2.0	0.05	0.5	1.0
Program P2	1.0	0.1	0.02	10.0	1.0	0.2	50.0	5.0	1.0
Arithmetic mean	1.0	5.05	10.01	5.05	1.0	1.1	25.03	2.75	1.0
Geometric mean	1.0	1.0	0.63	1.0	1.0	0.63	1.58	1.58	1.0
Total time	1.0	0.11	0.04	9.1	1.0	0.36	25.03	2.75	1.0

Figure 1.17 Execution times from Figure 1.15 normalized to each machine. The arithmetic mean performance varies depending on which is the reference machine. In column 2, B's execution time is five times longer than A's, although the reverse is true in column 4. In column 3, C is slowest, but in column 9, C is fastest. The geometric means are consistent independent of normalization—A and B have the same performance, and the execution time of C is 0.63 of A or B (1/1.58 is 0.63). Unfortunately, the total execution time of A is 10 times longer than that of B, and B in turn is about 3 times longer than C. As a point of interest, the relationship between the means of the same set of numbers is always harmonic mean ≤ geometric mean ≤ arithmetic mean.

was to avoid giving equal emphasis to the programs in our workload, but is this solution an improvement?

An additional drawback of using geometric mean as a method for summarizing performance for a benchmark suite (as SPEC CPU2000 does) is that it encourages hardware and software designers to focus their attention on the benchmarks where performance is easiest to improve rather than on the benchmarks that are slowest. For example, if some hardware or software improvement can cut the running time for a benchmark from 2 seconds to 1, the geometric mean will reward those designers with the same overall mark that it would give to designers who improve the running time on another benchmark in the suite from 10,000 seconds to 5000 seconds. Of course, everyone interested in running the second program thinks of the second batch of designers as their heroes and the first group as useless. Small programs are often easier to "crack," obtaining a large but unrepresentative performance improvement, and the use of geometric means rewards such behavior more than a measure that reflects total running time.

The ideal solution is to measure a real workload and weight the programs according to their frequency of execution. If this can't be done, then normalizing so that equal time is spent on each program on some machine at least makes the relative weightings explicit and will predict execution time of a workload with that mix. The problem above of unspecified inputs is best solved by specifying the inputs when comparing performance. If results must be normalized to a specific machine, first summarize performance with the proper weighted measure and then do the normalizing.

Lastly, we must remember that any summary measure necessarily loses information, especially when the measurements may vary widely. Thus, it is important both to ensure that the results of individual benchmarks, as well as the summary number, are available. Furthermore, the summary number should be used with caution, since the summary may not be the best indicator of performance for a customer's applications.

1.6 Quantitative Principles of Computer Design

Now that we have seen how to define, measure, and summarize performance, we can explore some of the guidelines and principles that are useful in design and analysis of computers. In particular, this section introduces some important observations about designing for performance and cost-performance, as well as two equations that we can use to evaluate design alternatives.

Make the Common Case Fast

Perhaps the most important and pervasive principle of computer design is to make the common case fast: In making a design trade-off, favor the frequent case over the infrequent case. This principle also applies when determining how to spend resources, since the impact on making some occurrence faster is higher if the occurrence is frequent. Improving the frequent event, rather than the rare event, will obviously help performance, too. In addition, the frequent case is often simpler and can be done faster than the infrequent case. For example, when adding two numbers in the CPU, we can expect overflow to be a rare circumstance and can therefore improve performance by optimizing the more common case of no overflow. This may slow down the case when overflow occurs, but if that is rare, then overall performance will be improved by optimizing for the normal case.

We will see many cases of this principle throughout this text. In applying this simple principle, we have to decide what the frequent case is and how much performance can be improved by making that case faster. A fundamental law, called *Amdahl's Law,* can be used to quantify this principle.

Amdahl's Law

The performance gain that can be obtained by improving some portion of a computer can be calculated using Amdahl's Law. Amdahl's Law states that the performance improvement to be gained from using some faster mode of execution is limited by the fraction of the time the faster mode can be used.

Amdahl's Law defines the *speedup* that can be gained by using a particular feature. What is speedup? Suppose that we can make an enhancement to a machine that will improve performance when it is used. Speedup is the ratio

$$\text{Speedup} = \frac{\text{Performance for entire task using the enhancement when possible}}{\text{Performance for entire task without using the enhancement}}$$

Alternatively,

$$\text{Speedup} = \frac{\text{Execution time for entire task without using the enhancement}}{\text{Execution time for entire task using the enhancement when possible}}$$

Speedup tells us how much faster a task will run using the machine with the enhancement as opposed to the original machine.

Amdahl's Law gives us a quick way to find the speedup from some enhancement, which depends on two factors:

1. *The fraction of the computation time in the original machine that can be converted to take advantage of the enhancement*—For example, if 20 seconds of the execution time of a program that takes 60 seconds in total can use an enhancement, the fraction is 20/60. This value, which we will call Fraction$_{\text{enhanced}}$, is always less than or equal to 1.

2. *The improvement gained by the enhanced execution mode; that is, how much faster the task would run if the enhanced mode were used for the entire program*—This value is the time of the original mode over the time of the

enhanced mode: If the enhanced mode takes 2 seconds for some portion of the program that can completely use the mode, while the original mode took 5 seconds for the same portion, the improvement is 5/2. We will call this value, which is always greater than 1, Speedup$_{enhanced}$.

The execution time using the original machine with the enhanced mode will be the time spent using the unenhanced portion of the machine plus the time spent using the enhancement:

$$\text{Execution time}_{new} = \text{Execution time}_{old} \times \left((1 - \text{Fraction}_{enhanced}) + \frac{\text{Fraction}_{enhanced}}{\text{Speedup}_{enhanced}} \right)$$

The overall speedup is the ratio of the execution times:

$$\text{Speedup}_{overall} = \frac{\text{Execution time}_{old}}{\text{Execution time}_{new}} = \frac{1}{(1 - \text{Fraction}_{enhanced}) + \frac{\text{Fraction}_{enhanced}}{\text{Speedup}_{enhanced}}}$$

Example   Suppose that we are considering an enhancement to the processor of a server system used for Web serving. The new CPU is 10 times faster on computation in the Web serving application than the original processor. Assuming that the original CPU is busy with computation 40% of the time and is waiting for I/O 60% of the time, what is the overall speedup gained by incorporating the enhancement?

Answer   Fraction$_{enhanced}$ = 0.4
Speedup$_{enhanced}$ = 10

$$\text{Speedup}_{overall} = \frac{1}{0.6 + \frac{0.4}{10}} = \frac{1}{0.64} \approx 1.56$$

Amdahl's Law expresses the law of diminishing returns: The incremental improvement in speedup gained by an additional improvement in the performance of just a portion of the computation diminishes as improvements are added. An important corollary of Amdahl's Law is that if an enhancement is only usable for a fraction of a task, we can't speed up the task by more than the reciprocal of 1 minus that fraction.

A common mistake in applying Amdahl's Law is to confuse "fraction of time converted to use an enhancement" and "fraction of time after enhancement is in use." If, instead of measuring the time that we *could use* the enhancement in a computation, we measure the time *after* the enhancement is in use, the results will be incorrect! (Try Exercise 1.3 to see how wrong.)

Amdahl's Law can serve as a guide to how much an enhancement will improve performance and how to distribute resources to improve cost-performance. The goal, clearly, is to spend resources proportional to where time is spent. Amdahl's Law is particularly useful for comparing the overall system performance of two alternatives, but it can also be applied to compare two CPU design alternatives, as the following example shows.

Example A common transformation required in graphics engines is square root. Implementations of floating-point (FP) square root vary significantly in performance, especially among processors designed for graphics. Suppose FP square root (FPSQR) is responsible for 20% of the execution time of a critical graphics benchmark. One proposal is to enhance the FPSQR hardware and speed up this operation by a factor of 10. The other alternative is just to try to make all FP instructions in the graphics processor run faster by a factor of 1.6; FP instructions are responsible for a total of 50% of the execution time for the application. The design team believes that they can make all FP instructions run 1.6 times faster with the same effort as required for the fast square root. Compare these two design alternatives.

Answer We can compare these two alternatives by comparing the speedups:

$$\text{Speedup}_{FPSQR} = \frac{1}{(1-0.2)+\frac{0.2}{10}} = \frac{1}{0.82} = 1.22$$

$$\text{Speedup}_{FP} = \frac{1}{(1-0.5)+\frac{0.5}{1.6}} = \frac{1}{0.8125} = 1.23$$

Improving the performance of the FP operations overall is slightly better because of the higher frequency.

In the above example, we needed to know the time consumed by the new and improved FP operations; often it is difficult to measure these times directly. In the next section, we will see another way of doing such comparisons based on the use of an equation that decomposes the CPU execution time into three separate components. If we know how an alternative affects these three components, we can determine its overall performance effect. Furthermore, it is often possible to build simulators that measure these components before the hardware is actually designed.

The CPU Performance Equation

Essentially all computers are constructed using a clock running at a constant rate. These discrete time events are called *ticks, clock ticks, clock periods, clocks, cycles,* or *clock cycles.* Computer designers refer to the time of a clock period by its duration (e.g., 1 ns) or by its rate (e.g., 1 GHz). CPU time for a program can then be expressed two ways:

CPU time = CPU clock cycles for a program × Clock cycle time or

$$\text{CPU time} = \frac{\text{CPU clock cycles for a program}}{\text{Clock rate}}$$

In addition to the number of clock cycles needed to execute a program, we can also count the number of instructions executed—the *instruction path length* or *instruction count* (IC). If we know the number of clock cycles and the instruction count, we can calculate the average number of *clock cycles per instruction* (CPI). Because it is easier to work with, and because we will deal with simple processors in this chapter, we use CPI. Designers sometimes also use *instructions per clock* (IPC), which is the inverse of CPI.

CPI is computed as

$$\text{CPI} = \frac{\text{CPU clock cycles for a program}}{\text{Instruction count}}$$

This CPU figure of merit provides insight into different styles of instruction sets and implementations, and we will use it extensively in the next four chapters.

By transposing instruction count in the above formula, clock cycles can be defined as IC × CPI. This allows us to use CPI in the execution time formula:

$$\text{CPU time} = \text{Instruction count} \times \text{Clock cycle time} \times \text{Cycles per instruction}$$

or

$$\text{CPU time} = \frac{\text{Instruction count} \times \text{Clock cycle time}}{\text{Clock rate}}$$

Expanding the first formula into the units of measurement and inverting the clock rate shows how the pieces fit together:

$$\frac{\text{Instructions}}{\text{Program}} \times \frac{\text{Clock cycles}}{\text{Instruction}} \times \frac{\text{Seconds}}{\text{Clock cycle}} = \frac{\text{Seconds}}{\text{Program}} = \text{CPU time}$$

As this formula demonstrates, CPU performance is dependent upon three characteristics: clock cycle (or rate), clock cycles per instruction, and instruction count. Furthermore, CPU time is *equally* dependent on these three characteristics: A 10% improvement in any one of them leads to a 10% improvement in CPU time.

Unfortunately, it is difficult to change one parameter in complete isolation from others because the basic technologies involved in changing each characteristic are interdependent:

■ *Clock cycle time*—Hardware technology and organization

■ *CPI*—Organization and instruction set architecture

■ *Instruction count*—Instruction set architecture and compiler technology

Luckily, many potential performance improvement techniques primarily improve one component of CPU performance with small or predictable impacts on the other two.

Sometimes it is useful in designing the CPU to calculate the number of total CPU clock cycles as

$$CPU \text{ clock cycles} = \sum_{i=1}^{n} IC_i \times CPI_i$$

where IC_i represents number of times instruction i is executed in a program and CPI_i represents the average number of instructions per clock for instruction i. This form can be used to express CPU time as

$$CPU \text{ time} = \left(\sum_{i=1}^{n} IC_i \times CPI_i \right) \times \text{Clock cycle time}$$

and overall CPI as

$$CPI = \frac{\sum_{i=1}^{n} IC_i \times CPI_i}{\text{Instruction count}} = \sum_{i=1}^{n} \frac{IC_i}{\text{Instruction count}} \times CPI_i$$

The latter form of the CPI calculation uses each individual CPI_i and the fraction of occurrences of that instruction in a program (i.e., $IC_i \div$ Instruction count). CPI_i should be measured and not just calculated from a table in the back of a reference manual since it must include pipeline effects, cache misses, and any other memory system inefficiencies.

Consider our earlier example, here modified to use measurements of the frequency of the instructions and of the instruction CPI values, which, in practice, are obtained by simulation or by hardware instrumentation.

Example   Suppose we have made the following measurements:

Frequency of FP operations (other than FPSQR) = 25%

Average CPI of FP operations = 4.0

Average CPI of other instructions = 1.33

Frequency of FPSQR = 2%

CPI of FPSQR = 20

Assume that the two design alternatives are to decrease the CPI of FPSQR to 2 or to decrease the average CPI of all FP operations to 2.5. Compare these two design alternatives using the CPU performance equation.

Answer   First, observe that only the CPI changes; the clock rate and instruction count remain identical. We start by finding the original CPI with neither enhancement:

$$CPI_{original} = \sum_{i=1}^{n} CPI_i \times \left(\frac{IC_i}{Instruction\ count}\right)$$

$$= (4 \times 25\%) + (1.33 \times 75\%) = 2.0$$

We can compute the CPI for the enhanced FPSQR by subtracting the cycles saved from the original CPI:

$$CPI_{with\ new\ FPSQR} = CPI_{original} - 2\% \times (CPI_{old\ FPSQR} - CPI_{of\ new\ FPSQR\ only})$$

$$= 2.0 - 2\% \times (20 - 2) = 1.64$$

We can compute the CPI for the enhancement of all FP instructions the same way or by summing the FP and non-FP CPIs. Using the latter gives us

$$CPI_{new\ FP} = (75\% \times 1.33) + (25\% \times 2.5) = 1.625$$

Since the CPI of the overall FP enhancement is slightly lower, its performance will be marginally better. Specifically, the speedup for the overall FP enhancement is

$$Speedup_{new\ FP} = \frac{CPU\ time_{original}}{CPU\ time_{new\ FP}} = \frac{IC \times Clock\ cycle \times CPI_{original}}{IC \times Clock\ cycle \times CPI_{new\ FP}}$$

$$= \frac{CPI_{original}}{CPI_{new\ FP}} = \frac{2.00}{1.625} = 1.23$$

Happily, this is the same speedup we obtained using Amdahl's Law on page 42. It is often possible to measure the constituent parts of the CPU performance equation. This is a key advantage for using the CPU performance equation versus Amdahl's Law in the previous example. In particular, it may be difficult to measure things such as the fraction of execution time for which a set of instructions is responsible. In practice this would probably be computed by summing the product of the instruction count and the CPI for each of the instructions in the set. Since the starting point is often individual instruction count and CPI measurements, the CPU performance equation is incredibly useful.

Measuring and Modeling the Components of the CPU Performance Equation

To use the CPU performance equation as a design tool, we need to be able to measure the various factors. For an existing processor, it is easy to obtain the execution time by measurement, and the clock speed is known. The challenge lies in discovering the instruction count or the CPI. Most newer processors include counters for both instructions executed and for clock cycles. By periodically monitoring these counters, it is also possible to attach execution time and instruction count to segments of the code, which can be helpful to programmers trying to understand and tune the performance of an application. Often, a designer or programmer will want to understand performance at a more fine-grained level than what is available from the hardware counters. For example, they may want to know why the CPI is what it is. In such cases, simulation techniques like those used for processors that are being designed are used.

There are three general classes of simulation techniques that are used. In general, the more sophisticated techniques yield more accuracy, particularly for more recent architectures, at the cost of longer execution time. The first and simplest technique, and hence the least costly, is profile-based, static modeling. In this technique a dynamic execution profile of the program, which indicates how often each instruction is executed, is obtained by one of three methods:

1. By using hardware counters on the processor, which are periodically saved. This technique often gives an approximate profile, but one that is within a few percent of exact.

2. By using instrumented execution, in which instrumentation code is compiled into the program. This code is used to increment counters, yielding an exact profile. (This technique can also be used to create a trace of memory addresses that are accessed, which is useful for other simulation techniques.)

3. By interpreting the program at the instruction set level, compiling instruction counts in the process.

Once the profile is obtained, it is used to analyze the program in a static fashion by looking at the code. Obviously, with the profile, the total instruction count is easy to obtain. It is also easy to get a detailed dynamic instruction mix telling what types of instructions were executed with what frequency. Finally, for simple processors, it is possible to compute an approximation to the CPI. This approximation is computed by modeling and analyzing the execution of each basic block (or straight-line code segment) and then computing an overall estimate of CPI or total compute cycles by multiplying the estimate for each basic block by the number of times it is executed. Although this simple model ignores memory behavior and has severe limits for modeling complex pipelines, it is a reasonable and very fast technique for modeling the performance of short, integer pipelines, ignoring the memory system behavior.

Trace-driven simulation is a more sophisticated technique for modeling performance and is particularly useful for modeling memory system performance. In trace-driven simulation, a trace of the memory references executed is created, usually either by simulation or by instrumented execution. The trace includes what instructions were executed (given by the instruction address), as well as the data addresses accessed.

Trace-driven simulation can be used in several different ways. The most common use is to model memory system performance, which can be done by simulating the memory system, including the caches and any memory management hardware using the address trace. A trace-driven simulation of the memory system can be combined with a static analysis of pipeline performance to obtain a reasonably accurate performance model for simple pipelined processors. For more complex pipelines, the trace data can be used to perform a more detailed analysis of the pipeline performance by simulation of the processor pipeline. Since the trace data allows a simulation of the exact ordering of instructions, higher accuracy can be achieved than with a static approach. Trace-driven simulation typically isolates the simulation of any pipeline behavior from the memory system. In particular, it assumes that the trace is completely independent of the memory system behavior. As we will see in Chapters 3 and 5, this is not the case for the most advanced processors—a third technique is needed.

The third technique, which is the most accurate and most costly, is execution-driven simulation. In execution-driven simulation a detailed simulation of the memory system and the processor pipeline are done simultaneously. This allows the exact modeling of the interaction between the two, which is critical, as we will see in Chapters 3 and 5.

There are many variations on these three basic techniques. We will see examples of these tools in later chapters and use various versions of them in the exercises.

Principle of Locality

Although Amdahl's Law is a theorem that applies to any system, other important fundamental observations come from properties of programs. The most important program property that we regularly exploit is *principle of locality:* Programs tend to reuse data and instructions they have used recently. A widely held rule of thumb is that a program spends 90% of its execution time in only 10% of the code. An implication of locality is that we can predict with reasonable accuracy what instructions and data a program will use in the near future based on its accesses in the recent past.

Principle of locality also applies to data accesses, though not as strongly as to code accesses. Two different types of locality have been observed. *Temporal locality* states that recently accessed items are likely to be accessed in the near future. *Spatial locality* says that items whose addresses are near one another tend to be referenced close together in time. We will see these principles applied in Chapter 5.

Take Advantage of Parallelism

Taking advantage of parallelism is one of the most important methods for improving performance. We give three brief examples, which are expounded on in later chapters. Our first example is the use of parallelism at the system level. To improve the throughput performance on a typical server benchmark, such as SPECWeb or TPC, multiple processors and multiple disks can be used. The workload of handling requests can then be spread among the CPUs or disks, resulting in improved throughput. This is the reason that scalability is viewed as a valuable asset for server applications.

At the level of an individual processor, taking advantage of parallelism among instructions is critical to achieving high performance. One of the simplest ways to do this is through pipelining. The basic idea behind pipelining, which is explained in more detail in Appendix A and is a major focus of Chapter 3, is to overlap the execution of instructions, so as to reduce the total time to complete a sequence of instructions. Viewed from the perspective of the CPU performance equation, we can think of pipelining as reducing the CPI by allowing instructions that take multiple cycles to overlap. A key insight that allows pipelining to work is that not every instruction depends on its immediate predecessor, and thus, executing the instructions completely or partially in parallel may be possible.

Parallelism can also be exploited at the level of detailed digital design. For example, set-associative caches use multiple banks of memory that are typically searched in parallel to find a desired item. Modern ALUs use carry-lookahead, which uses parallelism to speed the process of computing sums from linear to logarithmic in the number of bits per operand.

There are many different ways designers take advantage of parallelism. One common class of techniques is parallel computation of two or more *possible* outcomes, followed by late selection. This technique is used in carry select adders, in set-associative caches, and in handling branches in pipelines. Virtually every chapter in this book will have an example of how performance is enhanced through the exploitation of parallelism.

1.7 Putting It All Together: Performance and Price-Performance

In the "Putting It All Together" sections that appear near the end of every chapter, we show real examples that use the principles in that chapter. In this section we look at measures of performance and price-performance, first in desktop systems using the SPEC CPU benchmarks, then in servers using TPC-C as the benchmark, and finally in the embedded market using EEMBC as the benchmark.

Performance and Price-Performance for Desktop Systems

Although there are many benchmark suites for desktop systems, a majority of them are OS or architecture specific. In this section we examine the CPU performance and price-performance of a variety of desktop systems using the SPEC CPU2000 integer and floating-point suites. As mentioned earlier, SPEC CPU2000 summarizes CPU performance using a geometric mean normalized to a Sun system, with larger numbers indicating higher performance.

Each system was configured with one CPU, 512 MB of SDRAM (with ECC if available), approximately 20 GB of disk, a fast graphics system, and a 10/100M bit Ethernet connection. The seven systems we examined and their processors and price are shown in Figure 1.18. The wide variation in price is driven by a

Vendor	Model	Processor	Clock rate (MHz)	Price
Compaq	Presario 7000	AMD Athlon	1,400	$2,091
Dell	Precision 420	Intel Pentium III	1,000	$3,834
Dell	Precision 530	Intel Pentium 4	1,700	$4,175
HP	Workstation c3600	PA 8600	552	$12,631
IBM	RS6000 44P/170	IBM III-2	450	$13,889
Sun	Sunblade 100	UltraSPARC II-e	500	$2,950
Sun	Sunblade 1000	UltraSPARC III	750	$9,950

Figure 1.18   Seven different desktop systems from five vendors using seven different microprocessors showing the processor, its clock rate, and the selling price. All these systems are configured with 512 MB of ECC SDRAM, a high-end graphics system (which is *not* the highest-performance system available for the more expensive platforms), and approximately 20 GB of disk. Many factors are responsible for the wide variation in price despite these common elements. First, the systems offer different levels of expandability (with the Presario system being the least expandable, the Dell systems and Sunblade 100 being moderately expandable, and the HP, IBM, and Sunblade 1000 being very flexible and expandable). Second, the use of cheaper disks (ATA versus SCSI) and less expensive memory (PC memory versus custom DIMMs) has a significant impact. Third, the cost of the CPU varies by at least a factor of 2. In 2001 the Athlon sold for about $200, the Pentium III for about $240, and the Pentium 4 for about $500. Fourth, software differences (Linux or a Microsoft OS versus a vendor-specific OS) probably affect the final price. Fifth, the lower-end systems use PC commodity parts in others areas (fans, power supply, support chip sets), which lower costs. Finally, the commoditization effect, which we discussed in Section 1.4, is at work, especially for the Compaq and Dell systems. These prices were as of July 2001.

number of factors, including system expandability, the use of cheaper disks (ATA versus SCSI), less expensive memory (PC memory versus custom DIMMs), software differences (Linux or a Microsoft OS versus a vendor-specific OS), the cost of the CPU, and the commoditization effect, which we discussed in Section 1.4. (See the further discussion on price variation in the caption of Figure 1.18.)

Figure 1.19 shows the performance and the price-performance of these seven systems using SPEC CINT2000 as the metric. The Compaq system using the AMD Athlon CPU offers both the highest performance and the best price-performance, followed by the two Dell systems, which have comparable price-performance, although the Pentium 4 system is faster. The Sunblade 100 has the lowest performance, but somewhat better price-performance than the other UNIX-based workstation systems.

Figure 1.20 shows the performance and price-performance for the SPEC floating-point benchmarks. The floating-point instruction set enhancements in the Pentium 4 give it a clear performance advantage, although the Compaq Athlon-based system still has superior price-performance. The IBM, HP, and Sunblade 1000 all outperform the Dell 420 with a Pentium III, but the Dell system still offers better price-performance than the IBM, Sun, or HP workstations.

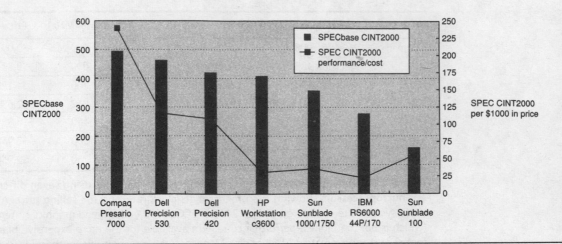

Figure 1.19 Performance and price-performance for seven systems are measured using SPEC CINT2000 as the benchmark. With the exception of the Sunblade 100 (Sun's low-end entry system), price-performance roughly parallels performance, contradicting the conventional wisdom—at least on the desktop—that higher-performance systems carry a disproportionate price premium. Price-performance is plotted as CINT2000 performance per $1000 in system cost. These performance numbers and prices were as of July 2001. The measurements are available online at *www.spec.org/osg/cpu2000/*.

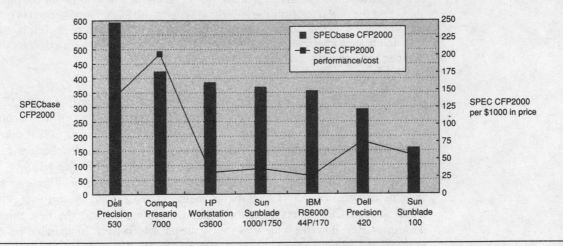

Figure 1.20 Performance and price-performance for seven systems are measured using SPEC CFP2000 as the benchmark. Price-performance is plotted as CFP2000 performance per $1000 in system cost. The dramatically improved floating-point performance of the Pentium 4 versus the Pentium III is clear in this figure. Price-performance partially parallels performance but not as clearly as in the case of the integer benchmarks. These performance numbers and prices were as of July 2001. The measurements are available online at *www.spec.org/osg/cpu2000/*.

Performance and Price-Performance for Transaction-Processing Servers

One of the largest server markets is online transaction processing (OLTP), which we described earlier. The standard industry benchmark for OLTP is TPC-C, which relies on a database system to perform queries and updates. Five factors make the performance of TPC-C particularly interesting. First, TPC-C is a reasonable approximation to a real OLTP application; although this makes benchmark setup complex and time-consuming, it also makes the results reasonably indicative of real performance for OLTP. Second, TPC-C measures total system performance, including the hardware, the operating system, the I/O system, and the database system, making the benchmark more predictive of real performance. Third, the rules for running the benchmark and reporting execution time are very complete, resulting in more comparable numbers. Fourth, because of the importance of the benchmark, computer system vendors devote significant effort to making TPC-C run well. Fifth, vendors are required to report both performance and price-performance, enabling us to examine both.

Because the OLTP market is large and quite varied, there is an incredible range of computing systems used for these applications, ranging from small single-processor servers to midrange multiprocessor systems to large-scale clusters consisting of tens to hundreds of processors. To allow an appreciation for this diversity and its range of performance and price-performance, we will examine six of the top results by performance (and the comparative price-performance) and six of the top results by price-performance (and the comparative performance). For TPC-C, performance is measured in transactions per minute (TPM), while price-performance is measured in TPM per dollar. Figure 1.21 shows the characteristics of a dozen systems whose performance or price-performance is near the top in one measure or the other.

Figure 1.22 charts the performance and price-performance of six of the highest-performing OLTP systems described in Figure 1.21. The IBM cluster system, consisting of 280 Pentium III processors, provides the highest overall performance, beating any other system by almost a factor of 3, as well as the best price-performance by just over a factor of 1.5. The other systems are all moderate-scale multiprocessors and offer fairly comparable performance and similar price-performance to the others in the group. Chapters 6 and 8 discuss the design of cluster and multiprocessor systems.

Figure 1.23 charts the performance and price-performance of the six OLTP systems from Figure 1.21 with the best price-performance. These systems are all multiprocessor systems, and, with the exception of the HP system, are based on Pentium III processors. Although the smallest system (the three-processor Dell system) has the best price-performance, several of the other systems offer better performance at about a factor of 0.65 of the price-performance. Notice that the systems with the best price-performance in Figure 1.23 average almost four times better in price-performance (TPM/$ = 99 versus 27) than the high-performance systems in Figure 1.22.

Vendor and system	CPUs	Database	OS	Price
IBM xSeries 370 c/s	280 Pentium III @ 900 MHz	Microsoft SQL Server 2000	Microsoft Windows Advanced Server	$15,543,346
Compaq AlphaServer GS 320	32 Alpha 21264 @ 1 GHz	Oracle 9i	Compaq Tru64 UNIX	$10,286,029
Fujitsu PRIMEPOWER 20000	48 SPARC64 GP @ 563 MHz	SymfoWARE Server Enterprise	Sun Solaris 8	$9,671,742
IBM pSeries 680 7017-S85	24 IBM RS64-IV @ 600 MHz	Oracle 8 v8.1.7.1	IBM AIX 4.3.3	$7,546,837
HP 9000 Enterprise Server	48 HP PA-RISC 8600 @ 552 MHz	Oracle8 v8.1.7.1	HP UX 11.i 64-bit	$8,522,104
IBM iSeries 400 840-2420	24 iSeries400 Model 840 @ 450 MHz	IBM DB2 for AS/400 V4	IBM OS/400 V4	$8,448,137
Dell PowerEdge 6400	3 Pentium III @ 700 MHz	Microsoft SQL Server 2000	Microsoft Windows 2000	$131,275
IBM xSeries 250 c/s	4 Pentium III @ 700 MHz	Microsoft SQL Server 2000	Microsoft Windows Advanced Server	$297,277
Compaq Proliant ML570 6/700 2	4 Pentium III @ 700 MHz	Microsoft SQL Server 2000	Microsoft Windows Advanced Server	$375,016
HP NetServer LH 6000	6 Pentium III @ 550 MHz	Microsoft SQL Server 2000	Microsoft Windows NT Enterprise	$372,805
NEC Express 5800/180	8 Pentium III @ 900 MHz	Microsoft SQL Server 2000	Microsoft Windows Advanced Server	$682,724
HP 9000 / L2000	4 PA-RISC 8500 @ 440 MHz	Sybase Adaptive Server	HP UX 11.0 64-bit	$368,367

Figure 1.21 The characteristics of a dozen OLTP systems with either high total performance (top half of the table) or superior price-performance (bottom half of the table). The IBM exSeries with 280 Pentium IIIs is a cluster, while all the other systems are tightly coupled multiprocessors. Surprisingly, none of the top performing systems by either measure are uniprocessors! The system descriptions and detailed benchmark reports are available at *www.tpc.org/*.

Performance and Price-Performance for Embedded Processors

Comparing performance and price-performance of embedded processors is more difficult than for the desktop or server environments because of several characteristics. First, benchmarking is in its comparative infancy in the embedded space. Although the EEMBC benchmarks represent a substantial advance in benchmark availability and benchmark practice, as we discussed earlier, these benchmarks have significant drawbacks. Equally importantly, in the embedded space, processors are often designed for a particular class of applications; such designs are often not measured outside of their application space, and when they are, they may not perform well. Finally, as mentioned earlier, cost and power are often the most important factors for an embedded application. Although we can partially measure cost by looking at the cost of the processor, other aspects of the design

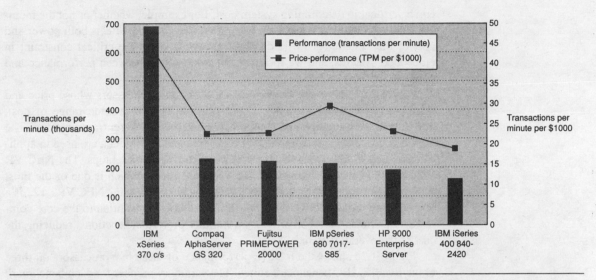

Figure 1.22 **The performance (measured in thousands of transactions per minute) and the price-performance (measured in transactions per minute per $1000) are shown for six of the highest-performing systems using TPC-C as the benchmark.** Interestingly, IBM occupies three of these six positions, with different hardware platforms (a cluster of Pentium IIIs, a Power III–based multiprocessor, and an AS 400–based multiprocessor.

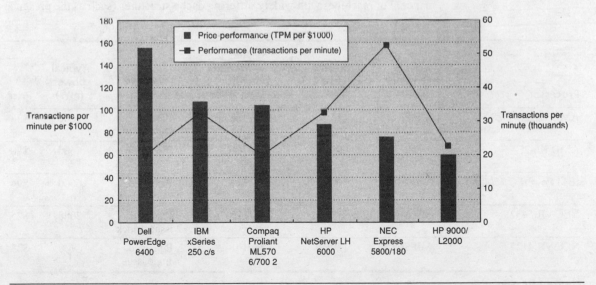

Figure 1.23 **Price-performance (plotted as transactions per minute per $1000 of system cost) and overall performance (plotted as thousands of transactions per minute).**

can be critical in determining system cost. For example, whether or not the memory controller and I/O control are integrated into the chip affects both power and cost of the system. As we said earlier, power is often the critical constraint in embedded systems, and we focus on the relationship between performance and power in the next section.

Figure 1.24 shows the characteristics of the five processors whose price and price-performance we examine. These processors span a wide range of cost, power, and performance and thus are used in very different applications. The high-end processors, such as the PowerPC 650 and AMD Elan, are used in applications such as network switches and possibly high-end laptops. The NEC VR 5432 series is a newer version of the VR 5400 series, which is one of the most heavily used processors in color laser printers. In contrast, the NEC VR 4122 is a low-end, low-power device used primarily in PDAs; in addition to the core computing functions, the 4122 provides a number of system functions, reducing the cost of the overall system.

Figure 1.25 shows the relative performance of these five processors on three of the five EEMBC benchmark suites. The summary number for each benchmark suite is proportional to the geometric mean of the individual performance measures for each benchmark in the suite (measured as iterations per second). The clock rate differences explain between 33% and 75% of the performance differences. For machines with similar organization (such as the AMD Elan SC520 and the NEC VR 4122), the clock rate is the primary factor in determining performance. For machines with widely differing cache structures (such as the presence

Processor	Instruction set	Processor clock rate (MHz)	Cache instruction/data on-chip secondary cache	Processor organization	Typical power (mW)	Price
AMD Elan SC520	x86	133	16K/16K	Pipelined: single issue	1600	$38
AMD K6-2E+	x86	500	32K/32K 128K	Pipelined: 3+ issues/clock	9600	$78
IBM PowerPC 750CX	PowerPC	500	32K/32K 128K	Pipelined: 4 issues/clock	6000	$94
NEC VR 5432	MIPS64	167	32K/32K	Pipelined: 2 issues/clock	2088	$25
NEC VR 4122	MIPS64	180	32K/16K	Pipelined: single issue	700	$33

Figure 1.24 **Five different embedded processors spanning a range of performance (more than a factor of 10, as we will see) and a wide range in price (roughly a factor of 4 and probably 50% higher than that if total system cost is considered).** The price does not include interface and support chips, which could significantly increase the deployed system cost. Likewise, the power indicated includes only the processor's typical power consumption (in milliwatts). These processors also differ widely in terms of execution capability, from a maximum of four instructions per clock to one! All the processors except the NEC VR 4122 include a hardware floating-point unit.

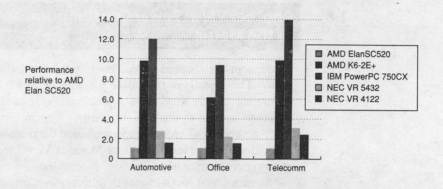

Figure 1.25 Relative performance of five different embedded processors for three of the five EEMBC benchmark suites. The performance is scaled relative to the AMD Elan SC520, so that the scores across the suites have a narrower range.

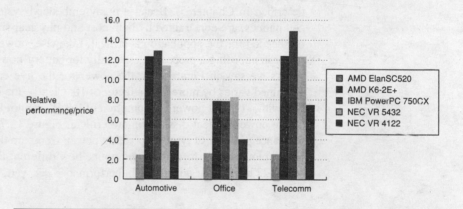

Figure 1.26 Relative price-performance of five different embedded processors for three of the five EEMBC benchmark suites, using only the price of the processor.

or absence of a secondary cache) or different pipelines, clock rate explains less of the performance difference.

Figure 1.26 shows the price-performance of these processors, where price is measured only by the processor cost. Here, the wide range in price narrows the performance differences, making the slower processors more cost-effective. If our cost analysis also included the system support chips, the differences would narrow even further, probably boosting the VR 5432 to the top in price-performance and making the VR 4122 at least competitive with the high-end IBM and AMD chips.

1.8 ▪ **Another View: Power Consumption and Efficiency as the Metric**

Throughout the chapters of this book, you will find sections entitled "Another View." These sections emphasize the way in which different segments of the computing market may solve a problem. For example, if the "Putting It All Together" section emphasizes the memory system for a desktop microprocessor, the "Another View" section may emphasize the memory system of an embedded application or a server. In this first "Another View" section, we look at the issue of power consumption in embedded processors.

As mentioned several times in this chapter, cost and power are often at least as important as performance in the embedded market. In addition to the cost of the processor module (which includes any required interface chips), memory is often the next most costly part of an embedded system. Recall that, unlike a desktop or server system, most embedded systems do not have secondary storage; instead, the entire application must reside in either FLASH or DRAM (as described in Chapter 5). Because many embedded systems, such as PDAs and cell phones, are constrained by both cost and physical size, the amount of memory needed for the application is critical. Likewise, power is often a determining factor in choosing a processor, especially for battery-powered systems.

As we saw in Figure 1.24, the power for the five embedded processors we examined varies by more than a factor of 10. Clearly, the high-performance AMD K6, with a typical power consumption of 9.3 W, cannot be used in environments where power or heat dissipation are critical. Figure 1.27 shows the relative performance per watt of typical operating power. Compare this figure to Figure 1.25, which plots raw performance, and notice how different the results are. The NEC VR 4122 has a clear advantage in performance per watt, but is the second lowest

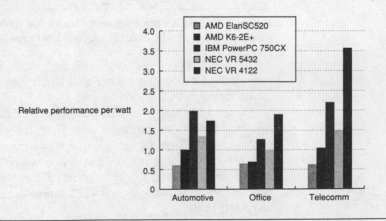

Figure 1.27 Relative performance per watt for the five embedded processors. The power is measured as typical operating power for the processor and does not include any interface chips.

performing processor! From the viewpoint of power consumption, the NEC VR 4122, which was designed for battery-based systems, is the big winner. The IBM PowerPC displays efficient use of power to achieve its high performance, although at 6 W typical, it is probably not suitable for most battery-based devices.

1.9   Fallacies and Pitfalls

The purpose of this section, which will be found in every chapter, is to explain some commonly held misbeliefs or misconceptions that you should avoid. We call such misbeliefs *fallacies*. When discussing a fallacy, we try to give a counter-example. We also discuss *pitfalls*—easily made mistakes. Often pitfalls are generalizations of principles that are true in a limited context. The purpose of these sections is to help you avoid making these errors in machines that you design.

Fallacy   *The relative performance of two processors with the same instruction set architecture (ISA) can be judged by clock rate or by the performance of a single benchmark suite.*

As processors have become faster and more sophisticated, processor performance in one application area can diverge from that in another area. Sometimes the instruction set architecture is responsible for this, but increasingly the pipeline structure and memory system are responsible. This also means that clock rate is not a good metric, even if the instruction sets are identical. Figure 1.28 shows the performance of a 1.7 GHz Pentium 4 relative to a 1 GHz Pentium III. The figure

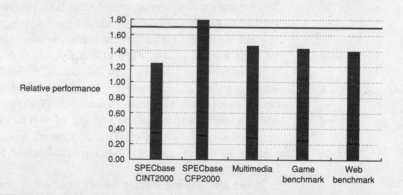

Figure 1.28   A comparison of the performance of the Pentium 4 (P4) relative to the Pentium III (P3) on five different sets of benchmark suites. The bars show the relative performance of a 1.7 GHz P4 versus a 1 GHz P3. The thick horizontal line at 1.7 shows how much faster a Pentium 4 at 1.7 GHz would be than a 1 GHz Pentium III assuming performance scaled linearly with clock rate. Of course, this line represents an idealized approximation to how fast a P3 would run. The first two sets of bars are the SPEC integer and floating-point suites. The third set of bars represents three multimedia benchmarks. The fourth set represents a pair of benchmarks based on the game Quake, and the final benchmark is the composite Webmark score, a PC-based Web benchmark.

also shows the performance of a hypothetical 1.7 GHz Pentium III assuming linear scaling of performance based on the clock rate. In all cases except the SPEC floating-point suite, the Pentium 4 delivers less performance per MHz than the Pentium III. As mentioned earlier, instruction set enhancements (the SSE2 extensions), which significantly boost floating-point execution rates, are probably responsible for the better performance of the Pentium 4 for these floating-point benchmarks.

Performance within a single processor implementation family (such as Pentium III) usually scales slower than clock speed because of the increased relative cost of stalls in the memory system. Across generations (such as the Pentium 4 and Pentium III) enhancements to the basic implementation usually yield performance that is somewhat better than what would be derived from just clock rate scaling. As Figure 1.28 shows, the Pentium 4 is usually slower than the Pentium III when performance is adjusted by linearly scaling the clock rate. This may partly derive from the focus on high clock rate as a primary design goal. We discuss both the differences between the Pentium III and Pentium 4 further in Chapter 3 as well as why the performance does not scale as fast as the clock rate does.

Fallacy   *Benchmarks remain valid indefinitely.*

Several factors influence the usefulness of a benchmark as a predictor of real performance, and some of these may change over time. A big factor influencing the usefulness of a benchmark is the ability of the benchmark to resist "cracking," also known as benchmark engineering or "benchmarksmanship." Once a benchmark becomes standardized and popular, there is tremendous pressure to improve performance by targeted optimizations or by aggressive interpretation of the rules for running the benchmark. Small kernels or programs that spend their time in a very small number of lines of code are particularly vulnerable.

For example, despite the best intentions, the initial SPEC89 benchmark suite included a small kernel, called matrix300, which consisted of eight different 300 × 300 matrix multiplications. In this kernel, 99% of the execution time was in a single line (see SPEC [1989]). Optimization of this inner loop by the compiler (using an idea called blocking, discussed in Chapter 5) for the IBM Powerstation 550 resulted in performance improvement by a factor of more than 9 over an earlier version of the compiler! This benchmark tested compiler performance and was not, of course, a good indication of overall performance, nor of this particular optimization.

Even after the elimination of this benchmark, vendors found methods to tune the performance of individual benchmarks by the use of different compilers or preprocessors, as well as benchmark-specific flags. Although the baseline performance measurements require the use of one set of flags for all benchmarks, the tuned or optimized performance does not. In fact, benchmark-specific flags are allowed, even if they are illegal in general and could lead to incorrect compilation! Allowing benchmark and even input-specific flags has led to long lists of options, as Figure 1.29 shows. This list of options, which is not significantly dif-

Peak: -v -g3 -arch ev6 -non_shared ONESTEP plus:

168.wupwise: f77 -fast -O4 -pipeline -unroll 2

171.swim: f90 -fast -O5 -transform_loops

172.mgrid: kf77 -O5 -transform_loops -tune ev6 -unroll 8

173.applu: f77 -fast -O5 -transform_loops -unroll 14

177.mesa: cc -fast -O4

178.galgel: kf90 -O4 -unroll 2 -ldxml RM_SOURCES = lapak.f90

179.art: kcc -fast -O4 -ckapargs='-arl=4 -ur=4' -unroll 10

183.equake: kcc -fast -ckapargs='-arl=4' -xtaso_short

187.facerec: f90 -fast -O4

188.ammp: cc -fast -O4 -xtaso_short

189.lucas: kf90 -fast -O5 -fkapargs='-ur=1' -unroll 1

191.fma3d: kf90 -O4

200.sixtrack: f90 -fast -O5 -transform_loops

301.apsi: kf90 -O5 -transform_loops -unroll 8 -fkapargs='-ur=1'

Figure 1.29 The tuning parameters for the SPEC CFP2000 report on an AlphaServer DS20E Model 6/667. This is the portion of the SPEC report for the tuned performance corresponding to that in Figure 1.14. These parameters describe the compiler options (four different compilers are used). Each line shows the option used for one of the SPEC CFP2000 benchmarks. Data from *www.spec.org/osg/cpu2000/results/res1999q4/cpu2000-19991130-00012.html.*

ferent from the option lists used by other vendors, is used to obtain the peak performance for the Compaq AlphaServer DS20E Model 6/667. The list makes it clear why the baseline measurements were needed. The performance difference between the baseline and tuned numbers can be substantial. For the SPEC CFP2000 benchmarks on the AlphaServer DS20E Model 6/667, the overall performance (which by SPEC CPU2000 rules is summarized by geometric mean) is 1.12 times higher for the peak numbers. As compiler technology improves, a system tends to achieve closer to peak performance using the base flags. Similarly, as the benchmarks improve in quality, they become less susceptible to highly application-specific optimizations. Thus, the gap between peak and base, which in early times was often 20%, has narrowed.

Ongoing improvements in technology can also change what a benchmark measures. Consider the benchmark gcc, considered one of the most realistic and challenging of the SPEC92 benchmarks. Its performance is a combination of CPU time and real system time. Since the input remains fixed and real system time is limited by factors, including disk access time, that improve slowly, an increasing amount of the run time is system time rather than CPU time. This may be appropriate. On the other hand, it may be appropriate to change the input over time, reflecting the desire to compile larger programs. In fact, the SPEC92 input was changed to include four copies of each input file used in SPEC89; although this increases run time, it may or may not reflect the way compilers are actually being used.

Over a long period of time, these changes may make even a well-chosen benchmark obsolete. For example, more than half the benchmarks added to the 1992 and 1995 SPEC CPU benchmark release were dropped from the next generation of the suite! To show how dramatically benchmarks must adapt over time, we summarize the status of the integer and FP benchmarks from SPEC89, -92, and -95 in Figure 1.30.

Pitfall *Comparing hand-coded assembly and compiler-generated, high-level language performance.*

In most applications of computers, hand-coding is simply not tenable. A combination of the high cost of software development and maintenance together with time-to-market pressures have made it impossible for many applications to consider assembly language. In parts of the embedded market, however, several factors have continued to encourage limited use of hand-coding, at least of key loops. The most important factors favoring this tendency are the importance of a few small loops to overall performance (particularly real-time performance) in some embedded applications, and the inclusion of instructions that can significantly boost performance of certain types of computations, but that compilers can not effectively use.

When performance is measured either by kernels or by applications that spend most of their time in a small number of loops, hand-coding of the critical parts of the benchmark can lead to large performance gains. In such instances, the performance difference between the hand-coded and machine-generated versions of a benchmark can be very large, as shown for two different machines in Figure 1.31. Both designers and users must be aware of this potentially large difference and not extrapolate performance for compiler-generated code from hand-coded benchmarks.

Fallacy *Peak performance tracks observed performance.*

The only universally true definition of peak performance is "the performance level a machine is guaranteed not to exceed." The gap between peak performance and observed performance is typically a factor of 10 or more in supercomputers. (See Appendix G for an explanation.) Since the gap is so large and can vary significantly by benchmark, peak performance is not useful in predicting observed performance unless the workload consists of small programs that normally operate close to the peak.

As an example of this fallacy, a small code segment using long vectors ran on the Hitachi S810/20 in 1.3 seconds and on the Cray X-MP in 2.6 seconds. Although this suggests the S810 is two times faster than the X-MP, the X-MP runs a program with more typical vector lengths two times faster than the S810. These data are shown in Figure 1.32.

Benchmark name	Integer or FP	SPEC89	SPEC92	SPEC95	SPEC2000
gcc	integer	adopted	modified	modified	modified
espresso	integer	adopted	modified	*dropped*	
li	integer	adopted	modified	modified	*dropped*
eqntott	integer	adopted	*dropped*		
spice	FP	adopted	modified	*dropped*	
doduc	FP	adopted	*dropped*		
nasa7	FP	adopted	*dropped*		
fpppp	FP	adopted		modified	*dropped*
matrix300	FP	adopted	*dropped*		
tomcatv	FP	adopted		modified	*dropped*
compress	integer		adopted	modified	*dropped*
sc	integer		adopted	*dropped*	
mdljdp2	FP		adopted	*dropped*	
wave5	FP		adopted	modified	*dropped*
ora	FP		adopted	*dropped*	
mdljsp2	FP		adopted	*dropped*	
alvinn	FP		adopted	*dropped*	
ear	FP		adopted	*dropped*	
swm256 (aka swim)	FP		adopted	modified	modified
su2cor	FP		adopted	modified	*dropped*
hydro2d	FP		adopted	modified	*dropped*
go	integer			adopted	*dropped*
m88ksim	integer			adopted	*dropped*
ijpeg	integer			adopted	*dropped*
perl	integer			adopted	modified
vortex	integer			adopted	modified
mgrid	FP			adopted	modified
applu	FP			adopted	*dropped*
apsi	FP			adopted	modified
turb3d	FP			adopted	*dropped*

Figure 1.30 The evolution of the SPEC benchmarks over time showing when benchmarks were adopted, modified, and dropped. All the programs in the 89, 92, and 95 releases are shown. "Modified" indicates that either the input or the size of the benchmark was changed, usually to increase its running time and avoid perturbation in measurement or domination of the execution time by some factor other than CPU time.

Machine	EEMBC benchmark set	Compiler-generated performance	Hand-coded performance	Ratio hand/ compiler
Trimedia 1300 @166 MHz	Consumer	23.3	110.0	4.7
BOPS Manta @ 136 MHz	Telecomm	2.6	225.8	86.8
TI TMS320C6203 @ 300 MHz	Telecomm	6.8	68.5	10.1

Figure 1.31 The performance of three embedded processors on C and hand-coded versions of portions of the EEMBC benchmark suite. In the case of the BOPS and TI processors, they also provide versions that are compiled but where the C is altered initially to improve performance and code generation; such versions can achieve most of the benefit from hand optimization at least for these machines and these benchmarks.

Measurement	Cray X-MP	Hitachi S810/20	Performance
A(i) = B(i) * C(i) + D(i) * E(i) (vector length 1000 done 100,000 times)	2.6 secs	1.3 secs	Hitachi two times faster
Vectorized FFT (vector lengths 64, 32, . . . , 2)	3.9 secs	7.7 secs	Cray two times faster

Figure 1.32 Measurements of peak performance and actual performance for the Hitachi S810/20 and the Cray X-MP. Note that the gap between peak and observed performance is large and can vary across benchmarks. Data from pages 18–20 of Lubeck, Moore, and Mendez [1985]. Also see "Fallacies and Pitfalls" in Appendix G.

Fallacy *The best design for a computer is the one that optimizes the primary objective without considering implementation.*

Although in a perfect world where implementation complexity and implementation time could be ignored, this might be true, design complexity is an important factor. Complex designs take longer to complete, prolonging time to market. Given the rapidly improving performance of computers, longer design time means that a design will be less competitive. The architect must be constantly aware of the impact of his design choices on the design time for both hardware and software. The many postponements of the availability of the Itanium processor (roughly a two-year delay from the initial target date) should serve as a topical reminder of the risks of introducing both a new architecture and a complex design. With processor performance increasing by just over 50% per year, each week delay translates to a 1% loss in relative performance!

Pitfall *Neglecting the cost of software in either evaluating a system or examining cost-performance.*

For many years, hardware was so expensive that it clearly dominated the cost of software, but this is no longer true. Software costs in 2001 could have been a large fraction of both the purchase and operational costs of a system. For example, for a medium-size database OLTP server, Microsoft OS software might run about $2000, while the Oracle software would run between $6000 and $9000 for a four-year, one-processor license. Assuming a four-year software lifetime means a total software cost for these two major components of between $8000 and $11,000. A midrange Dell server with 512 MB of memory, Pentium III at 1 GHz, and between 20 and 100 GB of disk would cost roughly the same amount as these two major software components—meaning that software costs are roughly 50% of the total system cost!

Alternatively, consider a professional desktop system, which can be purchased with 1 GHz Pentium III, 128 MB DRAM, 20 GB disk, and a 19-inch monitor for just under $1000. The software costs of a Windows OS and Office 2000 are about $300 if bundled with the system and about double that if purchased separately, so the software costs are somewhere between 23% and 38% of the total cost!

Pitfall   *Falling prey to Amdahl's Law.*

Virtually every practicing computer architect knows Amdahl's Law. Despite this, we almost all occasionally fall into the trap of expending tremendous effort optimizing some aspect of a system before we measure its usage. Only when the overall speedup is unrewarding do we recall that we should have measured the usage of that feature before we spent so much effort enhancing it!

Fallacy   *Synthetic benchmarks predict performance for real programs.*

This fallacy appeared in the first edition of this book, published in 1990. With the arrival and dominance of organizations such as SPEC and TPC, we thought perhaps the computer industry had learned a lesson and reformed its faulty practices, but the emerging embedded market has embraced Dhrystone as its most quoted benchmark! Hence, this fallacy survives.

The best known examples of synthetic benchmarks are Whetstone and Dhrystone. These are not real programs and, as such, may not reflect program behavior for factors not measured. Compiler and hardware optimizations can artificially inflate performance of these benchmarks but not of real programs. The other side of the coin is that because these benchmarks are not natural programs, they don't reward optimizations of behaviors that occur in real programs. Here are some examples:

▪ Optimizing compilers can discard 25% of the Dhrystone code; examples include loops that are only executed once, making the loop overhead instructions unnecessary. To address these problems the authors of the benchmark "require" both optimized and unoptimized code to be reported. In addition, they "forbid" the practice of inline-procedure expansion optimization, since Dhrystone's simple procedure structure allows elimination of all procedure calls at almost no increase in code size.

- Most Whetstone floating-point loops execute small numbers of times or include calls inside the loop. These characteristics are different from many real programs. As a result Whetstone underrewards many loop optimizations and gains little from techniques such as multiple issue (Chapter 3) and vectorization (Appendix G).

- Compilers can optimize a key piece of the Whetstone loop by noting the relationship between square root and exponential, even though this is very unlikely to occur in real programs. For example, one key loop contains the following FORTRAN code:

```
X = SQRT(EXP(ALOG(X)/T1))
```

It could be compiled as if it were

```
X = EXP(ALOG(X)/(2×T1))
```

since

$$\text{SQRT(EXP(X))} = \sqrt[2]{e^X} = e^{X/2} = \text{EXP(X/2)}$$

It would be surprising if such optimizations were ever invoked except in this synthetic benchmark. (Yet one reviewer of this book found several compilers that performed this optimization!) This single change converts all calls to the square root function in Whetstone into multiplies by 2, surely improving performance—if Whetstone is your measure.

Fallacy *MIPS is an accurate measure for comparing performance among computers.*

This fallacy also appeared in the first edition of this book, published in 1990. We initially thought it could be retired, but, alas, the embedded market not only uses Dhrystone as the benchmark of choice, but reports performance as "Dhrystone MIPS," a measure that this fallacy will show is problematic.

One alternative to time as the metric is MIPS, or *million instructions per second*. For a given program, MIPS is simply

$$\text{MIPS} = \frac{\text{Instruction count}}{\text{Execution time} \times 10^6} = \frac{\text{Clock rate}}{\text{CPI} \times 10^6}$$

Some find this rightmost form convenient since clock rate is fixed for a machine and CPI is usually a small number, unlike instruction count or execution time. Relating MIPS to time,

$$\text{Execution time} = \frac{\text{Instruction count}}{\text{MIPS} \times 10^6}$$

Since MIPS is a rate of operations per unit time, performance can be specified as the inverse of execution time, with faster machines having a higher MIPS rating.

The good news about MIPS is that it is easy to understand, especially by a customer, and faster machines means bigger MIPS, which matches intuition. The problem with using MIPS as a measure for comparison is threefold:

- MIPS is dependent on the instruction set, making it difficult to compare MIPS of computers with different instruction sets.

- MIPS varies between programs on the same computer.

- Most importantly, MIPS can vary inversely to performance!

The classic example of the last case is the MIPS rating of a machine with optional floating-point hardware. Since it generally takes more clock cycles per floating-point instruction than per integer instruction, floating-point programs using the optional hardware instead of software floating-point routines take less time but have a *lower* MIPS rating. Software floating point executes simpler instructions, resulting in a higher MIPS rating, but it executes so many more that overall execution time is longer.

MIPS is sometimes used by a single vendor (e.g., IBM) within a single set of machines designed for a given class of applications. In such cases, the use of MIPS is less harmful since relative differences among MIPS ratings of machines with the same architecture and the same applications are more likely to track relative performance differences.

To try to avoid the worst difficulties of using MIPS as a performance measure, computer designers began using relative MIPS, which we discuss in detail on page 72, and this is what the embedded market reports for Dhrystone. Although less harmful than an actual MIPS measurement, relative MIPS have their shortcomings (e.g., they are not really MIPS!), especially when measured using Dhrystone!

1.10 Concluding Remarks

This chapter has introduced a number of concepts that we will expand upon as we go through this book. The major ideas in instruction set architecture and the alternatives available will be the primary subjects of Chapter 2. Not only will we see the functional alternatives, we will also examine quantitative data that enable us to understand the trade-offs. The quantitative principle, *Make the common case fast,* will be a guiding light in this next chapter, and the CPU performance equation will be our major tool for examining instruction set alternatives. Chapter 2 concludes an examination of how instruction sets are used by programs.

In Chapter 2, we will include a section, "Crosscutting Issues," that specifically addresses interactions between topics addressed in different chapters. In that section within Chapter 2, we focus on the interactions between compilers and instruction set design. This "Crosscutting Issues" section will appear in all future chapters.

In Chapters 3 and 4 we turn our attention to instruction-level parallelism (ILP), of which pipelining is the simplest and most common form. Exploiting ILP is one of the most important techniques for building high-speed uniprocessors. The presence of two chapters reflects the fact that there are two rather different approaches to exploiting ILP. Chapter 3 begins with an extensive discussion of basic concepts that will prepare you not only for the wide range of ideas examined in both chapters, but also to understand and analyze new techniques that will be introduced in the coming years. Chapter 3 uses examples that span about 35 years, drawing from one of the first modern supercomputers (IBM 360/91) to the fastest processors in the market in 2001. It emphasizes what is called the dynamic or run time approach to exploiting ILP. Chapter 4 focuses on compile time approaches to exploiting ILP. These approaches were heavily used in the early 1990s and return again with the introduction of the Intel Itanium. Appendix A is a version of an introductory chapter on pipelining from the 1995 second edition of this text. For readers without much experience and background in pipelining, that appendix is a useful bridge between the basic topics explored in this chapter (which we expect to be review for many readers, including those of our more introductory text, *Computer Organization and Design: The Hardware/Software Interface*) and the advanced topics in Chapter 3.

In Chapter 5 we turn to the all-important area of memory system design. We will examine a wide range of techniques that conspire to make memory look infinitely large while still being as fast as possible. As in Chapters 3 and 4, we will see that hardware-software cooperation has become a key to high-performance memory systems, just as it has to high-performance pipelines.

Chapter 6 focuses on the issue of achieving higher performance through the use of multiple processors, or multiprocessors. Instead of using parallelism to overlap individual instructions, multiprocessing uses parallelism to allow multiple instruction streams to be executed simultaneously on different processors. Our focus is on the dominant form of multiprocessors, shared-memory multiprocessors, though we introduce other types as well and discuss the broad issues that arise in any multiprocessor. Here again, we explore a variety of techniques, focusing on the important ideas first introduced in the 1980s and 1990s.

In Chapters 7 and 8, we move away from a CPU-centric view and discuss issues in storage systems and interconnect. We apply a similar quantitative approach, but one based on observations of system behavior and using an end-to-end approach to performance analysis. Chapter 7 addresses the important issue of how to efficiently store and retrieve data using primarily lower-cost magnetic storage technologies. As we saw earlier, such technologies offer better cost per bit by a factor of 50–100 over DRAM. Magnetic storage is likely to remain advantageous wherever cost or nonvolatility (it keeps the information after the power is turned off) are important. In Chapter 7, our focus is on examining the performance of disk storage systems for typical I/O-intensive workloads, like the OLTP benchmarks we saw in this chapter. We extensively explore the idea of RAID-based systems, which use many small disks, arranged in a redundant fashion, to achieve both high performance and high availability. Chapter 8 discusses the primary interconnection technology used for I/O devices. This chapter explores the topic of system interconnect more broadly, including wide area and system area networks used to allow computers to communicate. Chapter 8 also describes clusters, which are growing in importance due to their suitability and efficiency for database and Web server applications.

1.11   Historical Perspective and References

If ... history ... teaches us anything, it is that man in his quest for knowledge and progress, is determined and cannot be deterred.

John F. Kennedy
address at Rice University (1962)

A section on historical perspective closes each chapter in the text. This section provides historical background on some of the key ideas presented in the chapter. We may trace the development of an idea through a series of machines or describe significant projects. If you're interested in examining the initial development of an idea or machine or interested in further reading, references are provided at the end of the section. In this historical section, we discuss the early development of digital computers and the development of performance measurement methodologies. The development of the key innovations in desktop, server, and embedded processor architectures are discussed in historical sections in virtually every chapter of the book.

The First General-Purpose Electronic Computers

J. Presper Eckert and John Mauchly at the Moore School of the University of Pennsylvania built the world's first fully operational electronic general-purpose computer. This machine, called ENIAC (Electronic Numerical Integrator and Calculator), was funded by the U.S. Army and became operational during World War II, but it was not publicly disclosed until 1946. ENIAC was used for computing artillery firing tables. The machine was enormous—100 feet long, $8^1/_2$ feet high, and several feet wide. Each of the 20 ten-digit registers was 2 feet long. In total, there were 18,000 vacuum tubes.

Although the size was three orders of magnitude bigger than the size of the average machines built today, it was more than five orders of magnitude slower, with an add taking 200 microseconds. The ENIAC provided conditional jumps and was programmable, which clearly distinguished it from earlier calculators. Programming was done manually by plugging up cables and setting switches and required from a half hour to a whole day. Data were provided on punched cards. The ENIAC was limited primarily by a small amount of storage and tedious programming.

In 1944, John von Neumann was attracted to the ENIAC project. The group wanted to improve the way programs were entered and discussed storing programs as numbers; von Neumann helped crystallize the ideas and wrote a memo proposing a stored-program computer called EDVAC (Electronic Discrete Variable Automatic Computer). Herman Goldstine distributed the memo and put von Neumann's name on it, much to the dismay of Eckert and Mauchly, whose names were omitted. This memo has served as the basis for the commonly used term *von Neumann computer*. Several early inventors in the computer field believe that this term gives too much credit to von Neumann, who conceptualized and wrote up the ideas, and too little to the engineers, Eckert and Mauchly, who worked on the machines. Like most historians, your authors (winners of the 2000 IEEE von Neumann Medal) believe that all three individuals played a key role in developing the stored-program computer. Von Neumann's role in writing up the ideas, in generalizing them, and in thinking about the programming aspects was critical in transferring the ideas to a wider audience.

In 1946, Maurice Wilkes of Cambridge University visited the Moore School to attend the latter part of a series of lectures on developments in electronic computers. When he returned to Cambridge, Wilkes decided to embark on a project to build a stored-program computer named EDSAC (Electronic Delay Storage Automatic Calculator). (The EDSAC used mercury delay lines for its memory; hence the phrase "delay storage" in its name.) The EDSAC became operational in 1949 and was the world's first full-scale, operational, stored-program computer [Wilkes, Wheeler, and Gill 1951; Wilkes 1985, 1995]. (A small prototype called the Mark I, which was built at the University of Manchester and ran in 1948, might be called the first operational stored-program machine.) The EDSAC was an accumulator-based architecture. This style of instruction set architecture remained popular until the early 1970s. (Chapter 2 starts with a brief summary of the EDSAC instruction set.)

In 1947, Eckert and Mauchly applied for a patent on electronic computers. The dean of the Moore School, by demanding the patent be turned over to the university, may have helped Eckert and Mauchly conclude they should leave. Their departure crippled the EDVAC project, which did not become operational until 1952.

Goldstine left to join von Neumann at the Institute for Advanced Study at Princeton in 1946. Together with Arthur Burks, they issued a report based on the 1944 memo [Burks, Goldstine, and von Newmann 1946]. The paper led to the IAS machine built by Julian Bigelow at Princeton's Institute for Advanced Study. It had a total of 1024 40-bit words and was roughly 10 times faster than ENIAC. The group thought about uses for the machine, published a set of reports, and encouraged visitors. These reports and visitors inspired the development of a number of new computers, including the first IBM computer, the 701, which was based on the IAS machine. The paper by Burks, Goldstine, and von Neumann was incredible for the period. Reading it today, you would never guess this landmark paper was written more than 50 years ago, as most of the architectural concepts seen in modern computers are discussed there (e.g., see the quote at the beginning of Chapter 5).

In the same time period as ENIAC, Howard Aiken was designing an electromechanical computer called the Mark-I at Harvard. The Mark-I was built by a team of engineers from IBM. He followed the Mark-I by a relay machine, the Mark-II, and a pair of vacuum tube machines, the Mark-III and Mark-IV. The Mark-III and Mark-IV were built after the first stored-program machines. Because they had separate memories for instructions and data, the machines were regarded as reactionary by the advocates of stored-program computers. The term

Harvard architecture was coined to describe this type of machine. Though clearly different from the original sense, this term is used today to apply to machines with a single main memory but with separate instruction and data caches.

The Whirlwind project [Redmond and Smith 1980] began at MIT in 1947 and was aimed at applications in real-time radar signal processing. Although it led to several inventions, its overwhelming innovation was the creation of magnetic core memory, the first reliable and inexpensive memory technology. Whirlwind had 2048 16-bit words of magnetic core. Magnetic cores served as the main memory technology for nearly 30 years.

Important Special-Purpose Machines

During the Second World War, there were major computing efforts in both Great Britain and the United States focused on special-purpose code-breaking computers. The work in Great Britain was aimed at decrypting messages encoded with the German Enigma coding machine. This work, which occurred at a location called Bletchley Park, led to two important machines. The first, an electromechanical machine, conceived of by Alan Turing, was called BOMB [see Good in Metropolis, Howlett, and Rota 1980]. The second, much larger and electronic machine, conceived and designed by Newman and Flowers, was called COLOSSUS [see Randall in Metropolis, Howlett, and Rota 1980]. These were highly specialized cryptanalysis machines, which played a vital role in the war by providing the ability to read coded messages, especially those sent to U-boats. The work at Bletchley Park was highly classified (indeed some of it is still classified), and so its direct impact on the development of ENIAC, EDSAC, and other computers is hard to trace, but it certainly had an indirect effect in advancing the technology and gaining understanding of the issues.

Similar work on special-purpose computers for cryptanalysis went on in the United States. The most direct descendent of this effort was a company, Engineering Research Associates (ERA) [see Thomash in Metropolis, Howlett, and Rota 1980], which was founded after the war to attempt to commercialize on the key ideas. ERA built several machines, which were sold to secret government agencies, and was eventually purchased by Sperry-Rand, which had earlier purchased the Eckert Mauchly Computer Corporation.

Another early set of machines that deserves credit was a group of special-purpose machines built by Konrad Zuse in Germany in the late 1930s and early 1940s [see Bauer and Zuse in Metropolis, Howlett, and Rota 1980]. In addition to producing an operating machine, Zuse was the first to implement floating point, which von Neumann claimed was unnecessary! His early machines used a mechanical store that was smaller than other electromechanical solutions of the time. His last machine was electromechanical but, because of the war, was never completed.

An important early contributor to the development of electronic computers was John Atanasoff, who built a small-scale electronic computer in the early

1940s [Atanasoff 1940]. His machine, designed at Iowa State University, was a special-purpose computer (called the ABC—Atanasoff Berry Computer) that was never completely operational. Mauchly briefly visited Atanasoff before he built ENIAC, and several of Atanasoff's ideas (e.g., using binary representation) likely influenced Mauchly. The presence of the Atanasoff machine, together with delays in filing the ENIAC patents (the work was classified, and patents could not be filed until after the war) and the distribution of von Neumann's EDVAC paper, were used to break the Eckert-Mauchly patent [Larson 1973]. Though controversy still rages over Atanasoff's role, Eckert and Mauchly are usually given credit for building the first working, general-purpose, electronic computer [Stern 1980]. Atanasoff, however, demonstrated several important innovations included in later computers. Atanasoff deserves much credit for his work, and he might fairly be given credit for the world's first special-purpose electronic computer and for possibly influencing Eckert and Mauchly.

Commercial Developments

In December 1947, Eckert and Mauchly formed Eckert-Mauchly Computer Corporation. Their first machine, the BINAC, was built for Northrop and was shown in August 1949. After some financial difficulties, the Eckert-Mauchly Computer Corporation was acquired by Remington-Rand, later called Sperry-Rand. Sperry-Rand merged the Eckert-Mauchly acquisition, ERA, and its tabulating business to form a dedicated computer division, called UNIVAC. UNIVAC delivered its first computer, the UNIVAC I, in June 1951. The UNIVAC I sold for $250,000 and was the first successful commercial computer—48 systems were built! Today, this early machine, along with many other fascinating pieces of computer lore, can be seen at the Computer Museum in Mountain View, California. Other places where early computing systems can be visited include the Deutsches Museum in Munich and the Smithsonian in Washington, D.C., as well as numerous online virtual museums.

IBM, which earlier had been in the punched card and office automation business, didn't start building computers until 1950. The first IBM computer, the IBM 701 based on von Neumann's IAS machine, shipped in 1952 and eventually sold 19 units [see Hurd in Metropolis, Howlett, and Rota 1980]. In the early 1950s, many people were pessimistic about the future of computers, believing that the market and opportunities for these "highly specialized" machines were quite limited. Nonetheless, IBM quickly became the most successful computer company. The focus on reliability and a customer- and market-driven strategy was key. Although the 701 and 702 were modest successes, IBM's follow-on machines, the 650, 704, and 705 (delivered in 1954 and 1955) were significant successes, each selling from 132 to 1800 computers.

Several books describing the early days of computing have been written by the pioneers [Wilkes 1985, 1995; Goldstine 1972], as well as Metropolis, Howlett, and Rota [1980], which is a collection of recollections by early pioneers. There are numerous independent histories, often built around the people involved [Slater 1987], as well as a journal, *Annals of the History of Computing,* devoted to the history of computing.

The history of some of the computers invented after 1960 can be found in Chapter 2 (the IBM 360, the DEC VAX, the Intel 80x86, and the early RISC machines), Chapters 3 and 4 (the pipelined processors, including Stretch and the CDC 6600), and Appendix G (vector processors including the TI ASC, CDC Star, and Cray processors).

Development of Quantitative Performance Measures: Successes and Failures

In the earliest days of computing, designers set performance goals—ENIAC was to be 1000 times faster than the Harvard Mark-I, and the IBM Stretch (7030) was to be 100 times faster than the fastest machine in existence. What wasn't clear, though, was how this performance was to be measured. In looking back over the years, it is a consistent theme that each generation of computers obsoletes the performance evaluation techniques of the prior generation.

The original measure of performance was time to perform an individual operation, such as addition. Since most instructions took the same execution time, the timing of one gave insight into the others. As the execution times of instructions in a machine became more diverse, however, the time for one operation was no longer useful for comparisons. To take these differences into account, an *instruction mix* was calculated by measuring the relative frequency of instructions in a computer across many programs. The Gibson mix [Gibson 1970] was an early popular instruction mix. Multiplying the time for each instruction times its weight in the mix gave the user the *average instruction execution time.* (If measured in clock cycles, average instruction execution time is the same as average CPI.) Since instruction sets were similar, this was a more accurate comparison than add times. From average instruction execution time, then, it was only a small step to MIPS (as we have seen, the one is the inverse of the other). MIPS had the virtue of being easy for the layperson to understand.

As CPUs became more sophisticated and relied on memory hierarchies and pipelining, there was no longer a single execution time per instruction; MIPS could not be calculated from the mix and the manual. The next step was benchmarking using kernels and synthetic programs. Curnow and Wichmann [1976] created the Whetstone synthetic program by measuring scientific programs written in Algol 60. This program was converted to FORTRAN and was widely used to characterize scientific program performance. An effort with similar goals to Whetstone, the Livermore FORTRAN Kernels, was made by McMahon [1986] and researchers at Lawrence Livermore Laboratory in an attempt to establish a benchmark for supercomputers. These kernels, however, consisted of loops from real programs.

As it became clear that using MIPS to compare architectures with different instruction sets would not work, a notion of relative MIPS was created. When the VAX-11/780 was ready for announcement in 1977, DEC ran small benchmarks that were also run on an IBM 370/158. IBM marketing referred to the 370/158 as a 1 MIPS computer, and since the programs ran at the same speed, DEC marketing called the VAX-11/780 a 1 MIPS computer. Relative MIPS for a machine M was defined based on some reference machine as

$$\text{MIPS}_M = \frac{\text{Performance}_M}{\text{Performance}_{\text{reference}}} \times \text{MIPS}_{\text{reference}}$$

The popularity of the VAX-11/780 made it a popular reference machine for relative MIPS, especially since relative MIPS for a 1 MIPS computer is easy to calculate: If a machine was five times faster than the VAX-11/780, for that benchmark its rating would be 5 relative MIPS. The 1 MIPS rating was unquestioned for four years, until Joel Emer of DEC measured the VAX-11/780 under a time-sharing load. He found that the VAX-11/780 native MIPS rating was 0.5. Subsequent VAXes that run 3 native MIPS for some benchmarks were therefore called 6 MIPS machines because they run six times faster than the VAX-11/780. By the early 1980s, the term MIPS was almost universally used to mean relative MIPS.

The 1970s and 1980s marked the growth of the supercomputer industry, which was defined by high performance on floating-point-intensive programs. Average instruction time and MIPS were clearly inappropriate metrics for this industry, hence the invention of MFLOPS (millions of floating-point operations per second), which effectively measured the inverse of execution time for a benchmark. Unfortunately customers quickly forget the program used for the rating, and marketing groups decided to start quoting peak MFLOPS in the supercomputer performance wars.

SPEC (System Performance and Evaluation Cooperative) was founded in the late 1980s to try to improve the state of benchmarking and make a more valid basis for comparison. The group initially focused on workstations and servers in the UNIX marketplace, and that remains the primary focus of these benchmarks today. The first release of SPEC benchmarks, now called SPEC89, was a substantial improvement in the use of more realistic benchmarks.

References

Amdahl, G. M. [1967]. "Validity of the single processor approach to achieving large scale computing capabilities," *Proc. AFIPS 1967 Spring Joint Computer Conf.* 30 (April), Atlantic City, N.J., 483–485.

Atanasoff, J. V. [1940]. "Computing machine for the solution of large systems of linear equations," Internal Report, Iowa State University, Ames.

Bell, C. G. [1984]. "The mini and micro industries," *IEEE Computer* 17:10 (October), 14–30.

Bell, C. G., J. C. Mudge, and J. E. McNamara [1978]. *A DEC View of Computer Engineering*, Digital Press, Bedford, Mass.

Burks, A. W., H. H. Goldstine, and J. von Neumann [1946]. "Preliminary discussion of the logical design of an electronic computing instrument," Report to the U.S. Army Ordnance Department, p. 1; also appears in *Papers of John von Neumann,* W. Aspray and A. Burks, eds., MIT Press, Cambridge, Mass., and Tomash Publishers, Los Angeles, Calif., 1987, 97–146.

Curnow, H. J., and B. A. Wichmann [1976]. "A synthetic benchmark," *The Computer J.,* 19:1, 43–49.

Flemming, P. J., and J. J. Wallace [1986]. "How not to lie with statistics: The correct way to summarize benchmarks results," *Comm. ACM* 29:3 (March), 218–221.

Fuller, S. H., and W. E. Burr [1977]. "Measurement and evaluation of alternative computer architectures," *Computer* 10:10 (October), 24–35.

Gibson, J. C. [1970]. "The Gibson mix," Rep. TR. 00.2043, IBM Systems Development Division, Poughkeepsie, N.Y. (Research done in 1959.)

Goldstine, H. H. [1972]. *The Computer: From Pascal to von Neumann,* Princeton University Press, Princeton, N.J.

Jain, R. [1991]. *The Art of Computer Systems Performance Analysis: Techniques for Experimental Design, Measurement, Simulation, and Modeling,* Wiley, New York.

Larson, E. R. [1973]. "Findings of fact, conclusions of law, and order for judgment," File No. 4-67, Civ. 138, *Honeywell v. Sperry-Rand and Illinois Scientific Development,* U.S. District Court for the State of Minnesota, Fourth Division (October 19).

Lubeck, O., J. Moore, and R. Mendez [1985]. "A benchmark comparison of three supercomputers: Fujitsu VP-200, Hitachi S810/20, and Cray X-MP/2," *Computer* 18:12 (December), 10–24.

McMahon, F. M. [1986]. "The Livermore FORTRAN kernels: A computer test of numerical performance range," Tech. Rep. UCRL-55745, Lawrence Livermore National Laboratory, Univ. of California, Livermore (December).

Metropolis, N., J. Howlett, and G-C Rota, eds. [1980]. *A History of Computing in the Twentieth Century,* Academic Press, New York.

Redmond, K. C., and T. M. Smith [1980]. *Project Whirlwind—The History of a Pioneer Computer,* Digital Press, Boston.

Shurkin, J. [1984]. *Engines of the Mind: A History of the Computer*, W. W. Norton, New York.

Slater, R. [1987]. *Portraits in Silicon,* MIT Press, Cambridge, Mass.

Smith, J. E. [1988]. "Characterizing computer performance with a single number," *Comm. ACM* 31:10 (October), 1202–1206.

SPEC [1989]. *SPEC Benchmark Suite Release 1.0* (October 2).

SPEC [1994]. *SPEC Newsletter* (June).

Stern, N. [1980]. "Who invented the first electronic digital computer?" *Annals of the History of Computing* 2:4 (October), 375–376.

Touma, W. R. [1993]. *The Dynamics of the Computer Industry: Modeling the Supply of Workstations and Their Components,* Kluwer Academic, Boston.

Weicker, R. P. [1984]. "Dhrystone: A synthetic systems programming benchmark," *Comm. ACM* 27:10 (October), 1013–1030.

Wilkes, M. V. [1985]. *Memoirs of a Computer Pioneer,* MIT Press, Cambridge, Mass.

Wilkes, M. V. [1995]. *Computing Perspectives,* Morgan Kaufmann, San Francisco.

Wilkes, M. V., D. J. Wheeler, and S. Gill [1951]. *The Preparation of Programs for an Electronic Digital Computer*, Addison-Wesley, Cambridge, Mass.

Exercises

Each exercise has a difficulty rating in square brackets and a list of the chapter sections it depends on in angle brackets. See the Preface for a description of the difficulty scale. Solutions to the "starred" exercises appear in Appendix B.

1.1 [15/15/15/15] <1.3, 1.4, 7.2> Computer system designers must be alert to the rapid change of computer technology. To see one example of how radically change can affect design, consider the evolution of DRAM and magnetic disk technologies since publication of the first edition of this text in 1990. At that time DRAM density had been improving for 10 years at a rate of about 60% per year, giving rise every third year to a new generation of DRAM chips with four times more capacity than before. Magnetic disk data recording density had been improving for 30 years at nearly 30% per year, doubling every three years.

   a. [15] <1.3> The first edition posed a question much like this. Assume that cost per megabyte for either type of storage is proportional to density, that 1990 is the start of the 4M bit DRAM generation, and that in 1990 DRAM costs 20 times more per megabyte than disk. Using the well-established historic density improvement rates, create a table showing projected relative cost of each DRAM generation and disk from 1990 for six generations. What conclusion can be drawn about the future of disk drives in computer designs and about the magnetic disk industry from this projection?

   b. [15] <1.4, 7.2> The conclusion supported by the result from part (a) is far from today's reality. Shortly before 1990 the change from inductive heads to thin film, and then magnetoresistive heads, allowed magnetic disk recording density to begin a 60% annual improvement trend, matching DRAM. Since about 1997, giant magnetoresistive effect heads have upped the rate to 100% per year, and, available to the mass market in 2001, antiferromagnetically coupled recording media should support or improve that rate for several years. Using data from Figures 1.5 and 7.4, plot the actual ratio of DRAM to disk price per unit of storage for each DRAM generation (3-year intervals) starting in 1983. Compare your answer with part (a) by including those data points on the graph. Assume that DRAM storage is built from the then-available chip size with the lowest cost per bit and that disk cost is the median cost for that year. Note that 1 GB = 1000 MB. Ignore the cost of any packaging, support hardware, and control hardware needed to incorporate DRAM and disk into a computer system.

   c. [15] <1.3> Not only price, but disk physical volume and mass improve with recording density. Today's standard laptop computer disk drive bay is 10 cm long and 7 cm wide. Assume that a 100 MB disk in 1990 occupied 500 cc (cubic centimeters) and massed 1000 g (grams). If disk volume and mass had improved only 30% per year since 1990, what would the height (neglect mechanical constraints on disk drive shape) and mass of a 30 GB laptop computer disk be today? For comparison, actual typical height and mass values for 2001 are 1.25 cm and 100 g.

d. [15] <1.3, 1.4> Increasing disk recording density expands the range of software applications possible at a given computer price point. High-quality desktop digital video editing capability is available in 2001 on a $1000 PC. Five minutes of digital video consumes about 1 GB of storage, so the 20 GB disk of the PC in Figure 1.9 provides reasonable capacity. If disk density had improved only at 30% per year since 1990, but other PC component costs shown in Figure 1.9 were unchanged and the ratio of retail price to component cost given in Figure 1.10 was unaffected, approximately how much more would a desktop video PC cost in 2001?

1.2 [20/10/10/10/15] <1.6> In this exercise, assume that we are considering enhancing a machine by adding vector hardware to it. When a computation is run in vector mode on the vector hardware, it is 10 times faster than the normal mode of execution. We call the percentage of time that could be spent using vector mode the *percentage of vectorization*.Vectors are discussed in Appendix G, but you don't need to know anything about how they work to answer this question!

a. [20] <1.6> Draw a graph that plots the speedup as a percentage of the computation performed in vector mode. Label the y-axis "Net speedup" and label the x-axis "Percent vectorization."

b. [10] <1.6> What percentage of vectorization is needed to achieve a speedup of 2?

c. [10] <1.6> What percentage of the computation run time is spent in vector mode if a speedup of 2 is achieved?

d. [10] <1.6> What percentage of vectorization is needed to achieve one-half the maximum speedup attainable from using vector mode?

e. [15] <1.6> Suppose you have measured the percentage of vectorization for programs to be 70%. The hardware design group says they can double the speed of the vector hardware with a significant additional engineering investment. You wonder whether the compiler crew could increase the use of vector mode as another approach to increasing performance. How much of an increase in the percentage of vectorization (relative to current usage) would you need to obtain the same performance gain as doubling vector hardware speed? Which investment would you recommend?

1.3 [15/10] <1.6> Assume—as in the Amdahl's Law example on page 41—that we make an enhancement to a computer that improves some mode of execution by a factor of 10. Enhanced mode is used 50% of the time, measured as a percentage of the execution time *when the enhanced mode is in use*. Recall that Amdahl's Law depends on the fraction of the original, *unenhanced* execution time that could make use of enhanced mode. Thus, we cannot directly use this 50% measurement to compute speedup with Amdahl's Law.

a. [15] <1.6> What is the speedup we have obtained from fast mode?

b. [10] <1.6> What percentage of the original execution time has been converted to fast mode?

✪ 1.4 [12/10/Discussion] <1.6> Amdahl's Law implies that the ultimate goal of high-performance computer system design should be an enhancement that offers arbitrarily large speedup for all of the task time. Perhaps surprisingly, this goal can be approached quite closely with real computers and tasks. Section 3.5 describes how some branch instructions can, with high likelihood, be executed in zero time with a hardware enhancement called a branch-target buffer. Arbitrarily large speedup can be achieved for complex computational tasks when more efficient algorithms are developed. A classic example from the field of digital signal processing is the discrete Fourier transform (DFT) and the more efficient fast Fourier transform (FFT). How these two transforms work is not important here. All we need to know is that they compute the same result, and with an input of n floating-point data values, a DFT algorithm will execute approximately n^2 floating-point instructions, while the FFT algorithm will execute approximately $n \log_2 n$ floating-point instructions.

a. [12] <1.6> Ignore instructions other than floating point. What is the speedup gained by using the FFT instead of the DFT for an input of $n = 2^k$ floating-point values in the range $8 \leq n \leq 1024$ and also in the limit as $n \rightarrow \infty$?

b. [10] <1.6> When $n = 1024$, what is the percentage reduction in the number of executed floating-point instructions when using the FFT rather than the DFT?

c. [Discussion] <1.6> Despite the speedup achieved by processors with a branch-target buffer, not only do processors without such a buffer remain in production, new processor designs without this enhancement are still developed. Yet, once the FFT became known, the DFT was abandoned. Certainly speedup is desirable. What reasons can you think of to explain this asymmetry in use of a hardware and a software enhancement, and what does your answer say about the economics of hardware and algorithm technologies?

1.5 [15] <1.6> Show that the problem statements in the examples on pages 42 and 44 describe identical situations and equivalent design alternatives.

✪ 1.6 [15] <1.9> Dhrystone is a well-known integer benchmark. Computer A is measured to perform D_A executions of the Dhrystone benchmark per second, and to achieve a millions of instructions per second rate of $MIPS_A$ while doing Dhrystone. Computer B is measured to perform D_B executions of the Dhrystone benchmark per second. What is the fallacy in calculating the MIPS rating of computer B as $MIPS_B = MIPS_A \times (D_B / D_A)$?

1.7 [15/15/8] <1.9> A certain benchmark contains 195,578 floating-point operations, with the details shown in Figure 1.33.

The benchmark was run on an embedded processor after compilation with optimization turned on. The embedded processor is based on a current RISC processor that includes floating-point function units, but the embedded processor does not include floating point for reasons of cost, power consumption, and lack of need for floating point by the target applications. The compiler allows floating-point instructions to be calculated with the hardware units or using software routines, depending on compiler flags. The benchmark took 1.08 seconds on the

Operation	Count
Add	82,014
Subtract	8,229
Multiply	73,220
Divide	21,399
Convert integer to FP	6,006
Compare	4,710
Total	195,578

Figure 1.33 Occurrences of floating-point operations.

RISC processor and 13.6 seconds using software on its embedded version. Assume that the CPI using the RISC processor was measured to be 10, while the CPI of the embedded version of the processor was measured to be 6.

a. [15] <1.9> What is the total number of instructions executed for both runs?

b. [15] <1.9> What is the MIPS rating for both runs?

c. [8] <1.9> On the average, how many integer instructions docs it take to perform a floating-point operation in software?

1.8   [15/10/15/15/15] <1.3, 1.4> This exercise estimates the complete packaged cost of a microprocessor using the die cost equation and adding in packaging and testing costs. We begin with a short description of testing cost and follow with a discussion of packaging issues.

Testing is the second term of the chip cost equation:

$$\text{Cost of integrated circuit} = \frac{\text{Cost of die} + \text{Cost of testing die} + \text{Cost of packaging}}{\text{Final test yield}}$$

Testing costs are determined by three components:

$$\text{Cost of testing die} = \frac{\text{Cost of testing per hour} \times \text{Average die test time}}{\text{Die yield}}$$

Since bad dies are discarded, die yield is in the denominator in the equation—the good must shoulder the costs of testing those that fail. (In practice, a bad die may take less time to test, but this effect is small, since moving the probes on the die is a mechanical process that takes a large fraction of the time.) Testing costs about $50 to $500 per hour, depending on the tester needed. High-end designs with many high-speed pins require the more expensive testers. For higher-end microprocessors test time would run $300 to $500 per hour. Die tests take about 5 to 90 seconds on average, depending on the simplicity of the die and the provisions to reduce testing time included in the chip.

The cost of a package depends on the material used, the number of pins, and the die area. The cost of the material used in the package is in part determined by the ability to dissipate heat generated by the die. For example, a *plastic quad flat pack* (PQFP) dissipating less than 1 W, with 208 or fewer pins, and containing a die up to 1 cm on a side costs $2 in 2001. A ceramic *pin grid array* (PGA) can handle 300 to 600 pins and a larger die with more power, but it costs $20 to $60. In addition to the cost of the package itself is the cost of the labor to place a die in the package and then bond the pads to the pins, which adds from a few cents to a dollar or two to the cost. Some good dies are typically lost in the assembly process, thereby further reducing yield. For simplicity we assume the final test yield is 1.0; in practice it is at least 0.95. We also ignore the cost of the final packaged test.

This exercise requires the information provided in Figure 1.34.

a. [15] <1.4> For each of the microprocessors in Figure 1.34, compute the number of good chips you would get per 20 cm wafer using the model on page 19. Assume a defect density of 0.5 defect per cm^2, a wafer yield of 95%, and $\alpha = 4$.

b. [10] <1.4> For each microprocessor in Figure 1.34, compute the cost per projected good die before packaging and testing. Use the number of good dies per wafer from part (a) of this exercise and the wafer cost from Figure 1.34.

c. [15] <1.3> Using the additional assumptions shown in Figure 1.35, compute the cost per good, tested, and packaged part using the costs per good die from part (b) of this exercise.

d. [15] <1.3> There are wide differences in defect densities between semiconductor manufacturers. Find the costs for the largest processor in Figure 1.34 (total cost including packaging), assuming defect densities are 0.3 per cm^2 and assuming that defect densities are 1.0 per cm^2.

e. [15] <1.3> The parameter α depends on the complexity of the process. Additional metal levels result in increased complexity. For example, α might be approximated by the number of interconnect levels. For the Digital 21064C with six levels of interconnect, estimate the cost of working, packaged, and tested die if $\alpha = 4$ and if $\alpha = 6$. Assume a defect density of 0.8 defects per cm^2.

Microprocessor	Die area (mm^2)	Pins	Technology	Estimated wafer cost ($)	Package
Alpha 21264C	115	524	CMOS, 0.18μ, 6M	4700	CLGA
Power3-II	163	1088	CMOS, 0.22μ, 6M	4000	SLC
Itanium	300	418	CMOS, 0.18μ, 6M	4900	PAC
MIPS R14000	204	527	CMOS, 0.25μ, 4M	3700	CPGA
UltraSPARC III	210	1368	CMOS, 0.15μ, 6M	5200	FC-LGA

Figure 1.34 Characteristics of microprocessors. About half of the pins are for power and ground connections. The technology entry is the process type, line width, and number of interconnect levels.

Package type	Pin count	Package cost ($)	Test time (secs)	Test cost per hour ($)
PAC	< 500	20	30	400
SLC	< 1100	20	20	420
Grid array (CLGA, CPGA, or FC-LGA)	< 500	20	20	400
Grid array (CLGA, CPGA, or FC-LGA)	< 1000	25	25	440
Grid array (CLGA, CPGA, or FC-LGA)	< 1500	30	30	480

Figure 1.35 Package and test characteristics.

1.9 [20/20] <1.4> On page 20 the concluding discussion about the die cost model claims that, for realistic die sizes and defect densities, die cost is better modeled as a function of (roughly) the die area squared rather than to the fourth power.

    a. [20] <1.4> Using the model and a spreadsheet, determine the cost of dies ranging in area from 0.5 to 4 cm^2 and assuming a defect density of 0.6 and α = 4. Next, use a mathematical analysis tool for fitting polynomial curves to fit the (die area, die cost) data pairs you computed in the spreadsheet. What is the lowest degree polynomial that is a close fit to the data?

    b. [20] <1.4> Suppose defect densities were much higher: say, 2 defects per cm^2. Now what is lowest degree polynomial that is a close fit?

✪ 1.10 [15/15/10] <1.5, 1.9> Assume the two programs in Figure 1.15 each execute 100 million floating-point operations during execution on each of the three machines. If performance is expressed as a rate, then the average that tracks total execution time is the *harmonic mean,*

$$\frac{n}{\sum_{i=1}^{n} \frac{1}{Rate_i}}$$

where Rate$_i$ is a function of $1/Time_i$, the execution time for the ith of n programs in the workload.

    a. [15] <1.5, 1.9> Calculate the MFLOPS rating of each program.

    b. [15] <1.5, 1.9> Calculate the arithmetic, geometric, and harmonic means of MFLOPS for each machine.

    c. [10] <1.5, 1.9> Which of the three means matches the relative performance of total execution time?

1.11 [12] <1.5> One reason people may incorrectly summarize rate data using an arithmetic mean is that it always gives an answer greater than or equal to the geometric mean. Show that for any two positive integers, a and b, the arithmetic mean is always greater than or equal to the geometric mean. When are the two equal?

1.12   [12] <1.5> For reasons similar to those in Exercise 1.11, some people use arithmetic mean instead of harmonic mean (see the definition of harmonic mean in Exercise 1.10). Show that for any two positive rates, r and s, the arithmetic mean is always greater than or equal to the harmonic mean. When are the two equal?

✪ 1.13   [10/10/10/10] <1.5> Sometimes we have a set of computer performance measurements that range from very slow to very fast execution. A single statistic, such as a mean, may not capture a useful sense of the data set as a whole. For example, the CPU pipeline and hard disk subsystem of a computer execute their respective basic processing steps at speeds that differ by a factor of typically 10^7. This is a speed difference in excess of that between a jet airliner in cruising flight (~1000 kilometers per hour) and a snail gliding on the long, thin leaf of an agapanthus (perhaps 1 meter per hour). Let's look at what happens when measurements with such a large range are summarized by a single number.

a. [10] <1.5> What are the arithmetic means of two sets of benchmark measurements, one with nine values of 10^7 and one value of 1 and the other set with nine values of 1 and one value of 10^7? How do these means compare with the data set medians? Which outlying data point affects the arithmetic mean more, a large or a small value?

b. [10] <1.5> What are the harmonic means (see Exercise 1.10 for the definition of harmonic mean) of the two sets of measurements specified in part (a)? How do these means compare with the data set medians? Which outlying data point affects the harmonic mean more, a large or a small value?

c. [10] <1.5> Which mean, arithmetic or harmonic, produces a statistic closest to the median?

d. [10] <1.5> Repeat parts (a) and (b) for two sets of 10 benchmark measurements with the outlying value only a factor of 2 larger or smaller. How representative of the entire set do the arithmetic and harmonic mean statistics seem for this narrow range of performance values?

1.14   [15/15] <1.5> A spreadsheet is useful for performing the computations of this exercise. Some of the results from the SPEC2000 Web site (*www.spec.org*) are shown in Figure 1.36. The *reference time* is the execution time for a particular computer system chosen by SPEC as a performance reference for all other tested systems. The *base ratio* is simply the run time for a benchmark divided into the reference time for that benchmark. The SPECfp_base2000 statistic is computed as the geometric mean of the base ratios. Let's see how a weighted arithmetic mean compares.

a. [15] <1.5> Calculate the weights for a workload so that running times on the reference computer will be equal for each of the 14 benchmarks in Figure 1.36.

SPEC CFP2000 program name	Reference time	Base ratio		
		Compaq AlphaServer ES40 Model 6/667	IBM eServer pSeries 640	Intel VC820
168.wupwise	1600	458	307	393
171.swim	3100	1079	227	406
172.mgrid	1800	525	284	246
173.applu	2100	386	311	244
177.mesa	1400	502	273	535
178.galgel	2900	445	380	295
179.art	2600	1238	924	379
183.equake	1300	220	528	233
187.facerec	1900	677	215	296
188.ammp	2200	405	272	283
189.lucas	2000	639	261	312
191.fma3d	2100	472	305	282
200.sixtrack	1100	273	205	169
301.apsi	2600	445	292	345
SPECfp_base2000 (geometric mean)		500	313	304

Figure 1.36 SPEC2000 performance for SPEC CFP2000. *Reference time* for each program is for a particular Sun Microsystems Ultra 10 computer configuration. *Base ratio* is the measured execution time of an executable generated by conservative compiler optimization, which is required to be identical for each program, divided into the reference time and is expressed as a percentage. SPECfp_base2000 is the geometric mean of the 14 base ratio values; it would be 100 for the reference computer system. The Compaq AlphaServer ES40 6/667 uses a 667 MHz Alpha 21164A microprocessor and an 8 MB off-chip tertiary cache. The IBM eServer pSeries 640 uses a 375 MHz Power3-II CPU and a 4 MB off-chip secondary cache. The Intel VC820 uses a 1000 MHz Pentium III processor with a 256 KB on-chip secondary cache. Data are from the SPEC Web site (*www.spec.orq*).

b. [15] <1.5> Using the weights computed in part (a) of this exercise, calculate the weighted arithmetic means of the execution times of the 14 programs in Figure 1.36.

1.15 [15/20/15] <1.5> "The only consistent and reliable measure of performance is the execution time of real programs" [page 25].

a. [15] <1.5> For the execution time of a real program on a given computer system to have a meaningful value, two conditions must be satisfied. One has to do with the conditions within the computer system at the time of measurement, and the other has to do with the measured program itself. What are the conditions?

b. [20] <1.5> Programs such as operating systems, Web servers, device drivers, and TCP/IP stacks are intended to either not terminate or terminate only upon an exceptional condition. Is throughput (work per unit time) a consistent and reliable performance measure for these programs? Why, or why not?

c. [15] <1.5> The fundamental unit of work that is of interest for programs such as Web servers and database systems is the transaction. Many computer systems are able to pipeline the processing of transactions, thus overlapping transaction execution times. What performance measurement error does the use of throughput rather than transaction execution time avoid?

✪ 1.16 [15/15/15] <1.6> Three enhancements with the following speedups are proposed for a new architecture:

$$Speedup_1 = 30$$

$$Speedup_2 = 20$$

$$Speedup_3 = 15$$

Only one enhancement is usable at a time.

a. [15] <1.6> If enhancements 1 and 2 are each usable for 25% of the time, what fraction of the time must enhancement 3 be used to achieve an overall speedup of 10?

b. [15] <1.6> Assume the enhancements can be used 25%, 35%, and 10% of the time for enhancements 1, 2, and 3, respectively. For what fraction of the reduced execution time is no enhancement in use?

c. [15] <1.6> Assume, for some benchmark, the possible fraction of use is 15% for each of enhancements 1 and 2 and 70% for enhancement 3. We want to maximize performance. If only one enhancement can be implemented, which should it be? If two enhancements can be implemented, which should be chosen?

1.17 [10/10/10/15/10] <1.6, 1.9> Your company has a benchmark that is considered representative of your typical applications. An embedded processor under consideration to support your task does not have a floating-point unit and must emulate each floating-point instruction by a sequence of integer instructions. This processor is rated at 120 MIPS on the benchmark. A third-party vendor offers a compatible coprocessor to boost performance. That coprocessor executes each floating-point instruction in hardware (i.e., no emulation is necessary). The processor/coprocessor combination rates 80 MIPS on the same benchmark. The following symbols are used to answer parts (a)–(e) of this exercise:

I—Number of integer instructions executed on the benchmark.

F—Number of floating-point instructions executed on the benchmark.

Y—Number of integer instructions to emulate one floating-point instruction.

W—Time to execute the benchmark on the processor alone.

B—Time to execute the benchmark on the processor/coprocessor combination.

a. [10] <1.6, 1.9> Write an equation for the MIPS rating of each configuration using the symbols above.

b. [10] <1.6> For the configuration without the coprocessor, we measure that $F = 8 \times 10^6$, $Y = 50$, and $W = 4$ seconds. Find I.

c. [10] <1.6> What is the value of B?

d. [15] <1.6, 1.9> What is the MFLOPS rating of the system with the coprocessor?

e. [10] <1.6, 1.9> Your colleague wants to purchase the coprocessor even though the MIPS rating for the configuration using the coprocessor is less than that of the processor alone. Is your colleague's evaluation correct? Defend your answer.

⭐ 1.18 [10/12] <1.6, 1.9> One problem cited with MFLOPS as a measure is that not all FLOPS are created equal. To overcome this problem, normalized or weighted MFLOPS measures were developed. Figure 1.37 shows how the authors of the "Livermore Loops" benchmark calculate the number of normalized floating-point operations per program according to the operations actually found in the source code. Thus, the *native MFLOPS* rating is not the same as the *normalized MFLOPS* rating reported in the supercomputer literature, which has come as a surprise to a few computer designers.

Let's examine the effects of this weighted MFLOPS measure. The SPEC CFP2000 171.swim program runs on the Compaq AlphaServer ES40 in 287 seconds. The number of floating-point operations executed in that program are listed in Figure 1.38.

a. [10] <1.6, 1.9> What is the native MFLOPS for 171.swim on a Compaq AlphaServer ES40?

b. [12] <1.6, 1.9> Using the conversions in Figure 1.37, what is the normalized MFLOPS?

1.19 [30] <1.5, 1.9> Devise a program in C that gets the peak MIPS rating for a computer. Run it on two machines to calculate the peak MIPS. Now run SPEC CINT2000 176.gcc on both machines. How well do peak MIPS predict performance of 176.gcc?

Real FP operations	Normalized FP operations
Add, Subtract, Compare, Multiply	1
Divide, Square root	4
Functions (Exponentiation, Sin, . . .)	8

Figure 1.37 Real versus normalized floating-point operations. The number of normalized floating-point operations per real operation in a program used by the authors of the Livermore FORTRAN kernels, or "Livermore Loops," to calculate MFLOPS. A kernel with one Add, one Divide, and one Sin would be credited with 13 normalized floating-point operations. Native MFLOPS won't give the results reported for other machines on that benchmark.

Floating-point operation	Times executed
load	77,033,084,546
store	22,823,523,329
copy	4,274,605,803
add	41,324,938,303
sub	21,443,753,876
mul	31,487,066,317
div	1,428,275,916
convert	11,760,563
Total	199,827,008,653

Figure 1.38 Floating-point operations in SPEC CFP2000 171.swim.

1.20 [30] <1.5, 1.9> Devise a program in C or FORTRAN that gets the peak MFLOPS rating for a computer. Run it on two machines to calculate the peak MFLOPS. Now run the SPEC CFP2000 171.swim benchmark on both machines. How well do peak MFLOPS predict performance of 171.swim?

1.21 [20/20/25] <1.7> Vendors often sell several models of a computer that have identical hardware with the sole exception of processor clock speed. The following questions explore the influence of clock speed on performance.

a. [20] <1.7> From the collection of computers with reported SPEC CFP2000 benchmark results at *www.spec.org/osg/cpu2000/results/*, choose a set of three computer models that are identical in tested configurations (both hardware and software) except for clock speed. For each pair of models, compare the clock speedup to the SPECint_base2000 benchmark speedup. How closely does benchmark performance track clock speed? Is this consistent with the description of the SPEC benchmarks on pages 28–30?

b. [20] <1.7> Now the workload for the computers in part (a) is as follows: a user launches a word-processing program, opens the file of an existing five-page text document, checks spelling, finds no errors, and finally prints the document to an inkjet printer. Suppose the execution time for this benchmark on the slowest clock rate model is 1 minute and 30 seconds, apportioned in this way: 5 seconds to load the word-processing program and the chosen document file from disk to memory, 5 seconds for the user to invoke spell checking, 1 second for spell checking to complete, 2 seconds for the user to absorb the information that there are no spelling errors, 5 seconds for the user to initiate the printing command, 2 seconds for the printing dialog box to appear, 2 seconds for the user to accept the default printing options and command that printing proceed, 8 seconds for the printer to start, and 1 minute to print the five pages.

User think time—the time it takes for a human to respond after waiting for a computer reply in interactive use—improves significantly when the computer can respond to a command quickly because the user maintains better mental focus. Assume that for computer response times less than 2 seconds, any computer response time improvement is matched by double that amount of improvement in the human response time, bounded by a 0.5 second minimum human response time.

What is the clock speedup and word-processing benchmark speedup for each pair of computer models? Discuss the importance of a faster processor for this workload.

c. [25] <1.7> Choose a desktop computer vendor that has a Web-based store and find the price for three systems that are configured identically except for processor clock rate. What is the relative price performance for each system if the workload execution time is determined only by processor clock speed ($ per MHz)? What is the relative price performance ($ per second) for each system if, during a workload execution time total of 100 seconds on the slowest system, the processor is busy 5% of the time and other system components and/or the user are busy the other 95% of the time?

1.22 [30] <1.5, 1.7> Find results from different benchmark sets, for example, PC versus SPEC benchmarks, and compare their performance measurements for two related processors, such as the Pentium III and Pentium 4. Discuss reasons for the differences in performance.

1.23 [20] <1.5, 1.8> Assume that typical power consumption for the 667 MHz Alpha 21164A, 375 MHz Power3-II, and 1000 MHz Pentium III processors is 50, 27, and 35 W, respectively. Using data from Figure 1.36 and scaling to the performance of the Pentium III, create a graph showing the relative performance and the relative performance per watt of these three processors for 171.swim, 183.equake, 301.apsi, and SPECfp_base2000.

1.24 [25] <1.4, 1.8> Design goals for a desktop computer system besides price and performance might include reducing size and noise. Assume that room air is available for cooling. Develop a simple model, similar to the cost model of Figure 1.10, that identifies the sources of additional system demands for power caused by a watt of processor power and includes the transition from passive, convective airflow to forced airflow cooling. Develop an analogous model showing the effect of processor power on system volume. Describe the effect that processor power consumption has on system noise and size.

1.25 [Discussion] <1.5> What is an interpretation of the geometric mean of execution times? What do you think are the advantages and disadvantages of using (a) total execution times versus (b) weighted arithmetic means of execution times using equal running time on the SPARC versus (c) geometric means of ratios of speed to the SPARC (used as the reference machine by SPEC2000)?

1.26   [30] <1.5> SPEC2000 programs are often compiled at levels of optimization that are almost never used by software that is sold commercially—and sometimes using compilers that no one would use in a real product. Rerun SPEC2000 programs on machines for which you can find official ratings, but this time run binaries of the programs compiled with simple optimization and no optimization. Does relative performance change? What do you conclude about the machines? About SPEC2000?

1.27   [Discussion] <1.5> PC benchmark suites use scripts to run programs as fast as possible, that is, with no user think time, the time a real user would spend understanding the current program output before providing the next user input. Also, to be sure to exercise new features of the latest version of the benchmark program, apparently they exercise every option once. What are the disadvantages of this approach? Can you think of compiler or architecture techniques that improve performance for real users but are penalized by this style of benchmarking?

1.28   [Discussion] <1.6> Amdahl's Law makes it clear that to deliver substantial performance improvement, a design enhancement must be usable a large fraction of the time. With this principle in mind, examine the table of contents for this text, determine the major themes of computer design that are covered and the ranking of specific techniques within the major topics, and discuss the extent to which Amdahl's Law is a useful dimension on which to organize the study of computer design.

2

Instruction Set Principles and Examples

A n   Add the number in storage location *n* into the accumulator.

E n   If the number in the accumulator is greater than or equal to zero execute next the order which stands in storage location *n*; otherwise proceed serially.

Z   Stop the machine and ring the warning bell.

Wilkes and Renwick
*Selection from the List of 18 Machine
Instructions for the EDSAC (1949)*

Introduction

In this chapter we concentrate on instruction set architecture—the portion of the computer visible to the programmer or compiler writer. This chapter introduces the wide variety of design alternatives available to the instruction set architect. In particular, this chapter focuses on five topics. First, we present a taxonomy of instruction set alternatives and give some qualitative assessment of the advantages and disadvantages of various approaches. Second, we present and analyze some instruction set measurements that are largely independent of a specific instruction set. Third, we discuss instruction set architecture of processors not aimed at desktops or servers: digital signal processors (DSPs) and media processors. DSPs and media processors are deployed in embedded applications, where cost and power are as important as performance, with an emphasis on real-time performance. As discussed in Chapter 1, real-time programmers often target worst-case performance to guarantee not missing regularly occurring events. Fourth, we address the issue of languages and compilers and their bearing on instruction set architecture. Finally, the "Putting It All Together" section shows how these ideas are reflected in the MIPS instruction set, which is typical of RISC architectures, and "Another View" presents the Trimedia TM32 CPU, an example of a media processor. We conclude with fallacies and pitfalls of instruction set design.

To illustrate the principles further, Appendices C through F give four examples of general-purpose RISC architectures (MIPS, PowerPC, Precision Architecture, SPARC), four embedded RISC processors (ARM, Hitachi SH, MIPS 16, Thumb), and three older architectures (80x86, IBM 360/370, and VAX). Before we discuss how to classify architectures, we need to say something about instruction set measurement.

Throughout this chapter, we examine a wide variety of architectural measurements. Clearly, these measurements depend on the programs measured and on the compilers used in making the measurements. The results should not be interpreted as absolute, and you might see different data if you did the measurement with a different compiler or a different set of programs. We believe that the measurements in this chapter are reasonably indicative of a class of typical applications. Many of the measurements are presented using a small set of benchmarks, so that the data can be reasonably displayed and the differences among programs can be seen. An architect for a new computer would want to analyze a much larger collection of programs before making architectural decisions. The measurements shown are usually *dynamic*—that is, the frequency of a measured event is weighed by the number of times that event occurs during execution of the measured program.

Before starting with the general principles, let's review the three application areas from the last chapter. *Desktop computing* emphasizes performance of programs with integer and floating-point data types, with little regard for program size or processor power consumption. For example, code size has never been reported in the four generations of SPEC benchmarks. *Servers* today are used primarily for database, file server, and Web applications, plus some time-sharing applications for many users. Hence, floating-point performance is much less important for performance than integers and character strings, yet virtually every server processor still includes floating-point instructions. *Embedded applications* value cost and power, so code size is important because less memory is both cheaper and lower power, and some classes of instructions (such as floating point) may be optional to reduce chip costs.

Thus, instruction sets for all three applications are very similar. Appendix C takes advantage of the similarities to describe eight instruction sets in one short appendix. In fact, the MIPS architecture that drives this chapter has been used successfully in desktops, servers, and embedded applications.

One successful architecture very different from RISC is the 80x86 (see Appendix D). Surprisingly, its success does not necessarily belie the advantages of a RISC instruction set. The commercial importance of binary compatibility with PC software combined with the abundance of transistors provided by Moore's Law led Intel to use a RISC instruction set internally while supporting an 80x86 instruction set externally. As we shall see in Section 3.10 of the next chapter, recent Intel microprocessors use hardware to translate from 80x86 instructions to RISC-like instructions and then execute the translated operations inside the chip. They maintain the illusion of 80x86 architecture to the programmer while allowing the computer designer to implement a RISC-style processor for performance.

DSPs and media processors, which can be used in embedded applications, emphasize real-time performance and often deal with infinite, continuous streams of data. Keeping up with these streams often means targeting worst-case performance to offer real-time guarantees. Architects of these computers also have a tradition of identifying a small number of important kernels that are critical to success, and hence are often supplied by the manufacturer. As a result of this heritage, these instruction set architectures include quirks that can improve performance for the targeted kernels but that no compiler will ever generate.

In contrast, desktop and server applications historically do not reward such eccentricities since they do not have as narrowly defined a set of important kernels, and since little of the code is hand-optimized. If a compiler cannot generate it, desktop and server programs generally won't use it. We'll see the impact of these different cultures on the details of the instruction set architectures of this chapter.

Given the increasing importance of media to desktop and embedded applications, a recent trend is to merge these cultures by adding DSP/media instructions to conventional architectures. Hand-coded library routines then try to deliver DSP/media performance using conventional desktop and media architectures, while compilers can generate code for the rest of the program using the conventional instruction set. Section 2.8 describes such extensions. Similarly, embedded applications are beginning to run more general-purpose code as they begin to include operating systems and more intelligent features.

Now that the background is set, we begin by exploring how instruction set architectures can be classified.

2.2 Classifying Instruction Set Architectures

The type of internal storage in a processor is the most basic differentiation, so in this section we will focus on the alternatives for this portion of the architecture. The major choices are a stack, an accumulator, or a set of registers. Operands may be named explicitly or implicitly: The operands in a *stack architecture* are implicitly on the top of the stack, and in an *accumulator architecture* one operand is implicitly the accumulator. The *general-purpose register architectures* have only explicit operands—either registers or memory locations. Figure 2.1 shows a block diagram of such architectures, and Figure 2.2 shows how the code sequence C = A + B would typically appear in these three classes of instruction sets. The explicit operands may be accessed directly from memory or may need to be first loaded into temporary storage, depending on the class of architecture and choice of specific instruction.

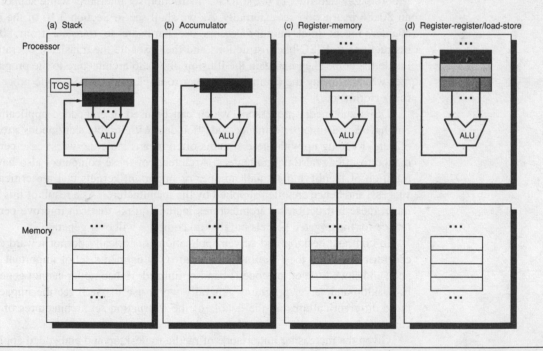

Figure 2.1 Operand locations for four instruction set architecture classes. The arrows indicate whether the operand is an input or the result of the ALU operation, or both an input and result. Lighter shades indicate inputs, and the dark shade indicates the result. In (a), a Top Of Stack register (TOS), points to the top input operand, which is combined with the operand below. The first operand is removed from the stack, the result takes the place of the second operand, and TOS is updated to point to the result. All operands are implicit. In (b), the Accumulator is both an implicit input operand and a result. In (c), one input operand is a register, one is in memory, and the result goes to a register. All operands are registers in (d) and, like the stack architecture, can be transferred to memory only via separate instructions: push or pop for (a) and load or store for (d).

Stack	Accumulator	Register (register-memory)	Register (load-store)
Push A	Load A	Load R1,A	Load R1,A
Push B	Add B	Add R3,R1,B	Load R2,B
Add	Store C	Store R3,C	Add R3,R1,R2
Pop C			Store R3,C

Figure 2.2   The code sequence for C = A + B for four classes of instruction sets. Note that the Add instruction has implicit operands for stack and accumulator architectures, and explicit operands for register architectures. It is assumed that A, B, and C all belong in memory and that the values of A and B cannot be destroyed. Figure 2.1 shows the Add operation for each class of architecture.

As the figures show, there are really two classes of register computers. One class can access memory as part of any instruction, called *register-memory* architecture, and the other can access memory only with load and store instructions, called *load-store* or *register-register* architecture. A third class, not found in computers shipping today, keeps all operands in memory and is called a *memory-memory* architecture. Some instruction set architectures have more registers than a single accumulator, but place restrictions on uses of these special registers. Such an architecture is sometimes called an *extended accumulator* or *special-purpose register* computer.

Although most early computers used stack or accumulator-style architectures, virtually every new architecture designed after 1980 uses a load-store register architecture. The major reasons for the emergence of general-purpose register (GPR) computers are twofold. First, registers—like other forms of storage internal to the processor—are faster than memory. Second, registers are more efficient for a compiler to use than other forms of internal storage. For example, on a register computer the expression $(A*B) - (B*C) - (A*D)$ may be evaluated by doing the multiplications in any order, which may be more efficient because of the location of the operands or because of pipelining concerns (see Chapter 3). Nevertheless, on a stack computer the hardware must evaluate the expression in only one order, since operands are hidden on the stack, and it may have to load an operand multiple times.

More importantly, registers can be used to hold variables. When variables are allocated to registers, the memory traffic reduces, the program speeds up (since registers are faster than memory), and the code density improves (since a register can be named with fewer bits than can a memory location).

As explained in Section 2.11, compiler writers would prefer that all registers be equivalent and unreserved. Older computers compromise this desire by dedicating registers to special uses, effectively decreasing the number of general-purpose registers. If the number of truly general-purpose registers is too small, trying to allocate variables to registers will not be profitable. Instead, the compiler will reserve all the uncommitted registers for use in expression evaluation.

The dominance of hand-optimized code in the DSP community has led to DSPs with many special-purpose registers and few general-purpose registers.

How many registers are sufficient? The answer, of course, depends on the effectiveness of the compiler. Most compilers reserve some registers for expression evaluation, use some for parameter passing, and allow the remainder to be allocated to hold variables. Just as people tend to be bigger than their parents, new instruction set architectures tend to have more registers than their ancestors.

Two major instruction set characteristics divide GPR architectures. Both characteristics concern the nature of operands for a typical arithmetic or logical instruction (ALU instruction). The first concerns whether an ALU instruction has two or three operands. In the three-operand format, the instruction contains one result operand and two source operands. In the two-operand format, one of the operands is both a source and a result for the operation. The second distinction among GPR architectures concerns how many of the operands may be memory addresses in ALU instructions. The number of memory operands supported by a typical ALU instruction may vary from none to three. Figure 2.3 shows combinations of these two attributes with examples of computers. Although there are seven possible combinations, three serve to classify nearly all existing computers. As we mentioned earlier, these three are register-register (also called load-store), register-memory, and memory-memory.

Figure 2.4 shows the advantages and disadvantages of each of these alternatives. Of course, these advantages and disadvantages are not absolutes: They are qualitative and their actual impact depends on the compiler and implementation strategy. A GPR computer with memory-memory operations could easily be ignored by the compiler and used as a register-register computer. One of the most pervasive architectural impacts is on instruction encoding and the number of instructions needed to perform a task. We will see the impact of these architectural alternatives on implementation approaches in Chapters 3 and 4.

Number of memory addresses	Maximum number of operands allowed	Type of architecture	Examples
0	3	Register-register	Alpha, ARM, MIPS, PowerPC, SPARC, SuperH, Trimedia TM5200
1	2	Register-memory	IBM 360/370, Intel 80x86, Motorola 68000, TI TMS320C54x
2	2	Memory-memory	VAX (also has three-operand formats)
3	3	Memory-memory	VAX (also has two-operand formats)

Figure 2.3 Typical combinations of memory operands and total operands per typical ALU instruction with examples of computers. Computers with no memory reference per ALU instruction are called load-store or register-register computers. Instructions with multiple memory operands per typical ALU instruction are called register-memory or memory-memory, according to whether they have one or more than one memory operand.

Type	Advantages	Disadvantages
Register-register (0, 3)	Simple, fixed-length instruction encoding. Simple code generation model. Instructions take similar numbers of clocks to execute (see App. A).	Higher instruction count than architectures with memory references in instructions. More instructions and lower instruction density leads to larger programs.
Register-memory (1, 2)	Data can be accessed without a separate load instruction first. Instruction format tends to be easy to encode and yields good density.	Operands are not equivalent since a source operand in a binary operation is destroyed. Encoding a register number and a memory address in each instruction may restrict the number of registers. Clocks per instruction vary by operand location.
Memory-memory (2, 2) or (3, 3)	Most compact. Doesn't waste registers for temporaries.	Large variation in instruction size, especially for three-operand instructions. In addition, large variation in work per instruction. Memory accesses create memory bottleneck. (Not used today.)

Figure 2.4 Advantages and disadvantages of the three most common types of general-purpose register computers. The notation (m, n) means m memory operands and n total operands. In general, computers with fewer alternatives simplify the compiler's task since there are fewer decisions for the compiler to make (see Section 2.11). Computers with a wide variety of flexible instruction formats reduce the number of bits required to encode the program. The number of registers also affects the instruction size since you need $\log_2$ (number of registers) for each register specifier in an instruction. Thus, doubling the number of registers takes 3 extra bits for a register-register architecture, or about 10% of a 32-bit instruction.

Summary: Classifying Instruction Set Architectures

Here and at the end of Sections 2.3 through 2.11 we summarize those characteristics we would expect to find in a new instruction set architecture, building the foundation for the MIPS architecture introduced in Section 2.12. From this section we should clearly expect the use of general-purpose registers. Figure 2.4, combined with Appendix A on pipelining, leads to the expectation of a register-register (also called load-store) version of a general-purpose register architecture.

With the class of architecture covered, the next topic is addressing operands.

2.3   Memory Addressing

Independent of whether the architecture is register-register or allows any operand to be a memory reference, it must define how memory addresses are interpreted and how they are specified. The measurements presented here are largely, but not completely, computer independent. In some cases the measurements are significantly affected by the compiler technology. These measurements have been made using an optimizing compiler, since compiler technology plays a critical role.

Interpreting Memory Addresses

How is a memory address interpreted? That is, what object is accessed as a function of the address and the length? All the instruction sets discussed in this book—except some DSPs—are byte addressed and provide access for bytes (8 bits), half words (16 bits), and words (32 bits). Most of the computers also provide access for double words (64 bits).

There are two different conventions for ordering the bytes within a larger object. *Little Endian* byte order puts the byte whose address is "x . . . x000" at the least-significant position in the double word (the little end). The bytes are numbered

7	6	5	4	3	2	1	0

Big Endian byte order puts the byte whose address is "x . . . x000" at the most-significant position in the double word (the big end). The bytes are numbered

0	1	2	3	4	5	6	7

When operating within one computer, the byte order is often unnoticeable—only programs that access the same locations as both, say, words and bytes can notice the difference. Byte order is a problem when exchanging data among computers with different orderings, however. Little Endian ordering also fails to match normal ordering of words when strings are compared. Strings appear "SDRAWKCAB" (backwards) in the registers.

A second memory issue is that in many computers, accesses to objects larger than a byte must be *aligned*. An access to an object of size s bytes at byte address A is aligned if $A \bmod s = 0$. Figure 2.5 shows the addresses at which an access is aligned or misaligned.

Why would someone design a computer with alignment restrictions? Misalignment causes hardware complications, since the memory is typically aligned on a multiple of a word or double-word boundary. A misaligned memory access may, therefore, take multiple aligned memory references. Thus, even in computers that allow misaligned access, programs with aligned accesses run faster.

Even if data are aligned, supporting byte, half-word, and word accesses requires an alignment network to align bytes, half words, and words in 64-bit registers. For example, in Figure 2.5, suppose we read a byte from an address with its three low-order bits having the value 4. We will need to shift right 3 bytes to align the byte to the proper place in a 64-bit register. Depending on the instruction, the computer may also need to sign-extend the quantity. Stores are easy: Only the addressed bytes in memory may be altered. On some computers a byte, half-word, and word operation does not affect the upper portion of a register. Although all the computers discussed in this book permit byte, half-word, and word accesses to memory, only the IBM 360/370, Intel 80x86, and VAX support ALU operations on register operands narrower than the full width.

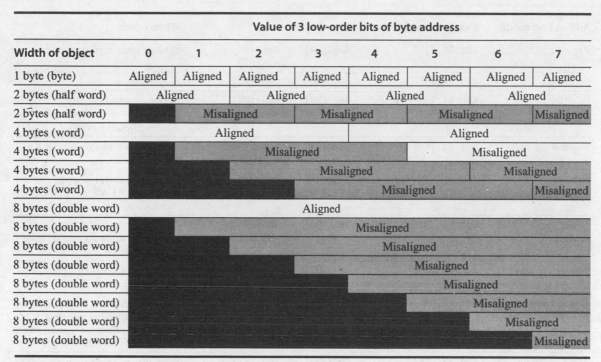

Width of object	Value of 3 low-order bits of byte address							
	0	1	2	3	4	5	6	7
1 byte (byte)	Aligned	Aligned	Aligned	Aligned	Aligned	Aligned	Aligned	Aligned
2 bytes (half word)	Aligned		Aligned		Aligned		Aligned	
2 bytes (half word)		Misaligned		Misaligned		Misaligned		Misaligned
4 bytes (word)	Aligned				Aligned			
4 bytes (word)		Misaligned				Misaligned		
4 bytes (word)			Misaligned				Misaligned	
4 bytes (word)				Misaligned				Misaligned
8 bytes (double word)	Aligned							
8 bytes (double word)		Misaligned						
8 bytes (double word)			Misaligned					
8 bytes (double word)				Misaligned				
8 bytes (double word)					Misaligned			
8 bytes (double word)						Misaligned		
8 bytes (double word)							Misaligned	
8 bytes (double word)								Misaligned

Figure 2.5 Aligned and misaligned addresses of byte, half-word, word, and double-word objects for byte-addressed computers. For each misaligned example some objects require two memory accesses to complete. Every aligned object can always complete in one memory access, as long as the memory is as wide as the object. The figure shows the memory organized as 8 bytes wide. The byte offsets that label the columns specify the low-order 3 bits of the address.

Now that we have discussed alternative interpretations of memory addresses, we can discuss the ways addresses are specified by instructions, called *addressing modes*.

Addressing Modes

Given an address, we now know what bytes to access in memory. In this subsection we will look at addressing modes—how architectures specify the address of an object they will access. Addressing modes specify constants and registers in addition to locations in memory. When a memory location is used, the actual memory address specified by the addressing mode is called the *effective address*.

Figure 2.6 shows all the data addressing modes that have been used in recent computers. Immediates or literals are usually considered memory addressing modes (even though the value they access is in the instruction stream), although registers are often separated. We have kept addressing modes that depend on the program counter, called *PC-relative addressing*, separate. PC-relative addressing

Addressing mode	Example instruction	Meaning	When used
Register	Add R4,R3	Regs[R4] ← Regs[R4] + Regs[R3]	When a value is in a register.
Immediate	Add R4,#3	Regs[R4] ← Regs[R4] + 3	For constants.
Displacement	Add R4,100(R1)	Regs[R4] ← Regs[R4] + Mem[100+Regs[R1]]	Accessing local variables (+ simulates register indirect, direct addressing modes).
Register indirect	Add R4,(R1)	Regs[R4] ← Regs[R4] + Mem[Regs[R1]]	Accessing using a pointer or a computed address.
Indexed	Add R3,(R1+R2)	Regs[R3] ← Regs[R3] +Mem[Regs[R1]+Regs[R2]]	Sometimes useful in array addressing: R1 = base of array; R2 = index amount.
Direct or absolute	Add R1,(1001)	Regs[R1] ← Regs[R1] + Mem[1001]	Sometimes useful for accessing static data; address constant may need to be large.
Memory indirect	Add R1,@(R3)	Regs[R1] ← Regs[R1] + Mem[Mem[Regs[R3]]]	If R3 is the address of a pointer p, then mode yields $*p$.
Autoincrement	Add R1,(R2)+	Regs[R1] ← Regs[R1] + Mem[Regs[R2]] Regs[R2] ← Regs[R2] + d	Useful for stepping through arrays within a loop. R2 points to start of array; each reference increments R2 by size of an element, d.
Autodecrement	Add R1,-(R2)	Regs[R2] ← Regs[R2] - d Regs[R1] ← Regs[R1] + Mem[Regs[R2]]	Same use as autoincrement. Autodecrement/-increment can also act as push/pop to implement a stack.
Scaled	Add R1,100(R2)[R3]	Regs[R1] ← Regs[R1] + Mem[100+Regs[R2] +Regs[R3]*d]	Used to index arrays. May be applied to any indexed addressing mode in some computers.

Figure 2.6 Selection of addressing modes with examples, meaning, and usage. In autoincrement/-decrement and scaled addressing modes, the variable d designates the size of the data item being accessed (i.e., whether the instruction is accessing 1, 2, 4, or 8 bytes). These addressing modes are only useful when the elements being accessed are adjacent in memory. RISC computers use displacement addressing to simulate register indirect with 0 for the address and to simulate direct addressing using 0 in the base register. In our measurements, we use the first name shown for each mode. The extensions to C used as hardware descriptions are defined on page 132 and on the back inside cover.

is used primarily for specifying code addresses in control transfer instructions, discussed in Section 2.9.

Figure 2.6 shows the most common names for the addressing modes, though the names differ among architectures. In this figure and throughout the book, we will use an extension of the C programming language as a hardware description notation. In this figure, only one non-C feature is used: The left arrow (←) is used for assignment. We also use the array Mem as the name for main memory and the array Regs for registers. Thus, Mem[Regs[R1]] refers to the contents of the memory location whose address is given by the contents of register 1 (R1). Later, we will introduce extensions for accessing and transferring data smaller than a word.

Addressing modes have the ability to significantly reduce instruction counts; they also add to the complexity of building a computer and may increase the average CPI (clock cycles per instruction) of computers that implement those modes. Thus, the usage of various addressing modes is quite important in helping the architect choose what to include.

Figure 2.7 shows the results of measuring addressing mode usage patterns in three programs on the VAX architecture. We use the old VAX architecture for a few measurements in this chapter because it has the richest set of addressing modes and the fewest restrictions on memory addressing. For example, Figure 2.6 shows all the modes the VAX supports. Most measurements in this chapter, however, will use the more recent register-register architectures to show how programs use instruction sets of current computers.

As Figure 2.7 shows, immediate and displacement addressing dominate addressing mode usage. Let's look at some properties of these two heavily used modes.

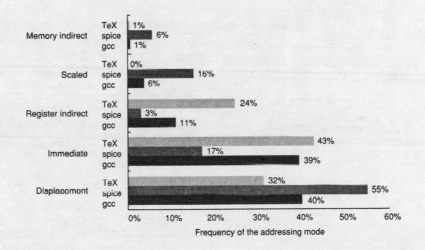

Figure 2.7 Summary of use of memory addressing modes (including immediates). These major addressing modes account for all but a few percent (0% to 3%) of the memory accesses. Register modes, which are not counted, account for one-half of the operand references, while memory addressing modes (including immediate) account for the other half. Of course, the compiler affects what addressing modes are used; see Section 2.11. The memory indirect mode on the VAX can use displacement, autoincrement, or autodecrement to form the initial memory address; in these programs, almost all the memory indirect references use displacement mode as the base. Displacement mode includes all displacement lengths (8, 16, and 32 bits). The PC-relative addressing modes, used almost exclusively for branches, are not included. Only the addressing modes with an average frequency of over 1% are shown. The data are from a VAX using three SPEC89 programs.

Displacement Addressing Mode

The major question that arises for a displacement-style addressing mode is that of the range of displacements used. Based on the use of various displacement sizes, a decision of what sizes to support can be made. Choosing the displacement field sizes is important because they directly affect the instruction length. Figure 2.8 shows the measurements taken on the data access on a load-store architecture using our benchmark programs. We look at branch offsets in Section 2.9—data accessing patterns and branches are different; little is gained by combining them, although in practice the immediate sizes are made the same for simplicity.

Immediate or Literal Addressing Mode

Immediates can be used in arithmetic operations, in comparisons (primarily for branches), and in moves where a constant is wanted in a register. The last case occurs for constants written in the code—which tend to be small—and for address constants, which tend to be large. For the use of immediates it is impor-

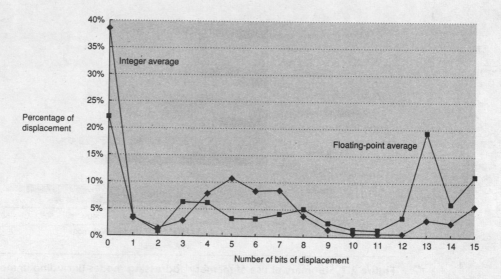

Figure 2.8 Displacement values are widely distributed. There are both a large number of small values and a fair number of large values. The wide distribution of displacement values is due to multiple storage areas for variables and different displacements to access them (see Section 2.11) as well as the overall addressing scheme the compiler uses. The x-axis is $\log_2$ of the displacement; that is, the size of a field needed to represent the magnitude of the displacement. Zero on the x-axis shows the percentage of displacements of value 0. The graph does not include the sign bit, which is heavily affected by the storage layout. Most displacements are positive, but a majority of the largest displacements (14+ bits) are negative. Since these data were collected on a computer with 16-bit displacements, they cannot tell us about longer displacements. These data were taken on the Alpha architecture with full optimization (see Section 2.11) for SPEC CPU2000, showing the average of integer programs (CINT2000) and the average of floating-point programs (CFP2000).

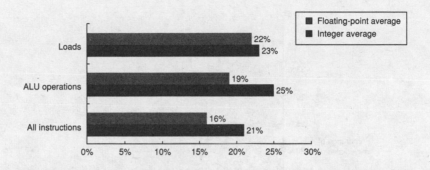

Figure 2.9 About one-quarter of data transfers and ALU operations have an immediate operand. The bottom bars show that integer programs use immediates in about one-fifth of the instructions, while floating-point programs use immediates in about one-sixth of the instructions. For loads, the load immediate instruction loads 16 bits into either half of a 32-bit register. Load immediates are not loads in a strict sense because they do not access memory. Occasionally a pair of load immediates is used to load a 32-bit constant, but this is rare. (For ALU operations, shifts by a constant amount are included as operations with immediate operands.) The programs and computer used to collect these statistics are the same as in Figure 2.8.

tant to know whether they need to be supported for all operations or for only a subset. Figure 2.9 shows the frequency of immediates for the general classes of integer operations in an instruction set.

Another important instruction set measurement is the range of values for immediates. Like displacement values, the size of immediate values affects instruction length. As Figure 2.10 shows, small immediate values are most heavily used. Large immediates are sometimes used, however, most likely in addressing calculations.

2.4   Addressing Modes for Signal Processing

To give a flavor of the different perspectives of different architecture cultures, here are two addressing modes that distinguish DSPs.

Since DSPs deal with infinite, continuous streams of data, they routinely rely on circular buffers. Hence, as data are added to the buffer, a pointer is checked to see if it is pointing to the end of the buffer. If not, the pointer is incremented to the next address; if it is, the pointer is set instead to the start of the buffer. Similar issues arise when emptying a buffer.

Every recent DSP has a *modulo* or *circular* addressing mode to handle this case automatically, our first novel DSP addressing mode. It keeps a start register and an end register with every address register, allowing the autoincrement and autodecrement addressing modes to reset when they reach the end of the buffer. One variation makes assumptions about the buffer size starting at an address that

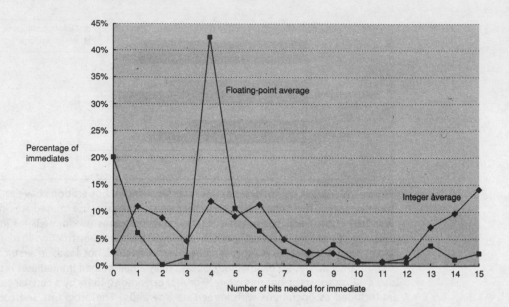

Figure 2.10 The distribution of immediate values. The *x*-axis shows the number of bits needed to represent the magnitude of an immediate value—0 means the immediate field value was 0. The majority of the immediate values are positive. About 20% were negative for CINT2000, and about 30% were negative for CFP2000. These measurements were taken on an Alpha, where the maximum immediate is 16 bits, for the same programs as in Figure 2.8. A similar measurement on the VAX, which supported 32-bit immediates, showed that about 20% to 25% of immediates were longer than 16 bits.

ends in "xxx00.00" and so uses just a single buffer length register per address register.

Even though DSPs are tightly targeted to a small number of algorithms, it is surprising that this next addressing mode is included for just one application: fast Fourier transform (FFT). FFTs start or end their processing with data shuffled in a particular order. For eight data items in a radix-2 FFT, the transformation is listed below, with addresses in parentheses shown in binary:

$$0\ (000_2) \quad => \quad 0\ (000_2)$$
$$1\ (001_2) \quad => \quad 4\ (100_2)$$
$$2\ (010_2) \quad => \quad 2\ (010_2)$$
$$3\ (011_2) \quad => \quad 6\ (110_2)$$
$$4\ (100_2) \quad => \quad 1\ (001_2)$$
$$5\ (101_2) \quad => \quad 5\ (101_2)$$
$$6\ (110_2) \quad => \quad 3\ (011_2)$$
$$7\ (111_2) \quad => \quad 7\ (111_2)$$

Without special support such address transformations would take an extra memory access to get the new address, or involve a fair amount of logical instructions to transform the address.

The DSP solution is based on the observation that the resulting binary address is simply the reverse of the initial address! For example, address 100_2 (4) becomes 001_2 (1). Hence, many DSPs have this second novel addressing mode— *bit reverse* addressing—whereby the hardware reverses the lower bits of the address, with the number of bits reversed depending on the step of the FFT algorithm.

As DSP programmers migrate toward larger programs and hence become more attracted to compilers, they have been trying to use the compiler technology developed for the desktop and embedded computers. Such compilers have no hope of taking high-level language code and producing these two addressing modes, so they are limited to assembly language programmers. As stated before, the DSP community routinely uses library routines, and hence programmers may benefit even if *they* write at a higher level.

Figure 2.11 shows the static frequency of data addressing modes in a DSP for a set of 54 library routines. This architecture has 17 addressing modes, yet the 6 modes also found in Figure 2.6 for desktop and server computers account for 95% of the DSP addressing. Despite measuring hand-coded routines to derive Figure 2.11, the use of novel addressing mode is sparse.

These results are for just one library for just one DSP; other libraries might use more addressing modes, and static and dynamic frequencies may differ. Yet Figure 2.11 still makes the point that there is often a mismatch between what programmers and compilers actually use versus what architects expect, and this is just as true for DSPs as it is for more traditional processors.

Summary: Memory Addressing

First, because of their popularity, we would expect a new architecture to support at least the following addressing modes: displacement, immediate, and register indirect. Figure 2.7 shows that they represent 75% to 99% of the addressing modes used in our SPEC measurements. Second, we would expect the size of the address for displacement mode to be at least 12–16 bits, since the caption in Figure 2.8 suggests these sizes would capture 75% to 99% of the displacements. Third, we would expect the size of the immediate field to be at least 8–16 bits. As the caption in Figure 2.10 suggests, these sizes would capture 50% to 80% of the immediates.

Desktop and server processors rely on compilers, and so addressing modes must match the ability of the compilers to use them, while historically DSPs rely on hand-coded libraries to exercise novel addressing modes. Even so, there are times when programmers find they do not need the clever tricks that architects thought would be useful—or tricks that other programmers promised that they would use. As DSPs head toward relying even more on compiled code, we expect increasing emphasis on simpler addressing modes.

Addressing mode	Assembly symbol	Percent
Immediate	#num	30.02%
Displacement	ARx(num)	10.82%
Register indirect	*ARx	17.42%
Direct	num	11.99%
Autoincrement, preincrement (increment register *before* using contents as address)	*+ARx	0
Autoincrement, postincrement (increment register *after* using contents as address)	*ARx+	18.84%
Autoincrement, preincrement with 16b immediate	*+ARx(num)	0.77%
Autoincrement, preincrement, with circular addressing	*ARx+%	0.08%
Autoincrement, postincrement with 16b immediate, with circular addressing	*ARx+(num)%	0
Autoincrement, postincrement by contents of AR0	*ARx+0	1.54%
Autoincrement, postincrement by contents of AR0, with circular addressing	*ARx+0%	2.15%
Autoincrement, postincrement by contents of AR0, with bit reverse addressing	*ARx+0B	0
Autodecrement, postdecrement (decrement register *after* using contents as address)	*ARx-	6.08%
Autodecrement, postdecrement, with circular addressing	*ARx-%	0.04%
Autodecrement, postdecrement by contents of AR0	*ARx-0	0.16%
Autodecrement, postdecrement by contents of AR0, with circular addressing	*ARx-0%	0.08%
Autodecrement, postdecrement by contents of AR0, with bit reverse addressing	*ARx-0B	0
Total		100.00%

Figure 2.11 Frequency of addressing modes for TI TMS320C54x DSP. The C54x has 17 data addressing modes, not counting register access, but the four found in MIPS account for 70% of the modes. Autoincrement and autodecrement, found in some RISC architectures, account for another 25% of the usage. These data were collected from a measurement of static instructions for the C-callable library of 54 DSP routines coded in assembly language. See *www.ti.com/sc/docs/products/dsp/c5000/c54x/54dsplib.htm.*

Having covered instruction set classes and decided on register-register architectures, plus the previous recommendations on data addressing modes, we next cover the sizes and meanings of data.

2.5   Type and Size of Operands

How is the type of an operand designated? Normally, encoding in the opcode designates the type of an operand—this is the method used most often. Alternatively, the data can be annotated with tags that are interpreted by the hardware. These tags specify the type of the operand, and the operation is chosen accordingly. Computers with tagged data, however, can only be found in computer museums.

Let's start with desktop and server architectures. Usually the type of an operand—integer, single-precision floating point, character, and so on—effectively gives its size. Common operand types include character (8 bits), half word (16 bits), word (32 bits), single-precision floating point (also 1 word), and double-precision floating point (2 words). Integers are almost universally represented as two's complement binary numbers. Characters are usually in ASCII, but the 16-bit Unicode (used in Java) is gaining popularity with the internationalization of computers. Until the early 1980s, most computer manufacturers chose their own floating-point representation. Almost all computers since that time follow the same standard for floating point, the IEEE standard 754. The IEEE floating-point standard is discussed in detail in Appendix H.

Some architectures provide operations on character strings, although such operations are usually quite limited and treat each byte in the string as a single character. Typical operations supported on character strings are comparisons and moves.

For business applications, some architectures support a decimal format, usually called *packed decimal* or *binary-coded decimal*—4 bits are used to encode the values 0–9, and 2 decimal digits are packed into each byte. Numeric character strings are sometimes called *unpacked decimal,* and operations—called *packing* and *unpacking*—are usually provided for converting back and forth between them.

One reason to use decimal operands is to get results that exactly match decimal numbers, as some decimal fractions do not have an exact representation in binary. For example, 0.10_{10} is a simple fraction in decimal, but in binary it requires an infinite set of repeating digits: $0.0001100110\overline{0011}\ldots_2$. Thus, calculations that are exact in decimal can be close but inexact in binary, which can be a problem for financial transactions. (See Appendix H to learn more about precise arithmetic.)

Our SPEC benchmarks use byte or character, half-word (short integer), word (integer), double-word (long integer), and floating-point data types. Figure 2.12 shows the dynamic distribution of the sizes of objects referenced from memory for these programs. The frequency of access to different data types helps in deciding what types are most important to support efficiently. Should the computer have a 64-bit access path, or would taking two cycles to access a double word be satisfactory? As we saw earlier, byte accesses require an alignment network: How important is it to support bytes as primitives? Figure 2.12 uses memory references to examine the types of data being accessed.

In some architectures, objects in registers may be accessed as bytes or half words. However, such access is very infrequent—on the VAX, it accounts for no more than 12% of register references, or roughly 6% of all operand accesses in these programs.

2.6   Operands for Media and Signal Processing

Graphics applications deal with 2D and 3D images. A common 3D data type is called a *vertex,* a data structure with four components: x-coordinate, y-coordinate, z-coordinate, and a fourth coordinate (w) to help with color or hidden surfaces. Three vertices specify a graphics primitive such as a triangle. Vertex values are usually 32-bit floating-point values.

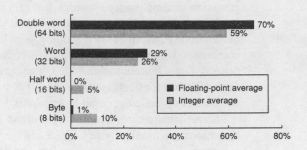

Figure 2.12 Distribution of data accesses by size for the benchmark programs. The double-word data type is used for double-precision floating point in floating-point programs and for addresses, since the computer uses 64-bit addresses. On a 32-bit address computer the 64-bit addresses would be replaced by 32-bit addresses, and so almost all double-word accesses in integer programs would become single-word accesses.

Assuming a triangle is visible, when it is rendered it is filled with pixels. *Pixels* are typically 32 bits, usually consisting of four 8-bit channels: R (red), G (green), B (blue), and A (which denotes the transparency of the surface or transparency of the pixel when the pixel is rendered).

DSPs add *fixed point* to the data types discussed so far. If you think of integers as having a binary point to the right of the least-significant bit, fixed point has a binary point just to the right of the sign bit. Hence, fixed-point data are fractions between −1 and +1.

Example Here are three simple 16-bit patterns:

0100 0000 0000 0000

0000 1000 0000 0000

0100 1000 0000 1000

What values do they represent if they are two's complement integers? Fixed-point numbers?

Answer Number representation tells us that the ith digit to the left of the binary point represents 2^{i-1} and the ith digit to the right of the binary point represents 2^{-i}. First assume these three patterns are integers. Then the binary point is to the far right, so they represent 2^{14}, 2^{11}, and $(2^{14} + 2^{11} + 2^3)$, or 16,384, 2048, and 18,440.

Fixed point places the binary point just to the right of the sign bit, so as fixed point these patterns represent 2^{-1}, 2^{-4}, and $(2^{-1} + 2^{-4} + 2^{-12})$. The fractions are 1/2, 1/16, and (2048 + 256 + 1)/4096 or 2305/4096, which represents about 0.50000, 0.06250, and 0.56274. Alternatively, for an n-bit two's complement, fixed-point number we could just divide the integer presentation by 2^{n-1} to derive the same results:

16,384/32,768 = 1/2, 2048/32,768 = 1/16, and 18,440/32,768 = 2305/4096.

Fixed point can be thought of as just low-cost floating point. It doesn't include an exponent in every word and have hardware that automatically aligns and normalizes operands. Instead, fixed point relies on the DSP programmer to keep the exponent in a separate variable and ensure that each result is shifted left or right to keep the answer aligned to that variable. Since this exponent variable is often shared by a set of fixed-point variables, this style of arithmetic is also called *blocked floating point,* since a block of variables has a common exponent.

To support such manual calculations, DSPs usually have some registers that are wider to guard against round-off error, just as floating-point units internally have extra guard bits. Figure 2.13 surveys four generations of DSPs, listing data sizes and width of the accumulating registers. Note that DSP architects are not bound by the powers of 2 for word sizes. Figure 2.14 shows the size of data operands for the TI TMS320C540x DSP.

Summary: Type and Size of Operands

From this section we would expect a new 32-bit architecture to support 8-, 16-, and 32-bit integers and 32-bit and 64-bit IEEE 754 floating-point data. A new 64-bit address architecture would need to support 64-bit integers as well. The level of support for decimal data is less clear, and it is a function of the intended use of the computer as well as the effectiveness of the decimal support. DSPs need wider accumulating registers than the size in memory to aid accuracy in fixed-point arithmetic.

Generation	Year	Example DSP	Data width	Accumulator width
1	1982	TI TMS32010	16 bits	32 bits
2	1987	Motorola DSP56001	24 bits	56 bits
3	1995	Motorola DSP56301	24 bits	56 bits
4	1998	TI TMS320C6201	16 bits	40 bits

Figure 2.13 Four generations of DSPs, their data width, and the width of the registers that reduces round-off error. Section 2.8 explains that multiply-accumulate operations use wide registers to avoid losing precision when accumulating double-length products [Bier 1997].

Data size	Memory operand in operation	Memory operand in data transfer
16 bits	89.3%	89.0%
32 bits	10.7%	11.0%

Figure 2.14 Size of data operands for TMS320C540x DSP. About 90% of operands are 16 bits. This DSP has two 40-bit accumulators. There are no floating-point operations, as is typical of many DSPs, so these data are all fixed-point integers. For details on these measurements, see the caption of Figure 2.11 on page 104.

We have reviewed instruction set classes and chosen the register-register class; reviewed memory addressing and selected displacement, immediate, and register indirect addressing modes; and selected the operand sizes and types above. Now we are ready to look at instructions that do the heavy lifting in the architecture.

2.7 Operations in the Instruction Set

The operators supported by most instruction set architectures can be categorized as in Figure 2.15. One rule of thumb across all architectures is that the most widely executed instructions are the simple operations of an instruction set. For example, Figure 2.16 shows 10 simple instructions that account for 96% of instructions executed for a collection of integer programs running on the popular Intel 80x86. Hence, the implementor of these instructions should be sure to make these fast, as they are the common case.

As mentioned before, the instructions in Figure 2.16 are found in every computer for every application—desktop, server, embedded—with the variations of

Operator type	Examples
Arithmetic and logical	Integer arithmetic and logical operations: add, subtract, and, or, multiple, divide
Data transfer	Loads-stores (move instructions on computers with memory addressing)
Control	Branch, jump, procedure call and return, traps
System	Operating system call, virtual memory management instructions
Floating point	Floating-point operations: add, multiply, divide, compare
Decimal	Decimal add, decimal multiply, decimal-to-character conversions
String	String move, string compare, string search
Graphics	Pixel and vertex operations, compression/decompression operations

Figure 2.15 Categories of instruction operators and examples of each. All computers generally provide a full set of operations for the first three categories. The support for system functions in the instruction set varies widely among architectures, but all computers must have some instruction support for basic system functions. The amount of support in the instruction set for the last four categories may vary from none to an extensive set of special instructions. Floating-point instructions will be provided in any computer that is intended for use in an application that makes much use of floating point. These instructions are sometimes part of an optional instruction set. Decimal and string instructions are sometimes primitives, as in the VAX or the IBM 360, or may be synthesized by the compiler from simpler instructions. Graphics instructions typically operate on many smaller data items in parallel, for example, performing eight 8-bit additions on two 64-bit operands.

Rank	80x86 instruction	Integer average (% total executed)
1	load	22%
2	conditional branch	20%
3	compare	16%
4	store	12%
5	add	8%
6	and	6%
7	sub	5%
8	move register-register	4%
9	call	1%
10	return	1%
Total		96%

Figure 2.16 The top 10 instructions for the 80x86. Simple instructions dominate this list and are responsible for 96% of the instructions executed. These percentages are the average of the five SPECint92 programs.

operations in Figure 2.15 largely depending on which data types that the instruction set includes.

2.8   Operations for Media and Signal Processing

Because media processing is judged by human perception, the data for multimedia operations is often much narrower than the 64-bit data word of modern desktop and server processors. For example, floating-point operations for graphics are normally in single precision, not double precision, and often at a precision less than required by IEEE 754. Rather than waste the 64-bit ALUs when operating on 32-bit, 16-bit, or even 8-bit integers, multimedia instructions can operate on several narrower data items at the same time. Thus, a *partitioned add* operation on 16-bit data with a 64-bit ALU would perform four 16-bit adds in a single clock cycle. The extra hardware cost is simply to prevent carries between the four 16-bit partitions of the ALU. For example, such instructions might be used for graphical operations on pixels.

These operations are commonly called *single-instruction multiple-data* (SIMD) or *vector* instructions. Chapter 6 and Appendix F describe the full machines that pioneered these architectures.

Most graphics multimedia applications use 32-bit floating-point operations. Some computers double peak performance of single-precision, floating-point operations; they allow a single instruction to launch two 32-bit operations on operands found side by side in a double-precision register. Just as in the prior case, the two partitions must be insulated to prevent operations on one half from affecting the other. Such floating-point operations are called *paired single operations*. For example, such an operation might be used for graphical transformations of vertices. This doubling in performance is typically accomplished by doubling the number of floating-point units, making it more expensive than just suppressing carries in integer adders.

Figure 2.17 summarizes the SIMD multimedia instructions found in several recent computers.

DSPs also provide operations found in the first three rows of Figure 2.15, but they change the semantics a bit. First, because they are often used in real-time applications, there is not an option of causing an exception on arithmetic overflow (otherwise it could miss an event); thus, the result will be used no matter what the inputs. To support such an unyielding environment, DSP architectures use *saturating arithmetic:* If the result is too large to be represented, it is set to the largest representable number, depending on the sign of the result. In contrast, two's complement arithmetic can add a small positive number to a large positive

Instruction category	Alpha MAX	HP PA-RISC MAX2	Intel Pentium MMX	PowerPC AltiVec	SPARC VIS
Add/subtract		4H	8B, 4H, 2W	16B, 8H, 4W	4H, 2W
Saturating add/sub		4H	8B, 4H	16B, 8H, 4W	
Multiply			4H	16B, 8H	
Compare	8B (>=)		8B, 4H, 2W (=, >)	16B, 8H, 4W (=, >, > =, <, <=)	4H, 2W (=, not=, >, <=)
Shift right/left		4H	4H, 2W	16B, 8H, 4W	
Shift right arithmetic		4H		16B, 8H, 4W	
Multiply and add				8H	
Shift and add (saturating)		4H			
And/or/xor	8B, 4H, 2W	8B, 4H, 2W	8B, 4H, 2W	16B, 8H, 4W	8B, 4H, 2W
Absolute difference	8B			16B, 8H, 4W	8B
Maximum/minimum	8B, 4W			16B, 8H, 4W	
Pack (2n bits → n bits)	2W → 2B, 4H → 4B	2*4H → 8B	4H → 4B, 2W → 2H	4W → 4B, 8H → 8B	2W → 2H, 2W → 2B, 4H → 4B
Unpack/merge	2B → 2W, 4B → 4H		2B → 2W, 4B → 4H	4B → 4W, 8B → 8H	4B → 4H, 2*4B → 8B
Permute/shuffle		4H		16B, 8H, 4W	

Figure 2.17 **Summary of multimedia support for desktop RISCs.** Note the diversity of support, with little in common across the five architectures. All are fixed-width operations, performing multiple narrow operations on either a 64-bit or 128-bit ALU. B stands for byte (8 bits), H for half word (16 bits), and W for word (32 bits). Thus, 8B means an operation on 8 bytes in a single instruction. Note that AltiVec assumes a 128-bit ALU, and the rest assume 64 bits. Pack and unpack use the notation 2*2W to mean 2 operands each with 2 words. This table is a simplification of the full multimedia architectures, leaving out many details. For example, HP MAX2 includes an instruction to calculate averages, and SPARC VIS includes instructions to set registers to constants. Also, this table does not include the memory alignment operation of AltiVec, MAX, and VIS.

number and end up with a negative result. DSP algorithms rely on saturating arithmetic and would be incorrect if run on a computer without it.

A second issue for DSPs is that there are several modes to round the wider accumulators into the narrower data words, just as the IEEE 754 has several rounding modes to choose from.

Finally, the targeted kernels for DSPs accumulate a series of products, and hence have a *multiply-accumulate* (MAC) instruction. MACs are key to dot product operations for vector and matrix multiplies. In fact, MACs/second is the primary peak performance metric that DSP architects brag about. The wide accumulators are used primarily to accumulate products, with rounding used when transferring results to memory.

Figure 2.18 shows the static mix of instructions for the TI TMS320C540x DSP for a set of library routines. This 16-bit architecture uses two 40-bit accumulators, plus a stack for passing parameters to library routines and for saving return addresses. DSP designers believe multiplies and MACs are more common for their applications than in desktop applications, and this static data supports that belief. Although not shown in the figure, 15% to 20% of the multiplies and MACs round the final sum. The C54 also has eight address registers that can be accessed via load and store instructions, as these registers are memory mapped—that is, each register also has a memory address. The larger number of stores is due in part to writing portions of the 40-bit accumulators to 16-bit words, and also to transfer between registers as their index registers also have memory addressees. There are no floating-point operations, as is typical of many DSPs, so these operations are all on fixed-point integers.

Summary: Operations in the Instruction Set and for Media and Signal Processing

From this section and the section preceding it, we see the importance and popularity of simple instructions: load, store, add, subtract, move register-register, and shift. DSPs add multiplies and multiply-accumulates to this simple set of primitives.

Reviewing where we are in the architecture space, we have looked at instruction classes and selected register-register. We selected displacement, immediate, and register indirect addressing and selected 8-, 16-, 32-, and 64-bit integers and 32- and 64-bit floating point. For operations we emphasize the simple list mentioned above. We are now ready to show how computers make decisions.

2.9   Instructions for Control Flow

Because the measurements of branch and jump behavior are fairly independent of other measurements and applications, we now examine the use of control flow instructions, which have little in common with the operations of the previous sections.

Instruction	Percent
store mem16	32.2%
load mem16	9.4%
add mem16	6.8%
call	5.0%
push mem16	5.0%
subtract mem16	4.9%
multiple-accumulate (MAC) mem16	4.6%
move mem-mem 16	4.0%
change status	3.7%
pop mem16	2.8%
conditional branch	2.6%
load mem32	2.5%
return	2.5%
store mem32	2.0%
branch	2.0%
repeat	2.0%
multiply	1.8%
NOP	1.5%
add mem32	1.3%
subtract mem32	0.9%
Total	**97.2%**

Figure 2.18 Mix of instructions for TMS320C540x DSP. As in Figure 2.16, simple instructions dominate this list of most frequent instructions. "Mem16" stands for a 16-bit memory operand, and "mem32" stands for a 32-bit memory operand. The large number of change status instructions is to set mode bits to affect instructions, essentially saving opcode space in these 16-bit instructions by keeping some of it in a status register. For example, status bits determine whether 32-bit operations operate in SIMD mode to produce 16-bit results in parallel or act as a single 32-bit result. For details on these measurements, see the caption of Figure 2.11.

There is no consistent terminology for instructions that change the flow of control. In the 1950s they were typically called *transfers*. Beginning in 1960 the name *branch* began to be used. Later, computers introduced additional names. Throughout this book we will use *jump* when the change in control is unconditional and *branch* when the change is conditional.

We can distinguish four different types of control flow change:

■ Conditional branches

■ Jumps

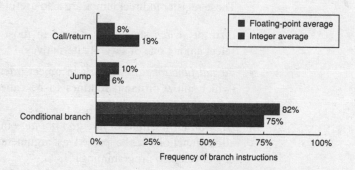

Figure 2.19 Breakdown of control flow instructions into three classes: calls or returns, jumps, and conditional branches. Conditional branches clearly dominate. Each type is counted in one of three bars. The programs and computer used to collect these statistics are the same as those in Figure 2.8.

- Procedure calls
- Procedure returns

We want to know the relative frequency of these events, as each event is different, may use different instructions, and may have different behavior. Figure 2.19 shows the frequencies of these control flow instructions for a load-store computer running our benchmarks.

Addressing Modes for Control Flow Instructions

The destination address of a control flow instruction must always be specified. This destination is specified explicitly in the instruction in the vast majority of cases—procedure return being the major exception, since for return the target is not known at compile time. The most common way to specify the destination is to supply a displacement that is added to the *program counter* (PC). Control flow instructions of this sort are called *PC-relative*. PC-relative branches or jumps are advantageous because the target is often near the current instruction, and specifying the position relative to the current PC requires fewer bits. Using PC-relative addressing also permits the code to run independently of where it is loaded. This property, called *position independence*, can eliminate some work when the program is linked and is also useful in programs linked dynamically during execution.

To implement returns and indirect jumps when the target is not known at compile time, a method other than PC-relative addressing is required. Here, there must be a way to specify the target dynamically, so that it can change at run time. This dynamic address may be as simple as naming a register that contains the target address; alternatively, the jump may permit any addressing mode to be used to supply the target address.

These register indirect jumps are also useful for four other important features:

- *Case* or *switch* statements, found in most programming languages (which select among one of several alternatives)

- *Virtual functions* or *methods* in object-oriented languages like C++ or Java (which allow different routines to be called depending on the type of the argument)

- *High-order functions* or *function pointers* in languages like C or C++ (which allow functions to be passed as arguments, giving some of the flavor of object-oriented programming)

- *Dynamically shared libraries* (which allow a library to be loaded and linked at run time only when it is actually invoked by the program rather than loaded and linked statically before the program is run)

In all four cases the target address is not known at compile time, and hence is usually loaded from memory into a register before the register indirect jump.

As branches generally use PC-relative addressing to specify their targets, an important question concerns how far branch targets are from branches. Knowing the distribution of these displacements will help in choosing what branch offsets to support, and thus will affect the instruction length and encoding. Figure 2.20 shows the distribution of displacements for PC-relative branches in instructions. About 75% of the branches are in the forward direction.

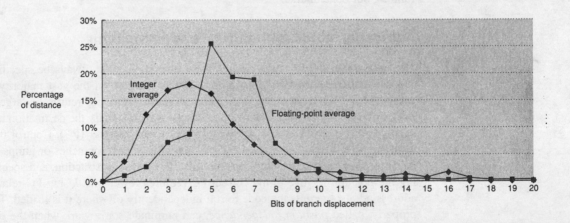

Figure 2.20 Branch distances in terms of number of instructions between the target and the branch instruction. The most frequent branches in the integer programs are to targets that can be encoded in 4–8 bits. This result tells us that short displacement fields often suffice for branches and that the designer can gain some encoding density by having a shorter instruction with a smaller branch displacement. These measurements were taken on a load-store computer (Alpha architecture) with all instructions aligned on word boundaries. An architecture that requires fewer instructions for the same program, such as a VAX, would have shorter branch distances. However, the number of bits needed for the displacement may increase if the computer has variable-length instructions to be aligned on any byte boundary. Figure 2.42 for Exercise 2.5 shows the accumulative distribution of these branch displacement data. The programs and computer used to collect these statistics are the same as those in Figure 2.8.

Conditional Branch Options

Since most changes in control flow are branches, deciding how to specify the branch condition is important. Figure 2.21 shows the three primary techniques in use today and their advantages and disadvantages.

One of the most noticeable properties of branches is that a large number of the comparisons are simple tests, and a large number are comparisons with zero. Thus, some architectures choose to treat these comparisons as special cases, especially if a *compare and branch* instruction is being used. Figure 2.22 shows the frequency of different comparisons used for conditional branching.

DSPs add another looping structure, usually called a *repeat* instruction. It allows a single instruction or a block of instructions to be repeated up to, say, 256 times. For example, the TMS320C54 dedicates three special registers to hold the block starting address, ending address, and repeat counter. The memory instructions in a repeat loop will typically have autoincrement or autodecrement addressing to access a vector. The goal of such instructions is to avoid loop overhead, which can be significant in the small loops of DSP kernels.

Procedure Invocation Options

Procedure calls and returns include control transfer and possibly some state saving; at a minimum the return address must be saved somewhere, sometimes in a special link register or just a GPR. Some older architectures provide a mechanism to save many registers, while newer architectures require the compiler to generate stores and loads for each register saved and restored.

Name	Examples	How condition is tested	Advantages	Disadvantages
Condition code (CC)	80x86, ARM, PowerPC, SPARC, SuperH	Tests special bits set by ALU operations, possibly under program control.	Sometimes condition is set for free.	CC is extra state. Condition codes constrain the ordering of instructions since they pass information from one instruction to a branch.
Condition register	Alpha, MIPS	Tests arbitrary register with the result of a comparison.	Simple.	Uses up a register.
Compare and branch	PA-RISC, VAX	Compare is part of the branch. Often compare is limited to subset.	One instruction rather than two for a branch.	May be too much work per instruction for pipelined execution.

Figure 2.21 The major methods for evaluating branch conditions, their advantages, and their disadvantages. Although condition codes can be set by ALU operations that are needed for other purposes, measurements on programs show that this rarely happens. The major implementation problems with condition codes arise when the condition code is set by a large or haphazardly chosen subset of the instructions, rather than being controlled by a bit in the instruction. Computers with compare and branch often limit the set of compares and use a condition register for more complex compares. Often, different techniques are used for branches based on floating-point comparison versus those based on integer comparison. This dichotomy is reasonable since the number of branches that depend on floating-point comparisons is much smaller than the number depending on integer comparisons.

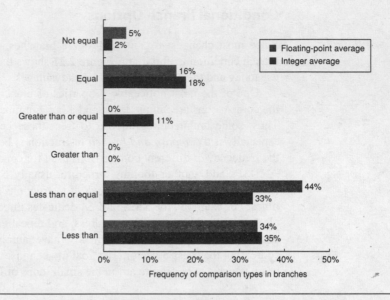

Figure 2.22 Frequency of different types of compares in conditional branches. Less than (or equal) branches dominate this combination of compiler and architecture. These measurements include both the integer and floating-point compares in branches. The programs and computer used to collect these statistics are the same as those in Figure 2.8.

There are two basic conventions in use to save registers: either at the call site or inside the procedure being called. *Caller saving* means that the calling procedure must save the registers that it wants preserved for access after the call, and thus the called procedure need not worry about registers. *Callee saving* is the opposite: the called procedure must save the registers it wants to use, leaving the caller unrestrained.

There are times when caller save must be used because of access patterns to globally visible variables in two different procedures. For example, suppose we have a procedure P1 that calls procedure P2, and both procedures manipulate the global variable x. If P1 had allocated x to a register, it must be sure to save x to a location known by P2 before the call to P2. A compiler's ability to discover when a called procedure may access register-allocated quantities is complicated by the possibility of separate compilation. Suppose P2 may not touch x but can call another procedure, P3, that may access x, yet P2 and P3 are compiled separately. Because of these complications, most compilers will conservatively caller save *any* variable that may be accessed during a call.

In the cases where either convention could be used, some programs will be more optimal with callee save and some will be more optimal with caller save. As a result, most real systems today use a combination of the two mechanisms. This convention is specified in an application binary interface (ABI) that sets down the basic rules as to which registers should be caller saved and which should be callee saved. Later in this chapter we will examine the mismatch between sophisticated instructions for automatically saving registers and the needs of the compiler.

Summary: Instructions for Control Flow

Control flow instructions are some of the most frequently executed instructions. Although there are many options for conditional branches, we would expect branch addressing in a new architecture to be able to jump to hundreds of instructions either above or below the branch. This requirement suggests a PC-relative branch displacement of at least 8 bits. We would also expect to see register indirect and PC-relative addressing for jump instructions to support returns as well as many other features of current systems.

We have now completed our instruction architecture tour at the level seen by an assembly language programmer or compiler writer. We are leaning toward a register-register architecture with displacement, immediate, and register indirect addressing modes. These data are 8-, 16-, 32-, and 64-bit integers and 32- and 64-bit floating-point data. The instructions include simple operations, PC-relative conditional branches, jump and link instructions for procedure call, and register indirect jumps for procedure return (plus a few other uses).

Now we need to select how to represent this architecture in a form that makes it easy for the hardware to execute.

2.10 Encoding an Instruction Set

Clearly, the choices mentioned above will affect how the instructions are encoded into a binary representation for execution by the processor. This representation affects not only the size of the compiled program; it affects the implementation of the processor, which must decode this representation to quickly find the operation and its operands. The operation is typically specified in one field, called the *opcode*. As we shall see, the important decision is how to encode the addressing modes with the operations.

This decision depends on the range of addressing modes and the degree of independence between opcodes and modes. Some older computers have one to five operands with 10 addressing modes for each operand (see Figure 2.6). For such a large number of combinations, typically a separate *address specifier* is needed for each operand: The address specifier tells what addressing mode is used to access the operand. At the other extreme are load-store computers with only one memory operand and only one or two addressing modes; obviously, in this case, the addressing mode can be encoded as part of the opcode.

When encoding the instructions, the number of registers and the number of addressing modes both have a significant impact on the size of instructions, as the register field and addressing mode field may appear many times in a single instruction. In fact, for most instructions many more bits are consumed in encoding addressing modes and register fields than in specifying the opcode. The architect must balance several competing forces when encoding the instruction set:

1. The desire to have as many registers and addressing modes as possible.

2. The impact of the size of the register and addressing mode fields on the average instruction size and hence on the average program size.

3. A desire to have instructions encoded into lengths that will be easy to handle in a pipelined implementation. (The importance of having easily decoded instructions is discussed in Chapters 3 and 4.) As a minimum, the architect wants instructions to be in multiples of bytes, rather than an arbitrary bit length. Many desktop and server architects have chosen to use a fixed-length instruction to gain implementation benefits while sacrificing average code size.

Figure 2.23 shows three popular choices for encoding the instruction set. The first we call *variable,* since it allows virtually all addressing modes to be with all operations. This style is best when there are many addressing modes and operations. The second choice we call *fixed,* since it combines the operation and the addressing mode into the opcode. Often fixed encoding will have only a single size for all instructions; it works best when there are few addressing modes and operations. The trade-off between variable encoding and fixed encoding is size of programs versus ease of decoding in the processor. Variable tries to use as few bits as possible to represent the program, but individual instructions can vary widely in both size and the amount of work to be performed.

Let's look at an 80x86 instruction to see an example of the variable encoding:

```
add EAX,1000(EBX)
```

The name add means a 32-bit integer add instruction with two operands, and this opcode takes 1 byte. An 80x86 address specifier is 1 or 2 bytes, specifying the source/destination register (EAX) and the addressing mode (displacement in this case) and base register (EBX) for the second operand. This combination takes 1 byte to specify the operands. When in 32-bit mode (see Appendix D), the size of the address field is either 1 byte or 4 bytes. Since 1000 is bigger than 2^8, the total length of the instruction is

$$1 + 1 + 4 = 6 \text{ bytes}$$

The length of 80x86 instructions varies between 1 and 17 bytes. 80x86 programs are generally smaller than the RISC architectures, which use fixed formats (see Appendix C).

Given these two poles of instruction set design of variable and fixed, the third alternative immediately springs to mind: Reduce the variability in size and work of the variable architecture but provide multiple instruction lengths to reduce code size. This *hybrid* approach is the third encoding alternative and we'll see examples shortly.

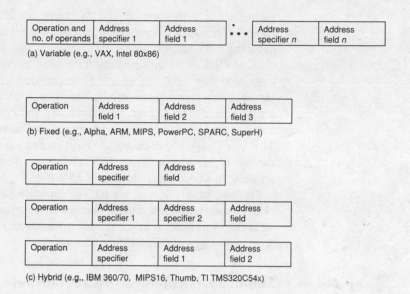

Figure 2.23 Three basic variations in instruction encoding: variable length, fixed length, and hybrid. The variable format can support any number of operands, with each address specifier determining the addressing mode and the length of the specifier for that operand. It generally enables the smallest code representation, since unused fields need not be included. The fixed format always has the same number of operands, with the addressing modes (if options exist) specified as part of the opcode (see also Figure C.3 in Appendix C). It generally results in the largest code size. Although the fields tend not to vary in their location, they will be used for different purposes by different instructions. The hybrid approach has multiple formats specified by the opcode, adding one or two fields to specify the addressing mode and one or two fields to specify the operand address (see also Figure D.7 in Appendix D).

Reduced Code Size in RISCs

As RISC computers started being used in embedded applications, the 32-bit fixed format became a liability since cost and hence smaller code are important. In response, several manufacturers offered a new hybrid version of their RISC instruction sets, with both 16-bit and 32-bit instructions. The narrow instructions support fewer operations, smaller address and immediate fields, fewer registers, and two-address format rather than the classic three-address format of RISC computers. Appendix C gives two examples, the ARM Thumb and MIPS MIPS16, which both claim a code size reduction of up to 40%.

In contrast to these instruction set extensions, IBM simply compresses its standard instruction set, and then adds hardware to decompress instructions as they are fetched from memory on an instruction cache miss. Thus, the instruction cache contains full 32-bit instructions, but compressed code is kept in main memory, ROMs, and the disk. The advantage of MIPS16 and Thumb is that instruction caches act as if they are about 25% larger, while IBM's CodePack means that compilers need not be changed to handle different instruction sets and instruction decoding can remain simple.

CodePack starts with run-length encoding compression on any PowerPC program, and then loads the resulting compression tables in a 2 KB table on chip. Hence, every program has its own unique encoding. To handle branches, which are no longer to an aligned word boundary, the PowerPC creates a hash table in memory that maps between compressed and uncompressed addresses. Like a TLB (see Chapter 5), it caches the most recently used address maps to reduce the number of memory accesses. IBM claims an overall performance cost of 10%, resulting in a code size reduction of 35% to 40%.

Hitachi simply invented a RISC instruction set with a fixed 16-bit format, called SuperH, for embedded applications (see Appendix C). It has 16 rather than 32 registers to make it fit the narrower format and fewer instructions, but otherwise looks like a classic RISC architecture.

Summary: Encoding an Instruction Set

Decisions made in the components of instruction set design discussed in previous sections determine whether the architect has the choice between variable and fixed instruction encodings. Given the choice, the architect more interested in code size than performance will pick variable encoding, and the one more interested in performance than code size will pick fixed encoding. The appendices give 11 examples of the results of architects' choices. In Chapters 3 and 4, the impact of variability on performance of the processor will be discussed further.

We have almost finished laying the groundwork for the MIPS instruction set architecture that will be introduced in Section 2.12. Before we do that, however, it will be helpful to take a brief look at compiler technology and its effect on program properties.

2.11 Crosscutting Issues: The Role of Compilers

Today almost all programming is done in high-level languages for desktop and server applications. This development means that since most instructions executed are the output of a compiler, an instruction set architecture is essentially a compiler target. In earlier times for these applications, and currently for DSPs, architectural decisions were often made to ease assembly language programming or for a specific kernel. Because the compiler will significantly affect the performance of a computer, understanding compiler technology today is critical to designing and efficiently implementing an instruction set.

Once it was popular to try to isolate the compiler technology and its effect on hardware performance from the architecture and its performance, just as it was popular to try to separate architecture from its implementation. This separation is essentially impossible with today's desktop compilers and computers. Architectural choices affect the quality of the code that can be generated for a computer and the complexity of building a good compiler for it, for better or for worse. For example, Section 2.14 shows the substantial performance impact on a DSP of compiling versus hand-optimizing the code.

In this section, we discuss the critical goals in the instruction set primarily from the compiler viewpoint. It starts with a review of the anatomy of current compilers. Next we discuss how compiler technology affects the decisions of the architect, and how the architect can make it hard or easy for the compiler to produce good code. We conclude with a review of compilers and multimedia operations, which unfortunately is a bad example of cooperation between compiler writers and architects.

The Structure of Recent Compilers

To begin, let's look at what optimizing compilers are like today. Figure 2.24 shows the structure of recent compilers.

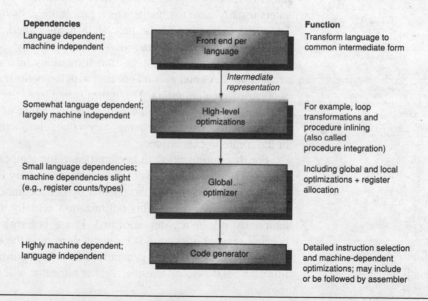

Figure 2.24 Compilers typically consist of two to four passes, with more highly optimizing compilers having more passes. This structure maximizes the probability that a program compiled at various levels of optimization will produce the same output when given the same input. The optimizing passes are designed to be optional and may be skipped when faster compilation is the goal and lower-quality code is acceptable. A *pass* is simply one phase in which the compiler reads and transforms the entire program. (The term *phase* is often used interchangeably with *pass*.) Because the optimizing passes are separated, multiple languages can use the same optimizing and code generation passes. Only a new front end is required for a new language.

A compiler writer's first goal is correctness—all valid programs must be compiled correctly. The second goal is usually speed of the compiled code. Typically, a whole set of other goals follows these two, including fast compilation, debugging support, and interoperability among languages. Normally, the passes in the compiler transform higher-level, more abstract representations into progressively lower-level representations. Eventually it reaches the instruction set. This structure helps manage the complexity of the transformations and makes writing a bug-free compiler easier.

The complexity of writing a correct compiler is a major limitation on the amount of optimization that can be done. Although the multiple-pass structure helps reduce compiler complexity, it also means that the compiler must order and perform some transformations before others. In the diagram of the optimizing compiler in Figure 2.24, we can see that certain high-level optimizations are performed long before it is known what the resulting code will look like. Once such a transformation is made, the compiler can't afford to go back and revisit all steps, possibly undoing transformations. Such iteration would be prohibitive, both in compilation time and in complexity. Thus, compilers make assumptions about the ability of later steps to deal with certain problems. For example, compilers usually have to choose which procedure calls to expand inline before they know the exact size of the procedure being called. Compiler writers call this problem the *phase-ordering problem*.

How does this ordering of transformations interact with the instruction set architecture? A good example occurs with the optimization called *global common subexpression elimination*. This optimization finds two instances of an expression that compute the same value and saves the value of the first computation in a temporary. It then uses the temporary value, eliminating the second computation of the common expression.

For this optimization to be significant, the temporary must be allocated to a register. Otherwise, the cost of storing the temporary in memory and later reloading it may negate the savings gained by not recomputing the expression. There are, in fact, cases where this optimization actually slows down code when the temporary is not register allocated. Phase ordering complicates this problem because register allocation is typically done near the end of the global optimization pass, just before code generation. Thus, an optimizer that performs this optimization *must* assume that the register allocator will allocate the temporary to a register.

Optimizations performed by modern compilers can be classified by the style of the transformation, as follows:

- *High-level optimizations* are often done on the source with output fed to later optimization passes.

- *Local optimizations* optimize code only within a straight-line code fragment (called a *basic block* by compiler people).

- *Global optimizations* extend the local optimizations across branches and introduce a set of transformations aimed at optimizing loops.

- *Register allocation* associates registers with operands.
- *Processor-dependent optimizations* attempt to take advantage of specific architectural knowledge.

Register Allocation

Because of the central role that register allocation plays, both in speeding up the code and in making other optimizations useful, it is one of the most important—if not the most important—of the optimizations. Register allocation algorithms today are based on a technique called *graph coloring*. The basic idea behind graph coloring is to construct a graph representing the possible candidates for allocation to a register and then to use the graph to allocate registers. Roughly speaking, the problem is how to use a limited set of colors so that no two adjacent nodes in a dependency graph have the same color. The emphasis in the approach is to achieve 100% register allocation of active variables. The problem of coloring a graph in general can take exponential time as a function of the size of the graph (NP-complete). There are heuristic algorithms, however, that work well in practice, yielding close allocations that run in near-linear time.

Graph coloring works best when there are at least 16 (and preferably more) general-purpose registers available for global allocation for integer variables and additional registers for floating point. Unfortunately, graph coloring does not work very well when the number of registers is small because the heuristic algorithms for coloring the graph are likely to fail.

Impact of Optimizations on Performance

It is sometimes difficult to separate some of the simpler optimizations—local and processor-dependent optimizations—from transformations done in the code generator. Examples of typical optimizations are given in Figure 2.25. The last column of Figure 2.25 indicates the frequency with which the listed optimizing transforms were applied to the source program.

Figure 2.26 shows the effect of various optimizations on instructions executed for two programs. In this case, optimized programs executed roughly 25% to 90% fewer instructions than unoptimized programs. The figure illustrates the importance of looking at optimized code before suggesting new instruction set features, since a compiler might completely remove the instructions the architect was trying to improve.

The Impact of Compiler Technology on the Architect's Decisions

The interaction of compilers and high-level languages significantly affects how programs use an instruction set architecture. There are two important questions: How are variables allocated and addressed? How many registers are needed to

Optimization name	Explanation	Percentage of the total number of optimizing transforms
High-level	*At or near the source level; processor-independent*	
Procedure integration	Replace procedure call by procedure body	N.M.
Local	*Within straight-line code*	
Common subexpression elimination	Replace two instances of the same computation by single copy	18%
Constant propagation	Replace all instances of a variable that is assigned a constant with the constant	22%
Stack height reduction	Rearrange expression tree to minimize resources needed for expression evaluation	N.M.
Global	*Across a branch*	
Global common subexpression elimination	Same as local, but this version crosses branches	13%
Copy propagation	Replace all instances of a variable A that has been assigned X (i.e., $A = X$) with X	11%
Code motion	Remove code from a loop that computes same value each iteration of the loop	16%
Induction variable elimination	Simplify/eliminate array addressing calculations within loops	2%
Processor-dependent	*Depends on processor knowledge*	
Strength reduction	Many examples, such as replace multiply by a constant with adds and shifts	N.M.
Pipeline scheduling	Reorder instructions to improve pipeline performance	N.M.
Branch offset optimization	Choose the shortest branch displacement that reaches target	N.M.

Figure 2.25 Major types of optimizations and examples in each class. These data tell us about the relative frequency of occurrence of various optimizations. The third column lists the static frequency with which some of the common optimizations are applied in a set of 12 small FORTRAN and Pascal programs. There are nine local and global optimizations done by the compiler included in the measurement. Six of these optimizations are covered in the figure, and the remaining three account for 18% of the total static occurrences. The abbreviation *N.M.* means that the number of occurrences of that optimization was not measured. Processor-dependent optimizations are usually done in a code generator, and none of those was measured in this experiment. The percentage is the portion of the static optimizations that are of the specified type. Data from Chow [1983] (collected using the Stanford UCODE compiler).

allocate variables appropriately? To address these questions, we must look at the three separate areas in which current high-level languages allocate their data:

■ The *stack* is used to allocate local variables. The stack is grown or shrunk on procedure call or return, respectively. Objects on the stack are addressed relative to the stack pointer and are primarily scalars (single variables) rather than

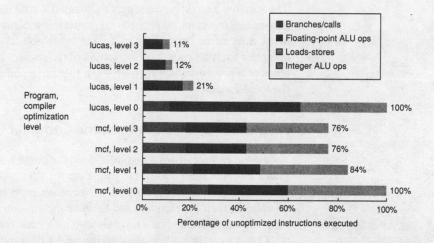

Figure 2.26 Change in instruction count for the programs lucas and mcf from the SPEC2000 as compiler optimization levels vary. Level 0 is the same as unoptimized code. Level 1 includes local optimizations, code scheduling, and local register allocation. Level 2 includes global optimizations, loop transformations (software pipelining), and global register allocation. Level 3 adds procedure integration. These experiments were performed on the Alpha compilers.

arrays. The stack is used for activation records, *not* as a stack for evaluating expressions. Hence, values are almost never pushed or popped on the stack.

- The *global data area* is used to allocate statically declared objects, such as global variables and constants. A large percentage of these objects are arrays or other aggregate data structures.

- The *heap* is used to allocate dynamic objects that do not adhere to a stack discipline. Objects in the heap are accessed with pointers and are typically not scalars.

Register allocation is much more effective for stack-allocated objects than for global variables, and register allocation is essentially impossible for heap-allocated objects because they are accessed with pointers. Global variables and some stack variables are impossible to allocate because they are *aliased*—there are multiple ways to refer to the address of a variable, making it illegal to put it into a register. (Most heap variables are effectively aliased for today's compiler technology.)

For example, consider the following code sequence, where & returns the address of a variable and * dereferences a pointer:

```
p = &a          -- gets address of a in p
a = ...         -- assigns to a directly
*p = ...        -- uses p to assign to a
...a...         -- accesses a
```

The variable a could not be register allocated across the assignment to *p without generating incorrect code. Aliasing causes a substantial problem because it is often difficult or impossible to decide what objects a pointer may refer to. A compiler must be conservative; some compilers will not allocate *any* local variables of a procedure in a register when there is a pointer that may refer to *one* of the local variables.

How the Architect Can Help the Compiler Writer

Today, the complexity of a compiler does not come from translating simple statements like A = B + C. Most programs are *locally simple,* and simple translations work fine. Rather, complexity arises because programs are large and globally complex in their interactions, and because the structure of compilers means decisions are made one step at a time about which code sequence is best.

Compiler writers often are working under their own corollary of a basic principle in architecture: *Make the frequent cases fast and the rare case correct.* That is, if we know which cases are frequent and which are rare, and if generating code for both is straightforward, then the quality of the code for the rare case may not be very important—but it must be correct!

Some instruction set properties help the compiler writer. These properties should not be thought of as hard-and-fast rules, but rather as guidelines that will make it easier to write a compiler that will generate efficient and correct code.

- *Provide regularity* —Whenever it makes sense, the three primary components of an instruction set—the operations, the data types, and the addressing modes—should be *orthogonal.* Two aspects of an architecture are said to be orthogonal if they are independent. For example, the operations and addressing modes are orthogonal if, for every operation to which one addressing mode can be applied, all addressing modes are applicable. This regularity helps simplify code generation and is particularly important when the decision about what code to generate is split into two passes in the compiler. A good counterexample of this property is restricting what registers can be used for a certain class of instructions. Compilers for special-purpose register architectures typically get stuck in this dilemma. This restriction can result in the compiler finding itself with lots of available registers, but none of the right kind!

- *Provide primitives, not solutions*—Special features that "match" a language construct or a kernel function are often unusable. Attempts to support high-level languages may work only with one language, or do more or less than is required for a correct and efficient implementation of the language. An example of how such attempts have failed is given in Section 2.14.

- *Simplify trade-offs among alternatives*—One of the toughest jobs a compiler writer has is figuring out what instruction sequence will be best for every segment of code that arises. In earlier days, instruction counts or total code size might have been good metrics, but—as we saw in the last chapter—this is no longer true. With caches and pipelining, the trade-offs have become very complex. Anything the designer can do to help the compiler writer understand the costs of alternative code sequences would help improve the code. One of the most difficult instances of complex trade-offs occurs in a register-memory architecture in deciding how many times a variable should be referenced before it is cheaper to load it into a register. This threshold is hard to compute and, in fact, may vary among models of the same architecture.

■ *Provide instructions that bind the quantities known at compile time as constants*—A compiler writer hates the thought of the processor interpreting at run time a value that was known at compile time. Good counterexamples of this principle include instructions that interpret values that were fixed at compile time. For instance, the VAX procedure call instruction (calls) dynamically interprets a mask saying what registers to save on a call, but the mask is fixed at compile time (see Section 2.14).

Compiler Support (or Lack Thereof) for Multimedia Instructions

Alas, the designers of the SIMD instructions that operate on several narrow data items in a single clock cycle consciously ignored the previous subsection. These instructions tend to be solutions, not primitives; they are short of registers; and the data types do not match existing programming languages. Architects hoped to find an inexpensive solution that would help some users, but in reality, only a few low-level graphics library routines use them.

The SIMD instructions are really an abbreviated version of an elegant architecture style that has its own compiler technology. As explained in Appendix G, *vector architectures* operate on vectors of data. Invented originally for scientific codes, multimedia kernels are often vectorizable as well. Hence, we can think of Intel's MMX or PowerPC's AltiVec as simply short vector computers: MMX with vectors of eight 8-bit elements, four 16-bit elements, or two 32-bit elements, and AltiVec with vectors twice that length. They are implemented as simply adjacent, narrow elements in wide registers.

These abbreviated architectures build the vector register size into the architecture: the sum of the sizes of the elements is limited to 64 bits for MMX and 128 bits for AltiVec. When Intel decided to expand to 128-bit vectors, it added a whole new set of instructions, called Streaming SIMD Extension (SSE).

The missing elegance from these architectures involves the specification of the vector length and the memory addressing modes. By making the vector width variable, these vectors seamlessly switch between different data widths simply by increasing the number of elements per vector. For example, vectors could have, say, 32 64-bit elements, 64 32-bit elements, 128 16-bit elements, and 256 8-bit elements. Another advantage is that the number of elements per vector register can vary between generations while remaining binary compatible. One generation might have 32 64-bit elements per vector register, and the next have 64 64-bit elements. (The number of elements per register is located in a status register.) The number of elements executed per clock cycle is also implementation dependent, and all run the same binary code. Thus, one generation might operate at 64 bits per clock cycle, and another at 256 bits per clock cycle.

A major advantage of vector computers is hiding latency of memory access by loading many elements at once and then overlapping execution with data transfer. The goal of vector addressing modes is to collect data scattered about memory, place them in a compact form so that they can be operated on efficiently, and then place the results back where they belong.

Over the years traditional vector computers added *strided addressing* and *gather/scatter addressing* to increase the number of programs that can be vectorized. Strided addressing skips a fixed number of words between each access, so sequential addressing is often called *unit stride addressing*. Gather and scatter find their addresses in another vector register: Think of it as register indirect addressing for vector computers. From a vector perspective, in contrast, these short-vector SIMD computers support only unit strided accesses: Memory accesses load or store all elements at once from a single wide memory location. Since the data for multimedia applications are often streams that start and end in memory, strided and gather/scatter addressing modes are essential to successful vectorization.

Example   As an example, compare a vector computer to MMX for color representation conversion of pixels from RGB (red green blue) to YUV (luminosity chrominance), with each pixel represented by 3 bytes. The conversion is just three lines of C code placed in a loop:

```
Y = ( 9798*R + 19235*G + 3736*B)/ 32768;
U = (-4784*R -  9437*G + 4221*B)/ 32768 + 128;
V = (20218*R - 16941*G - 3277*B)/ 32768 + 128;
```

A 64-bit-wide vector computer can calculate 8 pixels simultaneously. One vector computer for media with strided addresses takes

- 3 vector loads (to get RGB)
- 3 vector multiplies (to convert R)
- 6 vector multiply adds (to convert G and B)
- 3 vector shifts (to divide by 32,768)
- 2 vector adds (to add 128)
- 3 vector stores (to store YUV)

The total is 20 instructions to perform the 20 operations in the previous C code to convert 8 pixels [Kozyrakis 2000]. (Since a vector might have 32 64-bit elements, this code actually converts up to 32×8 or 256 pixels.)

In contrast, Intel's Web site shows that a library routine to perform the same calculation on 8 pixels takes 116 MMX instructions plus 6 80x86 instructions [Intel 2001]. This sixfold increase in instructions is due to the large number of instructions to load and unpack RGB pixels and to pack and store YUV pixels, since there are no strided memory accesses.

Having short, architecture-limited vectors with few registers and simple memory addressing modes makes it more difficult to use vectorizing compiler technology. Another challenge is that no programming language (yet) has support for operations on these narrow data. Hence, these SIMD instructions are commonly found only in hand-coded libraries.

Summary: The Role of Compilers

This section leads to several recommendations. First, we expect a new instruction set architecture to have at least 16 general-purpose registers—not counting separate registers for floating-point numbers—to simplify allocation of registers using graph coloring. The advice on orthogonality suggests that all supported addressing modes apply to all instructions that transfer data. Finally, the last three pieces of advice—provide primitives instead of solutions, simplify trade-offs between alternatives, don't bind constants at run time—all suggest that it is better to err on the side of simplicity. In other words, understand that less is more in the design of an instruction set. Alas, SIMD extensions are more an example of good marketing than outstanding achievement of hardware-software co-design.

2.12   Putting It All Together: The MIPS Architecture

In this section we describe a simple 64-bit load-store architecture called MIPS. The instruction set architecture of MIPS and RISC relatives was based on observations similar to those covered in the last sections. (In Section 2.16 we discuss how and why these architectures became popular.) Reviewing our expectations from each section, for desktop applications:

- *Section 2.2*—Use general-purpose registers with a load-store architecture.
- *Section 2.3*—Support these addressing modes: displacement (with an address offset size of 12–16 bits), immediate (size 8–16 bits), and register indirect.
- *Section 2.5*—Support these data sizes and types: 8-, 16-, 32-, and 64-bit integers and 64-bit IEEE 754 floating-point numbers.
- *Section 2.7*—Support these simple instructions, since they will dominate the number of instructions executed: load, store, add, subtract, move register-register, and shift.

- *Section 2.9*—Compare equal, compare not equal, compare less, branch (with a PC-relative address at least 8 bits long), jump, call, and return.

- *Section 2.10*—Use fixed instruction encoding if interested in performance, and use variable instruction encoding if interested in code size.

- *Section 2.11*—Provide at least 16 general-purpose registers, be sure all addressing modes apply to all data transfer instructions, and aim for a minimalist instruction set. This section didn't cover floating-point programs, but they often use separate floating-point registers. The justification is to increase the total number of registers without raising problems in the instruction format or in the speed of the general-purpose register file. This compromise, however, is not orthogonal.

We introduce MIPS by showing how it follows these recommendations. Like most recent computers, MIPS emphasizes

- a simple load-store instruction set
- design for pipelining efficiency (discussed in Appendix A), including a fixed instruction set encoding
- efficiency as a compiler target

MIPS provides a good architectural model for study, not only because of the popularity of this type of processor (see Chapter 1), but also because it is an easy architecture to understand. We will use this architecture again in Chapters 3 and 4, and it forms the basis for a number of exercises and programming projects.

In the 15 years since the first MIPS processor, there have been many versions of MIPS (see Appendix C). We will use a subset of what is now called MIPS64, which will often abbreviate to just MIPS, but the full instruction set is found in Appendix C.

Registers for MIPS

MIPS64 has 32 64-bit general-purpose registers (GPRs), named R0, R1, . . . , R31. GPRs are also sometimes known as *integer registers*. Additionally, there is a set of 32 floating-point registers (FPRs), named F0, F1, . . . , F31, which can hold 32 single-precision (32-bit) values or 32 double-precision (64-bit) values. (When holding one single-precision number, the other half of the FPR is unused.) Both single- and double-precision floating-point operations (32-bit and 64-bit) are provided. MIPS also includes instructions that operate on two single-precision operands in a single 64-bit floating-point register.

The value of R0 is always 0. We shall see later how we can use this register to synthesize a variety of useful operations from a simple instruction set.

A few special registers can be transferred to and from the general-purpose registers. An example is the floating-point status register, used to hold information about the results of floating-point operations. There are also instructions for moving between an FPR and a GPR.

Data Types for MIPS

The data types are 8-bit bytes, 16-bit half words, 32-bit words, and 64-bit double words for integer data and 32-bit single precision and 64-bit double precision for floating point. Half words were added because they are found in languages like C and popular in some programs, such as the operating systems, concerned about size of data structures. They will also become more popular if Unicode becomes widely used. Single-precision floating-point operands were added for similar reasons. (Remember the early warning that you should measure many more programs before designing an instruction set.)

The MIPS64 operations work on 64-bit integers and 32- or 64-bit floating point. Bytes, half words, and words are loaded into the general-purpose registers with either zeros or the sign bit replicated to fill the 64 bits of the GPRs. Once loaded, they are operated on with the 64-bit integer operations.

Addressing Modes for MIPS Data Transfers

The only data addressing modes are immediate and displacement, both with 16-bit fields. Register indirect is accomplished simply by placing 0 in the 16-bit displacement field, and absolute addressing with a 16-bit field is accomplished by using register 0 as the base register. Embracing zero gives us four effective modes, although only two are supported in the architecture.

MIPS memory is byte addressable with a 64-bit address. It has a mode bit that allows software to select either Big Endian or Little Endian. As it is a load-store architecture, all references between memory and either GPRs or FPRs are through loads or stores. Supporting the data types mentioned above, memory accesses involving GPRs can be to a byte, half word, word, or double word. The FPRs may be loaded and stored with single-precision or double-precision numbers. All memory accesses must be aligned.

MIPS Instruction Format

Since MIPS has just two addressing modes, these can be encoded into the opcode. Following the advice on making the processor easy to pipeline and decode, all instructions are 32 bits with a 6-bit primary opcode. Figure 2.27 shows the instruction layout. These formats are simple while providing 16-bit fields for displacement addressing, immediate constants, or PC-relative branch addresses.

Appendix C shows a variant of MIPS—called MIPS16—which has 16-bit and 32-bit instructions to improve code density for embedded applications. We will stick to the traditional 32-bit format in this book.

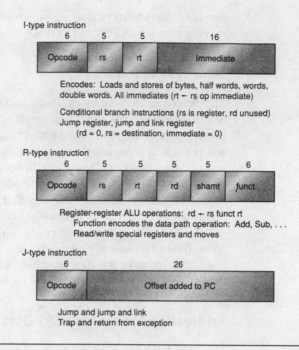

I-type instruction

6	5	5	16
Opcode	rs	rt	Immediate

Encodes: Loads and stores of bytes, half words, words, double words. All immediates (rt ← rs op immediate)

Conditional branch instructions (rs is register, rd unused)
Jump register, jump and link register
(rd = 0, rs = destination, immediate = 0)

R-type instruction

6	5	5	5	5	6
Opcode	rs	rt	rd	shamt	funct

Register-register ALU operations: rd ← rs funct rt
Function encodes the data path operation: Add, Sub, . . .
Read/write special registers and moves

J-type instruction

6	26
Opcode	Offset added to PC

Jump and jump and link
Trap and return from exception

Figure 2.27 Instruction layout for MIPS. All instructions are encoded in one of three types, with common fields in the same location in each format.

MIPS Operations

MIPS supports the list of simple operations recommended above plus a few others. There are four broad classes of instructions: loads and stores, ALU operations, branches and jumps, and floating-point operations.

Any of the general-purpose or floating-point registers may be loaded or stored, except that loading R0 has no effect. Figure 2.28 gives examples of the load and store instructions. Single-precision floating-point numbers occupy half a floating-point register. Conversions between single and double precision must be done explicitly. The floating-point format is IEEE 754 (see Appendix H). A list of all the MIPS instructions in our subset appears in Figure 2.31 (page 137).

To understand these figures we need to introduce a few additional extensions to our C description language presented initially on page 98:

- A subscript is appended to the symbol ← whenever the length of the datum being transferred might not be clear. Thus, $←_n$ means transfer an n-bit quantity. We use $x, y ← z$ to indicate that z should be transferred to x and y.

- A subscript is used to indicate selection of a bit from a field. Bits are labeled from the most-significant bit starting at 0. The subscript may be a single digit (e.g., Regs[R4]$_0$ yields the sign bit of R4) or a subrange (e.g., Regs[R3]$_{56..63}$ yields the least-significant byte of R3).

Example instruction	Instruction name	Meaning
LD R1,30(R2)	Load double word	$\text{Regs}[\text{R1}] \leftarrow_{64} \text{Mem}[30+\text{Regs}[\text{R2}]]$
LD R1,1000(R0)	Load double word	$\text{Regs}[\text{R1}] \leftarrow_{64} \text{Mem}[1000+0]$
LW R1,60(R2)	Load word	$\text{Regs}[\text{R1}] \leftarrow_{64} (\text{Mem}[60+\text{Regs}[\text{R2}]]_0)^{32} \#\# \text{Mem}[60+\text{Regs}[\text{R2}]]$
LB R1,40(R3)	Load byte	$\text{Regs}[\text{R1}] \leftarrow_{64} (\text{Mem}[40+\text{Regs}[\text{R3}]]_0)^{56} \#\#$ $\text{Mem}[40+\text{Regs}[\text{R3}]]$
LBU R1,40(R3)	Load byte unsigned	$\text{Regs}[\text{R1}] \leftarrow_{64} 0^{56} \#\# \text{Mem}[40+\text{Regs}[\text{R3}]]$
LH R1,40(R3)	Load half word	$\text{Regs}[\text{R1}] \leftarrow_{64} (\text{Mem}[40+\text{Regs}[\text{R3}]]_0)^{48} \#\#$ $\text{Mem}[40+\text{Regs}[\text{R3}]]\#\#\text{Mem}[41+\text{Regs}[\text{R3}]]$
L.S F0,50(R3)	Load FP single	$\text{Regs}[\text{F0}] \leftarrow_{64} \text{Mem}[50+\text{Regs}[\text{R3}]] \#\# 0^{32}$
L.D F0,50(R2)	Load FP double	$\text{Regs}[\text{F0}] \leftarrow_{64} \text{Mem}[50+\text{Regs}[\text{R2}]]$
SD R3,500(R4)	Store double word	$\text{Mem}[500+\text{Regs}[\text{R4}]] \leftarrow_{64} \text{Regs}[\text{R3}]$
SW R3,500(R4)	Store word	$\text{Mem}[500+\text{Regs}[\text{R4}]] \leftarrow_{32} \text{Regs}[\text{R3}]$
S.S F0,40(R3)	Store FP single	$\text{Mem}[40+\text{Regs}[\text{R3}]] \leftarrow_{32} \text{Regs}[\text{F0}]_{0..31}$
S.D F0,40(R3)	Store FP double	$\text{Mem}[40+\text{Regs}[\text{R3}]] \leftarrow_{64} \text{Regs}[\text{F0}]$
SH R3,502(R2)	Store half	$\text{Mem}[502+\text{Regs}[\text{R2}]] \leftarrow_{16} \text{Regs}[\text{R3}]_{48..63}$
SB R2,41(R3)	Store byte	$\text{Mem}[41+\text{Regs}[\text{R3}]] \leftarrow_{8} \text{Regs}[\text{R2}]_{56..63}$

Figure 2.28 The load and store instructions in MIPS. All use a single addressing mode and require that the memory value be aligned. Of course, both loads and stores are available for all the data types shown.

- The variable Mem, used as an array that stands for main memory, is indexed by a byte address and may transfer any number of bytes.

- A superscript is used to replicate a field (e.g., 0^{48} yields a field of zeros of length 48 bits).

- The symbol ## is used to concatenate two fields and may appear on either side of a data transfer.

A summary of the entire description language appears on the back inside cover. As an example, assuming that R8 and R10 are 64-bit registers:

$$\text{Regs}[\text{R10}]_{32..63} \leftarrow_{32} (\text{Mem}[\text{Regs}[\text{R8}]]_0)^{24} \#\# \text{Mem}[\text{Regs}[\text{R8}]]$$

means that the byte at the memory location addressed by the contents of register R8 is sign-extended to form a 32-bit quantity that is stored into the lower half of register R10. (The upper half of R10 is unchanged.)

All ALU instructions are register-register instructions. Figure 2.29 gives some examples of the arithmetic/logical instructions. The operations include simple arithmetic and logical operations: add, subtract, AND, OR, XOR, and shifts. Immediate forms of all these instructions are provided using a 16-bit sign-extended immediate. The operation LUI (load upper immediate) loads bits 32 through 47 of a register, while setting the rest of the register to 0. LUI allows a 32-bit constant to

Example instruction	Instruction name	Meaning
DADDU R1,R2,R3	Add unsigned	Regs[R1]←Regs[R2]+Regs[R3]
DADDIU R1,R2,#3	Add immediate unsigned	Regs[R1]←Regs[R2]+3
LUI R1,#42	Load upper immediate	Regs[R1]←0^{32}##42##0^{16}
DSLL R1,R2,#5	Shift left logical	Regs[R1]←Regs[R2]<<5
DSLT R1,R2,R3	Set less than	if (Regs[R2]<Regs[R3]) Regs[R1]←1 else Regs[R1]←0

Figure 2.29 Examples of arithmetic/logical instructions on MIPS, both with and without immediates.

be built in two instructions, or a data transfer using any constant 32-bit address in one extra instruction.

As mentioned above, R0 is used to synthesize popular operations. Loading a constant is simply an add immediate where one source operand is R0, and a register-register move is simply an add where one of the sources is R0. (We sometimes use the mnemonic LI, standing for load immediate, to represent the former, and the mnemonic MOV for the latter.)

MIPS Control Flow Instructions

MIPS provides compare instructions, which compare two registers to see if the first is less than the second. If the condition is true, these instructions place a 1 in the destination register (to represent true); otherwise they place the value 0. Because these operations "set" a register, they are called set-equal, set-not-equal, set-less-than, and so on. There are also immediate forms of these compares.

Control is handled through a set of jumps and a set of branches. Figure 2.30 gives some typical branch and jump instructions. The four jump instructions are differentiated by the two ways to specify the destination address and by whether or not a link is made. Two jumps use a 26-bit offset shifted 2 bits and then replace the lower 28 bits of the program counter (of the instruction sequentially following the jump) to determine the destination address. The other two jump instructions specify a register that contains the destination address. There are two flavors of jumps: plain jump and jump and link (used for procedure calls). The latter places the return address—the address of the next sequential instruction—in R31.

All branches are conditional. The branch condition is specified by the instruction, which may test the register source for zero or nonzero; the register may contain a data value or the result of a compare. There are also conditional branch instructions to test for whether a register is negative and for equality between two registers. The branch-target address is specified with a 16-bit signed offset that is shifted left two places and then added to the program counter, which

Example instruction	Instruction name	Meaning
J name	Jump	$PC_{36..63} \leftarrow$ name
JAL name	Jump and link	$Regs[R31] \leftarrow PC+4$; $PC_{36..63} \leftarrow$ name; $((PC+4)-2^{27}) \leq$ name $< ((PC+4)+2^{27})$
JALR R2	Jump and link register	$Regs[R31] \leftarrow PC+4$; $PC \leftarrow Regs[R2]$
JR R3	Jump register	$PC \leftarrow Regs[R3]$
BEQZ R4,name	Branch equal zero	if $(Regs[R4]==0)$ $PC \leftarrow$ name; $((PC+4)-2^{17}) \leq$ name $< ((PC+4)+2^{17})$
BNE R3,R4,name	Branch not equal zero	if $(Regs[R3]!= Regs[R4])$ $PC \leftarrow$ name; $((PC+4)-2^{17}) \leq$ name $< ((PC+4)+2^{17})$
MOVZ R1,R2,R3	Conditional move if zero	if $(Regs[R3]==0)$ $Regs[R1] \leftarrow Regs[R2]$

Figure 2.30 Typical control flow instructions in MIPS. All control instructions, except jumps to an address in a register, are PC-relative. Note that the branch distances are longer than the address field would suggest; since MIPS instructions are all 32 bits long, the byte branch address is multiplied by 4 to get a longer distance.

is pointing to the next sequential instruction. There is also a branch to test the floating-point status register for floating-point conditional branches, described later.

Chapters 3 and 4 show that conditional branches are a major challenge to pipelined execution; hence many architectures have added instructions to convert a simple branch into a conditional arithmetic instruction. MIPS included conditional move on zero or not zero. The value of the destination register either is left unchanged or is replaced by a copy of one of the source registers depending on whether or not the value of the other source register is zero.

MIPS Floating-Point Operations

Floating-point instructions manipulate the floating-point registers and indicate whether the operation to be performed is single or double precision. The operations MOV.S and MOV.D copy a single-precision (MOV.S) or double-precision (MOV.D) floating-point register to another register of the same type. The operations MFC1 and MTC1 move data between a single floating-point register and an integer register; moving a double-precision value to two integer registers requires two instructions. Conversions from integer to floating point are also provided, and vice versa.

The floating-point operations are add, subtract, multiply, and divide; a suffix D is used for double precision, and a suffix S is used for single precision (e.g., ADD.D, ADD.S, SUB.D, SUB.S, MUL.D, MUL.S, DIV.D, DIV.S). Floating-point compares set a bit in the special floating-point status register that can be tested with a pair of branches: BC1T and BC1F, branch floating-point true and branch floating-point false.

To get greater performance for graphics routines, MIPS64 has instructions that perform two 32-bit floating-point operations on each half of the 64-bit floating-point register. These *paired single* operations include ADD.PS, SUB.PS, MUL.PS, and DIV.PS. (They are loaded and stored using double-precision loads and stores.)

Giving a nod toward the importance of DSP applications, MIPS64 also includes both integer and floating-point multiply-add instructions: MADD, MADD.S, MADD.D, and MADD.PS. Unlike DSPs, the registers are all the same width in these combined operations. Figure 2.31 contains a list of a subset of MIPS64 operations and their meaning.

MIPS Instruction Set Usage

To give an idea which instructions are popular, Figure 2.32 shows the frequency of instructions and instruction classes for five SPECint92 programs, and Figure 2.33 shows the same data for five SPECfp92 programs. To give a more intuitive feeling, Figure 2.34 shows the data graphically for all instructions that are responsible on average for more than 1% of the instructions executed.

2.13   Another View: The Trimedia TM32 CPU

Media processor is a name given to a class of embedded processors that are dedicated to multimedia processing. Typically they are cost sensitive like embedded processors but follow the compiler orientation from desktop and server computing. Like DSPs, they operate on narrower data types than the desktop and must often deal with infinite, continuous streams of data. Figure 2.35 gives a list of media application areas and benchmark algorithms for media processors.

The Trimedia TM32 CPU is a representative of this class. As multimedia applications have considerable parallelism in the processing of these data streams, the instruction set architectures often look different from the desktop. The TM32 is intended for products like set-top boxes and advanced televisions.

First, there are many more registers: 128 32-bit registers, which contain either integer or floating-point data. Second, and not surprisingly, the TM32 offers the partitioned ALU or SIMD instructions to allow computations on multiple instances of narrower data, as described in Figure 2.17. Third, showing its heritage, for integers the TM32 offers both two's complement arithmetic favored by desktop processors and saturating arithmetic favored by DSPs. Figure 2.36 lists the operations found in the Trimedia TM32 CPU.

However, the most unusual feature from the perspective of the desktop is that the architecture allows the programmer to specify five independent operations to

Instruction type/opcode	Instruction meaning
Data transfers	*Move data between registers and memory, or between the integer and FP or special registers; only memory address mode is 16-bit displacement + contents of a GPR*
LB,LBU,SB	Load byte, load byte unsigned, store byte (to/from integer registers)
LH,LHU,SH	Load half word, load half word unsigned, store half word (to/from integer registers)
LW,LWU,SW	Load word, load word unsigned, store word (to/from integer registers)
LD,SD	Load double word, store double word (to/from integer registers)
L.S,L.D,S.S,S.D	Load SP float, load DP float, store SP float, store DP float
MFC0,MTC0	Copy from/to GPR to/from a special register
MOV.S,MOV.D	Copy one SP or DP FP register to another FP register
MFC1,MTC1	Copy 32 bits from/to FP registers to/from integer registers
Arithmetic/logical	*Operations on integer or logical data in GPRs; signed arithmetic trap on overflow*
DADD,DADDI,DADDU, DADDIU	Add, add immediate (all immediates are 16 bits); signed and unsigned
DSUB,DSUBU	Subtract; signed and unsigned
DMUL,DMULU,DDIV, DDIVU,MADD	Multiply and divide, signed and unsigned; multiply-add; all operations take and yield 64-bit values
AND,ANDI	And, and immediate
OR,ORI,XOR,XORI	Or, or immediate, exclusive or, exclusive or immediate
LUI	Load upper immediate; loads bits 32 to 47 of register with immediate, then sign-extends
DSLL,DSRL,DSRA,DSLLV, DSRLV,DSRAV	Shifts: both immediate (DS__) and variable form (DS__V); shifts are shift left logical, right logical, right arithmetic
SLT,SLTI,SLTU,SLTIU	Set less than, set less than immediate; signed and unsigned
Control	*Conditional branches and jumps; PC-relative or through register*
BEQZ,BNEZ	Branch GPR equal/not equal to zero; 16-bit offset from PC + 4
BEQ,BNE	Branch GPR equal/not equal; 16-bit offset from PC + 4
BC1T,BC1F	Test comparison bit in the FP status register and branch; 16-bit offset from PC + 4
MOVN,MOVZ	Copy GPR to another GPR if third GPR is negative, zero
J,JR	Jumps: 26-bit offset from PC + 4 (J) or target in register (JR)
JAL,JALR	Jump and link: save PC + 4 in R31, target is PC-relative (JAL) or a register (JALR)
TRAP	Transfer to operating system at a vectored address
ERET	Return to user code from an exception; restore user mode
Floating point	*FP operations on DP and SP formats*
ADD.D,ADD.S,ADD.PS	Add DP, SP numbers, and pairs of SP numbers
SUB.D,SUB.S,ADD.PS	Subtract DP, SP numbers, and pairs of SP numbers
MUL.D,MUL.S,MUL.PS	Multiply DP, SP floating point, and pairs of SP numbers
MADD.D,MADD.S,MADD.PS	Multiply-add DP, SP numbers and pairs of SP numbers
DIV.D,DIV.S,DIV.PS	Divide DP, SP floating point, and pairs of SP numbers
CVT._._	Convert instructions: CVT.x.y converts from type x to type y, where x and y are L (64-bit integer), W (32-bit integer), D (DP), or S (SP). Both operands are FPRs.
C.__.D,C.__.S	DP and SP compares: "__" = LT,GT,LE,GE,EQ,NE; sets bit in FP status register

Figure 2.31 Subset of the instructions in MIPS64. Figure 2.27 lists the formats of these instructions. SP = single precision; DP = double precision. This list can also be found on the page preceding the back inside cover.

Instruction	gap	gcc	gzip	mcf	perl	Integer average
load	26.5%	25.1%	20.1%	30.3%	28.7%	26%
store	10.3%	13.2%	5.1%	4.3%	16.2%	10%
add	21.1%	19.0%	26.9%	10.1%	16.7%	19%
sub	1.7%	2.2%	5.1%	3.7%	2.5%	3%
mul	1.4%	0.1%				0%
compare	2.8%	6.1%	6.6%	6.3%	3.8%	5%
load imm	4.8%	2.5%	1.5%	0.1%	1.7%	2%
cond branch	9.3%	12.1%	11.0%	17.5%	10.9%	12%
cond move	0.4%	0.6%	1.1%	0.1%	1.9%	1%
jump	0.8%	0.7%	0.8%	0.7%	1.7%	1%
call	1.6%	0.6%	0.4%	3.2%	1.1%	1%
return	1.6%	0.6%	0.4%	3.2%	1.1%	1%
shift	3.8%	1.1%	2.1%	1.1%	0.5%	2%
and	4.3%	4.6%	9.4%	0.2%	1.2%	4%
or	7.9%	8.5%	4.8%	17.6%	8.7%	9%
xor	1.8%	2.1%	4.4%	1.5%	2.8%	3%
other logical	0.1%	0.4%	0.1%	0.1%	0.3%	0%
load FP						0%
store FP						0%
add FP						0%
sub FP						0%
mul FP						0%
div FP						0%
mov reg-reg FP						0%
compare FP						0%
cond mov FP						0%
other FP						0%

Figure 2.32 MIPS dynamic instruction mix for five SPECint2000 programs. Note that integer register-register move instructions are included in the or instruction. Blank entries have the value 0.0%.

be issued at the same time. If there are not five independent instructions available for the compiler to schedule together—that is, the rest are dependent—then NOPs are placed in the leftover slots. This instruction coding technique is called, naturally enough, *very long instruction word* (VLIW), and it predates the Trimedia processors. VLIW is the subject of Chapter 4, so we will just give a preview of VLIW here. An example helps explain how the Trimedia TM32 CPU works,

Instruction	applu	art	equake	lucas	swim	FP average
load	13.8%	18.1%	22.3%	10.6%	9.1%	15%
store	2.9%		0.8%	3.4%	1.3%	2%
add	30.4%	30.1%	17.4%	11.1%	24.4%	23%
sub	2.5%		0.1%	2.1%	3.8%	2%
mul	2.3%			1.2%		1%
compare		7.4%	2.1%			2%
load imm	13.7%		1.0%	1.8%	9.4%	5%
cond branch	2.5%	11.5%	2.9%	0.6%	1.3%	4%
cond mov		0.3%	0.1%			0%
jump			0.1%			0%
call			0.7%			0%
return			0.7%			0%
shift	0.7%		0.2%	1.9%		1%
and			0.2%	1.8%		0%
or	0.8%	1.1%	2.3%	1.0%	7.2%	2%
xor		3.2%	0.1%			1%
other logical			0.1%			0%
load FP	11.4%	12.0%	19.7%	16.2%	16.8%	15%
store FP	4.2%	4.5%	2.7%	18.2%	5.0%	7%
add FP	2.3%	4.5%	9.8%	8.2%	9.0%	7%
sub FP	2.9%		1.3%	7.6%	4.7%	3%
mul FP	8.6%	4.1%	12.9%	9.4%	6.9%	8%
div FP	0.3%	0.6%	0.5%		0.3%	0%
mov reg-reg FP	0.7%	0.9%	1.2%	1.8%	0.9%	1%
compare FP		0.9%	0.6%	0.8%		0%
cond mov FP		0.6%		0.8%		0%
other FP				1.6%		0%

Figure 2.33 MIPS dynamic instruction mix for five programs from SPECfp2000. Note that integer register-register move instructions are included in the or instruction. Blank entries have the value 0.0%.

and one can be found in Chapter 4 on page 363–364. This section also compares the performance of the Trimedia TM32 CPU using the EEMBC benchmarks.

Given that the Trimedia TM32 CPU has longer instruction words and they often contain NOPs, Trimedia compacts its instructions in memory, decoding them to the full size when loaded into the cache.

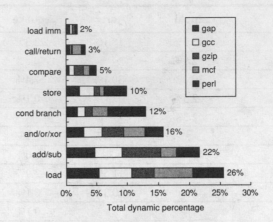

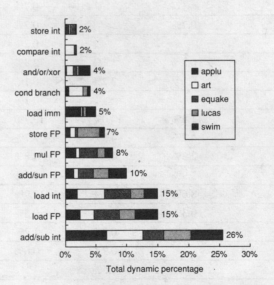

Figure 2.34 Graphical display of instructions executed of the five programs from SPECint2000 in Figure 2.32 (top) and the five programs from SPECfp2000 in Figure 2.33 (bottom). Just as in Figures 2.16 and 2.18, the most popular instructions are simple. These instruction classes collectively are responsible on average for 96% of instructions executed for SPECint2000 and 97% of instructions executed for SPECfp2000.

Figure 2.37 shows the TM32 CPU instruction mix for the EEMBC benchmarks. Using the unmodified source code, the instruction mix is similar to others, although there are more byte data transfers. If the C code is hand-tuned, it can extensively use SIMD instructions. Note the large number of pack and

Application area	Benchmarks
Data communication	Viterbi decoding
Audio coding	AC3 decode
Video coding	MPEG2 encode, DVD decode
Video processing	Layered natural motion, dynamic noise, reduction, peaking
Graphics	3D renderer library

Figure 2.35 Media processor application areas and example benchmarks. From Riemens et al. [1999]. This list shares only Viterbi decoding with the EEMBC benchmarks (see Figure 1.13 in Chapter 1), with the rest being generally larger programs than EEMBC.

Operation category	Examples	Number of operations	Comment
Load-store ops	ld8, ld16, ld32, limm, st8, st16, st32	33	signed, unsigned, register indirect, indexed, scaled addressing
Byte shuffles	shift right 1, 2, 3 bytes, select byte, merge, pack	11	SIMD type convert
Bit shifts	asl, asr, lsl, lsr, rol	10	shifts, SIMD
Multiplies and multimedia	mul, sum of products, sum of SIMD elements, multimedia, e.g., sum of products (FIR)	23	round, saturate, two's comp, SIMD
Integer arithmetic	add, sub, min, max, abs, average, bitand, bitor, bitxor, bitinv, bitandinv, eql, neq, gtr, geq, les, leq, sign-extend, zero-extend, sum of absolute differences	62	saturate, two's comp, unsigned, immediate, SIMD
Floating point	add, sub, neg, mul, div, sqrt, eql, neq, gtr, geq, les, leq, IEEE flags	42	scalar
Special ops	alloc, prefetch, copy back, read tag, read cache status, read counter	20	cache, special regs
Branch	jmpt, jmpf	6	(un)interruptible
Total		207	

Figure 2.36 List of operations and number of variations in Trimedia TM32 CPU. The data transfer opcodes include addressing modes in the count of operations, so the number is high compared to other architectures. SIMD means partitioned ALU operations of multiple narrow data items being operated on simultaneously in a 32-bit ALU; these include special operations for multimedia. The branches are delayed three slots.

merge instructions to align the data for the SIMD instructions. The cost in code size of these VLIW instructions is still a factor of 2 to 3 larger than MIPS *after* compaction.

Operation	Out of the box	Modified C source code
add word	26.5%	20.5%
load byte	10.4%	1.0%
subtract word	10.1%	1.1%
shift left arithmetic	7.8%	0.2%
store byte	7.4%	1.5%
multiply word	5.5%	0.4%
shift right arithmetic	3.6%	0.7%
and word	3.6%	6.8%
load word	3.5%	7.2%
load immediate	3.1%	1.6%
set greater than, equal	2.9%	1.3%
store word	2.0%	5.3%
jump	1.8%	0.8%
conditional branch	1.3%	1.0%
pack/merge bytes	2.6%	16.8%
SIMD sum of half-word products	0.0%	10.1%
SIMD sum of byte products	0.0%	7.7%
pack/merge half words	0.0%	6.5%
SIMD subtract half word	0.0%	2.9%
SIMD maximum byte	0.0%	1.9%
Total	92.2%	95.5%
TM32 CPU code size (bytes)	243,968	387,328
MIPS code size (bytes)	120,729	

Figure 2.37 TM32 CPU instruction mix running EEMBC consumer benchmark. The instruction mix for "out-of-the-box" C code is similar to general-purpose computers, with a higher emphasis on byte data transfers. The hand-optimized C code uses the SIMD instructions and the pack and merge instructions to align the data. The middle column shows the relative instruction mix for unmodified kernels, while the right column allows modification at the C level. These columns list all operations that were responsible for at least 1% of the total in one of the mixes. MIPS code size is for the Apogee compiler for the NEC VR5432.

2.14 Fallacies and Pitfalls

Architects have repeatedly tripped on common, but erroneous, beliefs. In this section we look at a few of them.

Pitfall *Designing a "high-level" instruction set feature specifically oriented to supporting a high-level language structure.*

Attempts to incorporate high-level language features in the instruction set have led architects to provide powerful instructions with a wide range of flexibility. However, often these instructions do more work than is required in the frequent case, or they don't exactly match the requirements of some languages. Many such efforts have been aimed at eliminating what in the 1970s was called the *semantic gap*. Although the idea is to supplement the instruction set with additions that bring the hardware up to the level of the language, the additions can generate what Wulf [1981] has called a *semantic clash:*

> . . . by giving too much semantic content to the instruction, the computer designer made it possible to use the instruction only in limited contexts. [p. 43]

More often the instructions are simply overkill—they are too general for the most frequent case, resulting in unneeded work and a slower instruction. Again, the VAX CALLS is a good example. CALLS uses a callee save strategy (the registers to be saved are specified by the callee), *but* the saving is done by the call instruction in the caller. The CALLS instruction begins with the arguments pushed on the stack, and then takes the following steps:

1. Align the stack if needed.

2. Push the argument count on the stack.

3. Save the registers indicated by the procedure call mask on the stack (as mentioned in Section 2.11). The mask is kept in the called procedure's code—this permits the callee to specify the registers to be saved by the caller even with separate compilation.

4. Push the return address on the stack, and then push the top and base of stack pointers (for the activation record).

5. Clear the condition codes, which sets the trap enable to a known state.

6. Push a word for status information and a zero word on the stack.

7. Update the two stack pointers.

8. Branch to the first instruction of the procedure.

The vast majority of calls in real programs do not require this amount of overhead. Most procedures know their argument counts, and a much faster linkage convention can be established using registers to pass arguments rather than the stack in memory. Furthermore, the CALLS instruction forces two registers to be used for linkage, while many languages require only one linkage register. Many attempts to support procedure call and activation stack management have failed to be useful, either because they do not match the language needs or because they are too general and hence too expensive to use.

The VAX designers provided a simpler instruction, JSB, that is much faster since it only pushes the return PC on the stack and jumps to the procedure. However, most VAX compilers use the more costly CALLS instructions. The call instructions were included in the architecture to standardize the procedure linkage convention. Other computers have standardized their calling convention by agreement among compiler writers and without requiring the overhead of a complex, very general procedure call instruction.

Fallacy *There is such a thing as a typical program.*

Many people would like to believe that there is a single "typical" program that could be used to design an optimal instruction set. For example, see the synthetic benchmarks discussed in Chapter 1. The data in this chapter clearly show that programs can vary significantly in how they use an instruction set. For example, Figure 2.38 shows the mix of data transfer sizes for four of the SPEC2000 programs: It would be hard to say what is typical from these four programs. The variations are even larger on an instruction set that supports a class of applications, such as decimal instructions, that are unused by other applications.

Pitfall *Innovating at the instruction set architecture to reduce code size without accounting for the compiler.*

Figure 2.39 shows the relative code sizes for four compilers for the MIPS instruction set. Whereas architects struggle to reduce code size by 30% to 40%, different compiler strategies can change code size by much larger factors. Similar to performance optimization techniques, the architect should start with the tightest code the compilers can produce before proposing hardware innovations to save space.

Pitfall *Expecting to get good performance from a compiler for DSPs.*

Figure 2.40 shows the performance improvement to be gained by using assembly language versus compiling from C for two Texas Instruments DSPs. Assembly

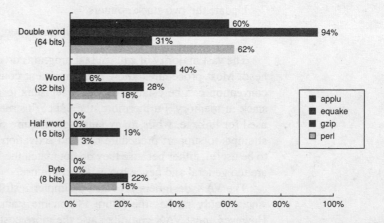

Figure 2.38 Data reference size of four programs from SPEC2000. Although you can calculate an average size, it would be hard to claim the average is typical of programs.

Compiler	Apogee Software: Version 4.1	Green Hills: Multi2000 Version 2.0	Algorithmics SDE4.0B	IDT/c 7.2.1
Architecture	MIPS IV	MIPS IV	MIPS 32	MIPS 32
Processor	NEC VR5432	NEC VR5000	IDT 32334	IDT 79RC32364
Autocorrelation kernel	1.0	2.1	1.1	2.7
Convolutional encoder kernel	1.0	1.9	1.2	2.4
Fixed-point bit allocation kernel	1.0	2.0	1.2	2.3
Fixed-point complex FFT kernel	1.0	1.1	2.7	1.8
Viterbi GSM decoder kernel	1.0	1.7	0.8	1.1
Geometric mean of five kernels	1.0	1.7	1.4	2.0

Figure 2.39   Code size relative to Apogee Software Version 4.1 C compiler for Telecom application of EEMBC benchmarks. The instruction set architectures are virtually identical, yet the code sizes vary by factors of 2. These results were reported February–June 2000.

TMS320C54 D ("C54") for DSPstone kernels	Ratio to assembly in execution time (> 1 means slower)	Ratio to assembly code space (> 1 means bigger)	TMS 320C6203 ("C62") for EEMBC Telecom kernels	Ratio to assembly in execution time (> 1 means slower)	Ratio to assembly code space (> 1 means bigger)
Convolution	11.8	16.5	Convolutional encoder	44.0	0.5
FIR	11.5	8.7	Fixed-point complex FFT	13.5	1.0
Matrix 1 × 3	7.7	8.1	Viterbi GSM decoder	13.0	0.7
FIR2dim	5.3	6.5	Fixed-point bit allocation	7.0	1.4
Dot product	5.2	14.1	Autocorrelation	1.8	0.7
LMS	5.1	0.7			
N real update	4.7	14.1			
IIR n biquad	2.4	8.6			
N complex update	2.4	9.8			
Matrix	1.2	5.1			
Complex update	1.2	8.7			
IIR one biquad	1.0	6.4			
Real update	0.8	15.6			
C54 geometric mean	3.2	7.8	C62 geometric mean	10.0	0.8

Figure 2.40   Ratio of execution time and code size for compiled code versus handwritten code for TMS320C54 DSPs on left (using the 14 DSPstone kernels) and Texas Instruments TMS 320C6203 on right (using the 6 EEMBC Telecom kernels). The geometric mean of performance improvements is 3.2:1 for C54 running DSPstone and 10.0:1 for the C62 running EEMBC. The compiler does a better job on code space for the C62, which is a VLIW processor, but the geometric mean of code size for the C54 is almost a factor of 8 larger when compiled. Modifying the C code gives much better results. The EEMBC results were reported May 2000. For DSPstone, see Ropers, Lollman, and Wellhausen [1999].

language programming gains factors of 3–10 in performance and factors of 1–8 in code size. This gain is large enough to lure DSP programmers away from high-level languages, despite their well-documented advantages in programmer productivity and software maintenance.

Fallacy *An architecture with flaws cannot be successful.*

The 80x86 provides a dramatic example: The instruction set architecture is one only its creators could love (see Appendix D). Succeeding generations of Intel engineers have tried to correct unpopular architectural decisions made in designing the 80x86. For example, the 80x86 supports segmentation, whereas all others picked paging; it uses extended accumulators for integer data, but other processors use general-purpose registers; and it uses a stack for floating-point data, when everyone else abandoned execution stacks long before.

Despite these major difficulties, the 80x86 architecture has been enormously successful. The reasons are threefold: first, its selection as the microprocessor in the initial IBM PC makes 80x86 binary compatibility extremely valuable. Second, Moore's Law provided sufficient resources for 80x86 microprocessors to translate to an internal RISC instruction set and then execute RISC-like instructions (see Section 3.10 in the next chapter). This mix enables binary compatibility with the valuable PC software base and performance on par with RISC processors. Third, the very high volumes of PC microprocessors means Intel can easily pay for the increased design cost of hardware translation. In addition, the high volumes allow the manufacturer to go up the learning curve, which lowers the cost of the product.

The larger die size and increased power for translation may be a liability for embedded applications, but it makes tremendous economic sense for the desktop. And its cost-performance in the desktop also makes it attractive for servers, with its main weakness for servers being 32-bit addresses: Companies already offer high-end servers with more than one terabyte (2^{40} bytes) of memory.

Fallacy *You can design a flawless architecture.*

All architecture design involves trade-offs made in the context of a set of hardware and software technologies. Over time those technologies are likely to change, and decisions that may have been correct at the time they were made look like mistakes. For example, in 1975 the VAX designers overemphasized the importance of code size efficiency, underestimating how important ease of decoding and pipelining would be five years later. An example in the RISC camp is delayed branch (see Appendix C). It was a simple matter to control pipeline hazards with five-stage pipelines, but a challenge for processors with longer pipelines that issue multiple instructions per clock cycle. In addition, almost all architectures eventually succumb to the lack of sufficient address space.

In general, avoiding such flaws in the long run would probably mean compromising the efficiency of the architecture in the short run, which is dangerous, since a new instruction set architecture must struggle to survive its first few years.

2.15   Concluding Remarks

The earliest architectures were limited in their instruction sets by the hardware technology of that time. As soon as the hardware technology permitted, computer architects began looking for ways to support high-level languages. This search led to three distinct periods of thought about how to support programs efficiently. In the 1960s, stack architectures became popular. They were viewed as being a good match for high-level languages—and they probably were, given the compiler technology of the day. In the 1970s, the main concern of architects was how to reduce software costs. This concern was met primarily by replacing software with hardware, or by providing high-level architectures that could simplify the task of software designers. The result was both the high-level language computer architecture movement and powerful architectures like the VAX, which has a large number of addressing modes, multiple data types, and a highly orthogonal architecture. In the 1980s, more sophisticated compiler technology and a renewed emphasis on processor performance saw a return to simpler architectures, based mainly on the load-store style of computer.

The following instruction set architecture changes occurred in the 1990s:

■ *Address size doubles*—The 32-bit address instruction sets for most desktop and server processors were extended to 64-bit addresses, expanding the width of the registers (among other things) to 64 bits. Appendix C gives three examples of architectures that have gone from 32 bits to 64 bits.

■ *Optimization of conditional branches via conditional execution*—In the next two chapters we see that conditional branches can limit the performance of aggressive computer designs. Hence, there was interest in replacing conditional branches with conditional completion of operations, such as conditional move (see Chapter 4), which was added to most instruction sets.

■ *Optimization of cache performance via prefetch*—Chapter 5 explains the increasing role of memory hierarchy in performance of computers, with a cache miss on some computers taking as many instruction times as page faults took on earlier computers. Hence, prefetch instructions were added to try to hide the cost of cache misses by prefetching (see Chapter 5).

■ *Support for multimedia*—Most desktop and embedded instruction sets were extended with support for multimedia and DSP applications, as discussed in this chapter.

■ *Faster floating-point operations*—Appendix H describes operations added to enhance floating-point performance, such as operations that perform a multiply and an add and paired single execution. (We include them in MIPS.)

Looking to the next decade, we see the following trends in instruction set design:

■ *Long instruction words*—The desire to achieve more instruction-level parallelism by changing the architecture to support wider instructions (see Chapter 4).

- *Increased conditional execution*—More support for conditional execution of operations to support greater speculation.

- *Blending of general-purpose and DSP architectures*—Parallel efforts between desktop and embedded processors to add DSP support versus extending DSP processors to make them better targets for compilers, suggesting a culture clash in the marketplace between general purpose and DSPs.

- *80x86 emulation*—Given the popularity of software for the 80x86 architecture, many companies are looking to see if changes to the instruction sets can significantly improve performance, cost, or power when emulating the 80x86 architecture.

Between 1970 and 1985 many thought the primary job of the computer architect was the design of instruction sets. As a result, textbooks of that era emphasize instruction set design, much as computer architecture textbooks of the 1950s and 1960s emphasized computer arithmetic. The educated architect was expected to have strong opinions about the strengths and especially the weaknesses of the popular computers. The importance of binary compatibility in quashing innovations in instruction set design was unappreciated by many researchers and textbook writers, giving the impression that many architects would get a chance to design an instruction set.

The definition of computer architecture today has been expanded to include design and evaluation of the full computer system—not just the definition of the instruction set and not just the processor—and hence there are plenty of topics for the architect to study. (You may have guessed this the first time you lifted this book!) Hence, the bulk of this book is on the design of computers versus instruction sets.

The many appendices may satisfy readers interested in instruction set architecture: Appendix C compares seven popular load-store computers with MIPS. Appendix D describes the most widely used instruction set, the Intel 80x86, and compares instruction counts for it with that of MIPS for several programs. For those interested in the historical computers, Appendix E summarizes the VAX architecture and Appendix F summarizes the IBM 360/370.

2.16   Historical Perspective and References

One's eyebrows should rise whenever a future architecture is developed with a stack- or register-oriented instruction set.

Meyers [1978, p 20]

The earliest computers, including the UNIVAC I, the EDSAC, and the IAS computers, were accumulator-based computers. The simplicity of this type of computer made it the natural choice when hardware resources were very constrained. The first general-purpose register computer was the Pegasus, built by Ferranti,

Ltd., in 1956. The Pegasus had eight general-purpose registers, with R0 always being zero. Block transfers loaded the eight registers from the drum memory.

Stack Architectures

In 1963, Burroughs delivered the B5000. The B5000 was perhaps the first computer to seriously consider software and hardware-software trade-offs. Barton and the designers at Burroughs made the B5000 a stack architecture (as described in Barton [1961]). Designed to support high-level languages such as ALGOL, this stack architecture used an operating system (MCP) written in a high-level language. The B5000 was also the first computer from a U.S. manufacturer to support virtual memory. The B6500, introduced in 1968 (and discussed in Hauck and Dent [1968]), added hardware-managed activation records. In both the B5000 and B6500, the top two elements of the stack were kept in the processor and the rest of the stack was kept in memory. The stack architecture yielded good code density, but only provided two high-speed storage locations. The authors of both the original IBM 360 paper [Amdahl, Blaauw, and Brooks 1964] and the original PDP-11 paper [Bell et al. 1970] argue against the stack organization. They cite three major points in their arguments against stacks:

1. Performance is derived from fast registers, not the way they are used.

2. The stack organization is too limiting and requires many swap and copy operations.

3. The stack has a bottom, and when placed in slower memory there is a performance loss.

Stack-based hardware fell out of favor in the late 1970s and, except for the Intel 80x86 floating-point architecture, essentially disappeared. For example, except for the 80x86, none of the computers listed in the SPEC report uses a stack.

In the 1990s, however, stack architectures received a shot in the arm with the success of the Java Virtual Machine (JVM). The JVM is a software interpreter for an intermediate language produced by Java compilers, called *Java bytecodes* [Lindholm and Yellin 1999]. The purpose of the interpreter is to provide software compatibility across many platforms, with the hope of "write once, run everywhere." Although the slowdown is about a factor of 10 due to interpretation, there are times when compatibility is more important than performance, such as when downloading a Java "applet" into an Internet browser.

Although a few have proposed hardware to directly execute the JVM instructions (see McGhan and O'Connor [1998]), thus far none of these proposals have been significant commercially. The hope instead is that *just in time* (JIT) Java compilers—which compile during run time to the native instruction set of the computer running the Java program—will overcome the performance penalty of interpretation. The popularity of Java has also led to compilers that compile directly into the native hardware instruction sets, bypassing the illusion of the Java bytecodes.

Computer Architecture Defined

IBM coined the term *computer architecture* in the early 1960s. Amdahl, Blaauw, and Brooks [1964] used the term to refer to the programmer-visible portion of the IBM 360 instruction set. They believed that a *family* of computers of the same architecture should be able to run the same software. Although this idea may seem obvious to us today, it was quite novel at that time. IBM, although it was the leading company in the industry, had five different architectures before the 360. Thus, the notion of a company standardizing on a single architecture was a radical one. The 360 designers hoped that defining a common architecture would bring six different divisions of IBM together. Their definition of architecture was

> . . . the structure of a computer that a machine language programmer must understand to write a correct (timing independent) program for that machine.

The term "machine language programmer" meant that compatibility would hold, even in machine language, while "timing independent" allowed different implementations. This architecture blazed the path for binary compatibility, which others have followed.

The IBM 360 was the first computer to sell in large quantities with both byte addressing using 8-bit bytes and general-purpose registers. The 360 also had register-memory and limited memory-memory instructions. Appendix F summarizes this instruction set.

In 1964, Control Data delivered the first supercomputer, the CDC 6600. As Thornton [1964] discusses, he, Cray, and the other 6600 designers were among the first to explore pipelining in depth. The 6600 was the first general-purpose, load-store computer. In the 1960s, the designers of the 6600 realized the need to simplify architecture for the sake of efficient pipelining. Microprocessor and minicomputer designers largely neglected this interaction between architectural simplicity and implementation during the 1970s, but it returned in the 1980s.

High-Level Language Computer Architecture

In the late 1960s and early 1970s, people realized that software costs were growing faster than hardware costs. McKeeman [1967] argued that compilers and operating systems were getting too big and too complex and taking too long to develop. Because of inferior compilers and the memory limitations of computers, most systems programs at the time were still written in assembly language. Many researchers proposed alleviating the software crisis by creating more powerful, software-oriented architectures. Tanenbaum [1978] studied the properties of high-level languages. Like other researchers, he found that most programs are simple. He then argued that architectures should be designed with this in mind and that they should optimize for program size and ease of compilation. Tanenbaum proposed a stack computer with frequency-encoded instruction formats to accomplish these goals. However, as we have observed, program size does not translate directly to cost-performance, and stack computers faded out shortly after this work.

Strecker's article [1978] discusses how he and the other architects at DEC responded to this by designing the VAX architecture. The VAX was designed to simplify compilation of high-level languages. Compiler writers had complained about the lack of complete orthogonality in the PDP-11. The VAX architecture was designed to be highly orthogonal and to allow the mapping of a high-level language statement into a single VAX instruction. Additionally, the VAX designers tried to optimize code size because compiled programs were often too large for available memories. Appendix E summarizes this instruction set.

The VAX-11/780 was the first computer announced in the VAX series. It is one of the most successful—and most heavily studied—computers ever built. The cornerstone of DEC's strategy was a single architecture, VAX, running a single operating system, VMS. This strategy worked well for over 10 years. The large number of papers reporting instruction mixes, implementation measurements, and analysis of the VAX makes it an ideal case study [Wiecek 1982; Clark and Levy 1982]. Bhandarkar and Clark [1991] give a quantitative analysis of the disadvantages of the VAX versus a RISC computer, essentially a technical explanation for the demise of the VAX.

While the VAX was being designed, a more radical approach, called *high-level language computer architecture* (HLLCA), was being advocated in the research community. This movement aimed to eliminate the gap between high-level languages and computer hardware—what Gagliardi [1973] called the "semantic gap"—by bringing the hardware "up to" the level of the programming language. Meyers [1982] provides a good summary of the arguments and a history of high-level language computer architecture projects.

HLLCA never had a significant commercial impact. The increase in memory size on computers eliminated the code size problems arising from high-level languages and enabled operating systems to be written in high-level languages. The combination of simpler architectures together with software offered greater performance and more flexibility at lower cost and lower complexity.

Reduced Instruction Set Computers

In the early 1980s, the direction of computer architecture began to swing away from providing high-level hardware support for languages. Ditzel and Patterson [1980] analyzed the difficulties encountered by the high-level language architectures and argued that the answer lay in simpler architectures. In another paper [Patterson and Ditzel 1980], these authors first discussed the idea of reduced instruction set computers (RISC) and presented the argument for simpler architectures. Clark and Strecker [1980], who were VAX architects, rebutted their proposal.

The simple load-store computers such as MIPS are commonly called RISC architectures. The roots of RISC architectures go back to computers like the 6600, where Thornton, Cray, and others recognized the importance of instruction set simplicity in building a fast computer. Cray continued his tradition of keeping computers simple in the CRAY-1. Commercial RISCs are built primarily on the work of three research projects: the Berkeley RISC processor, the IBM 801, and the Stanford MIPS processor. These architectures have attracted enormous industrial interest because of claims of a performance advantage of anywhere from two to five times over other computers using the same technology.

Begun in 1975, the IBM project was the first to start but was the last to become public. The IBM computer was designed as a 24-bit ECL minicomputer, while the university projects were both MOS-based, 32-bit microprocessors. John Cocke is considered the father of the 801 design. He received both the Eckert-Mauchly and Turing awards in recognition of his contribution. Radin [1982] describes the highlights of the 801 architecture. The 801 was an experimental project that was never designed to be a product. In fact, to keep down cost and complexity, the computer was built with only 24-bit registers.

In 1980, Patterson and his colleagues at Berkeley began the project that was to give this architectural approach its name (see Patterson and Ditzel [1980]). They built two computers called RISC-I and RISC-II. Because the IBM project was not widely known or discussed, the role played by the Berkeley group in promoting the RISC approach was critical to the acceptance of the technology. They also built one of the first instruction caches to support hybrid format RISCs (see Patterson et al. [1983]). It supported 16-bit and 32-bit instructions in memory but 32 bits in the cache. The Berkeley group went on to build RISC computers targeted toward Smalltalk, described by Ungar et al. [1984], and LISP, described by Taylor et al. [1986].

In 1981, Hennessy and his colleagues at Stanford published a description of the Stanford MIPS computer. Efficient pipelining and compiler-assisted scheduling of the pipeline were both important aspects of the original MIPS design. MIPS stood for Microprocessor without Interlocked Pipeline Stages, reflecting the lack of hardware to stall the pipeline, as the compiler would handle dependencies.

These early RISC computers—the 801, RISC-II, and MIPS—had much in common. Both university projects were interested in designing a simple computer that could be built in VLSI within the university environment. All three computers used a simple load-store architecture, fixed-format 32-bit instructions, and emphasized efficient pipelining. Patterson [1985] describes the three computers and the basic design principles that have come to characterize what a RISC computer is. Hennessy [1984] provides another view of the same ideas, as well as other issues in VLSI processor design.

In 1985, Hennessy published an explanation of the RISC performance advantage and traced its roots to a substantially lower CPI—under 2 for a RISC processor and over 10 for a VAX-11/780 (though not with identical workloads). A paper by Emer and Clark [1984] characterizing VAX-11/780 performance was instrumental in helping the RISC researchers understand the source of the performance advantage seen by their computers.

Since the university projects finished up, in the 1983–84 time frame, the technology has been widely embraced by industry. Many manufacturers of the early computers (those made before 1986) claimed that their products were RISC computers. These claims, however, were often born more of marketing ambition than of engineering reality.

In 1986, the computer industry began to announce processors based on the technology explored by the three RISC research projects. Moussouris et al. [1986] describe the MIPS R2000 integer processor, while Kane's book [1986] is a complete description of the architecture. Hewlett-Packard converted their existing minicomputer line to RISC architectures; Lee [1989] describes the HP Precision Architecture. IBM never directly turned the 801 into a product. Instead, the ideas were adopted for a new, low-end architecture that was incorporated in the IBM RT-PC and described in a collection of papers [Waters 1986]. In 1990, IBM announced a new RISC architecture (the RS 6000), which is the first superscalar RISC processor (see Chapter 4). In 1987, Sun Microsystems began delivering computers based on the SPARC architecture, a derivative of the Berkeley RISC-II processor; SPARC is described in Garner et al. [1988]. The PowerPC joined the forces of Apple, IBM, and Motorola. Appendix C summarizes several RISC architectures.

To help resolve the RISC versus traditional design debate, designers of VAX processors later performed a quantitative comparison of VAX and a RISC processor for implementations with comparable organizations. Their choices were the VAX 8700 and the MIPS M2000. The differing goals for VAX and MIPS have led to very different architectures. The VAX goals, simple compilers and code density, led to powerful addressing modes, powerful instructions, efficient instruction encoding, and few registers. The MIPS goals were high performance via pipelining, ease of hardware implementation, and compatibility with highly optimizing compilers. These goals led to simple instructions, simple addressing modes, fixed-length instruction formats, and a large number of registers.

Figure 2.41 shows the ratio of the number of instructions executed, the ratio of CPIs, and the ratio of performance measured in clock cycles. Since the organizations were similar, clock cycle times were assumed to be the same. MIPS executes about twice as many instructions as the VAX, while the CPI for the VAX is about six times larger than that for the MIPS. Hence, the MIPS M2000 has almost three times the performance of the VAX 8700. Furthermore, much less hardware is needed to build the MIPS processor than the VAX processor. This cost-performance gap is the reason the company that used to make the VAX has dropped it and is now making the Alpha, which is quite similar to MIPS. Bell and Strecker [1998] summarize the debate inside the company.

Looking back, only one complex instruction set computer (CISC) instruction set survived the RISC/CISC debate, and that one had binary compatibility with PC software. The volume of chips is so high in the PC industry that there is a sufficient revenue stream to pay the extra design costs—and sufficient resources due to Moore's Law—to build microprocessors that translate from CISC to RISC internally. Whatever loss in efficiency, due to longer pipeline stages and bigger die size to accommodate translation on the chip, was hedged by having a semiconductor fabrication line dedicated to producing just these microprocessors. The high volumes justify the economics of a fab line tailored to these chips.

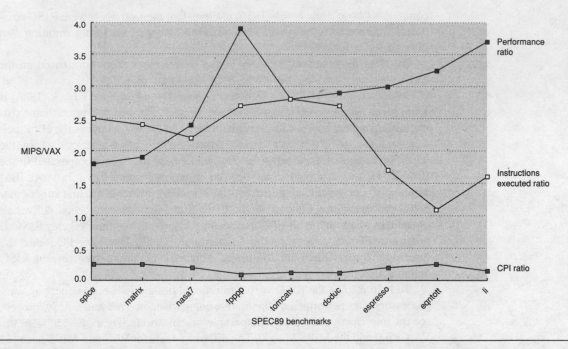

Figure 2.41 Ratio of MIPS M2000 to VAX 8700 in instructions executed and performance in clock cycles using SPEC89 programs. On average, MIPS executes a little over twice as many instructions as the VAX, but the CPI for the VAX is almost six times the MIPS CPI, yielding almost a threefold performance advantage. (Based on data from Bhandarkar and Clark [1991].)

Thus, in the desktop/server market, RISC computers use compilers to translate into RISC instructions and the remaining CISC computer uses hardware to translate into RISC instructions. One recent novel variation for the laptop market is the Transmeta Crusoe (see Section 4.8), which interprets 80x86 instructions and compiles on the fly into internal instructions.

The embedded market, which competes in cost and power, cannot afford the luxury of hardware translation and thus uses compilers and RISC architectures. More than twice as many 32-bit embedded microprocessors were shipped in 2000 than PC microprocessors, with RISC processors responsible for over 90% of that embedded market.

A Brief History of Digital Signal Processors

(Jeff Bier prepared this DSP history.)

In the late 1990s, digital signal-processing (DSP) applications, such as digital cellular telephones, emerged as one of the largest consumers of embedded computing power. Today, microprocessors specialized for DSP applications—sometimes called digital signal processors, DSPs, or DSP processors—are used in most of these applications. In 2000 this was a $6 billion market. Compared to other embedded computing applications, DSP applications are differentiated by the following:

- Computationally demanding, iterative numeric algorithms often composed of vector dot products, hence the importance of multiply and multiply-accumulate instructions

- Sensitivity to small numeric errors (for example, numeric errors may manifest themselves as audible noise in an audio device)

- Stringent real-time requirements

- "Streaming" data (typically, input data is provided from an analog-to-digital converter as an infinite stream; results are emitted in a similar fashion)

- High data bandwidth

- Predictable, simple (though often eccentric) memory access patterns

- Predictable program flow (typically characterized by nested loops)

In the 1970s there was strong interest in using DSP techniques in telecommunications equipment, such as modems and central office switches. The microprocessors of the day did not provide adequate performance, though. Fixed-function hardware proved effective in some applications, but lacked the flexibility and reusability of a programmable processor. Thus, engineers were motivated to adapt microprocessor technology to the needs of DSP applications.

The first commercial DSPs emerged in the early 1980s, about 10 years after Intel's introduction of the 4004. A number of companies, including Intel, developed early DSPs, but most of these early devices were not commercially successful. NEC's µPD7710, introduced in 1980, became the first merchant-market DSP to ship in volume quantities, but was hampered by weak development tools. AT&T's DSP1, also introduced in 1980, was limited to use within AT&T, but it spawned several generations of successful devices that AT&T soon began offering to other system manufacturers. In 1982, Texas Instruments introduced its first DSP, the TMS32010. Backed by strong tools and applications engineering support, the TI processor was a solid success.

Like the first microprocessors, these early DSPs had simple architectures. In contrast with their general-purpose cousins, though, DSPs adopted a range of specialized features to boost performance and efficiency in signal-processing tasks. For example, a single-cycle multiplier aided arithmetic performance. Specialized data paths streamlined multiply-accumulate operations and provided features to minimize numeric errors, such as saturation arithmetic. Separate program and data memories provided the memory bandwidth required to keep the relatively powerful data paths fed. Dedicated, specialized addressing hardware sped simple addressing operations, such as autoincrement addressing. Complex, specialized instruction sets allowed these processors to combine many operations in a single instruction, but only certain limited combinations of operations were supported.

From the mid-1980s to the mid-1990s, many new commercial DSP architectures were introduced. For the most part, these architectures followed a gradual, evolutionary path, adopting incremental improvements rather than fundamental innovations when compared with the earliest DSPs like the TMS32010. DSP application programs expanded from a few hundred lines of source code to tens of thousands of lines. Hence, the quality of development tools and the availability of off-the-shelf application software components became, for many users, more important than performance in selecting a processor. Today, chips based on these "conventional DSP" architectures still dominate DSP applications and are used in products such as cellular telephones, disk drives (for servo control), and consumer audio devices.

Early DSP architectures had proven effective, but the highly specialized and constrained instruction sets that gave them their performance and efficiency also created processors that were difficult targets for compiler writers. The performance and efficiency demands of most DSP applications could not be met by the resulting weak compilers, so much software—all software for some processors— was written in assembly language. As applications became larger and more complex, assembly language programming became less practical. Users also suffered from the incompatibility of many new DSP architectures with their predecessors, which forced them to periodically rewrite large amounts of existing application software.

In roughly 1995, architects of digital signal processors began to experiment with very different types of architectures, often adapting techniques from earlier high-performance general-purpose or scientific-application processor designs. These designers sought to further increase performance and efficiency, but to do so with architectures that would be better compiler targets, and that would offer a better basis for future compatible architectures. For example, in 1997, Texas Instruments announced the TMS320C62xx family, an eight-issue VLIW design boasting increased parallelism, a higher clock speed, and a radically simple, RISC-like instruction set. Other DSP architects adopted SIMD approaches, superscalar designs, chip multiprocessing, or a combination of these techniques. Therefore, DSP architectures today are more diverse than ever, and the rate of architectural innovation is increasing.

DSP architects were experimenting with new approaches, often adapting techniques from general-purpose processors. In parallel, designers of general-purpose processors (both those targeting embedded applications and those intended for computers) noticed that DSP tasks were becoming increasingly common in all kinds of microprocessor applications. In many cases, these designers added features to their architectures to boost performance and efficiency in DSP tasks. These features ranged from modest instruction set additions to extensive architectural retrofits. In some cases, designers created all-new architectures intended to encompass capabilities typically found in a DSP and those typically found in a general-purpose processor. Today, virtually every commercial 32-bit microprocessor architecture—from ARM to 80x86—has been subject to some kind of DSP-oriented enhancement.

Throughout the 1990s, an increasing number of system designers turned to system-on-chip devices. These are complex integrated circuits typically containing a processor core and a mix of memory, application-specific hardware (such as algorithm accelerators), peripherals, and I/O interfaces tuned for a specific application. An example is second-generation cellular phones. In some cases, chip manufacturers provide a complete complement of application software along with these highly integrated chips. These processor-based chips are often the solution of choice for relatively mature, high-volume applications. Though these chips are not sold as "processors," the processors inside them define their capabilities to a significant degree.

More information on the history of DSPs can be found in Boddie [2000], Stauss [1998], and Texas Instruments [2000].

Multimedia Support in Desktop Instruction Sets

Since every desktop microprocessor by definition has its own graphical displays, as transistor budgets increased it was inevitable that support would be added for graphics operations. The earliest color for PCs used 8 bits per pixel in the "256 color" format of VGA, which some PCs still support for compatibility. The next step was 16 bits per pixel by encoding R in 5 bits, G in 6 bits, and B in 5 bits. This format is called *high color* on PCs. On PCs the 32-bit format discussed earlier, with R, G, B, and A, is called *true color*.

The addition of speakers and microphones for teleconferencing and video games suggested support of sound as well. Audio samples of 16 bits are sufficient for most end users, but professional audio work uses 24 bits.

The architects of the Intel i860, which was justified as a graphical accelerator within the company, recognized that many graphics and audio applications would perform the same operation on vectors of these data. Although a vector unit was beyond the transistor budget of the i860 in 1989, by partitioning the carry chains within a 64-bit ALU, it could perform simultaneous operations on short vectors. It operated on eight 8-bit operands, four 16-bit operands, or two 32-bit operands. The cost of such partitioned ALUs was small. Applications that lend themselves to such support include MPEG (video), games like DOOM (3D graphics), Adobe Photoshop (digital photography), and teleconferencing (audio and image processing). Operations on four 8-bit operands were for pixels.

Like a virus, over time such multimedia support has spread to nearly every desktop microprocessor. HP was the first successful desktop RISC to include such support. The pair of single floating-point operations, which came later, are useful for operations on vertices.

These extensions have been called partitioned ALU, subword parallelism, vector, or SIMD (single instruction, multiple data). Since Intel marketing uses SIMD to describe the MMX extension of the 80x86, SIMD has become the popular name.

Summary

Prior to the RISC architecture movement, the major trend had been highly micro-coded architectures aimed at reducing the semantic gap and code size. DEC, with the VAX, and Intel, with the iAPX 432, were among the leaders in this approach.

Although those two computers have faded into history, one contemporary survives: the 80x86. This architecture did not have a philosophy about high-level language; it had a deadline. Since the iAPX 432 was late and Intel desperately needed a 16-bit microprocessor, the 8086 was designed in a few months. It was forced to be assembly language compatible with the 8-bit 8080, and assembly language was expected to be widely used with this architecture. Its saving grace has been its ability to evolve.

The 80x86 dominates the desktop with an 85% share, which is due in part to the importance of binary compatibility as a result of IBM's selection of the 8086 in the early 1980s. Rather than change the instruction set architecture, recent 80x86 implementations translate into RISC-like instructions internally and then execute them (see Section 3.10 in the next chapter). RISC processors dominate the embedded market with a similar market share because binary compatibility is unimportant, plus die size and power goals make hardware translation a luxury.

VLIW is currently being tested across the board, from DSPs to servers. Will code size be a problem in the embedded market, where the instruction memory in a chip could be bigger than the processor? Will VLIW DSPs achieve respectable cost-performance if compilers produce the code? Will the high power and large die of server VLIWs be successful, at a time when concern for power efficiency of servers is increasing? Once again an attractive feature of this field is that time will shortly tell how VLIW fares, and we should know answers to these questions by the fourth edition of this book.

References

Amdahl, G. M., G. A. Blaauw, and F. P. Brooks, Jr. [1964]. "Architecture of the IBM System 360," *IBM J. Research and Development* 8:2 (April), 87–101.

Barton, R. S. [1961]. "A new approach to the functional design of a computer," *Proc. Western Joint Computer Conf.,* 393–396.

Bell, G., R. Cady, H. McFarland, B. DeLagi, J. O'Laughlin, R. Noonan, and W. Wulf [1970]. "A new architecture for mini-computers: The DEC PDP-11," *Proc. AFIPS SJCC*, 657–675.

Bell, G., and W. D. Strecker [1998]. "Computer structures: What have we learned from the PDP-11?" *25 Years of the International Symposia on Computer Architecture (Selected Papers)*, ACM, 138–151.

Bhandarkar, D., and D. W. Clark [1991]. "Performance from architecture: Comparing a RISC and a CISC with similar hardware organizations," *Proc. Fourth Conf. on Architectural Support for Programming Languages and Operating Systems,* IEEE/ACM (April), Palo Alto, Calif., 310–319.

Bier, J. [1997]. "The evolution of DSP processors," presentation at U.C. Berkeley, November 14.

Boddie, J. R. [2000]. "History of DSPs," *www.lucent.com/micro/dsp/dsphist.html*.

Chow, F. C. [1983]. *A Portable Machine-Independent Global Optimizer—Design and Measurements,* Ph.D. thesis, Stanford Univ. (December).

Clark, D., and H. Levy [1982]. "Measurement and analysis of instruction set use in the VAX-11/780," *Proc. Ninth Symposium on Computer Architecture* (April), Austin, Tex., 9–17.

Clark, D., and W. D. Strecker [1980]. "Comments on 'the case for the reduced instruction set computer'," *Computer Architecture News* 8:6 (October), 34–38.

Crawford, J., and P. Gelsinger [1988]. *Programming the 80386,* Sybex Books, Alameda, Calif.

Ditzel, D. R., and D. A. Patterson [1980]. "Retrospective on high-level language computer architecture," *Proc. Seventh Annual Symposium on Computer Architecture,* La Baule, France (June), 97–104.

Emer, J. S., and D. W. Clark [1984]. "A characterization of processor performance in the VAX-11/780," *Proc. 11th Symposium on Computer Architecture* (June), Ann Arbor, Mich., 301–310.

Gagliardi, U. O. [1973]. "Report of workshop 4—software-related advances in computer hardware," *Proc. Symposium on the High Cost of Software,* Menlo Park, Calif., 99–120.

Game, M., and A. Booker [1999]. "CodePack code compression for PowerPC processors," *MicroNews,* 5:1, *www.chips.ibm.com/micronews/vol5_no1/codepack.html*.

Garner, R., A. Agarwal, F. Briggs, E. Brown, D. Hough, B. Joy, S. Kleiman, S. Munchnik, M. Namjoo, D. Patterson, J. Pendleton, and R. Tuck [1988]. "Scalable processor architecture (SPARC)," *COMPCON, IEEE* (March), San Francisco, 278–283.

Hauck, E. A., and B. A. Dent [1968]. "Burroughs' B6500/B7500 stack mechanism," *Proc. AFIPS SJCC,* 245–251.

Hennessy, J. [1984]. "VLSI processor architecture," *IEEE Trans. on Computers* C-33:11 (December), 1221–1246.

Hennessy, J. [1985]. "VLSI RISC processors," *VLSI Systems Design* VI:10 (October), 22–32.

Hennessy, J., N. Jouppi, F. Baskett, and J. Gill [1981]. "MIPS: A VLSI processor architecture," *Proc. CMU Conf. on VLSI Systems and Computations* (October), Computer Science Press, Rockville, Md.

Intel [2001]. "Using MMX instructions to convert RGB to YUV color conversion," *cedar.intel.com/cgi-bin/ids.dll/content/content.jsp?cntKey=Legacy::irtm_AP548_9996&cntType=IDS_EDITORIAL*.

Kane, G. [1986]. *MIPS R2000 RISC Architecture,* Prentice Hall, Englewood Cliffs, N.J.

Kozyrakis, C. [2000]. "Vector IRAM: A media-oriented vector processor with embedded DRAM," presentation at Hot Chips 12 Conf., Palo Alto, Calif, 13–15.

Lee, R. [1989]. "Precision architecture," *Computer* 22:1 (January), 78–91.

Levy, H., and R. Eckhouse [1989]. *Computer Programming and Architecture: The VAX,* Digital Press, Boston.

Lindholm, T., and F. Yellin [1999]. *The Java Virtual Machine Specification,* second edition, Addison-Wesley, Reading, Mass. Also available online at *java.sun.com/docs/books/vmspec/*.

Lunde, A. [1977]. "Empirical evaluation of some features of instruction set processor architecture," *Comm. ACM* 20:3 (March), 143–152.

McGhan, H., and M. O'Connor [1998]. "PicoJava: A direct execution engine for Java bytecode," *Computer* 31:10 (October), 22–30.

McKeeman, W. M. [1967]. "Language directed computer design," *Proc. 1967 Fall Joint Computer Conf.,* Washington, D.C., 413–417.

Meyers, G. J. [1978]. "The evaluation of expressions in a storage-to-storage architecture," *Computer Architecture News* 7:3 (October), 20–23.

Meyers, G. J. [1982]. *Advances in Computer Architecture,* second edition, Wiley, New York.

Moussouris, J., L. Crudele, D. Freitas, C. Hansen, E. Hudson, S. Przybylski, T. Riordan, and C. Rowen [1986]. "A CMOS RISC processor with integrated system functions," *Proc. COMPCON, IEEE* (March), San Francisco, 191.

Patterson, D. [1985]. "Reduced instruction set computers," *Comm. ACM* 28:1 (January), 8–21.

Patterson, D. A., and D. R. Ditzel [1980]. "The case for the reduced instruction set computer," *Computer Architecture News* 8:6 (October), 25–33.

Patterson, D. A., P. Garrison, M. Hill, D. Lioupis, C. Nyberg, T. Sippel, and K. Van Dyke [1983]. "Architecture of a VLSI instruction cache for a RISC," *10th Annual Int'l Conf. on Computer Architecture Conf. Proc.,* Stockholm, Sweden, June 13–16, 108–116.

Radin, G. [1982]. "The 801 minicomputer," *Proc. Symposium Architectural Support for Programming Languages and Operating Systems* (March), Palo Alto, Calif., 39–47.

Riemens, A., K. A. Vissers, R. J. Schutten, F. W. Sijstermans, G. J. Hekstra, and G. D. La Hei [1999]."Trimedia CPU64 application domain and benchmark suite," *Proc. 1999 IEEE Int'l Conf. on Computer Design: VLSI in Computers and Processors, ICCD'99,* Austin, Tex., October 10–13, 580–585.

Ropers, A., H. W. Lollman, and J. Wellhausen [1999]. "DSPstone: Texas Instruments TMS320C54x," Technical Report Nr. IB 315 1999/9-ISS-Version 0.9, Aachen University of Technology, *www.ert.rwth-aachen.de/Projekte/Tools/coal/dspstone_c54x /index.html.*

Strauss, W. [1998]. "DSP strategies 2002," *Forward Concepts, www.usadata.com /market_research/spr_05/spr_r127-005.htm.*

Strecker, W. D. [1978]. "VAX-11/780: A virtual address extension of the PDP-11 family," *Proc. AFIPS National Computer Conf.* 47, 967–980.

Tanenbaum, A. S. [1978]. "Implications of structured programming for machine architecture," *Comm. ACM* 21:3 (March), 237–246.

Taylor, G., P. Hilfinger, J. Larus, D. Patterson, and B. Zorn [1986]. "Evaluation of the SPUR LISP architecture," *Proc. 13th Symposium on Computer Architecture* (June), Tokyo.

Texas Instruments [2000]. "History of innovation: 1980s," *www.ti.com/corp/docs/company /history/1980s.shtml.*

Thornton, J. E. [1964]. "Parallel operation in Control Data 6600," *Proc. AFIPS Fall Joint Computer Conf., Part II,* 26, 33–40.

Ungar, D., R. Blau, P. Foley, D. Samples, and D. Patterson [1984]. "Architecture of SOAR: Smalltalk on a RISC," *Proc. 11th Symposium on Computer Architecture* (June), Ann Arbor, Mich., 188–197.

van Eijndhoven, J. T. J., F. W. Sijstermans, K. A. Vissers, E. J. D. Pol, M. I. A. Tromp, P. Struik, R. H. J. Bloks, P. van der Wolf, A. D. Pimentel, H. P. E. Vranken [1999]. "Trimedia CPU64 architecture," *Proc. 1999 IEEE Int'l Conf. on Computer Design: VLSI in Computers and Processors, ICCD'99,* Austin, Tex., October 10–13, 586–592.

Wakerly, J. [1989]. *Microcomputer Architecture and Programming,* Wiley, New York.

Waters, F., ed. [1986]. *IBM RT Personal Computer Technology,* IBM, Austin, Tex., SA 23-1057.

Wiecek, C. [1982]. "A case study of the VAX 11 instruction set usage for compiler execution," *Proc. Symposium on Architectural Support for Programming Languages and Operating Systems* (March), IEEE/ACM, Palo Alto, Calif., 177–184.

Wulf, W. [1981]. "Compilers and computer architecture," *Computer* 14:7 (July), 41–47.

Exercises

Solutions to the "starred" exercises appear in Appendix B.

2.1 [10/15] <2.2> For the following assume that values A, B, C, D, and E reside in memory. Also assume that instruction operation codes are represented in 8 bits, memory addresses are 64 bits, and register addresses are 6 bits.

   a. [10] <2.2> For each instruction set architecture shown in Figure 2.2, how many addresses, or names, appear in each instruction for the code to compute C = A + B, and what is the total code size?

   b. [15] <2.2> Some of the instruction set architectures in Figure 2.2 destroy operands in the course of computation. This loss of data values from processor internal storage has performance consequences. For each architecture in Figure 2.2, write the code sequence to compute C = A + B followed by D = A − E. In your code, mark each operand that is destroyed during execution and mark each "overhead" instruction that is included just to overcome this loss of data from processor internal storage. What is the total code size, the number of bytes of instructions and data moved to or from memory, the number of overhead instructions, and the number of overhead data bytes for each of your code sequences?

✪ 2.2 [15] <2.2> Some operations on two operands (subtraction, for example) are not commutative. What are the advantages and disadvantages of the stack, accumulator, and load-store architectures when executing noncommutative operations?

2.3 [15/15/10/10] <2.3> The value represented by the hexadecimal number 434F 4D50 5554 4552 is to be stored in an aligned 64-bit double word.

   a. [15] <2.3> Using the physical arrangement of the first row in Figure 2.5, write the value to be stored using Big Endian byte order. Next, interpret each byte as an ASCII character and below each byte write the corresponding character, forming the character string as it would be stored in Big Endian order.

   b. [15] <2.3> Using the same physical arrangement as in part (a), write the value to be stored using Little Endian byte order and below each byte write the corresponding ASCII character.

   c. [10] <2.3> What are the hexadecimal values of all misaligned 2-byte words that can be read from the given 64-bit double word when stored in Big Endian byte order?

   d. [10] <2.3> What are the hexadecimal values of all misaligned 4-byte words that can be read from the given 64-bit double word when stored in Little Endian byte order?

2.4 [20/15/15/20] <2.2, 2.3, 2.10> Your task is to compare the memory efficiency of four different styles of instruction set architectures. The architecture styles are

1. *Accumulator*—All operations occur between a single register and a memory location.

2. *Memory-memory*—All instruction addresses reference only memory locations.

3. *Stack*—All operations occur on top of the stack. Push and pop are the only instructions that access memory; all others remove their operands from the stack and replace them with the result. The implementation uses a hardwired stack for only the top two stack entries, which keeps the processor circuit very small and low cost. Additional stack positions are kept in memory locations, and accesses to these stack positions require memory references.

4. *Load-store*—All operations occur in registers, and register-to-register instructions have three register names per instruction.

To measure memory efficiency, make the following assumptions about all four instruction sets:

▪ All instructions are an integral number of bytes in length.

▪ The opcode is always 1 byte (8 bits).

▪ Memory accesses use direct, or absolute, addressing.

▪ The variables A, B, C, and D are initially in memory.

a. [20] <2.2, 2.3> Invent your own assembly language mnemonics (Figure 2.2 provides a useful sample to generalize), and for each architecture write the best equivalent assembly language code for this high-level language code sequence:

```
A = B + C;
B = A + C;
D = A - B;
```

b. [15] <2.3> Label each instance in your assembly codes for part (a) where a value is loaded from memory after having been loaded once. Also label each instance in your code where the result of one instruction is passed to another instruction as an operand, and further classify these events as involving storage within the processor or storage in memory.

c. [15] <2.10> Assume the given code sequence is from a small, embedded computer application, such as a microwave oven controller, that uses 16-bit memory addresses and data operands. If a load-store architecture is used, assume it has 16 general-purpose registers. For each architecture answer the following questions: How many instruction bytes are fetched? How many bytes of data are transferred from/to memory? Which architecture is most efficient as measured by code size? Which architecture is most efficient as measured by total memory traffic (code + data)?

d. [20] <2.10> Now assume a processor with 64-bit memory addresses and data operands. For each architecture answer the questions of part (c). How have the relative merits of the architectures changed for the chosen metrics?

2.5 [20/20/20] <2.3> We are designing instruction set formats for a load-store architecture and are trying to decide whether it is worthwhile to have multiple offset lengths for branches and memory references. The length of an instruction would be equal to 16 bits + offset length in bits, so ALU instructions will be 16 bits.

Figure 2.42 contains data on offset size for the Alpha architecture with full optimization for SPEC CPU2000. For instruction set frequencies, use the data for MIPS from the average of the five benchmarks for the load-store machine in Figure 2.32. Assume that the miscellaneous instructions are all ALU instructions that use only registers.

Number of offset magnitude bits	Cumulative data references	Cumulative branches
0	30.4%	0.1%
1	33.5%	2.8%
2	35.0%	10.5%
3	40.0%	22.9%
4	47.3%	36.5%
5	54.5%	57.4%
6	60.4%	72.4%
7	66.9%	85.2%
8	71.6%	90.5%
9	73.3%	93.1%
10	74.2%	95.1%
11	74.9%	96.0%
12	76.6%	96.8%
13	87.9%	97.4%
14	91.9%	98.1%
15	100%	98.5%
16	100%	99.5%
17	100%	99.8%
17	100%	99.9%
19	100%	100%
20	100%	100%
21	100%	100%

Figure 2.42 The second and third columns contain the cumulative percentage of the data references and branches, respectively, that can be accommodated with the corresponding number of bits of magnitude in the displacement. These are the average distances of all the integer and floating-point programs in Figure 2.8.

a. [20] <2.3> Suppose offsets are permitted to be 0, 8, 16, or 24 bits in length, including the sign bit. What is the average length of an executed instruction?

b. [20] <2.3> Suppose we want a fixed-length instruction and we chose a 24-bit instruction length (for everything, including ALU instructions). For every offset of longer than 8 bits, additional instruction(s) are required. Determine the number of instruction bytes fetched in this machine with fixed instruction size versus those fetched with a byte-variable-sized instruction as defined in part (a).

c. [20] <2.3> Now suppose we use a fixed offset length of 24 bits so that no additional instruction is ever required. How many instruction bytes would be required? Compare this result to your answer to part (b).

2.6 [15/10] <2.3> Several researchers have suggested that adding a register-memory addressing mode to a load-store machine might be useful. The idea is to replace sequences of

```
LOAD        R1,0(Rb)
ADD         R2,R2,R1
```

by

```
ADD         R2,0(Rb)
```

Assume the new instruction will cause the clock cycle to increase by 5%. Use the instruction frequencies for the gcc benchmark on the load-store machine from Figure 2.32. The new instruction affects only the clock cycle and not the CPI.

a. [15] <2.3> What percentage of the loads must be eliminated for the machine with the new instruction to have at least the same performance?

b. [10] <2.3> Show a situation in a multiple instruction sequence where a load of R1 followed immediately by a use of R1 (with some type of opcode) could not be replaced by a single instruction of the form proposed, assuming that the same opcode exists.

2.7 [25] <2.2–2.5> Find an instruction set manual for some older machine (libraries and private bookshelves are good places to look). Summarize the instruction set with the discriminating characteristics used in Figures 2.3 and 2.4. Write the code sequence for this machine for the statements in Exercise 2.1(b). The size of the data need not be the same as in Exercise 2.1(b) if the word size is smaller in the older machine.

✪ 2.8 [20] <2.2, 2.12> Consider the following fragment of C code:

```
for (i=0; i<=100; i++)
        {A[i] = B[i] + C;}
```

Assume that A and B are arrays of 64-bit integers, and C and i are 64-bit integers. Assume that all data values and their addresses are kept in memory (at addresses 0, 5000, 1500, and 2000 for A, B, C, and i, respectively) except when they are operated on. Assume that values in registers are lost between iterations of the loop.

Write the code for MIPS. How many instructions are required dynamically? How many memory-data references will be executed? What is the code size in bytes?

2.9 [20] <2.2, 2.12> For this question use the code sequence of Exercise 2.8, but put the scalar data—the value of i, the value of C, and the addresses of the array variables (but not the actual array)—in registers and keep them there whenever possible.

Write the code for MIPS. How many instructions are required dynamically? How many memory-data references will be executed? What is the code size in bytes?

2.10 [15] <2.12> When designing memory systems it becomes useful to know the frequency of memory reads versus writes and also accesses for instructions versus those for data. Using the average instruction mix information for MIPS in Figure 2.32, find

■ the percentage of all memory accesses for data

■ the percentage of data accesses that are reads

■ the percentage of all memory accesses that are reads

Ignore the size of a datum when counting accesses.

2.11 [18] <2.12> Compute the effective CPI for MIPS using Figure 2.32. Suppose we have made the following measurements of average CPI for instructions:

Instruction	Clock cycles
All ALU instructions	1.0
Loads-stores	1.4
Conditional branches	
Taken	2.0
Not taken	1.5
Jumps	1.2

Assume that 60% of the conditional branches are taken and that all instructions in the "other" category of Figure 2.32 are ALU instructions. Average the instruction frequencies of gap and gcc to obtain the instruction mix.

2.12 [20/10] <2.3, 2.12> Consider adding a new index addressing mode to MIPS. The addressing mode adds two registers and an 11-bit signed offset to get the effective address.

Our compiler will be changed so that code sequences of the form

```
ADD R1, R1, R2
LW  Rd, 100(R1)    (or store)
```

will be replaced with a load (or store) using the new addressing mode. Use the overall average instruction frequencies from Figure 2.32 in evaluating this addition.

a. [20] <2.3, 2.12> Assume that the addressing mode can be used for 10% of the displacement loads and stores (accounting for both the frequency of this type of address calculation and the shorter offset). What is the ratio of instruction count on the enhanced MIPS compared to the original MIPS?

b. [10] <2.3, 2.12> If the new addressing mode lengthens the clock cycle by 5%, which machine will be faster and by how much?

2.13 [30] <2.7> Many computer manufacturers now include tools or simulators that allow you to measure the instruction set usage of a user program. Among the methods in use are machine simulation, hardware-supported trapping, and a compiler technique that instruments the object code module by inserting counters. Find a processor available to you that includes such a tool. Use it to measure the instruction set mix for one of the SPEC CPU2000 benchmarks reported on in this chapter. Compare the results to those shown in this chapter.

✪ 2.14 [10/10] <2.8> One use of saturating arithmetic is for real-time applications that may fail their response time constraints if processor effort is diverted to handling arithmetic exceptions. Another benefit is that the result may be more desirable. Take, for example, an image array of 24-bit picture elements (pixels), each comprised of three 8-bit unsigned integers, representing red, green, and blue color brightness, that represent an image. Larger values are brighter.

a. [10] <2.8> Brighten the two pixels E5F1D7 and AAC4DE by adding 20 to each color component using unsigned arithmetic and ignoring overflow to maintain a fixed total instruction-processing time. The values are given in hexadecimal. What are the resulting pixel values? Are the pixels brightened?

b. [10] <2.8> Repeat part (a) but use saturating arithmetic instead. What are the resulting pixel values? Are the pixels brightened?

2.15 [20] <2.9> A condition code is a bit of processor state updated each time certain ALU operation(s) execute to reflect some aspect of the execution. For example, a subtract instruction may set a bit if the result is negative and reset it for a positive result. A later operation can refer to this specific "result sign" condition code bit to glean information about the subtract result, provided no other instruction of the set that updates the result sign condition code has executed in the meantime. The concept of dedicated condition codes can be generalized to an array of general-purpose condition bits. An instruction is encoded to use any one of the general-purpose condition bits, as selected by the compiler. What are the advantages and disadvantages of a collection of general-purpose condition bits as compared to those of dedicated condition codes (see Figure 2.21)?

2.16 [25/15] <2.7, 2.11> Find a C compiler and compile the code shown in Exercise 2.8 for one of the machines covered in this book. Compile the code both optimized and unoptimized.

a. [25] <2.7, 2.11> Find the instruction count, dynamic instruction bytes fetched, and data accesses done for both the optimized and unoptimized versions.

b. [15] <2.7, 2.11> Try to improve the code by hand and compute the same measures as in part (a) for your hand-optimized version.

2.17 [30/30] <2.7, 2.11> Small synthetic benchmarks can be very misleading when used for measuring instruction mixes. This is particularly true when these benchmarks are optimized. In this exercise, we want to explore these differences. This programming exercise can be done with any load-store machine.

a. Compile Whetstone with optimization. Compute the instruction mix for the top 20 most frequently executed instructions. How do the optimized and unoptimized mixes compare? How does the optimized mix compare to the mix for 171.swim from SPEC2000 on the same or a similar machine?

b. [30] <2.7, 2.11> Follow the same guidelines as for part (a), but this time use Dhrystone and compare it with gcc.

★ 2.18 [10] <2.11> Consider this high-level language code sequence of three statements:

```
A = B + C;
B = A + C;
D = A - B;
```

Use the technique of copy propagation (see Figure 2.25) to transform the code sequence to the point where no operand is a computed value. Note the instances in which the transformation has reduced the computational work of a statement and those cases where the work has increased. What does this suggest about the technical challenge faced in trying to satisfy the desire for optimizing compilers?

2.19 [20] <2.2, 2.10, 2.12> The design of MIPS provides for 32 general-purpose registers and 32 floating-point registers. If registers are good, are more registers better? List and discuss as many trade-offs as you can that should be considered by instruction set architecture designers examining whether to, and how much to, increase the numbers of MIPS registers.

2.20 [30] <2.3, 2.10, 2.12> MIPS has only a three-address format for its R-type register-register instructions. Many operations might use the same destination register as one of the sources. We could introduce a new instruction format into MIPS called R_2 that has only two addresses and is a total of 24 bits in length. By using this instruction type whenever an operation had only two different register operands, we could reduce the instruction bandwidth required for a program. Modify the MIPS simulator to count the frequency of register-register operations with only two different register operands. Using the benchmarks that come with the simulator, determine how much more instruction bandwidth MIPS requires than MIPS with the R_2 format.

2.21 [40] <2.2–2.12> Very long instruction word (VLIW) computers are discussed in Chapter 4, but increasingly DSPs and media processors are adopting this style of instruction set architecture. One example is the TI TMS320C6203. See if you can compare code size of VLIW to more traditional computers. One attempt would be to code a common kernel across several machines. Another would be to get access to compilers for each machine and compare code sizes. Based on your data, is VLIW an appropriate architecture for embedded applications? Why or why not?

2.22 [35] <2.2–2.8> GCC targets most modern instruction set architectures (see *www.gnu.org/software/gcc/gcc.html*). Create a version of gcc for several architectures that you have access to, such as 80x86, Alpha, MIPS, PowerPC, and SPARC. Then compile a subset of SPEC CPU2000 integer benchmarks and create a table of code sizes. Which architecture is best for each program?

2.23 [25] <App. C> How much do the instruction set variations among the RISC machines discussed in Appendix C affect performance? Choose at least three small programs (e.g., a sorting routine), and code these programs in MIPS and two other assembly languages. What is the resulting difference in instruction count?

2.24 [Discussion] <2.2–2.12> Where do instruction sets come from? Since the earliest computers date from just after World War II, it should be possible to derive the ancestry of the instructions in modern computers. This project will take a good deal of delving into libraries and perhaps contacting pioneers, but see if you can derive the ancestry of the instructions in, say, MIPS.

2.25 [Discussion] <2.2–2.15> What are the *economic* arguments (i.e., more machines sold) for and against changing instruction set architecture in desktop and server markets? What about embedded markets?

2.26 [Discussion] <1, 2> As we shall see in Chapter 3, many desktop microprocessors have a microinstruction set architecture (internal) that is different from the instruction set architecture (external) that software uses. For most such microprocessors, hardware translates each external instruction to internal instruction(s) when the instruction is fetched. However, at least one microprocessor uses an interpreter to translate instructions one at a time for the hardware and, when it detects frequently used code segments, invokes a compiler on the fly to compile those segments into optimized hardware instruction sequences and saves the compiled segments for reuse. List the pros and cons of each approach, commenting on at least the following issues: impact on clock cycle time, die size, code size, CPI, software compatibility, and execution time of the program.

3

Instruction-Level Parallelism and Its Dynamic Exploitation

"Who's first?"

"America."

"Who's second?"

"Sir, there is no second."

Dialog between two observers of the sailing race later named "The America's Cup" and run every few years— the inspiration for John Cocke's naming of the IBM research processor as "America." This processor was the precursor to the RS/6000 series and the first superscalar microprocessor.

Instruction-Level Parallelism: Concepts and Challenges

All processors since about 1985, including those in the embedded space, use pipelining to overlap the execution of instructions and improve performance. This potential overlap among instructions is called *instruction-level parallelism* (ILP) since the instructions can be evaluated in parallel. In this chapter and the next, we look at a wide range of techniques for extending the pipelining ideas by increasing the amount of parallelism exploited among instructions. This chapter is at a considerably more advanced level than the material in Appendix A. If you are not familiar with the ideas in Appendix A, you should review that appendix before venturing into this chapter.

We start this chapter by looking at the limitation imposed by data and control hazards and then turn to the topic of increasing the ability of the processor to exploit parallelism. This section introduces a large number of concepts, which we build on throughout these two chapters. While some of the more basic material in this chapter could be understood without all of the ideas in this section, this basic material is important to later sections of this chapter as well as to Chapter 4.

There are two largely separable approaches to exploiting ILP. This chapter covers techniques that are largely dynamic and depend on the hardware to locate the parallelism. The next chapter focuses on techniques that are static and rely much more on software. In practice, this partitioning between dynamic and static and between hardware-intensive and software-intensive is not clean, and techniques from one camp are often used by the other. Nonetheless, for exposition purposes, we have separated the two approaches and tried to indicate where an approach is transferable.

The dynamic, hardware-intensive approaches dominate the desktop and server markets and are used in a wide range of processors, including the Pentium III and 4; the Athlon; the MIPS R10000/12000; the Sun UltraSPARC III; the PowerPC 603, G3, and G4; and the Alpha 21264. The static, compiler-intensive approaches, which we focus on in the next chapter, have seen broader adoption in the embedded market than the desktop or server markets, although the new IA-64 architecture and Intel's Itanium use this more static approach.

In this section, we discuss features of both programs and processors that limit the amount of parallelism that can be exploited among instructions, as well as the critical mapping between program structure and hardware structure, which is key to understanding whether a program property will actually limit performance and under what circumstances.

Recall that the value of the CPI (cycles per instruction) for a pipelined processor is the sum of the base CPI and all contributions from stalls:

Pipeline CPI = Ideal pipeline CPI + Structural stalls + Data hazard stalls + Control stalls

The *ideal pipeline CPI* is a measure of the maximum performance attainable by the implementation. By reducing each of the terms of the right-hand side, we minimize the overall pipeline CPI and thus increase the IPC (instructions per clock). In this chapter we will see that the techniques we introduce to increase the ideal IPC can increase the importance of dealing with structural, data hazard, and control stalls. The equation above allows us to characterize the various techniques we examine in this chapter by what component of the overall CPI a technique reduces. Figure 3.1 shows the techniques we examine in this chapter and in the next, as well as the topics covered in the introductory material in Appendix A.

Before we examine these techniques in detail, we need to define the concepts on which these techniques are built. These concepts, in the end, determine the limits on how much parallelism can be exploited.

What Is Instruction-Level Parallelism?

All the techniques in this chapter and the next exploit parallelism among instructions. As we stated earlier, this type of parallelism is called instruction-level parallelism. The amount of parallelism available within a *basic block*—a straight-line code sequence with no branches in except to the entry and no branches out except at the exit—is quite small. For typical MIPS programs the average dynamic branch frequency is often between 15% and 25%, meaning that between four and seven instructions execute between a pair of branches. Since these instructions are likely to depend upon one another, the amount of overlap we can exploit within a basic block is likely to be much less than the average basic block size. To obtain substantial performance enhancements, we must exploit ILP across multiple basic blocks.

Technique	Reduces	Section
Forwarding and bypassing	Potential data hazard stalls	A.2
Delayed branches and simple branch scheduling	Control hazard stalls	A.2
Basic dynamic scheduling (scoreboarding)	Data hazard stalls from true dependences	A.8
Dynamic scheduling with renaming	Data hazard stalls and stalls from antidependences and output dependences	3.2
Dynamic branch prediction	Control stalls	3.4
Issuing multiple instructions per cycle	Ideal CPI	3.6
Speculation	Data hazard and control hazard stalls	3.7
Dynamic memory disambiguation	Data hazard stalls with memory	3.2, 3.7
Loop unrolling	Control hazard stalls	4.1
Basic compiler pipeline scheduling	Data hazard stalls	A.2, 4.1
Compiler dependence analysis	Ideal CPI, data hazard stalls	4.4
Software pipelining, trace scheduling	Ideal CPI, data hazard stalls	4.3
Compiler speculation	Ideal CPI, data, control stalls	4.4

Figure 3.1 The major techniques examined in Appendix A, Chapter 3, or Chapter 4 are shown together with the component of the CPI equation that the technique affects.

The simplest and most common way to increase the amount of parallelism available among instructions is to exploit parallelism among iterations of a loop. This type of parallelism is often called *loop-level parallelism*. Here is a simple example of a loop, which adds two 1000-element arrays, that is completely parallel:

```
for (i=1; i<=1000; i=i+1)
        x[i] = x[i] + y[i];
```

Every iteration of the loop can overlap with any other iteration, although within each loop iteration there is little or no opportunity for overlap.

There are a number of techniques we will examine for converting such loop-level parallelism into instruction-level parallelism. Basically, such techniques work by unrolling the loop either statically by the compiler (an approach we explore in the next chapter) or dynamically by the hardware (the subject of this chapter).

An important alternative method for exploiting loop-level parallelism is the use of vector instructions (see Appendix G). Essentially, a vector instruction operates on a sequence of data items. For example, the above code sequence could execute in four instructions on some vector processors: two instructions to load the vectors x and y from memory, one instruction to add the two vectors, and an instruction to store back the result vector. Of course, these instructions would be pipelined and have relatively long latencies, but these latencies may be overlapped. Vector instructions and the operation of vector processors are described in detail in the online Appendix G. Although the development of the vector ideas preceded many of the techniques we examine in these two chapters for exploiting ILP, processors that exploit ILP have almost completely replaced vector-based processors. Vector instruction sets, however, may see a renaissance, at least for use in graphics, digital signal processing, and multimedia applications.

Data Dependences and Hazards

Determining how one instruction depends on another is critical to determining how much parallelism exists in a program and how that parallelism can be exploited. In particular, to exploit instruction-level parallelism we must determine which instructions can be executed in parallel. If two instructions are *parallel,* they can execute simultaneously in a pipeline without causing any stalls, assuming the pipeline has sufficient resources (and hence no structural hazards exist). If two instructions are dependent they are not parallel and must be executed in order, though they may often be partially overlapped. The key in both cases is to determine whether an instruction is dependent on another instruction.

Data Dependences

There are three different types of dependences: data dependences (also called true data dependences), name dependences, and control dependences. An instruction *j* is *data dependent* on instruction *i* if either of the following holds:

- instruction *i* produces a result that may be used by instruction *j*, or
- instruction *j* is data dependent on instruction *k*, and instruction *k* is data dependent on instruction *i*.

The second condition simply states that one instruction is dependent on another if there exists a chain of dependences of the first type between the two instructions. This dependence chain can be as long as the entire program.

For example, consider the following code sequence that increments a vector of values in memory (starting at 0(R1) and with the last element at 8(R2)) by a scalar in register F2:

```
Loop:   L.D      F0,0(R1)     ;F0=array element
        ADD.D    F4,F0,F2     ;add scalar in F2
        S.D      F4,0(R1)     ;store result
        DADDUI   R1,R1,#-8    ;decrement pointer 8 bytes
        BNE      R1,R2,LOOP   ;branch R1!=R2
```

The data dependences in this code sequence involve both floating-point data:

```
Loop:   L.D      F0,0(R1)     ;F0=array element
        ADD.D    F4,F0,F2     ;add scalar in F2
        S.D      F4,0(R1)     ;store result
```

and integer data:

```
        DADDIU   R1,R1,-8     ;decrement pointer
                              ;8 bytes (per DW)
        BNE      R1,R2,Loop   ;branch R1!=zero
```

Both of the above dependent sequences, as shown by the arrows, have each instruction depending on the previous one. The arrows here and in following examples show the order that must be preserved for correct execution. The arrow points from an instruction that must precede the instruction that the arrowhead points to.

If two instructions are data dependent, they cannot execute simultaneously or be completely overlapped. The dependence implies that there would be a chain of one or more data hazards between the two instructions. Executing the instructions simultaneously will cause a processor with pipeline interlocks to detect a hazard and stall, thereby reducing or eliminating the overlap. In a processor without interlocks that relies on compiler scheduling, the compiler cannot schedule dependent instructions in such a way that they completely overlap, since the program will not execute correctly. The presence of a data dependence in an instruction sequence reflects a data dependence in the source code from which the instruction sequence was generated. The effect of the original data dependence must be preserved.

Dependences are a property of *programs*. Whether a given dependence results in an actual hazard being detected and whether that hazard actually causes a stall are properties of the *pipeline organization*. This difference is critical to understanding how instruction-level parallelism can be exploited.

In our example, there is a data dependence between the DADDIU and the BNE; this dependence causes a stall because we moved the branch test for the MIPS pipeline to the ID stage. Had the branch test stayed in EX, this dependence would not cause a stall. Of course, the branch delay would then still be two cycles, rather than one.

The presence of the dependence indicates the potential for a hazard, but the actual hazard and the *length of any stall* is a property of the pipeline. The importance of the data dependences is that a dependence (1) indicates the possibility of a hazard, (2) determines the order in which results must be calculated, and (3) sets an upper bound on how much parallelism can possibly be exploited. Such limits are explored in Section 3.8.

Since a data dependence can limit the amount of instruction-level parallelism we can exploit, a major focus of this chapter and the next is overcoming these limitations. A dependence can be overcome in two different ways: maintaining the dependence but avoiding a hazard, and eliminating a dependence by transforming the code. Scheduling the code is the primary method used to avoid a hazard without altering a dependence. In this chapter, we consider hardware schemes for scheduling code dynamically as it is executed. As we will see, some types of dependences can be eliminated, primarily by software, and in some cases by hardware techniques.

A data value may flow between instructions either through registers or through memory locations. When the data flow occurs in a register, detecting the dependence is reasonably straightforward since the register names are fixed in the instructions, although it gets more complicated when branches intervene and correctness concerns cause a compiler or hardware to be conservative.

Dependences that flow through memory locations are more difficult to detect since two addresses may refer to the same location but look different: For example, 100(R4) and 20(R6) may be identical. In addition, the effective address of a load or store may change from one execution of the instruction to another (so that 20(R4) and 20(R4) will be different), further complicating the detection of a dependence. In this chapter, we examine hardware for detecting data dependences that involve memory locations, but we will see that these techniques also have limitations. The compiler techniques for detecting such dependences are critical in uncovering loop-level parallelism, as we will see in the next chapter.

Name Dependences

The second type of dependence is a *name dependence*. A name dependence occurs when two instructions use the same register or memory location, called a *name,* but there is no flow of data between the instructions associated with that name. There are two types of name dependences between an instruction *i* that *precedes* instruction *j* in program order:

1. An *antidependence* between instruction *i* and instruction *j* occurs when instruction *j* writes a register or memory location that instruction *i* reads. The original ordering must be preserved to ensure that *i* reads the correct value.

2. An *output dependence* occurs when instruction *i* and instruction *j* write the same register or memory location. The ordering between the instructions must be preserved to ensure that the value finally written corresponds to instruction *j*.

Both antidependences and output dependences are name dependences, as opposed to true data dependences, since there is no value being transmitted between the instructions. Since a name dependence is not a true dependence, instructions involved in a name dependence can execute simultaneously or be reordered, if the name (register number or memory location) used in the instructions is changed so the instructions do not conflict. This renaming can be more easily done for register operands, where it is called *register renaming*. Register renaming can be done either statically by a compiler or dynamically by the hardware. Before describing dependences arising from branches, let's examine the relationship between dependences and pipeline data hazards.

Data Hazards

A hazard is created whenever there is a dependence between instructions, and they are close enough that the overlap caused by pipelining, or other reordering of instructions, would change the order of access to the operand involved in the dependence. Because of the dependence, we must preserve what is called *program order,* that is, the order that the instructions would execute in if executed sequentially one at a time as determined by the original source program. The goal of both our software and hardware techniques is to exploit parallelism by preserving program order *only where it affects the outcome of the program.* Detecting and avoiding hazards ensures that necessary program order is preserved.

Data hazards may be classified as one of three types, depending on the order of read and write accesses in the instructions. By convention, the hazards are named by the ordering in the program that must be preserved by the pipeline. Consider two instructions *i* and *j,* with *i* occurring before *j* in program order. The possible data hazards are

■ RAW (*read after write*)—*j* tries to read a source before *i* writes it, so *j* incorrectly gets the *old* value. This hazard is the most common type and corresponds to a true data dependence. Program order must be preserved to ensure that j receives the value from i. In the simple common five-stage static pipeline (see Appendix A), a load instruction followed by an integer ALU instruction that directly uses the load result will lead to a RAW hazard.

■ WAW *(write after write)*—j tries to write an operand before it is written by i. The writes end up being performed in the wrong order, leaving the value written by i rather than the value written by j in the destination. This hazard corresponds to an output dependence. WAW hazards are present only in pipelines that write in more than one pipe stage or allow an instruction to proceed even when a previous instruction is stalled. The classic five-stage integer pipeline used in Appendix A writes a register only in the WB stage and avoids this class of hazards, but this chapter explores pipelines that allow instructions to be reordered, creating the possibility of WAW hazards. WAW hazards can also exist between a short integer pipeline and a longer floating-point pipeline (see the pipelines in Sections A.5 and A.6 of Appendix A). For example, a floating-point multiply instruction that writes F4, shortly followed by a load of F4, could yield a WAW hazard, since the load could complete before the multiply completed.

■ WAR *(write after read)*—j tries to write a destination before it is read by i, so i incorrectly gets the *new* value. This hazard arises from an antidependence. WAR hazards cannot occur in most static issue pipelines—even deeper pipelines or floating-point pipelines—because all reads are early (in ID) and all writes are late (in WB). (See Appendix A to convince yourself.) A WAR hazard occurs either when there are some instructions that write results early in the instruction pipeline *and* other instructions that read a source late in the pipeline, or when instructions are reordered, as we will see in this chapter.

Note that the RAR *(read after read)* case is not a hazard.

Control Dependences

The last type of dependence is a *control dependence*. A control dependence determines the ordering of an instruction, i, with respect to a branch instruction so that the instruction i is executed in correct program order and only when it should be. Every instruction, except for those in the first basic block of the program, is control dependent on some set of branches, and, in general, these control dependences must be preserved to preserve program order. One of the simplest examples of a control dependence is the dependence of the statements in the "then" part of an if statement on the branch. For example, in the code segment

```
if p1 {
    S1;
};
if p2 {
    S2;
}
```

S1 is control dependent on p1, and S2 is control dependent on p2 but not on p1. In general, there are two constraints imposed by control dependences:

1. An instruction that is control dependent on a branch cannot be moved *before* the branch so that its execution *is no longer controlled* by the branch. For example, we cannot take an instruction from the then portion of an if statement and move it before the if statement.

2. An instruction that is not control dependent on a branch cannot be moved *after* the branch so that its execution *is controlled* by the branch. For example, we cannot take a statement before the if statement and move it into the then portion.

Control dependence is preserved by two properties in a simple pipeline, such as that in Chapter 1. First, instructions execute in program order. This ordering ensures that an instruction that occurs before a branch is executed before the branch. Second, the detection of control or branch hazards ensures that an instruction that is control dependent on a branch is not executed until the branch direction is known.

Although preserving control dependence is a useful and simple way to help preserve program order, the control dependence in itself is not the fundamental performance limit. We may be willing to execute instructions that should not have been executed, thereby violating the control dependences, *if* we can do so without affecting the correctness of the program. Control dependence is not the critical property that must be preserved. Instead, the two properties critical to program correctness—and normally preserved by maintaining both data and control dependence—are the *exception behavior* and the *data flow*.

Preserving the exception behavior means that any changes in the ordering of instruction execution must not change how exceptions are raised in the program. Often this is relaxed to mean that the reordering of instruction execution must not cause any new exceptions in the program. A simple example shows how maintaining the control and data dependences can prevent such situations. Consider this code sequence:

```
        DADDU     R2,R3,R4
        BEQZ      R2,L1
        LW        R1,0(R2)
L1:
```

In this case, it is easy to see that if we do not maintain the data dependence involving R2, we can change the result of the program. Less obvious is the fact that if we ignore the control dependence and move the load instruction before the branch, the load instruction may cause a memory protection exception. Notice that *no data dependence* prevents us from interchanging the BEQZ and the LW; it is only the control dependence. To allow us to reorder these instructions (and still preserve the data dependence), we would like to just ignore the exception when the branch is taken. In Section 3.7, we will look at a hardware technique, speculation, which allows us to overcome this exception problem. The next chapter looks at other techniques for the same problem.

The second property preserved by maintenance of data dependences and control dependences is the data flow. The data flow is the actual flow of data values among instructions that produce results and those that consume them. Branches make the data flow dynamic, since they allow the source of data for a given instruction to come from many points. Put another way, it is not sufficient to just maintain data dependences because an instruction may be data dependent on more than one predecessor. Program order is what determines which predecessor will actually deliver a data value to an instruction. Program order is ensured by maintaining the control dependences.

For example, consider the following code fragment:

```
        DADDU    R1,R2,R3
        BEQZ     R4,L
        DSUBU    R1,R5,R6
L:      ...

        OR       R7,R1,R8
```

In this example, the value of R1 used by the OR instruction depends on whether the branch is taken or not. Data dependence alone is not sufficient to preserve correctness. The OR instruction is data dependent on both the DADDU and DSUBU instructions, but preserving this order alone is insufficient for correct execution. Instead, when the instructions execute, the data flow must be preserved: If the branch is not taken, then the value of R1 computed by the DSUBU should be used by the OR, and if the branch is taken, the value of R1 computed by the DADDU should be used by the OR. By preserving the control dependence of the OR on the branch, we prevent an illegal change to the data flow. For similar reasons, the DSUBU instruction cannot be moved above the branch. Speculation, which helps with the exception problem, will also allow us to lessen the impact of the control dependence while still maintaining the data flow, as we will see in Section 3.7.

Sometimes we can determine that violating the control dependence cannot affect either the exception behavior or the data flow. Consider the following code sequence:

```
            DADDU    R1,R2,R3
            BEQZ     R12,skipnext
            DSUBU    R4,R5,R6
            DADDU    R5,R4,R9
skipnext:   OR       R7,R8,R9
```

Suppose we knew that the register destination of the DSUBU instruction (R4) was unused after the instruction labeled skipnext. (The property of whether a value will be used by an upcoming instruction is called *liveness*.) If R4 were unused, then changing the value of R4 just before the branch would not affect the data flow since R4 would be *dead* (rather than live) in the code region after skipnext. Thus, if R4 were dead and the existing DSUBU instruction could not generate an exception (other than those from which the processor resumes the same process), we could move the DSUBU instruction before the branch, since the data flow cannot be affected by this change. If the branch is taken, the DSUBU instruction will execute and will be useless, but it will not affect the program results. This type of code scheduling is sometimes called *speculation,* since the compiler is betting on the branch outcome; in this case, the bet is that the branch is usually not taken. More ambitious compiler speculation mechanisms are discussed in Chapter 4.

Control dependence is preserved by implementing control hazard detection that causes control stalls. Control stalls can be eliminated or reduced by a variety of hardware and software techniques. Delayed branches, which we saw in Chapter 1, can reduce the stalls arising from control hazards; scheduling a delayed branch requires that the compiler preserve the data flow.

The key focus of the rest of this chapter is on techniques that exploit instruction-level parallelism using hardware. The data dependences in a compiled program act as a limit on how much ILP can be exploited. The challenge is to approach that limit by trying to minimize the actual hazards and associated stalls that arise. The techniques we examine become ever more sophisticated in an attempt to exploit all the available parallelism while maintaining the necessary true data dependences in the code.

3.2 Overcoming Data Hazards with Dynamic Scheduling

A simple statically scheduled pipeline fetches an instruction and issues it, unless there was a data dependence between an instruction already in the pipeline and the fetched instruction that cannot be hidden with bypassing or forwarding. (Forwarding logic reduces the effective pipeline latency so that the certain dependences do not result in hazards.) If there is a data dependence that cannot be hidden, then the hazard detection hardware stalls the pipeline (starting with the instruction that uses the result). No new instructions are fetched or issued until the dependence is cleared.

In this section, we explore an important technique, called *dynamic scheduling,* in which the hardware rearranges the instruction execution to reduce the stalls while maintaining data flow and exception behavior. Dynamic scheduling offers several advantages: It enables handling some cases when dependences are unknown at compile time (e.g., because they may involve a memory reference), and it simplifies the compiler. Perhaps most importantly, it also allows code that was compiled with one pipeline in mind to run efficiently on a different pipeline. In Section 3.7, we will explore hardware speculation, a technique with significant performance advantages, which builds on dynamic scheduling. As we will see, the advantages of dynamic scheduling are gained at a cost of a significant increase in hardware complexity.

Although a dynamically scheduled processor cannot change the data flow, it tries to avoid stalling when dependences, which could generate hazards, are present. In contrast, static pipeline scheduling by the compiler (covered in the next chapter) tries to minimize stalls by separating dependent instructions so that they will not lead to hazards. Of course, compiler pipeline scheduling can also be used on code destined to run on a processor with a dynamically scheduled pipeline.

Dynamic Scheduling: The Idea

A major limitation of the simple pipelining techniques we discuss in Appendix A is that they all use in-order instruction issue and execution: Instructions are issued in program order, and if an instruction is stalled in the pipeline, no later instructions can proceed. Thus, if there is a dependence between two closely spaced instructions in the pipeline, this will lead to a hazard and a stall will result. If there are multiple functional units, these units could lie idle. If instruction j depends on a long-running instruction i, currently in execution in the pipeline, then all instructions after j must be stalled until i is finished and j can execute. For example, consider this code:

```
DIV.D    F0,F2,F4
ADD.D    F10,F0,F8
SUB.D    F12,F8,F14
```

The SUB.D instruction cannot execute because the dependence of ADD.D on DIV.D causes the pipeline to stall; yet SUB.D is not data dependent on anything in the pipeline. This hazard creates a performance limitation that can be eliminated by not requiring instructions to execute in program order.

In the classic five-stage pipeline developed in the first chapter, both structural and data hazards could be checked during instruction decode (ID): When an instruction could execute without hazards, it was issued from ID knowing that all data hazards had been resolved. To allow us to begin executing the SUB.D in the above example, we must separate the issue process into two parts: checking for any structural hazards and waiting for the absence of a data hazard. We can still check for structural hazards when we issue the instruction; thus, we still use in-order instruction issue (i.e., instructions issued in program order), but we want an instruction to begin execution as soon as its data operand is available. Thus, this pipeline does *out-of-order execution,* which implies *out-of-order completion.*

Out-of-order execution introduces the possibility of WAR and WAW hazards, which do not exist in the five-stage integer pipeline and its logical extension to an in-order floating-point pipeline. Consider the following MIPS floating-point code sequence:

```
DIV.D    F0,F2,F4
ADD.D    F6,F0,F8
SUB.D    F8,F10,F14
MUL.D    F6,F10,F8
```

There is an antidependence between the ADD.D and the SUB.D, and if the pipeline executes the SUB.D before the ADD.D (which is waiting for the DIV.D), it will violate the antidependence, yielding a WAR hazard. Likewise, to avoid violating output dependences, such as the write of F6 by MUL.D, WAW hazards must be handled. As we will see, both these hazards are avoided by the use of register renaming.

Out-of-order completion also creates major complications in handling exceptions. Dynamic scheduling with out-of-order completion must preserve exception behavior in the sense that *exactly* those exceptions that would arise if the program were executed in strict program order *actually* do arise. Dynamically scheduled processors preserve exception behavior by ensuring that no instruction can generate an exception until the processor knows that the instruction raising the exception will be executed; we will see shortly how this property can be guaranteed. Although exception behavior must be preserved, dynamically scheduled processors may generate *imprecise* exceptions. An exception is *imprecise* if the processor state when an exception is raised does not look exactly as if the instructions were executed sequentially in strict program order. Imprecise exceptions can occur because of two possibilities:

1. The pipeline may have *already completed* instructions that are *later* in program order than the instruction causing the exception.

2. The pipeline may have *not yet completed* some instructions that are *earlier* in program order than the instruction causing the exception.

Imprecise exceptions make it difficult to restart execution after an exception. Rather than address these problems in this section, we will discuss a solution that provides precise exceptions in the context of a processor with speculation in Section 3.7. For floating-point exceptions, other solutions have been used, as discussed in Appendix A.

To allow out-of-order execution, we essentially split the ID pipe stage of our simple five-stage pipeline into two stages:

1. *Issue*—Decode instructions, check for structural hazards.

2. *Read operands*—Wait until no data hazards, then read operands.

An instruction fetch stage precedes the issue stage and may fetch either into an instruction register or into a queue of pending instructions; instructions are then issued from the register or queue. The EX stage follows the read operands stage, just as in the five-stage pipeline. Execution may take multiple cycles, depending on the operation.

We will distinguish when an instruction *begins execution* and when it *completes execution;* between the two times, the instruction is *in execution*. Our pipeline allows multiple instructions to be in execution at the same time, and without this capability, a major advantage of dynamic scheduling is lost. Having multiple instructions in execution at once requires multiple functional units, pipelined functional units, or both. Since these two capabilities—pipelined functional units and multiple functional units—are essentially equivalent for the purposes of pipeline control, we will assume the processor has multiple functional units.

In a dynamically scheduled pipeline, all instructions pass through the issue stage in order (in-order issue); however, they can be stalled or bypass each other in the second stage (read operands) and thus enter execution out of order. *Scoreboarding* is a technique for allowing instructions to execute out of order when there are sufficient resources and no data dependences; it is named after the CDC 6600 scoreboard, which developed this capability. We focus on a more sophisticated technique, called *Tomasulo's algorithm,* that has several major enhancements over scoreboarding. The reader wishing a gentler introduction to these concepts may want to consult Appendix A, which thoroughly discusses scoreboarding and includes several examples.

Dynamic Scheduling Using Tomasulo's Approach

A key approach to allow execution to proceed in the presence of dependences was used by the IBM 360/91 floating-point unit. Invented by Robert Tomasulo, this scheme tracks when operands for instructions are available, to minimize RAW hazards, and introduces register renaming, to minimize WAW and RAW hazards. There are many variations on this scheme in modern processors, although the key concept of tracking instruction dependences to allow execution as soon as operands are available and renaming registers to avoid WAR and WAW hazards are common characteristics.

The IBM 360/91 was completed just before caches appeared in commercial processors. IBM's goal was to achieve high floating-point performance from an instruction set and from compilers designed for the entire 360 computer family, rather than from specialized compilers for the high-end processors. The 360 architecture had only four double-precision floating-point registers, which limits the effectiveness of compiler scheduling; this fact was another motivation for the Tomasulo approach. In addition, the IBM 360/91 had long memory accesses and long floating-point delays, which Tomasulo's algorithm was designed to overcome. At the end of the section, we will see that Tomasulo's algorithm can also support the overlapped execution of multiple iterations of a loop.

We explain the algorithm, which focuses on the floating-point unit and load-store unit, in the context of the MIPS instruction set. The primary difference between MIPS and the 360 is the presence of register-memory instructions in the latter processor. Because Tomasulo's algorithm uses a load functional unit, no significant changes are needed to add register-memory addressing modes. The IBM 360/91 also had pipelined functional units, rather than multiple functional units, but we describe the algorithm as if there were multiple functional units. It is a simple conceptual extension to also pipeline those functional units.

As we will see, RAW hazards are avoided by executing an instruction only when its operands are available. WAR and WAW hazards, which arise from name dependences, are eliminated by register renaming. *Register renaming* eliminates these hazards by renaming all destination registers, including those with a pending read or write for an earlier instruction, so that the out-of-order write does not affect any instructions that depend on an earlier value of an operand.

To better understand how register renaming eliminates WAR and WAW hazards, consider the following example code sequence that includes both a potential WAR and WAW hazard:

```
DIV.D    F0,F2,F4
ADD.D    F6,F0,F8
S.D      F6,0(R1)
SUB.D    F8,F10,F14
MUL.D    F6,F10,F8
```

There is an antidependence between the ADD.D and the SUB.D and an output dependence between the ADD.D and the MUL.D, leading to two possible hazards: a WAR hazard on the use of F8 by ADD.D and a WAW hazard since the ADD.D may finish later than the MUL.D. There are also three true data dependences: between the DIV.D and the ADD.D, between the SUB.D and the MUL.D, and between the ADD.D and the S.D.

These name dependences can both be eliminated by register renaming. For simplicity, assume the existence of two temporary registers, S and T. Using S and T, the sequence can be rewritten without any dependences as

```
DIV.D    F0,F2,F4
ADD.D    S,F0,F8
S.D      S,0(R1)
SUB.D    T,F10,F14
MUL.D    F6,F10,T
```

In addition, any subsequent uses of F8 must be replaced by the register T. In this code segment, the renaming process can be done statically by the compiler. Finding any uses of F8 that are later in the code requires either sophisticated compiler analysis or hardware support, since there may be intervening branches between the above code segment and a later use of F8. As we will see, Tomasulo's algorithm can handle renaming across branches.

In Tomasulo's scheme, register renaming is provided by the *reservation stations,* which buffer the operands of instructions waiting to issue, and by the issue logic. The basic idea is that a reservation station fetches and buffers an operand as soon as it is available, eliminating the need to get the operand from a register. In addition, pending instructions designate the reservation station that will provide their input. Finally, when successive writes to a register overlap in execution, only the last one is actually used to update the register. As instructions are issued, the register specifiers for pending operands are renamed to the names of the reservation station, which provides register renaming. Since there can be more reservation stations than real registers, the technique can even eliminate hazards arising from name dependences that could not be eliminated by a compiler. As we explore the components of Tomasulo's scheme, we will return to the topic of register renaming and see exactly how the renaming occurs and how it eliminates WAR and WAW hazards.

The use of reservation stations, rather than a centralized register file, leads to two other important properties. First, hazard detection and execution control are distributed: The information held in the reservation stations at each functional unit determine when an instruction can begin execution at that unit. Second, results are passed directly to functional units from the reservation stations where they are buffered, rather than going through the registers. This bypassing is done with a common result bus that allows all units waiting for an operand to be loaded simultaneously (on the 360/91 this is called the *common data bus,* or CDB). In pipelines with multiple execution units and issuing multiple instructions per clock, more than one result bus will be needed.

Figure 3.2 shows the basic structure of a Tomasulo-based MIPS processor, including both the floating-point unit and the load-store unit; none of the execution control tables are shown. Each reservation station holds an instruction that has been issued and is awaiting execution at a functional unit, and either the operand values for that instruction, if they have already been computed, or else the names of the reservation stations that will provide the operand values.

The load buffers and store buffers hold data or addresses coming from and going to memory and behave almost exactly like reservation stations, so we distinguish them only when necessary. The floating-point registers are connected by a pair of buses to the functional units and by a single bus to the store buffers. All results from the functional units and from memory are sent on the common data bus, which goes everywhere except to the load buffer. All reservation stations have tag fields, employed by the pipeline control.

Before we describe the details of the reservation stations and the algorithm, let's look at the steps an instruction goes through, just as we did for the five-stage pipeline of Appendix A. Since the structure is dramatically different, there are only three steps (though each one can now take an arbitrary number of clock cycles):

1. *Issue*—Get the next instruction from the head of the instruction queue, which is maintained in FIFO order to ensure the maintenance of correct data flow. If there is a matching reservation station that is empty, issue the instruction to the station with the operand values, if they are currently in the registers. If there is not an empty reservation station, then there is a structural hazard and the instruction stalls until a station or buffer is freed. If the operands are not in the registers, keep track of the functional units that will produce the operands. This step renames registers, eliminating WAR and WAW hazards.

2. *Execute*—If one or more of the operands is not yet available, monitor the common data bus while waiting for it to be computed. When an operand becomes available, it is placed into the corresponding reservation station. When all the operands are available, the operation can be executed at the corresponding functional unit. By delaying instruction execution until the operands are available, RAW hazards are avoided. Notice that several instructions

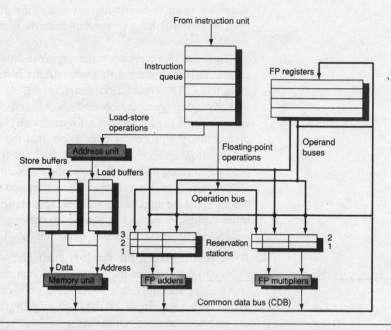

Figure 3.2 The basic structure of a MIPS floating-point unit using Tomasulo's algorithm. Instructions are sent from the instruction unit into the instruction queue from which they are issued in FIFO order. The reservation stations include the operation and the actual operands, as well as information used for detecting and resolving hazards. Load buffers have three functions: hold the components of the effective address until it is computed, track outstanding loads that are waiting on the memory, and hold the results of completed loads that are waiting for the CDB. Similarly, store buffers have three functions: hold the components of the effective address until it is computed, hold the destination memory addresses of outstanding stores that are waiting for the data value to store, and hold the address and value to store until the memory unit is available. All results from either the FP units or the load unit are put on the CDB, which goes to the FP register file as well as to the reservation stations and store buffers. The FP adders implement addition and subtraction, and the FP multipliers do multiplication and division.

could become ready in the same clock cycle for the same functional unit. Although independent functional units could begin execution in the same clock cycle for different instructions, if more than one instruction is ready for a single functional unit, the unit will have to choose among them. For the floating-point reservation stations, this choice may be made arbitrarily; loads and stores, however, present an additional complication.

Loads and stores require a two-step execution process. The first step computes the effective address when the base register is available, and the effective address is then placed in the load or store buffer. Loads in the load buffer execute as soon as the memory unit is available. Stores in the store buffer wait for the value to be stored before being sent to the memory unit. Loads and stores are maintained in program order through the effective address calculation, which will help to prevent hazards through memory, as we will see shortly.

To preserve exception behavior, no instruction is allowed to initiate execution until all branches that precede the instruction in program order have completed. This restriction guarantees that an instruction that causes an exception during execution really would have been executed. In a processor using branch prediction (as all dynamically scheduled processors do), this means that the processor must know that the branch prediction was correct before allowing an instruction after the branch to begin execution. It is possible by recording the occurrence of the exception, but not actually raising it, to allow execution of the instruction to start and not stall the instruction until it enters Write Result. As we will see, speculation provides a more flexible and more complete method to handle exceptions, so we will delay making this enhancement and show how speculation handles this problem later.

3. *Write result*—When the result is available, write it on the CDB and from there into the registers and into any reservation stations (including store buffers) waiting for this result. Stores also write data to memory during this step: When both the address and data value are available, they are sent to the memory unit and the store completes.

The data structures used to detect and eliminate hazards are attached to the reservation stations, to the register file, and to the load and store buffers with slightly different information attached to different objects. These tags are essentially names for an extended set of virtual registers used in renaming. In our example, the tag field is a 4-bit quantity that denotes one of the five reservation stations or one of the six load buffers. As we will see, this produces the equivalent of 11 registers that can be designated as result registers (as opposed to the 4 double-precision registers that the 360 architecture contains). In a processor with more real registers, we would want renaming to provide an even larger set of virtual registers. The tag field describes which reservation station contains the instruction that will produce a result needed as a source operand.

Once an instruction has issued and is waiting for a source operand, it refers to the operand by the reservation station number where the instruction that will write the register has been assigned. Unused values, such as zero, indicate that the operand is already available in the registers. Because there are more reservation stations than actual register numbers, WAW and WAR hazards are eliminated by renaming results using reservation station numbers. Although in Tomasulo's scheme the reservation stations are used as the extended virtual registers, other approaches could use a register set with additional registers or a structure like the reorder buffer, which we will see in Section 3.7.

In describing the operation of this scheme, we use a terminology taken from the CDC scoreboard scheme, showing the terminology used by the IBM 360/91 for historical reference. It is important to remember that the tags in the Tomasulo scheme refer to the buffer or unit that will produce a result; the register names are discarded when an instruction issues to a reservation station.

Each reservation station has seven fields:

- Op—The operation to perform on source operands S1 and S2.

- Qj, Qk—The reservation stations that will produce the corresponding source operand; a value of zero indicates that the source operand is already available in Vj or Vk, or is unnecessary. (The IBM 360/91 calls these SINKunit and SOURCEunit.)

- Vj, Vk—The value of the source operands. Note that only one of the V field or the Q field is valid for each operand. For loads, the Vk field is used to hold the offset field. (These fields are called SINK and SOURCE on the IBM 360/91.)

- A—Used to hold information for the memory address calculation for a load or store. Initially, the immediate field of the instruction is stored here; after the address calculation, the effective address is stored here.

- Busy—Indicates that this reservation station and its accompanying functional unit are occupied.

The register file has a field, Qi:

- Qi—The number of the reservation station that contains the operation whose result should be stored into this register. If the value of Qi is blank (or 0), no currently active instruction is computing a result destined for this register, meaning that the value is simply the register contents.

The load and store buffers each have a field, A, which holds the result of the effective address once the first step of execution has been completed.

In the next section, we will first consider some examples that show how these mechanisms work and then examine the detailed algorithm.

3.3   Dynamic Scheduling: Examples and the Algorithm

Before we examine Tomasulo's algorithm in detail, let's consider a few examples, which will help illustrate how the algorithm works.

Example   Show what the information tables look like for the following code sequence when only the first load has completed and written its result:

```
1.    L.D      F6,34(R2)
2.    L.D      F2,45(R3)
3.    MUL.D    F0,F2,F4
4.    SUB.D    F8,F2,F6
5.    DIV.D    F10,F0,F6
6.    ADD.D    F6,F8,F2
```

Answer The result is shown in the three tables in Figure 3.3. The numbers appended to the names add, mult, and load stand for the tag for that reservation station—Add1 is the tag for the result from the first add unit. In addition we have included an instruction status table. This table is included only to help you understand the algorithm; it is *not* actually a part of the hardware. Instead, the reservation station keeps the state of each operation that has issued.

		Instruction status		
Instruction		Issue	Execute	Write Result
L.D	F6,34(R2)	√	√	√
L.D	F2,45(R3)	√	√	
MUL.D	F0,F2,F4	√		
SUB.D	F8,F2,F6	√		
DIV.D	F10,F0,F6	√		
ADD.D	F6,F8,F2	√		

				Reservation stations			
Name	Busy	Op	Vj	Vk	Qj	Qk	A
Load1	no						
Load2	yes	Load					45 + Regs[R3]
Add1	yes	SUB		Mem[34 + Regs[R2]]	Load2		
Add2	yes	ADD			Add1	Load2	
Add3	no						
Mult1	yes	MUL		Regs[F4]	Load2		
Mult2	yes	DIV		Mem[34 + Regs[R2]]	Mult1		

				Register status				
Field	F0	F2	F4	F6	F8	F10	F12	...	F30
Qi	Mult1	Load2		Add2	Add1	Mult2			

Figure 3.3 Reservation stations and register tags shown when all of the instructions have issued, but only the first load instruction has completed and written its result to the CDB. The second load has completed effective address calculation, but is waiting on the memory unit. We use the array Regs[ ] to refer to the register file and the array Mem[ ] to refer to the memory. Remember that an operand is specified by either a Q field or a V field at any time. Notice that the ADD.D instruction, which has a WAR hazard at the WB stage, has issued and could complete before the DIV.D initiates.

Tomasulo's scheme offers two major advantages over earlier and simpler schemes: (1) the distribution of the hazard detection logic and (2) the elimination of stalls for WAW and WAR hazards.

The first advantage arises from the distributed reservation stations and the use of the CDB. If multiple instructions are waiting on a single result, and each instruction already has its other operand, then the instructions can be released simultaneously by the broadcast on the CDB. If a centralized register file were used, the units would have to read their results from the registers when register buses are available.

The second advantage, the elimination of WAW and WAR hazards, is accomplished by renaming registers using the reservation stations, and by the process of storing operands into the reservation station as soon as they are available. For example, in our code sequence in Figure 3.3 we have issued both the DIV.D and the ADD.D, even though there is a WAR hazard involving F6. The hazard is eliminated in one of two ways. First, if the instruction providing the value for the DIV.D has completed, then Vk will store the result, allowing DIV.D to execute independent of the ADD.D (this is the case shown).

On the other hand, if the L.D had not completed, then Qk would point to the Load1 reservation station, and the DIV.D instruction would be independent of the ADD.D. Thus, in either case, the ADD.D can issue and begin executing. Any uses of the result of the DIV.D would point to the reservation station, allowing the ADD.D to complete and store its value into the registers without affecting the DIV.D. We'll see an example of the elimination of a WAW hazard shortly. But let's first look at how our earlier example continues execution. In this example, and the ones that follow in this chapter, assume the following latencies: Load is 1 clock cycle, Add is 2 clock cycles, multiply is 10 clock cycles, and divide is 40 clock cycles.

Example Using the same code segment as in the previous example (page 189), show what the status tables look like when the MUL.D is ready to write its result.

Answer The result is shown in the three tables in Figure 3.4. Notice that ADD.D has completed since the operands of DIV.D were copied, thereby overcoming the WAR hazard. Notice that even if the load of F6 was delayed, the add into F6 could be executed without triggering a WAW hazard.

Tomasulo's Algorithm: The Details

Figure 3.5 gives the checks and steps that each instruction must go through. As mentioned earlier, loads and stores go through a functional unit for effective address computation before proceeding to independent load or store buffers. Loads take a second execution step to access memory and then go to Write Result to send the value from memory to the register file and/or any waiting reservation stations. Stores complete their execution in the Write Result stage, which writes the result to memory. Notice that all writes occur in Write Result, whether the

Instruction		Instruction status		
		Issue	Execute	Write Result
L.D	F6,34(R2)	√	√	√
L.D	F2,45(R3)	√	√	√
MUL.D	F0,F2,F4	√	√	
SUB.D	F8,F2,F6	√	√	√
DIV.D	F10,F0,F6	√		
ADD.D	F6,F8,F2	√	√	√

				Reservation stations				
Name	Busy	Op	Vj		Vk	Qj	Qk	A
Load1	no							
Load2	no							
Add1	no							
Add2	no							
Add3	no							
Mult1	yes	MUL	Mem[45 + Regs[R3]]		Regs[F4]			
Mult2	yes	DIV			Mem[34 + Regs[R2]]	Mult1		

				Register status				
Field	F0	F2	F4	F6	F8	F10	F12	...	F30
Qi	Mult1					Mult2			

Figure 3.4 Multiply and divide are the only instructions not finished.

destination is a register or memory. This restriction simplifies Tomasulo's algorithm and is critical to its extension with speculation in Section 3.7.

Tomasulo's Algorithm: A Loop-Based Example

To understand the full power of eliminating WAW and WAR hazards through dynamic renaming of registers, we must look at a loop. Consider the following simple sequence for multiplying the elements of an array by a scalar in F2:

```
Loop:   L.D      F0,0(R1)
        MUL.D    F4,F0,F2
        S.D      F4,0(R1)
        DADDUI   R1,R1,-8
        BNE      R1,R2,Loop; branches if R1≠R2
```

Instruction state		Wait until	Action or bookkeeping

Issue	FP Operation	Station r empty	if (RegisterStat[rs].Qi≠0)
			   {RS[r].Qj ← RegisterStat[rs].Qi}
			else {RS[r].Vj ← Regs[rs]; RS[r].Qj ← 0};
			if (RegisterStat[rt].Qi≠0)
			   {RS[r].Qk ← RegisterStat[rt].Qi
			else {RS[r].Vk ← Regs[rt]; RS[r].Qk ← 0};
			RS[r].Busy ← yes; RegisterStat[rd].Qi=r;

	Load or Store	Buffer r empty	if (RegisterStat[rs].Qi≠0) {RS[r].Qj ← RegisterStat[rs].Qi} else {RS[r].Vj ← Regs[rs]; RS[r].Qj ← 0}; RS[r].A ← imm; RS[r].Busy ← yes;
	Load only		RegisterStat[rt].Qi=r;
	Store only		if (RegisterStat[rt].Qi≠0) {RS[r].Qk ← RegisterStat[rs].Qi} else {RS[r].Vk ← Regs[rt]; RS[r].Qk ← 0};
Execute	FP Operation	(RS[r].Qj = 0) and (RS[r].Qk = 0)	Compute result: operands are in Vj and Vk
	Load-Store step 1	RS[r].Qj = 0 & r is head of load-store queue	RS[r].A ← RS[r].Vj + RS[r].A;
	Load step 2	Load step 1 complete	Read from Mem[RS[r].A]
Write result	FP Operation or Load	Execution complete at r & CDB available	∀x(if (RegisterStat[x].Qi=r) {Regs[x] ← result; RegisterStat[x].Qi ← 0}); ∀x(if (RS[x].Qj=r) {RS[x].Vj ← result;RS[x].Qj ← 0}); ∀x(if (RS[x].Qk=r) {RS[x].Vk ← result;RS[x].Qk ← 0}); RS[r].Busy ← no;
	Store	Execution complete at r & RS[r].Qk = 0	Mem[RS[r].A] ← RS[r].Vk; RS[r].Busy ← no;

Figure 3.5 Steps in the algorithm and what is required for each step. For the issuing instruction, rd is the destination, rs and rt are the source register numbers, imm is the sign-extended immediate field, and r is the reservation station or buffer that the instruction is assigned to. RS is the reservation station data structure. The value returned by an FP unit or by the load unit is called result. RegisterStat is the register status data structure (not the register file, which is Regs[]). When an instruction is issued, the destination register has its Qi field set to the number of the buffer or reservation station to which the instruction is issued. If the operands are available in the registers, they are stored in the V fields. Otherwise, the Q fields are set to indicate the reservation station that will produce the values needed as source operands. The instruction waits at the reservation station until both its operands are available, indicated by zero in the Q fields. The Q fields are set to zero either when this instruction is issued, or when an instruction on which this instruction depends completes and does its write back. When an instruction has finished execution and the CDB is available, it can do its write back. All the buffers, registers, and reservation stations whose value of Qj or Qk is the same as the completing reservation station update their values from the CDB and mark the Q fields to indicate that values have been received. Thus, the CDB can broadcast its result to many destinations in a single clock cycle, and if the waiting instructions have their operands, they can all begin execution on the next clock cycle. Loads go through two steps in Execute, and stores perform slightly differently during Write Result, where they may have to wait for the value to store. Remember that to preserve exception behavior, instructions should not be allowed to execute if a branch that is earlier in program order has not yet completed. Because any concept of program order is not maintained after the Issue stage, this restriction is usually implemented by preventing any instruction from leaving the Issue step, if there is a pending branch already in the pipeline. In Section 3.7, we will see how speculation support removes this restriction.

If we predict that branches are taken, using reservation stations will allow multiple executions of this loop to proceed at once. This advantage is gained without changing the code—in effect, the loop is unrolled dynamically by the hardware, using the reservation stations obtained by renaming to act as additional registers.

Let's assume we have issued all the instructions in two successive iterations of the loop, but none of the floating-point load-stores or operations has completed. The reservation stations, register status tables, and load and store buffers at this point are shown in Figure 3.6. (The integer ALU operation is ignored, and it is assumed the branch was predicted as taken.) Once the system reaches this state, two copies of the loop could be sustained with a CPI close to 1.0, provided

Instruction status				
Instruction	**From iteration**	**Issue**	**Execute**	**Write Result**
L.D F0,0(R1)	1	√	√	
MUL.D F4,F0,F2	1	√		
S.D F4,0(R1)	1	√		
L.D F0,0(R1)	2	√	√	
MUL.D F4,F0,F2	2	√		
S.D F4,0(R1)	2	√		

Reservation stations							
Name	**Busy**	**Op**	**Vj**	**Vk**	**Qj**	**Qk**	**A**
Load1	yes	Load					Regs[R1] + 0
Load2	yes	Load					Regs[R1] − 8
Add1	no						
Add2	no						
Add3	no						
Mult1	yes	MUL		Regs[F2]	Load1		
Mult2	yes	MUL		Regs[F2]	Load2		
Store1	yes	Store	Regs[R1]			Mult1	
Store2	yes	Store	Regs[R1] − 8			Mult2	

Register status									
Field	**F0**	**F2**	**F4**	**F6**	**F8**	**F10**	**F12**	**...**	**F30**
Qi	Load2		Mult2						

Figure 3.6 Two active iterations of the loop with no instruction yet completed. Entries in the multiplier reservation stations indicate that the outstanding loads are the sources. The store reservation stations indicate that the multiply destination is the source of the value to store.

the multiplies could complete in four clock cycles. As we will see later in this chapter, when extended with multiple instruction issue, Tomasulo's approach can sustain more than one instruction per clock.

A load and a store can safely be done in a different order, provided they access different addresses. If a load and a store access the same address, then either

- the load is before the store in program order and interchanging them results in a WAR hazard, or

- the store is before the load in program order and interchanging them results in a RAW hazard.

Similarly, interchanging two stores to the same address results in a WAW hazard.

Hence, to determine if a load can be executed at a given time, the processor can check whether any uncompleted store that precedes the load in program order shares the same data memory address as the load. Similarly, a store must wait until there are no unexecuted loads or stores that are earlier in program order and share the same data memory address.

To detect such hazards, the processor must have computed the data memory address associated with any earlier memory operation. A simple, but not necessarily optimal, way to guarantee that the processor has all such addresses is to perform the effective address calculations in program order. (We really only need keep the relative order between stores and other memory references; that is, loads can be reordered freely.)

Let's consider the situation of a load first. If we perform effective address calculation in program order, then when a load has completed effective address calculation, we can check whether there is an address conflict by examining the A field of all active store buffers. If the load address matches the address of any active entries in the store buffer, the load instruction is not sent to the load buffer until the conflicting store completes. (Some implementations bypass the value directly to the load from a pending store, reducing the delay for this RAW hazard.)

Stores operate similarly, except that the processor must check for conflicts in both the load buffers and the store buffers, since conflicting stores cannot be reordered with respect to either a load or a store. This dynamic disambiguation of addresses is an alternative to the techniques, discussed in the next chapter, that a compiler would use when interchanging a load and store.

A dynamically scheduled pipeline can yield very high performance, provided branches are predicted accurately—an issue we address in the next section. The major drawback of this approach is the complexity of the Tomasulo scheme, which requires a large amount of hardware. In particular, each reservation station must contain an associative buffer, which must run at high speed, as well as complex control logic. Lastly, the performance can be limited by the single CDB. Although additional CDBs can be added, each CDB must interact with each reservation station, and the associative tag-matching hardware would need to be duplicated at each station for each CDB.

In Tomasulo's scheme two different techniques are combined: the renaming of the architectural registers to a larger set of registers and the buffering of source operands from the register file. Source operand buffering resolves WAR hazards that arise when the operand is available in the registers. As we will see later, it is also possible to eliminate WAR hazards by the renaming of a register together with the buffering of a result until no outstanding references to the earlier version of the register remain. This approach will be used when we discuss hardware speculation.

Tomasulo's scheme is particularly appealing if the designer is forced to pipeline an architecture for which it is difficult to schedule code, that has a shortage of registers, or for which the designer wishes to obtain high performance without pipeline-specific compilation. On the other hand, the advantages of the Tomasulo approach versus compiler scheduling for an efficient single-issue pipeline are probably fewer than the costs of implementation. But, as processors become more aggressive in their issue capability and designers are concerned with the performance of difficult-to-schedule code (such as most nonnumeric code), techniques such as register renaming and dynamic scheduling become more important. Furthermore, the role of dynamic scheduling as a basis for hardware speculation has made this approach very popular in the past five years.

The key components for enhancing ILP in Tomasulo's algorithm are dynamic scheduling, register renaming, and dynamic memory disambiguation. It is difficult to assess the value of these features independently. When we examine the studies of ILP in Section 3.8, we will look at how these features affect the amount of parallelism discovered under ideal circumstances.

Corresponding to the dynamic hardware techniques for scheduling around data dependences are dynamic techniques for handling branches efficiently. These techniques are used for two purposes: to predict whether a branch will be taken and to find the target more quickly. *Hardware branch prediction,* the name for these techniques, is the next topic we discuss.

3.4 Reducing Branch Costs with Dynamic Hardware Prediction

The previous section described techniques for overcoming data hazards. The frequency of branches and jumps demands that we also attack the potential stalls arising from control dependences. Indeed, as the amount of ILP we attempt to exploit grows, control dependences rapidly become the limiting factor. Although schemes in this section are helpful in processors that try to maintain one instruction issue per clock, they are *crucial* to any processor that tries to issue more than one instruction per clock for two reasons. First, branches will arrive up to *n* times faster in an *n*-issue processor, and providing an instruction stream to the processor will probably require that we predict the outcome of branches. Second, Amdahl's Law reminds us that relative impact of the control stalls will be larger with the lower potential CPI in such machines.

In Appendix A, we will examine a variety of basic schemes (e.g., predict not taken and delayed branch) for dealing with branches. Those schemes are all static: The action taken does not depend on the dynamic behavior of the branch. This section focuses on using hardware to dynamically predict the outcome of a branch—the prediction will depend on the behavior of the branch at run time and will change if the branch changes its behavior during execution.

We start with a simple branch prediction scheme and then examine approaches that increase the accuracy of our branch prediction mechanisms. After that, we look at more elaborate schemes that try to find the instruction following a branch even earlier. The goal of all these mechanisms is to allow the processor to resolve the outcome of a branch early, thus preventing control dependences from causing stalls. The effectiveness of a branch prediction scheme depends not only on the accuracy, but also on the cost of a branch when the prediction is correct and when the prediction is incorrect. These branch penalties depend on the structure of the pipeline, the type of predictor, and the strategies used for recovering from misprediction.

Basic Branch Prediction and Branch-Prediction Buffers

The simplest dynamic branch-prediction scheme is a *branch-prediction buffer* or *branch history table*. A branch-prediction buffer is a small memory indexed by the lower portion of the address of the branch instruction. The memory contains a bit that says whether the branch was recently taken or not. This scheme is the simplest sort of buffer; it has no tags and is useful only to reduce the branch delay when it is longer than the time to compute the possible target PCs. We don't know, in fact, if the prediction is correct—it may have been put there by another branch that has the same low-order address bits. But this doesn't matter. The prediction is a hint that is assumed to be correct, and fetching begins in the predicted direction. If the hint turns out to be wrong, the prediction bit is inverted and stored back. Of course, this buffer is effectively a cache where every access is a hit, and, as we will see, the performance of the buffer depends on both how often the prediction is for the branch of interest and how accurate the prediction is when it matches. Before we analyze the performance, it is useful to make a small, but important, improvement in the accuracy of the branch-prediction scheme.

This simple 1-bit prediction scheme has a performance shortcoming: Even if a branch is almost always taken, we will likely predict incorrectly twice, rather than once, when it is not taken. The following example shows this.

Example   Consider a loop branch whose behavior is taken nine times in a row, then not taken once. What is the prediction accuracy for this branch, assuming the prediction bit for this branch remains in the prediction buffer?

Answer   The steady-state prediction behavior will mispredict on the first and last loop iterations. Mispredicting the last iteration is inevitable since the prediction bit will say taken (the branch has been taken nine times in a row at that point). The misprediction on the first iteration happens because the bit is flipped on prior execution of the last iteration of the loop, since the branch was not taken on that iteration. Thus, the prediction accuracy for this branch that is taken 90% of the time is only 80% (two incorrect predictions and eight correct ones). In general, for branches used to form loops—a branch is taken many times in a row and then not taken once—a 1-bit predictor will mispredict at twice the rate that the branch is not taken. It seems that we should expect that the accuracy of the predictor would at least match the taken branch frequency for these highly regular branches.

To remedy this, 2-bit prediction schemes are often used. In a 2-bit scheme, a prediction must miss twice before it is changed. Figure 3.7 shows the finite-state processor for a 2-bit prediction scheme.

The 2-bit scheme is actually a specialization of a more general scheme that has an n-bit saturating counter for each entry in the prediction buffer. With an n-bit counter, the counter can take on values between 0 and $2^n - 1$: When the counter is greater than or equal to one-half of its maximum value (2^{n-1}), the branch is predicted as taken; otherwise, it is predicted untaken. As in the 2-bit scheme, the counter is incremented on a taken branch and decremented on an

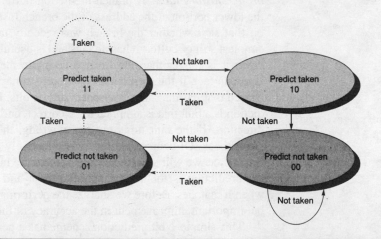

Figure 3.7 The states in a 2-bit prediction scheme. By using 2 bits rather than 1, a branch that strongly favors taken or not taken—as many branches do—will be mispredicted less often than with a 1-bit predictor. The 2 bits are used to encode the four states in the system. In a counter implementation, the counters are incremented when a branch is taken and decremented when it is not taken; the counters saturate at 00 or 11. One complication of the 2-bit scheme is that it updates the prediction bits more often than a 1-bit predictor, which only updates the prediction bit on a mispredict. Since we typically read the prediction bits on every cycle, a 2-bit predictor will typically need both a read and a write access port.

untaken branch. Studies of n-bit predictors have shown that the 2-bit predictors do almost as well, and thus most systems rely on 2-bit branch predictors rather than the more general n-bit predictors.

A branch-prediction buffer can be implemented as a small, special "cache" accessed with the instruction address during the IF pipe stage, or as a pair of bits attached to each block in the instruction cache and fetched with the instruction. If the instruction is decoded as a branch and if the branch is predicted as taken, fetching begins from the target as soon as the PC is known. Otherwise, sequential fetching and executing continue. If the prediction turns out to be wrong, the prediction bits are changed as shown in Figure 3.7.

Although this scheme is useful for most pipelines, the five-stage, classic pipeline finds out both whether the branch is taken and what the target of the branch is at roughly the same time, *assuming* no hazard in accessing the register specified in the conditional branch. (Remember that this is true for the five-stage pipeline because the branch does a compare of a register against zero during the ID stage, which is when the effective address is also computed.) Thus, this scheme does not help for the five-stage pipeline; we will explore a scheme that can work for such pipelines, and for machines issuing multiple instructions per clock, a little later. First, let's see how well branch prediction works in general.

What kind of accuracy can be expected from a branch-prediction buffer using 2 bits per entry on real applications? For the SPEC89 benchmarks a branch-prediction buffer with 4096 entries results in a prediction accuracy ranging from over 99% to 82%, or a *misprediction rate* of 1% to 18%, as shown in Figure 3.8. To show the differences more clearly, we plot misprediction frequency rather than prediction frequency. A 4K entry buffer, like that used for these results, is considered large; smaller buffers would have worse results.

Knowing just the prediction accuracy, as shown in Figure 3.8, is not enough to determine the performance impact of branches, even given the branch costs and penalties for misprediction. We also need to take into account the branch frequency, since the importance of accurate prediction is larger in programs with higher branch frequency. For example, the integer programs—li, eqntott, espresso, and gcc—have higher branch frequencies than those of the more easily predicted FP programs.

As we try to exploit more ILP, the accuracy of our branch prediction becomes critical. As we can see in Figure 3.8, the accuracy of the predictors for integer programs, which typically also have higher branch frequencies, is lower than for the loop-intensive scientific programs. We can attack this problem in two ways: by increasing the size of the buffer and by increasing the accuracy of the scheme we use for each prediction. A buffer with 4K entries is already large and, as Figure 3.9 shows, performs quite comparably to an infinite buffer. The data in Figure 3.9 make it clear that the hit rate of the buffer is not the limiting factor. As we mentioned above, simply increasing the number of bits per predictor without changing the predictor structure also has little impact. Instead, we need to look at how we might increase the accuracy of each predictor.

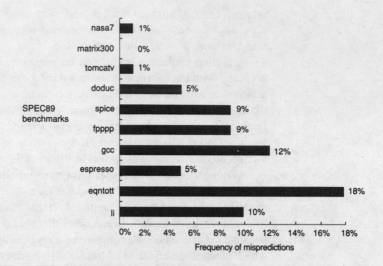

Figure 3.8 Prediction accuracy of a 4096-entry 2-bit prediction buffer for the SPEC89 benchmarks. The misprediction rate for the integer benchmarks (gcc, espresso, eqntott, and li) is substantially higher (average of 11%) than that for the FP programs (average of 4%). Even omitting the FP kernels (nasa7, matrix300, and tomcatv) still yields a higher accuracy for the FP benchmarks than for the integer benchmarks. These data, as well as the rest of the data in this section, are taken from a branch prediction study done using the IBM Power architecture and optimized code for that system. See Pan, So, and Rameh [1992].

Correlating Branch Predictors

These 2-bit predictor schemes use only the recent behavior of a single branch to predict the future behavior of that branch. It may be possible to improve the prediction accuracy if we also look at the recent behavior of *other* branches rather than just the branch we are trying to predict. Consider a small code fragment from the SPEC92 benchmark eqntott (the worst case for the 2-bit predictor):

```
if (aa==2)
        aa=0;
if (bb==2)
        bb=0;
if (aa!=bb) {
```

Here is the MIPS code that we would typically generate for this code fragment assuming that aa and bb are assigned to registers R1 and R2:

```
DSUBUI      R3,R1,#2
BNEZ        R3,L1       ;branch b1  (aa!=2)
DADD        R1,R0,R0    ;aa=0
```

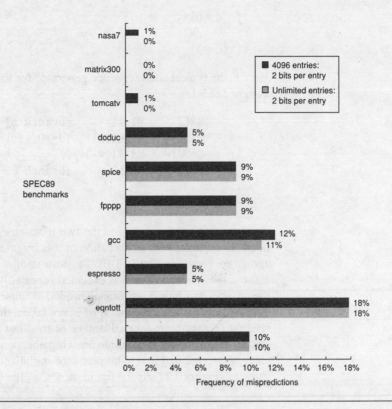

Figure 3.9 Prediction accuracy of a 4096-entry 2-bit prediction buffer versus an infinite buffer for the SPEC89 benchmarks.

```
L1:     DSUBUI      R3,R2,#2
        BNEZ        R3,L2       ;branch b2  (bb!=2)
        DADD        R2,R0,R0    ;bb=0
L2:     DSUBU       R3,R1,R2    ;R3=aa-bb
        BEQZ        R3,L3       ;branch b3  (aa==bb)
```

Let's label these branches b1, b2, and b3. The key observation is that the behavior of branch b3 is correlated with the behavior of branches b1 and b2. Clearly, if branches b1 and b2 are both not taken (i.e., if the conditions both evaluate to true and aa and bb are both assigned 0), then b3 will be taken, since aa and bb are clearly equal. A predictor that uses only the behavior of a single branch to predict the outcome of that branch can never capture this behavior.

Branch predictors that use the behavior of other branches to make a prediction are called *correlating predictors* or *two-level predictors*. To see how such predictors work, let's choose a simple hypothetical case. Consider the following simplified code fragment (chosen for illustrative purposes):

```
if (d==0)
      d=1;
if (d==1)
```

Here is the typical code sequence generated for this fragment, assuming that d is assigned to R1:

```
        BNEZ    R1,L1       ;branch b1     (d!=0)
        DADDIU  R1,R0,#1    ;d==0, so d=1
L1:     DADDIU  R3,R1,#-1
        BNEZ    R3,L2       ;branch b2     (d!=1)
...
L2:
```

The branches corresponding to the two if statements are labeled b1 and b2. The possible sequences for an execution of this fragment, assuming d has values 0, 1, and 2, are shown in Figure 3.10. To illustrate how a correlating predictor works, assume the sequence above is executed repeatedly and ignore other branches in the program (including any branch needed to cause the above sequence to repeat). From Figure 3.10, we see that if b1 is not taken, then b2 will be not taken. A correlating predictor can take advantage of this, but our standard predictor cannot. Rather than consider all possible branch paths, consider a sequence where d alternates between 2 and 0. A 1-bit predictor initialized to not taken has the behavior shown in Figure 3.11. As the figure shows, *all* the branches are mispredicted!

Initial value of d	d == 0?	b1	Value of d before b2	d == 1?	b2
0	yes	not taken	1	yes	not taken
1	no	taken	1	yes	not taken
2	no	taken	2	no	taken

Figure 3.10 Possible execution sequences for a code fragment.

d = ?	b1 prediction	b1 action	New b1 prediction	b2 prediction	b2 action	New b2 prediction
2	NT	T	T	NT	T	T
0	T	NT	NT	T	NT	NT
2	NT	T	T	NT	T	T
0	T	NT	NT	T	NT	NT

Figure 3.11 Behavior of a 1-bit predictor initialized to not taken. T stands for taken, NT for not taken.

Alternatively, consider a predictor that uses 1 bit of correlation. The easiest way to think of this is that every branch has two separate prediction bits: one prediction assuming the last branch executed was not taken and another prediction that is used if the last branch executed was taken. Note that, in general, the last branch executed is *not* the same instruction as the branch being predicted, although this can occur in simple loops consisting of a single basic block (since there are no other branches in the loops).

We write the pair of prediction bits together, with the first bit being the prediction if the last branch in the program is not taken and the second bit being the prediction if the last branch in the program is taken. The four possible combinations and the meanings are listed in Figure 3.12.

The action of the 1-bit predictor with 1 bit of correlation, when initialized to NT/NT, is shown in Figure 3.13.

In this case, the only misprediction is on the first iteration, when d = 2. The correct prediction of b1 is because of the choice of values for d, since b1 is not obviously correlated with the previous prediction of b2. The correct prediction of b2, however, shows the advantage of correlating predictors. Even if we had chosen different values for d, the predictor for b2 would correctly predict the case when b1 is not taken on every execution of b2 after one initial incorrect prediction.

The predictor in Figures 3.12 and 3.13 is called a (1,1) predictor since it uses the behavior of the last branch to choose from among a pair of 1-bit branch predictors. In the general case an (*m,n*) predictor uses the behavior of the last *m*

Prediction bits	Prediction if last branch not taken	Prediction if last branch taken
NT/NT	NT	NT
NT/T	NT	T
T/NT	T	NT
T/T	T	T

Figure 3.12 Combinations and meaning of the taken/not taken prediction bits. T stands for taken, NT for not taken.

d = ?	b1 prediction	b1 action	New b1 prediction	b2 prediction	b2 action	New b2 prediction
2	**NT/NT**	T	T/NT	**NT/NT**	T	NT/T
0	**T**/NT	NT	T/NT	NT/**T**	NT	NT/T
2	**T**/NT	T	T/NT	NT/**T**	T	NT/T
0	**T**/NT	NT	T/NT	NT/**T**	NT	NT/T

Figure 3.13 The action of the 1-bit predictor with 1 bit of correlation, initialized to not taken/not taken. T stands for taken, NT for not taken. The prediction used is shown in bold.

branches to choose from 2^m branch predictors, each of which is an n-bit predictor for a single branch. The attraction of this type of correlating branch predictor is that it can yield higher prediction rates than the 2-bit scheme and requires only a trivial amount of additional hardware. The simplicity of the hardware comes from a simple observation: The global history of the most recent m branches can be recorded in an m-bit shift register, where each bit records whether the branch was taken or not taken. The branch-prediction buffer can then be indexed using a concatenation of the low-order bits from the branch address with the m-bit global history. For example, Figure 3.14 shows a (2,2) predictor and how the prediction is accessed.

There is one subtle effect in this implementation. Because the prediction buffer is not a cache, the counters indexed by a single value of the global predictor may in fact correspond to different branches at some point in time. This insight is no different from our earlier observation that the prediction may not correspond to the current branch. In Figure 3.14 we draw the buffer as a two-dimensional object to ease understanding. In reality, the buffer can simply be implemented as a linear memory array that is 2 bits wide; the indexing is done by concatenating the global history bits and the number of required bits from the branch address. For the example in Figure 3.14, a (2,2) buffer with 64 total entries, the 4 low-order address bits of the branch (word address) and the 2 global bits form a 6-bit index that can be used to index the 64 counters.

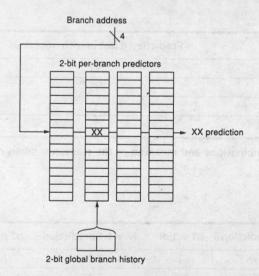

Figure 3.14 A (2,2) branch-prediction buffer uses a 2-bit global history to choose from among four predictors for each branch address. Each predictor is in turn a 2-bit predictor for that particular branch. The branch-prediction buffer shown here has a total of 64 entries; the branch address is used to choose four of these entries, and the global history is used to choose one of the four. The 2-bit global history can be implemented as a shifter register that simply shifts in the behavior of a branch as soon as it is known.

How much better do the correlating branch predictors work when compared with the standard 2-bit scheme? To compare them fairly, we must compare predictors that use the same number of state bits. The number of bits in an (m,n) predictor is

$$2^m \times n \times \text{Number of prediction entries selected by the branch address}$$

A 2-bit predictor with no global history is simply a (0,2) predictor.

Example   How many bits are in the (0,2) branch predictor we examined earlier? How many bits are in the branch predictor shown in Figure 3.14?

Answer   The earlier predictor had 4K entries selected by the branch address. Thus the total number of bits is

$$2^0 \times 2 \times 4K = 8K$$

The predictor in Figure 3.14 has

$$2^2 \times 2 \times 16 = 128 \text{ bits}$$

To compare the performance of a correlating predictor with that of our simple 2-bit predictor examined in Figure 3.8, we need to determine how many entries we should assume for the correlating predictor.

Example   How many branch-selected entries are in a (2,2) predictor that has a total of 8K bits in the prediction buffer?

Answer   We know that

$$2^2 \times 2 \times \text{Number of prediction entries selected by the branch} = 8K$$

Hence

$$\text{Number of prediction entries selected by the branch} = 1K$$

Figure 3.15 compares the performance of the earlier 2-bit simple predictor with 4K entries and a (2,2) predictor with 1K entries. As you can see, this predictor not only outperforms a simple 2-bit predictor with the same total number of state bits, it often outperforms a 2-bit predictor with an unlimited number of entries.

-    There is a wide spectrum of correlating predictors, with the (0,2) and (2,2) predictors being among the most interesting. The exercises ask you to explore the performance of a third extreme: a predictor that does not rely on the branch address. For example, a (12,2) predictor that has a total of 8K bits does not use

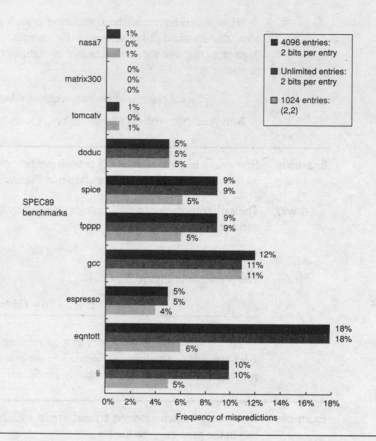

Figure 3.15 Comparison of 2-bit predictors. A noncorrelating predictor for 4096 bits is first, followed by a noncorrelating 2-bit predictor with unlimited entries and a 2-bit predictor with 2 bits of global history and a total of 1024 entries.

the branch address in indexing the predictor, but instead relies solely on the global branch history. Surprisingly, this degenerate case can outperform a noncorrelating 2-bit predictor if enough global history is used and the table is large enough!

Tournament Predictors: Adaptively Combining Local and Global Predictors

The primary motivation for correlating branch predictors came from the observation that the standard 2-bit predictor using only local information failed on some important branches and that, by adding global information, the performance could be improved. Tournament predictors take this insight to the next level, by using multiple predictors, usually one based on global information and one based on local information, and combining them with a selector. Tournament predictors can achieve both better accuracy at medium sizes (8K bits–32K bits) and also make use of very large numbers of prediction bits effectively.

Tournament predictors are the most popular form of *multilevel branch predictors*. A multilevel branch predictor use several levels of branch-prediction tables together with an algorithm for choosing among the multiple predictors; we will see several variations on multilevel predictors in this section. Existing tournament predictors use a 2-bit saturating counter per branch to choose among two different predictors. The four states of the counter dictate whether to use predictor 1 or predictor 2. The state transition diagram is shown in Figure 3.16.

The advantage of a tournament predictor is its ability to select the right predictor for the right branch. Figure 3.17 shows how the tournament predictor selects between a local and global predictor depending on the benchmark, as well as on the branch. The ability to choose between a prediction based on strictly local information and one incorporating global information on a per-branch basis is particularly critical in the integer benchmarks.

Figure 3.18 looks at the performance of three different predictors (a local 2-bit predictor, a correlating predictor, and a tournament predictor) for different numbers of bits using SPEC89 as the benchmark. As we saw earlier, the prediction capability of the local predictor does not improve beyond a certain size. The correlating predictor shows a significant improvement, and the tournament predictor generates slightly better performance.

An Example: The Alpha 21264 Branch Predictor

The 21264 uses the most sophisticated branch predictor in any processor as of 2001. The 21264 has a tournament predictor using 4K 2-bit counters indexed by

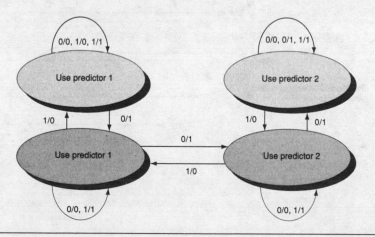

Figure 3.16   The state transition diagram for a tournament predictor has four states corresponding to which predictor to use. The counter is incremented whenever the "predicted" predictor is correct and the other predictor is incorrect, and it is decremented in the reverse situation.

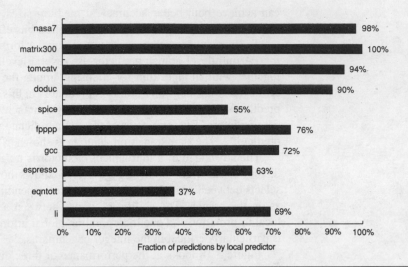

Figure 3.17 **The fraction of predictions coming from the local predictor for a tournament predictor using the SPEC89 benchmarks.** The tournament predictor selects between a local 2-bit predictor and a 2-bit local/global predictor, called gshare. Gshare is indexed by an exclusive or of the branch address bits and the global history; it performs similarly to the correlating predictor discussed earlier. In this case each predictor has 1024 entries, each 2 bits, for a total of 6K bits.

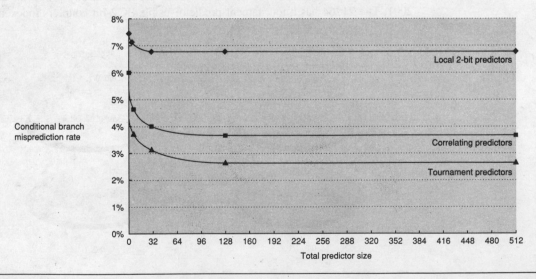

Figure 3.18 **The misprediction rate for three different predictors on SPEC89 as the total number of bits is increased.** The predictors are a local 2-bit predictor, a correlating predictor, which is optimally structured at each point in the graph, and a tournament predictor using the same structure as in Figure 3.17.

the local branch address to choose from among a global predictor and a local predictor. The global predictor also has 4K entries and is indexed by the history of the last 12 branches; each entry in the global predictor is a standard 2-bit predictor.

The local predictor consists of a two-level predictor. The top level is a local history table consisting of 1024 10-bit entries; each 10-bit entry corresponds to the most recent 10 branch outcomes for the entry. That is, if the branch was taken 10 or more times in a row, the entry in the local history table will be all 1s. If the branch is alternately taken and untaken, the history entry consists of alternating 0s and 1s. This 10-bit history allows patterns of up to 10 branches to be discovered and predicted. The selected entry from the local history table is used to index a table of 1K entries consisting of 3-bit saturating counters, which provide the local prediction. This combination, which uses a total of 29K bits, leads to high accuracy in branch prediction. For the SPECfp95 benchmarks there is less than 1 misprediction per 1000 completed instructions, and for SPECint95, there are about 11.5 mispredictions per 1000 completed instructions.

<table>
<tr><td>3.5</td><td></td></tr>
</table>

3.5   High-Performance Instruction Delivery

In a high-performance pipeline, especially one with multiple issue, predicting branches well is not enough; we actually have to be able to deliver a high-bandwidth instruction stream. In recent multiple-issue processors, this has meant delivering 4–8 instructions every clock cycle. To accomplish this, we consider three concepts in this section: a branch-target buffer, an integrated instruction fetch unit, and dealing with indirect branches by predicting return addresses.

Branch-Target Buffers

To reduce the branch penalty for our five-stage pipeline, we need to know from what address to fetch by the end of IF. This requirement means we must know whether the as-yet-undecoded instruction is a branch and, if so, what the next PC should be. If the instruction is a branch and we know what the next PC should be, we can have a branch penalty of zero. A branch-prediction cache that stores the predicted address for the next instruction after a branch is called a *branch-target buffer* or *branch-target cache*.

For the classic, five-stage pipeline, a branch-*prediction* buffer is accessed during the ID cycle, so that at the end of ID we know the branch-target address (since it is computed during ID), the fall-through address (computed during IF), and the prediction. Thus, by the end of ID we know enough to fetch the next predicted instruction. For a branch-*target* buffer, we access the buffer during the IF stage using the instruction address of the fetched instruction, a possible branch, to index the buffer. If we get a hit, then we know the predicted instruction address at the end of the IF cycle, which is one cycle earlier than for a branch-prediction buffer.

Because we are predicting the next instruction address and will send it out *before* decoding the instruction, we *must* know whether the fetched instruction is predicted as a taken branch. Figure 3.19 shows what the branch-target buffer looks like. If the PC of the fetched instruction matches a PC in the buffer, then the corresponding predicted PC is used as the next PC. In Chapter 5 we will discuss caches in much more detail; we will see that the hardware for this branch-target buffer is essentially identical to the hardware for a cache.

If a matching entry is found in the branch-target buffer, fetching begins immediately at the predicted PC. Note that (unlike a branch-prediction buffer) the entry must be for this instruction because the predicted PC will be sent out before it is known whether this instruction is even a branch. If we did not check whether the entry matched this PC, then the wrong PC would be sent out for instructions that were not branches, resulting in a slower processor. We only need to store the predicted-taken branches in the branch-target buffer, since an untaken branch follows the same strategy (fetch the next sequential instruction) as a nonbranch. Complications arise when we are using a 2-bit predictor, since this requires that we store information for both taken and untaken branches. One way to resolve this is to use both a target buffer and a prediction buffer, which is the solution used by several PowerPC processors. We assume that the buffer only holds PC-

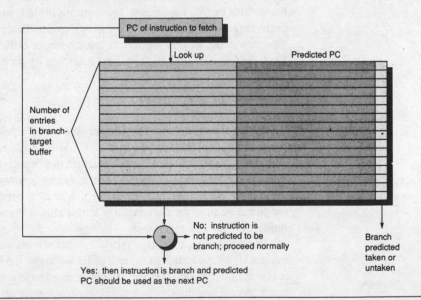

Figure 3.19 A branch-target buffer. The PC of the instruction being fetched is matched against a set of instruction addresses stored in the first column; these represent the addresses of known branches. If the PC matches one of these entries, then the instruction being fetched is a taken branch, and the second field, predicted PC, contains the prediction for the next PC after the branch. Fetching begins immediately at that address. The third field, which is optional, may be used for extra prediction state bits.

relative conditional branches, since this makes the target address a constant; it is not hard to extend the mechanism to work with indirect branches.

Figure 3.20 shows the steps followed when using a branch-target buffer and where these steps occur in the pipeline. From this we can see that there will be no branch delay if a branch-prediction entry is found in the buffer and is correct. Otherwise, there will be a penalty of at least two clock cycles. In practice, this penalty could be larger, since the branch-target buffer must be updated. We could assume that the instruction following a branch or at the branch target is not a branch, and do the update during that instruction time; however, this does complicate the control. Instead, we will take a two-clock-cycle penalty when the branch is not correctly predicted or when we get a miss in the buffer. Dealing with the mispredictions and misses is a significant challenge, since we typically will have to halt instruction fetch while we rewrite the buffer entry. Thus, we would like to make this process fast to minimize the penalty.

To evaluate how well a branch-target buffer works, we first must determine the penalties in all possible cases. Figure 3.21 contains this information.

Example   Determine the total branch penalty for a branch-target buffer assuming the penalty cycles for individual mispredictions from Figure 3.21. Make the following assumptions about the prediction accuracy and hit rate:

- Prediction accuracy is 90% (for instructions in the buffer).

- Hit rate in the buffer is 90% (for branches predicted taken).

Assume that 60% of the branches are taken.

Answer   We compute the penalty by looking at the probability of two events: the branch is predicted taken but ends up being not taken, and the branch is taken but is not found in the buffer. Both carry a penalty of two cycles.

Probability (branch in buffer, but actually not taken) = Percent buffer hit rate × Percent incorrect predictions
$$= 90\% \times 10\% = 0.09$$
Probability (branch not in buffer, but actually taken) = 10%
$$\text{Branch penalty} = (0.09 + 0.10) \times 2$$
$$\text{Branch penalty} = 0.38$$

This penalty compares with a branch penalty for delayed branches, which we evaluated in Chapter 1, of about 0.5 clock cycles per branch. Remember, though, that the improvement from dynamic branch prediction will grow as the branch delay grows; in addition, better predictors will yield a larger performance advantage.

One variation on the branch-target buffer is to store one or more *target instructions* instead of, or in addition to, the predicted *target address*. This variation has two potential advantages. First, it allows the branch-target buffer access to take longer than the time between successive instruction fetches, possibly

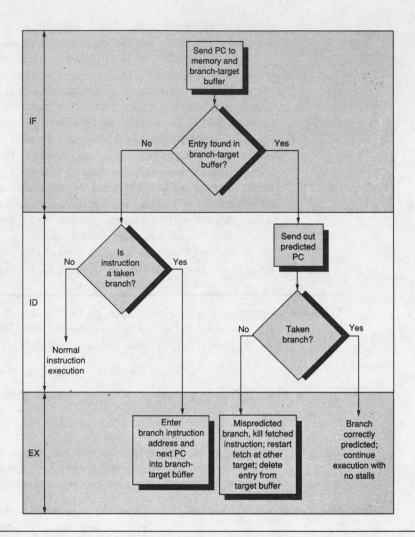

Figure 3.20 The steps involved in handling an instruction with a branch-target buffer. If the PC of an instruction is found in the buffer, then the instruction must be a branch that is predicted taken; thus, fetching immediately begins from the predicted PC in ID. If the entry is not found and it subsequently turns out to be a taken branch, it is entered in the buffer along with the target, which is known at the end of ID. If the entry is found, but the instruction turns out not to be a taken branch, it is removed from the buffer. If the instruction is a branch, is found, and is correctly predicted, then execution proceeds with no delays. If the prediction is incorrect, we suffer a one-clock-cycle delay fetching the wrong instruction and restart the fetch one clock cycle later, leading to a total mispredict penalty of two clock cycles. If the branch is not found in the buffer and the instruction turns out to be a branch, we will have proceeded as if the instruction were not a branch and can turn this into an assume-not-taken strategy. The penalty will differ depending on whether the branch is actually taken or not.

Instruction in buffer	Prediction	Actual branch	Penalty cycles
yes	taken	taken	0
yes	taken	not taken	2
no		taken	2
no		not taken	0

Figure 3.21 Penalties for all possible combinations of whether the branch is in the buffer and what it actually does, assuming we store only taken branches in the buffer. There is no branch penalty if everything is correctly predicted and the branch is found in the target buffer. If the branch is not correctly predicted, the penalty is equal to one clock cycle to update the buffer with the correct information (during which an instruction cannot be fetched) and one clock cycle, if needed, to restart fetching the next correct instruction for the branch. If the branch is not found and taken, a two-cycle penalty is encountered, during which time the buffer is updated.

allowing a larger branch-target buffer. Second, buffering the actual target instructions allows us to perform an optimization called *branch folding*. Branch folding can be used to obtain zero-cycle unconditional branches, and sometimes zero-cycle conditional branches. Consider a branch-target buffer that buffers instructions from the predicted path and is being accessed with the address of an unconditional branch. The only function of the unconditional branch is to change the PC. Thus, when the branch-target buffer signals a hit and indicates that the branch is unconditional, the pipeline can simply substitute the instruction from the branch-target buffer in place of the instruction that is returned from the cache (which is the unconditional branch). If the processor is issuing multiple instructions per cycle, then the buffer will need to supply multiple instructions to obtain the maximum benefit. In some cases, it may be possible to eliminate the cost of a conditional branch when the condition codes are preset.

Integrated Instruction Fetch Units

To meet the demands of multiple-issue processors many recent designers have chosen to implement an integrated instruction fetch unit, as a separate autonomous unit that feeds instructions to the rest of the pipeline. Essentially, this amounts to recognizing that characterizing instruction fetch as a simple single pipe stage given the complexities of multiple issue is no longer valid.

Instead, recent designs have used an integrated instruction fetch unit that integrates several functions:

1. *Integrated branch prediction*—The branch predictor becomes part of the instruction fetch unit and is constantly predicting branches, so as to drive the fetch pipeline.

2. *Instruction prefetch*—To deliver multiple instructions per clock, the instruction fetch unit will likely need to fetch ahead. The unit autonomously

manages the prefetching of instructions (see Chapter 5 for a discussion of techniques for doing this), integrating it with branch prediction.

3. *Instruction memory access and buffering*—When fetching multiple instructions per cycle a variety of complexities are encountered, including the difficulty that fetching multiple instructions may require accessing multiple cache lines. The instruction fetch unit encapsulates this complexity, using prefetch to try to hide the cost of crossing cache blocks. The instruction fetch unit also provides buffering, essentially acting as an on-demand unit to provide instructions to the issue stage as needed and in the quantity needed.

As designers try to increase the number of instructions executed per clock, instruction fetch will become an ever more significant bottleneck, and clever new ideas will be needed to deliver instructions at the necessary rate. One of the emerging ideas, called *trace caches,* is discussed in Chapter 5.

Return Address Predictors

Another method that designers have studied and included in many recent processors is a technique for predicting indirect jumps, that is, jumps whose destination address varies at run time. Although high-level language programs will generate such jumps for indirect procedure calls, select or case statements, and FORTRAN-computed gotos, the vast majority of the indirect jumps come from procedure returns. For example, for the SPEC89 benchmarks procedure returns account for 85% of the indirect jumps on average. For languages like C++ and Java, procedure returns are even more frequent. Thus, focusing on procedure returns seems appropriate.

Though procedure returns can be predicted with a branch-target buffer, the accuracy of such a prediction technique can be low if the procedure is called from multiple sites and the calls from one site are not clustered in time. To overcome this problem, the concept of a small buffer of return addresses operating as a stack has been proposed. This structure caches the most recent return addresses: pushing a return address on the stack at a call and popping one off at a return. If the cache is sufficiently large (i.e., as large as the maximum call depth), it will predict the returns perfectly. Figure 3.22 shows the performance of such a return buffer with 1–16 elements for a number of the SPEC benchmarks. We will use this type of return predictor when we examine the studies of ILP in Section 3.8.

Branch-prediction schemes are limited both by prediction accuracy and by the penalty for misprediction. As we have seen, typical prediction schemes achieve prediction accuracy in the range of 80% to 95%, depending on the type of program and the size of the buffer. In addition to trying to increase the accuracy of the predictor, we can try to reduce the penalty for misprediction. The penalty can be reduced by fetching from both the predicted and unpredicted direction. Fetching both paths requires that the memory system be dual-ported, have an interleaved cache, or fetch from one path and then the other. Although this adds cost to the system, it may be the only way to reduce branch penalties below a cer-

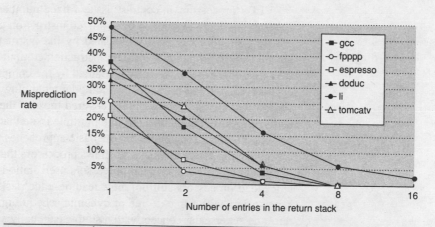

Figure 3.22   Prediction accuracy for a return address buffer operated as a stack. The accuracy is the fraction of return addresses predicted correctly. Since call depths are typically not large, with some exceptions, a modest buffer works well. On average returns account for 81% of the indirect jumps in these six benchmarks.

tain point. Caching addresses or instructions from multiple paths in the target buffer is another alternative that some processors have used.

We have seen a variety of software-based static schemes and hardware-based dynamic schemes for trying to boost the performance of our pipelined processor. These schemes attack both the data dependences (discussed in the previous subsections) and the control dependences (discussed in this subsection). Our focus to date has been on sustaining the throughput of the pipeline at one instruction per clock. In the next section we will look at techniques that attempt to exploit more parallelism by issuing multiple instructions in a clock cycle.

3.6   Taking Advantage of More ILP with Multiple Issue

The techniques of the previous two sections can be used to eliminate data and control stalls and achieve an ideal CPI of one. To improve performance further we would like to decrease the CPI to less than one. But the CPI cannot be reduced below one if we issue only one instruction every clock cycle.

The goal of the *multiple-issue processors*, discussed in this section, is to allow multiple instructions to issue in a clock cycle. Multiple-issue processors come in two basic flavors: *superscalar* processors and *VLIW* (very long instruction word) processors. Superscalar processors issue varying numbers of instructions per clock and are either statically scheduled (using compiler techniques covered in the next chapter) or dynamically scheduled (using techniques based on Tomasulo's algorithm). Statically scheduled processors use in-order execution, while dynamically scheduled processors use out-of-order execution.

VLIW processors, in contrast, issue a fixed number of instructions formatted either as one large instruction or as a fixed instruction packet with the parallelism among instructions explicitly indicated by the instruction (hence, they are also known as EPIC—explicitly parallel instruction computers). VLIW and EPIC processors are inherently statically scheduled by the compiler. The next chapter covers both VLIWs and the necessary compiler technology in detail, so between this chapter and the next, we will have covered most of the techniques for exploiting instruction-level parallelism through multiple issue that are in use in existing processors. Figure 3.23 summarizes the basic approaches to multiple issue and their distinguishing characteristics and shows processors that use each approach.

Although early superscalar processors used static instruction scheduling, and embedded processors still do, most leading-edge desktops and servers now use superscalars with some degree of dynamic scheduling. In this section, we introduce the superscalar concept with a simple, statically scheduled processor, which will require the techniques from the next chapter to achieve good efficiency. We then explore in detail a dynamically scheduled superscalar that builds on the Tomasulo scheme.

Statically Scheduled Superscalar Processors

In a typical superscalar processor, the hardware might issue from zero (since it may be stalled) to eight instructions in a clock cycle. In a statically scheduled superscalar, instructions issue in order and all pipeline hazards are checked for at issue time. The pipeline control logic must check for hazards among the instruc-

Common name	Issue structure	Hazard detection	Scheduling	Distinguishing characteristic	Examples
Superscalar (static)	dynamic	hardware	static	in-order execution	Sun UltraSPARC II/III
Superscalar (dynamic)	dynamic	hardware	dynamic	some out-of-order execution	IBM Power2
Superscalar (speculative)	dynamic	hardware	dynamic with speculation	out-of-order execution with speculation	Pentium III/4, MIPS R10K, Alpha 21264, HP PA 8500, IBM RS64III
VLIW/LIW	static	software	static	no hazards between issue packets	Trimedia, i860
EPIC	mostly static	mostly software	mostly static	explicit dependences marked by compiler	Itanium

Figure 3.23 The five primary approaches in use for multiple-issue processors and the primary characteristics that distinguish them. This chapter has focused on the hardware-intensive techniques, which are all some form of superscalar. The next chapter focuses on compiler-based approaches, which are either VLIW or EPIC. Figure 3.61, near the end of this chapter, provides more details on a variety of recent superscalar processors.

tions being issued in a given clock cycle, as well as among the issuing instructions and all those still in execution. If some instruction in the instruction stream is dependent (i.e., will cause a data hazard) or doesn't meet the issue criteria (i.e., will cause a structural hazard), only the instructions preceding that one in the instruction sequence will be issued. In contrast, in VLIWs, the compiler has complete responsibility for creating a package of instructions that can be simultaneously issued, and the hardware does not dynamically make any decisions about multiple issue. (As we will see, for example, the Intel IA-64 architecture relies on the programmer to describe the presence of register dependences within an issue packet.) Thus, we say that a superscalar processor has *dynamic* issue capability, and a VLIW processor has *static* issue capability.

Before we look at an example, let's explore the process of instruction issue in slightly more detail. Suppose we had a four-issue, static superscalar processor. During instruction fetch the pipeline would receive from one to four instructions from the instruction fetch unit, which may not always be able to deliver four instructions. We call this group of instructions received from the fetch unit that could *potentially* issue in one clock cycle the *issue packet*. Conceptually, the instruction fetch unit examines each instruction in the issue packet in program order. If an instruction would cause a structural hazard or a data hazard either due to an earlier instruction already in execution or due to an instruction earlier in the issue packet, then the instruction is not issued. This issue limitation results in zero to four instructions from the issue packet actually being issued in a given clock cycle. Although the instruction decode and issue process *logically* proceeds in sequential order through the instructions, in practice, the issue unit examines all the instructions in the issue packet at once, checks for hazards among the instructions in the packet and those in the pipeline, and decides which instructions can issue.

These issue checks are sufficiently complex that performing them in one cycle could mean that the issue logic determined the minimum clock cycle length. As a result, in many statically scheduled and *all* dynamically scheduled superscalars, the issue stage is split and pipelined, so that it can issue instructions every clock cycle.

This division is not, however, totally straightforward because the processor must also detect any hazards between the two packets of instructions while they are still in the issue pipeline. One approach is to use the first stage of the issue pipeline to decide how many instructions from the packet can issue simultaneously, ignoring instructions already issued, and use the second stage to examine hazards among the selected instructions and those that have already been issued. By splitting the issue pipe stage and pipelining it, the performance cost of superscalar instruction issue tends to be higher branch penalties, further increasing the importance of branch prediction.

As we increase the processor's issue rate, further pipelining of the issue stage could become necessary. Although breaking the issue stage into two stages is reasonably straightforward, it is less obvious how to pipeline it further. Thus, instruction issue is likely to be one limitation on the clock rate of superscalar processors.

A Statically Scheduled Superscalar MIPS Processor

What would the MIPS processor look like as a superscalar? For simplicity, let's assume two instructions can be issued per clock cycle and that one of the instructions can be a load, store, branch, or integer ALU operation, and the other can be any floating-point operation. Note that we consider loads and stores, including those to floating-point registers, as integer operations. As we will see, issue of an integer operation in parallel with a floating-point operation is much simpler and less demanding than arbitrary dual issue. This configuration is, in fact, very close to the organization used in the HP 7100 processor. Although high-end desktop processors now do four or more issues per clock, dual-issue superscalar pipelines are becoming common at the high end of the embedded processor market.

Issuing two instructions per cycle will require fetching and decoding 64 bits of instructions. Early superscalars often limited the placement of the instruction types; for example, the integer instruction must be first, but modern superscalars have dropped this restriction. Assuming the instruction placement is not limited, there are three steps involved in fetch and issue: fetch two instructions from the cache; determine whether zero, one, or two instructions can issue; and issue them to the correct functional unit.

Fetching two instructions is more complex than fetching one, since the instruction pair could appear anywhere in the cache block. Many processors will only fetch one instruction if the first instruction of the pair is the last word of a cache block. High-end superscalars generally rely on an independent instruction prefetch unit, as mentioned in the previous section and described further in Chapter 5.

For this simple superscalar, doing the hazard checking is relatively straightforward, since the restriction of one integer and one FP instruction eliminates most hazard possibilities within the issue packet, making it sufficient in many cases to look only at the opcodes of the instructions. The only difficulties that arise are when the integer instruction is a floating-point load, store, or move. This possibility creates contention for the floating-point register ports and may also create a new RAW hazard when the second instruction of the pair depends on the first (e.g., the first is an FP load and the second an FP operation, or the first is an FP operation and the second an FP store). This use of an issue restriction, which represents a structural hazard, to reduce the complexity of both hazard detection and pipeline structure is common in multiple-issue processors. (There is also the possibility of new WAR and WAW hazards across issue packet boundaries.)

Finally, the instructions chosen for execution are dispatched to their appropriate functional units. Figure 3.24 shows how the instructions look as they go into the pipeline in pairs; for simplicity the integer instruction is always shown first, although it may be the second instruction in the issue packet.

With this pipeline, we have substantially boosted the rate at which we can issue floating-point instructions. To make this worthwhile, however, we need either pipelined floating-point units or multiple independent units. Otherwise, the floating-point data path will quickly become the bottleneck, and the advantages gained by dual issue will be small.

Instruction type	Pipe stages							
Integer instruction	IF	ID	EX	MEM	WB			
FP instruction	IF	ID	EX	EX	EX	WB		
Integer instruction		IF	ID	EX	MEM	WB		
FP instruction		IF	ID	EX	EX	EX	WB	
Integer instruction			IF	ID	EX	MEM	WB	
FP instruction			IF	ID	EX	EX	EX	WB
Integer instruction				IF	ID	EX	MEM	WB
FP instruction				IF	ID	EX	EX	EX

Figure 3.24 Superscalar pipeline in operation. The integer and floating-point instructions are issued at the same time, and each executes at its own pace through the pipeline. This figure assumes that all the FP instructions are adds that take three execution cycles. This scheme will only improve the performance of programs with a large fraction of floating-point operations.

By issuing an integer and a floating-point operation in parallel, the need for additional hardware, beyond the enhanced hazard detection logic, is minimized—integer and floating-point operations use different register sets and different functional units on load-store architectures. Allowing FP loads and stores to issue with FP operations, a highly desirable capability for performance reasons, creates the need for an additional read/write port on the FP register file. In addition, because there are twice as many instructions in the pipeline, a larger set of bypass paths will be needed.

A final complication is maintaining a precise exception model. To see how imprecise exceptions can happen, consider the following:

- A floating-point instruction can finish execution after an integer instruction that is later in program order (e.g., when an FP instruction is the first instruction in an issue packet and both instructions are issued).

- The floating-point instruction exception could be detected after the integer instruction completed.

Left untouched, this situation would result in an imprecise exception because the integer instruction, which in program order follows the FP instruction that raised the exception, will have been completed. This situation represents a slight complication over those that can arise in a single-issue pipeline when the floating-point pipeline is deeper than the integer pipeline, but is no different than what we saw could arise with a dynamically scheduled pipeline. Several solutions are possible: early detection of FP exceptions (see Appendix A), the use of software mechanisms to restore a precise exception state before resuming execution, and delaying instruction completion until we know an exception is impossible (the speculation approach we cover in the next section uses this approach).

Maintaining the peak throughput for this dual-issue pipeline is much harder than it is for a single-issue pipeline. In our classic, five-stage pipeline, loads had a latency of one clock cycle, which prevented one instruction from using the result without stalling. In the superscalar pipeline, the result of a load instruction cannot be used on the *same* clock cycle or on the *next* clock cycle, and hence, the next three instructions cannot use the load result without stalling. The branch delay for a taken branch becomes either two or three instructions, depending on whether the branch is the first or second instruction of a pair.

To effectively exploit the parallelism available in a superscalar processor, more ambitious compiler or hardware scheduling techniques will be needed. In fact, without such techniques, a superscalar processor is likely to provide little or no additional performance.

In the next chapter, we will show how relatively simple compiler techniques suffice for a two-issue pipeline such as this one. Alternatively, we can employ an extension of Tomasulo's algorithm to schedule the pipeline, as the next section shows.

Multiple Instruction Issue with Dynamic Scheduling

Dynamic scheduling is one method for improving performance in a multiple instruction issue processor. When applied to a superscalar processor, dynamic scheduling has the traditional benefit of boosting performance in the face of data hazards, but it also allows the processor to potentially overcome the issue restrictions. Put another way, although the hardware may not be able to initiate execution of more than one integer and one FP operation in a clock cycle, dynamic scheduling can eliminate this restriction at instruction issue, at least until the hardware runs out of reservation stations.

Let's assume we want to extend Tomasulo's algorithm to support our two-issue superscalar pipeline. We do not want to issue instructions to the reservation stations out of order, since this could lead to a violation of the program semantics. To gain the full advantage of dynamic scheduling we should remove the constraint of issuing one integer and one FP instruction in a clock, but this will significantly complicate instruction issue.

Alternatively, we could use a simpler scheme: separate the data structures for the integer and floating-point registers, then simultaneously issue a floating-point instruction and an integer instruction to their respective reservation stations, as long as the two issued instructions do not access the same register set. Unfortunately, this approach bars issuing two instructions with a dependence in the same clock cycle, such as a floating-point load (an integer instruction) and a floating-point add. Rather than try to fix this problem, let's explore the general scheme for allowing the issue stage to handle two arbitrary instructions per clock.

Two different approaches have been used to issue multiple instructions per clock in a dynamically scheduled processor, and both rely on the observation that the key is assigning a reservation station and updating the pipeline control tables. One approach is to run this step in half a clock cycle, so that two instructions can be processed in one clock cycle. A second alternative is to build the logic necessary to handle two instructions at once, including any possible dependences between the instructions. Modern superscalar processors that issue four or more instructions per clock often include both approaches: They both pipeline and widen the issue logic.

There is one final issue to discuss before we look at an example: how should dynamic branch prediction be integrated into a dynamically scheduled pipeline. The IBM 360/91 used a simple static prediction scheme, but only allowed instructions to be fetched and issued (but not actually executed) until the branch had completed. In this section, we follow the same approach. In the next section, we will examine speculation, which takes this a step further and actually executes instructions based on branch predictions.

Assume that we have the most general implementation of a two-issue dynamically scheduled processor, meaning that it can issue any pair of instructions if there are reservation stations of the right type available. Because the interaction of the integer and floating-point instructions is crucial, we also extend Tomasulo's scheme to deal with both the integer and floating-point functional units and registers. Let's see how a simple loop executes on this processor.

Example Consider the execution of the following simple loop, which adds a scalar in F2 to each element of a vector in memory. Use a MIPS pipeline extended with Tomasulo's algorithm and with multiple issue:

```
Loop:   L.D       F0,0(R1)     ;F0=array element
        ADD.D     F4,F0,F2     ;add scalar in F2
        S.D       F4,0(R1)     ;store result
        DADDIU    R1,R1,#-8    ;decrement pointer
                               ;8 bytes (per DW)
        BNE       R1,R2,LOOP   ;branch R1!=R2
```

Assume that both a floating-point and an integer operation can be issued on every clock cycle, even if they are dependent. Assume one integer functional unit is used for both ALU operations and effective address calculations and a separate pipelined FP functional unit for each operation type. Assume that Issue and Write Results take one cycle each and that there is dynamic branch-prediction hardware and a separate functional unit to evaluate branch conditions. As in most dynamically scheduled processors, the presence of the Write Results stage means that the effective instruction latencies will be one cycle longer than in a simple in-order pipeline. Thus, the number of cycles of latency between a source instruction and an instruction consuming the result is one cycle for integer ALU operations, two cycles for loads, and three cycles for FP add. Create a table showing when each instruction issues, begins execution, and writes its result to the CDB for the first three iterations of the loop. Assume two CDBs and assume that branches single issue (no delayed branches) but that branch prediction is perfect. Also show the resource usage for the integer unit, the floating-point unit, the data cache, and the two CDBs.

Answer The loop will be dynamically unwound, and, whenever possible, instructions will be issued in pairs. The execution timing is shown in Figure 3.25. Figure 3.26 shows the resource utilization. The loop will continue to fetch and issue a new loop iteration every three clock cycles, and sustaining one iteration every three cycles would lead to an IPC of 5/3 = 1.67. The instruction execution rate, however, is lower: By looking at the Execute stage we can see that the sustained instruction completion rate is 15/16 = 0.94. Assuming the branches are perfectly predicted, the issue unit will eventually fill all the reservation stations and will stall.

The throughput improvement versus a single-issue pipeline is small because there is only one floating-point operation per iteration and, thus, the integer pipeline becomes a bottleneck. The performance could be enhanced by compiler techniques we will discuss in the next chapter. Alternatively, if the processor could

Iteration number	Instructions		Issues at	Executes	Memory access at	Write CDB at	Comment
1	L.D	F0,0(R1)	1	2	3	4	First issue
1	ADD.D	F4,F0,F2	1	5		8	Wait for L.D
1	S.D	F4,0(R1)	2	3	9		Wait for ADD.D
1	DADDIU	R1,R1,#-8	2	4		5	Wait for ALU
1	BNE	R1,R2,Loop	3	6			Wait for DADDIU
2	L.D	F0,0(R1)	4	7	8	9	Wait for BNE complete
2	ADD.D	F4,F0,F2	4	10		13	Wait for L.D
2	S.D	F4,0(R1)	5	8	14		Wait for ADD.D
2	DADDIU	R1,R1,#-8	5	9		10	Wait for ALU
2	BNE	R1,R2,Loop	6	11			Wait for DADDIU
3	L.D	F0,0(R1)	7	12	13	14	Wait for BNE complete
3	ADD.D	F4,F0,F2	7	15		18	Wait for L.D
3	S.D	F4,0(R1)	8	13	19		Wait for ADD.D
3	DAADIU	R1,R1,#-8	8	14		15	Wait for ALU
3	BNE	R1,R2,Loop	9	16			Wait for DADDIU

Figure 3.25 The clock cycle of issue, execution, and writing result for a dual-issue version of our Tomasulo pipeline. The Write Result stage does not apply to either stores or branches, since they do not write any registers. We assume a result is written to the CDB at the end of the clock cycle it is available in. This figure also assumes a wider CDB. For L.D and S.D, the execution is effective address calculation. For branches, the execute cycle shows when the branch condition can be evaluated and the prediction checked; we assume that this can happen as early as the cycle after issue, if the operands are available. Any instructions following a branch cannot start execution until after the branch condition has been evaluated. We assume one memory unit, one integer pipeline, and one FP adder. If two instructions could use the same functional unit at the same point, priority is given to the "older" instruction. Note that the load of the next iteration performs its memory access before the store of the current iteration.

Clock number	Integer ALU	FP ALU	Data cache	CDB
2	1/ L.D			
3	1 / S.D		1/ L.D	
4	1 / DADDIU			1/ L.D
5		1 / ADD.D		1 / DADDIU
6				
7	2 / L.D			
8	2 / S.D		2 / L.D	1 / ADD.D
9	2 / DADDIU		1 / S.D	2 / L.D
10		2 / ADD.D		2 / DADDIU
11				
12	3 / L.D			
13	3 / S.D		3 / L.D	2 / ADD.D
14	3 / DADDIU		2 / S.D	3 / L.D
15		3 / ADD.D		3 / DADDIU
16				
17				
18				3 / ADD.D
19			3 / S.D	
20				

Figure 3.26 Resource usage table for the example shown in Figure 3.25. The entry in each box shows the opcode and iteration number of the instruction that uses the functional unit heading the column at the clock cycle corresponding to the row. Only a single CDB is actually required and that is what we show.

execute more integer operations per cycle, larger improvements would be possible. A revised example demonstrates this potential improvement and the flexibility of dynamic scheduling to adapt to different hardware capabilities.

Example Consider the execution of the same loop on a two-issue processor, but, in addition, assume that there are separate integer functional units for effective address calculation and for ALU operations. Create a table as in Figure 3.25 for the first three iterations of the same loop and another table to show the resource usage.

Answer Figure 3.27 shows the improvement in performance: The loop executes in 5 clock cycles less (11 versus 16 execution cycles). The cost of this improvement is both a separate address adder and the logic to issue to it; note that, in contrast to the earlier example, a second CDB is needed. As Figure 3.28 shows this example has a higher instruction execution rate but lower efficiency as measured by the utilization of the functional units.

Iteration number	Instructions	Issues at	Executes	Memory access at	Write CDB at	Comment
1	L.D F0,0(R1)	1	2	3	4	First issue
1	ADD.D F4,F0,F2	1	5		8	Wait for L.D
1	S.D F4,0(R1)	2	3	9		Wait for ADD.D
1	DADDIU R1,R1,#-8	2	3		4	Executes earlier
1	BNE R1,R2,Loop	3	5			Wait for DADDIU
2	L.D F0,0(R1)	4	6	7	8	Wait for BNE complete
2	ADD.D F4,F0,F2	4	9		12	Wait for L.D
2	S.D F4,0(R1)	5	7	13		Wait for ADD.D
2	DADDIU R1,R1,#-8	5	6		7	Executes earlier
2	BNE R1,R2,Loop	6	8			Wait for DADDIU
3	L.D F0,0(R1)	7	9	10	11	Wait for BNE complete
3	ADD.D F4,F0,F2	7	12		15	Wait for L.D
3	S.D F4,0(R1)	8	10	16		Wait for ADD.D
3	DADDIU R1,R1,#-8	8	9		10	Executes earlier
3	BNE R1,R2,Loop	9	11			Wait for DADDIU

Figure 3.27 **The clock cycle of issue, execution, and writing result for a dual-issue version of our Tomasulo pipeline with separate functional units for integer ALU operations and effective address calculation, which also uses a wider CDB.** The extra integer ALU allows the DADDIU to execute earlier, in turn allowing the BNE to execute earlier, and, thereby, starting the next iteration earlier.

Three factors limit the performance (as shown in Figure 3.27) of the two-issue dynamically scheduled pipeline:

1. There is an imbalance between the functional unit structure of the pipeline and the example loop. This imbalance means that it is impossible to fully use the FP units. To remedy this, we would need fewer dependent integer operations per loop. The next point is a different way of looking at this limitation.

2. The amount of overhead per loop iteration is very high: two out of five instructions (the DADDIU and the BNE) are overhead. In the next chapter we look at how this overhead can be reduced.

3. The control hazard, which prevents us from starting the next L.D before we know whether the branch was correctly predicted, causes a one-cycle penalty on every loop iteration. The next section introduces a technique that addresses this limitation.

3.7   Hardware-Based Speculation

As we try to exploit more instruction-level parallelism, maintaining control dependences becomes an increasing burden. Branch prediction reduces the direct

Clock number	Integer ALU	Address adder	FP ALU	Data cache	CDB #1	CDB #2
2		1/ L.D				
3	1 / DADDIU	1 / S.D		1/ L.D		
4					1/L.D	1 / DADDIU
5			1 / ADD.D			
6	2 / DADDIU	2 / L.D				
7		2 / S.D		2 / L.D	2 / DADDIU	
8					1 / ADD.D	2 / L.D
9	3 / DADDIU	3 / L.D	2 / ADD.D	1 / S.D		
10		3 / S.D		3 / L.D	3 / DADDIU	
11					3 / L.D	
12			3 / ADD.D		2 / ADD.D	
13				2 / S.D		
14						
15						3 / ADD.D
16				3 / S.D		

Figure 3.28 Resource usage table for the example shown in Figure 3.27, using the same format as Figure 3.26.

stalls attributable to branches, but for a processor executing multiple instructions per clock, just predicting branches accurately may not be sufficient to generate the desired amount of instruction-level parallelism. A wide issue processor may need to execute a branch every clock cycle to maintain maximum performance. Hence, exploiting more parallelism requires that we overcome the limitation of control dependence. The performance of the pipeline in Figure 3.25 makes this clear: There is one stall cycle each loop iteration due to a branch hazard. In programs with more branches and more data-dependent branches, this penalty could be larger.

Overcoming control dependence is done by speculating on the outcome of branches and *executing* the program as if our guesses were correct. This mechanism represents a subtle, but important, extension over branch prediction with dynamic scheduling. In particular, with speculation, we fetch, issue, and *execute* instructions, as if our branch predictions were always correct; dynamic scheduling only fetches and issues such instructions. Of course, we need mechanisms to handle the situation where the speculation is incorrect. The next chapter discusses a variety of mechanisms for supporting speculation by the compiler. In this section, we explore *hardware speculation,* which extends the ideas of dynamic scheduling.

Hardware-based speculation combines three key ideas: dynamic branch prediction to choose which instructions to execute, speculation to allow the execution of instructions before the control dependences are resolved (with the ability to undo the effects of an incorrectly speculated sequence), and dynamic scheduling to deal with the scheduling of different combinations of basic blocks. (In comparison, dynamic scheduling without speculation only partially overlaps basic blocks because it requires that a branch be resolved before actually executing any instructions in the successor basic block.) Hardware-based speculation follows the predicted flow of data values to choose when to execute instructions. This method of executing programs is essentially a *data flow execution:* Operations execute as soon as their operands are available.

The approach we examine here, and the one implemented in a number of processors (PowerPC 603/604/G3/G4, MIPS R10000/R12000, Intel Pentium II/III/4, Alpha 21264, and AMD K5/K6/Athlon), is to implement speculative execution based on Tomasulo's algorithm. Just as with Tomasulo's algorithm, we explain hardware speculation in the context of the floating-point unit, but the ideas are easily applicable to the integer unit.

The hardware that implements Tomasulo's algorithm can be extended to support speculation. To do so, we must separate the bypassing of results among instructions, which is needed to execute an instruction speculatively, from the actual completion of an instruction. By making this separation, we can allow an instruction to execute and to bypass its results to other instructions, without allowing the instruction to perform any updates that cannot be undone, until we know that the instruction is no longer speculative. Using the bypassed value is like performing a speculative register read, since we do not know whether the instruction providing the source register value is providing the correct result until the instruction is no longer speculative. When an instruction is no longer speculative, we allow it to update the register file or memory; we call this additional step in the instruction execution sequence *instruction commit.*

The key idea behind implementing speculation is to allow instructions to execute out of order but to force them to commit *in order* and to prevent any irrevocable action (such as updating state or taking an exception) until an instruction commits. In the simple single-issue five-stage pipeline we could ensure that instructions committed in order, and only after any exceptions for that instruction had been detected, simply by moving writes to the end of the pipeline. When we add speculation, we need to separate the process of completing execution from instruction commit, since instructions may finish execution considerably before they are ready to commit. Adding this commit phase to the instruction execution sequence requires some changes to the sequence as well as an additional set of hardware buffers that hold the results of instructions that have finished execution but have not committed. This hardware buffer, which we call the *reorder buffer,* is also used to pass results among instructions that may be speculated.

The reorder buffer (ROB) provides additional registers in the same way as the reservation stations in Tomasulo's algorithm extend the register set. The ROB holds the result of an instruction between the time the operation associated with the instruction completes and the time the instruction commits. Hence, the ROB is a source of operands for instructions, just as the reservation stations provide operands in Tomasulo's algorithm. The key difference is that in Tomasulo's algorithm, once an instruction writes its result, any subsequently issued instructions will find the result in the register file. With speculation, the register file is not updated until the instruction commits (and we know definitively that the instruction should execute); thus, the ROB supplies operands in the interval between completion of instruction execution and instruction commit. The ROB is similar to the store buffer in Tomasulo's algorithm, and we integrate the function of the store buffer into the ROB for simplicity.

Each entry in the ROB contains four fields: the instruction type, the destination field, the value field, and the ready field. The instruction type field indicates whether the instruction is a branch (and has no destination result), a store (which has a memory address destination), or a register operation (ALU operation or load, which has register destinations). The destination field supplies the register number (for loads and ALU operations) or the memory address (for stores) where the instruction result should be written. The value field is used to hold the value of the instruction result until the instruction commits. We will see an example of ROB entries shortly. Finally, the ready field indicates that the instruction has completed execution, and the value is ready.

Figure 3.29 shows the hardware structure of the processor including the ROB. The ROB completely replaces the store buffers. Stores still execute in two steps, but the second step is performed by instruction commit. Although the renaming function of the reservation stations is replaced by the ROB, we still need a place to buffer operations (and operands) between the time they issue and the time they begin execution. This function is still provided by the reservation stations. Since every instruction has a position in the ROB until it commits, we tag a result using the ROB entry number rather than using the reservation station number. This tagging requires that the ROB assigned for an instruction must be tracked in the reservation station. Later in this section, we will explore an alternative implementation that uses extra registers for renaming and the ROB only to track when instructions can commit.

Here are the four steps involved in instruction execution:

1. *Issue*—Get an instruction from the instruction queue. Issue the instruction if there is an empty reservation station and an empty slot in the ROB; send the operands to the reservation station if they are available in either the registers or the ROB. Update the control entries to indicate the buffers are in use. The number of the ROB allocated for the result is also sent to the reservation station, so that the number can be used to tag the result when it is placed on the CDB. If either all reservations are full or the ROB is full, then instruction issue is stalled until both have available entries. This stage is sometimes called *dispatch* in a dynamically scheduled processor.

2. *Execute*—If one or more of the operands is not yet available, monitor the CDB while waiting for the register to be computed. This step checks for RAW hazards. When both operands are available at a reservation station, execute the operation. (Some dynamically scheduled processors call this step

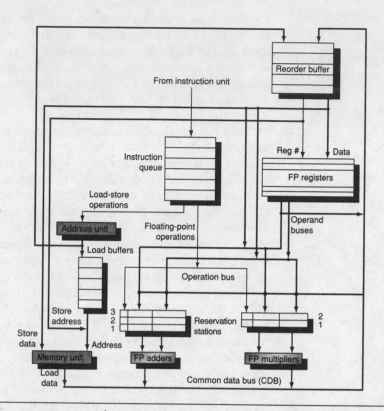

Figure 3.29 The basic structure of a MIPS FP unit using Tomasulo's algorithm and extended to handle speculation. Comparing this to Figure 3.2, which implemented Tomasulo's algorithm, the major change is the addition of the ROB and the elimination of the store buffer, whose function is integrated into the ROB. This mechanism can be extended to multiple issue by making the CDB wider to allow for multiple completions per clock.

"issue," but we use the name "execute," which was used in the first dynamically scheduled processor, the CDC 6600.) Instructions may take multiple clock cycles in this stage, and loads still require two steps in this stage. Stores need only have the base register available at this step, since execution for a store at this point is only effective address calculation.

3. *Write result*—When the result is available, write it on the CDB (with the ROB tag sent when the instruction issued) and from the CDB into the ROB, as well as to any reservation stations waiting for this result. Mark the reservation station as available. Special actions are required for store instructions. If the value to be stored is available, it is written into the Value field of the ROB entry for the store. If the value to be stored is not available yet, the CDB must be monitored until that value is broadcast, at which time the Value field of the ROB entry of the store is updated. For simplicity in our description, we

assume that this occurs during the Write Results stage of a store; we discuss relaxing this requirement later.

4. *Commit*—There are three different sequences of actions at commit depending on whether the committing instruction is a branch with an incorrect prediction, a store, or any other instruction (normal commit). The normal commit case occurs when an instruction reaches the head of the ROB and its result is present in the buffer; at this point, the processor updates the register with the result and removes the instruction from the ROB. Committing a store is similar except that memory is updated rather than a result register. When a branch with incorrect prediction reaches the head of the ROB, it indicates that the speculation was wrong. The ROB is flushed and execution is restarted at the correct successor of the branch. If the branch was correctly predicted, the branch is finished. Some machines call this commit phase "completion" or "graduation."

Once an instruction commits, its entry in the ROB is reclaimed and the register or memory destination is updated, eliminating the need for the ROB entry. If the ROB fills, we simply stop issuing instructions until an entry is made free. Now, let's examine how this scheme would work with the same example we used for Tomasulo's algorithm.

Example   Assume the same latencies for the floating-point functional units as in earlier examples: add is 2 clock cycles, multiply is 10 clock cycles, and divide is 40 clock cycles. Using the code segment below, the same one we used to generate Figure 3.4, show what the status tables look like when the MUL.D is ready to go to commit.

```
L.D      F6,34(R2)
L.D      F2,45(R3)
MUL.D    F0,F2,F4
SUB.D    F8,F6,F2
DIV.D    F10,F0,F6
ADD.D    F6,F8,F2
```

Answer   The result is shown in the three tables in Figure 3.30. Notice that although the SUB.D instruction has completed execution, it does not commit until the MUL.D commits. The reservation stations and register status field contain the same basic information that they did for Tomasulo's algorithm (see page 189 for a description of those fields). The differences are that reservation station numbers are replaced with ROB entry numbers in the Qj and Qk fields, as well as in the register status fields, and we have added the Dest field to the reservation stations. The Dest field designates the ROB number that is the destination for the result produced by this reservation station entry.

The above example illustrates the key important difference between a processor with speculation and a processor with dynamic scheduling. Compare the content of Figure 3.30 with that of Figure 3.4, which shows the same code sequence in operation on a processor with Tomasulo's algorithm. The key difference is that, in the example above, no instruction after the earliest uncompleted instruction (MUL.D above) is allowed to complete. In contrast, in Figure 3.4 the SUB.D and ADD.D instructions have also completed.

Reservation stations

Name	Busy	Op	Vj	Vk	Qj	Qk	Dest	A
Load1	no							
Load2	no							
Add1	no							
Add2	no							
Add3	no							
Mult1	no	MUL.D	Mem[45 + Regs[R3]]	Regs[F4]			#3	
Mult2	yes	DIV.D		Mem[34 + Regs[R2]]	#3		#5	

Reorder buffer

Entry	Busy	Instruction		State	Destination	Value
1	no	L.D	F6,34(R2)	Commit	F6	Mem[34 + Regs[R2]]
2	no	L.D	F2,45(R3)	Commit	F2	Mem[45 + Regs[R3]]
3	yes	MUL.D	F0,F2,F4	Write result	F0	#2 × Regs[F4]
4	yes	SUB.D	F8,F6,F2	Write result	F8	#1 – #2
5	yes	DIV.D	F10,F0,F6	Execute	F10	
6	yes	ADD.D	F6,F8,F2	Write result	F6	#4 + #2

FP register status

Field	F0	F1	F2	F3	F4	F5	F6	F7	F8	F10
Reorder #	3						6		4	5
Busy	yes	no	no	no	no	no	yes	...	yes	yes

Figure 3.30 At the time the MUL.D is ready to commit, only the two L.D instructions have committed, although several others have completed execution. The MUL.D is at the head of the ROB, and the two L.D instructions are there only to ease understanding. The SUB.D and ADD.D instructions will not commit until the MUL.D instruction commits, although the results of the instructions are available and can be used as sources for other instructions. The DIV.D is in execution, but has not completed solely due to its longer latency than MUL.D. The Value column indicates the value being held; the format #X is used to refer to a value field of ROB entry X. Reorder buffers 1 and 2 are actually completed, but are shown for informational purposes. We do not show the entries for the load-store queue, but these entries are kept in order.

One implication of this difference is that the processor with the ROB can dynamically execute code while maintaining a precise interrupt model. For example, if the MUL.D instruction caused an interrupt, we could simply wait until it reached the head of the ROB and take the interrupt, flushing any other pending instructions. Because instruction commit happens in order, this yields a precise exception. By contrast, in the example using Tomasulo's algorithm, the SUB.D and ADD.D instructions could both complete before the MUL.D raised the exception. The result is that the registers F8 and F6 (destinations of the SUB.D and ADD.D instructions) could be overwritten, and the interrupt would be imprecise. Some users and architects have decided that imprecise floating-point exceptions are acceptable in high-performance processors, since the program will likely terminate; see Appendix H for further discussion of this topic. Other types of exceptions, such as page faults, are much more difficult to accommodate if they are imprecise, since the program must transparently resume execution after handling such an exception. The use of a ROB with in-order instruction commit provides precise exceptions, in addition to supporting speculative execution, as the next example shows.

Example   Consider the code example used earlier for Tomasulo's algorithm and shown in Figure 3.6 in execution:

```
Loop:    L.D        F0,0(R1)
         MUL.D      F4,F0,F2
         S.D        F4,0(R1)
         DADDIU     R1,R1,#-8
         BNE        R1,R2,Loop      ;branches if R1≠R2
```

Assume that we have issued all the instructions in the loop twice. Let's also assume that the L.D and MUL.D from the first iteration have committed and all other instructions have completed execution. Normally, the store would wait in the ROB for both the effective address operand (R1 in this example) and the value (F4 in this example). Since we are only considering the floating-point pipeline, assume the effective address for the store is computed by the time the instruction is issued.

Answer   The result is shown in the two tables in Figure 3.31.

Because neither the register values nor any memory values are actually written until an instruction commits, the processor can easily undo its speculative actions when a branch is found to be mispredicted. Suppose that in the previous example (see Figure 3.31), the branch BNE is not taken the first time. The instructions prior to the branch will simply commit when each reaches the head of the ROB; when the branch reaches the head of that buffer, the buffer is simply cleared and the processor begins fetching instructions from the other path.

		Reorder buffer				
Entry	Busy	Instruction		State	Destination	Value
1	no	L.D	F0,0(R1)	Commit	F0	Mem[0 + Regs[R1]]
2	no	MUL.D	F4,F0,F2	Commit	F4	#1 × Regs[F2]
3	yes	S.D	F4,0(R1)	Write result	0 + Regs[R1]	#2
4	yes	DADDIU	R1,R1,#-8	Write result	R1	Regs[R1] − 8
5	yes	BNE	R1,R2,Loop	Write result		
6	yes	L.D	F0,0(R1)	Write result	F0	Mem[#4]
7	yes	MUL.D	F4,F0,F2	Write result	F4	#6 × Regs[F2]
8	yes	S.D	F4,0(R1)	Write result	0 + #4	#7
9	yes	DADDIU	R1,R1,#-8	Write result	R1	#4 − 8
10	yes	BNE	R1,R2,Loop	Write result		

	FP register status								
Field	F0	F1	F2	F3	F4	F5	F6	F7	F8
Reorder #	6				7				
Busy	yes	no	no	no	yes	no	no	. . .	no

Figure 3.31 Only the L.D and MUL.D instructions have committed, although all the others have completed execution. Hence, no reservation stations are busy and none are shown. The remaining instructions will be committed as fast as possible. The first two reorder buffers are empty, but are shown for completeness.

In practice, machines that speculate try to recover as early as possible after a branch is mispredicted. This recovery can be done by clearing the ROB for all entries that appear after the mispredicted branch, allowing those that are before the branch in the ROB to continue, and restarting the fetch at the correct branch successor. In speculative processors, however, performance is more sensitive to the branch-prediction mechanisms, since the impact of a misprediction will be higher. Thus, all the aspects of handling branches—prediction accuracy, misprediction detection, and misprediction recovery—increase in importance.

Exceptions are handled by not recognizing the exception until it is ready to commit. If a speculated instruction raises an exception, the exception is recorded in the ROB. If a branch misprediction arises and the instruction should not have been executed, the exception is flushed along with the instruction when the ROB is cleared. If the instruction reaches the head of the ROB, then we know it is no longer speculative and the exception should really be taken. We can also try to handle exceptions as soon as they arise and all earlier branches are resolved, but this is more challenging in the case of exceptions than for branch mispredict and, because it occurs less frequently, not as critical.

Figure 3.32 shows the steps of execution for an instruction, as well as the conditions that must be satisfied to proceed to the step and the actions taken. We show

Status	Wait until	Action or bookkeeping

Issue
all
instructions
	Reservation
	station (r)
	and
	ROB (b)
	both available
		`if (RegisterStat[rs].Busy)/*in-flight instr. writes rs*/`
		`{h ← RegisterStat[rs].Reorder;`
		`  if (ROB[h].Ready)/* Instr completed already */`
		`     {RS[r].Vj ← ROB[h].Value; RS[r].Qj ← 0;}`
		`  else {RS[r].Qj ← h;} /* wait for instruction */`
		`} else {RS[r].Vj ← Regs[rs]; RS[r].Qj ← 0;};`
		`RS[r].Busy ← yes; RS[r].Dest ← b;`
		`ROB[b].Instruction ← opcode; ROB[b].Dest ← rd;ROB[b].Ready ← no;`

FP
operations
and stores
		`if (RegisterStat[rt].Busy) /*in-flight instr writes rt*/`
		`{h ← RegisterStat[rt].Reorder;`
		`  if (ROB[b].Ready) /* Instr completed already */`
		`     {RS[r].Vk ← ROB[h].Value; RS[r].Qk ← 0;}`
		`  else {RS[r].Qk ← h;} /* Wait for instruction */`
		`} else {RS[r].Vk ← Regs[rt]; RS[r].Qk ← 0;};`

FP operations		`RegisterStat[rd].Qi=b; RegisterStat[rd].Busy ← yes;` `ROB[b].Dest ← rd;`
Loads		`RS[r].A ← imm; RegisterStat[rt].Qi=b;` `RegisterStat[rt].Busy ← yes; ROB[b].Dest ← rt;`
Stores		`RS[r].A ← imm;`
Execute FP op	(RS[r].Qj = 0) and (RS[r].Qk = 0)	Compute results—operands are in Vj and Vk
Load step1	(RS[r].Qj = 0) and there are no stores earlier in the queue	`RS[r].A ← RS[r].Vj + RS[r].A;`
Load step 2	Load step 1 done and all stores earlier in ROB have different address	Read from Mem[RS[r].A]
Store	(RS[r].Qj = 0) and store at queue head	`ROB[h].Address ← RS[r].Vj + RS[r].A;`

Write result
all but store
	Execution done at *r*
	and CDB available.
		`b ← RS[r].Reorder; RS[r].Busy ← no;`
		`∀x(if (RS[x].Qj=b) {RS[x].Vj ← result; RS[x].Qj ← 0});`
		`∀x(if (RS[x].Qk=b) {RS[x].Vk ← result; RS[x].Qk ← 0});`
		`ROB[b].Value ← result; ROB[b].Ready ← yes;`

Store	Execution done at *r* and (RS[r].Qk = 0)	`ROB[h].Value ← RS[r].Vk;`

Commit	Instruction is at the
	head of the ROB
	(entry h) and
	ROB[h].ready = yes
		`d = ROB[h].Dest; /* register dest, if exists */`
		`if (ROB[h].Instruction==Branch)`
		`  {if (branch is mispredicted)`
		`    {clear ROB[h], RegisterStat; fetch branch dest;};}`
		`else if (ROB[h].Instruction==Store)`
		`      {Mem[ROB[h].Address] ← ROB[h].Value;}`
		`else /* put the result in the register destination */`
		`    {Regs[d] ← ROB[h].Value;};`
		`ROB[h].Busy ← no; /* free up ROB entry */`
		`/* free up dest register if no one else writing it */`
		`if (RegisterStat[d].Qi==h) {RegisterStat[d].Busy ← no;};`

Figure 3.32 Steps in the algorithm and what is required for each step. For the issuing instruction, rd is the destination, rs and rt are the sources, r is the reservation station allocated, and b is the assigned ROB entry. RS is the reservation station data structure. The value returned by a reservation station is called the result. RegisterStat is the register data structure, Regs represents the actual registers, and ROB is the reorder buffer data structure.

the case where mispredicted branches are not resolved until commit. Although speculation seems like a simple addition to dynamic scheduling, a comparison of Figure 3.32 with the comparable figure for Tomasulo's algorithm (see Figure 3.5) shows that speculation adds significant complications to the control. In addition, remember that branch mispredictions are somewhat more complex as well.

There is an important difference in how stores are handled in a speculative processor versus in Tomasulo's algorithm. In Tomasulo's algorithm, a store can update memory when it reaches Write Results (which ensures that the effective address has been calculated) and the data value to store is available. In a speculative processor, a store updates memory only when it reaches the head of the ROB. This difference ensures that memory is not updated until an instruction is no longer speculative.

Figure 3.32 has one significant simplification for stores, which is unneeded in practice. Figure 3.32 requires stores to wait in the Write Results stage for the register source operand whose value is to be stored; the value is then moved from the Vk field of the store's reservation station to the Value field of the store's ROB entry. In reality, however, the value to be stored need not arrive until *just before* the store commits and can be placed directly into the store's ROB entry by the sourcing instruction. This is accomplished by having the hardware track when the source value to be stored is available in the store's ROB entry and searching the ROB on every instruction completion to look for dependent stores. This addition is not complicated, but adding it has two effects: We would need to add a field to the ROB and Figure 3.32, which is already in a small font, would no longer fit on one page! Although Figure 3.32 makes this simplification, in our examples, we will allow the store to pass through the Write Results stage and simply wait for the value to be ready when it commits.

Like Tomasulo's algorithm, we must avoid hazards through memory. WAW and WAR hazards through memory are eliminated with speculation because the actual updating of memory occurs in order, when a store is at the head of the ROB, and hence, no earlier loads or stores can still be pending. RAW hazards through memory are maintained by two restrictions:

1. not allowing a load to initiate the second step of its execution if any active ROB entry occupied by a store has a Destination field that matches the value of the A field of the load, and

2. maintaining the program order for the computation of an effective address of a load with respect to all earlier stores.

Together, these two restrictions ensure that any load that accesses a memory location written to by an earlier store cannot perform the memory access until the store has written the data. Some speculative machines will actually bypass the value from the store to the load directly, when such a RAW hazard occurs.

Although this explanation of speculative execution has focused on floating point, the techniques easily extend to the integer registers and functional units, as we will see in the "Putting It All Together" section. Indeed, speculation may be more useful in integer programs, since such programs tend to have code where the branch behavior is less predictable. Additionally, these techniques can be extended to work in a multiple-issue processor by allowing multiple instructions to issue and commit every clock. In fact, speculation is probably most interesting in such processors, since less ambitious techniques can probably exploit sufficient ILP within basic blocks when assisted by a compiler.

Multiple Issue with Speculation

A speculative processor can be extended to multiple issue using the same techniques we employed when extending a Tomasulo-based processor in Section 3.6. The same techniques for implementing the instruction issue unit can be used: We process multiple instructions per clock assigning reservation stations and reorder buffers to the instructions.

The two challenges of multiple issue with Tomasulo's algorithm—instruction issue and monitoring the CDBs for instruction completion—become the major challenges for multiple issue with speculation. In addition, to maintain throughput of greater than one instruction per cycle, a speculative processor must be able to handle multiple instruction commits per clock cycle. To show how speculation can improve performance in a multiple-issue processor, consider the following example using speculation.

Example Consider the execution of the following loop, which searches an array, on a two-issue processor, once without speculation and once with speculation:

```
Loop:   LD      R2,0(R1)      ;R2=array element
        DADDIU  R2,R2,#1      ;increment R2
        SD      R2,0(R1)      ;store result
        DADDIU  R1,R1,#4      ;increment pointer
        BNE     R2,R3,LOOP    ;branch if not last element
```

Assume that there are separate integer functional units for effective address calculation, for ALU operations, and for branch condition evaluation. Create a table as in Figure 3.27 for the first three iterations of this loop for both machines. Assume that up to two instructions of any type can commit per clock.

Answer Figures 3.33 and 3.34 show the performance for a two-issue dynamically scheduled processor, without and with speculation. In this case, where a branch is a key potential performance limitation, speculation helps significantly. The third branch in the speculative processor executes in clock cycle 13, while it executes in clock cycle 19 on the nonspeculative pipeline. Because the completion rate on the nonspeculative pipeline is falling behind the issue rate rapidly, the nonspeculative pipeline will stall when a few more iterations are issued. The performance of the nonspeculative processor could be improved by allowing load instructions to

Iteration number	Instructions		Issues at clock cycle number	Executes at clock cycle number	Memory access at clock cycle number	Write CDB at clock cycle number	Comment
1	LD	R2,0(R1)	1	2	3	4	First issue
1	DADDIU	R2,R2,#1	1	5		6	Wait for LW
1	SD	R2,0(R1)	2	3	7		Wait for DADDIU
1	DADDIU	R1,R1,#4	2	3		4	Execute directly
1	BNE	R2,R3,LOOP	3	7			Wait for DADDIU
2	LD	R2,0(R1)	4	8	9	10	Wait for BNE
2	DADDIU	R2,R2,#1	4	11		12	Wait for LW
2	SD	R2,0(R1)	5	9	13		Wait for DADDIU
2	DADDIU	R1,R1,#4	5	8		9	Wait for BNE
2	BNE	R2,R3,LOOP	6	13			Wait for DADDIU
3	LD	R2,0(R1)	7	14	15	16	Wait for BNE
3	DADDIU	R2,R2,#1	7	17		18	Wait for LW
3	SD	R2,0(R1)	8	15	19		Wait for DADDIU
3	DADDIU	R1,R1,#4	8	14		15	Wait for BNE
3	BNZ	R2,R3,LOOP	9	19			Wait for DADDIU

Figure 3.33 The time of issue, execution, and writing result for a dual-issue version of our pipeline *without* speculation. Note that the L.D following the BNE cannot start execution earlier, because it must wait until the branch outcome is determined. This type of program, with data-dependent branches that cannot be resolved earlier, shows the strength of speculation. Separate functional units for address calculation, ALU operations, and branch condition evaluation allow multiple instructions to execute in the same cycle.

complete effective address calculation before a branch is decided, but unless speculative memory accesses are allowed, this improvement will gain only one clock per iteration.

The previous example clearly shows how speculation can be advantageous when there are data-dependent branches, which otherwise would limit performance. This advantage depends, however, on accurate branch prediction. Incorrect speculation will not improve performance, but will, in fact, typically harm performance.

Design Considerations for Speculative Machines

In this section we briefly examine a number of important considerations that arise in speculative machines.

Iteration number	Instructions		Issues at clock number	Executes at clock number	Read access at clock number	Write CDB at clock number	Commits at clock number	Comment
1	LD	R2,0(R1)	1	2	3	4	5	First issue
1	DADDIU	R2,R2,#1	1	5		6	7	Wait for LW
1	SD	R2,0(R1)	2	3			7	Wait for DADDIU
1	DADDIU	R1,R1,#4	2	3		4	8	Commit in order
1	BNE	R2,R3,LOOP	3	7			8	Wait for DADDIU
2	LD	R2,0(R1)	4	5	6	7	9	No execute delay
2	DADDIU	R2,R2,#1	4	8		9	10	Wait for LW
2	SD	R2,0(R1)	5	6			10	Wait for DADDIU
2	DADDIU	R1,R1,#4	5	6		7	11	Commit in order
2	BNE	R2,R3,LOOP	6	10			11	Wait for DADDIU
3	LD	R2,0(R1)	7	8	9	10	12	Earliest possible
3	DADDIU	R2,R2,#1	7	11		12	13	Wait for LW
3	SD	R2,0(R1)	8	9			13	Wait for DADDIU
3	DADDIU	R1,R1,#4	8	9		10	14	Executes earlier
3	BNE	R2,R3,LOOP	9	13			14	Wait for DADDIU

Figure 3.34 The time of issue, execution, and writing result for a dual-issue version of our pipeline *with* speculation. Note that the L.D following the BNE can start execution early because it is speculative.

Register Renaming versus Reorder Buffers

One alternative to the use of a ROB is the explicit use of a larger physical set of registers combined with register renaming. This approach builds on the concept of renaming used in Tomasulo's algorithm and extends it. In Tomasulo's algorithm, the values of the *architecturally visible registers* (R0, . . . , R31 and F0, . . . , F31) are contained, at any point in execution, in some combination of the register set and the reservation stations. With the addition of speculation, register values may also temporarily reside in the ROB. In either case, if the processor does not issue new instructions for a period of time, all existing instructions will commit, and the register values will appear in the register file, which directly corresponds to the architecturally visible registers.

In the register-renaming approach, an extended set of physical registers is used to hold both the architecturally visible registers as well as temporary values. Thus, the extended registers replace the function of both the ROB and the reservation stations. During instruction issue, a renaming process maps the names of architectural registers to physical register numbers in the extended register set, allocating a new unused register for the destination. WAW and WAR hazards are avoided by renaming of the destination register, and speculation recovery is handled because a physical register holding an instruction destination does not become the architectural register until the instruction commits. The renaming map is a simple data structure that supplies the physical register number of the register that currently corresponds to the specified architectural register. This structure is similar in structure and function to the register status table in Tomasulo's algorithm.

One question you may be asking is, How do we ever know which registers are the architectural registers if they are constantly changing? Most of the time when the program is executing it does not matter. There are clearly cases, however, where another process, such as the operating system, must be able to know exactly where the contents of a certain architectural register resides. To understand how this capability is provided, assume the processor does not issue instructions for some period of time. Then eventually all instructions in the pipeline will commit, and the mapping between the architecturally visible registers and physical registers will become stable. At that point, a subset of the physical registers contains the architecturally visible registers, and the value of any physical register not associated with an architectural register is unneeded. It is then easy to move the architectural registers to a fixed subset of physical registers so that the values can be communicated to another process.

An advantage of the renaming approach versus the ROB approach is that instruction commit is simplified, since it requires only two simple actions: record that the mapping between an architectural register number and physical register number is no longer speculative, and free up any physical registers being used to hold the "older" value of the architectural register. In a design with reservation stations, a station is freed up when the instruction using it completes execution, and a ROB is freed up when the corresponding instruction commits.

With register renaming, deallocating registers is more complex, since before we free up a physical register, we must know that it no longer corresponds to an architectural register, and that no further uses of the physical register are outstanding. A physical register corresponds to an architectural register until the architectural register is rewritten, causing the renaming table to point elsewhere. That is, if no renaming entry points to a particular physical register, then it no longer corresponds to an architectural register. There may, however, still be uses of the physical register outstanding. The processor can determine whether this is the case by examining the source register specifiers of all instructions in the functional unit queues. If a given physical register does not appear as a source and it is not designated as an architectural register, it may be reclaimed and reallocated.

Alternatively, the processor can simply wait until another instruction that writes the same architectural register commits. At that point, there can be no further uses of the older value outstanding. Although this method may tie up a physical register slightly longer than necessary, it is easy to implement and hence is used in the MIPS R10000.

In addition to simplifying instruction commit, a renaming approach means that instruction issue need not examine both the ROB and the register file for an operand, since all results are in the register file. One possibly disconcerting aspect of the renaming approach is that the "real" architectural registers are never fixed but constantly change according to the contents of a renaming map. Although this complicates the design and debugging, it is not inherently problematic and is an accepted fact in many newer implementations. It is sometimes even made architecturally visible, as we will see in the IA-64 architecture in the next chapter.

The PowerPC 603/604 series, the MIPS R10000/12000, the Alpha 21264, and the Pentium II, III, and 4 all use register renaming, adding from 20 to 80 extra registers. Since all results are allocated a new virtual register until they commit, these extra registers replace a primary function of the ROB and largely determine how many instructions may be in execution (between issue and commit) at one time.

How Much to Speculate

One of the significant advantages of speculation is its ability to uncover events that would otherwise stall the pipeline early, such as cache misses. This potential advantage, however, comes with a significant potential disadvantage: The processor may speculate that some costly exceptional event occurs and begin processing the event, when in fact, the speculation was incorrect.

To maintain some of the advantage, while minimizing the disadvantages, most pipelines with speculation will allow only low-cost exceptional events (such as a first-level cache miss) to be handled in speculative mode. If an expensive exceptional event occurs, such as a second-level cache miss or a translation lookaside buffer (TLB) miss, the processor will wait until the instruction causing the event is no longer speculative before handling the event. Although this may slightly degrade the performance of some programs, it avoids significant performance losses in others, especially those that suffer from a high frequency of such events coupled with less than excellent branch prediction.

Speculating through Multiple Branches

In the examples we have considered so far, it has been possible to resolve a branch before having to speculate on another. Three different situations can benefit from speculating on multiple branches simultaneously: a very high branch frequency, significant clustering of branches, and long delays in functional units. In the first two cases, achieving high performance may mean that multiple branches are speculated, and it may even mean handling more than one branch per clock. Database programs, and other less structured integer computations, often exhibit these properties, making speculation on multiple branches important. Likewise, long delays in functional units can raise the importance of speculating on multiple branches as a way to avoid stalls from the longer pipeline delays.

Speculating on multiple branches slightly complicates the process of speculation recovery, but is straightforward otherwise. A more complex technique is predicting and speculating on more than one branch per cycle. The IBM Power2 could resolve two branches per cycle but did not speculate on any other instructions. As of 2001, no processor has yet combined full speculation with resolving multiple branches per cycle, but we can expect that this capability will be needed in the future.

Of course, all the techniques described in the next chapter and in this one cannot take advantage of more parallelism than is provided by the application. The question of how much parallelism is available, and under what circumstances, has been hotly debated and is the topic of the next section.

3.8 Studies of the Limitations of ILP

Exploiting ILP to increase performance began with the first pipelined processors in the 1960s. In the 1980s and 1990s, these techniques were key to achieving rapid performance improvements. The question of how much ILP exists is critical to our long-term ability to enhance performance at a rate that exceeds the increase in speed of the base integrated circuit technology. On a shorter scale, the critical question of what is needed to exploit more ILP is crucial to both computer designers and compiler writers. The data in this section also provide us with a way to examine the value of ideas that we have introduced in this chapter, including memory disambiguation, register renaming, and speculation.

In this section we review one of the studies done of these questions. Section 3.15 describes several studies, including the source for the data in this section (Wall's 1993 study). All these studies of available parallelism operate by making a set of assumptions and seeing how much parallelism is available under those assumptions. The data we examine here are from a study that makes the fewest assumptions; in fact, the ultimate hardware model is probably unrealizable. Nonetheless, all such studies assume a certain level of compiler technology, and some of these assumptions could affect the results, despite the use of incredibly ambitious hardware. In addition, new ideas may invalidate the very basic assumptions of this and other studies; for example, value prediction, a technique we discuss at the end of this section, may allow us to overcome the limit of data dependences.

In the future, advances in compiler technology together with significantly new and different hardware techniques may be able to overcome some limitations assumed in these studies; however, it is unlikely that such advances *when coupled with realistic hardware* will overcome all these limits in the near future. Instead, developing new hardware and software techniques to overcome the limits seen in these studies will continue to be one of the most important challenges in computer design.

The Hardware Model

To see what the limits of ILP might be, we first need to define an ideal processor. An ideal processor is one where all artificial constraints on ILP are removed. The only limits on ILP in such a processor are those imposed by the actual data flows through either registers or memory.

The assumptions made for an ideal or perfect processor are as follows:

1. *Register renaming*—There are an infinite number of virtual registers available, and hence all WAW and WAR hazards are avoided and an unbounded number of instructions can begin execution simultaneously.

2. *Branch prediction*—Branch prediction is perfect. All conditional branches are predicted exactly.

3. *Jump prediction*—All jumps (including jump register used for return and computed jumps) are perfectly predicted. When combined with perfect branch prediction, this is equivalent to having a processor with perfect speculation and an unbounded buffer of instructions available for execution.

4. *Memory address alias analysis*—All memory addresses are known exactly and a load can be moved before a store provided that the addresses are not identical.

Assumptions 2 and 3 eliminate *all* control dependences. Likewise, assumptions 1 and 4 eliminate *all but the true* data dependences. Together, these four assumptions mean that *any* instruction in the program's execution can be scheduled on the cycle immediately following the execution of the predecessor on which it depends. It is even possible, under these assumptions, for the *last* dynamically executed instruction in the program to be scheduled on the very first cycle! Thus, this set of assumptions subsumes both control and address speculation and implements them as if they were perfect.

Initially, we examine a processor that can issue an unlimited number of instructions at once looking arbitrarily far ahead in the computation. For all the processor models we examine, there are no restrictions on what types of instructions can execute in a cycle. For the unlimited-issue case, this means there may be an unlimited number of loads or stores issuing in one clock cycle. In addition, all functional unit latencies are assumed to be one cycle, so that any sequence of dependent instructions can issue on successive cycles. Latencies longer than one cycle would decrease the number of issues per cycle, although not the number of instructions under execution at any point. (The instructions in execution at any point are often referred to as *in flight*.)

Finally, we assume perfect caches, which is equivalent to saying that all loads and stores always complete in one cycle. This assumption allows our study to focus on fundamental limits to ILP. The resulting data, however, will be very optimistic because realistic caches would significantly reduce the amount of ILP that could be successfully exploited, even if the rest of the processor were perfect!

Of course, this processor is on the edge of unrealizable. For example, the Alpha 21264 is one of the most advanced superscalar processors announced to date. The 21264 issues up to four instructions per clock and initiates execution on up to six (with significant restrictions on the instruction type, e.g., at most two load-stores), supports a large set of renaming registers (41 integer and 41 floating point, allowing up to 80 instructions in flight), and uses a large tournament-style branch predictor. After looking at the parallelism available for the perfect processor, we will examine the impact of restricting various features.

To measure the available parallelism, a set of programs was compiled and optimized with the standard MIPS optimizing compilers. The programs were instrumented and executed to produce a trace of the instruction and data references. Every instruction in the trace is then scheduled as early as possible, limited only by the data dependences. Since a trace is used, perfect branch prediction and perfect alias analysis are easy to do. With these mechanisms, instructions may be scheduled much earlier than they would otherwise, moving across large numbers of instructions on which they are not data dependent, including branches, since branches are perfectly predicted.

Figure 3.35 shows the average amount of parallelism available for six of the SPEC92 benchmarks. Throughout this section the parallelism is measured by the average instruction issue rate (remember that all instructions have a one-cycle latency), which is the ideal IPC. Three of these benchmarks (fpppp, doduc, and tomcatv) are floating-point intensive, and the other three are integer programs. Two of the floating-point benchmarks (fpppp and tomcatv) have extensive parallelism, which could be exploited by a vector computer or by a multiprocessor (the structure in fpppp is quite messy, however, since some hand transformations have been done on the code). The doduc program has extensive parallelism, but the parallelism does not occur in simple parallel loops as it does in fpppp and tomcatv. The program li is a LISP interpreter that has many short dependences.

In the next few sections, we restrict various aspects of this processor to show what the effects of various assumptions are before looking at some ambitious but realizable processors.

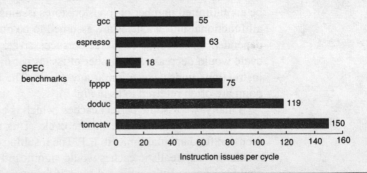

Figure 3.35 ILP available in a perfect processor for six of the SPEC92 benchmarks. The first three programs are integer programs, and the last three are floating-point programs. The floating-point programs are loop-intensive and have large amounts of loop-level parallelism.

Limitations on the Window Size and Maximum Issue Count

To build a processor that even comes close to perfect branch prediction and perfect alias analysis requires extensive dynamic analysis, since static compile time
schemes cannot be perfect. Of course, most realistic dynamic schemes will not be
perfect, but the use of dynamic schemes will provide the ability to uncover parallelism that cannot be analyzed by static compile time analysis. Thus, a dynamic
processor might be able to more closely match the amount of parallelism uncovered by our ideal processor.

How close could a real dynamically scheduled, speculative processor come to
the ideal processor? To gain insight into this question, consider what the perfect
processor must do:

1. Look arbitrarily far ahead to find a set of instructions to issue, predicting all
   branches perfectly.

2. Rename all register uses to avoid WAR and WAW hazards.

3. Determine whether there are any data dependences among the instructions in
   the issue packet; if so, rename accordingly.

4. Determine if any memory dependences exist among the issuing instructions
   and handle them appropriately.

5. Provide enough replicated functional units to allow all the ready instructions
   to issue.

Obviously, this analysis is quite complicated. For example, to determine
whether n issuing instructions have any register dependences among them,
assuming all instructions are register-register and the total number of registers is
unbounded, requires

$$2n - 2 + 2n - 4 + \ldots + 2 = 2 \sum_{i=1}^{n-1} i = 2\frac{(n-1)n}{2} = n^2 - n$$

comparisons. Thus, to detect dependences among the next 2000 instructions—the
default size we assume in several figures—requires almost *4 million* comparisons! Even issuing only 50 instructions requires 2450 comparisons. This cost
obviously limits the number of instructions that can be considered for issue at
once.

In existing and near-term processors, the costs are not quite so high, since we
need only detect dependence pairs and the limited number of registers allows different solutions. Furthermore, in a real processor, issue occurs in order, and
dependent instructions are handled by a renaming process that accommodates
dependent renaming in one clock. Once instructions are issued, the detection of
dependences is handled in a distributed fashion by the reservation stations or
scoreboard.

The set of instructions that is examined for simultaneous execution is called
the *window*. Each instruction in the window must be kept in the processor, and the

number of comparisons required every clock is equal to the maximum completion rate times the window size times the number of operands per instruction (today typically $6 \times 80 \times 2 = 960$), since every pending instruction must look at every completing instruction for either of its operands. Thus, the total window size is limited by the required storage, the comparisons, and a limited issue rate, which makes a larger window less helpful. To date, the window size has been in the range of 32–126, which can require over 2000 comparisons. The HP PA 8600 reportedly has over 7000 comparators!

The window size directly limits the number of instructions that begin execution in a given cycle. In practice, real processors will have a more limited number of functional units (e.g., no processor has handled more than two memory references per clock or more than two FP operations), as well as limited numbers of buses and register access ports, which serve as limits on the number of instructions initiated in the same clock. Thus, the maximum number of instructions that may issue, begin execution, or commit in the same clock cycle is usually much smaller than the window size.

Obviously, the number of possible implementation constraints in a multiple-issue processor is large, including issues per clock, functional units and unit latency, register file ports, functional unit queues (which may be fewer than units), issue limits for branches, and limitations on instruction commit. Each of these acts as a constraint on the ILP. Rather than try to understand each of these effects, however, we will focus on limiting the size of the window, with the understanding that all other restrictions would further reduce the amount of parallelism that can be exploited.

Figures 3.36 and 3.37 show the effects of restricting the size of the window from which an instruction can execute; the *only* difference in the two graphs is the format—the data are identical. As we can see in Figure 3.36, the amount of parallelism uncovered falls sharply with decreasing window size. In 2001, the most advanced processors have window sizes in the range of 64–128, but these window sizes are not strictly comparable to those shown in Figure 3.36 for two reasons. First, the functional units are pipelined, reducing the effective window size compared to the case where all units have single-cycle latency. Second, in real processors the window must also hold any memory references waiting on a cache miss, which are not considered in this model, since it assumes a perfect, single-cycle cache access.

As we can see in Figure 3.37, the integer programs do not contain nearly as much parallelism as the floating-point programs. This result is to be expected. Looking at how the parallelism drops off in Figure 3.37 makes it clear that the parallelism in the floating-point cases is coming from loop-level parallelism. The fact that the amount of parallelism at low window sizes is not that different among the floating-point and integer programs implies a structure where there are dependences within loop bodies, but few dependences between loop iterations in programs such as tomcatv. At small window sizes, the processors simply cannot see the instructions in the next loop iteration that could be issued in parallel with instructions from the current iteration. This case is an example of where better compiler technology (see the next chapter) could uncover higher amounts of ILP,

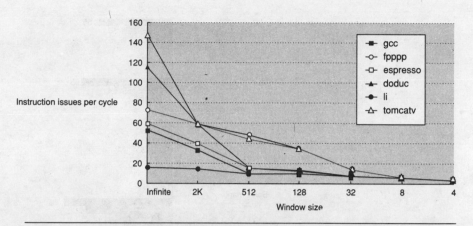

Figure 3.36 The effects of reducing the size of the window. The window is the group of instructions from which an instruction can execute. The start of the window is the earliest uncompleted instruction (remember that instructions complete in one cycle), and the last instruction in the window is determined by the window size. The instructions in the window are obtained by perfectly predicting branches and selecting instructions until the window is full.

since it could find the loop-level parallelism and schedule the code to take advantage of it, even with small window sizes.

We know that large window sizes are impractical and inefficient, and the data in Figures 3.36 and 3.37 tell us that issue rates will be considerably reduced with realistic windows. Thus we will assume a base window size of 2K entries and a maximum issue capability of 64 instructions per clock for the rest of this analysis. As we will see in the next few sections, when the rest of the processor is not perfect, a 2K window and a 64-issue limitation do not constrain the amount of ILP the processor can exploit.

The Effects of Realistic Branch and Jump Prediction

Our ideal processor assumes that branches can be perfectly predicted: The outcome of any branch in the program is known before the first instruction is executed! Of course, no real processor can ever achieve this. Figures 3.38 and 3.39 show the effects of more realistic prediction schemes in two different formats. Our data are for several different branch-prediction schemes, varying from perfect to no predictor. We assume a separate predictor is used for jumps. Jump predictors are important primarily with the most accurate branch predictors, since the branch frequency is higher and the accuracy of the branch predictors dominates.

The five levels of branch prediction shown in these figures are

1. *Perfect*—All branches and jumps are perfectly predicted at the start of execution.

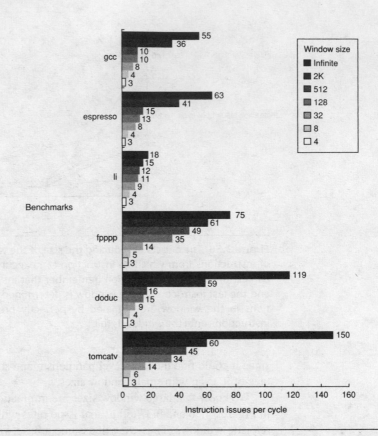

Figure 3.37 The effect of window size shown by each application by plotting the average number of instruction issues per clock cycle. The most interesting observation is that at modest window sizes, the amount of parallelism found in the integer and floating-point programs is similar.

2. *Tournament-based branch predictor*—The prediction scheme uses a correlating 2-bit predictor and a noncorrelating 2-bit predictor together with a selector, which chooses the best predictor for each branch. The prediction buffer contains 2^{13} (8K) entries, each consisting of three 2-bit fields, two of which are predictors and the third a selector. The correlating predictor is indexed using the exclusive-or of the branch address and the global branch history. The noncorrelating predictor is the standard 2-bit predictor indexed by the branch address. The selector table is also indexed by the branch address and specifies whether the correlating or noncorrelating predictor should be used. The selector is incremented or decremented just as we would for a standard 2-bit predictor. This predictor, which uses a total of 48K bits, outperforms both the correlating and noncorrelating predictors, achieving an average accuracy of 97% for these six SPEC benchmarks; this predictor is comparable in strat-

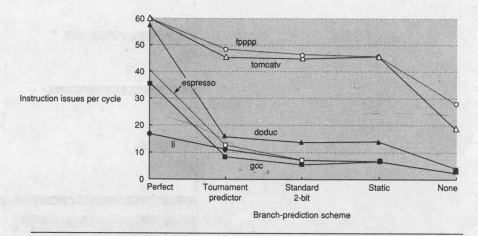

Figure 3.38 The effect of branch-prediction schemes. This graph shows the impact of going from a perfect model of branch prediction (all branches predicted correctly arbitrarily far ahead), to various dynamic predictors (selective and 2-bit), to compile time, profile-based prediction, and finally to using no predictor. The predictors are described precisely in the text.

egy and somewhat larger than the best predictors in use in 2001. Jump prediction is done with a pair of 2K-entry predictors, one organized as a circular buffer for predicting returns and one organized as a standard predictor and used for computed jumps (as in case statement or computed gotos). These jump predictors are nearly perfect.

3. *Standard 2-bit predictor with 512 2-bit entries*—In addition, we assume a 16-entry buffer to predict returns.

4. *Static*—A static predictor uses the profile history of the program and predicts that the branch is always taken or always not taken based on the profile.

5. *None*—No branch prediction is used, though jumps are still predicted. Parallelism is largely limited to within a basic block.

Since we do *not* charge additional cycles for a mispredicted branch, the only effect of varying the branch prediction is to vary the amount of parallelism that can be exploited across basic blocks by speculation. Figure 3.40 shows the accuracy of the three realistic predictors for the conditional branches for the subset of SPEC92 benchmarks we include here. By comparison, Figure 3.61, near the end of this chapter, shows the size and type of branch predictor in recent high-performance processors.

Figure 3.39 shows that the branch behavior of two of the floating-point programs is much simpler than the other programs, primarily because these two programs have many fewer branches and the few branches that exist are more predictable. This property allows significant amounts of parallelism to be

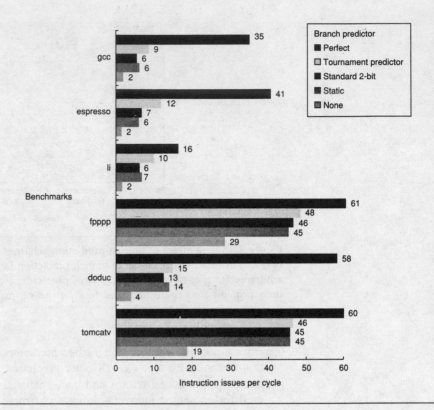

Figure 3.39 The effect of branch-prediction schemes sorted by application. This graph highlights the differences among the programs with extensive loop-level parallelism (tomcatv and fpppp) and those without (the integer programs and doduc).

exploited with realistic prediction schemes. In contrast, for all the integer programs and for doduc, the FP benchmark with the least loop-level parallelism, even the difference between perfect branch prediction and the ambitious selective predictor is dramatic. Like the window size data, these figures tell us that to achieve significant amounts of parallelism in integer programs, the processor must select and execute instructions that are widely separated. When branch prediction is not highly accurate, the mispredicted branches become a barrier to finding the parallelism.

As we have seen, branch prediction is critical, especially with a window size of 2K instructions and an issue limit of 64. For the rest of the studies, in addition to the window and issue limit, we assume as a base a more ambitious tournament predictor that uses two levels of prediction and a total of 8K entries. This predictor, which requires more than 150K bits of storage (roughly four times the largest predictor to date), slightly outperforms the selective predictor described above (by about 0.5–1%). We also assume a pair of 2K jump and return predictors, as described above.

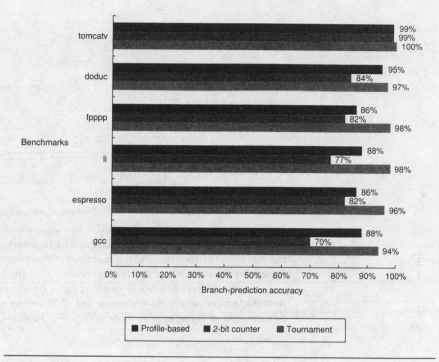

Figure 3.40 **Branch-prediction accuracy for the conditional branches in the SPEC92 subset.**

The Effects of Finite Registers

Our ideal processor eliminates all name dependences among register references using an infinite set of physical registers. To date, the Alpha 21264 has provided the largest number of extended registers: 41 integer and 41 FP registers, in addition to 32 integer and 32 floating-point architectural registers. Figures 3.41 and 3.42 show the effect of reducing the number of registers available for renaming, again using the same data in two different forms. Both the FP and GP registers are increased by the number of registers shown on the axis or in the legend.

At first, the results in these figures might seem somewhat surprising: You might expect that name dependences should only slightly reduce the parallelism available. Remember though, exploiting large amounts of parallelism requires evaluating many independent threads of execution. Thus, many registers are needed to hold live variables from these threads. Figure 3.41 shows that the impact of having only a finite number of registers is significant if extensive parallelism exists. Although these graphs show a large impact on the floating-point programs, the impact on the integer programs is small primarily because the limitations in window size and branch prediction have limited the ILP substantially, making renaming less valuable. In addition, notice that the reduction in available parallelism is significant even if 64 additional integer and 64 additional FP registers are

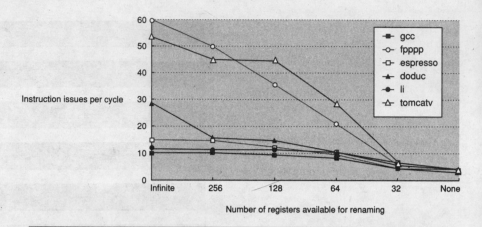

Figure 3.41 The effect of finite numbers of registers available for renaming. Both the number of FP registers and the number of GP registers are increased by the number shown on the x-axis. The effect is most dramatic on the FP programs, although having only 32 extra GP and 32 extra FP registers has a significant impact on all the programs. As stated earlier, we assume a window size of 2K entries and a maximum issue width of 64 instructions. "None" implies no extra registers available.

available for renaming, which is comparable to the number of extra registers available on any existing processor as of 2001.

Although register renaming is obviously critical to performance, an infinite number of registers is not practical. Thus, for the next section, we assume that there are 256 integer and 256 FP registers available for renaming—far more than any anticipated processor has.

The Effects of Imperfect Alias Analysis

Our optimal model assumes that it can perfectly analyze all memory dependences, as well as eliminate all register name dependences. Of course, perfect alias analysis is not possible in practice: The analysis cannot be perfect at compile time, and it requires a potentially unbounded number of comparisons at run time (since the number of simultaneous memory references is unconstrained). Figures 3.43 and 3.44 show the impact of three other models of memory alias analysis, in addition to perfect analysis. The three models are

1. *Global/stack perfect*—This model does perfect predictions for global and stack references and assumes all heap references conflict. This model represents an idealized version of the best compiler-based analysis schemes currently in production. Recent and ongoing research on alias analysis for pointers should improve the handling of pointers to the heap in the future.

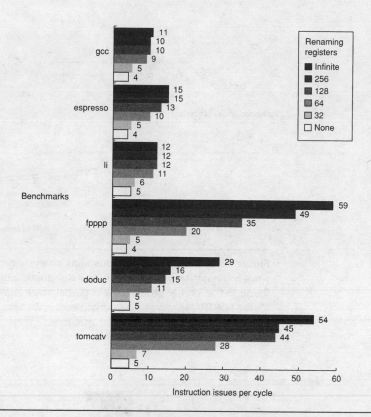

Figure 3.42 The reduction in available parallelism is significant when fewer than an unbounded number of renaming registers are available. For the integer programs, the impact of having more than 64 registers is not seen here. To use more than 64 registers requires uncovering lots of parallelism, which for the integer programs requires essentially perfect branch prediction.

2. *Inspection*—This model examines the accesses to see if they can be determined not to interfere at compile time. For example, if an access uses R10 as a base register with an offset of 20, then another access that uses R10 as a base register with an offset of 100 cannot interfere. In addition, addresses based on registers that point to different allocation areas (such as the global area and the stack area) are assumed never to alias. This analysis is similar to that performed by many existing commercial compilers, though newer compilers can do better, at least for loop-oriented programs.

3. *None*—All memory references are assumed to conflict.

As you might expect, for the FORTRAN programs (where no heap references exist), there is no difference between perfect and global/stack perfect analysis. The global/stack perfect analysis is optimistic, since no compiler could ever find

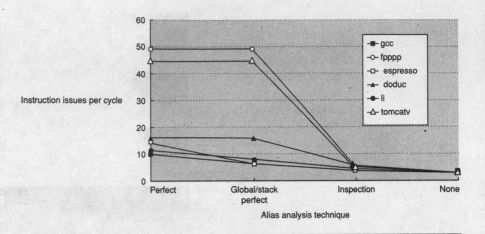

Figure 3.43 The effect of various alias analysis techniques on the amount of ILP. Anything less than perfect analysis has a dramatic impact on the amount of parallelism found in the integer programs, and global/stack analysis is perfect (and unrealizable) for the FORTRAN programs. As we said earlier, we assume a maximum issue width of 64 instructions and a window of 2K instructions.

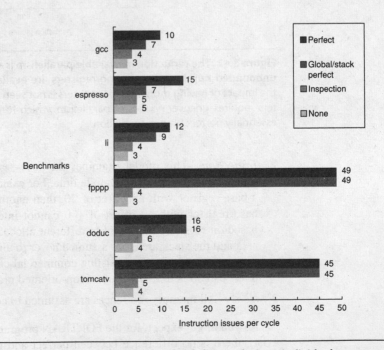

Figure 3.44 The effect of varying levels of alias analysis on individual programs.

all array dependences exactly. The fact that perfect analysis of global and stack references is still a factor of two better than inspection indicates that either sophisticated compiler analysis or dynamic analysis on the fly will be required to obtain much parallelism. In practice, dynamically scheduled processors rely on dynamic memory disambiguation and are limited by three factors:

1. To implement perfect dynamic disambiguation for a given load, we must know the memory addresses of all earlier stores that have not yet committed, since a load may have a dependence through memory on a store. One technique for reducing this limitation on in-order address calculation is memory address speculation. With memory address speculation, the processor either assumes that no such memory dependences exist or uses a hardware prediction mechanism to predict if a dependence exists, stalling the load if a dependence is predicted. Of course, the processor can be wrong about the absence of the dependence, so we need a mechanism to discover if a dependence truly exists and to recover if so. To discover if a dependence exists, the processor examines the destination address of each completing store that is earlier in program order than the given load. If a dependence that should have been enforced occurs, the processor uses the speculative restart mechanism to redo the load and the following instructions. (We will see how this type of address speculation can be supported with instruction set extensions in the next chapter.)

2. Only a small number of memory references can be disambiguated per clock cycle.

3. The number of the load-store buffers determines how much earlier or later in the instruction stream a load or store may be moved.

Both the number of simultaneous disambiguations and the number of the load-store buffers will affect the clock cycle time.

<table>
<tr><td>3.9</td></tr>
</table>

Limitations on ILP for Realizable Processors

In this section we look at the performance of processors with ambitious levels of hardware support equal to or better than what is likely in the next few years. In particular we assume the following fixed attributes:

1. Up to 64 instruction issues per clock with *no* issue restrictions. As we discuss later, the practical implications of very wide issue widths on clock rate, logic complexity, and power may be the most important limitation on exploiting ILP.

2. A tournament predictor with 1K entries and a 16-entry return predictor. This predictor is fairly comparable to the best predictors in 2001; the predictor is not a primary bottleneck.

3. Perfect disambiguation of memory references done dynamically—this is ambitious but perhaps attainable for small window sizes (and hence small issue rates and load-store buffers) or through a memory dependence predictor.

4. Register renaming with 64 additional integer and 64 additional FP registers, exceeding the largest number available on any processor in 2001 (41 and 41 in the Alpha 21264), but probably easily reachable within two or three years.

Figures 3.45 and 3.46 show the result for this configuration as we vary the window size. This configuration is more complex and expensive than any existing implementations, especially in terms of the number of instruction issues, which is more than 10 times larger than the largest number of issues available on any processor in 2001. Nonetheless, it gives a useful bound on what future implementations might yield. The data in these figures are likely to be very optimistic for another reason. There are no issue restrictions among the 64 instructions: They may all be memory references. No one would even contemplate this capability in a processor in the near future. Unfortunately, it is quite difficult to bound the performance of a processor with reasonable issue restrictions; not only is the space of possibilities quite large, but the existence of issue restrictions requires that the parallelism be evaluated with an accurate instruction scheduler, making the cost of studying processors with large numbers of issues very expensive.

In addition, remember that in interpreting these results, cache misses and nonunit latencies have not been taken into account, and both these effects will have significant impact (see the exercises).

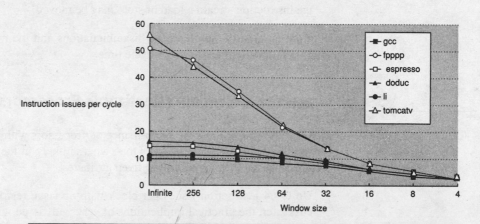

Figure 3.45 The amount of parallelism available for a wide variety of window sizes and a fixed implementation with up to 64 issues per clock. Although there are fewer rename registers than the window size, the fact that all operations have zero latency, and that the number of rename registers equals the issue width, allows the processor to exploit parallelism within the entire window. In a real implementation, the window size and the number of renaming registers must be balanced to prevent one of these factors from overly constraining the issue rate.

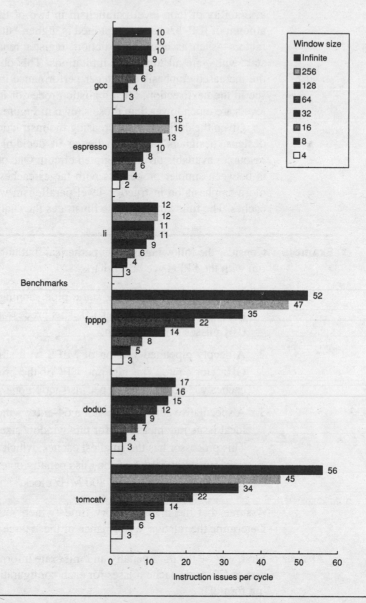

Figure 3.46 **The amount of parallelism available versus the window size for a variety of integer and floating-point programs with up to 64 arbitrary instruction issues per clock.**

Figure 3.45 shows the parallelism versus window size. The most startling observation is that with the realistic processor constraints listed above, the effect of the window size for the integer programs is not as severe as for FP programs. This result points to the key difference between these two types of programs. The availability of loop-level parallelism in two of the FP programs means that the amount of ILP that can be exploited is higher, but that for integer programs other factors—such as branch prediction, register renaming, and less parallelism to start with—are all important limitations. This observation is critical because of the increased emphasis on integer performance in the last few years. As we will see in the next section, for a realistic processor in 2001, the actual performance levels are much lower than those shown in Figure 3.45.

Given the difficulty of increasing the instruction rates with realistic hardware designs, designers face a challenge in deciding how best to use the limited resources available on an integrated circuit. One of the most interesting trade-offs is between simpler processors with larger caches and higher clock rates versus more emphasis on instruction-level parallelism with a slower clock and smaller caches. The following example illustrates the challenges.

Example   Consider the following three hypothetical, but not atypical, processors, which we run with the SPEC gcc benchmark:

1. A simple MIPS two-issue static pipe running at a clock rate of 1 GHz and achieving a pipeline CPI of 1.0. This processor has a cache system that yields 0.01 misses per instruction.

2. A deeply pipelined version of MIPS with slightly smaller caches and a 1.2 GHz clock rate. The pipeline CPI of the processor is 1.2, and the smaller caches yield 0.015 misses per instruction on average.

3. A speculative superscalar with a 64-entry window. It achieves one-half of the ideal issue rate measured for this window size. (Use the data in Figure 3.45.) This processor has the smallest caches, which lead to 0.02 misses per instruction, but it hides 10% of the miss penalty on every miss by dynamic scheduling. This processor has an 800 MHz clock.

Assume that the main memory time (which sets the miss penalty) is 100 ns. Determine the relative performance of these three processors.

Answer   First, we use the miss penalty and miss rate information to compute the contribution to CPI from cache misses for each configuration. We do this with the following formula:

$$\text{Cache CPI} = \text{Misses per instruction} \times \text{Miss penalty}$$

We need to compute the miss penalties for each system:

$$\text{Miss penalty} = \frac{\text{Memory access time}}{\text{Clock cycle}}$$

The clock cycle times for the processors are 1 ns, 0.83 ns, and 1.25 ns, respectively. Hence, the miss penalties are

$$\text{Miss penalty}_1 = \frac{100 \text{ ns}}{1 \text{ ns}} = 100 \text{ cycles}$$

$$\text{Miss penalty}_2 = \frac{100 \text{ ns}}{0.83 \text{ ns}} = 120 \text{ cycles}$$

$$\text{Miss penalty}_3 = \frac{0.9 \times 100 \text{ ns}}{1.25 \text{ ns}} = 72 \text{ cycles}$$

Applying this for each cache:

$$\text{Cache CPI}_1 = 0.01 \times 100 = 1.0$$
$$\text{Cache CPI}_2 = 0.015 \times 120 = 1.8$$
$$\text{Cache CPI}_3 = 0.02 \times 72 = 1.44$$

We know the pipeline CPI contribution for everything but processor 3; its pipeline CPI is given by

$$\text{Pipeline CPI}_3 = \frac{1}{\text{Issue rate}} = \frac{1}{9 \times 0.5} = \frac{1}{4.5} = 0.22$$

Now we can find the CPI for each processor by adding the pipeline and cache CPI contributions.

$$\text{CPI}_1 = 1.0 + 1.0 = 2.0$$
$$\text{CPI}_2 = 1.2 + 1.8 = 3.0$$
$$\text{CPI}_3 = 0.22 + 1.44 = 1.66$$

Since this is the same architecture we can compare instruction execution rates to determine relative performance:

$$\text{Instruction execution rate} = \frac{\text{CR}}{\text{CPI}}$$

$$\text{Instruction execution rate}_1 = \frac{1000 \text{ MHz}}{2} = 500 \text{ MIPS}$$

$$\text{Instruction execution rate}_2 = \frac{1200 \text{ MHz}}{3.0} = 400 \text{ MIPS}$$

$$\text{Instruction execution rate}_3 = \frac{800 \text{ MHz}}{1.66} = 482 \text{ MIPS}$$

In this example, the moderate-issue processor looks best. Of course, the designer building either system 2 or system 3 will probably be alarmed by the large fraction of the system performance lost to cache misses. In Chapter 5 we'll see the most common solution to this problem: adding another level of caches.

Beyond the Limits of This Study

Like any limit study, the study we have examined in this section has its own limitations. We divide these into two classes: limitations that arise even for the perfect speculative processor and limitations that arise for one or more realistic models. Of course, all the limitations in the first class apply to the second. The most important limitations that apply even to the perfect model are

1. *WAR and WAW hazards through memory*—The study eliminated WAW and WAR hazards through register renaming, but not in memory usage. Although at first glance it might appear that such circumstances are rare (especially WAW hazards), they arise due to the allocation of stack frames. A called procedure reuses the memory locations of a previous procedure on the stack, and this can lead to WAW and WAR hazards that are unnecessarily limiting. Austin and Sohi [1992] examine this issue.

2. *Unnecessary dependences*—With infinite numbers of registers, all but true register data dependences are removed. There are, however, dependences arising from either recurrences or code generation conventions that introduce unnecessary true data dependences. One example of these is the dependence on the control variable in a simple do loop: Since the control variable is incremented on every loop iteration, the loop contains at least one dependence. As we show in the next chapter, loop unrolling and aggressive algebraic optimization can remove such dependent computation. Wall's study includes a limited amount of such optimizations, but applying them more aggressively could lead to increased amounts of ILP. In addition, certain code generation conventions introduce unneeded dependences, in particular the use of return address registers and a register for the stack pointer (which is incremented and decremented in the call/return sequence). Wall removes the effect of the return address register, but the use of a stack pointer in the linkage convention can cause "unnecessary" dependences. Postiff et al. [1999] explored the advantages of removing this constraint.

3. *Overcoming the data flow limit*—A recently proposed idea to boost ILP, which goes beyond the capability of the study above, is *value prediction*. Value prediction consists of predicting data values and speculating on the prediction. There are two obvious uses of this scheme: predicting data values and speculating on the result, and predicting address values for memory alias elimination. The latter affects parallelism only under less than perfect circumstances, as we discuss shortly.

Value prediction has possibly the most potential for increasing ILP. *Data value prediction and speculation* predicts data values and uses them in destination instructions speculatively. Such speculation allows multiple dependent instructions to be executed in the same clock cycle, thus increasing the potential ILP. To be effective, however, data values must be predicted very accurately, since they will be used by consuming instructions, just as if they were correctly computed. Thus, inaccurate prediction will lead to incorrect speculation and recovery, just as when branches are mispredicted.

One insight that gives some hope is that certain instructions produce the same values with high frequency, so it may be possible to selectively predict values for certain instructions with high accuracy. Obviously, perfect data value prediction would lead to infinite parallelism, since every value of every instruction could be predicted a priori.

Thus, studying the effect of value prediction in true limit studies is difficult and has not yet been done. Several studies have examined the role of value prediction in exploiting ILP in more realistic processors (e.g., Lipasti, Wilkerson, and Shen [1996]). The extent to which general value prediction will be used in real processors remains unclear at the present.

For a less than perfect processor, there are several ideas, that have been proposed, which could expose more ILP. We mention the two most important here:

1. *Address value prediction and speculation*—This technique predicts memory address values and speculates by reordering loads and stores. It eliminates the need to compute effective addresses to determine whether memory references can be reordered, and could provide better aliasing analysis than any practical scheme. Because we need not actually predict data values, but only determine if effective addresses are identical, this type of prediction can be accomplished by simpler techniques. Recent processors include limited versions of this technique, and it can be expected that future implementations of address value prediction may yield an approximation to perfect alias analysis, allowing processors to eliminate this limit to exploiting ILP.

2. *Speculating on multiple paths*—This idea was discussed by Lam and Wilson [1992] and explored in the study covered in this section. By speculating on multiple paths, the cost of incorrect recovery is reduced and more parallelism can be uncovered. It only makes sense to evaluate this scheme for a limited number of branches because the hardware resources required grow exponentially. Wall [1993] provides data for speculating in both directions on up to eight branches. Whether such schemes ever become practical, or whether it will always be better to devote the equivalent silicon area to better branch predictors remains to be seen. In Chapter 6, we discuss thread-level parallelism and the use of speculative threads.

It is critical to understand that none of the limits in this section are fundamental in the sense that overcoming them requires a change in the laws of physics! Instead, they are practical limitations that imply the existence of some formidable barriers to exploiting additional ILP. These limitations—whether they be window size, alias detection, or branch prediction—represent challenges for designers and researchers to overcome! As we discuss in the concluding remarks, there are a variety of other practical issues that may actually be the more serious limits to exploiting ILP in future processors.

3.10   Putting It All Together: The P6 Microarchitecture

The Intel P6 microarchitecture forms the basis for the Pentium Pro, Pentium II, and Pentium III. In addition to some specialized instruction set extensions (MMX and SSE), these three processors differ in clock rate, cache architecture, and memory interface, as summarized in Figure 3.47.

The P6 microarchitecture is a dynamically scheduled processor that translates each IA-32 instruction to a series of micro-operations (uops) that are executed by the pipeline; the uops are similar to typical RISC instructions. Up to three IA-32 instructions are fetched, decoded, and translated into uops every clock cycle. If an IA-32 instruction requires more than four uops, it is implemented by a microcoded sequence that generates the necessary uops in multiple clock cycles. The maximum number of uops that may be generated per clock cycle is six, with four allocated to the first IA-32 instruction and one uop slot to each of the remaining two IA-32 instructions.

The uops are executed by an out-of-order speculative pipeline using register renaming and a ROB. This pipeline is very similar to that in Section 3.7, except that the functional unit capability and the sizes of buffers are different. Up to three uops per clock can be renamed and dispatched to the reservation stations; instruction commit can also complete up to three uops per clock. The pipeline is structured in 14 stages composed of the following:

■ Eight stages are used for in-order instruction fetch, decode, and dispatch. The next instruction is selected during fetch using a 512-entry, two-level branch predictor. The decode and issue stages including register renaming (using 40 virtual registers) and dispatch to one of 20 reservation stations and to one of 40 entries in the ROB.

■ Three stages are used for out-of-order execution in one of five separate functional units (integer unit, FP unit, branch unit, memory address unit, and memory access unit). The execution pipeline is from 1 cycle (for simple integer ALU operations) to 32 cycles for FP divide. The issue rate and latency of some typical operations appear in Figure 3.48.

■ Three stages are used for instruction commit.

Processor	First ship date	Clock rate range	L1 cache	L2 cache
Pentium Pro	1995	100–200 MHz	8 KB instr. + 8 KB data	256 KB–1024 KB
Pentium II	1998	233–450 MHz	16 KB instr. + 16 KB data	256 KB–512 KB
Pentium II Xeon	1999	400–450 MHz	16 KB instr. + 16 KB data	512 KB–2 MB
Celeron	1999	500–900 MHz	16 KB instr. + 16 KB data	128 KB
Pentium III	1999	450–1100 MHz	16 KB instr. + 16 KB data	256 KB–512 KB
Pentium III Xeon	2000	700–900 MHz	16 KB instr. + 16 KB data	1 MB–2 MB

Figure 3.47 **The Intel processors based on the P6 microarchitecture and their important differences.** In the Pentium Pro, the processor and specialized cache SRAMs were integrated into a multichip module. In the Pentium II, standard SRAMs are used. In the Pentium III, there is either an on-chip 256 KB L2 cache or an off-chip 512 KB cache. The Xeon versions are intended for server applications; they use an off-chip L2 and support multiprocessing. The Pentium II added the MMX instruction extension, while the Pentium III added the SSE extensions.

Instruction name	Pipeline stages	Repeat rate
Integer ALU	1	1
Integer load	3	1
Integer multiply	4	1
FP add	3	1
FP multiply	5	2
FP divide (64-bit)	32	32

Figure 3.48 The latency and repeat rate for common uops in the P6 microarchitecture. A repeat rate of 1 means that the unit is fully pipelined, and a repeat rate of 2 means that operations can start every other cycle.

Figure 3.49 shows a high-level picture of the pipeline, the throughput of each stage, and the capacity of buffers between stages. A stage will not achieve its throughput if either the input buffer cannot supply enough operands or the output buffer lacks capacity. In addition, internal restrictions or dynamic events (such as a cache miss) can cause a stall within all the units. For example, an instruction cache miss will prevent the instruction fetch stage from generating 16 bytes of instructions; similarly, three instructions can be decoded only under certain restrictions in how they map to uops.

Performance of the Pentium Pro Implementation

This section looks at some performance measurements for the Pentium Pro implementation. The Pentium Pro has the smallest set of primary caches among the P6-based microprocessors; it has, however, a high-bandwidth interface to the secondary caches. Thus, while we would expect more performance to be lost to

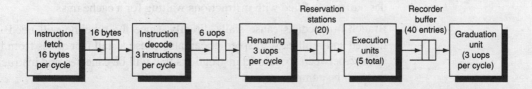

Figure 3.49 The P6 processor pipeline showing the throughput of each stage and the total buffering provided between stages. The buffering provided is either as bytes (before instruction decoding), as uops (after decoding and translation), as reservation station entries (after issue), or as reorder buffer entries (after execution). There are five execution units, each of which can potentially initiate a new uop every cycle (though some are not fully pipelined as shown in Figure 3.48). Recall that during renaming an instruction reserves a reorder buffer entry, so that stalls can occur during renaming/issue when the reorder buffer is full. Notice that the instruction fetch unit can fill the entire prefetch buffer in one cycle; if the buffer is partially full, fewer bytes will be fetched.

cache misses than on the Pentium II, the relatively faster and higher-bandwidth secondary caches should reduce this effect somewhat. The measurements in this section use a 200 MHz Pentium Pro with a 256 KB secondary cache and a 66 MHz main memory bus. The data for this section comes from a study by Bhandarkar and Ding [1997] that uses SPEC CPU95 as the benchmark set.

Understanding the performance of a dynamically scheduled processor is complex. To see why, consider first that the actual CPI will be significantly greater than the ideal CPI, which in the case of the P6 architecture is 0.33. If the effective CPI is, for example, 0.66, then the processor can fall behind, achieving a CPI of 1, during some part of the execution and subsequently catch up by issuing and graduating two instructions per clock. Furthermore, consider how stalls actually occur in dynamically scheduled, speculative processors. Since cache misses are overlapped, branch outcomes are speculated, and data dependences are dynamically scheduled around, what does a stall actually mean? In the limit, stalls occur when the processor fails to commit its full complement of instructions in a clock cycle.

Of course, the lack of instructions to complete means that, somewhere earlier in the pipeline, some instructions failed to make progress (or in the limit, failed to even issue). This blockage can occur for a combination of several reasons in the Pentium Pro:

1. Less than three IA-32 instructions could be fetched because of instruction cache misses.

2. Less than three instructions could issue because one of the three IA-32 instructions generated more than the allocated number of uops (four for the first instruction and one for each of the other two).

3. Not all the micro-operations generated in a clock cycle could issue because of a shortage of reservation stations or reorder buffers.

4. A data dependence led to a stall because every reservation station or the reorder buffer was filled with instructions that are dependent.

5. A data cache miss led to a stall because every reservation station or the reorder buffer was filled with instructions waiting for a cache miss.

6. Branch mispredicts cause stalls directly, since the pipeline will need to be flushed and refilled. A mispredict can also cause a stall that arises from interference between speculated instructions that will be canceled and instructions that will be completed.

Because of the ability to overlap potential stall cycles from multiple sources, it is difficult to assign the cost of a stall cycle to any single cause. Instead, we will look at the contributions to stalls and conclude by showing that the actual CPI is less than what would be observed if no overlap of stalls were possible.

Stalls in the Decode Cycle

To start, let's look at the rate at which instructions are fetched and issued. Although the processor attempts to fetch three instructions every cycle, it cannot maintain this rate if the instruction cache generates a miss, if one of the instructions requires more than the number of micro-operations available to it, or if the six-entry uop issue buffer is full. Figure 3.50 shows the fraction of time in which 0, 1, 2, or 3 IA-32 instructions are decoded.

Figure 3.51 breaks out the stalls at decode time according to whether they are due to instruction cache stalls, which lead to less than three instructions available to decode, or resource capacity limitations, which means that a lack of reservation stations or reorder buffers prevents a uop from issuing. Failure to issue a uop eventually leads to a full uop buffer (recall that it has six entries), which then blocks instruction decode.

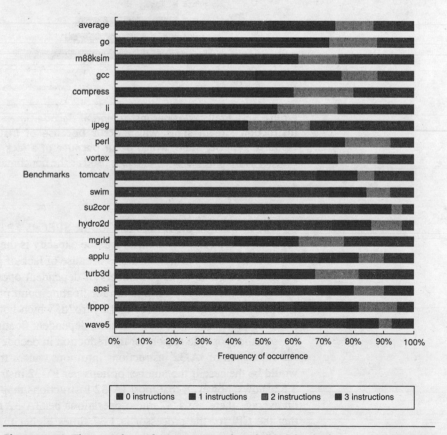

Figure 3.50 The number of instructions decoded each clock varies widely and depends upon a variety of factors, including the instruction cache miss rate, the instruction decode rate, and the downstream execution rate. On average for these benchmarks, 0.87 instructions are decoded per cycle.

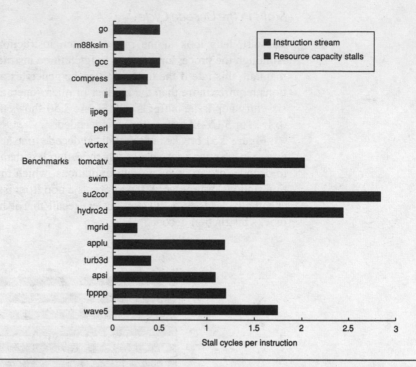

Figure 3.51 Stall cycles per instruction at decode time and the breakdown due to instruction stream stalls, which occur because of instruction cache misses, or resource capacity stalls, which occur because of a lack of reservation stations or reorder buffer entries. SPEC CPU95 is used as the benchmark suite for this and the rest of the measurements in this section.

The instruction cache miss rate for the SPEC95 FP benchmarks is small, and, for most of the FP benchmarks, resource capacity is the primary cause of decode stalls. The resource limitation arises because of lack of progress further down the pipeline, due either to large numbers of dependent operations or to long latency operations; the latter is a limitation for floating-point programs in particular. For example, the programs su2cor and hydro2d, which both have large numbers of resource stalls, also have long-running, dependent floating-point calculations.

Another possible reason for the reduction in decode throughput could be that the expansion of IA-32 instructions into uops causes the uop buffer to fill. This would be the case if the number of uops per IA-32 instruction were large. Figure 3.52 shows, however, that most IA-32 instructions map to a single uop, and that on average there are 1.37 micro-operations per IA-32 instruction (which means that the CPI for the processor is 1.37 times higher than the CPI of the micro-operations). Surprisingly, the integer programs take slightly more micro-operations per IA-32 instruction on average than the floating-point programs!

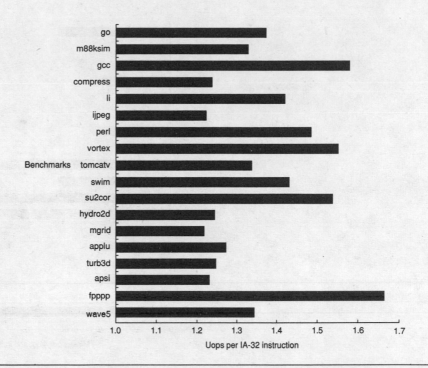

Figure 3.52 The number of micro-operations per IA-32 instruction. Other than fpppp, the integer programs typically require more uops. Most instructions will take only one uop, and, thus, the uop buffer fills primarily because of delays in the execution unit.

Data Cache Behavior

Figure 3.53 shows the number of first-level (L1) and second-level (L2) cache misses per thousand instructions. The L2 misses, although smaller in number, cost more than five times as much as L1 misses and, thus, dominate in some applications. Instruction cache misses are a minor effect in most of the programs. Although the speculative, out-of-order pipeline may be effective at hiding stalls due to L1 data misses, it cannot hide the long latency L2 cache misses, and L2 miss rates and effective CPI track similarly.

Branch Performance and Speculation Costs

Branch-target addresses are predicted with a 512-entry branch-target buffer (BTB), based on the two-level adaptive scheme of Yeh and Patt, which is similar to the predictor described on page 206. If the BTB does not hit, a static prediction is used: backward branches are predicted taken (and have a one-cycle penalty if correctly predicted) and forward branches are predicted not taken (and have no

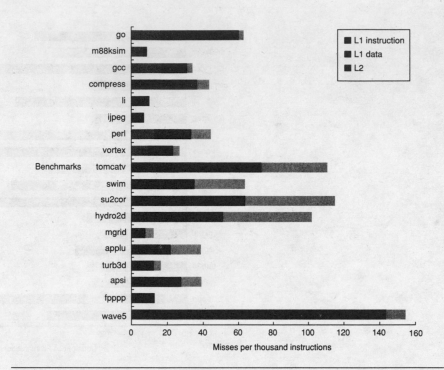

Figure 3.53 The number of misses per thousand instructions for the primary (L1) and secondary (L2) caches. Recall that the primary consists of a pair of 8 KB caches and the secondary is 256 KB. Because the cost of a secondary cache is about five times higher, the potential stalls from L2 cache misses are more serious than a simple frequency comparison would show.

penalty if correctly predicted). Branch mispredicts have both a direct performance penalty, which is between 10 and 15 cycles, and an indirect penalty due to the overhead of incorrectly speculated instructions, which is essentially impossible to measure. (Sometimes misspeculated instructions can result in a performance advantage, but this is likely to be rare.) Figure 3.54 shows the fraction of branches mispredicted either because of BTB misses or because of incorrect predictions. On average about 20% of the branches either miss or are mispredicted and use the simple static predictor rule.

To understand the secondary effects arising from speculation that will be canceled, Figure 3.55 plots the average number of speculated uops that do not commit. On average about 1.2 times as many uops issue as commit. By factoring in the branch frequency and the mispredict rates, we find that, on average, each mispredicted branch issues 20 uops that will later be canceled. Unfortunately, accessing the exact costs of incorrectly speculated operations is virtually impossible, since they may cost nothing (if they do not block the progress of other instructions) or may be very costly.

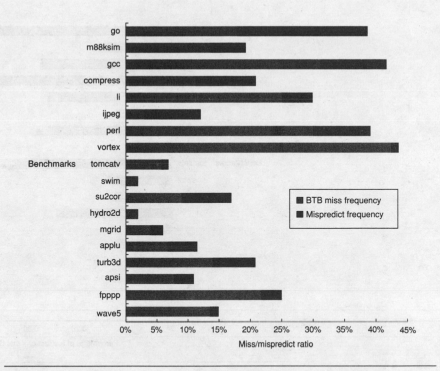

Figure 3.54 The BTB miss frequency dominates the mispredict frequency, arguing for a larger predictor, even at the cost of a slightly higher mispredict rate.

Putting the Pieces Together: Overall Performance of the P6 Pipeline

Overall performance depends on the rate at which instructions actually complete and commit. Figure 3.56 shows the fraction of the time that zero, one, two, or three uops commit. On average, one uop commits per cycle, but, as Figure 3.56 shows, 23% of the time three uops commit in a cycle. This distribution demonstrates the ability of a dynamically scheduled pipeline to fall behind (on 55% of the cycles, no uops commit) and later catch up (31% of the cycles have two or three uops committing).

Figure 3.57 sums up all the possible issue and stall cycles per IA-32 instruction and compares it to the actual measured CPI on the processor. The uop cycles in Figure 3.57 are the number of cycles per instruction assuming that the processor sustains three uops per cycle and accounting for the number of uops required per IA-32 instruction for that benchmark. The sum of the issue cycles plus stalls exceeds the actual measured CPI by an average of 1.37, varying from 1.0 to 1.75. This difference arises from the ability of the dynamically scheduled pipeline to overlap and hide different classes of stalls arising in different types of programs. The average CPI is 1.15 for the SPECint programs and 2.0 for the SPECFP programs. The P6 microarchitecture is clearly designed to focus on integer programs.

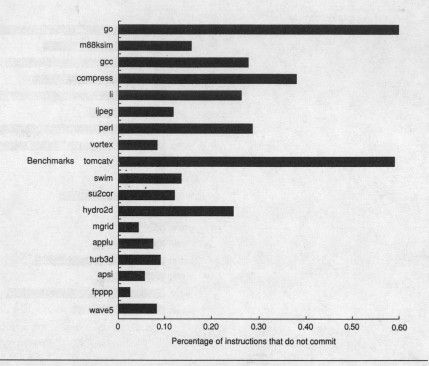

Figure 3.55 The "speculation factor" can be thought of as the fraction of issued instructions that do not commit. For the benchmarks with high speculation factors (> 30%), there are almost certainly some negative performance effects.

The Pentium III versus the Pentium 4

The microarchitecture of the Pentium 4, which is called NetBurst, is similar to that of the Pentium III (called the P6 microarchitecture): Both fetch up to three IA-32 instructions per cycle, decode them into micro-ops, and send the uops to an out-of-order execution engine that can graduate up to three uops per cycle. There are, however, many differences that are designed to allow the NetBurst microarchitecture to operate at a significantly higher clock rate than the P6 microarchitecture and to help maintain or close the peak to sustained execution throughput. Among the most important of these are the following:

▪ NetBurst has a much deeper pipeline. P6 requires about 10 clock cycles from the time a simple add instruction is fetched until the availability of its results. In comparison, NetBurst takes about 20 cycles, including 2 cycles reserved simply to drive results across the chip!

▪ NetBurst uses register renaming (like the MIPS R10K and the Alpha 21264) rather than the reorder buffer, which is used in P6. Use of register renaming allows many more outstanding results (potentially up to 128) in NetBurst versus the 40 that are permitted in P6.

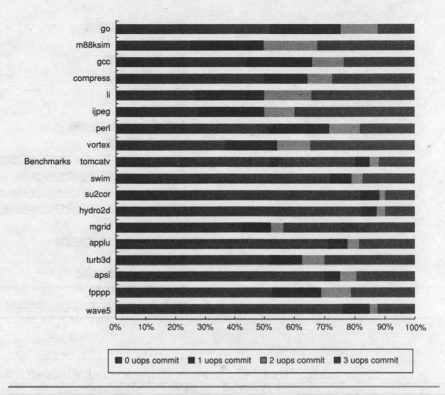

Figure 3.56 The breakdown in how often zero, one, two, or three uops commit in a cycle. The average number of uop completions per cycle is distributed as 0 completions, 55% of the cycles; 1 completion, 13% of the cycles; 2 completions, 8% of the cycles; and 3 completions, 23% of the cycles.

- There are seven integer execution units in NetBurst versus five in P6. The additions are an additional integer ALU and an additional address computation unit.

- An aggressive ALU (operating at twice the clock rate) and an aggressive data cache lead to lower latencies for the basic ALU operations (effectively one-half a clock cycle in NetBurst versus one in P6) and for data loads (effectively two cycles in NetBurst versus three in P6). These high-speed functional units are critical to lowering the potential increase in stalls from the very deep pipeline.

- NetBurst uses a sophisticated trace cache (see Chapter 5) to improve instruction fetch performance, while P6 uses a conventional prefetch buffer and instruction cache.

- NetBurst has a branch-target buffer that is eight times larger and has an improved prediction algorithm.

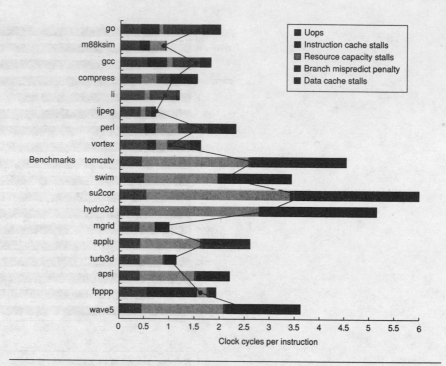

Figure 3.57 **The actual CPI (shown as a line) is lower than the sum of the number of uop cycles plus all stalls.** The uop cycles assume that three uops are completed every cycle and include the number of uops per instruction for the specific benchmark. All other stalls are the actual number of stall cycles. (TLB stalls that contribute less than 0.1 stalls/cycle are omitted.) The overall CPI is lower than the sum of the uop cycles plus stalls through the use of dynamic scheduling.

- NetBurst has a level 1 data cache that is 8 KB compared to P6's 16 KB L1 data cache. NetBurst's larger level 2 cache (256 KB) with higher bandwidth should offset this disadvantage.

- NetBurst implements the new SSE2 floating-point instructions that allow two floating operations per instruction; these operations are structured as a 128-bit SIMD or short-vector structure. As we saw in Chapter 1, this gives Pentium 4 a considerable advantage over Pentium III on floating-point code.

A Brief Performance Comparison of the Pentium III and Pentium 4

As we saw in Figure 1.28 in the first chapter, the Pentium 4 at 1.7 GHz outperforms the Pentium III at 1 GHz by a factor of 1.26 for SPEC CINT2000 and 1.8 for SPEC CFP2000. Figure 3.58 shows the performance of the Pentium III and Pentium 4 on four of the SPEC benchmarks that are in both SPEC95 and SPEC2000. The floating-point benchmarks clearly take advantage of the new instruction set extensions and yield an advantage of 1.6–1.7 above clock rate scaling.

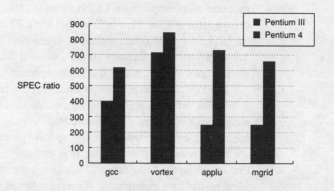

Figure 3.58   The performance of the Pentium 4 for four SPEC2000 benchmarks (two integer, gcc and vortex, and two floating point, applu and mgrid) exceeds the Pentium III by a factor of between 1.2 and 2.9. This exceeds the purely clock speed advantage for the floating-point benchmarks and is less than the clock speed advantage for the integer programs.

For the two integer benchmarks, the situation is somewhat different. In both cases the Pentium 4 delivers less than linear scaling with the increase in clock rate. If we assume the instruction counts are identical for integer codes on the two processors, then the CPI for the two integer benchmarks is higher on the Pentium 4 (by a factor of 1.1 for gcc and a factor of 1.5 for vortex). Looking at the data for the Pentium Pro, we can see that these benchmarks have relatively low level 2 miss rates and that they hide much of their level 1 miss penalty through dynamic scheduling and speculation. Thus, it is likely that the deeper pipeline and larger pipeline stall penalties on the Pentium 4 lead to a higher CPI for these two programs and reduce some of the gain from the high clock rate.

One interesting question is, Why did the designers at Intel decide on the approach they took for the Pentium 4? On the surface, the alternative of doubling the issue rate of the Pentium III, as opposed to doubling the pipeline depth and the clock rate, looks at least as attractive. Of course, there are numerous changes between the two architectures, making an exact analysis of the trade-offs difficult. Furthermore, because of the changes in the floating-point instruction set, a comparison of the two pipeline organizations needs to focus on integer performance.

There are two sources of performance loss that arise if we compare the deeper pipeline of the Pentium 4 with that of the Pentium III. The first is the increase in clock overhead that occurs due to increased clock skew and jitter. This overhead is given by the difference between the ideal clock speed and the achieved clock speed. In comparable technologies, the Pentium 4 clock rate is between 1.7 and 1.8 times higher than the Pentium III clock rate. This range represents between 85% and 90% of the ideal clock rate, which is 2 times higher.

The second source of performance loss is the increase in CPI that arises from the deeper pipeline. We can estimate this by taking the ratio in clock rate versus the ratio in achieved overall performance. Using SPECint as the performance measure and comparing a 1 GHz Pentium III to a 1.7 GHz Pentium 4, the performance ratio is 1.26. This tells us that the CPI for SPECint on the Pentium 4 must be 1.7/1.26 = 1.34 times higher, or alternatively that the Pentium 4 is about 1.26/ 1.7 = 74% of the efficiency of the Pentium III. Of course, some of this loss is in the memory system, rather than in the pipeline.

The key question is whether doubling the issue width would result in a greater than 1.26 times overall performance gain. This is a very difficult question to answer, since we must account for the improvement in pipeline CPI, the relative increase in cost of memory stalls, and the potential clock rate impact of a processor with twice the issue width. It is unlikely, looking at the data in Section 3.9, that doubling the issue rate will achieve better than a factor of 1.5 improvement in ideal instruction throughput. When combined with the potential impact on clock rate and the memory system costs, it appears that the choice of the Intel Pentium 4 designers to favor a deeper pipeline rather than wider issue is at least a reasonable design choice.

3.11 Another View: Thread-Level Parallelism

Throughout this chapter, our discussion has focused on exploiting parallelism in programs by finding and using the parallelism among instructions within the program. Although this approach has the great advantage that it is reasonably transparent to the programmer, as we have seen, ILP can be quite limited or hard to exploit in some applications. Furthermore, there may be significant parallelism occurring naturally at a higher level in the application that cannot be exploited with the approaches discussed in this chapter. For example, an online transaction-processing system has natural parallelism among the multiple queries and updates that are presented by requests. These queries and updates can be processed mostly in parallel, since they are largely independent of one another. Similarly, embedded applications often have natural high-level parallelism. For example, a processor in a network router can exploit parallelism among independent packets.

This higher-level parallelism is called *thread-level parallelism* (TLP) because it is logically structured as separate threads of execution. A *thread* is a separate process with its own instructions and data. A thread may represent a process that is part of a parallel program consisting of multiple processes, or it may represent an independent program on its own. Each thread has all the state (instructions, data, PC, register state, and so on) necessary to allow it to execute. Unlike instruction-level parallelism, which exploits implicit parallel operations within a loop or straight-line code segment, thread-level parallelism is explicitly represented by the use of multiple threads of execution that are inherently parallel.

Thread-level parallelism is an important alternative to instruction-level parallelism primarily because it could be more cost-effective to exploit than instruction-level parallelism. There are many important applications where thread-level parallelism occurs naturally, as it does in many server applications. In other cases, the software is being written from scratch, and expressing the inherent parallelism is easy, as is true in some embedded applications. Chapter 6 explores multiprocessors and the support they provide for thread-level parallelism.

The investment required to program applications to expose thread-level parallelism makes it costly to switch the large established base of software to multiprocessors. This is especially true for desktop applications, where the natural parallelism that is present in many server environments is harder to find. Thus, despite the potentially greater efficiency of exploiting thread-level parallelism, it is likely that ILP-based approaches will continue to be the primary focus for desktop-oriented processors.

3.12   Crosscutting Issues: Using an ILP Data Path to Exploit TLP

Thread-level and instruction-level parallelism exploit two different kinds of parallel structure in a program. One natural question to ask is whether it is possible for a processor oriented at instruction-level parallelism to exploit thread-level parallelism.

The motivation for this question comes from the observation that a data path designed to exploit higher amounts of ILP will find that functional units are often idle because of either stalls or dependences in the code. Could the parallelism among threads be used as a source of independent instructions that might keep the processor busy during stalls? Could this thread-level parallelism be used to employ the functional units that would otherwise lie idle when insufficient ILP exists?

Multithreading, and a variant called *simultaneous multithreading,* take advantage of these insights by using thread-level parallelism either as the primary form of parallelism exploitation—for example, on top of a simple pipelined processor—or as a method that works in conjunction with ILP mechanisms. In both cases, multiple threads are being executed within a single processor by duplicating the thread-specific state (program counter, registers, and so on) and sharing the other processor resources by multiplexing them among the threads. Since multithreading is a method for exploiting thread-level parallelism, we discuss it in more depth in Chapter 6.

3.13   Fallacies and Pitfalls

Our first fallacy has two parts: First, simple rules do not hold, and, second, the choice of benchmarks plays a major role.

Fallacy   *Processors with lower CPIs will always be faster.*

Fallacy   *Processors with faster clock rates will always be faster.*

Although a lower CPI is certainly better, sophisticated pipelines typically have slower clock rates than processors with simple pipelines. In applications with limited ILP or where the parallelism cannot be exploited by the hardware resources, the faster clock rate often wins. But, when significant ILP exists, a processor that exploits lots of ILP may be better.

The IBM Power3 processor is designed for high-performance FP and is capable of sustaining four instructions per clock, including two FP and two load-store instructions. The Power3-II offers a 400 MHz clock rate in 2001 and achieves a SPEC CINT2000 peak rating of 249 and a SPEC CFP2000 peak rating of 344. The Pentium III has a comparably aggressive integer pipeline but has less aggressive FP units. An 800 MHz Pentium III in 2001 achieves a SPEC CINT2000 peak rating of 344 and a SPEC CFP2000 peak rating of 237.

Thus, the faster clock rate of the Pentium III (800 MHz versus 400 MHz) leads to an integer rating that is 1.38 times higher than the Power3, but the more aggressive FP pipeline of the Power3 (and a better instruction set for floating point) leads to a lower CPI. If we assume comparable instruction counts, the Power3 CPI must be almost three times better than that of the Pentium III for the SPEC FP2000 benchmarks, leading to an overall performance advantage of 1.45.

Of course, this fallacy is nothing more than a restatement of a pitfall from Chapter 2 about comparing processors using only one part of the performance equation.

Pitfall *Emphasizing an improvement in CPI by increasing issue rate while sacrificing clock rate can lead to lower performance.*

The TI SuperSPARC design is a flexible multiple-issue processor capable of issuing up to three instructions per cycle. It had a 1994 clock rate of 60 MHz. The HP PA 7100 processor is a simple dual-issue processor (integer and FP combination) with a 99 MHz clock rate in 1994. The HP processor is faster on all the SPEC92 benchmarks except two of the integer benchmarks and one FP benchmark, as shown in Figure 3.59. On average, the two processors are close on integer, but the HP processor is about 1.5 times faster on the FP benchmarks. Of course, differences in compiler technology, detailed trade-offs in the processor (including the cache size and memory organization), and the implementation technology could all contribute to the performance differences.

The potential of multiple-issue techniques has caused *many* designers to focus on improving CPI while possibly not focusing adequately on the trade-off in cycle time incurred when implementing these sophisticated techniques. This inclination arises at least partially because it is easier with good simulation tools to evaluate the impact of enhancements that affect CPI than it is to evaluate the cycle time impact.

There are two factors that lead to this outcome. First, it is difficult to know the clock rate impact of an approach until the design is well under way, and then it may be too late to make large changes in the organization. Second, the design simulation tools available for determining and improving CPI are generally better than those available for determining and improving cycle time.

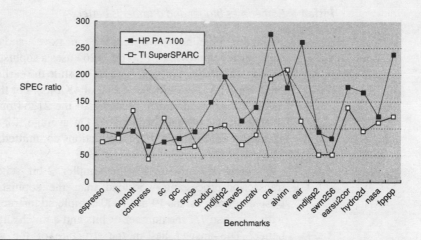

Figure 3.59 The performance of a 99 MHz HP PA 7100 processor versus a 60 MHz SuperSPARC. The comparison is based on 1994 measurements.

In understanding the complex interaction between cycle time and various organizational approaches, the experience of the designers seems to be one of the most valuable factors. With ever more complex designs, however, even the best designers find it hard to understand the complex trade-offs between clock rate and other organizational decisions. At the end of Section 3.14, we will see the opposite problem: how emphasizing a high clock rate, obtained through a deeper pipeline, can lead to degraded CPI and a lower performance gain than might be expected based solely on the higher clock rate.

Pitfall   *Improving only one aspect of a multiple-issue processor and expecting overall performance improvement.*

This pitfall is simply a restatement of Amdahl's Law. A designer might simply look at a design, see a poor branch-prediction mechanism, and improve it, expecting to see significant performance improvements. The difficulty is that many factors limit the performance of multiple-issue machines, and improving one aspect of a processor often exposes some other aspect that previously did not limit performance.

We can see examples of this in the data on ILP. For example, looking just at the effect of branch prediction in Figure 3.39, we can see that going from a standard 2-bit predictor to a tournament predictor significantly improves the parallelism in espresso (from an issue rate of 7 to an issue rate of 12). If the processor provides only 32 registers for renaming, however, the amount of parallelism is limited to 5 issues per clock cycle, even with a branch-prediction scheme better than either alternative.

Pitfall *Sometimes bigger and dumber is better.*

Advanced pipelines have focused on novel and increasingly sophisticated schemes for improving CPI. The 21264 uses a sophisticated tournament predictor with a total of 29K bits (see page 207), while the earlier 21164 uses a simple 2-bit predictor with 2K entries (or a total of 4K bits). For the SPEC95 benchmarks, the more sophisticated branch predictor of the 21264 outperforms the simpler 2-bit scheme on all but one benchmark. On average, for SPECint95, the 21264 has 11.5 mispredictions per 1000 instructions committed, while the 21164 has about 16.5 mispredictions.

Somewhat surprisingly, the simpler 2-bit scheme works better for the transaction-processing workload than the sophisticated 21264 scheme (17 mispredictions versus 19 per 1000 completed instructions)! How can a predictor with less than 1/7 the number of bits and a much simpler scheme actually work better? The answer lies in the structure of the workload. The transaction-processing workload has a very large code size (more than an order of magnitude larger than any SPEC95 benchmark) with a large branch frequency. The ability of the 21164 predictor to hold twice as many branch predictions based on purely local behavior (2K versus the 1K local predictor in the 21264) seems to provide a slight advantage.

This pitfall also reminds us that different applications can produce different behaviors. As processors become more sophisticated, including specific microarchitectural features aimed at some particular program behavior, it is likely that different applications will see more divergent behavior.

3.14 Concluding Remarks

The tremendous interest in multiple-issue organizations came about because of an interest in improving performance without affecting the standard uniprocessor programming model. Although taking advantage of ILP is conceptually simple, the design problems are amazingly complex in practice. It is extremely difficult to achieve the performance you might expect from a simple first-level analysis.

The trade-offs between increasing clock speed and decreasing CPI through multiple issue are extremely hard to quantify. In the 1995 edition of this book, we stated:

> Although you might expect that it is possible to build an advanced multiple-issue processor with a high clock rate, a factor of 1.5 to 2 in clock rate has consistently separated the highest clock rate processors and the most sophisticated multiple-issue processors. It is simply too early to tell whether this difference is due to fundamental implementation trade-offs, or to the difficulty of dealing with the complexities in multiple-issue processors, or simply a lack of experience in implementing such processors.

Given the availability of the Alpha 21264 at 800 MHz, the Pentium III at 1.1 GHz, the AMD Athlon at 1.3 GHz, and the Pentium 4 at 2 GHz, it is clear that the limitation was primarily our understanding of how to build such processors. It is also likely that the first generation of CAD tools, which were used for more than 2 million logic transistors, represented a limitation.

One insight that was clear in 1995 and remains clear in 2001 is that the peak to sustained performance ratios for multiple-issue processors are often quite large and typically grow as the issue rate grows. Thus, increasing the clock rate by X is almost always a better choice than increasing the issue width by X, although often the clock rate increase may rely largely on deeper pipelining, substantially narrowing the advantage. This insight probably played a role in motivating Intel to pursue a deeper pipeline for the Pentium 4, rather than trying to increase the issue width. Recall, however, the fundamental observation we made in Chapter 1 about the improvement in semiconductor technologies: The number of transistors available grows faster than the speed of the transistors. Thus, a strategy that focuses only on deeper pipelining may not be the best use of the technology in the long run.

Rather than embracing dramatic new approaches in microarchitecture, the last five years have focused on raising the clock rates of multiple-issue machines and narrowing the gap between peak and sustained performance. The dynamically scheduled, multiple-issue processors announced in the last two years (the Alpha 21264, the Pentium III and 4, and the AMD Athlon) have the same basic structure and similar sustained issue rates (three to four instructions per clock) as the first dynamically scheduled, multiple-issue processors announced in 1995! But the clock rates are 4 to 8 times higher, the caches are 2 to 4 times bigger, there are 2 to 4 times as many renaming registers, and twice as many load-store units! The result is performance that is 6 to 10 times higher.

All the leading-edge desktop and server processors are large, complex chips with more than 15 million transistors per processor. Notwithstanding, a simple two-way superscalar that issues FP instructions in parallel with integer instructions, or dual-issues integer instructions (but not memory references), can probably be built with little impact on clock rate and with a tiny die size (in comparison to today's processors). Such a processor should perform well with a higher sustained to peak ratio than the high-end wide-issue processors and can be amazingly cost-effective. As a result, the high end of the embedded space has recently moved to multiple-issue processors!

Whether approaches based primarily on faster clock rates, simpler hardware, and more static scheduling or approaches using more sophisticated hardware to achieve lower CPI will win out is difficult to say and may depend on the benchmarks.

Practical Limitations on Exploiting More ILP

Independent of the method used to exploit ILP, there are potential limitations that arise from employing more transistors. When the number of transistors employed is increased, the clock period is often determined by wire delays encountered both in distributing the clock and in the communication path of critical signals, such as those that signal exceptions. These delays make it more difficult to employ increased numbers of transistors to exploit more ILP, while also increasing the clock rate. These problems are sometimes overcome by adding additional stages, which are reserved just for communicating signals across longer wires. The Pentium 4 does this. These increased clock stages, however, can lead to more stalls and a higher CPI, since they increase pipeline latency. We saw exactly this phenomenon when comparing the Pentium 4 to the Pentium III.

Although the limitations explored in Section 3.8 act as significant barriers to exploiting more ILP, it may be that more basic challenges would prevent the efficient exploitation of additional ILP, even if it could be uncovered. For example, doubling the issue rates above the current rates of 4 instructions per clock will probably require a processor to sustain three or four memory accesses per cycle and probably resolve two or three branches per cycle. In addition, supplying 8 instructions per cycle will probably require fetching 16, speculating through multiple branches, and accessing roughly 20 registers per cycle. None of this is impossible, but whether it can be done while simultaneously maintaining clock rates exceeding 2 GHz is an open question and will surely be a significant challenge for any design team!

Equal in importance to the CPI versus clock rate trade-off are realistic limitations on power. Recall that dynamic power is proportional to the product of the number of switching transistors and the switching rate. A microprocessor trying to achieve both a low CPI and a high CR fights both of these factors. Achieving an improved CPI means more instructions in flight and more transistors switching every clock cycle.

Two factors make it likely that the switching transistor count grows faster than performance. The first is the gap between peak issue rates and sustained performance, which continues to grow. Since the number of transistors switching is likely to be proportional to the peak issue rate, and the performance is proportional to the sustained rate, the growing performance gap translates to increasing transistor switches per unit of performance. Second, issuing multiple instructions incurs some overhead in logic that grows as the issue rate grows. This logic is responsible for instruction issue analysis, including dependence checking, register renaming, and similar functions. The combined result is that, without voltage reductions to decrease power, lower CPIs are likely to lead to lower ratios of performance per watt.

A similar conundrum applies to attempts to increase clock rate. Of course, increasing the clock rate will increase transistor switching frequency and directly increase power consumption. As we saw in the Pentium 4 discussion, a deeper pipeline structure can be used to achieve a clock rate increase that exceeds what could be obtained just from improvements in transistor speed. Deeper pipelines, however, incur additional power penalties, resulting from several sources. The most important of these is the simple observation that a deeper pipeline means more operations are in flight every clock cycle, which means more transistors are switching, which means more power!

What is key to understand is the extent to which this potential growth in power caused by an increase in both the switching frequency and number of transistors switching is offset by a reduction in the operating voltage. Although this relationship is complex to understand, we can look at the results empirically and draw some conclusions.

The Pentium III and Pentium 4 provide an opportunity to examine this issue. As discussed on page 268, the Pentium 4 has a much deeper pipeline and can exploit more ILP than the Pentium III, although its basic peak issue rate is the same. The operating voltage of the Pentium 4 at 1.7 GHz is slightly higher than a 1 GHz Pentium III: 1.75 V versus 1.70 V. The power difference, however, is much larger: The 1.7 GHz Pentium 4 consumes 64 W typical, while the 1 GHz Pentium III consumes only 30 W by comparison. Figure 3.60 shows the effective performance of a 1.7 GHz Pentium 4 per watt relative to the performance per watt of a 1 GHz Pentium III using the same benchmarks presented in Figure 1.28 in the first chapter. Clearly, while the Pentium 4 is faster, its higher clock rate, deeper pipeline, and higher sustained execution rate make it significantly less power efficient. Whether the decreased power efficiency of the Pentium 4 relative to the Pentium III is a deep issue and unlikely to be overcome, or whether it is an artifact of the two implementations is a key question that will probably be settled in future implementations. What is clear is that neither deeper pipelines nor wider issue rates can circumvent the need to consume more power to improve performance.

More generally, the question of how best to exploit parallelism remains open. Clearly ILP will continue to play a big role because of its smaller impact on programmers and applications when compared to an explicitly parallel model using multiple threads and parallel processors. What sort of parallelism computer architects will employ as they try to achieve higher performance levels, and what type of parallelism programmers will accept, are hard to predict. Likewise, it is unclear whether vectors will play a larger role in processors designed for multimedia and DSP applications, or whether such processors will rely on limited SIMD and ILP approaches. We will return to these questions in the next chapter as well as in Chapter 6.

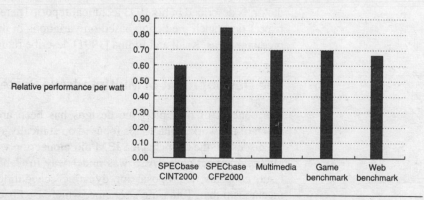

Figure 3.60 The relative performance per watt of the Pentium 4 is 15% to 40% less than the Pentium III on these five sets of benchmarks.

3.15 Historical Perspective and References

This section describes some of the major advances in dynamically scheduled pipelines and ends with some of the recent literature on multiple-issue processors. Ideas such as data flow computation derived from observations that programs were limited by data dependence. The history of basic pipelining and the CDC 6600, the first dynamically scheduled processor, are contained in Appendix A.

The IBM 360 Model 91: A Landmark Computer

The IBM 360/91 introduced many new concepts, including tagging of data, register renaming, dynamic detection of memory hazards, and generalized forwarding. Tomasulo's algorithm is described in his 1967 paper. Anderson, Sparacio, and Tomasulo [1967] describe other aspects of the processor, including the use of branch prediction. Many of the ideas in the 360/91 faded from use for nearly 25 years before being broadly resurrected in the 1990s. Unfortunately, the 360/91 was not successful, and only a handful were sold. The complexity of the design made it late to the market and allowed the Model 85, which was the first IBM processor with a cache, to outperform the 91.

Branch-Prediction Schemes

The 2-bit dynamic hardware branch-prediction scheme was described by J. E. Smith [1981]. Ditzel and McLellan [1987] describe a novel branch-target buffer for CRISP, which implements branch folding. The correlating predictor we examine was described by Pan, So, and Rameh [1992]. Yeh and Patt [1992, 1993] generalized the correlation idea and described multilevel predictors that use branch histories for each branch, similar to the local history predictor used in the 21264. McFarling's tournament prediction scheme, which he refers to as a combined predictor, is described in his 1993 technical report. There are a variety of more recent papers on branch prediction based on variations in the multilevel and correlating predictor ideas. Kaeli and Emma [1991] describe return address prediction.

The Development of Multiple-Issue Processors

The concept of multiple-issue designs has been around for a while, although much of the work in the 1970s focused on statically scheduled approaches, which we discuss in the next chapter. IBM did pioneering work on multiple issue. In the 1960s, a project called ACS was under way in California. It included multiple-issue concepts, a proposal for dynamic scheduling (although with a simpler mechanism than Tomasulo's scheme, which used backup registers), and fetching down both branch paths. The project originally started as a new architecture to follow Stretch and surpass the CDC 6600/6800. ACS started in New York but was moved to California, later changed to be S/360 compatible, and eventually canceled. John Cocke was one of the intellectual forces behind the team that included a number of IBM veterans and younger contributors, many of whom went on to other important roles in IBM and elsewhere: Jack Bertram, Ed Sussenguth, Gene Amdahl, Herb Schorr, Fran Allen, Lynn Conway, and Phil Dauber, among others. While the compiler team published many of their ideas and had great influence outside IBM, the architecture ideas were not widely disseminated at that time. The most complete accessible documentation of this important project is at *www.cs.clemson.edu/~mark/acs.html,* which includes interviews with the ACS veterans and pointers to other sources. Sussenguth [1999] is a good overview of ACS.

More than 10 years after ACS was canceled, John Cocke made a new proposal for a superscalar processor that dynamically made issue decisions; he and Tilak Agerwala described the key ideas in several talks in the mid-1980s and coined the term *superscalar.* He called the design America; it is described by Agerwala and Cocke [1987]. The IBM Power1 architecture (the RS/6000 line) is based on these ideas (see Bakoglu et al. [1989]).

J. E. Smith [1984] and his colleagues at Wisconsin proposed the decoupled approach that included multiple issue with limited dynamic pipeline scheduling. A key feature of this processor is the use of queues to maintain order among a class of instructions (such as memory references) while allowing it to slip behind or ahead of another class of instructions. The Astronautics ZS-1 described by Smith et al. [1987] embodies this approach with queues to connect the load-store unit and the operation units. The Power2 design uses queues in a similar fashion. J. E. Smith [1989] also describes the advantages of dynamic scheduling and compares that approach to static scheduling.

The concept of speculation has its roots in the original 360/91, which performed a very limited form of speculation. The approach used in recent processors combines the dynamic scheduling techniques of the 360/91 with a buffer to allow in-order commit. Smith and Pleszkun [1988] explored the use of buffering to maintain precise interrupts and described the concept of a reorder buffer. Sohi [1990] describes adding renaming and dynamic scheduling, making it possible to use the mechanism for speculation. Patt and his colleagues were early proponents of aggressive reordering and speculation. They focused on checkpoint and restart mechanisms and pioneered an approach called HPSm, which is also an extension of Tomasulo's algorithm [Hwu and Patt 1986].

The use of speculation as a technique in multiple-issue processors was evaluated by Smith, Johnson, and Horowitz [1989] using the reorder buffer technique; their goal was to study available ILP in nonscientific code using speculation and multiple issue. In a subsequent book, Johnson [1990] describes the design of a speculative superscalar processor. Johnson later led the AMD K-5 design, one of the first speculative superscalars.

Studies of ILP and Ideas to Increase ILP

A series of early papers, including Tjaden and Flynn [1970] and Riseman and Foster [1972], concluded that only small amounts of parallelism could be available at the instruction level without investing an enormous amount of hardware.

These papers dampened the appeal of multiple instruction issue for more than 10 years. Nicolau and Fisher [1984] published a paper based on their work with trace scheduling and asserted the presence of large amounts of potential ILP in scientific programs.

Since then there have been many studies of the available ILP. Such studies have been criticized since they presume some level of both hardware support and compiler technology. Nonetheless, the studies are useful to set expectations as well as to understand the sources of the limitations. Wall has participated in several such studies, including Jouppi and Wall [1989], Wall [1991], and Wall [1993]. Although the early studies were criticized as being conservative (e.g., they didn't include speculation), the last study is by far the most ambitious study of ILP to date and the basis for the data in Section 3.8. Sohi and Vajapeyam [1989] give measurements of available parallelism for wide-instruction-word processors. Smith, Johnson, and Horowitz [1989] also used a speculative superscalar processor to study ILP limits. At the time of their study, they anticipated that the processor they specified was an upper bound on reasonable designs. Recent and upcoming processors, however, are likely to be at least as ambitious as their processor.

Lam and Wilson [1992] looked at the limitations imposed by speculation and showed that additional gains are possible by allowing processors to speculate in multiple directions, which requires more than one PC. (Such schemes cannot exceed what perfect speculation accomplishes, but they help close the gap between realistic prediction schemes and perfect prediction.) Wall's 1993 study includes a limited evaluation of this approach (up to eight branches are explored).

Going Beyond the Data Flow Limit

One other approach that has been explored in the literature is the use of value prediction. Value prediction can allow speculation based on data values. There have been a number of studies of the use of value prediction. Lipasti and Shen published two papers in 1996 evaluating the concept of value prediction and its potential impact on ILP exploitation. Sodani and Sohi [1997] approach the same problem from the viewpoint of reusing the values produced by instructions. Moshovos et al. [1997] show that deciding when to speculate on values, by tracking whether such speculation has been accurate in the past, is important to achieving performance gains with value speculation. Moshovos and Sohi [1997] and Chrysos and Emer [1998] focus on predicting memory dependences and using this information to eliminate the dependence through memory. González and González [1998], Babbay and Mendelson [1998], and Calder, Reinman, and Tullsen [1999] are more recent studies of the use of value prediction. This area is currently highly active, with new results being published in every conference.

Recent Advanced Microprocessors

The years 1994–95 saw the announcement of wide superscalar processors (three or more issues per clock) by every major processor vendor: Intel Pentium Pro and

Pentium II (these processors share the same core pipeline architecture, described by Colwell and Steck [1995]); AMD K-5, K-6, and Athlon; Sun UltraSPARC (see Lauterbach and Horel [1999]); Alpha 21164 (see Edmondson et. al [1995]) and 21264 (see Kessler [1999]); MIPS R10000 and R12000 (see Yeager et al. [1996]); PowerPC 603, 604, 620 (see Diep, Nelson, and Shen [1995]); and HP 8000 (Kumar [1997]). The latter part of the decade (1996–2000), saw second generations of much of these processors (Pentium III, AMD Athlon, Alpha 21264, among others). The second generation, although similar in issue rate, could sustain a lower CPI and provided much higher clock rates. All included dynamic scheduling, and almost universally supported speculation. In practice, many factors, including the implementation technology, the memory hierarchy, the skill of the designers, and the type of applications benchmarked, all play a role in determining which approach is best. Figure 3.61 shows the most interesting processors of the past few years and their characteristics.

References

Agerwala, T., and J. Cocke [1987]. "High performance reduced instruction set processors," IBM Tech. Rep. (March).

Anderson, D. W., F. J. Sparacio, and R. M. Tomasulo [1967]. "The IBM 360 Model 91: Processor philosophy and instruction handling," *IBM J. Research and Development* 11:1 (January), 8–24.

Austin, T. M., and G. Sohi [1992]. "Dynamic dependency analysis of ordinary programs," *Proc. 19th Symposium on Computer Architecture* (May), Gold Coast, Australia, 342–351.

Babbay, F., and A. Mendelson [1998]. "Using value prediction to increase the power of speculative execution hardware," *ACM Trans. on Computer Systems* 16:3 (August), 234–270.

Bakoglu, H. B., G. F. Grohoski, L. E. Thatcher, J. A. Kaeli, C. R. Moore, D. P. Tattle, W. E. Male, W. R. Hardell, D. A. Hicks, M. Nguyen Phu, R. K. Montoye, W. T. Glover, and S. Dhawan [1989]. "IBM second-generation RISC processor organization," *Proc. Int'l Conf. on Computer Design,* IEEE (October), Rye, N.Y., 138–142.

Bhandarkar, D., and D. W. Clark [1991]. "Performance from architecture: Comparing a RISC and a CISC with similar hardware organizations," *Proc. Fourth Conf. on Architectural Support for Programming Languages and Operating Systems,* IEEE/ACM (April), Palo Alto, Calif., 310–319.

Bhandarkar, D., and J. Ding [1997]. "Performance characterization of the Pentium Pro processor," *Proc. Third Int'l Symposium on High Performance Computer Architecture,* IEEE (February), San Antonio, 288–297.

Bloch, E. [1959]. "The engineering design of the Stretch computer," *Proc. Fall Joint Computer Conf.,* 48–59.

Bucholtz, W. [1962]. *Planning a Computer System: Project Stretch,* McGraw-Hill, New York.

Calder, B., G. Reinman, and D. Tullsen [1999]. "Selective value prediction". *Proc. 26th Int'l Symposium on Computer Architecture (ISCA),* Atlanta, June.

Chen, T. C. [1980]. "Overlap and parallel processing," in *Introduction to Computer Architecture,* H. Stone, ed., Science Research Associates, Chicago, 427–486.

Processor	System ship	Maximum current CR (MHz)	Power (W)	Transistors (M)	Window size	Rename registers (int/FP)	Issue rate: maximum/ memory/ integer/FP/ branch	Branch-predict buffer	Pipe stages (int/load)
MIPS R14000	2000	400	25	7	48	32/32	4/1/2/2/1	2K × 2	6
UltraSPARC III	2001	900	65	29	N.A.	None	4/1/4/3/1	16K × 2	14/15
Pentium III	2000	1000	30	24	40	Total: 40	3/2/2/1/1	512 entries	12/14
Pentium 4	2001	1700	64	42	126	Total: 128	3/2/3/2/1	4K × 2	22/24
HP PA 8600	2001	552	60	130	56	Total: 56	4/2/2/2/1	2K × 2	7/9
Alpha 21264B	2001	833	75	15	80	41/41	4/2/4/2/1	multilevel (see p. 207)	7/9
PowerPC 7400 (G4)	2000	450	5	7	5	6/6	3/1/2/1/1	512 × 2	4/5
AMD Athlon	2001	1330	76	37	72	36/36	3/2/3/3/1	4K × 9	9/11
IBM Power3-II	2000	450	36	23	32	16/24	4/2/2/2/2	2K × 2	7/8

Figure 3.61 Recent high-performance processors and their characteristics. The window size column shows the size of the buffer available for instructions and, hence, the maximum number of instructions in flight. Both the Pentium III and the Athlon schedule micro-operations, and the window is the maximum number of micro-operations in execution. The IBM, HP, and UltraSPARC processors support dynamic issue, but not speculation. To read more about these processors the following references are useful: *IBM Journal of Research and Development* (contains issues on Power and PowerPC designs), the *Digital Technical Journal* (contains issues on various Alpha processors), and the proceedings of the Hot Chips Symposium (annual meeting at Stanford, which reviews the newest microprocessors), the International Solid State Circuits Conference, the annual Microprocessor Forum meetings, and the annual International Symposium on Computer Architecture. Much of the data in this table came from Microprocessor Report online April 30, 2001.

Chrysos, G. Z., and J. S. Emer [1998]. "Memory dependence prediction using store sets," *Proc. 25th Int'l Symposium on Computer Architecture (ISCA)*, June, Barcelona, 142–153.

Clark, D. W. [1987]. "Pipelining and performance in the VAX 8800 processor," *Proc. Second Conf. on Architectural Support for Programming Languages and Operating Systems*, IEEE/ACM (March), Palo Alto, Calif., 173–177.

Colwell, R. P., and R. Steck [1995]. "A 0.6um BiCMOS processor with dynamic execution." *Proc. of Int'l Symposium on Solid State Circuits*, 176–177.

Cvetanovic, Z., and R. E. Kessler [2000]. "Performance analysis of the Alpha 21264-based Compaq ES40 system," *Proc. 27th Symposium on Computer Architecture* (June), Vancouver, Canada, 192–202.

Davidson, E. S. [1971]. "The design and control of pipelined function generators," *Proc. Conf. on Systems, Networks, and Computers*, IEEE (January), Oaxtepec, Mexico, 19–21.

Davidson, E. S., A. T. Thomas, L. E. Shar, and J. H. Patel [1975]. "Effective control for pipelined processors," *COMPCON, IEEE* (March), San Francisco, 181–184.

Diep, T. A., C. Nelson, and J. P. Shen [1995]. "Performance evaluation of the PowerPC 620 microarchitecture," *Proc. 22nd Symposium on Computer Architecture* (June), Santa Margherita, Italy.

Ditzel, D. R., and H. R. McLellan [1987]. "Branch folding in the CRISP microprocessor: Reducing the branch delay to zero," *Proc. 14th Symposium on Computer Architecture* (June), Pittsburgh, 2–7.

Edmondson, J. H., P. I. Rubinfield, R. Preston, and V. Rajagopalan [1995]. "Superscalar instruction execution in the 21164 Alpha microprocessor," *IEEE Micro* 15:2, 33–43.

Emer, J. S., and D. W. Clark [1984]. "A characterization of processor performance in the VAX-11/780," *Proc. 11th Symposium on Computer Architecture* (June), Ann Arbor, Mich., 301–310.

Foster, C. C., and E. M. Riseman [1972]. "Percolation of code to enhance parallel dispatching and execution," *IEEE Trans. on Computers* C-21:12 (December), 1411–1415.

González, J., and A. González [1998]. "Limits of instruction level parallelism with data speculation," *Proc. of the VECPAR Conf.*, 585–598.

Heinrich, J. [1993]. *MIPS R4000 User's Manual*, Prentice Hall, Englewood Cliffs, N.J.

Hwu, W.-M., and Y. Patt [1986]. "HPSm, a high performance restricted data flow architecture having minimum functionality," *Proc. 13th Symposium on Computer Architecture* (June), Tokyo, 297–307.

IBM [1990]. "The IBM RISC System/6000 processor" (collection of papers), *IBM J. Research and Development* 34:1 (January).

Johnson, M. [1990]. *Superscalar Microprocessor Design*, Prentice Hall, Englewood Cliffs, N.J.

Jordan, H. F. [1983]. "Performance measurements on HEP: A pipelined MIMD computer," *Proc. 10th Symposium on Computer Architecture* (June), 207–212.

Jouppi, N. P., and D. W. Wall [1989]. "Available instruction-level parallelism for superscalar and superpipelined processors," *Proc. Third Conf. on Architectural Support for Programming Languages and Operating Systems*, IEEE/ACM (April), Boston, 272–282.

Kaeli, D. R., and P. G. Emma [1991]. "Branch history table prediction of moving target branches due to subroutine returns," *Proc. 18th Int'l Symposium on Computer Architecture (ISCA)*, Toronto, May, 34–42.

Keller, R. M. [1975]. "Look-ahead processors," *ACM Computing Surveys* 7:4 (December), 177–195.

Kessler, R. [1999]. "The Alpha 21264 microprocessor," *IEEE Micro* 19:2 (March/April) 24–36.

Killian, E. [1991]. "MIPS R4000 technical overview—64 bits/100 MHz or bust," *Hot Chips III Symposium Record* (August), Stanford University, 1.6–1.19.

Kogge, P. M. [1981]. *The Architecture of Pipelined Computers*, McGraw-Hill, New York.

Kumar, A. [1997]. "The HP PA-8000 RISC CPU," *IEEE Micro* 17:2 (March/April).

Kunkel, S. R., and J. E. Smith [1986]. "Optimal pipelining in supercomputers," *Proc. 13th Symposium on Computer Architecture* (June), Tokyo, 404–414.

Lam, M. S., and R. P. Wilson [1992]. "Limits of control flow on parallelism," *Proc. 19th Symposium on Computer Architecture* (May), Gold Coast, Australia, 46–57.

Lauterbach G., and T. Horel [1999]. "UltraSPARC-III: Designing third generation 64-bit performance," *IEEE Micro* 19:3 (May/Junc).

Lipasti, M. H., and J. P. Shen [1996]. "Exceeding the dataflow limit via value prediction," *Proc. 29th Annual ACM/IEEE Int'l Symposium on Microarchitecture* (December).

Lipasti, M. H., C. B. Wilkerson, and J. P. Shen [1996]. "Value locality and load value prediction," *Proc. Seventh Symposium on Architectural Support for Programming Languages and Operating Systems* (October), 138–147.

McFarling, S. [1993]. "Combining branch predictors," WRL Technical Note TN-36 (June), Digital Western Research Laboratory, Palo Alto, Calif.

Moshovos, A., S. Breach, T. N. Vijaykumar, and G. S. Sohi [1997]. "Dynamic speculation and synchronization of data dependences," *Proc. 24th Int'l Symposium on Computer Architecture (ISCA),* June, Boulder, Colo.

Moshovos, A., and G. S. Sohi [1997]. "Streamlining inter-operation memory communication via data dependence prediction," *Proc. 30th Annual Int'l Symposium on Microarchitecture (MICRO-30),* December, 235–245.

Nicolau, A., and J. A. Fisher [1984]. "Measuring the parallelism available for very long instruction word architectures," *IEEE Trans. on Computers* C-33:11 (November), 968–976.

Pan, S.-T., K. So, and J. T. Rameh [1992]. "Improving the accuracy of dynamic branch prediction using branch correlation," *Proc. Fifth Conf. on Architectural Support for Programming Languages and Operating Systems,* IEEE/ACM (October), Boston, 76–84.

Postiff, M.A., D. A. Greene, G. S. Tyson, and T. N. Mudge [1992]. "The limits of instruction level parallelism in SPEC95 applications," *Computer Architecture News* 27:1 (March), 31–40.

Ramamoorthy, C. V., and H. F. Li [1977]. "Pipeline architecture," *ACM Computing Surveys* 9:1 (March), 61–102.

Riseman, E. M., and C. C. Foster [1972]. "Percolation of code to enhance parallel dispatching and execution," *IEEE Trans. on Computers* C-21:12 (December), 1411–1415.

Rymarczyk, J. [1982]. "Coding guidelines for pipelined processors," *Proc. Symposium on Architectural Support for Programming Languages and Operating Systems,* IEEE/ACM (March), Palo Alto, Calif., 12–19.

Sites, R. [1979]. *Instruction Ordering for the CRAY-1 Computer,* Tech. Rep. 78-CS-023 (July), Dept. of Computer Science, Univ. of Calif., San Diego.

Smith, A., and J. Lee [1984]. "Branch prediction strategies and branch-target buffer design," *Computer* 17:1 (January), 6–22.

Smith, J. E. [1981]. "A study of branch prediction strategies," *Proc. Eighth Symposium on Computer Architecture* (May), Minneapolis, 135–148.

Smith, J. E. [1984]. "Decoupled access/execute computer architectures," *ACM Trans. on Computer Systems* 2:4 (November), 289–308.

Smith, J. E. [1989]. "Dynamic instruction scheduling and the Astronautics ZS-1," *Computer* 22:7 (July), 21–35.

Smith, J. E., G. E. Dermer, B. D. Vanderwarn, S. D. Klinger, C. M. Rozewski, D. L. Fowler, K. R. Scidmore, and J. P. Laudon [1987]. "The ZS-1 central processor," *Proc. Second Conf. on Architectural Support for Programming Languages and Operating Systems,* IEEE/ACM (March), Palo Alto, Calif., 199–204.

Smith, J. E., and A. R. Pleszkun [1988]. "Implementing precise interrupts in pipelined processors," *IEEE Trans. on Computers* 37:5 (May), 562–573. This paper is based on an earlier paper that appeared in *Proc. 12th Symposium on Computer Architecture,* June 1988.

Smith, M. D., M. Horowitz, and M. S. Lam [1992]. "Efficient superscalar performance through boosting," *Proc. Fifth Conf. on Architectural Support for Programming Languages and Operating Systems* (October), Boston, IEEE/ACM, 248–259.

Smith, M. D., M. Johnson, and M. A. Horowitz [1989]. "Limits on multiple instruction issue," *Proc. Third Conf. on Architectural Support for Programming Languages and Operating Systems,* IEEE/ACM (April), Boston, 290–302.

Sodani, A., and G. Sohi [1997]. "Dynamic Instruction Reuse," *Proc. 24th Int'l Symposium on Computer Architecture* (June).

Sohi, G. S. [1990]. "Instruction issue logic for high-performance, interruptible, multiple functional unit, pipelined computers," *IEEE Trans. on Computers* 39:3 (March), 349–359.

Sohi, G. S., and S. Vajapeyam [1989]. "Tradeoffs in instruction format design for horizontal architectures," *Proc. Third Conf. on Architectural Support for Programming Languages and Operating Systems,* IEEE/ACM (April), Boston, 15–25.

Sussenguth, E. [1999]. "IBM's ACS-1 Machine," *IEEE Computer* 22:11 (November).

Thorlin, J. F. [1967]. "Code generation for PIE (parallel instruction execution) computers," *Proc. Spring Joint Computer Conf.,* 27.

Thornton, J. E. [1964]. "Parallel operation in the Control Data 6600," *Proc. AFIPS Fall Joint Computer Conf., Part II,* 26, 33–40.

Thornton, J. E. [1970]. *Design of a Computer, the Control Data 6600,* Scott, Foresman, Glenview, Ill.

Tjaden, G. S., and M. J. Flynn [1970]. "Detection and parallel execution of independent instructions," *IEEE Trans. on Computers* C-19:10 (October), 889–895.

Tomasulo, R. M. [1967]. "An efficient algorithm for exploiting multiple arithmetic units," *IBM J. Research and Development* 11:1 (January), 25–33.

Wall, D. W. [1991]. "Limits of instruction-level parallelism," *Proc. Fourth Conf. on Architectural Support for Programming Languages and Operating Systems* (April), Santa Clara, Calif., IEEE/ACM, 248–259.

Wall, D. W. [1993]. *Limits of Instruction-Level Parallelism,* Research Rep. 93/6, Western Research Laboratory, Digital Equipment Corp. (November).

Weiss, S., and J. E. Smith [1984]. "Instruction issue logic for pipelined supercomputers," *Proc. 11th Symposium on Computer Architecture* (June), Ann Arbor, Mich., 110–118.

Weiss, S., and J. E. Smith [1987]. "A study of scalar compilation techniques for pipelined supercomputers," *Proc. Second Conf. on Architectural Support for Programming Languages and Operating Systems* (March), IEEE/ACM, Palo Alto, Calif., 105–109.

Weiss, S., and J. E. Smith [1994]. *Power and PowerPC,* Morgan Kaufmann, San Francisco.

Yeager, K. [1996]. "The MIPS R10000 superscalar microprocessor," *IEEE Micro* 16:2 (April), 28–40.

Yeh, T., and Y. N. Patt [1992]. "Alternative implementations of two-level adaptive branch prediction," *Proc. 19th Int'l Symposium on Computer Architecture* (May), Gold Coast, Australia, 124–134.

Yeh, T., and Y. N. Patt [1993]. "A comparison of dynamic branch predictors that use two levels of branch history," *Proc. 20th Symposium on Computer Architecture* (May), San Diego, 257–266.

Exercises

Solutions to the "starred" exercises appear in Appendix B.

3.1 [12/12/12/15] <3.1, 3.2, 3.3, 3.6> For the following code fragment, assume that all data references are shown, that all values are defined before use, and that only b and c are used again after this segment. You may ignore any possible exceptions. The individual statements are numbered to provide an easy reference.

```
1. if (a > c) {
2.      d = d + 5;
3.      a = b + d + e;}
   } else {
4.      e = e + 2;
5.      f = f + 2;
6.      c = c + f;
   }
7. b = a + f;
```

a. [12] <3.1> List the control dependences. For each control dependence, tell whether the dependent statement can be scheduled before the if statement based on the data references.

b. [12] <3.1, 3.2, 3.3, 3.6> Assume a dynamically scheduled, multiple-issue processor without speculation and with a window that is holding the entire code fragment. Find the data dependences and use this information to make a list of the successive groups of statements that are issued together.

c. [12] <3.1> It is given that only the values b and c are live after the code segment. If it is known that a value is not live at some point in the code, then the statement that defines that value can be deleted without changing the program meaning. Find any values that are not live within the given code fragment, and list the statement(s) that a compiler with this information could delete.

d. [15] <3.1, 3.2, 3.3, 3.6> How does the result for part (c) affect the ILP achieved by the processor of part (b)? What does this illustrate about measuring computer performance factors such as ILP, making hardware design choices, and compiler technology?

✪ 3.2 [15/15] <3.1, 3.2> This chapter examines hardware approaches for exploiting instruction-level parallelism. This exercise asks how well hardware can find and exploit ILP.

Consider the following four MIPS code fragments each containing two instructions:

```
i.        DADDI   R1,R1,#4
          LD      R2,7(R1)

ii.       DADD    R3,R1,R2
          SD      R2,7(R1)
```

iii.   SD   R2,7(R1)
            S.D   F2,200(R7)

iv.   BEZ   R1,place
            SD   R1,7(R1)

a. [15] <3.1> For each code fragment (i) to (iv) identify each type of dependence that exists or that may exist (a fragment may have no dependences) and describe what data flow, name reuse, or control structure causes or would cause the dependence. For a dependence that may exist, describe the source of the ambiguity and identify the time at which that uncertainty is resolved.

b. [15] <3.2> For each code fragment, discuss whether dynamic scheduling is, may be, or is not sufficient to allow out-of-order execution of the fragment.

3.3 [12/15] <3.1, A> Consider the following MIPS assembly code.

```
LD    R1,45(R2)
DADD  R7,R1,R5
DSUB  R8,R1,R6
OR    R9,R5,R1
BNEZ  R7,target
DADD  R10,R8,R5
XOR   R2,R3,R4
```

a. [12] <3.1> Identify each dependence by type; list the two instructions involved; identify which instruction is dependent; and, if there is one, name the storage location involved.

b. [15] <3.1, A> Use information about the MIPS five-stage pipeline from Appendix A and assume a register file that writes in the first half of the clock cycle and reads in the second half-cycle forwarding. Which of the dependences that you found in part (a) become hazards and which do not? Why?

3.4 [20/15/20/15/15] <1, 2, 3.1> Stack and accumulator instruction set architectures (see Figures 2.1 and 2.2) were common in the early days of electronic computers. Processors for both can be implemented with a small number of logic gates. With the technology of the time, vacuum tubes, only small circuits had reasonable cost and acceptable reliability. Solid-state integration of extremely inexpensive, highly reliable transistors has made very large circuits feasible. Current processors use the register-register (load-store) instruction set architecture, which requires more gates to build. Increased feasible circuit size could explain growing use of the load-store ISA, but is that sufficient to explain the absence of new generations of stack and accumulator processors? The following explores other possible reasons: cost, clock speed, dependences, and opportunity for instruction scheduling.

a. [20] <1, 2> Chapter 1 presents a model for integrated circuit die cost that shows cost escalates rapidly with increasing die area. The essential core circuit of a stack processor (ALU, two stack positions, control logic, and data paths) or of an accumulator processor (ALU, accumulator, control logic, and data paths) is smaller than the essential core circuit of a register-register processor (ALU, set of at least three registers for operands and result, control logic, and data paths). For current processors, investigate how much die area is devoted to functions other than the essential core execution logic and what reliability is achieved. Discuss how much cost and reliability advantage stack or accumulator designs would have with respect to current load-store processor designs if they could cut essential core execution logic area by 10%, by 50%, and by more than 99%.

b. [15] <2> Consider the block diagram circuits shown in Figure 2.1 for the stack, accumulator, and load-store ISAs. How might achievable clock speeds differ among the processor circuits?

c. [20] <2, 3.1> Consider the following simple computation:

```
C = A + B
E = D - C
```

Using Figure 2.2 as a start, write instruction sequences to perform the computation on stack, accumulator, and load-store architectures. Assume that the stack architecture subtracts the next-to-top-of-stack from the top-of-stack. Assume that the accumulator architecture subtracts a memory location from the accumulator. Use distinct registers for all data values in the load-store sequence. Carefully examine your code to find the dependences. For each dependence, list its type, the two instructions involved, which instruction is dependent, and the storage location involved. Rank the architectures by their potential to exploit instruction-level parallelism.

d. [15] <2, 3.1> For your code in part (c), describe the different instruction schedules that a compiler could produce for each architecture.

e. [15] <1, 2, 3.1> Which of the factors examined in parts (a) through (d)—cost, clock speed, dependences, and opportunity for instruction scheduling—explain the dominance of today's processor designs by the register-register (load-store) ISA and why are these factors critical?

★ 3.5 [15/15/15/15/12] <3.3> This exercise examines the basic Tomasulo algorithm. Answer the following questions based upon the tabular description of the algorithm given in Figure 3.5.

a. [15] <3.3> For each row of the table, state (1) whether that row could apply simultaneously to more than one program instruction (ILP); (2) whether the Tomasulo algorithm allows ILP for that row; (3) if ILP is not allowed, how that restriction is enforced; and (4) if ILP is allowed, what if anything could prevent achieving the maximum ILP present in the program.

b. [15] <3.3> Which one of rs and rt holds the name of the base address register for a load or store instruction? Explain your answer in sufficient detail to be a proof.

c. [15] <3.3> In the terminology of the table, write the function(s) performed by the Address unit in Figure 3.2.

d. [15] <3.3> Write the table entries required to support integer ALU operation instructions.

e. [12] <3.3> Consider how branch instructions affect the instruction processing described in the table. Show the modifications to the table necessary to take the presence of branch instructions in the program into account.

3.6 [20/25/25] <3.2, 3.3, 3.6, 3.7> In this exercise, we will look at how variations on Tomasulo's algorithm perform when running a common vector loop. The loop is the so-called DAXPY loop (double-precision aX plus Y) and is the central operation in Gaussian elimination. The following code implements the operation Y = aX + Y for a vector of length 100. Initially, R1 = 0 and F0 contains a.

```
foo:    L.D       F2,0(R1)      ;load X(i)
        MUL.D     F4,F2,F0      ;multiply a*X(i)
        L.D       F6,0(R2)      ;load Y(i)
        ADD.D     F6,F4,F6      ;add a*X(i) + Y(i)
        S.D       F6,0(R2)      ;store Y(i)
        DADDUI    R1,R1,#8      ;increment X index
        DADDUI    R2,R2,#8      ;increment Y index
        DSGTUI    R3,R1,#800    ;test if done
        BEQZ      R3,foo        ;loop if not done
```

The pipeline function units are described in Figure 3.62.

Assume the following:

■ Function units are not pipelined.

■ There is no forwarding between function units; results are communicated by the CDB.

■ The execution stage (EX) does both the effective address calculation and the memory access for loads and stores. Thus the pipeline is IF / ID / IS / EX / WB.

■ Loads take 1 clock cycle.

■ The issue (IS) and write result (WB) stages each take 1 clock cycle.

FU type	Cycles in EX	Number of FUs	Number of reservation stations
Integer	1	1	5
FP adder	4	1	3
FP multiplier	15	1	2

Figure 3.62 Information about pipeline function units.

- There are 5 load buffer slots and 5 store buffer slots.
- Assume that the BNEQZ instruction takes 0 clock cycles.

a. [20] <3.2, 3.3> For this problem use the single-issue Tomasulo MIPS pipeline of Figure 3.2 with the pipeline latencies from Figure 3.63. Show the number of stall cycles for each instruction and what clock cycle each instruction begins execution (i.e., enters its first EX cycle) for three iterations of the loop. How many clock cycles does each loop iteration take? Report your answer in the form of a table like that in Figure 3.25.

b. [25] <3.6> Use the MIPS code for DAXPY above and a fully pipelined FPU with the latencies of Figure 3.63. Assume a two-issue Tomasulo's algorithm for the hardware with one integer unit taking one execution cycle (a latency of 0 cycles to use) for all integer operations. Show the number of stall cycles for each instruction and what clock cycle each instruction begins execution (i.e., enters its first EX cycle) for three iterations of the loop. Show your answer in the form of a table like that in Figure 3.25.

c. [25] <3.7> Using the MIPS code for DAXPY above, assume Tomasulo's algorithm with speculation as shown in Figure 3.29. Assume the latencies shown in Figure 3.63. Assume that there are separate integer function units for effective address calculation, for ALU operations, and for branch condition evaluation. Create a table as in Figure 3.34 for the first three iterations of this loop.

3.7 [15/15] <3.2, 3.3> Tomasulo's algorithm has a disadvantage: Only one result can complete per clock, per CDB.

a. [15] <3.2> Use the hardware configuration from Figure 3.2 and the FP latencies from Figure 3.63. Find a code sequence of no more than 10 instructions where Tomasulo's algorithm must stall due to CDB contention. Indicate where this occurs in your sequence.

b. [15] <3.2, 3.3> Generalize your result from part (a) by describing the characteristic of any code sequence that will eventually experience structural hazard stall given *n* CDBs.

Instruction producing result	Instruction using result	Latency in clock cycles
FP multiply	FP ALU op	6
FP add	FP ALU op	4
FP multiply	FP store	5
FP add	FP store	3
Integer operation (including load)	Any	0

Figure 3.63 Pipeline latencies where latency is number of cycles between producing and consuming instruction.

3.8 [20] <3.4> Branch-prediction buffers are indexed using the low-order address bits of the branch instruction. Assume now that some other subset of address bits is chosen. Discuss the effects on buffer operation.

★ 3.9 [15/15/15] <3.4> Increasing the size of a branch-prediction buffer means that it is less likely that two branches in a program will share the same predictor. A single predictor predicting a single branch instruction is generally more accurate than is that same predictor serving more than one branch instruction.

    a. [15] <3.4> List a sequence of branch taken and not taken actions to show a simple example of 1-bit predictor sharing that reduces misprediction rate.

    b. [15] <3.4> List a sequence of branch taken and not taken actions that show a simple example of how sharing a 1-bit predictor increases misprediction.

    c. [15] <3.4> Discuss why the sharing of branch predictors can be expected to increase mispredictions for the long instruction execution sequences of actual programs.

3.10 [15] <3.4> Construct a version of the table in Figure 3.13 on page 203 assuming the 1-bit predictors are initialized to NT, the correlation bit is initialized to T, and the value of **d** (leftmost column of the table) alternates 1, 2, 1, 2. Also, note and count the instances of misprediction.

3.11 [20/15/15/15] <3.4> Figure 3.15 on page 206 and Figure 3.18 on page 208 show that the prediction accuracy of a local 2-bit predictor improves very slowly with increasing branch-prediction buffer size, once size exceeds some amount. Because prediction buffers must be of finite size, two or more branches may be mapped to the same buffer entry. While it is possible for sharing to improve branch prediction by accidentally allowing sharing of information between related branches, typically the sharing results in destructive interference. For the following, assume that prediction accuracy is always worse when branches share a predictor.

    a. [20] <3.4> For a branch-prediction buffer implementing a given type of predictor, what characteristic of any program guarantees that prediction accuracy as a function of increasing buffer size must eventually become constant (i.e., independent of buffer size)? *Hint:* examine the contents of and compare the prediction accuracy of branch-prediction buffers of different sizes on a simple code fragment such as the following:

```
Loop:    DSUBI  R1,R1,#1
         BNEZ   R1,Loop
         LD     R10,0(R3)
```

    b. [15] <3.4> Figure 3.15 shows that, to within the precision of the measurements, the SPEC89 benchmarks nasa7, tomcatv, and gcc were the only programs to have less branch misprediction when buffer size increased from 4096 entries to infinite. Based on the answer to part (a), what quantitative measure can you infer about the machine instruction count of the executable codes for these four benchmarks?

c. [15] <3.4> Can you infer anything similar to the result in part (b) about the instruction counts of the other seven benchmarks?

d. [15] <3.4> How might an optimizing compiler improve prediction accuracy for the other seven benchmarks in part (c) and when would this be and not be possible?

3.12 [30] <3.4> Implement a simulator to evaluate the performance of a branch-prediction buffer that does not store branches that are predicted as untaken. Consider the following prediction schemes: a 1-bit predictor storing only predicted-taken branches, a 2-bit predictor storing all the branches, a scheme with a target buffer that stores only predicted-taken branches, and a 2-bit prediction buffer. Explore different sizes for the buffers, keeping the total number of bits (assuming 32-bit addresses) the same for all schemes. Determine what the branch penalties are, using Figure 3.21 as a guideline. How do the different schemes compare both in prediction accuracy and in branch cost?

3.13 [30] <3.4> Implement a simulator to evaluate various branch-prediction schemes. You can use the instruction portion of a set of cache traces to simulate the branch-prediction buffer. Pick a set of table sizes (e.g., 1K bits, 2K bits, 8K bits, and 16K bits). Determine the performance of both (0,2) and (2,2) predictors for the various table sizes. Also compare the performance of the degenerate predictor that uses no branch address information for these table sizes. Determine how large the table must be for the degenerate predictor to perform as well as a (0,2) predictor with 256 entries.

✪ 3.14 [15] <3.5> Suppose we have a deeply pipelined processor, for which we implement a branch-target buffer for the conditional branches only. Assume that the misprediction penalty is always 4 cycles and the buffer miss penalty is always 3 cycles. Assume 90% hit rate and 90% accuracy, and 15% branch frequency. How much faster is the processor with the branch-target buffer versus a processor that has a fixed 2-cycle branch penalty? Assume a base CPI without branch stalls of 1.

3.15 [10/15] <3.5> Consider a branch-target buffer that has penalties of 0, 2, and 2 clock cycles for correct conditional branch prediction, incorrect prediction, and a buffer miss, respectively. Consider a branch-target buffer design that distinguishes conditional and unconditional branches, storing the target address for a conditional branch and the target instruction for an unconditional branch.

a. [10] <3.5> What is the penalty in clock cycles when an unconditional branch is found in the buffer?

b. [15] <3.5> Determine the improvement from branch folding for unconditional branches. Assume a 90% hit rate, an unconditional branch frequency of 5%, and a 2-cycle penalty for a buffer miss. How much improvement is gained by this enhancement? How high must the hit rate be for this enhancement to provide a performance gain?

3.16 [10/20/20/20/20/15] <3.1, 3.6> This exercise explores variations on the theme of the example on page 221. Each part of this exercise lists changes to make to the set of assumptions given in the example. For parts (b) through (d) do the following: (i) produce a new version of the table in Figure 3.25 covering enough iterations to reach a steady-state condition, (ii) compute a value for the sustained instruction completion rate, and (iii) provide any other information requested in that part.

Make the following two assumptions also:

- There is only one memory access port.
- If there is contention for a resource, then the earliest instruction in program order is given access to that resource.

a. [10] <3.1, 3.6> What structural hazards occur in the example?

b. [20] <3.6> Assume that there are two integer functional units. Describe any structural hazards and compare them to the case for the original example.

c. [20] <3.6> Assume that three instructions may issue simultaneously (but the BNE still issues separately). Describe any structural hazards.

d. [20] <3.6> Assume branches are speculated and issue with another instruction. Assume that branch prediction is perfect. Count and describe the structural hazards.

e. [20] <3.6> Assume branches are speculated and issue with another instruction. Assume that branch prediction is perfect. Assume that there are two integer functional units.

f. [15] <3.6> Discuss the relative magnitude of performance benefit derived from adding an integer functional unit, increasing issue width, and supporting speculation. Comment on the potential for synergy between various enhancements.

★ 3.17 [10/20/15] <3.6> To keep the issue step of the statically scheduled superscalar MIPS processor quite simple, an issue limit of one integer and one floating-point instruction per clock was imposed. Let's remove this restriction and see how issue step workload grows with increasing multiple-issue capability. Assume a five-stage superscalar pipeline (IF, ID, EX, MEM, WB) with no issue restrictions and no structural hazards. Also, regardless of instruction, each stage always takes just 1 clock cycle to complete its task, and an instruction may have up to two operands and one result.

a. [10] <3.6> The ID stage must check for what type(s) of data dependences?

b. [20] <3.6> For a two-issue design with 32 integer registers and 32 floating-point registers, how many bits must be brought to comparators in the ID stage and how many comparisons must be performed during each clock cycle to check just for data hazards? How many if the issue width is doubled?

c. [15] <3.6> Let the issue limit be n instructions, and assume the total number of registers is unbounded. How many comparisons, as a function of n, must be performed to check just for data hazards?

3.18   [25] <3.7> Consider the execution of the following loop, which searches an array, on a single-issue processor, first with dynamic scheduling and then with speculation:

```
Loop:    LD      R2,0(R1)     ;R2=array element
         DADDI   R2,R2,#1     ;increment R2
         SD      R2,0(R1)     ;store result
         DADDI   R1,R1,#4     ;decrement pointer
         BNEZ    R2,LOOP      ;branch if last element!=0
```

Assume that there are separate integer functional units for effective address calculation, for ALU operations, and for branch condition evaluation. Create a table as in Figure 3.27 for the first three iterations of this loop for both machines. Assume that one instruction can commit per clock.

3.19   [15] <3.7> Use of a speculative technique may decrease performance. This is certainly true in particular when a speculative guess is wrong; performance at that point in the program is less than it would have been without speculation. However, it can also be true in general, that is, for a substantial workload such as an entire program. For a speculative technique to improve performance in general, what mathematical condition must be true? *Hint:* Construct a model in terms of speculation costs, benefits, and frequencies.

✪ 3.20   [15] <1.6, 3.7> When an instruction is correctly speculated, what is the effect on the three factors comprising the CPU time formula (from Chapter 1): dynamic instruction count, average clocks per instruction, and clock cycle time? When speculation is incorrect, it is possible for CPU time to increase. Which factor(s) of the CPU time formula best model this increase and why?

✪ 3.21   [15] <3.7> Consider the speculative Tomasulo processor shown in Figure 3.28 on page 225. Assume that the ROB has three buffer entries, named 0, 1, and 2. For the following code fragment, assume that ADD.D, SUB.D, and ADDI instructions execute for 1 cycle, and MUL.D executes for 10 cycles. Assume that the processor has sufficient function units to avoid stalling instruction issue.

```
ADD.D    F0, F8, F8
MUL.D    F2, F8, F8
SUB.D    F4, F0, F2
DADDI    R10,R12,R12
```

Fill in the table below to show ROB contents and history as it would exist on the cycle that the ADDI instruction writes its result. Assume that F8 and R12 are initialized and that the ROB is initially empty. (One table entry is already filled in to provide a fixed starting point for your answer.) Because a ROB is implemented as a circular queue, the entry number labels repeat modulo 3 reading down the table. If a ROB entry would be reallocated during the simulated execution time, write the details of the new allocation in the next available correspondingly numbered table row. Use the rightmost column to indicate if the instruction has been committed.

	ROB fields			Committed?
Entry	Instruction	Destination	Value	Yes/no
0	ADD.D			
1				
2				
0				
1				
2				

3.22 [20/15] <3.5, 3.7> Consider our speculative processor from Section 3.7. Since the reorder buffer contains a value field, you might think that the value field of the reservation stations could be eliminated.

a. [20] <3.5, 3.7> Show an example where this is the case and an example where the value field of the reservation stations is still needed. Use the speculative machine shown in Figure 3.29. Show MIPS code for both examples. How many value fields are needed in each reservation station?

b. [15] <3.5, 3.7> Find a modification to the rules for instruction commit that allows elimination of the value fields in the reservation station. What are the negative side effects of such a change?

3.23 [25] <3.7> Our implementation of speculation uses a reorder buffer and introduces the concept of instruction commit, delaying commit and the irrevocable updating of the registers until we know an instruction will complete. There are two other possible implementation techniques, both originally developed as a method for preserving precise interrupts when issuing out of order. One idea introduces a future file that keeps future values of a register; this idea is similar to the reorder buffer. An alternative is to keep a history buffer that records values of registers that have been speculatively overwritten.

Design a speculative processor like the one in Section 3.7 but using a history buffer. Show the state of the processor, including the contents of the history buffer, for the example in Figure 3.31. Show the changes needed to Figure 3.32 for a history buffer implementation. Describe exactly how and when entries in the history buffer are read and written, including what happens on an incorrect speculation.

3.24 [15/25] <3.8, 3.9> Aggressive hardware support for ILP is detailed at the beginning of Section 3.9. Keeping such a processor from stalling due to lack of work requires an average instruction fetch rate, f, that equals the average instruction completion rate, c. Achieving a high fetch rate is challenging in the presence of cache misses. Branches add to the difficulty and are ignored in this exercise. To explore just how challenging, model the average instruction memory access time as $h + mp$, where h is the time in clock cycles for a successful cache access, m is the rate of unsuccessful cache access, and p is the extra time, or penalty, in clock cycles to fetch from main memory instead of the cache.

a. [15] <3.8, 3.9> Write an equation for the number of instructions that the processor must attempt to fetch each clock cycle to achieve on average fetch rate $f = c$.

b. [25] <3.8, 3.9> Using a program with suitable graphing capability, such as a spreadsheet, plot the equation from part (a) for $0.01 \leq m \leq 0.1$, $10 \leq p \leq 100$, $1 \leq h \leq 2$ and a completion rate of 4 instructions per clock cycle. Comment on the importance of low average memory access time to the feasibility of achieving even modest average fetch rates.

3.25 [45] <3.2, 3.3> One benefit of a dynamically scheduled processor is its ability to tolerate changes in latency or issue capability without requiring recompilation. This capability was a primary motivation behind the 360/91 implementation of Tomasulo's algorithm. The purpose of this programming assignment is to evaluate this effect. Implement a version of Tomasulo's algorithm for MIPS to issue one instruction per clock; your implementation should also be capable of in-order issue. Assume fully pipelined functional units and the execution times in Figure 3.64.

Choose 5–10 small FP benchmarks (with loops) to run; compare the performance with and without dynamic scheduling. Try scheduling the loops by hand and see how close you can get with the statically scheduled processor to the dynamically scheduled results.

Change the processor to the configuration shown in Figure 3.65. Rerun the loops and compare the performance of the dynamically scheduled processor and the statically scheduled processor.

3.26 [45] <3.6> Perform the investigation of Exercise 3.25 but for a multiple-issue version of Tomasulo's algorithm. Use and/or adapt appropriate simulation tools.

3.27 [30/30] <3.8, 3.9> This exercise involves a programming assignment to evaluate what types of parallelism might be expected in more modest, and more realistic, processors than those studied in Section 3.8. These studies will require execution traces. You may be able to find traces or obtain them from a tracing program. For simplicity, assume perfect caches. For a more ambitious project, assume a real cache. To simplify the task, make the following assumptions:

■ Assume perfect branch and jump prediction: hence you can use the trace as the input to the window, without having to consider branch effects—the trace is perfect.

■ Assume there are 64 spare integer and 64 spare floating-point registers; this is easily implemented by stalling the issue of the processor whenever there are more live registers required.

■ Assume a window size of 64 instructions (the same for alias detection). Use greedy scheduling of instructions in the window. That is, at any clock cycle, pick for execution the first n instructions in the window that meet the issue constraints.

Unit	Execution time (clocks)
Integer	7
Branch	9
Load-store	11
FP add	13
FP mul	15
FP divide	17

Figure 3.64 Execution times for functional unit pipelines.

Unit	Execution time (clocks)
Integer	19
Branch	21
Load-store	23
FP add	25
FP mul	27
FP divide	29

Figure 3.65 Execution times for functional units, configuration 2.

a. [30] <3.8, 3.9> Determine the effect of limited instruction issue by performing the following experiments:

- Vary the issue count from 4 to16 instructions per clock.

- Assuming eight issues per clock, determine the effect of restricting the processor to two memory references per clock.

b. [30] <3.8, 3.9> Determine the impact of latency in instructions. Remember that with limited issue and a greedy scheduler, the impact of latency effects will be greater. Assume the following latency models for a processor that issues up to 16 instructions per clock:

- Model 1: All latencies are 1 clock.

- Model 2: Load latency and branch latency are 1 clock; all FP latencies are 2 clocks.

- Model 3: Load and branch latency is 2 clocks; all FP latencies are 5 clocks.

3.28 [Discussion] <3.2, 3.3> There is a subtle problem that must be considered when implementing Tomasulo's algorithm. It might be called the "two ships passing in the night problem." What happens if an instruction is being passed to a reservation station during the same clock period as one of its operands is going onto the common data bus? Before an instruction is in a reservation station, the operands are fetched from the register file; but once it is in the station, the operands are always obtained from the CDB. Since the instruction and its operand tag are in transit to the reservation station, the tag cannot be matched against the tag on the CDB. So there is a possibility that the instruction will then sit in the reservation station forever waiting for its operand, which it just missed. How might this problem be solved? You might consider subdividing one of the steps in the algorithm into multiple parts. (This intriguing problem is courtesy of J. E. Smith.)

3.29   [Discussion] <3.3, 3.7> Dynamic instruction scheduling requires a considerable investment in hardware. In return, this capability allows the hardware to run programs that could not be run at full speed with only compile time, static scheduling. What trade-offs should be taken into account in trying to decide between a dynamically and a statically scheduled implementation? What situations in either hardware technology or program characteristics are likely to favor one approach or the other? Most speculative schemes rely on dynamic scheduling; how does speculation affect the arguments in favor of dynamic scheduling?

3.30   [Discussion] <3.5> A branch-target buffer offers potential performance gains, but at a cost. Power consumption and clock cycle time may be critical design issues for a processor. Discuss the effect that a branch-target buffer has on these parameters as a function of buffer size. How is this BTB effect on power and clock cycle time similar to or different from that of other pipeline structures, such as the register file or ALU? What ways can you think of to improve the benefits of a BTB while at the same time meeting or exceeding power consumption and clock cycle time goals?

3.31   [Discussion] <3.6, A> Discuss the advantages and disadvantages of a superscalar implementation and a superpipelined implementation in the context of MIPS. What types of ILP favor each approach? What other concerns would you consider in choosing which type of processor to build? How does speculation affect the results?

4

Exploiting Instruction-Level Parallelism with Software Approaches

Processors are being produced with the potential for very many parallel operations on the instruction level.... Far greater extremes in instruction-level parallelism are on the horizon.

J. Fisher
*[1981], in the paper that inaugurated
the term "instruction-level parallelism"*

One of the surprises about IA-64 is that we hear no claims of high frequency, despite claims that an EPIC processor is less complex than a superscalar processor. It's hard to know why this is so, but one can speculate that the overall complexity involved in focusing on CPI, as IA-64 does, makes it hard to get high megahertz.

M. Hopkins
*[2000], in a commentary on the IA-64 architecture,
a joint development of HP and Intel designed to
achieve dramatic increases in the exploitation
of ILP while retaining a simple architecture,
which would allow higher performance*

Basic Compiler Techniques for Exposing ILP

This chapter starts by examining the use of compiler technology to improve the performance of pipelines and simple multiple-issue processors. These techniques are crucial for processors that use static issue, and they are often important even for processors that make dynamic issue decisions but use static scheduling. After applying these concepts to reducing stalls from data hazards in single-issue pipelines, we examine the use of compiler-based techniques for branch prediction. Armed with this more powerful compiler technology, we examine the design and performance of multiple-issue processors using static issuing or scheduling. Sections 4.4 and 4.5 examine more advanced software and hardware techniques, designed to enable a processor to exploit more instruction-level parallelism. Section 4.7, "Putting It All Together," examines the IA-64 architecture and its first implementation, Itanium. Two different static, VLIW-style processors are covered in Section 4.8, "Another View."

Basic Pipeline Scheduling and Loop Unrolling

To keep a pipeline full, parallelism among instructions must be exploited by finding sequences of unrelated instructions that can be overlapped in the pipeline. To avoid a pipeline stall, a dependent instruction must be separated from the source instruction by a distance in clock cycles equal to the pipeline latency of that source instruction. A compiler's ability to perform this scheduling depends both on the amount of ILP available in the program and on the latencies of the functional units in the pipeline. Throughout this chapter we will assume the FP unit latencies shown in Figure 4.1, unless different latencies are explicitly stated. We assume the standard five-stage integer pipeline, so that branches have a delay of one clock cycle. We assume that the functional units are fully pipelined or replicated (as many times as the pipeline depth), so that an operation of any type can be issued on every clock cycle and there are no structural hazards.

Instruction producing result	Instruction using result	Latency in clock cycles
FP ALU op	Another FP ALU op	3
FP ALU op	Store double	2
Load double	FP ALU op	1
Load double	Store double	0

Figure 4.1 Latencies of FP operations used in this chapter. The first column shows the originating instruction type. The second column is the type of the consuming instruction. The last column is the number of intervening clock cycles needed to avoid a stall. These numbers are similar to the average latencies we would see on an FP unit. The latency of a floating-point load to a store is zero, since the result of the load can be bypassed without stalling the store. We will continue to assume an integer load latency of 1 and an integer ALU operation latency of 0.

In this subsection, we look at how the compiler can increase the amount of available ILP by unrolling loops. This example serves both to illustrate an important technique as well as to motivate the more powerful program transformations described later in this chapter. We will rely on an example similar to the one we used in the last chapter, adding a scalar to a vector:

```
for (i=1000; i>0; i=i-1)
    x[i] = x[i] + s;
```

We can see that this loop is parallel by noticing that the body of each iteration is independent. We will formalize this notion later in this chapter and describe how we can test whether loop iterations are independent at compile time. First, let's look at the performance of this loop, showing how we can use the parallelism to improve its performance for a MIPS pipeline with the latencies shown above.

The first step is to translate the above segment to MIPS assembly language. In the following code segment, R1 is initially the address of the element in the array with the highest address, and F2 contains the scalar value s. Register R2 is precomputed, so that 8(R2) is the last element to operate on.

The straightforward MIPS code, not scheduled for the pipeline, looks like this:

```
Loop:   L.D     F0,0(R1)      ;F0=array element
        ADD.D   F4,F0,F2      ;add scalar in F2
        S.D     F4,0(R1)      ;store result
        DADDUI  R1,R1,#-8     ;decrement pointer
                              ;8 bytes (per DW)
        BNE     R1,R2,Loop    ;branch R1!=R2
```

Let's start by seeing how well this loop will run when it is scheduled on a simple pipeline for MIPS with the latencies from Figure 4.1.

Example Show how the loop would look on MIPS, both scheduled and unscheduled, including any stalls or idle clock cycles. Schedule for delays both from floating-point operations and from the delayed branch.

Answer Without any scheduling, the loop will execute as follows:

			Clock cycle issued
Loop:	L.D	F0,0(R1)	1
	stall		2
	ADD.D	F4,F0,F2	3
	stall		4
	stall		5
	S.D	F4,0(R1)	6
	DADDUI	R1,R1,#-8	7
	stall		8
	BNE	R1,R2,Loop	9
	stall		10

This code requires 10 clock cycles per iteration. We can schedule the loop to obtain only one stall:

```
Loop:   L.D      F0,0(R1)
        DADDUI   R1,R1,#-8
        ADD.D    F4,F0,F2
        stall
        BNE      R1,R2,Loop  ;delayed branch
        S.D      F4,8(R1)    ;altered & interchanged with DADDUI
```

Execution time has been reduced from 10 clock cycles to 6. The stall after ADD.D is for use by the S.D.

Notice that to schedule the delayed branch, the compiler had to determine that it could swap the DADDUI and S.D by changing the address to which the S.D stored: The address was 0(R1) and is now 8(R1). This change is not trivial, since most compilers would see that the S.D instruction depends on the DADDUI and would refuse to interchange them. A smarter compiler, capable of limited symbolic optimization, could figure out the relationship and perform the interchange. The chain of dependent instructions from the L.D to the ADD.D and then to the S.D determines the clock cycle count for this loop. This chain must take at least 6 cycles because of dependencies and pipeline latencies.

In the above example, we complete one loop iteration and store back one array element every 6 clock cycles, but the actual work of operating on the array element takes just 3 (the load, add, and store) of those 6 clock cycles. The remaining 3 clock cycles consist of loop overhead—the DADDUI and BNE—and a stall. To eliminate these 3 clock cycles we need to get more operations within the loop relative to the number of overhead instructions.

A simple scheme for increasing the number of instructions relative to the branch and overhead instructions is *loop unrolling*. Unrolling simply replicates the loop body multiple times, adjusting the loop termination code.

Loop unrolling can also be used to improve scheduling. Because it eliminates the branch, it allows instructions from different iterations to be scheduled together. In this case, we can eliminate the data use stall by creating additional independent instructions within the loop body. If we simply replicated the instructions when we unrolled the loop, the resulting use of the same registers could prevent us from effectively scheduling the loop. Thus, we will want to use different registers for each iteration, increasing the required register count.

Example   Show our loop unrolled so that there are four copies of the loop body, assuming R1 is initially a multiple of 32, which means that the number of loop iterations is a multiple of 4. Eliminate any obviously redundant computations and do not reuse any of the registers.

Answer   Here is the result after merging the DADDUI instructions and dropping the unnecessary BNE operations that are duplicated during unrolling. Note that R2 must now be set so that 32(R2) is the starting address of the last four elements.

```
Loop:   L.D     F0,0(R1)
        ADD.D   F4,F0,F2
        S.D     F4,0(R1)        ;drop DADDUI & BNE
        L.D     F6,-8(R1)
        ADD.D   F8,F6,F2
        S.D     F8,-8(R1)       ;drop DADDUI & BNE
        L.D     F10,-16(R1)
        ADD.D   F12,F10,F2
        S.D     F12,-16(R1)     ;drop DADDUI & BNE
        L.D     F14,-24(R1)
        ADD.D   F16,F14,F2
        S.D     F16,-24(R1)
        DADDUI  R1,R1,#-32
        BNE     R1,R2,Loop
```

We have eliminated three branches and three decrements of R1. The addresses on the loads and stores have been compensated to allow the DADDUI instructions on R1 to be merged. This optimization may seem trivial, but it is not; it requires symbolic substitution and simplification. We will see more general forms of these optimizations that eliminate dependent computations in Section 4.4.

Without scheduling, every operation in the unrolled loop is followed by a dependent operation and thus will cause a stall. This loop will run in 28 clock cycles—each L.D has 1 stall, each ADD.D 2, the DADDUI 1, the branch 1, plus 14 instruction issue cycles—or 7 clock cycles for each of the four elements. Although this unrolled version is currently slower than the *scheduled* version of the original loop, this will change when we schedule the unrolled loop. Loop unrolling is normally done early in the compilation process, so that redundant computations can be exposed and eliminated by the optimizer.

In real programs we do not usually know the upper bound on the loop. Suppose it is n, and we would like to unroll the loop to make k copies of the body. Instead of a single unrolled loop, we generate a pair of consecutive loops. The first executes ($n \bmod k$) times and has a body that is the original loop. The second is the unrolled body surrounded by an outer loop that iterates (n/k) times. For large values of n, most of the execution time will be spent in the unrolled loop body.

In the previous example, unrolling improves the performance of this loop by eliminating overhead instructions, although it increases code size substantially. How will the unrolled loop perform when it is scheduled for the pipeline described earlier?

Example Show the unrolled loop in the previous example after it has been scheduled for the pipeline with the latencies shown in Figure 4.1.

```
Answer   Loop:  L.D      F0,0(R1)
                L.D      F6,-8(R1)
                L.D      F10,-16(R1)
                L.D      F14,-24(R1)
                ADD.D    F4,F0,F2
                ADD.D    F8,F6,F2
                ADD.D    F12,F10,F2
                ADD.D    F16,F14,F2
                S.D      F4,0(R1)
                S.D      F8,-8(R1)
                DADDUI   R1,R1,#-32
                S.D      F12,16(R1)
                BNE      R1,R2,Loop
                S.D      F16,8(R1);8-32 = -24
```

The execution time of the unrolled loop has dropped to a total of 14 clock cycles, or 3.5 clock cycles per element, compared with 7 cycles per element before scheduling and 6 cycles when scheduled but not unrolled.

The gain from scheduling on the unrolled loop is even larger than on the original loop. This increase arises because unrolling the loop exposes more computation that can be scheduled to minimize the stalls; the code above has no stalls. Scheduling the loop in this fashion necessitates realizing that the loads and stores are independent and can be interchanged.

Summary of the Loop Unrolling and Scheduling Example

Throughout this chapter we will look at a variety of hardware and software techniques that allow us to take advantage of instruction-level parallelism to fully utilize the potential of the functional units in a processor. The key to most of these techniques is to know when and how the ordering among instructions may be changed. In our example we made many such changes, which to us, as human beings, were obviously allowable. In practice, this process must be performed in a methodical fashion either by a compiler or by hardware. To obtain the final unrolled code we had to make the following decisions and transformations:

1. Determine that it was legal to move the S.D after the DADDUI and BNE, and find the amount to adjust the S.D offset.

2. Determine that unrolling the loop would be useful by finding that the loop iterations were independent, except for the loop maintenance code.

3. Use different registers to avoid unnecessary constraints that would be forced by using the same registers for different computations.

4. Eliminate the extra test and branch instructions and adjust the loop termination and iteration code.

5. Determine that the loads and stores in the unrolled loop can be interchanged by observing that the loads and stores from different iterations are independent. This transformation requires analyzing the memory addresses and finding that they do not refer to the same address.

6. Schedule the code, preserving any dependences needed to yield the same result as the original code.

The key requirement underlying all of these transformations is an understanding of how an instruction depends on another and how the instructions can be changed or reordered given the dependences. Before examining how these techniques work for higher issue rate pipelines, let us examine how the loop unrolling and scheduling techniques affect data dependences.

Example Show how the process of optimizing the loop overhead by unrolling the loop actually eliminates data dependences. In this example and those used in the remainder of this chapter, we use nondelayed branches for simplicity; it is easy to extend the examples to use delayed branches.

Answer Here is the unrolled but unoptimized code with the extra DADDUI instructions, but without the branches. (Eliminating the branches is another type of transformation, since it involves control rather than data.) The arrows show the data dependences that are within the unrolled body and involve the DADDUI instructions. The underlined registers are the dependent uses.

```
Loop:   L.D      F0,0(R1)
        ADD.D    F4,F0,F2
        S.D      F4,0(R1)
        DADDUI   R1,R1,#-8;drop BNE
        L.D      F6,0(R1)
        ADD.D    F8,F6,F2
        S.D      F8,0(R1)
        DADDUI   R1,R1,#-8;drop BNE
        L.D      F10,0(R1)
        ADD.D    F12,F10,F2
        S.D      F12,0(R1)
        DADDUI   R1,R1,#-8;drop BNE
        L.D      F14,0(R1)
        ADD.D    F16,F14,F2
        S.D      F16,0(R1)
        DADDUI   R1,R1,#-8
        BNE      R1,R2,LOOP
```

As the arrows show, the DADDUI instructions form a dependent chain that involves the DADDUI, L.D, and S.D instructions. This chain forces the body to execute in order, as well as making the DADDUI instructions necessary, which increases the instruction count. The compiler removes this dependence by symbolically computing the intermediate values of R1 and folding the computation into the offset of the L.D and S.D instructions and by changing the final DADDUI into a decrement by 32. This transformation makes the three DADDUI unnecessary, and the compiler can remove them. There are other types of dependences in this code, as the next few examples show.

Example   Unroll our example loop, eliminating the excess loop overhead, but using the same registers in each loop copy. Indicate both the data and name dependences within the body. Show how renaming eliminates name dependences that reduce parallelism.

Answer   Here's the loop unrolled but with the same registers in use for each copy. The data dependences are shown with gray arrows and the name dependences with black arrows. As in earlier examples, the direction of the arrow indicates the ordering that must be preserved for correct execution of the code:

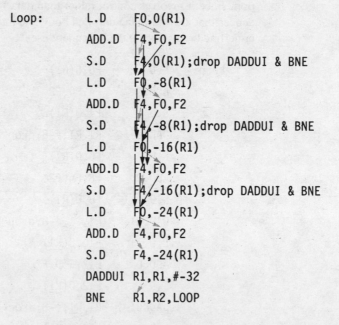

```
Loop:      L.D      F0,0(R1)
           ADD.D    F4,F0,F2
           S.D      F4,0(R1);drop DADDUI & BNE
           L.D      F0,-8(R1)
           ADD.D    F4,F0,F2
           S.D      F4,-8(R1);drop DADDUI & BNE
           L.D      F0,-16(R1)
           ADD.D    F4,F0,F2
           S.D      F4,-16(R1);drop DADDUI & BNE
           L.D      F0,-24(R1)
           ADD.D    F4,F0,F2
           S.D      F4,-24(R1)
           DADDUI   R1,R1,#-32
           BNE      R1,R2,LOOP
```

The name dependences force the instructions in the loop to be almost completely ordered, allowing only the order of the L.D following each S.D to be interchanged. When the registers used for each copy of the loop body are renamed, only the true dependences within each body remain:

```
Loop:      L.D      F0,0(R1).
           ADD.D    F4,F0,F2
           S.D      F4,0(R1);drop DADDUI & BNE
           L.D      F6,-8(R1)
           ADD.D    F8,F6,F2
           S.D      F8,-8(R1);drop DADDUI & BNE
           L.D      F10,-16(R1)
           ADD.D    F12,F10,F2
           S.D      F12,-16(R1);drop DADDUI & BNE
           L.D      F14,-24(R1)
           ADD.D    F16,F14,F2
           S.D      F16,-24(R1)
           DADDUI   R1,R1,#-32
           BNE      R1,R2,LOOP
```

With the renaming, the copies of each loop body become independent and can be overlapped or executed in parallel. This renaming process can be performed either by the compiler or in hardware, as we saw in the last chapter.

There are three different types of limits to the gains that can be achieved by loop unrolling: a decrease in the amount of overhead amortized with each unroll, code size limitations, and compiler limitations. Let's consider the question of loop overhead first. When we unrolled the loop four times, it generated sufficient parallelism among the instructions that the loop could be scheduled with no stall cycles. In fact, in 14 clock cycles, only 2 cycles were loop overhead: the DSUBI, which maintains the index value, and the BNE, which terminates the loop. If the loop is unrolled eight times, the overhead is reduced from 1/2 cycle per original iteration to 1/4. Exercise 4.3 asks you to compute the theoretically optimal number of times to unroll this loop for a random number of iterations.

A second limit to unrolling is the growth in code size that results. For larger loops, the code size growth may be a concern either in the embedded space where memory may be at a premium or if the larger code size causes a decrease in the instruction cache miss rate. We return to the issue of code size when we consider more aggressive techniques for uncovering instruction-level parallelism in Section 4.4.

Another factor often more important than code size is the potential shortfall in registers that is created by aggressive unrolling and scheduling. This secondary effect that results from instruction scheduling in large code segments is called *register pressure*. It arises because scheduling code to increase ILP causes the number of live values to increase. After aggressive instruction scheduling, it may not be possible to allocate all the live values to registers. The transformed code, while theoretically faster, may lose some or all of its advantage, because it generates a shortage of registers. Without unrolling, aggressive scheduling is sufficiently limited by branches so that register pressure is rarely a problem. The combination of unrolling and aggressive scheduling can, however, cause this problem. The problem becomes especially challenging in multiple-issue machines that require the exposure of more independent instruction sequences whose execution can be overlapped. In general, the use of sophisticated high-level transformations, whose potential improvements are hard to measure before detailed code generation, has led to significant increases in the complexity of modern compilers.

Loop unrolling is a simple but useful method for increasing the size of straight-line code fragments that can be scheduled effectively. This transformation is useful in a variety of processors, from simple pipelines like those in MIPS to the statically scheduled superscalars we described in the last chapter, as we will see now.

Using Loop Unrolling and Pipeline Scheduling with Static Multiple Issue

We begin by looking at a simple two-issue, statically scheduled superscalar MIPS pipeline from the last chapter, using the pipeline latencies from Figure 4.1 and the same example code segment we used for the single-issue examples above. This processor can issue two instructions per clock cycle: One of the instructions can be a load, store, branch, or integer ALU operation, and the other can be any floating-point operation.

Recall that this pipeline did not generate a significant performance enhancement for the previous example because of the limited ILP in a given loop iteration. Let's see how loop unrolling and pipeline scheduling can help.

Example   Unroll and schedule the loop used in the earlier examples and shown on page 305.

Answer   To schedule this loop without any delays, we will need to unroll the loop to make five copies of the body. After unrolling, the loop will contain five each of L.D, ADD.D, and S.D; one DADDUI; and one BNE. The unrolled and scheduled code is shown in Figure 4.2.

This unrolled superscalar loop now runs in 12 clock cycles per iteration, or 2.4 clock cycles per element, versus 3.5 for the scheduled and unrolled loop on the ordinary MIPS pipeline. In this example, the performance of the superscalar MIPS is limited by the balance between integer and floating-point computation. Every floating-point instruction is issued together with an integer instruction, but there are not enough floating-point instructions to keep the floating-point pipeline full. When scheduled, the original loop ran in 6 clock cycles per iteration. We have improved on that by a factor of 2.5, more than half of which came from loop unrolling. Loop unrolling took us from 6 to 3.5 (a factor of 1.7), while superscalar execution gave us a factor of 1.5 improvement.

	Integer instruction	FP instruction	Clock cycle
Loop:	L.D F0,0(R1)		1
	L.D F6,-8(R1)		2
	L.D F10,-16(R1)	ADD.D F4,F0,F2	3
	L.D F14,-24(R1)	ADD.D F8,F6,F2	4
	L.D F18,-32(R1)	ADD.D F12,F10,F2	5
	S.D F4,0(R1)	ADD.D F16,F14,F2	6
	S.D F8,-8(R1)	ADD.D F20,F18,F2	7
	S.D F12,-16(R1)		8
	DADDUI R1,R1,#-40		9
	S.D F16,16(R1)		10
	BNE R1,R2,Loop		11
	S.D F20,8(R1)		12

Figure 4.2 The unrolled and scheduled code as it would look on a superscalar MIPS.

4.2 Static Branch Prediction

In Chapter 3, we examined the use of dynamic branch predictors. Static branch predictors are sometimes used in processors where the expectation is that branch behavior is highly predictable at compile time; static prediction can also be used to assist dynamic predictors.

In Appendix A, we will discuss an architectural feature that supports static branch predication, namely, delayed branches. Delayed branches expose a pipeline hazard so that the compiler can reduce the penalty associated with the hazard. As we saw, the effectiveness of this technique partly depends on whether we correctly guess which way a branch will go. Being able to accurately predict a branch at compile time is also helpful for scheduling data hazards. Loop unrolling is one simple example of this; another example arises from conditional selection branches. Consider the following code segment:

```
        LD      R1,0(R2)
        DSUBU   R1,R1,R3
        BEQZ    R1,L
        OR      R4,R5,R6
        DADDU   R10,R4,R3
L:      DADDU   R7,R8,R9
```

The dependence of the DSUBU and BEQZ on the LD instruction means that a stall will be needed after the LD. Suppose we knew that this branch was almost always taken and that the value of R7 was not needed on the fall-through path. Then we could increase the speed of the program by moving the instruction DADD R7,R8,R9 to the position after the LD. Correspondingly, if we knew the branch was rarely taken and that the value of R4 was not needed on the taken path, then we could contemplate moving the OR instruction after the LD. In addition, we can also use the information to better schedule any branch delay, since choosing how to schedule the delay depends on knowing the branch behavior. We will return to this topic in Section 4.4, when we discuss global code scheduling.

To perform these optimizations, we need to predict the branch statically when we compile the program. There are several different methods to statically predict branch behavior. The simplest scheme is to predict a branch as taken. This scheme has an average misprediction rate that is equal to the untaken branch frequency, which for the SPEC programs is 34%. Unfortunately, the misprediction rate ranges from not very accurate (59%) to highly accurate (9%).

A better alternative is to predict on the basis of branch direction, choosing backward-going branches to be taken and forward-going branches to be not taken. For some programs and compilation systems, the frequency of forward taken branches may be significantly less than 50%, and this scheme will do better than just predicting all branches as taken. In the SPEC programs, however, more than half of the forward-going branches are taken. Hence, predicting all branches as taken is the better approach. Even for other benchmarks or compilers, direction-based prediction is unlikely to generate an overall misprediction rate of less than 30% to 40%. An enhancement of this technique was explored by Ball and Larus [1993]; their approach uses program context information and generates more accurate predictions than a simple scheme based solely on branch direction.

A still more accurate technique is to predict branches on the basis of profile information collected from earlier runs. The key observation that makes this worthwhile is that the behavior of branches is often bimodally distributed; that is, an individual branch is often highly biased toward taken or untaken. Figure 4.3 shows the success of branch prediction using this strategy. The same input data were used for runs and for collecting the profile; other studies have shown that changing the input so that the profile is for a different run leads to only a small change in the accuracy of profile-based prediction.

Although we can derive the prediction accuracy of a predicted-taken strategy and measure the accuracy of the profile scheme, as in Figure 4.3, the wide range of frequency of conditional branches in these programs, from 3% to 24%, means that the overall frequency of a mispredicted branch varies widely. Figure 4.4 shows the number of instructions executed between mispredicted branches for both a profile-based and a predicted-taken strategy. The number varies widely, both because of the variation in accuracy and the variation in branch frequency. On average, the predicted-taken strategy has 20 instructions per mispredicted branch and the profile-based strategy has 110. These averages, however, are very different for integer and FP programs, as the data in Figure 4.4 show.

Static branch behavior is useful for scheduling instructions when the branch delays are exposed by the architecture (either delayed or canceling branches), for assisting dynamic predictors (as we will see in the IA-64 architecture in Section 4.7), and for determining which code paths are more frequent, which is a key step in code scheduling (see Section 4.4, page 332).

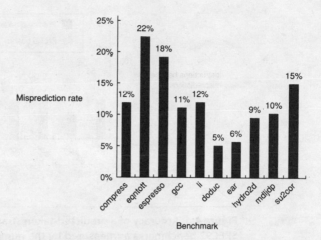

Figure 4.3 **Misprediction rate on SPEC92 for a profile-based predictor varies widely but is generally better for the FP programs, which have an average misprediction rate of 9% with a standard deviation of 4%, than for the integer programs, which have an average misprediction rate of 15% with a standard deviation of 5%.** The actual performance depends on both the prediction accuracy and the branch frequency, which varies from 3% to 24%; we will examine the combined effect in Figure 4.4.

4.3   Static Multiple Issue: The VLIW Approach

Superscalar processors decide on the fly how many instructions to issue. A statically scheduled superscalar must check for any dependences between instructions in the issue packet as well as between any issue candidate and any instruction already in the pipeline. As we have seen in Section 4.1, a statically scheduled superscalar requires significant compiler assistance to achieve good performance. In contrast, a dynamically scheduled superscalar requires less compiler assistance, but has significant hardware costs.

An alternative to the superscalar approach is to rely on compiler technology not only to minimize the potential data hazard stalls, but to actually format the instructions in a potential issue packet so that the hardware need not check explicitly for dependences. The compiler may be required to ensure that dependences within the issue packet cannot be present or, at a minimum, indicate when a dependence may be present. Such an approach offers the potential advantage of simpler hardware while still exhibiting good performance through extensive compiler optimization.

The first multiple-issue processors that required the instruction stream to be explicitly organized to avoid dependences used wide instructions with multiple operations per instruction. For this reason, this architectural approach was named VLIW (very long instruction word), denoting that the instructions, since they contained several instructions, were very wide (64 to 128 bits, or more). The basic architectural concepts and compiler technology are the same whether

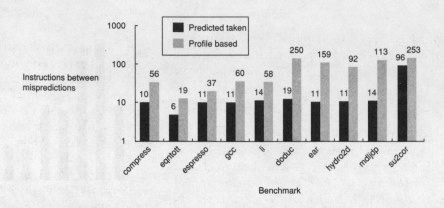

Figure 4.4 Accuracy of a predicted-taken strategy and a profile-based predictor for SPEC92 benchmarks as measured by the number of instructions executed between mispredicted branches and shown on a log scale. The average number of instructions between mispredictions is 20 for the predicted-taken strategy and 110 for the profile-based prediction; however, the standard deviations are large: 27 instructions for the predicted-taken strategy and 85 instructions for the profile-based scheme. This wide variation arises because programs such as su2cor have both low conditional branch frequency (3%) and predictable branches (85% accuracy for profiling), although eqntott has eight times the branch frequency with branches that are nearly 1.5 times *less* predictable. The difference between the FP and integer benchmarks as groups is large. For the predicted-taken strategy, the average distance between mispredictions for the integer benchmarks is 10 instructions, and for the FP programs it is 30 instructions. With the profile scheme, the distance between mispredictions for the integer benchmarks is 46 instructions, and for the FP benchmarks it is 173 instructions.

multiple operations are organized into a single instruction, or whether a set of instructions in an issue packet is preconfigured by a compiler to exclude dependent operations (since the issue packet can be thought of as a very large instruction). Early VLIWs were quite rigid in their instruction formats and effectively required recompilation of programs for different versions of the hardware.

To reduce this inflexibility and enhance the performance of the approach, several innovations have been incorporated into more recent architectures of this type, while still requiring the compiler to do most of the work of finding and scheduling instructions for parallel execution. This second generation of VLIW architectures is the approach being pursued for desktop and server markets.

In the remainder of this section, we look at the basic concepts in a VLIW architecture. Section 4.4 introduces additional compiler techniques that are required to achieve good performance for compiler-intensive approaches, and Section 4.5 describes hardware innovations that improve flexibility and performance of explicitly parallel approaches. Finally, Section 4.7 describes how the Intel IA-64 supports explicit parallelism.

The Basic VLIW Approach

VLIWs use multiple, independent functional units. Rather than attempting to issue multiple, independent instructions to the units, a VLIW packages the multiple operations into one very long instruction, or requires that the instructions in the issue packet satisfy the same constraints. Since there is no fundamental difference in the two approaches, we will just assume that multiple operations are placed in one instruction, as in the original VLIW approach. Since the burden for choosing the instructions to be issued simultaneously falls on the compiler, the hardware in a superscalar to make these issue decisions is unneeded.

Since this advantage of a VLIW increases as the maximum issue rate grows, we focus on a wider-issue processor. Indeed, for simple two-issue processors, the overhead of a superscalar is probably minimal. Many designers would probably argue that a four-issue processor has manageable overhead, but as we saw in the last chapter, this overhead grows with issue width.

Because VLIW approaches make sense for wider processors, we choose to focus our example on such an architecture. For example, a VLIW processor might have instructions that contain five operations, including one integer operation (which could also be a branch), two floating-point operations, and two memory references. The instruction would have a set of fields for each functional unit—perhaps 16 to 24 bits per unit, yielding an instruction length of between 112 and 168 bits.

To keep the functional units busy, there must be enough parallelism in a code sequence to fill the available operation slots. This parallelism is uncovered by unrolling loops and scheduling the code within the single larger loop body. If the unrolling generates straight-line code, then *local scheduling* techniques, which operate on a single basic block, can be used. If finding and exploiting the parallelism requires scheduling code across branches, a substantially more complex *global scheduling* algorithm must be used. Global scheduling algorithms are not only more complex in structure, but they also must deal with significantly more complicated trade-offs in optimization, since moving code across branches is expensive. In the next section, we will discuss *trace scheduling,* one of these global scheduling techniques developed specifically for VLIWs. In Section 4.5, we will examine hardware support that allows some conditional branches to be eliminated, extending the usefulness of local scheduling and enhancing the performance of global scheduling.

For now, let's assume we have a technique to generate long, straight-line code sequences, so that we can use local scheduling to build up VLIW instructions and instead focus on how well these processors operate.

Example   Suppose we have a VLIW that could issue two memory references, two FP operations, and one integer operation or branch in every clock cycle. Show an unrolled version of the loop x[i] = x[i] + s (see page 305 for the MIPS code) for such a processor. Unroll as many times as necessary to eliminate any stalls. Ignore the branch delay slot.

Memory reference 1	Memory reference 2	FP operation 1	FP operation 2	Integer operation/branch
L.D F0,0(R1)	L.D F6,-8(R1)			
L.D F10,-16(R1)	L.D F14,-24(R1)			
L.D F18,-32(R1)	L.D F22,-40(R1)	ADD.D F4,F0,F2	ADD.D F8,F6,F2	
L.D F26,-48(R1)		ADD.D F12,F10,F2	ADD.D F16,F14,F2	
		ADD.D F20,F18,F2	ADD.D F24,F22,F2	
S.D F4,0(R1)	S.D F8,-8(R1)	ADD.D F28,F26,F2		
S.D F12,-16(R1)	S.D F16,-24(R1)			DADDUI R1,R1,#-56
S.D F20,24(R1)	S.D F24,16(R1)			
S.D F28,8(R1)				BNE R1,R2,Loop

Figure 4.5 VLIW instructions that occupy the inner loop and replace the unrolled sequence. This code takes 9 cycles assuming no branch delay; normally the branch delay would also need to be scheduled. The issue rate is 23 operations in 9 clock cycles, or 2.5 operations per cycle. The efficiency, the percentage of available slots that contained an operation, is about 60%. To achieve this issue rate requires a larger number of registers than MIPS would normally use in this loop. The VLIW code sequence above requires at least eight FP registers, while the same code sequence for the base MIPS processor can use as few as two FP registers or as many as five when unrolled and scheduled. In the superscalar example in Figure 4.2, six registers were needed.

Answer   The code is shown in Figure 4.5. The loop has been unrolled to make seven copies of the body, which eliminates all stalls (i.e., completely empty issue cycles), and runs in 9 cycles. This code yields a running rate of seven results in 9 cycles, or 1.29 cycles per result, nearly twice as fast as the two-issue superscalar of Section 4.1 that used unrolled and scheduled code.

For the original VLIW model, there are both technical and logistical problems. The technical problems are the increase in code size and the limitations of lockstep operation. Two different elements combine to increase code size substantially for a VLIW. First, generating enough operations in a straight-line code fragment requires ambitiously unrolling loops (as in earlier examples), thereby increasing code size. Second, whenever instructions are not full, the unused functional units translate to wasted bits in the instruction encoding. In Figure 4.5, we saw that only about 60% of the functional units were used, so almost half of each instruction was empty. In most VLIWs, an instruction may need to be left completely empty if no operations can be scheduled.

To combat this code size increase, clever encodings are sometimes used. For example, there may be only one large immediate field for use by any functional unit. Another technique is to compress the instructions in main memory and expand them when they are read into the cache or are decoded. We will see techniques to reduce code size increases in both Sections 4.7 and 4.8.

Early VLIWs operated in lockstep; there was no hazard detection hardware at all. This structure dictated that a stall in any functional unit pipeline must cause the entire processor to stall, since all the functional units must be kept synchronized. Although a compiler may be able to schedule the deterministic functional units to prevent stalls, predicting which data accesses will encounter a cache stall and scheduling them is very difficult. Hence, caches needed to be blocking and to cause *all* the functional units to stall. As the issue rate and number of memory references becomes large, this synchronization restriction becomes unacceptable. In more recent processors, the functional units operate more independently, and the compiler is used to avoid hazards at issue time, while hardware checks allow for unsynchronized execution once instructions are issued.

Binary code compatibility has also been a major logistical problem for VLIWs. In a strict VLIW approach, the code sequence makes use of both the instruction set definition and the detailed pipeline structure, including both functional units and their latencies. Thus, different numbers of functional units and unit latencies require different versions of the code. This requirement makes migrating between successive implementations, or between implementations with different issue widths, more difficult than it is for a superscalar design. Of course, obtaining improved performance from a new superscalar design may require recompilation. Nonetheless, the ability to run old binary files is a practical advantage for the superscalar approach.

One possible solution to this migration problem, and the problem of binary code compatibility in general, is object-code translation or emulation. This technology is developing quickly and could play a significant role in future migration schemes. Another approach is to temper the strictness of the approach so that binary compatibility is still feasible. This later approach is used in the IA-64 architecture, as we will see in Section 4.7.

The major challenge for all multiple-issue processors is to try to exploit large amounts of ILP. When the parallelism comes from unrolling simple loops in FP programs, the original loop probably could have been run efficiently on a vector processor (described in Appendix G). It is not clear that a multiple-issue processor is preferred over a vector processor for such applications; the costs are similar, and the vector processor is typically the same speed or faster. The potential advantages of a multiple-issue processor versus a vector processor are twofold. First, a multiple-issue processor has the potential to extract some amount of parallelism from less regularly structured code, and, second, it has the ability to use a more conventional, and typically less expensive, cache-based memory system. For these reasons multiple-issue approaches have become the primary method for taking advantage of instruction-level parallelism, and vectors have become primarily an extension to these processors.

4.4 Advanced Compiler Support for Exposing and Exploiting ILP

In this section we discuss compiler technology for increasing the amount of parallelism that we can exploit in a program. We begin by defining when a loop is parallel and how a dependence can prevent a loop from being parallel. We also discuss techniques for eliminating some types of dependences. As we will see in later sections, hardware support for these compiler techniques can greatly increase their effectiveness. This section serves as an introduction to these techniques. We do not attempt to explain the details of ILP-oriented compiler techniques, since that would take hundreds of pages, rather than the 20 we have allotted. Instead, we view this material as providing general background that will enable the reader to have a basic understanding of the compiler techniques used to exploit ILP in modern computers.

Detecting and Enhancing Loop-Level Parallelism

Loop-level parallelism is normally analyzed at the source level or close to it, while most analysis of ILP is done once instructions have been generated by the compiler. Loop-level analysis involves determining what dependences exist among the operands in a loop across the iterations of that loop. For now, we will consider only data dependences, which arise when an operand is written at some point and read at a later point. Name dependences also exist and may be removed by renaming techniques like those we used earlier.

The analysis of loop-level parallelism focuses on determining whether data accesses in later iterations are dependent on data values produced in earlier iterations; such a dependence is called a *loop-carried dependence*. Most of the examples we considered in Section 4.1 have no loop-carried dependences and, thus, are loop-level parallel. To see that a loop is parallel, let us first look at the source representation:

```
for (i=1000; i>0; i=i-1)
        x[i] = x[i] + s;
```

In this loop, there is a dependence between the two uses of x[i], but this dependence is within a single iteration and is not loop carried. There is a dependence between successive uses of i in different iterations, which is loop carried, but this dependence involves an induction variable and can be easily recognized and eliminated. We saw examples of how to eliminate dependences involving induction variables during loop unrolling in Section 4.1, and we will look at additional examples later in this section.

Because finding loop-level parallelism involves recognizing structures such as loops, array references, and induction variable computations, the compiler can do this analysis more easily at or near the source level, as opposed to the machine-code level. Let's look at a more complex example.

Example   Consider a loop like this one:

```
for (i=1; i<=100; i=i+1) {
        A[i+1] = A[i] + C[i];   /* S1 */
        B[i+1] = B[i] + A[i+1]; /* S2 */
}
```

Assume that A, B, and C are distinct, nonoverlapping arrays. (In practice, the arrays may sometimes be the same or may overlap. Because the arrays may be passed as parameters to a procedure, which includes this loop, determining whether arrays overlap or are identical often requires sophisticated, interprocedural analysis of the program.) What are the data dependences among the statements S1 and S2 in the loop?

Answer   There are two different dependences:

1. S1 uses a value computed by S1 in an earlier iteration, since iteration i computes A[i+1], which is read in iteration i+1. The same is true of S2 for B[i] and B[i+1].

2. S2 uses the value, A[i+1], computed by S1 in the same iteration.

These two dependences are different and have different effects. To see how they differ, let's assume that only one of these dependences exists at a time. Because the dependence of statement S1 is on an earlier iteration of S1, this dependence is loop carried. This dependence forces successive iterations of this loop to execute in series.

The second dependence above (S2 depending on S1) is within an iteration and is not loop carried. Thus, if this were the only dependence, multiple iterations of the loop could execute in parallel, as long as each pair of statements in an iteration were kept in order. We saw this type of dependence in an example in Section 4.1, where unrolling was able to expose the parallelism.

It is also possible to have a loop-carried dependence that does not prevent parallelism, as the next example shows.

Example   Consider a loop like this one:

```
for (i=1; i<=100; i=i+1) {
    A[i] = A[i] + B[i];    /* S1 */
    B[i+1] = C[i] + D[i];  /* S2 */
}
```

What are the dependences between S1 and S2? Is this loop parallel? If not, show how to make it parallel.

Answer   Statement S1 uses the value assigned in the previous iteration by statement S2, so there is a loop-carried dependence between S2 and S1. Despite this loop-carried dependence, this loop can be made parallel. Unlike the earlier loop, this dependence is not circular: neither statement depends on itself, and although S1 depends on S2, S2 does not depend on S1. A loop is parallel if it can be written without a cycle in the dependences, since the absence of a cycle means that the dependences give a partial ordering on the statements.

Although there are no circular dependences in the above loop, it must be transformed to conform to the partial ordering and expose the parallelism. Two observations are critical to this transformation:

1. There is no dependence from S1 to S2. If there were, then there would be a cycle in the dependences and the loop would not be parallel. Since this other dependence is absent, interchanging the two statements will not affect the execution of S2.

2. On the first iteration of the loop, statement S1 depends on the value of B[1] computed prior to initiating the loop.

These two observations allow us to replace the loop above with the following code sequence:

```
A[1] = A[1] + B[1];
for (i=1; i<=99; i=i+1) {
    B[i+1] = C[i] + D[i];
    A[i+1] = A[i+1] + B[i+1];
}
B[101] = C[100] + D[100];
```

The dependence between the two statements is no longer loop carried, so that iterations of the loop may be overlapped, provided the statements in each iteration are kept in order.

Our analysis needs to begin by finding all loop-carried dependences. This dependence information is *inexact,* in the sense that it tells us that such a dependence *may* exist. Consider the following example:

```
for (i=1;i<=100;i=i+1) {
    A[i] = B[i] + C[i]
    D[i] = A[i] * E[i]
}
```

The second reference to A in this example need not be translated to a load instruction, since we know that the value is computed and stored by the previous statement; hence, the second reference to A can simply be a reference to the register into which A was computed. Performing this optimization requires knowing that the two references are *always* to the same memory address and that there is no intervening access to the same location. Normally, data dependence analysis only tells that one reference *may* depend on another; a more complex analysis is required to determine that two references *must be* to the exact same address. In the example above, a simple version of this analysis suffices, since the two references are in the same basic block.

Often loop-carried dependences are in the form of a *recurrence:*

```
for (i=2;i<=100;i=i+1) {
    Y[i] = Y[i-1] + Y[i];
}
```

A recurrence is when a variable is defined based on the value of that variable in an earlier iteration, often the one immediately preceding, as in the above fragment. Detecting a recurrence can be important for two reasons: Some architectures (especially vector computers) have special support for executing recurrences, and some recurrences can be the source of a reasonable amount of parallelism. To see how the latter can be true, consider this loop:

```
for (i=6;i<=100;i=i+1) {
    Y[i] = Y[i-5] + Y[i];
}
```

On the iteration i, the loop references element $i - 5$. The loop is said to have a *dependence distance* of 5. Many loops with carried dependences have a dependence distance of 1. The larger the distance, the more potential parallelism can be obtained by unrolling the loop. For example, if we unroll the first loop, with a dependence distance of 1, successive statements are dependent on one another; there is still some parallelism among the individual instructions, but not much. If we unroll the loop that has a dependence distance of 5, there is a sequence of five statements that have no dependences, and thus much more ILP. Although many loops with loop-carried dependences have a dependence distance of 1, cases with larger distances do arise, and the longer distance may well provide enough parallelism to keep a processor busy.

Finding Dependences

Finding the dependences in a program is an important part of three tasks: (1) good scheduling of code, (2) determining which loops might contain parallelism, and (3) eliminating name dependences. The complexity of dependence analysis arises because of the presence of arrays and pointers in languages like C or C++, or pass-by-reference parameter passing in FORTRAN. Since scalar variable references explicitly refer to a name, they can usually be analyzed quite easily, with aliasing because of pointers and reference parameters causing some complications and uncertainty in the analysis.

How does the compiler detect dependences in general? Nearly all dependence analysis algorithms work on the assumption that array indices are *affine*. In simplest terms, a one-dimensional array index is affine if it can be written in the form $a \times i + b$, where a and b are constants and i is the loop index variable. The index of a multidimensional array is affine if the index in each dimension is affine. Sparse array accesses, which typically have the form x[y[i]], are one of the major examples of nonaffine accesses.

Determining whether there is a dependence between two references to the same array in a loop is thus equivalent to determining whether two affine functions can have the same value for different indices between the bounds of the loop. For example, suppose we have stored to an array element with index value $a \times i + b$ and loaded from the same array with index value $c \times i + d$, where i is the for-loop index variable that runs from m to n. A dependence exists if two conditions hold:

1. There are two iteration indices, j and k, both within the limits of the for loop. That is, $m \leq j \leq n, m \leq k \leq n$.

2. The loop stores into an array element indexed by $a \times j + b$ and later fetches from that *same* array element when it is indexed by $c \times k + d$. That is, $a \times j + b = c \times k + d$.

In general, we cannot determine whether a dependence exists at compile time. For example, the values of $a, b, c,$ and d may not be known (they could be values in other arrays), making it impossible to tell if a dependence exists. In other cases, the dependence testing may be very expensive but decidable at compile time. For example, the accesses may depend on the iteration indices of multiple nested loops. Many programs, however, contain primarily simple indices where $a, b, c,$ and d are all constants. For these cases, it is possible to devise reasonable compile time tests for dependence.

As an example, a simple and sufficient test for the absence of a dependence is the *greatest common divisor* (GCD) test. It is based on the observation that if a loop-carried dependence exists, then GCD (c,a) must divide $(d - b)$. (Recall that an integer, x, *divides* another integer, y, if we get an integer quotient when we do the division y/x and there is no remainder.)

Example   Use the GCD test to determine whether dependences exist in the following loop:

```
for (i=1; i<=100; i=i+1) {
    X[2*i+3] = X[2*i] * 5.0;
}
```

Answer   Given the values $a = 2, b = 3, c = 2,$ and $d = 0$, then GCD(a,c) = 2, and $d - b = -3$. Since 2 does not divide -3, no dependence is possible.

The GCD test is sufficient to guarantee that no dependence exists (you can show this in Exercise 4.14); however, there are cases where the GCD test succeeds but no dependence exists. This can arise, for example, because the GCD test does not take the loop bounds into account.

In general, determining whether a dependence actually exists is NP-complete. In practice, however, many common cases can be analyzed precisely at low cost. Recently, approaches using a hierarchy of exact tests increasing in generality and cost have been shown to be both accurate and efficient. (A test is *exact* if it precisely determines whether a dependence exists. Although the general case is NP-complete, there exist exact tests for restricted situations that are much cheaper.)

In addition to detecting the presence of a dependence, a compiler wants to classify the type of dependence. This classification allows a compiler to recognize name dependences and eliminate them at compile time by renaming and copying.

Example   The following loop has multiple types of dependences. Find all the true dependences, output dependences, and antidependences, and eliminate the output dependences and antidependences by renaming.

```
for (i=1; i<=100; i=i+1) {
    Y[i] = X[i] / c; /* S1 */
    X[i] = X[i] + c; /* S2 */
    Z[i] = Y[i] + c; /* S3 */
    Y[i] = c - Y[i]; /* S4 */
}
```

Answer   The following dependences exist among the four statements:

1. There are true dependences from S1 to S3 and from S1 to S4 because of Y[i]. These are not loop carried, so they do not prevent the loop from being considered parallel. These dependences will force S3 and S4 to wait for S1 to complete.

2. There is an antidependence from S1 to S2, based on X[i].

3. There is an antidependence from S3 to S4 for Y[i].

4. There is an output dependence from S1 to S4, based on Y[i].

The following version of the loop eliminates these false (or pseudo) dependences.

```
for (i=1; i<=100; i=i+1 {
    /* Y renamed to T to remove output dependence */
    T[i] = X[i] / c;
    /* X renamed to X1 to remove antidependence */
    X1[i] = X[i] + c;
    /* Y renamed to T to remove antidependence */
    Z[i] = T[i] + c;
    Y[i] = c - T[i];
}
```

After the loop, the variable X has been renamed X1. In code that follows the loop, the compiler can simply replace the name X by X1. In this case, renaming does not require an actual copy operation but can be done by substituting names or by register allocation. In other cases, however, renaming will require copying.

Dependence analysis is a critical technology for exploiting parallelism. At the instruction level it provides information needed to interchange memory references when scheduling, as well as to determine the benefits of unrolling a loop. For detecting loop-level parallelism, dependence analysis is the basic tool. Effectively compiling programs to either vector computers or multiprocessors depends critically on this analysis. The major drawback of dependence analysis is that it applies only under a limited set of circumstances, namely, among references within a single loop nest and using affine index functions. Thus, there are a wide variety of situations in which array-oriented dependence analysis *cannot* tell us what we might want to know, including the following:

- When objects are referenced via pointers rather than array indices (but see discussion below)

- When array indexing is indirect through another array, which happens with many representations of sparse arrays

- When a dependence may exist for some value of the inputs, but does not exist in actuality when the code is run since the inputs never take on those values

- When an optimization depends on knowing more than just the possibility of a dependence, but needs to know on *which* write of a variable does a read of that variable depend

To deal with the issue of analyzing programs with pointers, another type of analysis, often called *points-to* analysis, is required (see Wilson and Lam [1995]). The key question that we want answered from dependence analysis of pointers is whether two pointers can designate the same address. In the case of complex dynamic data structures, this problem is extremely difficult. For example, we may want to know whether two pointers can reference the *same* node in a list at a given point in a program, which in general is undecidable and in practice is extremely difficult to answer. We may, however, be able to answer a simpler question: Can two pointers designate nodes in the *same* list, even if they may be separate nodes? This more restricted analysis can still be quite useful in scheduling memory accesses performed through pointers.

The basic approach used in points-to analysis relies on information from three major sources:

1. Type information, which restricts what a pointer can point to.

2. Information derived when an object is allocated or when the address of an object is taken, which can be used to restrict what a pointer can point to. For example, if p always points to an object allocated in a given source line and q never points to that object, then p and q can never point to the same object.

3. Information derived from pointer assignments. For example, if p may be assigned the value of q, then p may point to anything q points to.

There are several cases where analyzing pointers has been successfully applied and is extremely useful:

- When pointers are used to pass the address of an object as a parameter, it is possible to use points-to analysis to determine the possible set of objects referenced by a pointer. One important use is to determine if two pointer parameters may designate the same object.

- When a pointer can point to one of several types, it is sometimes possible to determine the type of the data object that a pointer designates at different parts of the program.

- It is often possible to separate out pointers that may only point to a local object versus a global one.

There are two different types of limitations that affect our ability to do accurate dependence analysis for large programs. The first type of limitation arises from restrictions in the analysis algorithms. Often, we are limited by the lack of applicability of the analysis rather than a shortcoming in dependence analysis per se. For example, dependence analysis for pointers is essentially impossible for programs that use pointers in arbitrary fashion—for example, by doing arithmetic on pointers.

The second limitation is the need to analyze behavior across procedure boundaries to get accurate information. For example, if a procedure accepts two parameters that are pointers, determining whether the values could be the same requires analyzing across procedure boundaries. This type of analysis, called *interprocedural analysis,* is much more difficult and complex than analysis within a single procedure. Unlike the case of analyzing array indices within a single loop nest, points-to analysis usually requires an interprocedural analysis. The reason for this is simple. Suppose we are analyzing a program segment with two pointers; if the analysis does not know anything about the two pointers at the start of the program segment, it must be conservative and assume the worst case. The worst case is that the two pointers *may* designate the same object, but they are not *guaranteed* to designate the same object. This worst case is likely to propagate through the analysis, producing useless information. In practice, getting fully accurate interprocedural information is usually too expensive for real programs. Instead, compilers usually use approximations in interprocedural analysis. The result is that the information may be too inaccurate to be useful.

Modern programming languages that use strong typing, such as Java, make the analysis of dependences easier. At the same time the extensive use of procedures to structure programs, as well as abstract data types, makes the analysis more difficult. Nonetheless, we expect that continued advances in analysis algorithms, combined with the increasing importance of pointer dependency analysis, will mean that there is continued progress on this important problem.

Eliminating Dependent Computations

Compilers can reduce the impact of dependent computations so as to achieve more ILP. The key technique is to eliminate or reduce a dependent computation by back substitution, which increases the amount of parallelism and sometimes increases the amount of computation required. These techniques can be applied both within a basic block and within loops, and we describe them differently.

Within a basic block, algebraic simplifications of expressions and an optimization called *copy propagation,* which eliminates operations that copy values, can be used to simplify sequences like the following:

```
DADDUI      R1,R2,#4
DADDUI      R1,R1,#4
```

to

```
DADDUI      R1,R2,#8
```

assuming this is the only use of R1. In fact, the techniques we used to reduce multiple increments of array indices during loop unrolling and to move the increments across memory addresses in Section 4.1 are examples of this type of optimization.

In these examples, computations are actually eliminated, but it also possible that we may want to increase the parallelism of the code, possibly even increasing the number of operations. Such optimizations are called *tree height reduction,* since they reduce the height of the tree structure representing a computation, making it wider but shorter. Consider the following code sequence:

```
ADD         R1,R2,R3
ADD         R4,R1,R6
ADD         R8,R4,R7
```

Notice that this sequence requires at least three execution cycles, since all the instructions depend on the immediate predecessor. By taking advantage of associativity, we can transform the code and rewrite it as

```
ADD         R1,R2,R3
ADD         R4,R6,R7
ADD         R8,R1,R4
```

This sequence can be computed in two execution cycles. When loop unrolling is used, opportunities for these types of optimizations occur frequently.

Although arithmetic with unlimited range and precision is associative, computer arithmetic is not associative, for either integer arithmetic, because of limited range, or floating-point arithmetic, because of both range and precision. Thus, using these restructuring techniques can sometimes lead to erroneous behavior, although such occurrences are rare. For this reason, most compilers require that optimizations that rely on associativity be explicitly enabled.

When loops are unrolled, this sort of algebraic optimization is important to reduce the impact of dependences arising from recurrences. *Recurrences* are expressions whose value on one iteration is given by a function that depends on the previous iterations. When a loop with a recurrence is unrolled, we may be able to algebraically optimize the unrolled loop, so that the recurrence need only be evaluated once per unrolled iteration. One common type of recurrence arises from an explicit program statement, such as

```
sum = sum + x;
```

Assume we unroll a loop with this recurrence five times. If we let the value of x on these five iterations be given by x1, x2, x3, x4, and x5, then we can write the value of sum at the end of each unroll as

```
sum = sum + x1 + x2 + x3 + x4 + x5;
```

If unoptimized this expression requires five dependent operations, but it can be rewritten as

```
sum = ((sum + x1) + (x2 + x3)) + (x4 + x5);
```

which can be evaluated in only three dependent operations.

Recurrences also arise from implicit calculations, such as those associated with array indexing. Each array index translates to an address that is computed based on the loop index variable. Again, with unrolling and algebraic optimization, the dependent computations can be minimized.

Software Pipelining: Symbolic Loop Unrolling

We have already seen that one compiler technique, loop unrolling, is useful to uncover parallelism among instructions by creating longer sequences of straight-line code. There are two other important techniques that have been developed for this purpose: *software pipelining* and *trace scheduling*.

Software pipelining is a technique for reorganizing loops such that each iteration in the software-pipelined code is made from instructions chosen from different iterations of the original loop. This approach is most easily understood by looking at the scheduled code for the superscalar version of MIPS, which appeared in Figure 4.2. The scheduler in this example essentially interleaves instructions from different loop iterations, so as to separate the dependent instructions that occur within a single loop iteration. By choosing instructions from different iterations, dependent computations are separated from one another by an entire loop body, increasing the possibility that the unrolled loop can be scheduled without stalls.

A software-pipelined loop interleaves instructions from different iterations without unrolling the loop, as illustrated in Figure 4.6. This technique is the software counterpart to what Tomasulo's algorithm does in hardware. The software-pipelined loop for the earlier example would contain one load, one add, and one store, each from a different iteration. There is also some start-up code that is needed before the loop begins as well as code to finish up after the loop is completed. We will ignore these in this discussion, for simplicity; the topic is addressed in Exercise 4.10.

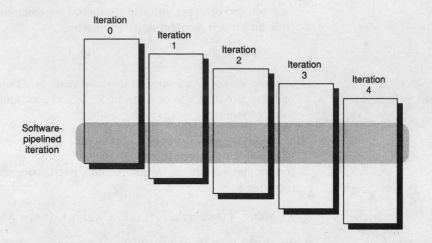

Figure 4.6 A software-pipelined loop chooses instructions from different loop iterations, thus separating the dependent instructions within one iteration of the original loop. The start-up and finish-up code will correspond to the portions above and below the software-pipelined iteration.

Example Show a software-piplined version of this loop, which increments all the elements of an array whose starting address is in R1 by the contents of F2:

```
Loop:     L.D       F0,0(R1)
          ADD.D     F4,F0,F2
          S.D       F4,0(R1)
          DADDUI    R1,R1,#-8
          BNE       R1,R2,Loop
```

You may omit the start-up and clean-up code.

Answer Software pipelining symbolically unrolls the loop and then selects instructions from each iteration. Since the unrolling is symbolic, the loop overhead instructions (the DADDUI and BNE) need not be replicated. Here's the body of the unrolled loop without overhead instructions, highlighting the instructions taken from each iteration:

```
Iteration i:      L.D       F0,0(R1)
                  ADD.D     F4,F0,F2
                  S.D       F4,0(R1)
Iteration i+1:    L.D       F0,0(R1)
                  ADD.D     F4,F0,F2
                  S.D       F4,0(R1)
Iteration i+2:    L.D       F0,0(R1)
                  ADD.D     F4,F0,F2
                  S.D       F4,0(R1)
```

The selected instructions from different iterations are then put together in the loop with the loop control instructions:

```
Loop:   S.D     F4,16(R1)     ;stores into M[i]
        ADD.D   F4,F0,F2      ;adds to M[i-1]
        L.D     F0,0(R1)      ;loads M[i-2]
        DADDUI  R1,R1,#-8
        BNE     R1,R2,Loop
```

This loop can be run at a rate of 5 cycles per result, ignoring the start-up and clean-up portions, and assuming that DADDUI is scheduled before the ADD.D and that the L.D instruction, with an adjusted offset, is placed in the branch delay slot. Because the load and store are separated by offsets of 16 (two iterations), the loop should run for two fewer iterations. (We address this and the start-up and clean-up portions in Exercise 4.10.) Notice that the reuse of registers (e.g., F4, F0, and R1) requires the hardware to avoid the WAR hazards that would occur in the loop. This hazard should not be a problem in this case, since no data-dependent stalls should occur.

By looking at the unrolled version we can see what the start-up code and finish-up code will need to be. For start-up, we will need to execute any instructions that correspond to iteration 1 and 2 that will not be executed. These instructions are the L.D for iterations 1 and 2 and the ADD.D for iteration 1. For the finish-up code, we need to execute any instructions that will not be executed in the final two iterations. These include the ADD.D for the last iteration and the S.D for the last two iterations.

Register management in software-pipelined loops can be tricky. The previous example is not too hard since the registers that are written on one loop iteration are read on the next. In other cases, we may need to increase the number of iterations between when we issue an instruction and when the result is used. This increase is required when there are a small number of instructions in the loop body and the latencies are large. In such cases, a combination of software pipelining and loop unrolling is needed. An example of this is shown in Exercise 4.11.

Software pipelining can be thought of as *symbolic* loop unrolling. Indeed, some of the algorithms for software pipelining use loop-unrolling algorithms to figure out how to software-pipeline the loop. The major advantage of software pipelining over straight loop unrolling is that software pipelining consumes less code space. Software pipelining and loop unrolling, in addition to yielding a better scheduled inner loop, each reduce a different type of overhead. Loop unrolling reduces the overhead of the loop—the branch and counter update code. Software pipelining reduces the time when the loop is not running at peak speed to once per loop at the beginning and end. If we unroll a loop that does 100 iterations a constant number of times, say, 4, we pay the overhead $100/4 = 25$ times—every time the inner unrolled loop is initiated. Figure 4.7 shows this behavior graphically. Because these techniques attack two different types of overhead, the best performance can come from doing both. In practice, compilation using software

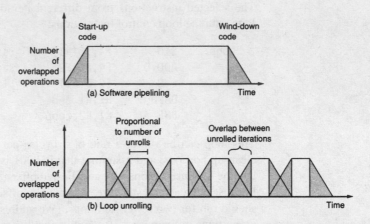

Figure 4.7 The execution pattern for (a) a software-pipelined loop and (b) an unrolled loop. The shaded areas are the times when the loop is not running with maximum overlap or parallelism among instructions. This occurs once at the beginning and once at the end for the software-pipelined loop. For the unrolled loop it occurs m/n times if the loop has a total of m iterations and is unrolled n times. Each block represents an unroll of n iterations. Increasing the number of unrollings will reduce the start-up and clean-up overhead. The overhead of one iteration overlaps with the overhead of the next, thereby reducing the impact. The total area under the polygonal region in each case will be the same, since the total number of operations is just the execution rate multiplied by the time.

pipelining is quite difficult for several reasons: Many loops require significant transformation before they can be software pipelined, the trade-offs in terms of overhead versus efficiency of the software-pipelined loop are complex, and the issue of register management creates additional complexities. To help deal with the last two of these issues, the IA-64 added extensive hardware support for software pipelining. Although this hardware can make it more efficient to apply software pipelining, it does not eliminate the need for complex compiler support, or the need to make difficult decisions about the best way to compile a loop.

Global Code Scheduling

In Section 4.1 we examined the use of loop unrolling and code scheduling to improve ILP. The techniques in Section 4.1 work well when the loop body is straight-line code, since the resulting unrolled loop looks like a single basic block. Similarly, software pipelining works well when the body is a single basic block, since it is easier to find the repeatable schedule. When the body of an unrolled loop contains internal control flow, however, scheduling the code is much more complex. In general, effective scheduling of a loop body with internal control flow will require moving instructions across branches, which is global code scheduling. In this section, we first examine the challenge and limitations of global code scheduling. In Section 4.5 we examine hardware support for eliminating control flow within an inner loop; then, we examine two compiler techniques that can be used when eliminating the control flow is not a viable approach.

Global code scheduling aims to compact a code fragment with internal control structure into the shortest possible sequence that preserves the data and control dependences. The data dependences force a partial order on operations, while the control dependences dictate instructions across which code cannot be easily moved. Data dependences are overcome by unrolling and, in the case of memory operations, using dependence analysis to determine if two references refer to the same address. Finding the shortest possible sequence for a piece of code means finding the shortest sequence for the *critical path,* which is the longest sequence of dependent instructions.

Control dependences arising from loop branches are reduced by unrolling. Global code scheduling can reduce the effect of control dependences arising from conditional nonloop branches by moving code. Since moving code across branches will often affect the frequency of execution of such code, effectively using global code motion requires estimates of the relative frequency of different paths. Although global code motion cannot guarantee faster code, if the frequency information is accurate, the compiler can determine whether such code movement is likely to lead to faster code.

Global code motion is important since many inner loops contain conditional statements. Figure 4.8 shows a typical code fragment, which may be thought of as an iteration of an unrolled loop, and highlights the more common control flow.

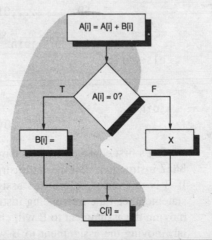

Figure 4.8 A code fragment and the common path shaded with gray. Moving the assignments to B or C requires a more complex analysis than for straight-line code. In this section we focus on scheduling this code segment efficiently without hardware assistance. Predication or conditional instructions, which we discuss in the next section, provide another way to schedule this code.

Effectively scheduling this code could require that we move the assignments to B and C to earlier in the execution sequence, before the test of A. Such global code motion must satisfy a set of constraints to be legal. In addition, the movement of the code associated with B, unlike that associated with C, is speculative: It will speed the computation up only when the path containing the code would be taken.

To perform the movement of B, we must ensure that neither the data flow nor the exception behavior is changed. Compilers avoid changing the exception behavior by not moving certain classes of instructions, such as memory references, that can cause exceptions. In Section 4.5, we will see how hardware support allows for more opportunities for speculative code motion as well as removes control dependences. Although such enhanced support for speculation can make it possible to explore more opportunities, the difficulty of choosing how to best compile the code remains complex.

How can the compiler ensure that the assignments to B and C can be moved without affecting the data flow? To see what's involved, let's look at a typical code generation sequence for the flowchart in Figure 4.8. Assuming that the addresses for A, B, C are in R1, R2, and R3, respectively, here is such a sequence:

```
          LD       R4,0(R1)      ;load A
          LD       R5,0(R2)      ;load B
          DADDU    R4,R4,R5      ;Add to A
          SD       R4,0(R1)      ;Store A
          ...
          BNEZ     R4,elsepart   ;Test A
          ...                    ;then part
          SD       ...,0(R2)     ;Stores to B
          ...
          J        join          ;jump over else
elsepart: ...                    ;else part
          X                      ;code for X
          ...
join:     ...                    ;after if
          SD       ...,0(R3)     ;store C[i]
```

Let's first consider the problem of moving the assignment to B to before the BNEZ instruction. Call the last instruction to assign to B before the if statement i. If B is referenced before it is assigned either in code segment X or after the if statement, call the referencing instruction j. If there is such an instruction j, then moving the assignment to B will change the data flow of the program. In particular, moving the assignment to B will cause j to become data dependent on the moved version of the assignment to B rather than on i, on which j originally depended. You could imagine more clever schemes to allow B to be moved even when the value is used: For example, in the first case, we could make a shadow copy of B before the if statement and use that shadow copy in X. Such schemes are usually avoided, both because they are complex to implement and because they will slow down the program if the trace selected is not optimal and the operations end up requiring additional instructions to execute.

Moving the assignment to C up to before the first branch requires two steps. First, the assignment is moved over the join point of the else part into the portion corresponding to the then part. This movement makes the instructions for C control dependent on the branch and means that they will not execute if the else path, which is the infrequent path, is chosen. Hence, instructions that were data dependent on the assignment to C, and which execute after this code fragment, will be affected. To ensure the correct value is computed for such instructions, a copy is made of the instructions that compute and assign to C on the else path. Second, we can move C from the then part of the branch across the branch condition, if it does not affect any data flow into the branch condition. If C is moved to before the if test, the copy of C in the else branch can usually be eliminated, since it will be redundant.

We can see from this example that global code scheduling is subject to many constraints. This observation is what led designers to provide hardware support to make such code motion easier, and Section 4.5 explores such support in detail.

Global code scheduling also requires complex trade-offs to make code motion decisions. For example, assuming that the assignment to B can be moved before the conditional branch (possibly with some compensation code on the alternative branch), will this movement make the code run faster? The answer is, possibly! Similarly, moving the copies of C into the if and else branches makes the code initially bigger! Only if the compiler can successfully move the computation across the if test will there be a likely benefit.

Consider the factors that the compiler would have to consider in moving the computation and assignment of B:

■ What are the relative execution frequencies of the then case and the else case in the branch? If the then case is much more frequent, the code motion may be beneficial. If not, it is less likely, although not impossible, to consider moving the code.

■ What is the cost of executing the computation and assignment to B above the branch? It may be that there are a number of empty instruction issue slots in the code above the branch and that the instructions for B can be placed into these slots that would otherwise go empty. This opportunity makes the computation of B "free" at least to first order.

■ How will the movement of B change the execution time for the then case? If B is at the start of the critical path for the then case, moving it may be highly beneficial.

■ Is B the best code fragment that can be moved above the branch? How does it compare with moving C or other statements within the then case?

■ What is the cost of the compensation code that may be necessary for the else case? How effectively can this code be scheduled, and what is its impact on execution time?

As we can see from this *partial* list, global code scheduling is an extremely complex problem. The trade-offs depend on many factors, and individual decisions to globally schedule instructions are highly interdependent. Even choosing which instructions to start considering as candidates for global code motion is complex!

To try to simplify this process, several different methods for global code scheduling have been developed. The two methods we briefly explore here rely on a simple principle: focus the attention of the compiler on a straight-line code segment representing what is estimated to be the most frequently executed code path. Unrolling is used to generate the straight-line code, but, of course, the complexity arises in how conditional branches are handled. In both cases, they are effectively straightened by choosing and scheduling the most frequent path.

Trace Scheduling: Focusing on the Critical Path

Trace scheduling is useful for processors with a large number of issues per clock, where conditional or predicated execution (see Section 4.5) is inappropriate or unsupported, and where simple loop unrolling may not be sufficient by itself to uncover enough ILP to keep the processor busy. Trace scheduling is a way to organize the global code motion process, so as to simplify the code scheduling by incurring the costs of possible code motion on the less frequent paths. Because it can generate *significant* overheads on the designated infrequent path, it is best used where profile information indicates significant differences in frequency between different paths and where the profile information is highly indicative of program behavior independent of the input. Of course, this limits its effective applicability to certain classes of programs.

There are two steps to trace scheduling. The first step, called *trace selection,* tries to find a likely sequence of basic blocks whose operations will be put together into a smaller number of instructions; this sequence is called a *trace.* Loop unrolling is used to generate long traces, since loop branches are taken with high probability. Additionally, by using static branch prediction, other conditional branches are also chosen as taken or not taken, so that the resultant trace is a straight-line sequence resulting from concatenating many basic blocks. If, for example, the program fragment shown in Figure 4.8 corresponds to an inner loop with the highlighted path being much more frequent, and the loop were unwound four times, the primary trace would consist of four copies of the shaded portion of the program, as shown in Figure 4.9.

Once a trace is selected, the second process, called *trace compaction,* tries to squeeze the trace into a small number of wide instructions. Trace compaction is code scheduling; hence, it attempts to move operations as early as it can in a sequence (trace), packing the operations into as few wide instructions (or issue packets) as possible.

The advantage of the trace scheduling approach is that it simplifies the decisions concerning global code motion. In particular, branches are viewed as jumps into or out of the selected trace, which is assumed to be the most probable path.

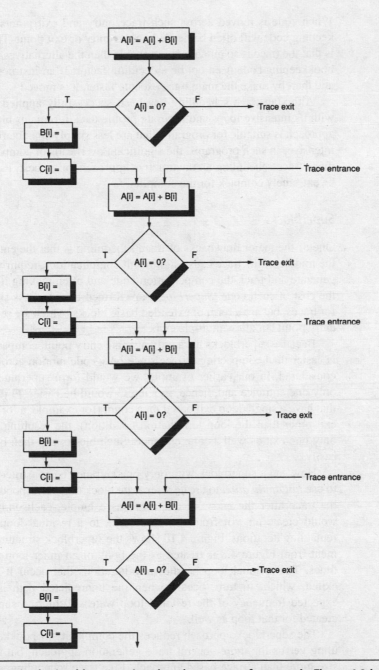

Figure 4.9 This trace is obtained by assuming that the program fragment in Figure 4.8 is the inner loop and unwinding it four times, treating the shaded portion in Figure 4.8 as the likely path. The trace exits correspond to jumps off the frequent path, and the trace entrances correspond to returns to the trace.

When code is moved across such trace entry and exit points, additional book-keeping code will often be needed on the entry or exit point. The key assumption is that the trace is so much more probable than the alternatives that the cost of the bookkeeping code need not be a deciding factor: If an instruction can be moved and thereby make the main trace execute faster, it is moved.

Although trace scheduling has been successfully applied to scientific code with its intensive loops and accurate profile data, it remains unclear whether this approach is suitable for programs that are less simply characterized and less loop-intensive. In such programs, the significant overheads of compensation code may make trace scheduling an unattractive approach, or, at best, its effective use will be extremely complex for the compiler.

Superblocks

One of the major drawbacks of trace scheduling is that the entries and exits into the middle of the trace cause significant complications, requiring the compiler to generate and track the compensation code and often making it difficult to assess the cost of such code. *Superblocks* are formed by a process similar to that used for traces, but are a form of extended basic blocks, which are restricted to a single entry point but allow multiple exits.

Because superblocks have only a single entry point, compacting a superblock is easier than compacting a trace since only code motion across an exit need be considered. In our earlier example, we would form superblocks that contained only one entrance and, hence, moving C would be easier. Furthermore, in loops that have a single loop exit based on a count (for example, a for loop with no loop exit other than the loop termination condition), the resulting superblocks have only one exit as well as one entrance. Such blocks can then be scheduled more easily.

How can a superblock with only one entrance be constructed? The answer is to use *tail duplication* to create a separate block that corresponds to the portion of the trace after the entry. In our previous example, each unrolling of the loop would create an exit from the superblock to a residual loop that handles the remaining iterations. Figure 4.10 shows the superblock structure if the code fragment from Figure 4.8 is treated as the body of an inner loop and unrolled four times. The residual loop handles any iterations that occur if the superblock is exited, which, in turn, occurs when the unpredicted path is selected. If the expected frequency of the residual loop were still high, a superblock could be created for that loop as well.

The superblock approach reduces the complexity of bookkeeping and scheduling versus the more general trace generation approach, but may enlarge code size more than a trace-based approach. Like trace scheduling, superblock scheduling may be most appropriate when other techniques (e.g., if conversion) fail. Even in such cases, assessing the cost of code duplication may limit the usefulness of the approach and will certainly complicate the compilation process.

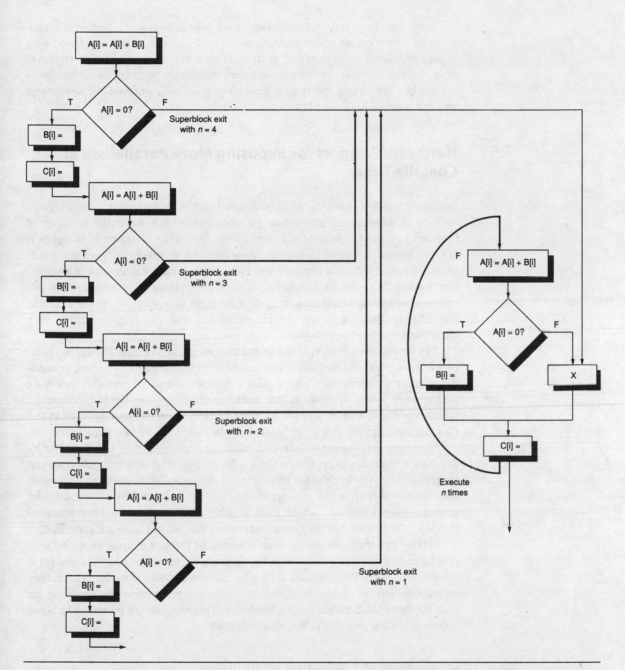

Figure 4.10 This superblock results from unrolling the code in Figure 4.8 four times and creating a superblock.

Loop unrolling, software pipelining, trace scheduling, and superblock scheduling all aim at trying to increase the amount of ILP that can be exploited by a processor issuing more than one instruction on every clock cycle. The effectiveness of each of these techniques and their suitability for various architectural approaches are among the hottest topics being actively pursued by researchers and designers of high-speed processors.

4.5 Hardware Support for Exposing More Parallelism at Compile Time

Techniques such as loop unrolling, software pipelining, and trace scheduling can be used to increase the amount of parallelism available when the behavior of branches is fairly predictable at compile time. When the behavior of branches is not well known, compiler techniques alone may not be able to uncover much ILP. In such cases, the control dependences may severely limit the amount of parallelism that can be exploited. Similarly, potential dependences between memory reference instructions could prevent code movement that would increase available ILP. This section introduces several techniques that can help overcome such limitations.

The first is an extension of the instruction set to include *conditional* or *predicated instructions*. Such instructions can be used to eliminate branches, converting a control dependence into a data dependence and potentially improving performance. Such approaches are useful with either the hardware-intensive schemes of the last chapter or the software-intensive approaches discussed in this chapter, since in both cases, predication can be used to eliminate branches.

Hardware speculation with in-order commit preserved exception behavior by detecting and raising exceptions only at commit time when the instruction was no longer speculative. To enhance the ability of the *compiler* to speculatively move code over branches, while still preserving the exception behavior, we consider several different methods, which include either explicit checks for exceptions or techniques to ensure that only those exceptions that should arise are generated.

Finally, the hardware speculation schemes of the last chapter provided support for reordering loads and stores, by checking for potential address conflicts at run time. To allow the compiler to reorder loads and stores when it suspects they do not conflict, but cannot be absolutely certain, a mechanism for checking for such conflicts can be added to the hardware. This mechanism permits additional opportunities for memory reference speculation.

Conditional or Predicated Instructions

The concept behind conditional instructions is quite simple: An instruction refers to a condition, which is evaluated as part of the instruction execution. If the condition is true, the instruction is executed normally; if the condition is false, the execution continues as if the instruction were a no-op. Many newer architectures include some form of conditional instructions. The most common example of such an instruction is conditional move, which moves a value from one register to another if the condition is true. Such an instruction can be used to completely eliminate a branch in simple code sequences.

Example   Consider the following code:

```
if (A==0) {S=T;}
```

Assuming that registers R1, R2, and R3 hold the values of A, S, and T, respectively, show the code for this statement with the branch and with the conditional move.

Answer   The straightforward code using a branch for this statement is (remember that we are assuming normal rather than delayed branches)

```
        BNEZ    R1,L
        ADDU    R2,R3,R0
L:
```

Using a conditional move that performs the move only if the third operand is equal to zero, we can implement this statement in one instruction:

```
        CMOVZ   R2,R3,R1
```

The conditional instruction allows us to convert the control dependence present in the branch-based code sequence to a data dependence. (This transformation is also used for vector computers, where it is called *if conversion*.) For a pipelined processor, this moves the place where the dependence must be resolved from near the front of the pipeline, where it is resolved for branches, to the end of the pipeline, where the register write occurs.

One obvious use for conditional move is to implement the absolute value function: A = abs (B), which is implemented as if (B<0) {A=-B;) else {A=B;}. This if statement can be implemented as a pair of conditional moves, or as one unconditional move (A=B) and one conditional move (A=-B).

In the example above or in the compilation of absolute value, conditional moves are used to change a control dependence into a data dependence. This enables us to eliminate the branch and possibly improve the pipeline behavior. As issue rates increase, designers are faced with one of two choices: execute multiple branches per clock cycle or find a method to eliminate branches to avoid this requirement. Handling multiple branches per clock is complex, since one branch must be control dependent on the other. The difficulty of accurately predicting two branch outcomes, updating the prediction tables, and executing the correct sequence has so far caused most designers to avoid processors that execute multiple branches per clock. Conditional moves and predicated instructions provide a way of reducing the branch pressure. In addition, a conditional move can often eliminate a branch that is hard to predict, increasing the potential gain.

Conditional moves are the simplest form of conditional or predicated instructions, and although useful for short sequences, have limitations. In particular, using conditional move to eliminate branches that guard the execution of large blocks of code can be inefficient, since many conditional moves may need to be introduced.

To remedy the inefficiency of using conditional moves, some architectures support full predication, whereby the execution of all instructions is controlled by a predicate. When the predicate is false, the instruction becomes a no-op. Full predication allows us to simply convert large blocks of code that are branch dependent. For example, an if-then-else statement within a loop can be entirely converted to predicated execution, so that the code in the then case executes only if the value of the condition is true, and the code in the else case executes only if the value of the condition is false. Predication is particularly valuable with global code scheduling, since it can eliminate nonloop branches, which significantly complicate instruction scheduling.

Predicated instructions can also be used to speculatively move an instruction that is time critical, but may cause an exception if moved before a guarding branch. Although it is possible to do this with conditional move, it is more costly, as we explore in Exercises 4.16 and 4.17.

Example   Here is a code sequence for a two-issue superscalar that can issue a combination of one memory reference and one ALU operation, or a branch by itself, every cycle:

First instruction slot	Second instruction slot
LW R1,40(R2)	ADD R3,R4,R5
	ADD R6,R3,R7
BEQZ R10,L	
LW R8,0(R10)	
LW R9,0(R8)	

This sequence wastes a memory operation slot in the second cycle and will incur a data dependence stall if the branch is not taken, since the second LW after the branch depends on the prior load. Show how the code can be improved using a predicated form of LW.

Answer   Call the predicated version load word LWC and assume the load occurs unless the third operand is 0. The LW immediately following the branch can be converted to an LWC and moved up to the second issue slot:

First instruction slot	Second instruction slot
LW R1,40(R2)	ADD R3,R4,R5
LWC R8,0(R10),R10	ADD R6,R3,R7
BEQZ R10,L	
LW R9,0(R8)	

This improves the execution time by several cycles since it eliminates one instruction issue slot and reduces the pipeline stall for the last instruction in the sequence. Of course, if the compiler mispredicted the branch, the predicated instruction will have no effect and will not improve the running time. This is why the transformation is speculative.

If the sequence following the branch were short, the entire block of code might be converted to predicated execution and the branch eliminated.

When we convert an entire code segment to predicated execution or speculatively move an instruction and make it predicted, we remove a control dependence. Correct code generation and the conditional execution of predicated instructions ensure that we maintain the data flow enforced by the branch. To ensure that the exception behavior is also maintained, a predicated instruction must not generate an exception if the predicate is false. The property of not causing exceptions is quite critical, as the previous example shows: If register R10 contains zero, the instruction LW R8,0(R10) executed unconditionally is likely to cause a protection exception, and this exception should not occur. Of course, if the condition is satisfied (i.e., R10 is not zero), the LW may still cause a legal and resumable exception (e.g., a page fault), and the hardware must take the exception when it knows that the controlling condition is true.

The major complication in implementing predicated instructions is deciding when to annul an instruction. Predicated instructions may either be annulled during instruction issue or later in the pipeline before they commit any results or raise an exception. Each choice has a disadvantage. If predicated instructions are annulled early in the pipeline, the value of the controlling condition must be known early to prevent a stall for a data hazard. Since data-dependent branch conditions, which tend to be less predictable, are candidates for conversion to predicated execution, this choice can lead to more pipeline stalls. Because of this potential for data hazard stalls, no design with predicated execution (or conditional move) annuls instructions early. Instead, all existing processors annul instructions later in the pipeline, which means that annulled instructions will consume functional unit resources and potentially have a negative impact on performance. A variety of other pipeline implementation techniques, such as forwarding, interact with predicated instructions, further complicating the implementation.

Predicated or conditional instructions are extremely useful for implementing short alternative control flows, for eliminating some unpredictable branches, and for reducing the overhead of global code scheduling. Nonetheless, the usefulness of conditional instructions is limited by several factors:

■ Predicated instructions that are annulled (i.e., whose conditions are false) still take some processor resources. An annulled predicated instruction requires fetch resources at a minimum, and in most processors functional unit execution time. Therefore, moving an instruction across a branch and making it conditional will slow the program down whenever the moved instruction would not have been normally executed. Likewise, predicating a control-dependent portion of code and eliminating a branch may slow down the processor if that code would not have been executed. An important exception to these situations occurs when the cycles used by the moved instruction when it is not performed would have been idle anyway (as in the earlier superscalar example). Moving an instruction across a branch or converting a code segment to predicated execution is essentially speculating on the outcome of the branch. Conditional instructions make this easier but do not eliminate the execution time taken by an incorrect guess. In simple cases, where we trade a conditional move for a branch and a move, using conditional moves or predication is almost always better. When longer code sequences are made conditional, the benefits are more limited.

■ Predicated instructions are most useful when the predicate can be evaluated early. If the condition evaluation and predicated instructions cannot be separated (because of data dependences in determining the condition), then a conditional instruction may result in a stall for a data hazard. With branch prediction and speculation, such stalls can be avoided, at least when the branches are predicted accurately.

■ The use of conditional instructions can be limited when the control flow involves more than a simple alternative sequence. For example, moving an instruction across multiple branches requires making it conditional on both branches, which requires two conditions to be specified or requires additional instructions to compute the controlling predicate. If such capabilities are not present, the overhead of if conversion will be larger, reducing its advantage.

■ Conditional instructions may have some speed penalty compared with unconditional instructions. This may show up as a higher cycle count for such instructions or a slower clock rate overall. If conditional instructions are more expensive, they will need to be used judiciously.

For these reasons, many architectures have included a few simple conditional instructions (with conditional move being the most frequent), but only a few architectures include conditional versions for the majority of the instructions. The MIPS, Alpha, PowerPC, SPARC, and Intel x86 (as defined in the Pentium processor) all support conditional move. The IA-64 architecture supports full predication for all instructions, as we will see in Section 4.7.

Compiler Speculation with Hardware Support

As we saw earlier in this chapter, many programs have branches that can be accurately predicted at compile time either from the program structure or by using a profile. In such cases, the compiler may want to speculate either to improve the scheduling or to increase the issue rate. Predicated instructions provide one method to speculate, but they are really more useful when control dependences can be completely eliminated by if conversion. In many cases, we would like to move speculated instructions not only before the branch, but before the condition evaluation, and predication cannot achieve this.

As pointed out earlier, to speculate ambitiously requires three capabilities:

1. The ability of the compiler to find instructions that, with the possible use of register renaming, can be speculatively moved and not affect the program data flow

2. The ability to ignore exceptions in speculated instructions, until we know that such exceptions should really occur

3. The ability to speculatively interchange loads and stores, or stores and stores, which may have address conflicts

The first of these is a compiler capability, while the last two require hardware support, which we explore next.

Hardware Support for Preserving Exception Behavior

To speculate ambitiously, we must be able to move any type of instruction and still preserve its exception behavior. The key to being able to do this is to observe that the results of a speculated sequence that is mispredicted will not be used in the final computation, and such a speculated instruction should not cause an exception.

There are four methods that have been investigated for supporting more ambitious speculation without introducing erroneous exception behavior:

1. The hardware and operating system cooperatively ignore exceptions for speculative instructions. As we will see later, this approach preserves exception behavior for correct programs, but not for incorrect ones. This approach may be viewed as unacceptable for some programs, but it has been used, under program control, as a "fast mode" in several processors.

2. Speculative instructions that never raise exceptions are used, and checks are introduced to determine when an exception should occur.

3. A set of status bits, called *poison bits,* are attached to the result registers written by speculated instructions when the instructions cause exceptions. The poison bits cause a fault when a normal instruction attempts to use the register.

4. A mechanism is provided to indicate that an instruction is speculative, and the hardware buffers the instruction result until it is certain that the instruction is no longer speculative.

To explain these schemes, we need to distinguish between exceptions that indicate a program error and would normally cause termination, such as a memory protection violation, and those that are handled and normally resumed, such as a page fault. Exceptions that can be resumed can be accepted and processed for speculative instructions just as if they were normal instructions. If the speculative instruction should not have been executed, handling the unneeded exception may have some negative performance effects, but it cannot cause incorrect execution. The cost of these exceptions may be high, however, and some processors use hardware support to avoid taking such exceptions, just as processors with hardware speculation may take some exceptions in speculative mode, while avoiding others until an instruction is known not to be speculative.

Exceptions that indicate a program error should not occur in correct programs, and the result of a program that gets such an exception is not well defined, except perhaps when the program is running in a debugging mode. If such exceptions arise in speculated instructions, we cannot take the exception until we know that the instruction is no longer speculative.

In the simplest method for preserving exceptions, the hardware and the operating system simply handle all resumable exceptions when the exception occurs and simply return an undefined value for any exception that would cause termination. If the instruction generating the terminating exception was not speculative, then the program is in error. Note that instead of terminating the program, the program is allowed to continue, although it will almost certainly generate incorrect results. If the instruction generating the terminating exception is speculative, then the program may be correct and the speculative result will simply be unused; thus, returning an undefined value for the instruction cannot be harmful. This scheme can never cause a correct program to fail, no matter how much speculation is done. An incorrect program, which formerly might have received a terminating exception, will get an incorrect result. This is acceptable for some programs, assuming the compiler can also generate a normal version of the program, which does not speculate and can receive a terminating exception.

Example   Consider the following code fragment from an if-then-else statement of the form

```
if (A==0) A = B; else A = A+4;
```

where A is at 0(R3) and B is at 0(R2):

```
            LD      R1,0(R3)    ;load A
            BNEZ    R1,L1       ;test A
            LD      R1,0(R2)    ;then clause
            J       L2          ;skip else
    L1:     DADDI   R1,R1,#4    ;else clause
    L2:     SD      R1,0(R3)    ;store A
```

Assume the then clause is *almost always* executed. Compile the code using compiler-based speculation. Assume R14 is unused and available.

Answer   Here is the new code:

```
        LD      R1,0(R3)    ;load A
        LD      R14,0(R2)   ;speculative load B
        BEQZ    R1,L3       ;other branch of the if
        DADDI   R14,R1,#4   ;the else clause
L3:     SD      R14,0(R3)   ;nonspeculative store
```

The then clause is completely speculated. We introduce a temporary register to avoid destroying R1 when B is loaded; if the load is speculative, R14 will be useless. After the entire code segment is executed, A will be in R14. The else clause could have also been compiled speculatively with a conditional move, but if the branch is highly predictable and low cost, this might slow the code down, since two extra instructions would always be executed as opposed to one branch.

In such a scheme, it is not necessary to know that an instruction is speculative. Indeed, it is helpful only when a program is in error and receives a terminating exception on a normal instruction; in such cases, if the instruction were not marked as speculative, the program could be terminated.

In this method for handling speculation, as in the next one, renaming will often be needed to prevent speculative instructions from destroying live values. Renaming is usually restricted to register values. Because of this restriction, the targets of stores cannot be destroyed and stores cannot be speculative. The small number of registers and the cost of spilling will act as one constraint on the amount of speculation. Of course, the major constraint remains the cost of executing speculative instructions when the compiler's branch prediction is incorrect.

A second approach to preserving exception behavior when speculating introduces speculative versions of instructions that do not generate terminating exceptions and instructions to check for such exceptions. This combination preserves the exception behavior exactly.

Example   Show how the previous example can be coded using a speculative load (sLD) and a speculation check instruction (SPECCK) to completely preserve exception behavior. Assume R14 is unused and available.

Answer   Here is the code that achieves this:

```
        LD      R1,0(R3)    ;load A
        sLD     R14,0(R2)   ;speculative, no termination
        BNEZ    R1,L1       ;test A
        SPECCK  0(R2)       ;perform speculation check
        J       L2          ;skip else
L1:     DADDI   R14,R1,#4   ;else clause
L2:     SD      R14,0(R3)   ;store A
```

Notice that the speculation check requires that we maintain a basic block for the then case. If we had speculated only a portion of the then case, then a basic block representing the then case would exist in any event. More importantly, notice that checking for a possible exception requires extra code.

A third approach for preserving exception behavior tracks exceptions as they occur but postpones any terminating exception until a value is actually used, preserving the occurrence of the exception, although not in a completely precise fashion. The scheme is simple: A poison bit is added to every register, and another bit is added to every instruction to indicate whether the instruction is speculative. The poison bit of the destination register is set whenever a speculative instruction results in a terminating exception; all other exceptions are handled immediately. If a speculative instruction uses a register with a poison bit turned on, the destination register of the instruction simply has its poison bit turned on. If a normal instruction attempts to use a register source with its poison bit turned on, the instruction causes a fault. In this way, any program that would have generated an exception still generates one, albeit at the first instance where a result is used by an instruction that is not speculative. Since poison bits exist only on register values and not memory values, stores are never speculative and thus trap if either operand is "poison."

Example Consider the code fragment from page 346 and show how it would be compiled with speculative instructions and poison bits. Show where an exception for the speculative memory reference would be recognized. Assume R14 is unused and available.

Answer Here is the code (an s preceding the opcode indicates a speculative instruction):

```
        LD      R1,0(R3)      ;load A
        sLD     R14,0(R2)     ;speculative load B
        BEQZ    R1,L3         ;
        DADDI   R14,R1,#4     ;
L3:     SD      R14,0(R3)     ;exception for speculative LW
```

If the speculative sLD generates a terminating exception, the poison bit of R14 will be turned on. When the nonspeculative SW instruction occurs, it will raise an exception if the poison bit for R14 is on.

One complication that must be overcome is how the OS saves the user registers on a context switch if the poison bit is set. A special instruction is needed to save and reset the state of the poison bits to avoid this problem.

The fourth and final approach listed earlier relies on a hardware mechanism that operates like a reorder buffer. In such an approach, instructions are marked by the compiler as speculative and include an indicator of how many branches the instruction was speculatively moved across and what branch action (taken/not taken) the compiler assumed. This last piece of information basically tells the hardware the location of the code block where the speculated instruction origi- nally was. In practice, most of the benefit of speculation is gained by allowing movement across a single branch, and, thus, only 1 bit saying whether the specu- lated instruction came from the taken or not taken path is required. Alternatively, the original location of the speculative instruction is marked by a *sentinel,* which tells the hardware that the earlier speculative instruction is no longer speculative and values may be committed.

All instructions are placed in a reorder buffer when issued and are forced to commit in order, as in a hardware speculation approach. (Notice, though, that no actual speculative branch prediction or dynamic scheduling occurs.) The reorder buffer tracks when instructions are ready to commit and delays the "write-back" portion of any speculative instruction. Speculative instructions are not allowed to commit until the branches that have been speculatively moved over are also ready to commit, or, alternatively, until the corresponding sentinel is reached. At that point, we know whether the speculated instruction should have been executed or not. If it should have been executed and it generated a terminating exception, then we know that the program should be terminated. If the instruction should not have been executed, then the exception can be ignored. Notice that the compiler, rather than the hardware, has the job of register renaming to ensure correct usage of the speculated result, as well as correct program execution.

Hardware Support for Memory Reference Speculation

Moving loads across stores is usually done when the compiler is certain the addresses do not conflict. As we saw with the examples in Section 4.1, such trans- formations are critical to reducing the critical path length of a code segment. To allow the compiler to undertake such code motion when it cannot be absolutely certain that such a movement is correct, a special instruction to check for address conflicts can be included in the architecture. The special instruction is left at the original location of the load instruction (and acts like a guardian), and the load is moved up across one or more stores.

When a speculated load is executed, the hardware saves the address of the accessed memory location. If a subsequent store changes the location before the check instruction, then the speculation has failed. If the location has not been touched, then the speculation is successful. Speculation failure can be handled in two ways. If only the load instruction was speculated, then it suffices to redo the load at the point of the check instruction (which could supply the target register in addition to the memory address). If additional instructions that depended on the load were also speculated, then a fix-up sequence that reexecutes all the specu- lated instructions starting with the load is needed. In this case, the check instruc- tion specifies the address where the fix-up code is located.

In this section we have seen a variety of hardware assist mechanisms. Such mechanisms are key to achieving good support with the compiler-intensive approaches of this chapter. In addition, several of them can be easily integrated in the hardware-intensive approaches of the previous chapter and provide additional benefits.

4.6 Crosscutting Issues: Hardware versus Software Speculation Mechanisms

The hardware-intensive approaches to speculation in the previous chapter and the software approaches of this chapter provide alternative approaches to exploiting ILP. Some of the trade-offs, and the limitations, for these approaches are listed below:

▪ To speculate extensively, we must be able to disambiguate memory references. This capability is difficult to do at compile time for integer programs that contain pointers. In a hardware-based scheme, dynamic run time disambiguation of memory addresses is done using the techniques we saw earlier for Tomasulo's algorithm. This disambiguation allows us to move loads past stores at run time. Support for speculative memory references can help overcome the conservatism of the compiler, but unless such approaches are used carefully, the overhead of the recovery mechanisms may swamp the advantages.

▪ Hardware-based speculation works better when control flow is unpredictable, and when hardware-based branch prediction is superior to software-based branch prediction done at compile time. These properties hold for many integer programs. For example, a good static predictor has a misprediction rate of about 16% for four major integer SPEC92 programs, and a hardware predictor has a misprediction rate of under 10%. Because speculated instructions may slow down the computation when the prediction is incorrect, this difference is significant. One result of this difference is that even statically scheduled processors normally include dynamic branch predictors.

▪ Hardware-based speculation maintains a completely precise exception model even for speculated instructions. Recent software-based approaches have added special support to allow this as well.

▪ Hardware-based speculation does not require compensation or bookkeeping code, which is needed by ambitious software speculation mechanisms.

▪ Compiler-based approaches may benefit from the ability to see further in the code sequence, resulting in better code scheduling than a purely hardware-driven approach.

▪ Hardware-based speculation with dynamic scheduling does not require different code sequences to achieve good performance for different implementations of an architecture. Although this advantage is the hardest to quantify, it may be the most important in the long run. Interestingly, this was one of the motivations for the IBM 360/91. On the other hand, more recent explicitly parallel architectures, such as IA-64, have added flexibility that reduces the hardware dependence inherent in a code sequence.

The major disadvantage of supporting speculation in hardware is the complexity and additional hardware resources required. This hardware cost must be evaluated against both the complexity of a compiler for a software-based approach and the amount and usefulness of the simplifications in a processor that relies on such a compiler. We return to this topic in the concluding remarks.

Some designers have tried to combine the dynamic and compiler-based approaches to achieve the best of each. Such a combination can generate interesting and obscure interactions. For example, if conditional moves are combined with register renaming, a subtle side effect appears. A conditional move that is annulled must still copy a value to the destination register, since it was renamed earlier in the instruction pipeline. These subtle interactions complicate the design and verification process and can also reduce performance. For example, in the Alpha 21264 this problem is overcome by mapping each conditional instruction to two instructions in the pipeline.

4.7   Putting It All Together: The Intel IA-64 Architecture and Itanium Processor

This section is an overview of the Intel IA-64 architecture and the initial implementation, the Itanium processor.

The Intel IA-64 Instruction Set Architecture

The IA-64 is a RISC-style, register-register instruction set, but with many novel features designed to support compiler-based exploitation of ILP. Our focus here is on the unique aspects of the IA-64 ISA. Most of these aspects have been discussed already in this chapter, including predication, compiler-based parallelism detection, and support for memory reference speculation.

The IA-64 Register Model

The components of the IA-64 register state are

- 128 64-bit general-purpose registers, which as we will see shortly are actually 65 bits wide

- 128 82-bit floating-point registers, which provide two extra exponent bits over the standard 80-bit IEEE format

- 64 1-bit predicate registers

- 8 64-bit branch registers, which are used for indirect branches

- a variety of registers used for system control, memory mapping, performance counters, and communication with the OS

The integer registers are configured to help accelerate procedure calls using a register stack mechanism similar to that developed in the Berkeley RISC-I processor and used in the SPARC architecture. Registers 0–31 are always accessible and are addressed as 0–31. Registers 32–128 are used as a register stack, and each procedure is allocated a set of registers (from 0 to 96) for its use. The new register stack frame is created for a called procedure by renaming the registers in hardware; a special register called the current frame pointer (CFM) points to the set of registers to be used by a given procedure. The frame consists of two parts: the local area and the output area. The local area is used for local storage, while the output area is used to pass values to any called procedure. The alloc instruction specifies the size of these areas. Only the integer registers have register stack support.

On a procedure call, the CFM pointer is updated so that R32 of the called procedure points to the first register of the output area of the called procedure. This update enables the parameters of the caller to be passed into the addressable registers of the callee. The callee executes an alloc instruction to allocate both the number of required local registers, which include the output registers of the caller, and the number of output registers needed for parameter passing to a called procedure. Special load and store instructions are available for saving and restoring the register stack, and special hardware (called the *register stack engine*) handles overflow of the register stack.

In addition to the integer registers, there are three other sets of registers: the floating-point registers, the predicate registers, and the branch registers. The floating-point registers are used for floating-point data, and the branch registers are used to hold branch destination addresses for indirect branches. The predication registers hold predicates, which control the execution of predicated instructions; we describe the predication mechanism later in this section.

Both the integer and floating-point registers support register rotation for registers 32–128. Register rotation is designed to ease the task of allocating registers in software-pipelined loops, a problem that we discussed in Section 4.4. In addition, when combined with the use of predication, it is possible to avoid the need for unrolling and for separate prologue and epilogue code for a software-pipelined loop. This capability reduces the code expansion incurred to use software pipelining and makes the technique usable for loops with smaller numbers of iterations, where the overheads would traditionally negate many of the advantages.

Instruction Format and Support for Explicit Parallelism

The IA-64 architecture is designed to achieve the major benefits of a VLIW approach—implicit parallelism among operations in an instruction and fixed formatting of the operation fields—while maintaining greater flexibility than a VLIW normally allows. This combination is achieved by relying on the compiler to detect ILP and schedule instructions into parallel instruction slots, but adding flexibility in the formatting of instructions and allowing the compiler to indicate when an instruction cannot be executed in parallel with its successors.

Execution unit slot	Instruction type	Instruction description	Example instructions
I-unit	A	Integer ALU	add, subtract, and, or, compare
	I	Non-ALU integer	integer and multimedia shifts, bit tests, moves
M-unit	A	Integer ALU	add, subtract, and, or, compare
	M	Memory access	Loads and stores for integer/FP registers
F-unit	F	Floating point	Floating-point instructions
B-unit	B	Branches	Conditional branches, calls, loop branches
L + X	L + X	Extended	Extended immediates, stops and no-ops

Figure 4.11 The five execution unit slots in the IA-64 architecture and what instructions types they may hold are shown. A-type instructions, which correspond to integer ALU instructions, may be placed in either an I-unit or M-unit slot. L + X slots are special, as they occupy two instruction slots; L + X instructions are used to encode 64-bit immediates and a few special instructions. L + X instructions are executed either by the I-unit or the B-unit.

The IA-64 architecture uses two different concepts to achieve the benefits of implicit parallelism and ease of instruction decode. Implicit parallelism is achieved by placing instructions into *instruction groups,* while the fixed formatting of multiple instructions is achieved through the introduction of a concept called a *bundle,* which contains three instructions. Let's start by defining an instruction group.

An instruction group is a sequence of consecutive instructions with no register data dependences among them (there are a few minor exceptions). All the instructions in a group could be executed in parallel, if sufficient hardware resources existed and if any dependences through memory were preserved. An instruction group can be arbitrarily long, but the compiler must *explicitly* indicate the boundary between one instruction group and another. This boundary is indicated by placing a *stop* between two instructions that belong to different groups. To understand how stops are indicated, we must first explain how instructions are placed into bundles.

IA-64 instructions are encoded in bundles, which are 128 bits wide. Each bundle consists of a 5-bit template field and three instructions, each 41 bits in length. To simplify the decoding and instruction issue process, the template field of a bundle specifies what types of execution units each instruction in the bundle requires. Figure 4.11 shows the five different execution unit types and describes what instruction classes they may hold, together with some examples.

The 5-bit template field within each bundle describes *both* the presence of any stops associated with the bundle and the execution unit type required by each instruction within the bundle. Figure 4.12 shows the possible formats that the template field encodes and the position of any stops it specifies. The bundle formats can specify only a subset of all possible combinations of instruction types and stops. To see how the bundle works, let's consider an example.

Template	Slot 0	Slot 1	Slot 2
0	M	I	I
1	M	I	I
2	M	I	I
3	M	I	I
4	M	L	X
5	M	L	X
8	M	M	I
9	M	M	I
10	M	M	I
11	M	M	I
12	M	F	I
13	M	F	I
14	M	M	F
15	M	M	F
16	M	I	B
17	M	I	B
18	M	B	B
19	M	B	B
22	B	B	B
23	B	B	B
24	M	M	B
25	M	M	B
28	M	F	B
29	M	F	B

Figure 4.12 The 24 possible template values (8 possible values are reserved) and the instruction slots and stops for each format. Stops are indicated by heavy lines and may appear within and/or at the end of the bundle. For example, template 9 specifies that the instruction slots are M, M, and I (in that order) and that the only stop is between this bundle and the next. Template 11 has the same type of instruction slots but also includes a stop after the first slot. The L + X format is used when slot 1 is L and slot 2 is X.

Example   Unroll the array increment example, x[i] = x[i] + s (introduced on page 305), seven times (see page 317 for the unrolled code) and place the instructions into bundles, first ignoring pipeline latencies (to minimize the number of bundles) and then scheduling the code to minimize stalls. In scheduling the code assume one bundle executes per clock and that any stalls cause the entire bundle to be stalled. Use the pipeline latencies from Figure 4.1. Use MIPS instruction mnemonics for simplicity.

Answer The two different versions are shown in Figure 4.13. Although the latencies are different from those in Itanium, the most common bundle, MMF, must be issued by itself in Itanium, just as our example assumes.

Bundle template	Slot 0	Slot 1	Slot 2	Execute cycle (1 bundle/cycle)
9: M M I	L.D F0,0(R1)	L.D F6,-8(R1)		1
14: M M F	L.D F10,-16(R1)	L.D F14,-24(R1)	ADD.D F4,F0,F2	3
15: M M F	L.D F18,-32(R1)	L.D F22,-40(R1)	ADD.D F8,F6,F2	4
15: M M F	L.D F26,-48(R1)	S.D F4,0(R1)	ADD.D F12,F10,F2	6
15: M M F	S.D F8,-8(R1)	S.D F12,-16(R1)	ADD.D F16,F14,F2	9
15: M M F	S.D F16,-24(R1)		ADD.D F20,F18,F2	12
15: M M F	S.D F20,-32(R1)		ADD.D F24,F22,F2	15
15: M M F	S.D F24,-40(R1)		ADD.D F28,F26,F2	18
12: M M F	S.D F28,-48(R1)	DADDUI R1,R1,#-56	BNE R1,R2,Loop	21

(a) The code scheduled to minimize the number of bundles

Bundle template	Slot 0	Slot 1	Slot 2	Execute cycle (1 bundle/cycle)
8: M M I	L.D F0,0(R1)	L.D F6,-8(R1)		1
9: M M I	L.D F10,-16(R1)	L.D F14,-24(R1)		2
14: M M F	L.D F18,-32(R1)	L.D F22,-40(R1)	ADD.D F4,F0,F2	3
14: M M F	L.D F26,-48(R1)		ADD.D F8,F6,F2	4
15: M M F			ADD.D F12,F10,F2	5
14: M M F		S.D F4,0(R1)	ADD.D F16,F14,F2	6
14: M M F		S.D F8,-8(R1)	ADD.D F20,F18,F2	7
15: M M F		S.D F12,-16(R1)	ADD.D F24,F22,F2	8
14: M M F		S.D F16,-24(R1)	ADD.D F28,F26,F2	9
9: M M I	S.D F20,-32(R1)	S.D F24,-40(R1)		11
8: M M I	S.D F28,-48(R1)	DADDUI R1,R1,#-56	BNE R1,R2,Loop	12

(b) The code scheduled to minimize the number of cycles assuming one bundle executed per cycle

Figure 4.13 The IA-64 instructions, including bundle bits and stops, for the unrolled version of x[i] = x[i] + s, when unrolled seven times and scheduled (a) to minimize the number of instruction bundles and (b) to minimize the number of cycles (assuming that a hazard stalls an entire bundle). Blank entries indicate unused slots, which are encoded as no-ops. The absence of stops indicates that some bundles could be executed in parallel. Minimizing the number of bundles yields 9 bundles versus the 11 needed to minimize the number of cycles. The scheduled version executes in just over half the number of cycles. Version (a) fills 85% of the instruction slots, while (b) fills 70%. The number of empty slots in the scheduled code and the use of bundles may lead to code sizes that are much larger than other RISC architectures.

Instruction Set Basics

Before turning to the special support for speculation, we briefly discuss the major instruction encodings and survey the instructions in each of the five primary instruction classes (A, I, M, F, and B). Each IA-64 instruction is 41 bits in length. The high-order 4 bits, together with the bundle bits that specify the execution unit slot, are used as the major opcode. (That is, the 4-bit opcode field is reused across the execution field slots, and it is appropriate to think of the opcode as being 4 bits + the M, F, I, B, L + X designation.) The low-order 6 bits of every instruction are used for specifying the predicate register that guards the instruction (see the next subsection).

Figure 4.14 summarizes most of the major instruction formats, other than the multimedia instructions, and gives examples of the instructions encoded for each format.

Predication and Speculation Support

The IA-64 architecture provides comprehensive support for predication: Nearly every instruction in the IA-64 architecture can be predicated. An instruction is predicated by a specifying a predicate register, whose identity is placed in the lower 6 bits of each instruction field. Because nearly all instructions can be predicated, both if conversion and code motion have lower overhead than they would with only limited support for conditional instructions. One consequence of full predication is that a conditional branch is simply a branch with a guarding predicate!

Predicate registers are set using compare or test instructions. A compare instruction specifies one of ten different comparison tests and two predicate registers as destinations. The two predicate registers are written either with the result of the comparison (0 or 1) and the complement, or with some logical function that combines the two tests (such as and) and the complement. This capability allows multiple comparisons to be done in one instruction.

Speculation support in the IA-64 architecture consists of separate support for control speculation, which deals with deferring exception for speculated instructions, and memory reference speculation, which supports speculation of load instructions.

Deferred exception handling for speculative instructions is supported by providing the equivalent of poison bits. For the GPRs, these bits are called NaTs (Not a Thing), and this extra bit makes the GPRs effectively 65 bits wide. For the FP registers this capability is obtained using a special value, NaTVal (Not a Thing Value); this value is encoded using a significand of 0 and an exponent outside of the IEEE range. Only speculative load instructions generate such values, but all instructions that do not affect memory will cause a NaT or NaTVal to be propagated to the result register. (There are both speculative and nonspeculative loads; the latter can only raise immediate exceptions and cannot defer them.) Floating-point exceptions are not handled through this mechanism, but use floating-point status registers to record exceptions.

Instruction type	Number of formats	Representative instructions	Extra opcode bits	GPRs/ FPRs	Immediate bits	Other/comment
A	8	add, subtract, and, or	9	3	0	
		shift left and add	7	3	0	2-bit shift count
		ALU immediates	9	2	8	
		add immediate	3	2	14	
		add immediate	0	2	22	
		compare	4	2	0	2 predicate register destinations
		compare immediate	3	1	8	2 predicate register destinations
I	29	shift R/L variable	9	3	0	Many multimedia instructions use this format.
		test bit	6	3	6-bit field specifier	2 predicate register destinations
		move to BR	6	1	9-bit branch predict	branch register specifier
M	46	integer/FP load and store, line prefetch	10	2	0	speculative/ nonspeculative
		integer/FP load and store, and line prefetch and post-increment by immediate	9	2	8	speculative/ nonspeculative
		integer/FP load prefetch and register postincrement	10	3		speculative/ nonspeculative
		integer/FP speculation check	3	1	21 in two fields	
B	9	PC-relative branch, counted branch	7	0	21	
		PC-relative call	4	0	21	1 branch register
F	15	FP arithmetic	2	4		
		FP compare	2	2		2 6-bit predicate regs
L + X	4	move immediate long	2	1	64	

Figure 4.14 A summary of some of the instruction formats of the IA-64 ISA. The major opcode bits and the guarding predication register specifier add 10 bits to every instruction. The number of formats indicated for each instruction class in the second column (a total of 111) is a strict interpretation: A different use of a field, even of the same size, is considered a different format. The number of formats that actually have *different field sizes* is one-third to one-half as large. Some instructions have unused bits that are reserved; we have not included those in this table. Immediate bits include the sign bit. The branch instructions include prediction bits, which are used when the predictor does not have a valid prediction. Only one of the many formats for the multimedia instructions is shown in this table.

A deferred exception can be resolved in two different ways. First, if a nonspeculative instruction, such as a store, receives a NaT or NaTVal as a source operand, it generates an immediate and unrecoverable exception. Alternatively, a chk.s instruction can be used to detect the presence of NaT or NaTVal and branch to a routine designed by the compiler to recover from the speculative operation. Such a recovery approach makes more sense for memory reference speculation.

The inability to store the contents of instructions with NaT or NaTVal set would make it impossible for the OS to save the state of the processor. Thus, IA-64 includes special instructions to save and restore registers that do not cause an exception for a NaT or NaTVal and also save and restore the NaT bits.

Memory reference support in the IA-64 uses a concept called *advanced loads*. An advanced load is a load that has been speculatively moved above store instructions on which it is potentially dependent. To speculatively perform a load, the ld.a (for advanced load) instruction is used. Executing this instruction creates an entry in a special table, called the *ALAT*. The ALAT stores both the register destination of the load and the address of the accessed memory location. When a store is executed, an associative lookup against the active ALAT entries is performed. If there is an ALAT entry with the same memory address as the store, the ALAT entry is marked as invalid.

Before any nonspeculative instruction (i.e., a store) uses the value generated by an advanced load or a value derived from the result of an advanced load, an explicit check is required. The check specifies the destination register of the advanced load. If the ALAT for that register is still valid, the speculation was legal and the only effect of the check is to clear the ALAT entry. If the check fails, the action taken depends on which of two different types of checks was employed. The first type of check is an instruction ld.c, which simply causes the data to be reloaded from memory at that point. An ld.c instruction is used when *only* the load is advanced. The alternative form of a check, chk.a, specifies the address of a fix-up routine that is used to reexecute the load *and any other* speculated code that depended on the value of the load.

The Itanium Processor

The Itanium processor is the first implementation of the IA-64 architecture. It became available in mid-2001 with an 800 MHz clock. The processor core is capable of up to six issues per clock, with up to three branches and two memory references. The memory hierarchy consists of a three-level cache. The first level uses split instruction and data caches; floating-point data are not placed in the first-level cache. The second and third levels are unified caches, with the third level being an off-chip 4 MB cache placed in the same container as the Itanium die.

Functional Units and Instruction Issue

There are nine functional units in the Itanium processor: two I-units, two M-units, three B-units, and two F-units. All the functional units are pipelined. Figure 4.15

Instruction	Latency
Integer load	1
Floating-point load	9
Correctly predicted taken branch	0–3
Mispredicted branch	9
Integer ALU operations	0
FP arithmetic	4

Figure 4.15 The latency of some typical instructions on Itanium. The latency is defined as the smallest number of intervening instructions between two dependent instructions. Integer load latency assumes a hit in the first-level cache. FP loads always bypass the primary cache, so the latency is equal to the access time of the second-level cache. There are some minor restrictions for some of the functional units, but these primarily involve the execution of infrequent instructions.

gives the pipeline latencies for some typical instructions. In addition, when a result is bypassed from one unit to another, there is usually at least one additional cycle of delay.

Itanium has an instruction issue window that contains up to two bundles at any given time. With this window size, Itanium can issue up to six instructions in a clock. In the worst case, if a bundle is split when it is issued, the hardware could see as few as four instructions: one from the first bundle to be executed and three from the second bundle. Instructions are allocated to functional units based on the bundle bits, ignoring the presence of no-ops or predicated instructions with untrue predicates. In addition, when issue to a functional unit is blocked because the next instruction to be issued needs an already committed unit, the resulting bundle is split. A split bundle still occupies one of the two bundle slots, even if it has only one instruction remaining. Further, there are several Itanium-dependent restrictions that cause a bundle to be split and issue a stop. For example, an MMF bundle, which contains two memory type instructions and a floating-point type instruction, always generates a split before this bundle and after this bundle. This issue limitation means that a sequence of MMF bundles (like those in our earlier example shown in Figure 4.13) can execute at most three instructions per clock, even if no data dependences are present and no cache misses occur.

The Itanium processor uses a 10-stage pipeline divided into four major parts:

■ *Front-end (stages IPG, Fetch, and Rotate)*—Prefetches up to 32 bytes per clock (two bundles) into a prefetch buffer, which can hold up to eight bundles (24 instructions). Branch prediction is done using a multilevel adaptive predictor like that in the P6 microarchitecture we saw in Chapter 3.

■ *Instruction delivery (stages EXP and REN)*—Distributes up to six instructions to the nine functional units. Implements register renaming for both rotation and register stacking.

■ *Operand delivery (WLD and REG)*—Accesses the register file, performs register bypassing, accesses and updates a register scoreboard, and checks predicate dependences. The scoreboard is used to detect when individual instructions can proceed, so that a stall of one instruction in a bundle need not cause the entire bundle to stall. (As we saw in Figure 4.13, stalling the entire bundle leads to poor performance unless the instructions are carefully scheduled.)

■ *Execution (EXE, DET, and WRB)*—Executes instructions through ALUs and load-store units, detects exceptions and posts NaTs, retires instructions, and performs write back.

Remarkably, the Itanium has many of the features more commonly associated with the dynamically scheduled pipelines described in the last chapter: strong emphasis on branch prediction, register renaming, scoreboarding, a deep pipeline with many stages before execution (to handle instruction alignment, renaming, etc.), and several stages following execution to handle exception detection. It is somewhat surprising that an approach whose goal is to rely on compiler technology and simpler hardware seems to be at least as complex as the dynamically scheduled processors we saw in the last chapter!

Itanium Performance

Figure 4.16 shows the performance of an 800 MHz Itanium versus a 1 GHz Alpha 21264 and a 2 GHz Pentium 4 for SPECint. The Itanium has only about 60% of the performance of the Pentium 4 and 68% of the performance of the Alpha 21264. What is perhaps even more surprising is that even if we normalize for clock rate, the Itanium has still only about 85% of the performance of the Alpha 21264, which is an older design in an older technology with about 20% less power consumption, despite its higher clock rate!

The SPECfp benchmarks reveal a different story, as we can see in Figure 4.17. Overall, the Itanium processor is 1.08 times faster than the Pentium 4 and about 1.20 times faster than the Alpha 21264, at a clock rate that is only 40% to 80% as high. For floating-point applications, the Itanium looks like a very competitive processor. As we saw in Chapter 3, floating-point benchmarks exploit higher degrees of ILP well and also can make effective use of an aggressive memory system, including a large L3 cache. Both of these factors probably play a role.

There are two unusual aspects of the SPECfp performance measurements. First, the Itanium gains its performance advantage over the Pentium 4 primarily on the strength of its performance on one benchmark (art), where it is over four times faster than the Pentium 4. If that benchmark were excluded, the Pentium 4 would outperform the Itanium for SPECfp. The other unusual aspect of this performance data is that the Alpha processor shows a large gap of almost 30% between tuned and base performance for SPECfp. This compares to a gap between base and peak for the Itanium system of 0% and for the Pentium 4 system of 3%. Looking at the benchmark-specific flags for the Alpha system, which

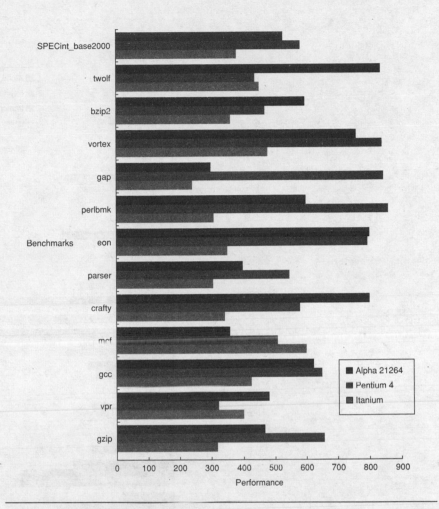

Figure 4.16 The SPECint benchmark set shows that the Itanium is considerably slower than either the Alpha 21264 or the Pentium 4. The Itanium system is a Hewlett-Packard server rx4610 with an 800 MHz Itanium and a 4 MB off-chip, L3 cache. The Alpha system is a 1 GHz Compaq AlphaServer GS320 with only an on-chip L2 cache. The Pentium 4 system is a 2 GHz Compaq Precision 330 workstation with a 256 KB on-chip L2 cache. The overall SPECint_base2000 number is computed as the geometric mean of the individual ratios.

primarily describe loop-unrolling optimizations, it appears that this difference is due to compiler immaturity for the Alpha system. If the base performance could be brought to 95% of the peak performance, the Alpha system would have the highest SPECfp rating among these three processors.

As we mentioned in the last chapter, power may be the most difficult hurdle in future processors and in achieving their performance goals. The limitations on power seem to be serious independently of how ILP is exploited, whether through

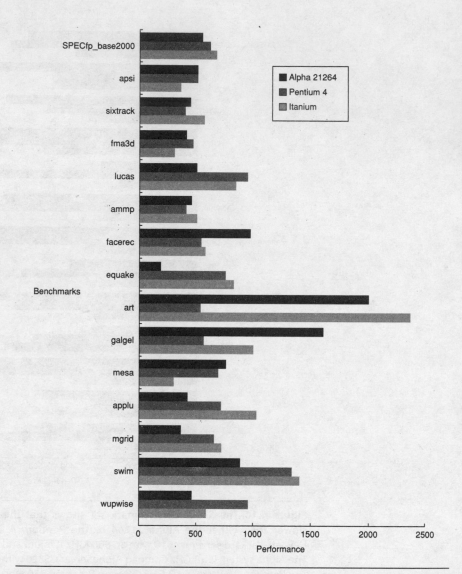

Figure 4.17 The SPECfp benchmark set shows that the Itanium is somewhat faster than either the Alpha 21264 or the Pentium 4. The Itanium system is a Hewlett-Packard server rx4610 with one 800 MHz Itanium processor enabled and a 4 MB off-chip, L3 cache. The Alpha system is a Compaq AlphaServer GS320 with a 1 GHz Alpha 21264. The Pentium 4 system is a 2 GHz Compaq Precision 330 workstation and like the Alpha system has only the on-chip L2 caches. The overall SPECfp_base2000 number is computed as the geometric mean of the individual ratios.

pipelining and faster clock rates or through wider issue. The SPECfp data confirm this view. Although the Itanium achieves better floating-point performance than either the Alpha 21264 or the Pentium 4, its floating-point performance per watt is no better than that of the Alpha 21264 and only 56% of the Pentium 4!

4.8   Another View: ILP in the Embedded and Mobile Markets

The Trimedia and Crusoe chips represent interesting approaches to applying the VLIW concepts in the embedded space. The Trimedia CPU is perhaps the closest current processor to a "classic" VLIW processor; it also supports a mechanism for compressing instructions while they are in main memory and the instruction cache and decompressing them during instruction fetch. This approach addresses the code size disadvantages of a VLIW processor, which would be especially troublesome in the embedded space. In contrast, the Crusoe processor uses software translation from the x86 architecture to a VLIW processor, achieving lower power consumption than typical x86 processors, which is key for Crusoe's target market—mobile applications.

The Trimedia TM32 Architecture

The Trimedia TM32 CPU is a classic VLIW architecture: Every instruction contains five operations, and the processor is completely statically scheduled. In particular, the compiler is responsible for explicitly including no-ops both within an instruction—when an operation field cannot be used—and between dependent instructions. The processor does not detect hazards, which if present will lead to incorrect execution. To reduce the cost of explicit no-ops in code size, the Trimedia processor compresses the code stream until the instructions are fetched from the instruction cache when they are expanded.

A Trimedia instruction consists of five operation slots, each able to specify an operation to one functional unit or an immediate field. Each individual operation in an instruction is predicated with a single register value, which if 0 causes *that* operation in the instruction to be canceled. The compiler must ensure that when multiple branches are included in an instruction, *at most* one predicate is true. Loads can be freely speculated in the Trimedia architecture, since they do not generate exceptions. (There is no support for paged virtual memory.)

The mapping between instruction slots and units is limited, both for instruction encoding reasons and to simply instruction dispatch. As Figure 4.18 shows, there are 23 functional units of 11 different types. An instruction can specify any combination that will fit within the restrictions on the five fields.

To see how this VLIW processor operates, let's look at an example.

Example   First compile the loop for the following C code into MIPS instructions, and then show what it might look like if the Trimedia processor's operations fields were the same as MIPS instructions. (In fact, the Trimedia operation types are very close to MIPS instructions in capability.) Assume the functional unit capacities and latencies shown in Figure 4.18.

Functional unit	Unit latency	Operation slots					Typical operations performed by functional unit
		1	2	3	4	5	
ALU	0	yes	yes	yes	yes	yes	integer add/subtract/compare, logicals
DMem	2				yes	yes	loads and stores
DMemSpec	2					yes	cache invalidate, prefetch, allocate
Shifter	0	yes	yes				shifts and rotates
DSPALU	1	yes		yes			simple DSP arithmetic operations
DSPMul	2		yes	yes			DSP operations with multiplication
Branch	3		yes	yes	yes		branches and jumps
FALU	2	yes			yes		FP add, subtract
IFMul	2		yes	yes			integer and FP multiply
FComp	0			yes			FP compare
FTough	16		yes				FP divide, square root

Figure 4.18 There are 23 functional units of 11 different types in the Trimedia CPU. This table shows the type of operations executed by each functional unit and the instruction slots available for specifying a particular functional unit. The number of instruction slots available for specifying a unit is equal to the number of copies of that unit. Hence, there are five ALU units and two FALU units.

```
void sum (int a[], int b[], int c[], int n)
{        int i;
         for (i=0; i<n; i++)
                c[i] = a[i]+b[i];
}
```

Unroll the loop so there are up to four copies of the body, if needed.

Answer   Figure 4.19 shows the MIPS code before and after unrolling. Figure 4.20 shows the code for the Trimedia processor. (We assume that R30 contains the address of the first instruction in the sequence.) A standard MIPS processor needs 20 32-bit instructions for the unrolled loop and the Trimedia processor takes 8 instructions, meaning that 1/2 of the VLIW operation slots are full. The importance of compressing the code stream in the Trimedia CPU is clear from this example. As Figure 2.37 in Chapter 2 showed, even after compression, Trimedia code is two to three times larger than MIPS code.

Figure 4.21 shows the performance and code size of the TM1300, a 166 MHz implementation of the TM32 architecture, and the NEC VR5000, a 250 MHz version of the MIPS-32 architecture using the EEMBC consumer benchmarks or measurements. The performance, which is plotted with columns on the left axis, and code size, which is plotted with lines on the right axis, are both shown relative to the NEC VR4122, a low-end embedded processor implementing the MIPS

```
Loop:   LD      R11,R0(R4)      # R11 = a[i]
        LD      R12,R0(R5)      # R12 = b[i]
        DADDU   R17,R11,R12     # R17 = a[i]+b[i]
        SD      R17,0(R6)       # c[i] = a[i]+b[i]
        DADDIU  R4,R4,8         # R4 = next a[] address
        DADDIU  R5,R5,8         # R5 = next b[] address
        DADDIU  R6,R6,8         # R6 = next c[] address
        BNE     R4,R7,Loop      # if not last go to Loop
```

(a) The MIPS code before unrolling

```
Loop:   LD      R11,0(R4))      # load a[i]
        LD      R12,R0(R5))     # load b[i]
        DADDU   R17,R11,R12     # load b[i]
        SD      R17,0(R6)       # c[i] = a[i]+b[i]
        LD      R14,8(R4)       # load a[i]
        LD      R15,8(R5)       # load b[i]
        DADDU   R18,R14,R15     # a[i]+b[i]
        SD      R18,8(R6)       # c[i] = a[i]+b[i]
        LD      R19,16(R4)      # load a[i]
        LD      R20,16(R5)      # load b[i]
        DADDU   R21,R19,R20     # a[i]+b[i]
        SD      R21,16(R6)      # c[i] = a[i]+b[i]
        LD      R22,24(R4)      # load a[i]
        LD      R23,24(R5)      # load b[i]
        DADDU   R24,R22,R23     # a[i]+b[i]
        SD      R24,24(R6)      # c[i] = a[i]+b[i]
        DADDIU  R4,R4,32        # R4 = next a[] address
        DADDIU  R5,R5,32        # R5 = next b[] address
        DADDIU  R6,R6,32        # R6 = next c[] address
        BNE     R4,R7,Loop      # if not last go to Loop
```

(b) The MIPS code after unrolling four times and optimizing the code but not scheduling it (for simplicity, we have assumed that n is a multiple of four)

Figure 4.19 The MIPS code for the integer vector sum shown in part (a) before unrolling and in part (b) after unrolling four times. These code sequences assume that the starting addresses of a, b, and c are in registers R4, R5, and R6, and that R7 contains the address of a[n].

instruction set. Two different performance measurements are shown for the TM1300. The "out-of-box" measurement allows no changes to the source; the optimized version allows changes, including hand-coding. In the case of the TM1300, only source code medications and pragmas, which supply directions to the compiler, are used. The optimized TM1300 result is almost five times faster overall than the out-of-the-box result when the performance is summarized by the geometric mean. The out-of-the-box result for the TM1300 is 1.6 times faster than the VR5000.

Slot 1	Slot 2	Slot 3	Slot 4	Slot 5
			LD R11,0(R4)	LD R12,R0(R5)
DADDUI R25,R6,32			LD R14,8(R4)	LD R15,8(R5)
SETEQ R25,R25,R7			LD R19,16(R4)	LD R20,16(R5)
DADDU R17,R11,R12	DADDIU R4,R4,32		LD R22,24(R4)	LD R23,24(R5)
DADDU R18,R14,R15	JMPF R25,R30		SD R17,0(R6)	
DADDU R21,R19,R20	DADDIU R5,R5,32		SD R18,8(R6)	
DADDU R24,R22,R23			SD R21,16(R6)	
DADDIU R6,R6,32			SD R24,24(R6)	

Figure 4.20 The Trimedia code for a simple loop summing two vectors to generate a third makes good use of multiple memory ports but still contains a large fraction of idle slots. Loops with more computation within the body would make better use of the available operation slots. The DADDUI and SETEQ operations in the second and third instruction (first slot) serve to compute the loop termination test. The DADDUI duplicates a later add, so that the computation can be done early enough to schedule the branch and fill the three branch delay slots. The loop branch uses the JMPF instruction that tests a register (R25) and branches to an address specified by another register (R30).

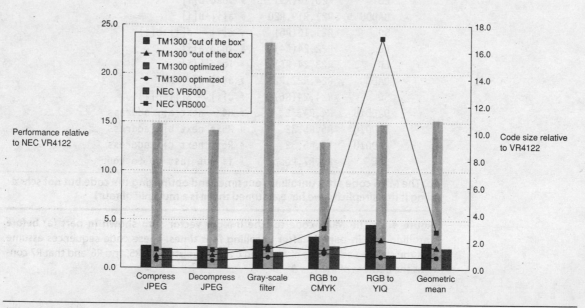

Figure 4.21 The performance and the code size for the EEMBC consumer benchmarks run on the Trimedia TM1300 and the NEC VR5000 and shown relative to the performance and code size for the low-end NEC VR4122. The columns and the left axis show the performance of the processors normalized to the out-of-the-box performance of the NEC VR4122. The TM1300 has a clock speed of 166 MHz, and results are shown for a version with no source code changes (the "out-of-the-box" version) and with a set of changes at the source level (the "optimized" version) consisting of code changes and pragmas, which is then compiled. The lines and the right axis show the code size relative to the out-of-the-box NEC VR4122 using the Green Hills compiler. The measurements all come from the EEMBC Web site: *www.eembc.org/benchmark/benchmain.asp.*

One cost that is paid for this performance gain is a significant increase in code size. The code size of the out-of-the-box version of the benchmarks on the TM1300 is twice as large overall as the code size on the VR5000. For the TM1300 optimized version, the code size is four times larger than the VR5000 version. Imagine how much larger the code size might be if code compression techniques were not used in the TM32 architecture.

This trade-off between code size and performance illustrates a fundamental difference in the design objectives of the MIPS and TM32 architectures. The MIPS architecture is a general-purpose architecture with some extensions for the embedded market. The TM32 architecture is an architecture designed for specific classes of embedded applications. The much larger code size of the TM32 would simply make it unsuitable for many market segments, and its specialized instruction set might not have significant performance benefits. On the other hand, its high performance for certain important functions, especially those in media processing, may allow it to be used in place of special-purpose chips designed for a single function, such as JPEG compression or image conversion. By replacing several special-purpose, dedicated chips with a single programmable processor, system cost might be reduced.

The Transmeta Crusoe Processor

The Crusoe processor is a VLIW processor designed for the low-power marketplace, especially mobile PCs and mobile Internet appliances. What makes it most unusual is that it achieves instruction set compatibility with the x86 instruction set through a software system that translates from the x86 instruction set to the VLIW instruction set implemented by Crusoe.

Instruction Set Basics

The Crusoe processor is a reasonably straightforward VLIW with in-order execution. Instructions come in two sizes: 64 bits (containing two operations) and 128 bits (containing four operations).

There are five different types of operation slots:

1. *ALU operations*—Typical RISC ALU operations with three integer register operands, each specifying one of 64 integer registers.

2. *Compute*—This slot may specify any integer ALU operation (there are two integer ALUs in the data path), a floating-point operation (using the 32 floating-point registers), or a multimedia operation.

3. *Memory*—A load or store operation.

4. *Branch*—A branch instruction.

5. *Immediate*—A 32-bit immediate used by another operation in this instruction.

There are two different 128-bit instruction formats, characterized by what operation slots they have:

Memory	Compute	ALU	Immediate

Memory	Compute	ALU	Branch

The Crusoe processor uses a simple in-order, 6-stage pipeline for integer instructions—two fetch stages, decode, register read, execute, and register write back—and a 10-stage pipeline for floating point, which has four extra execute stages.

Software Translation and Hardware Support

The software responsible for implementing the x86 instruction set uses a variety of techniques to establish a balance between execution speed and translation time. Initially, and for lowest overhead execution, the x86 code can be interpreted on an instruction-by-instruction basis. If a code segment is executed several times, it can be translated into an equivalent Crusoe code sequence, and the translation can be cached. The unit of translation is at least a basic block, since we know that if any instruction is executed in the block, they will all be executed. Translating an entire block both improves the translated code quality and reduces the translation overhead, since the translator need only be called once per basic block. Even a quick translation of a basic block can produce acceptable results, since simple code scheduling can be done during the translation.

One of the major challenges of a software-based implementation of an instruction set is maintaining the exception behavior of the original ISA while achieving good performance. In particular, achieving good performance often means reordering operations that correspond to instructions in the original program, which means that operations will be executed in a different order than in a strict sequential interpretation. This reordering is crucial to obtaining good performance when the target is a VLIW. Hence, just as other VLIW processors have found it useful to have support for speculative reordering, such support is important in Crusoe.

The Crusoe support for speculative reordering consists of four major parts: a shadowed register file, a program-controlled store buffer, memory alias detection hardware with speculative loads, and a conditional move instruction (called select) that is used to do if conversion on x86 code sequences.

The shadowed register file and the program-controlled store buffer allow operations to be executed in a different order while ensuring that permanent state is not committed until no exceptions are possible. Of the integer registers, 48 are shadowed; of the floating-point registers, 16. The shadow registers are used to hold the precise state and are updated only when a translated sequence that may correspond to several x86 instructions has been executed without an exception. To indicate that the shadow registers should be updated, a commit is executed, which has no overhead since every instruction has a bit used to indicate that a commit should be executed at the end of the instruction. If an exception occurs, the primary register set (called the working registers) can be restored from the shadow registers using a rollback operation. This mechanism allows out-of-order completion of register writes without sacrificing the precise exception model of the x86.

One of the most novel features of the Crusoe processor is the program-controlled write buffer. Stores generally cause irrevocable state update. Thus, in the dynamically scheduled pipelines of Chapter 3, stores are committed in order. Similarly, in the IA-64 architecture, stores are not speculated, since the state update cannot be undone. The Crusoe architecture provides a novel solution to this scheme: It includes the ability to control when the write buffer is allowed to update the memory. A gate instruction causes all stores to be held in the buffer, until a commit is executed. A rollback will cause the buffer to be flushed. This feature allows for speculative store execution without violating the exception model.

By using special speculative loads and stores (similar to the ld.s and chk.s mechanisms in IA-64) together with the rollback capability, the software translator can speculatively reorder loads and stores. The ldp instruction indicates a speculative load, whose effective address is stored in a special cache. A special store, stam, indicates a store that a load was moved across; if the ldp and stam touch the same address, then the speculative load was incorrect. A rollback is initiated, and the code sequence is reexecuted starting at the x86 instruction that followed the last gate.

This combination can also be used to do speculative data reuse in the case where a store intervenes between two loads that the compiler believes are to the same address. By making the first load an ldp and the store a stam, the translator can then reuse the value of the first load, knowing that if the store was to the same address as the load, it would cause a trap. The resulting trap can then reexecute the sequence using a more conservative interpretation.

Performance Measures

Since the aim of the Crusoe processor is to achieve competitive performance at low power, benchmarks that measure both performance and power are critical. Because Crusoe depends on realistic behavior to tune the code translation process, it will not perform in a predictive manner when benchmarked using simple but unrealistic scripts. Unfortunately, existing standard benchmarks use simple scripts that do not necessarily reflect actual user behavior (for benchmarks such as Microsoft Office) in terms of both repetition and timing. To remedy this factor, Transmeta has proposed a new set of benchmark scripts. Unfortunately, these scripts have not been released and endorsed by either a group of vendors or an independent entity.

Instead of including such results, Figure 4.22 summarizes the results of benchmarks whose behavior is well known (both are multimedia benchmarks).

| Workload description | Power consumption for the workload (W) | | Relative consumption TM 3200/Mobile Pentium III |
	Mobile Pentium III @ 500 MHz, 1.6V	TM 3200 @ 400 MHz 1.5V	
MP3 playback	0.672	0.214	0.32
DVD playback	1.13	0.479	0.42

Figure 4.22 The energy performance of the processor and memory interface modules using two multimedia benchmarks is shown for the Mobile Pentium III and the Transmeta 3200. Both these chips are available in more recent versions that have additional power management features.

Since the execution time is constrained by real-time constraints, the execution times are identical, and we compare only the power required.

Although processor power differences can certainly affect battery life, with new processors designed to reduce energy consumption, the processor is often a minor contributor to overall energy usage. Figure 4.23 shows power measurements for a typical laptop based on a Mobile Pentium III. As you can see, small differences in processor power consumption are unlikely to make a large difference in overall power usage.

4.9 Fallacies and Pitfalls

Fallacy *There is a simple approach to multiple-issue processors that yields high performance without a significant investment in silicon area or design complexity.*

This is a fallacy in the sense that many designers have believed it and committed significant effort to trying to find this "silver bullet" approach. Although it is possible to build relatively simple multiple-issue processors, as issue rates increase, the gap between peak and sustained performance grows quickly. This gap has forced designers to explore sophisticated techniques for maintaining performance (dynamic scheduling, hardware and software support for speculation, more flexible issue, sophisticated instruction prefetch, and branch prediction). As Figure 4.24—which includes data on Itanium, Pentium III and 4, and Alpha 21264—shows, the result is uniformly high transistor counts, as well as high power consumption. See if you can match the characteristics to the processor without reading the answer in the caption!

In addition to the hardware complexity, it has become clear that compiling for processors with significant amounts of ILP has become extremely complex. Not only must the compiler support a wide set of sophisticated transformation, but tuning the compiler to achieve good performance across a wide set of benchmarks appears to be very difficult.

Major system	Component	Power (W)	Percent of total power
Processor	Low-power Pentium III	0.8	8%
	Processor interface/memory controller	0.65	6%
	Memory	0.1	1%
	Graphics	0.5	5%
I/O	Hard drive	0.65	6%
	DVD drive	2.51	24%
	Audio	0.5	5%
	Control and other	1.3	12%
	TFT display	2.8	27%
Power	Power supply	0.72	7%
Total		10.43	100%

Figure 4.23 Power distribution inside a laptop during DVD playback shows that the processor subsystem consumes only 20% of the power! The I/O subsystem consumes an astonishing 74% of the power, with the display and DVD drive alone responsible for more than 50% of the total system power. The lesson for laptop users is clear: Do not use your disk drive and keep your display off! These data were measured by Intel and are available on their Web site.

Issue rate: total/ memory/integer/ FP/branch	Maximum clock rate available (in mid-2001)	Transistors with/ without caches	On-chip caches: first level and second level	Power (W)	SPECbase CPU2000 int/fp
4/2/4/2/1	1 GHz	15 M/6 M	64 KB + 64 KB	107	561/643
3/2/2/1/1	2 GHz	42 M/23M	12K entries + 8 KB 256 KB	67	636/648
3/2/2/1/1	1 GHz	28 M/9.5 M	16 KB + 16 KB 256 KB	36	454/329
6/2/2/2/3	0.8 GHz	25 M/17 M	16K + 16K 96 KB	130	379/714

Figure 4.24 The key characteristics of four recent multiple-issue microprocessors show significant dramatic variety. The processors vary from a dynamically scheduled speculative processor to a statically scheduled multiple-issue processor to a VLIW. They range in die size from just over 100 mm^2 to almost 300 mm^2 and in power from 36 W to just under 130 W, although the integrated circuit processes differ significantly. The SPEC numbers are the highest official numbers reported as of August 2001, and the clock rate of that system is shown. Can you guess what these four processors are?

Answer: Alpha 21264, Intel Pentium 4, Intel Pentium III, Intel Itanium.

Obtaining good performance is also affected by design decisions at the system level, and such choices can be complex. For example, for the first machine in Figure 4.24 the highest SPECint number comes from a 1 GHz part, but the highest SPECfp number comes from a system with an 833 MHz part!

Concluding Remarks

The EPIC approach is based on the application of massive resources. These resources include more load-store, computational, and branch units, as well as larger, lower-latency caches than would be required for a superscalar processor. Thus, IA-64 gambles that, in the future, power will not be the critical limitation, and that massive resources, along with the machinery to exploit them, will not penalize performance with their adverse effect on clock speed, path length, or CPI factors.

M. Hopkins [2000]
in a commentary on the EPIC approach
and the IA-64 architecture

The relative merits of software-intensive and hardware-intensive approaches to exploiting ILP continue to be debated. Over time, it appears that advantageous elements from the "enemy camp" are slowly being incorporated into each approach. Examples include the following:

"Software" techniques in hardware-centric approaches	"Hardware" techniques in software-intensive approaches
▪ Support for conditional instructions	▪ Scoreboard scheduling of instructions
▪ Prefetch instructions and other cache "hints"	▪ Dynamic branch prediction
▪ Branch prediction hints	▪ Rollback or trap-and-fix-up support for speculation
▪ Special support for speculative (nonexcepting) loads	▪ Hardware for checking speculated load correctness

Initially, the software-intensive and hardware-intensive approaches were quite different, and the ability to manage the complexity of the hardware-intensive approaches was in doubt. The development of several high-performance dynamic speculation processors, which have high clock rates, has eased this concern. The complexity of the IA-64 architecture and the Itanium design has indicated to many designers that it is unlikely that a software-intensive approach will produce processors that are much faster, much smaller (in transistor count or die size), much simpler, or much more power efficient. Similarly, the development of compilers for these processors has proved challenging. Although it is likely that both future compilers for IA-64 and future implementations will be more effective, the IA-64 architecture does *not* appear to represent a significant breakthrough in scaling ILP or in avoiding the problems of complexity and power consumption in high-performance processors.

As both approaches have proven to have advantages, each has tended to incorporate techniques from the other. It remains unclear whether the two approaches will continue to move toward the middle, or whether a new architectural approach that truly combines the best of each will be developed.

The alternative to trying to continue to push uniprocessors to exploit ILP is to look toward multiprocessors, the topic of Chapter 6. Looking toward multiprocessors to take advantage of parallelism overcomes a fundamental problem in ILP processors: building a cost-effective memory system. A multiprocessor memory system is inherently multiported and, as we will see, can even be distributed in a larger processor.

Using multiprocessors to exploit parallelism encounters two difficulties. First, it is likely that the software model will need to change. Second, multiprocessors may have difficulty in exploiting fine-grained, low-level parallelism. Although it appears clear that using a large number of processors requires new programming approaches, using a smaller number of processors efficiently could be based on compiler or language approaches, or might even be used for multiple independent processes. Exploiting the type of fine-grained parallelism that a compiler can easily uncover can be quite difficult in a multiprocessor, since the processors are relatively far apart. Simultaneous multithreading (see Chapter 6) may be the intermediate step between ILP and true multiprocessing.

In 2000, IBM announced the first commercial single-chip, general-purpose multiprocessor, the IBM Power4, which contains two Power3 processors and an integrated second-level cache, for a total transistor count of 174 million! Because the Power4 chip also contains a memory interface, a third-level cache interface, and a direct multiprocessor interconnect, IBM used the Power4 to build an eight-processor module using four Power4 chips. The module has a total size of about 64 in^2 and is capable of a peak performance of 32 billion floating-point operations per second! The challenge for multiprocessors appears to be the same as for ILP-intensive uniprocessors: Translate this enormous peak performance into delivered performance on real applications. In the case of the IBM design, the intended market is large-scale servers, where the available application parallelism may make a multiprocessor attractive.

The embedded world actually delivered multiple processors on a die first! The TI TMS320C80 provides four DSPs and a RISC processor, which acts as controller, on a single die. Likewise, several embedded versions of MIPS processors use multiple processors per die. The obvious parallelism in embedded applications and the lack of stringent software compatibility requirements may allow the embedded world to embrace on-chip multiprocessing faster than the desktop environment. We will return to this discussion in Chapter 6.

4.11   Historical Perspective and References

This section describes the historical development of multiple-issue approaches, beginning with static multiple issue and proceeding to the most recent work leading to IA-64. Similarly, we look at the long history of compiler technology in this area.

The Development of Multiple-Issue Processors

Most of the early multiple-issue processors followed an LIW or VLIW design approach. Charlesworth [1981] reports on the Floating Point Systems AP-120B, one of the first wide-instruction processors containing multiple operations per instruction. Floating Point Systems applied the concept of software pipelining in both a compiler and by handwriting assembly language libraries to use the processor efficiently. Since the processor was an attached processor, many of the difficulties of implementing multiple issue in general-purpose processors, for example, virtual memory and exception handling, could be ignored.

The Stanford MIPS processor had the ability to place two operations in a single instruction, although this capability was dropped in commercial variants of the architecture, primarily for performance reasons. Along with his colleagues at Yale, Fisher [1983] proposed creating a processor with a very wide instruction (512 bits) and named this type of processor a VLIW. Code was generated for the processor using trace scheduling, which Fisher [1981] had developed originally for generating horizontal microcode. The implementation of trace scheduling for the Yale processor is described by Fisher et al. [1984] and by Ellis [1986]. The Multiflow processor (see Colwell et al. [1987]) was based on the concepts developed at Yale, although many important refinements were made to increase the practicality of the approach. Among these was a controllable store buffer that provided support for a form of speculation. Although more than 100 Multiflow processors were sold, a variety of problems, including the difficulties of introducing a new instruction set from a small company and the competition provided from commercial RISC microprocessors that changed the economics in the minicomputer market, led to the failure of Multiflow as a company.

Around the same time as Multiflow, Cydrome was founded to build a VLIW-style processor (see Rau et al. [1989]), which was also unsuccessful commercially. Dehnert, Hsu, and Bratt [1989] explain the architecture and performance of the Cydrome Cydra 5, a processor with a wide-instruction word that provides dynamic register renaming and additional support for software pipelining. The Cydra 5 is a unique blend of hardware and software, including conditional instructions and register rotation, aimed at extracting ILP. Cydrome relied on more hardware than the Multiflow processor and achieved competitive performance primarily on vector-style codes. In the end, Cydrome suffered from problems similar to those of Multiflow and was not a commercial success. Both Multiflow and Cydrome, although unsuccessful as commercial entities, produced a number of people with extensive experience in exploiting ILP as well as advanced compiler technology; many of those people have gone on to incorporate their experience and the pieces of the technology in newer processors. Fisher and Rau [1993] edited a comprehensive collection of papers covering the hardware and software of these two important processors.

Rau had also developed a scheduling technique called *polycyclic scheduling,* which is a basis for most software-pipelining schemes (see Rau, Glaeser, and Picard [1982]). Rau's work built on earlier work by Davidson and his colleagues on the design of optimal hardware schedulers for pipelined processors. Other historical LIW processors have included the Apollo DN 10000 and the Intel i860, both of which could dual-issue FP and integer operations.

One of the interesting approaches used in early VLIW processors, such as the AP-120B and i860, was the idea of a pipeline organization that requires operations to be "pushed through" a functional unit and the results to be caught at the end of the pipeline. In such processors, operations advance only when another operation pushes them from behind (in sequence). Furthermore, an instruction specifies the destination for an instruction issued earlier that will be pushed out of the pipeline when this new operation is pushed in. Such an approach has the advantage that it does not specify a result destination when an operation first issues but only when the result register is actually written. This separation eliminates the need to detect WAW and WAR hazards in the hardware. The disadvantage is that it increases code size since no-ops may be needed to push results out when there is a dependence on an operation that is still in the pipeline and no other operations of that type are immediately needed. Instead of the "push-and-catch" approach used in these two processors, almost all designers have chosen to use *self-draining pipelines* that specify the destination in the issuing instruction and in which an issued instruction will complete without further action. The advantages in code density and simplifications in code generation seem to outweigh the advantages of the more unusual structure.

Compiler Technology and Hardware Support for Scheduling

Loop-level parallelism and dependence analysis was developed primarily by D. Kuck and his colleagues at the University of Illinois in the 1970s. They also coined the commonly used terminology of *antidependence* and *output dependence* and developed several standard dependence tests, including the GCD and Banerjee tests. The latter test was named after Uptal Banerjee and comes in a variety of flavors. Recent work on dependence analysis has focused on using a variety of exact tests ending with a linear programming algorithm called Fourier-Motzkin. D. Maydan and W. Pugh both showed that the sequences of exact tests were a practical solution.

In the area of uncovering and scheduling ILP, much of the early work was connected to the development of VLIW processors, described earlier. Lam [1988] developed algorithms for software pipelining and evaluated their use on Warp, a wide-instruction-word processor designed for special-purpose applications. Weiss and Smith [1987] compare software pipelining versus loop unrolling as techniques for scheduling code on a pipelined processor. Rau [1994] developed modulo scheduling to deal with the issues of software-pipelining loops and simultaneously handling register allocation.

Support for speculative code scheduling was explored in a variety of contexts, including several processors that provided a mode in which exceptions were ignored, allowing more aggressive scheduling of loads (e.g., the MIPS TFP processor [Hsu 1994]). Several groups explored ideas for more aggressive hardware support for speculative code scheduling. For example, Smith, Horowitz, and Lam [1992] created a concept called boosting that contains a hardware facility for supporting speculation but provides a checking and recovery mechanism, similar to those in IA-64 and Crusoe. The sentinel scheduling idea, which is also similar to the speculate-and-check approach used in both Crusoe and the IA-64 architectures, was developed jointly by researchers at the University of Illinois and HP Laboratories (see Mahlke et al. [1992]).

In the early 1990s, Wen-Mei Hwu and his colleagues at the University of Illinois developed a compiler framework, called IMPACT (see Chang et. al. [1991]), for exploring the interaction between multiple-issue architectures and compiler technology. This project led to several important ideas, including superblock scheduling (see Hwu et al. [1993]); extensive use of profiling for guiding a variety of optimizations (e.g., procedure inlining); and the use of a special buffer (similar to the ALAT or program-controlled store buffer) for compile-aided memory conflict detection (see Gallagher et al. [1994]). They also explored the performance trade-offs between partial and full support for predication in Mahlke et al. [1995].

The early RISC processors all had delayed branches, a scheme inspired from microprogramming, and several studies on compile time branch prediction were inspired by delayed branch mechanisms. McFarling and Hennessy [1986] did a quantitative comparison of a variety of compile time and run time branch-prediction schemes. Fisher and Freudenberger [1992] evaluated a range of compile time branch-prediction schemes using the metric of distance between mispredictions.

EPIC and the IA-64 Development

The roots of the EPIC approach lie in earlier attempts to build LIW and VLIW machines—especially those at Cydrome and Multiflow—and in a long history of compiler work that continued after these companies failed at HP, the University of Illinois, and elsewhere. Insights gained from that work led designers at HP to propose a VLIW-style, 64-bit architecture to follow the HP PA RISC architecture. Intel was looking for a new architecture to replace the x86 (now called IA-32) architecture and to provide 64-bit capability. In 1995, they formed a partnership to design a new architecture, IA-64, and build processors based on it. Itanium is the first such processor. A description of the IA-64 architecture is available online at *devresource.hp.com/devresource/Docs/Refs/IA64ISA/*. A description of the highlights of the Itanium processor is available at *www.intel .com/design/itanium/microarch_ovw/index.htm*.

References

Ball, T., and J. R. Larus [1993]. "Branch prediction for free," *Proc. SIGPLAN 1993 Conf. on Programming Language Design and Implementation,* June, 300–313.

Chang, P. P., S. A. Mahlke, W. Y. Chen, N. J. Warter, and W. W. Hwu [1991]. "IMPACT: An architectural framework for multiple-instruction-issue processors," *Proc. 18th Int'l Symposium on Computer Architecture* (May), 266–275.

Charlesworth, A. E. [1981]. "An approach to scientific array processing: The architecture design of the AP-120B/FPS-164 family," *Computer* 14:9 (September), 18–27.

Colwell, R. P., R. P. Nix, J. J. O'Donnell, D. B. Papworth, and P. K. Rodman [1987]. "A VLIW architecture for a trace scheduling compiler," *Proc. Second Conf. on Architectural Support for Programming Languages and Operating Systems,* IEEE/ACM (March), Palo Alto, Calif., 180–192.

Davidson, E. S. [1971]. "The design and control of pipelined function generators," *Proc. Conf. on Systems, Networks, and Computers,* IEEE (January), Oaxtepec, Mexico, 19–21.

Davidson, E. S., A. T. Thomas, L. E. Shar, and J. H. Patel [1975]. "Effective control for pipelined processors," *COMPCON, IEEE* (March), San Francisco, 181–184.

Dehnert, J. C., P. Y.-T. Hsu, and J. P. Bratt [1989]. "Overlapped loop support on the Cydra 5," *Proc. Third Conf. on Architectural Support for Programming Languages and Operating Systems* (April), IEEE/ACM, Boston, 26–39.

Ellis, J. R. [1986]. *Bulldog: A compiler for VLIW architectures,* MIT Press, Cambridge, Mass.

Fisher, J. A. [1981]. "Trace scheduling: A technique for global microcode compaction," *IEEE Trans. on Computers* 30:7 (July), 478–490.

Fisher, J. A. [1983]. "Very long instruction word architectures and ELI-512," *Proc. Tenth Symposium on Computer Architecture* (June), Stockholm, 140–150.

Fisher, J. A., J. R. Ellis, J. C. Ruttenberg, and A. Nicolau [1984]. "Parallel processing: A smart compiler and a dumb processor," *Proc. SIGPLAN Conf. on Compiler Construction* (June), Palo Alto, Calif., 11–16.

Fisher, J. A., and S. M. Freudenberger [1992]. "Predicting conditional branches from previous runs of a program," *Proc. Fifth Conf. on Architectural Support for Programming Languages and Operating Systems,* IEEE/ACM (October), Boston, 85–95.

Fisher, J. A., and B. R. Rau [1993]. *Journal of Supercomputing* (January), Kluwer.

Foster, C. C., and E. M. Riseman [1972]. "Percolation of code to enhance parallel dispatching and execution," *IEEE Trans. on Computers* C-21:12 (December), 1411–1415.

Gallagher, D. M., W. Y. Chen, S. A. Mahlke, J. C. Gyllenhaal, and W.W. Hwu [1994]. "Dynamic memory disambiguation using the memory conflict buffer," *Proc. Sixth Int'l Conf. on Architectural Support for Programming Languages and Operating Systems* (October), Santa Clara, Calif., 183–193.

Hopkins, M. [2000]. "A critical look at IA-64: Massive resources, massive ILP, but can it deliver?" *Microprocessor Report* (February).

Hsu, P. [1994]. "Designing the TFP microprocessor," *IEEE Micro* 18:2 (April), 2333.

Hwu, W. W., S. A. Mahlke, W. Y. Chen, P. P. Chang, N. J. Warter, R. A. Bringmann, R. O. Ouellette, R. E. Hank, T. Kiyohara, G. E. Haab, J. G. Holm, and D. M. Lavery [1993]. "The superblock: An effective technique for VLIW and superscalar compilation," *J. Supercomputing* 7:1, 2 (March), 229–248.

Lam, M. [1988]. "Software pipelining: An effective scheduling technique for VLIW processors," *SIGPLAN Conf. on Programming Language Design and Implementation,* ACM (June), Atlanta, Ga., 318–328.

Mahlke, S. A., W. Y. Chen, W.-M. Hwu, B. R. Rau, and M. S. Schlansker [1992]. "Sentinel scheduling for VLIW and superscalar processors," *Proc. Fifth Conf. on Architec-*

tural Support for Programming Languages and Operating Systems (October), Boston, IEEE/ACM, 238–247.

Mahlke, S. A., R. E. Hank, J. E. McCormick, D. I. August, and W. W. Hwu [1995]. "A comparison of full and partial predicated execution support for ILP processors," *Proc. 22nd Annual Int'l Symposium on Computer Architecture* (June), Santa Margherita Ligure, Italy, 138–149.

McFarling, S., and J. Hennessy [1986]. "Reducing the cost of branches," *Proc. 13th Symposium on Computer Architecture* (June), Tokyo, 396–403.

Nicolau, A., and J. A. Fisher [1984]. "Measuring the parallelism available for very long instruction word architectures," *IEEE Trans. on Computers* C-33:11 (November), 968–976.

Rau, B. R. [1994]. "Iterative modulo scheduling: An algorithm for software pipelining loops," *Proc. 27th Annual Int'l Symposium on Microarchitecture* (November), San Jose, Calif., 63–74.

Rau, B. R., C. D. Glaeser, and R. L. Picard [1982]. "Efficient code generation for horizontal architectures: Compiler techniques and architectural support," *Proc. Ninth Symposium on Computer Architecture* (April), 131–139.

Rau, B. R., D. W. L. Yen, W. Yen, and R. A. Towle [1989]. "The Cydra 5 departmental supercomputer: Design philosophies, decisions, and trade-offs," *IEEE Computers* 22:1 (January), 12–34.

Riseman, E. M., and C. C. Foster [1972]. "Percolation of code to enhance parallel dispatching and execution," *IEEE Trans. on Computers* C-21:12 (December), 1411–1415.

Smith, M. D., M. Horowitz, and M. S. Lam [1992]. "Efficient superscalar performance through boosting," *Proc. Fifth Conf. on Architectural Support for Programming Languages and Operating Systems* (October), Boston, IEEE/ACM, 248–259.

Thorlin, J. F. [1967]. "Code generation for PIE (parallel instruction execution) computers," *Proc. Spring Joint Computer Conf.,* 27.

Weiss, S., and J. E. Smith [1987]. "A study of scalar compilation techniques for pipelined supercomputers," *Proc. Second Conf. on Architectural Support for Programming Languages and Operating Systems* (March), IEEE/ACM, Palo Alto, Calif., 105–109.

Wilson, R. P., and M. S. Lam [1995]. "Efficient context-sensitive pointer analysis for C programs," *Proc. ACM SIGPLAN'95 Conf. on Programming Language Design and Implementation,* La Jolla, Calif., June, 1–12.

Exercises

Solutions to the "starred" exercises appear in Appendix B.

⊛ 4.1 [15/10] <4.1, A.4> If we assume the set of latencies in Figure 4.1 and that a result can always be forwarded, then a specific structure for some of the CPU pipeline is implied. Assume the CPU uses the standard five-stage IF/ID/EX/Mem/WB pipeline.

a. [15] <4.1, A.4> Using a style similar to that of Figures A.23 and A.31 in Appendix A, draw a block diagram showing only the implied portions of the pipeline. Label each component and data path in your diagram and show the number of clock cycles each functional unit requires.

b. [10] <4.1, A.4> For each functional unit in your part (a) diagram, which row(s) of Figure 4.1 provide the information to determine the number of clock cycles needed for that functional unit to complete its operation?

4.2 [15/15] <4.1> This chapter examines software approaches for exploiting instruction-level parallelism. This exercise asks how well software can find and exploit ILP. Chapter 3 presents hardware techniques for exposing and exploiting ILP. Exercise 3.2 is a reprise of this ILP analysis, but from a hardware perspective.

Consider the following four MIPS code fragments, each containing two instructions:

```
i.        DADDI R1,R1,#4
          LD R2,7(R1)

ii.       DADD R3,R1,R2
          SD 7(R1),R2

iii.      SD 7(R1),R2
          S.D 200(R7),F2

iv.       BEZ R1,place
          SD 7(R1),R1
```

a. [15] <4.1> For each code fragment (i)–(iv) identify each type of dependence that a compiler will find (a fragment may have no dependences) and describe what data flow, name reuse, or control structure causes the dependence.

b. [15] <4.1> Assuming nonspeculative execution, for each code fragment discuss whether a compiler could schedule the two instructions.

4.3 [20/15/15] <2.12, 4.1> Consider the simple loop in Section 4.1. Assume the number of iterations is unknown, but large.

a. [20] <4.1> Find the theoretically optimal number of unrollings using the latencies in Figure 4.1. *Hint:* Recall that you will need two loops: one unrolled and one not!

b. [15] <2.12, 4.1> What is the actual maximum number of times the simple loop in Section 4.1 can be unrolled using the given MIPS code? What is the limiting resource? Show how to increase the number of times the loop may be unrolled by transforming the MIPS code to make less intensive use of the limiting resource. How much does this transformation improve performance?

c. [15] <2.12, 4.1> For the MIPS instruction set, what additional parameters limit the number of times this loop can be unrolled? *Hint:* When you find one limiting parameter, assume that the resource it defines is unlimited, look for an additional parameter, and repeat as needed.

4.4 [15] <4.1> Section 4.1 presents a technique for unrolling loops where the unrolling factor is not statically known to be a factor of the number of loop iterations. For a factor of k, the technique constructs two consecutive loops that iterate (n mod k) and (n/k) times, respectively. Find a technique to use just a single loop containing the unrolled body iterated $\lceil n/k \rceil$ times. What restrictions are there on the use of this technique? When does this technique perform better than the general, two-consecutive-loops technique? Can a compiler employ this technique?

✪ **4.5** [15] <4.1> List all the dependences (output, anti, and true) in the following code fragment. Indicate whether the true dependences are loop carried or not. Show why the loop is not parallel.

```
for (i=2;i<100;i=i+1) {
        a[i] = b[i] + a[i];    /* S1 */
        c[i-1] = a[i] + d[i];  /* S2 */
        a[i-1] = 2 * b[i];     /* S3 */
        b[i+1] = 2 * b[i];     /* S4 */
}
```

4.6 [15] <4.1> Here is an unusual loop. First, list the dependences and then rewrite the loop so that it is parallel.

```
for (i=1;i<100;i=i+1) {
        a[i] = b[i] + c[i];    /* S1 */
        b[i] = a[i] + d[i];    /* S2 */
        a[i+1] = a[i] + e[i];  /* S3 */
}
```

✪ **4.7** [20/12] <4.1> The following loop is a dot product (assuming the running sum in F2 is initially 0) and contains a recurrence. Assume the pipeline latencies from Figure 4.1 and a 1-cycle delayed branch.

```
foo:    L.D      F0,0(R1)      ;load X[i]
        L.D      F4,0(R2)      ;load Y[i]
        MUL.D    F0,F0,F4      ;multiply X[i]*Y[i]
        ADD.D    F2,F0,F2      ;add sum = sum + X[i]*Y[i]
        DADDUI   R1,R1,#-8     ;decrement X index
        DADDUI   R2,R2,#-8     ;decrement Y index
        BNEZ     R1,foo        ;loop if not done
```

a. [20] <4.1> Assume a single-issue pipeline. Despite the fact that the loop is not parallel, it can be scheduled with no delays. Unroll the following loop a sufficient number of times to schedule it without any delays. Show the schedule after eliminating any redundant overhead instructions. *Hint:* An additional transformation of the code is needed to schedule without delay.

b. [12] <4.1> Show the schedule of the transformed code from part (a) for the processor in Figure 4.2. For an issue capability that is 100% greater, how much faster is the loop body?

4.8 [15/15] <4.1> The following loop computes $Y[i] = a \times X[i] + Y[i]$, the key step in a Gaussian elimination. Assume the pipeline latencies from Figure 4.1 and a 1-cycle delayed branch.

```
loop:   L.D      F0,0(R1)      ;load X[i]
        MUL.D    F0,F0,F2      ;multiply a*X[i]
        L.D      F4,0(R2)      ;load Y[i]
        ADD.D    F0,F0,F4      ;add a*X[i]+Y[i]
        S.D      0(R2),F0      ;store Y[i]
```

```
        DSUBUI      R1,R1,#8        ;decrement X index
        DSUBUI      R2,R2,#8        ;decrement Y index
        BNEZ        R1,loop         ;loop if not done
```

a. [15] <4.1> Assume a single-issue pipeline. Unroll the loop as many times as necessary to schedule it without any delays, collapsing the loop overhead instructions. Show the schedule. What is the execution time per element?

b. [15] <4.1> Assume a dual-issue processor as in Figure 4.2. Unroll the loop as many times as necessary to schedule it without any delays, collapsing the loop overhead instructions. Show the schedule. What is the execution time per element? How many instruction issue slots are unused?

4.9 [20/15/20/15/15] <1.5, 4.1, 4.3, 4.4> In this exercise, we look at how some software techniques can extract ILP in a common vector loop. The following loop is the so-called DAXPY loop (double-precision *aX* plus *Y;* discussed in Appendix G) and the central operation in Gaussian elimination. The following code implements the DAXPY operation, $Y = a \times X + Y$, for a vector length 100.

```
bar:    L.D         F2,0(R1)        ;load X(i)
        MUL.D       F4,F2,F0        ;multiply a*X(i)
        L.D         F6,0(R2)        ;load Y(i)
        ADD.D       F6,F4,F6        ;add a*X(i) + Y(i)
        S.D         0(R2),F6        ;store Y(i)
        DADDUI      R1,R1,#8        ;increment X index
        DADDUI      R2,R2,#8        ;increment Y index
        DSGTUI      R3,R1,#800      ;test if done
        BEQZ        R3,bar          ;loop if not done
```

For (a)–(e) assume the pipeline latencies from Figure 4.1 and a 1-cycle delayed branch that resolves in the ID stage. Assume that integer operations issue and complete in 1 clock cycle and that their results are fully bypassed.

a. [20] <1.5, 4.1> Assume a single-issue pipeline. Show how the loop would look both unscheduled by the compiler and after compiler scheduling for both floating-point operation and branch delays, including any stalls or idle clock cycles (see the example on page 305). What is the execution time per element of the result vector, Y, unscheduled and scheduled? How much faster must the clock be for processor hardware alone to match the performance improvement achieved by the scheduling compiler (neglect the possible increase in the number of clock cycles necessary for memory system access effects of higher processor clock speed on memory system performance)?

b. [15] <4.1> Assume a single-issue pipeline. Unroll the loop as many times as necessary to schedule it without any stalls, collapsing the loop overhead instructions. How many times must the loop be unrolled? Show the instruction schedule. What is the execution time per element of the result vector? What is the major contribution to the reduction in time per element?

c. [20] <4.3> Assume a VLIW processor with instructions that contain five operations, as shown in Figure 4.5. We will compare two degrees of loop unrolling. First, unroll the loop 4 times to extract ILP, and schedule it without any stalls (i.e., completely empty issue cycles), collapsing the loop overhead instructions, and then repeat the process but unroll the loop 10 times. Ignore the branch delay slot. Show the two schedules. What is the execution time per element of the result vector for each schedule? What percent of the operation slots are used in each schedule? How much does the size of the code differ between the two schedules? What is the total register demand for the two schedules?

d. [15] <4.4> Assume a family of VLIW processors designed for different price-performance points in the marketplace. The budget version of the processor has latencies greater than those in Figure 4.1. What will happen if the code for your answer to part (c) is executed on the low-cost processor? How could you eliminate any undesirable behavior?

e. [15] <4.4> Assume a single-issue pipeline. Show the schedule for a software-pipelined version of the DAXPY loop. You may omit the start-up and clean-up code. What is the execution time per element of the result vector?

4.10 [20/20] <4.4> In this exercise we finish the compiler code transformation started in the software-pipelining loop example on page 330.

a. [20] <4.4> Starting with the solution loop body given in the example, write code for the complete software-pipelined loop by adding the start-up and finish-up code. Assume that there will be a large number of iterations executed. You need not show code to initialize the loop induction variable and the scalar increment value. Using the latencies in Figure 4.1 and assuming a 1-cycle branch delay, write an expression for the total time for the software-pipelined loop to increment all elements of the array.

b. [20] <4.4> The original loop in the example may execute only one iteration. Write code for the complete software-pipelined loop that allows one, two, or as many iterations as needed for the array size. Then, for your final answer, schedule and possibly further transform your code so that it can execute with only two stalls, and show where those stalls occur. Assume the latencies in Figure 4.1, and use delayed branches that always execute the instruction in the 1-cycle branch delay slot.

4.11 [20] <4.4> Consider the loop that we software-pipelined on page 330. Suppose the latency of the ADD.D was 5 cycles. The software-pipelined loop now has a stall. Show how this loop can be written using both software pipelining and loop unrolling to eliminate any stalls. The loop should be unrolled as few times as possible (once is enough). Show the loop start-up and clean-up code.

✪ 4.12 [15] <4.4> Here is a simple code fragment:

```
for (i=2;i<=100;i+=2)
    a[i] = a[50*i+1];
```

To use the GCD test, this loop must first be "normalized"—written so that the index starts at 1 and increments by 1 on every iteration. Write a normalized version of the loop (change the indices as needed), then use the GCD test to see if there is a dependence.

4.13   [15] <4.4> Here is another loop:

```
for (i=2,i<=n/2;i+=2)
    a[i] = a[i] + a[i + n/2];
```

Normalize the loop. Does the GCD test detect a dependence? Is there a loop-carried, true dependence in this loop? Explain.

4.14   [25] <4.4> Show that if there is a true dependence between the two array elements $A(a \times i + b)$ and $A(c \times i + d)$, then $GCD(c,a)$ divides $(d - b)$.

4.15   [15] <4.5> It is common in scientific codes for array elements to be addressed based on the element values in an index array. Consider the following loop:

```
for (i=1,i<=n,i+=1)
    a[x[i]] = a[x[i]] + b[x[i]];
```

The array subscripts are not affine, so the GCD test cannot be used. However, the loop may still be parallel, so additional compiler tests may be valuable. What condition on the index array x[] will make the loop parallel? Be as general in your answer as you can. *Hint:* Think of the loop as adding the elements of one linked list to the corresponding elements of another linked list.

4.16   [15/15/15] <4.5> Consider the following code fragment from an if-then-else statement of the form

```
if (A==0) A = B; else A = A+4;
```

where A is at 0(R3) and B is at 0(R2):

```
        LD      R1,0(R3)      ;load A
        BNEZ    R1,L1         ;test A
        LD      R1,0(R2)      ;then clause
        J       L2            ;skip else
L1:     DADDI   R1,R1,#4      ;else clause
L2:     SD      0(R3),R1      ;store A
```

In the following assume a standard single-issue MIPS pipeline, branch resolution in the ID stage, delayed branches, and forwarding.

a.   [15] <4.5> Assume conditional load instructions LWZ Rd,x(Rs1),Rs2 and LWNZ Rd,x(Rs1),Rs2 that do not load unless the value of Rs2 is zero or not zero, respectively. Compile the code using a conditional load and write it showing any stall cycles that would occur in the pipeline. Compare the clock cycles and register use to that of the original code fragment.

b.   [15] <4.5> Boosting supports compiler speculation via a load instruction LW+ that includes a flag of the compiler prediction for the branch on which the load depends. If the prediction flag matches the branch resolution result, then the loaded value is written to the register. Compile the code using a boosted load and write it showing any stall cycles that would occur in the pipeline. Compare the clock cycles and register use to that of the original code fragment.

c. [15] <4.5> Compile the code using compiler-based speculation for both the then and else clauses and write it showing any stall cycles that would occur in the pipeline. Assume conditional move instructions CMVZ Rd,Rs1,Rs2 and CMVNZ Rd,Rs1,Rs2 that move the contents of register Rs1 to register Rd if Rs2 is equal to or not equal to zero, respectively. Compare the clock cycles and register use to that of the original code fragment.

✪ 4.17   [15] <4.5> Perform the same transformation (moving up the branch) as the example on page 342, but using only conditional move. Be careful that your loads, which are no longer control dependent, cannot raise an exception if they should not have been executed!

4.18   [15/15] <4.5> In this exercise we will investigate how predication affects the form and execution of pipelined instructions. Conditional execution of instructions is traditionally implemented with branches. For example, the MIPS instruction

```
DADD R1,R2,R3        ;R1=R2+R3
```

is unconditional. Its execution is made conditional on the value in register R8 by writing

```
        BNEZ R8,place ;if(R8==0)
        DADD R1,R2,R3 ;then{ R1=R2+R3 }
place:
```

If predicated, however, the instruction form could be

```
        (R8) ADD R1,R2,R3 ;if(R8){ R1=R2+R3 }
place:
```

with control of execution of the ADD an integral part of the instruction itself, thus eliminating a control dependence between what was before two instructions. If R8 has been set to the value true, then the ADD computes the sum and places it in the result register; otherwise the ADD behaves like a NOP, computing no result and leaving R1 unchanged.

Assume a set of 1-bit predicate registers that are set by a compare instruction of the form

```
    (qp) CMP.NE pT,pF=R8,R0
```

This compare (written with mnemonic CMP) is itself predicated on the truth value of the qualifying predicate, qp. This example uses a not equal (.NE) comparison relation to match the code fragment above; other relations may be available. If qp is true, the CMP.NE sets the 1-bit predicate registers pT and pF such that pT=(R8!=R0) and pF!=(R8!=R0). That is, pT is assigned the truth value of the statement "R8 is not equal to R0," and pF is assigned the complement of the truth value of that same statement. If qp is false, the CMP.NE behaves as would a NOP instruction.

a. [15] <4.5> Using predicated instructions, write the following code fragment as a single basic block (assuming the SUB instruction is the only entry point for the code). You may assume that any compare instruction you use is not itself predicated.

```
        DSUB R1,R13,R14
        BNEZ R1,L1
        DADDI R2,R2,#1
        SD 0(R7),R2
        J L2
L1:     MUL.D F0,F0,F2
        ADD.D F0,F4
        S.D 0(R8),F0
L2:
```

b. [15] <4.5> What are all the dependences in the code given in part (a), and what are the dependences in the code for your answer to part (a)? How do they differ, and what is the advantage for performance of the predicated code?

4.19 [15/12/12] <4.5, 4.7> See the description of predicated instructions in the preceding exercise, then answer the following questions.

a. [15] <4.5, 4.7> Write the following code without branches. Use predicated MIPS instructions.

```
if (A>B) then { X=1;}
else {
        if (C<D) then { X=2;}
        else { X=3;} }
```

b. [12] <4.7> Where would an IA-64 compiler place stop(s) in the answer to part (a)?

c. [12] <4.7> What are the possible sequences of instruction bundle templates (see Figure 4.12) for the answer to part (a)? Assume that the first instruction begins a bundle.

✪ 4.20 [10] <4.5> Predicated instructions cannot eliminate a branch instruction when that branch is part of what kind of program structure?

4.21 [15]<4.7> A compiler for IA-64 has generated the following sequence of three instructions:

```
        L.D F0,0(R1)   ;F0=Mem[0+R1]
(p1)    DADD R1,R2,R3  ;if (p1) then R1=R2+R3
(p2)    DSUB R5,R1,R4  ;if (p2) then R5=R1-R4
```

where p1 and p2 are two predicate registers that are set earlier in the program. Assume that the three instructions are to form a bundle. What are the possible templates that the compiler could use for the bundle (see Figure 4.12), and under what circumstances would each template be chosen?

4.22 [20] <4.7> A compound conditional joins more than two values by Boolean operators, for example, X&&Y&&Z. If predicate-generating compare instructions can be ganged together to simultaneously update a single predicate register, then compound conditionals can be computed more rapidly. Consider a parallel computation of an && only compound condition (a conjunction term). If the predicate register were initialized to true, then simultaneous writes by only those compare instructions determining that their comparison should set the predicate to false (zero) is readily supportable in hardware. There will be no contention from trying to set the predicate simultaneously to conflicting values. A parallel not-equal compare to update pT might be written

```
(qp) CMP.NE.AND pT=Rx,R0
```

where R0 always contains zero and .AND denotes that the write by this compare to predicate register pT will occur only if this compare finds pT is false. Initialize a predicate register to true, and then use the parallel compare instruction to transform the following code into a single block of predicated instructions and form it into as few bundles as possible, as in Figure 4.13 on page 355.

```
if (X && Y && Z) then { A=A+1;}
else { A=A+2;}
```

4.23 [10/20/10] <4.1, 4.5, 4.7, 5.10, 5.11> The example on page 342 uses a speculative load instruction to move a load above its guarding branch instruction. Consider the following code:

```
instr. 1                    ;arbitrary instruction
instr. 2                    ;next instruction in block
. . .                       ;intervening instructions
BEQZ        R1, null        ;check for null pointer
L.D         F2,0(R1)        ;load using pointer
ADD.D       F4,F0,F2        ;dependent ADD.D
. . .
null:  . . .                ;handle null pointer
```

a. [10] <4.5> Write the above code using a speculative load (sL.D) and a speculation check instruction (SPECCK) to preserve exception behavior. Where should the L.D move to best hide its potentially long latency?

b. [20] <4.1, 4.5, 4.7> Assume a speculation check instruction that branches to recovery code. Write the above code speculating on both the load and the dependent add. Use a speculative load, a nonspeculative add, a check instruction, and the block of recovery code. How should the speculated load and add be scheduled with respect to each other?

c. [10] <5.10, 5.11> What type(s) of load exceptions could the SPECCK protect for in part (a)? What type of load exception will trigger the recovery code in part (b)?

✪ 4.24 [15] <4.7> An advanced load address table (ALAT) holds the effective address of a load that has been moved before a preceding store, which may or may not have the same or overlapping effective address. For which processor, the one of Figure 4.1 or the IA-64 described in Figure 4.15, is an ALAT most beneficial and why?

4.25 [15] <4.8> Why might speculation and predication be of less value in the embedded computer marketplace than in the server or desktop arena? What are the market niches where they will be least valued?

4.26 [20] <4.1, 4.4, 4.5> Branches are the target of considerable effort for dynamically scheduled processors. For statically scheduled processors, loop unrolling, trace scheduling, superblocks, and predication all attempt to reduce the negative effects of branches on performance. Construct a comparison of these four techniques. For each technique include a description of its best-suited branch characteristics, suitable program structures, needed hardware support, complexity of compiler support, effect on code size, effect on fetching, and other meaningful distinguishing features.

4.27 [Discussion] <3.2–3.7, 4.1–4.5> Dynamic instruction scheduling requires a considerable investment in hardware. In return, this capability allows the hardware to run programs that could not be run at full speed with only compile time, static scheduling. What trade-offs should be taken into account in trying to decide between a dynamically and a statically scheduled implementation? What situations in either hardware technology or program characteristics are likely to favor one approach or the other? Most speculative schemes rely on dynamic scheduling; how does speculation affect the arguments in favor of dynamic scheduling? Many static schemes incorporate predication; how do branch behavior and program structure affect the arguments in favor of predication?

4.28 [Discussion] <3.2, 3.3, 4.5> Consider combining the static and dynamic ILP techniques of predicated instructions and the Tomasulo algorithm. How might predicated instructions be handled in each of the three steps of the Tomasulo algorithm (see Section 3.2)? For each approach that you can devise, clearly define how it is implemented, discuss its performance potential, list what additional hardware support is necessary if any, tell whether the approach involves speculative execution or not, and identify whether dependences on the predicate behave as data or control dependences. Do you think the two techniques work together well?

4.29 [Discussion] <4.3–4.5> Discuss the advantages and disadvantages of a superscalar implementation and a VLIW approach in the context of MIPS. What levels of ILP favor each approach? What other concerns would you consider in choosing which type of processor to build? How does speculation affect the results?

4.30 [Discussion] <3, 4> Investigate the delivered clock speeds for various processors using primarily hardware techniques for exploiting ILP and for processors focused on software techniques for exploiting ILP. Try to determine the reasons for any differences in clock speeds. Examine available benchmark results to see how they do or do not correlate closely with clock speed.

5

Memory Hierarchy
Design

Ideally one would desire an indefinitely large memory capacity such that any particular ...word would be immediately available....We are ...forced to recognize the possibility of constructing a hierarchy of memories, each of which has greater capacity than the preceding but which is less quickly accessible.

A. W. Burks, H. H. Goldstine, and J. von Neumann
Preliminary Discussion of the Logical Design of an
Electronic Computing Instrument (1946)

Introduction

Computer pioneers correctly predicted that programmers would want unlimited amounts of fast memory. An economical solution to that desire is a *memory hierarchy,* which takes advantage of locality and cost-performance of memory technologies. The *principle of locality,* presented in the first chapter, says that most programs do not access all code or data uniformly (see Section 1.6, page 47). This principle, plus the guideline that smaller hardware is faster, led to hierarchies based on memories of different speeds and sizes. Figure 5.1 shows a multilevel memory hierarchy, including typical sizes and speeds of access.

Since fast memory is expensive, a memory hierarchy is organized into several levels—each smaller, faster, and more expensive per byte than the next lower level. The goal is to provide a memory system with cost almost as low as the cheapest level of memory and speed almost as fast as the fastest level. The levels of the hierarchy usually subset one another. All data in one level are also found in the level below, and all data in that lower level are found in the one below it, and so on until we reach the bottom of the hierarchy.

Note that each level maps addresses from a slower, larger memory to a smaller but faster memory higher in the hierarchy. As part of address mapping, the memory hierarchy is given the responsibility of address checking; hence protection schemes for scrutinizing addresses are also part of the memory hierarchy.

The importance of the memory hierarchy has increased with advances in performance of processors. For example, in 1980 microprocessors were often designed without caches, while in 2001 many come with two levels of caches on the chip. As noted in Chapter 1, microprocessor performance improved 35% per year until 1986, and 55% per year since 1987. Figure 5.2 plots CPU performance projections against the historical performance improvement in time to access main memory. Clearly, there is a processor-memory performance gap that computer architects must try to close.

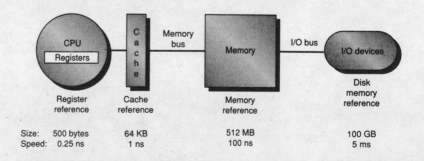

Figure 5.1 The levels in a typical memory hierarchy in embedded, desktop, and server computers. As we move farther away from the CPU, the memory in the level below becomes slower and larger. Note that the time units change by factors of 10—from picoseconds to milliseconds—and that the size units change by factors of 1000—from bytes to terabytes. Figure 5.3 shows more parameters for desktops and small servers.

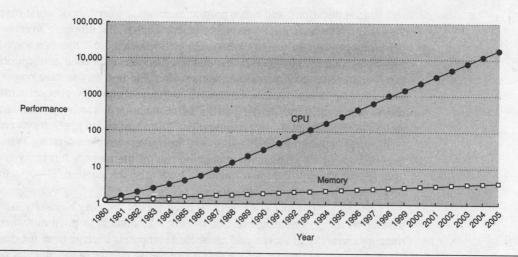

Figure 5.2 Starting with 1980 performance as a baseline, the gap in performance between memory and CPUs is plotted over time. Note that the vertical axis must be on a logarithmic scale to record the size of the CPU-DRAM performance gap. The memory baseline is 64 KB DRAM in 1980, with three years to the next generation and a 7% per year performance improvement in latency (see Figure 5.30 on page 456). The CPU line assumes a 1.35 improvement per year until 1986, and a 1.55 improvement thereafter.

This chapter describes the many ideas invented to overcome the processor-memory performance gap. To put these abstract ideas into practice, throughout the chapter we show examples from the four levels of the memory hierarchy in a computer using the Alpha 21264 microprocessor. Toward the end of the chapter we evaluate the impact of these levels on performance using the SPEC95 benchmark programs.

The 21264 is a microprocessor designed for desktops and servers. Even these two related classes of computers have different concerns in a memory hierarchy. Desktop computers are primarily running one application at a time on top of an operating system for a single user, whereas server computers may typically have hundreds of users running potentially dozens of applications simultaneously. These characteristics result in more context switches, which effectively increase compulsory miss rates. Thus, desktop computers are concerned more with average latency from the memory hierarchy, whereas server computers are also concerned about memory bandwidth. Although protection is important on desktop computers to deter programs from clobbering each other, server computers must prevent one user from accessing another's data, and hence the importance of protection escalates. Server computers also tend to be much larger, with more memory and disk storage, and hence often run much larger applications. In 2001 virtually all servers can be purchased as multiprocessors with hundreds of disks, which places even greater bandwidth demands on the memory hierarchy.

The memory hierarchy of the embedded computers is often quite different from that of the desktop and server. First, embedded computers are often used in real-time applications, and hence programmers must worry about worst-case performance. This concern is problematic for caches that improve average-case performance, but can degrade worst-case performance; we'll mention some techniques to address this later in the chapter. Second, embedded applications are often concerned about power and battery life. The best way to save power is to have less hardware. Hence, embedded computers may not choose hardware-intensive optimizations in the quest of better memory hierarchy performance, as would most desktop and server computers. Third, embedded applications are typically only running one application and use a very simple operating system, if they use one at all. Hence, the protection role of the memory hierarchy is often diminished. Finally, the main memory itself may be quite small—less than 1 MB—and there is often no disk storage.

This chapter is a tour of the general principles of memory hierarchy using the desktop as the generic example, but we will take detours to point out where the memory hierarchy of servers and embedded computers diverge from the desktop. Toward the end of the chapter we will pause for two views of the memory hierarchy in addition to the Alpha 21264: the Sony Playstation 2 and the Sun Fire 6800 server. Our first stop is a review.

5.2 Review of the ABCs of Caches

Cache: a safe place for hiding or storing things.

Webster's New World Dictionary of the American Language
Second College Edition (1976)

This section is a quick review of cache basics, covering the following 36 terms:

cache	fully associative	write allocate
virtual memory	dirty bit	unified cache
memory stall cycles	block offset	misses per instruction
direct mapped	write back	block
valid bit	data cache	locality
block address	hit time	address trace
write through	cache miss	set
instruction cache	page fault	random replacement
average memory access time	miss rate	index field
cache hit	n-way set associative	no-write allocate
page	least-recently used	write buffer
miss penalty	tag field	write stall

Readers who know the meaning of such terms should skip to "An Example: The Alpha 21264 Data Cache" on page 403, or even further to Section 5.3, "Cache Performance," on page 406. (If this review goes too quickly, you might want to look at Chapter 7 in *Computer Organization and Design,* which we wrote for readers with less experience.)

For those interested in a review, two particularly important levels of the memory hierarchy are cache and virtual memory.

Cache is the name given to the first level of the memory hierarchy encountered once the address leaves the CPU. Since the principle of locality applies at many levels, and taking advantage of locality to improve performance is popular, the term *cache* is now applied whenever buffering is employed to reuse commonly occurring items. Examples include *file caches, name caches,* and so on.

When the CPU finds a requested data item in the cache, it is called a *cache hit.* When the CPU does not find a data item it needs in the cache, a *cache miss* occurs. A fixed-size collection of data containing the requested word, called a *block,* is retrieved from the main memory and placed into the cache. *Temporal locality* tells us that we are likely to need this word again in the near future, so it is useful to place it in the cache where it can be accessed quickly. Because of *spatial locality,* there is a high probability that the other data in the block will be needed soon.

The time required for the cache miss depends on both the latency and bandwidth of the memory. Latency determines the time to retrieve the first word of the block, and bandwidth determines the time to retrieve the rest of this block. A cache miss is handled by hardware and causes processors following in-order execution to pause, or stall, until the data are available.

Similarly, not all objects referenced by a program need to reside in main memory. If the computer has *virtual memory,* then some objects may reside on disk. The address space is usually broken into fixed-size blocks, called *pages.* At any time, each page resides either in main memory or on disk. When the CPU references an item within a page that is not present in the cache or main memory, a *page fault* occurs, and the entire page is moved from the disk to main memory. Since page faults take so long, they are handled in software and the CPU is not stalled. The CPU usually switches to some other task while the disk access occurs. The cache and main memory have the same relationship as the main memory and disk.

Figure 5.3 shows the range of sizes and access times of each level in the memory hierarchy for computers ranging from high-end desktops to low-end servers.

Cache Performance Review

Because of locality and the higher speed of smaller memories, a memory hierarchy can substantially improve performance. One method to evaluate cache performance is to expand our CPU execution time equation from Chapter 1. We now account for the number of cycles during which the CPU is stalled waiting for a

Level	1	2	3	4
Name	registers	cache	main memory	disk storage
Typical size	< 1 KB	< 16 MB	< 16 GB	> 100 GB
Implementation technology	custom memory with multiple ports, CMOS	on-chip or off-chip CMOS SRAM	CMOS DRAM	magnetic disk
Access time (ns)	0.25–0.5	0.5–25	80–250	5,000,000
Bandwidth (MB/sec)	20,000–100,000	5000–10,000	1000–5000	20–150
Managed by	compiler	hardware	operating system	operating system/operator
Backed by	cache	main memory	disk	CD or tape

Figure 5.3 The typical levels in the hierarchy slow down and get larger as we move away from the CPU for a large workstation or small server. Embedded computers might have no disk storage, and much smaller memories and caches. The access times increase as we move to lower levels of the hierarchy, which makes it feasible to manage the transfer less responsively. The implementation technology shows the typical technology used for these functions. The access time is given in nanoseconds for typical values in 2001; these times will decrease over time. Bandwidth is given in megabytes per second between levels in the memory hierarchy. Bandwidth for disk storage includes both the media and the buffered interfaces.

memory access, which we call the *memory stall cycles*. The performance is then the product of the clock cycle time and the sum of the CPU cycles and the memory stall cycles:

$$\text{CPU execution time} = (\text{CPU clock cycles} + \text{Memory stall cycles}) \times \text{Clock cycle time}$$

This equation assumes that the CPU clock cycles include the time to handle a cache hit, and that the CPU is stalled during a cache miss. Section 5.3 reexamines this simplifying assumption.

The number of memory stall cycles depends on both the number of misses and the cost per miss, which is called the *miss penalty:*

$$\text{Memory stall cycles} = \text{Number of misses} \times \text{Miss penalty}$$

$$= IC \times \frac{\text{Misses}}{\text{Instruction}} \times \text{Miss penalty}$$

$$= IC \times \frac{\text{Memory accesses}}{\text{Instruction}} \times \text{Miss rate} \times \text{Miss penalty}$$

The advantage of the last form is that the components can be easily measured. We already know how to measure instruction count. (For speculative CPUs, we only count instructions that commit in IC.) Measuring the number of memory references per instruction can be done in the same fashion; every instruction requires an instruction access, and we can easily decide if it also requires a data access.

Note that we calculated miss penalty as an average, but we will use it below as if it were a constant. The memory behind the cache may be busy at the time of the miss because of prior memory requests or memory refresh (see Section 5.9).

The number of clock cycles also varies at interfaces between different clocks of the processor, bus, and memory. Thus, please remember that using a single number for miss penalty is a simplification.

The component *miss rate* is simply the fraction of cache accesses that result in a miss (i.e., number of accesses that miss divided by number of accesses). Miss rates can be measured with cache simulators that take an *address trace* of the instruction and data references, simulate the cache behavior to determine which references hit and which miss, and then report the hit and miss totals. Some microprocessors provide hardware to count the number of misses and memory references, which is a much easier and faster way to measure miss rate.

The formula above is an approximation since the miss rates and miss penalties are often different for reads and writes. Memory stall clock cycles could then be defined in terms of the number of memory accesses per instruction, miss penalty (in clock cycles) for reads and writes, and miss rate for reads and writes:

$$\text{Memory stall clock cycles} = \text{IC} \times \text{Reads per instruction} \times \text{Read miss rate} \times \text{Read miss penalty}$$
$$+ \text{IC} \times \text{Writes per instruction} \times \text{Write miss rate} \times \text{Write miss penalty}$$

We normally simplify the complete formula by combining the reads and writes and finding the average miss rates and miss penalty for reads *and* writes:

$$\text{Memory stall clock cycles} = \text{IC} \times \frac{\text{Memory accesses}}{\text{Instruction}} \times \text{Miss rate} \times \text{Miss penalty}$$

The miss rate is one of the most important measures of cache design, but, as we will see in later sections, not the only measure.

Example   Assume we have a computer where the clocks per instruction (CPI) is 1.0 when all memory accesses hit in the cache. The only data accesses are loads and stores, and these total 50% of the instructions. If the miss penalty is 25 clock cycles and the miss rate is 2%, how much faster would the computer be if all instructions were cache hits?

Answer   First compute the performance for the computer that always hits:

$$\text{CPU execution time} = (\text{CPU clock cycles} + \text{Memory stall cycles}) \times \text{Clock cycle}$$
$$= (\text{IC} \times \text{CPI} + 0) \times \text{Clock cycle}$$
$$= \text{IC} \times 1.0 \times \text{Clock cycle}$$

Now for the computer with the real cache, first we compute memory stall cycles:

$$\text{Memory stall cycles} = \text{IC} \times \frac{\text{Memory accesses}}{\text{Instruction}} \times \text{Miss rate} \times \text{Miss penalty}$$
$$= \text{IC} \times (1 + 0.5) \times 0.02 \times 25$$
$$= \text{IC} \times 0.75$$

where the middle term $(1 + 0.5)$ represents one instruction access and 0.5 data accesses per instruction. The total performance is thus

$$\text{CPU execution time}_{\text{cache}} = (\text{IC} \times 1.0 + \text{IC} \times 0.75) \times \text{Clock cycle}$$
$$= 1.75 \times \text{IC} \times \text{Clock cycle}$$

The performance ratio is the inverse of the execution times:

$$\frac{\text{CPU execution time}_{\text{cache}}}{\text{CPU execution time}} = \frac{1.75 \times \text{IC} \times \text{Clock cycle}}{1.0 \times \text{IC} \times \text{Clock cycle}}$$
$$= 1.75$$

The computer with no cache misses is 1.75 times faster.

Some designers prefer measuring miss rate as *misses per instruction* rather than misses per memory reference. These two are related:

$$\frac{\text{Misses}}{\text{Instruction}} = \frac{\text{Miss rate} \times \text{Memory accesses}}{\text{Instruction count}} = \text{Miss rate} \times \frac{\text{Memory accesses}}{\text{Instruction}}$$

The latter formula is useful when you know the average number of memory accesses per instruction because it allows you to convert miss rate into misses per instruction, and vice versa. For example, we can turn the miss rate per memory reference in the previous example into misses per instruction:

$$\frac{\text{Misses}}{\text{Instruction}} = \text{Miss rate} \times \frac{\text{Memory accesses}}{\text{Instruction}} = 0.02 \times 1.5 = 0.030$$

By the way, misses per instruction are often reported as misses per 1000 instructions to show integers instead of fractions. Thus, the answer above could also be expressed as 30 misses per 1000 instructions.

The advantage of misses per instruction is that it is independent of the hardware implementation. For example, the 21264 fetches about twice as many instructions as are actually committed, which can artificially reduce the miss rate if measured as misses per memory reference rather than per instruction. The drawback is that misses per instruction is architecture dependent; for example, the average number of memory accesses per instruction may be very different for an 80x86 versus MIPS. Thus, misses per instruction are most popular with architects working with a single computer family, although the similarity of RISC architectures allows one to give insights into others.

Example   To show equivalency between the two miss rate equations, let's redo the example above, this time assuming a miss rate per 1000 instructions of 30. What is memory stall time in terms of instruction count?

Answer   Recomputing the memory stall cycles:

$$\text{Memory stall cycles} = \text{Number of misses} \times \text{Miss penalty}$$

$$= \text{IC} \times \frac{\text{Misses}}{\text{Instruction}} \times \text{Miss penalty}$$

$$= \text{IC} / 1000 \times \frac{\text{Misses}}{\text{Instruction} \times 1000} \times \text{Miss penalty}$$

$$= \text{IC} / 1000 \times 30 \times 25$$

$$= \text{IC} / 1000 \times 750$$

$$= \text{IC} \times 0.75$$

We get the same answer as on page 395.

Four Memory Hierarchy Questions

We continue our introduction to caches by answering the four common questions for the first level of the memory hierarchy:

Q1: Where can a block be placed in the upper level? (*block placement*)

Q2: How is a block found if it is in the upper level? (*block identification*)

Q3: Which block should be replaced on a miss? (*block replacement*)

Q4: What happens on a write? (*write strategy*)

The answers to these questions help us understand the different trade-offs of memories at different levels of a hierarchy; hence we ask these four questions on every example.

Q1: Where Can a Block Be Placed in a Cache?

Figure 5.4 shows that the restrictions on where a block is placed create three categories of cache organization:

■ If each block has only one place it can appear in the cache, the cache is said to be *direct mapped*. The mapping is usually

(Block address) MOD *(Number of blocks in cache)*

■ If a block can be placed anywhere in the cache, the cache is said to be *fully associative*.

■ If a block can be placed in a restricted set of places in the cache, the cache is *set associative*. A *set* is a group of blocks in the cache. A block is first mapped onto a set, and then the block can be placed anywhere within that set. The set is usually chosen by *bit selection;* that is,

(Block address) MOD *(Number of sets in cache)*

If there are *n* blocks in a set, the cache placement is called *n-way set associative*.

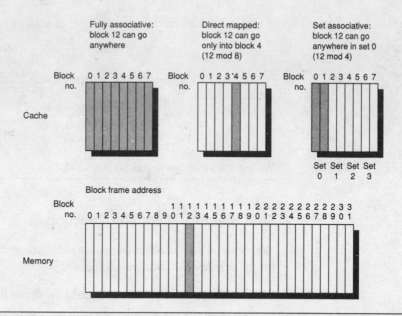

Figure 5.4 This example cache has eight block frames and memory has 32 blocks. The three options for caches are shown left to right. In fully associative, block 12 from the lower level can go into any of the eight block frames of the cache. With direct mapped, block 12 can only be placed into block frame 4 (12 modulo 8). Set associative, which has some of both features, allows the block to be placed anywhere in set 0 (12 modulo 4). With two blocks per set, this means block 12 can be placed either in block 0 or in block 1 of the cache. Real caches contain thousands of block frames and real memories contain millions of blocks. The set-associative organization has four sets with two blocks per set, called *two-way set associative*. Assume that there is nothing in the cache and that the block address in question identifies lower-level block 12.

The range of caches from direct mapped to fully associative is really a continuum of levels of set associativity. Direct mapped is simply one-way set associative, and a fully associative cache with *m* blocks could be called "*m*-way set associative." Equivalently, direct mapped can be thought of as having *m* sets, and fully associative as having one set.

The vast majority of processor caches today are direct mapped, two-way set associative, or four-way set associative, for reasons we will see shortly.

Q2: How Is a Block Found If It Is in the Cache?

Caches have an address tag on each block frame that gives the block address. The tag of every cache block that might contain the desired information is checked to see if it matches the block address from the CPU. As a rule, all possible tags are searched in parallel because speed is critical.

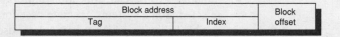

Figure 5.5 The three portions of an address in a set-associative or direct-mapped cache. The tag is used to check all the blocks in the set, and the index is used to select the set. The block offset is the address of the desired data within the block. Fully associative caches have no index field.

There must be a way to know that a cache block does not have valid information. The most common procedure is to add a *valid bit* to the tag to say whether or not this entry contains a valid address. If the bit is not set, there cannot be a match on this address.

Before proceeding to the next question, let's explore the relationship of a CPU address to the cache. Figure 5.5 shows how an address is divided. The first division is between the *block address* and the *block offset*. The block frame address can be further divided into the *tag field* and the *index field*. The block offset field selects the desired data from the block, the index field selects the set, and the tag field is compared against it for a hit. Although the comparison could be made on more of the address than the tag, there is no need because of the following:

- The offset should not be used in the comparison, since the entire block is present or not, and hence all block offsets result in a match by definition.

- Checking the index is redundant, since it was used to select the set to be checked. An address stored in set 0, for example, must have 0 in the index field or it couldn't be stored in set 0; set 1 must have an index value of 1; and so on. This optimization saves hardware and power by reducing the width of memory size for the cache tag.

If the total cache size is kept the same, increasing associativity increases the number of blocks per set, thereby decreasing the size of the index and increasing the size of the tag. That is, the tag-index boundary in Figure 5.5 moves to the right with increasing associativity, with the end point of fully associative caches having no index field.

Q3: Which Block Should Be Replaced on a Cache Miss?

When a miss occurs, the cache controller must select a block to be replaced with the desired data. A benefit of direct-mapped placement is that hardware decisions are simplified—in fact, so simple that there is no choice: Only one block frame is checked for a hit, and only that block can be replaced. With fully associative or set-associative placement, there are many blocks to choose from on a miss. There are three primary strategies employed for selecting which block to replace:

- *Random*—To spread allocation uniformly, candidate blocks are randomly selected. Some systems generate pseudorandom block numbers to get reproducible behavior, which is particularly useful when debugging hardware.

- *Least-recently used* (LRU)—To reduce the chance of throwing out information that will be needed soon, accesses to blocks are recorded. Relying on the past to predict the future, the block replaced is the one that has been unused for the longest time. LRU relies on a corollary of locality: If recently used blocks are likely to be used again, then a good candidate for disposal is the least-recently used block.

- *First in, first out* (FIFO)—Because LRU can be complicated to calculate, this approximates LRU by determining the *oldest* block rather than the LRU.

A virtue of random replacement is that it is simple to build in hardware. As the number of blocks to keep track of increases, LRU becomes increasingly expensive and is frequently only approximated. Figure 5.6 shows the difference in miss rates between LRU, random, and FIFO replacement.

Q4: What Happens on a Write?

Reads dominate processor cache accesses. All instruction accesses are reads, and most instructions don't write to memory. Figure 2.32 in Chapter 2 suggests a mix of 10% stores and 37% loads for MIPS programs, making writes 10%/(100% + 37% + 10%) or about 7% of the overall memory traffic. Of the *data cache* traffic, writes are 10%/(37% + 10%) or about 21%. Making the common case fast means optimizing caches for reads, especially since processors traditionally wait for reads to complete but need not wait for writes. Amdahl's Law (Section 1.6) reminds us, however, that high-performance designs cannot neglect the speed of writes.

	Associativity								
	Two-way			Four-way			Eight-way		
Size	LRU	Random	FIFO	LRU	Random	FIFO	LRU	Random	FIFO
16 KB	114.1	117.3	115.5	111.7	115.1	113.3	109.0	111.8	110.4
64 KB	103.4	104.3	103.9	102.4	102.3	103.1	99.7	100.5	100.3
256 KB	92.2	92.1	92.5	92.1	92.1	92.5	92.1	92.1	92.5

Figure 5.6 Data cache misses per 1000 instructions comparing least-recently used, random, and first in, first out replacement for several sizes and associativities. There is little difference between LRU and random for the largest-size cache, with LRU outperforming the others for smaller caches. FIFO generally outperforms random in the smaller cache sizes. These data were collected for a block size of 64 bytes for the Alpha architecture using 10 SPEC2000 benchmarks. Five are from SPECint2000 (gap, gcc, gzip, mcf, and perl) and five are from SPECfp2000 (applu, art, equake, lucas, and swim). We will use this computer and these benchmarks in most figures in this chapter.

Fortunately, the common case is also the easy case to make fast. The block can be read from the cache at the same time that the tag is read and compared, so the block read begins as soon as the block address is available. If the read is a hit, the requested part of the block is passed on to the CPU immediately. If it is a miss, there is no benefit—but also no harm in desktop and server computers; just ignore the value read. Embedded's emphasis on power generally means avoiding unnecessary work, which might lead the designer to separate data read from address check so that data is not read on a miss.

Such optimism is not allowed for writes. Modifying a block cannot begin until the tag is checked to see if the address is a hit. Because tag checking cannot occur in parallel, writes normally take longer than reads. Another complexity is that the processor also specifies the size of the write, usually between 1 and 8 bytes; only that portion of a block can be changed. In contrast, reads can access more bytes than necessary without fear; once again, embedded designers might weigh the power benefits of reading less.

The write policies often distinguish cache designs. There are two basic options when writing to the cache:

- *Write through*—The information is written to both the block in the cache *and* to the block in the lower-level memory.

- *Write back*—The information is written only to the block in the cache. The modified cache block is written to main memory only when it is replaced.

To reduce the frequency of writing back blocks on replacement, a feature called the *dirty bit* is commonly used. This status bit indicates whether the block is *dirty* (modified while in the cache) or *clean* (not modified). If it is clean, the block is not written back on a miss, since identical information to the cache is found in lower levels.

Both write back and write through have their advantages. With write back, writes occur at the speed of the cache memory, and multiple writes within a block require only one write to the lower-level memory. Since some writes don't go to memory, write back uses less memory bandwidth, making write back attractive in multiprocessors that are common in servers. Since write back uses the rest of the memory hierarchy and memory buses less than write through, it also saves power, making it attractive for embedded applications.

Write through is easier to implement than write back. The cache is always clean, so unlike write back read misses never result in writes to the lower level. Write through also has the advantage that the next lower level has the most current copy of the data, which simplifies data coherency. Data coherency (see Section 5.12) is important for multiprocessors and for I/O, which we examine in Chapters 6 and 7.

As we will see, I/O and multiprocessors are fickle: They want write back for processor caches to reduce the memory traffic and write through to keep the cache consistent with lower levels of the memory hierarchy.

When the CPU must wait for writes to complete during write through, the CPU is said to *write stall*. A common optimization to reduce write stalls is a *write buffer,* which allows the processor to continue as soon as the data are written to the buffer, thereby overlapping processor execution with memory updating. As we will see shortly, write stalls can occur even with write buffers.

Since the data are not needed on a write, there are two options on a write miss:

■ *Write allocate* —The block is allocated on a write miss, followed by the write hit actions above. In this natural option, write misses act like read misses.

■ *No-write allocate*—This apparently unusual alternative is write misses do *not* affect the cache. Instead, the block is modified only in the lower-level memory.

Thus, blocks stay out of the cache in no-write allocate until the program tries to read the blocks, but even blocks that are only written will still be in the cache with write allocate. Let's look at an example.

Example   Assume a fully associative write-back cache with many cache entries that starts empty. Below is a sequence of five memory operations (the address is in square brackets):

```
Write Mem[100];
WriteMem[100];
Read Mem[200];
WriteMem[200];
WriteMem[100].
```

What are the number of hits and misses when using no-write allocate versus write allocate?

Answer   For no-write allocate, the address 100 is not in the cache, and there is no allocation on write, so the first two writes will result in misses. Address 200 is also not in the cache, so the read is also a miss. The subsequent write to address 200 is a hit. The last write to 100 is still a miss. The result for no-write allocate is four misses and one hit.

For write allocate, the first accesses to 100 and 200 are misses, and the rest are hits since 100 and 200 are both found in the cache. Thus, the result for write allocate is two misses and three hits.

Either write miss policy could be used with write through or write back. Normally, write-back caches use write allocate, hoping that subsequent writes to that block will be captured by the cache. Write-through caches often use no-write allocate. The reasoning is that even if there are subsequent writes to that block, the writes must still go to the lower-level memory, so what's to be gained?

An Example: The Alpha 21264 Data Cache

To give substance to these ideas, Figure 5.7 shows the organization of the data cache in the Alpha 21264 microprocessor that is found in the Compaq Alpha-Server ES40, one of several models that use it. The cache contains 65,536 (64K) bytes of data in 64-byte blocks with two-way set-associative placement, write back, and write allocate on a write miss.

Let's trace a cache hit through the steps of a hit as labeled in Figure 5.7. (The four steps are shown as circled numbers.) As we will see later (Figure 5.36), the 21264 processor presents a 48-bit virtual address to the cache for tag comparison, which is simultaneously translated into a 44-bit physical address. (It also optionally supports 43-bit virtual addresses with 41-bit physical addresses.)

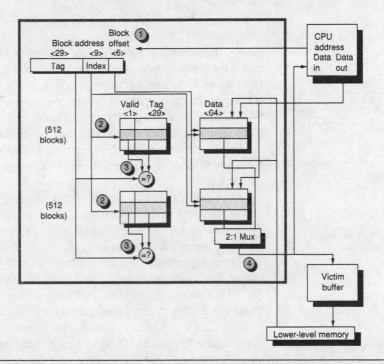

Figure 5.7 The organization of the data cache in the Alpha 21264 microprocessor. The 64 KB cache is two-way set associative with 64-byte blocks. The 9-bit index selects among 512 sets. The four steps of a read hit, shown as circled numbers in order of occurrence, label this organization. Three bits of the block offset join the index to supply the RAM address to select the proper 8 bytes. Thus, the cache holds two groups of 4096 64-bit words, with each group containing half of the 512 sets. Although not exercised in this example, the line from lower-level memory to the cache is used on a miss to load the cache. The size of address leaving the CPU is 44 bits because it is a physical address and not a virtual address. Figure 5.36 on page 466 explains how the Alpha maps from virtual to physical for a cache access.

The reason Alpha doesn't use all 64 bits of virtual address is that its designers don't think anyone needs that big of a virtual address space yet, and the smaller size simplifies the Alpha virtual address mapping. The designers planned to grow the virtual address in future microprocessors.

The physical address coming into the cache is divided into two fields: the 38-bit block address and the 6-bit block offset ($64 = 2^6$ and $38 + 6 = 44$). The block address is further divided into an address tag and cache index. Step 1 shows this division.

The cache index selects the tag to be tested to see if the desired block is in the cache. The size of the index depends on cache size, block size, and set associativity. For the 21264 cache the set associativity is set to two, and we calculate the index as follows:

$$2^{\text{Index}} = \frac{\text{Cache size}}{\text{Block size} \times \text{Set associativity}} = \frac{65,536}{64 \times 2} = 512 = 2^9$$

Hence, the index is 9 bits wide, and the tag is $38 - 9$ or 29 bits wide. Although that is the index needed to select the proper block, 64 bytes is much more than the CPU wants to consume at once. Hence, it makes more sense to organize the data portion of the cache memory 8 bytes wide, which is the natural data word of the 64-bit Alpha processor. Thus, in addition to 9 bits to index the proper cache block, 3 more bits from the block offset are used to index the proper 8 bytes.

Index selection is step 2 in Figure 5.7. The two tags are compared and the winner is selected. (Section 5.10 explains how the 21264 handles virtual address translation.)

After reading the two tags from the cache, they are compared to the tag portion of the block address from the CPU. This comparison is step 3 in the figure. To be sure the tag contains valid information, the valid bit must be set or else the results of the comparison are ignored.

Assuming one tag does match, the final step is to signal the CPU to load the proper data from the cache by using the winning input from a 2:1 multiplexor. The 21264 allows 3 clock cycles for these four steps, so the instructions in the following 2 clock cycles would wait if they tried to use the result of the load.

Handling writes is more complicated than handling reads in the 21264, as it is in any cache. If the word to be written is in the cache, the first three steps are the same. Since the 21264 executes out of order, only after it signals that the instruction has committed and the cache tag comparison indicates a hit are the data written to the cache.

So far we have assumed the common case of a cache hit. What happens on a miss? On a read miss, the cache sends a signal to the processor telling it the data are not yet available, and 64 bytes are read from the next level of the hierarchy. The path to the next lower level in the 21264 is 16 bytes wide. In the 667 MHz AlphaServer ES40 it takes 2.25 ns per transfer, or 9 ns for all 64 bytes. Since the data cache is set associative, there is a choice on which block to replace. The 21264 does *round-robin* selection, also called first in, first out (FIFO), dedicating a bit for every two blocks to remember where to go next. Unlike LRU, which selects the block that was referenced longest ago, round-robin selects the block that was filled longest ago. Round-robin is easier to implement since it is only updated on a miss rather than on every hit. Replacing a block means updating the data, the address tag, the valid bit, and the round-robin bit.

Since the 21264 uses write back, the old data block could have been modified, and hence it cannot simply be discarded. The 21264 keeps 1 dirty bit per block to record if the block was written. If the "victim" was modified, its data and address are sent to the Victim Buffer. (This structure is similar to a *write buffer* in other computers.) The 21264 has space for eight victim blocks. In parallel with other cache actions, it writes victim blocks to the next level of the hierarchy. If the Victim Buffer is full, the cache must wait.

A write miss is very similar to a read miss, since the 21264 allocates a block on a read or a write miss.

We have seen how it works, but the *data* cache cannot supply all the memory needs of the processor: The processor also needs instructions. Although a single cache could try to supply both, it can be a bottleneck. For example, when a load or store instruction is executed, the pipelined processor will simultaneously request both a data word *and* an instruction word. Hence, a single cache would present a structural hazard for loads and stores, leading to stalls. One simple way to conquer this problem is to divide it: One cache is dedicated to instructions and another to data. Separate caches are found in most recent processors, including the Alpha 21264. Hence, it has a 64 KB instruction cache as well as the 64 KB data cache.

The CPU knows whether it is issuing an instruction address or a data address, so there can be separate ports for both, thereby doubling the bandwidth between the memory hierarchy and the CPU. Separate caches also offer the opportunity of optimizing each cache separately: Different capacities, block sizes, and associativities may lead to better performance. (In contrast to the instruction caches and data caches of the 21264, the terms *unified* or *mixed* are applied to caches that can contain either instructions or data.)

Figure 5.8 shows that instruction caches have lower miss rates than data caches. Separating instructions and data removes misses due to conflicts between instruction blocks and data blocks, but the split also fixes the cache space devoted to each type. Which is more important to miss rates? A fair comparison of separate instruction and data caches to unified caches requires the total cache size to be the same. For example, a separate 16 KB instruction cache and 16 KB data cache should be compared to a 32 KB unified cache. Calculating the average miss rate with separate instruction and data caches necessitates knowing the percentage of memory references to each cache. Figure 2.32 on page 138 suggests the split is 100%/(100% + 26% + 10%) or about 74% instruction references to (26% + 10%)/(100% + 26% + 10%) or about 26% data references. Splitting affects performance beyond what is indicated by the change in miss rates, as we will see shortly.

Size	Instruction cache	Data cache	Unified cache
8 KB	8.16	44.0	63.0
16 KB	3.82	40.9	51.0
32 KB	1.36	38.4	43.3
64 KB	0.61	36.9	39.4
128 KB	0.30	35.3	36.2
256 KB	0.02	32.6	32.9

Figure 5.8 Miss per 1000 instructions for instruction, data, and unified caches of different sizes. The percentage of instruction references is about 74%. The data are for two-way associative caches with 64-byte blocks for the same computer and benchmarks as Figure 5.6.

5.3   Cache Performance

Because instruction count is independent of the hardware, it is tempting to evaluate CPU performance using that number. As we saw in Chapter 1, however, such indirect performance measures have waylaid many a computer designer. The corresponding temptation for evaluating memory hierarchy performance is to concentrate on miss rate because it, too, is independent of the speed of the hardware. As we will see, miss rate can be just as misleading as instruction count. A better measure of memory hierarchy performance is the *average memory access time:*

$$\text{Average memory access time} = \text{Hit time} + \text{Miss rate} \times \text{Miss penalty}$$

where *Hit time* is the time to hit in the cache; we have seen the other two terms before. The components of average access time can be measured either in absolute time—say, 0.25–1.0 nanoseconds on a hit—or in the number of clock cycles that the CPU waits for the memory—such as a miss penalty of 75–100 clock cycles. Remember that average memory access time is still an indirect measure of performance; although it is a better measure than miss rate, it is not a substitute for execution time.

This formula can help us decide between split caches and a unified cache.

Example   Which has the lower miss rate: a 16 KB instruction cache with a 16 KB data cache or a 32 KB unified cache? Use the miss rates in Figure 5.8 to help calculate the correct answer, assuming 36% of the instructions are data transfer instructions. Assume a hit takes 1 clock cycle and the miss penalty is 100 clock cycles. A load or store hit takes 1 extra clock cycle on a unified cache if there is only one cache port to satisfy two simultaneous requests. Using the pipelining terminology of the previous chapter, the unified cache leads to a structural hazard. What is the average memory access time in each case? Assume write-through caches with a write buffer and ignore stalls due to the write buffer.

Answer   First let's convert misses per 1000 instructions into miss rates. Solving the general formula from above, the miss rate is

$$\text{Miss rate} = \frac{\dfrac{\text{Misses}}{1000 \text{ Instructions}} / 1000}{\dfrac{\text{Memory accesses}}{\text{Instruction}}}$$

Since every instruction access has exactly one memory access to fetch the instruction, the instruction miss rate is

$$\text{Miss rate}_{16 \text{ KB instruction}} = \frac{3.82/1000}{1.00} = 0.004$$

Since 36% of the instructions are data transfers, the data miss rate is

$$\text{Miss rate}_{16 \text{ KB data}} = \frac{40.9/1000}{0.36} = 0.114$$

The unified miss rate needs to account for instruction and data accesses:

$$\text{Miss rate}_{32 \text{ KB unified}} = \frac{43.3/1000}{1.00 + 0.36} = 0.0318$$

As stated above, about 74% of the memory accesses are instruction references. Thus, the overall miss rate for the split caches is

$$(74\% \times 0.004) + (26\% \times 0.114) = 0.0324$$

Thus, a 32 KB unified cache has a slightly lower effective miss rate than two 16 KB caches.

The average memory access time formula can be divided into instruction and data accesses:

Average memory access time

$= \%$ instructions $\times$ (Hit time + Instruction miss rate $\times$ Miss penalty)

$+ \%$ data $\times$ (Hit time + Data miss rate $\times$ Miss penalty)

Therefore, the time for each organization is

Average memory access time$_{\text{split}}$

$= 74\% \times (1 + 0.004 \times 100) + 26\% \times (1 + 0.114 \times 100)$

$= (74\% \times 1.38) + (26\% \times 12.36) = 1.023 + 3.214 = 4.24$

Average memory access time$_{\text{unified}}$

$= 74\% \times (1 + 0.0318 \times 100) + 26\% \times (1 + 1 + 0.0318 \times 100)$

$= (74\% \times 4.18) + (26\% \times 5.18) = 3.096 + 1.348 = 4.44$

Hence, the split caches in this example—which offer two memory ports per clock cycle, thereby avoiding the structural hazard—have a better average memory access time than the single-ported unified cache despite having a worse effective miss rate.

Average Memory Access Time and Processor Performance

An obvious question is whether average memory access time due to cache misses predicts processor performance.

First, there are other reasons for stalls, such as contention due to I/O devices using memory. Designers often assume that all memory stalls are due to cache misses, since the memory hierarchy typically dominates other reasons for stalls. We use this simplifying assumption here, but beware to account for *all* memory stalls when calculating final performance.

Second, the answer depends also on the CPU. If we have an in-order execution CPU (see Chapter 3), then the answer is basically yes. The CPU stalls during misses, and the memory stall time is strongly correlated to average memory access time. Let's make that assumption for now, but we'll return to out-of-order CPUs in the next subsection.

As stated in the previous section, we can model CPU time as

CPU time = (CPU execution clock cycles + Memory stall clock cycles) × Clock cycle time

This formula raises the question whether the clock cycles for a cache hit should be considered part of CPU execution clock cycles or part of memory stall clock cycles. Although either convention is defensible, the most widely accepted is to include hit clock cycles in CPU execution clock cycles.

We can now explore the impact of caches on performance.

Example   Let's use an in-order execution computer for the first example, such as the Ultra-SPARC III (see Section 5.15). Assume the cache miss penalty is 100 clock cycles, and all instructions normally take 1.0 clock cycles (ignoring memory stalls). Assume the average miss rate is 2%, there is an average of 1.5 memory references per instruction, and the average number of cache misses per 1000 instructions is 30. What is the impact on performance when behavior of the cache is included? Calculate the impact using both misses per instruction and miss rate.

Answer $$\text{CPU time} = \text{IC} \times \left(\text{CPI}_{\text{execution}} + \frac{\text{Memory stall clock cycles}}{\text{Instruction}} \right) \times \text{Clock cycle time}$$

The performance, including cache misses, is

$$\text{CPU time}_{\text{with cache}} = \text{IC} \times (1.0 + (30/1000 \times 100)) \times \text{Clock cycle time}$$
$$= \text{IC} \times 4.00 \times \text{Clock cycle time}$$

Now calculating performance using miss rate:

$$\text{CPU time} = \text{IC} \times \left(\text{CPI}_{\text{execution}} + \text{Miss rate} \times \frac{\text{Memory accesses}}{\text{Instruction}} \times \text{Miss penalty} \right) \times \text{Clock cycle time}$$

$$\begin{aligned} \text{CPU time}_{\text{with cache}} &= \text{IC} \times (1.0 + (1.5 \times 2\% \times 100)) \times \text{Clock cycle time} \\ &= \text{IC} \times 4.00 \times \text{Clock cycle time} \end{aligned}$$

The clock cycle time and instruction count are the same, with or without a cache. Thus, CPU time increases fourfold, with CPI from 1.00 for a "perfect cache" to 4.00 with a cache that can miss. Without any memory hierarchy at all the CPI would increase again to $1.0 + 100 \times 1.5$ or 151—a factor of almost 40 times longer than a system with a cache!

As this example illustrates, cache behavior can have enormous impact on performance. Furthermore, cache misses have a double-barreled impact on a CPU with a low CPI and a fast clock:

1. The lower the $\text{CPI}_{\text{execution}}$, the higher the *relative* impact of a fixed number of cache miss clock cycles.

2. When calculating CPI, the cache miss penalty is measured in CPU clock cycles for a miss. Therefore, even if memory hierarchies for two computers are identical, the CPU with the higher clock rate has a larger number of clock cycles per miss and hence a higher memory portion of CPI.

The importance of the cache for CPUs with low CPI and high clock rates is thus greater, and, consequently, greater is the danger of neglecting cache behavior in assessing performance of such computers. Amdahl's Law strikes again!

Although minimizing average memory access time is a reasonable goal—and we will use it in much of this chapter—keep in mind that the final goal is to reduce CPU execution time. The next example shows how these two can differ.

Example What is the impact of two different cache organizations on the performance of a CPU? Assume that the CPI with a perfect cache is 2.0, the clock cycle time is 1.0 ns, there are 1.5 memory references per instruction, the size of both caches is 64 KB, and both have a block size of 64 bytes. One cache is direct mapped and the other is two-way set associative. Figure 5.7 shows that for set-associative caches we must add a multiplexor to select between the blocks in the set depending on the tag match. Since the speed of the CPU is tied directly to the speed of a cache hit, assume the CPU clock cycle time must be stretched 1.25 times to accommodate the selection multiplexor of the set-associative cache. To the first approximation, the cache miss penalty is 75 ns for either cache organization. (In practice, it is normally rounded up or down to an integer number of clock cycles.) First, calculate the average memory access time and then CPU performance. Assume the hit time is 1 clock cycle, the miss rate of a direct-mapped 64 KB cache is 1.4%, and the miss rate for a two-way set-associative cache of the same size is 1.0%.

Answer   Average memory access time is

$$\text{Average memory access time} = \text{Hit time} + \text{Miss rate} \times \text{Miss penalty}$$

Thus, the time for each organization is

$$\text{Average memory access time}_{1\text{-way}} = 1.0 + (.014 \times 75) = 2.05 \text{ ns}$$
$$\text{Average memory access time}_{2\text{-way}} = 1.0 \times 1.25 + (.010 \times 75) = 2.00 \text{ ns}$$

The average memory access time is better for the two-way set-associative cache. CPU performance is

$$\text{CPU time} = \text{IC} \times \left(\text{CPI}_{\text{execution}} + \frac{\text{Misses}}{\text{Instruction}} \times \text{Miss penalty} \right) \times \text{Clock cycle time}$$

$$= \text{IC} \times \Big[(\text{CPI}_{\text{execution}} \times \text{Clock cycle time})$$

$$+ \left(\text{Miss rate} \times \frac{\text{Memory accesses}}{\text{Instruction}} \times \text{Miss penalty} \times \text{Clock cycle time} \right) \Big]$$

Substituting 75 ns for (Miss penalty × Clock cycle time), the performance of each cache organization is

$$\text{CPU time}_{1\text{-way}} = \text{IC} \times (2 \times 1.0 + (1.5 \times 0.014 \times 75)) = 3.58 \times \text{IC}$$
$$\text{CPU time}_{2\text{-way}} = \text{IC} \times (2 \times 1.0 \times 1.25 + (1.5 \times 0.010 \times 75)) = 3.63 \times \text{IC}$$

and relative performance is

$$\frac{\text{CPU time}_{2\text{-way}}}{\text{CPU time}_{1\text{-way}}} = \frac{3.63 \times \text{Instruction count}}{3.58 \times \text{Instruction count}} = \frac{3.63}{3.58} = 1.01$$

In contrast to the results of average memory access time comparison, the direct-mapped cache leads to slightly better average performance because the clock cycle is stretched for *all* instructions for the two-way set-associative case, even if there are fewer misses. Since CPU time is our bottom-line evaluation, and since direct mapped is simpler to build, the preferred cache is direct mapped in this example.

Miss Penalty and Out-of-Order Execution Processors

For an out-of-order execution processor, how do you define "miss penalty"? Is it the full latency of the miss to memory, or is it just the "exposed" or nonoverlapped latency when the processor must stall? This question does not arise in processors that stall until the data miss completes.

Let's redefine memory stalls to lead to a new definition of miss penalty as nonoverlapped latency:

$$\frac{\text{Memory stall cycles}}{\text{Instruction}} = \frac{\text{Misses}}{\text{Instruction}} \times (\text{Total miss latency} - \text{Overlapped miss latency})$$

Similarly, as some out-of-order CPUs stretch the hit time, that portion of the performance equation could be divided by total hit latency less overlapped hit latency. This equation could be further expanded to account for contention for memory resources in an out-of-order processor by dividing total miss latency into latency without contention and latency due to contention. Let's just concentrate on miss latency.

We now have to decide the following:

- *Length of memory latency*—What to consider as the start and the end of a memory operation in an out-of-order processor

- *Length of latency overlap*—What is the start of overlap with the processor (or equivalently, when do we say a memory operation is stalling the processor)

Given the complexity of out-of-order execution processors, there is no single correct definition.

Since only committed operations are seen at the retirement pipeline stage, we say a processor is stalled in a clock cycle if it does not retire the maximum possible number of instructions in that cycle. We attribute that stall to the first instruction that could not be retired. This definition is by no means foolproof. For example, applying an optimization to improve a certain stall time may not always improve execution time because another type of stall—hidden behind the targeted stall—may now be exposed.

For latency, we could start measuring from the time the memory instruction is queued in the instruction window, or when the address is generated, or when the instruction is actually sent to the memory system. Any option works as long as it is used in a consistent fashion.

Example   Let's redo the example above, but this time we assume the processor with the longer clock cycle time supports out-of-order execution yet still has a direct-mapped cache. Assume 30% of the 75 ns miss penalty can be overlapped; that is, the average CPU memory stall time is now 52.5 ns.

Answer   Average memory access time for the out-of-order (OOO) computer is

$$\text{Average memory access time}_{1\text{-way,OOO}} = 1.0 \times 1.25 + (0.014 \times 52.5) = 1.99 \text{ ns}$$

The performance of the OOO cache is

$$\text{CPU time}_{1\text{-way,OOO}} = \text{IC} \times (2 \times 1.0 \times 1.25 + (1.5 \times 0.014 \times 52.5)) = 3.60 \times \text{IC}$$

Hence, despite a much slower clock cycle time and the higher miss rate of a direct-mapped cache, the out-of-order computer can be slightly faster if it can hide 30% of the miss penalty.

In summary, although the state of the art in defining and measuring memory stalls for out-of-order processors is not perfect and is relatively complex, be aware of the issues because they significantly affect performance.

Improving Cache Performance

To help summarize this section and to act as a handy reference, Figure 5.9 lists the cache equations in this chapter.

The increasing gap between CPU and main memory speeds shown in Figure 5.2 has attracted the attention of many architects. A bibliographic search for the years 1989–2001 revealed more than 5000 research papers on the subject of caches. Your authors' job was to survey all 5000 papers, decide what is and is not worthwhile, translate the results into a common terminology, reduce the

$$2^{\text{index}} = \frac{\text{Cache size}}{\text{Block size} \times \text{Set associativity}}$$

$$\text{CPU execution time} = (\text{CPU clock cycles} + \text{Memory stall cycles}) \times \text{Clock cycle time}$$

$$\text{Memory stall cycles} = \text{Number of misses} \times \text{Miss penalty}$$

$$\text{Memory stall cycles} = \text{IC} \times \frac{\text{Misses}}{\text{Instruction}} \times \text{Miss penalty}$$

$$\frac{\text{Misses}}{\text{Instruction}} = \text{Miss rate} \times \frac{\text{Memory accesses}}{\text{Instruction}}$$

$$\text{Average memory access time} = \text{Hit time} + \text{Miss rate} \times \text{Miss penalty}$$

$$\text{CPU execution time} = \text{IC} \times \left(\text{CPI}_{\text{execution}} + \frac{\text{Memory stall clock cycles}}{\text{Instruction}} \right) \times \text{Clock cycle time}$$

$$\text{CPU execution time} = \text{IC} \times \left(\text{CPI}_{\text{execution}} + \frac{\text{Misses}}{\text{Instruction}} \times \text{Miss penalty} \right) \times \text{Clock cycle time}$$

$$\text{CPU execution time} = \text{IC} \times \left(\text{CPI}_{\text{execution}} + \text{Miss rate} \times \frac{\text{Memory accesses}}{\text{Instruction}} \times \text{Miss penalty} \right) \times \text{Clock cycle time}$$

$$\frac{\text{Memory stall cycles}}{\text{Instruction}} = \frac{\text{Misses}}{\text{Instruction}} \times (\text{Total miss latency} - \text{Overlapped miss latency})$$

$$\text{Average memory access time} = \text{Hit time}_{\text{L1}} + \text{Miss rate}_{\text{L1}} \times (\text{Hit time}_{\text{L2}} + \text{Miss rate}_{\text{L2}} \times \text{Miss penalty}_{\text{L2}})$$

$$\frac{\text{Memory stall cycles}}{\text{Instruction}} = \frac{\text{Misses}_{\text{L1}}}{\text{Instruction}} \times \text{Hit time}_{\text{L2}} + \frac{\text{Misses}_{\text{L2}}}{\text{Instruction}} \times \text{Miss penalty}_{\text{L2}}$$

Figure 5.9 Summary of performance equations in this chapter. The first equation calculates the cache index size, and the rest help evaluate performance. The final two equations deal with multilevel caches, which are explained early in the next section. They are included here to help make the figure a useful reference.

results to their essence, write in an intriguing fashion, and provide just the right amount of detail!

Fortunately, this task was simplified by our long-standing policy of only including ideas in this book that have made their way into commercially viable computers. In computer architecture, many ideas look much better on paper than in silicon.

The average memory access time formula gave us a framework to present the surviving cache optimizations for improving cache performance or power:

$$\text{Average memory access time} = \text{Hit time} + \text{Miss rate} \times \text{Miss penalty}$$

Hence, we organize 17 cache optimizations into four categories:

- Reducing the miss penalty (Section 5.4): multilevel caches, critical word first, read miss before write miss, merging write buffers, and victim caches

- Reducing the miss rate (Section 5.5): larger block size, larger cache size, higher associativity, way prediction and pseudoassociativity, and compiler optimizations

- Reducing the miss penalty or miss rate via parallelism (Section 5.6): non-blocking caches, hardware prefetching, and compiler prefetching

- Reducing the time to hit in the cache (Section 5.7): small and simple caches, avoiding address translation, pipelined cache access, and trace caches

Figure 5.26 on page 449 concludes with a summary of the implementation complexity and the performance benefits of the 17 techniques presented.

5.4   Reducing Cache Miss Penalty

Reducing cache misses has been the traditional focus of cache research, but the cache performance formula assures us that improvements in miss penalty can be just as beneficial as improvements in miss rate. Moreover, Figure 5.2 shows that technology trends have improved the speed of processors faster than DRAMs, making the relative cost of miss penalties increase over time.

We give five optimizations here to address increasing miss penalty. Perhaps the most interesting optimization is the first, which adds more levels of caches to reduce miss penalty.

First Miss Penalty Reduction Technique: Multilevel Caches

Many techniques to reduce miss penalty affect the CPU. This technique ignores the CPU, concentrating on the interface between the cache and main memory.

The performance gap between processors and memory leads the architect to this question: Should I make the cache faster to keep pace with the speed of CPUs, or make the cache larger to overcome the widening gap between the CPU and main memory?

One answer is, both. Adding another level of cache between the original cache and memory simplifies the decision. The first-level cache can be small enough to match the clock cycle time of the fast CPU. Yet the second-level cache can be large enough to capture many accesses that would go to main memory, thereby lessening the effective miss penalty.

Although the concept of adding another level in the hierarchy is straightforward, it complicates performance analysis. Definitions for a second level of cache are not always straightforward. Let's start with the definition of *average memory access time* for a two-level cache. Using the subscripts L1 and L2 to refer, respectively, to a first-level and a second-level cache, the original formula is

$$\text{Average memory access time} = \text{Hit time}_{L1} + \text{Miss rate}_{L1} \times \text{Miss penalty}_{L1}$$

and

$$\text{Miss penalty}_{L1} = \text{Hit time}_{L2} + \text{Miss rate}_{L2} \times \text{Miss penalty}_{L2}$$

so

$$\text{Average memory access time} = \text{Hit time}_{L1} + \text{Miss rate}_{L1}$$
$$\times (\text{Hit time}_{L2} + \text{Miss rate}_{L2} \times \text{Miss penalty}_{L2})$$

In this formula, the second-level miss rate is measured on the leftovers from the first-level cache. To avoid ambiguity, these terms are adopted here for a two-level cache system:

■ *Local miss rate*—This rate is simply the number of misses in a cache divided by the total number of memory accesses to this cache. As you would expect, for the first-level cache it is equal to Miss rate_{L1}, and for the second-level cache it is Miss rate_{L2}.

■ *Global miss rate*—The number of misses in the cache divided by the total number of memory accesses generated by the CPU. Using the terms above, the global miss rate for the first-level cache is still just Miss rate_{L1}, but for the second-level cache it is $\text{Miss rate}_{L1} \times \text{Miss rate}_{L2}$.

This local miss rate is large for second-level caches because the first-level cache skims the cream of the memory accesses. This is why the global miss rate is the more useful measure: It indicates what fraction of the memory accesses that leave the CPU go all the way to memory.

Here is a place where the misses per instruction metric shines. Instead of confusion about local or global miss rates, we just expand memory stalls per instruction to add the impact of a second-level cache.

$$\text{Average memory stalls per instruction} = \text{Misses per instruction}_{L1} \times \text{Hit time}_{L2}$$
$$+ \text{Misses per instruction}_{L2} \times \text{Miss penalty}_{L2}$$

Example   Suppose that in 1000 memory references there are 40 misses in the first-level cache and 20 misses in the second-level cache. What are the various miss rates?

Assume the miss penalty from the L2 cache to memory is 100 clock cycles, the hit time of the L2 cache is 10 clock cycles, the hit time of L1 is 1 clock cycle, and there are 1.5 memory references per instruction. What is the average memory access time and average stall cycles per instruction? Ignore the impact of writes.

Answer   The miss rate (either local or global) for the first-level cache is 40/1000 or 4%. The local miss rate for the second-level cache is 20/40 or 50%. The global miss rate of the second-level cache is 20/1000 or 2%. Then

$$\text{Average memory access time} = \text{Hit time}_{L1} + \text{Miss rate}_{L1} \times (\text{Hit time}_{L2} + \text{Miss rate}_{L2} \times \text{Miss penalty}_{L2})$$
$$= 1 + 4\% \times (10 + 50\% \times 100) = 1 + 4\% \times 60 = 3.4 \text{ clock cycles}$$

To see how many misses we get per instruction, we divide 1000 memory references by 1.5 memory references per instruction, which yields 667 instructions. Thus, we need to multiply the misses by 1.5 to get the number of misses per 1000 instructions. We have 40×1.5 or 60 L1 misses, and 20×1.5 or 30 L2 misses, per 1000 instructions. For average memory stalls per instruction, assuming the misses are distributed uniformly between instructions and data:

$$\text{Average memory stalls per instruction} = \text{Misses per instruction}_{L1} \times \text{Hit time}_{L2} + \text{Misses per instruction}_{L2}$$
$$\times \text{Miss penalty}_{L2} = (60/1000) \times 10 + (30/1000)$$
$$\times 100 = 0.060 \times 10 + 0.030 \times 100 = 3.6 \text{ clock cycles}$$

If we subtract the L1 hit time from AMAT and then multiply by the average number of memory references per instruction, we get the same average memory stalls per instruction:

$$(3.4 - 1.0) \times 1.5 = 2.4 \times 1.5 = 3.6 \text{ clock cycles}$$

As this example shows, there is less confusion with multilevel caches when calculating using misses per instruction versus miss rates.

Note that these formulas are for combined reads and writes, assuming a write-back first-level cache. Obviously, a write-through first-level cache will send *all* writes to the second level, not just the misses, and a write buffer might be used.

Figures 5.10 and 5.11 show how miss rates and relative execution time change with the size of a second-level cache for one design. From these figures we can gain two insights. The first is that the global cache miss rate is very similar to the single cache miss rate of the second-level cache, provided that the second-level cache is much larger than the first-level cache. Hence, our intuition and knowledge about the first-level caches apply. The second insight is that the local cache rate is *not* a good measure of secondary caches; it is a function of the miss rate of the first-level cache, and hence can vary by changing the first-level cache. Thus, the global cache miss rate should be used when evaluating second-level caches.

With these definitions in place, we can consider the parameters of second-level caches. The foremost difference between the two levels is that the speed of the first-level cache affects the clock rate of the CPU, while the speed of the second-level cache only affects the miss penalty of the first-level cache. Thus, we

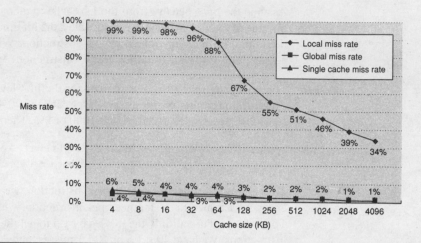

Figure 5.10 Miss rates versus cache size for multilevel caches. Second-level caches *smaller* than the sum of the two 64 KB first-level caches make little sense, as reflected in the high miss rates. After 256 KB the single cache is within 10% of the global miss rates. The miss rate of a single-level cache versus size is plotted against the local miss rate and global miss rate of a second-level cache using a 32 KB first-level cache. The L2 caches (unified) were two-way set associative with LRU replacement. Each had split L1 instruction and data caches that were 64 KB two-way set associative with LRU replacement. The block size for both L1 and L2 caches was 64 bytes. Data were collected as in Figure 5.6.

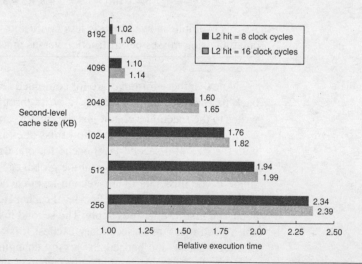

Figure 5.11 Relative execution time by second-level cache size. The two bars are for different clock cycles for an L2 cache hit. The reference execution time of 1.00 is for an 8192 KB second-level cache with a 1-clock-cycle latency on a second-level hit. These data were collected the same way as in Figure 5.10, using a simulator to imitate the Alpha 21264.

can consider many alternatives in the second-level cache that would be ill chosen for the first-level cache. There are two major questions for the design of the second-level cache: Will it lower the average memory access time portion of the CPI, and how much does it cost?

The initial decision is the size of a second-level cache. Since everything in the first-level cache is likely to be in the second-level cache, the second-level cache should be much bigger than the first. If second-level caches are just a little bigger, the local miss rate will be high. This observation inspires the design of huge second-level caches—the size of main memory in older computers! One question is whether set associativity makes more sense for second-level caches.

Example   Given the data below, what is the impact of second-level cache associativity on its miss penalty?

- Hit time$_{L2}$ for direct mapped = 10 clock cycles.
- Two-way set associativity increases hit time by 0.1 clock cycles to 10.1 clock cycles.
- Local miss rate$_{L2}$ for direct mapped = 25%.
- Local miss rate$_{L2}$ for two-way set associative = 20%.
- Miss penalty$_{L2}$ = 100 clock cycles.

Answer   For a direct-mapped second-level cache, the first-level cache miss penalty is

$$\text{Miss penalty}_{1\text{-way L2}} = 10 + 25\% \times 100 = 35.0 \text{ clock cycles}$$

Adding the cost of associativity increases the hit cost only 0.1 clock cycles, making the new first-level cache miss penalty

$$\text{Miss penalty}_{2\text{-way L2}} = 10.1 + 20\% \times 100 = 30.1 \text{ clock cycles}$$

In reality, second-level caches are almost always synchronized with the first-level cache and CPU. Accordingly, the second-level hit time must be an integral number of clock cycles. If we are lucky, we shave the second-level hit time to 10 cycles; if not, we round up to 11 cycles. Either choice is an improvement over the direct-mapped second-level cache:

$$\text{Miss penalty}_{2\text{-way L2}} = 10 + 20\% \times 100 = 30.0 \text{ clock cycles}$$
$$\text{Miss penalty}_{2\text{-way L2}} = 11 + 20\% \times 100 = 31.0 \text{ clock cycles}$$

Now we can reduce the miss penalty by reducing the *miss rate* of the second-level caches.

Another consideration concerns whether data in the first-level cache is in the second-level cache. *Multilevel inclusion* is the natural policy for memory hierarchies: L1 data are always present in L2. Inclusion is desirable because consistency between I/O and caches (or among caches in a multiprocessor) can be determined just by checking the second-level cache (see Section 6.10).

One drawback to inclusion is that measurements can suggest smaller blocks for the smaller first-level cache and larger blocks for the larger second-level cache. For example, the Pentium 4 has 64-byte blocks in its L1 caches and 128-byte blocks in its L2 cache. Inclusion can still be maintained with more work on a second-level miss. The second-level cache must invalidate all first-level blocks that map onto the second-level block to be replaced, causing a slightly higher first-level miss rate. To avoid such problems, many cache designers keep the block size the same in all levels of caches.

However, what if the designer can only afford an L2 cache that is slightly bigger than the I 1 cache? Should a significant portion of its space be used as a redundant copy of the L1 cache? In such cases a sensible opposite policy is *multi-level exclusion:* L1 data is *never* found in an L2 cache. Typically, with exclusion a cache miss in L1 results in a swap of blocks between L1 and L2 instead of a replacement of an L1 block with an L2 block. This policy prevents wasting space in the L2 cache. For example, the AMD Athlon chip obeys the exclusion property since it has two 64 KB L1 caches and only a 256 KB L2 cache.

As these issues illustrate, although a novice might design the first- and second-level caches independently, the designer of the first-level cache has a simpler job given a compatible second-level cache. It is less of a gamble to use a write through, for example, if there is a write-back cache at the next level to act as a backstop for repeated writes.

The essence of all cache designs is balancing fast hits and few misses. For second-level caches, there are many fewer hits than in the first-level cache, so the emphasis shifts to fewer misses. This insight leads to much larger caches and techniques to lower the miss rate, described in Section 5.5, such as higher associativity and larger blocks.

Second Miss Penalty Reduction Technique: Critical Word First and Early Restart

Multilevel caches require extra hardware to reduce the miss penalty, but not this second technique. It is based on the observation that the CPU normally needs just one word of the block at a time. This strategy is impatience: Don't wait for the full block to be loaded before sending the requested word and restarting the CPU. Here are two specific strategies:

■ *Critical word first*—Request the missed word first from memory and send it to the CPU as soon as it arrives; let the CPU continue execution while filling the rest of the words in the block. Critical-word-first fetch is also called *wrapped* fetch and *requested word first*.

■ *Early restart*—Fetch the words in normal order, but as soon as the requested word of the block arrives, send it to the CPU and let the CPU continue execution.

Generally these techniques only benefit designs with large cache blocks, since the benefit is low unless blocks are large. The problem is that given spatial locality, there is more than random chance that the next miss is to the remainder of the block. In such cases, the effective miss penalty is the time from the miss until the second piece arrives.

Example   Let's assume a computer has a 64-byte cache block, an L2 cache that takes 11 clock cycles to get the critical 8 bytes, and then 2 clock cycles per 8 bytes to fetch the rest of the block. (These parameters are similar to the AMD Athlon.) Calculate the average miss penalty for critical word first, assuming that there will be no other accesses to the rest of the block until it is completely fetched. Then calculate assuming the following instructions read data sequentially 8 bytes at a time from the rest of the block. Compare the times with and without critical word first.

Answer   The average miss penalty is 11 clock cycles for critical word first. The Athlon can issue two loads per clock cycle, which is faster than the L2 cache can supply data. Thus, it would take $11 + (8 - 1)$ times 2 or 25 clock cycles for the CPU to sequentially read a full cache block. Without critical word first, it would take 25 clock cycles to load the block, and then 8/2 or 4 clocks to issue the loads, giving 29 clock cycles total.

As this example illustrates, the benefits of critical word first and early restart depend on the size of the block and the likelihood of another access to the portion of the block that has not yet been fetched.

The next technique takes overlap between the CPU and cache miss penalty even further to reduce the average miss penalty.

Third Miss Penalty Reduction Technique: Giving Priority to Read Misses over Writes

This optimization serves reads before writes have been completed. We start with looking at the complexities of a write buffer.

With a write-through cache the most important improvement is a write buffer (page 402) of the proper size. Write buffers, however, do complicate memory accesses because they might hold the updated value of a location needed on a read miss.

Example   Look at this code sequence:

```
SW  R3, 512(R0)    ;M[512] ← R3       (cache index 0)
LW  R1, 1024(R0)   ;R1 ← M[1024]      (cache index 0)
LW  R2, 512(R0)    ;R2 ← M[512]       (cache index 0)
```

Assume a direct-mapped, write-through cache that maps 512 and 1024 to the same block, and a four-word write buffer. Will the value in R2 always be equal to the value in R3?

Answer   Using the terminology from Chapter 3, this is a read-after-write data hazard in memory. Let's follow a cache access to see the danger. The data in R3 are placed into the write buffer after the store. The following load uses the same cache index and is therefore a miss. The second load instruction tries to put the value in location 512 into register R2; this also results in a miss. If the write buffer hasn't completed writing to location 512 in memory, the read of location 512 will put the old, wrong value into the cache block, and then into R2. Without proper precautions, R3 would not be equal to R2!

The simplest way out of this dilemma is for the read miss to wait until the write buffer is empty. The alternative is to check the contents of the write buffer on a read miss, and if there are no conflicts and the memory system is available, let the read miss continue. Virtually all desktop and server processors use the latter approach, giving reads priority over writes.

The cost of writes by the processor in a write-back cache can also be reduced. Suppose a read miss will replace a dirty memory block. Instead of writing the dirty block to memory, and then reading memory, we could copy the dirty block to a buffer, then read memory, and *then* write memory. This way the CPU read, for which the processor is probably waiting, will finish sooner. Similar to the previous situation, if a read miss occurs, the processor can either stall until the buffer is empty or check the addresses of the words in the buffer for conflicts.

Fourth Miss Penalty Reduction Technique: Merging Write Buffer

This technique also involves write buffers, this time improving their efficiency.

Write-through caches rely on write buffers, as all stores must be sent to the next lower level of the hierarchy. As mentioned above, even write-back caches use a simple buffer when a block is replaced. If the write buffer is empty, the data and the full address are written in the buffer, and the write is finished from the CPU's perspective; the CPU continues working while the write buffer prepares to write the word to memory. If the buffer contains other modified blocks, the addresses can be checked to see if the address of this new data matches the address of a valid write buffer entry. If so, the new data are combined with that entry, called *write merging*.

If the buffer is full and there is no address match, the cache (and CPU) must wait until the buffer has an empty entry. This optimization uses the memory more efficiently since multiword writes are usually faster than writes performed one word at a time.

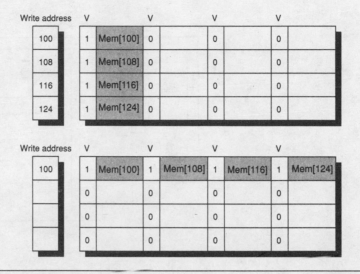

Figure 5.12 **To illustrate write merging, the write buffer on top does not use it while the write buffer on the bottom does.** The four writes are merged into a single buffer entry with write merging; without it, the buffer is full even though three-fourths of each entry is wasted. The buffer has four entries, and each entry holds four 64-bit words. The address for each entry is on the left, with valid bits (V) indicating whether or not the next sequential 8 bytes are occupied in this entry. (Without write merging, the words to the right in the upper part of the figure would only be used for instructions that wrote multiple words at the same time.)

The optimization also reduces stalls due to the write buffer being full. Figure 5.12 shows a write buffer with and without write merging. Assume we had four entries in the write buffer, and each entry could hold four 64-bit words. Without this optimization, four stores to sequential addresses would fill the buffer at one word per entry, even though these four words when merged exactly fit within a single entry of the write buffer.

Note that input/output device registers are often mapped into the physical address space, as is the case of the 21264. These I/O addresses cannot allow write merging because separate I/O registers may not act like an array of words in memory. For example, they may require one address and data word per register rather than multiword writes using a single address.

Fifth Miss Penalty Reduction Technique: Victim Caches

One approach to lower the miss penalty is to remember what was discarded in case it is needed again. Since the discarded data has already been fetched, it can be used again at small cost.

Such "recycling" requires a small, fully associative cache between a cache and its refill path. Figure 5.13 shows the organization. This *victim cache* contains

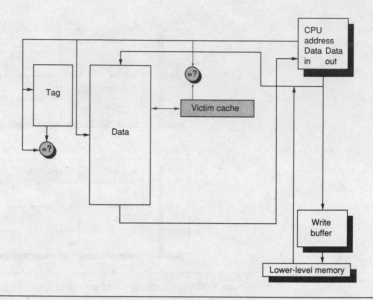

Figure 5.13 Placement of victim cache in the memory hierarchy. Although it reduces the miss penalty, the victim cache is aimed at reducing the damage done by conflict misses, described in the next section. Jouppi [1990] found the four-entry victim cache could reduce the miss penalty for 20% to 95% of conflict misses.

only blocks that are discarded from a cache because of a miss—"victims"—and are checked on a miss to see if they have the desired data before going to the next lower-level memory. If it is found there, the victim block and cache block are swapped. The AMD Athlon has a victim cache with eight entries.

Jouppi [1990] found that victim caches of one to five entries are effective at reducing misses, especially for small, direct-mapped data caches. Depending on the program, a four-entry victim cache might remove one-quarter of the misses in a 4 KB direct-mapped data cache.

Summary of Miss Penalty Reduction Techniques

The processor-memory performance gap of Figure 5.2 determines the miss penalty, and as the gap grows so does the number of techniques that try to close it. We present five in this section. The first technique follows the proverb "the more the merrier": Assuming the principle of locality will keep applying recursively, just keep adding more levels of increasingly larger caches until you are happy. The second technique is impatience: It retrieves the word of the block that caused the miss rather than waiting for the full block to arrive. The next technique is preference. It gives priority to reads over writes since the processor generally waits for reads but continues after launching writes. The fourth technique is companionship, combining writes to sequential words into a single block to create a more efficient transfer to memory. Finally comes a cache equivalent of recycling, as a victim cache keeps a few discarded blocks available for when the fickle primary cache wants a word that it recently discarded. All these techniques help with miss penalty, but multilevel caches are probably the most important.

Testimony of the importance of miss penalty is that most desktop and server computers use the first four optimizations. Yet most cache research has concentrated on reducing the miss rate, so that is where we go in the next section.

5.5   Reducing Miss Rate

The classical approach to improving cache behavior is to reduce miss rates, and we present five techniques to do so. To gain better insights into the causes of misses, we first start with a model that sorts all misses into three simple categories:

- *Compulsory*—The very first access to a block *cannot* be in the cache, so the block must be brought into the cache. These are also called *cold-start misses* or *first-reference misses*.

- *Capacity*—If the cache cannot contain all the blocks needed during execution of a program, capacity misses (in addition to compulsory misses) will occur because of blocks being discarded and later retrieved.

- *Conflict*—If the block placement strategy is set associative or direct mapped, conflict misses (in addition to compulsory and capacity misses) will occur because a block may be discarded and later retrieved if too many blocks map to its set. These misses are also called *collision misses* or *interference misses*. The idea is that hits in a fully associative cache that become misses in an *n*-way set-associative cache are due to more than *n* requests on some popular sets.

Figure 5.14 shows the relative frequency of cache misses, broken down by the "three C's." Compulsory misses are those that occur in an infinite cache. Capacity misses are those that occur in a fully associative cache. Conflict misses are those that occur going from fully associative to eight-way associative, four-way associative, and so on. Figure 5.15 presents the same data graphically. The top graph shows absolute miss rates; the bottom graph plots the percentage of all the misses by type of miss as a function of cache size.

To show the benefit of associativity, conflict misses are divided into misses caused by each decrease in associativity. Here are the four divisions of conflict misses and how they are calculated:

- *Eight-way*—Conflict misses due to going from fully associative (no conflicts) to eight-way associative

- *Four-way*—Conflict misses due to going from eight-way associative to four-way associative

- *Two-way*—Conflict misses due to going from four-way associative to two-way associative

Cache size (KB)	Degree associative	Total miss rate	Miss rate components (relative percent) *(sum = 100% of total miss rate)*					
			Compulsory		Capacity		Conflict	
4	1-way	0.098	0.0001	0.1%	0.070	72%	0.027	28%
4	2-way	0.076	0.0001	0.1%	0.070	93%	0.005	7%
4	4-way	0.071	0.0001	0.1%	0.070	99%	0.001	1%
4	8-way	0.071	0.0001	0.1%	0.070	100%	0.000	0%
8	1-way	0.068	0.0001	0.1%	0.044	65%	0.024	35%
8	2-way	0.049	0.0001	0.1%	0.044	90%	0.005	10%
8	4-way	0.044	0.0001	0.1%	0.044	99%	0.000	1%
8	8-way	0.044	0.0001	0.1%	0.044	100%	0.000	0%
16	1-way	0.049	0.0001	0.1%	0.040	82%	0.009	17%
16	2-way	0.041	0.0001	0.2%	0.040	98%	0.001	2%
16	4-way	0.041	0.0001	0.2%	0.040	99%	0.000	0%
16	8-way	0.041	0.0001	0.2%	0.040	100%	0.000	0%
32	1-way	0.042	0.0001	0.2%	0.037	89%	0.005	11%
32	2-way	0.038	0.0001	0.2%	0.037	99%	0.000	0%
32	4-way	0.037	0.0001	0.2%	0.037	100%	0.000	0%
32	8-way	0.037	0.0001	0.2%	0.037	100%	0.000	0%
64	1-way	0.037	0.0001	0.2%	0.028	77%	0.008	23%
64	2-way	0.031	0.0001	0.2%	0.028	91%	0.003	9%
64	4-way	0.030	0.0001	0.2%	0.028	95%	0.001	4%
64	8-way	0.029	0.0001	0.2%	0.028	97%	0.001	2%
128	1-way	0.021	0.0001	0.3%	0.019	91%	0.002	8%
128	2-way	0.019	0.0001	0.3%	0.019	100%	0.000	0%
128	4-way	0.019	0.0001	0.3%	0.019	100%	0.000	0%
128	8-way	0.019	0.0001	0.3%	0.019	100%	0.000	0%
256	1-way	0.013	0.0001	0.5%	0.012	94%	0.001	6%
256	2-way	0.012	0.0001	0.5%	0.012	99%	0.000	0%
256	4-way	0.012	0.0001	0.5%	0.012	99%	0.000	0%
256	8-way	0.012	0.0001	0.5%	0.012	99%	0.000	0%
512	1-way	0.008	0.0001	0.8%	0.005	66%	0.003	33%
512	2-way	0.007	0.0001	0.9%	0.005	71%	0.002	28%
512	4-way	0.006	0.0001	1.1%	0.005	91%	0.000	8%
512	8-way	0.006	0.0001	1.1%	0.005	95%	0.000	4%

Figure 5.14 Total miss rate for each size cache and percentage of each according to the "three C's." Compulsory misses are independent of cache size, while capacity misses decrease as capacity increases, and conflict misses decrease as associativity increases. Figure 5.15 shows the same information graphically. Note that the 2:1 cache rule of thumb (inside front cover) is supported by the statistics in this table through 128 KB: A direct-mapped cache of size N has about the same miss rate as a two-way set-associative cache of size N/2. Caches larger than 128 KB do not prove that rule. Note that the Capacity column is also the fully associative miss rate. Data were collected as in Figure 5.6 using LRU replacement.

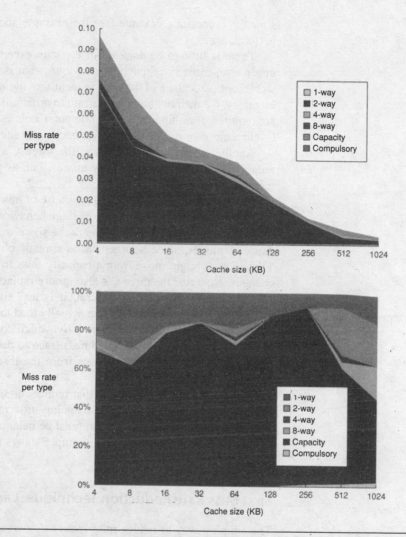

Figure 5.15 Total miss rate (top) and distribution of miss rate (bottom) for each size cache according to the three C's for the data in Figure 5.14. The top diagram is the actual data cache miss rates, while the bottom diagram shows the percentage in each category. (Space allows the graphs to show one extra cache size than can fit in Figure 5.14.)

▪   *One-way*—Conflict misses due to going from two-way associative to one-way associative (direct mapped)

As we can see from the figures, the compulsory miss rate of the SPEC2000 programs is very small, as it is for many long-running programs.

Having identified the three C's, what can a computer designer do about them? Conceptually, conflicts are the easiest: Fully associative placement avoids all conflict misses. Full associativity is expensive in hardware, however, and may slow the processor clock rate (see the example above), leading to lower overall performance.

There is little to be done about capacity except to enlarge the cache. If the upper-level memory is much smaller than what is needed for a program, and a significant percentage of the time is spent moving data between two levels in the hierarchy, the memory hierarchy is said to *thrash*. Because so many replacements are required, thrashing means the computer runs close to the speed of the lower-level memory, or maybe even slower because of the miss overhead.

Another approach to improving the three C's is to make blocks larger to reduce the number of compulsory misses, but, as we will see, large blocks can increase other kinds of misses.

The three C's give insight into the cause of misses, but this simple model has its limits; it gives you insight into average behavior but may not explain an individual miss. For example, changing cache size changes conflict misses as well as capacity misses, since a larger cache spreads out references to more blocks. Thus, a miss might move from a capacity miss to a conflict miss as cache size changes. Note that the three C's also ignore replacement policy, since it is difficult to model and since, in general, it is less significant. In specific circumstances the replacement policy can actually lead to anomalous behavior, such as poorer miss rates for larger associativity, which contradicts the three C's model. (Some have proposed using an address trace to determine optimal placement in memory to avoid placement misses from the three C's model; we've not followed that advice here.)

Alas, many of the techniques that reduce miss rates also increase hit time or miss penalty. The desirability of reducing miss rates using the five techniques presented in the rest of this section must be balanced against the goal of making the whole system fast. This first example shows the importance of a balanced perspective.

First Miss Rate Reduction Technique: Larger Block Size

The simplest way to reduce miss rate is to increase the block size. Figure 5.16 shows the trade-off of block size versus miss rate for a set of programs and cache sizes. Larger block sizes will reduce compulsory misses. This reduction occurs because the principle of locality has two components: temporal locality and spatial locality. Larger blocks take advantage of spatial locality.

At the same time, larger blocks increase the miss penalty. Since they reduce the number of blocks in the cache, larger blocks may increase conflict misses and even capacity misses if the cache is small. Clearly, there is little reason to increase the block size to such a size that it *increases* the miss rate. There is also no benefit to reducing miss rate if it increases the average memory access time. The increase in miss penalty may outweigh the decrease in miss rate.

Example   Figure 5.17 shows the actual miss rates plotted in Figure 5.16. Assume the memory system takes 80 clock cycles of overhead and then delivers 16 bytes every 2

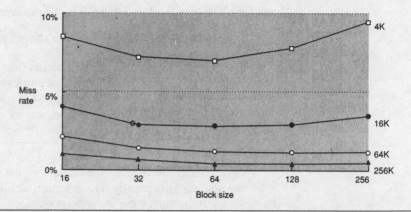

Figure 5.16   Miss rate versus block size for five different-sized caches. Note that miss rate actually goes up if the block size is too large relative to the cache size. Each line represents a cache of different size. Figure 5.17 shows the data used to plot these lines. Unfortunately, SPEC2000 traces would take too long if block size were included, so these data are based on SPEC92 on a DECstation 5000 [Gee et al. 1993].

	Cache size			
Block size	4K	16K	64K	256K
16	8.57%	3.94%	2.04%	1.09%
32	7.24%	2.87%	1.35%	0.70%
64	7.00%	2.64%	1.06%	0.51%
128	7.78%	2.77%	1.02%	0.49%
256	9.51%	3.29%	1.15%	0.49%

Figure 5.17   Actual miss rate versus block size for five different-sized caches in Figure 5.16. Note that for a 4 KB cache, 256-byte blocks have a higher miss rate than 32-byte blocks. In this example, the cache would have to be 256 KB in order for a 256-byte block to decrease misses.

clock cycles. Thus, it can supply 16 bytes in 82 clock cycles, 32 bytes in 84 clock cycles, and so on. Which block size has the smallest average memory access time for each cache size in Figure 5.17?

Answer   Average memory access time is

$$\text{Average memory access time} = \text{Hit time} + \text{Miss rate} \times \text{Miss penalty}$$

If we assume the hit time is 1 clock cycle independent of block size, then the access time for a 16-byte block in a 1 KB cache is

$$\text{Average memory access time} = 1 + (15.05\% \times 82) = 13.341 \text{ clock cycles}$$

and for a 256-byte block in a 256 KB cache the average memory access time is

$$\text{Average memory access time} = 1 + (0.49\% \times 112) = 1.549 \text{ clock cycles}$$

Figure 5.18 shows the average memory access time for all block and cache sizes between those two extremes. The boldfaced entries show the fastest block size for a given cache size: 32 bytes for 4 KB and 64 bytes for the larger caches. These sizes are, in fact, popular block sizes for processor caches today (see Figure 5.57 on page 505).

As in all of these techniques, the cache designer is trying to minimize both the miss rate and the miss penalty. The selection of block size depends on both the latency and bandwidth of the lower-level memory. High latency and high bandwidth encourage large block size since the cache gets many more bytes per miss for a small increase in miss penalty. Conversely, low latency and low bandwidth encourage smaller block sizes since there is little time saved from a larger block. For example, twice the miss penalty of a small block may be close to the penalty of a block twice the size. The larger number of small blocks may also reduce conflict misses. Note that Figures 5.16 and 5.18 show the difference between selecting a block size based on minimizing miss rate versus minimizing average memory access time.

After seeing the positive and negative impact of larger block size on compulsory and capacity misses, the next two subsections look at the potential of higher capacity and higher associativity.

Second Miss Rate Reduction Technique: Larger Caches

The obvious way to reduce capacity misses in Figures 5.14 and 5.15 is to increase capacity of the cache. The obvious drawback is longer hit time and higher cost. This technique has been especially popular in off-chip caches: The size of second-

Block size	Miss penalty	Cache size			
		4K	**16K**	**64K**	**256K**
16	82	8.027	4.231	2.673	1.894
32	84	**7.082**	3.411	2.134	1.588
64	88	7.160	**3.323**	**1.933**	**1.449**
128	96	8.469	3.659	1.979	1.470
256	112	11.651	4.685	2.288	1.549

Figure 5.18 Average memory access time versus block size for five different-sized caches in Figure 5.16. Block sizes of 32 and 64 bytes dominate. The smallest average time per cache size is boldfaced.

or third-level caches in 2001 equals the size of main memory in desktop computers from the first edition of this book, only a decade before!

Third Miss Rate Reduction Technique: Higher Associativity

Figures 5.14 and 5.15 show how miss rates improve with higher associativity. There are two general rules of thumb that can be gleaned from these figures. The first is that eight-way set associative is for practical purposes as effective in reducing misses for these sized caches as fully associative. You can see the difference by comparing the eight-way entries to the capacity miss column in Figure 5.14, since capacity misses are calculated using fully associative caches. The second observation, called the *2:1 cache rule of thumb* and found on the front inside cover, is that a direct-mapped cache of size N has about the same miss rate as a two-way set-associative cache of size $N/2$. This held for cache sizes less than 128 KB.

Like many of these examples, improving one aspect of the average memory access time comes at the expense of another. Increasing block size reduces miss rate while increasing miss penalty, and greater associativity can come at the cost of increased hit time (see Figure 5.24 in Section 5.7). Hence, the pressure of a fast processor clock cycle encourages simple cache designs, but the increasing miss penalty rewards associativity, as the following example suggests.

Example   Assume higher associativity would increase the clock cycle time as listed below:

$$\text{Clock cycle time}_{2\text{-way}} = 1.36 \times \text{Clock cycle time}_{1\text{-way}}$$
$$\text{Clock cycle time}_{4\text{-way}} = 1.44 \times \text{Clock cycle time}_{1\text{-way}}$$
$$\text{Clock cycle time}_{8\text{-way}} = 1.52 \times \text{Clock cycle time}_{1\text{-way}}$$

Assume that the hit time is 1 clock cycle, that the miss penalty for the direct-mapped case is 25 clock cycles to an L2 cache that never misses, and that the miss penalty need not be rounded to an integral number of clock cycles. Using Figure 5.14 for miss rates, for which cache sizes are each of these three statements true?

$$\text{Average memory access time}_{8\text{-way}} < \text{Average memory access time}_{4\text{-way}}$$
$$\text{Average memory access time}_{4\text{-way}} < \text{Average memory access time}_{2\text{-way}}$$
$$\text{Average memory access time}_{2\text{-way}} < \text{Average memory access time}_{1\text{-way}}$$

Answer   Average memory access time for each associativity is

$$\text{Average memory access time}_{8\text{-way}} = \text{Hit time}_{8\text{-way}} + \text{Miss rate}_{8\text{-way}} \times \text{Miss penalty}_{8\text{-way}} = 1.52 + \text{Miss rate}_{8\text{-way}} \times 25$$
$$\text{Average memory access time}_{4\text{-way}} = 1.44 + \text{Miss rate}_{4\text{-way}} \times 25$$
$$\text{Average memory access time}_{2\text{-way}} = 1.36 + \text{Miss rate}_{2\text{-way}} \times 25$$
$$\text{Average memory access time}_{1\text{-way}} = 1.00 + \text{Miss rate}_{1\text{-way}} \times 25$$

The miss penalty is the same time in each case, so we leave it as 25 clock cycles. For example, the average memory access time for a 4 KB direct-mapped cache is

$$\text{Average memory access time}_{1\text{-way}} = 1.00 + (0.133 \times 25) = 3.44$$

and the time for a 512 KB, eight-way set-associative cache is

$$\text{Average memory access time}_{8\text{-way}} = 1.52 + (0.006 \times 25) = 1.66$$

Using these formulas and the miss rates from Figure 5.14, Figure 5.19 shows the average memory access time for each cache and associativity. The figure shows that the formulas in this example hold for caches less than or equal to 8 KB for up to four-way associativity. Starting with 16 KB, the greater hit time of larger associativity outweighs the time saved due to the reduction in misses.

Note that we did not account for the slower clock rate on the rest of the program in this example, thereby understating the advantage of direct-mapped cache.

Fourth Miss Rate Reduction Technique: Way Prediction and Pseudoassociative Caches

Another approach reduces conflict misses and yet maintains the hit speed of direct-mapped cache. In *way prediction,* extra bits are kept in the cache to predict the way, or block within the set of the *next* cache access. This prediction means the multiplexor is set early to select the desired block, and only a single tag comparison is performed that clock cycle. A miss results in checking the other blocks for matches in subsequent clock cycles.

Cache size (KB)	Associativity			
	One-way	Two-way	Four-way	Eight-way
4	3.44	3.25	3.22	**3.28**
8	2.69	2.58	2.55	**2.62**
16	2.23	**2.40**	**2.46**	**2.53**
32	2.06	**2.30**	**2.37**	**2.45**
64	1.92	**2.14**	**2.18**	**2.25**
128	1.52	**1.84**	**1.92**	**2.00**
256	1.32	**1.66**	**1.74**	**1.82**
512	1.20	**1.55**	**1.59**	**1.66**

Figure 5.19 Average memory access time using miss rates in Figure 5.14 for parameters in the example. Boldface type means that this time is higher than the number to the left; that is, higher associativity *increases* average memory access time.

The Alpha 21264 uses way prediction in its two-way set-associative instruction cache. Added to each block of the instruction cache is a block predictor bit. The bit is used to select which of the two blocks to try on the *next* cache access. If the predictor is correct, the instruction cache latency is 1 clock cycle. If not, it tries the other block, changes the way predictor, and has a latency of 3 clock cycles. (The latency of the 21264 data cache, which is very similar to its instruction cache, is also 3 clock cycles.) Simulations using SPEC95 suggested set prediction accuracy is in excess of 85%, so way prediction saves pipeline stages in more than 85% of the instruction fetches.

In addition to improving performance, way prediction can reduce power for embedded applications. By only supplying power to the half of the tags that are expected to be used, the MIPS R4300 series lowers power consumption with the same benefits.

A related approach is called *pseudoassociative* or *column associative*. Accesses proceed just as in the direct-mapped cache for a hit. On a miss, however, before going to the next lower level of the memory hierarchy, a second cache entry is checked to see if it matches there. A simple way is to invert the most significant bit of the index field to find the other block in the "pseudoset."

Pseudoassociative caches then have one fast and one slow hit time—corresponding to a regular hit and a pseudohit—in addition to the miss penalty. Figure 5.20 shows the relative times. One danger would be if many fast hit times of the direct-mapped cache became slow hit times in the pseudoassociative cache. The performance would then be *degraded* by this optimization. Hence, it is important to indicate for each set which block should be the fast hit and which should be the slow one. One way is simply to make the upper one fast and swap the contents of the blocks. Another danger is that the miss penalty may become slightly longer, adding the time to check another cache entry.

Fifth Miss Rate Reduction Technique: Compiler Optimizations

Thus far our techniques to reduce misses have required changes to or additions to the hardware: larger blocks, larger caches, higher associativity, or pseudoassociativity. This final technique reduces miss rates without any hardware changes.

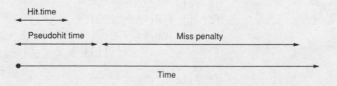

Figure 5.20 Relationship between regular hit time, pseudohit time, and miss penalty. Basically, pseudoassociativity offers a normal hit and a slow hit rather than more misses.

This magical reduction comes from optimized software—the hardware designer's favorite solution! The increasing performance gap between processors and main memory has inspired compiler writers to scrutinize the memory hierarchy to see if compile time optimizations can improve performance. Once again research is split between improvements in instruction misses and improvements in data misses.

Code can easily be rearranged without affecting correctness; for example, reordering the procedures of a program might reduce instruction miss rates by reducing conflict misses. McFarling [1989] looked at using profiling information to determine likely conflicts between groups of instructions. Reordering the instructions reduced misses by 50% for a 2 KB direct-mapped instruction cache with 4-byte blocks, and by 75% in an 8 KB cache. McFarling got the best performance when it was possible to prevent some instructions from ever entering the cache. Even without that feature, optimized programs on a direct-mapped cache missed less than unoptimized programs on an eight-way set-associative cache of the same size.

Another code optimization aims for better efficiency from long cache blocks. Aligning basic blocks so that the entry point is at the beginning of a cache block decreases the chance of a cache miss for sequential code.

Data have even fewer restrictions on location than code. The goal of such transformations is to try to improve the spatial and temporal locality of the data. For example, array calculations can be changed to operate on all the data in a cache block rather than blindly striding through arrays in the order the programmer happened to place the loop.

To give a feeling of this type of optimization, we will show two examples, transforming the C code by hand to reduce cache misses.

Loop Interchange

Some programs have nested loops that access data in memory in nonsequential order. Simply exchanging the nesting of the loops can make the code access the data in the order they are stored. Assuming the arrays do not fit in the cache, this technique reduces misses by improving spatial locality; reordering maximizes use of data in a cache block before they are discarded.

```
/* Before */
for (j = 0; j < 100; j = j+1)
      for (i = 0; i < 5000; i = i+1)
            x[i][j] = 2 * x[i][j];

/* After */
for (i = 0; i < 5000; i = i+1)
    for (j = 0; j < 100; j = j+1)
          x[i][j] = 2 * x[i][j];
```

The original code would skip through memory in strides of 100 words, while the revised version accesses all the words in one cache block before going to the next block. This optimization improves cache performance without affecting the number of instructions executed.

Blocking

This optimization tries to reduce misses via improved temporal locality. We are again dealing with multiple arrays, with some arrays accessed by rows and some by columns. Storing the arrays row by row (*row major order*) or column by column (*column major order*) does not solve the problem because both rows and columns are used in every iteration of the loop. Such orthogonal accesses mean that transformations such as loop interchange are not helpful.

Instead of operating on entire rows or columns of an array, blocked algorithms operate on submatrices or *blocks*. The goal is to maximize accesses to the data loaded into the cache before the data are replaced. The code example below, which performs matrix multiplication, helps motivate the optimization:

```
/* Before */
for (i = 0; i < N; i = i+1)
        for (j = 0; j < N; j = j+1)
                {r = 0;
                for (k = 0; k < N; k = k + 1)
                        r = r + y[i][k]*z[k][j];
                x[i][j] = r;
                };
```

The two inner loops read all N by N elements of z, read the same N elements in a row of y repeatedly, and write one row of N elements of x. Figure 5.21 gives a

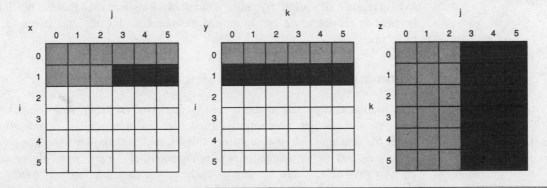

Figure 5.21 **A snapshot of the three arrays x, y, and z when i = 1.** The age of accesses to the array elements is indicated by shade: white means not yet touched, light means older accesses, and dark means newer accesses. Compared to Figure 5.22, elements of y and z are read repeatedly to calculate new elements of x. The variables i, j, and k are shown along the rows or columns used to access the arrays.

snapshot of the accesses to the three arrays. A dark shade indicates a recent access, a light shade indicates an older access, and white means not yet accessed.

The number of capacity misses clearly depends on N and the size of the cache. If it can hold all three N by N matrices, then all is well, provided there are no cache conflicts. If the cache can hold one N by N matrix and one row of N, then at least the ith row of y and the array z may stay in the cache. Less than that and misses may occur for both x and z. In the worst case, there would be $2N^3 + N^2$ memory words accessed for N^3 operations.

To ensure that the elements being accessed can fit in the cache, the original code is changed to compute on a submatrix of size B by B. Two inner loops now compute in steps of size B rather than the full length of x and z. B is called the *blocking factor*. (Assume x is initialized to zero.)

```
/* After */
for (jj = 0; jj < N; jj = jj+B)
for (kk = 0; kk < N; kk = kk+B)
for (i = 0; i < N; i = i+1)
        for (j = jj; j < min(jj+B,N); j = j+1)
            {r = 0;
             for (k = kk; k < min(kk+B,N); k = k + 1)
                    r = r + y[i][k]*z[k][j];
             x[i][j] = x[i][j] + r;
            };
```

Figure 5.22 illustrates the accesses to the three arrays using blocking. Looking only at capacity misses, the total number of memory words accessed is $2N^3/B + N^2$. This total is an improvement by about a factor of B. Hence, blocking exploits a combination of spatial and temporal locality, since y benefits from spatial locality and z benefits from temporal locality.

Although we have aimed at reducing cache misses, blocking can also be used to help register allocation. By taking a small blocking size such that the block can be held in registers, we can minimize the number of loads and stores in the program.

Summary of Reducing Cache Miss Rate

This section first presented the three C's model of cache misses: compulsory, capacity, and conflict. This intuitive model led to three obvious optimizations: larger block size to reduce compulsory misses, larger cache size to reduce capacity misses, and higher associativity to reduce conflict misses. Since higher associativity may affect cache hit time or cache power consumption, way prediction checks only a piece of the cache for hits and then on a miss checks the rest. The final technique is the favorite of the hardware designer, leaving cache optimizations to the compiler.

The increasing processor-memory gap has meant that cache misses are a primary cause of lower than expected performance. As a result, both algorithms and

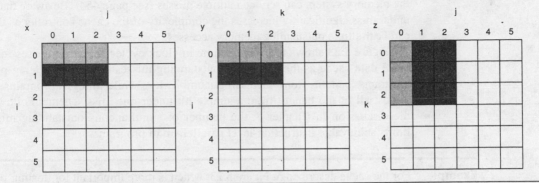

Figure 5.22 The age of accesses to the arrays x, y, and z. Note in contrast to Figure 5.21 the smaller number of elements accessed.

compilers are changing from the traditional focus of reducing operations to reducing cache misses.

The next section increases performance by having the processor and memory hierarchy operate in parallel, with compilers again playing a significant role in orchestrating this parallelism.

5.6   Reducing Cache Miss Penalty or Miss Rate via Parallelism

This section describes three techniques that overlap the execution of instructions with activity in the memory hierarchy. The first creates a memory hierarchy to match the out-of-order processors, but the second and third work with any type of processor. Although popular in desktop and server computers, the emphasis on efficiency in power and silicon area of embedded computers means such techniques are only found in embedded computers if they are small and reduce power.

First Miss Penalty/Rate Reduction Technique: Nonblocking Caches to Reduce Stalls on Cache Misses

For pipelined computers that allow out-of-order completion (Chapter 3), the CPU need not stall on a cache miss. For example, the CPU could continue fetching instructions from the instruction cache while waiting for the data cache to return the missing data. A *nonblocking cache* or *lockup-free cache* escalates the potential benefits of such a scheme by allowing the data cache to continue to supply cache hits during a miss. This "hit under miss" optimization reduces the effective miss penalty by being helpful during a miss instead of ignoring the requests of the CPU. A subtle and complex option is that the cache may further lower the effective miss penalty if it can overlap multiple misses: a "hit under multiple miss" or "miss under miss" optimization. The second option is beneficial only if the memory system can service multiple misses (see page 454). Be aware that hit under miss significantly increases the complexity of the cache controller as there can be multiple outstanding memory accesses.

Figure 5.23 shows the average time in clock cycles for cache misses for an 8 KB data cache as the number of outstanding misses is varied. Floating-point programs benefit from increasing complexity, while integer programs get almost all of the benefit from a simple hit-under-one-miss scheme. Following the discussion in Chapter 3, the number of simultaneous outstanding misses limits achievable instruction-level parallelism in programs.

Example For the cache described in Figure 5.23, which is more important for floating-point programs: two-way set associativity or hit under one miss? What about integer programs? Assume the following average miss rates for 8 KB data caches: 11.4% for floating-point programs with a direct-mapped cache, 10.7% for these programs with a two-way set-associative cache, 7.4% for integer programs with a direct-mapped cache, and 6.0% for integer programs with a two-way set-associative cache. Assume the average memory stall time is just the product of the miss rate and the miss penalty.

Answer The numbers for Figure 5.23 were based on a miss penalty of 16 clock cycles assuming an L2 cache. Although this is low for a miss penalty (we'll see how in the next subsection), let's stick with it for consistency. For floating-point programs the average memory stall times are

$$\text{Miss rate}_{DM} \times \text{Miss penalty} = 11.4\% \times 16 = 1.84$$

$$\text{Miss rate}_{2\text{-way}} \times \text{Miss penalty} = 10.7\% \times 16 = 1.71$$

The memory stalls of two-way are thus 1.71/1.84 or 93% of direct-mapped cache. The caption of Figure 5.23 says hit under one miss reduces the average memory stall time to 76% of a blocking cache. Hence, for floating-point programs, the direct-mapped data cache supporting hit under one miss gives better performance than a two-way set-associative cache that blocks on a miss.

For integer programs the calculation is

$$\text{Miss rate}_{DM} \times \text{Miss penalty} = 7.4\% \times 16 = 1.18$$

$$\text{Miss rate}_{2\text{-way}} \times \text{Miss penalty} = 6.0\% \times 16 = 0.96$$

The memory stalls of two-way are thus 0.96/1.18 or 81% of direct-mapped cache. The caption of Figure 5.23 says hit under one miss reduces the average memory stall time to 81% of a blocking cache, so the two options give about the same performance for integer programs. One advantage of hit under miss is that it cannot affect the hit time, as associativity can.

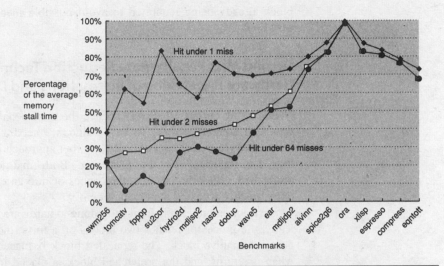

Figure 5.23 Ratio of the average memory stall time for a blocking cache to hit-under-miss schemes as the number of outstanding misses is varied for 18 SPEC92 programs. The hit-under-64-misses line allows one miss for every register in the processor. The first 14 programs are floating-point programs: the average for hit under 1 miss is 76%, for 2 misses is 51%, and for 64 misses is 39%. The final four are integer programs, and the three averages are 81%, 78%, and 78%, respectively. These data were collected for an 8 KB direct-mapped data cache with 32-byte blocks and a 16-clock-cycle miss penalty, which today would imply a second-level cache. These data were generated using the VLIW Multiflow compiler, which scheduled loads away from use [Farkas and Jouppi 1994].

The real difficulty with performance evaluation of nonblocking caches is that a cache miss does not necessarily stall the CPU. As mentioned on page 410, in this case it is difficult to judge the impact of any single miss, and hence difficult to calculate the average memory access time. As was the case of a second miss to the remaining block with critical word first earlier, the effective miss penalty is not the sum of the misses but the nonoverlapped time that the CPU is stalled. In general, out-of-order CPUs are capable of hiding the miss penalty of an L1 data cache miss that hits in the L2 cache, but are not capable of hiding a significant fraction of an L2 cache miss. Changing the program to pipeline L2 misses can help, especially to a banked memory system (see Section 5.8).

Chapter 1 discusses the pros and cons of execution-driven simulation versus trace-driven simulation. Cache studies involving out-of-order CPUs use execution-driven simulation to evaluate innovations, as avoiding a cache miss that is completely hidden by dynamic issue does not help performance.

An added complexity of multiple outstanding misses is that it is now possible for there to be more than one miss request to the same block. For example, with 64-byte blocks there could be a miss to address 1000 and then later a miss to address 1032. Thus, the hardware must check on misses to be sure it is not to a block already being requested to avoid possible incoherency problems and to save time.

Second Miss Penalty/Rate Reduction Technique: Hardware Prefetching of Instructions and Data

Nonblocking caches effectively reduce the miss penalty by overlapping execution with memory access. To have value, we need a processor that can allow instructions to execute out of order. Another approach is to prefetch items before they are requested by the processor. Both instructions and data can be prefetched, either directly into the caches or into an external buffer that can be more quickly accessed than main memory.

Instruction prefetch is frequently done in hardware outside of the cache. Typically, the processor fetches two blocks on a miss: the requested block and the next consecutive block. The requested block is placed in the instruction cache when it returns, and the prefetched block is placed into the instruction stream buffer. If the requested block is present in the instruction stream buffer, the original cache request is canceled, the block is read from the stream buffer, and the next prefetch request is issued.

Jouppi [1990] found that a single instruction stream buffer would catch 15% to 25% of the misses from a 4 KB direct-mapped instruction cache with 16-byte blocks. With 4 blocks in the instruction stream buffer, the hit rate improves to about 50%, and with 16 blocks to 72%.

A similar approach can be applied to data accesses. Jouppi found that a single data stream buffer caught about 25% of the misses from the 4 KB direct-mapped cache. Instead of having a single stream, there could be multiple stream buffers beyond the data cache, each prefetching at different addresses. Jouppi found that four data stream buffers increased the data hit rate to 43%. Palacharla and Kessler [1994] looked at a set of scientific programs and considered stream buffers that could handle either instructions or data. They found that eight stream buffers could capture 50% to 70% of all misses from a processor with two 64 KB four-way set-associative caches, one for instructions and the other for data.

The UltraSPARC III uses such a prefetch scheme. A prefetch cache remembers the address used to prefetch the data. If a load hits in the prefetch cache, the block is read from the prefetch cache, and the next prefetch request is issued. It calculates the "stride" of the next prefetched block using the difference between the current address and the previous address. There can be up to eight simultaneous prefetches in the UltraSPARC III.

Example   What is the effective miss rate of the UltraSPARC III using prefetching? How much bigger a data cache would be needed in the UltraSPARC III to match the average access time if prefetching were removed? It has a 64 KB data cache. Assume prefetching reduces the data miss rate by 20%.

Answer   We assume it takes 1 extra clock cycle if the data miss the cache but are found in the prefetch buffer. Here is our revised formula:

$$\text{Average memory access time}_{\text{prefetch}} = \text{Hit time} + \text{Miss rate} \times \text{Prefetch hit rate} \times 1$$
$$+ \text{Miss rate} \times (1 - \text{Prefetch hit rate}) \times \text{Miss penalty}$$

Let's assume the prefetch hit rate is 20%. Figure 5.8 on page 406 gives the misses per 1000 instructions for a 64 KB data cache as 36.9. To convert to a miss rate, if we assume 22% data references, the rate is

$$\frac{36.9}{1000 \times 22/100} = \frac{36.9}{220}$$

or 16.7%. Assume the hit time is 1 clock cycle and the miss penalty is 15 clock cycles since UltraSPARC III has an L2 cache:

$$\text{Average memory access time}_{\text{prefetch}} = 1 + (16.7\% \times 20\% \times 1) + (16.7\% \times (1 - 20\%) \times 15)$$
$$= 1 + 0.034 + 2.013 = 3.046$$

To find the effective miss rate with the equivalent performance, we start with the original formula and solve for the miss rate:

$$\text{Average memory access time} = \text{Hit time} + \text{Miss rate} \times \text{Miss penalty}$$
$$\text{Miss rate} = \frac{\text{Average memory access time} - \text{Hit time}}{\text{Miss penalty}}$$
$$\text{Miss rate} = \frac{3.046 - 1}{15} = \frac{2.046}{15} = 13.6\%$$

Our calculation suggests that the effective miss rate of prefetching with a 64 KB cache is 13.6%. Figure 5.8 gives the misses per 1000 instructions of a 256 KB data cache as 32.6, yielding a miss rate of 32.6/(22% × 1000) or 14.8%. If the prefetching reduces the miss rate by 20%, then a 64 KB data cache with prefetching outperforms a 256 KB cache without it.

Prefetching relies on utilizing memory bandwidth that otherwise would be unused, but if it interferes with demand misses, it can actually lower performance. Help from compilers can reduce useless prefetching.

Third Miss Penalty/Rate Reduction Technique: Compiler-Controlled Prefetching

An alternative to hardware prefetching is for the compiler to insert prefetch instructions to request the data before they are needed. There are two flavors of prefetch:

- *Register prefetch* will load the value into a register.
- *Cache prefetch* loads data only into the cache and not the register.

Either of these can be *faulting* or *nonfaulting;* that is, the address does or does not cause an exception for virtual address faults and protection violations. Nonfaulting prefetches simply turn into no-ops if they would normally result in an exception. Using this terminology, a normal load instruction could be considered a "faulting register prefetch instruction."

The most effective prefetch is "semantically invisible" to a program: It doesn't change the contents of registers and memory, *and* it cannot cause virtual memory faults. Most processors today offer nonfaulting cache prefetches. This section assumes nonfaulting cache prefetch, also called *nonbinding* prefetch.

Prefetching makes sense only if the processor can proceed while the prefetched data are being fetched; that is, the caches do not stall but continue to supply instructions and data while waiting for the prefetched data to return. As you would expect, the data cache for such computers is normally nonblocking.

Like hardware-controlled prefetching, the goal is to overlap execution with the prefetching of data. Loops are the important targets, as they lend themselves to prefetch optimizations. If the miss penalty is small, the compiler just unrolls the loop once or twice, and it schedules the prefetches with the execution. If the miss penalty is large, it uses software pipelining (page 329 in Chapter 4) or unrolls many times to prefetch data for a future iteration.

Issuing prefetch instructions incurs an instruction overhead, however, so care must be taken to ensure that such overheads do not exceed the benefits. By concentrating on references that are likely to be cache misses, programs can avoid unnecessary prefetches while improving average memory access time significantly.

Example   For the code below, determine which accesses are likely to cause data cache misses. Next, insert prefetch instructions to reduce misses. Finally, calculate the number of prefetch instructions executed and the misses avoided by prefetching. Let's assume we have an 8 KB direct-mapped data cache with 16-byte blocks, and it is a write-back cache that does write allocate. The elements of a and b are 8 bytes long since they are double-precision floating-point arrays. There are 3 rows and 100 columns for a and 101 rows and 3 columns for b. Let's also assume they are not in the cache at the start of the program.

```
for (i = 0; i < 3; i = i+1)
        for (j = 0; j < 100; j = j+1)
                a[i][j] = b[j][0] * b[j+1][0];
```

Answer   The compiler will first determine which accesses are likely to cause cache misses; otherwise, we will waste time on issuing prefetch instructions for data that would be hits. Elements of a are written in the order that they are stored in memory, so a will benefit from spatial locality: The even values of j will miss and the odd values will hit. Since a has 3 rows and 100 columns, its accesses will lead to $3 \times \left\lceil \dfrac{100}{2} \right\rceil$, or 150 misses.

The array b does not benefit from spatial locality since the accesses are not in the order it is stored. The array b does benefit twice from temporal locality: The same elements are accessed for each iteration of i, and each iteration of j uses the same value of b as the last iteration. Ignoring potential conflict misses, the misses due to b will be for b[j+1][0] accesses when i = 0, and also the first access to b[j][0] when j = 0. Since j goes from 0 to 99 when i = 0, accesses to b lead to 100 + 1, or 101 misses.

Thus, this loop will miss the data cache approximately 150 times for a plus 101 times for b, or 251 misses.

To simplify our optimization, we will not worry about prefetching the first accesses of the loop. These may be already in the cache, or we will pay the miss penalty of the first few elements of a or b. Nor will we worry about suppressing the prefetches at the end of the loop that try to prefetch beyond the end of a (a[i][100] . . . a[i][106]) and the end of b (b[101][0]. . . b[107][0]). If these were faulting prefetches, we could not take this luxury. Let's assume that the miss penalty is so large we need to start prefetching at least, say, seven iterations in advance. (Stated alternatively, we assume prefetching has no benefit until the eighth iteration.) We underline the changes to the code above needed to add prefetching.

```
for (j = 0; j < 100; j = j+1) {
    prefetch(b[j+7][0]);
    /* b(j,0) for 7 iterations later */
    prefetch(a[0][j+7]);
    /* a(0,j) for 7 iterations later */
    a[0][j] = b[j][0] * b[j+1][0];};
for (i = 1; i < 3; i = i+1)
    for (j = 0; j < 100; j = j+1) {
        prefetch(a[i][j+7]);
        /* a(i,j) for +7 iterations */
        a[i][j] = b[j][0] * b[j+1][0];}
```

This revised code prefetches a[i][7] through a[i][99] and b[7][0] through b[100][0], reducing the number of nonprefetched misses to

- 7 misses for elements b[0][0], b[1][0], . . . , b[6][0] in the first loop
- 4 misses ($\lceil 7/2 \rceil$) for elements a[0][0], a[0][1], . . . , a[0][6] in the first loop (spatial locality reduces misses to one per 16-byte cache block)
- 4 misses ($\lceil 7/2 \rceil$) for elements a[1][0], a[1][1], . . . , a[1][6] in the second loop
- 4 misses ($\lceil 7/2 \rceil$) for elements a[2][0], a[2][1], . . . , a[2][6] in the second loop

or a total of 19 nonprefetched misses. The cost of avoiding 232 cache misses is executing 400 prefetch instructions, likely a good trade-off.

Example   Calculate the time saved in the example above. Ignore instruction cache misses and assume there are no conflict or capacity misses in the data cache. Assume that prefetches can overlap with each other and with cache misses, thereby transferring at the maximum memory bandwidth. Here are the key loop times ignoring cache misses: The original loop takes 7 clock cycles per iteration, the first prefetch loop takes 9 clock cycles per iteration, and the second prefetch loop takes 8 clock cycles per iteration (including the overhead of the outer for loop). A miss takes 100 clock cycles.

Answer   The original doubly nested loop executes the multiply 3×100 or 300 times. Since the loop takes 7 clock cycles per iteration, the total is 300×7 or 2100 clock cycles plus cache misses. Cache misses add 251×100 or 25,100 clock cycles, giving a total of 27,200 clock cycles. The first prefetch loop iterates 100 times; at 9 clock cycles per iteration the total is 900 clock cycles plus cache misses. They add 11×100 or 1100 clock cycles for cache misses, giving a total of 2000. The second loop executes 2×100 or 200 times, and at 8 clock cycles per iteration it takes 1600 clock cycles plus 8×100 or 800 clock cycles for cache misses. This gives a total of 2400 clock cycles. From the prior example we know that this code executes 400 prefetch instructions during the $2000 + 2400$ or 4400 clock cycles to execute these two loops. If we assume that the prefetches are completely overlapped with the rest of the execution, then the prefetch code is 27,200/4400 or 6.2 times faster.

In addition to the nonfaulting prefetch loads, the 21264 offers prefetches to help with writes. In the example above, we prefetched a[i][j+7] even though we were not going to read the data. We just wanted it in the cache so that we could write over it. If an aligned cache block is being written in full, the write hint instruction tells the cache to allocate the block but not to bother loading the data, as the CPU will write over it. In the previous example, if the array a were properly aligned and padded, such an instruction could replace the instructions prefetching a with the write hint instructions, thereby saving hundreds of memory accesses. Since these write hints do have side effects, care would also have to be taken not to access memory outside of the memory allocated for a.

Although array optimizations are easy to understand, modern programs are more likely to use pointers. Luk and Mowry [1999] have demonstrated that compiler-based prefetching can sometimes be extended to pointers as well. Of 10 programs with recursive data structures, prefetching all pointers when a node is visited improved performance by 4% to 31% in half the programs. On the other hand, the remaining programs were still within 2% of their original performance. The issue is both whether prefetches are to data already in the cache and whether they occur early enough for the data to arrive by the time it is needed.

Summary of Reducing Cache Miss Penalty/Miss Rate via Parallelism

This section first covered nonblocking caches, which enable out-of-order processors. In general, such processors hide cache misses to L1 caches that hit in the L2 cache, but not a complete L2 cache miss. However, if miss under miss is supported, nonblocking caches can take advantage of more bandwidth behind the cache by having several outstanding misses operating at once for programs with sufficient instruction-level parallelism.

The hardware and software prefetching techniques leverage excess memory bandwidth for performance by trying to anticipate the needs of a cache. Although speculation may not make sense for power-sensitive embedded applications, it normally does for desktop and server computers. The potential success of prefetching is either lower miss penalty, or if it is started far in advance of need, reduction of the miss rate. This ambiguity of whether it helps miss rate or miss penalty is one reason it is included in a separate section.

Now that we have spent 30 pages on techniques that reduce cache miss penalties or miss rates in Sections 5.4 to 5.6, it is time to look at reducing the final component of average memory access time.

5.7   Reducing Hit Time

Hit time is critical because it affects the clock rate of the processor; in many processors today the cache access time limits the clock cycle rate, even for processors that take multiple clock cycles to access the cache. Hence, a fast hit time is multiplied in importance beyond the average memory access time formula because it helps everything. This section gives four general techniques.

First Hit Time Reduction Technique: Small and Simple Caches

A time-consuming portion of a cache hit is using the index portion of the address to read the tag memory and then compare it to the address. Our guideline from Chapter 1 suggests that smaller hardware is faster, and a small cache certainly helps the hit time. It is also critical to keep the cache small enough to fit on the same chip as the processor to avoid the time penalty of going off chip. The second suggestion is to keep the cache simple, such as using direct mapping (see page 429). A main benefit of direct-mapped caches is that the designer can overlap the tag check with the transmission of the data. This effectively reduces hit time. Hence, the pressure of a fast clock cycle encourages small and simple cache designs for first-level caches. For second-level caches, some designs strike a compromise by keeping the tags on chip and the data off chip, promising a fast tag check, yet providing the greater capacity of separate memory chips.

One approach to determining the impact on hit time in advance of building a chip is to use CAD tools. CACTI is a program to estimate the access time of alternative cache structures on CMOS microprocessors within 10% of more detailed CAD tools. For a given minimum feature size, it estimates the hit time of caches as you vary cache size, associativity, and number of read/write ports. Figure 5.24 shows the estimated impact on hit time as cache size and associativity are varied. Depending on cache size, for these parameters the model suggests that hit time for direct mapped is 1.2–1.5 times faster than two-way set associative; two-way is 1.02–1.11 times faster than four-way; and four-way is 1.0–1.08 times faster than fully associative (except for a 256 KB cache, which is 1.19 times faster).

Although the amount of on-chip cache increased with new generations of microprocessors, the size of the L1 caches has recently not increased between generations. The L1 caches are the same size for the Alpha 21264 and 21364, UltraSPARC II and III, and AMD K6 and Athlon. The L1 data cache size is actually reduced from 16 KB in the Pentium III to 8 KB in the Pentium 4. The emphasis recently is on fast clock time while hiding L1 misses with dynamic execution and using L2 caches to avoid going to memory.

Second Hit Time Reduction Technique: Avoiding Address Translation during Indexing of the Cache

Even a small and simple cache must cope with the translation of a virtual address from the CPU to a physical address to access memory. As described in Section 5.10, processors treat main memory as just another level of the memory hierarchy, and thus the address of the virtual memory that exists on disk must be mapped onto the main memory.

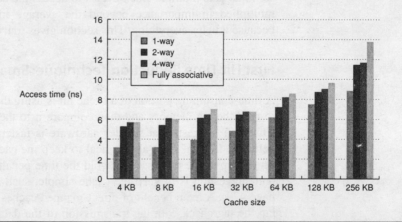

Figure 5.24 Access times as size and associativity vary in a CMOS cache. These data are based on Spice runs used to validate the CACTI model 2.0 by Reinman and Jouppi [1999]. They assumed 0.80-micron feature size, a single read/write port, 32 address bits, 64 output bits, and 32-byte blocks. The median ratios of access time relative to the direct-mapped caches are 1.36, 1.44, and 1.52 for 2-way, 4-way, and 8-way associative caches, respectively.

The guideline of making the common case fast suggests that we use virtual addresses for the cache, since hits are much more common than misses. Such caches are termed *virtual caches,* with *physical cache* used to identify the traditional cache that uses physical addresses. As we will shortly see, it is important to distinguish two tasks: indexing the cache and comparing addresses. Thus, the issues are whether a virtual or physical address is used to index the cache and whether a virtual or physical address is used in the tag comparison. Full virtual addressing for both indices and tags eliminates address translation time from a cache hit. Then why doesn't everyone build virtually addressed caches?

One reason is protection. Page-level protection is checked as part of the virtual to physical address translation, and it must be enforced no matter what. One solution is to copy the protection information from the TLB on a miss, add a field to hold it, and check it on every access to the virtually addressed cache.

Another reason is that every time a process is switched, the virtual addresses refer to different physical addresses, requiring the cache to be flushed. Figure 5.25 shows the impact on miss rates of this flushing. One solution is to increase the width of the cache address tag with a *process-identifier tag* (PID). If the operating system assigns these tags to processes, it only need flush the cache when a PID is recycled; that is, the PID distinguishes whether or not the data in the cache are for this program. Figure 5.25 shows the improvement in miss rates by using PIDs to avoid cache flushes.

A third reason why virtual caches are not more popular is that operating systems and user programs may use two different virtual addresses for the same physical address. These duplicate addresses, called *synonyms* or *aliases,* could result in two copies of the same data in a virtual cache; if one is modified, the other will have the wrong value. With a physical cache this wouldn't happen, since the accesses would first be translated to the same physical cache block.

Hardware solutions to the synonym problem, called *antialiasing,* guarantee every cache block a unique physical address. The Alpha 21264 uses a 64 KB instruction cache with an 8 KB page and two-way set associativity, hence the hardware must handle aliases involved with the two virtual address bits in the set index. It avoids aliases by simply checking all eight possible locations on a miss—two blocks in four sets—to be sure that none match the physical address of the data being fetched. If one is found, it is invalidated, so when the new data are loaded into the cache their physical address is guaranteed to be unique.

Software can make this problem much easier by forcing aliases to share some address bits. The version of UNIX from Sun Microsystems, for example, requires all aliases to be identical in the last 18 bits of their addresses; this restriction is called *page coloring*. Note that page coloring is simply set-associative mapping applied to virtual memory: The 4 KB (2^{12}) pages are mapped using 64 (2^6) sets to ensure that the physical and virtual addresses match in the last 18 bits. This restriction means a direct-mapped cache that is 2^{18} (256K) bytes or smaller can never have duplicate physical addresses for blocks. From the perspective of the cache, page coloring effectively increases the page offset, as software guarantees that the last few bits of the virtual and physical page address are identical.

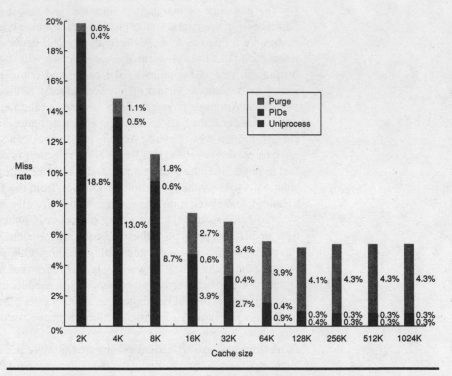

Figure 5.25 Miss rate versus virtually addressed cache size of a program measured three ways: without process switches (uniprocess), with process switches using a process-identifier tag (PID), and with process switches but without PIDs (purge). PIDs increase the uniprocess absolute miss rate by 0.3% to 0.6% and save 0.6% to 4.3% over purging. Agarwal [1987] collected these statistics for the Ultrix operating system running on a VAX, assuming direct-mapped caches with a block size of 16 bytes. Note that the miss rate goes up from 128K to 256K. Such nonintuitive behavior can occur in caches because changing size changes the mapping of memory blocks onto cache blocks, which can change the conflict miss rate.

The final area of concern with virtual addresses is I/O. I/O typically uses physical addresses and thus would require mapping to virtual addresses to interact with a virtual cache. (The impact of I/O on caches is further discussed in Section 5.12.)

One alternative to get the best of both virtual and physical caches is to use part of the page offset—the part that is identical in both virtual and physical addresses—to index the cache. At the same time as the cache is being read using that index, the virtual part of the address is translated, and the tag match uses physical addresses.

This alternative allows the cache read to begin immediately, and yet the tag comparison is still with physical addresses. The limitation of this *virtually indexed, physically tagged* alternative is that a direct-mapped cache can be no bigger than the page size. For example, in the data cache in Figure 5.7 on page 403, the index is 9 bits and the cache block offset is 6 bits. To use this trick, the virtual page size would have to be at least $2^{(9+6)}$ bytes or 32 KB. If not, a portion of the index must be translated from virtual to physical address.

Associativity can keep the index in the physical part of the address and yet still support a large cache. Recall that the size of the index is controlled by this formula:

$$2^{\text{Index}} = \frac{\text{Cache size}}{\text{Block size} \times \text{Set associativity}}$$

For example, doubling associativity and doubling the cache size does not change the size of the index. The Pentium III, with 8 KB pages, avoids translation with its 16 KB cache by using 2-way set associativity. The IBM 3033 cache, as an extreme example, is 16-way set associative, even though studies show there is little benefit to miss rates above 8-way set associativity. This high associativity allows a 64 KB cache to be addressed with a physical index, despite the handicap of 4 KB pages in the IBM architecture.

Third Hit Time Reduction Technique: Pipelined Cache Access

The final technique is simply to pipeline cache access so that the effective latency of a first-level cache hit can be multiple clock cycles, giving fast cycle time and slow hits. For example, the pipeline for the Pentium takes 1 clock cycle to access the instruction cache, for the Pentium Pro through Pentium III it takes 2 clocks, and for the Pentium 4 it takes 4 clocks. This split increases the number of pipeline stages, leading to greater penalty on mispredicted branches and more clock cycles between the issue of the load and the use of the data (see Appendix A).

Note that this technique in reality increases the bandwidth of instructions rather than decreasing the actual latency of a cache hit.

Fourth Hit Time Reduction Technique: Trace Caches

A challenge in the effort to find instruction-level parallelism beyond four instructions per cycle is to supply enough instructions every cycle without dependencies. One solution is called a *trace cache*. Instead of limiting the instructions in a static cache block to spatial locality, a trace cache finds a dynamic sequence of instructions *including taken branches* to load into a cache block.

The name comes from the cache blocks containing dynamic traces of the executed instructions as determined by the CPU rather than containing static sequences of instructions as determined by memory. Hence, the branch prediction is folded into the cache and must be validated along with the addresses to have a valid fetch. The Intel NetBurst microarchitecture, which is the foundation of the Pentium 4 and its successors, uses a trace cache.

Clearly, trace caches have much more complicated address mapping mechanisms, as the addresses are no longer aligned to power of 2 multiples of the word size. However, they have other benefits for utilization of the data portion of the instruction cache. Very long blocks in conventional caches may be entered from a taken branch, and hence the first portion of the block would occupy space in the cache that might not be fetched. Similarly, such blocks may be exited by taken branches, so the last portion of the block might be wasted. Given that taken branches or jumps are 1 in 5 to 10 instructions, space utilization is a real problem for processors like the AMD Athlon, whose 64-byte block would likely include 16–24 80x86 instructions. The trend toward even greater instruction issue should make the problem worse. Trace caches store instructions only from the branch entry point to the exit of the trace, thereby avoiding such header and trailer overhead.

The downside of trace caches is that they store the same instructions multiple times in the instruction cache. Conditional branches making different choices result in the same instructions being part of separate traces, which each occupy space in the cache.

Cache Optimization Summary

The techniques in Sections 5.4–5.7 to improve miss rate, miss penalty, and hit time generally impact the other components of the average memory access equation as well as the complexity of the memory hierarchy. Figure 5.26 summarizes these techniques and estimates the impact on complexity, with + meaning that the technique improves the factor, − meaning it hurts that factor, and blank meaning it has no impact. Generally no technique helps more than one category.

5.8   Main Memory and Organizations for Improving Performance

Main memory is the next level down in the hierarchy. Main memory satisfies the demands of caches and serves as the I/O interface, as it is the destination of input as well as the source for output. Performance measures of main memory emphasize both latency and bandwidth. (Memory bandwidth is the number of bytes read or written per unit time.) Traditionally, main memory latency (which affects the cache miss penalty) is the primary concern of the cache, while main memory bandwidth is the primary concern of I/O and multiprocessors. The relationship of main memory and multiprocessors is discussed in Chapter 6, and the relationship of main memory and I/O is discussed in Chapter 7.

Although caches are interested in low-latency memory, it is generally easier to improve memory bandwidth with new organizations than it is to reduce latency. With the popularity of second-level caches and their larger block sizes, main memory bandwidth becomes important to caches as well. In fact, cache designers increase block size to take advantage of the high memory bandwidth.

The previous sections describe what can be done with cache organization to reduce this CPU-DRAM performance gap, but simply making caches larger or adding more levels of caches may not be a cost-effective way to eliminate the

Technique	Miss penalty	Miss rate	Hit time	Hardware complexity	Comment
Multilevel caches	+			2	Costly hardware; harder if block size L1 ≠ L2; widely used
Critical word first and early restart	+			2	Widely used
Giving priority to read misses over writes	+			1	Trivial for uniprocessor, and widely used
Merging write buffer	+			1	Used with write through; in 21164, UltraSPARC III; widely used
Victim caches	+	+		2	AMD Athlon has eight entries
Larger block size	−	+		0	Trivial; Pentium 4 L2 uses 128 bytes
Larger cache size		+	−	1	Widely used, especially for L2 caches
Higher associativity		+	−	1	Widely used
Way-predicting caches		+		2	Used in I-cache of UltraSPARC III; D-cache of MIPS R4300 series
Pseudoassociative		+		2	Used in L2 of MIPS R10000
Compiler techniques to reduce cache misses		+		0	Software is a challenge; some computers have compiler option
Nonblocking caches	+			3	Used with all out-of-order CPUs
Hardware prefetching of instructions and data	+	+		2 instr., 3 data	Many prefetch instructions; UltraSPARC III prefetches data
Compiler-controlled prefetching	+	+		3	Needs nonblocking cache too; several processors support it
Small and simple caches		−	+	0	Trivial; widely used
Avoiding address translation during indexing of the cache			+	2	Trivial if small cache; used in Alpha 21164, UltraSPARC III
Pipelined cache access			+	1	Widely used
Trace cache			+	3	Used in Pentium 4

Figure 5.26 Summary of cache optimizations showing impact on cache performance and complexity for the techniques in Sections 5.4–5.7. Although generally a technique helps only one factor, prefetching can reduce misses if done sufficiently early; if not, it can reduce miss penalty. + means that the technique improves the factor, − means it hurts that factor, and blank means it has no impact. The complexity measure is subjective, with 0 being the easiest and 3 being a challenge.

gap. Innovative organizations of main memory are needed as well. In this section we examine techniques for organizing memory to improve bandwidth.

Let's illustrate these organizations with the case of satisfying a cache miss. Assume the performance of the basic memory organization is

- 4 clock cycles to send the address
- 56 clock cycles for the access time per word
- 4 clock cycles to send a word of data

Given a cache block of 4 words, and that a word is 8 bytes, the miss penalty is $4 \times (4 + 56 + 4)$ or 256 clock cycles, with a memory bandwidth of 1/8 byte (32/256) per clock cycle. These values are our default case.

Figure 5.27 shows some of the options to faster memory systems. The next three solutions assume generic memory technology, which we explore in the next section. The simplest approach to increasing memory bandwidth, then, is to make the memory wider; we examine this first.

First Technique for Higher Bandwidth: Wider Main Memory

First-level caches are often organized with a physical width of 1 word because most CPU accesses are that size; see Figure 5.27(a). Doubling or quadrupling the width of the cache and the memory will therefore double or quadruple the memory bandwidth. With a main memory width of 2 words, the miss penalty in our example would drop from 4×64 or 256 clock cycles as calculated earlier to 2×64 or 128 clock cycles. The reason is at twice the width we need half the memory accesses, and each takes 64 clock cycles. At 4 words wide the miss penalty is just 1×64 clock cycles. The bandwidth is then 1/4 byte per clock cycle at 2 words wide and 1/2 byte per clock cycle when the memory is 4 words wide.

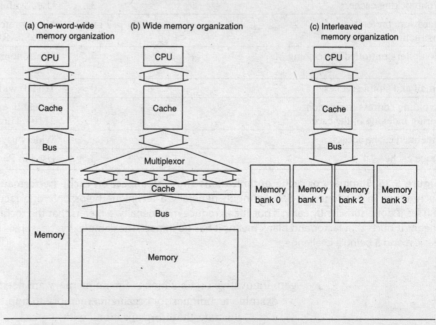

Figure 5.27 Three examples of bus width, memory width, and memory interleaving to achieve higher memory bandwidth. (a) The simplest design, with everything the width of one word; (b) a wider memory, bus, and L2 cache with a narrow L1 cache; (c) a narrow bus and cache with an interleaved memory.

There is cost in the wider connection between the CPU and memory, typically called a memory *bus*. CPUs will still access the cache a word at a time, so there now needs to be a multiplexor between the cache and the CPU—and that multiplexor may be on the critical timing path. Second-level caches can help since the multiplexing can be between first- and second-level caches, not on the critical path; see Figure 5.27(b).

Since main memory is traditionally expandable by the customer, a drawback to wide memory is that the minimum increment is doubled or quadrupled when the width is doubled or quadrupled. In addition, memories with error correction have difficulties with writes to a portion of the protected block, such as a byte. The rest of the data must be read so that the new error correction code can be calculated and stored when the data are written. (Section 5.15 describes error correction on the Sun Fire 6800 server.) If the error correction is done over the full width, the wider memory will increase the frequency of such "read-modify-write" sequences because more writes become partial block writes. Many designs of wider memory have separate error correction every word since most writes are that size.

Second Technique for Higher Bandwidth: Simple Interleaved Memory

Increasing width is one way to improve bandwidth, but another is to take advantage of the potential parallelism of having many chips in a memory system. Memory chips can be organized in *banks* to read or write multiple words at a time rather than a single word. In general, the purpose of interleaved memory is to try to take advantage of the potential memory bandwidth of *all* the chips in the system; in contrast, most memory systems activate only the chips containing the needed words. The two philosophies affect the power of the memory system, leading to different decisions depending on the relative importance of power versus performance.

The banks are often 1 word wide so that the width of the bus and the cache need not change, but sending addresses to several banks permits them all to read simultaneously. Figure 5.27(c) shows this organization. For example, sending an address to four banks (with access times shown on page 449) yields a miss penalty of $4 + 56 + (4 \times 4)$ or 76 clock cycles, giving a bandwidth of about 0.4 bytes per clock cycle. Banks are also valuable on writes. Although back-to-back writes would normally have to wait for earlier writes to finish, banks allow 1 clock cycle for each write, provided the writes are not destined to the same bank. Such a memory organization is especially important for write through.

The mapping of addresses to banks affects the behavior of the memor system. The previous example assumes the addresses of the four banks are interleaved at the word level: Bank 0 has all words whose address modulo 4 is 0, bank 1 has all words whose address modulo 4 is 1, and so on. Figure 5.28 shows this interleaving.

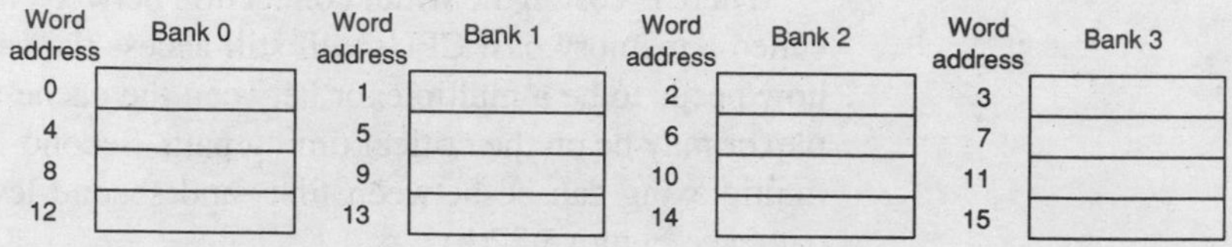

Figure 5.28 Four-way interleaved memory. This example assumes word addressing: With byte addressing and 8 bytes per word, each of these addresses would be multiplied by 8.

This mapping is referred to as the *interleaving factor. Interleaved memory* normally means banks of memory that are word interleaved. This interleaving optimizes sequential memory accesses. A cache read miss is an ideal match to word-interleaved memory, because the words in a block are read sequentially. Write-back caches make writes as well as reads sequential, getting even more efficiency from word-interleaved memory.

Example What can interleaving and wide memory buy? Consider the following description of a computer and its cache performance:

Block size = 1 word

Memory bus width = 1 word

Miss rate = 3%

Memory accesses per instruction = 1.2

Cache miss penalty = 64 cycles (as above)

Average cycles per instruction (ignoring cache misses) = 2

If we change the block size to 2 words, the miss rate falls to 2%, and a 4-word block has a miss rate of 1.2%. What is the improvement in performance of interleaving two ways and four ways versus doubling the width of memory and the bus, assuming the access times on page 449?

Answer The CPI for the base computer using 1-word blocks is

$$2 + (1.2 \times 3\% \times 64) = 4.30$$

Since the clock cycle time and instruction count won't change in this example, we can calculate performance improvement by just comparing CPI.

Increasing the block size to 2 words gives the following options:

64-bit bus and memory, no interleaving = $2 + (1.2 \times 2\% \times 2 \times 64) = 5.07$

64-bit bus and memory, interleaving = $2 + (1.2 \times 2\% \times (4 + 56 + 8)) = 3.63$

128-bit bus and memory, no interleaving = $2 + (1.2 \times 2\% \times 1 \times 64) = 3.54$

Thus, doubling the block size slows down the straightforward implementation (5.07 versus 4.30), while interleaving or wider memory is 1.19 or 1.22 times faster, respectively. If we increase the block size to four, the following is obtained:

64-bit bus and memory, no interleaving $= 2 + (1.2 \times 1.2\% \times 4 \times 64) = 5.69$

64-bit bus and memory, interleaving $= 2 + (1.2 \times 1.2\% \times (4 + 56 + 16)) = 3.09$

128-bit bus and memory, no interleaving $= 2 + (1.2 \times 1.2\% \times 2 \times 64) = 3.84$

Again, the larger block hurts performance for the simple case (5.69 versus 4.30), although the interleaved 64-bit memory is now fastest—1.39 times faster versus 1.12 for the wider memory and bus.

This subsection has shown that interleaved memory is logically a wide memory, except that accesses to banks are staged over time to share internal resources—the memory bus in this example.

How many banks should be included? One metric, used in vector computers, is as follows:

Number of banks $\geq$ Number of clock cycles to access word in bank

The memory system goal is to deliver information from a new bank each clock cycle for sequential accesses. To see why this formula holds, imagine there were fewer banks than clock cycles to access a word in a 64-bit bank, say, 8 banks with an access time of 10 clock cycles. After 10 clock cycles the CPU could get a word from bank 0, and then bank 0 would begin fetching the next desired word as the CPU received the following 7 words from the other 7 banks. At clock cycle 18 the CPU would be at the door of bank 0, waiting for it to supply the next word. The CPU would have to wait until clock cycle 20 for the word to appear. Hence, we want more banks than clock cycles to access a bank to avoid waiting.

We will discuss conflicts on nonsequential accesses to banks in the following subsection. For now, we note that having many banks reduces the chance of these bank conflicts.

Ironically, as capacity per memory chip increases, there are fewer chips in the same-sized memory system, making multiple banks much more expensive. For example, a 512 MB main memory takes 256 memory chips of $4M \times 4$ bits, easily organized into 16 banks of 16 memory chips. However, it takes only sixteen $64M \times 4$-bit memory chips for 64 MB, making one bank the limit. Many manufacturers will want to have a small memory option in the baseline model. This shrinking number of chips is the main disadvantage of interleaved memory banks. Chips organized with wider paths, such as $16M \times 16$ bits, postpone this weakness.

A second disadvantage of memory banks is again the difficulty of main memory expansion. Either the memory system must support multiple generations of memory chips, or the memory controller changes the interleaving based on the size of physical memory, or both.

Third Technique for Higher Bandwidth: Independent Memory Banks

The original motivation for memory banks was higher memory bandwidth by interleaving sequential accesses. This hardware is not much more difficult since the banks can share address lines with a memory controller, enabling each bank to use the data portion of the memory bus.

A generalization of interleaving is to allow multiple independent accesses, where multiple memory controllers allow banks (or sets of word-interleaved banks) to operate independently. Each bank needs separate address lines and possibly a separate data bus. For example, an input device may use one controller and one bank, the cache read may use another, and a cache write may use a third. Nonblocking caches (page 435) allow the CPU to proceed beyond a cache miss, potentially allowing multiple cache misses to be serviced simultaneously. Such a design only makes sense with memory banks; otherwise the multiple reads will be serviced by a single memory port and get only a small benefit of overlapping access with transmission. Multiprocessors that share a common memory provide further motivation for memory banks (see Chapter 6).

Independent of memory technology, higher bandwidth is available using memory banks, by making memory and its bus wider, or doing both. The next section examines the underlying memory technology.

5.9   Memory Technology

… the one single development that put computers on their feet was the invention of a reliable form of memory, namely, the core memory.… Its cost was reasonable, it was reliable and, because it was reliable, it could in due course be made large. [p. 209]

Maurice Wilkes
Memoirs of a Computer Pioneer (1985)

The previous section described ways to organize memory chips; this section describes the technology inside the memory chips. Before describing the options, let's go over the performance metrics.

Memory latency is traditionally quoted using two measures—access time and cycle time. *Access time* is the time between when a read is requested and when the desired word arrives, while *cycle time* is the minimum time between requests to memory. One reason that cycle time is greater than access time is that the memory needs the address lines to be stable between accesses.

DRAM Technology

The main memory of virtually every desktop or server computer sold since 1975 is composed of semiconductor DRAMs. As early DRAMs grew in capacity, the cost of a package with all the necessary address lines was an issue. The solution was to multiplex the address lines, thereby cutting the number of address pins in half. Figure 5.29 shows the basic DRAM organization. One half of the address is sent first, called the *row access strobe* (RAS). It is followed by the other half of the address, sent during the *column access strobe* (CAS). These names come from the internal chip organization, since the memory is organized as a rectangular matrix addressed by rows and columns.

An additional requirement of DRAM derives from the property signified by its first letter, *D*, for *dynamic*. To pack more bits per chip, DRAMs use only a single transistor to store a bit. Reading that bit can disturb the information, however. To prevent loss of information, each bit must be "refreshed" periodically. Fortunately, all the bits in a row can be refreshed simultaneously just by reading that row. Hence, every DRAM in the memory system must access every row within a certain time window, such as 8 milliseconds. Memory controllers include hardware to periodically refresh the DRAMs.

This requirement means that the memory system is occasionally unavailable because it is sending a signal telling every chip to refresh. The time for a refresh is typically a full memory access (RAS and CAS) for each row of the DRAM. Since the memory matrix in a DRAM is conceptually square, the number of steps in a refresh is usually the square root of the DRAM capacity. DRAM designers try to keep time spent refreshing to less than 5% of the total time.

Earlier sections presented main memory as if operated like a Swiss train, consistently delivering the goods exactly according to schedule. Refresh belies that myth, since some accesses take much longer than others do. Thus, refresh is another reason for variability of memory latency and hence cache miss penalty.

Amdahl suggested a rule of thumb that memory capacity should grow linearly with CPU speed to keep a balanced system, so that a 1000 MIPS processor

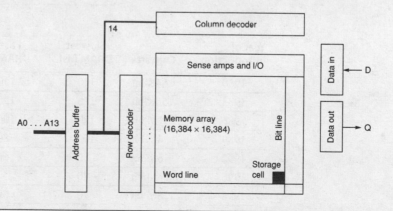

Figure 5.29 Internal organization of a 64M bit DRAM. DRAMs often use banks of memory arrays internally and select between them. For example, instead of one 16,384 × 16,384 memory, a DRAM might use 256 1024 × 1024 arrays or 16 2048 × 2048 arrays.

should have 1000 MB of memory. CPU designers rely on DRAMs to supply that demand: In the past they expected a fourfold improvement in capacity every three years, or 55% per year. Unfortunately, the performance of DRAMs is growing at a much slower rate. Figure 5.30 shows a performance improvement in row access time, which is related to latency, of about 5% per year. The CAS or data transfer time, which is related to bandwidth, is growing at more than twice that rate.

Although we have been talking about individual chips, DRAMs are commonly sold on small boards called *dual inline memory modules* (DIMMs). DIMMs typically contain 4 to 16 DRAMs. They are normally organized to be 8 bytes wide for desktop systems.

In addition to the DIMM packaging and the new interfaces to improve the data transfer time, discussed in the following subsections, the biggest change to DRAMs has been a slowing down in capacity growth. For 20 years DRAMs obeyed Moore's Law, bringing out a new chip with four times the capacity every three years. As a result of a slowing in demand for DRAMs, since 1998 new chips only double capacity every two years. In 2001, this new slower pace shows no sign of changing.

Just as virtually all desktop or server computers since 1975 used DRAMs for main memory, virtually all use SRAM for cache, the topic of the next subsection.

SRAM Technology

In contrast to DRAMs are SRAMs—the first letter standing for *static*. The dynamic nature of the circuits in DRAM require data to be written back after being read; hence the difference between the access time and the cycle time as

Year of introduction	Chip size	Row access strobe (RAS)		Column access strobe (CAS)/ data transfer time (ns)	Cycle time (ns)
		Slowest DRAM (ns)	Fastest DRAM (ns)		
1980	64K bit	180	150	75	250
1983	256K bit	150	120	50	220
1986	1M bit	120	100	25	190
1989	4M bit	100	80	20	165
1992	16M bit	80	60	15	120
1996	64M bit	70	50	12	110
1998	128M bit	70	50	10	100
2000	256M bit	65	45	7	90
2002	512M bit	60	40	5	80

Figure 5.30 Times of fast and slow DRAMs with each generation. Performance improvement of row access time is about 5% per year. The improvement by a factor of 2 in column access accompanied the switch from NMOS DRAMs to CMOS DRAMs.

well as the need to refresh. SRAMs typically use six transistors per bit to prevent the information from being disturbed when read.

This difference in refresh alone can make a difference for embedded applications. Devices often go into low power or standby mode for long periods. SRAM needs only minimal power to retain the charge in standby mode, but DRAMs must continue to be refreshed occasionally so as to not lose information.

In DRAM designs the emphasis is on cost per bit and capacity, while SRAM designs are concerned with speed and capacity. (Because of this concern, SRAM address lines are not multiplexed.) Thus, unlike DRAMs, there is no difference between access time and cycle time. For memories designed in comparable technologies, the capacity of DRAMs is roughly 4 to 8 times that of SRAMs. The cycle time of SRAMs is 8 to 16 times faster than DRAMs, but they are also 8 to 16 times as expensive.

Embedded Processor Memory Technology: ROM and Flash

Embedded computers usually have small memories, and most do not have a disk to act as nonvolatile storage. Two memory technologies are found in embedded computers to address this problem.

The first is *read-only memory* (ROM). ROM is programmed at the time of manufacture, needing only a single transistor per bit to represent 1 or 0. ROM is used for the embedded program and for constants, often included as part of a larger chip.

In addition to being nonvolatile, ROM is also indestructible; nothing the computer can do can modify the contents of this memory. Hence, ROM also provides a level of protection to the code of embedded computers. Since address-based protection is often not enabled in embedded processors, ROM can fulfill an important role.

The second memory technology offers nonvolatility but allows the memory to be modified. *Flash memory* allows the embedded device to alter nonvolatile memory after the system is manufactured, which can shorten product development. Flash memory, described on page 689 in Chapter 7, allows reading at almost DRAM speeds, but writing flash is 10 to 100 times slower. In 2001, the DRAM capacity per chip and the megabytes per dollar is about four to eight times greater than flash memory.

Improving Memory Performance in a Standard DRAM Chip

As Moore's Law continues to supply more transistors and as the processor-memory gap increases pressure on memory performance, some of the ideas of the previous section have made their way inside the DRAM chip. Generally the idea has been for greater bandwidth, often at the cost of greater latency. This subsection presents techniques that take advantage of the nature of DRAMs.

As mentioned earlier, a DRAM access is divided into row access and column access. DRAMs must buffer a row of bits inside the DRAM for the column access, and this row is usually the square root of the DRAM size—8K bits for 64M bits, 16K bits for 256M bits, and so on.

Although presented logically as a single monolithic array of memory bits, the internal organization of DRAM actually consists of many memory modules. For a variety of manufacturing reasons, these modules are usually 1–4M bits. Thus, if you were to examine a 256M bit DRAM under a microscope, you might see 128 memory arrays, each of 2M bits, on the chip. This large number of arrays internally presents the opportunity to provide much higher bandwidth off chip.

To improve bandwidth, there have been a variety of evolutionary innovations over time. The first was timing signals that allow repeated accesses to the row buffer without another row access time, typically called *fast page mode*. Such a buffer comes naturally, as each array will buffer 1024 to 2048 bits for each access.

The second major change is that conventional DRAMs have an asynchronous interface to the memory controller, and hence every transfer involves overhead to synchronize with the controller. The solution was to add a clock signal to the DRAM interface, so that the repeated transfers would not bear that overhead. This optimization is called *synchronous DRAM* (SDRAM). SDRAMs typically also have a programmable register to hold the number of bytes requested, and hence can send many bytes over several cycles per request.

In 2001 the bus rates are 100–150 MHz. SDRAM DIMMs of these speeds are called PC100, PC133, and PC 150, based on the clock speed of the individual chip. Multiplying the 8-byte width of the DIMM times the clock rate, the peak speed per memory module is 800–1200 MB/sec.

The third major DRAM innovation to increase bandwidth is to transfer data on both the rising edge and falling edge of the DRAM clock signal, thereby doubling the peak data rate. This optimization is called *double data rate* (DDR). The bus speeds for these DRAMs are also 100–150 MHz, but these DDR DIMMs are confusingly labeled by the peak *DIMM* bandwidth. The name PC1600 comes from 100 MHz × 2 × 8 bytes or 1600 MB/sec, 133 MHz leads to PC2100, 150 MHz yields PC2400, and so on.

In each of the three cases the advantage of such optimizations is that they add a small amount of logic to exploit the high internal DRAM bandwidth, adding little cost to the system while achieving a significant improvement in bandwidth. Unlike traditional interleaved memories, there is no danger in using such a mode as DRAM chips increase in capacity.

Improving Memory Performance via a New DRAM Interface: RAMBUS

Recently new breeds of DRAMs have been produced that further optimize the interface between the DRAM and CPU. The company RAMBUS takes the standard DRAM core and provides a new interface, making a single chip act more like a memory system than a memory component: Each chip has interleaved memory and a high-speed interface. RAMBUS licenses its technology to companies that use its interface, both DRAM and microprocessor manufacturers.

The first-generation RAMBUS interface dropped RAS/CAS, replacing it with a bus that allows other accesses over the bus between the sending of the address and return of the data. It is typically called *RDRAM*. (Such a bus is called a *packet-switched bus* or *split-transaction* bus, described in Chapters 7 and 8.) This bus allows a single chip to act as a memory bank. A chip can return a variable amount of data from a single request, and even perform its own refresh. RDRAM offered a byte-wide interface and was one of the first DRAMs to use a clock signal. It also transfers on both edges of its clock. Inside each chip were four banks, each with their own row buffer. To run at its 300 MHz clock, the RAMBUS bus is limited to be no more than 4 inches long. Typically a microprocessor uses a single RAMBUS channel, so just one RDRAM is transferring at a time.

The second-generation RAMBUS interface, called *direct RDRAM* (DRDRAM), offers up to 1.6 GB/sec of bandwidth from a single DRAM. Innovations in this interface include separate row- and column-command buses instead of the conventional multiplexing; an 18-bit data bus; expanding from 4 to 16 internal banks per RDRAM to reduce bank conflicts; increasing the number of row buffers from 4 to 8; increasing the clock to 400 MHz; and a much more sophisticated controller on chip. Because of the separation of data, row, and column buses, three transactions can be performed simultaneously.

RAMBUS helped set the new optimistic naming trend, calling the 350 MHz part PC700, the 400 MHz part PC800, and so on. Since each chip is 2 bytes wide, the peak chip bandwidth of PC700 is 1400 MB/sec, PC800 is 1600 MB/sec, and so on. RAMBUS chips are not sold in DIMMs but in "RIMMs," which are similar in size but incompatible with DIMMs. RIMMs are designed to have a single RAMBUS chip on the RIMM supply the memory bandwidth needs of the computer and are not interchangeable with DIMMs.

Comparing RAMBUS and DDR SDRAM

How does the RAMBUS interface compare in cost and performance when placed in a system? Most main memory systems already use SDRAM to get more bits per memory access, in the hope of reducing the CPU-DRAM performance gap. Since most computers use memory in DIMM packages, which are typically at least 64 bits wide, the DIMM memory bandwidth is closer to what RAMBUS provides than you might expect when just comparing DRAM chips.

The one note of caution is that performance of cache-based systems is based in part on latency to the first byte and in part on the bandwidth to deliver the rest of the bytes in the block. Although these innovations help with the latter case, none help with latency. Amdahl's Law reminds us of the limits of accelerating one piece of the problem while ignoring another part.

In addition to performance, the new breed of DRAMs such as RDRAM and DRDRAM have a price premium over traditional DRAMs to provide the greater bandwidth since these chips are larger. The question over time is how much more. In 2001 it is factor of 2; Section 5.16 has a detailed price-performance evaluation.

The marketplace will determine whether the more radical DRAMs such as RAMBUS will become popular for main memory, or whether the price premium restricts them to niche markets.

5.10 Virtual Memory

... a system has been devised to make the core drum combination appear to the programmer as a single level store, the requisite transfers taking place automatically.

Kilburn et al. [1962]

At any instant in time computers are running multiple processes, each with its own address space. (Processes are described in the next section.) It would be too expensive to dedicate a full address space worth of memory for each process, especially since many processes use only a small part of their address space. Hence, there must be a means of sharing a smaller amount of physical memory among many processes. One way to do this, *virtual memory,* divides physical memory into blocks and allocates them to different processes. Inherent in such an approach must be a *protection* scheme that restricts a process to the blocks belonging only to that process. Most forms of virtual memory also reduce the time to start a program, since not all code and data need be in physical memory before a program can begin.

Although protection provided by virtual memory is essential for current computers, sharing is not the reason that virtual memory was invented. If a program became too large for physical memory, it was the programmer's job to make it fit. Programmers divided programs into pieces, then identified the pieces that were mutually exclusive, and loaded or unloaded these *overlays* under user program control during execution. The programmer ensured that the program never tried to access more physical main memory than was in the computer, and that the proper overlay was loaded at the proper time. As you can well imagine, this responsibility eroded programmer productivity.

Virtual memory was invented to relieve programmers of this burden; it automatically manages the two levels of the memory hierarchy represented by main memory and secondary storage. Figure 5.31 shows the mapping of virtual memory to physical memory for a program with four pages.

In addition to sharing protected memory space and automatically managing the memory hierarchy, virtual memory also simplifies loading the program for execution. Called *relocation,* this mechanism allows the same program to run in any location in physical memory. The program in Figure 5.31 can be placed anywhere in physical memory or disk just by changing the mapping between them. (Prior to the popularity of virtual memory, processors would include a relocation register just for that purpose.) An alternative to a hardware solution would be software that changed all addresses in a program each time it was run.

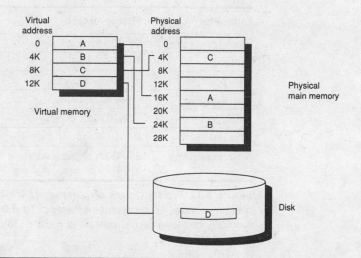

Figure 5.31   The logical program in Its contiguous virtual address space is shown on the left. It consists of four pages A, B, C, and D. The actual location of three of the blocks is in physical main memory and the other is located on the disk.

Several general memory hierarchy ideas from Chapter 1 about caches are analogous to virtual memory, although many of the terms are different. *Page* or *segment* is used for block, and *page fault* or *address fault* is used for miss. With virtual memory, the CPU produces *virtual addresses* that are translated by a combination of hardware and software to *physical addresses,* which access main memory. This process is called *memory mapping* or *address translation.* Today, the two memory hierarchy levels controlled by virtual memory are DRAMs and magnetic disks. Figure 5.32 shows a typical range of memory hierarchy parameters for virtual memory.

There are further differences between caches and virtual memory beyond those quantitative ones mentioned in Figure 5.32:

■ Replacement on cache misses is primarily controlled by hardware, while virtual memory replacement is primarily controlled by the operating system. The longer miss penalty means it's more important to make a good decision, so the operating system can be involved and take time deciding what to replace.

■ The size of the processor address determines the size of virtual memory, but the cache size is independent of the processor address size.

■ In addition to acting as the lower-level backing store for main memory in the hierarchy, secondary storage is also used for the file system. In fact, the file system occupies most of secondary storage. It is not normally in the address space.

Parameter	First-level cache	Virtual memory
Block (page) size	16–128 bytes	4096–65,536 bytes
Hit time	1–3 clock cycles	50–150 clock cycles
Miss penalty	8–150 clock cycles	1,000,000–10,000,000 clock cycles
(access time)	(6–130 clock cycles)	(800,000–8,000,000 clock cycles)
(transfer time)	(2–20 clock cycles)	(200,000–2,000,000 clock cycles)
Miss rate	0.1–10%	0.00001–0.001%
Address mapping	25–45 bit physical address to 14–20 bit cache address	32–64 bit virtual address to 25–45 bit physical address

Figure 5.32 Typical ranges of parameters for caches and virtual memory. Virtual memory parameters represent increases of 10–1,000,000 times over cache parameters. Normally first-level caches contain at most 1 MB of data, while physical memory contains 32 MB to 1 TB.

Virtual memory also encompasses several related techniques. Virtual memory systems can be categorized into two classes: those with fixed-size blocks, called *pages*, and those with variable-size blocks, called *segments*. Pages are typically fixed at 4096 to 65,536 bytes, while segment size varies. The largest segment supported on any processor ranges from 2^{16} bytes up to 2^{32} bytes; the smallest segment is 1 byte. Figure 5.33 shows how the two approaches might divide code and data.

The decision to use paged virtual memory versus segmented virtual memory affects the CPU. Paged addressing has a single fixed-size address divided into page number and offset within a page, analogous to cache addressing. A single address does not work for segmented addresses; the variable size of segments requires 1 word for a segment number and 1 word for an offset within a segment, for a total of 2 words. An unsegmented address space is simpler for the compiler.

The pros and cons of these two approaches have been well documented in operating systems textbooks; Figure 5.34 summarizes the arguments. Because of the replacement problem (the third line of the figure), few computers today use pure segmentation. Some computers use a hybrid approach, called *paged segments*, in which a segment is an integral number of pages. This simplifies replacement because memory need not be contiguous, and the full segments need not be in main memory. A more recent hybrid is for a computer to offer multiple page sizes, with the larger sizes being powers of 2 times the smallest page size. The IBM 405CR embedded processor, for example, allows 1 KB, 4 KB ($2^2 \times 1$ KB), 16 KB ($2^4 \times 1$ KB), 64 KB ($2^6 \times 1$ KB), 256 KB ($2^8 \times 1$ KB), 1024 KB ($2^{10} \times 1$ KB), and 4096 KB ($2^{12} \times 1$ KB) to act as a single page.

Four Memory Hierarchy Questions Revisited

We are now ready to answer the four memory hierarchy questions for virtual memory.

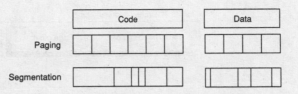

Figure 5.33 Example of how paging and segmentation divide a program.

	Page	**Segment**
Words per address	One	Two (segment and offset)
Programmer visible?	Invisible to application programmer	May be visible to application programmer
Replacing a block	Trivial (all blocks are the same size)	Hard (must find contiguous, variable-size, unused portion of main memory)
Memory use inefficiency	Internal fragmentation (unused portion of page)	External fragmentation (unused pieces of main memory)
Efficient disk traffic	Yes (adjust page size to balance access time and transfer time)	Not always (small segments may transfer just a few bytes)

Figure 5.34 Paging versus segmentation. Both can waste memory, depending on the block size and how well the segments fit together in main memory. Programming languages with unrestricted pointers require both the segment and the address to be passed. A hybrid approach, called *paged segments,* shoots for the best of both worlds: Segments are composed of pages, so replacing a block is easy, yet a segment may be treated as a logical unit.

Q1: Where Can a Block Be Placed in Main Memory?

The miss penalty for virtual memory involves access to a rotating magnetic storage device and is therefore quite high. Given the choice of lower miss rates or a simpler placement algorithm, operating systems designers normally pick lower miss rates because of the exorbitant miss penalty. Thus, operating systems allow blocks to be placed anywhere in main memory. According to the terminology in Figure 5.4 (page 398), this strategy would be labeled fully associative.

Q2: How Is a Block Found If It Is in Main Memory?

Both paging and segmentation rely on a data structure that is indexed by the page or segment number. This data structure contains the physical address of the block. For segmentation, the offset is added to the segment's physical address to obtain the final physical address. For paging, the offset is simply concatenated to this physical page address (see Figure 5.35).

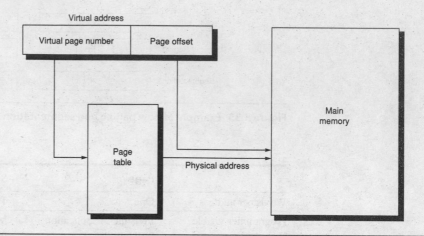

Figure 5.35 The mapping of a virtual address to a physical address via a page table.

This data structure, containing the physical page addresses, usually takes the form of a *page table.* Indexed by the virtual page number, the size of the table is the number of pages in the virtual address space. Given a 32-bit virtual address, 4 KB pages, and 4 bytes per page table entry, the size of the page table would be $(2^{32}/2^{12}) \times 2^2 = 2^{22}$ or 4 MB.

To reduce the size of this data structure, some computers apply a hashing function to the virtual address. The hash allows the data structure to be the length of the number of *physical* pages in main memory. This number could be much smaller than the number of virtual pages. Such a structure is called an *inverted page table.* Using the previous example, a 512 MB physical memory would only need 1 MB (8×512 MB/4 KB) for an inverted page table; the extra 4 bytes per page table entry are for the virtual address. The HP/Intel IA-64 covers both bases by offering both traditional pages tables *and* inverted page tables, leaving the choice of mechanism to the operating system programmer.

To reduce address translation time, computers use a cache dedicated to these address translations, called a *translation lookaside buffer,* or simply *translation buffer,* described in more detail shortly.

Q3: Which Block Should Be Replaced on a Virtual Memory Miss?

As mentioned earlier, the overriding operating system guideline is minimizing page faults. Consistent with this guideline, almost all operating systems try to replace the least-recently used (LRU) block because if the past predicts the future, that is the one less likely to be needed.

To help the operating system estimate LRU, many processors provide a *use bit* or *reference bit,* which is logically set whenever a page is accessed. (To reduce work, it is actually set only on a translation buffer miss, which is described shortly.) The operating system periodically clears the use bits and later records them so it can determine which pages were touched during a particular time period. By keeping track in this way, the operating system can select a page that is among the least-recently referenced.

Q4: What Happens on a Write?

The level below main memory contains rotating magnetic disks that take millions of clock cycles to access. Because of the great discrepancy in access time, no one has yet built a virtual memory operating system that writes through main memory to disk on every store by the CPU. (This remark should not be interpreted as an opportunity to become famous by being the first to build one!) Thus, the write strategy is always write back.

Since the cost of an unnecessary access to the next-lower level is so high, virtual memory systems usually include a dirty bit. It allows blocks to be written to disk only if they have been altered since being read from the disk.

Techniques for Fast Address Translation

Page tables are usually so large that they are stored in main memory and are sometimes paged themselves. Paging means that every memory access logically takes at least twice as long, with one memory access to obtain the physical address and a second access to get the data. This cost is far too dear.

One remedy is to remember the last translation, so that the mapping process is skipped if the current address refers to the same page as the last one. A more general solution is to again rely on the principle of locality; if the accesses have locality, then the *address translations* for the accesses must also have locality. By keeping these address translations in a special cache, a memory access rarely requires a second access to translate the data. This special address translation cache is referred to as a *translation lookaside buffer* (TLB), also called a *translation buffer* (TB).

A TLB entry is like a cache entry where the tag holds portions of the virtual address and the data portion holds a physical page frame number, protection field, valid bit, and usually a use bit and dirty bit. To change the physical page frame number or protection of an entry in the page table, the operating system must make sure the old entry is not in the TLB; otherwise, the system won't behave properly. Note that this dirty bit means the corresponding *page* is dirty, not that the address translation in the TLB is dirty nor that a particular block in the data cache is dirty. The operating system resets these bits by changing the value in the page table and then invalidating the corresponding TLB entry. When the entry is reloaded from the page table, the TLB gets an accurate copy of the bits.

Figure 5.36 shows the Alpha 21264 data TLB organization, with each step of the translation labeled. The TLB uses fully associative placement; thus, the translation begins (steps 1 and 2) by sending the virtual address to all tags. Of course, the tag must be marked valid to allow a match. At the same time, the type of memory access is checked for a violation (also in step 2) against protection information in the TLB.

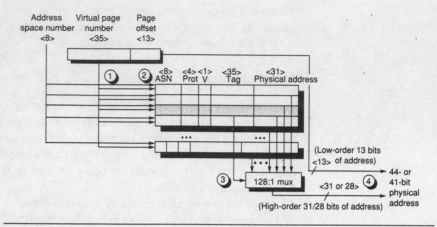

Figure 5.36 Operation of the Alpha 21264 data TLB during address translation. The four steps of a TLB hit are shown as circled numbers. The address space number (ASN) is used like a PID for virtual caches, in that the TLB is not flushed on a context switch, but only when ASNs are recycled. The next fields of an entry are protection permissions (Prot) and the valid bit (V). Note that there is no specific reference, use bit, or dirty bit. Hence, a page replacement algorithm such as LRU must rely on disabling reads and writes occasionally to record reads and writes to pages to measure usage and whether or not pages are dirty. The advantage of these omissions is that the TLB need not be written during normal memory accesses nor during a TLB miss. Alpha 21264 has an option of either 44-bit or 41-bit physical addresses. This TLB has 128 entries.

To reduce TLB misses due to context switches, each entry has an 8-bit address space number (ASN), which plays the same role as the PID mentioned in Figure 5.25 on page 446. If the context switching returns to the process with the same ASN, it can still match the TLB. Thus, the process ASN and the *page table entry* (PTE) ASN must also match for a valid tag.

For reasons similar to those in the cache case, there is no need to include the 13 bits of the Alpha 21264 page offset in the TLB. The matching tag sends the corresponding physical address through effectively a 128:1 multiplexor (step 3). The page offset is then combined with the physical page frame to form a full physical address (step 4). The address size is 44 or 41 bits depending on a physical address mode bit (see Section 5.11).

Address translation can easily be on the critical path determining the clock cycle of the processor, so the 21264 uses a virtually addressed instruction cache; thus the TLB is only accessed during an instruction cache miss.

Selecting a Page Size

The most obvious architectural parameter is the page size. Choosing the page is a question of balancing forces that favor a larger page size versus those favoring a smaller size. The following favor a larger size:

- The size of the page table is inversely proportional to the page size; memory (or other resources used for the memory map) can therefore be saved by making the pages bigger.

- As mentioned in Section 5.7, a larger page size can allow larger caches with fast cache hit times.

- Transferring larger pages to or from secondary storage, possibly over a network, is more efficient than transferring smaller pages.

- The number of TLB entries is restricted, so a larger page size means that more memory can be mapped efficiently, thereby reducing the number of TLB misses.

It is for this final reason that recent microprocessors have decided to support multiple page sizes; for some programs, TLB misses can be as significant on CPI as the cache misses.

The main motivation for a smaller page size is conserving storage. A small page size will result in less wasted storage when a contiguous region of virtual memory is not equal in size to a multiple of the page size. The term for this unused memory in a page is *internal fragmentation*. Assuming that each process has three primary segments (text, heap, and stack), the average wasted storage per process will be 1.5 times the page size. This amount is negligible for computers with hundreds of megabytes of memory and page sizes of 4 KB to 8 KB. Of course, when the page sizes become very large (more than 32 KB), lots of storage (both main and secondary) may be wasted, as well as I/O bandwidth. A final concern is process start-up time; many processes are small, so a large page size would lengthen the time to invoke a process.

Summary of Virtual Memory and Caches

With virtual memory, TLBs, first-level caches, and second-level caches all mapping portions of the virtual and physical address space, it can get confusing what bits go where. Figure 5.37 gives a hypothetical example going from a 64-bit virtual address to a 41-bit physical address with two levels of cache. This L1 cache is virtually indexed, physically tagged since both the cache size and the page size are 8 KB. The L2 cache is 4 MB. The block size for both is 64 bytes.

First, the 64-bit virtual address is logically divided into a virtual page number and page offset. The former is sent to the TLB to be translated into a physical address, and the high bit of the latter is sent to the L1 cache to act as an index. If the TLB match is a hit, then the physical page number is sent to the L1 cache tag to check for a match. If it matches, it's an L1 cache hit. The block offset then selects the word for the CPU.

If the L1 cache check results in a miss, the physical address is then used to try the L2 cache. The middle portion of the physical address is used as an index to the 4 MB L2 cache. The resulting L2 cache tag is compared to the upper part of the physical address to check for a match. If it matches, we have an L2 cache hit,

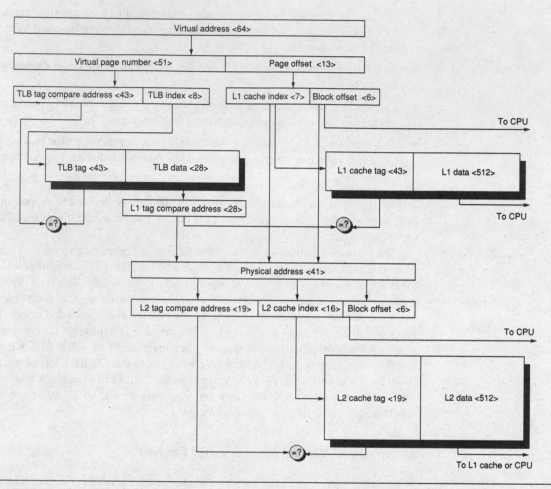

Figure 5.37 The overall picture of a hypothetical memory hierarchy going from virtual address to L2 cache access. The page size is 8 KB. The TLB is direct mapped with 256 entries. The L1 cache is a direct-mapped 8 KB, and the L2 cache is a direct-mapped 4 MB. Both use 64-byte blocks. The virtual address is 64 bits and the physical address is 41 bits. The primary difference between this simple figure and a real cache, as in Figure 5.43, is replication of pieces of this figure.

and the data are sent to the CPU, which uses the block offset to select the desired word. On an L2 miss, the physical address is then used to get the block from memory.

Although this is a simple example, the major difference between this drawing and a real cache is replication. First, there is only one L1 cache. When there are two L1 caches, the top half of the diagram is duplicated. Note this would lead to two TLBs, which is typical. Hence, one cache and TLB is for instructions, driven from the PC, and one cache and TLB is for data, driven from the effective address. The second simplification is that all the caches and TLBs are direct mapped. If any were n-way set associative, then we would replicate each set of tag memory, comparators, and data memory n times and connect data memories with an n:1 multiplexor to select a hit. Of course, if the total cache size remained the same, the cache index would also shrink by n bits according to the formula in Figure 5.9 on page 412.

5.11   Protection and Examples of Virtual Memory

The invention of multiprogramming, where a computer would be shared by several programs running concurrently, led to new demands for protection and sharing among programs. These demands are closely tied to virtual memory in computers today, and so we cover the topic here along with two examples of virtual memory.

Multiprogramming leads to the concept of a *process*. Metaphorically, a process is a program's breathing air and living space—that is, a running program plus any state needed to continue running it. Time-sharing is a variation of multiprogramming that shares the CPU and memory with several interactive users at the same time, giving the illusion that all users have their own computers. Thus, at any instant it must be possible to switch from one process to another. This exchange is called a *process switch* or *context switch*.

A process must operate correctly whether it executes continuously from start to finish, or it is interrupted repeatedly and switched with other processes. The responsibility for maintaining correct process behavior is shared by designers of the computer and the operating system. The computer designer must ensure that the CPU portion of the process state can be saved and restored. The operating system designer must guarantee that processes do not interfere with each others' computations.

The safest way to protect the state of one process from another would be to copy the current information to disk. However, a process switch would then take seconds—far too long for a time-sharing environment.

This problem is solved by operating systems partitioning main memory so that several different processes have their state in memory at the same time. This division means that the operating system designer needs help from the computer designer to provide protection so that one process cannot modify another. Besides protection, the computers also provide for sharing of code and data between processes, to allow communication between processes or to save memory by reducing the number of copies of identical information.

Protecting Processes

The simplest protection mechanism is a pair of registers that checks every address to be sure that it falls between the two limits, traditionally called *base* and *bound*. An address is valid if

$$\text{Base} \leq \text{Address} \leq \text{Bound}$$

In some systems, the address is considered an unsigned number that is always added to the base, so the limit test is just

$$(\text{Base} + \text{Address}) \leq \text{Bound}$$

If user processes are allowed to change the base and bounds registers, then users can't be protected from each other. The operating system, however, must be able to change the registers so that it can switch processes. Hence, the computer designer has three more responsibilities in helping the operating system designer protect processes from each other:

1. Provide at least two modes, indicating whether the running process is a user process or an operating system process. This latter process is sometimes called a *kernel* process, a *supervisor* process, or an *executive* process.

2. Provide a portion of the CPU state that a user process can use but not write. This state includes the base/bound registers, a user/supervisor mode bit(s), and the exception enable/disable bit. Users are prevented from writing this state because the operating system cannot control user processes if users can change the address range checks, give themselves supervisor privileges, or disable exceptions.

3. Provide mechanisms whereby the CPU can go from user mode to supervisor mode and vice versa. The first direction is typically accomplished by a *system call,* implemented as a special instruction that transfers control to a dedicated location in supervisor code space. The PC is saved from the point of the system call, and the CPU is placed in supervisor mode. The return to user mode is like a subroutine return that restores the previous user/supervisor mode.

Base and bound constitute the minimum protection system, while virtual memory offers a more fine-grained alternative to this simple model. As we have seen, the CPU address must be mapped from virtual to physical address. This mapping provides the opportunity for the hardware to check further for errors in the program or to protect processes from each other. The simplest way of doing this is to add permission flags to each page or segment. For example, since few programs today intentionally modify their own code, an operating system can detect accidental writes to code by offering read-only protection to pages. This page-level protection can be extended by adding user/kernel protection to prevent a user program from trying to access pages that belong to the kernel. As long as the CPU provides a read/write signal and a user/kernel signal, it is easy for the address translation hardware to detect stray memory accesses before they can do damage. Such reckless behavior simply interrupts the CPU and invokes the operating system.

Processes are thus protected from one another by having their own page tables, each pointing to distinct pages of memory. Obviously, user programs must be prevented from modifying their page tables or protection would be circumvented.

Protection can be escalated, depending on the apprehension of the computer designer or the purchaser. *Rings* added to the CPU protection structure expand memory access protection from two levels (user and kernel) to many more. Like a military classification system of top secret, secret, confidential, and unclassified, concentric rings of security levels allow the most trusted to access anything, the second most trusted to access everything except the innermost level, and so on. The "civilian" programs are the least trusted and, hence, have the most limited range of accesses. There may also be restrictions on what pieces of memory can contain code—execute protection—and even on the entrance point between the levels. The Intel Pentium protection structure, which uses rings, is described later in this section. It is not clear whether rings are an improvement in practice over the simple system of user and kernel modes.

As the designer's apprehension escalates to trepidation, these simple rings may not suffice. Restricting the freedom given a program in the inner sanctum requires a new classification system. Instead of a military model, the analogy of this system is to keys and locks: A program can't unlock access to the data unless it has the key. For these keys, or *capabilities*, to be useful, the hardware and operating system must be able to explicitly pass them from one program to another without allowing a program itself to forge them. Such checking requires a great deal of hardware support if time for checking keys is to be kept low.

A Paged Virtual Memory Example: The Alpha Memory Management and the 21264 TLB

The Alpha architecture uses a combination of segmentation and paging, providing protection while minimizing page table size. With 48-bit virtual addresses, the 64-bit address space is first divided into three segments: *seg0* (bits 63–47 = 0 . . . 00), *kseg* (bits 63–46 = 0 . . . 10), and *seg1* (bits 63–46 = 1 . . . 11). kseg is reserved for the operating system kernel, has uniform protection for the whole space, and does not use memory management. User processes use seg0, which is mapped into pages with individual protection. Figure 5.38 shows the layout of seg0 and seg1. seg0 grows from address 0 upward, while seg1 grows downward to 0. Many systems today use some such combination of predivided segments and paging. This approach provides many advantages: Segmentation divides the

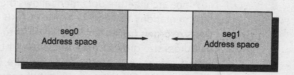

Figure 5.38 The organization of seg0 and seg1 in the Alpha. User processes live in seg0, while seg1 is used for portions of the page tables. seg0 includes a downward-growing stack, text, and data and an upward-growing heap.

address space and conserves page table space, while paging provides virtual memory, relocation, and protection.

Even with this division, the size of page tables for the 64-bit address space is alarming. Hence, the Alpha uses a three-level hierarchical page table to map the address space to keep the size reasonable. Figure 5.39 shows address translation in the Alpha. The addresses for each of these page tables come from three "level" fields, labeled level1, level2, and level3. Address translation starts with adding the level1 address field to the page table base register and then reading memory

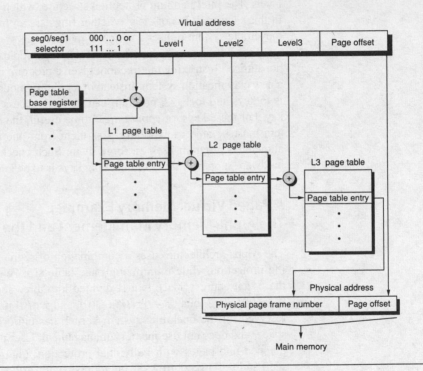

Figure 5.39 The mapping of an Alpha virtual address. The 21264's virtual memory implementation with three page table levels supports an effective physical address size of 41 bits (allowing access up to 2^{40} bytes of memory and 2^{40} I/O addresses). Each page table is exactly one page long, so each level field is n bits wide, where 2^n = page size/8. The Alpha architecture document allows the page size to grow from 8 KB in the current implementations to 16 KB, 32 KB, or 64 KB in the future. The virtual address for each page size grows from the original 43 bits to 47, 51, or 55 bits, and the maximum physical address size grows from the current 41 bits to 45, 47, or 48 bits. The 21264 also can support a four-level page table structure (with a level 0 page table field in virtual address bits 43–52) that can allow full access to its 44-bit physical address and 48-bit virtual address while keeping page sizes to 8 KB. That mode is not depicted here. In addition, the size depends on the operating system. VMS does not require kseg like UNIX does, so VMS could reach the entire 44-bit physical address space with three-level page tables. The 41-bit physical address restriction comes from the fact that some operating systems need the kseg section.

from this location to get the base of the second-level page table. The level2 address field is in turn added to this newly fetched address, and memory is accessed again to determine the base of the third page table. The level3 address field is added to this base address, and memory is read using this sum to (finally) get the physical address of the page being referenced. This address is concatenated with the page offset to get the full physical address. Each page table in the Alpha architecture is constrained to fit within a single page. The first three levels (0, 1, and 2) use physical addresses that need no further translation, but level3 is mapped virtually. These normally hit the TLB, but if not, the table is accessed a second time with physical addresses.

The Alpha uses a 64-bit PTE in each of these page tables. The first 32 bits contain the physical page frame number, and the other half includes the following five protection fields:

■ *Valid*—Says that the page frame number is valid for hardware translation

■ *User read enable*—Allows user programs to read data within this page

■ *Kernel read enable*—Allows the kernel to read data within this page

■ *User write enable*—Allows user programs to write data within this page

■ *Kernel write enable*—Allows the kernel to write data within this page

In addition, the PTE has fields reserved for systems software to use as it pleases. Since the Alpha goes through three levels of tables on a TLB miss, there are three potential places to check protection restrictions. The Alpha obeys only the bottom-level PTE, checking the others only to be sure the valid bit is set.

Since the PTEs are 8 bytes long, the page tables are exactly one page long, and the Alpha 21264 has 8 KB pages, each page table has 1024 PTEs. Each of the three level fields are 10 bits long and the page offset is 13 bits. This derivation leaves $64 - (3 \times 10 + 13)$ or 21 bits to be defined. If this is a seg0 address, the most-significant bit of the level 1 field is a 0, and for seg1 the two most-significant bits of the level 1 field are 11_{two}. Alpha requires all bits to the left of the level 1 field to be identical. For seg0 these 21 bits are all zeros, and for seg1 they are all ones. This restriction means the 21264 virtual addresses are really much shorter than the full 64 bits found in registers.

The maximum virtual address and physical address is then tied to the page size. The original architecture document allows for the Alpha to expand the minimum page size from 8 KB up to 64 KB, thereby increasing the virtual address to $3 \times 13 + 16$ or 55 bits and the maximum physical address to $32 + 16$ or 48 bits. In fact, the upcoming 21364 supports both. It will be interesting to see whether or not operating systems accommodate such expansion plans.

Although we have explained translation of legal addresses, what prevents the user from creating illegal address translations and getting into mischief? The page tables themselves are protected from being written by user programs. Thus, the user can try any virtual address, but by controlling the page table entries the operating system controls what physical memory is accessed. Sharing of memory

Parameter	Description
Block size	1 PTE (8 bytes)
Hit time	1 clock cycle
Miss penalty (average)	20 clock cycles
TLB size	same for instruction and data TLBs: 128 PTEs per TLB, each of which can map 1, 8, 64, or 512 pages
Block selection	round-robin
Write strategy	(not applicable)
Block placement	fully associative

Figure 5.40 Memory hierarchy parameters of the Alpha 21264 TLB.

between processes is accomplished by having a page table entry in each address space point to the same physical memory page.

The Alpha 21264 employs two TLBs to reduce address translation time, one for instruction accesses and another for data accesses. Figure 5.40 shows the important parameters. The Alpha allows the operating system to tell the TLB that contiguous sequences of pages can act as one: The options are 8, 64, and 512 times the minimum page size. Thus, the variable page size of a PTE mapping makes the match more challenging, as the size of the space being mapped in the PTE also must be checked to determine the match. Figure 5.36 describes the data TLB.

Memory management in the Alpha 21264 is typical of most desktop or server computers today, relying on page-level address translation and correct operation of the operating system to provide safety to multiple processes sharing the computer. In the next subsection we see a protection scheme for individuals who want to trust the operating system as little as possible.

A Segmented Virtual Memory Example: Protection in the Intel Pentium

The second system is the most dangerous system a man ever designs. . . . The general tendency is to over-design the second system, using all the ideas and frills that were cautiously sidetracked on the first one.

F. P. Brooks, Jr.
The Mythical Man-Month (1975)

The original 8086 used segments for addressing, yet it provided nothing for virtual memory or for protection. Segments had base registers but no bound registers and no access checks, and before a segment register could be loaded the corresponding segment had to be in physical memory. Intel's dedication to virtual memory and protection is evident in the successors to the 8086 (today called IA-32), with a few fields extended to support larger addresses. This protection scheme is elaborate, with many details carefully designed to try to avoid security loopholes. The next few pages highlight a few of the Intel safeguards; if you find the reading difficult, imagine the difficulty of implementing them!

The first enhancement is to double the traditional two-level protection model: the Pentium has four levels of protection. The innermost level (0) corresponds to Alpha kernel mode and the outermost level (3) corresponds to Alpha user mode. The IA-32 has separate stacks for each level to avoid security breaches between the levels. There are also data structures analogous to Alpha page tables that contain the physical addresses for segments, as well as a list of checks to be made on translated addresses.

The Intel designers did not stop there. The IA-32 divides the address space, allowing both the operating system and the user access to the full space. The IA-32 user can call an operating system routine in this space and even pass parameters to it while retaining full protection. This safe call is not a trivial action, since the stack for the operating system is different from the user's stack. Moreover, the IA-32 allows the operating system to maintain the protection level of the *called* routine for the parameters that are passed to it. This potential loophole in protection is prevented by not allowing the user process to ask the operating system to access something indirectly that it would not have been able to access itself. (Such security loopholes are called *Trojan horses*.)

The Intel designers were guided by the principle of trusting the operating system as little as possible, while supporting sharing and protection. As an example of the use of such protected sharing, suppose a payroll program writes checks and also updates the year-to-date information on total salary and benefits payments. Thus, we want to give the program the ability to read the salary and year-to-date information, and modify the year-to-date information but not the salary. We will see the mechanism to support such features shortly. In the rest of this subsection, we will look at the big picture of the IA-32 protection and examine its motivation.

Adding Bounds Checking and Memory Mapping

The first step in enhancing the Intel processor was getting the segmented addressing to check bounds as well as supply a base. Rather than a base address, as in the 8086, segment registers in the IA-32 contain an index to a virtual memory data structure called a *descriptor table*. Descriptor tables play the role of page tables in the Alpha. On the IA-32 the equivalent of a page table entry is a *segment descriptor*. It contains fields found in PTEs:

- *Present bit*—Equivalent to the PTE valid bit, used to indicate this is a valid translation

- *Base field*—Equivalent to a page frame address, containing the physical address of the first byte of the segment

- *Access bit*—Like the reference bit or use bit in some architectures that is helpful for replacement algorithms

- *Attributes field*—Specifies the valid operations and protection levels for operations that use this segment

There is also a *limit field,* not found in paged systems, which establishes the upper bound of valid offsets for this segment. Figure 5.41 shows examples of IA-32 segment descriptors.

IA-32 provides an optional paging system in addition to this segmented addressing. The upper portion of the 32-bit address selects the segment descriptor, and the middle portion is an index into the page table selected by the descriptor. We describe below the protection system that does not rely on paging.

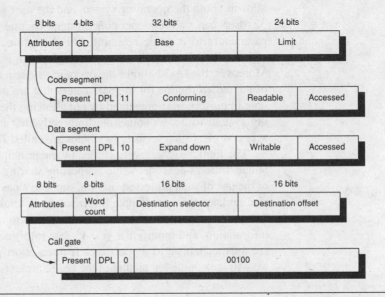

Figure 5.41 The IA-32 segment descriptors are distinguished by bits in the attributes field. *Base, limit, present, readable,* and *writable* are all self-explanatory. D gives the default addressing size of the instructions: 16 bits or 32 bits. G gives the granularity of the segment limit: 0 means in bytes and 1 means in 4 KB pages. G is set to 1 when paging is turned on to set the size of the page tables. DPL means *descriptor privilege level*—this is checked against the code privilege level to see if the access will be allowed. *Conforming* says the code takes on the privilege level of the code being called rather than the privilege level of the caller; it is used for library routines. The *expand-down field* flips the check to let the base field be the high-water mark and the limit field be the low-water mark. As you might expect, this is used for stack segments that grow down. *Word count* controls the number of words copied from the current stack to the new stack on a call gate. The other two fields of the call gate descriptor, *destination selector* and *destination offset,* select the descriptor of the destination of the call and the offset into it, respectively. There are many more than these three segment descriptors in the IA-32 protection model.

Adding Sharing and Protection

To provide for protected sharing, half of the address space is shared by all processes and half is unique to each process, called *global address space* and *local address space,* respectively. Each half is given a descriptor table with the appropriate name. A descriptor pointing to a shared segment is placed in the global descriptor table, while a descriptor for a private segment is placed in the local descriptor table.

A program loads an IA-32 segment register with an index to the table *and* a bit saying which table it desires. The operation is checked according to the attributes in the descriptor, the physical address being formed by adding the offset in the CPU to the base in the descriptor, provided the offset is less than the limit field. Every segment descriptor has a separate 2-bit field to give the legal access level of this segment. A violation occurs only if the program tries to use a segment with a lower protection level in the segment descriptor.

We can now show how to invoke the payroll program mentioned above to update the year-to-date information without allowing it to update salaries. The program could be given a descriptor to the information that has the writable field clear, meaning it can read but not write the data. A trusted program can then be supplied that will only write the year-to-date information. It is given a descriptor with the writable field set (Figure 5.41). The payroll program invokes the trusted code using a code segment descriptor with the conforming field set. This setting means the called program takes on the privilege level of the code being called rather than the privilege level of the caller. Hence, the payroll program can read the salaries and call a trusted program to update the year-to-date totals, yet the payroll program cannot modify the salaries. If a Trojan horse exists in this system, to be effective it must be located in the trusted code whose only job is to update the year-to-date information. The argument for this style of protection is that limiting the scope of the vulnerability enhances security.

Adding Safe Calls from User to OS Gates and Inheriting Protection Level for Parameters

Allowing the user to jump into the operating system is a bold step. How, then, can a hardware designer increase the chances of a safe system without trusting the operating system or any other piece of code? The IA-32 approach is to restrict where the user can enter a piece of code, to safely place parameters on the proper stack, and to make sure the user parameters don't get the protection level of the called code.

To restrict entry into others' code, the IA-32 provides a special segment descriptor, or *call gate,* identified by a bit in the attributes field. Unlike other descriptors, call gates are full physical addresses of an object in memory; the offset supplied by the CPU is ignored. As stated above, their purpose is to prevent the user from randomly jumping anywhere into a protected or more privileged code segment. In our programming example, this means the only place the payroll program can invoke the trusted code is at the proper boundary. This restriction is needed to make conforming segments work as intended.

What happens if caller and callee are "mutually suspicious," so that neither trusts the other? The solution is found in the word count field in the bottom descriptor in Figure 5.41. When a call instruction invokes a call gate descriptor, the descriptor copies the number of words specified in the descriptor from the local stack onto the stack corresponding to the level of this segment. This copying allows the user to pass parameters by first pushing them onto the local stack. The hardware then safely transfers them onto the correct stack. A return from a call gate will pop the parameters off both stacks and copy any return values to the proper stack. Note that this model is incompatible with the current practice of passing parameters in registers.

This scheme still leaves open the potential loophole of having the operating system use the user's address, passed as parameters, with the operating system's security level, instead of with the user's level. The IA-32 solves this problem by dedicating 2 bits in every CPU segment register to the *requested protection level*. When an operating system routine is invoked, it can execute an instruction that sets this 2-bit field in all address parameters with the protection level of the user that called the routine. Thus, when these address parameters are loaded into the segment registers, they will set the requested protection level to the proper value. The IA-32 hardware then uses the requested protection level to prevent any foolishness: No segment can be accessed from the system routine using those parameters if it has a more privileged protection level than requested.

Summary: Protection on the Alpha versus the IA-32

If the IA-32 protection model looks harder to build than the Alpha model, that's because it is. This effort must be especially frustrating for the IA-32 engineers, since few customers use the elaborate protection mechanism. In addition, the fact that the protection model is a mismatch for the simple paging protection of UNIX-like systems means it will be used only by someone writing an operating system especially for this computer.

In the last edition we wondered whether the popularity of the Internet would lead to demands for increased support for security, and hence put this elaborate protection model to good use. Despite widely documented security breaches and the ubiquity of this architecture, no one has proposed a new operating system to leverage the 80x86 protection features.

5.12 Crosscutting Issues: The Design of Memory Hierarchies

This section describes four topics discussed in other chapters that are fundamental to memory hierarchy design.

Superscalar CPU and Number of Ports to the Cache

One complexity of the advanced designs of Chapters 3 and 4 is that multiple instructions can be issued within a single clock cycle. Clearly, if there is not sufficient peak bandwidth from the cache to match the peak demands of the instructions, there is little benefit to designing such parallelism in the processor. Some processors increase complexity of instruction fetch by allowing instructions to be issued to be found on any boundary instead of, say, a multiple of 4 words. As mentioned above, similar reasoning applies to CPUs that want to continue executing instructions on a cache miss: Clearly, the memory hierarchy must also be nonblocking or the CPU cannot benefit.

For example, the UltraSPARC III fetches up to four instructions per clock cycle, and executes up to four, with up to two being loads or stores. Hence, the instruction cache must deliver 128 bits per clock cycle and the data cache must support two 64-bit accesses per clock cycle.

Speculative Execution and the Memory System

Inherent in CPUs that support speculative execution or conditional instructions is the possibility of generating invalid addresses that would not occur without speculative execution. Not only would this be incorrect behavior if exceptions were taken, the benefits of speculative execution would be swamped by false exception overhead. Hence, the memory system must identify speculatively executed instructions and conditionally executed instructions and suppress the corresponding exception.

By similar reasoning, we cannot allow such instructions to cause the cache to stall on a miss because again unnecessary stalls could overwhelm the benefits of speculation. Hence, these CPUs must be matched with nonblocking caches (see page 435).

In reality, the penalty of an L2 miss is so large that compilers normally only speculate on L1 misses. Figure 5.23 on page 437 shows that for some well-behaved scientific programs the compiler can sustain multiple outstanding L2 misses so as to effectively cut the L2 miss penalty. Once again, for this to work the memory system behind the cache must match the desires of the compiler in number of simultaneous memory accesses.

Combining the Instruction Cache with Instruction Fetch and Decode Mechanisms

With Moore's Law continuing to offer more transistors and increasing demands for instruction-level parallelism and clock rate, increasingly the instruction cache and first part of instruction execution are merging (see Chapter 3).

The leading example is the NetBurst microarchitecture of the Pentium 4 and its successors. Not only does it use a trace cache (see page 447), which combines branch prediction with instruction fetch, it also stores the internal RISC operations (see Chapter 3) in the trace cache. Hence, cache hits save 5 of 25 pipeline stages for decoding and translation. The downside of caching decoded instructions is impact on die size. It appears on the die that the 12000 RISC operations in the trace cache take the equivalent of 96 KB of SRAM, which suggests that the RISC operations are about 64 bits long. 80x86 instructions would surely be two to three times more efficient.

Embedded computers also have bigger instructions in the cache, but for another reason. Given the importance of code size for such applications, several keep a compressed version of the instruction in main memory and then expand to the full size in the instruction cache (see page 119 in Chapter 2.)

Embedded Computer Caches and Real-Time Performance

As mentioned before, embedded computers often are placed in real-time environments where a set of tasks must be completed every time period. In such situations performance variability is of more concern than average-case performance. Since caches were invented to improve average-case performance at the cost of greater variability, they would seem to be a problem for real-time computing.

In practice, instruction caches are widely used in embedded computers since most code has predictable behavior. Data caches then are the real issue.

To cope with that challenge, some embedded computers allow a portion of the cache to be "locked down." That is, a portion of the cache acts like a small scratchpad memory under program control. In a set-associative data cache, one block of an entry would be locked down while the others could still buffer accesses to main memory. If it was direct mapped, then every address that maps onto that locked-down block would result in a miss and later is passed to the CPU.

Embedded Computer Caches and Power

Although caches were invented to reduce memory access time, they also save power. It is much more power efficient to access on-chip memory than it is to drive the pins of the chip, drive the memory bus, activate the external memory chips, and then make the return trip.

To further improve power efficiency of caches on chip, some of the optimizations in Sections 5.4–5.7 are reoriented for power. For example, the MIPS 4300 uses way prediction to only power half of the address-checking hardware for its two-way set-associative cache.

I/O and Consistency of Cached Data

Because of caches, data can be found in memory and in the cache. As long as the CPU is the sole device changing or reading the data and the cache stands between the CPU and memory, there is little danger in the CPU seeing the old or *stale* copy. I/O devices give the opportunity for other devices to cause copies to be inconsistent or for other devices to read the stale copies. Figure 5.42 illustrates the problem, generally referred to as the *cache coherency* problem.

The question is this: Where does the I/O occur in the computer—between the I/O device and the cache or between the I/O device and main memory? If input puts data into the cache and output reads data from the cache, both I/O and the CPU see the same data, and the problem is solved. The difficulty in this approach is that it interferes with the CPU. I/O competing with the CPU for cache access will cause the CPU to stall for I/O. Input may also interfere with the cache by displacing some information with new data that is unlikely to be accessed soon. For example, on a page fault the CPU may need to access a few words in a page, but a

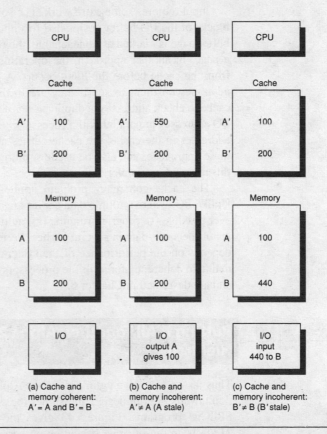

Figure 5.42 The cache coherency problem. A′ and B′ refer to the cached copies of A and B in memory. In (a) cache and main memory are in a coherent state. In (b) we assume a write-back cache when the CPU writes 550 into A. Now A′ has the value, but the value in memory has the old, stale value of 100. If an output used the value of A from memory, it would get the stale data. In (c) the I/O system inputs 440 into the memory copy of B, so now B′ in the cache has the old, stale data.

program is not likely to access every word of the page if it was loaded into the cache. Given the integration of caches onto the same integrated circuit, it is also difficult for that interface to be visible.

The goal for the I/O system in a computer with a cache is to prevent the stale-data problem while interfering with the CPU as little as possible. Many systems, therefore, prefer that I/O occur directly to main memory, with main memory acting as an I/O buffer. If a write-through cache were used, then memory would have an up-to-date copy of the information, and there would be no stale-data issue for output. (This benefit is a reason processors used write through.) Alas, write through is usually found today only in first-level data caches backed by an L2 cache that uses write back. Even embedded caches avoid write through for reasons of power efficiency.

Input requires some extra work. The software solution is to guarantee that no blocks of the I/O buffer designated for input are in the cache. In one approach, a buffer page is marked as noncachable; the operating system always inputs to such a page. In another approach, the operating system flushes the buffer addresses from the cache before the input occurs. A hardware solution is to check the I/O addresses on input to see if they are in the cache. To avoid slowing down the cache to check addresses, a duplicate set of tags may be used to allow checking of I/O addresses in parallel with processor cache accesses. If there is a match of I/O addresses in the cache, the cache entries are invalidated to avoid stale data. All these approaches can also be used for output with write-back caches. More about this is found in Chapter 7.

The cache coherency problem applies to multiprocessors as well as I/O. Unlike I/O, where multiple data copies are a rare event—one to be avoided whenever possible—a program running on multiple processors will *want* to have copies of the same data in several caches. Performance of a multiprocessor program depends on the performance of the system when sharing data. The protocols to maintain coherency for multiple processors are called *cache coherency protocols,* and are described in Chapter 6.

5.13 Putting It All Together: Alpha 21264 Memory Hierarchy

Thus far we have given glimpses of the Alpha 21264 memory hierarchy; this section unveils the full design and shows the performance of its components for the SPEC95 programs. Figure 5.43 gives the overall picture of this design. The 21264 is an out-of-order execution processor that fetches up to four instructions per clock cycle and executes up to six instructions per clock cycle. It uses either a 48-bit virtual address and a 44-bit physical address, or a 43-bit virtual address and a 41-bit physical address; thus far, all systems just use 41 bits. In either case, Alpha halves the physical address space, with the lower half for memory addresses and the upper half for I/O addresses. For the rest of this section, we assume use of the 43-bit virtual address and the 41-bit physical address.

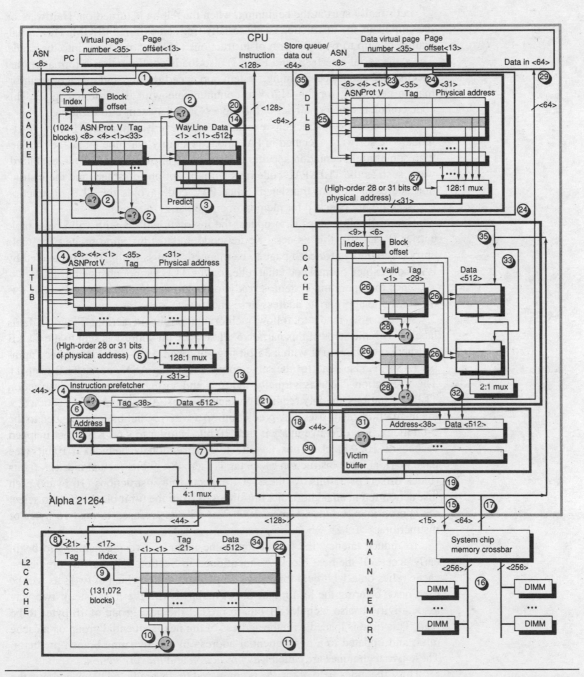

Figure 5.43 The overall picture of the Alpha 21264 memory hierarchy. Individual components can be seen in greater detail in Figures 5.7 (page 403) and 5.36 (page 466). The instruction cache is virtually indexed and tagged, but the data cache has a virtual index but physical tags. Hence, every data address must be sent to the data TLB at the same time as it is sent to the data cache. Both the instruction and data TLBs have 128 entries. Each TLB entry can map a page of size 8 KB, 64 KB, 512 KB, or 4 MB. The 21264 supports a 48-bit or 43-bit virtual address and a 44-bit or 41-bit physical address.

Let's really start at the beginning, when the Alpha is turned on. Hardware on the chip loads the instruction cache serially from an external PROM. This initialization fills up to 64 KB worth of instructions (16K instructions) into the cache. The same serial interface (and PROM) also loads configuration information that specifies L2 cache speed/timing, system port speed/timing, and much other information necessary for the 21264 to communicate with the external logic. This code completes the remainder of the processor and system initialization.

The preloaded instructions execute in privileged architecture library (PAL) mode. The software executed in PAL mode is simply machine language routines with some implementation-specific extensions to allow access to low-level hardware, such as the TLB. PAL code runs with exceptions disabled, and the instruction addresses are not translated. Since PAL code avoids the TLB, instruction accesses are not checked for memory management violations.

One of the first steps is to update the instruction TLB with valid page table entries (PTEs) for this process. Kernel code updates the appropriate page table entry (in memory) for each page to be mapped. A miss in the TLB is handled by PAL code, since normal code that relies on the TLB cannot change the TLB.

Once the operating system is ready to begin executing a user process, it sets the PC to the appropriate address in segment seg0.

We are now ready to follow memory hierarchy in action: Figure 5.43 is labeled with the steps of this narrative. First, a 12-bit address is sent to the 64 KB instruction cache, along with a 35-bit page number. An 8-bit address space number (ASN) is also sent, for the same purpose as using ASNs in the TLB (step 1). The instruction cache is virtually indexed and virtually tagged, so instruction TLB translations are only required on cache misses. As mentioned in Section 5.5, the instruction cache uses way prediction, so a way-predict bit is prepended to the 9-bit index. The effective index is then 10 bits, similar to a 64 KB direct-mapped cache with 1024 blocks. Thus, the effective instruction cache index is 10 bits (see page 404), and the instruction cache tag is then 48 – 9 bits (actual index) – 6 bits (block offset) or 33 bits. As the 21264 expects four instructions (16 bytes) each instruction fetch, an additional 2 bits are used from the 6-bit block offset to select the appropriate 16 bytes. Hence, 10 + 2 or 12 bits are used to read 16 bytes of instructions.

To reduce latency, the instruction cache includes two mechanisms to begin early access of the next block. As mentioned in Section 5.5, the way-predicting cache relies on a 1-bit field for every 16 bytes to predict which of two sets will be used next, offering the hit time of direct mapped with the miss rate of two-way associativity. It also includes 11 bits to predict the next group of 16 bytes to be read. This field is loaded with the address of the next sequential group on a cache miss, and updated to a nonsequential address by the dynamic branch predictor. These two techniques are called *way prediction* and *line prediction*.

Thus, the index field of the PC is compared to the predicted block address, the tag field of the PC is compared to the address from the tag portion of the cache, and the 8-bit process ASN to the tag ASN field (step 2). The valid bit is also checked. If any field has the wrong value, it is a miss. On a hit in the instruction cache, the proper fetch block is supplied, and the next way and line prediction is loaded to read the next block (step 3). There is also a protection field in the tag, to ensure that instruction fetch does not violate protection barriers. The instruction stream access is now done.

An instruction cache miss causes a simultaneous check of the instruction TLB and the instruction prefetcher (step 4). The fully associative TLB simultaneously searches all 128 entries to find a match between the address and a valid PTE (step 5). In addition to translating the address, the TLB checks to see if the PTE demands that this access result in an exception and if the address space number of the processor matches the address space number in the field. An exception might occur either if this access violates the protection on the page or if the page is not in main memory. If the desired instruction address is found in the instruction prefetcher (step 6), the instructions are (eventually) supplied directly by the prefetcher (step 7). Otherwise, if there is no TLB exception, an access to the second-level cache is started (step 8).

In the case of a complete miss, the second-level cache continues trying to fetch the block. The 21264 microprocessor is designed to work with direct-mapped second-level caches from 1 MB to 16 MB. For this section we use the memory system of the 667 MHz Compaq AlphaServer ES40, a shared-memory system with from one to four processors. It has a 444 MHz, 8 MB direct-mapped second-level cache. (The data rate is 444 MHz; the L2 SRAM parts use the double data rate technique of DRAMs, so they are clocked at only half that rate.) The L2 index is

$$2^{\text{Index}} = \frac{\text{Cache size}}{\text{Block size} \times \text{Set associativity}} = \frac{8192\text{K}}{64 \times 1} = 128\text{K} = 2^{17}$$

so the 35-bit block address (41-bit physical address – 6-bit block offset) is divided into an 18-bit tag and a 17-bit index (step 9). The cache controller reads the tag from that index, and if it matches and is valid (step 10), it returns the critical 16 bytes (step 11), with the remaining 48 bytes of the cache block supplied 16 bytes per 2.25 ns. The 21264 L2 interface does not require that the L2 cache clock be an integer multiple of the processor clock, so it can be loaded in faster than the 3.00 ns that you might expect from a 667 MHz processor. At the same time, a request is made for the next sequential 64-byte block (step 12), which is loaded into the instruction prefetcher in the next 6 clock cycles (step 13). Each miss can cause a prefetch of up to four cache blocks. An instruction cache miss costs approximately 15 CPU cycles (22 ns), depending on clock alignments.

By the way, the instruction prefetcher does not rely on the TLB for address translation. It simply increments the physical address of the miss by 64 bytes, checking to make sure that the new address is within the same page. If the incremented address crosses a page boundary, then the prefetch is suppressed. To save time, the prefetched instructions are passed around the CPU and then written to the instruction cache while the instructions execute in the CPU (step 14).

If the instruction is not found in the secondary cache, the physical address command is sent to the ES40 system chip set via four consecutive transfer cycles on a narrow, 15-bit outbound address bus (step 15). The address and command use the address bus for 8 CPU cycles. The ES40 connects the microprocessor to memory via a crossbar to one of two 256-bit memory buses to service the request (step 16). Each bus contains a variable number of DIMMs. The size and number of DIMMs can vary to give a total of 32 GB of memory in the 667 MHz ES40. Since the 21264 provides single error correction/double error detection checking on data cache (see Section 5.15), L2 cache, buses, and main memory, the data buses actually include an additional 32 bits for ECC bits.

Although the crossbar has two 256-bit buses, the path to the microprocessor is much narrower—64 data bits. Thus, the 21264 has two off-chip paths: 128 data bits for the L2 cache and 64 data bits for the memory crossbar. Separate paths allow a point-to-point connection and hence a high clock rate interface for both the L2 cache and the crossbar.

The total latency of the instruction miss that is serviced by main memory is approximately 130 CPU cycles for the critical instructions. The system logic fills the remainder of the 64-byte cache block at a rate of 8 bytes per 2 CPU cycles (step 17).

Since the second-level cache is a write-back cache, any miss can lead to an old block being written back to memory. The 21264 places this "victim" block into a victim file (step 18), as it does with a victim dirty block in the data cache, to get out of the way of new data when the new cache reference determined first read the L2 cache, that is, the original instruction fetch read that missed (step 8). The 21264 sends the address of the victim out the system address bus following the address of the new request (step 19). The system chip set later extracts the victim data and writes it to the memory DIMMs.

The new data are loaded into the instruction cache as soon as they arrive (step 20). It also goes into a (L1) victim buffer (step 21) and is later written to the L2 cache (step 22). The victim buffer is of size 8, so many victims can be queued before being written back either to the L2 or to memory. The 21264 can also manage up to 8 simultaneous cache block misses, allowing it to hit under 8 misses as described in Section 5.4.

If this initial instruction is a load, the data address is also sent to the data cache. It is 64 KB, two-way set associative, and write back with a 64-byte block size. Unlike the instruction cache, the data cache is virtually indexed and *physically* tagged. Thus, the page frame of the instruction's data address is sent to the data TLB (step 23) at the same time the 9-bit index (plus an additional 3 bits to select the appropriate 8 bytes) from the virtual address is sent to the data cache (step 24). The data TLB is a fully associative cache containing 128 PTEs (step 25), each of which represents page sizes from 8 KB to 4 MB. A TLB miss will trap to PAL code to load the valid PTE for this address. In the worst case, the page is not in memory, and the operating system gets the page from disk, just as before. Since millions of instructions could execute during a page fault, the operating system will swap in another process if one is waiting to run.

The index field of the address is sent to both sets of the data cache (step 26). Assuming that we have a valid PTE in the data TLB (step 27), the two tags and valid bits are compared to the physical page frame (step 28), with a match sending the desired 8 bytes to the CPU (step 29). A miss goes to the second-level cache, which proceeds similarly to an instruction miss (step 30), except that it must check the victim buffer first to be sure the block is not there (step 31).

As mentioned in Section 5.7, the data cache can be virtually addressed and physically tagged. On a miss, the cache controller must check for a synonym (two different virtual addresses that reference the same physical address). Hence, the data cache tags are examined in parallel with the L2 cache tags during an L2 lookup. As the minimum page size is 8 KB or 13 bits and the cache index plus block offset is 15 bits, the cache must check 2^2 or 4 blocks per set for synonyms. If it finds a synonym, the offending block is invalidated. This guarantees that a cache block can reside in one of the eight possible data cache locations at any given time.

A write-back victim can be produced on a data cache miss. The victim data are extracted from the data cache simultaneously with the fill of the data cache with the L2 data and sent to the victim buffer (step 32).

In the case of an L2 miss, the fill data from the system is written directly into the (L1) data cache (step 33). The L2 is written only with L1 victims (step 34). They appear either because they were modified by the CPU or because they had been loaded from memory directly into the data cache but not yet written into the L2 cache.

Suppose the instruction is a store instead of a load. When the store issues, it does a data cache lookup just like a load. A store miss causes the block to be filled into the data cache very much as with a load miss. The store does not update the cache until later, after it is known to be nonspeculative. During this time the store resides in a store queue, part of the out-of-order control mechanism of the CPU. Stores write from the store queue into the data cache on idle cache cycles (step 35). The data cache is ECC protected, so a read-modify-write operation is required to update the data cache on stores.

Performance of the 21264 Memory Hierarchy

How well does the 21264 work? The bottom line in this evaluation is the percentage of time lost while the CPU is waiting for the memory hierarchy. The major components are the instruction and data caches, instruction and data TLBs, and the secondary cache. Alas, in an out-of-order execution processor like the 21264, it is very hard to isolate the time waiting for memory, since a memory stall for one instruction may be completely hidden by successful completion of a later instruction.

How well does out-of-order perform compared with in-order? Figure 5.44 shows relative performance for SPECint2000 benchmarks for the out-of-order 21264 and its predecessor, the in-order Alpha 21164. The clock rates are similar in the figure, but differences include the on-chip caches (two 64 KB L1 caches versus two 8 KB L1 caches plus one 96 KB L2 cache). The miss rate for the 21164 on-chip L2 cache is also plotted in the figure along with the miss rate of a 1MB cache. Figure 5.44 shows that speedup generally tracks its miss rate; the higher the 21164 miss rate, the higher the speedup of the 21264 over the 21164.

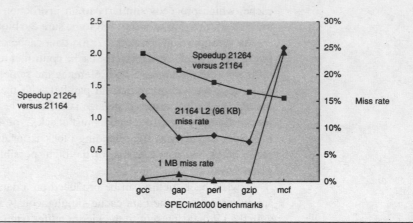

Figure 5.44 Alpha 21264/21164 performance speedup versus miss rates for SPECint2000. The left axis shows the speedup of the out-of-order 21264 is greatest with the highest miss rate of the 21164 L2 cache (right axis) as long as the access is a hit in the 21264 L2 cache. If it misses the L2 cache of the 21264, out-of-order execution is not as helpful. The 21264 is running at 500 MHz, and the earlier 21164 is running at 533 MHz.

The only exception is mcf, which is also the only program with a high miss rate for the 1 MB cache.

This result is likely explained by the 21264's ability to continue to execute during cache misses that stall the 21164 but hit in the L2 cache of the 21264. If the miss also misses in the L2 cache, then the 21264 must also stall, hence the lower speedup for mcf.

Figure 5.45 shows the CPI and various misses per 1000 instructions for a benchmark similar to TPC-C on a commercial database and the SPEC95 programs. Clearly, the SPEC95 programs do not tax the 21264 memory hierarchy, with instruction cache misses per instruction of 0.001% to 0.343% and second-level cache misses per instruction of 0.001% to 1%. The commercial benchmark does exercise the memory hierarchy more, with misses per instruction of 1.1% and 0.7%, respectively.

How do the CPIs compare to the peak rate of 0.25, or 4 instructions per clock cycle? For SPEC95 the 21264 completes almost 2 instructions per clock cycle, with an average CPI of 0.55 to 0.59. For the database benchmark, the combination of higher miss rates for caches and TLBs and a higher branch misprediction rate (not shown) yields a CPI of 2.23, or less than 1 instruction every 2 clock cycles. This factor of 4 slowdown in CPI suggests that microprocessors designed to be used in servers may see much heavier demands on the memory systems than do microprocessors for desktops.

| Program | CPI | Cache misses per 1000 instructions | | TLB misses per 1000 instructions |
		I-cache	L2 cache	I-TLB
TPC-C-like	2.23	11.15	7.30	1.21
go	0.58	0.53	0.00	0.00
m88ksim	0.38	0.16	0.04	0.01
gcc	0.63	3.43	0.25	0.30
compress	0.70	0.00	0.40	0.00
li	0.49	0.07	0.00	0.01
ijpeg	0.49	0.03	0.02	0.01
perl	0.56	1.66	0.09	0.26
vortex	0.58	1.19	0.63	1.98
Average SPECint95	0.55	0.88	0.18	0.03
tomcatv	0.52	0.01	5.16	0.12
swim	0.40	0.00	5.99	0.10
su2cor	0.59	0.03	1.64	0.11
hydro2d	0.64	0.01	0.46	0.19
mgrid	0.44	0.02	0.05	0.10
applu	0.94	0.01	10.20	0.18
turb3d	0.44	0.01	1.60	0.10
apsi	0.67	0.05	0.01	0.04
fpppp	0.52	0.13	0.00	0.00
wave5	0.74	0.07	1.72	0.89
Average SPECfp95	0.59	0.03	2.68	0.09

Figure 5.45 CPI and misses per 1000 instructions for running a TPC-C-like database workload and the SPEC95 benchmarks (see Chapter 1) on the Alpha 21264 in the Compaq ES40. In addition to the worse miss rates shown here, the TPC-C-like benchmark also has a branch misprediction rate of about 19 per 1000 instructions retired. This rate is 1.7 times worse than the average SPECint95 program and 25 times worse than the average SPECfp95. Since the 21264 uses an out-of-order instruction execution, the statistics are calculated as the number of misses per 1000 instructions successfully committed. Cvetanovic and Kessler [2000] collected these data, but unfortunately did not include miss rates of the L1 data cache or data TLB. Note that their hardware performance monitor could not isolate the benefits of successful hardware prefetching to the instruction cache. Hence, compulsory misses are likely very low.

5.14 | ### Another View: The Emotion Engine of the Sony Playstation 2

Desktop computers and servers rely on the memory hierarchy to reduce average access time to relatively static data, but there are embedded applications where data are often a continuous stream. In such applications there is still spatial locality, but temporal locality is much more limited.

To give another look at memory performance beyond the desktop, this section examines the microprocessor at the heart of the Sony Playstation 2. As, we will see, the steady stream of graphics and audio demanded by electronic games leads to a different approach to memory design. The style is high bandwidth via many dedicated independent memories.

Figure 5.46 shows the three C's for the MP3 decode kernel. Compared to the SPEC2000 results in Figure 5.15 on page 425, much smaller caches capture the misses for multimedia applications. Hence, we expect small caches.

Figure 5.47 shows a block diagram of the Sony Playstation 2 (PS2). Not surprisingly for a game machine, there are interfaces for video, sound, and a DVD player. Surprisingly, there are two standard computer I/O buses, USB and IEEE 1394, a PCMCIA slot as found in portable PCs, and a modem. These additions suggest Sony has greater plans for the PS2 beyond traditional games. Although it appears that the I/O processor (IOP) simply handles the I/O devices and the game console, it includes a 34 MHz MIPS processor that also acts as the emulation computer to run games for earlier Sony Playstations. It also connects to a standard PC audio card to provide the sound for the games.

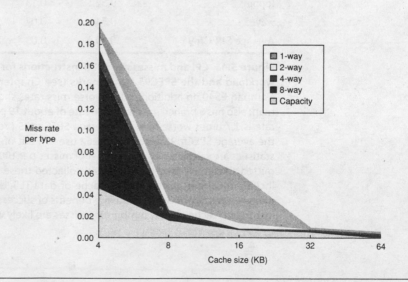

Figure 5.46 Three C's for MPEG3 decode. A two-way set-associative, 16 KB data cache has a total miss rate of 0.013, compared to 0.041 in Figure 5.14 on page 424. The compulsory misses are too small to see on the graph. (From Hughes et al. [2001].)

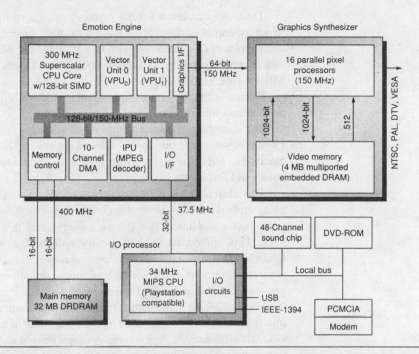

Figure 5.47 Block diagram of the Sony Playstation 2. The 10 DMA channels orchestrate the transfers between all the small memories on the chip, which when completed all head toward the Graphics Interface so as to be rendered by the Graphics Synthesizer. The Graphics Synthesizer uses DRAM on chip to provide an entire frame buffer plus graphics processors to perform the rendering desired based on the display commands given from the Emotion Engine. The embedded DRAM allows 1024-bit transfers between the pixel processors and the display buffer. The Superscalar CPU is a 64-bit MIPS III with two-instruction issue, and comes with a 2-way set-associative, 16 KB instruction cache; a 2-way set-associative, 8 KB data cache; and 16 KB of scratchpad memory. It has been extended with 128-bit SIMD instructions for multimedia applications (see Chapter 2). Vector Unit 0 is primarily a DSP-like coprocessor for the CPU (see Chapter 2), which can operate on 128-bit registers in SIMD manner between 8 bits and 32 bits per word. It has 4 KB of instruction memory and 4 KB of data memory. Vector Unit 1 has similar functions to VPU0, but it normally operates independently of the CPU and contains 16 KB of instruction memory and 16 KB of data memory. All three units can communicate over the 128-bit system bus, but there is also a 128-bit dedicated path between the CPU and VPU0 and a 128-bit dedicated path between VPU1 and the Graphics Interface. Although VPU0 and VPU1 have identical microarchitectures, the differences in memory size and units to which they have direct connections affect the roles that they take in a game. At 0.25-micron line widths, the Emotion Engine chip uses 13.5M transistors and is 225 mm^2, and the Graphics Synthesizer is 279 mm^2. To put this in perspective, the Alpha 21264 microprocessor in 0.25-micron technology is about 160 mm^2 and uses 15M transistors. (This figure is based on Figure 1 in "Sony's Emotionally Charged Chip," *Microprocessor Report* 13:5.)

Thus, one challenge for the memory system of this embedded application is to act as source or destination for the extensive number of I/O devices. The PS2 designers met this challenge with two PC800 (400 MHz) DRDRAM chips using two channels, offering 32 MB of storage and a peak memory bandwidth of 3.2 MB/sec (see Section 5.8).

What's left in the figure are basically two big chips: the Graphics Synthesizer and the Emotion Engine.

The Graphics Synthesizer takes rendering commands from the Emotion Engine in what are commonly called *display lists*. These are lists of 32-bit commands that tell the renderer what shape to use and where to place them, plus what colors and textures to fill them.

This chip also has the highest bandwidth portion of the memory system. By using embedded DRAM on the Graphics Synthesizer, the chip contains the full video buffer *and* has a 2048-bit-wide interface so that pixel filling is not a bottleneck. This embedded DRAM greatly reduces the bandwidth demands on the DRDRAM. It illustrates a common technique found in embedded applications: separate memories dedicated to individual functions to inexpensively achieve greater memory bandwidth for the entire system.

The remaining large chip is the Emotion Engine, and its job is to accept inputs from the IOP and create the display lists of a video game to enable 3D video transformations in real time. A major insight shaped the design of the Emotion Engine: Generally, in a racing car game there are foreground objects that are constantly changing and background objects that change less in reaction to the events, although the background can be most of the screen. This observation led to a split of responsibilities.

The CPU works with VPU0 as a tightly coupled coprocessor, in that every VPU0 instruction is a standard MIPS coprocessor instruction, and the addresses are generated by the MIPS CPU. VPU0 is called a vector processor, but it is similar to 128-bit SIMD extensions for multimedia found in several desktop processors (see Chapter 2).

VPU1, in contrast, fetches its own instructions and data and acts in parallel with CPU-VPU0, acting more like a traditional vector unit. With this split, the more flexible CPU-VPU0 handles the foreground action and the VPU1 handles the background. Both deposit their resulting display lists into the Graphics Interface to send the lists to the Graphics Synthesizer.

Thus, the programmers of the Emotion Engine have three processor sets to choose from to implement their programs: the traditional 64-bit MIPS architecture including a floating-point unit, the MIPS architecture extended with multimedia instructions (VPU0), and an independent vector processor (VPU1). To accelerate MPEG decoding, there is another coprocessor (Image Processing Unit) that can act independent of the other two.

With this split of function, the question then is how to connect the units together, how to make the data flow between units, and how to provide the memory bandwidth needed by all these units. As mentioned earlier, the Emotion Engine designers chose many dedicated memories. The CPU has a 16 KB scratchpad memory (SPRAM) in addition to a 16 KB instruction cache and an 8 KB data cache. VPU0 has a 4 KB instruction memory and a 4 KB data memory, and VPU1 has a 16 KB instruction memory and a 16 KB data memory. Note that these are four *memories,* not caches of a larger memory elsewhere. In each memory the latency is just 1 clock cycle. VPU1 has more memory than VPU0 because it creates the bulk of the display lists and because it largely acts independently.

The programmer organizes all memories as two double buffers, one pair for the incoming DMA data and one pair for the outgoing DMA data. The programmer then uses the various processors to transform the data from the input buffer to the output buffer. To keep the data flowing among the units, the programmer next sets up the 10 DMA channels, taking care to meet the real-time deadline for realistic animation of 15 frames per second.

Figure 5.48 shows that this organization supports two main operating modes: serial, where CPU/VPU0 acts as a preprocessor on what to give VPU1 for it to create for the Graphics Interface using the scratchpad memory as the buffer; and parallel, where both the CPU/VPU0 and VPU1 create display lists. The display lists and the Graphics Synthesizer have multiple context identifiers to distinguish the parallel display lists to produce a coherent final image.

All units in the Emotion Engine are linked by a common 150 MHz, 128-bit-wide bus. To offer greater bandwidth, there are also two dedicated buses: a 128-bit path between the CPU and VPU0 and a 128-bit path between VPU1 and the Graphics Interface. The programmer also chooses which bus to use when setting up the DMA channels.

Taking the big picture, if a server-oriented designer had been given the problem, we might see a single common bus with many local caches and cache coherent mechanisms to keep data consistent. In contrast, the Playstation 2 followed the tradition of embedded designers and has at least nine distinct memory modules. To keep the data flowing in real time from memory to the display, the PS2

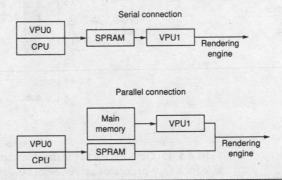

Figure 5.48 Two modes of using Emotion Engine organization. The first mode divides the work between the two units, and then allows the Graphics Interface to properly merge the display lists. The second mode uses CPU/VPU0 as a filter of what to send to VPU1, which then does all the display lists. It is up to the programmer to choose between serial and parallel data flow. SPRAM is the scratchpad memory.

uses dedicated memories, dedicated buses, and DMA channels. Coherency is the responsibility of the programmer, and given the continuous flow from main memory to the graphics interface and the real-time requirements, programmer-controlled coherency works well for this application.

5.15 Another View: The Sun Fire 6800 Server

The Sun Fire 6800 is a midrange multiprocessor server with particular attention paid to the memory system. The emphasis of this server is cost-performance for both commercial computing and running database applications such as data warehousing and data mining, as well as high-performance computing. This server also includes special features to improve availability and maintainability.

Given these goals, what should be the size of the caches? Looking at the SPEC2000 results in Figure 5.17 on page 427 suggests miss rates of 0.5% for a 1 MB data cache, with infinitesimal instruction cache miss rates at those sizes. It would seem that a 1 MB off-chip cache should be sufficient.

Commercial workloads, however, get very different results. Figure 5.49 shows the impact on the off-chip cache for an Alpha 21164 server running commercial workloads, which reveals three differences. First, unlike the results for SPEC2000, commercial workloads running database applications have significant misses just for instructions with a 1 MB cache. The reason is that the code size of commercial databases is measured in millions of lines of code, unlike any SPEC2000 benchmark. Second, note that capacity and conflict misses remain significant until the cache size becomes 4–8 MB. Even compulsory misses lead to

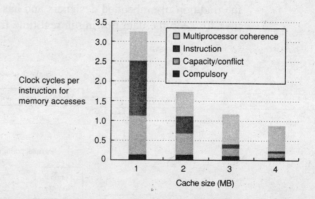

Figure 5.49 **Clock cycles per instruction for memory accesses versus off-chip cache size for a four-processor server.** Note how much higher the performance impact is for large caches than for the SPEC2000 programs in Figure 5.15 on page 425. The workload includes the Oracle commercial database engine for the online transaction-processing (OLTP) and decision support systems and the AltaVista search engine for the Web index search. These data were collected by Barroso, Gharachorloo, and Bugnion [1998] using the Alpha 21164 microprocessor.

a measurably higher CPI because servers often run many processes, which results in many context switches and thus more compulsory misses. Finally, there is a new category of misses in a multiprocessor—those due to having to keep all the caches of a multiprocessor coherent, a problem mentioned in Section 5.12. These are sometimes called *coherency misses,* adding a fourth C to our three C's model from Section 5.5. Chapter 6 explains a good deal more about coherence or sharing traffic in multiprocessors. The data suggest that commercial workloads need considerably bigger off-chip caches than does SPEC2000.

Figure 5.50 shows the essential characteristics of the Sun Fire 6800 that the designers selected. Note the 8 MB L2 cache, which is in response to the commercial needs.

The microprocessor that drives this server is the UltraSPARC III. One striking feature of the chip is the number of pins: 1368 in a Ball Grid Array. Figure 5.51 shows how one chip could use so many pins. The L2 cache bus operates at

Category	Quantity
Processors	2–24 UltraSPARC III processors
Processor clock rate	900 MHz
Pipeline	14 stages
Superscalar	4-issue, 4-way sustained
L1 I-cache	32 KB, 4-way set associative, pseudorandom replacement
L1 I-cache latency	2 clocks
L1 D-cache	64 KB, 4-way set associative; write through, no-write allocate, pseudorandom replacement
L1 D-cache latency	2 clocks
L1 I/D miss penalty	20 ns (15–18 clock cycles, depending on clock rate)
L2 cache	8 MB, direct mapped; write back, write allocate, multilevel inclusion
L2 miss penalty	220–280 ns (198–252 clock cycles, depending whether memory is local)
Write cache	2 KB, 4-way set associative, LRU, 64-byte block, no-write allocate
Prefetch cache	2 KB, 4-way set associative, LRU, 64-byte block
Block size	32 bytes
Processor address space	64 bits
Maximum memory	8 GB/processor, or up to 192 GB total
System bus, peak speed	Sun Fire Interconnect, 9.6 GB/sec
I/O cards	up to 8 66 MHz, 64-bit PCI; 24 33 MHz, 64-bit PCI
Domains	1–4
Processor power	70 W at 750 MHz
Processor package	1368 pin flip-chip ceramic Ball Grid Array
Processor technology	29M transistors (75% SRAM cache), die size is 217 mm^2; 0.15 micron, 7-layer CMOS

Figure 5.50 Technical summary of Sun Fire 6800 server and UltraSPARC III microprocessor.

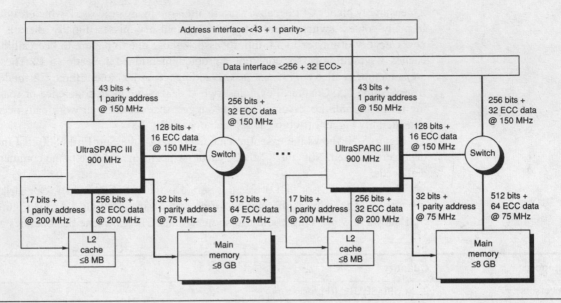

Figure 5.51 Sun Fire 6800 server block diagram. Note the large number of wide memory paths per processor. Up to 24 processors can be connected. Up to 12 share a single Sun Fire Data Interconnect. With more than 12, a second data interconnect is added. The number of separate paths to different memories are 256 data pins + 32 bits of error correction code (ECC) and 17 address bits + 1 bit parity for the off-chip L2 cache (200 MHz); 43 address pins + 1 bit of parity for addresses to external main memory; 32 address pins + 1 bit of parity for addresses to local main memory; 128 data pins + 16 bits of ECC to a data switch (150 MHz); 256 data pins + 32 bits of ECC between the data switch and the data interconnect (150 MHz); and 512 data pins + 64 bits of ECC between the data switch and local memory (75 MHz).

200 MHz, local memory at 75 MHz, and the rest operate at 150 MHz. The combination of UltraSPARC III and the data switch yields a peak bandwidth to off-chip memory of 11 GB/sec.

Note that the several wide buses include error correction bits in Figure 5.51. Error correction codes enable buses and memories to both detect and correct errors. The idea is to calculate and store parity over different subsets of the bits in the protected word. When parity does not match, it indicates an error. By looking at which of the overlapping subsets have a parity error and which don't, it is possible to determine the bit that failed. The Sun Fire ECC was also designed to detect any pair of bit errors, and also to detect if a whole DRAM chip failed, turning all the bits of an 8-bit-wide chip to 0. Such codes are generally classified as *single error correcting/double error detecting* (SEC/DED). The UltraSPARC sends these ECC bits between the memory chips and the microprocessor, so that errors that occur on the high-speed buses are also detected and corrected.

In addition to several wide buses for memory bandwidth, the designers of UltraSPARC were concerned about latency. Hence, the chip includes a DRAM controller on the chip, which they claim saved 80 ns of latency. The result is 220 ns to the local memory and 280 ns to the nonlocal memory. (This server supports nonuniform memory access shared memory, described in Chapter 6.) Since memory is connected directly to the processor to lower latency, its size is a function of the number of processors. The limit in 2001 is 8 GB per processor.

For similar latency reasons, UltraSPARC also includes the tags for the L2 cache on chip. The designers claim this saved 10 clock cycles off a miss. At a total of almost 90 KB of tags, it is comparable in size to the data cache.

The on-chip caches are both four-way set associative, with the instruction cache being 32 KB and the data cache being 64 KB. The block size for these caches is 32 bytes. To reduce latency to the data cache, it combines an address adder with the word line decoder. This combination largely eliminates the adder's latency. Compared to UltraSPARC II at the same cache size and clock rate, sum-addressed memory reduced latency from 3 to 2 clock cycles.

The L1 data cache uses write through (no-write allocate) and the L2 cache uses write back (write allocate). Both L1 caches provide parity to detect errors; since the data cache is write through, there is always a redundant copy of the data elsewhere, so parity errors only require prefetching the good data. The memory system behind the cache supports to up 15 outstanding memory accesses.

Between the two levels of cache is a 2 KB write cache. The write cache acts as a write buffer and merges writes to consecutive locations. It keeps a bit per byte to indicate if it is valid and does not read the block from the L2 cache when the block is allocated. Often the entire block is written, thereby avoiding a read access to the L2 cache. The designers claim more than 90% of the time UltraSPARC III can merge a store into an existing dirty block of the write cache. The write cache is also a convenient place to calculate ECC.

UltraSPARC III handles address translation with multiple levels of on-chip TLBs, with the smaller ones being fastest. A cache access starts with a virtual address selecting four blocks and four microtags, which checks 8 bits of the virtual address to select the set. In parallel with the cache access, the 64-bit virtual address is translated to the 43-bit physical address using two TLBs: a 16-entry fully associative cache and a 128-entry four-way set-associative cache. The physical address is then compared to the cache full tag, and only if they match is a cache hit allowed to proceed.

To get even more memory performance, UltraSPARC III also has a data prefetch cache, essentially the same as the streaming buffers described in Section 5.6. It supports up to eight prefetch requests initiated either by hardware or by software. The prefetch cache remembers the address used to prefetch the data. If a load hits in the prefetch cache, it automatically prefetches the next load address. It calculates the stride using the current address and the previous address. Each prefetch entry is 64 bytes, and it is filled in 14 clock cycles from the L2 cache. Loads from the prefetch cache complete at the rate of 2 every 3 clock cycles versus 2 every 4 clock cycles from the data cache. This multiported memory can support two 8-byte reads and one 16-byte write every clock cycle.

In addition to prefetching data, UltraSPARC III has a small instruction prefetch buffer of 32 bytes that tries to stay one block ahead of the instruction decoder. On an instruction cache miss, two blocks are requested: one for the instruction cache and one for the instruction prefetch buffer. The buffer is then used to fill the cache if a sequential access also misses. In addition to parity and ECC to help with dependability, the Sun Fire 6800 server offers up to four dynamic system domains. This option allows the computer to be divided into quarters or halves, with each piece running its own version of the operating system independently. Thus, a hardware or software failure in one piece does not affect applications running on the rest of the computer. The "dynamic" portion of the name means the reconfiguration can occur without rebooting the system.

To help diagnose problems, every UltraSPARC III has an 8-bit "back door" bus that runs independently from the main buses. If the system bus has an error, processors can still boot and run diagnostic programs over this back door bus to diagnose the problem.

Among the other availability features of the 6800 is a redundant path between the processors. Each system has two networks to connect the 24 processors together, so that if one fails, the system still works. Similarly, each Sun Fire Interconnect has two crossbar chips to link it to the processor board, so that one crossbar chip can fail and yet the board can still communicate. There are also dual redundant system controllers that monitor server operation, and so they are able to notify administrators when problems are detected. Administrators can use the controllers to remotely initiate diagnostics and corrective actions.

In summary, the Sun Fire 6800 server and its processor pay much greater attention to dependability, memory latency and bandwidth, and system scalability than do desktop computers and processors.

5.16 Fallacies and Pitfalls

As the most naturally quantitative of the computer architecture disciplines, memory hierarchy would seem to be less vulnerable to fallacies and pitfalls. Yet we were limited here not by lack of warnings, but by lack of space!

Fallacy *Predicting cache performance of one program from another.*

Figure 5.52 shows the instruction miss rates and data miss rates for three programs from the SPEC2000 benchmark suite as cache size varies. Depending on the program, the data misses per thousand instructions for a 4096 KB cache is 9, 2, or 90, and the instruction misses per thousand instructions for a 4 KB cache is 55, 19, or 0.0004. Figure 5.45 on page 489 shows that commercial programs such as databases will have significant miss rates even in an 8 MB second-level cache, which is generally not the case for the SPEC programs. Similarly, MPEG3 decode in Figure 5.46 on page 490 fits entirely in a 64 KB data cache, while SPEC doesn't get such low miss rates until 1024 KB. Clearly, generalizing cache performance from one program to another is unwise.

Pitfall *Simulating enough instructions to get accurate performance measures of the memory hierarchy.*

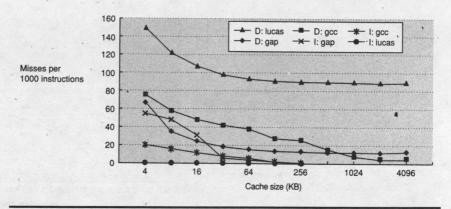

Figure 5.52 Instruction and data misses per 1000 instructions as cache size varies from 4 KB to 4096 KB. Instruction misses for gcc are 30,000 to 40,000 times larger than lucas, and conversely, data misses for lucas are 2 to 60 times larger than gcc. The programs gap, gcc, and lucas are from the SPEC2000 benchmark suite. These data are from the same experiment as in Figure 5.10.

There are really three pitfalls here. One is trying to predict performance of a large cache using a small trace. Another is that a program's locality behavior is not constant over the run of the entire program. The third is that a program's locality behavior may vary depending on the input.

Figure 5.53 shows the cumulative average instruction misses per thousand instructions for five inputs to a single SPEC2000 program. For these inputs, the average memory rate for the first 1.9 billion instructions is very different from the average miss rate for the rest of the execution.

The first edition of this book included another example of this pitfall. The compulsory miss ratios were erroneously high (e.g., 1%) because of tracing too few memory accesses. A program with a compulsory cache miss ratio of 1% running on a computer accessing memory 10 million times per second (at the time of the first edition) would access hundreds of megabytes of memory per second:

$$\frac{10,000,000 \text{ accesses}}{\text{Second}} \times \frac{0.01 \text{ misses}}{\text{Access}} \times \frac{32 \text{ bytes}}{\text{Miss}} \times \frac{60 \text{ seconds}}{\text{Minute}} = \frac{192,000,000 \text{ bytes}}{\text{Minute}}$$

Data on typical page fault rates and process sizes do not support the conclusion that memory is touched at this rate.

Pitfall *Too small an address space.*

Just five years after DEC and Carnegie Mellon University collaborated to design the new PDP-11 computer family, it was apparent that their creation had a fatal flaw. An architecture announced by IBM six years *before* the PDP-11 was still thriving, with minor modifications, 25 years later. And the DEC VAX, criticized for including unnecessary functions, sold millions of units after the PDP-11 went out of production. Why?

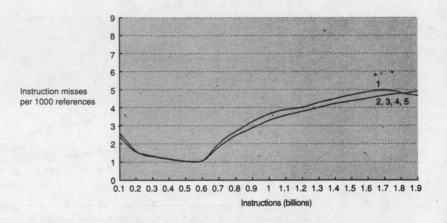

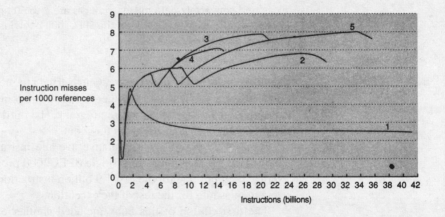

Figure 5.53 Instruction misses per 1000 references for five inputs to perl benchmark from SPEC2000. There is little variation in misses and little difference between the five inputs for the first 1.9 billion instructions, but running to completion shows how misses vary over the life of the program and how they depend on the input. The top graph shows the running average misses for the first 1.9 billion instructions, which starts at about 2.5 and ends at about 4.7 misses per 1000 references for all five inputs. The bottom graph shows the running average misses to run to completion, which takes 16–41 billion instructions depending on the input. After the first 1.9 billion instructions, the misses per 1000 references vary from 2.4 to 7.9 depending on the input. The simulations were for the Alpha processor using separate L1 caches for instructions and data, each 2-way 64 KB with LRU, and a unified 1 MB direct-mapped L2 cache.

The fatal flaw of the PDP-11 was the size of its addresses (16 bits) as compared to the address sizes of the IBM 360 (24 to 31 bits) and the VAX (32 bits). Address size limits the program length, since the size of a program and the amount of data needed by the program must be less than $2^{Address\ size}$ The reason the address size is so hard to change is that it determines the minimum width of anything that can contain an address: PC, register, memory word, and effective-address arithmetic. If there is no plan to expand the address from the start, then the chances of successfully changing address size are so slim that it normally means the end of that computer family. Bell and Strecker [1976] put it like this:

> There is only one mistake that can be made in computer design that is difficult to recover from—not having enough address bits for memory addressing and memory management. The PDP-11 followed the unbroken tradition of nearly every known computer. [p. 2]

A partial list of successful computers that eventually starved to death for lack of address bits includes the PDP-8, PDP-10, PDP-11, Intel 8080, Intel 8086, Intel 80186, Intel 80286, Motorola 6800, AMI 6502, Zilog Z80, CRAY-1, and CRAY X-MP.

Even the venerable 80x86 line is showing danger signs, with Intel justifying migration to IA-64 in part to provide a larger flat address space than 32 bits, and AMD proposing its own 64-bit address extension called x86-64.

As we expected, by this third edition every desktop and server microprocessor manufacturer offers computers with 64-bit flat addresses. DSPs and embedded applications, however, may yet be condemned to repeat history as memories grow and desired functions multiply.

Pitfall   *Emphasizing memory bandwidth in DRAMs versus memory latency.*

Direct RDRAM offers up to 1.6 GB/sec of bandwidth from a single DRAM. When announced, the peak bandwidth was eight times faster than individual conventional SDRAM chips.

PCs do most memory accesses through a two-level cache hierarchy, so it is unclear how much benefit is gained from high bandwidth without also improving memory latency. According to Pabst [2000], when comparing PCs with 400 MHz DRDRAMs to PCs with 133 MHz SDRAM, for office applications they had identical average performance. For games, DRDRAM was 1% to 2% faster. For professional graphics applications, it was 10% to 15% faster. The tests used an 800 MHz Pentium III (which integrates a 256 KB L2 cache), chip sets that support a 133 MHz system bus, and 128 MB of main memory.

One measure of the RDRAM cost is about a 20% larger die for the same capacity compared to SDRAM. DRAM designers use redundant rows and columns to significantly improve yield on the memory portion of the DRAM, so a much larger interface might have a disproportionate impact on yield. Yields are a closely guarded secret, but prices are not. Figure 5.54 compares prices of various versions of DRAM, in memory modules and in systems. Using this evaluation, in 2000 the price is about a factor of 2 to 3 higher for RDRAM.

RDRAM is at its strongest in small memory systems that need high bandwidth. The low cost of the Sony Playstation 2, for example, limits the amount of memory in the system to just two chips, yet its graphics has an appetite for high memory bandwidth. RDRAM is at its weakest in servers, where the large number of DRAM chips needed in even the minimal memory configuration makes it easy to achieve high bandwidth with ordinary DRAMs.

	Modules		Dell XPS PCs					
ECC?	No ECC	ECC	No ECC			ECC		
Label	DIMM	RIMM	A	B	B – A	C	D	D – C
Memory or system?	DRAM		System		DRAM	System		DRAM
Memory size (MB)	256	256	128	512	384	128	512	384
SDRAM PC100	$175	$259	$1519	$2139	$620	$1559	$2269	$710
DRDRAM PC700	$725	$826	$1689	$3009	$1320	$1789	$3409	$1620
Price ratio DRDRAM/SDRAM	4.1	3.2	1.1	1.4	2.1	1.1	1.5	2.3

Figure 5.54 Comparison of price of SDRAM versus DRDRAM in memory modules and in systems in 2000. DRDRAM memory modules cost about a factor of 4 more without ECC and 3 more with ECC. Looking at the cost of the extra 384 MB of memory in PCs in going from 128 MB to 512 MB, DRDRAM costs twice as much. Except for differences in bandwidths of the DRAMs, the systems were identically configured. The Dell XPS PCs were identical except for memory: 800 MHz Pentium III, 20 GB ATA disk, 48X CD-ROM, 17-inch monitor, and Microsoft Windows 95/98 and Office 98. The module prices were the lowest found at pricewatch.com in June 2000. By September 2001 PC800 DRDRAM cost $76 for 256 MB, while PC100 to PC150 SDRAM cost $15 to $23, or about a factor of 3.3 to 5.0 less expensive. (In September 2001 Dell did not offer systems whose only difference was type of DRAMs; hence we stick with the comparison from 2000.)

Pitfall *Delivering high memory bandwidth in a cache-based system.*

Caches help with average cache memory latency but may not deliver high memory bandwidth to an application that needs it. Figure 5.55 shows the top 10 results from the Stream benchmark as of 2001, which measures bandwidth to copy data [McCalpin 2001]. The NEC SX 5 offers up to 16,384 SDRAM memory banks to achieve its top ranking.

Only three computers rely on data caches, and they are the three slowest of the top 10, about a factor of a hundred slower than the fastest processor. Stated another way, a processor from 1988—the Cray Y-MP—still has a factor of 10 in memory bandwidth advantage over cache-based processors from 2001.

Pitfall *Ignoring the impact of the operating system on the performance of the memory hierarchy.*

Figure 5.56 shows the memory stall time due to the operating system spent on three large workloads. About 25% of the stall time is either spent in misses in the operating system or results from misses in the application programs because of interference with the operating system.

Pitfall *Relying on the operating systems to change the page size over time.*

The Alpha architects had an elaborate plan to grow the architecture over time by growing its page size, even building it into the size of its virtual address. When it

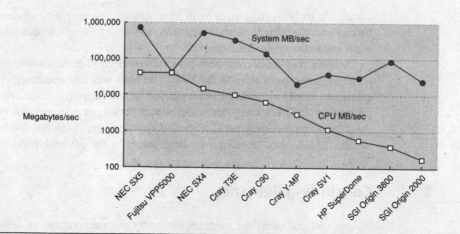

Figure 5.55 **Top 10 in memory bandwidth as measured by the copy portion of the stream benchmark [McCalpin 2001].** Note that the last three computers are the only cache-based systems on the list, and that six of the top seven are vector computers. Systems use between 8 and 256 processors to achieve higher memory bandwidth. System bandwidth is bandwidth of all CPUs collectively. CPU bandwidth is simply system bandwidth divided by the number of CPUs. The STREAM benchmark is a simple synthetic benchmark program that measures sustainable memory bandwidth (in MB/sec) for simple vector kernels. It specifically works with data sets much larger than the available cache on any given system.

	Misses		% time due to application misses		% time due directly to OS misses				% time OS
Workload	% in applications	% in OS	Inherent application misses	OS conflicts with applications	OS instruction misses	Data misses for migration	Data misses in block operations	Rest of OS misses	misses and application conflicts
Pmake	47%	53%	14.1%	4.8%	10.9%	1.0%	6.2%	2.9%	25.8%
Multipgm	53%	47%	21.6%	3.4%	9.2%	4.2%	4.7%	3.4%	24.9%
Oracle	73%	27%	25.7%	10.2%	10.6%	2.6%	0.6%	2.8%	26.8%

(The three columns "% time due to application misses" and "% time due directly to OS misses" fall under the group heading "Time".)

Figure 5.56 **Misses and time spent in misses for applications and operating system.** The operating system adds about 25% to the execution time of the application. Each CPU has a 64 KB instruction cache and a two-level data cache with 64 KB in the first level and 256 KB in the second level; all caches are direct mapped with 16-byte blocks. Collected on Silicon Graphics POWER station 4D/340, a multiprocessor with four 33 MHz R3000 CPUs running three application workloads under a UNIX System V—Pmake: a parallel compile of 56 files; Multipgm: the parallel numeric program MP3D running concurrently with Pmake and a five-screen edit session; and Oracle: running a restricted version of the TP-1 benchmark using the Oracle database. (Data from Torrellas, Gupta, and Hennessy [1992].)

came time to grow page sizes with later Alphas, the operating system designers balked and the virtual memory system was revised to grow the address space while maintaining the 8 KB page.

Architects of other computers noticed very high TLB miss rates, and so added multiple, larger page sizes to the TLB. The hope was that operating systems programmers would allocate an object to the largest page that made sense, thereby preserving TLB entries. After a decade of trying, most operating systems use these "superpages" only for handpicked functions: mapping the display memory or other I/O devices, or using very large pages for the database code.

5.17 Concluding Remarks

Figure 5.57 compares the memory hierarchy of microprocessors aimed at desktop, server, and embedded applications. The L1 caches are similar across applications, with the primary differences being L2 cache size, die size, processor clock rate, and instructions issued per clock.

In contrast to showing the state of the art in a given year, Figure 5.58 shows evolution over a decade of the memory hierarchy of Alpha microprocessors and systems. The primary change between the Alpha 21064 and 21364 is the hundredfold increase in on-chip cache size, which tries to compensate for the sixfold increase in main memory latency as measured in instructions.

The difficulty of building a memory system to keep pace with faster CPUs is underscored by the fact that the raw material for main memory is the same as that found in the cheapest computer. It is the principle of locality that saves us here—its soundness is demonstrated at all levels of the memory hierarchy in current computers, from disks to TLBs. One question is whether increasing scale breaks any of our assumptions. Are L3 caches bigger than prior main memories a cost-effective solution? Do 8 KB pages makes sense with terabyte main memories?

The design decisions at all these levels interact, and the architect must take the whole system view to make wise decisions. The primary challenge for the memory hierarchy designer is in choosing parameters that work well together, not in inventing new techniques. The increasingly fast CPUs are spending a larger fraction of time waiting for memory, which has led to new inventions that have increased the number of choices: prefetching, cache-aware compilers, and increasing page size. Fortunately, there tends to be a technological "sweet spot" in balancing cost, performance, power, and complexity: Missing the target wastes performance, power, hardware, design time, debug time, or possibly all five. Architects hit the target by careful, quantitative analysis.

5.18 Historical Perspective and References

Although the pioneers of computing knew of the need for a memory hierarchy and coined the term, the automatic management of two levels was first proposed by Kilburn et al. [1962]. It was demonstrated with the Atlas computer at the

MPU	AMD Athlon	Intel Pentium III	Intel Pentium 4	IBM PowerPC 405CR	Sun UltraSPARC III
Instruction set architecture	80x86	80x86	80x86	PowerPC	SPARC v9
Intended application	desktop	desktop, server	desktop	embedded core	server
CMOS process	0.18	0.18	0.18	0.25	0.15
Die size (mm^2)	128	106–385	217	37	210
Instructions issued/clock	3	3	3 RISC ops	1	4
Clock rate (2001)	1400 MHz	900–1200 MHz	2000 MHz	266 MHz	900 MHz
Instruction cache	64 KB, 2-way set associative	16 KB, 2-way set associative	12000 RISC op trace cache (~96 KB)	16 KB, 2-way set associative	32 KB, 4-way set associative
Latency (clocks)	3	3	4	1	2
Data cache	64 KB, 2-way set associative	16 KB, 2-way set associative	8 KB, 4-way set associative	8 KB, 2-way set associative	64 KB, 4-way set associative
Latency (clocks)	3	3	2	1	2
TLB entries (I/D/L2 TLB)	280/288	32/64	128	4/8/64	128/512
Minimum page size	8 KB	8 KB	8 KB	1 KB	8 KB
On-chip L2 cache	256 KB, 16-way set associative	256–2048 KB, 8-way set associative	256 KB, 8-way set associative	—	—
Off-chip L2 cache	—	—	—	—	8 MB, 1-way set associative
Latency (clocks)	11	7	?	—	15
Block size (L1/L2, bytes)	64	32	64/128	32	32
Memory bus width (bits)	64	64	64	64	128
Memory bus clock	133 MHz	133 MHz	400 MHz	133 MHz	150 MHz

Figure 5.57 Desktop, embedded, and server microprocessors in 2001. From a memory hierarchy perspective, the primary differences between applications is L2 cache. There is no L2 cache for embedded, 256 KB on chip for desktop, and servers use 2 MB on chip or 8 MB off chip. The processor clock rates also vary: 266 MHz for embedded, 900 MHz for servers, and 1200–2000 MHz for desktop. The Intel Pentium III includes the Xeon chip set for multiprocessor servers. It has the same processor core as the standard Pentium III, but a much larger on-chip L2 cache (up to 2 MB) and die size (385 mm^2) but a slower clock rate (900 MHz).

University of Manchester. This computer appeared the year *before* the IBM 360 was announced. Although IBM planned for its introduction with the next generation (System/370), the operating system TSS wasn't up to the challenge in 1970. Virtual memory was announced for the 370 family in 1972, and it was for this computer that the term "translation lookaside buffer" was coined [Case and Padegs 1978]. The only computers today without virtual memory are a few supercomputers, embedded processors, and older personal computers.

CPU	21064	21164	21264	21364
CMOS process feature size	0.68	0.50	0.35	0.18
Clock rate (initial)	200	300	525	~1000
First system ship date	3000/800	8400 5/300	ES40	2002–2003?
CPI gcc (SPECint92/95)	2.51	1.27	0.63	~0.6
Instruction cache	8 KB, 1-way	8 KB, 1-way	64 KB, 2-way	64 KB, 2-way
Latency (clocks)	2	2	2 or 3	2 or 3
Data cache	8 KB, 1-way, write through	8 KB, 1-way, write through	64 KB, 2-way, write back	64 KB, 2-way, write back
Latency	2	2	3	3
Write/victim buffer	4 blocks	6 blocks	8 blocks	32 blocks
Block size (bytes, all caches)	32	32	32 or 64	64
Virtual/physical address size	43/34	43/40	48/44 or 43/41	48/44 or 43/41
Page size	8 KB	8 KB	8 KB	8 KB or 64 KB
Instruction TLB	12-entry, fully associative	48-entry, fully associative	128-entry, fully associative	128-entry, fully associative
Data TLB	32-entry, fully associative	64-entry, fully associative	128-entry, fully associative	128-entry, fully associative
Path width off chip (bits)	128	128	128 to L2, 64 to memory	128?
On-chip unified L2 cache	—	96 KB, 3-way, write back	—	1536 KB, 6-way, write back
Latency (clocks)	—	7	—	12
Off-chip unified L2 or L3 cache	2 MB, 1-way, write back	4 MB, 1-way, write back	8 MB, 1-way, write back	—
Latency (clocks)	5	12	16	—
Memory size	.008–1 GB	0.125–14 GB	0.5–32 GB	0.5–4 GB/processor
Latency (clocks)	68	80	122	~90
Latency (instructions)	27	63	194	~150

Figure 5.58 Four generations of Alpha microprocessors and systems. Instruction latency was calculated by dividing the latency in clock cycles by average CPI for SPECint programs. The 21364 integrates a large on-chip cache and a memory controller to connect directly to DRDRAM chips, thereby significantly lowering memory latency. The large on-chip cache and low latency to memory make an off-chip cache unnecessary. A network allows processors to access nonlocal memory with nonuniform access times (see Chapter 6): 30 clocks per network hop, so 120 clocks in the nearest group of 4 and 200 in a group of 16. Memory latency in instructions is calculated by dividing clocks by average CPI.

Both the Atlas and the IBM 360 provided protection on pages, and the GE 645 was the first system to provide paged segmentation. The earlier Burroughs computers provided virtual memory using segmentation, similar to the segmented address scheme of the Intel 8086. The 80286, the first 80x86 to have the protection mechanisms described on pages 474–478, was inspired by the Multics protection software that ran on the GE 645. Over time, computers evolved more elaborate mechanisms. The most elaborate mechanism was *capabilities,* which reached its highest interest in the late 1970s and early 1980s [Fabry 1974; Wulf, Levin, and Harbison 1981]. Wilkes [1982], one of the early workers on capabilities, had this to say:

> Anyone who has been concerned with an implementation of the type just described [capability system], or has tried to explain one to others, is likely to feel that complexity has got out of hand. It is particularly disappointing that the attractive idea of capabilities being tickets that can be freely handed around has become lost. . . .
>
> Compared with a conventional computer system, there will inevitably be a cost to be met in providing a system in which the domains of protection are small and frequently changed. This cost will manifest itself in terms of additional hardware, decreased runtime speed, and increased memory occupancy. It is at present an open question whether, by adoption of the capability approach, the cost can be reduced to reasonable proportions. [p. 112]

Today there is little interest in capabilities either from the operating systems or the computer architecture communities, despite growing interest in protection and security.

Bell and Strecker [1976] reflected on the PDP-11 and identified a small address space as the only architectural mistake that is difficult to recover from. At the time of the creation of PDP-11, core memories were increasing at a very slow rate. In addition, competition from 100 other minicomputer companies meant that DEC might not have a cost-competitive product if every address had to go through the 16-bit data path twice; hence, the architect's decision to add only 4 more address bits than found in the predecessor of the PDP-11.

The architects of the IBM 360 were aware of the importance of address size and planned for the architecture to extend to 32 bits of address. Only 24 bits were used in the IBM 360, however, because the low-end 360 models would have been even slower with the larger addresses in 1964. Unfortunately, the architects didn't reveal their plans to the software people, and programmers who stored extra information in the upper 8 "unused" address bits foiled the expansion effort. (Apple made a similar mistake 20 years later with the 24-bit address in the Motorola 68000, which required a procedure to later determine "32-bit clean" programs for the Macintosh when later 68000s used the full 32-bit virtual address.) Virtually every computer since then will check to make sure the unused bits stay unused, and trap if the bits have the wrong value.

A few years after the Atlas paper, Wilkes published the first paper describing the concept of a cache [1965]:

> The use is discussed of a fast core memory of, say, 32,000 words as slave to a slower core memory of, say, one million words in such a way that in practical cases the effective access time is nearer that of the fast memory than that of the slow memory. [p. 270]

This two-page paper describes a direct-mapped cache. Although this is the first publication on caches, the first implementation was probably a direct-mapped instruction cache built at the University of Cambridge. It was based on tunnel diode memory, the fastest form of memory available at the time. Wilkes states that G. Scarott suggested the idea of a cache memory.

Subsequent to that publication, IBM started a project that led to the first commercial computer with a cache, the IBM 360/85 [Liptay 1968]. Gibson [1967] describes how to measure program behavior as memory traffic as well as miss rate and shows how the miss rate varies between programs. Using a sample of 20 programs (each with 3 million references!), Gibson also relied on average memory access time to compare systems with and without caches. This precedent is more than 30 years old, and yet many used miss rates until the early 1990s.

Conti, Gibson, and Pitkowsky [1968] describe the resulting performance of the 360/85. The 360/91 outperforms the 360/85 on only 3 of the 11 programs in the paper, even though the 360/85 has a slower clock cycle time (80 ns versus 60 ns), less memory interleaving (4 versus 16), and a slower main memory (1.04 microsecond versus 0.75 microsecond). This paper was also the first to use the term "cache."

Others soon expanded the cache literature. Strecker [1976] published the first comparative cache design paper examining caches for the PDP-11. Smith [1982] later published a thorough survey paper, using the terms "spatial locality" and "temporal locality"; this paper has served as a reference for many computer designers.

Although most studies relied on simulations, Clark [1983] used a hardware monitor to record cache misses of the VAX-11/780 over several days. Clark and Emer [1985] later compared simulations and hardware measurements for translations.

Hill [1987] proposed the three C's used in Section 5.5 to explain cache misses. Jouppi [1998] retrospectively says that Hill's three C's model led directly to his invention of the victim cache to take advantage of faster direct-mapped caches and yet avoid most of the cost of conflict misses. Sugumar and Abraham [1993] argue that the baseline cache for the three C's model should use optimal replacement; this eliminates the anomalies of LRU-based miss classification, and allows conflict misses to be broken down into those caused by mapping and those caused by a nonoptimal replacement algorithm.

One of the first papers on nonblocking caches is by Kroft [1981]. Kroft [1998] later explained that he was the first to design a computer with a cache at Control Data Corporation, and when using old concepts for new mechanisms, he hit upon the idea of allowing his two-ported cache to continue to service other accesses on a miss.

Baer and Wang [1988] did one of the first examinations of the multilevel inclusion property. Wang, Baer, and Levy [1989] then produced an early paper on performance evaluation of multilevel caches. Later, Jouppi and Wilton [1994] proposed multilevel exclusion for multilevel caches on chip.

In addition to victim caches, Jouppi [1990] also examined prefetching via streaming buffers. His work was extended by Farkas, Jouppi, and Chow [1995] to streaming buffers that work well with nonblocking loads and speculative execution for in-order processors, and later Farkas et al. [1997] showed that while out-of-order processors can tolerate unpredictable latency better, they still benefit. They also refined memory bandwidth demands of stream buffers.

Proceedings of the Symposium on Architectural Support for Compilers and Operating Systems (ASPLOS) and the International Computer Architecture Symposium (ISCA) from the 1990s are filled with papers on caches. (In fact, some wags claimed ISCA really stood for the International *Cache* Architecture Symposium.)

This chapter relies on the measurements of SPEC2000 benchmarks collected by Cantin and Hill [2001]. There are several other papers used in this chapter that are cited in the captions of the figures that use the data: Agarwal and Pudar [1993]; Barroso, Gharachorloo, and Bugnion [1998]; Farkas and Jouppi [1994]; Jouppi [1990]; Lam, Rothberg, and Wolf [1991]; Lebeck and Wood [1994]; McCalpin [2001]; Mowry, Lam, and Gupta [1992]; and Torrellas, Gupta, and Hennessy [1992].

The Alpha architecture is described in detail by Bhandarkar [1995] and by Sites [1992]. Sources of information on the 21264 are Compaq [1999], Cvetanovic and Kessler [2000], and Kessler [1999]. Two Emotion Engine references are Kunimatsu et al. [2000] and Oka and Suzuoki [1999]. Information on the Sun Fire 6800 server is found primarily on Sun's Web site, but Horel and Lauterbach [1999] and Heald et al. [2000] published detailed information on UltraSPARC III.

References

Agarwal, A. [1987]. *Analysis of Cache Performance for Operating Systems and Multiprogramming*, Ph.D. thesis, Stanford Univ., Tech. Rep. No. CSL-TR-87-332 (May).

Agarwal, A., and S. D. Pudar [1993]. "Column-associative caches: A technique for reducing the miss rate of direct-mapped caches," 20th Annual Int'l Symposium on Computer Architecture ISCA '20, San Diego, Calif., May 16–19. *Computer Architecture News* 21:2 (May), 179–190.

Baer, J.-L., and W.-H. Wang [1988]. "On the inclusion property for multi-level cache hierarchies," *Proc. 15th Annual Symposium on Computer Architecture* (May–June), Honolulu, 73–80.

Barroso, L. A., K. Gharachorloo, and E. Bugnion [1998]. "Memory system characterization of commercial workloads," *Proc. 25th Int'l Symposium on Computer Architecture,* Barcelona (July), 3–14.

Bell, C. G,. and W. D. Strecker [1976]. "Computer structures: What have we learned from the PDP-11?," *Proc. Third Annual Symposium on Computer Architecture* (January), Pittsburgh, 1–14.

Bhandarkar, D. P. [1995]. *Alpha Architecture Implementations,* Digital Press, Newton, Mass.

Borg, A., R. E. Kessler, and D. W. Wall [1990]. "Generation and analysis of very long address traces," *Proc. 17th Annual Int'l Symposium on Computer Architecture,* Seattle, Wash., May 28–31, 270–279.

Cantin, J. F., and M. D. Hill [2001]. *Cache Performance for Selected SPEC CPU2000 Benchmarks, www.jfred.org/cache-data.html* (June).

Case, R. P., and A. Padegs [1978]. "The architecture of the IBM System/370," *Communications of the ACM* 21:1, 73–96. Also appears in D. P. Siewiorek, C. G. Bell, and A. Newell, *Computer Structures: Principles and Examples,* McGraw-Hill, New York (1982), 830–855.

Clark, D. W. [1983]. "Cache performance of the VAX-11/780," *ACM Trans. on Computer Systems* 1:1, 24–37.

Clark, D. W., and J. S. Emer [1985]. "Performance of the VAX-11/780 translation buffer: Simulation and measurement," *ACM Trans. on Computer Systems* 3:1 (February), 31–62.

Compaq Computer Corporation [1999]. *Compiler Writer's Guide for the Alpha 21264,* Order Number EC-RJ66A-TE, June, *www1.support.compaq.com/alpha-tools/documentation/current/21264_EV67/ec-rj66a-te_comp_writ_gde_for_alpha21264.pdf*.

Conti, C., D. H. Gibson, and S. H. Pitkowsky [1968]. "Structural aspects of the System/360 Model 85, Part I: General organization," *IBM Systems J.* 7:1, 2–14.

Crawford, J., and P. Gelsinger [1988]. *Programming the 80386,* Sybex, Alameda, Calif.

Cvetanovic, Z., and R.E. Kessler [2000]. "Performance analysis of the Alpha 21264-based Compaq ES40 system," *Proc. 27th Annual Int'l Symposium on Computer Architecture*, Vancouver, Canada, June 10–14, IEEE Computer Society Press, 192–202.

Fabry, R. S. [1974]. "Capability based addressing," *Comm. ACM* 17:7 (July), 403–412.

Farkas, K. I., P. Chow, N. P. Jouppi, and Z. Vranesic [1997]. "Memory-system design considerations for dynamically-scheduled processors," *Proc. 24th Annual Int'l Symposium on Computer Architecture,* Denver, Col., June 2–4, 133–143.

Farkas, K. I., and N. P. Jouppi [1994]. "Complexity/performance trade-offs with non-blocking loads," *Proc. 21st Annual Int'l Symposium on Computer Architecture*, Chicago (April).

Farkas, K. I., N. P. Jouppi, and P. Chow [1995]. "How useful are non-blocking loads, stream buffers and speculative execution in multiple issue processors?," *Proc. First IEEE Symposium on High-Performance Computer Architecture,* Raleigh, N.C., January 22–25, 78–89.

Gao, Q. S. [1993]. "The Chinese remainder theorem and the prime memory system," 20th Annual Int'l Symposium on Computer Architecture ISCA '20, San Diego, Calif., May 16–19, *Computer Architecture News* 21:2 (May), 337–340.

Gee, J. D., M. D. Hill, D. N. Pnevmatikatos, and A. J. Smith [1993]. "Cache performance of the SPEC92 benchmark suite," *IEEE Micro* 13:4 (August), 17–27.

Gibson, D. H. [1967]. "Considerations in block-oriented systems design," *AFIPS Conf. Proc.* 30, SJCC, 75–80.

Handy, J. [1993]. *The Cache Memory Book*, Academic Press, Boston.

Heald, R., K. Aingaran, C. Amir, M. Ang, M. Boland, A. Das, P. Dixit, G. Gouldsberry, J. Hart, T. Horel, W.-J. Hsu, J. Kaku, C. Kim, S. Kim, F. Klass, H. Kwan, R. Lo, H. McIntyre, A. Mehta, D. Murata, S. Nguyen, Y.-P. Pai, S. Patel, K. Shin, K. Tam, S. Vishwanthaiah, J. Wu, G. Yee, and H. You [2000]. "Implementation of third-generation SPARC V9 64-b microprocessor," *ISSCC Digest of Technical Papers,* 412–413 and slide supplement.

Hill, M. D. [1987]. *Aspects of Cache Memory and Instruction Buffer Performance*, Ph.D. thesis, University of Calif. at Berkeley, Computer Science Division, Tech. Rep. UCB/CSD 87/381 (November).

Hill, M. D. [1988]. "A case for direct mapped caches," *Computer* 21:12 (December), 25–40.

Horel, T., and G. Lauterbach [1999]. "UltraSPARC-III: Designing third-generation 64-bit performance," *IEEE Micro* 19:3 (May–June), 73–85.

Hughes, C. J., P. Kaul, S. V. Adve, R. Jain, C. Park, and J. Srinivasan [2001]. "Variability in the execution of multimedia applications and implications for architecture, "*Proc. 28th Annual Int'l Symposium on Computer Architecture,* Goteborg, Sweden, June 30– July 4, 254–265.

Jouppi, N. P. [1990]. "Improving direct-mapped cache performance by the addition of a small fully-associative cache and prefetch buffers," *Proc. 17th Annual Int'l Symposium on Computer Architecture,* 364–73.

Jouppi, N. P. [1998]. "Retrospective: Improving direct-mapped cache performance by the addition of a small fully-associative cache and prefetch buffers," *25 Years of the Int'l Symposia on Computer Architecture (Selected Papers)*, ACM, 71–73.

Jouppi, N. P., and S. J. E. Wilton [1994]. "Trade-offs in two-level on-chip caching," *Proc. 21st Annual Int'l Symposium on Computer Architecture,* Chicago, April 18– 21, 34–45.

Kesslcr, R. E. [1999]. "The Alpha 21264 microprocessor," *IEEE Micro* 19:2 (March/ April), 24–36.

Kilburn, T., D. B. G. Edwards, M. J. Lanigan, and F. H. Sumner [1962]. "One-level storage system," *IRE Trans. on Electronic Computers* EC-11 (April) 223–235. Also appears in D. P. Siewiorek, C. G. Bell, and A. Newell, *Computer Structures: Principles and Examples* (1982), McGraw-Hill, New York, 135–148.

Kroft, D. [1981]. "Lockup-free instruction fetch/prefetch cache organization," *Proc. Eighth Annual Symposium on Computer Architecture* (May 12–14), Minneapolis, 81–87.

Kroft, D. [1998]. "Retrospective: Lockup-free instruction fetch/prefetch cache organization," *25 Years of the Int'l Symposia on Computer Architecture (Selected Papers),* ACM, 20–21.

Kunimatsu, A., N. Ide, T. Sato, Y. Endo, H. Murakami, T. Kamei, M. Hirano, F. Ishihara, H. Tago, M. Oka, A. Ohba, T. Yutaka, T. Okada, and M. Suzuoki [2000]. "Vector unit architecture for emotion synthesis," *IEEE Micro* 20:2 (March–April), 40–47.

Lam, M. S., E. E. Rothberg, and M. E. Wolf [1991]. "The cache performance and optimizations of blocked algorithms," Fourth Int'l Conf. on Architectural Support for Programming Languages and Operating Systems, Santa Clara, Calif., April 8–11. *SIGPLAN Notices* 26:4 (April), 63–74.

Lebeck, A. R., and D. A. Wood [1994]. "Cache profiling and the SPEC benchmarks: A case study," *Computer* 27:10 (October), 15–26.

Liptay, J. S. [1968]. "Structural aspects of the System/360 Model 85, Part II: The cache," *IBM Systems J.* 7:1, 15–21.

Luk, C.-K., and T. C Mowry [1999]. "Automatic compiler-inserted prefetching for pointer-based applications," *IEEE Trans. on Computers,* 48:2 (February), 134–141.

McCalpin, J. D. [2001]. *STREAM: Sustainable Memory Bandwidth in High Performance Computers, www.cs.virginia.edu/stream/.*

McFarling, S. [1989]. "Program optimization for instruction caches," *Proc. Third Int'l Conf. on Architectural Support for Programming Languages and Operating Systems* (April 3–6), Boston, 183–191.

Mowry, T. C., S. Lam, and A. Gupta [1992]. "Design and evaluation of a compiler algorithm for prefetching," Fifth Int'l Conf. on Architectural Support for Programming Languages and Operating Systems (ASPLOS-V), Boston, October 12–15, *SIGPLAN Notices* 27:9 (September), 62–73.

Oka, M., and M. Suzuoki [1999]. "Designing and programming the emotion engine," *IEEE Micro* 19:6 (November–December), 20–28.

Pabst, T. [2000]. "Performance showdown at 133 MHz FSB—the best platform for coppermine," *www6.tomshardware.com/mainboard/00q1/000302/*.

Palacharla, S., and R. E. Kessler [1994]. "Evaluating stream buffers as a secondary cache replacement," *Proc. 21st Annual Int'l Symposium on Computer Architecture*, Chicago, April 18–21, 24–33.

Przybylski, S. A. [1990]. *Cache Design: A Performance-Directed Approach*, Morgan Kaufmann, San Francisco.

Przybylski, S. A., M. Horowitz, and J. L. Hennessy [1988]. "Performance trade-offs in cache design," *Proc. 15th Annual Symposium on Computer Architecture* (May–June), Honolulu, 290–298.

Reinman, G., and N. P. Jouppi. [1999]. "Extensions to CACTI," *research.compaq.com /wrl/people/jouppi/CACTI.html*.

Saavedra-Barrera, R. H. [1992]. *CPU Performance Evaluation and Execution Time Prediction Using Narrow Spectrum Benchmarking*, Ph.D. dissertation, University of Calif., Berkeley (May).

Samples, A. D., and P. N. Hilfinger [1988]. "Code reorganization for instruction caches," Tech. Rep. UCB/CSD 88/447 (October), University of Calif., Berkeley.

Sites, R. L. (ed.) [1992]. *Alpha Architecture Reference Manual*, Digital Press, Burlington, Mass.

Smith, A. J. [1982]. "Cache memories," *Computing Surveys* 14:3 (September), 473–530.

Smith, J. E., and J. R. Goodman [1983]. "A study of instruction cache organizations and replacement policies," *Proc. 10th Annual Symposium on Computer Architecture* (June 5–7), Stockholm, 132–137.

Stokes, J. [2000]. "Sound and Vision: A Technical Overview of the Emotion Engine," *arstechnica.com/reviews/1q00/playstation2/ee-1.html*.

Strecker, W. D. [1976]. "Cache memories for the PDP-11?," *Proc. Third Annual Symposium on Computer Architecture* (January), Pittsburgh, 155–158.

Sugumar, R. A, and S. G. Abraham [1993]. "Efficient simulation of caches under optimal replacement with applications to miss characterization," *1993 ACM Sigmetrics Conf. on Measurement and Modeling of Computer Systems*, Santa Clara, Calif., May 17–21, 24–35.

Torrellas, J., A. Gupta, and J. Hennessy [1992]. "Characterizing the caching and synchronization performance of a multiprocessor operating system," Fifth Int'l Conf. on Architectural Support for Programming Languages and Operating Systems (ASPLOS-V), Boston, October 12–15, *SIGPLAN Notices* 27:9 (September), 162–174.

Wang, W.-H., J.-L. Baer, and H. M. Levy [1989]. "Organization and performance of a two-level virtual-real cache hierarchy," *Proc. 16th Annual Symposium on Computer Architecture* (May 28–June 1), Jerusalem, 140–148.

Wilkes, M. [1965]. "Slave memories and dynamic storage allocation," *IEEE Trans. Electronic Computers* EC-14:2 (April), 270–271.

Wilkes, M. V. [1982]. "Hardware support for memory protection: Capability implementations," *Proc. Symposium on Architectural Support for Programming Languages and Operating Systems* (March 1–3), Palo Alto, Calif., 107–116.

Wulf, W. A., R. Levin, and S. P. Harbison [1981]. *Hydra/C.mmp: An Experimental Computer System*, McGraw-Hill, New York.

Exercises

Solutions to "starred" exercises appear in Appendix B.

⭐ 5.1 [15/15/12/12] <5.1, 5.2> Let's try to show how you can make *unfair* benchmarks. Here are two machines with the same processor and main memory but different cache organizations. Assume that both processors run at 2 GHz, have a CPI of 1, and have a cache (read) miss time of 100 ns. Further, assume that writing a 32-bit word to main memory requires 100 ns (for the write-through cache), and that writing a 32-byte block requires 200 ns (for the write-back cache). The caches are unified—they contain both instructions and data, and each cache has a total capacity of 64 KB, not including tags and status bits.

The cache on system A is two-way set associative and has 32-byte blocks. It is write through and does not allocate a block on a write miss.

The cache on system B is direct mapped and has 32-byte blocks. It is write back and allocates a block on a write miss.

a. [15] <5.1, 5.2> Describe a program that makes system A run as fast as possible relative to system B's speed.

b. [15] <5.1, 5.2> Describe a program that makes system B run as fast as possible relative to system A's speed.

c. [12] <5.1, 5.2> How much faster is the program in part (a) on system A as compared to system B?

d. [12] <5.1, 5.2> How much faster is the program in part (b) on system B as compared to system A?

5.2 [15/10/12/12/12/12/12/12/12/12/12] <5.3, 5.4> In this exercise, we will run a program to evaluate the behavior of a memory system. The key is having accurate timing and then having the program stride through memory to invoke different levels of the hierarchy. Below is the code in C for UNIX systems. The first part is a procedure that uses a standard UNIX utility to get an accurate measure of the user CPU time; this procedure may need to change to work on some systems. The second part is a nested loop to read and write memory at different strides and cache sizes. To get accurate cache timing, this code is repeated many times. The third part times the nested loop overhead only so that it can be subtracted from overall measured times to see how long the accesses were. The last part prints the time per access as the size and stride varies. You may need to change CACHE_MAX depending on the question you are answering and the size of memory on the system you are measuring. The code below was taken from a program written by Andrea Dusseau of U.C. Berkeley, and was based on a detailed description found in Saavedra-Barrera [1992].

```
#include <stdio.h>
#include <sys/times.h>
#include <sys/types.h>
#include <time.h>
#define CACHE_MIN (1024) /* smallest cache */
```

```
#define CACHE_MAX (1024*1024) /* largest cache */
#define SAMPLE 10 /* to get a larger time sample */
#ifndef CLK_TCK
#define CLK_TCK 60 /* number clock ticks per second */
#endif
int x[CACHE_MAX]; /* array going to stride through */
double get_seconds() { /* routine to read time */
    struct tms rusage;
    times(&rusage); /* UNIX utility: time in clock ticks */
    return (double) (rusage.tms_utime)/CLK_TCK;
}
void main() {
int register i, index, stride, limit, temp;
int steps, tsteps, csize;
double sec0, sec; /* timing variables */
for (csize=CACHE_MIN; csize <= CACHE_MAX; csize=csize*2)
    for (stride=1; stride <= csize/2; stride=stride*2) {
        sec = 0; /* initialize timer */
        limit = csize-stride+1; /* cache size this loop */
        steps = 0;
            do { /* repeat until collect 1 second */
        sec0 = get_seconds(); /* start timer */
        for (i=SAMPLE*stride;i!=0;i=i-1) /* larger sample */
            for (index=0; index < limit; index=index+stride)
                x[index] = x[index] + 1; /* cache access */
        steps = steps + 1; /* count while loop iterations */
        sec = sec + (get_seconds() - sec0);/* end timer */
        } while (sec < 1.0); /* until collect 1 second */

        /* Repeat empty loop to subtract loop overhead */
        tsteps = 0; /* used to match no. while iterations */
            do { /* repeat until same no. iterations as above */
        sec0 = get_seconds(); /* start timer */
        for (i=SAMPLE*stride;i!=0;i=i-1) /* larger sample */
            for (index=0; index < limit; index=index+stride)
                temp = temp + index; /* dummy code */
        tsteps = tsteps + 1; /* count while iterations */
        sec = sec - (get_seconds() - sec0);/* - overhead */
        } while (tsteps<steps); /* until = no. iterations */
        printf("Size:%7d Stride:%7d read+write:%14.0f ns\n",
            csize*sizeof(int), stride*sizeof(int), (double)
            sec*1e9/(steps*SAMPLE*stride*((limit-1)/stride+1)));
    }; /* end of both outer for loops */
}
```

The program above assumes that program addresses track physical addresses, which is true on the few machines that use virtually addressed caches, such as the

Alpha 21264. In general, virtual addresses tend to follow physical addresses shortly after rebooting, so you may need to reboot the machine in order to get smooth lines in your results.

To answer the questions below, assume that the sizes of all components of the memory hierarchy are powers of 2.

a. [15] <5.3, 5.4> Plot the experimental results with elapsed time on the y-axis and the memory stride on the x-axis. Use logarithmic scales for both axes, and draw a line for each cache size.

b. [10] <5.3, 5.4> How many levels of cache are there?

c. [12] <5.3, 5.4> What are the overall size and block size of the first-level cache? *Hint:* Assume that the size of the page is much larger than the size of a block in a second-level cache (if there is one), and the size of a second-level cache block is greater than or equal to the size of a block in a first-level cache.

d. [12] <5.3, 5.4> What are the overall size and block size of the second-level cache, if there is one?

e. [12] <5.3, 5.4> What is the associativity of the first-level cache? What is the associativity of the second-level cache, if there is one?

f. [12] <5.3, 5.4> What is the system page size?

g. [12] <5.3, 5.4> How many entries are there in the TLB?

h. [12] <5.3, 5.4> What are the miss penalties for the first-level cache and (if present) second-level cache?

i. [12] <5.3, 5.4> What is the time for a page fault to secondary memory (i.e., disk)? *Hint:* Disk accesses have latencies measured in milliseconds.

j. [12] <5.3, 5.4> What is the miss penalty for the TLB?

k. [12] <5.3, 5.4> Is there anything else you have discovered about the memory hierarchy from these measurements?

5.3 [10/10/10] <5.2> Figure 5.59 shows the output from running the program in Exercise 5.2 on a Sun Blade 1000 server, which has separate L1 instruction and data caches and a unified L2 cache.

a. [10] <5.2> How big is the cache?

b. [10] <5.2> What is the block size in the cache?

c. [15] <5.2> What is the miss penalty for the L1 cache? L2 cache? Additional memory hierarchy level(s)?

d. [20] <5.2> What might explain the access time behavior shown for very large strides?

5.4 [10/10/10/10/15/20] <5.2> You are building a system around a processor with in-order execution that runs at 1.1 GHz and has a CPI of 0.7 excluding memory accesses. The only instructions that read or write data from memory are loads (20% of all instructions) and stores (5% of all instructions).

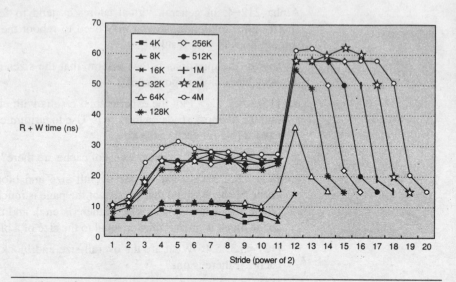

Figure 5.59 **Results of running program in Exercise 5.2 on a Sun Blade 1000.**

The memory system for this computer is composed of a split L1 cache that imposes no penalty on hits. Both the I-cache and D-cache are direct mapped and hold 32 KB each. The I-cache has a 2% miss rate and 32-byte blocks, and the D-cache is write through with a 5% miss rate and 16-byte blocks. There is a write buffer on the D-cache that eliminates stalls for 95% of all writes.

The 512 KB write-back, unified L2 cache has 64-byte blocks and an access time of 15 ns. It is connected to the L1 cache by a 128-bit data bus that runs at 266 MHz and can transfer one 128-bit word per bus cycle. Of all memory references sent to the L2 cache in this system, 80% are satisfied without going to main memory. Also, 50% of all blocks replaced are dirty.

The 128-bit-wide main memory has an access latency of 60 ns, after which any number of bus words may be transferred at the rate of one per cycle on the 128-bit-wide 133 MHz main memory bus.

a. [10] <5.2> What is the average memory access time for instruction accesses?

b. [10] <5.2> What is the average memory access time for data reads?

c. [10] <5.2> What is the average memory access time for data writes?

d. [10] <5.2> What is the overall CPI, including memory accesses?

e. [15] <5.2> You are considering replacing the 1.1 GHz CPU with one that runs at 2.1 GHz, but is otherwise identical. How much faster does the system run with a faster processor? Assume the L1 cache still has no hit penalty, and that the speed of the L2 cache, main memory, and buses remains the same in absolute terms (e.g., the L2 cache still has a 15 ns access time and a 266 MHz bus connecting it to the CPU and L1 cache).

f. [20] <5.2> If you want to make your system run faster, which part of the memory system would you improve? Graph the change in overall system performance holding all parameters fixed except the one that you're improving. Parameters you might consider improving include L2 cache speed, bus speeds, main memory speed, and L1 and L2 hit rates. Based on these graphs, how could you best improve overall system performance with minimal cost?

5.5 [10/15/15/25] <3, 4, 5.2> Converting miss rate (misses per reference) into misses per instruction relies upon two factors: references per instruction fetched and the fraction of fetched instructions that actually commits.

a. [10] <3, 4, 5.2> The formula for misses per instruction on page 396 is written first in terms of three factors: miss rate, memory accesses, and instruction count. Each of these factors represents actual events. What is different about writing misses per instruction as miss rate times the factor *memory accesses per instruction*?

b. [15] <5.2> Speculative processors will fetch instructions that do not commit. The formula for misses per instruction on page 396 refers to misses per instruction on the execution path, that is, only the instructions that must actually be executed to carry out the program. Convert the formula for misses per instruction on page 396 into one that uses only miss rate, references per instruction fetched, and fraction of fetched instructions that commit. Why rely upon these factors rather than those in the formula on page 396?

c. [15] <3, 4, 5.2> The conversion in part (b) could yield an incorrect value to the extent that the value of the factor references per instruction fetched is not equal to the number of references for any particular instruction. Rewrite the formula of part (b) to correct this deficiency.

d. [25] <3, 4, 5.2> Simulate a SPEC95 or SPEC2000 benchmark using Simple-Scalar (*www.cs.wisc.edu/~mscalar/simplescalar.html*), first using in-order execution and then using out-of-order execution. Does miss rate vary between the two executions?

✪ 5.6 [20] <5.1, 5.3> In systems with a write-through L1 cache backed by a write-back L2 cache instead of main memory, a merging write buffer can be simplified. Explain how this can be done. Are there situations where having a full write buffer (instead of the simple version you've just proposed) could be helpful?

5.7 [20] <5.3, 5.4> A cache may use a write buffer to reduce write latency and a victim cache to hold recently evicted (nondirty) blocks. Would there be any advantages to combining the two into a single piece of hardware? Would there be any disadvantages?

5.8 [20] <5.6> Improve on the compiler prefetch example found on pages 440–441. Try to eliminate both the number of extraneous prefetches and the number of nonprefetched cache misses. Calculate the performance of this refined version using the parameters in the example.

5.9 [25/25/25/25] <5.4> Use an instruction simulator and cache simulator such as SimpleScalar (*www.cs.wisc.edu/~mscalar/simplescalar.html*) to calculate the effectiveness of early restart and out-of-order fetch. What is the distribution of block offsets for the first accesses to blocks as block size increases from 4 words to 64 words by factors of 2 for the following (assume two-way set-associative caches):

a. [25] <5.4> A 128 KB instruction-only cache?

b. [25] <5.4> A 128 KB data-only cache?

c. [25] <5.4> A 256 KB unified cache?

d. [25] <5.4> A split 128/128 L1 cache with a 1 MB L2 cache? Assume that the L2 cache has 64-word blocks, and that both the L1 and L2 cache can fetch out of order.

5.10 [30/30] <3, 4, 5> Use an out-of-order, superscalar simulator such as SimpleScalar (*www.cs.wisc.edu/~mscalar/simplescalar.html*) and a simple benchmark for the following:

a. [30] <3, 4, 5> Run the benchmark and find the hit rates for a memory system with a level 1 cache ranging from 64 KB to 256 KB and a level 2 cache ranging from 512 KB to 4 MB assuming that instructions are executed in order and issued at most one per cycle (in other words, the CPU is not really out of order and superscalar).

b. [30] <3, 4, 5> Run the same program on the same range of memory systems on an out-of-order, four-way instruction issue processor with two integer units, one floating-point unit, and one memory unit. How do the hit rates vary from the in-order case?

5.11 [25] <3, 4, 5> Let's study the impact of out-of-order execution on temporal locality in an L1 data cache. Use an out-of-order, superscalar simulator such as SimpleScalar (*www.cs.wisc.edu/~mscalar/simplescalar.html*) and a simple benchmark. Then vary the out-of-orderliness by changing the size of the load and store queues and measure the miss rate as a function of associativity. What do your results indicate about the number of conflict misses and CPU execution model?

5.12 [20/20/15/25] <5.5> Smith and Goodman [1983] found that for a given small size, a direct-mapped instruction cache consistently outperformed a fully associative instruction cache using LRU replacement.

a. [20] <5.5> Explain how this would be possible. (*Hint:* You can't explain this with the three C's model because it "ignores" replacement policy.)

b. [20] <5.5> Explain where replacement policy fits into the three C's model, and explain why this means that misses caused by a replacement policy are "ignored"—or, more precisely, cannot in general be definitively classified—by the three C's model.

c. [15] <5.5> Are there any replacement policies for the fully associative cache that would outperform the direct-mapped cache? Ignore the policy of "do what a direct-mapped cache would do."

d. [25] <5.5> Use a cache simulator to see if Smith and Goodman's results hold for memory reference traces that you have access to. If they do not hold, why not?

5.13 [15/20] <5.2, 5.5> McFarling [1989] found that the best memory hierarchy performance occurred when it was possible to prevent some instructions from entering the cache (see page 432).

a. [15] <5.5> Explain why McFarling's result could be true.

b. [20] <5.2, 5.5> The four memory hierarchy questions (Section 5.2) form a model for describing cache designs. Where does a cache that does not always *read-allocate* fit or not fit into this model?

5.14 [20/15/20/15/15] <1.4, 3.3, 5.5> Way prediction allows an associative cache to provide the hit time of a direct-mapped cache. The MIPS R10K processor uses way prediction to achieve a different goal: reduce the cost of the chip package.

The R10K hardware includes an on-chip L1 cache, on-chip L2 tag comparison circuitry, and an on-chip L2 way prediction table. L2 tag information is brought on chip to detect an L2 hit or miss. The way prediction table contains 8K 1-bit entries, each corresponding to two L2 cache blocks. L2 cache storage is built externally to the processor package, must be two-way associative, and may have one of several block sizes.

a. [20] <1.4, 5.5> How can way prediction reduce the number of pins needed on the R10K package to read L2 tags and data, and what is the impact on performance compared to a package with a full complement of pins to interface to the L2 cache?

b. [15] <5.5> What is the performance drawback of just using the same smaller number of pins but not including way prediction?

c. [20] <5.5> Assume that the R10K uses most-recently used way prediction. What are reasonable design choices for the cache state update(s) to make when the desired data is in the predicted way, the desired data is in the non-predicted way, and the desired data is not in the secondary cache?

d. [15] <5.5> If a 512 KB L2 cache has 64-byte blocks, how many way prediction table entries are needed? How would the R10K support this need?

e. [15] <3.3, 5.5> For a 4 MB L2 cache with 128-byte blocks, how is the usefulness of the R10K way prediction table analogous to that of a branch history table?

5.15 [25/20] <5.5> Simulating a single process workload gives miss rates that are lower than those seen in real computer systems.

a. [25] <5.5> Write a program that merges traces written by an instruction simulator such as SimpleScalar (*www.cs.wisc.edu/~mscalar/simplescalar.html*) and produces a stream of references that more accurately reflects a real computer workload. SimpleScalar has a precompiled set of SPEC95 benchmarks that may be useful for this exercise.

    b. [20] <5.5> Run the resulting traces through a cache simulator for various cache sizes. How does the miss rate for the merged traces differ from the miss rate from running the programs sequentially?

★ 5.16 [15/15] <5.5, 5.6> As caches increase in size, blocks often increase in size as well.

    a. [15] <5.5, 5.6> If a large instruction cache has larger data blocks, is there still a need for prefetching? Explain the interaction between prefetching and increased block size in instruction caches.

    b. [15] <5.5, 5.6> Is there a need for data prefetch instructions when data blocks get larger? Explain.

5.17 [15/20] <5.10, 5.13> The Alpha 21264 uses a fully associative cache with 128 entries for its TLB. This arrangement is very flexible, but can lead to performance issues.

    a. [15] <5.10> Fully associative caches are often slow and/or difficult to build. How could you build a TLB from a two-way set-associative cache? What drawbacks are there to using a set-associative cache rather than a fully associative cache for the TLB?

    b. [20] <5.10, 5.13> The 21264 TLB supports multiple page sizes. Could a memory system using a two-way set-associative TLB support multiple page sizes? Explain.

5.18 [15/15] <5.7, 5.10> The 21264 uses a virtually addressed instruction cache, removing the TLB from the critical path on instruction fetches. The use of virtually addressed caches can reduce time to fetch data from the cache, but can lead to problems (as discussed in Section 5.7).

    a. [15] <5.7, 5.10> The 21264 eliminates aliases in the virtually addressed cache by checking eight different locations on each access. Other systems use page coloring to do the same thing. Is this really necessary for instruction caches? Explain.

    b. [15] <5.7, 5.10> Virtually addressed caches often need to have more tag bits than physically addressed caches, both because virtual addresses are often longer than physical addresses and because virtually addressed caches need to store additional tag bits to distinguish cached blocks from different processes. How much added overhead does this contribute? Assume 64-bit virtual addresses, 8-bit process identifiers, and a physical memory that can hold up to 64 GB of main memory (i.e., physical tags need only be large enough to handle 36-bit physical addresses). How does overhead vary for different cache block sizes?

★ 5.19 [15/15/15/15/15/15] <5.10, 5.11> Some memory systems handle TLB misses in software (as an exception), while others use hardware for TLB misses.

    a. [15] <5.10, 5.11> What are the trade-offs between these two methods for handling TLB misses?

b. [15] <5.10, 5.11> Will TLB miss handling in software always be slower than TLB miss handling in hardware? Explain.

c. [15] <5.10, 5.11> Are there page table structures that would be difficult to handle in hardware, but possible in software? Are there any such structures that would be difficult for software to handle but easy for hardware to manage?

d. [15] <5.10, 5.11> Use the data from Figure 5.45 to calculate the penalty to CPI for TLB misses on the following workloads assuming hardware TLB handlers require 10 cycles per miss and software TLB handlers take 30 cycles per miss: (50% gcc, 25% perl, 25% ijpeg), (30% swim, 30% wave5, 20% hydro2d, 10% gcc).

e. [15] <5.10, 5.11> Are the TLB miss times in part (d) realistic? Discuss.

f. [15] <5.10, 5.11> Why are TLB miss rates for floating-point programs generally higher than those for integer programs?

5.20 [25/25/25/25/20] <5.10> How big should a TLB be? TLB misses are usually very fast (fewer than 10 instructions plus the cost of an exception), so it may not be worth having a huge TLB just to lower TLB miss rate a bit. Using the Simple-Scalar simulator (*www.cs.wisc.edu/~mscalar/simplescalar.html*) and one or more SPEC95 benchmarks, calculate the TLB miss rate and the TLB overhead (in percentage of time wasted handling TLB misses) for the following TLB configurations. Assume that each TLB miss requires 20 instructions.

a. [25] <5.10> 128 entries, two-way set associative, 4 KB to 64 KB pages (going by powers of 2).

b. [25] <5.10> 256 entries, two-way set associative, 4 KB to 64 KB pages (going by powers of 2).

c. [25] <5.10> 512 entries, two-way set associative, 4 KB to 64 KB pages (going by powers of 2).

d. [25] <5.10> 1024 entries, two-way set associative, 4 KB to 64 KB pages (going by powers of 2).

e. [20] <5.10> What would be the effect on TLB miss rate and overhead for a multitasking environment? How would the context switch frequency affect the overhead?

5.21 [15/20/20] <5.11> It is possible to provide more flexible protection than that in the Intel Pentium architecture by using a protection scheme similar to that used in the HP-PA architecture. In such a scheme each page table entry contains a "protection ID" (key) along with access rights for the page, as shown below. On each reference, the CPU compares the protection ID in the page table entry with those stored in each of four protection ID registers (access to these registers requires that the CPU be in supervisor mode). If there is no match for the protection ID in the page table entry or if the access is not a permitted access (writing to a read-only page, for example), an exception is generated.

Protection ID	Permissions	Physical page number	Valid?	Dirty?	Used?

a. [15] <5.11> How could a process have more than four valid protection IDs at any given time? In other words, suppose a process wished to have 10 protection IDs simultaneously. Propose a mechanism by which this could be done (perhaps with help from software).

b. [20] <5.11> Explain how this model could be used to facilitate the construction of operating systems from relatively small pieces of code that can't overwrite each other (microkernels). What advantages might such an operating system have over a monolithic operating system in which any code in the OS can write to any memory location?

c. [20] <5.11> A simple design change to this system would allow two protection IDs for each page table entry, one for read access and the other for either write or execute access (the field is unused if neither the writable nor executable bit is set). What advantages might there be from having different protection IDs for read and write capabilities? *Hint:* Could this make it easier to share data and code between processes?

Protection ID 1	Protection ID 2	Executable?	Writable?	Physical page number	Valid?	Dirty?	Used?

5.22   [25/25/25] <5.16> One of the common pitfalls in memory system design is simulating too few references. Using your favorite simulator and several different traces, show the following:

a. [25] <5.16> Instruction cache miss rate versus trace length for varying sizes of instruction cache. Use a fixed trace and the same associativity and block size for each cache size—the point here is to measure the effect of using too short of a trace. Discuss the reasons for the different measured miss rates.

b. [25] <5.16> Data cache miss rate versus trace length for varying sizes of data cache. Perform the same analysis as in part (a).

c. [25] <5.16> Using your results, can you give a rule of thumb for how long of a simulation is necessary for a given cache size? How does this answer relate to the issues raised in Exercise 5.15 (i.e., how are short traces related to context switch issues)?

5.23   [15/15/10/10] <5.5, 5.16> Compulsory misses can distort the miss rate measured using a trace that is too short.

a. [15] <5.5, 5.16> The first 100,000 instruction references of a program are simulated on an 8 KB direct-mapped cache with 16-byte blocks, and a total of 600 misses occur. How many of the misses could be compulsory?

b. [15] <5.5, 5.16> Assume that to complete, the program from which the 100,000 initial references were taken executes for another 900,000 references. Assume no compulsory misses occur after the initial 100,000 references; that is, the cache initialization transient ended some time during the first 100,000 references. What range of miss rate is it possible to measure for the combination of this cache and this complete program?

c. [10] <5.5> If the simulated cache design has fewer blocks, what is the effect on the range of possible measured miss rate?

d. [10] <5.5, 5.16> If the simulated memory reference trace is lengthened, what is the effect on the range of possible measured miss rate?

5.24 [15/20/25/25/20/15/15] <5.2, 5.16> The miss behavior of a complete program may be quite different from that for any one segment (see Figure 5.53). Further, the entire memory reference trace of a program or set of programs may include billions and billions of addresses, requiring more time or more computing resources to simulate than is available. Under certain assumptions the magnitude of cache simulation work can be substantially reduced while maintaining accurate results. This exercise explores the limits of reduction.

a. [15] <5.16> To reduce simulation time and effort, traces should be as short as possible, but not shorter. How short can a trace be without being so short that it is impossible to establish a miss rate? (*Hint:* State your answer in the form of a necessary trace characteristic rather than as a specific trace length.) Note that to obtain good precision of measured miss rate, a trace should be perhaps a factor of 10 "longer" than your minimum.

b. [20] <5.2, 5.16> The miss rate data reported and discussed in the text are for an entire cache. If a cache has a large number of sets, it may be accurate to assume that any subset of sets has the same miss rate as does the entire cache. How should a trace be prepared to exploit this observation? By what maximum factor could simulation effort be reduced? In practice, 10% of sets are simulated (essentially a 90% reduction in trace size) to obtain good statistical confidence in the results, but how could you quantify the error introduced by this technique?

c. [25] <5.2> Simulation of many cache designs—size, number of sets, associativity—is needed before an informed decision on which one design to build can be made. For a *stacking* replacement policy, the contents of a set for a k-way associative cache includes, at any point during trace simulation, the contents of sets for all j-way associative caches, for $j < k$, provided the caches all have the same block size and number of sets. Further, if the blocks of the k-way set are ordered from "least replaceable" to "most replaceable," then the first j blocks in the k-way set are precisely the blocks that would be held at that exact time in a j-way associative cache, and their order represents exactly the same "least replaceable" to "most replaceable" labeling that the j-way cache would ascribe to each block. Thus, the blocks of the k-way set can be arranged in a stack from which, starting at the top, all j-way set contents can be found. LRU is an example of a stacking replacement policy.

For a fixed block size, a fixed number of sets, and a stacking replacement policy, a single simulation run can produce miss rates for one-way through k-way associative cache designs. Describe an algorithm to accomplish this economical simulation. Detail the data structure(s), any data structure maintenance, hit and miss event counting, and the formula for generating the set of cache miss rate results of your method. Is there any error introduced by using only a single run? How much reduction in simulation effort might reasonably be expected?

d. [25] <5.2> Consider all blocks that map into one set of a cache of size N. For a cache of size $2N$, these same blocks all map into exactly two sets, assuming block size and associativity are the same. How can you extend the algorithm of part (c) for stacking replacement policy caches to use a single simulation run for multiple numbers of sets as well as multiple associativities? Is there any error introduced by using only a single run? How much reduction in simulation effort might reasonably be expected for this combined run?

e. [20] <5.2> Running a complete memory reference trace through a cache simulator means simulating many cache hits. While hits are good news, it is the misses that we need to know about. Prove that the same number of misses would be counted by a simulation of a k-way set-associative cache with s sets, block size b, and a stacking replacement policy on a given memory reference trace and by a simulation of that same cache on a stripped version of the given trace produced by retaining only those references that would be misses in a direct-mapped cache with s sets and block size b.

f. [15] <5.2> By how much does the trace stripping technique of part (e) reduce the simulation effort required for a k-way cache?

g. [15] <5.2> Can the techniques of parts (b), (d), and (e) be combined? Why or why not?

✪ 5.25 [Discussion] <3, 5> Designing caches for out-of-order (OOO) superscalar CPUs is difficult for several reasons. Clearly, the cache will need to be nonblocking and may need to cope with several outstanding misses. However, the access pattern for OOO superscalar processors differs from that generated by in-order execution. What are the differences, and how might they affect cache design for OOO processors?

5.26 [Discussion] <5.8> Few computers today take advantage of the extra security available with gates and rings found in a CPU like the Intel Pentium. Construct a scenario where the computer industry would switch over to this model of protection. What (if any) would be the cost of doing so, other than the costs of modifying the operating system kernel to use gates and rings?

5.27 [Discussion] <5.7, 5.8> Some people have argued that with increasing capacity of memory storage per chip, virtual memory is an idea whose time has passed, and they expect to see it dropped from future computers. Find reasons for and against this argument.

5.28 [Discussion] <5> A hypothetical new technology, magnetic RAM (MRAM), has been proposed. MRAM will have cost and density similar to that of DRAM, but will retain data even after power is removed. However, there is a drawback to MRAM: The amount of energy needed to write a bit (by switching the magnetic orientation of a small area of magnetic material) is higher than that needed to set a bit in DRAM. As a result, MRAM designers must trade off write rate and data density: For a given density there is a maximum write rate beyond which the chip will melt. Propose uses for MRAM that would employ a dense, but slow to update memory. Are there applications for MRAM that would use a less dense but faster write memory?

5.29   [Discussion] <3, 4, 5> As we saw in Chapters 3 and 4, the time needed to execute a single instruction has fallen dramatically over the past few years, thanks to techniques such as pipelining, superscalar execution, and VLIW organization. However, memory access speeds have not kept up. As a result, memory access times may soon dominate program execution times (if they don't already). What is the impact of these changes on other computer science research areas such as algorithms, data structures, operating systems, and compilers? Find textbooks that suggest solutions to problems appropriate for older systems where processing time is the bottleneck, and suggest changes that might be more appropriate for newer systems in which the memory system is the bottleneck.

6

Multiprocessors and Thread-Level Parallelism

The turning away from the conventional organization came in the middle 1960s, when the law of diminishing returns began to take effect in the effort to increase the operational speed of a computer.... Electronic circuits are ultimately limited in their speed of operation by the speed of light ... and many of the circuits were already operating in the nanosecond range.

W. Jack Bouknight et al.
The Illiac IV System (1972)

... sequential computers are approaching a fundamental physical limit on their potential computational power. Such a limit is the speed of light ...

Angel L. DeCegama
The Technology of Parallel Processing, Volume I (1989)

... today's multiprocessors ... are nearing an impasse as technologies approach the speed of light. Even if the components of a sequential processor could be made to work this fast, the best that could be expected is no more than a few million instructions per second.

David Mitchell
The Transputer: The Time Is Now (1989)

6.1 Introduction

As the quotations that open this chapter show, the view that advances in uniprocessor architecture were nearing an end has been widely held at varying times. To counter this view, we observe that during the period 1985–2000, uniprocessor performance growth, driven by the microprocessor, was at its highest rate since the first transistorized computers in the late 1950s and early 1960s.

On balance, though, we believe that parallel processors will definitely have a bigger role in the future. This view is driven by three observations. First, since microprocessors are likely to remain the dominant uniprocessor technology, the logical way to improve performance beyond a single processor is by connecting multiple microprocessors together. This combination is likely to be more cost-effective than designing a custom processor. Second, it is unclear whether the pace of architectural innovation that has been based for more than 15 years on increased exploitation of instruction-level parallelism can be sustained indefinitely. As we saw in Chapters 3 and 4, modern multiple-issue processors have become incredibly complex, and the performance increases achieved through increasing complexity, increasing silicon, and increasing power seem to be diminishing. Third, there appears to be slow but steady progress on the major obstacle to widespread use of parallel processors, namely, software. This progress is probably faster in the server and embedded markets, as we discussed in Chapters 3 and 4. Server and embedded applications exhibit natural parallelism that can be exploited without some of the burdens of rewriting a gigantic software base. This is more of a challenge in the desktop space.

We, however, are extremely reluctant to predict the death of advances in uniprocessor architecture. Indeed, we believe that the rapid rate of performance growth will continue at least for the next five years. Whether this pace of innovation can be sustained longer is difficult to predict but hard to bet against. Nonetheless, if the pace of progress in uniprocessors does slow down, multiprocessor architectures will become increasingly attractive.

That said, we are left with two problems. First, multiprocessor architecture is a large and diverse field, and much of the field is in its youth, with ideas coming and going and, until very recently, more architectures failing than succeeding. Given that we are already on page 528, full coverage of the multiprocessor design space and its trade-offs would require another volume. (Indeed, Culler, Singh, and Gupta [1999] cover *only* multiprocessors in their 1000-page book!) Second, such coverage would necessarily entail discussing approaches that may not stand the test of time, something we have largely avoided to this point. For these reasons, we have chosen to focus on the mainstream of multiprocessor design: multiprocessors with small to medium numbers of processors (≤ 128). Such designs vastly dominate in terms of both units and dollars. We will pay only slight attention to the larger-scale multiprocessor design space (≥ 128 processors). At the present, the future architecture of such multiprocessors is unsettled, and even the viability of that marketplace is in doubt. We will return to this topic briefly at the end of the chapter, in Section 6.15.

A Taxonomy of Parallel Architectures

We begin this chapter with a taxonomy so that you can appreciate both the breadth of design alternatives for multiprocessors and the context that has led to the development of the dominant form of multiprocessors. We briefly describe the alternatives and the rationale behind them; a longer description of how these different models were born (and often died) can be found in the historical perspective at the end of the chapter.

The idea of using multiple processors both to increase performance and to improve availability dates back to the earliest electronic computers. About 30 years ago, Flynn [1966] proposed a simple model of categorizing all computers that is still useful today. He looked at the parallelism in the instruction and data streams called for by the instructions at the most constrained component of the multiprocessor, and placed all computers into one of four categories:

1. *Single instruction stream, single data stream* (SISD)—This category is the uniprocessor.

2. *Single instruction stream, multiple data streams* (SIMD)—The same instruction is executed by multiple processors using different data streams. Each processor has its own data memory (hence multiple data), but there is a single instruction memory and control processor, which fetches and dispatches instructions. The multimedia extensions we considered in Chapter 2 are a limited form of SIMD parallelism. Vector architectures are the largest class of processors of this type.

3. *Multiple instruction streams, single data stream* (MISD)—No commercial multiprocessor of this type has been built to date, but may be in the future. Some special-purpose stream processors approximate a limited form of this (there is only a single data stream that is operated on by successive functional units).

4. *Multiple instruction streams, multiple data streams* (MIMD)—Each processor fetches its own instructions and operates on its own data. The processors are often off-the-shelf microprocessors.

This is a coarse model, as some multiprocessors are hybrids of these categories. Nonetheless, it is useful to put a framework on the design space.

As discussed in the historical perspectives, many of the early multiprocessors were SIMD, and the SIMD model received renewed attention in the 1980s, and except for vector processors, was gone by the mid-1990s. MIMD has clearly emerged as the architecture of choice for general-purpose multiprocessors. Two factors are primarily responsible for the rise of the MIMD multiprocessors:

1. MIMDs offer flexibility. With the correct hardware and software support, MIMDs can function as single-user multiprocessors focusing on high performance for one application, as multiprogrammed multiprocessors running many tasks simultaneously, or as some combination of these functions.

2. MIMDs can build on the cost-performance advantages of off-the-shelf microprocessors. In fact, nearly all multiprocessors built today use the same microprocessors found in workstations and single-processor servers.

With an MIMD, each processor is executing its own instruction stream. In many cases, each processor executes a different process. Recall from the last chapter that a process is a segment of code that may be run independently, and that the state of the process contains all the information necessary to execute that program on a processor. In a multiprogrammed environment, where the processors may be running independent tasks, each process is typically independent of the processes on other processors.

It is also useful to be able to have multiple processors executing a single program and sharing the code and most of their address space. When multiple processes share code and data in this way, they are often called *threads*. Today, the term *thread* is often used in a casual way to refer to multiple loci of execution that may run on different processors, even when they do not share an address space.

To take advantage of an MIMD multiprocessor with *n* processors, we must usually have at least *n* threads or processes to execute. The independent threads are typically identified by the programmer or created by the compiler. Since the parallelism in this situation is contained in the threads, it is called *thread-level parallelism*.

Threads may vary from large-scale, independent processes—for example, independent programs running in a multiprogrammed fashion on different processors—to parallel iterations of a loop, automatically generated by a compiler and each executing for perhaps less than a thousand instructions. Although the size of a thread is important in considering how to exploit thread-level parallelism efficiently, the important qualitative distinction is that such parallelism is identified at a high level by the software system and that the threads consist of hundreds to millions of instructions that may be executed in parallel. In contrast, instruction-level parallelism is identified primarily by the hardware, although with software help in some cases, and is found and exploited one instruction at a time.

Existing MIMD multiprocessors fall into two classes, depending on the number of processors involved, which in turn dictate a memory organization and interconnect strategy. We refer to the multiprocessors by their memory organization because what constitutes a small or large number of processors is likely to change over time.

The first group, which we call *centralized shared-memory architectures,* has at most a few dozen processors in 2000. For multiprocessors with small processor counts, it is possible for the processors to share a single centralized memory and to interconnect the processors and memory by a bus. With large caches, the bus and the single memory, possibly with multiple banks, can satisfy the memory demands of a small number of processors. By replacing a single bus with multiple buses, or even a switch, a centralized shared-memory design can be scaled to a few dozen processors. Although scaling beyond that is technically conceivable, sharing a centralized memory, even organized as multiple banks, becomes less attractive as the number of processors sharing it increases.

Because there is a single main memory that has a symmetric relationship to all processors and a uniform access time from any processor, these multiprocessors are often called *symmetric (shared-memory) multiprocessors* (SMPs), and this style of architecture is sometimes called *uniform memory access* (UMA). This type of centralized shared-memory architecture is currently by far the most popular organization. Figure 6.1 shows what these multiprocessors look like. The architecture of such multiprocessors is the topic of Section 6.3.

The second group consists of multiprocessors with physically distributed memory. To support larger processor counts, memory must be distributed among the processors rather than centralized; otherwise the memory system would not be able to support the bandwidth demands of a larger number of processors without incurring excessively long access latency. With the rapid increase in processor performance and the associated increase in a processor's memory bandwidth requirements, the scale of multiprocessor for which distributed memory is preferred over a single, centralized memory continues to decrease in number (which is another reason not to use small and large scale). Of course, the larger number of processors raises the need for a high bandwidth interconnect, of which we will see examples in Chapter 8. Both direct interconnection networks (i.e., switches) and indirect networks (typically multidimensional meshes) are used. Figure 6.2 shows what these multiprocessors look like.

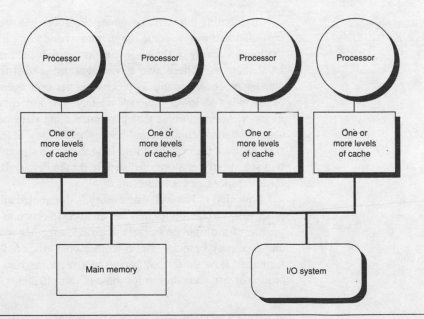

Figure 6.1 Basic structure of a centralized shared-memory multiprocessor. Multiple processor-cache subsystems share the same physical memory, typically connected by a bus. In larger designs, multiple buses, or even a switch may be used, but the key architectural property—uniform access time to all memory from all processors—remains.

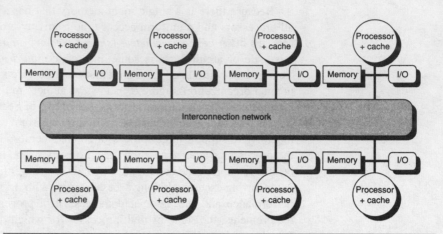

Figure 6.2 The basic architecture of a distributed-memory multiprocessor consists of individual nodes containing a processor, some memory, typically some I/O, and an interface to an interconnection network that connects all the nodes. Individual nodes may contain a small number of processors, which may be interconnected by a small bus or a different interconnection technology, which is less scalable than the global interconnection network.

Distributing the memory among the nodes has two major benefits. First, it is a cost-effective way to scale the memory bandwidth if most of the accesses are to the local memory in the node. Second, it reduces the latency for accesses to the local memory. These two advantages make distributed memory attractive at smaller processor counts as processors get ever faster and require more memory bandwidth and lower memory latency. The key disadvantage for a distributed-memory architecture is that communicating data between processors becomes somewhat more complex and has higher latency, at least when there is no contention, because the processors no longer share a single, centralized memory. As we will see shortly, the use of distributed memory leads to two different paradigms for interprocessor communication.

Typically, I/O as well as memory is distributed among the nodes of the multiprocessor, and the nodes may be small SMPs (two to eight processors). Although the use of multiple processors in a node together with a memory and a network interface may be quite useful from a cost-efficiency viewpoint, it is not fundamental to how these multiprocessors work, and so we will focus on the one-processor-per-node design for most of this chapter.

Models for Communication and Memory Architecture

As discussed earlier, any large-scale multiprocessor must use multiple memories that are physically distributed with the processors. There are two alternative architectural approaches that differ in the method used for communicating data among processors.

In the first method, communication occurs through a shared address space. That is, the physically separate memories can be addressed as one logically shared address space, meaning that a memory reference can be made by any processor to any memory location, assuming it has the correct access rights. These multiprocessors are called *distributed shared-memory* (DSM) architectures. The term *shared memory* refers to the fact that the *address space* is shared; that is, the same physical address on two processors refers to the same location in memory. Shared memory does *not* mean that there is a single, centralized memory. In contrast to the symmetric shared-memory multiprocessors, also known as UMAs (uniform memory access), the DSM multiprocessors are also called NUMAs (nonuniform memory access), since the access time depends on the location of a data word in memory.

Alternatively, the address space can consist of multiple private address spaces that are logically disjoint and cannot be addressed by a remote processor. In such multiprocessors, the same physical address on two different processors refers to two different locations in two different memories. Each processor-memory module is essentially a separate computer; therefore, these parallel processors have been called *multicomputers*. A multicomputer can even consist of completely separate computers connected on a local area network, which today are popularly called *clusters*. For applications that require little or no communication and can make use of separate memories, such clusters of processors, whether using a standardized or customized interconnect, can form a very cost-effective approach (see Section 8.10).

With each of these organizations for the address space, there is an associated communication mechanism. For a multiprocessor with a shared address space, that address space can be used to communicate data implicitly via load and store operations; hence the name *shared memory* for such multiprocessors. For a multiprocessor with multiple address spaces, communication of data is done by explicitly passing messages among the processors. Therefore, these multiprocessors are often called *message-passing multiprocessors*.

In message-passing multiprocessors, communication occurs by sending messages that request action or deliver data, just as with the network protocols discussed in Section 8.2. For example, if one processor wants to access or operate on data in a remote memory, it can send a message to request the data or to perform some operation on the data. In such cases, the message can be thought of as a *remote procedure call* (RPC). When the destination processor receives the message, either by polling for it or via an interrupt, it performs the operation or access on behalf of the remote processor and returns the result with a reply message. This type of message passing is also called *synchronous,* since the initiating processor sends a request and waits until the reply is returned before continuing. Software systems have been constructed to encapsulate the details of sending and receiving messages, including passing complex arguments or return values, presenting a clean RPC facility to the programmer.

Communication can also occur from the viewpoint of the writer of data rather than the reader, and this can be more efficient when the processor producing data knows which other processors will need the data. In such cases, the data can be sent directly to the consumer process without having to be requested first. It is often possible to perform such message sends asynchronously, allowing the sender process to continue immediately. Often the receiver will want to block if it tries to receive the message before it has arrived; in other cases, the reader may check whether a message is pending before actually trying to perform a blocking receive. Also the sender must be prepared to block if the receiver has not yet consumed an earlier message and no buffer space is available. The message-passing facilities offered in different multiprocessors are fairly diverse. To ease program portability, standard message-passing libraries (for example, message-passing interface, or MPI) have been proposed. Such libraries sacrifice some performance to achieve a common interface.

Performance Metrics for Communication Mechanisms

Three performance metrics are critical in any communication mechanism:

1. *Communication bandwidth*—Ideally the communication bandwidth is limited by processor, memory, and interconnection bandwidths, rather than by some aspect of the communication mechanism. The bisection bandwidth (see Section 8.5) is determined by the interconnection network. The bandwidth in or out of a single node, which is often as important as bisection bandwidth, is affected both by the architecture within the node and by the communication mechanism. How does the communication mechanism affect the communication bandwidth of a node? When communication occurs, resources within the nodes involved in the communication are tied up or occupied, preventing other outgoing or incoming communication. When this occupancy is incurred for each word of a message, it sets an absolute limit on the communication bandwidth. This limit is often lower than what the network or memory system can provide. Occupancy may also have a component that is incurred for each communication event, such as an incoming or outgoing request. In the latter case, the occupancy limits the communication rate, and the impact of the occupancy on overall communication bandwidth depends on the size of the messages.

2. *Communication latency*—Ideally the latency is as low as possible. As we will see in Chapter 8,

$$\text{Communication latency} = \text{Sender overhead} + \text{Time of flight} \\ + \text{Transmission time} + \text{Receiver overhead}$$

Time of flight is fixed and transmission time is determined by the interconnection network. The software and hardware overheads in sending and receiving messages are largely determined by the communication mechanism and its implementation. Why is latency crucial? Latency affects both performance and how easy it is to program a multiprocessor. Unless latency is hidden, it directly affects performance either by tying up processor resources or by causing the processor to wait. Overhead and occupancy are closely related, since many forms of overhead also tie up some part of the node, incurring an occupancy cost, which in turn limits bandwidth. Key features of a communication mechanism may directly affect overhead and occupancy. For example, how is the destination address for a remote communication named, and how is protection implemented? When naming and protection mechanisms are provided by the processor, as in a shared address space, the additional overhead is small. Alternatively, if these mechanisms must be provided by the operating system for each communication, this increases the overhead and occupancy costs of communication, which in turn reduce bandwidth and increase latency.

3. *Communication latency hiding*—How well can the communication mechanism hide latency by overlapping communication with computation or with other communication? Although measuring this is not as simple as measuring the first two metrics, it is an important characteristic that can be quantified by measuring the running time on multiprocessors with the same communication latency but different support for latency hiding. We will see examples of latency-hiding techniques for shared memory in Sections 6.8 and 6.10. Although hiding latency is certainly a good idea, it poses an additional burden on the software system and ultimately on the programmer. Furthermore, the amount of latency that can be hidden is application dependent. Thus, it is usually best to reduce latency wherever possible.

Each of these performance measures is affected by the characteristics of the communications needed in the application. The size of the data items being communicated is the most obvious, since it affects both latency and bandwidth in a direct way, as well as affecting the efficacy of different latency-hiding approaches. Similarly, the regularity in the communication patterns affects the cost of naming and protection, and hence the communication overhead. In general, mechanisms that perform well with smaller as well as larger data communication requests, and irregular as well as regular communication patterns, are more flexible and efficient for a wider class of applications. Of course, in considering any communication mechanism, designers must consider cost as well as performance.

Advantages of Different Communication Mechanisms

Each of these two primary communication mechanisms has its advantages. For shared-memory communication, advantages include

■ Compatibility with the well-understood mechanisms in use in centralized multiprocessors, which all use shared-memory communication. The OpenMP consortium (see *www.openmp.org* for description) has proposed a standardized programming interface for shared-memory multiprocessors.

■ Ease of programming when the communication patterns among processors are complex or vary dynamically during execution. Similar advantages simplify compiler design.

- The ability to develop applications using the familiar shared-memory model, focusing attention only on those accesses that are performance critical.

- Lower overhead for communication and better use of bandwidth when communicating small items. This arises from the implicit nature of communication and the use of memory mapping to implement protection in hardware, rather than through the I/O system.

- The ability to use hardware-controlled caching to reduce the frequency of remote communication by supporting automatic caching of all data, both shared and private. As we will see, caching reduces both latency and contention for accessing shared data. This advantage also comes with a disadvantage, which we mention below.

The major advantages for message-passing communication include the following:

- The hardware can be simpler, especially by comparison with a scalable shared-memory implementation that supports coherent caching of remote data.

- Communication is explicit, which means it is simpler to understand; in shared-memory models, it can be difficult to know when communication is occurring and when it is not, as well as how costly the communication is.

- Explicit communication focuses programmer attention on this costly aspect of parallel computation, sometimes leading to improved structure in a multiprocessor program.

- Synchronization is naturally associated with sending messages, reducing the possibility for errors introduced by incorrect synchronization.

- It makes it easier to use sender-initiated communication, which may have some advantages in performance.

Of course, the desired communication model can be created on top of a hardware model that supports either of these mechanisms. Supporting message passing on top of shared memory is considerably easier: Because messages essentially send data from one memory to another, sending a message can be implemented by doing a copy from one portion of the address space to another. The major difficulties arise from dealing with messages that may be misaligned and of arbitrary length in a memory system that is normally oriented toward transferring aligned blocks of data organized as cache blocks. These difficulties can be overcome either with small performance penalties in software or with essentially no penalties, using a small amount of hardware support.

Supporting shared memory efficiently on top of hardware for message passing is much more difficult. Without explicit hardware support for shared memory, all shared-memory references need to involve the operating system to provide address translation and memory protection, as well as to translate memory references into message sends and receives. Loads and stores usually move small amounts of data, so the high overhead of handling these communications in software severely limits the range of applications for which the performance of software-based shared memory is acceptable. An ongoing area of research is the exploration of when a software-based model is acceptable and whether a software-based mechanism is usable for the highest level of communication in a hierarchically structured system. One possible direction is the use of virtual memory mechanisms to share objects at the page level, a technique called *shared virtual memory;* we discuss this approach in Section 6.10.

In distributed-memory multiprocessors, the memory model and communication mechanisms distinguish the multiprocessors. Originally, distributed-memory multiprocessors were built with message passing, since it was clearly simpler and many designers and researchers did not believe that a shared address space could be built with distributed memory. Shared-memory communication has been supported in virtually every multiprocessor designed since 1995. What hardware communication mechanisms will be supported in the very largest multiprocessors, called *massively parallel processors* (MPPs), which typically have far more than 100 processors, is unclear; shared memory, message passing, and hybrid approaches are all contenders. Despite the symbolic importance of the MPPs, such multiprocessors are a small portion of the market and have little or no influence on the mainstream multiprocessors with tens of processors. We will return to a discussion of the possibilities and trends for MPPs in the concluding remarks and historical perspective at the end of this chapter.

SMPs, which we focus on in Section 6.3, vastly dominate DSM multiprocessors in terms of market size (both units and dollars) and will probably be the architecture of choice for on-chip multiprocessors. For moderate-scale multiprocessors (> 8 processors) long-term technical trends favor distributing memory, which is also likely to be the dominant approach when on-chip SMPs are used as the building blocks in the future. These distributed shared-memory multiprocessors are a natural extension of the centralized multiprocessors that dominate the market, so we discuss these architectures in Section 6.5. In contrast, multicomputers or message-passing multiprocessors build on advances in network technology and are described in Chapter 8. Since the technologies employed were well described in the last chapter, we focus our attention on shared-memory approaches in the rest of this chapter.

Challenges of Parallel Processing

Two important hurdles, both explainable with Amdahl's Law, make parallel processing challenging. The first has to do with the limited parallelism available in programs, and the second arises from the relatively high cost of communications. Limitations in available parallelism make it difficult to achieve good speedups in any parallel processor, as our first example shows.

Example   Suppose you want to achieve a speedup of 80 with 100 processors. What fraction of the original computation can be sequential?

Answer   Amdahl's Law is

$$\text{Speedup} = \frac{1}{\dfrac{\text{Fraction}_{\text{enhanced}}}{\text{Speedup}_{\text{enhanced}}} + (1 - \text{Fraction}_{\text{enhanced}})}$$

For simplicity in this example, assume that the program operates in only two modes: parallel with all processors fully used, which is the enhanced mode, or serial with only one processor in use. With this simplification, the speedup in enhanced mode is simply the number of processors, while the fraction of enhanced mode is the time spent in parallel mode. Substituting into the previous equation:

$$80 = \frac{1}{\dfrac{\text{Fraction}_{\text{parallel}}}{100} + (1 - \text{Fraction}_{\text{parallel}})}$$

Simplifying this equation yields

$$0.8 \times \text{Fraction}_{\text{parallel}} + 80 \times (1 - \text{Fraction}_{\text{parallel}}) = 1$$

$$80 - 79.2 \times \text{Fraction}_{\text{parallel}} = 1$$

$$\text{Fraction}_{\text{parallel}} = \frac{80 - 1}{79.2}$$

$$\text{Fraction}_{\text{parallel}} = 0.9975$$

Thus to achieve a speedup of 80 with 100 processors, only 0.25% of original computation can be sequential. Of course, to achieve linear speedup (speedup of *n* with *n* processors), the entire program must usually be parallel with no serial portions. (One exception to this is *superlinear speedup* that occurs due to the increased memory and cache available when the processor count is increased. This effect is usually not very large and rarely scales linearly with processor count.) In practice, programs do not just operate in fully parallel or sequential mode, but often use less than the full complement of the processors when running in parallel mode. Exercise 6.1 asks you to extend Amdahl's Law to deal with such a case.

The second major challenge in parallel processing involves the large latency of remote access in a parallel processor. In existing shared-memory multiprocessors, communication of data between processors may cost anywhere from 100 clock cycles to over 1000 clock cycles, depending on the communication mechanism, the type of interconnection network, and the scale of the multiprocessor. Figure 6.3 shows the typical round-trip delays to retrieve a word from a remote memory for several different shared-memory parallel processors.

The effect of long communication delays is clearly substantial. Let's consider a simple example.

Multiprocessor	Year shipped	SMP or NUMA	Maximum processors	Interconnection network	Typical remote memory access time (ns)
Sun Starfire servers	1996	SMP	64	multiple buses	500
SGI Origin 3000	1999	NUMA	512	fat hypercube	500
Cray T3E	1996	NUMA	2048	2-way 3D torus	300
HP V series	1998	SMP	32	8 × 8 crossbar	1000
Compaq AlphaServer GS	1999	SMP	32	switched buses	400

Figure 6.3 Typical remote access times to retrieve a word from a remote memory in shared-memory multiprocessors.

Example   Suppose we have an application running on a 32-processor multiprocessor, which has a 400 ns time to handle reference to a remote memory. For this application, assume that all the references except those involving communication hit in the local memory hierarchy, which is slightly optimistic. Processors are stalled on a remote request, and the processor clock rate is 1 GHz. If the base IPC (assuming that all references hit in the cache) is 2, how much faster is the multiprocessor if there is no communication versus if 0.2% of the instructions involve a remote communication reference?

Answer   It is simpler to first calculate the CPI. The effective CPI for the multiprocessor with 0.2% remote references is

$$CPI = \text{Base CPI} + \text{Remote request rate} \times \text{Remote request cost}$$

$$= \frac{1}{\text{Base IPC}} + 0.2\% \times \text{Remote request cost}$$

$$= 0.5 + 0.2\% \times \text{Remote request cost}$$

The remote request cost is

$$\frac{\text{Remote access cost}}{\text{Cycle time}} = \frac{400\text{ns}}{1\text{ ns}} = 400 \text{ cycles}$$

Hence we can compute the CPI:

$$CPI = 0.5 + 0.8 = 1.3$$

The multiprocessor with all local references is $1.3/0.5 = 2.6$ times faster. In practice, the performance analysis is much more complex, since some fraction of the noncommunication references will miss in the local hierarchy and the remote access time does not have a single constant value. For example, the cost of a remote reference could be quite a bit worse, since contention caused by many references trying to use the global interconnect can lead to increased delays.

These problems—insufficient parallelism and long-latency remote communication—are the two biggest challenges in using multiprocessors. The problem of inadequate application parallelism must be attacked primarily in software with new algorithms that can have better parallel performance. Reducing the impact of long remote latency can be attacked both by the architecture and by the programmer. For example, we can reduce the frequency of remote accesses with either hardware mechanisms, such as caching shared data, or software mechanisms, such as restructuring the data to make more accesses local. We can try to tolerate the latency by using prefetching or multithreading, which we examined in Chapters 4 and 5.

Much of this chapter focuses on techniques for reducing the impact of long remote communication latency. For example, Sections 6.3 and 6.5 discuss how caching can be used to reduce remote access frequency, while maintaining a coherent view of memory. Section 6.7 discusses synchronization, which, because it inherently involves interprocessor communication, is an additional potential bottleneck. Section 6.8 talks about latency-hiding techniques and memory consistency models for shared memory. Before we wade into these topics, it is helpful to have some understanding of the characteristics of parallel applications, both for better comprehension of the results we show using some of these applications and to gain a better understanding of the challenges in writing efficient parallel programs.

6.2 Characteristics of Application Domains

In earlier chapters, we examined the performance and characteristics of applications with only a small amount of insight into the structure of the applications. For understanding the key elements of uniprocessor performance, such as caches and pipelining, general knowledge of an application is often adequate, although we saw that deeper application knowledge was necessary to exploit higher levels of ILP.

In parallel processing, the additional performance-critical characteristics—such as load balance, synchronization, and sensitivity to memory latency—typically depend on high-level characteristics of the application. These characteristics include factors like how data are distributed, the structure of a parallel algorithm, and the spatial and temporal access patterns to data. Therefore at this point we take the time to examine the three different classes of workloads.

The three different domains of multiprocessor workloads we explore are a commercial workload, consisting of transaction processing, decision support, and web searching; a multiprogrammed workload with operating systems behavior included; and a workload consisting of individual parallel programs from the technical computing domain.

A Commercial Workload

Our commercial workload consists of three applications:

1. An online transaction-processing (OLTP) workload modeled after TPC-B (which has similar memory behavior to its newer cousin TPC-C) and using Oracle 7.3.2 as the underlying database. The workload consists of a set of client processes that generate requests and a set of servers that handle them. The server processes consume 85% of the user time, with the remaining going to the clients. Although the I/O latency is hidden by careful tuning and enough requests to keep the CPU busy, the server processes typically block for I/O after about 25,000 instructions.

2. A decision support system (DSS) workload based on TPC-D and also using Oracle 7.3.2 as the underlying database. The workload includes only 6 of the 17 read queries in TPC-D, although the 6 queries examined in the benchmark span the range of activities in the entire benchmark. To hide the I/O latency, parallelism is exploited both within queries, where parallelism is detected during a query formulation process, and across queries. Blocking calls are much less frequent than in the OLTP benchmark; the 6 queries average about 1.5 million instructions before blocking.

3. A Web index search (AltaVista) benchmark based on a search of a memory-mapped version of the AltaVista database (200 GB). The inner loop is heavily optimized. Because the search structure is static, little synchronization is needed among the threads.

The fraction of time spent in user mode, in the kernel, and in the idle loop are shown in Figure 6.4. The frequency of I/O increases both the kernel time and the idle time (see the OLTP entry, which has the largest I/O to computation ratio). AltaVista, which maps the entire search database into memory and has been extensively tuned, shows the least kernel or idle time.

Benchmark	% time user mode	% time kernel	% time CPU idle
OLTP	71	18	11
DSS (range for the six queries)	82–94	3–5	4–13
DSS (average across all queries)	87	3.7	9.3
AltaVista	> 98	< 1	<1

Figure 6.4 **The distribution of execution time in the commercial workloads.** The OLTP benchmark has the largest fraction of both OS time and CPU idle time (which is I/O wait time). The DSS benchmark shows much less OS time, since it does less I/O, but still more than 9% idle time. The extensive tuning of the AltaVista search engine is clear in these measurements. The data for this workload were collected by Barroso, Gharachorloo, and Bugnion [1998] on a four-processor AlphaServer 4100.

Multiprogramming and OS Workload

For small-scale multiprocessors we will also look at a multiprogrammed workload consisting of both user activity and OS activity. The workload used is two independent copies of the compile phase of the Andrew benchmark. The compile phase consists of a parallel make using eight processors. The workload runs for 5.24 seconds on eight processors, creating 203 processes and performing 787 disk requests on three different file systems. The workload is run with 128 MB of memory, and no paging activity takes place.

The workload has three distinct phases: compiling the benchmarks, which involves substantial compute activity; installing the object files in a library; and removing the object files. The last phase is completely dominated by I/O and only two processes are active (one for each of the runs). In the middle phase, I/O also plays a major role and the CPU is largely idle.

Because both CPU idle time and instruction cache performance are important in this workload, we examine these two issues here, focusing on the data cache performance later in the chapter. For the workload measurements, we assume the following memory and I/O systems:

- *Level 1 instruction cache*—32 KB, two-way set associative with a 64-byte block, 1 clock cycle hit time

- *Level 1 data cache*—32 KB, two-way set associative with a 32-byte block, 1 clock cycle hit time

- *Level 2 cache*—1 MB unified, two-way set associative with a 128-byte block, hit time 10 clock cycles

- *Main memory*—Single memory on a bus with an access time of 100 clock cycles

- *Disk system*—Fixed-access latency of 3 ms (less than normal to reduce idle time)

Figure 6.5 shows how the execution time breaks down for the eight processors using the parameters just listed. Execution time is broken into four compo-

	User execution	Kernel execution	Synchronization wait	CPU idle (waiting for I/O)
% instructions executed	27	3	1	69
% execution time	27	7	2	64

Figure 6.5 The distribution of execution time in the multiprogrammed parallel make workload. The high fraction of idle time is due to disk latency when only one of the eight processors is active. These data and the subsequent measurements for this workload were collected with the SimOS system [Rosenblum et al. 1995]. The actual runs and data collection were done by M. Rosenblum, S. Herrod, and E. Bugnion of Stanford University.

nents: idle—execution in the kernel mode idle loop; user—execution in user code; synchronization—execution or waiting for synchronization variables; and kernel—execution in the OS that is neither idle nor in synchronization access.

Unlike the parallel scientific workload, this multiprogramming workload has a significant instruction cache performance loss, at least for the OS. The instruction cache miss rate in the OS for a 64-byte block size, two-way set-associative cache varies from 1.7% for a 32 KB cache to 0.2% for a 256 KB cache. User-level instruction cache misses are roughly one-sixth of the OS rate, across the variety of cache sizes.

Scientific/Technical Applications

Our scientific/technical parallel workload consists of two applications and two computational kernels. The kernels are an FFT (fast Fourier transformation) and an LU decomposition, which were chosen because they represent commonly used techniques in a wide variety of applications and have performance characteristics typical of many parallel scientific applications. In addition, the kernels have small code segments whose behavior we can understand and directly track to specific architectural characteristics. Like many scientific applications, I/O is essentially nonexistent in this workload.

The two applications that we use in this chapter are Barnes and Ocean, which represent two important but very different types of parallel computation. We briefly describe each of these applications and kernels and characterize their basic behavior in terms of parallelism and communication. We describe how the problem is decomposed for a distributed shared-memory multiprocessor; certain data decompositions that we describe are not necessary on multiprocessors that have a single, centralized memory.

The FFT Kernel

The FFT is the key kernel in applications that use spectral methods, which arise in fields ranging from signal processing to fluid flow to climate modeling. The FFT application we study here is a one-dimensional version of a parallel algorithm for a complex number FFT. It has a sequential execution time for n data points of $n \log n$. The algorithm uses a high radix (equal to $\sqrt{n}$) that minimizes communication. The measurements shown in this chapter are collected for a million-point input data set.

There are three primary data structures: the input and output arrays of the data being transformed and the roots of unity matrix, which is precomputed and only read during the execution. All arrays are organized as square matrices. The six steps in the algorithm are as follows:

1. Transpose data matrix.

2. Perform 1D FFT on each row of data matrix.

3. Multiply the roots of unity matrix by the data matrix and write the result in the data matrix.

4. Transpose data matrix.

5. Perform 1D FFT on each row of data matrix.

6. Transpose data matrix.

The data matrices and the roots of unity matrix are partitioned among processors in contiguous chunks of rows, so that each processor's partition falls in its own local memory. The first row of the roots of unity matrix is accessed heavily by all processors and is often replicated, as we do, during the first step of the algorithm just shown. The data transposes ensure good locality during the individual FFT steps, which would otherwise access nonlocal data.

The only communication is in the transpose phases, which require all-to-all communication of large amounts of data. Contiguous subcolumns in the rows assigned to a processor are grouped into blocks, which are transposed and placed into the proper location of the destination matrix. Every processor transposes one block locally and sends one block to each of the other processors in the system. Although there is no reuse of individual words in the transpose, with long cache blocks it makes sense to block the transpose to take advantage of the spatial locality afforded by long blocks in the source matrix.

The LU Kernel

LU is an LU factorization of a dense matrix and is representative of many dense linear algebra computations, such as QR factorization, Cholesky factorization, and eigenvalue methods. For a matrix of size $n \times n$ the running time is n^3 and the parallelism is proportional to n^2. Dense LU factorization can be performed efficiently by blocking the algorithm, using the techniques in Chapter 5, which leads to highly efficient cache behavior and low communication. After blocking the algorithm, the dominant computation is a dense matrix multiply that occurs in the innermost loop. The block size is chosen to be small enough to keep the cache miss rate low, and large enough to reduce the time spent in the less parallel parts of the computation. Relatively small block sizes (8×8 or 16×16) tend to satisfy both criteria.

Two details are important for reducing interprocessor communication. First, the blocks of the matrix are assigned to processors using a 2D tiling: the $\frac{n}{B} \times \frac{n}{B}$ (where each block is $B \times B$) matrix of blocks is allocated by laying a grid of size $p \times p$ over the matrix of blocks in a cookie-cutter fashion until all the blocks are allocated to a processor. Second, the dense matrix multiplication is performed by the processor that owns the *destination* block. With this blocking and allocation scheme, communication during the reduction is both regular and predictable. For the measurements in this chapter, the input is a 512×512 matrix and a block of 16×16 is used.

A natural way to code the blocked LU factorization of a 2D matrix in a shared address space is to use a 2D array to represent the matrix. Because blocks are allocated in a tiled decomposition, and a block is not contiguous in the address space in a 2D array, it is very difficult to allocate blocks in the local memories of the processors that own them. The solution is to ensure that blocks assigned to a processor are allocated locally and contiguously by using a 4D array (with the first two dimensions specifying the block number in the 2D grid of blocks, and the next two specifying the element in the block).

The Barnes Application

Barnes is an implementation of the Barnes-Hut n-body algorithm solving a problem in galaxy evolution. *N-body algorithms* simulate the interaction among a large number of bodies that have forces interacting among them. In this instance the bodies represent collections of stars and the force is gravity. To reduce the computational time required to model completely all the individual interactions among the bodies, which grow as n^2, n-body algorithms take advantage of the fact that the forces drop off with distance. (Gravity, for example, drops off as $1/d^2$, where d is the distance between the two bodies.) The Barnes-Hut algorithm takes advantage of this property by treating a collection of bodies that are "far away" from another body as a single point at the center of mass of the collection and with mass equal to the collection. If the body is far enough from any body in the collection, then the error introduced will be negligible. The collections are structured in a hierarchical fashion, which can be represented in a tree. This algorithm yields an $n \log n$ running time with parallelism proportional to n.

The Barnes-Hut algorithm uses an octree (each node has up to eight children) to represent the eight cubes in a portion of space. Each node then represents the collection of bodies in the subtree rooted at that node, which we call a *cell*. Because the density of space varies and the leaves represent individual bodies, the depth of the tree varies. The tree is traversed once per body to compute the net force acting on that body. The force calculation algorithm for a body starts at the root of the tree. For every node in the tree it visits, the algorithm determines if the center of mass of the cell represented by the subtree rooted at the node is "far enough away" from the body. If so, the entire subtree under that node is approximated by a single point at the center of mass of the cell, and the force this center of mass exerts on the body is computed. On the other hand, if the center of mass is not far enough away, the cell must be "opened" and each of its subtrees visited. The distance between the body and the cell, together with the error tolerances, determines which cells must be opened. This force calculation phase dominates the execution time. This chapter takes measurements using 16K bodies; the criterion for determining whether a cell needs to be opened is set to the middle of the range typically used in practice.

Obtaining effective parallel performance on Barnes-Hut is challenging because the distribution of bodies is nonuniform and changes over time, making partitioning the work among the processors and maintenance of good locality of reference difficult. We are helped by two properties: (1) the system evolves slowly, and (2) because gravitational forces fall off quickly, with high probability, each cell requires touching a small number of other cells, most of which were used on the last time step. The tree can be partitioned by allocating each processor a subtree. Many of the accesses needed to compute the force on a body in the subtree will be to other bodies in the subtree. Since the amount of work associated with a subtree varies (cells in dense portions of space will need to access more cells), the size of the subtree allocated to a processor is based on some measure of the work it has to do (e.g., how many other cells does it need to visit), rather than just on the number of nodes in the subtree. By partitioning the octree representation, we can obtain good load balance and good locality of reference, while keeping the partitioning cost low. Although this partitioning scheme results in good locality of reference, the resulting data references tend to be for small amounts of data and are unstructured. Thus this scheme requires an efficient implementation of shared-memory communication.

The Ocean Application

Ocean simulates the influence of eddy and boundary currents on large-scale flow in the ocean. It uses a restricted red-black Gauss-Seidel multigrid technique to solve a set of elliptical partial differential equations. *Red-black Gauss-Seidel* is an iteration technique that colors the points in the grid so as to consistently update each point based on previous values of the adjacent neighbors. *Multigrid methods* solve finite difference equations by iteration using hierarchical grids. Each grid in the hierarchy has fewer points than the grid below and is an approximation to the lower grid. A finer grid increases accuracy and thus the rate of convergence, while requiring more execution time, since it has more data points. Whether to move up or down in the hierarchy of grids used for the next iteration is determined by the rate of change of the data values. The estimate of the error at every time step is used to decide whether to stay at the same grid, move to a coarser grid, or move to a finer grid. When the iteration converges at the finest level, a solution has been reached. Each iteration has n^2 work for an $n \times n$ grid and the same amount of parallelism.

The arrays representing each grid are dynamically allocated and sized to the particular problem. The entire ocean basin is partitioned into square subgrids (as close as possible) that are allocated in the portion of the address space corresponding to the local memory of the individual processors, which are assigned responsibility for the subgrid. For the measurements in this chapter we use an input that has 130×130 grid points. There are five steps in a time iteration. Since data are exchanged between the steps, all the processors present synchronize at the end of each step before proceeding to the next. Communication occurs when the boundary points of a subgrid are accessed by the adjacent subgrid in nearest-neighbor fashion.

Computation/Communication for the Parallel Programs

A key characteristic in determining the performance of parallel programs is the ratio of computation to communication. If the ratio is high, it means the application has lots of computation for each datum communicated. As we saw in Section 6.1, communication is the costly part of parallel computing; therefore, high computation-to-communication ratios are very beneficial. In a parallel processing environment, we are concerned with how the ratio of computation to communication changes as we increase either the number of processors, the size of the problem, or both. Knowing how the ratio changes as we increase the processor count sheds light on how well the application can be sped up. Because we are often interested in running larger problems, it is vital to understand how changing the data set size affects this ratio.

To understand what happens quantitatively to the computation-to-communication ratio as we add processors, consider what happens separately to computation and to communication as we either add processors or increase problem size. Figure 6.6 shows that as we add processors, for these applications, the amount of computation per processor falls proportionately and the amount of communication per processor falls more slowly. As we increase the problem size, the computation scales as the $O(\ )$ complexity of the algorithm dictates. Communication scaling is more complex and depends on details of the algorithm; we describe the basic phenomena for each application in the caption of Figure 6.6.

Application	Scaling of computation	Scaling of communication	Scaling of computation-to-communication
FFT	$\dfrac{n\log n}{p}$	$\dfrac{n}{p}$	$\log n$
LU	$\dfrac{n}{p}$	$\dfrac{\sqrt{n}}{\sqrt{p}}$	$\dfrac{\sqrt{n}}{\sqrt{p}}$
Barnes	$\dfrac{n\log n}{p}$	approximately $\dfrac{\sqrt{n}(\log n)}{\sqrt{p}}$	approximately $\dfrac{\sqrt{n}}{\sqrt{p}}$
Ocean	$\dfrac{n}{p}$	$\dfrac{\sqrt{n}}{\sqrt{p}}$	$\dfrac{\sqrt{n}}{\sqrt{p}}$

Figure 6.6　Scaling of computation, of communication, and of the ratio are critical factors in determining performance on parallel multiprocessors. In this table p is the increased processor count and n is the increased data set size. Scaling is on a per-processor basis. The computation scales up with n at the rate given by $O(\ )$ analysis and scales down linearly as p is increased. Communication scaling is more complex. In FFT all data points must interact, so communication increases with n and decreases with p. In LU and Ocean, communication is proportional to the boundary of a block, so it scales with data set size at a rate proportional to the side of a square with n points, namely, $\sqrt{n}$; for the same reason communication in these two applications scales inversely to $\sqrt{p}$. Barnes has the most complex scaling properties. Because of the fall-off of interaction between bodies, the basic number of interactions among bodies, which require communication, scales as $\sqrt{n}$. An additional factor of $\log n$ is needed to maintain the relationships among the bodies. As processor count is increased, communication scales inversely to $\sqrt{p}$.

The overall computation-to-communication ratio is computed from the individual growth rate in computation and communication. In general, this ratio rises slowly with an increase in data set size and decreases as we add processors. This reminds us that performing a fixed-size problem with more processors leads to increasing inefficiencies because the amount of communication among processors grows. It also tells us how quickly we must scale data set size as we add processors, to keep the fraction of time in communication fixed. The following example illustrates these trade-offs.

Example   Suppose we know that for a given multiprocessor the Ocean application spends 20% of its execution time waiting for communication when run on four processors. Assume that the cost of each communication event is independent of processor count, which is not true in general, since communication costs rise with processor count. How much faster might we expect Ocean to run on a 32-processor machine with the same problem size? What fraction of the execution time is spent on communication in this case? How much larger a problem should we run if we want the fraction of time spent communicating to be the same?

Answer   The computation-to-communication ratio for Ocean is $\sqrt{n}/\sqrt{p}$, so if the problem size is the same, the communication frequency scales by $\sqrt{p}$. This means that communication time increases by $\sqrt{8}$. We can use a variation on Amdahl's Law, recognizing that the computation is decreased but the communication time is increased. If T_4 is the total execution time for 4 processors, then the execution time for 32 processors is

$$T_{32} = \text{Compute time} + \text{Communicaton time}$$

$$= \frac{0.8 \times T_4}{8} + (0.2 \times T_4) \times \sqrt{8}$$

$$= 0.1 \times T_4 + 0.57 \times T_4 = 0.67 \times T_4$$

Hence the speedup is

$$\text{Speedup} = \frac{T_4}{T_{32}} = \frac{T_4}{0.67 \times T_4} = 1.49$$

and the fraction of time spent in communication goes from 20% to $0.57/0.67 = 85\%$.

For the fraction of the communication time to remain the same, we must keep the computation-to-communication ratio the same, so the problem size must scale at the same rate as the processor count. Notice that because we have changed the problem size, we cannot fairly compare the speedup of the original problem and the scaled problem. We will return to the critical issue of scaling applications for multiprocessors in Sections 6.10 and 6.14.

| **6.3** | # Symmetric Shared-Memory Architectures |

Multis are a new class of computers based on multiple microprocessors. The small size, low cost, and high performance of microprocessors allow design and construction of computer structures that offer significant advantages in manufacture, price-performance ratio, and reliability over traditional computer families. . . . Multis are likely to be the basis for the next, the fifth, generation of computers. [p. 463]

Bell [1985]

As we saw in Chapter 5, the use of large, multilevel caches can substantially reduce the memory bandwidth demands of a processor. If the main memory bandwidth demands of a single processor are reduced, multiple processors may be able to share the same memory. Starting in the 1980s, this observation, combined with the emerging dominance of the microprocessor, motivated many designers to create small-scale multiprocessors where several processors shared a single physical memory connected by a shared bus. This type of design is called symmetric shared memory because each processor has the same relationship to one single shared memory. Because of the small size of the processors and the significant reduction in the requirements for bus bandwidth achieved by large caches, such symmetric multiprocessors are extremely cost-effective, provided that a sufficient amount of memory bandwidth exists. Early designs of such multiprocessors were able to place an entire CPU and cache subsystem on a board, which plugged into the bus backplane. More recent designs have placed up to four processors per board, and a recent announcement by IBM includes two processors on the same die. Figure 6.1 shows a simple diagram of such a multiprocessor.

Small-scale, shared-memory machines usually support the caching of both shared and private data. *Private data* are used by a single processor, while *shared data* are used by multiple processors, essentially providing communication among the processors through reads and writes of the shared data. When a private item is cached, its location is migrated to the cache, reducing the average access time as well as the memory bandwidth required. Since no other processor uses the data, the program behavior is identical to that in a uniprocessor. When shared data are cached, the shared value may be replicated in multiple caches. In addition to the reduction in access latency and required memory bandwidth, this replication also provides a reduction in contention that may exist for shared data items that are being read by multiple processors simultaneously. Caching of shared data, however, introduces a new problem: cache coherence.

What Is Multiprocessor Cache Coherence?

As we saw in Chapter 6, the introduction of caches caused a coherence problem for I/O operations, since the view of memory through the cache could be different from the view of memory obtained through the I/O subsystem. The same problem exists in the case of multiprocessors because the view of memory held by two different processors is through their individual caches. Figure 6.7 illustrates the problem and shows how two different processors can have two different values for the same location. This difficulty is generally referred to as the *cache coherence problem*.

Informally, we could say that a memory system is coherent if any read of a data item returns the most recently written value of that data item. This definition, although intuitively appealing, is vague and simplistic; the reality is much more complex. This simple definition contains two different aspects of memory system behavior, both of which are critical to writing correct shared-memory programs. The first aspect, called *coherence,* defines what values can be returned by a read. The second aspect, called *consistency,* determines when a written value will be returned by a read. Let's look at coherence first.

A memory system is coherent if

1. A read by a processor P to a location X that follows a write by P to X, with no writes of X by another processor occurring between the write and the read by P, always returns the value written by P.

2. A read by a processor to location X that follows a write by another processor to X returns the written value if the read and write are sufficiently separated in time and no other writes to X occur between the two accesses.

3. Writes to the same location are *serialized;* that is, two writes to the same location by any two processors are seen in the same order by all processors. For example, if the values 1 and then 2 are written to a location, processors can never read the value of the location as 2 and then later read it as 1.

The first property simply preserves program order—we expect this property to be true even in uniprocessors. The second property defines the notion of what it means to have a coherent view of memory: If a processor could continuously read an old data value, we would clearly say that memory was incoherent.

Time	Event	Cache contents for CPU A	Cache contents for CPU B	Memory contents for location X
0				1
1	CPU A reads X	1		1
2	CPU B reads X	1	1	1
3	CPU A stores 0 into X	0	1	0

Figure 6.7 The cache coherence problem for a single memory location (X), read and written by two processors (A and B). We initially assume that neither cache contains the variable and that X has the value 1. We also assume a write-through cache; a write-back cache adds some additional but similar complications. After the value of X has been written by A, A's cache and the memory both contain the new value, but B's cache does not, and if B reads the value of X, it will receive 1!

The need for write serialization is more subtle, but equally important. Suppose we did not serialize writes, and processor P1 writes location X followed by P2 writing location X. Serializing the writes ensures that every processor will see the write done by P2 at some point. If we did not serialize the writes, it might be the case that some processor could see the write of P2 first and then see the write of P1, maintaining the value written by P1 indefinitely. The simplest way to avoid such difficulties is to serialize writes, so that all writes to the same location are seen in the same order; this property is called *write serialization.*

Although the three properties just described are sufficient to ensure coherence, the question of when a written value will be seen is also important. To see why, observe that we cannot require that a read of X instantaneously see the value written for X by some other processor. If, for example, a write of X on one processor precedes a read of X on another processor by a very small time, it may be impossible to ensure that the read returns the value of the data written, since the written data may not even have left the processor at that point. The issue of exactly *when* a written value must be seen by a reader is defined by a *memory consistency model*—a topic discussed in Section 6.8.

Coherence and consistency are complementary: Coherence defines the behavior of reads and writes to the same memory location, while consistency defines the behavior of reads and writes with respect to accesses to other memory locations. For simplicity, and because we cannot explain the problem in full detail at this point, assume that we require that a write does not complete until all processors have seen the effect of the write and that the processor does not change the order of any write with any other memory access. This allows the processor to reorder reads, but forces the processor to finish a write in program order. We will rely on this assumption until we reach Section 6.8, where we will see exactly the meaning of this definition, as well as the alternatives.

Basic Schemes for Enforcing Coherence

The coherence problem for multiprocessors and I/O, although similar in origin, has different characteristics that affect the appropriate solution. Unlike I/O, where multiple data copies are a rare event—one to be avoided whenever possible—a program running on multiple processors will normally have copies of the same data in several caches. In a coherent multiprocessor, the caches provide both *migration* and *replication* of shared data items.

Coherent caches provide migration, since a data item can be moved to a local cache and used there in a transparent fashion. This migration reduces both the latency to access a shared data item that is allocated remotely and the bandwidth demand on the shared memory.

Coherent caches also provide replication for shared data that are being simultaneously read, since the caches make a copy of the data item in the local cache. Replication reduces both latency of access and contention for a read shared data item. Supporting this migration and replication is critical to performance in accessing shared data. Thus, rather than trying to solve the problem by avoiding it in software, small-scale multiprocessors adopt a hardware solution by introducing a protocol to maintain coherent caches.

The protocols to maintain coherence for multiple processors are called *cache coherence protocols*. Key to implementing a cache coherence protocol is tracking the state of any sharing of a data block. There are two classes of protocols, which use different techniques to track the sharing status, in use:

■ *Directory based*—The sharing status of a block of physical memory is kept in just one location, called the *directory;* we focus on this approach in Section 6.5, when we discuss scalable shared-memory architecture.

■ *Snooping*—Every cache that has a copy of the data from a block of physical memory also has a copy of the sharing status of the block, and no centralized state is kept. The caches are usually on a shared-memory bus, and all cache controllers monitor or *snoop* on the bus to determine whether or not they have a copy of a block that is requested on the bus. We focus on this approach in this section.

Snooping protocols became popular with multiprocessors using microprocessors and caches attached to a single shared memory because these protocols can use a preexisting physical connection—the bus to memory—to interrogate the status of the caches.

Snooping Protocols

There are two ways to maintain the coherence requirement described in the previous subsection. One method is to ensure that a processor has exclusive access to a data item before it writes that item. This style of protocol is called a *write invalidate protocol* because it invalidates other copies on a write. It is by far the most common protocol, both for snooping and for directory schemes. Exclusive access ensures that no other readable or writable copies of an item exist when the write occurs: All other cached copies of the item are invalidated.

Figure 6.8 shows an example of an invalidation protocol for a snooping bus with write-back caches in action. To see how this protocol ensures coherence, consider a write followed by a read by another processor: Since the write requires exclusive access, any copy held by the reading processor must be invalidated (hence the protocol name). Thus, when the read occurs, it misses in the cache and is forced to fetch a new copy of the data. For a write, we require that the writing processor have exclusive access, preventing any other processor from being able to write simultaneously. If two processors do attempt to write the same data simultaneously, one of them wins the race (we'll see how we decide who wins shortly), causing the other processor's copy to be invalidated. For the other processor to complete its write, it must obtain a new copy of the data, which must now contain the updated value. Therefore, this protocol enforces write serialization.

The alternative to an invalidate protocol is to update all the cached copies of a data item when that item is written. This type of protocol is called a *write update*

Processor activity	Bus activity	Contents of CPU A's cache	Contents of CPU B's cache	Contents of memory location X
				0
CPU A reads X	Cache miss for X	0		0
CPU B reads X	Cache miss for X	0	0	0
CPU A writes a 1 to X	Invalidation for X	1		0
CPU B reads X	Cache miss for X	1	1	1

Figure 6.8   An example of an invalidation protocol working on a snooping bus for a single cache block (X) with write-back caches. We assume that neither cache initially holds X and that the value of X in memory is 0. The CPU and memory contents show the value after the processor and bus activity have both completed. A blank indicates no activity or no copy cached. When the second miss by B occurs, CPU A responds with the value canceling the response from memory. In addition, both the contents of B's cache and the memory contents of X are updated. This update of memory, which occurs when a block becomes shared, is typical in most protocols and simplifies the protocol, as we will see shortly.

Processor activity	Bus activity	Contents of CPU A's cache	Contents of CPU B's cache	Contents of memory location X
				0
CPU A reads X	Cache miss for X	0		0
CPU B reads X	Cache miss for X	0	0	0
CPU A writes a 1 to X	Write broadcast of X	1	1	1
CPU B reads X		1	1	1

Figure 6.9   An example of a write update or broadcast protocol working on a snooping bus for a single cache block (X) with write-back caches. We assume that neither cache initially holds X and that the value of X in memory is 0. The CPU and memory contents show the value after the processor and bus activity have both completed. A blank indicates no activity or no copy cached. When CPU A broadcasts the write, both the cache in CPU B and the memory location of X are updated.

or *write broadcast* protocol. To keep the bandwidth requirements of this protocol under control it is useful to track whether or not a word in the cache is shared—that is, contained in other caches. If it is not, then there is no need to broadcast or update any other caches. Figure 6.9 shows an example of a write update protocol in operation. In the decade since these protocols were developed, invalidate has emerged as the winner for the vast majority of designs. To understand why, let's look at the qualitative performance differences.

The performance differences between write update and write invalidate protocols arise from three characteristics:

1. Multiple writes to the same word with no intervening reads require multiple write broadcasts in an update protocol, but only one initial invalidation in a write invalidate protocol.

2. With multiword cache blocks, each word written in a cache block requires a write broadcast in an update protocol, although only the first write to any word in the block needs to generate an invalidate in an invalidation protocol. An invalidation protocol works on cache blocks, while an update protocol must work on individual words (or bytes, when bytes are written). It is possible to try to merge writes in a write broadcast scheme, just as we did for write buffers in Chapter 5, but the basic difference remains.

3. The delay between writing a word in one processor and reading the written value in another processor is usually less in a write update scheme, since the written data are immediately updated in the reader's cache (assuming that the reading processor has a copy of the data). By comparison, in an invalidation protocol, the reader is invalidated first, then later reads the data and is stalled until a copy can be read and returned to the processor.

Because bus and memory bandwidth is usually the commodity most in demand in a bus-based multiprocessor and invalidation protocols generate less bus and memory traffic, invalidation has become the protocol of choice for almost all multiprocessors. Update protocols also cause problems for memory consistency models, reducing the potential performance gains of update, mentioned in point 3, even further. In designs with very small processor counts (two, or at most, four) where the processors are tightly coupled (perhaps even on the same chip), the larger bandwidth demands of update may be acceptable. Nonetheless, given the trends in increasing processor performance and the related increase in bandwidth demands, we can expect update schemes to be used very infrequently. For this reason, we will focus only on invalidate protocols for the rest of the chapter.

Basic Implementation Techniques

The key to implementing an invalidate protocol in a small-scale multiprocessor is the use of the bus to perform invalidates. To perform an invalidate the processor simply acquires bus access and broadcasts the address to be invalidated on the bus. All processors continuously snoop on the bus, watching the addresses. The processors check whether the address on the bus is in their cache. If so, the corresponding data in the cache are invalidated.

The serialization of access enforced by the bus also forces serialization of writes, since when two processors compete to write to the same location, one must obtain bus access before the other. The first processor to obtain bus access will cause the other processor's copy to be invalidated, causing writes to be strictly serialized. One implication of this scheme is that a write to a shared data item cannot complete until it obtains bus access.

In addition to invalidating outstanding copies of a cache block that is being written into, we also need to locate a data item when a cache miss occurs. In a write-through cache, it is easy to find the recent value of a data item, since all written data are always sent to the memory, from which the most recent value of a data item can always be fetched. (Write buffers can lead to some additional complexities, which are discussed in Section 6.8.)

For a write-back cache, however, the problem of finding the most recent data value is harder, since the most recent value of a data item can be in a cache rather than in memory. Happily, write-back caches can use the same snooping scheme both for cache misses and for writes: Each processor snoops every address placed on the bus. If a processor finds that it has a dirty copy of the requested cache block, it provides that cache block in response to the read request and causes the memory access to be aborted. Since write-back caches generate lower requirements for memory bandwidth, they are greatly preferable in a multi-processor, despite the slight increase in complexity. Therefore, we focus on implementation with write-back caches.

The normal cache tags can be used to implement the process of snooping, and the valid bit for each block makes invalidation easy to implement. Read misses, whether generated by an invalidation or by some other event, are also straightforward since they simply rely on the snooping capability. For writes we'd like to know whether any other copies of the block are cached because, if there are no other cached copies, then the write need not be placed on the bus in a write-back cache. Not sending the write reduces both the time taken by the write and the required bandwidth.

To track whether or not a cache block is shared we can add an extra state bit associated with each cache block, just as we have a valid bit and a dirty bit. By adding a bit indicating whether the block is shared, we can decide whether a write must generate an invalidate. When a write to a block in the shared state occurs, the cache generates an invalidation on the bus and marks the block as private. No further invalidations will be sent by that processor for that block. The processor with the sole copy of a cache block is normally called the *owner* of the cache block.

When an invalidation is sent, the state of the owner's cache block is changed from shared to unshared (or exclusive). If another processor later requests this cache block, the state must be made shared again. Since our snooping cache also sees any misses, it knows when the exclusive cache block has been requested by another processor and the state should be made shared.

Every bus transaction must check the cache-address tags, which could potentially interfere with CPU cache accesses. This potential interference is reduced by one of two techniques: duplicating the tags or employing a multilevel cache with *inclusion,* whereby the levels closer to the CPU are a subset of those further away. If the tags are duplicated, then the CPU and the snooping activity may proceed in parallel. Of course, on a cache miss the processor needs to arbitrate for and update both sets of tags. Likewise, if the snoop finds a matching tag entry, it needs to arbitrate for and access both sets of cache tags (to perform an invalidate or to update the shared bit), as well as possibly the cache data array to retrieve a copy of a block. Thus with duplicate tags the processor only needs to be stalled when it does a cache access at the same time that a snoop has detected a copy in the cache. Furthermore, snooping activity is delayed only when the cache is dealing with a miss.

If the CPU uses a multilevel cache with the inclusion property, then every entry in the primary cache is required to be in the secondary cache. Thus the snoop activity can be directed to the second-level cache, while most of the processor's activity is directed to the primary cache. If the snoop gets a hit in the secondary cache, then it must arbitrate for the primary cache to update the state and possibly retrieve the data, which usually requires a stall of the processor. Since many multiprocessors use a multilevel cache to decrease the bandwidth demands of the individual processors, this solution has been adopted in many designs. Sometimes it may even be useful to duplicate the tags of the secondary cache to further decrease contention between the CPU and the snooping activity. We discuss the inclusion property in more detail in Section 6.10.

An Example Protocol

A bus-based coherence protocol is usually implemented by incorporating a finite-state controller in each node. This controller responds to requests from the processor and from the bus, changing the state of the selected cache block, as well as using the bus to access data or to invalidate it. Figure 6.10 shows the requests generated by the processor-cache module in a node, in the top half of the table, as well as those coming from the bus, in the bottom half of the table. For simplicity, the protocol we explain does not distinguish between a write hit and a write miss to a shared cache block: In both cases, we treat such an access as a write miss. When the write miss is placed on the bus, any processors with copies of the cache block invalidate it. In a write-back cache, if the block is exclusive in just one cache, that cache also writes back the block. Treating write hits to shared blocks as cache misses reduces the number of different bus transactions and simplifies the controller. In more sophisticated protocols, these "misses" are treated as upgrade requests that generate a bus transaction and an invalidate, but do not actually transfer the data, since the copy in the cache is up to date.

Figure 6.11 shows a finite-state transition diagram for a single cache block using a write invalidation protocol and a write-back cache. For simplicity, the three states of the protocol are duplicated to represent transitions based on CPU requests (on the left, which corresponds to the top half of the table in Figure 6.10), as opposed to transitions based on bus requests (on the right, which corresponds to the bottom half of the table in Figure 6.10). Boldface type is used to distinguish the bus actions, as opposed to the conditions on which a state transition depends. The state in each node represents the state of the selected cache block specified by the processor or bus request.

Request	Source	State of addressed cache block	Function and explanation
Read hit	processor	shared or exclusive	Read data in cache.
Read miss	processor	invalid	Place read miss on bus.
Read miss	processor	shared	Address conflict miss: place read miss on bus.
Read miss	processor	exclusive	Address conflict miss: write back block, then place read miss on bus.
Write hit	processor	exclusive	Write data in cache.
Write hit	processor	shared	Place write miss on bus.
Write miss	processor	invalid	Place write miss on bus.
Write miss	processor	shared	Address conflict miss: place write miss on bus.
Write miss	processor	exclusive	Address conflict miss: write back block, then place write miss on bus.
Read miss	bus	shared	No action; allow memory to service read miss.
Read miss	bus	exclusive	Attempt to share data: place cache block on bus and change state to shared.
Write miss	bus	shared	Attempt to write shared block; invalidate the block.
Write miss	bus	exclusive	Attempt to write block that is exclusive elsewhere: write back the cache block and make its state invalid.

Figure 6.10 The cache coherence mechanism receives requests from both the processor and the bus and responds to these based on the type of request, whether it hits or misses in the cache, and the state of the cache block specified in the request. For read or write misses snooped from the bus, an action is required *only* if the read or write addresses match a block in the cache and the block is valid. Placing a write miss on the bus when a write hits in the shared state ensures an exclusive copy, although the data need not actually be transferred. This is referred to as an upgrade, and some protocols distinguish it from a write miss to avoid the data transfer.

All of the states in this cache protocol would be needed in a uniprocessor cache, where they would correspond to the invalid, valid (and clean), and dirty states. All of the state changes indicated by arcs in the left half of Figure 6.11 would be needed in a write-back uniprocessor cache; the only difference in a multiprocessor with coherence is that the controller must generate a write miss when the controller has a write hit for a cache block in the shared state. The state changes represented by the arcs in the right half of Figure 6.11 are needed only for coherence and would not appear at all in a uniprocessor cache controller.

In reality, there is only one finite-state machine per cache, with stimuli coming either from the attached CPU or from the bus. Figure 6.12 shows how the state transitions in the right half of Figure 6.11 are combined with those in the left half of the figure to form a single state diagram for each cache block.

To understand why this protocol works, observe that any valid cache block is either in the shared state in multiple caches or in the exclusive state in exactly one cache. Any transition to the exclusive state (which is required for a processor to write to the block) requires a write miss to be placed on the bus, causing all caches to make the block invalid. In addition, if some other cache had the

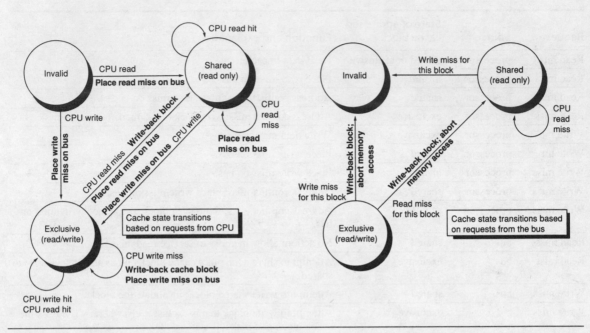

Figure 6.11 A write invalidate, cache coherence protocol for a write-back cache showing the states and state transitions for each block in the cache. The cache states are shown in circles with any access permitted by the CPU without a state transition shown in parentheses under the name of the state. The stimulus causing a state change is shown on the transition arcs in regular type, and any bus actions generated as part of the state transition are shown on the transition arc in bold. The stimulus actions apply to a block in the cache, not to a specific address in the cache. Hence, a read miss to a block in the shared state is a miss for that cache block but for a different address. The left side of the diagram shows state transitions based on actions of the CPU associated with this cache; the right side shows transitions based on operations on the bus. A read miss in the exclusive or shared state and a write miss in the exclusive state occur when the address requested by the CPU does not match the address in the cache block. Such a miss is a standard cache replacement miss. An attempt to write a block in the shared state always generates a miss, even if the block is present in the cache, since the block must be made exclusive. Whenever a bus transaction occurs, all caches that contain the cache block specified in the bus transaction take the action dictated by the right half of the diagram. The protocol assumes that memory provides data on a read miss for a block that is clean in all caches. In actual implementations, these two sets of state diagrams are combined. This protocol is somewhat simpler than those in use in existing multiprocessors.

block in exclusive state, that cache generates a write back, which supplies the block containing the desired address. Finally, if a read miss occurs on the bus to a block in the exclusive state, the owning cache also makes its state shared, forcing a subsequent write to require exclusive ownership.

The actions in gray in Figure 6.12, which handle read and write misses on the bus, are essentially the snooping component of the protocol. One other property that is preserved in this protocol, and in most other protocols, is that any memory block in the shared state is always up to date in the memory. This simplifies the implementation, as we will see in detail in Section 6.7.

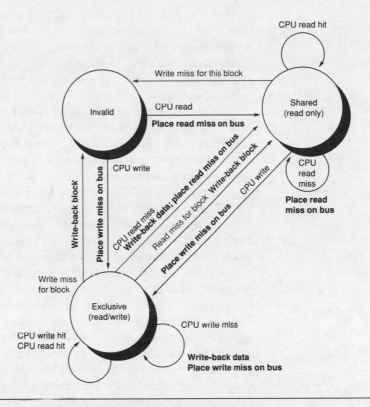

Figure 6.12 Cache coherence state diagram with the state transitions induced by the local processor shown in black and by the bus activities shown in gray. As in Figure 6.11, the activities on a transition are shown in bold.

Although our simple cache protocol is correct, it omits a number of complications that make the implementation much trickier. The most important of these is that the protocol assumes that operations are *atomic*—that is, an operation can be done in such a way that no intervening operation can occur. For example, the protocol described assumes that write misses can be detected, acquire the bus, and receive a response as a single atomic action. In reality this is not true. Similarly, if we used a split transaction bus (see Section 7.3), as most modern bus-based multiprocessors do, then even read misses would also not be atomic.

Nonatomic actions introduce the possibility that the protocol can *deadlock,* meaning that it reaches a state where it cannot continue. Appendix I deals with these complex issues, showing how the protocol can be modified to deal with nonatomic writes without introducing deadlock.

As stated earlier, this coherence protocol is actually simpler than those used in practice. There are two major simplifications. First, in this protocol all transitions to the exclusive state generate a write miss on the bus, and we assume that the requesting cache always fills the block with the contents returned. This simplifies the detailed implementation. Most real protocols distinguish between a write miss and a write hit, which can occur when the cache block is initially in the shared state. Such misses are called *ownership* or *upgrade* misses, since they involve changing the state of the block, but do not actually require a data fetch. To support such state changes, the protocol uses an *invalidate operation,* in addition to a write miss. With such operations, however, the actual implementation of the protocol becomes slightly more complex.

The second major simplification is that many multiprocessors distinguish between a cache block that is really shared and one that exists in the clean state in exactly one cache. This addition of a "clean and private" state eliminates the need to generate a bus transaction on a write to such a block. Another enhancement in wide use allows other caches to supply data on a miss to a shared block.

Constructing small-scale (two to four processors) bus-based multiprocessors has become very easy. Many modern microprocessors provide basic support for cache coherency and also allow the construction of a shared-memory bus by direct connection of the external memory bus of two processors. These capabilities reduce the number of chips required to build a small-scale multiprocessor. For example, the Intel Pentium III Xeon and Pentium 4 Xeon processors are designed for use in cache-coherent multiprocessors and have an external interface that supports snooping and allows two processors to be directly connected. They also have larger on-chip caches to reduce bus utilization. A system chip set containing an external memory controller is used to connect the shared processor memory bus with a set of memory chips. The memory controller also implements the coherency protocol. Since different-size multiprocessors generate different demands for bus bandwidth, Intel has two different system chip sets designed for dual-processor systems and for midrange systems (two to four processors). A small-scale multiprocessor may be built with only two additional system chips: the memory controller mentioned earlier and an I/O hub chip that interfaces standard I/O buses, such as PCI, to the memory bus.

The next section examines the performance of these protocols for our parallel and multiprogrammed workloads; the value of these extensions to a basic protocol will be clear when we examine the performance.

6.4 Performance of Symmetric Shared-Memory Multiprocessors

In a bus-based multiprocessor using an invalidation protocol, several different phenomena combine to determine performance. In particular, the overall cache performance is a combination of the behavior of uniprocessor cache miss traffic and the traffic caused by communication, which results in invalidations and subsequent cache misses. Changing the processor count, cache size, and block size can affect these two components of the miss rate in different ways, leading to overall system behavior that is a combination of the two effects.

In Chapter 5, we saw how breaking the uniprocessor miss rate into the three C's classification could provide insight into both application behavior and potential improvements to the cache design. Similarly, the misses that arise from inter-processor communication, which are often called *coherence misses,* can be broken into two separate sources.

The first source is the so-called true sharing misses that arise from the communication of data through the cache coherence mechanism. In an invalidation-based protocol, the first write by a processor to a shared cache block causes an invalidation to establish ownership of that block. Additionally, when another processor attempts to read a modified word in that cache block, a miss occurs and the resultant block is transferred. Both these misses are classified as true sharing misses since they directly arise from the sharing of data among processors.

The second effect, called *false sharing,* arises from the use of an invalidation-based coherence algorithm with a single valid bit per cache block. False sharing occurs when a block is invalidated (and a subsequent reference causes a miss) because some word in the block, other than the one being read, is written into. If the word written into is actually used by the processor that received the invalidate, then the reference was a true sharing reference and would have caused a miss independent of the block size or position of words. If, however, the word being written and the word read are different and the invalidation does not cause a new value to be communicated, but only causes an extra cache miss, then it is a false sharing miss. In a false sharing miss, the block is shared, but no word in the cache is actually shared, and the miss would not occur if the block size were a single word. The following example makes the sharing patterns clear.

Example   Assume that words x1 and x2 are in the same cache block, which is in the shared state in the caches of P1 and P2. Assuming the following sequence of events, identify each miss as a true sharing miss, a false sharing miss, or a hit. Any miss that would occur if the block size were one word is designated a true sharing miss.

Time	P1	P2
1	Write x1	
2		Read x2
3	Write x1	
4		Write x2
5	Read x2	

Answer   Here are classifications by time step:

1. This event is a true sharing miss, since x1 was read by P2 and needs to be invalidated from P2.

2. This event is a false sharing miss, since x2 was invalidated by the write of x1 in P1, but that value of x1 is not used in P2.

3. This event is a false sharing miss, since the block containing x1 is marked shared due to the read in P2, but P2 did not read x1. The cache block containing x1 will be in the shared state after the read by P2; a write miss is required to obtain exclusive access to the block. In some protocols this will be handled as an *upgrade request,* which generates a bus invalidate, but does not transfer the cache block.

4. This event is a false sharing miss for the same reason as step 3.

5. This event is a true sharing miss, since the value being read was written by P2.

True sharing and false sharing miss rates can be affected by a variety of changes in the cache architecture. Thus, we will find it useful to decompose not only the uniprocessor and multiprocessor miss rates, but also the true sharing and false sharing miss rates.

Performance Measurements of the Commercial Workload

The performance measurements of the commercial workload, which we examine in this section, were taken either on an AlphaServer 4100 or using a configurable simulator modeled after the AlphaServer 4100. The AlphaServer 4100 used for these measurements has four processors, each of which is an Alpha 21164 running at 300 MHz. Each processor has a three-level cache hierarchy:

- L1 consists of a pair of 8 KB direct-mapped on-chip caches, one for instruction and one for data. The block size is 32 bytes, and the data cache is write through to L2, using a write buffer.

- L2 is a 96 KB on-chip unified three-way set-associative cache with a 32-byte block size, using write back.

- L3 is an off-chip, combined, direct-mapped 2 MB cache with 64-byte blocks also using write back.

The latency for an access to L2 is 7 cycles, to L3 it is 21 cycles, and to main memory it is 80 clock cycles (typical without contention). Cache-to-cache transfers, which occur on a miss to an exclusive block held in another cache, require 125 clock cycles. All the measurements shown in this section were collected by Barroso, Gharachorloo, and Bugnion [1998].

We start by looking at the overall CPU execution for these benchmarks on the four-processor system; as discussed on page 541, these benchmarks include substantial I/O time, which is ignored in the CPU time measurements. We group the six DSS queries as a single benchmark, reporting the average behavior. The effective CPI varies widely for these benchmarks, from a CPI of 1.3 for the AltaVista Web search, to an average CPI of 1.6 for the DSS workload, to 7.0 for the OLTP workload. Figure 6.13 shows how the execution time breaks down into instruction execution, cache and memory system access time, and other stalls (which are primarily pipeline resource stalls, but also include TLB and branch mispredict

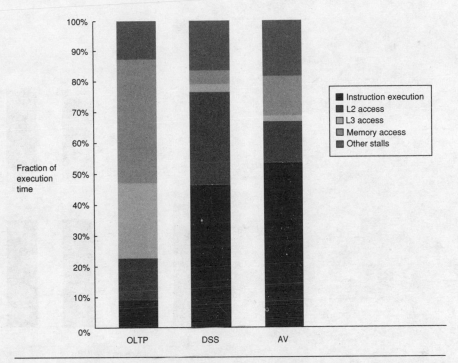

Figure 6.13   The execution time breakdown for the three programs (OLTP, DSS, and AltaVista) in the commercial workload. The DSS numbers are the average across six different queries. The CPI varies widely from a low of 1.3 for AltaVista, to 1.61 for the DSS queries, to 7.0 for Oracle. (Individually, the DSS queries show a CPI range of 1.3 to 1.9.) Other stalls include resource stalls (implemented with replay traps on the 21164), branch mispredict, memory barrier, and TLB misses. For these benchmarks, resource-based pipeline stalls are the dominant factor. These data combine the behavior of user and kernel accesses. Only OLTP has a significant fraction of kernel accesses, and the kernel accesses tend to be better behaved than the user accesses!

stalls). Although the performance of the DSS and AltaVista workloads is reasonable, the performance of the OLTP workload is very poor, due to a poor performance of the memory hierarchy.

Since the OLTP workload demands the most from the memory system with large numbers of expensive L3 misses, we focus on examining the impact of L3 cache size, processor count, and block size on the OLTP benchmark. Figure 6.14 shows the effect of increasing the cache size, using two-way set-associative caches, which reduces the large number of conflict misses. The execution time is improved as the L3 cache grows due to the reduction in L3 misses. The idle time also grows, reducing some of the performance gains. This growth occurs because with fewer memory system stalls, more server processes are needed to cover the I/O latency. The workload could be retuned to increase the computation/communication balance, holding the idle time in check.

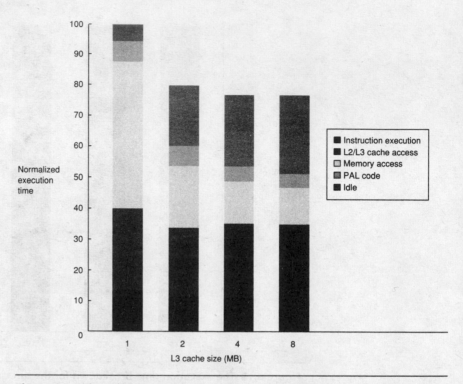

Figure 6.14 The relative performance of the OLTP workload as the size of the L3 cache, which is set as two-way set associative, from 1 MB to 8 MB. Interestingly, the performance of the 1 MB, two-way set-associative cache is very similar to the direct-mapped 2 MB cache that is used in the AlphaServer 4100.

To better understand how the L3 miss rate responds, we ask, What factors contribute to the L3 miss rate, and how do they change as the L3 cache grows? Figure 6.15 shows these data, displaying the number of memory access cycles contributed per instruction from five sources. The two largest sources of memory access cycles (due to L3 misses) with a 1 MB L3 are instruction and capacity/conflict misses. With a larger L3 these two sources shrink to be minor contributors. Unfortunately, the cold, false sharing, and true sharing misses are unaffected by a larger L3. Thus, at 4 and 8 MB, the true sharing misses generate the dominant fraction of the misses.

Clearly, increasing the cache size eliminates most of the uniprocessor misses, while leaving the multiprocessor misses untouched. How does increasing the processor count affect different types of misses? Figure 6.16 shows these data assuming a base configuration with a 2 MB, two-way set-associative L3 cache. As we might expect, the increase in the true sharing miss rate, which is not compensated for by any decrease in the uniprocessor misses, leads to an overall increase in the memory access cycles per instruction.

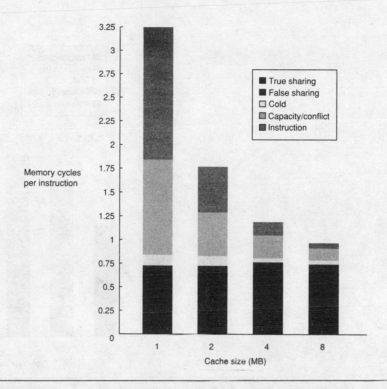

Figure 6.15 The contributing causes of memory access cycles shift as the cache size is increased. The L3 cache is simulated as two-way set associative.

The final question we examine is whether increasing the block size, which should decrease the instruction and cold miss rate and, within limits, also reduce the capacity/conflict miss rate, is helpful for this workload. Figure 6.17 shows the number of misses per 1000 instructions as the block size is increased from 32 to 256. Increasing the block size from 32 to 256 affects four of the miss rate components:

- The true sharing miss rate decreases by more than a factor of 2, indicating locality in the true sharing patterns.

- The cold start miss rate significantly decreases, as we would expect.

- The conflict/capacity misses show a small decrease (a factor of 1.26 compared to a factor of 8 increase in block size), indicating that the spatial locality is not high in the uniprocessor misses.

- The false sharing miss rate, although small in absolute terms, nearly doubles.

The lack of a significant effect on the instruction miss rate is startling and clearly indicates that the large instruction footprint has very poor spatial locality! Overall, increasing the block size of the of the third-level cache to 128 or possibly 256 bytes seems appropriate.

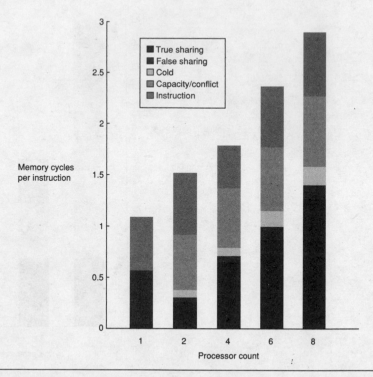

Figure 6.16 The contribution to memory access cycles increases as processor count increases primarily due to increased true sharing. The cold misses slightly increase since each processor must now handle more cold misses.

Performance of the Multiprogramming and OS Workload

In this subsection we examine the cache performance of the multiprogrammed workload as the cache size and block size are changed. The workload remains the same as described in the previous section: two independent parallel makes, each using up to eight processors. Because of differences between the behavior of the kernel and that of the user processes, we keep these two components separate. Remember, though, that the user processes execute more than eight times as many instructions, so that the overall miss rate is determined primarily by the miss rate in user code, which, as we will see, is often one-fifth of the kernel miss rate.

Figure 6.18 shows the data miss rate versus data cache size for the kernel and user components. The misses can be broken into three significant classes:

- Compulsory, or cold, misses represent the first access to this block by this processor and are significant in this workload.

- Coherence misses represent misses due to invalidations.

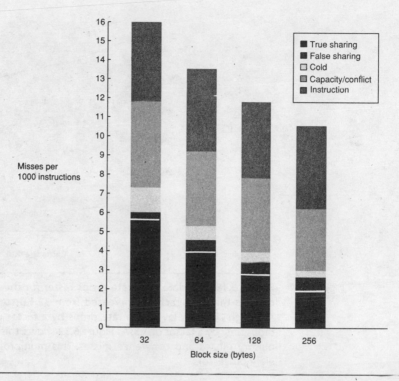

Figure 6.17 The number of misses per 1000 instructions drops steadily as the block size of the L3 cache is increased, making a good case for an L3 block size of at least 128 bytes. The L3 cache is a 2 MB, two-way set associative.

- Normal capacity misses include misses caused by interference between the OS and the user process and between multiple user processes. Conflict misses are included in this category.

For this workload the behavior of the operating system is more complex than the user processes for two reasons. First, the kernel initializes all pages before allocating them to a user, which significantly increases the compulsory component of the kernel's miss rate. Second, the kernel actually shares data and thus has a nontrivial coherence miss rate. In contrast, user processes cause coherence misses only when the process is scheduled on a different processor; this component of the miss rate is small. Figure 6.19 shows the breakdown of the kernel miss rate as the cache size is increased.

Increasing the block size is likely to have beneficial effects for this workload, since a larger fraction of the misses arise from compulsory and capacity, both of which can be potentially improved with larger block sizes. Since coherence misses are relatively rarer, the negative effects of increasing block size should be small. Figure 6.20 shows how the miss rate for the kernel and user references changes as the block size is increased, assuming a 32 KB two-way set-associative

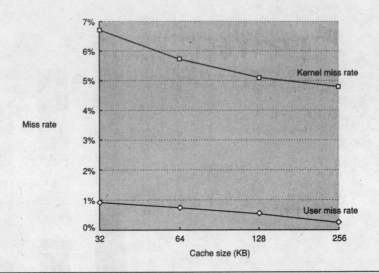

Figure 6.18 **The data miss rate drops faster for the user code than for the kernel code as the data cache is increased from 32 KB to 256 KB with a 32-byte block.** Although the user-level miss rate drops by a factor of 3, the kernel-level miss rate drops only by a factor of 1.3. As Figure 6.19 shows, this is due to a higher rate of compulsory misses and coherence misses. This multiprogramming workload is run on eight processors.

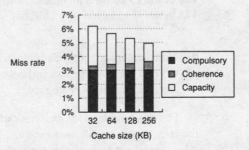

Figure 6.19 **The components of the kernel data miss rate change as the data cache size is increased from 32 KB to 256 KB, when the multiprogramming workload is run on eight processors.** The compulsory miss rate component stays constant, since it is unaffected by cache size. The capacity component drops by more than a factor of 2, while the coherence component nearly doubles. The increase in coherence misses occurs because the probability of a miss being caused by an invalidation increases with cache size, since fewer entries are bumped due to capacity.

data cache. Figure 6.21 confirms that, for the kernel references, the largest improvement is the reduction of the compulsory miss rate. The absence of large increases in the coherence miss rate as block size is increased means that false sharing effects are insignificant.

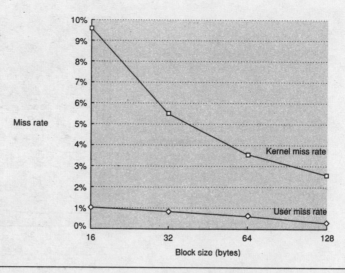

Figure 6.20 Miss rate for the multiprogramming workload drops steadily as the block size is increased for a 32 KB two-way set-associative data cache and an eight-CPU multiprocessor. As we might expect based on the higher compulsory component in the kernel, the improvement in miss rate for the kernel references is larger (almost a factor of 4 for the kernel references when going from 16-byte to 128-byte blocks versus just under a factor of 3 for the user references).

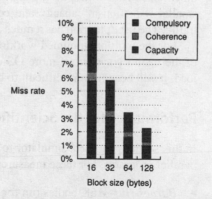

Figure 6.21 As we would expect, the increasing block size substantially reduces the compulsory miss rate in the kernel references. It also has a significant impact on the capacity miss rate, decreasing it by a factor of 2.4 over the range of block sizes. The increased block size has a small reduction in coherence traffic, which appears to stabilize at 64 bytes, with no change in the coherence miss rate in going to 128-byte lines. Because there are not significant reductions in the coherence miss rate as the block size increases, the fraction of the miss rate due to coherence grows from about 7% to about 15%.

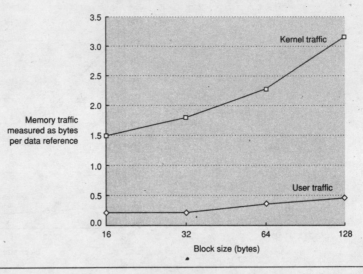

Figure 6.22 The number of bytes needed per data reference grows as block size is increased for both the kernel and user components. It is interesting to compare this chart against the same chart for the parallel program workload shown in Figure 6.26.

If we examine the number of bytes needed per data reference, as in Figure 6.22, we see that the kernel has a higher traffic ratio that grows quickly with block size. This is despite the significant reduction in compulsory misses; the smaller reduction in capacity and coherence misses drives an increase in total traffic. The user program has a much smaller traffic ratio that grows very slowly.

For the multiprogrammed workload, the OS is a much more demanding user of the memory system. If more OS or OS-like activity is included in the workload, it will become very difficult to build a sufficiently capable memory system.

Performance for the Scientific/Technical Workload

In this section, we use a simulator to study the performance of our four scientific parallel programs. For these measurements, the problem sizes are as follows:

- *Barnes-Hut*—16K bodies run for six time steps (the accuracy control is set to 1.0, a typical, realistic value)
- *FFT*—1 million complex data points
- *LU*—A 512×512 matrix is used with 16×16 blocks
- *Ocean*—A 130×130 grid with a typical error tolerance

In looking at the miss rates as we vary processor count, cache size, and block size, we decompose the total miss rate into *coherence misses* and normal uniprocessor misses. The normal uniprocessor misses consist of capacity, conflict, and compulsory misses. We label these misses as capacity misses because that is the dominant cause for these benchmarks. For these measurements, we include as a coherence miss any write misses needed to upgrade a block from shared to exclusive, even though no one is sharing the cache block. This measurement reflects a protocol that does not distinguish between a private and shared cache block.

Figure 6.23 shows the data miss rates for our four applications, as we increase the number of processors from 1 to 16, while keeping the problem size constant. As we increase the number of processors, the total amount of cache increases, usually causing the capacity misses to drop. In contrast, increasing the processor count usually causes the amount of communication to increase, in turn causing the coherence misses to rise. The magnitude of these two effects differs by application.

In FFT, the capacity miss rate drops (from nearly 7% to just over 5%) but the coherence miss rate increases (from about 1% to about 2.7%), leading to a constant overall miss rate. Ocean shows a combination of effects, including some that relate to the partitioning of the grid and how grid boundaries map to cache blocks. For a typical 2D grid code the communication-generated misses are proportional to the boundary of each partition of the grid, while the capacity misses are proportional to the area of the grid. Therefore, increasing the total amount of cache while keeping the total problem size fixed will have a more significant effect on the capacity miss rate, at least until each subgrid fits within an individual processor's cache. The significant jump in miss rate between one and two processors occurs because of conflicts that arise from the way in which the multiple grids are mapped to the caches. This conflict is present for direct-mapped and two-way set-associative caches, but fades at higher associativities. Such conflicts are not unusual in array-based applications, especially when there are multiple grids in use at once. In Barnes and LU the increase in processor count has little effect on the miss rate, sometimes causing a slight increase and sometimes causing a slight decrease.

Increasing the cache size usually has a beneficial effect on performance, since it reduces the frequency of costly cache misses. Figure 6.24 illustrates the change in miss rate as cache size is increased for 16 processors, showing the portion of the miss rate due to coherence misses and to uniprocessor capacity misses. Two effects can lead to a miss rate that does not decrease—at least not as quickly as we might expect—as cache size increases: inherent communication and plateaus in the miss rate. Inherent communication leads to a certain frequency of coherence misses that are not significantly affected by increasing cache size. Thus if the cache size is increased while maintaining a fixed problem size, the coherence miss rate eventually limits the decrease in cache miss rate. This effect is most obvious in Barnes, where the coherence miss rate essentially becomes the entire miss rate.

A less important effect is a temporary plateau in the capacity miss rate that arises when the application has some fraction of its data present in cache but some significant portion of the data set does not fit in the cache or in caches that are slightly bigger. In LU, a very small cache (about 4 KB) can capture the pair of

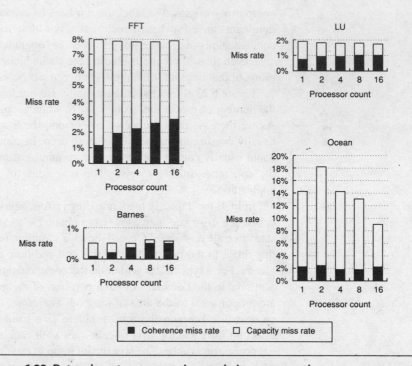

Figure 6.23 Data miss rates can vary in nonobvious ways as the processor count is increased from 1 to 16. The miss rates include both coherence and capacity miss rates. The compulsory misses in these benchmarks are all very small and are included in the capacity misses. Most of the misses in these applications are generated by accesses to data that are potentially shared, although in the applications with larger miss rates (FFT and Ocean), it is the capacity misses rather than the coherence misses that comprise the majority of the miss rate. Data are potentially shared if they are allocated in a portion of the address space used for shared data. In all except Ocean, the potentially shared data are heavily shared, while in Ocean only the boundaries of the subgrids are actually shared, although the entire grid is treated as a potentially shared data object. Of course, since the boundaries change as we increase the processor count (for a fixed-size problem), different amounts of the grid become shared. The anomalous increase in capacity miss rate for Ocean in moving from 1 to 2 processors arises because of conflict misses in accessing the subgrids. In all cases except Ocean, the fraction of the cache misses caused by coherence transactions rises when a fixed-size problem is run on an increasing number of processors. In Ocean, the coherence misses initially fall as we add processors due to a large number of misses that are write ownership misses to data that are potentially, but not actually, shared. As the subgrids begin to fit in the aggregate cache (around 16 processors), this effect lessens. The single processor numbers include write upgrade misses, which occur in this protocol even if the data are not actually shared, since they are in the shared state. For all these runs, the cache size is 64 KB, two-way set associative, with 32-byte blocks. Notice that the scale on the y-axis for each benchmark is different, so that the behavior of the individual benchmarks can be seen clearly.

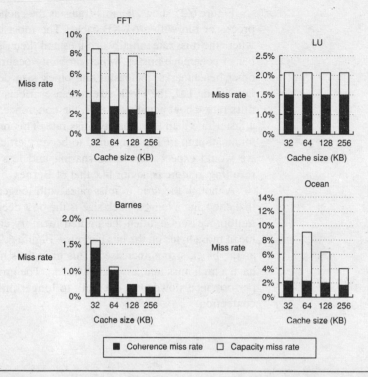

Figure 6.24 The miss rate usually drops as the cache size is increased, although coherence misses dampen the effect. The block size is 32 bytes and the cache is two-way set associative. The processor count is fixed at 16 processors. Observe that the scale for each graph is different.

16×16 blocks used in the inner loop; beyond that the next big improvement in capacity miss rate occurs when both matrices fit in the caches, which occurs when the total cache size is between 4 MB and 8 MB. This effect, sometimes called a *working set effect,* is partly at work between 32 KB and 128 KB for FFT, where the capacity miss rate drops only 0.3%. Beyond that cache size, a faster decrease in the capacity miss rate is seen, as a major data structure begins to reside in the cache. These plateaus are common in programs that deal with large arrays in a structured fashion.

Increasing the block size is another way to change the miss rate in a cache. In uniprocessors, larger block sizes are often optimal with larger caches. In multi-processors, two new effects come into play: a reduction in spatial locality for shared data and a potential increase in miss rate due to false sharing. Several stud-ies have shown that shared data have lower spatial locality than unshared data. Poorer locality means that, for shared data, fetching larger blocks is less effective than in a uniprocessor because the probability is higher that the block will be replaced before all its contents are referenced. Likewise, increasing the basic size also increases the potential frequency of false sharing, increasing the miss rate.

Figure 6.25 shows the miss rates as the cache block size is increased for a 16-processor run with a 64 KB cache. The most interesting behavior is in Barnes, where the miss rate initially declines and then rises due to an increase in the number of coherence misses, which probably occurs because of false sharing. In the other benchmarks, increasing the block size decreases the overall miss rate. In Ocean and LU, the block size increase affects both the coherence and capacity miss rates about equally. In FFT, the coherence miss rate is actually decreased at a faster rate than the capacity miss rate. This reduction occurs because the communication in FFT is structured to be very efficient. In less optimized programs, we would expect more false sharing and less spatial locality for shared data, resulting in more behavior like that of Barnes.

Although the drop in miss rates with longer blocks may lead you to believe that choosing a longer block size is the best decision, the bottleneck in bus-based multiprocessors is often the limited memory and bus bandwidth. Larger blocks mean more bytes on the bus per miss. Figure 6.26 shows the growth in bus traffic as the block size is increased. This growth is most serious in the programs that have a high miss rate, especially Ocean. The growth in traffic can actually lead to performance slowdowns due both to longer miss penalties and to increased bus contention.

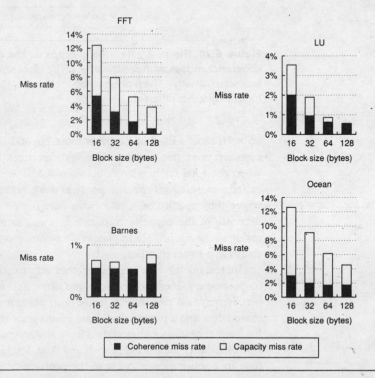

Figure 6.25 The data miss rate drops as the cache block size is increased. All these results are for a 16-processor run with a 64 KB cache and two-way set associativity. Once again we use different scales for each benchmark.

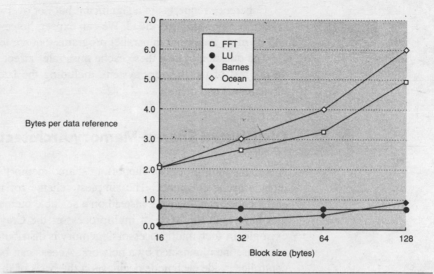

Bytes per data reference

Figure 6.26 Bus traffic for data misses climbs steadily as the block size in the data cache is increased. The factor of 3 increase in traffic for Ocean is the best argument against larger block sizes. Remember that our protocol treats ownership or upgrade misses the same as other misses, slightly increasing the penalty for large cache blocks; in both Ocean and FFT this simplification accounts for less than 10% of the traffic.

Summary: Performance of Snooping Cache Schemes

In this section we examined the cache performance of three very different workloads. We saw that the coherence traffic can introduce new behaviors in the memory system that do not respond as easily to changes in cache size or block size that are normally used to improve uniprocessor cache performance.

In the commercial workload, the performance of the Web searching and DSS benchmarks is reasonable (CPI of 1.3 and 1.6, respectively), while the OLTP benchmark is much worse (CPI = 7.0). For OLTP, the large instruction working set demands a large cache to achieve acceptable performance. Increasing the cache size reduces the execution time, but is limited by the true and false sharing misses, which do not decrease as the cache grows. Similarly, increasing the processor counts increases true and false sharing, leading to an increase in memory access cycles. Fortunately, this workload responds favorably to an increase in block size, although the instruction miss rate remains similar. For these large workloads, it appears that very large (≥ 4 MB) off-chip caches with large block sizes (64–128 bytes) could work reasonably well.

In the multiprogrammed workload, the user and OS portions perform very differently, although neither has significant coherence traffic. In the OS portion, the compulsory and capacity contributions to the miss rate are much larger, leading to overall miss rates that are comparable to the worst programs in the parallel program workload. User cache performance, on the other hand, is very good and compares to the best programs in the parallel program workload.

Coherence requests are a significant but not overwhelming component in the scientific processing workload. We can expect, however, that coherence requests will be more important in parallel programs that are less optimized.

The question of how these cache miss rates affect CPU performance depends on the rest of the memory system, including the latency and bandwidth of the interconnect and memory.

6.5   Distributed Shared-Memory Architectures

A scalable multiprocessor supporting shared memory could choose to exclude or include cache coherence. The simplest scheme for the hardware is to exclude cache coherence, focusing instead on a scalable memory system. Several companies have built this style of multiprocessor; the Cray T3D/E is the best known example. In such multiprocessors, memory is distributed among the nodes and all nodes are interconnected by a network. Access can be either local or remote—a controller inside each node decides, on the basis of the address, whether the data reside in the local memory or in a remote memory. In the latter case a message is sent to the controller in the remote memory to access the data.

These systems have caches, but to prevent coherence problems, shared data are marked as uncacheable and only private data are kept in the caches. Of course, software can still explicitly cache the value of shared data by copying the data from the shared portion of the address space to the local private portion of the address space that is cached. Coherence is then controlled by software. The advantage of such a mechanism is that little hardware support is required, although support for features such as block copy may be useful, since remote accesses fetch only single words (or double words) rather than cache blocks.

There are several disadvantages to this approach. First, compiler mechanisms for transparent software cache coherence are very limited. The techniques that currently exist apply primarily to programs with well-structured loop-level parallelism or a very strict form of object-oriented programming, and these techniques have significant overhead arising from explicitly copying data. For irregular problems or problems involving dynamic data structures and pointers (including operating systems, for example), compiler-based software cache coherence is currently impractical. The basic difficulty is that software-based coherence algorithms must be conservative: Every block that *might* be shared must be treated as if it *is* shared. Being conservative results in excess coherence overhead because the compiler cannot predict the actual sharing accurately enough. Due to the complexity of the possible interactions, asking programmers to deal with coherence is unworkable.

Second, without cache coherence, the multiprocessor loses the advantage of being able to fetch and use multiple words in a single cache block for close to the cost of fetching one word. The benefits of spatial locality in shared data cannot be leveraged when single words are fetched from a remote memory for each reference. Support for a DMA mechanism among memories can help, but such mechanisms are often either costly to use (since they may require OS intervention) or expensive to implement (since special-purpose hardware support and a buffer are needed). For message-passing programs, however, such mechanisms can be extremely useful, since programmers can overcome the usage penalties by using large messages.

Third, mechanisms for tolerating latency such as prefetch are more useful when they can fetch multiple words, such as a cache block, and where the fetched data remain coherent; we will examine this advantage in more detail later.

These disadvantages are magnified by the large latency of access to remote memory versus a local cache. For example, on the Cray T3E a local cache access has a latency of 2 cycles and is pipelined. A remote memory access takes up to 400 processor clock cycles for a remote memory using the 450 MHz Alpha processor in the T3E-900.

For these reasons, cache coherence is an accepted requirement in small-scale multiprocessors. For larger-scale architectures, there are new challenges to extending the cache-coherent shared-memory model. Although the bus can certainly be replaced with a more scalable interconnection network (e.g., the Sun Enterprise servers use up to four buses), and we could certainly distribute the memory so that the memory bandwidth could also be scaled, the lack of scalability of the snooping coherence scheme needs to be addressed.

A snooping protocol requires communication with all caches on every cache miss, including writes of potentially shared data. The absence of any centralized data structure that tracks the state of the caches is both the fundamental advantage of a snooping-based scheme, since it allows it to be inexpensive, as well as its Achilles' heel when it comes to scalability. For example, with only 16 processors, a block size of 64 bytes, and a 512 KB data cache, the total bus bandwidth demand (ignoring stall cycles) for the four programs in the scientific/technical workload ranges from about 1 GB/sec (for Barnes) to about 42 GB/sec (for FFT), assuming a processor that sustains a data reference every 1 ns, which is what a 2001 superscalar processor with nonblocking caches might generate. In comparison, the Sun Enterprise system with the Starfire interconnect, the highest-bandwidth SMP system in 2001, can support about 12 GB/sec of random accesses for the 16×16 crossbar and has a maximum bandwidth of 21.3 GB/sec at the memory system. Although the cache size used in these simulations is moderate (but large enough to eliminate much of the uniprocessor miss traffic), so is the problem size.

Alternatively, we could build scalable shared-memory architectures that include cache coherency. The key is to find an alternative coherence protocol to the snooping protocol. One alternative protocol is a *directory protocol*. A directory keeps the state of every block that may be cached. Information in the directory includes which caches have copies of the block, whether it is dirty, and so on. (Section 6.11 on page 622 describes a hybrid approach that uses directories to extend a snooping protocol.)

Existing directory implementations associate an entry in the directory with each memory block. In typical protocols, the amount of information is proportional to the product of the number of memory blocks and the number of processors. This overhead is not a problem for multiprocessors with less than about 200 processors because the directory overhead will be tolerable. For larger multiprocessors, we need methods to allow the directory structure to be efficiently scaled. The methods that have been proposed either try to keep information for fewer blocks (e.g., only those in caches rather than all memory blocks) or try to keep fewer bits per entry.

To prevent the directory from becoming the bottleneck, directory entries can be distributed along with the memory, so that different directory accesses can go to different locations, just as different memory requests go to different memories. A distributed directory retains the characteristic that the sharing status of a block is always in a single known location. This property is what allows the coherence protocol to avoid broadcast. Figure 6.27 shows how our distributed-memory multiprocessor looks with the directories added to each node.

Directory-Based Cache Coherence Protocols: The Basics

Just as with a snooping protocol, there are two primary operations that a directory protocol must implement: handling a read miss and handling a write to a shared, clean cache block. (Handling a write miss to a shared block is a simple combination of these two.) To implement these operations, a directory must track the state of each cache block. In a simple protocol, these states could be the following:

■ *Shared*—One or more processors have the block cached, and the value in memory is up to date (as well as in all the caches).

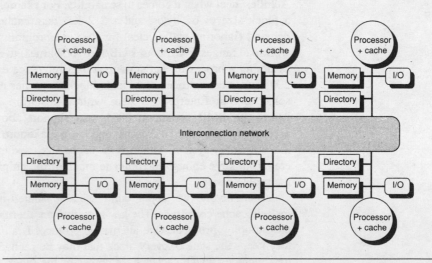

Figure 6.27 A directory is added to each node to implement cache coherence in a distributed-memory multiprocessor. Each directory is responsible for tracking the caches that share the memory addresses of the portion of memory in the node. The directory may communicate with the processor and memory over a common bus, as shown, or it may have a separate port to memory, or it may be part of a central node controller through which all intranode and internode communications pass.

- *Uncached*—No processor has a copy of the cache block.

- *Exclusive*—Exactly one processor has a copy of the cache block, and it has written the block, so the memory copy is out of date. The processor is called the *owner* of the block.

In addition to tracking the state of each cache block, we must track the processors that have copies of the block when it is shared, since they will need to be invalidated on a write. The simplest way to do this is to keep a bit vector for each memory block. When the block is shared, each bit of the vector indicates whether the corresponding processor has a copy of that block. We can also use the bit vector to keep track of the owner of the block when the block is in the exclusive state. For efficiency reasons, we also track the state of each cache block at the individual caches.

The states and transitions for the state machine at each cache are identical to what we used for the snooping cache, although the actions on a transition are slightly different. We make the same simplifying assumptions that we made in the case of the snooping cache: Attempts to write data that are not exclusive in the writer's cache always generate write misses, and the processors block until an access completes. Since the interconnect is no longer a bus and since we want to avoid broadcast, there are two additional complications. First, we cannot use the interconnect as a single point of arbitration, a function the bus performed in the snooping case. Second, because the interconnect is message oriented (unlike the bus, which is transaction oriented), many messages must have explicit responses.

Before we see the protocol state diagrams, it is useful to examine a catalog of the message types that may be sent between the processors and the directories. Figure 6.28 shows the type of messages sent among nodes. The *local node* is the node where a request originates. The *home node* is the node where the memory location and the directory entry of an address reside. The physical address space is statically distributed, so the node that contains the memory and directory for a given physical address is known. For example, the high-order bits may provide the node number, while the low-order bits provide the offset within the memory on that node. The local node may also be the home node. The directory must be accessed when the home node is the local node, since copies may exist in yet a third node, called a *remote node*.

A remote node is the node that has a copy of a cache block, whether exclusive (in which case it is the only copy) or shared. A remote node may be the same as either the local node or the home node. In such cases, the basic protocol does not change, but interprocessor messages may be replaced with intraprocessor messages.

In this section, we assume a simple model of memory consistency. To minimize the type of messages and the complexity of the protocol, we make an assumption that messages will be received and acted upon in the same order they are sent. This assumption may not be true in practice and can result in additional complications, some of which we address in Section 6.8 when we discuss memory consistency models. In this section, we use this assumption to ensure that invalidates sent by a processor are honored immediately.

Message type	Source	Destination	Message contents	Function of this message
Read miss	local cache	home directory	P, A	Processor P has a read miss at address A; request data and make P a read sharer.
Write miss	local cache	home directory	P, A	Processor P has a write miss at address A; request data and make P the exclusive owner.
Invalidate	home directory	remote cache	A	Invalidate a shared copy of data at address A.
Fetch	home directory	remote cache	A	Fetch the block at address A and send it to its home directory; change the state of A in the remote cache to shared.
Fetch/invalidate	home directory	remote cache	A	Fetch the block at address Á and send it to its home directory; invalidate the block in the cache.
Data value reply	home directory	local cache	D	Return a data value from the home memory.
Data write back	remote cache	home directory	A, D	Write back a data value for address A.

Figure 6.28 The possible messages sent among nodes to maintain coherence, along with the source and destination node, the contents (where P = requesting processor number, A = requested address, and D = data contents), and the function of the message. The first two messages are miss requests sent by the local cache to the home. The third through fifth messages are messages sent to a remote cache by the home when the home needs the data to satisfy a read or write miss request. Data value replies are used to send a value from the home node back to the requesting node. Data value write backs occur for two reasons: when a block is replaced in a cache and must be written back to its home memory, and also in reply to fetch or fetch/invalidate messages from the home. Writing back the data value whenever the block becomes shared simplifies the number of states in the protocol, since any dirty block must be exclusive and any shared block is always available in the home memory.

An Example Directory Protocol

The basic states of a cache block in a directory-based protocol are exactly like those in a snooping protocol, and the states in the directory are also analogous to those we showed earlier. Thus we can start with simple state diagrams that show the state transitions for an individual cache block and then examine the state diagram for the directory entry corresponding to each block in memory. As in the snooping case, these state transition diagrams do not represent all the details of a coherence protocol; however, the actual controller is highly dependent on a number of details of the multiprocessor (message delivery properties, buffering structures, and so on). In this section we present the basic protocol state diagrams. The knotty issues involved in implementing these state transition diagrams are examined in Appendix I, along with similar problems that arise for snooping caches.

Figure 6.29 shows the protocol actions to which an individual cache responds. We use the same notation as in the last section, with requests coming from outside the node in gray and actions in bold. The state transitions for an individual cache are caused by read misses, write misses, invalidates, and data fetch requests; these operations are all shown in Figure 6.29. An individual cache also generates read and write miss messages that are sent to the home directory. Read and write misses require data value replies, and these events wait for replies before changing state.

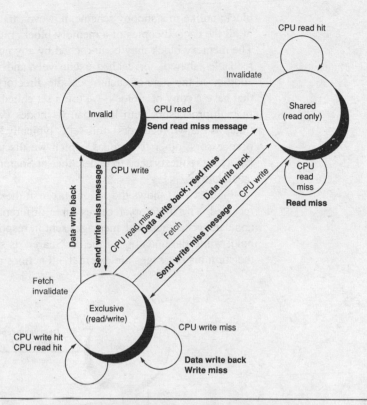

Figure 6.29 State transition diagram for an individual cache block in a directory-based system. Requests by the local processor are shown in black and those from the home directory are shown in gray. The states are identical to those in the snooping case, and the transactions are very similar, with explicit invalidate and write-back requests replacing the write misses that were formerly broadcast on the bus. As we did for the snooping controller, we assume that an attempt to write a shared cache block is treated as a miss; in practice, such a transaction can be treated as an ownership request or upgrade request and can deliver ownership without requiring that the cache block be fetched.

The operation of the state transition diagram for a cache block in Figure 6.29 is essentially the same as it is for the snooping case: The states are identical, and the stimulus is almost identical. The write miss operation, which was broadcast on the bus in the snooping scheme, is replaced by the data fetch and invalidate operations that are selectively sent by the directory controller. Like the snooping protocol, any cache block must be in the exclusive state when it is written, and any shared block must be up to date in memory.

In a directory-based protocol, the directory implements the other half of the coherence protocol. A message sent to a directory causes two different types of actions: updates of the directory state and sending additional messages to satisfy the request. The states in the directory represent the three standard states for a block; unlike in a snoopy scheme, however, the directory state indicates the state of all the cached copies of a memory block, rather than for a single cache block. The memory block may be uncached by any node, cached in multiple nodes and readable (shared), or cached exclusively and writable in exactly one node. In addition to the state of each block, the directory must track the set of processors that have a copy of a block; we use a set called *Sharers* to perform this function. In multiprocessors with less than 64 nodes (which may represent two to four times as many processors), this set is typically kept as a bit vector. In larger multiprocessors, other techniques, which we discuss in Exercise 6.16, are needed. Directory requests need to update the set Sharers and also read the set to perform invalidations.

Figure 6.30 shows the actions taken at the directory in response to messages received. The directory receives three different requests: read miss, write miss, and data write back. The messages sent in response by the directory are shown in bold, while the updating of the set Sharers is shown in bold italics. Because all the stimulus messages are external, all actions are shown in gray. Our simplified

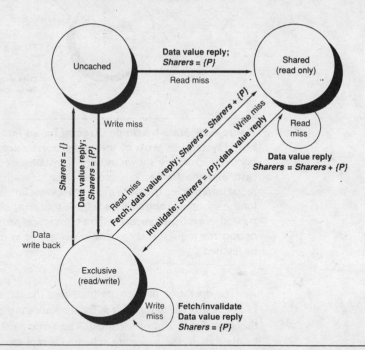

Figure 6.30 The state transition diagram for the directory has the same states and structure as the transition diagram for an individual cache. All actions are in gray because they are all externally caused. Bold indicates the action taken by the directory in response to the request. Bold italics indicate an action that updates the sharing set, Sharers, as opposed to sending a message.

protocol assumes that some actions are atomic, such as requesting a value and sending it to another node; a realistic implementation cannot use this assumption.

To understand these directory operations, let's examine the requests received and actions taken state by state. When a block is in the uncached state, the copy in memory is the current value, so the only possible requests for that block are

- *Read miss*—The requesting processor is sent the requested data from memory and the requestor is made the only sharing node. The state of the block is made shared.

- *Write miss*—The requesting processor is sent the value and becomes the sharing node. The block is made exclusive to indicate that the only valid copy is cached. Sharers indicates the identity of the owner.

When the block is in the shared state, the memory value is up to date, so the same two requests can occur:

- *Read miss*—The requesting processor is sent the requested data from memory and the requesting processor is added to the sharing set.

- *Write miss*—The requesting processor is sent the value. All processors in the set Sharers are sent invalidate messages, and the Sharers set is to contain the identity of the requesting processor. The state of the block is made exclusive.

When the block is in the exclusive state, the current value of the block is held in the cache of the processor identified by the set Sharers (the owner), so there are three possible directory requests:

- *Read miss*—The owner processor is sent a data fetch message, which causes the state of the block in the owner's cache to transition to shared and causes the owner to send the data to the directory, where it is written to memory and sent back to the requesting processor. The identity of the requesting processor is added to the set Sharers, which still contains the identity of the processor that was the owner (since it still has a readable copy).

- *Data write back*—The owner processor is replacing the block and therefore must write it back. This write back makes the memory copy up to date (the home directory essentially becomes the owner), the block is now uncached, and the Sharers set is empty.

- *Write miss*—The block has a new owner. A message is sent to the old owner, causing the cache to invalidate the block and send the value to the directory, from which it is sent to the requesting processor, which becomes the new owner. Sharers is set to the identity of the new owner, and the state of the block remains exclusive.

This state transition diagram in Figure 6.30 is a simplification, just as it was in the snooping cache case. In the directory case it is a larger simplification, since our assumption that bus transactions are atomic no longer applies. Appendix I explores these issues in depth.

In addition, the directory protocols used in real multiprocessors contain additional optimizations. In particular, in this protocol when a read or write miss occurs for a block that is exclusive, the block is first sent to the directory at the home node. From there it is stored into the home memory and also sent to the original requesting node. Many of the protocols in use in commercial multiprocessors forward the data from the owner node to the requesting node directly (as well as performing the write back to the home). Such optimizations often add complexity by increasing the possibility of deadlock and by increasing the types of messages that must be handled.

6.6   Performance of Distributed Shared-Memory Multiprocessors

The performance of a directory-based multiprocessor depends on many of the same factors that influence the performance of bus-based multiprocessors (e.g., cache size, processor count, and block size), as well as the distribution of misses to various locations in the memory hierarchy. The location of a requested data item depends on both the initial allocation and the sharing patterns. We start by examining the basic cache performance of our scientific/technical workload and then look at the effect of different types of misses.

Because the multiprocessor is larger and has longer latencies than our snooping-based multiprocessor, we begin with a slightly larger cache (128 KB) and a larger block size of 64 bytes.

In distributed-memory architectures, the distribution of memory requests between local and remote is key to performance because it affects both the consumption of global bandwidth and the latency seen by requests. Therefore, for the figures in this section we separate the cache misses into local and remote requests. In looking at the figures, keep in mind that, for these applications, most of the remote misses that arise are coherence misses, although some capacity misses can also be remote, and in some applications with poor data distribution such misses can be significant (see the pitfall on page 643).

As Figure 6.31 shows, the miss rates with these cache sizes are not affected much by changes in processor count, with the exception of Ocean, where the miss rate rises at 64 processors. This rise results from two factors: an increase in mapping conflicts in the cache that occur when the grid becomes small, which leads to a rise in local misses, and an increase in the number of the coherence misses, which are all remote.

Figure 6.32 shows how the miss rates change as the cache size is increased, assuming a 64-processor execution and 64-byte blocks. These miss rates decrease at rates that we might expect, although the dampening effect caused by little or no reduction in coherence misses leads to a slower decrease in the remote misses than in the local misses. By the time we reach the largest cache size shown, 512 KB, the remote miss rate is equal to or greater than the local miss rate. Larger caches would amplify this trend.

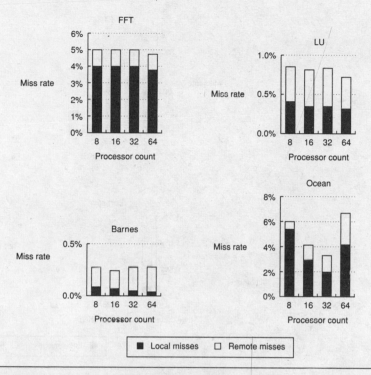

Figure 6.31 The data miss rate is often steady as processors are added for these benchmarks. Because of its grid structure, Ocean has an initially decreasing miss rate, which rises when there are 64 processors. For Ocean, the local miss rate drops from 5% at 8 processors to 2% at 32, before rising to 4% at 64. The remote miss rate in Ocean, driven primarily by communication, rises monotonically from 1% to 2.5%. Note that to show the detailed behavior of each benchmark, different scales are used on the y-axis. The cache for all these runs is 128 KB, two-way set associative, with 64-byte blocks. Remote misses include any misses that require communication with another node, whether to fetch the data or to deliver an invalidate. In particular, in this figure and other data in this section, the measurement of remote misses includes write upgrade misses where the data are up to date in the local memory but cached elsewhere and, therefore, require invalidations to be sent. Such invalidations do indeed generate remote traffic, but may or may not delay the write, depending on the consistency model (see Section 6.8).

We examine the effect of changing the block size in Figure 6.33. Because these applications have good spatial locality, increases in block size reduce the miss rate, even for large blocks, although the performance benefits for going to the largest blocks are small. Furthermore, most of the improvement in miss rate comes from a reduction in the local misses.

Rather than plot the memory traffic, Figure 6.34 plots the number of bytes required per data reference versus block size, breaking the requirement into local and global bandwidth. In the case of a bus, we can simply aggregate the demands

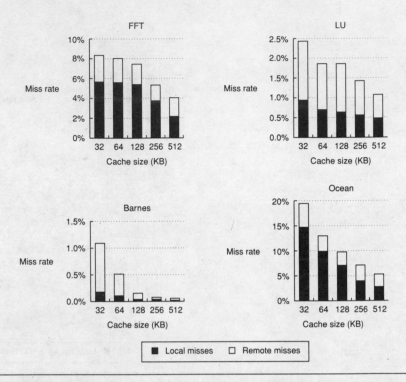

Figure 6.32 Miss rates decrease as cache sizes grow. Steady decreases are seen in the local miss rate, while the remote miss rate declines to varying degrees, depending on whether the remote miss rate had a large capacity component or was driven primarily by communication misses. In all cases, the decrease in the local miss rate is larger than the decrease in the remote miss rate. The plateau in the miss rate of FFT, which we mentioned in the last section, ends once the cache exceeds 128 KB. These runs were done with 64 processors and 64-byte cache blocks.

of each processor to find the total demand for bus and memory bandwidth. For a scalable interconnect, we can use the data in Figure 6.34 to compute the required per-node global bandwidth and the estimated bisection bandwidth, as the next example shows.

Example   Assume a 64-processor multiprocessor with 1 GHz processors that sustain one memory reference per processor clock. For a 64-byte block size, the remote miss rate is 0.7%. Find the per-node and estimated bisection bandwidth for FFT. Assume that the processor does not stall for remote memory requests; this might be true if, for example, all remote data were prefetched. How do these bandwidth requirements compare to various interconnection technologies?

Answer   The per-node bandwidth is simply the number of data bytes per reference times the reference rate: 0.7% × 1 GB/sec × 64 = 448 MB/sec. This rate is somewhat

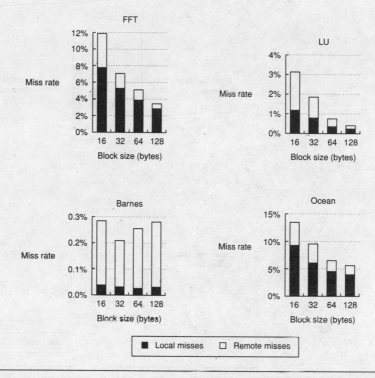

Figure 6.33 Data miss rate versus block size assuming a 128 KB cache and 64 processors in total. Although difficult to see, the coherence miss rate in Barnes actually rises for the largest block size, just as in the last section.

higher than the hardware sustainable transfer rate for the CrayT3E (using a block prefetch) and lower than that for an SGI Origin 3000 (1.6 GB/processor pair). The FFT per-node bandwidth demand exceeds the bandwidth sustainable from the fastest standard networks by more than a factor of 5.

FFT performs all-to-all communication, so the bisection bandwidth is equal to the number of processors times the per-node bandwidth, or about 64 x 448 MB/sec = 28.7 GB/sec. The SGI Origin 3000 with 64 processors has a bisection bandwidth of about 50 GB/sec. No standard networking technology comes close.

The previous example looked at the bandwidth demands. The other key issue for a parallel program is remote memory access time, or latency. To get insight into this, we use a simple example of a directory-based multiprocessor. Figure 6.35 shows the parameters we assume for our simple multiprocessor model. It assumes that the time to first word for a local memory access is 85 processor cycles and that the path to local memory is 16 bytes wide, while the network interconnect is 4 bytes wide. This model ignores the effects of contention, which are probably not too serious in the parallel benchmarks we examine, with the

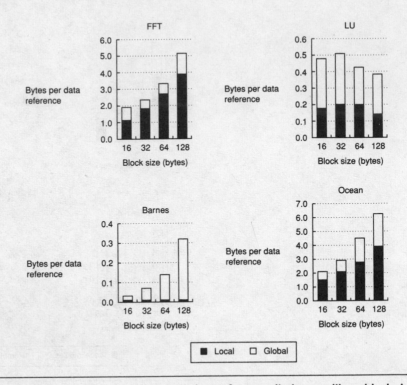

Figure 6.34 The number of bytes per data reference climbs steadily as block size is increased. These data can be used to determine the bandwidth required per node both internally and globally. The data assume a 128 KB cache for each of 64 processors.

Characteristic	Processor clock cycles ≤ 16 processors	Processor clock cycles 17–64 processors
Cache hit	1	1
Cache miss to local memory	85	85
Cache miss to remote home directory	125	150
Cache miss to remotely cached data (three-hop miss)	140	170

Figure 6.35 Characteristics of the example directory-based multiprocessor. Misses can be serviced locally (including from the local directory), at a remote home node, or using the services of both the home node and another remote node that is caching an exclusive copy. This last case is called a three-hop miss and has a higher cost because it requires interrogating both the home directory and a remote cache. Note that this simple model does not account for invalidation time, but does include some factor for increasing interconnect time. These remote access latencies are based on those in an SGI Origin 3000, the fastest scalable interconnect system in 2001, and assume a 500 MHz processor.

possible exception of FFT, which uses all-to-all communication. Contention could have a serious performance impact in other workloads.

Figure 6.36 shows the cost in cycles for the average memory reference, assuming the parameters in Figure 6.35. Only the latencies for each reference

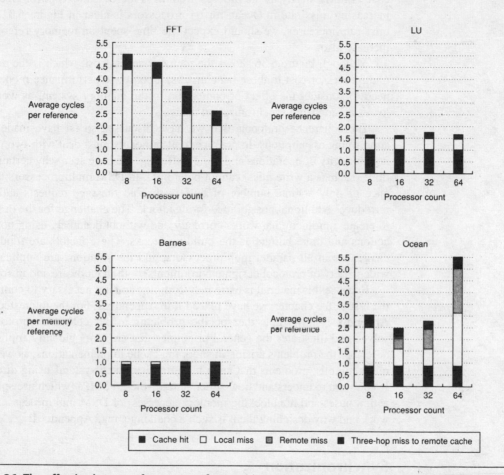

Figure 6.36 The effective latency of memory references in a DSM multiprocessor depends both on the relative frequency of cache misses and on the location of the memory where the accesses are served. These plots show the memory access cost (a metric called average memory access time in Chapter 5) for each of the benchmarks for 8, 16, 32, and 64 processors, assuming a 512 KB data cache that is two-way set associative with 64-byte blocks. The average memory access cost is composed of four different types of accesses, with the cost of each type given in Figure 6.35. For the Barnes and LU benchmarks, the low miss rates lead to low overall access times. In FFT, the higher access cost is determined by a higher local miss rate (1–4%) and a significant three-hop miss rate (1%). The improvement in FFT comes from the reduction in local miss rate from 4% to 1%, as the aggregate cache increases. Ocean shows the biggest change in the cost of memory accesses, and the highest overall cost at 64 processors. The high cost is driven primarily by a high local miss rate (average 1.6%). The memory access cost drops from 8 to 16 processors as the grids more easily fit in the individual caches. At 64 processors, the data set size is too small to map properly and both local misses and coherence misses rise, as we saw in Figure 6.31.

type are counted. Each bar indicates the contribution from cache hits, local misses, remote misses, and three-hop remote misses. The cost is influenced by the total frequency of cache misses and upgrades, as well as by the distribution of the location where the miss is satisfied. The cost for a remote memory reference is fairly steady as the processor count is increased, except for Ocean. The increasing miss rate in Ocean for 64 processors is clear in Figure 6.31. As the miss rate increases, we should expect the time spent on memory references to increase also.

Although Figure 6.36 shows the memory access cost, which is the dominant multiprocessor cost in these benchmarks, a complete performance model would need to consider the effect of contention in the memory system, as well as the losses arising from synchronization delays.

The coherence protocols that we have discussed so far have made several simplifying assumptions. In practice, real protocols must deal with two realities: nonatomicity of operations and finite buffering. We have seen why certain operations (such as a write miss) cannot be atomic. In DSM multiprocessors the presence of only a finite number of buffers to hold message requests and replies introduces additional possibilities for deadlock. The challenge for the designer is to create a protocol that works correctly and without deadlock, using nonatomic actions and finite buffers as the building blocks. These factors are fundamental challenges in all parallel multiprocessors, and the solutions are applicable to a wide variety of protocol design environments, both in hardware and in software.

Because this material is extremely complex and not necessary to comprehend the rest of the chapter, we have placed it in Appendix I. For the interested reader, Appendix I shows how the specific problems in our coherence protocols are solved and illustrates the general principles that are more globally applicable. It describes the problems arising in snooping cache implementations, as well as the more complex problems that arise in more distributed systems using directories. If you want to understand how either state-of-the-art SMPs (which use split transaction buses and nonblocking memory accesses) or DSM multiprocessors really work and why designing them is such a challenge, read Appendix I!

6.7 Synchronization

Synchronization mechanisms are typically built with user-level software routines that rely on hardware-supplied synchronization instructions. For smaller multiprocessors or low-contention situations, the key hardware capability is an uninterruptible instruction or instruction sequence capable of atomically retrieving and changing a value. Software synchronization mechanisms are then constructed using this capability. For example, we will see how very efficient spin locks can be built using a simple hardware synchronization instruction and the coherence mechanism. In larger-scale multiprocessors or high-contention situations, synchronization can become a performance bottleneck because contention introduces additional delays and because latency is potentially greater in such a multiprocessor. We will see how contention can arise in implementing some common user-level synchronization operations and examine more powerful hardware-supported synchronization primitives that can reduce contention as well as latency.

We begin by examining the basic hardware primitives, then construct several well-known synchronization routines with the primitives, and then turn to performance problems in larger multiprocessors and solutions for those problems.

Basic Hardware Primitives

The key ability we require to implement synchronization in a multiprocessor is a set of hardware primitives with the ability to atomically read and modify a memory location. Without such a capability, the cost of building basic synchronization primitives will be too high and will increase as the processor count increases. There are a number of alternative formulations of the basic hardware primitives, all of which provide the ability to atomically read and modify a location, together with some way to tell if the read and write were performed atomically. These hardware primitives are the basic building blocks that are used to build a wide variety of user-level synchronization operations, including things such as locks and barriers. In general, architects do not expect users to employ the basic hardware primitives, but instead expect that the primitives will be used by system programmers to build a synchronization library, a process that is often complex and tricky. Let's start with one such hardware primitive and show how it can be used to build some basic synchronization operations.

One typical operation for building synchronization operations is the *atomic exchange,* which interchanges a value in a register for a value in memory. To see how to use this to build a basic synchronization operation, assume that we want to build a simple lock where the value 0 is used to indicate that the lock is free and 1 is used to indicate that the lock is unavailable. A processor tries to set the lock by doing an exchange of 1, which is in a register, with the memory address corresponding to the lock. The value returned from the exchange instruction is 1 if some other processor had already claimed access and 0 otherwise. In the latter case, the value is also changed to 1, preventing any competing exchange from also retrieving a 0.

For example, consider two processors that each try to do the exchange simultaneously: This race is broken since exactly one of the processors will perform the exchange first, returning 0, and the second processor will return 1 when it does the exchange. The key to using the exchange (or swap) primitive to implement synchronization is that the operation is atomic: The exchange is indivisible and two simultaneous exchanges will be ordered by the write serialization mechanisms. It is impossible for two processors trying to set the synchronization variable in this manner to both think they have simultaneously set the variable.

There are a number of other atomic primitives that can be used to implement synchronization. They all have the key property that they read and update a memory value in such a manner that we can tell whether or not the two operations executed atomically. One operation, present in many older multiprocessors, is *test-and-set,* which tests a value and sets it if the value passes the test. For example, we could define an operation that tested for 0 and set the value to 1, which can be used in a fashion similar to how we used atomic exchange. Another atomic synchronization primitive is *fetch-and-increment:* It returns the value of a memory location and atomically increments it. By using the value 0 to indicate that the synchronization variable is unclaimed, we can use fetch-and-increment, just as we used exchange. There are other uses of operations like fetch-and-increment, which we will see shortly.

A slightly different approach to providing this atomic read-and-update operation has been used in some recent multiprocessors. Implementing a single atomic memory operation introduces some challenges, since it requires both a memory read and a write in a single, uninterruptible instruction. This requirement complicates the implementation of coherence, since the hardware cannot allow any other operations between the read and the write, and yet must not deadlock.

An alternative is to have a pair of instructions where the second instruction returns a value from which it can be deduced whether the pair of instructions was executed as if the instructions were atomic. The pair of instructions is effectively atomic if it appears as if all other operations executed by any processor occurred before or after the pair. Thus, when an instruction pair is effectively atomic, no other processor can change the value between the instruction pair.

The pair of instructions includes a special load called a *load linked* or *load locked* and a special store called a *store conditional*. These instructions are used in sequence: If the contents of the memory location specified by the load linked are changed before the store conditional to the same address occurs, then the store conditional fails. If the processor does a context switch between the two instructions, then the store conditional also fails. The store conditional is defined to return a value indicating whether or not the store was successful. Since the load linked returns the initial value and the store conditional returns 1 if it succeeds and 0 otherwise, the following sequence implements an atomic exchange on the memory location specified by the contents of R1:

```
try:    OR      R3,R4,R0        ;mov exchange value
        LL      R2,0(R1)        ;load linked
        SC      R3,0(R1)        ;store conditional
        BEQZ    R3,try          ;branch store fails
        MOV     R4,R2           ;put load value in R4
```

At the end of this sequence the contents of R4 and the memory location specified by R1 have been atomically exchanged (ignoring any effect from delayed branches). Any time a processor intervenes and modifies the value in memory between the LL and SC instructions, the SC returns 0 in R3, causing the code sequence to try again.

An advantage of the load linked/store conditional mechanism is that it can be used to build other synchronization primitives. For example, here is an atomic fetch-and-increment:

```
try:    LL      R2,0(R1)        ;load linked
        DADDUI  R3,R2,#1        ;increment
        SC      R3,0(R1)        ;store conditional
        BEQZ    R3,try          ;branch store fails
```

These instructions are typically implemented by keeping track of the address specified in the LL instruction in a register, often called the *link register*. If an interrupt occurs, or if the cache block matching the address in the link register is invalidated (for example, by another SC), the link register is cleared. The SC instruction simply checks that its address matches that in the link register. If so, the SC succeeds; otherwise, it fails. Since the store conditional will fail after either another attempted store to the load linked address or any exception, care must be taken in choosing what instructions are inserted between the two instructions. In particular, only register-register instructions can safely be permitted; otherwise, it is possible to create deadlock situations where the processor can never complete the SC. In addition, the number of instructions between the load linked and the store conditional should be small to minimize the probability that either an unrelated event or a competing processor causes the store conditional to fail frequently.

Implementing Locks Using Coherence

Once we have an atomic operation, we can use the coherence mechanisms of a multiprocessor to implement *spin locks*—locks that a processor continuously tries to acquire, spinning around a loop until it succeeds. Spin locks are used when a programmer expects the lock to be held for a very short amount of time and when she wants the process of locking to be low latency when the lock is available. Because spin locks tie up the processor, waiting in a loop for the lock to become free, they are inappropriate in some circumstances.

The simplest implementation, which we would use if there were no cache coherence, would keep the lock variables in memory. A processor could continually try to acquire the lock using an atomic operation, say, exchange, and test whether the exchange returned the lock as free. To release the lock, the processor simply stores the value 0 to the lock. Here is the code sequence to lock a spin lock whose address is in R1 using an atomic exchange:

```
        DADDUI  R2,R0,#1
lockit: EXCH    R2,0(R1)        ;atomic exchange
        BNEZ    R2,lockit       ;already locked?
```

If our multiprocessor supports cache coherence, we can cache the locks using the coherence mechanism to maintain the lock value coherently. Caching locks has two advantages. First, it allows an implementation where the process of "spinning" (trying to test and acquire the lock in a tight loop) could be done on a local cached copy rather than requiring a global memory access on each attempt to acquire the lock. The second advantage comes from the observation that there is often locality in lock accesses: that is, the processor that used the lock last will use it again in the near future. In such cases, the lock value may reside in the cache of that processor, greatly reducing the time to acquire the lock.

Obtaining the first advantage—being able to spin on a local cached copy rather than generating a memory request for each attempt to acquire the lock—requires a change in our simple spin procedure. Each attempt to exchange in the loop directly above requires a write operation. If multiple processors are attempting to get the lock, each will generate the write. Most of these writes will lead to write misses, since each processor is trying to obtain the lock variable in an exclusive state.

Thus we should modify our spin lock procedure so that it spins by doing reads on a local copy of the lock until it successfully sees that the lock is available. Then it attempts to acquire the lock by doing a swap operation. A processor first reads the lock variable to test its state. A processor keeps reading and testing until the value of the read indicates that the lock is unlocked. The processor then races against all other processes that were similarly "spin waiting" to see who can lock the variable first. All processes use a swap instruction that reads the old value and stores a 1 into the lock variable. The single winner will see the 0, and the losers will see a 1 that was placed there by the winner. (The losers will continue to set the variable to the locked value, but that doesn't matter.) The winning processor executes the code after the lock and, when finished, stores a 0 into the lock variable to release the lock, which starts the race all over again. Here is the code to perform this spin lock (remember that 0 is unlocked and 1 is locked):

```
lockit:  LD      R2,0(R1)      ;load of lock
         BNEZ    R2,lockit     ;not available-spin
         DADDUI  R2,R0,#1      ;load locked value
         EXCH    R2,0(R1)      ;swap
         BNEZ    R2,lockit     ;branch if lock wasn't 0
```

Let's examine how this "spin lock" scheme uses the cache coherence mechanisms. Figure 6.37 shows the processor and bus or directory operations for multiple processes trying to lock a variable using an atomic swap. Once the processor with the lock stores a 0 into the lock, all other caches are invalidated and must fetch the new value to update their copy of the lock. One such cache gets the copy of the unlocked value (0) first and performs the swap. When the cache miss of other processors is satisfied, they find that the variable is already locked, so they must return to testing and spinning.

This example shows another advantage of the load linked/store conditional primitives: The read and write operations are explicitly separated. The load linked need not cause any bus traffic. This fact allows the following simple code sequence, which has the same characteristics as the optimized version using exchange (R1 has the address of the lock):

Step	Processor P0	Processor P1	Processor P2	Coherence state of lock	Bus/directory activity
1	Has lock	Spins, testing if lock = 0	Spins, testing if lock = 0	Shared	None
2	Set lock to 0	(Invalidate received)	(Invalidate received)	Exclusive (P0)	Write invalidate of lock variable from P0
3		Cache miss	Cache miss	Shared	Bus/directory services P2 cache miss; write back from P0
4		(Waits while bus/ directory busy)	Lock = 0	Shared	Cache miss for P2 satisfied
5		Lock = 0	Executes swap, gets cache miss	Shared	Cache miss for P1 satisfied
6		Executes swap, gets cache miss	Completes swap: returns 0 and sets Lock = 1	Exclusive (P2)	Bus/directory services P2 cache miss; generates invalidate
7		Swap completes and returns 1, and sets Lock = 1	Enter critical section	Exclusive (P1)	Bus/directory services P1 cache miss; generates write back
8		Spins, testing if lock = 0			None

Figure 6.37 Cache coherence steps and bus traffic for three processors, P0, P1, and P2. This figure assumes write invalidate coherence. P0 starts with the lock (step 1). P0 exits and unlocks the lock (step 2). P1 and P2 race to see which reads the unlocked value during the swap (steps 3–5). P2 wins and enters the critical section (steps 6 and 7), while P1's attempt fails so it starts spin waiting (steps 7 and 8). In a real system, these events will take many more than 8 clock ticks, since acquiring the bus and replying to misses takes much longer.

```
lockit:  LL      R2,0(R1)     ;load linked
         BNEZ    R2,lockit    ;not available-spin
         DADDUI  R2,R0,#1     ;locked value
         SC      R2,0(R1)     ;store
         BEQZ    R2,lockit    ;branch if store fails
```

The first branch forms the spinning loop; the second branch resolves races when two processors see the lock available simultaneously.

Although our spin lock scheme is simple and compelling, it has difficulty scaling up to handle many processors because of the communication traffic generated when the lock is released. The next subsection discusses these problems in more detail, as well as techniques to overcome these problems in larger multiprocessors.

Synchronization Performance Challenges

To understand why the simple spin lock scheme of the previous subsection does not scale well, imagine a large multiprocessor with all processors contending for the same lock. The directory or bus acts as a point of serialization for all the processors, leading to lots of contention, as well as traffic. The following example shows how bad things can be.

Example   Suppose there are 10 processors on a bus that each try to lock a variable simultaneously. Assume that each bus transaction (read miss or write miss) is 100 clock cycles long. You can ignore the time of the actual read or write of a lock held in the cache, as well as the time the lock is held (they won't matter much!). Determine the number of bus transactions required for all 10 processors to acquire the lock, assuming they are all spinning when the lock is released at time 0. About how long will it take to process the 10 requests? Assume that the bus is totally fair so that every pending request is serviced before a new request and that the processors are equally fast.

Answer   When i processes are contending for the lock, they perform the following sequence of actions, each of which generates a bus transaction:

> i load linked operations to access the lock
>
> i store conditional operations to try to lock the lock
>
> 1 store (to release the lock)

Thus for i processes, there are a total of $2i + 1$ bus transactions. Note that this assumes that the critical section time is negligible, so that the lock is released before any other processors whose store conditional failed attempt another load linked.

Thus, for n processes, the total number of bus operations is:

$$\sum_{i=1}^{n} (2i + 1) = n(n + 1) + n = n^2 + 2n$$

For 10 processes there are 120 bus transactions requiring 12,000 clock cycles or 120 clock cycles per lock acquisition!

The difficulty in this example arises from contention for the lock and serialization of lock access, as well as the latency of the bus access. (The fairness property of the bus actually makes things worse, since it delays the processor that claims the lock from releasing it; unfortunately, for any bus arbitration scheme some worst-case scenario does exist.) The key advantages of spin locks—that they have low overhead in terms of bus or network cycles and offer good performance when locks are reused by the same processor—are both lost in this example. We will consider alternative implementations in the next section, but before we do that, let's consider the use of spin locks to implement another common high-level synchronization primitive.

Barrier Synchronization

One additional common synchronization operation in programs with parallel loops is a *barrier*. A barrier forces all processes to wait until all the processes reach the barrier and then releases all of the processes. A typical implementation of a barrier can be done with two spin locks: one to protect a counter that tallies the processes arriving at the barrier and one to hold the processes until the last process arrives at the barrier. To implement a barrier we usually use the ability to spin on a variable until it satisfies a test; we use the notation spin(condition) to indicate this. Figure 6.38 is a typical implementation, assuming that lock and unlock provide basic spin locks and total is the number of processes that must reach the barrier.

In practice, another complication makes barrier implementation slightly more complex. Frequently a barrier is used within a loop, so that processes released from the barrier would do some work and then reach the barrier again. Assume that one of the processes never actually leaves the barrier (it stays at the spin operation), which could happen if the OS scheduled another process, for example. Now it is possible that one process races ahead and gets to the barrier again before the last process has left. The "fast" process then traps the remaining "slow" process in the barrier by resetting the flag release. Now all the processes will wait infinitely at the next instance of this barrier because one process is trapped at the last instance, and the number of processes can never reach the value of total.

The important observation in this example is that the programmer did nothing wrong. Instead, the implementer of the barrier made some assumptions about forward progress that cannot be assumed. One obvious solution to this is to count

```
lock (counterlock);/* ensure update atomic */
if (count==0) release=0;/* first=>reset release */
count = count + 1;/* count arrivals */
unlock(counterlock);/* release lock */
if (count==total) {/* all arrived */
      count=0;/* reset counter */
      release=1;/* release processes */
}
else {/* more to come */
      spin (release==1);/* wait for arrivals */
}
```

Figure 6.38 Code for a simple barrier. The lock counterlock protects the counter so that it can be atomically incremented. The variable count keeps the tally of how many processes have reached the barrier. The variable release is used to hold the processes until the last one reaches the barrier. The operation spin (release==1) causes a process to wait until all processes reach the barrier.

```
local_sense =! local_sense; /* toggle local_sense */
lock (counterlock);/* ensure update atomic */
count=count+1;/* count arrivals */
if (count==total) {/* all arrived */
      count=0;/* reset counter */
      release=local_sense;/* release processes */
}
unlock (counterlock);/* unlock */
spin (release==local_sense);/* wait for signal */
}
```

Figure 6.39 Code for a sense-reversing barrier. The key to making the barrier reusable is the use of an alternating pattern of values for the flag release, which controls the exit from the barrier. If a process races ahead to the next instance of this barrier while some other processes are still in the barrier, the fast process cannot trap the other processes, since it does not reset the value of release as it did in Figure 6.38.

the processes as they exit the barrier (just as we did on entry) and not to allow any process to reenter and reinitialize the barrier until all processes have left the prior instance of this barrier. This extra step would significantly increase the latency of the barrier and the contention, which as we will see shortly are already large. An alternative solution is a *sense-reversing barrier,* which makes use of a private per-process variable, local_sense, which is initialized to 1 for each process. Figure 6.39 shows the code for the sense-reversing barrier. This version of a barrier is safely usable; as the next example shows, however, its performance can still be quite poor.

Example Suppose there are 10 processors on a bus that each try to execute a barrier simultaneously. Assume that each bus transaction is 100 clock cycles, as before. You can ignore the time of the actual read or write of a lock held in the cache as the time to execute other nonsynchronization operations in the barrier implementation. Determine the number of bus transactions required for all 10 processors to reach the barrier, be released from the barrier, and exit the barrier. Assume that the bus is totally fair, so that every pending request is serviced before a new request and that the processors are equally fast. Don't worry about counting the processors out of the barrier. How long will the entire process take?

Answer We assume that load linked and store conditional are used to implement lock and unlock. Figure 6.40 shows the sequence of bus events for a processor to traverse the barrier, assuming that the first process to grab the bus does not have the lock. There is a slight difference for the last process to reach the barrier, as described in the caption.

Event	Number of times for process i	Corresponding source line	Comment
LL counterlock	i	`lock (counterlock);`	All processes try for lock.
Store conditional	i	`lock (counterlock);`	All processes try for lock.
LD count	1	`count=count+1;`	Successful process.
Load linked	$i-1$	`lock (counterlock);`	Unsuccessful process; try again.
SD count	1	`count=count+1;`	Miss to get exclusive access.
SD counterlock	1	`unlock(counterlock);`	Miss to get the lock.
LD release	2	`spin (release==local_sense);/`	Read release: misses initially and when finally written.

Figure 6.40 Here are the actions, which require a bus transaction, taken when the ith process reaches the barrier. The last process to reach the barrier requires one less bus transaction, since its read of release for the spin will hit in the cache!

For the ith process, the number of bus transactions is: $3i + 4$. The last process to reach the barrier requires one less. Thus, for n processes, the number of bus transactions is

$$\left(\sum_{i=1}^{n} (3i + 4) \right) - 1 = \frac{3n^2 + 11n}{2} - 1$$

For 10 processes, this is 204 bus cycles or 20,400 clock cycles! Our barrier operation takes almost twice as long as the 10-processor lock-unlock sequence.

As we can see from these examples, synchronization performance can be a real bottleneck when there is substantial contention among multiple processes. When there is little contention and synchronization operations are infrequent, we are primarily concerned about the latency of a synchronization primitive—that is, how long it takes an individual process to complete a synchronization operation. Our basic spin lock operation can do this in two bus cycles: one to initially read the lock and one to write it. We could improve this to a single bus cycle by a variety of methods. For example, we could simply spin on the swap operation. If the lock were almost always free, this could be better, but if the lock were not free, it would lead to lots of bus traffic, since each attempt to lock the variable would lead to a bus cycle. In practice, the latency of our spin lock is not quite as bad as we have seen in this example, since the write miss for a data item present in the cache is treated as an upgrade and will be cheaper than a true read miss.

The more serious problem in these examples is the serialization of each process's attempt to complete the synchronization. This serialization is a problem when there is contention because it greatly increases the time to complete the synchronization operation. For example, if the time to complete all 10 lock and unlock operations depended only on the latency in the uncontended case, then it would take 1000 rather than 15,000 cycles to complete the synchronization operations. The barrier situation is as bad, and in some ways worse, since it is highly likely to incur contention. The use of a bus interconnect exacerbates these problems, but serialization could be just as serious in a directory-based multiprocessor, where the latency would be large. The next subsection presents some solutions that are useful when either the contention is high or the processor count is large.

Synchronization Mechanisms for Larger-Scale Multiprocessors

What we would like are synchronization mechanisms that have low latency in uncontended cases and that minimize serialization in the case where contention is significant. We begin by showing how software implementations can improve the performance of locks and barriers when contention is high; we then explore two basic hardware primitives that reduce serialization while keeping latency low.

Software Implementations

The major difficulty with our spin lock implementation is the delay due to contention when many processes are spinning on the lock. One solution is to artificially delay processes when they fail to acquire the lock. The best performance is obtained by increasing the delay exponentially whenever the attempt to acquire the lock fails. Figure 6.41 shows how a spin lock with *exponential back-off* is

```
            DADDUI    R3,R0,#1      ;R3 = initial delay
lockit:     LL        R2,0(R1)      ;load linked
            BNEZ      R2,lockit     ;not available-spin
            DADDUI    R2,R2,#1      ;get locked value
            SC        R2,0(R1)      ;store conditional
            BNEZ      R2,gotit      ;branch if store succeeds
            DSLL      R3,R3,#1      ;increase delay by factor of 2
            PAUSE     R3            ;delays by value in R3
            J         lockit
gotit:      use data protected by lock
```

Figure 6.41 A spin lock with exponential back-off. When the store conditional fails, the process delays itself by the value in R3. The delay can be implemented by decrementing a copy of the value in R3 until it reaches 0. The exact timing of the delay is multiprocessor dependent, although it should start with a value that is approximately the time to perform the critical section and release the lock. The statement pause R3 should cause a delay of R3 of these time units. The value in R3 is increased by a factor of 2 every time the store conditional fails, which causes the process to wait twice as long before trying to acquire the lock again. The small variations In the rate at which competing processors execute instructions are usually sufficient to ensure that processes will not continually collide. If the natural perturbation in execution time was insufficient, R3 could be initialized with a small random value, increasing the variance in the successive delays and reducing the probability of successive collisions.

implemented. Exponential back-off is a common technique for reducing contention in shared resources, including access to shared networks and buses (see Sections 8.5–8.7). This implementation still attempts to preserve low latency when contention is small by not delaying the initial spin loop. The result is that if many processes are waiting, the back-off does not affect the processes on their first attempt to acquire the lock. We could also delay that process, but the result would be poorer performance when the lock was in use by only two processes and the first one happened to find it locked.

Another technique for implementing locks is to use queuing locks. Queuing locks work by constructing a queue of waiting processors; whenever a processor frees up the lock, it causes the next processor in the queue to attempt access. This eliminates contention for a lock when it is freed. We show how queuing locks operate in the next section using a hardware implementation, but software implementations using arrays can achieve most of the same benefits (see Exercise 6.25). Before we look at hardware primitives, let's look at a better mechanism for barriers.

Our barrier implementation suffers from contention both during the *gather* stage, when we must atomically update the count, and at the *release* stage, when all the processes must read the release flag. The former is more serious because it requires exclusive access to the synchronization variable and thus creates much more serialization; in comparison, the latter generates only read contention. We can reduce the contention by using a *combining tree,* a structure where multiple requests are locally combined in tree fashion. The same combining tree can be used to implement the release process, reducing the contention there; we leave the last step for the exercises.

Our combining tree barrier uses a predetermined n-ary tree structure. We use the variable k to stand for the fan-in; in practice $k = 4$ seems to work well. When the kth process arrives at a node in the tree, we signal the next level in the tree. When a process arrives at the root, we release all waiting processes. As in our earlier example, we use a sense-reversing technique. A tree-based barrier, as shown in Figure 6.42, uses a tree to combine the processes and a single signal to release the barrier. Exercises 6.23 and 6.24 ask you to analyze the time for the combining barrier versus the noncombining version. Some MPPs (e.g., the T3D and CM-5) have also included hardware support for barriers, but more recent machines have relied on software libraries for this support.

Hardware Primitives

In this subsection we look at two hardware synchronization primitives. The first primitive deals with locks, while the second is useful for barriers and a number of other user-level operations that require counting or supplying distinct indices. In both cases we can create a hardware primitive where latency is essentially identical to our earlier version, but with much less serialization, leading to better scaling when there is contention.

```
struct node{/* a node in the combining tree */
      int counterlock; /* lock for this node */
      int count; /* counter for this node */
      int parent; /* parent in the tree = 0..P-1 except for root */
};
struct node tree [0..P-1]; /* the tree of nodes */
int local_sense; /* private per processor */
int release; /* global release flag */

/* function to implement barrier */
barrier (int mynode, int local_sense) {
      lock (tree[mynode].counterlock); /* protect count */
      tree[mynode].count=tree[mynode].count+1;
            /* increment count */
      if (tree[mynode].count==k) {/* all arrived at mynode */
            if (tree[mynode].parent >=0) {
                  barrier(tree[mynode].parent);
            } else{
                  release = local_sense;
            };
            tree[mynode].count = 0; /* reset for the next time */
      unlock (tree[mynode].counterlock); /* unlock */
      spin (release==local_sense); /* wait */
};
/* code executed by a processor to join barrier */
local_sense =! local_sense;
barrier (mynode);
```

Figure 6.42 An implementation of a tree-based barrier reduces contention considerably. The tree is assumed to be prebuilt statically using the nodes in the array tree. Each node in the tree combines *k* processes and provides a separate counter and lock, so that at most *k* processes contend at each node. When the *k*th process reaches a node in the tree, it goes up to the parent, incrementing the count at the parent. When the count in the parent node reaches *k*, the release flag is set. The count in each node is reset by the last process to arrive. Sense-reversing is used to avoid races as in the simple barrier. The value of tree[root].parent should be set to –1 when the tree is initially built.

The major problem with our original lock implementation is that it introduces a large amount of unneeded contention. For example, when the lock is released all processors generate both a read and a write miss, although at most one processor can successfully get the lock in the unlocked state. This sequence happens on each of the 10 lock/unlock sequences, as we saw in the example on page 596.

We can improve this situation by explicitly handing the lock from one waiting processor to the next. Rather than simply allowing all processors to compete every time the lock is released, we keep a list of the waiting processors and hand the lock to one explicitly, when its turn comes. This sort of mechanism has been called a *queuing lock*. Queuing locks can be implemented either in hardware, which we describe here, or in software using an array to keep track of the waiting processes. The basic concepts are the same in either case. Our hardware implementation assumes a directory-based multiprocessor where the individual processor caches are addressable. In a bus-based multiprocessor, a software implementation would be more appropriate and would have each processor using a different address for the lock, permitting the explicit transfer of the lock from one process to another.

How does a queuing lock work? On the first miss to the lock variable, the miss is sent to a synchronization controller, which may be integrated with the memory controller (in a bus-based system) or with the directory controller. If the lock is free, it is simply returned to the processor. If the lock is unavailable, the controller creates a record of the node's request (such as a bit in a vector) and sends the processor back a locked value for the variable, which the processor then spins on. When the lock is freed, the controller selects a processor to go ahead from the list of waiting processors. It can then either update the lock variable in the selected processor's cache or invalidate the copy, causing the processor to miss and fetch an available copy of the lock.

Example How many bus transactions and how long does it take to have 10 processors lock and unlock the variable using a queuing lock that updates the lock on a miss? Make the other assumptions about the system the same as those in the earlier example on page 596.

Answer For n processors, each will initially attempt a lock access, generating a bus transaction, one will succeed and free up the lock, for a total of $n + 1$ transactions for the first processor. Each subsequent processor requires two bus transactions, one to receive the lock and one to free it up. Thus, the total number of bus transactions is $(n + 1) + 2(n - 1) = 3n - 1$. Note that the number of bus transactions is now linear in the number of processors contending for the lock, rather than quadratic, as it was with the spin lock we examined earlier. For 10 processors, this requires 29 bus cycles or 2900 clock cycles.

There are a couple of key insights in implementing such a queuing lock capability. First, we need to be able to distinguish the initial access to the lock, so we can perform the queuing operation, and also the lock release, so we can provide the lock to another processor. The queue of waiting processes can be implemented by a variety of mechanisms. In a directory-based multiprocessor, this queue is akin to the sharing set, and similar hardware can be used to implement the directory and queuing lock operations. One complication is that the hardware must be prepared to reclaim such locks, since the process that requested the lock may have been context-switched and may not even be scheduled again on the same processor.

Queuing locks can be used to improve the performance of our barrier operation (see Exercise 6.19). Alternatively, we can introduce a primitive that reduces the amount of time needed to increment the barrier count, thus reducing the serialization at this bottleneck, which should yield comparable performance to using queuing locks. One primitive that has been introduced for this and for building other synchronization operations is *fetch-and-increment,* which atomically fetches a variable and increments its value. The returned value can be either the incremented value or the fetched value. Using fetch-and-increment we can dramatically improve our barrier implementation, compared to the simple code-sensing barrier.

Example   Write the code for the barrier using fetch-and-increment. Making the same assumptions as in our earlier example and also assuming that a fetch-and-increment operation, which returns the incremented value, takes 100 clock cycles, determine the time for 10 processors to traverse the barrier. How many bus cycles are required?

Answer   Figure 6.43 shows the code for the barrier. For *n* processors, this implementation requires *n* fetch-and-increment operations, *n* cache misses to access the count, and *n* cache misses for the release operation for a total of 3*n* bus transactions. For 10 processors, this is 30 bus transactions or 3000 clock cycles. Like the queueing lock, the time is linear in the number of processors. Of course, fetch-and-increment can also be used in implementing the combining tree barrier, reducing the serialization at each node in the tree.

As we have seen, synchronization problems can become quite acute in larger-scale multiprocessors. When the challenges posed by synchronization are combined with the challenges posed by long memory latency and potential load imbalance in computations, we can see why getting efficient usage of large-scale parallel processors is very challenging.

```
local_sense =! local_sense; /* toggle local_sense */
fetch_and_increment(count);/* atomic update */
if (count==total) {/* all arrived */
      count=0;/* reset counter */
      release=local_sense;/* release processes */
}
else {/* more to come */
      spin (release==local_sense);/* wait for signal */
}
```

Figure 6.43 Code for a sense-reversing barrier using fetch-and-increment to do the counting.

6.8   Models of Memory Consistency: An Introduction

Cache coherence ensures that multiple processors see a consistent view of memory. It does not answer the question of *how* consistent the view of memory must be. By "how consistent" we mean, when must a processor see a value that has been updated by another processor? Since processors communicate through shared variables (used both for data values and for synchronization), the question boils down to this: In what order must a processor observe the data writes of another processor? Since the only way to "observe the writes of another processor" is through reads, the question becomes, What properties must be enforced among reads and writes to different locations by different processors?

Although the question of how consistent memory must be seems simple, it is remarkably complicated, as we can see with a simple example. Here are two code segments from processes P1 and P2, shown side by side:

```
P1:      A = 0;                    P2:      B = 0;
         .....                              .....
         A = 1;                             B = 1;
L1:      if (B == 0) ...           L2:      if (A == 0)...
```

Assume that the processes are running on different processors, and that locations A and B are originally cached by both processors with the initial value of 0. If writes always take immediate effect and are immediately seen by other processors, it will be impossible for *both* if statements (labeled L1 and L2) to evaluate their conditions as true, since reaching the if statement means that either A or B must have been assigned the value 1. But suppose the write invalidate is delayed, and the processor is allowed to continue during this delay; then it is possible that both P1 and P2 have not seen the invalidations for B and A (respectively) *before* they attempt to read the values. The question is, Should this behavior be allowed, and if so, under what conditions?

The most straightforward model for memory consistency is called *sequential consistency*. Sequential consistency requires that the result of any execution be the same as if the memory accesses executed by each processor were kept in order and the accesses among different processors were arbitrarily interleaved. Sequential consistency eliminates the possibility of some nonobvious execution in the previous example because the assignments must be completed before the if statements are initiated.

The simplest way to implement sequential consistency is to require a processor to delay the completion of any memory access until all the invalidations caused by that access are completed. Of course, it is equally effective to delay the next memory access until the previous one is completed. Remember that memory consistency involves operations among different variables: the two accesses that must be ordered are actually to different memory locations. In our example, we must delay the read of A or B (A == 0 or B == 0) until the previous write has completed (B = 1 or A = 1). Under sequential consistency, we cannot, for example, simply place the write in a write buffer and continue with the read. Although sequential consistency presents a simple programming paradigm, it reduces potential performance, especially in a multiprocessor with a large number of processors or long interconnect delays, as we can see in the following example.

Example   Suppose we have a processor where a write miss takes 40 cycles to establish ownership, 10 cycles to issue each invalidate after ownership is established, and 50 cycles for an invalidate to complete and be acknowledged once it is issued. Assuming that four other processors share a cache block, how long does a write miss stall the writing processor if the processor is sequentially consistent? Assume that the invalidates must be explicitly acknowledged before the directory controller knows they are completed. Suppose we could continue executing after obtaining ownership for the write miss without waiting for the invalidates; how long would the write take?

Answer   When we wait for invalidates, each write takes the sum of the ownership time plus the time to complete the invalidates. Since the invalidates can overlap, we need only worry about the last one, which starts $10 + 10 + 10 + 10 = 40$ cycles after ownership is established. Hence the total time for the write is $40 + 40 + 50 = 130$ cycles. In comparison, the ownership time is only 40 cycles. With appropriate write buffer implementations it is even possible to continue before ownership is established.

To provide better performance, researchers and architects have explored two different routes. First, they developed ambitious implementations that preserve sequential consistency but use latency-hiding techniques to reduce the penalty; we discuss these in Section 6.10. Second, they developed less restrictive memory consistency models that allow for faster hardware. Such models can affect how the programmer sees the multiprocessor, so before we discuss these less restrictive models, let's look at what the programmer expects.

The Programmer's View

Although the sequential consistency model has a performance disadvantage, from the viewpoint of the programmer it has the advantage of simplicity. The challenge is to develop a programming model that is simple to explain and yet allows a high-performance implementation.

One such programming model that allows us to have a more efficient implementation is to assume that programs are *synchronized*. A program is synchronized if all access to shared data is ordered by synchronization operations. A data reference is ordered by a synchronization operation if, in every possible execution, a write of a variable by one processor and an access (either a read or a write) of that variable by another processor are separated by a pair of synchronization operations, one executed after the write by the writing processor and one executed before the access by the second processor. Cases where variables may be updated without ordering by synchronization are called *data races* because the execution outcome depends on the relative speed of the processors, and like races in hardware design, the outcome is unpredictable, which leads to another name for synchronized programs: *data-race-free*.

As a simple example, consider a variable being read and updated by two different processors. Each processor surrounds the read and update with a lock and an unlock, both to ensure mutual exclusion for the update and to ensure that the read is consistent. Clearly, every write is now separated from a read by the other processor by a pair of synchronization operations: one unlock (after the write) and one lock (before the read). Of course, if two processors are writing a variable with no intervening reads, then the writes must also be separated by synchronization operations.

It is a broadly accepted observation that most programs are synchronized. This observation is true primarily because if the accesses were unsynchronized, the behavior of the program would be quite difficult to determine because the speed of execution would determine which processor won a data race and thus affect the results of the program. Even with sequential consistency, reasoning about such programs is very difficult. Programmers could attempt to guarantee ordering by constructing their own synchronization mechanisms, but this is extremely tricky, can lead to buggy programs, and may not be supported architecturally, meaning that they may not work in future generations of the multiprocessor. Instead, almost all programmers will choose to use synchronization libraries that are correct and optimized for the multiprocessor and the type of synchronization. Finally, the use of standard synchronization primitives ensures that even if the architecture implements a more relaxed consistency model than sequential consistency, a synchronized program will behave as if the hardware implemented sequential consistency.

Relaxed Consistency Models: The Basics

The key idea in relaxed consistency models is to allow reads and writes to complete out of order, but to use synchronization operations to enforce ordering, so that a synchronized program behaves as if the processor were sequentially consistent. There are a variety of relaxed models that are classified according to what orderings they relax. The three major sets of orderings that are relaxed are

1. The W→R ordering, which yields a model known as total store ordering or processor consistency. Because this ordering retains ordering among writes, many programs that operate under sequential consistency operate under this model, without additional synchronization.

2. The W→W ordering, which yields a model known as partial store order.

3. The R→W and R→R orderings, which yield a variety of models including weak ordering, the Alpha consistency model, the PowerPC consistency model, and release consistency, depending on the details of the ordering restrictions and how synchronization operations enforce ordering.

By relaxing these orderings, the processor can possibly obtain significant performance advantages. There are, however, many complexities in describing relaxed consistency models, including the advantages and complexities of relaxing different orders, defining precisely what it means for a write to complete, and deciding when processors can see values that the processor itself has written. For more information about the complexities, implementation issues, and performance potential from relaxed models, we highly recommend the excellent tutorial by Adve and Gharachorloo [1996].

Final Remarks on Consistency Models

At the present time, many multiprocessors being built support some sort of relaxed consistency model, varying from processor consistency to release consistency. Since synchronization is highly multiprocessor specific and error prone, the expectation is that most programmers will use standard synchronization libraries and will write synchronized programs, making the choice of a weak consistency model invisible to the programmer and yielding higher performance.

An alternative viewpoint, which we discuss more extensively in the next section (specifically on page 619), argues that with speculation much of the performance advantage of relaxed consistency models can be obtained with sequential or processor consistency.

A key part of this argument in favor of relaxed consistency revolves around the role of the compiler and its ability to optimize memory access to potentially shared variables. This topic is also discussed on page 618.

6.9 Multithreading: Exploiting Thread-Level Parallelism within a Processor

Multithreading allows multiple threads to share the functional units of a single processor in an overlapping fashion. To permit this sharing, the processor must duplicate the independent state of each thread. For example, a separate copy of the register file, a separate PC, and a separate page table are required for each thread. The memory itself can be shared through the virtual memory mechanisms, which already support multiprogramming. In addition, the hardware must support the ability to change to a different thread relatively quickly; in particular, a thread switch should be much more efficient than a process switch, which typically requires hundreds to thousands of processor cycles.

There are two main approaches to multithreading. *Fine-grained multithreading* switches between threads on each instruction, causing the execution of multiple threads to be interleaved. This interleaving is often done in a round-robin fashion, skipping any threads that are stalled at that time. To make fine-grained multithreading practical, the CPU must be able to switch threads on every clock cycle. One key advantage of fine-grained multithreading is that it can hide the throughput losses that arise from both short and long stalls, since instructions from other threads can be executed when one thread stalls. The primary disadvantage of fine-grained multithreading is that it slows down the execution of the individual threads, since a thread that is ready to execute without stalls will be delayed by instructions from other threads.

Coarse-grained multithreading was invented as an alternative to fine-grained multithreading. Coarse-grained multithreading switches threads only on costly stalls, such as level 2 cache misses. This change relieves the need to have thread switching be essentially free and is much less likely to slow down the execution of an individual thread, since instructions from other threads will only be issued when a thread encounters a costly stall. Coarse-grained multithreading suffers, however, from a major drawback: It is limited in its ability to overcome throughput losses, especially from shorter stalls. This limitation arises from the pipeline start-up costs of coarse-grained multithreading. Because a CPU with coarse-grained multithreading issues instructions from a single thread, when a stall occurs, the pipeline must be emptied or frozen. The new thread that begins executing after the stall must fill the pipeline before instructions will be able to complete. Because of this start-up overhead, coarse-grained multithreading is much more useful for reducing the penalty of high-cost stalls, where pipeline refill is negligible compared to the stall time.

The next subsection explores a variation on fine-grained multithreading that enables a superscalar processor to exploit ILP and multithreading in an integrated and efficient fashion. Section 6.12 examines a commercial processor using coarse-grained multithreading.

Simultaneous Multithreading: Converting Thread-Level Parallelism into Instruction-Level Parallelism

Simultaneous multithreading (SMT) is a variation on multithreading that uses the resources of a multiple-issue, dynamically scheduled processor to exploit TLP at the same time it exploits ILP. The key insight that motivates SMT is that modern multiple-issue processors often have more functional unit parallelism available than a single thread can effectively use. Furthermore, with register renaming and dynamic scheduling, multiple instructions from independent threads can be issued without regard to the dependences among them; the resolution of the dependences can be handled by the dynamic scheduling capability.

Figure 6.44 conceptually illustrates the differences in a processor's ability to exploit the resources of a superscalar for the following processor configurations:

- A superscalar with no multithreading support
- A superscalar with coarse-grained multithreading
- A superscalar with fine-grained multithreading
- A superscalar with simultaneous multithreading

In the superscalar without multithreading support, the use of issue slots is limited by a lack of ILP, a topic we discussed extensively in Chapter 3. In addition, a major stall, such as an instruction cache miss, can leave the entire processor idle.

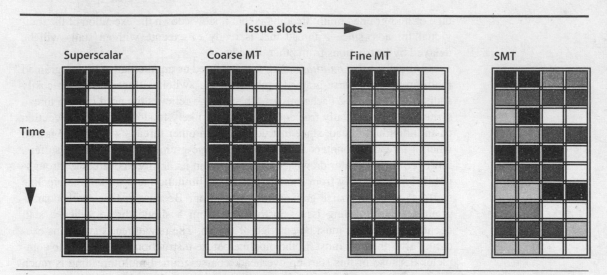

Figure 6.44 How four different approaches use the issue slots of a superscalar processor. The horizontal dimension represents the instruction issue capability in each clock cycle. The vertical dimension represents a sequence of clock cycles. An empty (white) box indicates that the corresponding issue slot is unused in that clock cycle. The shades of grey and black correspond to four different threads in the multithreading processors. Black is also used to indicate the occupied issue slots in the case of the superscalar without multithreading support. The additional pipeline start-up effects for coarse MT, which are not illustrated in this figure, would lead to further loss in throughput for coarse MT.

In the coarse-grained multithreaded superscalar, the long stalls are partially hidden by switching to another thread that uses the resources of the processor. Although this reduces the number of completely idle clock cycles, within each clock cycle, the ILP limitations still lead to idle cycles. Furthermore, in a coarse-grained multithreaded processor, since thread switching only occurs when there is a stall and the new thread has a start-up period, there are likely to be some fully idle cycles remaining.

In the fine-grained case, the interleaving of threads eliminates fully empty slots. Because only one thread issues instructions in a given clock cycle, however, ILP limitations still lead to a significant number of idle slots within individual clock cycles.

In the SMT case, thread-level parallelism (TLP) and instruction-level parallelism (ILP) are exploited simultaneously, with multiple threads using the issue slots in a single clock cycle. Ideally, the issue slot usage is limited by imbalances in the resource needs and resource availability over multiple threads. In practice, other factors—including how many active threads are considered, finite limitations on buffers, the ability to fetch enough instructions from multiple threads, and practical limitations of what instruction combinations can issue from one thread and from multiple threads—can also restrict how many slots are used. Although Figure 6.44 greatly simplifies the real operation of these processors, it does illustrate the potential performance advantages of multithreading in general and SMT in particular.

As mentioned earlier, simultaneous multithreading uses the insight that a dynamically scheduled processor already has many of the hardware mechanisms needed to support the integrated exploitation of TLP through multithreading. In particular, dynamically scheduled superscalars have a large set of virtual registers that can be used to hold the register sets of independent threads (assuming separate renaming tables are kept for each thread). Because register renaming provides unique register identifiers, instructions from multiple threads can be mixed in the data path without confusing sources and destinations across the threads. This observation leads to the insight that multithreading can be built on top of an out-of-order processor by adding a per-thread renaming table, keeping separate PCs, and providing the capability for instructions from multiple threads to commit. There are complications in handling instruction commit, since we would like instructions from independent threads to be able to commit independently. The independent commitment of instructions from separate threads can be supported by logically keeping a separate reorder buffer for each thread.

Design Challenges in SMT Processors

Because a dynamically scheduled superscalar processor is likely to have a deep pipeline, SMT will be unlikely to gain much in performance if it were coarse-grained. Since SMT will likely make sense only in a fine-grained implementation, we must worry about the impact of fine-grained scheduling on single-thread performance. This effect can be minimized by having a preferred thread, which still permits multithreading to preserve some of its performance advantage with a smaller compromise in single-thread performance. At first glance, it might appear that a preferred-thread approach sacrifices neither throughput nor single-thread performance. Unfortunately, with a preferred thread, the processor is likely to sacrifice some throughput when the preferred thread encounters a stall. The reason is that the pipeline is less likely to have a mix of instructions from several threads, resulting in greater probability that either empty slots or a stall will occur, although simulation results have shown that the use of a preferred thread has only a small performance impact. Nonetheless, throughput is maximized by having a sufficient number of independent threads to hide all stalls in any combination of threads.

Unfortunately, mixing many threads will inevitably compromise the execution time of individual threads. Similar problems exist in instruction fetch. To maximize single-thread performance, we should fetch as far ahead as possible in that single thread (possibly on both paths after a branch) and always have the fetch unit free when a branch is mispredicted and a miss occurs in the prefetch buffer. Unfortunately, this limits the number of instructions available for scheduling from other threads, reducing throughput. All multithreaded processors must seek to balance this trade-off, which, as we have seen, is a classic trade-off in computer systems.

In practice, the problems of dividing resources and balancing single-thread and multiple-thread performance turn out not to be as challenging as they sound, at least for current superscalar back ends. In particular, for current machines that issue four to eight instructions per cycle, it probably suffices to have a small number of active threads, and an even smaller number of "preferred" threads. Whenever possible, the processor acts on behalf of a preferred thread. This starts with prefetching instructions: Whenever the prefetch buffers for the preferred threads are not full, instructions are fetched for those threads. Only when the preferred-thread buffers are full is the instruction unit directed to prefetch for other threads. Note that having two preferred threads means that we are simultaneously prefetching for two instruction streams, and this adds complexity to the instruction fetch unit and the instruction cache. Similarly, the instruction issue unit can direct its attention to the preferred threads, considering other threads only if the preferred threads are stalled and cannot issue. In practice, having four to eight threads and two to four preferred threads is likely to completely utilize the capability of a superscalar back end that is roughly double the capability of those available in 2001.

There are a variety of other design challenges for an SMT processor, including the following:

- Dealing with a larger register file needed to hold multiple contexts

- Maintaining low overhead on the clock cycle, particularly in critical steps such as instruction issue, where more candidate instructions need to be considered, and in instruction completion, where choosing what instructions to commit may be challenging (the complexity of instruction commit has been avoided in most proposed SMT designs by only committing instructions from a single thread in any single clock cycle)

- Ensuring that the cache conflicts generated by the simultaneous execution of multiple threads do not cause significant performance degradation

In viewing these problems, two observations are important. First, in many cases, the potential performance overhead due to multithreading is small, and simple choices work well enough. Second, the efficiency of current superscalars is low enough that there is room for significant improvement, even at the cost of some overhead. SMT appears to be the most promising way to achieve that improvement in throughput.

Because SMT exploits thread-level parallelism on a multiple-issue superscalar, it is most likely to be included in high-end processors targeted at server markets. In addition, it is likely that there will be some mode to restrict the multithreading, so as to maximize the performance of a single thread.

Potential Performance Advantages from SMT

A key question is how much performance can be gained by implementing SMT. Since this question is likely to be of increasing interest as superscalar processors become wider and more aggressive, we will explore the performance in such a context. Figure 6.45 outlines the features of an aggressive SMT design incorporated into an aggressive superscalar, which might be achievable in 2004 or 2005.

Processor characteristic	Capability
Integer functional units	6, including up to 4 loads/stores per cycle
Pipeline depth	9 stages
Floating-point functional units	4 (all general purpose)
Instruction queues	32 entries each for integer and floating point
Renaming registers	100 each for integer and floating point (in addition to the architectural registers)
Commit capability	Up to 12 instructions per cycle
TLB	128 entries each for instructions and data
Primary instruction cache	128 KB, 2-way set associative, single ported, 2-cycle fill penalty, 32 outstanding misses (shared with the primary data cache)
Primary data cache	128 KB, 2-way set associative, dual ported, 2-cycle fill penalty
L2 cache	16 MB, direct-mapped, 20-cycle latency, fully pipelined
L1-L2 bus/refill	256 bits wide, 2-cycle latency
Store buffer	32 entries
Memory system	90-cycle latency, fully pipelined, connected with a 128-bit-wide, 4-cycle latency bus
Branch predictor	Tournament predictor with 4K local predictor indexed by a history table with 2K entries, an 8K global predictor, and a selector table with 8K entries
Branch-target buffer	1K entries, 4-way set associative
Hardware contexts for SMT	8
Fetch policy	8 instructions per clock, from up to 2 contexts

Figure 6.45 The processor configuration for the evaluation of an SMT extension starts with an aggressive superscalar that has roughly double the capacity of existing superscalar processors in 2001. The SMT extensions include support for eight contexts and the ability to fetch simultaneously from up to two contexts.

Figure 6.46 shows the advantage in throughput, measured as instructions per clock, of adding the SMT capability with eight contexts to the superscalar processor described in Figure 6.45, assuming there is no clock cycle penalty for adding the SMT extension. The benchmarks include a multiprogrammed execution of a subset of the SPEC benchmarks, as well as a Web server and the database and decision support benchmarks that we examined in Sections 6.2 and 6.4. A fuller discussion of the benchmarks appears in the caption.

The gains in throughput from the addition of SMT are fairly impressive, ranging from a factor of 1.7 to 4.2 and averaging 3.0. To better understand where these gains are coming from, Figure 6.47 plots several utilization and hit rate measures. As you might expect, the SMT processor shows considerably higher utilization of both the fetch unit and the functional units. The branch-prediction

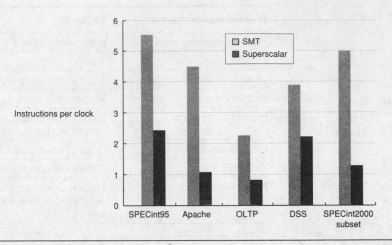

Figure 6.46 **The performance advantage gained by adding an eight-context SMT capability to the superscalar processor described in Figure 6.45, in terms of instructions per clock.** The benchmarks include two multiprogrammed workloads: one consisting of the SPECint95 benchmarks and the other consisting of eight of the SPECint2000 benchmarks (all except gzip and vpr). Apache is an open source http server, while the OLTP and DSS benchmarks are those described and used earlier in Sections 6.2 and 6.4. The data in this figure and the next are courtesy of the SMT group at the University of Washington, led by Susan Eggers and Hank Levy. Special simulations for these data were performed by Steve Swanson and Luke McDowell.

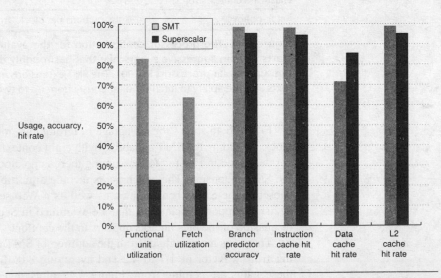

Figure 6.47 A comparison of the SMT processor to the base superscalar processor in several key measures: utilization of the functional units and fetch unit, accuracy of the branch predictor, and hit rates of the primary and secondary caches.

accuracy and instruction cache hit rates both show surprises: better performance for the SMT processor. The data cache performs slightly worse with SMT, as we might expect, while the L2 cache performs slightly better, probably because it is sufficiently large to hold the working set of multiple threads.

In interpreting these impressive performance gains, several characteristics should be kept in mind. First, the base superscalar is fairly aggressive: It has large primary caches, an aggressive secondary cache, and large numbers of functional units. Using only instruction-level parallelism, it is simply unable to exploit all the available hardware. Indeed, it is unlikely that a designer would build such a superscalar without a plan, such as the use of SMT, for exploiting thread-level parallelism on that processor. In addition, the SMT extension is also quite aggressive, with a total of eight contexts and the ability to fetch from two contexts simultaneously. This combination leads to a significant gain through the exploitation of available thread-level parallelism by the SMT extensions. In the near future it is unlikely that an SMT extension would show this much advantage, either because no designer will choose to build such an aggressive superscalar implementation or because the SMT extensions will not be as aggressive as those simulated above.

Prior to deciding to abandon the Alpha architecture in mid-2001, Compaq had announced that the Alpha 21464 would have SMT capability when it became available in 2002. In July 2001, Intel announced that a future processor based on the Pentium 4 microarchitecture and targeted at the server market, most likely Pentium 4 Xeon, would support SMT, initially with two-thread implementation. Intel claims a 30% improvement in throughput for server applications with this new support. In addition to having two contexts, another possible reason for these smaller performance gains is that instruction issue capability is segregated by thread. Simulation results have shown that sharing everything (issue slots, functional units, renaming registers) is key to maximizing SMT performance.

6.10   Crosscutting Issues

Because multiprocessors redefine many system characteristics (e.g., performance assessment, memory latency, and the importance of scalability), they introduce interesting design problems that cut across the spectrum, affecting both hardware and software. In this section we give several examples, including measuring and reporting the performance of multiprocessors, enhancing latency tolerance in memory systems, and a method for using virtual memory support to implement shared memory.

Memory System Issues

As we have seen in this chapter, memory system issues are at the core of the design of shared-memory multiprocessors. Indeed, multiprocessing introduces many new memory system complications that do not exist in uniprocessors. In this subsection we look at four implementation issues that have a significant impact on the design and implementation of a memory system in a multiprocessor context.

Inclusion and Its Implementation

Many multiprocessors use multilevel cache hierarchies to reduce both the demand on the global interconnect and the latency of cache misses. If the cache also provides *multilevel inclusion*—every level of cache hierarchy is a subset of the level further away from the processor—then we can use the multilevel structure to reduce the contention between coherence traffic and processor traffic, as explained earlier. Thus most multiprocessors with multilevel caches enforce the inclusion property. This restriction is also called the *subset property* because each cache is a subset of the cache below it in the hierarchy.

At first glance, preserving the multilevel inclusion property seems trivial. Consider a two-level example: Any miss in L1 either hits in L2 or generates a miss in L2, causing it to be brought into both L1 and L2. Likewise, any invalidate that hits in L2 must be sent to L1, where it will cause the block to be invalidated if it exists.

The catch is what happens when the block sizes of L1 and L2 are different. Choosing different block sizes is quite reasonable, since L2 will be much larger and have a much longer latency component in its miss penalty, and thus will want to use a larger block size. What happens to our "automatic" enforcement of inclusion when the block sizes differ? A block in L2 represents multiple blocks in L1, and a miss in L2 causes the replacement of data that is equivalent to multiple L1 blocks. For example, if the block size of L2 is four times that of L1, then a miss in L2 will replace the equivalent of four L1 blocks. Let's consider a detailed example.

Example   Assume that L2 has a block size four times that of L1. Show how a miss for an address that causes a replacement in L1 and L2 can lead to violation of the inclusion property.

Answer   Assume that L1 and L2 are direct mapped and that the block size of L1 is b bytes and the block size of L2 is $4b$ bytes. Suppose L1 contains two blocks with starting addresses x and $x + b$ and that $x \bmod 4b = 0$, meaning that x also is the starting address of a block in L2; then that single block in L2 contains the L1 blocks x, $x + b$, $x + 2b$, and $x + 3b$. Suppose the processor generates a reference to block y that maps to the block containing x in both caches and hence misses. Since L2 missed, it fetches $4b$ bytes and replaces the block containing x, $x + b$, $x + 2b$, and $x + 3b$, while L1 takes b bytes and replaces the block containing x. Since L1 still contains $x + b$, but L2 does not, the inclusion property no longer holds.

To maintain inclusion with multiple block sizes, we must probe the higher levels of the hierarchy when a replacement is done at the lower level to ensure that any words replaced in the lower level are invalidated in the higher-level caches. Most systems chose this solution rather than the alternative of not relying on inclusion and snooping the higher-level caches. In Exercise 6.32, we explore inclusion further and show that similar problems exist if the associativity of the levels is different. Baer and Wang [1988] describe the advantages and challenges of inclusion in detail.

Nonblocking Caches and Latency Hiding

We saw the idea of nonblocking or lockup-free caches in Chapter 5, where the concept was used to reduce cache misses by overlapping them with execution and by pipelining misses. There are additional benefits in the multiprocessor case. The first is that the miss penalties are likely to be larger, meaning there is more latency to hide, and the opportunity for pipelining misses is also probably larger, since the memory and interconnect system can often handle multiple outstanding memory references also.

Second, a multiprocessor needs nonblocking caches to take advantage of weak consistency models. For example, to implement a model like processor consistency requires that writes be nonblocking with respect to reads so that a processor can continue either immediately, by buffering the write, or as soon as it establishes ownership of the block and updates the cache. Relaxed consistency models allow further reordering of misses, but nonblocking caches are needed to take full advantage of this flexibility.

Finally, nonblocking support is critical to implementing prefetching. Prefetching, which we also discussed in Chapter 5, is even more important in multiprocessors than in uniprocessors, again due to longer memory latencies. In Chapter 5 we described why it is important that prefetches not affect the semantics of the program, since this allows them to be inserted anywhere in the program without changing the results of the computation.

In a multiprocessor, maintaining the absence of any semantic impact from the use of prefetches requires that prefetched data be kept coherent. A prefetched value is kept coherent if, when the value is actually accessed by a load instruction, the most recently written value is returned, even if that value was written after the prefetch. This result is exactly the property that cache coherence gives us for other variables in memory. A prefetch that brings a data value closer, and guarantees that on the actual memory access to the data (a load of the prefetched value) the most recent value of the data item is obtained, is called *nonbinding*, since the data value is not bound to a local copy, which would be incoherent. By contrast, a prefetch that moves a data value into a general-purpose register is binding, since the register value is a new variable, as opposed to a cache block, which is a coherent copy of a variable. A nonbinding prefetch maintains the coherence properties of any other value in memory, while a binding prefetch appears more like a register load, since it removes the data from the coherent address space.

Why is nonbinding prefetch critical? Consider a simple but typical example: a data value written by one processor and used by another. In this case, the consumer would like to prefetch the value as early as possible; but suppose the producing process is delayed for some reason. Then the prefetch may fetch the old value of the data item. If the prefetch is nonbinding, the copy of the old data is invalidated when the value is written, maintaining coherence. If the prefetch is binding, however, then the old, incoherent value of the data is used by the prefetching process. Because of the long memory latencies, a prefetch may need to be placed a hundred or more instructions earlier than the data use if we aim to hide the entire latency. This requirement makes the nonbinding property vital to ensure coherent usage of the prefetch in multiprocessors.

Implementing prefetch requires the same sort of support that a lockup-free cache needs, since there are multiple outstanding memory accesses. This requirement causes several complications:

1. A local node will need to keep track of the multiple outstanding accesses, since the replies may return in a different order than they were sent. This accounting can be handled by adding tags to the requests, or by incorporating the address of the memory block in the reply.

2. Before issuing a request (either a normal fetch or a prefetch), the node must ensure that it has not already issued a request for the same block, since two write requests for the same block could lead to incorrect operation of the protocol. For example, if the node issues a write prefetch to a block, while it has a write miss or write prefetch outstanding, both our snooping protocol and directory protocol can fail to operate properly.

3. Our implementation of the directory and snooping controllers assumes that the processor stalls on a miss. Stalling allows the cache controller to simply wait for a reply when it has generated a request. With a nonblocking cache or with prefetching, a processor can generate additional requests while it is waiting for replies. This complicates the directory and snooping controllers; Appendix I shows how these issues can be addressed.

Compiler Optimization and the Consistency Model

Another reason for defining a model for memory consistency is to specify the range of legal compiler optimizations that can be performed on shared data. In explicitly parallel programs, unless the synchronization points are clearly defined and the programs are synchronized, the compiler could not interchange a read and a write of two different shared data items because such transformations might affect the semantics of the program. This prevents even relatively simple optimizations, such as register allocation of shared data, because such a process usually interchanges reads and writes. In implicitly parallelized programs—for example, those written in High Performance FORTRAN (HPF)—programs must be synchronized and the synchronization points are known, so this issue does not arise.

Using Speculation to Hide Latency in Strict Consistency Models

As we saw in Chapters 4 and 5, speculation can be used to hide memory latency. It can also be used to hide latency arising from a strict consistency model, giving much of the benefit of a relaxed memory model. The key idea is for the processor to use dynamic scheduling to reorder memory references, letting them possibly execute out of order. Executing the memory references out of order may generate violations of sequential consistency, which might affect the execution of the program. This possibility is avoided by using the delayed commit feature of a speculative processor. Assume the coherency protocol is based on invalidation. If the processor receives an invalidation for a memory reference before the memory reference is committed, the processor uses speculation recovery to back out the computation and restart with the memory reference whose address was invalidated.

If the reordering of memory requests by the processor yields an execution order that could result in an outcome that differs from what would have been seen under sequential consistency, the processor will redo the execution. The key to using this approach is that the processor need only guarantee that the result would be the same as if all accesses were completed in order, and it can achieve this by detecting when the results might differ. The approach is attractive because the speculative restart will rarely be triggered. It will only be triggered when there are unsynchronized accesses that actually cause a race [Gharachorloo, Gupta, and Hennessy 1992].

Hill [1998] advocates the combination of sequential or processor consistency together with speculative execution as the consistency model of choice. His argument has three parts. First, an aggressive implementation of either sequential consistency or processor consistency will gain most of the advantage of a more relaxed model. Second, such an implementation adds very little to the implementation cost of a speculative processor. Third, such an approach allows the programmer to reason using the simpler programming models of either sequential or processor consistency.

The MIPS R10000 design team had this insight in the mid-1990s and used the R10000's out-of-order capability to support this type of aggressive implementation of sequential consistency. Hill's arguments are likely to motivate others to follow this approach.

One open question is how successful compiler technology will be in optimizing memory references to shared variables. The state of optimization technology and the fact that shared data are often accessed via pointers or array indexing have limited the use of such optimizations. If this technology became available and led to significant performance advantages, compiler writers would want to be able to take advantage of a more relaxed programming model.

Using Virtual Memory Support to Build Shared Memory

Suppose we wanted to support a shared address space among a group of workstations connected to a network. One approach is to use the virtual memory mechanism and operating system (OS) support to provide shared memory. This approach, which was first explored more than 10 years ago, has been called *distributed virtual memory* (DVM) or *shared virtual memory* (SVM). The key observation that this idea builds on is that the virtual memory hardware has the ability to control access to portions of the address space for both reading and writing. By using the hardware to check and intercept accesses and the operating system to ensure coherence, we can create a coherent, shared address space across the distributed memory of multiple processors.

In SVM, pages become the units of coherence, rather than cache blocks. The OS can allow pages to be replicated in read-only fashion, using the virtual memory support to protect the pages from writing. When a process attempts to write such a page, it traps to the operating system. The operating system on that processor can then send messages to the OS on each node that shares the page, requesting that the page be invalidated. Just as in a directory system, each page has a home node, and the operating system running in that node is responsible for tracking who has copies of the page.

The mechanisms are quite similar to those at work in coherent shared memory. The key differences are that the unit of coherence is a page and that software is used to implement the coherence algorithms. It is exactly these two differences that lead to the major performance differences. A page is considerably bigger than a cache block, and the possibilities for poor usage of a page and for false sharing are very high. Such events can lead to much less stable performance and sometimes even lower performance than a uniprocessor. Because the coherence algorithms are implemented in software, they have much higher overhead.

The result of this combination is that shared virtual memory has become an acceptable substitute for loosely coupled message passing, since in both cases the frequency of communication must be low, and communication that is structured in larger blocks is favored. Distributed virtual memory is not currently competitive with schemes that have hardware-supported, coherent memory, such as the distributed shared-memory schemes we examined in Section 6.5. Most programs written for coherent shared memory cannot be run efficiently on shared virtual memory without changes.

Several factors could change the attractiveness of shared virtual memory. Better implementation and small amounts of hardware support could reduce the overhead in the operating system. Compiler technology, as well as the use of smaller or multiple page sizes, could allow the system to reduce the disadvantages of coherence at a page-level granularity. The concept of software-supported shared memory remains an active area of research, and such techniques may play an important role in connecting more loosely coupled multiprocessors, such as networks of workstations.

Performance Measurement of Parallel Processors

One of the most controversial issues in parallel processing has been how to measure the performance of parallel processors. Of course, the straightforward answer is to measure a benchmark as supplied and to examine wall-clock time. Measuring wall-clock time obviously makes sense; in a parallel processor, measuring CPU time can be misleading because the processors may be idle but unavailable for other uses.

Users and designers are often interested in knowing not just how well a multiprocessor performs with a certain fixed number of processors, but also how the performance scales as more processors are added. In many cases, it makes sense to scale the application or benchmark, since if the benchmark is unscaled, effects arising from limited parallelism and increases in communication can lead to results that are pessimistic when the expectation is that more processors will be used to solve larger problems. Thus, it is often useful to measure the speedup as processors are added both for a fixed-size problem and for a scaled version of the problem, providing an unscaled and a scaled version of the speedup curves. The choice of how to measure the uniprocessor algorithm is also important to avoid anomalous results, since using the parallel version of the benchmark may understate the uniprocessor performance and thus overstate the speedup, as discussed with an example in Section 6.14.

Once we have decided to measure scaled speedup, the question is *how* to scale the application. Let's assume that we have determined that running a benchmark of size n on p processors makes sense. The question is how to scale the benchmark to run on $m \times p$ processors. There are two obvious ways to scale the problem: (1) keeping the amount of memory used per processor constant and (2) keeping the total execution time, assuming perfect speedup, constant. The first method, called *memory-constrained scaling,* specifies running a problem of size $m \times n$ on $m \times p$ processors. The second method, called *time-constrained scaling,* requires that we know the relationship between the running time and the problem size, since the former is kept constant. For example, suppose the running time of the application with data size n on p processors is proportional to n^2/p. Then with time-constrained scaling, the problem to run is the problem whose ideal running time on $m \times p$ processors is still n^2/p. The problem with this ideal running time has size $\sqrt{m} \times n$.

Example   Suppose we have a problem whose execution time for a problem of size n is proportional to n^3. Suppose the actual running time on a 10-processor multiprocessor is 1 hour. Under the time-constrained and memory-constrained scaling models, find the size of the problem to run and the effective running time for a 100-processor multiprocessor.

Answer   For the time-constrained problem, the ideal running time is the same, 1 hour, so the problem size is $\sqrt[3]{10} \times n$ or 2.15 times larger than the original. For memory-constrained scaling, the size of the problem is $10n$ and the ideal execution time is $10^3/10$, or 100 hours! Since most users will be reluctant to run a problem on an order of magnitude more processors for 100 times longer, this size problem is probably unrealistic.

In addition to the scaling methodology, there are questions as to how the program should be scaled when increasing the problem size affects the quality of the result. Often, we must change other application parameters to deal with this effect. As a simple example, consider the effect of time to convergence for solving a differential equation. This time typically increases as the problem size increases, since, for example, we often require more iterations for the larger problem. Thus when we increase the problem size, the total running time may scale faster than the basic algorithmic scaling would indicate.

For example, suppose that the number of iterations grows as the log of the problem size. Then for a problem whose algorithmic running time is linear in the size of the problem, the effective running time actually grows proportional to n log n. If we scaled from a problem of size m on 10 processors, purely algorithmic scaling would allow us to run a problem of size 10 m on 100 processors. Accounting for the increase in iterations means that a problem of size $k \times m$, where k log k = 10, will have the same running time on 100 processors. This problem size yields a scaling of 5.72 m, rather than 10 m.

In practice, scaling to deal with error requires a good understanding of the application and may involve other factors, such as error tolerances (for example, it affects the cell-opening criteria in Barnes-Hut). In turn, such effects often significantly affect the communication or parallelism properties of the application as well as the choice of problem size.

Scaled speedup is not the same as unscaled (or true) speedup; confusing the two has led to erroneous claims (e.g., see the fallacy on page 638). Scaled speedup has an important role, but only when the scaling methodology is sound and the results are clearly reported as using a scaled version of the application. Singh, Hennessy, and Gupta [1993] describe these issues in detail.

6.11 Putting It All Together: Sun's Wildfire Prototype

In Sections 6.3 and 6.5 we examined centralized memory architectures (also known as SMPs or symmetric multiprocessors) and distributed-memory architectures (also known as DSMs or distributed shared-memory multiprocessors). SMPs have the advantage of maintaining a single, centralized memory with uniform access time, and although cache hit rates are crucial, memory placement is not. In comparison, DSMs have a nonuniform memory architecture and memory placement can be important; in return, they can achieve far greater scalability.

The question is whether there is a way to combine the advantages of the two approaches: maximizing the uniform memory access property while simultaneously allowing greater scalability. The answer is a partial yes, if we accept some compromises on the uniformity of the memory model and some limits of scalability. The machine we discuss in this section, an experimental prototype multiprocessor called Wildfire, built by Sun Microsystems, attempts to do exactly this.

One key motivation for an approach that maximizes the uniformity of memory access while accepting some limits on scalability is the rising importance of OLTP and Web server markets for large-scale multiprocessors. In comparison to scientific applications, which played a key role in driving both SMP and DSM development, commercial server applications have both less predictable memory access patterns and less demand for scalability to hundreds or thousands of processors.

The Wildfire Architecture

Wildfire attempts to maximize the benefits of SMP, while allowing scalability by creating a DSM architecture using large SMPs as the nodes. The individual nodes in the Wildfire design are Sun E series multiprocessors (E6x00, E5x00, E4x00, or E3x00). Our measurements in this section are all done with E6000 multiprocessors as the nodes. An E6000 can accept up to 15 processors or I/O boards on the Gigaplane bus interconnect, which supports 50 million bus transactions per second and up to 112 outstanding transactions and has a peak bandwidth of 3.2 GB/sec. Each processor board contains 2 UltraSPARC III processors.

Wildfire can connect two to four E6000 multiprocessors by replacing one dual-processor (or I/O) board with a Wildfire Interface (WFI) board, yielding up to 112 processors (4×28), as shown in Figure 6.48. The WFI board supports one coherent address space across all four multiprocessor nodes, with the two high-order address bits used to designate which node contains a memory address. Hence, Wildfire is a cache-coherent nonuniform memory access architecture (cc-NUMA) with large nodes. Within each node of 28 processors, memory is uniformly accessible; only processes that span nodes need to worry about the nonuniformity in memory access times.

The WFI plugs into the bus and sees all memory requests; it implements the global coherence across up to four nodes. Each WFI has three ports that connect to up to three additional Wildfire nodes, each with a dual directional 800 MB/sec

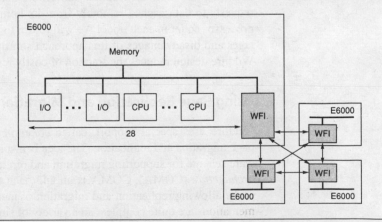

Figure 6.48 The Wildfire architecture uses a bus-based Sun Enterprise server as its building blocks. The WFI replaces a processor or I/O board and provides internode coherency and communication, as well as hardware support for page replication.

connection. WFI uses a simple directory scheme, similar to that discussed in Section 6.7. To keep the amount of directory state small, the directory is actually a cache, which is backed by the main memory in the node. When a miss occurs, the request is routed to the home node for the requested address. When the request arrives at the WFI of the home node, the WFI does a directory lookup. If the address is cached locally or clean in memory, a bus transaction is used to retrieve it. If the requested data is cached exclusively in a remote node, a request is sent to that remote node, where the WFI on that node generates a bus request to fetch the data. When the data are returned from either the remote owner or the home node, it is placed on the bus by the WFI and returned to the requesting processor.

We can see from this discussion one major disadvantage of this design: Each remote request requires either four or five bus transactions. Two transactions are required at the local node and two or three others are required elsewhere, depending on where the data are cached:

- If the referenced data are cached only in the home node, then two additional bus transactions in the home are sufficient to retrieve the data.

- If the referenced data are cached exclusively in a third remote node, then two bus transactions are required at the remote node and one is required at the home node (to write the shared data back into the home memory).

These are one-way transactions, and the E6000 bus is a split transaction bus, so even a normal memory access takes two bus transactions. Nonetheless, there is an increase in the required bus bandwidth of between 1.5 and 2.5. This increase means that the processor count at which the buses within the nodes become saturated is lowered by a factor of at least 1.5, so that if a 28-processor design saturated the bus bandwidth of an E6000, a four-node Wildfire design could accommodate about 18 processors per node before saturating the bus bandwidth, assuming an even distribution of remote requests. A significant fraction of requests to data cached remotely from its home would further lower the useful processor count in each node. We will return to a further discussion of the advantages and disadvantages of this approach shortly, but first, let us look at how the Wildfire design reduces the fraction of costly remote memory accesses.

Using Page Replication and Migration to Reduce NUMA Effects

Wildfire uses special support, called *coherent memory replication* (CMR), for page migration and replication. The idea is inspired by a more sophisticated hardware scheme for supporting migration and replication, called *cache-only memory architecture* (COMA). COMA is an approach that treats all main memory as a cache allowing replication and migration of memory blocks. Full COMA implementations are quite complex, so a variety of simplifications have been proposed. CMR is based on one of these simplifications called Simple COMA (S-COMA). S-COMA, like CMR, uses page-level mechanisms for migrating and replicating pages in memory, although coherence is still maintained at the cache-block level.

We discuss the COMA ideas, as well as other approaches to migration and replication, in more detail in Section 6.16.

To decide when to replicate or migrate pages, CMR uses a set of page counters that record the frequency of misses to remote pages. Migration is preferred when a page is primarily used by a node other than the one where the page is currently allocated. Replication is useful when multiple nodes share a page; the drawback of replication is that it requires extra memory. When the node sizes in a DSM are small, page migration and replication can lead to both excessive overhead for moving pages and excessive memory overhead from duplication of pages. With the large nodes in Wildfire, however, page-level migration and replication are much more attractive.

CMR, like S-COMA, maintains coherence at the unit of a cache block, rather than at the page level. This choice is important for two reasons. First, maintaining coherence at the page level is likely to lead to a significant number of false sharing misses; we saw this increase in false sharing misses with increases in block size in Section 6.3. Second, the large size of a page means that even true sharing misses are likely to end up moving many bytes of data that are never used. These two drawbacks have limited the usefulness of the shared virtual memory approach, which we discussed on page 620. CMR avoids these problems by making the unit of coherence a cache block and by selectively migrating and replicating some pages, while leaving others as standard NUMA pages that are accessed remotely when a cache miss occurs.

In addition to the page counters that the operating system uses to decide when to migrate or replicate a page, CMR requires special support to map between physical and virtual addresses of replicated pages. First, when a page is replicated the page tables are changed to refer to the local physical memory address of the duplicated page. To maintain coherence, however, a miss to this page must be sent to the home node to check the directory entry in that node. Thus, the WFI maintains a structure that maps the address of a replicated page (the local physical address) to its original physical address (called the global address) and generates the appropriate remote memory request, just as if the page were never replicated. When a write-back request or invalidation request is received, the global address must be translated to the local address, and the WFI maintains such a mapping for all pages that have been replicated. By maintaining these two maps, pages can be replicated while maintaining coherence at the unit of a cache block, which increases the usefulness of page replication.

Performance of Wildfire

In this subsection we look at the performance of the Wildfire prototype, starting first with basic performance measures such as latency for memory accesses and bandwidth and then turning to application performance. Since Wildfire is a research prototype, rather than a product, its performance evaluation for applications is limited, but some interesting experiments that evaluate the use of page migration and replication are available.

Basic Performance Measures: Latency and Bandwidth

To better understand the design trade-offs between DSM architectures with nodes that have small, medium, and large processor counts, we compare the latency and bandwidth measurements of two different machines: the Sun Wildfire and the SGI Origin 2000.

The SGI Origin 2000 is a highly scalable cc-NUMA architecture capable of accommodating up to 2048 processors. Each node consists of a pair of MIPS R1000 processors sharing a single memory module. An interface processor called the Hub (see Figure 6.49) provides an interface to the memory and directory in each node and implements the coherence protocol. The Hub interfaces directly to the routing chip, which provides a hypercube interconnection network that maintains a bisection bandwidth of 200 MB/sec per processor. The high dimension of the router also reduces hop counts leading to a lower ratio of remote to local access.

The Origin and Wildfire designs have significantly different motivations, so a comparison of the design trade-offs must acknowledge this fact. Among the most important differences are the following:

- They have different ranges of scalability. Origin can scale to thousands of processors, while the Wildfire design can scale to 112. Practically, the Wildfire design limit is likely to be closer to 64–80 processors, since bus bandwidth limits and the need for I/O boards will reduce the effective size of each node.

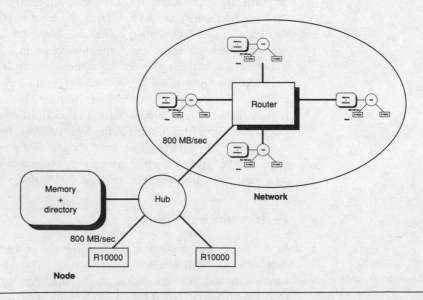

Figure 6.49 The SGI Origin 2000 uses an architecture that contains two processors per node and a scalable interconnection network that can handle up to 2048 processors. A higher-dimension network leads to scalable bisection bandwidth and a low ratio per out-of-node and in-node references.

- The Origin is designed primarily, though not exclusively, for scientific computation, and the Wildfire design is oriented primarily to commercial processing. For the Origin design, this means that scalable bandwidth is crucial, and for the Wildfire design, it means that hiding more of the NUMA-ness is crucial.

- The processors are also different in ways that affect both the bandwidth and latency of the nodes, including the block sizes of the L2 caches. We try to reduce this artifact by supplying multiple comparison numbers (e.g., latency to restart and back-to-back worst-case latency).

In Figure 6.50 we compare a variety of latency measurements for the two machines, showing the variation arising both from local versus remote accesses and the variation arising from the cache organization. The first portion of the table concentrates on local memory accesses, which remain within one node. We compare both the restart latency, which is the time from miss detection to pipeline restart, and a worst-case, back-to-back measurement, which is measured by a sequence of dependent loads. The performance differences arise from the cache architecture (including a factor of 2 difference in block size), the pipeline architecture, and the main memory access time. Local memory latency also depends on the state of the cache block. We show three cases:

1. The accessed block is unowned or it is in the shared state.

2. The accessed block is owned exclusively but clean, which requires that the block be invalidated.

3. The accessed block is owned and dirty, which requires that the block be retrieved from the cache to satisfy the miss.

These 6 combinations (3 possible states of the target block × 2 possible miss timings) are the most likely cases of a local miss, although there are several other possibilities. These latencies are primarily dominated by choices in the microprocessor design (such as minimizing time to restart or minimizing total miss time) as well as in the local memory system and coherence implementation. These choices increase the difficulty in comparing memory latency for a multiprocessor, since some of these design choices affect the remote latencies as well.

The second section of the table compares the remote access times under a variety of different circumstances but all assuming that the home address is in a different node and that any cached copies are in the home node. For these numbers we use restart latency and consider the two most probable coherence states for a remotely accessed datum: unowned and dirty. The first two entries describe the time to access a datum whose home is in the nearest node; for the Wildfire system all remote nodes are equidistant, while for the Origin, the nearest node is one router hop away. The second pair of numbers deals with the latency when the home is as far away as possible for Origin. Finally, the third and last pair provide the average latency for a uniform distribution of the home address across a multiprocessor with 128 processors.

Characteristic	How measured?	Target status?	Sun Wildfire	SGI Origin 2000
Local memory latency	restart	unowned	342	338
Local memory latency	back-to-back	unowned	330	472
Local memory latency	restart	exclusive	362	656
Local memory latency	back-to-back	exclusive	350	707
Local memory latency	restart	dirty	482	892
Local memory latency	back-to-back	dirty	470	1036
Remote memory latency to nearest node	restart	unowned	1774	570
Remote memory latency to nearest node	restart	dirty	2162	1128
Remote memory latency to furthest node (< 128)	restart	unowned	1774	1219
Remote memory latency to furthest node (< 128)	restart	dirty	2162	1787
Average remote memory latency processors (< 128)	restart	unowned	1774	973
Average remote memory latency: processors (< 128)	restart	dirty	2162	1531
Average memory latency all processors (< 128)	restart	unowned	1416	963
Average memory latency all processors (< 128)	restart	dirty	1742	1520
Three-hop miss to nearest node	restart	dirty	2550	953
Three-hop miss to furthest node (worst case)	restart	dirty	2550	1967
Average three-hop miss	restart	dirty	2550	1582

Figure 6.50 **A comparison of memory access latencies (in ns) between the Sun Wildfire prototype (using E6000 nodes) and an SGI Origin 2000 shows significant differences in both local and remote access times.** This table has four parts, corresponding to local memory accesses (which are within the node), remote memory access involving only the requesting and home node, average memory latency for the combination of local and remote (but not three-hop) misses, and three-hop latencies. The second column describes whether the latency is measured by time to restart the pipeline or by the back-to-back miss cost. For local accesses we show both; for remote accesses, we show the restart latency, which is the more likely case. The third column indicates the state of the remote data. "Unowned" means that they are in the shared or invalid state in the other caches. "Exclusive" means exclusive but clean, which requires an intervention to be completed before the memory access can complete, so that write serialization may be maintained. "Dirty" indicates that the data are exclusive and have been updated; an access, therefore, requires retrieving the data from the cache. In the local case, we show all three possibilities, to show the effect of the processor architecture (e.g., intervention cost and cache block size both affect the access times), while for remote accesses we show the unowned and dirty cases, which are likely to be the most frequent.

The fourth set of numbers deals with three-hop misses, assuming that the owner is in a different node from either the home or the originating node. Here the most likely case is that the data are dirty, and we show the restart latency for this case under the best, worst, and average assumptions.

From these measurements, we can see several of the trade-offs at work in a design that uses large nodes versus one that uses smaller nodes. Large nodes increase the number of processors reachable with a local access, but also typically have a longer remote access time. The latter is driven primarily by the higher overhead of acquiring access to the bus either for the directory or to access a remote cached copy. Of course, access latency is only part of the picture; bandwidth is also affected by these design decisions.

As Figure 6.51 shows, the pipeline memory bandwidth can be measured in many different ways. The Origin design supports greater memory bandwidth by every measure except local bandwidth to dirty data. Local bandwidth and bisection bandwidth are almost three times higher on a per-processor basis for Origin.

Application Performance of Wildfire

In this subsection, we examine the performance of Wildfire, first on an OLTP application and then on a scientific application. We look at both the basic performance of the architecture versus alternatives such as a strict SMP or a small-node NUMA and then consider the effect of Wildfire's support for replication and migration.

Characteristic	Sun Wildfire (MB/sec)	SGI Origin 2000 (MB/sec)
Pipelined local memory bandwidth: unowned data	312	554
Pipelined local memory bandwidth: exclusive data	266	340
Pipelined local memory bandwidth: dirty data	246	182
Total local memory bandwidth (per node)	2,700	631
Local memory bandwidth per processor	96	315
Aggregate local memory bandwidth (all nodes, 112 processors)	10,800	39,088
Remote memory bandwidth, unowned data		508
Remote three-hop bandwidth, dirty data		238
Total bisection bandwidth (112 processors)	9,600	25,600
Bisection bandwidth per processor (112 processors)	86	229

Figure 6.51 A comparison of memory bandwidth measurements (in MB/sec) between the Sun Wildfire prototype (using E6000 nodes) and an SGI Origin 2000 shows significant differences in both local and remote memory bandwidth. The first section of the table compares pipelined local memory bandwidth, which is defined as the sustainable bandwidth for independent accesses generated by a single processor; like restart latency, this measure depends on the state of the addressed cache block. The second section of the table compares the total local memory bandwidth (i.e., within a node) on a per-processor basis and systemwide. The third section compares the memory bandwidth for remote accesses, both a two-hop access to an unowned cache block and a three-hop access to a dirty cache block. The final section compares the total bisection bandwidth for the entire system and on a per-processor basis.

Performance of the OLTP Workload

In this study an OLTP application supporting 900 warehouses was run on a 16-processor E6000 and on a two-node, 16-processor Wildfire configuration. I/O was supplied by 240 disks connected by fiber channel. To examine the performance of Wildfire and the effect of its support for replication and migration, we consider six system alternatives:

1. Ideal SMP. A 16-processor SMP design, modeled using the E6000.

2. Wildfire with CMR and locality scheduling. A two-node, 16-processor Wildfire with replication and migration enabled and using the locality scheduling in the OS.

3. Wildfire with CMR only.

4. Wildfire base with neither CMR nor locality scheduling.

5. Unoptimized Wildfire with poor data placement. Poor data placement is modeled by assuming that 50% of the cache misses are remote, which in practice is unrealistic.

6. Unoptimized Wildfire with thin nodes (two processors per node) and poor data placement. This system assumes Wildfire's interconnection characteristics, but with eight two-processor nodes. Poor data placement is modeled by assuming that 87.5% (i.e., 14/16) of the cache misses are remote, which in practice is unrealistic.

To examine performance we first look at the fraction of cache misses satisfied within a node. Figure 6.52 shows the fraction of local accesses for each of these configurations. For this OLTP application the Wildfire optimizations improve the fraction of local accesses by a factor of 1.23 over unoptimized Wildfire, bringing the fraction of local accesses to 87%.

Figure 6.53 shows how these changes in local versus remote access fractions translate to performance for this OLTP application. The performance of each system in Figure 6.53 is relative to the E6000; however, as we will see when we examine a scientific application, the E6000 can encounter performance losses from bus contention at 16 processors, so that, in fact, the performance of the E6000 does not represent an upper bound for a multiprocessor using 16 of the same processors. The E6000 performance is probably within 10–20% of contention-free performance for this benchmark. As we can see from the data, the penalty for off-node accesses translates directly to reduced performance. The next subsection examines how Wildfire performs for a scientific application.

Performance of Wildfire on a Scientific Application

In this subsection we examine a performance study of Wildfire using a red-black finite difference solver to solve a two-dimensional Poisson equation for a square grid. In this implementation, each 2×2 block of grid points is assigned either a red or black color, so that the overall grid looks like a checkerboard. Red data

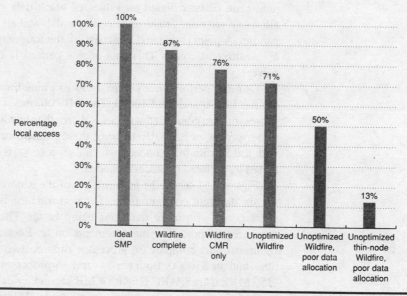

Figure 6.52 The fraction of local accesses (defined as within the node) is shown for six different configurations, ranging from an ideal SMP (with only one node and 16 processors), to four configurations with 8-processor nodes, to a configuration with thin 2-processor nodes. The fraction of remote accesses is set as a parameter for the two rightmost data points, while the other numbers are measured.

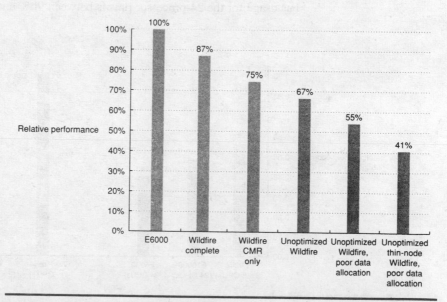

Figure 6.53 The performance of the OLTP application using 16 processors is highest for the E6000 and drops off as remote memory accesses become a major performance loss.

points are updated based on values of black data points and vice versa, which allows all red points to be updated in parallel and all black points to be updated in parallel. A point is updated by accessing the four neighboring points (all of which are a different color). This data access pattern is common in two-dimensional solvers.

Our first performance comparisons examine the performance of Wildfire versus the E6000 and the E10000. The E10000 uses a two-level interconnect. Four processors are connected with a 4×4 crossbar to four memory modules, creating a four-processor SMP. Up to 16 of these four-processor nodes can be connected with the Starfire interconnect, which uses a 16×16 crossbar. Coherence is maintained by a global broadcast scheme.

Figure 6.54 shows the performance of the generalized red-black (GRB) solver for six different configurations. The performance is given in terms of iterations per second, with more iterations being better. The leftmost group of columns compares 24-processor measurements on an E6000, E10000, and Wildfire; the rightmost bars compare 36-processor runs on two different Wildfire configurations and an E10000. Both the 24- and 36-processor runs use the same processor (250 MHz UltraSPARC II) with 4 MB secondary caches.

The 24-processor runs include a 3-node Wildfire configuration (with an 8-processor E6000 in each Wildfire node), a 6-node E10000, and a 24-processor E6000. The performance differences among the 24-processor runs on Wildfire, the E10000, and the E6000 arise primarily from bus and interconnect differences. The global broadcast of the E10000 has nontrivial overhead. Thus, despite the fact that the E10000 interconnect has performance equal to that of Wildfire, the performance of Wildfire is about 1.17 times better. For the E6000, the measured bus usage for the 24-processor runs is between 90% and 100%, leading to a sig-

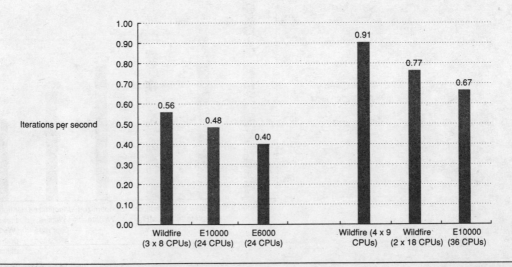

Figure 6.54 Performance for the red-black solver measured as iterations per second for three different 24-processor and three different 36-processor machines. Iterations per second is directly proportional to performance.

nificant bottleneck and lengthened memory access time. Overall, Wildfire has a performance advantage of about 1.39 versus the E6000. Equally importantly, these measurements tell us that configurations of Wildfire with larger processor counts per node will not have good performance, at least for applications with behavior similar to this solver. The 36-processor runs confirm this view.

The 36-processor runs compare three alternatives: a 9-node E10000, a 2×18 configuration of Wildfire (each Wildfire node is an 18-processor E6000), and a 4×9 configuration of Wildfire (each Wildfire node is a 9-processor E6000). The most interesting comparison here involves the 36-processor versus 24-processor results. The E10000 shows a slower than linear speedup (1.4 in run time versus 1.5 in processor count). The Wildfire results are more interesting; the 4×9 configuration also shows faster than linear speedup versus the 24-processor result. The 2×18 configuration, however, shows speedup that is slower than linear (1.38 versus 1.5), most probably because the bus has become a major bottleneck.

How well do the migration and replication capabilities of Wildfire work for scientific applications? To examine this question, this solver was executed starting with a memory allocation that placed all the data on a single node. Wildfire's migration and replication capabilities were used to allow data to migrate and replicate to one of the other nodes. Figure 6.55 shows the performance in iterations

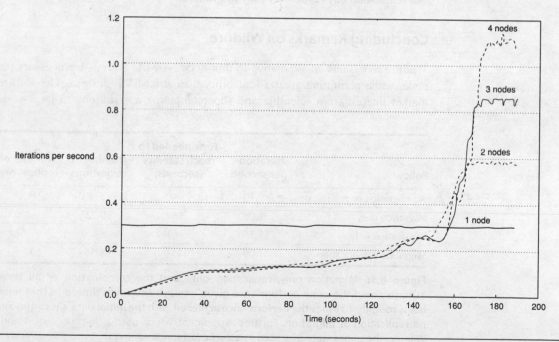

Figure 6.55 The replication and migration support of Wildfire allows an application to start with a pathological memory allocation (all memory on one node) and converge to a stable allocation that gives nearly linear speedup. The final iterations/second number shows that the 96-processor, 4-node version achieves 90% of linear speedup. As expected, the 2-node runs converge slightly faster than 3- or 4-node runs.

per second over time for a 1-, 2-, 3-, and 4-node Wildfire, each with 24 processors/node. As shown, the 2-, 3-, and 4-node runs converge to stable and best performance after somewhere between 120 and 180 seconds. Since during the initial time period, the application averages about 0.2 iterations per second, it requires between 600 and 900 iterations to reach the stable performance levels.

Although the eventual convergence to a good operating point from an initial pathological memory allocation is impressive, the number of iterations required is rather large and leaves open the question of how well the migration and replication strategies might work in problems where the memory allocation continued to change over time.

A key question is, What are the relative benefits of migration and replication? Figure 6.56 examines this question by showing the iteration rate and time to reach that rate. We also show the number of replications and migrations. The primary conclusion we can draw from the performance of these three cases is that the stable performance level for migration is competitive with the combination of migration and replication. Since supporting migration had much lower hardware costs than supporting replication (because the reverse memory maps are not needed), a design that supports migration may be equally or more cost-effective than supporting both migration and replication. The large data set coupled with well-defined access patterns by the "owner" of each portion of the grid means that replication buys little over only migration.

Concluding Remarks on Wildfire

Wildfire represents an alternative to thin-node NUMAs with 2–4 processors per node, while permitting greater scalability than strict SMP designs. The shift in market interest from scientific and supercomputing applications to large-scale

Policy	Iterations per second	Time needed to reach stability (seconds)	Number of migrations	Number of replications
No migration or replication	0.10	0	0	0
Migration only	1.06	154	99,251	
Replication only	1.15	61		98.545
Migration + replication	1.09	151	98,543	85

Figure 6.56 Migration only, replication only, and the combination of all three achieve about the same performance given enough execution time, and that number is roughly 10 times the performance achieved with the initial data allocation and no replication or migration. For this experiment, which used a 96-processor, 4-node Wildfire, the pages were allocated in a cyclic fashion, meaning that roughly 25% were allocated to the correct location initially. A large data set size (16K x 8K) that exceeds the capacity of the secondary caches leads to a high miss rate, which requires migration, replication, or careful initial data placement to reduce the miss penalty.

servers for database and Web applications may favor a fat-node design with 8–16 processors per node. There are two primary reasons for this:

1. Although a moderate range of scalability, up to a few hundred processors, may be of interest, the "sweet spot" of the server market is likely to be tens of processors. Few, if any, customers will express interest in the thousand-processor machines that are a key part of the supercomputer marketplace.

2. The memory access patterns of commercial applications tend to have less sharing and less predictable sharing and data access. The lower rates of sharing are key because a fat-node design will tend to have lower bisection bandwidth per processor than a thin-node design. Since a fat-node design has somewhat less dependence on exact memory allocation and data placement, it is likely to perform better for applications with irregular or changing data access patterns. Furthermore, fat nodes make it easier for migration and replication to work well.

The drawbacks of a fat-node design are essentially the dual of its advantages. These include less scalability, lower bisection bandwidth per processor, and higher internode latencies. For applications that require significant amounts of internode communication even with fat nodes, a fat-node design will face a more challenging programming and optimization task, since the ratio of local to remote access times is likely to be quite a bit larger. To read more on Wildfire, see Hagersten and Koster [1998] and Noordergraaf and van der Pas [1999], which are also the sources for the data in this section.

Considering the growing significance of the commercial server market with its less predictable memory access patterns, its reduced emphasis on ultimate scalability, and its lower interprocess communication requirements, it is likely the "plump" node designs will become more attractive. Growing processor demands and avoidance of bus limits are likely to lead to designs with 4–8 processors per node rather than the 16–24 limit in Wildfire. Although fatter nodes are likely to be beneficial, the nonuniform access time to memory cannot be ignored when the local node provides SMP-style access to only 3–7 other nodes.

| 6.12 | **Another View: Multithreading in a Commercial Server** |

Dynamic scheduling can be used to make a single program run faster, as we saw in the Pentium III. Alternatively, multithreading can use a different form of dynamic scheduling (scheduling across multiple threads) to increase the throughput of multiple simultaneously executing programs. This is the approach used in the IBM RS64 III.

The IBM RS64 III processor, also called Pulsar, is a PowerPC microprocessor that supports two different IBM product lines: the RS/6000 series, where it is called the RS64 III processor, and the AS/400 series, where it is called the A50.

Both product lines are aimed at commercial servers and focus on throughput in common commercial applications.

Motivated by the observation that such applications encounter high cache and TLB miss rates and thus degraded CPI, the designers decided to include a multi-threading capability to enhance throughput and make use of the processor during long TLB or cache miss stalls. In deciding how to support multithreading, the designers considered three facts:

1. The Pulsar processor, which was based on the earlier Northstar, is a statically scheduled processor.

2. The performance penalty for multithreading must be small both in silicon area and in clock rate.

3. Single-thread performance on Pulsar must not suffer.

This combination of considerations led to a multithreading architecture with the following characteristics:

▪ Pulsar supports precisely two threads; this minimizes both the incremental silicon area and the potential clock rate impact.

▪ The multithreading is coarsely scheduled; that is, threads are not interleaved, instead a thread switch occurs only when a long latency stall is encountered. Coarse multithreading was chosen to maximize single-thread performance and make use of the statically scheduled pipeline structure, which makes SMT an impractical choice.

To implement the multithreading architecture, Pulsar includes two copies of the register files and PC register, which resulted in relatively minor silicon over-head (< 10%). In addition, a special register that determines the maximum number of cycles between a thread switch ensures that no thread is ever completely starved for cycles. The overall architecture provides a significant improvement in multithreaded throughput, a key metric for the commercial server workloads. The Pulsar microprocessor is the first widely available, mainline microprocessor to support multithreading; it is likely that future microprocessors will include such a capability either through a coarse-grained form or using the SMT approach.

6.13   Another View: Embedded Multiprocessors

Multiprocessors are now common in server environments, and several desktop multiprocessors are available from vendors, such as Sun, Compaq, and Apple. In the embedded space, a number of special-purpose designs have used customized multiprocessors, including the Sony Playstation described in Chapters 2 and 5. Many special-purpose embedded designs consist of a general-purpose program-mable processor with special-purpose, finite-state machines that are used for stream-oriented I/O. In applications ranging from computer graphics and media processing to telecommunications, this style of special-purpose multiprocessor is becoming common. Although the interprocessor interactions in such designs are highly regimented and relatively simple—consisting primarily of a simple communication channel—because much of the design is committed to silicon, ensuring that the communication protocols among the input/output processors and the general-purpose processor are correct is a major challenge in such designs.

More recently, we have seen the first appearance, in the embedded space, of embedded multiprocessors built from several general-purpose processors. These multiprocessors have been focused primarily on the high-end telecommunications and networking market, where scalability is critical. An example of such a design is the MXP processor designed by empowerTel Networks for use in voice-over-IP systems. The MXP processor consists of four main components:

- An interface to serial voice streams, including support for handling jitter
- Support for fast packet routing and channel lookup
- A complete Ethernet interface, including the MAC layer
- Four MIPS32 R4000-class processors, each with their own caches (a total of 48 KB or 12 KB per processor)

The MIPS processors are used to run the code responsible for maintaining the voice-over-IP channels, including the assurance of quality of service, echo cancellation, simple compression, and packet encoding. Since the goal is to run as many independent voice streams as possible, a multiprocessor is an ideal solution.

Because of the small size of the MIPS cores, the entire chip takes only 13.5M transistors. Future generations of the chip are expected to handle more voice channels, as well as do more sophisticated echo cancellation, voice activity detection, and more sophisticated compression.

We expect that multiprocessing will become widespread in the embedded computing arena in the future for two primary reasons. First, the issues of binary software compatibility, which plague desktop and server systems, are less relevant in the embedded space. Often software in an embedded application is written from scratch for an application or significantly modified. Second, the applications often have natural parallelism, especially at the high end of the embedded space. Examples of this natural parallelism abound in applications such as a set-top box, a network switch, or a game system. The lower barriers to use of thread-level parallelism together with the greater sensitivity to die cost (and hence efficient use of silicon) will likely lead to more ready adoption of multiprocessing in the embedded space, as the application needs grow to demand more performance.

6.14 Fallacies and Pitfalls

Given the lack of maturity in our understanding of parallel computing, there are many hidden pitfalls that will be uncovered either by careful designers or by unfortunate ones. Given the large amount of hype that has surrounded multiprocessors, especially at the high end, common fallacies abound. We have included a selection of these.

Pitfall *Measuring performance of multiprocessors by linear speedup versus execution time.*

"Mortar shot" graphs—plotting performance versus number of processors showing linear speedup, a plateau, and then a falling off—have long been used to judge the success of parallel processors. Although speedup is one facet of a parallel program, it is not a direct measure of performance. The first question is the power of the processors being scaled: A program that linearly improves performance to equal 100 Intel 486s may be slower than the sequential version on a workstation. Be especially careful of floating-point-intensive programs; processing elements without hardware assist may scale wonderfully but have poor collective performance.

Comparing execution times is fair only if you are comparing the best algorithms on each computer. Comparing the identical code on two processors may seem fair, but it is not; the parallel program may be slower on a uniprocessor than a sequential version. Developing a parallel program will sometimes lead to algorithmic improvements, so that comparing the previously best known sequential program with the parallel code—which seems fair—will not compare equivalent algorithms. To reflect this issue, the terms *relative speedup* (same program) and *true speedup* (best program) are sometimes used.

Results that suggest *superlinear* performance, when a program on *n* processors is more than *n* times faster than the equivalent uniprocessor, may indicate that the comparison is unfair, although there are instances where "real" superlinear speedups have been encountered. For example, when Ocean is run on two processors, the combined cache produces a small superlinear speedup (2.1 versus 2.0).

In summary, comparing performance by comparing speedups is at best tricky and at worst misleading. Comparing the speedups for two different multiprocessors does not necessarily tell us anything about the relative performance of the multiprocessors. Even comparing two different algorithms on the same multiprocessor is tricky, since we must use true speedup, rather than relative speedup, to obtain a valid comparison.

Fallacy *Amdahl's Law doesn't apply to parallel computers.*

In 1987, the head of a research organization claimed that Amdahl's Law (see Section 1.6) had been broken by an MIMD multiprocessor. This statement hardly meant, however, that the law has been overturned for parallel computers; the neglected portion of the program will still limit performance. To understand the basis of the media reports, let's see what Amdahl [1967] originally said:

> A fairly obvious conclusion which can be drawn at this point is that the effort expended on achieving high parallel processing rates is wasted unless it is accompanied by achievements in sequential processing rates of very nearly the same magnitude. [p. 483]

One interpretation of the law was that since portions of every program must be sequential, there is a limit to the useful economic number of processors—say, 100. By showing linear speedup with 1000 processors, this interpretation of Amdahl's Law was disproved.

The basis for the statement that Amdahl's Law had been "overcome" was the use of scaled speedup. The researchers scaled the benchmark to have a data set size that is 1000 times larger and compared the uniprocessor and parallel execution times of the scaled benchmark. For this particular algorithm the sequential portion of the program was constant independent of the size of the input, and the rest was fully parallel—hence, linear speedup with 1000 processors.

We have already described the dangers of relating scaled speedup as true speedup. Additional problems with this sort of scaling methodology, which can result in unrealistic running times, were examined in Section 6.10.

Fallacy　*Linear speedups are needed to make multiprocessors cost-effective.*

It is widely recognized that one of the major benefits of parallel computing is to offer a "shorter time to solution" than the fastest uniprocessor. Many people, however, also hold the view that parallel processors cannot be as cost-effective as uniprocessors unless they can achieve perfect linear speedup. This argument says that because the cost of the multiprocessor is a linear function of the number of processors, anything less than linear speedup means that the ratio of performance/cost decreases, making a parallel processor less cost-effective than using a uniprocessor.

The problem with this argument is that cost is not only a function of processor count, but also depends on memory and I/O. The effect of including memory in the system cost was pointed out by Wood and Hill [1995], and we use an example from their article to demonstrate the effect of looking at a complete system. They compare a uniprocessor server, the Challenge DM (a deskside unit with 1 processor and up to 6 GB of memory), against a multiprocessor Challenge XL, a rack-mounted, bus-based multiprocessor holding up to 32 processors. (The XL also has faster processors than those of the Challenge DM—150 MHz versus 100 MHz—but we will ignore this difference.)

First, Wood and Hill introduce a cost function: $cost\,(p, m)$, which equals the list price of a multiprocessor with p processors and m megabytes of memory. For the Challenge DM:

$$cost(1, m) \; = \; \$38,400 + \$100 \times m$$

For the Challenge XL:

$$cost(p, m) \; = \; \$81,600 + \$20,000 \times p + \$100 \times m$$

Suppose our computation requires 1 GB of memory on either multiprocessor. Then the cost of the DM is $140,800, while the cost of the Challenge XL is $184,000 + $20,000 × p.

For different numbers of processors, we can compute what speedups are necessary to make the use of parallel processing on the XL *more* cost-effective than that of the uniprocessor. For example, the cost of an 8-processor XL is $344,000, which is about 2.5 times higher than the DM, so if we have a speedup on 8 processors of more than 2.5, the multiprocessor is actually *more* cost-effective than the uniprocessor. If we are able to achieve linear speedup, the 8-processor XL system is actually more than 3 times more cost-effective! Things get better with more processors: On 16 processors, we need to achieve a speedup of only 3.6, or less than 25% parallel efficiency, to make the multiprocessor as cost-effective as the uniprocessor.

The use of a multiprocessor may involve some additional memory overhead, although this number is likely to be small for a shared-memory architecture. If we assume an extremely conservative number of 100% overhead (i.e., double the memory is required on the multiprocessor), the 8-processor multiprocessor needs to achieve a speedup of 3.2 to break even, and the 16-processor multiprocessor needs to achieve a speedup of 4.3 to break even.

Surprisingly, the XL can even be cost-effective when compared against a headless workstation used as a server. For example, the cost function for a Challenge S, which can have at most 256 MB of memory, is

$$cost(1, m) = \$16,600 + \$100 \times m$$

For problems small enough to fit in 256 MB of memory on both multiprocessors, the XL breaks even with a speedup of 6.3 on 8 processors and 10.1 on 16 processors.

In comparing the cost-performance of two computers, we must be sure to include accurate assessments of both total system cost and what performance is achievable. For many applications with larger memory demands, such a comparison can dramatically increase the attractiveness of using a multiprocessor.

Fallacy *Multiprocessors are "free."*

This fallacy has two different interpretations, and both are erroneous. The first is, given that modern microprocessors contain support for snooping caches, we can build small-scale, bus-based multiprocessors for no additional cost in dollars (other than the microprocessor cost) or sacrifice of performance. Many designers believed this to be true and have even tried to build multiprocessors to prove it.

To understand why this doesn't work, you need to compare a design with no multiprocessing extensibility against a design that allows for a moderate level of multiprocessing (say, two to four processors). The two- to four-processor design requires some sort of bus and a coherence controller that is more complicated than the simple memory controller required for the uniprocessor design. Furthermore, the memory access time is almost always faster in the uniprocessor case, since the processor can be directly connected to memory with only a simple single-master bus. Thus the strictly uniprocessor solution typically has better performance and lower cost than the one-processor configuration of even a very small multiprocessor.

It also became popular in the 1980s to believe that the multiprocessor design was free in the sense that an MP could be quickly constructed from state-of-the-art microprocessors and then quickly updated using newer processors as they became available. This viewpoint ignores the complexity of cache coherence and the challenge of designing high-bandwidth, low-latency memory systems, which for modern processors is extremely difficult. Moreover, there is additional software effort: Compilers, operating systems, and debuggers all must be adapted for a parallel system. The next two fallacies are closely related to this one.

Fallacy   *Scalability is almost free.*

The goal of scalable parallel computing was a focus of much of the research and a significant segment of the high-end multiprocessor development from the mid-1980s through the late 1990s. In the first half of that period, it was widely held that you could build scalability into a multiprocessor and then simply offer the multiprocessor at any point on the scale from a small to large number of processors without sacrificing cost-effectiveness. The difficulty with this view is that multiprocessors that scale to larger processor counts require substantially more investment (in both dollars and design time) in the interprocessor communication network, as well as in aspects such as operating system support, reliability, and reconfigurability.

As an example, consider the Cray T3E, which uses a 3D torus capable of scaling to 2048 processors as an interconnection network. At 128 processors, it delivers a peak bisection bandwidth of 38.4 GB/sec, or 300 MB/sec per processor. But for smaller configurations, the Compaq AlphaServer ES40 can accept up to 4 processors and has 5.6 GB/sec of interconnect bandwidth, or almost four times the bandwidth per processor. Furthermore, the cost per CPU in a Cray T3E is several times higher than the cost in the ES40.

The cost of scalability can be seen even in more limited design ranges, such as the Sun Enterprise server line, which all use the same basic Ultraport interconnect, scaling the amount of interconnect for different systems. For example, the 4-processor Enterprise 450 places all 4 processors on a single board and uses an onboard crossbar. The midrange system, designed to support 6 to 30 processors, uses a single address bus and a 32-byte-wide data bus to connect the processors. The Enterprise 10000 series uses four address buses (memory address interleaved) and a 16×16 crossbar to connect the processors. Although the solution gives better scalability across the product range than forcing the low-end systems to accommodate four address buses and a multiboard crossbar, the cost of the interconnect system grows faster than linear as the number of processors grows, leading to a higher per-processor cost for the 6000 series versus the 450 and for the 10000 series versus the 6000 series.

Scalability is also not free in software: To build software applications that scale requires significantly more attention to load balance, locality, potential contention for shared resources, and the serial (or partly parallel) portions of the program. Obtaining scalability for real applications, as opposed to toys or small kernels, across factors of more than 10 in processor count, is a *major* challenge. In the future, better compiler technology and performance analysis tools may help with this critical problem.

Pitfall *Not developing the software to take advantage of, or optimize for, a multiprocessor architecture.*

There is a long history of software lagging behind on massively parallel processors, possibly because the software problems are much harder. Two examples from mainstream, bus-based multiprocessors illustrate the difficulty of developing software for new multiprocessors. The first has to do with not being able to take advantage of a potential architectural capability, and the second arises from the need to optimize the software for a multiprocessor.

The Sun SPARCCenter was an earlier bus-based multiprocessor with one or two buses. Memory is distributed on the boards with the processors to create a simple building block consisting of processor, cache, and memory. With this structure, the multiprocessor could also have a fast local access and use the bus only to access remote memory. The Sun operating system, however, was not able to deal with the NUMA (nonuniform memory access) aspect of memory, including such issues as controlling where memory was allocated (local versus global). If memory pages were allocated randomly, then successive runs of the same application could have substantially different performance, and the benefits of fast local access might be small or nonexistent. In addition, providing both a remote and a local access path to memory slightly complicated the design because of timing. Since neither the system software nor the application software would have been able to take advantage of faster local memory and the design was believed to be more complicated, the designers decided to require all requests to go over the bus.

Our second example shows the subtle kinds of problems that can arise when software designed for a uniprocessor is adapted to a multiprocessor environment. The SGI operating system protects the page table data structure with a single lock, assuming that page allocation is infrequent. In a uniprocessor, this does not represent a performance problem. In a multiprocessor, it can become a major performance bottleneck for some programs. Consider a program that uses a large number of pages that are initialized at start-up, which UNIX does for statically allocated pages. Suppose the program is parallelized so that multiple processes allocate the pages. Because page allocation requires the use of the page table data structure, which is locked whenever it is in use, even an OS kernel that allows multiple threads in the OS will be serialized if the processes all try to allocate their pages at once (which is exactly what we might expect at initialization time!).

This page table serialization eliminates parallelism in initialization and has significant impact on overall parallel performance. This performance bottleneck persists even under multiprogramming. For example, suppose we split the parallel program apart into separate processes and run them, one process per processor, so that there is no sharing between the processes. (This is exactly what one user did, since he reasonably believed that the performance problem was due to unintended sharing or interference in his application.) Unfortunately, the lock still serializes all the processes—so even the multiprogramming performance is poor. This pitfall indicates the kind of subtle but significant performance bugs that can arise when software runs on multiprocessors. Like many other key software components, the OS algorithms and data structures must be rethought in a multiprocessor context. Placing locks on smaller portions of the page table effectively eliminates the problem.

Pitfall   *Neglecting data distribution in a distributed shared-memory multiprocessor.*

Consider the Ocean benchmark running on a 32-processor DSM architecture. As Figure 6.31 (page 585) shows, the miss rate is 3.1% for a 64 KB cache. Because the grid used for the calculation is allocated in a tiled fashion (as described on page 546), 2.5% of the accesses are local capacity misses and 0.6% are remote communication misses needed to access data at the boundary of each grid. Assuming a 50-cycle local memory access cost and a 150-cycle remote memory access cost, the average miss has a cost of 69.3 cycles.

If the grid was allocated in a straightforward fashion by round-robin allocation of the pages, we could expect $1/32$ of the misses to be local and the rest to be remote, which would lead to a local miss rate of $31\% \times 1/32 = 0.1\%$ and a remote miss rate of 3.0%, for an average miss cost of 146.7 cycles. If the average CPI without cache misses is 0.6, and 45% of the instructions are data references, the version with tiled allocation is

$$\frac{0.6 + 45\% \times 3.1\% \times 146.7}{0.6 + 45\% \times 3.1\% \times 69.3} = \frac{0.6 + 2.05}{0.6 + 0.97} = \frac{2.65}{1.57} = 1.69 \text{ times faster}$$

This analysis only considers latency and assumes that contention effects do not lead to increased latency, which is very optimistic. Round-robin is also not the worst possible data allocation: If the grid fit in a subset of the memory and was allocated to only a subset of the nodes, contention for memory at those nodes could easily lead to a difference in performance of more than a factor of 2.

6.15   Concluding Remarks

For over a decade prophets have voiced the contention that the organization of a single computer has reached its limits and that truly significant advances can be made only by interconnection of a multiplicity of computers in such a manner as to permit cooperative solution.... Demonstration is made of the continued validity of the single processor approach. [p. 483]

Amdahl [1967]

The dream of building computers by simply aggregating processors has been around since the earliest days of computing. Progress in building and using effective and efficient parallel processors, however, has been slow. This rate of progress has been limited by difficult software problems as well as by a long process of evolving architecture of multiprocessors to enhance usability and improve efficiency. We have discussed many of the software challenges in this chapter, including the difficulty of writing programs that obtain good speedup due to Amdahl's Law, dealing with long remote access or communication latencies, and minimizing the impact of synchronization. The wide variety of different architectural approaches and the limited success and short life of many of the architectures to date has compounded the software difficulties. We discuss the history of the development of these multiprocessors in Section 6.16.

Despite this long and checkered past, progress in the last 15 years leads to some reasons to be optimistic about the future of parallel processing and multiprocessors. This optimism is based on a number of observations about this progress and the long-term technology directions:

- The use of parallel processing in some domains is beginning to be understood. Probably first among these is the domain of scientific and engineering computation. This application domain has an almost limitless thirst for more computation. It also has many applications that have lots of natural parallelism. Nonetheless, it has not been easy: Programming parallel processors even for these applications remains very challenging. Another important, and much larger (in terms of market size), application area is large-scale database and transaction-processing systems. This application domain also has extensive natural parallelism available through parallel processing of independent requests, but its needs for large-scale computation, as opposed to purely access to large-scale storage systems, are less well understood. There are also several contending architectural approaches that may be viable—a point we discuss shortly.

- It is now widely held that the most effective way to build a computer that offers more performance than that achieved with a single-chip microprocessor is by building a multiprocessor or a cluster that leverages the significant price-performance advantages of mass-produced microprocessors.

- Multiprocessors are highly effective for multiprogrammed workloads, which are often the dominant use of mainframes and large servers, as well as for file servers or Web servers, which are effectively a restricted type of parallel workload. In the future, such workloads may well constitute a large portion of the market for higher-performance multiprocessors. When a workload wants to share resources, such as file storage, or can efficiently time-share a resource, such as a large memory, a multiprocessor can be a very efficient host. Furthermore, the OS software needed to efficiently execute multiprogrammed workloads is commonplace.

- More recently, multiprocessors have proved very effective for certain intensive commercial workloads, such as OLTP (assuming the system supports enough I/O to be CPU limited), DSS applications (where query optimization is critical), and large-scale, Web searching applications. For commercial applications with undemanding communication requirements, little need for very large memories (typically used to cache databases), or limited demand for computation, clusters are likely to be more cost-effective than multiprocessors. The commercial space is currently a mix of clusters of basic PCs, SMPs, and clustered SMPs, with different architectural styles appearing to hold some lead in different application spaces.

- On-chip multiprocessing appears to be growing in importance for two reasons. First, in the embedded market where natural parallelism often exists, such approaches are an obvious alternative to faster, and possibly less silicon-efficient, processors. Second, diminishing returns in high-end microprocessor design will encourage designers to pursue on-chip multiprocessing as a potentially more cost-effective direction. We explore the challenges to this direction at the end of this section.

Although there is reason to be optimistic about the growing importance of multiprocessors, many areas of parallel architecture remain unclear. Two particularly important questions are, How will the largest-scale multiprocessors (the massively parallel processors, or MPPs) be built?, and What is the role of multiprocessing as a long-term alternative to higher-performance uniprocessors?

The Future of MPP Architecture

Hennessy and Patterson should move MPPs to Chapter 11.

Jim Gray
when asked about coverage of MPPs in the
second edition of this book, alluding to
Chapter 11 bankruptcy protection in U.S. law (1995)

Small-scale multiprocessors built using snooping bus schemes are extremely cost-effective. Microprocessors traditionally have even included much of the logic for cache coherence in the processor chip, and several allow the buses of two or more processors to be directly connected—implementing a coherent bus with no additional logic. With modern integration levels, multiple processors can be placed on a board, on a single multichip module (MCM), or even within a single die (as we saw in Section 6.13) resulting in a highly cost-effective multiprocessor. Recent microprocessors have been including support for DSM approaches, making it possible to connect small to moderate numbers of processors with little overhead. It is premature to predict that such architectures will dominate the middle range of processor counts (16–64), but it appears at present that this approach is the most attractive.

What is totally unclear at present is how the very largest multiprocessors will be constructed. The difficulties that designers face include the relatively small market for very large multiprocessors (> 64 nodes and often > $5 million) and the need for multiprocessors that scale to larger processor counts to be extremely cost-effective at the lower processor counts where most of the multiprocessors will be sold. At the present there appear to be four slightly different alternatives for large-scale multiprocessors:

1. Large-scale multiprocessors that simply scale up naturally, using proprietary interconnect and communications controller technology. This approach has been followed in multiprocessors like the Cray T3E and the SGI Origin. There are two primary difficulties with such designs. First, the multiprocessors are not cost-effective at small scales, where the cost of scalability is not valued. Second, these multiprocessors have programming models that are incompatible, in varying degrees, with the mainstream of smaller and midrange multiprocessors.

2. Large-scale multiprocessors constructed from clusters of midrange multiprocessors with combinations of proprietary and standard technologies to interconnect such multiprocessors. The Wildfire design is just such a system. This cluster approach gets its cost-effectiveness through the use of cost-optimized building blocks. In some approaches, the basic architectural model (e.g., coherent shared memory) is extended. Many companies offer a high-end version of such a machine, including HP, Sun, and SGI. Due to the two-level nature of the design, the programming model sometimes must be changed from shared memory to message passing or to a different variation on shared memory, among clusters. The migration and replication features in Wildfire offer a way to minimize this disadvantage. This class of machines has made important inroads, especially in commercial applications.

3. Designing clustered multicomputers that use off-the-shelf uniprocessor nodes and a custom interconnect. The advantage of such a design is the cost-effectiveness of the standard uniprocessor node, which is often a repackaged workstation; the disadvantage is that the programming model will probably need to be message passing even at very small node counts. In some application environments where little or no sharing occurs, this may be acceptable. In addition, the cost of the interconnect, because it is custom, can be significant, making the multiprocessor costly, especially at small node counts. The IBM SP-2 is the best example of this approach today.

4. Designing a cluster using *all* off-the-shelf components, which promises the lowest cost. The leverage in this approach lies in the use of commodity technology everywhere: in the processors (PC or workstation nodes), in the interconnect (high-speed local area network technology, such as ATM or Gigabit Ethernet), and in the software (standard operating systems and programming languages). Of course, such multiprocessors will use message passing, and communication is likely to have higher latency and lower bandwidth than in

the alternative designs. Like the previous class of designs, for applications that do not need high bandwidth or low-latency communication, this approach can be extremely cost-effective. Web servers, for example, may be a good match to these multicomputers, as we will see for the Google cluster in Chapter 8.

Each of these approaches has advantages and disadvantages, and the importance of the shortcomings of any one approach is dependent on the application class. In 2001 it is unclear which if any of these models will win out for larger-scale multiprocessors, although the growth of the market for Web servers has made "racks of PCs" the dominant form at least by processor count. It is likely that the current bifurcation by market and scale will continue for some time, although in some area a hybridization of these ideas may emerge, given the similarity in several of the approaches.

The Future of Microprocessor Architecture

As we saw in Chapters 3 and 4, architects are using ever more complex techniques to try to exploit more instruction-level parallelism. As we also saw in those chapters, the prospects for finding ever-increasing amounts of instruction-level parallelism in a manner that is efficient to exploit are somewhat limited. Likewise, there are increasingly difficult problems to be overcome in building memory hierarchies for high-performance processors. Of course, continued technology improvements will allow us to continue to advance clock rate. But the use of technology improvements that allow a faster gate speed alone is not sufficient to maintain the incredible growth of performance that the industry has experienced for over 15 years. Maintaining a rapid rate of performance growth will depend to an increasing extent on exploiting the dramatic growth in effective silicon area, which will continue to grow much faster than the basic speed of the process technology.

Unfortunately, for almost 10 years, increases in performance have come at the cost of ever-increasing inefficiencies in the use of silicon area, external connections, and power. This diminishing-returns phenomenon has only recently (as of 2001) appeared to have slowed the rate of performance growth. Whether or not this slowdown is temporary is unclear. What is clear is that we cannot sustain the rapid rate of performance improvements without significant new innovations in computer architecture.

Unlike the prophets quoted at the beginning of the chapter, we do not believe that we are about to "hit a brick wall" in our attempts to improve single-processor performance. Instead, we may see a gradual slowdown in performance growth, especially for integer performance, with the eventual growth being limited primarily by improvements in the speed of the technology. When these limitations will become serious is hard to say, but possibly as early as 2005 and likely by 2010. Even if such a slowdown were to occur, performance might well be expected to grow at the annual rate of 1.35 that we saw prior to 1985 at least until fundamental limitations in silicon become serious in the 2015 time frame.

Furthermore, we do not want to rule out the possibility of a breakthrough in uniprocessor design. In the early 1980s, many people predicted the end of growth in uniprocessor performance, only to see the arrival of RISC technology and an unprecedented 15-year growth in performance averaging 1.5 times per year!

With this in mind, we cautiously ask whether the long-term direction will be to use increased silicon to build multiple processors on a single chip. Such a direction is appealing from the architecture viewpoint—it offers a way to scale performance without increasing hardware complexity. It also offers an approach to easing some of the challenges in memory system design, since a distributed memory can be used to scale bandwidth while maintaining low latency for local accesses. The challenge lies in software and in what architecture innovations may be used to make the software easier.

In 2000, IBM announced the first commercial chips with two general-purpose processors on a single die, the Power4 processor. Each Power4 contains two Power3 microprocessors, a shared secondary cache, an interface to an off-chip tertiary cache or main memory, and a chip-to-chip communication system, which allows a four-processor crossbar-connected module to be built with no additional logic. Using four Power4 chips and the appropriate DRAMs, an eight-processor system can be integrated onto a board about 8 inches on a side. The board would contain 700 million transistors, not including the third-level cache or main memory, and would have a peak instruction execution rate of 32 billion instructions per second!

Evolution versus Revolution and the Challenges to Paradigm Shifts in the Computer Industry

Figure 6.57 shows what we mean by the *evolution-revolution spectrum* of computer architecture innovation. To the left are ideas that are invisible to the user (presumably excepting better cost, better performance, or both) and are at the evolutionary end of the spectrum. At the other end are revolutionary architecture ideas. These are the ideas that require new applications from programmers who must learn new programming languages and models of computation, and must invent new data structures and algorithms.

Revolutionary ideas are easier to get excited about than evolutionary ideas, but to be adopted they must have a much higher payoff. Caches are an example of an evolutionary improvement. Within five years after the first publication about caches, almost every computer company was designing a computer with a cache. The RISC ideas were nearer to the middle of the spectrum, for it took more than eight years for most companies to have a RISC product and more than 15 years for the last holdout to announce their product. Most multiprocessors have tended to the revolutionary end of the spectrum, with the largest-scale multiprocessors (MPPs) being more revolutionary than others. Most programs written to use multiprocessors as parallel engines have been written especially for that class of multiprocessors, if not for the specific architecture.

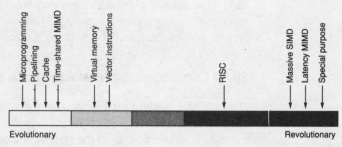

User compatibility	Binary	Upward binary	Assembly	High-level language	New programs, extended or new HLL, new algorithms
Example	VAX-11/780 vs. 8800	Intel 8086 vs. 80286 vs. 80386 vs. 80486	MIPS 1000 vs. DEC 3100	Sun 3 vs. Sun 4	SISD vs. Intel Paragon
Difference	Microcode, TLB, caches, pipelining, MIMD	Some new instructions	Byte order (Big vs. Little Endian)	Full instruction set (same data representation)	Algorithms, extended HLL, programs

Figure 6.57 The evolution-revolution spectrum of computer architecture. The second through fourth columns are distinguished from the final column in that applications and operating systems can be ported from other computers rather than written from scratch. For example, RISC is listed in the middle of the spectrum because user compatibility is only at the level of high-level languages, while microprogramming allows binary compatibility, and latency-oriented MIMDs require changes to algorithms and extending HLLs. Time-shared MIMD means MIMDs justified by running many independent programs at once, while latency MIMD means MIMDs intended to run a single program faster.

The challenge for both hardware and software designers that would propose that multiprocessors and parallel processing become the norm, rather than the exception, is the disruption to the established base of programs. There are two possible ways this paradigm shift could be facilitated: if parallel processing offers the only alternative to enhance performance, and if advances in hardware and software technology can construct a gentle ramp that allows the movement to parallel processing, at least with small numbers of processors, to be more evolutionary.

6.16   Historical Perspective and References

There is a tremendous amount of history in parallel processing; in this section we divide our discussion by both time period and architecture. We start with the SIMD approach and the Illiac IV. We then turn to a short discussion of some other early experimental multiprocessors and progress to a discussion of some of the great debates in parallel processing. Next we discuss the historical roots of the present multiprocessors and conclude by discussing recent advances.

SIMD Computers: Several Attempts, No Lasting Successes

The cost of a general multiprocessor is, however, very high and further design options were considered which would decrease the cost without seriously degrading the power or efficiency of the system. The options consist of recentralizing one of the three major components. . . . Centralizing the [control unit] gives rise to the basic organization of [an] . . . array processor such as the Illiac IV.

Bouknight et al. [1972]

The SIMD model was one of the earliest models of parallel computing, dating back to the first large-scale multiprocessor, the Illiac IV. The key idea in that multiprocessor, as in more recent SIMD multiprocessors, is to have a single instruction that operates on many data items at once, using many functional units.

The earliest ideas on SIMD-style computers are from Unger [1958] and Slotnick, Borck, and McReynolds [1962]. Slotnick's Solomon design formed the basis of the Illiac IV, perhaps the most infamous of the supercomputer projects. Although successful in pushing several technologies that proved useful in later projects, it failed as a computer. Costs escalated from the $8 million estimate in 1966 to $31 million by 1972, despite construction of only a quarter of the planned multiprocessor. Actual performance was at best 15 MFLOPS, versus initial predictions of 1000 MFLOPS for the full system [Hord 1982]. Delivered to NASA Ames Research in 1972, the computer took three more years of engineering before it was usable. These events slowed investigation of SIMD, with Danny Hillis [1985] resuscitating this style in the Connection Machine, which had 65,636 1-bit processors.

Real SIMD computers need to have a mixture of SISD and SIMD instructions. There is an SISD host computer to perform operations such as branches and address calculations that do not need parallel operation. The SIMD instructions are broadcast to all the execution units, each of which has its own set of registers. For flexibility, individual execution units can be disabled during an SIMD instruction. In addition, massively parallel SIMD multiprocessors rely on interconnection or communication networks to exchange data between processing elements.

SIMD works best in dealing with arrays in for loops. Hence, to have the opportunity for massive parallelism in SIMD there must be massive amounts of data, or *data parallelism*. SIMD is at its weakest in case statements, where each execution unit must perform a different operation on its data, depending on what data it has. The execution units with the wrong data are disabled so that the proper units can continue. Such situations essentially run at $1/n$th performance, where n is the number of cases.

The basic trade-off in SIMD multiprocessors is performance of a processor versus number of processors. Recent multiprocessors emphasize a large degree of parallelism over performance of the individual processors. The Connection Multiprocessor 2, for example, offered 65,536 single-bit-wide processors, while the Illiac IV had 64 64-bit processors.

After being resurrected in the 1980s, first by Thinking Machines and then by MasPar, the SIMD model has once again been put to bed as a general-purpose multiprocessor architecture, for two main reasons. First, it is too inflexible. A number of important problems cannot use such a style of multiprocessor, and the architecture does not scale down in a competitive fashion; that is, small-scale SIMD multiprocessors often have worse cost-performance compared with that of the alternatives. Second, SIMD cannot take advantage of the tremendous performance and cost advantages of microprocessor technology. Instead of leveraging this low-cost technology, designers of SIMD multiprocessors must build custom processors for their multiprocessors.

Although SIMD computers have departed from the scene as general-purpose alternatives, this style of architecture will continue to have a role in special-purpose designs. Many special-purpose tasks are highly data parallel and require a limited set of functional units. Thus designers can build in support for certain operations, as well as hardwire interconnection paths among functional units. Such organizations are often called *array processors,* and they are useful for tasks like image and signal processing.

Other Early Experiments

It is difficult to distinguish the first MIMD multiprocessor. Surprisingly, the first computer from the Eckert-Mauchly Corporation, for example, had duplicate units to improve availability. Holland [1959] gave early arguments for multiple processors.

Two of the best-documented multiprocessor projects were undertaken in the 1970s at Carnegie Mellon University. The first of these was C.mmp [Wulf and Bell 1972; Wulf and Harbison 1978], which consisted of 16 PDP-11s connected by a crossbar switch to 16 memory units. It was among the first multiprocessors with more than a few processors, and it had a shared-memory programming model. Much of the focus of the research in the C.mmp project was on software, especially in the OS area. A later multiprocessor, Cm* [Swan et al. 1977], was a cluster-based multiprocessor with a distributed memory and a nonuniform access time. The absence of caches and a long remote access latency made data placement critical. This multiprocessor and a number of application experiments are well described by Gehringer, Siewiorek, and Segall [1987]. Many of the ideas in these multiprocessors would be reused in the 1980s when the microprocessor made it much cheaper to build multiprocessors.

Great Debates in Parallel Processing

The quotes at the beginning of this chapter give the classic arguments for abandoning the current form of computing, and Amdahl [1967] gave the classic reply in support of continued focus on the IBM 360 architecture. Arguments for the advantages of parallel execution can be traced back to the 19th century [Menabrea 1842]! Yet the effectiveness of the multiprocessor for reducing latency of individual important programs is still being explored. Aside from these debates about the advantages and limitations of parallelism, several hot debates have focused on how to build multiprocessors.

It's hard to predict the future, yet in 1989 Gordon Bell made two predictions for 1995. We included these predictions in the first edition of the book, when the outcome was completely unclear. We discuss them in this section, together with an assessment of the accuracy of the prediction.

The first was that a computer capable of sustaining a teraFLOPS—one million MFLOPS—would be constructed by 1995, either using a multicomputer with 4K to 32K nodes or a Connection Multiprocessor with several million processing elements [Bell 1989]. To put this prediction in perspective, each year the Gordon Bell Prize acknowledges advances in parallelism, including the fastest real program (highest MFLOPS). In 1989 the winner used an eight-processor Cray Y-MP to run at 1680 MFLOPS. On the basis of these numbers, multiprocessors and programs would have to have improved by a factor of 3.6 each year for the fastest program to achieve 1 TFLOPS in 1995. In 1999, the first Gordon Bell prize winner crossed the 1 TFLOPS bar. Using a 5832-processor IBM RS/6000 SST system designed specially for Livermore Laboratories, they achieved 1.18 TFLOPS on a shock wave simulation. This ratio represents a year-to-year improvement of 1.93, which is still quite impressive.

What has become recognized since 1989 is that although we may have the technology to build a TFLOPS multiprocessor, it is not clear that the machine is cost-effective, except perhaps for a few very specialized and critically important applications related to national security. We estimated in 1990 that to achieve 1 TFLOPS would require a machine with about 5000 processors and would cost about $100 million. The 5832-processor IBM system at Livermore cost $110 million. As might be expected, improvements in the performance of individual microprocessors both in cost and performance directly affect the cost and performance of large-scale multiprocessors, but a 5000-processor system will cost more than 5000 times the price of a desktop system using the same processor.

The second Bell prediction concerned the number of data streams in supercomputers shipped in 1995. Danny Hillis believed that although supercomputers with a small number of data streams may be the best sellers, the biggest multiprocessors would be multiprocessors with many data streams, and these would perform the bulk of the computations. Bell bet Hillis that in the last quarter of calendar year 1995 more sustained MFLOPS would be shipped in multiprocessors using few data streams (≤ 100) rather than many data streams (≥ 1000). This bet concerned only supercomputers, defined as multiprocessors costing more than $1 million and used for scientific applications. Sustained MFLOPS was defined for this bet as the number of floating-point operations per *month,* so availability of multiprocessors affects their rating.

In 1989, when this bet was made, it was totally unclear who would win. In 1995, a survey of the current publicly known supercomputers showed only six multiprocessors in existence in the world with more than 1000 data streams, so Bell's prediction was a clear winner. In fact, in 1995, much smaller microprocessor-based multiprocessors (≤ 20 processors) were becoming dominant. In 1995, a survey of the 500 highest-performance multiprocessors in use (based on Linpack ratings), called the Top 500, showed that the largest number of multiprocessors were bus-based shared-memory multiprocessors! By 2000, the picture had become less clear: The top four vendors were IBM (144 SP systems), Sun (121 Enterprise systems), SGI (62 Origin systems), and Cray (54 T3E systems). Although IBM holds the largest number of spots, almost all the other systems on the TOP 500 list are shared-memory systems or clusters of such systems.

More Recent Advances and Developments

With the primary exception of the parallel vector multiprocessors (see Appendix G), all other recent MIMD computers have been built from off-the-shelf microprocessors using a bus and logically central memory or an interconnection network and a distributed memory. A number of experimental multiprocessors built in the 1980s further refined and enhanced the concepts that form the basis for many of today's multiprocessors.

The Development of Bus-Based Coherent Multiprocessors

Although very large mainframes were built with multiple processors in the 1960s and 1970s, multiprocessors did not become highly successful until the 1980s. Bell [1985] suggests the key was that the smaller size of the microprocessor allowed the memory bus to replace the interconnection network hardware, and that portable operating systems meant that multiprocessor projects no longer required the invention of a new operating system. In this paper, Bell defines the terms *multiprocessor* and *multicomputer* and sets the stage for two different approaches to building larger-scale multiprocessors.

The first bus-based multiprocessor with snooping caches was the Synapse N + 1 described by Frank [1984]. Goodman [1983] wrote one of the first papers to describe snooping caches. The late 1980s saw the introduction of many commercial bus-based, snooping cache architectures, including the Silicon Graphics 4D/240 [Baskett, Jermoluk, and Solomon 1988], the Encore Multimax [Wilson 1987], and the Sequent Symmetry [Lovett and Thakkar 1988]. The mid-1980s saw an explosion in the development of alternative coherence protocols, and Archibald and Baer [1986] provide a good survey and analysis, as well as references to the original papers. Figure 6.58 summarizes several snooping cache coherence protocols and shows some multiprocessors that have used or are using that protocol.

Name	Protocol type	Memory write policy	Unique feature	Multiprocessors using
Write Once	Write invalidate	Write back after first write	First snooping protocol described in literature	
Synapse N + 1	Write invalidate	Write back	Explicit state where memory is the owner	Synapse multiprocessors; first cache-coherent multiprocessors available
Berkeley (MOESI)	Write invalidate	Write back	Owned shared state	Berkeley SPUR multiprocessor; Sun Enterprise servers
Illinois (MESI)	Write invalidate	Write back	Clean private state; can supply data from any cache with a clean copy	SGI Power and Challenge series
"Firefly"	Write broadcast	Write back when private, write through when shared	Memory updated on broadcast	No current multiprocessors; SPARCCenter 2000 closest

Figure 6.58 Five snooping protocols summarized. Archibald and Baer [1986] use these names to describe the five protocols, and Eggers [1989] summarizes the similarities and differences as shown in this figure. The Firefly protocol was named for the experimental DEC Firefly multiprocessor, in which it appeared. The alternative names for protocols are based on the states they support: M = Modified, E = Exclusive (private clean), S = Shared, I = Invalid, O = Owner (shared dirty).

The early 1990s saw the beginning of an expansion of such systems with the use of very wide, high-speed buses (the SGI Challenge system used a 256-bit, packet-oriented bus supporting up to 8 processor boards and 32 processors) and later, the use of multiple buses and crossbar interconnects, for example, in the Sun SPARCCenter and Enterprise systems (Charlesworth [1998] discusses the interconnect architecture of these multiprocessors). In 2001, the Sun Enterprise servers represent the primary example of large-scale (> 16 processors), symmetric multiprocessors in active use.

Toward Large-Scale Multiprocessors

In the effort to build large-scale multiprocessors, two different directions were explored: message-passing multicomputers and scalable shared-memory multiprocessors. Although there had been many attempts to build mesh and hypercube-connected multiprocessors, one of the first multiprocessors to successfully bring together all the pieces was the Cosmic Cube built at Caltech [Seitz 1985]. It introduced important advances in routing and interconnect technology and substantially reduced the cost of the interconnect, which helped make the multicomputer viable. The Intel iPSC 860, a hypercube-connected collection of i860s, was based on these ideas. More recent multiprocessors, such as the Intel Paragon, have used networks with lower dimensionality and higher individual links. The Paragon also employed a separate i860 as a communications controller in each node, although a number of users have found it better to use both i860 processors for computation as well as communication. The Thinking Multiprocessors CM-5 made use of off-the-shelf microprocessors and a fat tree interconnect (see Chapter 8). It provided user-level access to the communication channel, thus significantly improving communication latency. In 1995, these two multiprocessors represented the state of the art in message-passing multicomputers.

Early attempts at building a scalable shared-memory multiprocessor include the IBM RP3 [Pfister et al. 1985], the NYU Ultracomputer [Schwartz 1980; Elder et al. 1985], the University of Illinois Cedar project [Gajksi et al. 1983], and the BBN Butterfly and Monarch [BBN Laboratories 1986; Rettberg et al. 1990]. These multiprocessors all provided variations on a nonuniform distributed-memory model (and hence are distributed shared-memory, or DSM, multiprocessors), but did not support cache coherence, which substantially complicated programming. The RP3 and Ultracomputer projects both explored new ideas in synchronization (fetch-and-operate) as well as the idea of combining references in the network. In all four multiprocessors, the interconnect networks turned out to be more costly than the processing nodes, raising problems for smaller versions of the multiprocessor. The Cray T3D/E (see Arpaci et al. [1995] for an evaluation of the T3D and Scott [1996] for a description of the T3E enhancements) builds on these ideas, using a noncoherent shared address space but building on the advances in interconnect technology developed in the multicomputer domain (see Scott and Thorson [1996]).

Extending the shared-memory model with scalable cache coherence was done by combining a number of ideas. Directory-based techniques for cache coherence were actually known before snooping cache techniques. In fact, the first cache coherence protocols actually used directories, as described by Tang [1976] and implemented in the IBM 3081. Censier and Feautrier [1978] described a directory coherence scheme with tags in memory. The idea of distributing directories with the memories to obtain a scalable implementation of cache coherence was first described by Agarwal et al. [1988] and served as the basis for the Stanford DASH multiprocessor (see Lenoski et al. [1990, 1992]), which was the first operational cache-coherent DSM multiprocessor. DASH was a "plump" node cc-NUMA machine that used four-processor SMPs as its nodes, interconnecting them in a style similar to that of Wildfire but using a more scalable two-dimensional grid rather than a crossbar for the interconnect.

The Kendall Square Research KSR-1 [Burkhardt et al. 1992] was the first commercial implementation of scalable coherent shared memory. It extended the basic DSM approach to implement a concept called *cache-only memory architecture* (COMA), which makes the main memory a cache. Like the Wildfire CMR scheme, in the KSR-1 memory blocks could be replicated in the main memories of each node with hardware support to handle the additional coherence requirements for these replicated blocks. (The KSR-1 was not strictly a pure COMA because it did not migrate the home location of a data item, but always kept a copy at home. Essentially, it implemented only replication.)

In parallel, researchers at the Swedish Institute for Computer Science [Hagersten, Landin, and Haridi 1992] developed a concept called DDM (Data Diffusion Machine), which is a true COMA, since all memory operates as a cache and a memory block does not exist in a predefined node. The absence of a designated home for a memory block significantly complicates the protocols, since it means that there is no static lookup scheme to find the location and status of a block. Furthermore, a true COMA must contend with the problem of finding a place to move a memory block when it conflicts with another block for the same location in memory (which happens because the memory is a cache with a limited associativity). In the event that the displaced block is the last copy of a memory block, which in itself may be difficult to know precisely, the displaced block must be migrated to some other memory location, since it cannot be destroyed (as it is the only copy of the data). This migration process can be very complex, requiring a potentially unbounded number of memory blocks to be displaced!

Although no pure COMA machines were ever built, the COMA idea has inspired many variations. COMA-F, or Flat COMA, was proposed by Stenström, Joe, and Gupta [1992] as a simpler alternative to the original COMA proposals. By allocating a home location, COMA-F eliminated the need for multilevel hierarchical lookups and possible displacement misses, since the block status could always be looked up in the home and the home location always had space for the block. Saulsbury et al. [1995] proposed Simple COMA (S-COMA), which implemented COMA using the virtual memory mechanisms for replication and migration, rather than hardware support at the cache level. Reactive NUMA [Falsafi and Wood 1997] is a proposal to develop a protocol that merges the best of cc-NUMA protocols with S-COMA protocols. At the same time, several groups (see Chandra et al. [1994] and Soundararajan et al. [1996]) explored the use of page-level replication and migration, both to assist in reducing remote misses and as an alternative to other schemes such as strict COMA or remote access caches. Wildfire builds on many of these ideas to create a blend of hardware and software mechanisms.

The Convex Exemplar implemented scalable coherent shared memory using a two-level architecture: At the lowest level eight-processor modules are built using a crossbar. A ring can then connect up to 32 of these modules, for a total of 256 processors (see Thekkath et al. [1997] for an evaluation). Laudon and Lenoski [1997] describe the SGI Origin, which was first delivered in 1996 and is closely based on the original Stanford DASH machine, although including a number of innovations for scalability and ease of programming. Origin uses a bit vector for the directory structure, which is either 16 or 32 bits long. Each bit represents a node, which consists of two processors; a coarse bit vector representation allows each bit to represent up to 8 nodes for a total of 1024 processors. As Galles [1996] describes, a high-performance fat hypercube is used for the global interconnect. Hristea, Lenoski, and Keen [1997] is a thorough evaluation of the performance of the Origin memory system.

More recent research has focused on enhanced scalability for cache-coherent designs, flexible and adaptable techniques for implementing coherency, and approaches that merge hardware and software schemes. The MIT Alewife machine [Agarwal et al. 1995] incorporated several innovations including processor support for multithreading and the use of cooperative mechanisms for handling coherence. The Stanford FLASH multiprocessor [Kuskin et al. 1994; Gibson et al. 2000] makes use of a programmable processor that implements the coherence scheme, as well as alternative schemes for message passing, synchronization primitives, or performance instrumentation. Reinhardt and his colleagues at the University of Wisconsin [Reinhardt, Larus, and Wood 1994] explored an alternative for a combination of user and base software and hardware support for coherent shared memory. The Star-T [Nikhil, Papadopoulos, and Arvind 1992] and Star-T Voyager [Ang et al. 1998] projects at MIT explored the use of multithreading and combining customized and commodity approaches to building scalable multiprocessors.

Developments in Synchronization and Consistency Models

A wide variety of synchronization primitives have been proposed for shared-memory multiprocessors. Mellor-Crummey and Scott [1991] provide an overview of the issues as well as efficient implementations of important primitives, such as locks and barriers. An extensive bibliography supplies references to other important contributions, including developments in spin locks, queuing locks, and barriers.

Lamport [1979] introduced the concept of sequential consistency and what correct execution of parallel programs means. Dubois, Scheurich, and Briggs [1988] introduced the idea of weak ordering (originally in 1986). In 1990, Adve and Hill provided a better definition of weak ordering and also defined the concept of data-race-free; at the same conference, Gharachorloo and his colleagues [1990] introduced release consistency and provided the first data on the performance of relaxed consistency models. More relaxed consistency models have been widely adopted in microprocessor architectures, including the Sun SPARC, Alpha, and IA-64. Adve and Gharachorloo [1996] is an excellent tutorial on memory consistency and the differences among these models.

Other References

The concept of using virtual memory to implement a shared address space among distinct machines was pioneered in Kai Li's Ivy system in 1988. There have been subsequent papers exploring both hardware support issues, software mechanisms, and programming issues. Amza et al. [1996] describe a system built on workstations using a new consistency model, Kontothanassis et al. [1997] describe a software shared-memory scheme using remote writes, and Erlichson et al. [1996] describe the use of shared virtual memory to build large-scale multiprocessors using SMPs as nodes.

There is an almost unbounded amount of information on multiprocessors and multicomputers: Conferences, journal papers, and even books seem to appear faster than any single person can absorb the ideas. No doubt many of these papers will go unnoticed—not unlike the past. Most of the major architecture conferences contain papers on multiprocessors. An annual conference, Supercomputing

XY (where X and Y are the last two digits of the year), brings together users, architects, software developers, and vendors and publishes the proceedings in book, CD-ROM, and online (see *www.scXY.org*) form. Two major journals, *Journal of Parallel and Distributed Computing* and the *IEEE Transactions on Parallel and Distributed Systems,* contain papers on all aspects of parallel processing. Several books focusing on parallel processing are included in the following references, with Culler, Singh, and Gupta [1999] being the most recent, large-scale effort. For years, Eugene Miya of NASA Ames has collected an online bibliography of parallel-processing papers. The bibliography, which now contains more than 35,000 entries, is available online at *liinwww.ira.uka.de/bibliography/Parallel /Eugene/index.html.*

In addition to documenting the discovery of concepts now used in practice, these references also provide descriptions of many ideas that have been explored and found wanting, as well as ideas whose time has just not yet come.

Multithreading and Simultaneous Multithreading

The concept of multithreading dates back to one of the earliest transistorized computers, the TX-2. TX-2 was one of the earliest transistorized computers and is also famous for being the computer on which Ivan Sutherland created Sketchpad, the first computer graphics system. TX-2 was built at MIT's Lincoln Laboratory and became operational in 1959. It used multiple threads to support fast context switching to handle I/O functions. Clark [1957] describes the basic architecture, and Forgie [1957] describes the I/O architecture. Multithreading was also used in the CDC 6600, where a fine-grained multithreading scheme with interleaved scheduling among threads was used as the architecture of the I/O processors. The HEP processor, a pipelined multiprocessor designed by Denelcor and shipped in 1982, used fine-grained multithreading to hide the pipeline latency as well as to hide the latency to a large memory shared among all the processors. Because the HEP had no cache, this hiding of memory latency was critical. Burton Smith, one of the primary architects, describes the HEP architecture in a 1978 paper, and Jordan [1983] published a performance evaluation. The Tera processor extends the multithreading ideas and is described by Alverson et al. in a 1992 paper.

In the late 1980s and early 1990s, researchers explored the concept of coarse-grained multithreading (also called block multithreading) as a way to tolerate latency, especially in multiprocessor environments. The SPARCLE processor in the Alewife system used such a scheme, switching threads whenever a high-latency exceptional event, such as a long cache miss, occurred. Agarwal et al. describe SPARCLE in a 1993 paper. The IBM Pulsar processor uses similar ideas.

By the early 1990s, several research groups had arrived at two key insights. First, they realized that fine-grained multithreading was needed to get the maximum performance benefit, since in a coarse-grained approach, the overhead of thread switching and thread start-up (e.g., filling the pipeline from the new thread) negated much of the performance advantage (see Laudon, Gupta, and

Horowitz 1994). Second, several groups realized that to effectively use large numbers of functional units would require both ILP and thread-level parallelism (TLP). These insights led to several architectures that used combinations of multithreading and multiple issue. Wolfe and Shen [1991] describe an architecture called XIMD that statically interleaves threads scheduled for a VLIW processor. Hirata et al. [1992] describe a proposed processor for media use that combines a static supersealar pipeline with support for multithreading; they report speedups from combining both forms of parallelism. Keckler and Dally [1992] combine static scheduling of ILP and dynamic scheduling of threads for a processor with multiple functional units. The question of how to balance the allocation of functional units between ILP and TLP and how to schedule the two forms of parallelism remained open.

When it became clear in the mid-1990s that dynamically scheduled superscalars would be delivered shortly, several research groups proposed using the dynamic scheduling capability to mix instructions from several threads on the fly. Yamamoto et al. [1994] appears to be the first such proposal, though the simulation results for their multithreaded superscalar architecture use simplistic assumptions. This work was quickly followed by Tullsen, Eggers, and Levy [1995], which was the first realistic simulation assessment and coined the term *simultaneous multithreading*. Subsequent work by the same group together with industrial coauthors addressed many of the open questions about SMT. For example, Tullsen et al. [1996] addressed questions about the challenges of scheduling ILP versus TLP. Lo et al. [1997] is an extensive discussion of the SMT concept and an evaluation of its performance potential, and Lo et. al. [1998] evaluates database performance on an SMT processor.

References

Adve, S. V., and K. Gharachorloo [1996]. "Shared memory consistency models: A tutorial," *IEEE Computer* 29:12 (December), 66–76.

Adve, S. V., and M. D. Hill [1990]. "Weak ordering—a new definition," *Proc. 17th Int'l Symposium on Computer Architecture* (June), Seattle, Wash., 2–14.

Agarwal, A., R. Bianchini, D. Chaiken, K. Johnson, and D. Kranz [1995]. "The MIT Alewife machine: Architecture and performance," *Int'l Symposium on Computer Architecture* (Denver, Colo.), June, 2–13.

Agarwal, A., J. L. Hennessy, R. Simoni, and M. A. Horowitz [1988]. "An evaluation of directory schemes for cache coherence," *Proc. 15th Int'l Symposium on Computer Architecture* (June), 280–289.

Agarwal, A., J. Kubiatowicz, D. Kranz, B.-H. Lim, D. Yeung, G. D'Souza, and M. Parkin [1993]. "Sparcle: An evolutionary processor design for large-scale multiprocessors," *IEEE Micro* 13 (June), 48–61.

Almasi, G. S., and A. Gottlieb [1989]. *Highly Parallel Computing,* Benjamin/Cummings, Redwood City, Calif.

Alverson, G., R. Alverson, D. Callahan, B. Koblenz, A. Porterfield, and B. Smith [1992]. "Exploiting heterogeneous parallelism on a multithreaded multiprocessor," *Proc. 1992 Int'l Conf. on Supercomputing* (November), 188–197.

Amdahl, G. M. [1967]. "Validity of the single processor approach to achieving large scale computing capabilities," *Proc. AFIPS Spring Joint Computer Conf.* 30, Atlantic City, N.J. (April), 483–485.

Amza C., A. L. Cox, S. Dwarkadas, P. Keleher, H. Lu, R. Rajamony, W. Yu, and W. Zwaenepoel [1996]. "Treadmarks: Shared memory computing on networks of workstations," *IEEE Computer* 29(2) (February), 18–28.

Ang, B., D. Chiou, D. Rosenband, M. Ehrlich, L. Rudolph, and Arvind [1998]. "StarT-Voyager: A flexible platform for exploring scalable SMP issues," *Proc. of SC'98*, Orlando, Fla., November.

Archibald, J., and J.-L. Baer [1986]. "Cache coherence protocols: Evaluation using a multiprocessor simulation model," *ACM Trans. on Computer Systems* 4:4 (November), 273–298.

Arpaci, R. H., D. E. Culler, A. Krishnamurthy, S. G. Steinberg, and K. Yelick [1995]. "Empirical evaluation of the CRAY-T3D: A compiler perspective," *Proc. Int'l Symposium on Computer Architecture* (June), Italy.

Baer J-L., and W-H. Wang [1988]. "On the inclusion properties for multi-level cache hierarchies," *Proc. 15th Annual Int'l Symposium on Computer Architecture* (May–June), Honolulu, 73–80.

Barroso, L.A., K. Gharachorloo, and E. Bugnion [1998]. "Memory system characterization of commercial workloads," *Proc. 25th Int'l Symposium on Computer Architecture,* Barcelona (July), 3–14.

Baskett, F., T. Jermoluk, and D. Solomon [1988]. "The 4D-MP graphics superworkstation: Computing + graphics = 40 MIPS + 40 MFLOPS and 10,000 lighted polygons per second," *Proc. COMPCON Spring,* San Francisco, 468–471.

BBN Laboratories [1986]. "Butterfly parallel processor overview," Tech. Rep. 6148, BBN Laboratories, Cambridge, Mass.

Bell, C. G. [1985]. "Multis: A new class of multiprocessor computers," *Science* 228 (April 26), 462–467.

Bell, C. G. [1989]. "The future of high performance computers in science and engineering," *Comm.* ACM 32:9 (September), 1091–1101.

Bouknight, W. J, S. A. Deneberg, D. E. McIntyre, J. M. Randall, A. H. Sameh, and D. L. Slotnick [1972]. "The Illiac IV system," *Proc. IEEE* 60:4, 369–379. Also appears in D. P. Siewiorek, C. G. Bell, and A. Newell, *Computer Structures: Principles and Examples,* McGraw-Hill, New York (1982), 306–316.

Burkhardt, H., III, S. Frank, B. Knobe, and J. Rothnie [1992]. "Overview of the KSR1 computer system," Tech. Rep. KSR-TR-9202001, Kendall Square Research, Boston (February).

Censier, L., and P. Feautrier [1978]. "A new solution to coherence problems in multicache systems," *IEEE Trans. on Computers* C-27:12 (December), 1112–1118.

Chandra, R., S. Devine, B. Verghese, A. Gupta, and M. Rosenblum [1994]. "Scheduling and page migration for multiprocessor compute servers," Sixth Int'l Conf. on Architectural Support for Programming Languages and Operating Systems (ASPLOS-VI), ACM, Santa Clara, Calif., October, 12–24.

Charlesworth, A. [1998]. "Starfire: Extending the SMP envelope," *IEEE Micro* 18:1 (January/February), 39–49.

Clark, W. A. [1957]. "The Lincoln TX-2 computer development," *Proc. Western Joint Computer Conference* (February), Institute of Radio Engineers, Los Angeles, 143–145.

Culler, D. E., J. P. Singh, and A. Gupta [1999]. *Parallel Computer Architecture: A Hardware/Software Approach,* Morgan Kaufmann, San Francisco.

Dubois, M., C. Scheurich, and F. Briggs [1988]. "Synchronization, coherence, and event ordering," *IEEE Computer* 9-21 (February).

Eggers, S. [1989]. *Simulation Analysis of Data Sharing in Shared Memory Multiprocessors*, Ph.D. thesis, Univ. of California, Berkeley. Computer Science Division Tech. Rep. UCB/CSD 89/501 (April).

Elder, J., A. Gottlieb, C. K. Kruskal, K. P. McAuliffe, L. Randolph, M. Snir, P. Teller, and J. Wilson [1985]. "Issues related to MIMD shared-memory computers: The NYU Ultracomputer approach," *Proc. 12th Int'l Symposium on Computer Architecture* (June), Boston, 126–135.

Erlichson, A., N. Nuckolls, G. Chesson, and J. L. Hennessy [1996]. "SoftFLASH: Analyzing the performance of clustered distributed virtual shared memory," *Proc. 7th Symposium on Architectural Support for Programming Languages and Operating Systems (ASPLOS-VII)*, October, 210–220.

Falsafi, B., and D. A. Wood [1997]. "Reactive NUMA: A design for unifying S-COMA and CC-NUMA," *Proc. 24th Int'l Symposium on Computer Architecture*, June, Denver, Colo., 229–240.

Flynn, M. J. [1966]. "Very high-speed computing systems," *Proc. IEEE* 54:12 (December), 1901–1909.

Forgie, J. W. [1957]. "The Lincoln TX-2 input-output system," *Proc. Western Joint Computer Conference* (February), Institute of Radio Engineers, Los Angeles, 156–160.

Frank, S. J. [1984]. "Tightly coupled multiprocessor systems speed memory access time," *Electronics* 57:1 (January), 164–169.

Gajski, D., D. Kuck, D. Lawrie, and A. Sameh [1983]. "CEDAR—a large scale multiprocessor," *Proc. Int'l Conf. on Parallel Processing* (August), 524–529.

Galles, M. [1996]. "Scalable pipelined interconnect for distributed endpoint routing: The SGI SPIDER chip," *Proc. Hot Interconnects '96*, Stanford University, August.

Gehringer, E. F., D. P. Siewiorek, and Z. Segall [1987]. *Parallel Processing: The Cm* Experience*, Digital Press, Bedford, Mass.

Gharachorloo, K., A. Gupta, and J. L. Hennessy [1992]. "Hiding memory latency using dynamic scheduling in shared-memory multiprocessors," *Proc. 19th Annual Int'l Symposium on Computer Architecture*, Gold Coast, Australia, June.

Gharachorloo, K., D. Lenoski, J. Laudon, P. Gibbons, A. Gupta, and J. L. Hennessy [1990]. "Memory consistency and event ordering in scalable shared-memory multiprocessors," *Proc. 17th Int'l Symposium on Computer Architecture* (June), Seattle, Wash., 15–26.

Gibson, J., R. Kunz, D. Ofelt, M. Horowitz, J. Hennessy, and M. Heinrich [2000]. "FLASH vs. (simulated) FLASH: Closing the simulation loop," *Proc. 9th Conf. on Architectural Support for Programming Languages and Operating Systems* (November), San Jose, Calif., 49–58.

Goodman, J. R. [1983]. "Using cache memory to reduce processor memory traffic," *Proc. 10th Int'l Symposium on Computer Architecture* (June), Stockholm, Sweden, 124–131.

Hagersten E., and M. Koster [1998]. "WildFire: A scalable path for SMPs," *Proc. Fifth Int'l Symposium on High Performance Computer Architecture*.

Hagersten, E., A. Landin, and S. Haridi [1992]. "DDM—a cache-only memory architecture," *IEEE Computer* 25:9 (September), 44–54.

Hill, M. D. [1998]. "Multiprocessors should support simple memory consistency models," *IEEE Computer* 31:8 (August), 28–34.

Hillis, W. D. [1985]. *The Connection Multiprocessor,* MIT Press, Cambridge, Mass.

Hirata, H., K. Kimura, S. Nagamine, Y. Mochizuki, A. Nishimura, Y. Nakase, and T. Nishizawa [1992]. "An elementary processor architecture with simultaneous instruction issuing from multiple threads," *Proc. 19th Annual Int'l Symposium on Computer Architecture* (May), 136–145.

Hockney, R. W., and C. R. Jesshope [1988]. *Parallel Computers-2, Architectures, Programming and Algorithms,* Adam Hilger Ltd., Bristol, England.

Holland, J. H. [1959]. "A universal computer capable of executing an arbitrary number of subprograms simultaneously," *Proc. East Joint Computer Conf.* 16, 108–113.

Hord, R. M. [1982]. *The Illiac-IV, The First Supercomputer,* Computer Science Press, Rockville, Md.

Hristea, C., D. Lenoski, and J. Keen [1997]. "Measuring memory hierarchy performance of cache-coherent multiprocessors using micro benchmarks," *Proc. Supercomputing 97,* San Jose, Calif., November.

Hwang, K. [1993]. *Advanced Computer Architecture and Parallel Programming,* McGraw-Hill, New York.

Jordan, H. F. [1983]. "Performance measurements on HEP—a pipelined MIMD computer," *Proc. 10th Int'l Symposium on Computer Architecture* (June), Stockholm, 207–212.

Keckler, S. W., and W. J. Dally [1992]. "Processor coupling: Integrating compile time and runtime scheduling for parallelism," *Proc. 19th Annual Int'l Symposium on Computer Architecture* (May), 202–213.

Kontothanassis, L., G. Hunt, R. Stets, N. Hardavellas, M. Cierniak, S. Parthasarathy, W. Meira, S. Dwarkadas, and M. Scott [1997]. "VM-based shared memory on low-latency, remote-memory-access networks," *Proc. 24th Annual Int'l. Symposium on Computer Architecture (*June), Denver, Colo.

Kuskin, J., D. Ofelt, M. Heinrich, J. Heinlein, R. Simoni, K. Gharachorloo, J. Chapin, D. Nakahira, J. Baxter, M. Horowitz, A. Gupta, M. Rosenblum, and J. L. Hennessy [1994]. "The Stanford FLASH multiprocessor," *Proc. 21st Int'l Symposium on Computer Architecture,* Chicago, April.

Lamport, L. [1979]. "How to make a multiprocessor computer that correctly executes multiprocess programs," *IEEE Trans. on Computers* C-28:9 (September), 241–248.

Laudon, J., A. Gupta, and M. Horowitz [1994]. "Interleaving: A multithreading technique targeting multiprocessors and workstations," *Proc. Sixth Int'l Conf. on Architectural Support for Programming Languages and Operating Systems* (October), Boston, 308–318.

Laudon, J., and D. Lenoski [1997]. "The SGI Origin: A ccNUMA highly scalable server," *Proc. 24th Int'l Symposium on Computer Architecture* (June), Denver, Colo., 241–251.

Lenoski, D., J. Laudon, K. Gharachorloo, A. Gupta, and J. L. Hennessy [1990]. "The Stanford DASH multiprocessor," *Proc. 17th Int'l Symposium on Computer Architecture* (June), Seattle, Wash., 148–159.

Lenoski, D., J. Laudon, K. Gharachorloo, W.-D. Weber, A. Gupta, J. L. Hennessy, M. A. Horowitz, and M. Lam [1992]. "The Stanford DASH multiprocessor," *IEEE Computer* 25:3 (March).

Li, K. [1988]. "IVY: A shared virtual memory system for parallel computing," *Proc. 1988 Int'l Conf. on Parallel Processing,* Pennsylvania State University Press.

Lo, J., L. Barroso, S. Eggers, K. Gharachorloo, H. Levy, and S. Parekh [1998]. "An analysis of database workload performance on simultaneous multithreaded processors," *Proc. 25th Int'l Symposium on Computer Architecture* (June), 39–50.

Lo, J., S. Eggers, J. Emer, H. Levy, R. Stamm, and D. Tullsen [1997]. "Converting thread-level parallelism into instruction-level parallelism via simultaneous multithreading," *ACM Transactions on Computer Systems* 15:2 (August), 322–354.

Lovett, T., and S. Thakkar [1988]. "The Symmetry multiprocessor system," *Proc. 1988 Int'l Conf. of Parallel Processing*, University Park, Penn., 303–310.

Mellor-Crummey, J. M., and M. L. Scott [1991]. "Algorithms for scalable synchronization on shared-memory multiprocessors," *ACM Trans. on Computer Systems* 9:1 (February), 21–65.

Menabrea, L. F. [1842]. "Sketch of the analytical engine invented by Charles Babbage," *Bibiothèque Universelle de Genève* (October).

Mitchell, D. [1989]. "The Transputer: The time is now," *Computer Design* (RISC supplement), 40–41.

Miya, E. N. [1985]. "Multiprocessor/distributed processing bibliography," *Computer Architecture News* (ACM SIGARCH) 13:1, 27–29.

Nikhil, R. S., G. M. Papadopoulos, and Arvind [1992]. "*T: A multithreaded massively parallel architecture," *Proc. 19th Int'l Symposium on Computer Architecture,* Gold Coast, Australia, May, 156–167.

Noordergraaf, L., and R. van der Pas [1999]. "Performance experiences on Sun's WildFire prototype," *Proc. Supercomputing 99,* Portland, Ore., November.

Pfister, G. F., W. C. Brantley, D. A. George, S. L. Harvey, W. J. Kleinfekder, K. P. McAuliffe, E. A. Melton, V. A. Norton, and J. Weiss [1985]. "The IBM research parallel processor prototype (RP3): Introduction and architecture," *Proc. 12th Int'l Symposium on Computer Architecture* (June), Boston, 764–771.

Reinhardt, S. K., J. R. Larus, and D. A. Wood [1994]. "Tempest and Typhoon: User-level shared memory," *Proc. 21st Annual Int'l Symposium on Computer Architecture,* Chicago, April, 325–336.

Rettberg, R. D., W. R. Crowther, P. P. Carvey, and R. S. Towlinson [1990]. "The Monarch parallel processor hardware design," *IEEE Computer* 23:4 (April).

Rosenblum, M., S. A. Herrod, E. Witchel, and A. Gupta [1995]. "Complete computer simulation: The SimOS approach," in *IEEE Parallel and Distributed Technology* (now called *Concurrency*) 4:3, 34–43.

Saulsbury, A., T. Wilkinson, J. Carter, and A. Landin [1995]. "An argument for Simple COMA," *Proc. First Conf. on High Performance Computer Architectures* (January), Raleigh, N. C., 276–285.

Schwartz, J. T. [1980]. "Ultracomputers," *ACM Trans. on Programming Languages and Systems* 4:2, 484–521.

Scott, S. L. [1996]. "Synchronization and communication in the T3E multiprocessor," *Proc. Architectural Support for Programming Languages and Operating Systems (ASPLOS-VII),* Cambridge, Mass., October, 26–36.

Scott, S. L., and G. M. Thorson [1996]. "The Cray T3E network: Adaptive routing in a high performance 3D torus," *Proc. Symposium on High Performance Interconnects (Hot Interconnects 4),* Stanford University, August, 14–156.

Seitz, C. L. [1985]. "The Cosmic Cube (concurrent computing)," *Communications of the ACM* 28:1 (January), 22–33.

Singh, J. P., J. L. Hennessy, and A. Gupta [1993]. "Scaling parallel programs for multiprocessors: Methodology and examples," *Computer* 26:7 (July), 22–33.

Slotnick, D. L., W. C. Borck, and R. C. McReynolds [1962]. "The Solomon computer," *Proc. Fall Joint Computer Conf.* (December), Philadelphia, 97–107.

Smith, B. J. [1978]. "A pipelined, shared resource MIMD computer," *Proc. 1978 ICPP* (August), 6–8.

Soundararajan, V., M. Heinrich, B. Verghese, K. Gharachorloo, A. Gupta, and J. L. Hennessy [1998]. "Flexible use of memory for replication/migration in cache-coherent DSM multiprocessors," *Proc. 25th Int'l Symposium on Computer Architecture* (June), Barcelona, 342–355.

Stenström, P., T. Joe, and A. Gupta [1992]. "Comparative performance evaluation of cache-coherent NUMA and COMA architectures," *Proc. 19th Annual Int'l Symposium on Computer Architecture,* May, Queensland, Australia, 80–91.

Stone, H. [1991]. *High Performance Computers,* Addison-Wesley, New York.

Swan, R. J., A. Bechtolsheim, K. W. Lai, and J. K. Ousterhout [1977]. "The implementation of the Cm* multi-microprocessor," *Proc. AFIPS National Computing Conf.,* 645–654.

Swan, R. J., S. H. Fuller, and D. P. Siewiorek [1977]. "Cm*—a modular, multimicroprocessor," *Proc. AFIPS National Computer Conf.* 46, 637–644.

Tang, C. K. [1976]. "Cache design in the tightly coupled multiprocessor system," *Proc. AFIPS National Computer Conf.,* New York (June), 749–753.

Thekkath, R., A. P. Singh, J. P. Singh, S. John, and J. L. Hennessy [1997]. "An evaluation of a commercial CC-NUMA architecture—the CONVEX Exemplar SPP1200," *Proc. 11th Int'l Parallel Processing Symposium (IPPS '97),* Geneva, Switzerland, April.

Tullsen, D. M., S. J. Eggers, J. S. Emer, H. M. Levy, J. L. Lo, and R. L. Stamm [1996]. "Exploiting choice: Instruction fetch and issue on an implementable simultaneous multithreading processor," *Proc. 23rd Annual Int'l Symposium on Computer Architecture* (May), 191–202.

Tullsen, D. M., S. J. Eggers, and H. M. Levy [1995]. "Simultaneous multithreading: Maximizing on-chip parallelism," *Proc. 22nd Int'l Symposium on Computer Architecture* (June), 392–403.

Unger, S. H. [1958]. "A computer oriented towards spatial problems," *Proc. Institute of Radio Engineers* 46:10 (October), 1744–1750.

Wilson, A. W., Jr. [1987]. "Hierarchical cache/bus architecture for shared-memory multiprocessors," *Proc. 14th Int'l Symposium on Computer Architecture* (June), Pittsburgh, 244–252.

Wood, D. A., and M. D. Hill [1995]. "Cost-effective parallel computing," *IEEE Computer* 28:2 (February).

Wolfe, A., and J. P. Shen [1991]. "A variable instruction stream extension to the VLIW architecture." *Proc. Fourth Conference on Architectural Support for Programming Languages and Operating Systems* (April), Santa Clara, Calif., 2–14.

Wulf, W., and C. G. Bell [1972]. "C.mmp—A multi-mini-processor," *Proc. AFIPS Fall Joint Computing Conf.* 41, part 2, 765–777.

Wulf, W., and S. P. Harbison [1978]. "Reflections in a pool of processors—an experience report on C.mmp/Hydra," *Proc. AFIPS 1978 National Computing Conf.* 48 (June), Anaheim, Calif., 939–951.

Yamamoto, W., M. J. Serrano, A. R. Talcott, R. C. Wood, and M. Nemirosky [1994]. "Performance estimation of multistreamed, superscalar processors," *Proc. 27th Hawaii Int'l Conf. on System Sciences* (January), I:195–204.

Exercises

Solutions to the "starred" exercises appear in Appendix B.

6.1 [15] <6.1> Assume that we have a function for an application of the form F(i,p), which gives the fraction of time that exactly i processors are usable given that a total of p processors are available. This means that

$$\sum_{i=1}^{p} F(i,p) = 1$$

Assume that when i processors are in use, the application runs i times faster. Rewrite Amdahl's Law so that it gives the speedup as a function of p for some application.

6.2 [10] <6.1, 6.2> The Transaction Processing Council (TPC) has several different benchmarks. Visit their Web site at *www.tpc.org* and look at the top 10 performers in each benchmark class. Determine whether each of the top 10 configurations is a multiprocessor, and if so, what type (e.g., SMP, NUMA, cluster). Does the ordering look different if price-performance is used as the metric?

6.3 [10] <6.1, 6.2> The Top 500 list categorizes the fastest scientific machines in the world according to their performance on the Linpack benchmark. Visit their Web site at *www.top500.org* and look at the top 100 performers (there are many repeats of a particular vendor product, since individual supercomputer sites rather than a product are counted). Determine how many different supercomputer products occur among the top 100 configurations and what type (e. g., SMP, NUMA, cluster) each different supercomputer is. Try to obtain cost information and see how the data change when cost-performance is considered.

✪ 6.4 [15] <6.3> In small bus-based multiprocessors, write-through caches are sometimes used. One reason is that a write-through cache has a slightly simpler coherence protocol. Show how the basic snooping cache coherence protocol of Figure 6.12 on page 559 can be changed for a write-through cache. From the viewpoint of an implementor, what is the major hardware functionality that is not needed with a write-through cache compared with a write-back cache?

6.5 [20] <6.3> Add a clean exclusive state to the basic snooping cache coherence protocol (Figure 6.12 on page 559). Show the protocol in the format of Figure 6.12.

6.6 [15] <6.3> One proposed solution for the problem of false sharing is to add a valid bit per word (or even for each byte). This would allow the protocol to invalidate a word without removing the entire block, letting a cache keep a portion of a block in its cache while another processor writes a different portion of the block. What extra complications are introduced into the basic snooping cache coherence protocol (Figure 6.12) if this capability is included? Remember to consider all possible protocol actions.

6.7 [12/10/15] <6.3> The performance differences for write invalidate and write update schemes can arise from both bandwidth consumption and latency. Assume a memory system with 64-byte cache blocks. Ignore the effects of contention.

a. [12] <6.3> Write two parallel code sequences to illustrate the bandwidth differences between invalidate and update schemes. One sequence should make update look much better and the other should make invalidate look much better.

b. [10] <6.3> Write a parallel code sequence to illustrate the latency advantage of an update scheme versus an invalidate scheme.

c. [15] <6.3> Show, by example, that when contention is included, the latency of update may actually be worse. Assume a bus-based multiprocessor with 50-cycle memory and snoop transactions.

6.8 [15/10] <6.2, 6.4> This exercise studies the impact of aggressive techniques to exploit instruction-level parallelism in the processor when used in the design of shared-memory multiprocessor systems. Consider two systems identical except for the processor. System A uses a processor with a simple single-issue in-order pipeline, while system B uses a processor with four-way issue, out-of-order execution and a reorder buffer with 64 entries. For four benchmarks—online transaction processing, decision support systems, LU, and FFT—system B gives a speedup of 1.5, 2.5, 2.9, and 2.4, respectively, over system A.

a. [15] <6.4> Following the convention of Figure 6.13, let us divide the execution time into instruction execution, cache access, memory access, and other stalls. How would you expect each of these components to differ between system A and system B?

b. [10] <6.2, 6.4> Based on the discussion of the behavior of OLTP workloads in Section 6.4, what is the important difference between the OLTP workload and the other benchmarks that limits benefit from a more aggressive processor design?

6.9 [15] <6.4> How would you change the code of an application to avoid false sharing? What might be done by a compiler and what might require programmer directives?

✪ 6.10 [15] <6.5> Assume a directory-based cache coherence protocol. The directory currently has information that indicates that processor P1 has the data in "exclusive" mode. If the directory now gets a request for the same cache block from processor P1, what could this mean? What should the directory controller do? (Such cases are called "race conditions" and are the reasons why coherence protocols are so hard to design and verify.)

6.11 [20] <6.5> As we discussed earlier, the directory controller can send invalidates for lines that have been replaced by the local cache controller. To avoid such messages, and to keep the directory consistent, replacement hints are used. Such messages tell the controller that a block has been replaced. Modify the directory coherence protocol of Section 6.5 to use such replacement hints.

6.12 [12/10/12/15] <6.4, 6.6> One possible approach to achieving the scalability of distributed shared memory and the cost-effectiveness of a bus design is to combine the two approaches, using a set of processors with memories attached directly to the processors and interconnected with a bus. The argument in favor of such a design is that the use of local memories and a coherence scheme with limited broadcast results in a reduction in bus traffic, allowing the bus to be used for a larger number of processors.

Assume the following characteristics for a machine with 64-byte cache blocks:

Total data miss rate (assume instruction miss rate is negligible)	2%
% misses to private data (used only by this processor)	60%
% misses to shared data that is unowned in a remote cache/memory	20%
% misses to shared data that is dirty in a remote cache	80%

Assume a local memory miss takes 100 ns until processor restart. For remote misses that must use the bus, use the E6000 (Wildfire) restart memory miss times from the top portion of Figure 6.50.

a. [12] <6.4, 6.6> Find the average miss time for this design.

b. [10] <6.4, 6.6> Assume a 1 GHz clock rate, a CPI of 1.0 when the cache hit rate is 100%, and that a load or store is issued every other clock cycle. If the processor is stalled during a cache miss until processor restart, what is the effective CPI? What is the effective rate at which loads or stores are issued from the processor?

c. [12] <6.4, 6.6> Assume a split-transaction bus with a request and acknowledge for all bus transactions. If a bus request or acknowledge requires 16 bytes of bus bandwidth and a data transfer requires a total of 80 bytes, what is the bandwidth demand on the shared bus per processor?

d. [15] <6.4, 6.6> Split-transaction buses are quite complex in practice, and the only accurate way to assess their bandwidth limitations is often by measurement. Using the results from part (b) and the assumptions from part (c) about bandwidth requirements, determine how many processors could share a bus with the bandwidth characteristics of the E6000 (Wildfire) bus as shown in the top portion of Figure 6.51. Assume that the processors should not consume more than 80% of the unowned or exclusive data bandwidth.

✪ 6.13 [12/10/12] <6.4, 6.6, 6.11> In this exercise, we compare the design of the Sun Wildfire to the Sun Origin on the basis of memory latency and bandwidth. For this exercise, use the latency measurements to processor restart from Figure 6.50 and the bandwidth measurements in Figure 6.51. Assume a 64-processor design with 16 processors per Wildfire node. Assume that remote accesses are uniformly distributed. (Remember that this affects Wildfire and the Origin differently!).

a. [12] <6.6, 6.11> For the remote access time outside of an Origin or Wildfire node, use the average remote latency for less than 128 nodes from the second section of Figure 6.50. Assuming that 80% of the remote misses are to dirty lines, find the average remote memory access time for Wildfire and Origin.

b. [10] <6.4, 6.6, 6.11> What should the fraction of dirty remote requests be to minimize the difference in remote access time between Wildfire and the Origin? What does this tell you about the design of the cache system within a node?

c. [12] <6.4, 6.11> Compare the local memory bandwidth of the Origin and E6000 nodes using the data in the top of Figure 6.51. Assuming accesses are either unowned or dirty, for what fraction of dirty accesses will the bandwidth of the two designs be the same?

6.14 [15/15/20] <6.6> A key design question in DSM multiprocessors is how big to make the nodes in the design. In Origin, each node contains two processors, while in Wildfire a node contains more processors, with 16 to 20 being a likely target. This choice represents a complex design trade-off: When each node is larger, more accesses use the first level of interconnect, which is usually faster, but larger nodes typically impose a higher burden on accesses that must go remote. Throughout this exercise assume a total of 128 processors, and assume the goal is to minimize the remote access time. A spreadsheet will make this exercise much easier!

Assume the following local and remote access times:

Intranode access time with n processors per node ($n \geq 2$)	$300 + 20\,(n-1)$ ns
Average remote access time	Local memory access time $+ 100 + 100 \times \sqrt{\dfrac{128}{n}}$

a. [15] <6.6> Assuming a uniform distribution of remote accesses, find the optimum node size for this multiprocessor.

b. [15] <6.6> A one-processor node could have a considerably lower local memory access time. Does there exist a one-processor node design that is faster than the optimal node size from part (a)? If so, what must the local memory access time be? If not, how would you change this design if you wanted to use a one-processor node design?

c. [20] <6.6> Now consider optimizing node size for best average memory access time. Suppose the memory accesses are not uniformly distributed, but heavily biased toward a nearest neighbor structure. The probability of a nearest neighbor being in the same node is given by the following:

Processors per node	Fraction within node
2–3	25%
4–7	50%
8–15	62.5%
16–31	75%
31–63	87.5%
≥ 64	100%

If this is the only improvement gained from a nearest neighbor allocation, find the optimal node size, assuming that 60% of the remote accesses are nearest neighbor.

6.15 [20] <6.6> In reality, a nearest neighbor access pattern also conveys advantages by reducing the time to access a remote node. Assume that if the nearest neighbor is not in the same node, then the access time is Local memory access time + 200. Now find the optimal node size assuming 60% of the remote accesses are nearest neighbor.

6.16 [20/15/30] <6.5> One downside of a straightforward implementation of directories using fully populated bit vectors is that the total size of the directory information scales as the product: Processor count × Memory blocks. If memory is grown linearly with processor count, then the total size of the directory grows quadratically in the processor count. In practice, because the directory needs only 1 bit per memory block (which is typically 32–128 bytes), this problem is not serious for small to moderate processor counts. For example, assuming a 128-byte block, the amount of directory storage compared to main memory is Processor count/ 1024, or about 10% additional storage with 100 processors. This problem can be avoided by observing that we only need to keep an amount of information that is proportional to the cache size of each processor. We explore some solutions in these exercises.

a. [20] <6.5> One method to obtain a scalable directory protocol is to organize the multiprocessor as a logical hierarchy with the processors at the leaves of the hierarchy and directories positioned at the root of each subtree. The directory at each subtree root records which descendents cache which memory blocks, as well as which memory blocks with a home in that subtree are cached outside of the subtree. Compute the amount of storage needed to record the processor information for the directories, assuming that each directory is fully associative. Your answer should incorporate both the number of nodes at each level of the hierarchy as well as the total number of nodes.

b. [15] <6.5> Assume that each level of the hierarchy in part (a) has a lookup cost of 50 cycles plus a cost to access the data or cache of 50 cycles, when the point is reached. We want to compute the AMAT (average memory access time—see Chapter 5) for a 64-processor multiprocessor with four-node subtrees. Use the data from the Ocean benchmark run on 64 processors (Figure 6.31) and assume that all noncoherence misses occur within a sub-tree node and that coherence misses are uniformly distributed across the multiprocessor. Find the AMAT for this multiprocessor. What does this say about hierarchies?

c. [30] <6.5> An alternative approach to implementing directory schemes is to implement bit vectors that are not dense. There are two such strategies: one reduces the number of bit vectors needed, and the other reduces the number of bits per vector. Using traces, you can compare these schemes. First, implement the directory as a four-way set-associative cache storing full bit vectors, but only for the blocks that are cached outside of the home node. If a directory cache miss occurs, choose a directory entry and invalidate the entry. Second, implement the directory so that every entry has 8 bits. If a block is cached in only one node outside of its home, this field contains the node number. If the block is cached in more than one node outside its home, this field is a bit vector with each bit indicating a group of eight processors, at least one of which caches the block. Using traces of 64-processor execution, simulate the behavior of these two schemes. Assume a perfect cache for nonshared references, so as to focus on coherency behavior. Determine the number of extraneous invalidations as the directory cache size is increased.

6.17   [10] <6.3–6.6> Some systems do not use multiprocessing for performance. Instead they run the same program in lockstep on multiple processors. What potential benefit is possible on such multiprocessors?

✪ 6.18   [15] <6.7> Some multiprocessors have implemented a special broadcast coherence protocol just for locks, sometimes even using a different bus. Evaluate the performance of the spin lock in the example on page 596 assuming a write broadcast protocol.

6.19   [15] <6.7> Implement the barrier in Figure 6.39 on page 598, using queuing locks. Compare the performance to the spin lock barrier.

✪ 6.20   [15] <6.7> Implement the barrier in Figure 6.39 on page 598, using fetch-and-increment. Compare the performance to the spin lock barrier.

6.21   [15] <6.7> Implement the barrier in Figure 6.42 on page 602, so that barrier release is also done with a combining tree.

6.22   [15] <6.7> One performance optimization commonly used is to pad synchronization variables to not have any other useful data in the same cache line as the synchronization variable. Construct a pathological example when not doing this can hurt performance. Assume a snoopy write invalidate protocol.

✪ 6.23   [15] <6.7> Find the time for n processes to synchronize using a standard barrier. Assume that the time for a single process to update the count and release the lock is c.

6.24   [15] <6.7> Find the time for n processes to synchronize using a combining tree barrier. Assume that the time for a single process to update the count and release the lock is c.

6.25   [25] <6.7> Implement a software version of the queuing lock for a bus-based system. Using the model in the example on page 596, how long does it take for 20 processors to acquire and release the lock? You need only count bus cycles.

6.26   [15/15/15] <6.4, 6.5, 6.7> Prefetching is a technique that allows the "consumer" of data to request the data to its cache *before* it needs them. With multiprocessors, we can think of the "dual" of this technique where the "producer" of the data "evicts" the data from its cache *after* it is done with them. An extension of such "postflushes" could be to send the data to the next processor that needs the data, in cases where that can be determined.

a. [15] <6.4, 6.7> When is prefetching likely to be applicable? When is producer-initiated communication likely to be beneficial? Would producer-initiated communication be applicable in the context of the queuing locks and tree barriers discussed in Section 6.7?

b. [15] <6.7> Assume a shared-memory multiprocessor system that takes 100 cycles for a memory access and 300 cycles for a cache-to-cache transfer. A program running on this machine spends 60% of its time stalled on memory accesses and 20% of its time stalled on synchronization. Of these memory stalls, 20% are due to producer-consumer data access patterns where the writer of data can identify the processor that will read the value next. In these cases, producer-initiated communication can directly transfer data to the cache of the next processor needing the data. This will reduce the latency of these memory accesses from 300 cycles for a cache-to-cache transfer to 1 cycle for a cache hit. Another 30% of the memory stalls are due to migratory data patterns where data move from one processor to another, but the migration path is unclear to the source processor. In this case, a producer-initiated communication primitive, such as "postflush," can reduce the latency of the memory access from 300 cycles to 100 cycles. Further assume that all the synchronization is due to tree barriers and that the tree barrier overhead can be reduced by 40% with producer-initiated communication. Assuming no other overheads, what is the reduction in execution time with producer-initiated communication?

c. [15] <6.5> What memory system and program code changes are required for implementing producer-initiated communication?

6.27 [20/30] <6.2–6.7> Both researchers and industry designers have explored the idea of having the capability to explicitly transfer data between memories. The argument in favor of such facilities is that the programmer can achieve better overlap of computation and communication by explicitly moving data when they are available. The first part of this exercise explores the potential on paper; the second explores the use of such facilities on real multiprocessors.

a. [20] <6.2–6.7> Assume that cache misses stall the processor, and that block transfer occurs into the local memory of a DSM node. Assume that remote misses cost 100 cycles and that local misses cost 40 cycles. Assume that each DMA transfer has an overhead of 10 cycles. Assuming that all the coherence traffic can be replaced with DMA into main memory followed by a cache miss, find the potential improvement for Ocean running on 64 processors (Figure 6.31).

b. [30] <6.2–6.7> Find a multiprocessor that implements both shared memory (coherent or incoherent) and a simple DMA facility. Implement a blocked matrix multiply using only shared memory and using the DMA facilities with shared memory. Is the latter faster? How much? What factors make the use of a block data transfer facility attractive?

6.28 [10/12/10/12] <6.8> As discussed in Section 6.8, the memory consistency model provides a specification of how the memory system will appear to the programmer. Consider the following code segment, where the initial values are A = flag = C = 0.

```
P1              P2
A = 2000        while (flag == 1) {;}
flag = 1        C = A
```

a. [10] <6.8> At the end of the code segment, what is the value you would expect for C?

b. [12] <6.8> A system with a general-purpose interconnection network, a directory-based cache coherence protocol, and support for nonblocking loads generates a result where C is 0. Describe a scenario where this result is possible.

c. [10] <6.8> If you wanted to make the system sequentially consistent, what are the key constraints you need to impose?

d. [12] <6.8> Assume a processor supports a relaxed memory consistency model. A relaxed consistency model requires synchronization to be explicitly identified. Assume that the processor supports a "barrier" instruction (e.g., the SPARC instruction set), which ensures that all memory operations preceding the barrier instruction complete before any memory operations following the barrier are allowed to begin. Where would you include barrier instructions in the above code segment to ensure that you get the "intuitive results" of sequential consistency?

6.29 [10/10/10] <6.9> The following results are seen from a simulation study of five floating-point benchmarks and two integer benchmarks from the SPEC92 suite. The branch misprediction rate nearly doubles from 5% to 9.1% going from 1 thread to 8 threads in an SMT processor. However, the wrong-path instructions fetched (on a misprediction) drops from 24% on a single-threaded processor to 7% on an 8-thread processor.

a. [10] <6.9> What causes the increase in branch misprediction rate?

b. [10] <6.9> Why is there a decrease in the number of wrong-path instructions fetched even though there is an increase in branch misprediction rates? (*Hint:* This is related to the scheduling of threads.)

c. [10] <6.9> Based on these numbers, what conclusions can you draw about the conflicts caused due to contention and interference on various resources in a multithreaded processor?

✪ 6.30 [15] <6.9> On page 612 one of the design challenges listed for SMT processors is ensuring that cache conflicts generated by the simultaneous execution of multiple threads do not cause significant performance degradation (often referred to as destructive cache interference). However, a simulation study of the online transaction-processing workload, OLTP, on an 8-threaded SMT processor shows a decrease in instruction cache miss rate from 14% to 9%. When is such a decrease, called constructive cache interference, likely to happen?

6.31 [15/15/10] <6.9> One of the important design decisions with an SMT processor is the heuristic to identify the "preferred thread." The following problem illustrates some of the challenges with this.

An eight-way SMT processor is running a multithreaded version of a parallel program. The processor uses the heuristic of giving preference to a thread that has the fewest instructions in the decode, rename, and instruction queues.

a. [15] <6.9> What are the advantages with this heuristic?

b. [15] <6.9> Craft a scenario where this heuristic may lead to a particular thread not being scheduled. (This is called starvation.)

c. [10] <6.9> What other heuristics can you think of to schedule the preferred thread?

6.32 [25] <6.10> Prove that in a two-level cache hierarchy, where L1 is closer to the processor, inclusion is maintained with no extra action if L2 has at least as much associativity as L1, both caches use LRU replacement, and both caches have the same block size.

6.33 [15] <6.10> The key differences, with respect to a hardware shared-memory system, of a shared virtual memory (SVM) system are (1) the longer latency of remote memory accesses through the OS handler and over the LAN, and (2) the larger units of coherence (pages instead of cache blocks). How are these two key differences likely to affect the performance and operation of the system? What are ways to address each negative effect?

⭐ **6.34** [10/15] <6.10> Consider a multiprocessor on a chip with four CPU cores. Each core has a 64 KB first-level cache, and the chip includes a 1 MB second-level cache.

a. [10] <6.10> If the system implements multilevel inclusion between the L1 and L2 caches, what is the upper bound on the capacity of the L2 that is wasted with duplicate data?

b. [15] <6.10> To avoid the potential waste of second-level cache capacity due to multilevel inclusion, the system designer may decide to forgo maintaining the inclusion property. In this case, blocks that are replaced in an L1 cache cause a write back to the L2 cache. What optimization discussed in Chapter 5 is this similar to? What other changes would you require to minimize contention for the L1 cache?

6.35 [20] <6.5, 6.11> As we saw in "Putting It All Together" and in "Fallacies and Pitfalls," data distribution can be important when an application has a nontrivial private data miss rate caused by capacity misses. This problem can be attacked with compiler technology (distributing the data in blocks) or through architectural support, as we saw in the description of CMR on Wildfire.

Assume that we have two DSM multiprocessors: one with CMR support and one without such support. Both multiprocessors have one processor per node, and remote coherence misses, which are uniformly distributed, take 1 μs. Assume that all capacity misses on the CMR multiprocessor hit in the local memory and require 250 ns. Assume that capacity misses take 200 ns when they are local on the DSM multiprocessor without CMR and 800 ns otherwise. Using the Ocean data for 32 processors (Figure 6.23), find what fraction of the capacity misses on the DSM multiprocessor must be local if the performance of the two multiprocessors is identical.

6.36 [15] <6.13> In contrast to the MXP chip that includes four similar MIPS 32 processors (discussed in Section 6.13), some embedded processors may support multiprocessing between nonuniform (heterogeneous) processor cores. For example, consider a DSP chip that includes a three-way issue master processor, two VLIW processors with support for special-purpose DSP primitives, and an intelligent DMA and memory controller, in addition to several on-chip DRAM banks. (Many commercial DSP processors exist with similar configurations; for example, the TI TMS 320C82.)

Discuss the trade-offs of writing parallel applications for such a heterogeneous system compared to writing parallel applications for the MXP configuration. What are the implications on binary software compatibility for future generations?

6.37 [Discussion] <6> When trying to perform detailed performance evaluation of a multiprocessor system, system designers use one of three tools: analytical models, trace-driven simulation, and execution-driven simulation. Analytical models use mathematical expressions to model the behavior of programs. Trace-driven simulations run the applications on a real machine and generate a trace, typically of memory operations. These traces can then be replayed through a cache simulator or a simulator with a simple processor model to predict the performance of the system when various parameters are changed. Execution-driven simulators simulate the entire execution including maintaining an equivalent structure for the processor state, and so on. What are the accuracy/speed trade-offs between these approaches?

6.38 [Discussion] <6.11> Construct a scenario whereby a truly revolutionary architecture—pick your favorite candidate—will play a significant role. *Significant* is defined as 10% of the computers sold, 10% of the users, 10% of the money spent on computers, or 10% of some other figure of merit.

6.39 [30] <6.3–6.7, 6.11> Using an available shared-memory multiprocessor, see if you can determine the organization and latencies of its memory hierarchy. For each level of the hierarchy, you can look at the total size, block size, and associativity, as well as the latency of each level of the hierarchy. If the multiprocessor uses a nonbus interconnection network, see if you can discover the topology and latency characteristics of the network. Try to make a table like that in Figure 6.50 for the machine. The lmbench (*www.bitmover.com/lmbench/*) and stream (*www. cs.virginia.edu/stream/*) benchmarks may prove useful in this exercise.

6.40 [30] <6.3–6.7, 6.11> Perform Exercise 6.39 but looking at the bandwidth characteristics rather than latency. See if you can prepare a table like that in Figure 6.51. Extend the table by looking at the effect of strided accesses, as well as sequential and unrelated accesses.

6.41 [40] <6.2, 6.10, 6.14> A multiprocessor or cluster is typically marketed using programs that can scale performance linearly with the number of processors. The project here is to port programs written for one multiprocessor to the others and to measure their absolute performance and how it changes as you change the number of processors. What changes need to be made to improve performance of the ported programs on each multiprocessor? What is the ratio of processor performance according to each program?

6.42 [35] <6.2, 6.10, 6.14> Instead of trying to create fair benchmarks, invent programs that make one multiprocessor or cluster look terrible compared with the others, and also programs that always make one look better than the others. It would be an interesting result if you couldn't find a program that made one multiprocessor or cluster look worse than the others. What are the key performance characteristics of each organization?

6.43 [40] <6.2, 6.10, 6.14> Multiprocessors and clusters usually show performance increases as you increase the number of processors, with the ideal being n times speedup for n processors. The goal of this biased benchmark is to make a program that gets worse performance as you add processors. For example, this means that one processor on the multiprocessor or cluster runs the program fastest, two are slower, four are slower than two, and so on. What are the key performance characteristics for each organization that give inverse linear speedup?

6.44 [50] <6.2, 6.10, 6.14> Networked workstations can be considered multicomputers or clusters, albeit with somewhat slower, though perhaps cheaper, communication relative to computation. Port some cluster benchmarks to a network using remote procedure calls for communication. How well do the benchmarks scale on the network versus the cluster? What are the practical differences between networked workstations and a commercial cluster, such as the IBM-SP series?

6.45 [50] <6.3, 6.4, 6.5, 6.8> Implement parallel versions of two·standard algorithms—matrix multiply and mergesort—for a shared-memory architecture that supports a relaxed memory consistency model. You will have to decide on a suitable partitioning of the computation, a suitable data layout across the processors, and implement the necessary synchronization to ensure correctness. Use a publicly available simulator, such as RSIM (*www.ece.rice.edu/~rsim*), to measure the speedups you get for various processor sizes. Experiment with various cache sizes, different latency parameters, and different working set sizes. Experiment with different cache coherence protocols. Vary the parameters to model both UMA and NUMA systems. How does that affect your experiments?

7

Storage Systems

I/O certainly has been lagging in the last decade.

Seymour Cray
Public lecture (1976)

Also, I/O needs a lot of work.

David Kuck
*Keynote address, 15th Annual
Symposium on Computer
Architecture* (1988)

Combining bandwidth and storage … enables swift and reliable access
to the ever expanding troves of content on the proliferating disks and
… repositories of the Internet. … the capacity of storage arrays of all
kinds is rocketing ahead of the advance of computer performance.

George Gilder
*"The End Is Drawing Nigh"
Forbes ASAP* (April 4, 2000)

Introduction

Input/output has been the orphan of computer architecture. Historically neglected by CPU enthusiasts, the prejudice against I/O is institutionalized in the most widely used performance measure, CPU time (page 25). The performance of a computer's I/O system cannot be measured by CPU time, which by definition ignores I/O. The second-class citizenship of I/O is even apparent in the label *peripheral* applied to I/O devices.

This attitude is contradicted by common sense. A computer without I/O devices is like a car without wheels—you can't get very far without them. And while CPU time is interesting, response time—the time between when the user types a command and when results appear—is surely a better measure of performance. The customer who pays for a computer cares about response time, even if the CPU designer doesn't.

Does I/O Performance Matter?

Some suggest that the prejudice against I/O is well founded. I/O speed doesn't matter, they argue, since there is always another process to run while one process waits for a peripheral.

There are several points to make in reply. First, this is an argument that performance is measured as *throughput*—number of tasks completed per hour—versus response time. Plainly, if users didn't care about response time, interactive software never would have been invented, and there would be no workstations or personal computers today; Section 7.7 gives experimental evidence of the importance of response time. It may also be expensive to rely on running other processes, since paging traffic from process switching might actually increase I/O. Furthermore, with mobile devices and desktop computing, there is only one person per computer and thus fewer processes than in time-sharing. Many times the only waiting process is the human being! Moreover, applications such as transaction processing (Section 7.7) place strict limits on response time as part of the performance analysis.

I/O's revenge is at hand. Suppose response time is just 10% longer than CPU time. First we speed up the CPU by a factor of 10, while neglecting I/O. Amdahl's Law tells us the speedup is only 5 times, half of what we would have achieved if both were sped up tenfold. Similarly, making the CPU 100 times faster without improving the I/O would obtain a speedup of only 10 times, squandering 90% of the potential. If, as predicted in Chapter 1, performance of CPUs improves at 55% per year and I/O did not improve, every task would become I/O bound. There would be no reason to buy faster CPUs—and no jobs for CPU designers. Thus, I/O performance increasingly limits system performance and effectiveness.

Does CPU Performance Matter?

Moore's Law leads to both large, fast CPUs but also to very small, cheap CPUs. Especially for systems using the latter CPU, it is increasingly unlikely that the most important goal is keeping the CPU busy versus keeping I/O devices busy, as the bulk of the costs may not be with the CPU.

This change in importance is also reflected by the names of our times. The 1960s to 1980s were called the Computing Revolution; the period since 1990 has been called the Information Age, with concerns focused on advances in information technology versus raw computational power.

This shift in focus from computation to communication and storage of information emphasizes reliability and scalability as well as cost-performance. To reflect the increasing importance of I/O, the third edition of this book has twice as many I/O chapters as the first edition and half as many on instruction set architecture. This chapter covers storage I/O and the next covers communication I/O. Although two chapters cannot fully vindicate I/O, they may at least atone for some of the sins of the past and restore some balance.

Does Performance Matter?

After 15 years of doubling processor performance every 18 months, processor performance is not the problem it once was. Many would find highly dependable systems much more attractive than faster versions of today's systems with today's level of unreliability. Although it is frustrating when a program crashes, people become hysterical if they lose their data. Hence, storage systems are typically held to a higher standard of dependability than the rest of the computer. Because of traditional demands placed on storage—and because a new century needs new challenges—this chapter defines reliability, availability, and dependability and shows how to improve them.

Dependability is the bedrock of storage, yet it also has its own rich performance theory—queuing theory—that balances throughput versus response time. The software that determines which processor features get used is the compiler, but the operating system usurps that role for storage.

Thus, storage has a different, multifaceted culture from processors, yet it is still found within the architecture tent. We start our exploration of storage with the hardware building blocks.

7.2   Types of Storage Devices

Rather than discuss the characteristics of all storage devices, we will concentrate on those most commonly found: magnetic disks, magnetic tapes, automated tape libraries, CDs, and DVDs. As these I/O devices are generally too large for embedded applications, we conclude with a description of Flash memory, a storage device commonly used in portable devices. (Experienced readers should skip the following subsections with which they are already familiar.)

Magnetic Disks

I think Silicon Valley was misnamed. If you look back at the dollars shipped in products in the last decade, there has been more revenue from magnetic disks than from silicon. They ought to rename the place Iron Oxide Valley.

Al Hoagland
one of the pioneers of magnetic disks (1982)

Despite repeated attacks by new technologies, magnetic disks have dominated non-volatile storage since 1965. Magnetic disks play two roles in computer systems:

- Long-term, nonvolatile storage for files, even when no programs are running
- A level of the memory hierarchy below main memory used as a backing store for virtual memory during program execution (see Section 5.10)

In this section, we are not talking about floppy disks, but the original "hard" disks.

As descriptions of magnetic disks can be found in countless books, we will only list the essential characteristics, with the terms illustrated in Figure 7.1. (Readers who recall these terms might want to skip to the section entitled "The Future of Magnetic Disks" on page 684; those interested in more detail should

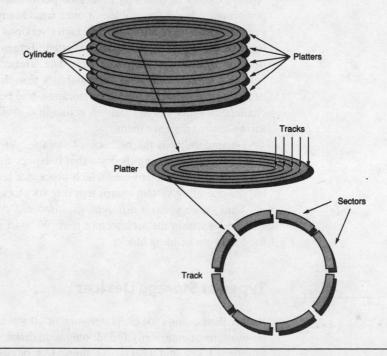

Figure 7.1 Disks are organized into platters, tracks, and sectors. Both sides of a platter are coated so that information can be stored on both surfaces. A cylinder refers to a track at the same position on every platter.

see Hospodor and Hoagland [1993]). A magnetic disk consists of a collection of *platters* (generally 1 to 12), rotating on a spindle at 3600 to 15,000 revolutions per minute (RPM). These platters are metal or glass disks covered with magnetic recording material on both sides, so 10 platters have 20 recording surfaces. Disk diameters in 2001 vary by almost a factor of 4, from 1.0 to 3.5 inches, although more than 95% of sales are either 2.5- or 3.5-inch diameter disks. Traditionally, the biggest disks have the highest performance, and the smallest disks have the lowest price per disk drive. Price per gigabyte often goes to the disks sold in highest volume, which today are 3.5-inch disks.

The disk surface is divided into concentric circles, designated *tracks*. There are typically 5000 to 30,000 tracks on each surface. Each track in turn is divided into *sectors* that contain the information; a track might have 100 to 500 sectors. A sector is the smallest unit that can be read or written. IBM mainframes allow users to select the size of the sectors, although most systems fix their size, typically at 512 bytes of data. The sequence recorded on the magnetic media is a sector number, a gap, the information for that sector including error correction code, a gap, the sector number of the next sector, and so on. Occasionally people forget this sequence—confusing the recording density with the density that a user's data can be stored—leading to fallacies about disks (see Section 7.14).

In the past, all tracks had the same number of sectors; the outer tracks, which are longer, recorded information at a much lower density than the inner tracks. Recording more sectors on the outer tracks than on the inner tracks, called *constant bit density,* is the standard today. This name is misleading, as the bit density is not really constant. Typically, the inner tracks are recorded at the highest density and the outer tracks at the lowest, but the outer tracks might record, say, 1.7 times more bits despite being 2.1 times longer.

Figure 7.2 shows the characteristics of three magnetic disks in 2000. Large-diameter drives have many more gigabytes to amortize the cost of electronics, so the traditional wisdom used to be that they had the lowest cost per gigabyte. This advantage can be offset, however, if the small drives have much higher sales volume, which lowers manufacturing costs. The 3.5-inch drive, which is the largest surviving drive in 2001, also has the highest sales volume, so it unquestionably has the best price per gigabyte.

To read and write information into a sector, a movable *arm* containing a *read/write head* is located over each surface. Rather than represent each recorded bit individually, groups of bits are recorded using a run-length-limited code. Run-length-limited codes ensure that there is both a minimum and maximum number of bits in a group that the reader must decipher before seeing synchronization signals, which enables higher recording density as well as reducing error rates. The arms for all surfaces are connected together and move in conjunction, so that all arms are over the same track of all surfaces. The term *cylinder* is used to refer to all the tracks under the arms at a given point on all surfaces.

To read or write a sector, the disk controller sends a command to move the arm over the proper track. This operation is called a *seek,* and the time to move the arm to the desired track is called *seek time.*

Characteristics	Seagate Cheetah ST173404LC Ultra160 SCSI Drive	IBM Travelstar 32GH DJSA-232 ATA-4 Drive	IBM 1 GB Microdrive DSCM-11000
Disk diameter (inches)	3.5	2.5	1.0
Formatted data capacity (GB)	73.4	32.0	1.0
Cylinders	14,100	21,664	7,167
Disks	12	4	1
Recording surfaces (or heads)	24	8	2
Bytes per sector	512–4,096	512	512
Average sectors per track (512 byte)	≈ 424	≈ 360 (256–469)	≈ 140
Maximum areal density (Gb/sq.in.)	6.0	14.0	15.2
Rotation speed (RPM)	10,033	5,411	3,600
Average seek random cylinder to cylinder (read/write) (ms)	5.6/6.2	12.0	12.0
Minimum seek (read/write) (ms)	0.6/0.9	2.5	1.0
Maximum seek (ms)	14.0/15.0	23.0	19.0
Data transfer rate (MB/sec)	27–40	11–21	2.6–4.2
Link speed to disk buffer (MB/sec)	160	67	13
Power idle/operating (W)	16.4/23.5	2.0/2.6	0.5/0.8
Buffer size (MB)	4.0	2.0	0.125
Size: height × width × depth (inches)	1.6 × 4.0 × 5.8	0.5 × 2.7 × 3.9	0.2 × 1.4 × 1.7
Weight (pounds)	2.00	0.34	0.035
Rated MTTF (powered-on hours)	1,200,000	(see caption)	(see caption)
Percentage of powered-on hours (POH) per month	100%	45%	20%
Percentage of POH seeking, reading, writing	90%	20%	20%
Load/unload cycles (disk powered on/off)	250 per year	300,000	300,000
Nonrecoverable read errors per bits read	< 1 per 10^{15}	< 1 per 10^{13}	< 1 per 10^{13}
Seek errors	< 1 per 10^{7}	not available	not available
Shock tolerance: operating, not operating	10 G, 175 G	150 G, 700 G	175 G, 1500 G
Vibration tolerance: operating, not operating (sine-swept, 0 to peak)	5–400 Hz @ 0.5 G, 22–400 Hz @ 2 G	5–500 Hz @ 1G, 2.5–500 Hz @ 5 G	5–500 Hz @ 1 G, 10–500 Hz @ 5 G

Figure 7.2 Characteristics of three magnetic disks of 2000. To help the reader gain intuition about disks, this table gives typical values for disk parameters. The 2.5-inch drive is a factor of 6 to 9 better in weight, size, and power than the 3.5-inch drive. The 1.0-inch drive is a factor of 10 to 11 better than the 2.5-inch drive in weight and size, and a factor of 3–4 better in power. Note that 3.5-inch drives are designed to be used almost continuously, and so are rarely turned on and off, while the smaller drives spend most of their time unused and thus are turned on and off repeatedly. In addition, these mobile drives must handle much larger shocks and vibrations, especially when turned off. These requirements affect the relative cost of these drives. Note that IBM no longer quotes MTBF for 2.5-inch drives, but when they last did it was 300,000 hours. IBM quotes the service life as 5 years or 20,000 powered-on hours, whichever is first. The service life for the 1.0-inch drives is 5 years or 8800 powered-on hours, whichever is first.

Average seek time is the subject of considerable misunderstanding. Disk manufacturers report minimum seek time, maximum seek time, and average seek time in their manuals. The first two are easy to measure, but the average was open to wide interpretation. The industry decided to calculate average seek time as the sum of the time for all possible seeks divided by the number of possible seeks. Average seek times are advertised to be 5 ms to 12 ms. Depending on the application and operating system, however, the actual average seek time may be only 25% to 33% of the advertised number. The explanation is locality of disk references. Section 7.14 has a detailed example.

The time for the requested sector to rotate under the head is the *rotation latency* or *rotational delay*. The average latency to the desired information is obviously halfway around the disk; if a disk rotates at 10,000 RPM, the average rotation time is therefore

$$\text{Average rotation time} = \frac{0.5}{10,000 \text{ RPM}} = \frac{0.5}{(10,000/60) \text{ RPS}} = 0.0030 \text{ sec} = 3.0 \text{ ms}$$

Note that there are two mechanical components to a disk access. It takes several milliseconds on average for the arm to move over the desired track and several milliseconds on average for the desired sector to rotate under the read/write head. A simple performance model is to allow one-half rotation of the disk to find the desired data after the proper track is found. Of course, the disk is always spinning, so seeking and rotating actually overlap.

The next component of disk access, *transfer time*, is the time it takes to transfer a block of bits, typically a sector, under the read/write head. This time is a function of the block size, disk size, rotation speed, recording density of the track, and speed of the electronics connecting the disk to computer. Transfer rates in 2001 range from 3 MB per second for the 3600 RPM, 1-inch drives to 65 MB per second for the 15,000 RPM, 3.5-inch drives.

Between the disk controller and main memory is a hierarchy of controllers and data paths, whose complexity varies. For example, whenever the transfer time is a small portion of the time of a full access, the designer will want to disconnect the memory device during the access so that other devices can transfer their data. (The default is to hold the data path for the full access.) This desire is true for high-performance disk controllers and, as we shall see later, for buses and networks.

There is also a desire to amortize this long access by reading more than simply what is requested; this is called *read ahead*. Read ahead is another case of computer designs trying to leverage spatial locality to enhance performance (see Chapter 5). The hope is that a nearby request will be for the nearby sectors, which will already be available. These sectors go into buffers on the disk that act as a cache. As Figure 7.2 shows, the size of this buffer varies from 0.125 to 4 MB. The hit rate presumably comes solely from spatial locality, but disk-caching algorithms are proprietary and so their techniques and hit rates are unknown. Transfers to and from the buffer operate at the speed of the I/O bus versus the speed of the disk media. In 2001, the I/O bus speeds vary from 80 to 320 MB per second.

To handle the complexities of disconnect/connect and read ahead, there is usually, in addition to the disk drive, a device called a *disk controller*. Thus, the final component of disk access time is *controller time,* which is the overhead the controller imposes in performing an I/O access. When referring to the performance of a disk in a computer system, the time spent waiting for a disk to become free (*queuing delay*) is added to this time.

Example   What is the average time to read or write a 512-byte sector for a disk? The advertised average seek time is 5 ms, the transfer rate is 40 MB/sec, it rotates at 10,000 RPM, and the controller overhead is 0.1 ms. Assume the disk is idle so that there is no queuing delay. In addition, calculate the time assuming the advertised seek time is three times longer than the measured seek time.

Answer   Average disk access is equal to average seek time + average rotational delay + transfer time + controller overhead. Using the calculated average seek time, the answer is

$$5 \text{ ms} + \frac{0.5}{10,000 \text{ RPM}} + \frac{0.5 \text{ KB}}{40.0 \text{ MB/sec}} + 0.1 \text{ ms} = 5.0 + 3.0 + 0.013 + 0.1 = 8.11 \text{ ms}$$

Assuming the measured seek time is 33% of the calculated average, the answer is

$$1.67 \text{ ms} + 3.0 \text{ ms} + 0.013 \text{ ms} + 0.1 \text{ ms} = 4.783 \text{ ms}$$

Note that only 0.013/4.783 or 0.3% of the time is the disk transferring data in this example. Even page-sized transfers often take less than 5%, so disks normally spend most of their time waiting for the head to get over the data rather than reading or writing the data.

Many disks today are shipped in *disk arrays*. These arrays contain dozens of disks and may look like a single large disk to the computer. Hence, there is often another level to the storage hierarchy, the *array controller*. They are often key in dependability and performance of storage systems, implementing functions such as RAID (see Section 7.5) and caching (see Section 7.12).

The Future of Magnetic Disks

The disk industry has concentrated on improving the capacity of disks. Improvement in capacity is customarily expressed as improvement in *areal density,* measured in bits per square inch:

$$\text{Areal density} = \frac{\text{Tracks}}{\text{Inch}} \text{ on a disk surface} \times \frac{\text{Bits}}{\text{Inch}} \text{ on a track}$$

Through about 1988 the rate of improvement of areal density was 29% per year, thus doubling density every three years. Between then and about 1996, the rate improved to 60% per year, quadrupling density every three years and matching the traditional rate of DRAMs. From 1997 to 2001 the rate increased to 100%, or doubling every year. In 2001, the highest density in commercial products is 20 billion bits per square inch, and the lab record is 60 billion bits per square inch.

Cost per gigabyte has dropped at least as fast as areal density has increased, with smaller drives playing the larger role in this improvement. Figure 7.3 plots price per personal computer disk between 1983 and 2000, showing both the rapid drop in price and the increase in capacity. Figure 7.4 translates these costs into price per gigabyte, showing that it has improved by a factor of 10,000 over those 17 years. Notice the much quicker drop in prices per disk over time, reflecting a faster decrease in price per gigabyte.

Because it is more efficient to spin smaller mass, smaller-diameter disks save power as well as volume. In 2001, 3.5-inch or 2.5-inch drives are the leading technology. In the largest drives, rotation speeds have improved from the 3600

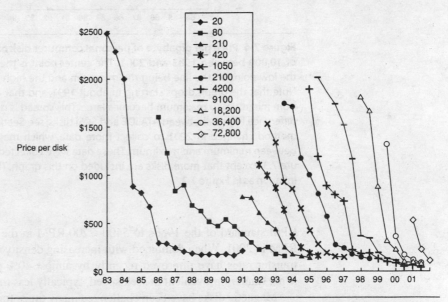

Figure 7.3 Price per personal computer disk by capacity (in megabytes) between 1983 and 2001. Note that later the price declines become steeper as the industry increases its rate of improvement from 30% per year to 100% per year. The capacity per disk increased almost 4000 times in 18 years. Although disks come in many sizes, we picked a small number of fixed sizes to show the trends. The price was adjusted to get a consistent disk capacity (e.g., shrinking the price of an 86 MB disk by 80/86 to get a point for the 80 MB line). The prices are in July 2001 dollars, adjusted for inflation using the Producer Price Index for manufacturing industries. The prices through 1995 were collected by Mike Dahlin from advertisements from the January and July editions of *Byte* magazine, using the lowest price of a disk of a particular size in that issue. Between January 1996 and January 2000, the advertisements come from *PC Magazine*, as *Byte* ceased publication. Since July 2000, the results came from biannual samples of price watch.com. (See *www.cs.utexas.edu/users/dahlin/techTrends/data/diskPrices*.)

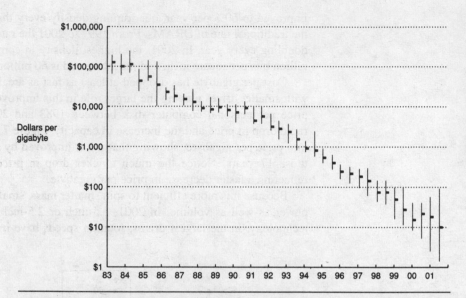

Figure 7.4 Price per gigabyte of personal computer disk over time, dropping a factor of 10,000 between 1983 and 2001. The center point is the median price per GB, with the low point on the line being the minimum and the high point being the maximum. Note that the graph drops starting in about 1991, and that in January 1997 the spread from minimum to maximum becomes large. This spread is due in part to the increasing difference in price between ATA.IDE and SCSI disks; see Section 7.14. The data collection method changed in 2001 to collect more data, which may explain the larger spread between minimum and maximum. These data were collected in the same way as for Figure 7.3, except that more disks are included on this graph. The prices were adjusted for inflation as in Figure 7.3.

RPM standard of the 1980s to 5400–7200 RPM in the 1990s to 10,000–15,000 RPM in 2001. When combined with increasing density (bits per inch on a track), transfer rates have improved recently by almost 40% per year. There has been some small improvement in seek speed, typically less than 10% per year.

Magnetic disks have been challenged many times for supremacy of secondary storage. One reason has been the fabled *access time gap* between disks and DRAM, as shown in Figure 7.5. DRAM latency is about 100,000 times less than disk, although bandwidth is only about 50 times larger. That performance gain costs 100 times more per gigabyte in 2001.

Many have tried to invent a technology cheaper than DRAM but faster than disk to fill that gap, but thus far, all have failed. So far, challengers have never had a product to market at the right time. By the time a new product would ship, DRAMs and disks have made advances as predicted earlier, costs have dropped accordingly, and the challenging product is immediately obsolete.

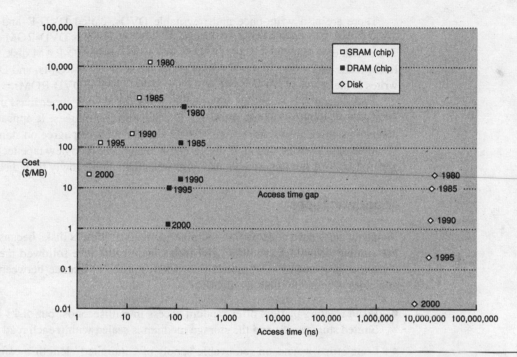

Figure 7.5 Cost versus access time for SRAM, DRAM, and magnetic disk in 1980, 1985, 1990, 1995, and 2000. The two-order-of-magnitude gap in cost and access times between semiconductor memory and rotating magnetic disks has inspired a host of competing technologies to try to fill it. So far, such attempts have been made obsolete before production by improvements in magnetic disks, DRAMs, or both. Note that between 1990 and 2000 the cost per megabyte of SRAM and DRAM chips made less improvement, while disk cost made dramatic improvement.

Optical Disks

One challenger to magnetic disks is *optical compact disks,* or *CDs,* and its successor, called *digital video discs* and then *digital versatile discs* or just *DVDs.* Both the *CD-ROM* and *DVD-ROM* are removable and inexpensive to manufacture, but they are read-only mediums. These 4.7-inch diameter disks hold 0.65 and 4.7 GB, respectively, although some DVDs write on both sides to double their capacity. Their high capacity and low cost have led to CD-ROMs and DVD-ROMs replacing floppy disks as the favorite medium for distributing software and other types of computer data.

The popularity of CDs and music that can be downloaded from the Web led to a market for rewritable CDs, conveniently called CD-RW, and write-once CDs, called CD-R. In 2001, there is a small cost premium for drives that can record on CD-RW. The media itself costs about $0.20 per CD-R disk or $0.60 per CD-RW disk. CD-RWs and CD-Rs read at about half the speed of CD-ROMs and CD-RWs and CD-Rs write at about a quarter the speed of CD-ROMs.

There are also write-once and rewritable DVDs, called DVD-R and (alas) DVD-RAM. Rewritable DVD drives cost 10 times as much as DVD-ROM drives. The media cost is about $10 per DVD-R disk to $15 per DVD-RAM disk. DVD-RAM reads and writes at about a third of the speed of DVD-ROMs, and DVD-R writes at the speed of DVD-RAM and reads at the speed of DVD-ROMs.

As CDs and DVDs are the replaceable media for the consumer mass market, their rate of improvement is governed by standards committees. It appears that magnetic storage grows more quickly than human beings can agree on standards. Writable optical disks may have the potential to compete with new tape technologies for archival storage, as tape also improves much more slowly than disks.

Magnetic Tapes

Magnetic tapes have been part of computer systems as long as disks because they use similar technology as disks, and hence historically have followed the same density improvements. The inherent cost-performance difference between disks and tapes is based on their geometries:

- Fixed rotating platters offer random access in milliseconds, but disks have a limited storage area and the storage medium is sealed within each reader.

- Long strips wound on removable spools of "unlimited" length mean many tapes can be used per reader, but tapes require sequential access that can take seconds.

One of the limits of tapes had been the speed at which the tapes can spin without breaking or jamming. A technology called *helical scan tapes* solves this problem by keeping the tape speed the same but recording the information on a diagonal to the tape with a tape reader that spins much faster than the tape is moving. This technology increases recording density by about a factor of 20 to 50. Helical scan tapes were developed for low-cost VCRs and camcorders, which brought down the cost of the tapes and readers.

One drawback to tapes is that they wear out. Helical tapes last for hundreds of passes, while the traditional longitudinal tapes wear out in thousands to millions of passes. The helical scan read/write heads also wear out quickly, typically rated for 2000 hours of continuous use. Finally, there are typically long rewind, eject, load, and spin-up times for helical scan tapes. In the archival backup market, such performance characteristics have not mattered, and hence there has been more engineering focus on increasing density than on overcoming these limitations.

Traditionally, tapes enjoyed a 10–100 times advantage over disks in price per gigabyte and were the technology of choice for disk backups. In 2001, it appears that tapes are falling behind the rapid advance in disk technology. Whereas in the past the contents of several disks could be stored on a single tape, the largest disk has greater capacity than the largest tapes. Amazingly, the prices of magnetic disks and tape media have crossed: in 2001, the price of a 40 GB IDE disk is about the same as the price of a 40 GB tape!

In the past, the claim was that magnetic tapes must track disks since innovations in disks must help tapes. This claim was important, because tapes are a small market and cannot afford a separate large research and development effort. One reason the market is small is that PC owners generally do not back up disks onto tape, and so while PCs are by far the largest market for disks, PCs are a small market for tapes.

Recently the argument has changed to the claim that tapes have compatibility requirements that are not imposed on disks; tape readers must read or write the current and previous generation of tapes, and must read the last four generations of tapes. As disks are a closed system, the disk heads need only read the platters that are enclosed with them, and this advantage explains why disks are improving at rates that are much more rapid.

In addition to the issue of capacity, another challenge is recovery time. Tapes are also not keeping up in bandwidth with disks. Thus, as disks continue to grow, it is not only more expensive to use tapes for backups, it will also take much longer to recover if a disaster occurs. This growing gap between rate of improvement in disks and tapes calls into question the sensibility of tape backup for disk storage.

Some bold organizations get rid of tapes altogether, using networks and remote disks to replicate the data geographically. The sites are picked so that disasters would not take out both sites, enabling instantaneous recovery time. These sites typically use a file system that does not overwrite data, which allows accidentally discarded files to be recovered. Such a solution depends on advances in disk capacity and network bandwidth to make economic sense, but these two are getting much more investment and hence have better records of accomplishment than tape.

Automated Tape Libraries

Tape capacities are enhanced by inexpensive robots to automatically load and store tapes, offering a new level of storage hierarchy. These *nearline* tapes mean access to terabytes of information in tens of seconds, without the intervention of a human operator. Figure 7.6 shows the Storage Technologies Corporation (STC) PowderHorn, which loads up to 6000 tapes, giving a total capacity of 300 TB. Putting this capacity into perspective, the Library of Congress is estimated to have 30 TB of text, if books could be magically transformed into ASCII characters.

There are many versions of tape libraries, but these mechanical marvels are not as reliable as other parts of the computer; it is not uncommon for tape libraries to have failure rates a factor of 10 higher than other storage devices.

Flash Memory

Embedded devices also need nonvolatile storage, but premiums placed on space and power normally lead to the use of Flash memory instead of magnetic recording. Flash memory is also used as a rewritable ROM in embedded systems,

Figure 7.6 The StorageTek PowderHorn 9310. This storage silo holds 2000–6000 tape cartridges per library storage module (LSM); using the 9840 cartridge, the total uncompressed capacity is 300 TB. Each cartridge holds 20 GB of uncompressed data. Depending on the block size and compression, readers transfer at 1.6–7.7 MB/sec in tests, with a peak speed of 20 MB/sec of compressed data. Each LSM has up to 10 tape readers and can exchange up to 450 cartridges per hour. One LSM is 7.7 feet tall, 10.7 feet in diameter, uses about 1.1 kilowatts, and weighs 8200 pounds. Sixteen LSMs can be linked together to pass cartridges between modules, increasing storage capacity another order of magnitude. (Courtesy Storage Technology Corp.)

typically to allow software to be upgraded without having to replace chips. Applications are typically prohibited from writing to Flash memory in such circumstances.

Like EEPROM (electrically erasable and programmable read-only memory), Flash memory is written by inducing the tunneling of charge from transistor gain to a floating gate. The floating gate acts as a potential well that stores the charge, and the charge cannot move from there without applying an external force. The primary difference between EEPROM and Flash memory is that Flash restricts writes to multikilobyte blocks, increasing memory capacity per chip by reducing area dedicated to control.

Compared to disks, Flash memories offer low power consumption (less than 50 milliwatts), can be sold in small sizes, and offer read access times comparable to DRAMs. In 2001, a 16M bit Flash memory has a 65 ns access time, and a 128M bit Flash memory has a 150 ns access time. Some memories even borrow the page mode access acceleration from DRAM to bring the time per word down in block transfers to 25–40 ns. Unlike DRAMs, writing is much slower and more complicated, sharing characteristics with the older electrically programmable read-only memories (EPROM) and EEPROM. A block of Flash memory is first electrically erased, and then written with 0s and 1s.

If the logical data are smaller than the Flash block size, the good data that should survive must be copied to another block before the old block can be erased. Thus, information is organized in Flash as linked lists of blocks. Such concerns lead to software that collects good data into fewer blocks so that the rest can be erased. The linked list structure is also used by some companies to map out bad blocks and offer reduced memory parts at half price rather than discard flawed chips.

The electrical properties of Flash memory are not as well understood as DRAM. Each company's experience, including whether it manufactured EPROM or EEPROM before Flash, affects the organization that it selects. The two basic types of Flash are based on whether the building blocks for the bits are NOR or NAND gates. NOR Flash devices in 2001 typically take 1–2 sec to erase 64 KB to 128 KB blocks, while NAND Flash devices take 5–6 ms to erase smaller blocks of 4 KB to 8 KB. Programming takes 10 μs per byte for NOR devices and 1.5 μs per byte for NAND devices. The number of times bits can be erased and still retain information is also often limited, typically about 100,000 cycles for NOR devices and 1,000,000 for some NAND devices.

An example illustrates read and write performance of Flash versus disks.

Example   Compare the time to read and write a 64 KB block to Flash memory and magnetic disk. For Flash, assume it takes 65 ns to read 1 byte, 1.5 μs to write 1 byte, and 5 ms to erase 4 KB. For disk, use the parameters of the Microdrive in Figure 7.2. Assume the measured seek time is one-third of the calculated average, the controller overhead is 0.1 ms, and the data are stored in the outer tracks, giving it the fastest transfer rate.

Answer   Average disk access is equal to average seek time + average rotational delay + transfer time + controller overhead. The average time to read or write 64 KB in a Microdrive disk is

$$\frac{12 \text{ ms}}{3} + \frac{0.5}{3600 \text{ RPM}} + \frac{64 \text{ KB}}{4.2 \text{ MB/sec}} + 0.1 \text{ ms} = 4.0 + 8.3 + 14.9 + 0.1 = 27.3 \text{ ms}$$

To read 64 KB in Flash you simply divide the 64 KB by the read bandwidth:

$$\text{Flash read time} = \frac{64 \text{ KB}}{1 \text{B}/65 \text{ ns}} = 4,259,840 \text{ ns} = 4.3 \text{ ms}$$

To write 64 KB, first erase it and then divide 64 KB by the write bandwidth:

$$\text{Flash write time} = \frac{64 \text{ KB}}{4 \text{KB}/5 \text{ ms}} + \frac{64 \text{ KB}}{1 \text{B}/1.5 \text{ μs}} = 80 \text{ ms} + 98,304 \text{ μs} = 178.3 \text{ ms}$$

Thus, Flash memory is about 6 times faster than disk for reading 64 KB, and disk is about 6 times faster than Flash memory for writing 64 KB. Note that this example assumes the Microdrive is already operating. If it was powered off to save energy, we should add time for it to resume.

The price per megabyte of Flash memory is about 6 times more than DRAM in 2001, making it 600 times more expensive per megabyte than disk. Of course Flash does have its uses, for example, when the designer may need only tens of megabytes or less of storage, not provided economically by disks.

Now that we have described several storage devices, we must discover how to connect them to a computer.

7.3   Buses—Connecting I/O Devices to CPU/Memory

In a computer system, the various subsystems must have interfaces to one another; for instance, the memory and CPU need to communicate, and so do the CPU and I/O devices. This communication is commonly done using a *bus*. The bus serves as a shared communication link between the subsystems. The two major advantages of the bus organization are low cost and versatility. By defining a single interconnection scheme, new devices can be added easily and peripherals may even be moved between computer systems that use a common bus. The cost of a bus is low, since a single set of wires is shared among multiple devices.

The major disadvantage of a bus is that it creates a communication bottleneck, possibly limiting the maximum I/O throughput. When I/O must pass through a central bus, this bandwidth limitation is as real as—and sometimes more severe than—memory bandwidth. In server systems, where I/O is frequent, designing a bus system capable of meeting the demands of the processor is a major challenge.

As Moore's Law marches on, buses are increasingly being replaced by networks and switches (see Section 7.10). To avoid the bus bottleneck, some I/O devices are connected to computers via *storage area networks* (SANs). SANs are covered in the next chapter, so this section concentrates on buses.

One reason bus design is so difficult is that the maximum bus speed is largely limited by physical factors: the length of the bus and the number of devices (and, hence, bus loading). These physical limits prevent arbitrary bus speedup. The desire for high I/O rates (low latency) and high I/O throughput can also lead to conflicting design requirements.

Buses were traditionally classified as *CPU-memory buses* or *I/O buses*. I/O buses may be lengthy, may have many types of devices connected to them, have a wide range in the data bandwidth of the devices connected to them, and normally follow a bus standard. CPU-memory buses, on the other hand, are short, generally high speed, and matched to the memory system to maximize memory-CPU bandwidth. During the design phase, the designer of a CPU-memory bus knows all the types of devices that must connect together, while the I/O bus designer must accept devices varying in latency and bandwidth capabilities. To lower costs, some computers have a single bus for both memory and I/O devices. In the quest for higher I/O performance, some buses are a hybrid of the two. For example, PCI is relatively short and is used to connect to more traditional I/O buses via bridges that speak both PCI on one end and the I/O bus protocol on the other. To indicate its intermediate state, such buses are sometimes called *mezzanine buses*.

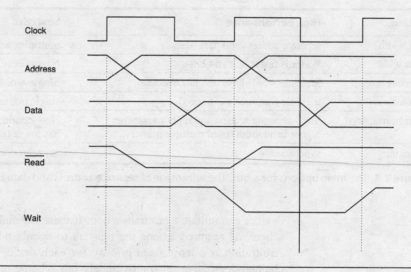

Clock

Address

Data

Read

Wait

Figure 7.7 Typical bus read transaction. The diagonal lines show when the data are changing with respect to the clock signal. This bus is synchronous. The read begins when the not read signal is asserted, and data are not ready until the wait signal is deasserted. The vertical bar shows when the data are ready to be read by the CPU.

Let's review a typical *bus transaction*, as seen in Figure 7.7. A bus transaction includes two parts: sending the address and receiving or sending the data. Bus transactions are usually defined by what they do to memory: A *read* transaction transfers data from memory (to either the CPU or an I/O device), and a *write* transaction writes data to the memory.

In a read transaction, the address is first sent down the bus to the memory, together with the appropriate control signals indicating a read. In Figure 7.7, this means asserting the read signal. The memory responds by returning the data on the bus with the appropriate control signals, in this case deasserting the wait signal. A write transaction requires that the CPU or I/O device sends both address and data and requires no return of data. Usually the CPU must wait between sending the address and receiving the data on a read, but the CPU often does not wait between sending the address and sending the data on writes.

Bus Design Decisions

The design of a bus presents several options, as Figure 7.8 shows. Like the rest of the computer system, decisions depend on cost and performance goals. The first three options in the figure are clear—separate address and data lines, wider data lines, and multiple-word transfers all give higher performance at more cost.

The next item in the table concerns the number of *bus masters*. These devices can initiate a read or write transaction; the CPU, for instance, is always a bus master. A bus has multiple masters when there are multiple CPUs or when I/O

Option	High performance	Low cost
Bus width	separate address and data lines	multiplex address and data lines
Data width	Wider is faster (e.g., 64 bits).	Narrower is cheaper (e.g., 8 bits).
Transfer size	Multiple words have less bus overhead.	Single-word transfer is simpler.
Bus masters	multiple (requires arbitration)	single master (no arbitration)
Split transaction?	Yes—separate request and reply packets get higher bandwidth (need multiple masters).	No—continuous connection is cheaper and has lower latency.
Clocking	synchronous	asynchronous

Figure 7.8 The main options for a bus. The advantage of separate address and data buses is primarily on writes.

devices can initiate a bus transaction. If there are multiple masters, an arbitration scheme is required among the masters to decide which one gets the bus next. Arbitration is often a fixed priority for each device, as is the case with daisy-chained devices, or an approximately fair scheme that randomly chooses which master gets the bus.

With multiple masters, a bus can offer higher bandwidth by using packets, as opposed to holding the bus for the full transaction. This technique is called *split transactions*. (Some systems call this ability *connect/disconnect*, a *pipelined bus*, a *pended bus*, or a *packet-switched bus*; the next chapter goes into more detail on packet switching.) Figure 7.9 shows the split-transaction bus. The idea is to divide bus events into requests and replies, so that the bus can be used in the time between the request and the reply.

The read transaction is broken into a read-request transaction that contains the address and a memory-reply transaction that contains the data. Each transaction must now be tagged so that the CPU and memory can tell which reply is for

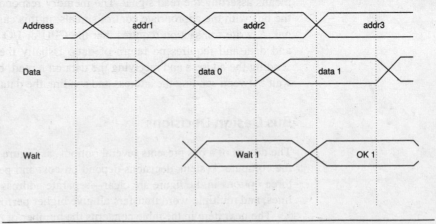

Figure 7.9 A split-transaction bus. Here the address on the bus corresponds to a later memory access.

which request. Split transactions make the bus available for other masters while the memory reads the words from the requested address. It also normally means that the CPU must arbitrate for the bus to send the data, and the memory must arbitrate for the bus to return the data. Thus, a split-transaction bus has higher bandwidth, but it usually has higher latency than a bus that is held during the complete transaction.

The final item in Figure 7.8, *clocking*, concerns whether a bus is synchronous or asynchronous. If a bus is *synchronous*, it includes a clock in the control lines and a fixed protocol for sending address and data relative to the clock. Since little or no logic is needed to decide what to do next, these buses can be both fast and inexpensive. They have two major disadvantages, however. Because of clock-skew problems, synchronous buses cannot be long, and everything on the bus must run at the same clock rate. Some buses allow multiple-speed devices on a bus, but they all run at the rate of the slowest device. CPU-memory buses are typically synchronous.

An *asynchronous* bus, on the other hand, is not clocked. Instead, self-timed, handshaking protocols are used between bus sender and receiver. Figure 7.10 shows the steps of a master performing a write on an asynchronous bus.

Asynchrony makes it much easier to accommodate a variety of devices and to lengthen the bus without worrying about clock skew or synchronization problems. If a synchronous bus can be used, it is usually faster than an asynchronous bus because it avoids the overhead of synchronizing the bus for each transaction. The choice of synchronous versus asynchronous bus has implications not only for data bandwidth, but also for an I/O system's physical distance and the number of devices that can be connected to the bus. Hence, I/O buses are more likely to be

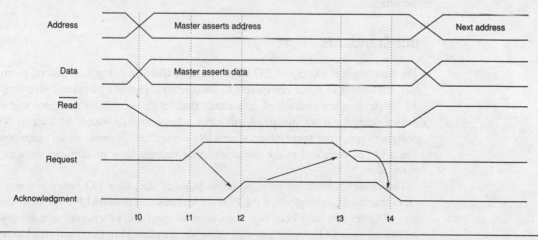

Figure 7.10 A master performs a write on an asynchronous bus. The state of the transaction at each time step is as follows. The master has obtained control and asserts address, read/write, and data. It then waits a specified amount of time for slaves to decode target: t1: master asserts request line; t2: slave asserts ack, indicating data received; t3: master releases req; t4: slave releases ack.

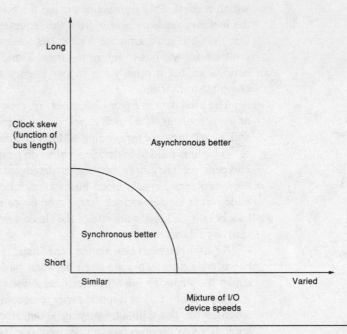

Figure 7.11 Preferred bus type as a function of length/clock skew and variation in I/O device speed. Synchronous is best when the distance is short and the I/O devices on the bus all transfer at similar speeds.

asynchronous than are memory buses. Figure 7.11 suggests when to use one over the other.

Bus Standards

The number and variety of I/O devices are flexible on many computers, permitting customers to tailor computers to their needs. The I/O bus is the interface to which devices are connected. Standards that let the computer designer and I/O device designer work independently play a large role in buses. As long as both designers meet the requirements, any I/O device can connect to any computer. The I/O bus standard is the document that defines how to connect devices to computers.

Machines sometimes grow to be so popular that their I/O buses become de facto standards; examples are the PDP-11 Unibus and the IBM PC-AT Bus. Once many I/O devices have been built for a popular machine, other computer designers will build their I/O interface so that those devices can plug into their machines as well. Sometimes standards also come from an explicit standards effort on the part of I/O device makers. Ethernet is an example of a standard that resulted from the cooperation of manufacturers. If standards are successful, they are eventually blessed by a sanctioning body like ANSI or IEEE. A recent variation on traditional standards bodies is trade associations. In that case a limited number of companies agree to produce a standard without cooperating with standards bodies, yet it is still done by committee. PCI is one example of a trade association standard.

Examples of Buses

Figures 7.12 to 7.14 summarize characteristics of common desktop I/O buses, I/O buses found in embedded devices, and CPU-memory interconnects found in servers.

	IDE/Ultra ATA	SCSI	PCI	PCI-X
Data width (primary)	16 bits	8 or 16 bits (wide)	32 or 64 bits	32 or 64 bits
Clock rate	up to 100 MHz	10 MHz (Fast), 20 MHz (Ultra), 40 MHz (Ultra2), 80 MHz (Ultra3 or Ultra160), 160 MHz (Ultra4 or Ultra320)	33 or 66 MHz	66, 100, 133 MHz
Number of bus masters	1	multiple	multiple	multiple
Bandwidth, peak	200 MB/sec	320 MB/sec	533 MB/sec	1066 MB/sec
Clocking	asynchronous	asynchronous	synchronous	synchronous
Standard	—	ANSI X3.131	—	—

Figure 7.12 Summary of parallel I/O buses. Peripheral Component Interconnect (PCI) and PCI Extended (PCI-X) connect main memory to peripheral devices. IDE/ATA and SCSI compete as interfaces to storage devices. Integrated Drive Electronics (IDE) is an early disk standard that connects two disks to a PC. It has been extended by AT-bus Attachment (ATA) to be both wider and faster. Small Computer System Interconnect (SCSI) connects up to 7 devices for 8-bit buses and up to 15 devices for 16-bit buses. They can even be different speeds, but they run at the rate of the slowest device. The peak bandwidth of an SCSI bus is the width (1 or 2 bytes) times the clock rate (10 to 160 MHz). Most SCSI buses today are 16 bits.

	I^{2}C	1-wire	RS-232	SPI
Data width (primary)	1 bit	1 bit	2 bits	1 bit
Signal wires	2	1	9 or 25	3
Clock rate	0.4–10 MHz	asynchronous	0.040 MHz or asynchronous	asynchronous
Number of bus masters	multiple	multiple	multiple	multiple
Bandwidth, peak	0.4–3.4 Mbits/sec	0.014 Mbits/sec	0.192 Mbit /sec	1 Mbit/sec
Clocking	asynchronous	asynchronous	asynchronous	asynchronous
Standard	none	none	EIA, ITU-T V.21	none

Figure 7.13 Summary of serial I/O buses, often used in embedded computers. I^{2}C was invented by Phillips in the early 1980s. 1-wire was developed by Dallas Semiconductor. RS-232 was introduced in 1962. SPI was created by Motorola in the early 1980s.

	HP HyperPlane Crossbar	IBM SP	Sun Gigaplane-XB
Data width (primary)	64 bits	128 bits	128 bits
Clock rate	120 MHz	111 MHz	83.3 MHz
Number of bus masters	multiple	multiple	multiple
Bandwidth per port, peak	960 MB/sec	1,700 MB/sec	1,300 MB/sec
Bandwidth total, peak	7,680 MB/sec	14,200 MB/sec	10,667 MB/sec
Clocking	synchronous	synchronous	synchronous
Standard	none	none	none

Figure 7.14 **Summary of CPU-memory interconnects found in 2001 servers.** These servers use crossbar switches to connect processors together instead of a shared bus interconnect. Each bus connects up to four processors and memory controllers, and then the crossbar connects the buses together. The number of slots in the crossbar is 16, 8, and 16, respectively.

Interfacing Storage Devices to the CPU

Having described I/O devices and looked at some of the issues of the connecting bus, we are ready to discuss the CPU end of the interface. The first question is where the physical connection of the I/O bus should be made. The two choices are connecting the bus to memory or to the cache. In this section, we examine the more usual case in which the I/O bus is connected to the main memory bus. Figure 7.15 shows a typical organization for desktops. In low-cost systems, the I/O bus *is* the memory bus; this means an I/O command on the bus could interfere with a CPU instruction fetch, for example.

Once the physical interface is chosen, the question becomes, How does the CPU address an I/O device that it needs to send or receive data? The most common practice is called *memory-mapped* I/O. In this scheme, portions of the machine's address space are assigned to I/O devices. Reads and writes to those addresses may cause data to be transferred; some portion of the I/O space may also be set aside for device control, so commands to the device are just accesses to those memory-mapped addresses.

The alternative practice is to use dedicated I/O opcodes in the CPU. In this case, the CPU sends a signal that this address is for I/O devices. Examples of computers with I/O instructions are the Intel 80x86 and the IBM 370 computers. I/O opcodes have been waning in popularity.

No matter which addressing scheme is selected, each I/O device has registers to provide status and control information. Through either loads and stores in memory-mapped I/O or through special instructions, the CPU sets flags to determine the operation the I/O device will perform.

Any I/O event is rarely a single operation. For example, the DEC LP11 line printer has two I/O device registers: one for status information and one for data to be printed. The status register contains a *done bit,* set by the printer when it has printed a character, and an *error bit,* indicating that the printer is jammed or out

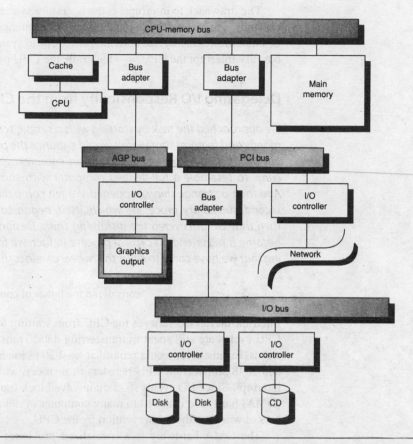

Figure 7.15 A typical interface of I/O devices and an I/O bus to the CPU-memory bus.

of paper. Each byte of data to be printed is put into the data register; the CPU must then wait until the printer sets the done bit before it can place another character in the buffer.

This simple interface, in which the CPU periodically checks status bits to see if it is time for the next I/O operation, is called *polling*. As you might expect, CPUs are so much faster than I/O devices that polling may waste a lot of CPU time. A huge fraction of the CPU cycles must be dedicated to interrogating the I/O device rather than performing useful computation. This inefficiency was recognized long ago, leading to the invention of interrupts that notify the CPU when it is time to service the I/O device.

Interrupt-driven I/O, used by most systems for at least some devices, allows the CPU to work on some other process while waiting for the I/O device. For example, the LP11 has a mode that allows it to interrupt the CPU whenever the done bit or error bit is set. In general-purpose applications, interrupt-driven I/O is the key to multitasking operating systems and good response times.

The drawback to interrupts is the operating system overhead on each event. In real-time applications with hundreds of I/O events per second, this overhead can be intolerable. One hybrid solution for real-time systems is to use a clock to periodically interrupt the CPU, at which time the CPU polls all I/O devices.

Delegating I/O Responsibility from the CPU

We approached the task by starting with a simple scheme and then adding commands and features that we felt would enhance the power of the machine. Gradually the [display] processor became more complex.... Finally the display processor came to resemble a full-fledged computer with some special graphics features. And then a strange thing happened. We felt compelled to add to the processor a second, subsidiary processor, which, itself, began to grow in complexity. It was then that we discovered the disturbing truth. Designing a display processor can become a never-ending cyclical process. In fact, we found the process so frustrating that we have come to call it the "wheel of reincarnation."

Ivan Sutherland
considered the father of computer graphics (1968)

Interrupt-driven I/O relieves the CPU from waiting for every I/O event, but many CPU cycles are still spent in transferring data. Transferring a disk block of 2048 words, for instance, would require at least 2048 loads from disk to CPU registers and 2048 stores from CPU registers to memory, as well as the overhead for the interrupt. Since I/O events so often involve block transfers, *direct memory access* (DMA) hardware is added to many computer systems to allow transfers of numbers of words without intervention by the CPU.

The DMA hardware is a specialized processor that transfers data between memory and an I/O device while the CPU goes on with other tasks. Thus, it is external to the CPU and must act as a master on the bus. The CPU first sets up the DMA registers, which contain a memory address and number of bytes to be transferred. More sophisticated DMA devices support *scatter/gather*, whereby a DMA device can write or read data from a list of separate addresses. Once the DMA transfer is complete, the DMA controller interrupts the CPU. There may be multiple DMA devices in a computer system; for example, DMA is frequently part of the controller for an I/O device.

Increasing the intelligence of the DMA device can further unburden the CPU. Devices called *I/O processors* (or *channel controllers*) operate either from fixed programs or from programs downloaded by the operating system. The operating system typically sets up a queue of *I/O control blocks* that contain information such as data location (source and destination) and data size. The I/O processor then takes items from the queue, doing everything requested and sending a single interrupt when the task specified in the I/O control blocks is complete. Whereas the LP11 line printer would cause 4800 interrupts to print a 60-line by 80-character page, an I/O processor could save 4799 of those interrupts.

I/O processors are similar to multiprocessors in that they facilitate several processes being executed simultaneously in the computer system. I/O processors are less general than CPUs, however, since they have dedicated tasks, and thus the parallelism they enable is much more limited. In addition, an I/O processor doesn't normally change information, as a CPU does, but just moves information from one place to another.

Embedded computers are characterized by a rich variety of DMA devices and I/O controllers. For example, Figure 7.16 shows the Au1000, a MIPS processor for embedded applications, which includes about 10 DMA channels and 20 I/O device controllers on chip.

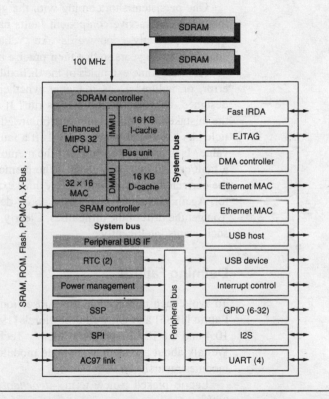

Figure 7.16 The Alchemy Semiconductor Au1000. Embedded devices typically have many DMAs and I/O interconnections, as illustrated in the Au1000. Eight DMA channels are included along with a separate IrDA DMA controller for networking. On-chip controllers include an SDRAM memory controller, a static RAM controller, two Ethernet MAC layer controllers, USB host and device controllers, two interrupt controllers, two 32-bit GPIO buses, and several embedded bus controllers: four UARTs, an SPI, an SSP, an I2S, and an AC97. This MIPS 32 core operates from 200 MHz, at 1.25 V and 200 mW for the whole chip, to 500 MHz, at 1.8 V and 900 mW. The on-chip system bus operates at 1/2 to 1/5 of the MIPS core clock rate.

Now that we have covered the basic types of storage devices and ways to connect them to the CPU, we are ready to look at ways to evaluate the performance of storage systems.

Reliability, Availability, and Dependability

Although people may be willing to live with a computer that occasionally crashes and forces all programs to be restarted, they insist that their information is never lost. The prime directive for storage is then to remember information, no matter what happens.

One persistent shortcoming with the general topic of making computer systems that can survive component faults has been confusion over terms. Consequently, perfectly good words like "reliability" and "availability" have been abused over the years so that their precise meaning is unclear.

Here are some examples of the difficulties. Is a programming mistake a fault, error, or failure? Does it matter whether we are talking about when it was designed, or when the program is run? If the running program doesn't exercise the mistake, is it still a fault/error/failure? Try another one. Suppose an alpha particle hits a DRAM memory cell. Is it a fault/error/failure if it doesn't change the value? Is it a fault/error/failure if the memory doesn't access the changed bit? Did a fault/error/failure still occur if the memory had error correction and delivered the corrected value to the CPU? A third example is a mistake by a human operator. Again, the same issues arise about data change, latency, and observability. You get the drift of the difficulties. Clearly, we need precise definitions to discuss such events intelligently.

Defining Failure

To avoid such imprecision, this subsection is based on the terminology used by Laprie [1985] and Gray and Siewiorek [1991], endorsed by IFIP working group 10.4 and the IEEE Computer Society Technical Committee on Fault Tolerance. We talk about a system as a single module, but the terminology applies to submodules recursively.

Laprie picked a new term—*dependability*—to have a clean slate to work with:

Computer system *dependability* is the quality of delivered service such that reliance can justifiably be placed on this service. The *service* delivered by a system is its observed *actual behavior* as perceived by other system(s) interacting with this system's users. Each module also has an ideal *specified behavior,* where a *service specification* is an agreed description of the expected behavior. A system *failure* occurs when the actual behavior deviates from the specified behavior. The failure occurred because of an *error,* a defect in that module. The cause of an error is a *fault.*

When a fault occurs it creates a *latent error,* which becomes *effective* when it is activated; when the error actually affects the delivered service, a failure occurs. The time between the occurrence of an error and the resulting failure is the *error latency.* Thus, an error is the manifestation *in the system* of a fault, and a failure is the manifestation *on the service* of an error. [p. 3]

Let's go back to our motivating examples above. A programming mistake is a *fault.* The consequence is an *error* (or *latent error*) in the software. Upon activation, the error becomes *effective.* When this effective error produces erroneous data that affect the delivered service, a *failure* occurs.

An alpha particle hitting a DRAM can be considered a fault. If it changes the memory, it creates an error. The error will remain latent until the affected memory word is read. If the effective word error affects the delivered service, a failure occurs. (If ECC corrected the error, a failure would not occur.)

A mistake by a human operator is a fault. The resulting altered data is an error. It is latent until activated, and so on as before.

To clarify, the relation between faults, errors, and failures is as follows:

- A fault creates one or more latent errors.

- The properties of errors are (1) a latent error becomes effective once activated; (2) an error may cycle between its latent and effective states; (3) an effective error often propagates from one component to another, thereby creating new errors. Thus, an effective error either is a formerly latent error in that component or has propagated from another error in that component or from elsewhere.

- A component failure occurs when the error affects the delivered service.

- These properties are recursive and apply to any component in the system.

We can now return to see how Laprie defines reliability and availability. Users perceive a system alternating between two states of delivered service with respect to the service specification:

1. *Service accomplishment,* where the service is delivered as specified

2. *Service interruption,* where the delivered service is different from the specified service

Transitions between these two states are caused by failures (from state 1 to state 2) or *restorations* (2 to 1). Quantifying these transitions leads to the two main measures of dependability:

- *Module reliability* is a measure of the continuous service accomplishment (or, equivalently, of the time to failure) from a reference initial instant. Hence, the mean time to failure (MTTF) of disks in Figure 7.2 is a reliability measure. The reciprocal of MTTF is a rate of failures. If a collection of modules have exponentially distributed lifetimes (see Section 7.7), the overall failure rate of the collection is the sum of the failure rates of the modules. Service interruption is measured as mean time to repair (MTTR).

■ *Module availability* is a measure of the service accomplishment with respect to the alternation between the two states of accomplishment and interruption. For nonredundant systems with repair, module availability is statistically quantified as

$$\text{Module availability} = \frac{\text{MTTF}}{(\text{MTTF} + \text{MTTR})}$$

Note that reliability and availability are now quantifiable metrics, rather than synonyms for dependability. *Mean time between failures* (MTBF) is simply the sum of MTTF + MTTR. Although MTBF is widely used, MTTF is often the more appropriate term.

Example   Assume a disk subsystem with the following components and MTTF:

■ 10 disks, each rated at 1,000,000-hour MTTF

■ 1 SCSI controller, 500,000-hour MTTF

■ 1 power supply, 200,000-hour MTTF

■ 1 fan, 200,000-hour MTTF

■ 1 SCSI cable, 1,000,000-hour MTTF

Using the simplifying assumptions that the components lifetimes are exponentially distributed—which means that the age of the component is not important in probability of failure—and that failures are independent, compute the MTTF of the system as a whole.

Answer   The sum of the failure rates is

$$\text{Failure rate}_{\text{system}} = 10 \times \frac{1}{1,000,000} + \frac{1}{500,000} + \frac{1}{200,000} + \frac{1}{200,000} + \frac{1}{1,000,000}$$

$$= \frac{10 + 2 + 5 + 5 + 1}{1,000,000 \text{ hours}} = \frac{23}{1,000,000 \text{ hours}}$$

The MTTF for the system is just the inverse of the failure rate:

$$\text{MTTF}_{\text{system}} = \frac{1}{\text{Failure rate}_{\text{system}}} = \frac{1,000,000 \text{ hours}}{23} = 43,500 \text{ hours}$$

or just under 5 years.

Classifying faults and fault tolerance techniques may aid with understanding. Gray and Siewiorek classify faults into four categories according to their cause:

1. *Hardware faults*—Devices that fail

2. *Design faults*—Faults in software (usually) and hardware design (occasionally)

3. *Operation faults*—Mistakes by operations and maintenance personnel

4. *Environmental faults*—Fire, flood, earthquake, power failure, and sabotage

Faults are also classified by their duration into transient, intermittent, and permanent [Nelson 1990]. *Transient faults* exist for a limited time and are not recurring. *Intermittent faults* cause a system to oscillate between faulty and fault-free operation. *Permanent faults* do not correct themselves with the passing of time.

Gray and Siewiorek divide improvements in module reliability into *valid construction* and *error correction.* Validation removes faults before the module is completed, ensuring that the module conforms to its specified behavior. Error correction occurs by having redundancy in designs to tolerate faults. *Latent error processing* describes the practice of trying to detect and repair errors before they become effective, such as preventative maintenance. *Effective error processing* describes correction of the error after it becomes effective, either by *masking* the error or by *recovering* from the error. Error correction, such as that used in disk sectors, can mask errors. Error recovery is either *backward* (returning to a previous correct state, such as with checkpoint-restart) or *forward* (constructing a new correct state, such as by resending a disk block).

Taking a slightly different view, Laprie divides reliability improvements into four methods:

1. *Fault avoidance*—How to prevent, by *construction,* fault occurrence

2. *Fault tolerance*—How to provide, by *redundancy,* service complying with the service specification in spite of faults having occurred or that are occurring

3. *Error removal*—How to minimize, by *verification,* the presence of latent errors

4. *Error forecasting*—How to estimate, by *evaluation,* the presence, creation, and consequences of errors

7.5   RAID: Redundant Arrays of Inexpensive Disks

An innovation that improves both dependability and performance of storage systems is *disk arrays.* One argument for arrays is that potential throughput can be increased by having many disk drives and, hence, many disk arms, rather than one large drive with one disk arm. For example, Figure 7.32 on page 733 shows how NFS throughput increases as the systems expand from 67 disks to 433 disks. Simply spreading data over multiple disks, called *striping,* automatically forces accesses to several disks. (Although arrays improve throughput, latency is not necessarily improved.) The drawback to arrays is that with more devices, dependability decreases: N devices generally have $1/N$ the reliability of a single device.

Although a disk array would have more faults than a smaller number of larger disks when each disk has the same reliability, dependability can be improved by adding redundant disks to the array to tolerate faults. That is, if a single disk fails, the lost information can be reconstructed from redundant information. The only danger is in having another disk fail between the time the first disk fails and the time it is replaced (termed *mean time to repair,* or MTTR). Since the *mean time to failure* (MTTF) of disks is tens of years, and the MTTR is measured in hours, redundancy can make the measured reliability of 100 disks much higher than that of a single disk. These systems have become known by the acronym *RAID,* standing originally for *redundant array of inexpensive disks,* although some have renamed it to *redundant array of independent disks* (see Section 7.16).

The several approaches to redundancy have different overhead and performance. Figure 7.17 shows the standard RAID levels. It shows how eight disks of user data must be supplemented by redundant or check disks at each RAID level. It also shows the minimum number of disk failures that a system would survive.

One problem is discovering when a disk faults. Fortunately, magnetic disks provide information about their correct operation. As mentioned in Section 7.2, extra check information is recorded in each sector to discover errors within that sector. As long as we transfer at least one sector and check the error detection information when reading sectors, electronics associated with disks will, with very high probability, discover when a disk fails or loses information.

Another issue in the design of RAID systems is decreasing the mean time to repair. This reduction is typically done by adding *hot spares* to the system—extra disks that are not used in normal operation. When a failure occurs on an active disk in a RAID, an idle hot spare is first pressed into service. The data missing

RAID level		Minimum number of disk faults survived	Example data disks	Corresponding check disks	Corporations producing RAID products at this level
0	Nonredundant striped	0	8	0	widely used
1	Mirrored	1	8	8	EMC, Compaq (Tandem), IBM
2	Memory-style ECC	1	8	4	
3	Bit-interleaved parity	1	8	1	Storage Concepts
4	Block-interleaved parity	1	8	1	Network Appliance
5	Block-interleaved distributed parity	1	8	1	widely used
6	P + Q redundancy	2	8	2	

Figure 7.17 RAID levels, their fault tolerance, and their overhead in redundant disks. The paper that introduced the term *RAID* [Patterson, Gibson, and Katz 1987] used a numerical classification that has become popular. In fact, the nonredundant disk array is often called RAID 0, indicating the data are striped across several disks but without redundancy. Note that mirroring (RAID 1) in this instance can survive up to eight disk failures provided only one disk of each mirrored pair fails; worst case is both disks in a mirrored pair. RAID 6 has a regular RAID 5 parity block across drives along with a second parity block on another drive. RAID 6 allows failure of any two drives, which is beyond the survival capability of RAID 5. In 2001, there may be no commercial implementations of RAID 2 or RAID 6; the rest are found in a wide range of products. RAID 0 + 1, 1 + 0, 01, and 10 are discussed in the text.

from the failed disk are then reconstructed onto the hot spare using the redundant data from the other RAID disks. If this process is performed automatically, MTTR is significantly reduced because waiting for the operator in the repair process is no longer the pacing item (see Section 7.9).

A related issue is *hot swapping*. Systems with hot swapping allow components to be replaced without shutting down the computer. Hence, a system with hot spares and hot swapping need never go offline; the missing data are constructed immediately onto spares, and the broken component is replaced to replenish the spare pool.

We cover here the most popular of these RAID levels; for more detail, see Chen et al. [1994].

No Redundancy (RAID 0)

This notation refers to a disk array in which data are striped but there is no redundancy to tolerate disk failure. Striping across a set of disks makes the collection appear to software as a single large disk, which simplifies storage management. It also improves performance for large accesses, since many disks can operate at once. Video-editing systems, for example, often stripe their data.

RAID 0 is something of a misnomer as there is no redundancy, it is not in the original RAID taxonomy, and striping predates RAID. However, RAID levels are often left to the operator to set when creating a storage system, and RAID 0 is often listed as one of the options. Hence, the term RAID 0 has become widely used.

Mirroring (RAID 1)

This traditional scheme for tolerating disk failure, called *mirroring* or *shadowing*, uses twice as many disks as does RAID 0. Whenever data are written to one disk, those data are also written to a redundant disk, so that there are always two copies of the information. If a disk fails, the system just goes to the "mirror" to get the desired information. Mirroring is the most expensive RAID solution, since it requires the most disks.

One issue is how mirroring interacts with striping. Suppose you had, say, four disks worth of data to store and eight physical disks to use. Would you create four pairs of disks—each organized as RAID 1—and then stripe data across the four RAID 1 pairs? Alternatively, would you create two sets of four disks—each organized as RAID 0—and then mirror writes to both RAID 0 sets? The RAID terminology has evolved to call the former RAID 1 + 0 or RAID 10 ("striped mirrors") and the latter RAID 0 + 1 or RAID 01 ("mirrored stripes").

Bit-Interleaved Parity (RAID 3)

The cost of higher availability can be reduced to $1/N$, where N is the number of disks in a *protection group*. Rather than have a complete copy of the original data for each disk, we need only add enough redundant information to restore the lost information on a failure. Reads or writes go to all disks in the group, with one extra disk to hold the check information in case there is a failure. RAID 3 is popular in applications with large data sets, such as multimedia and some scientific codes.

Parity is one such scheme. Readers unfamiliar with parity can think of the redundant disk as having the sum of all the data in the other disks. When a disk fails, then you subtract all the data in the good disks from the parity disk; the remaining information must be the missing information. Parity is simply the sum modulo two. The assumption behind this technique is that failures are so rare that taking longer to recover from failure but reducing redundant storage is a good trade-off.

Just as direct-mapped associative placement in caches can be considered a special case of set-associative placement (see Section 5.2), the mirroring can be considered the special case of one data disk and one parity disk ($N = 1$). Parity can be accomplished in this case by duplicating the data, so mirrored disks have the advantage of simplifying parity calculation. Duplicating data also means that the controller can improve read performance by reading from the disk of the pair that has the shortest seek distance. This optimization means the arms are no longer synchronized, however, and thus writes must now wait for the arm with the longer seek. Of course, the redundancy of $N = 1$ has the highest overhead for increasing disk availability.

Block-Interleaved Parity and Distributed Block-Interleaved Parity (RAID 4 and RAID 5)

Both these levels use the same ratio of data disks and check disks as RAID 3, but they access data differently. The parity is stored as blocks and associated with a set of data blocks.

In RAID 3, every access went to all disks. Some applications would prefer to do smaller accesses, allowing independent accesses to occur in parallel. That is the purpose of the next RAID levels. Since error detection information in each sector is checked on reads to see if data are correct, such "small reads" to each disk can occur independently as long as the minimum access is one sector.

Writes are another matter. It would seem that each small write would demand that all other disks be accessed to read the rest of the information needed to recalculate the new parity, as in Figure 7.18. A "small write" would require reading the old data and old parity, adding the new information, and then writing the new parity to the parity disk and the new data to the data disk.

The key insight to reduce this overhead is that parity is simply a sum of information; by watching which bits change when we write the new information, we need only change the corresponding bits on the parity disk. Figure 7.18 shows the shortcut. We must read the old data from the disk being written, compare old data to the new data to see which bits change, read the old parity, change the corresponding bits, then write the new data and new parity. Thus, the small write involves four disk accesses to two disks instead of accessing all disks. This organization is RAID 4.

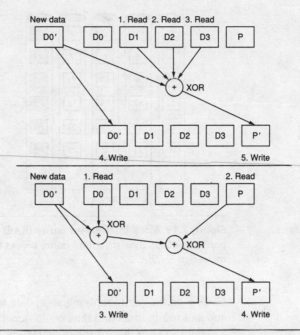

Figure 7.18 Small write update on RAID 3 versus RAID 4/RAID 5. This optimization for small writes reduces the number of disk accesses as well as the number of disks occupied. This figure assumes we have four blocks of data and one block of parity. The straightforward RAID 3 parity calculation at the top of the figure reads blocks D1, D2, and D3 before adding block D0′ to calculate the new parity P′. (In case you were wondering, the new data D0′ comes directly from the CPU, so disks are not involved in reading it.) The RAID 4/RAID 5 shortcut at the bottom reads the old value D0 and compares it to the new value D0′ to see which bits will change. You then read to old parity P and then change the corresponding bits to form P′. The logical function exclusive or does exactly what we want. This example replaces three disk reads (D1, D2, D3) and two disk writes (D0′, P′) involving all the disks for two disk reads (D0, P) and two disk writes (D0′, P′), which involve just two disks. Increasing the size of the parity group increases the savings of the shortcut.

RAID 4 efficiently supports a mixture of large reads, large writes, small reads, and small writes. One drawback to the system is that the parity disk must be updated on every write, so it is the bottleneck for back-to-back writes. To fix the parity-write bottleneck, the parity information can be spread throughout all the disks so that there is no single bottleneck for writes. The distributed parity organization is RAID 5.

Figure 7.19 shows how data are distributed in RAID 4 versus RAID 5. As the organization on the right shows, in RAID 5 the parity associated with each row of data blocks is no longer restricted to a single disk. This organization allows multiple writes to occur simultaneously as long as the stripe units are not located in the same disks. For example, a write to block 8 on the right must also access its parity block P2, thereby occupying the first and third disks. A second write to

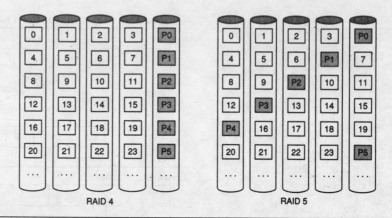

Figure 7.19 Block-interleaved parity (RAID 4) versus distributed block-interleaved parity (RAID 5). By distributing parity blocks to all disks, some small writes can be performed in parallel.

block 5 on the right, implying an update to its parity block P1, accesses the second and fourth disks and thus could occur at the same time as the write to block 8. Those same writes to the organization on the left would result in changes to blocks P1 and P2, both on the fifth disk, which would be a bottleneck.

P + Q Redundancy (RAID 6)

Parity-based schemes protect against a single self-identifying failure. When a single failure correction is not sufficient, parity can be generalized to have a second calculation over the data and another check disk of information. This second check block allows recovery from a second failure. (This second check must be more complicated than simple parity; see Blaum [1994] for details.) Thus, the storage overhead is twice that of RAID 5. The small write shortcut of Figure 7.18 works as well, except now there are six disk accesses instead of four to update both P and Q information.

RAID Summary

The higher throughput, measured either as megabytes per second or as I/Os per second, as well the ability to recover from failures make RAID attractive. When combined with the advantages of smaller size and lower power of small-diameter drives, RAIDs now dominate large-scale storage systems.

7.6 Errors and Failures in Real Systems

Publications of real error rates are rare for two reasons. First, academics rarely have access to significant hardware resources to measure. Second, industrial researchers are rarely allowed to publish failure information for fear that it would be used against their companies in the marketplace. Following are four exceptions.

Berkeley's Tertiary Disk

The Tertiary Disk project at the University of California created an art image server for the Fine Arts Museums of San Francisco. This database consists of high-quality images of over 70,000 artworks. The database was stored on a cluster, which consisted of 20 PCs containing 368 disks connected by a switched Ethernet. It occupied seven 7-foot-high racks.

Figure 7.20 shows the failure rates of the various components of Tertiary Disk. In advance of building the system, the designers assumed that data disks would be the least reliable part of the system, as they are both mechanical and plentiful. Next would be the IDE disks, since there were fewer of them, then the power supplies, followed by integrated circuits. They assumed that passive devices like cables would scarcely ever fail.

Component	Total in system	Total failed	Percentage failed
SCSI controller	44	1	2.3%
SCSI cable	39	1	2.6%
SCSI disk	368	7	1.9%
IDE disk	24	6	25.0%
Disk enclosure—backplane	46	13	28.3%
Disk enclosure—power supply	92	3	3.3%
Ethernet controller	20	1	5.0%
Ethernet switch	2	1	50.0%
Ethernet cable	42	1	2.3%
CPU/motherboard	20	0	0%

Figure 7.20 Failures of components in Tertiary Disk over 18 months of operation. For each type of component, the table shows the total number in the system, the number that failed, and the percentage failure rate. Disk enclosures have two entries in the table because they had two types of problems, backplane integrity failure and power supply failure. Since each enclosure had two power supplies, a power supply failure did not affect availability. This cluster of 20 PCs, contained in seven 7-foot-high, 19-inch-wide racks, hosts 368 8.4 GB, 7200 RPM, 3.5-inch IBM disks. The PCs are P6-200MHz with 96 MB of DRAM each. They run FreeBSD 3.0 and the hosts are connected via switched 100 Mbit/second Ethernet. All SCSI disks are connected to two PCs via double-ended SCSI chains to support RAID 1. The primary application is called the Zoom Project, which in 1998 was the world's largest art image database, with 72,000 images. See Talagala et al. [2000].

Figure 7.20 shatters those assumptions. Since the designers followed the manufacturer's advice of making sure the disk enclosures had reduced vibration and good cooling, the data disks were very reliable. In contrast, the PC chassis containing the IDE disks did not afford the same environmental controls. (The IDE disks did not store data, but helped the application and operating system to boot the PCs.) Figure 7.20 shows that the SCSI backplane, cables, and Ethernet cables were no more reliable than the data disks themselves!

As Tertiary Disk was a large system with many redundant components, it had the potential to survive this wide range of failures. Components were connected and mirrored images were placed so that no single failure could make any image unavailable. This strategy, which initially appeared to be overkill, proved to be vital.

This experience also demonstrated the difference between transient faults and hard faults. *Transient faults* are faults that come and go, at least temporarily fixing themselves. *Hard faults* stop the device from working properly and will continue to misbehave until repaired. Virtually all the failures in Figure 7.20 appeared first as transient faults. It was up to the operator to decide if the behavior was so poor that they needed to be replaced or if they could continue. In fact, the word "failure" was not used; instead, the group borrowed terms normally used for dealing with problem employees, with the operator deciding whether a problem component should or should not be "fired." Section 7.14 gives examples of transient and hard failures.

Tandem

The next example comes from industry. Gray [1990] collected data on faults for Tandem Computers, which was one of the pioneering companies in fault-tolerant computing. Figure 7.21 graphs the faults that caused system failures between 1985 and 1989 in absolute faults per system and in percentage of faults encountered. The data show a clear improvement in the reliability of hardware and maintenance. Disks in 1985 needed yearly service by Tandem, but they were replaced by disks that needed no scheduled maintenance. Shrinking numbers of chips and connectors per system plus software's ability to tolerate hardware faults reduced hardware's contribution to only 7% of failures by 1989. And when hardware was at fault, software embedded in the hardware device (firmware) was often the culprit. The data indicate that software in 1989 was the major source of reported outages (62%), followed by system operations (15%).

The problem with any such statistics is that these data only refer to what is reported; for example, environmental failures due to power outages were not reported to Tandem because they were seen as a local problem. Data on operation faults is very difficult to collect because it relies on the operators to report personal mistakes, which may affect the opinion of their managers, which in turn can affect job security and pay raises. Gray believes both environmental faults and operator faults are underreported. His study concluded that achieving higher availability requires improvement in software quality and software fault tolerance, simpler operations, and tolerance of operational faults.

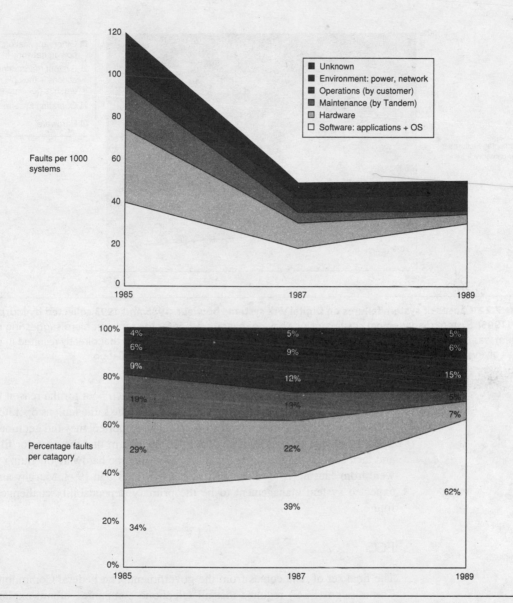

Figure 7.21 Faults in Tandem between 1985 and 1989. Gray [1990] collected these data for the fault-tolerant Tandem computers based on reports of component failures by customers.

VAX

The next example is also from industry. Murphy and Gent [1995] measured faults in VAX systems. They classified faults as hardware, operating system, system management, or application/networking. Figure 7.22 shows their data for 1985 and 1993. They tried to improve the accuracy of data on operator faults by having

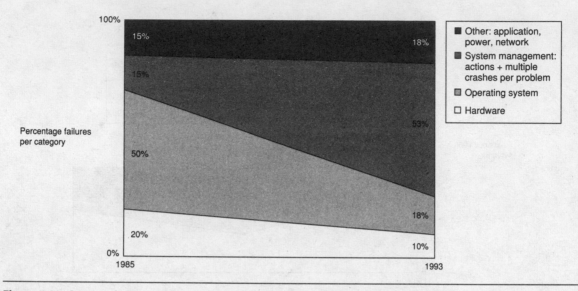

Figure 7.22 Causes of system failures on Digital VAX systems between 1985 and 1993 collected by Murphy and Gent [1995]. System management crashes include having several crashes for the same problem, suggesting that the problem was difficult for the operator to diagnose. It also included operator actions that directly resulted in crashes, such as giving parameters bad values, bad configurations, and bad application installation.

the system automatically prompt the operator on each boot for the reason for that reboot. They also classified consecutive crashes to the same fault as operator fault. Although they believe operator error is still underreported, they did get more accurate information than did Gray, who relied on a form that the operator filled out and then sent up the management chain. Note that the hardware/operating system went from causing 70% of the failures in 1985 to 28% in 1993. Murphy and Gent expected system management to be the primary dependability challenge in the future.

FCC

The final set of data comes from the government. The Federal Communications Commission (FCC) requires that all telephone companies submit explanations when they experience an outage that affects at least 30,000 people or lasts 30 minutes. These detailed disruption reports do not suffer from the self-reporting problem of earlier figures, as investigators determine the cause of the outage rather than operators of the equipment. Kuhn [1997] studied the causes of outages between 1992 and 1994, and Enriquez [2001] did a follow-up study for the first half of 2001. In addition to reporting number of outages, the FCC data include the number of customers affected and how long they were affected. Hence, we can look at the size and scope of failures, rather than assuming that all are equally important. Figure 7.23 plots the absolute and relative number of customer-outage minutes for those years, broken into four categories:

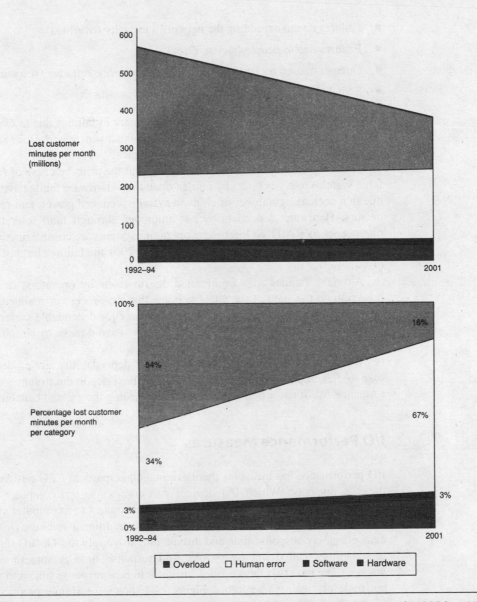

Figure 7.23 Failures in the public switched telephone network (PSTN) according to the FCC in 1992–94 and 2001. Note that, in both absolute and relative terms, overload outages shrank and outages due to human error increased, with human error responsible for two-thirds of the outages for this graph in 2001. These charts leave out two categories collected by Kuhn [1997] and Enriquez [2001], vandalism and nature. Vandalism is less than 1% of customer minutes and was not included because it was too small to plot. Nature is a very significant cause of outages in PSTN, as fires and floods can be extensive and their damage takes a while to repair. Nature was not included because it has little relevance for indication of failures in computer systems. Customer minutes multiplies the number of customers potentially affected by the length of the outage to indicate the size of the outage. Enriquez [2001] also reports blocked calls, which means calls that could not be made due to the outage. Blocked calls differentiate impact of outages during the middle of the day versus in 2001 the middle of the night. Blocked-call data also suggests human error is the most important challenge for outages.

- Failures due to exceeding the network's capacity (overload)
- Failures due to people (human error)
- Outages caused by faults in the telephone network software (software)
- Switch failure, cable failure, and power failure (hardware)

Although there was a significant improvement in failures due to overloading of the network over the years, failures due to humans increased, from about one-third to two-thirds of the customer-outage minutes.

These four examples and others suggest that the primary cause of failures in large systems today is faults by human operators. Hardware faults have declined due to a decreasing number of chips in systems, reduced power, and fewer connectors. Hardware dependability has improved through fault tolerance techniques such as RAID. At least some operating systems are considering reliability implications before adding new features, so in 2001 the failures largely occurred elsewhere.

Although failures may be initiated due to faults by operators, it is a poor reflection on the state of the art of systems that the process of maintenance and upgrading are so error prone. Thus, the challenge for dependable systems of the future is either to tolerate faults by operators or to avoid faults by simplifying the tasks of system administration.

We have now covered the bedrock issue of dependability, giving definitions, case studies, and techniques to improve it. The next step in the storage tour is performance. We'll cover performance metrics, queuing theory, and benchmarks.

7.7   I/O Performance Measures

I/O performance has measures that have no counterparts in CPU design. One of these is diversity: Which I/O devices can connect to the computer system? Another is capacity: How many I/O devices can connect to a computer system?

In addition to these unique measures, the traditional measures of performance, namely, response time and throughput, also apply to I/O. (I/O throughput is sometimes called *I/O bandwidth,* and response time is sometimes called *latency.*) The next two figures offer insight into how response time and throughput trade off against each other. Figure 7.24 shows the simple producer-server model. The producer creates tasks to be performed and places them in a buffer; the server takes tasks from the first in, first out buffer and performs them.

Response time is defined as the time a task takes from the moment it is placed in the buffer until the server finishes the task. Throughput is simply the average number of tasks completed by the server over a time period. To get the highest possible throughput, the server should never be idle, and thus the buffer should never be empty. Response time, on the other hand, counts time spent in the buffer and is therefore minimized by the buffer being empty.

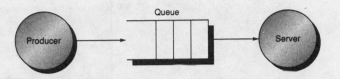

Figure 7.24 The traditional producer-server model of response time and throughput. Response time begins when a task is placed in the buffer and ends when it is completed by the server. Throughput is the number of tasks completed by the server in unit time.

Another measure of I/O performance is the interference of I/O with CPU execution. Transferring data may interfere with the execution of another process. There is also overhead due to handling I/O interrupts. Our concern here is how much longer a process will take because of I/O for another process.

Throughput versus Response Time

Figure 7.25 shows throughput versus response time (or latency) for a typical I/O system. The knee of the curve is the area where a little more throughput results in much longer response time or, conversely, a little shorter response time results in much lower throughput.

How does the architect balance these conflicting demands? If the computer is interacting with human beings, Figure 7.26 suggests an answer. This figure presents the results of two studies of interactive environments: one keyboard oriented and one graphical. An interaction, or *transaction*, with a computer is divided into three parts:

1. *Entry time*—The time for the user to enter the command. The graphics system in Figure 7.26 required 0.25 seconds on average to enter a command versus 4.0 seconds for the keyboard system.

2. *System response time*—The time between when the user enters the command and the complete response is displayed.

3. *Think time*—The time from the reception of the response until the user begins to enter the next command.

The sum of these three parts is called the *transaction time*. Several studies report that user productivity is inversely proportional to transaction time; *transactions per hour* are a measure of the work completed per hour by the user.

The results in Figure 7.26 show that reduction in response time actually decreases transaction time by more than just the response time reduction. Cutting system response time by 0.7 seconds saves 4.9 seconds (34%) from the conventional transaction and 2.0 seconds (70%) from the graphics transaction. This implausible result is explained by human nature: People need less time to think when given a faster response.

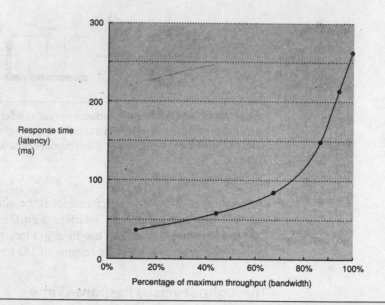

Figure 7.25 Throughput versus response time. Latency is normally reported as response time. Note that the minimum response time achieves only 11% of the throughput, while the response time for 100% throughput takes seven times the minimum response time. Note that the independent variable in this curve is implicit: to trace the curve, you typically vary load (concurrency). Chen et al. [1990] collected these data for an array of magnetic disks.

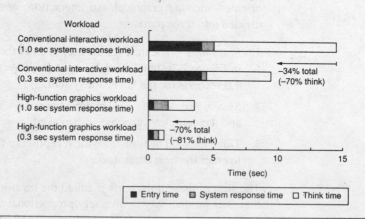

Figure 7.26 A user transaction with an interactive computer divided into entry time, system response time, and user think time for a conventional system and graphics system. The entry times are the same, independent of system response time. The entry time was 4 seconds for the conventional system and 0.25 seconds for the graphics system. (From Brady [1986].)

Whether these results are explained as a better match to the human attention span or getting people "on a roll," several studies report this behavior. In fact, as computer response times drop below 1 second, productivity seems to make a more than linear jump. Figure 7.27 compares transactions per hour (the inverse of transaction time) of a novice, an average engineer, and an expert performing physical design tasks on graphics displays. System response time magnified talent: A novice with subsecond system response time was as productive as an experienced professional with slower response, and the experienced engineer in turn could outperform the expert with a similar advantage in response time. In all cases the number of transactions per hour jumps more than linearly with subsecond response time.

Since humans may be able to get much more work done per day with better response time, it is possible to attach an economic benefit to lowering response time into the subsecond range [IBM 1982]. This assessment helps the architect decide how to tip the balance between response time and throughput.

Although these studies were on older machines, people's patience has not changed. It is still a problem today because response times are often still much longer than a second, even if hardware is 1000 times faster. Examples of long delays include starting an application on a desktop PC due to many disk I/Os, or network delays when clicking on Web links.

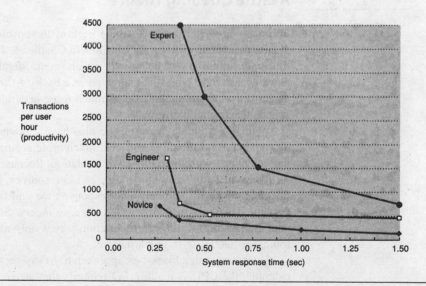

Figure 7.27 Transactions per hour versus computer response time for a novice, experienced engineer, and expert doing physical design on a graphics system. *Transactions per hour* are a measure of productivity. (From IBM [1982].)

I/O benchmark	Response time restriction	Throughput metric
TPC-C: Complex Query OLTP	≥ 90% of transaction must meet response time limit; 5 seconds for most types of transactions	new order transactions per minute
TPC-W: Transactional Web benchmark	≥ 90% of Web interactions must meet response time limit; 3 seconds for most types of Web interactions	Web interactions per second
SPECsfs97	average response time ≤ 40 ms	NFS operations per second

Figure 7.28 Response time restrictions for three I/O benchmarks.

Response Time versus Throughput in Benchmarks

I/O benchmarks offer another perspective on the response time versus throughput trade-off. Figure 7.28 shows the response time restrictions for three I/O benchmarks. The two reporting approaches report maximum throughput given either that 90% of response times must be less than a limit or that the average response time must be less than a limit.

7.8   A Little Queuing Theory

In processor design we have simple back-of-the-envelope calculations of performance associated with the CPI formula in Chapter 1. The next step in accuracy is full-scale simulation of the system, which is considerably more work. In I/O systems we also have a best-case analysis as a back-of-the-envelope calculation, and again full-scale simulation is also much more accurate and much more work to calculate expected performance.

With I/O systems, however, we also have a mathematical tool to guide I/O design that is a little more work and much more accurate than best-case analysis, but much less work than full-scale simulation. Because of the probabilistic nature of I/O events and because of sharing of I/O resources, we can give a set of simple theorems that will help calculate response time and throughput of an entire I/O system. This helpful field is called *queuing theory*. Since there are many books and courses on the subject, this section serves only as a first introduction to the topic; see Section 7.16 to learn more.

Let's start with a black-box approach to I/O systems, as in Figure 7.29. In our example, the CPU is making I/O requests that arrive at the I/O device, and the requests "depart" when the I/O device fulfills them.

We are usually interested in the long term, or steady state, of a system rather than in the initial start-up conditions. Suppose we weren't. Although there is a mathematics that helps (Markov chains), except for a few cases, the only way to solve the resulting equations is simulation. Since the purpose of this section is to show something a little harder than back-of-the-envelope calculations but less

Figure 7.29 Treating the I/O system as a black box. This leads to a simple but important observation: If the system is in steady state, then the number of tasks entering the system must equal the number of tasks leaving the system. This *flow-balanced* state is necessary but not sufficient for steady state. If the system has been observed or measured for a sufficiently long time and mean waiting times stabilize, then we say that the system has reached steady state.

than simulation, we won't cover such analyses here. (See the references at the end of this chapter for more details.)

Hence, in this section we make the simplifying assumption that we are evaluating systems with multiple independent requests for I/O service that are in equilibrium: the input rate must be equal to the output rate. We also assume there is a steady supply of tasks, for in many real systems the task consumption rate is determined by system characteristics such as capacity. TPC-C is one example.

This leads us to *Little's Law,* which relates the average number of tasks in the system, the average arrival rate of new tasks, and the average time to perform a task:

$$\text{Mean number of tasks in system} = \text{Arrival rate} \times \text{Mean response time}$$

Little's Law applies to any system in equilibrium, as long as nothing inside the black box is creating new tasks or destroying them. Note that the arrival rate and the response time must use the same time unit; inconsistency in time units is a common cause of errors.

Let's try to derive Little's Law. Assume we observe a system for $\text{Time}_{observe}$ minutes. During that observation, we record how long it took each task to be serviced, and then sum those times. The number of tasks completed during $\text{Time}_{observe}$ is Number_{task}, and the sum of the times each task spends in the system is $\text{Time}_{accumulated}$. Then

$$\text{Mean number of tasks in system} = \frac{\text{Time}_{accumulated}}{\text{Time}_{observe}}$$

$$\text{Mean response time} = \frac{\text{Time}_{accumulated}}{\text{Number}_{tasks}}$$

Algebra lets us split the first formula:

$$\frac{\text{Time}_{accumulated}}{\text{Time}_{observe}} = \frac{\text{Time}_{accumulated}}{\text{Number}_{tasks}} \times \frac{\text{Number}_{tasks}}{\text{Time}_{observe}}$$

Since the following definitions hold

$$\text{Mean number of tasks in system} = \frac{\text{Time}_{\text{accumulated}}}{\text{Time}_{\text{observe}}}$$

$$\text{Mean response time} = \frac{\text{Time}_{\text{accumulated}}}{\text{Number}_{\text{tasks}}}$$

$$\text{Arrival rate} = \frac{\text{Number}_{\text{tasks}}}{\text{Time}_{\text{observe}}}$$

if we substitute these three definitions into the previous formula, and swap the resulting two terms on the right-hand side, we get Little's Law:

$$\text{Mean number of tasks in system} = \text{Arrival rate} \times \text{Mean response time}$$

This simple equation is surprisingly powerful, as we shall see.

If we open the black box, we see Figure 7.30. The area where the tasks accumulate, waiting to be serviced, is called the *queue,* or *waiting line,* and the device performing the requested service is called the *server.* Until we get to the last two pages of this section, we assume a single server.

Little's Law and a series of definitions lead to several useful equations:

- $\text{Time}_{\text{server}}$—Average time to service a task; average service rate is $1/\text{Time}_{\text{server}}$, traditionally represented by the symbol μ in many queuing texts.

- $\text{Time}_{\text{queue}}$—Average time per task in the queue.

- $\text{Time}_{\text{system}}$—Average time/task in the system, or the response time, the sum of $\text{Time}_{\text{queue}}$ and $\text{Time}_{\text{server}}$

- Arrival rate—Average number of arriving tasks/second, traditionally represented by the symbol λ in many queuing texts.

- $\text{Length}_{\text{server}}$—Average number of tasks in service.

- $\text{Length}_{\text{queue}}$—Average length of queue.

- $\text{Length}_{\text{system}}$—Average number of tasks in system, the sum of $\text{Length}_{\text{queue}}$ and $\text{Length}_{\text{server}}$.

One common misunderstanding can be made clearer by these definitions: whether the question is how long a task must wait in the queue before service

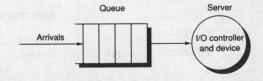

Figure 7.30 The single-server model for this section. In this situation, an I/O request "departs" by being completed by the server.

starts (Time$_{queue}$) or how long a task takes until it is completed (Time$_{system}$). The latter term is what we mean by response time, and the relationship between the terms is Time$_{system}$ = Time$_{queue}$ + Time$_{server}$.

The mean number of tasks in service (Length$_{server}$) is simply Arrival rate × Time$_{server}$, which is Little's Law. Server utilization is simply the mean number of tasks being serviced divided by the service rate. For a single server, the service rate is 1/Time$_{server}$. Server utilization (and, in this case, the mean number of tasks per server) is simply

$$\text{Server utilization} = \text{Arrival rate} \times \text{Time}_{server}$$

The value must be between 0 and 1; otherwise there would be more tasks arriving than could be serviced, violating our assumption that the system is in equilibrium. Note that this formula is just a restatement of Little's Law. Utilization is also called *traffic intensity* and is represented by the symbol ρ in many texts.

Example   Suppose an I/O system with a single disk gets on average 50 I/O requests per second. Assume the average time for a disk to service an I/O request is 10 ms. What is the utilization of the I/O system?

Answer   Using the equation above, with 10 ms represented as 0.01 seconds:

$$\text{Server utilization} = \text{Arrival rate} \times \text{Time}_{server} = \frac{50}{\text{sec}} \times 0.01\,\text{sec} = 0.50$$

Therefore, the I/O system utilization is 0.5.

How the queue delivers tasks to the server is called the *queue discipline*. The simplest and most common discipline is *first in, first out* (FIFO). If we assume FIFO, we can relate time waiting in the queue to the mean number of tasks in the queue:

$$\text{Time}_{queue} = \text{Length}_{queue} \times \text{Timeserver} + \text{Mean time to complete service of task}$$
when new task arrives if server is busy

That is, the time in the queue is the number of tasks in the queue times the mean service time plus the time it takes the server to complete whatever task is being serviced when a new task arrives. (There is one more restriction about the arrival of tasks, which we reveal on page 725.)

The last component of the equation is not as simple as it first appears. A new task can arrive at any instant, so we have no basis to know how long the existing task has been in the server. Although such requests are random events, if we know something about the distribution of events, we can predict performance.

To estimate the last component of the formula we need to know a little about distributions of *random variables*. A variable is random if it takes one of a specified set of values with a specified probability; that is, you cannot know exactly what its next value will be, but you may know the probability of all possible values.

Requests for service from an I/O system can be modeled by a random variable because the operating system is normally switching between several processes that generate independent I/O requests. We also model I/O service times by a random variable given the probabilistic nature of disks in terms of seek and rotational delays.

One way to characterize the distribution of values of a random variable with discrete values is a *histogram,* which divides the range between the minimum and maximum values into subranges called *buckets*. Histograms then plot the number in each bucket as columns. Histograms work well for distributions that are discrete values—for example, the number of I/O requests. For distributions that are not discrete values, such as time waiting for an I/O request, we have two choices. Either we need a curve to plot the values over the full range, so that we can accurately estimate the value, or we need a very fine time unit so that we get a very large number of buckets to accurately estimate time. For example, a histogram can be built of disk service times measured in intervals of 10 μs although disk service times are truly continuous.

Hence, to be able to solve the last part of the previous equation we need to characterize the distribution of this random variable. The mean time and some measure of the variance are sufficient for that characterization.

For the first term, we use the *arithmetic mean time* (see page 36 in Chapter 1 for a slightly different version of the formula). Let's first assume after measuring the number of occurrences, say, n_i, of tasks, you could compute frequency of occurrence of task i:

$$f_i = n_i \bigg/ \left(\sum_{i=1}^{n} n_i \right)$$

Then arithmetic mean is

$$\text{Arithmetic mean time} = f_1 \times T_1 + f_2 \times T_2 + \ldots + f_n \times T_n$$

where T_i is the time for task i and f_i is the frequency of occurrence of task i.

To characterize variability about the mean, many people use the standard deviation. Let's use the *variance* instead, which is simply the square of the standard deviation, as it will help us with characterizing the probability distribution. Given the arithmetic mean, the variance can be calculated as

$$\text{Variance} = (f_1 \times T_1^2 + f_2 \times T_2^2 + \ldots + f_n \times T_n^2) - \text{Arithmetic mean time}^2$$

It is important to remember the units when computing variance. Let's assume the distribution is of time. If time is on the order of 100 milliseconds, then squaring it yields 10,000 square milliseconds. This unit is certainly unusual. It would be more convenient if we had a unitless measure.

To avoid this unit problem, we use the *squared coefficient of variance,* traditionally called C^2:

$$C^2 = \frac{\text{Variance}}{\text{Arithmetic mean time}^2}$$

We can solve for C, the coefficient of variance, as

$$C = \frac{\sqrt{\text{Variance}}}{\text{Arithmetic mean time}} = \frac{\text{Standard deviation}}{\text{Arithmetic mean time}}$$

We are trying to characterize random events, but to be able to predict performance we need a distribution of random events where the mathematics is tractable. The most popular such distribution is the *exponential distribution*, which has a C value of 1.

Note that we are using a constant to characterize variability about the mean. The invariance of C over time reflects the property that the history of events has no impact on the probability of an event occurring now. This forgetful property is called *memoryless*, and this property is an important assumption used to predict behavior using these models. (Suppose this memoryless property did not exist; then we would have to worry about the exact arrival times of requests relative to each other, which would make the mathematics considerably less tractable!)

One of the most widely used exponential distributions is called a *Poisson distribution*, named after the mathematician Simeon Poisson. It is used to characterize random events in a given time interval and has several desirable mathematical properties. The Poisson distribution is described by the following equation (called the probability mass function):

$$\text{probability}(k) = \frac{e^{-a} \times a^k}{k!}$$

where a = Rate of events × Elapsed time. If interarrival times are exponentially distributed and we use arrival rate from above for rate of events, the number of arrivals in a time interval t is a *Poisson process*, which has the Poisson distribution with a = Arrival rate × t. As mentioned on page 723, the equation for Time_{server} has another restriction on task arrival: It holds only for Poisson processes.

Finally, we can answer the question about the length of time a new task must wait for the server to complete a task, called the *average residual service time*, which again assumes Poisson arrivals:

Average residual service time = $1/2 \times$ Weighted mean time $\times (1 + C^2)$

Although we won't derive this formula, we can appeal to intuition. When the distribution is not random and all possible values are equal to the average, the standard deviation is 0 and so C is 0. The average residual service time is then just half the average service time, as we would expect. If the distribution is random and it is Poisson, then C is 1 and the average residual service time equals the weighted mean time.

Example Using the definitions and formulas above, derive the average time waiting in the queue (Time_{queue}) in terms of the average service time (Time_{server}) and server utilization.

Answer All tasks in the queue (Length$_{queue}$) ahead of the new task must be completed before the task can be serviced; each takes on average Time$_{server}$. If a task is at the server, it takes average residual service time to complete. The chance the server is busy is *server utilization;* hence the expected time for service is Server utilization × Average residual service time. This leads to our initial formula:

$$\text{Time}_{queue} = \text{Length}_{queue} \times \text{Time}_{server}$$
$$+ \text{Server utilization} \times \text{Average residual service time}$$

Replacing average residual service time by its definition and Length$_{queue}$ by Arrival rate × Time$_{queue}$ yields

$$\text{Time}_{queue} = \text{Server utilization} \times (1/2 \times \text{Time}_{server} \times (1 + C^2))$$
$$+ (\text{Arrival rate} \times \text{Time}_{queue}) \times \text{Time}_{server}$$

Since this section is concerned with exponential distributions, C^2 is 1. Thus

$$\text{Time}_{queue} = \text{Server utilization} \times \text{Time}_{server} + (\text{Arrival rate} \times \text{Time}_{queue}) \times \text{Time}_{server}$$

Rearranging the last term, let us replace Arrival rate × Time$_{server}$ by Server utilization:

$$\text{Time}_{queue} = \text{Server utilization} \times \text{Time}_{server} + (\text{Arrival rate} \times \text{Time}_{server}) \times \text{Time}_{queue}$$
$$= \text{Server utilization} \times \text{Time}_{server} + \text{Server utilization} \times \text{Time}_{queue}$$

Rearranging terms and simplifying gives us the desired equation:

$$\text{Time}_{queue} = \text{Server utilization} \times \text{Time}_{server} + \text{Server utilization} \times \text{Time}_{queue}$$
$$\text{Time}_{queue} - \text{Server utilization} \times \text{Time}_{queue} = \text{Server utilization} \times \text{Time}_{server}$$
$$\text{Time}_{queue} \times (1 - \text{Server utilization}) = \text{Server utilization} \times \text{Time}_{server}$$
$$\text{Time}_{queue} = \text{Time}_{server} \times \frac{\text{Server utilization}}{(1 - \text{Server utilization})}$$

Little's Law can be applied to the components of the black box as well, since they must also be in equilibrium:

$$\text{Length}_{queue} = \text{Arrival rate} \times \text{Time}_{queue}$$

If we substitute for Time$_{queue}$ from above, we get

$$\text{Length}_{queue} = \text{Arrival rate} \times \text{Time}_{server} \times \frac{\text{Server utilization}}{(1 - \text{Server utilization})}$$

Since Arrival rate × Time$_{server}$ = Server utilization, we can simplify further:

$$\text{Length}_{queue} = \text{Server utilization} \times \frac{\text{Server utilization}}{(1 - \text{Server utilization})} = \frac{\text{Server utilization}^2}{(1 - \text{Server utilization})}$$

Example   For the system in the example on page 723, which has a server utilization of 0.5, what is the mean number of I/O requests in the queue?

Answer   Using the equation above,

$$\text{Length}_{queue} = \frac{\text{Server utilization}^2}{(1 - \text{Server utilization})} = \frac{0.5^2}{(1 - 0.5)} = \frac{0.25}{0.50} = 0.5$$

So there are 0.5 requests on average in the queue.

As mentioned earlier, these equations and this section are based on an area of applied mathematics called queuing theory, which offers equations to predict behavior of such random variables. Real systems are too complex for queuing theory to provide exact analysis, and hence queuing theory works best when only approximate answers are needed.

Queuing theory makes a sharp distinction between past events, which can be characterized by measurements using simple arithmetic, and future events, which are predictions requiring more sophisticated mathematics. In computer systems, we commonly predict the future from the past; one example is least-recently used block replacement (see Chapter 5). Hence, the distinction between measurements and predicted distributions is often blurred; we use measurements to verify the type of distribution and then rely on the distribution thereafter.

Let's review the assumptions about the queuing model:

- The system is in equilibrium.

- The times between two successive requests arriving, called the *interarrival times,* are exponentially distributed, which characterizes the arrival rate mentioned earlier.

- The number of sources of requests is unlimited. (This is called an *infinite population model* in queuing theory; finite population models are used when arrival rates vary with the number of jobs already in the system.)

- The server can start on the next job immediately after finishing with the prior one.

- There is no limit to the length of the queue, and it follows the first in, first out order discipline, so all tasks in line must be completed.

- There is one server.

Such a queue is called *M/M/1:*

M = exponentially random request arrival ($C^2 = 1$), with M standing for A. A. Markov, the mathematician who defined and analyzed the memoryless processes mentioned earlier

M = exponentially random request arrival ($C^2 = 1$), with M again for Markov

1 = single server

The M/M/1 model is a simple and widely used model.

The assumption of exponential distribution is commonly used in queuing examples for three reasons, one good, one fair, and one bad. The good reason is that a superposition of many arbitrary distributions acts as an exponential distribution. Many times in computer systems, a particular behavior is the result of many components interacting, so an exponential distribution of interarrival times is the right model. The fair reason is that when variability is unclear, an exponential distribution with intermediate variability (C = 1) is a safer guess than low variability (C ≈ 0) or high variability (large C). The bad reason is that the math is simpler if you assume exponential distributions.

Let's put queuing theory to work in a few examples.

Example Suppose a processor sends 10 disk I/Os per second, these requests are exponentially distributed, and the average service time of an older disk is 20 ms. Answer the following questions:

1. On average, how utilized is the disk?

2. What is the average time spent in the queue?

3. What is the average response time for a disk request, including the queuing time and disk service time?

Answer Let's restate these facts:

Average number of arriving tasks/second is 40.

Average disk time to service a task is 20 ms (0.02 sec).

The server utilization is then

$$\text{Server utilization} = \text{Arrival rate} \times \text{Time}_{server} = 40 \times 0.02 = 0.8$$

Since the service times are exponentially distributed, we can use the simplified formula for the average time spent waiting in line:

$$\text{Time}_{queue} = \text{Time}_{server} \times \frac{\text{Server utilization}}{(1 - \text{Server utilization})}$$

$$= 20 \text{ ms} \times \frac{0.8}{1 - 0.8} = 20 \times \frac{0.8}{0.2} = 20 \times 4 = 80 \text{ ms}$$

The average response time is

$$\text{Time}_{queue} + \text{Time}_{server} = 80 + 20 \text{ ms} = 100 \text{ ms}$$

Thus, on average we spend 80% of our time waiting in the queue!

Example Suppose we get a new, faster disk. Recalculate the answers to the questions above, assuming the disk service time is 10 ms.

Answer   The disk utilization is then

$$\text{Server utilization} = \text{Arrival rate} \times \text{Time}_{server} = 40 \times 0.01 = 0.4$$

The formula for the average time spent waiting in line:

$$\text{Time}_{queue} = \text{Time}_{server} \times \frac{\text{Server utilization}}{(1 - \text{Server utilization})}$$

$$= 10 \text{ ms} \times \frac{0.4}{1-0.4} = 10 \times \frac{0.4}{0.6} = 10 \times \frac{2}{3} = 6.7 \text{ ms}$$

The average response time is 10 + 6.7 ms or 16.7 ms, 6.0 times faster than the old response time even though the new service time is only 2.0 times faster.

Thus far, we have been assuming a single server, such as a single disk. Many real systems have multiple disks and hence could use multiple servers. Such a system is called an *M/M/m* model in queuing theory.

Let's give the same formulas for the M/M/m queue, using $N_{servers}$ to represent the number of servers. The first two formulas are easy:

$$\text{Utilization} = \frac{\text{Arrival rate} \times \text{Time}_{server}}{N_{servers}}$$

$$\text{Length}_{queue} = \text{Arrival rate} \times \text{Time}_{queue}$$

The time waiting in the queue is

$$\text{Time}_{queue} = \text{Time}_{server} \times \frac{P_{tasks \geq N_{servers}}}{N_{servers} \times (1 - \text{Utilization})}$$

This formula is related to the one for M/M/1, except we replace utilization of a single server with the probability that a task will be queued as opposed to being immediately serviced, and divide the time in queue by the number of servers. Alas, calculating the probability of jobs being in the queue when there are $N_{servers}$ is much more complicated. First, the probability that there are no tasks in the system is

$$\text{Prob}_{0 \text{ tasks}} = \left[1 + \frac{(N_{servers} \times \text{Utilization})^{N_{servers}}}{N_{servers}! \times (1 - \text{Utilization})} + \sum_{n=1}^{N_{servers}-1} \frac{(N_{servers} \times \text{Utilization})^{n}}{n!} \right]^{-1}$$

Then the probability there are as many or more tasks than we have servers is

$$\text{Prob}_{tasks \geq N_{servers}} = \frac{N_{servers} \times \text{Utilization}^{N_{servers}}}{N_{servers}! \times (1 - \text{Utilization})} \times \text{Prob}_{0 \text{ tasks}}$$

Note that if $N_{servers}$ is 1, $\text{Prob}_{task \geq N_{servers}}$ simplifies back to Utilization, and we get the same formula as for M/M/1. Let's try an example.

Example   Suppose instead of a new, faster disk, we add a second slow disk, and duplicate the data so that reads can be serviced by either disk. Let's assume that the requests are all reads. Recalculate the answers to the earlier questions, this time using an M/M/m queue.

Answer   The average utilization of the two disks is then

$$\text{Server utilization} = \frac{\text{Arrival rate} \times \text{Time}_{\text{server}}}{N_{\text{servers}}} = \frac{40 \times 0.02}{2} = 0.4$$

We first calculate the probability of no tasks in the queue:

$$\text{Prob}_{0\ \text{tasks}} = \left[1 + \frac{(2 \times \text{Utilization})^2}{2! \times (1 - \text{Utilization})} + \sum_{n=1}^{1} \frac{(2 \times \text{Utilization})^n}{n!}\right]^{-1}$$

$$= \left[1 + \frac{(2 \times 0.4)^2}{2 \times (1 - 0.4)} + (2 \times 0.4)\right]^{-1} = \left[1 + \frac{0.640}{1.2} + 0.800\right]^{-1}$$

$$= [1 + 0.533 + 0.800]^{-1} = 2.333^{-1}$$

We use this result to calculate the probability of tasks in the queue:

$$\text{Prob}_{\text{tasks} \geq N_{\text{servers}}} = \frac{2 \times \text{Utilization}^2}{2! \times (1 - \text{Utilization})} \times \text{Prob}_{0\ \text{tasks}}$$

$$= \frac{(2 \times 0.4)^2}{2 \times (1 - 0.4)} \times 2.333^{-1} = \frac{0.640}{1.2} \times 2.333^{-1}$$

$$= 0.533/2.333 = 0.229$$

Finally, the time waiting in the queue:

$$\text{Time}_{\text{queue}} = \text{Time}_{\text{server}} \times \frac{\text{Prob}_{\text{tasks} \geq N_{\text{servers}}}}{N_{\text{servers}} \times (1 - \text{Utilization})}$$

$$= 0.020 \times \frac{0.229}{2 \times (1 - 0.4)} = 0.020 \times \frac{0.229}{1.2}$$

$$= 0.020 \times 0.190 = 0.0038$$

The average response time is 20 + 3.8 ms or 23.8 ms. For this workload, two disks cut the queue waiting time by a factor of 21 over a single slow disk and a factor of 1.75 versus a single fast disk. The mean service time of a system with a single fast disk, however, is still 1.4 times faster than one with two disks since the disk service time is 2.0 times faster.

Section 7.11 and the exercises have other examples using queuing theory to predict performance.

Benchmarks of Storage Performance and Availability

The prior subsection tries to predict the performance of storage subsystems. We also need to measure the performance of real systems to collect the values of parameters needed for prediction, to determine if the queuing theory assumptions hold, and to suggest what to do if the assumptions don't hold. Benchmarks help.

Transaction-Processing Benchmarks

Transaction processing (TP, or OLTP for online transaction processing) is chiefly concerned with *I/O rate* (the number of disk accesses per second), as opposed to *data rate* (measured as bytes of data per second). TP generally involves changes to a large body of shared information from many terminals, with the TP system guaranteeing proper behavior on a failure. Suppose, for example, a bank's computer fails when a customer tries to withdraw money. The TP system would guarantee that the account is debited if the customer received the money *and* that the account is unchanged if the money was not received. Airline reservations systems as well as banks are traditional customers for TP.

As mentioned in Chapter 1, two dozen members of the TP community conspired to form a benchmark for the industry and, to avoid the wrath of their legal departments, published the report anonymously [Anon. et al. 1985]. This report led to the *Transaction Processing Council,* which in turn has led to seven benchmarks since its founding.

Figure 7.31 summarizes these benchmarks. Let's describe TPC-C to give a flavor of these benchmarks. TPC-C uses a database to simulate an order-entry environment of a wholesale supplier, including entering and delivering orders, recording payments, checking the status of orders, and monitoring the level of stock at the warehouses. It runs five concurrent transactions of varying complexity, and the database includes nine tables with a scalable range of records and

Benchmark	Data size (GB)	Performance metric	Date of first results
A: debit credit (retired)	0.1–10	transactions per second	July 1990
B: batch debit credit (retired)	0.1–10	transactions per second	July 1991
C: complex query OLTP	100–3000 (minimum 0.07 * tpm)	new order transactions per minute	September 1992
D: decision support (retired)	100, 300, 1000	queries per hour	December 1995
H: ad hoc decision support	100, 300, 1000	queries per hour	October 1999
R: business reporting decision support	1000	queries per hour	August 1999
W: transactional Web benchmark	≈ 50, 500	Web interactions per second	July 2000

Figure 7.31 Transaction Processing Council benchmarks. The summary results include both the performance metric and the price-performance of that metric. TPC-A, TPC-B, and TPC-D were retired.

customers. TPC-C is measured in transactions per minute (tpmC) and in price of system, including hardware, software, and three years of maintenance support.

These TPC benchmarks were either the first, and in some cases still the only ones, that have these unusual characteristics:

- *Price is included with the benchmark results.* The cost of hardware, software, and three-year maintenance agreements is included in a submission, which enables evaluations based on price-performance as well as high performance.

- *The data set generally must scale in size as the throughput increases.* The benchmarks are trying to model real systems, in which the demand on the system and the size of the data stored in it increase together. It makes no sense, for example, to have thousands of people per minute access hundreds of bank accounts.

- *The benchmark results are audited.* Before results can be submitted, they must be approved by a certified TPC auditor, who enforces the TPC rules that try to make sure that only fair results are submitted. Results can be challenged and disputes resolved by going before the TPC.

- *Throughput is the performance metric, but response times are limited.* For example, with TPC-C, 90% of the New-Order transaction response times must be less than 5 seconds.

- *An independent organization maintains the benchmarks.* Dues collected by TPC pay for an administrative structure including a Chief Operating Office. This organization settles disputes, conducts mail ballots on approval of changes to benchmarks, holds board meetings, and so on.

SPEC System-Level File Server (SFS) and Web Benchmarks

The SPEC benchmarking effort is best known for its characterization of processor performance, but it has created benchmarks for other fields as well. In 1990 seven companies agreed on a synthetic benchmark, called SFS, to evaluate systems running the Sun Microsystems network file service (NFS). This benchmark was upgraded to SFS 2.0 (also called SPECSFS97) to include support for NSF version 3, using TCP in addition to UDP as the transport protocol, and making the mix of operations more realistic. Measurements on NFS systems led to a synthetic mix of reads, writes, and file operations. SFS supplies default parameters for comparative performance. For example, half of all writes are done in 8 KB blocks and half are done in partial blocks of 1, 2, or 4 KB. For reads, the mix is 85% full blocks and 15% partial blocks.

Like TPC-C, SFS scales the amount of data stored according to the reported throughput: For every 100 NFS operations per second, the capacity must increase by 1 GB. It also limits the average response time, in this case to 40 ms. Figure 7.32 shows average response time versus throughput for four systems. Unfortunately, unlike the TPC benchmarks, SFS does not normalize for different price configurations. The fastest system in Figure 7.32 has seven times the number of

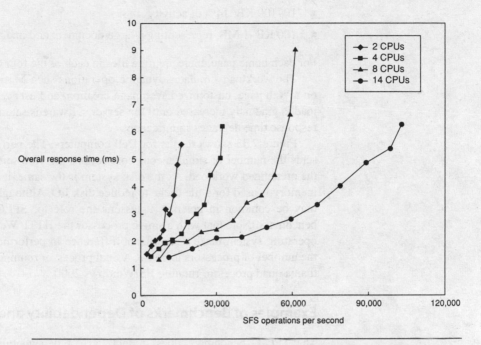

Figure 7.32 SPECSFS97 performance for four EMC Celerra 507 NFS servers: 2, 4, 8, and 14 CPUs provided 15,723, 32,049, 61,809, and 104,607 ops per second. Each processor had its own file system running across about 30 disks. Reported in June 2000, these systems all used DART v2.1.15.200 operating systems, 700 MHz Pentium III microprocessors, 0.5 GB of DRAM per processor, and Seagate Cheetah 36 GB disks. The total number of disks per system was 67, 133, 265, and 433, respectively. These disks were connected using six Symmetrix Model 8430 disk controllers. The 40 ms average response time limit imposed by SPECSFS97 was not an issue for these machines. The benchmark was retired in June 2001 after bugs were uncovered that affect the comparability of results, which is a serious bug for a benchmark! For more information, see *www.spec.org/osg/sfs97/sfs97_notice.html*.

CPUs and disks as the slowest system, but SPEC leaves it to you to calculate price versus performance. As performance scaled to new heights, SPEC discovered bugs in the benchmark that impact the amount of work done during the measurement periods. Hence, it was retired in June 2001.

SPECWeb is a benchmark for evaluating the performance of World Wide Web servers. The SPECWeb99 workload simulates accesses to a Web service provider, where the server supports home pages for several organizations. Each home page is a collection of files ranging in size from small icons to large documents and images, with some files being more popular than others. The workload defines four sizes of files and their frequency of activity:

■ Less than 1 KB, representing a small icon: 35% of activity

■ 1–10 KB: 50% of activity

- 10–100 KB: 14% of activity
- 100 KB–1 MB, representing a large document and image: 1% of activity

For each home page, there are nine files in each of the four classes.

The workload simulates dynamic operations such as rotating advertisements on a Web page, customized Web page creation, and user registration. The workload is gradually increased until the server software is saturated with hits and the response time degrades significantly.

Figure 7.33 shows results for Dell computers. The performance result represents the number of simultaneous connections the Web server can support using the predefined workload. As the disk system is the same, it appears that the large memory is used for a file cache to reduce disk I/O. Although memory of this size may be common in practice, it lessens the role for SPECWeb99 as a storage benchmark. Note that with a single processor the HTTP Web server software and operating system make a significant difference in performance, which grows as the number of processors increase. A dual processor running TUX/Linux is faster than a quad processor running IIS/Windows 2000.

Examples of Benchmarks of Dependability and Availability

The TPC-C benchmark does in fact have a dependability requirement. The benchmarked system must be able to handle a single disk failure, which means in practice that all submitters are running some RAID organization in their storage system.

Relatively recent efforts have focused on the effectiveness of fault tolerance in systems. Brown and Patterson [2000] propose that availability be measured by examining the variations in system quality-of-service metrics over time as faults are injected into the system. For a Web server the obvious metrics are performance (measured as requests satisfied per second) and degree of fault tolerance (measured as the number of faults that can be tolerated by the storage subsystem, network connection topology, and so forth).

System Name	Result	CPUs	Result/CPU	HTTP Version/OS	Pentium III	DRAM (GB)
PowerEdge 2400/667	732	1	732	IIS 5.0/Windows 2000	667 MHz EB	2
PowerEdge 2400/667	1270	1	1270	TUX 1.0/Red Hat Linux 6.2	667 MHz EB	2
PowerEdge 4400/800	1060	2	530	IIS 5.0/Windows 2000	800 MHz EB	4
PowerEdge 4400/800	2200	2	1100	TUX 1.0/Red Hat Linux 6.2	800 MHz EB	4
PowerEdge 6400/700	1598	4	400	IIS 5.0/Windows 2000	700 MHz Xeon	8
PowerEdge 6400/700	4200	4	1050	TUX 1.0/Red Hat Linux 6.2	700 MHz Xeon	8

Figure 7.33 SPECWeb99 results in 2000 for Dell computers. Each machine uses five 9 GB, 10,000 RPM disks except the fifth system, which has seven disks. The first four have 256 KB of L2 cache, while the last two have 2 MB of L2 cache.

The initial experiment injected a single fault—such as a disk sector write error—and recorded the system's behavior as reflected in the quality-of-service metrics. The example compared software RAID implementations provided by Linux, Solaris, and Windows 2000 Server. SPECWeb99 was used to provide a workload and to measure performance. To inject faults, one of the SCSI disks in the software RAID volume was replaced with an emulated disk. It was just a PC running software with a special SCSI controller that makes the combination of PC, controller, and software appear to other devices on the SCSI bus as a disk drive. The disk emulator allowed the injection of faults. The faults injected included a variety of transient disk faults, such as correctable read errors, and permanent faults, such as disk media failures on writes.

Figure 7.34 shows the behavior of each system under different faults. The two top graphs show Linux (on the left) and Solaris (on the right). Both systems automatically reconstruct data onto a hot spare disk immediately when a disk failure is detected. As can be seen in the figure, Linux reconstructs slowly and Solaris reconstructs quickly. Windows is shown at the bottom; a single disk failed so the data are still available, but this system does not begin reconstructing on the hot spare until the operator gives permission. Linux and Solaris, in contrast, start reconstruction upon the fault injection.

As RAID systems can lose data if a second disk fails before completing reconstruction, the longer the reconstruction (MTTR), the lower the availability (see Section 7.5). Increased reconstruction speed implies decreased application performance, however, as reconstruction steals I/O resources from running applications. Thus, there is a policy choice between taking a performance hit during reconstruction, or lengthening the window of vulnerability and thus lowering the predicted MTTF.

Although none of the tested systems documented their reconstruction policies outside of the source code, even a single fault injection was able to give insight into those policies. The experiments revealed that both Linux and Solaris initiate automatic reconstruction of the RAID volume onto a hot spare when an active disk is taken out of service due to a failure. Although Windows supports RAID reconstruction, the reconstruction must be initiated manually. Thus, without human intervention, a Windows system will not rebuild redundancy after a first failure and will remain susceptible to a second failure indefinitely, which increases the window of vulnerability.

The fault injection experiments also provided insight into other availability policies of Linux, Solaris, and Windows 2000 concerning automatic spare utilization, reconstruction rates, transient errors, and so on. Again, no system documented their policies.

In terms of managing transient faults, the fault injection experiments revealed that Linux's software RAID implementation takes an opposite approach than do the RAID implementations in Solaris and Windows. The Linux implementation is paranoid—it would rather shut down a disk in a controlled manner at the first error, rather than wait to see if the error is transient. In contrast, Solaris and Windows are more forgiving—they ignore most transient faults with the expectation

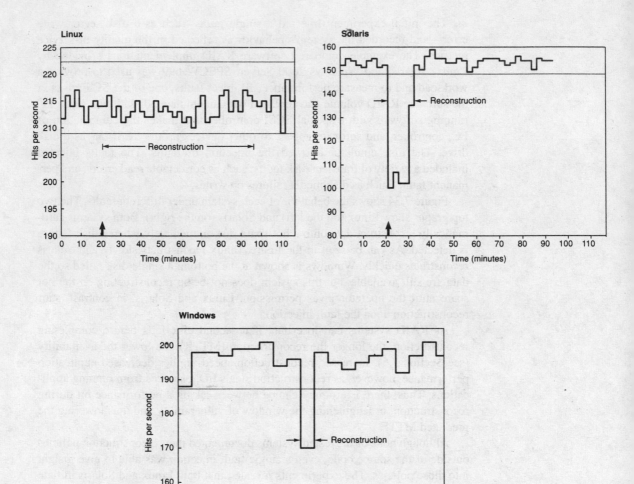

Figure 7.34 Availability benchmark for software RAID systems on the same computer running Red Hat 6.0 Linux, Solaris 7, and Windows 2000 operating systems. Note the difference in philosophy on speed of reconstruction of Linux versus Windows and Solaris. The *y*-axis is behavior in hits per second running SPECWeb99. The arrow indicates time of fault insertion. The lines at the top give the 99% confidence interval of performance before the fault is inserted. A 99% confidence interval means that if the variable is outside of this range, the probability is only 1% that this value would appear.

that they will not recur. Thus, these systems are substantially more robust to transients than the Linux system. Note that both Windows and Solaris do log the transient faults, ensuring that the errors are reported even if not acted upon. When faults were not transient, the systems behaved similarly.

Considering real failure data, none of the observed policies is particularly good, regardless of reconstruction behavior. Talagala and Patterson [1999] report that transient SCSI errors are frequent in a large system—such as the 368-disk Tertiary Disk farm—yet rarely do they indicate that a disk must be replaced. The logs covering 368 disks for 11 months indicate that 13 disks reported transient hardware errors but only 2 actually required replacement. In this situation, Linux's policy would have incorrectly wasted 11 disks and 11 spares, or 6% of the array. If there were not enough spares, data could have been lost despite no true disk failures. Equally poor would have been the response of Solaris or Windows, as these systems most likely would have ignored the stream of intermittent transient errors from the 2 truly defective disks, requiring administrator intervention to take them offline.

Future directions in availability benchmarking include characterizing a realistic fault workload, injecting multiple faults, and applying the technique to other fault-tolerant systems.

7.10   Crosscutting Issues

Thus far, we have ignored the role of the operating system in storage. In a manner analogous to the way compilers use an instruction set, operating systems determine what I/O techniques implemented by the hardware will actually be used.

For example, many I/O controllers used in early UNIX systems were 16-bit microprocessors. To avoid problems with 16-bit addresses in controllers, UNIX was changed to limit the maximum I/O transfer to 63 KB or less. Thus, a new I/O controller designed to efficiently transfer 1 MB files would never see more than 63 KB at a time under early UNIX, no matter how large the files.

The operating system enforces the protection between processes, which must include I/O activity as well as memory accesses. Since I/O is typically between a device and memory, the operating system must ensure safety.

DMA and Virtual Memory

Given the use of virtual memory, there is the matter of whether DMA should transfer using virtual addresses or physical addresses. Here are a couple of problems with DMA using physically mapped I/O:

- Transferring a buffer that is larger than one page will cause problems, since the pages in the buffer will not usually be mapped to sequential pages in physical memory.

- Suppose DMA is ongoing between memory and a frame buffer, and the operating system removes some of the pages from memory (or relocates them). The DMA would then be transferring data to or from the wrong page of memory.

One answer is for the operating system to guarantee that those pages touched by DMA devices are in physical memory for the duration of the I/O, and the pages are said to be *pinned* into main memory. Note that the addresses for a scatter/gather DMA transfer probably come from the page table.

To ensure protection often the operating system will copy user data into the kernel address space and then transfer between the kernel address space to the I/O device. Relentless copying of data is often the price paid for protection. If DMA supports scatter/gather, the operating system may be able to create a list of addresses and transfer sizes to reduce some of the overhead of copying.

Another answer is *virtual DMA*. It allows the DMA to use virtual addresses that are mapped to physical addresses during the DMA. Thus, a buffer could be sequential in virtual memory, but the pages can be scattered in physical memory, and the virtual addresses provide the protection of other processes. The operating system would update the address tables of a DMA if a process is moved using virtual DMA. Figure 7.35 shows address translation registers added to the DMA device.

Asynchronous I/O and Operating Systems

As mentioned in Section 7.2, disks typically spend much more time in mechanical delays than in transferring data. Thus, a natural path to higher I/O performance is parallelism, trying to get many disks to simultaneously access data for a program.

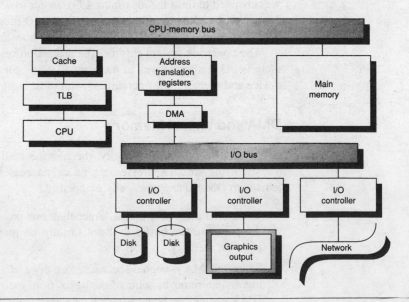

Figure 7.35 Virtual DMA requires a register for each page to be transferred in the DMA controller, showing the protection bits and the physical page corresponding to each virtual page.

The straightforward approach to I/O is to request data and then start using it. The operating system then switches to another process until the desired data arrive, and then the operating system switches back to the requesting process. Such a style is called *synchronous I/O*—the process waits until the data have been read from disk.

The alternative model is for the process to continue after making a request, and it is not blocked until it tries to read the requested data. Such *asynchronous I/O* allows the process to continue making requests so that many I/O requests can be operating simultaneously. Asynchronous I/O shares the same philosophy as caches in out-of-order CPUs, which achieve greater bandwidth by having multiple outstanding events.

Block Servers versus Filers

The operating system typically provides the file abstraction on top of blocks stored on the disk. The terms *logical units, logical volumes,* and *physical volumes* are related terms used in Microsoft and UNIX systems to refer to subset collections of disk blocks. A logical unit is the element of storage exported from a disk array, usually constructed from a subset of the array's disks. A logical unit appears to the server as a single virtual "disk." In a RAID disk array, the logical unit is configured as a particular RAID layout, such as RAID 5. A physical volume is the device file used by the file system to access a logical unit. A logical volume provides a level of virtualization that enables the file system to split the physical volume across multiple pieces or to stripe data across multiple physical volumes. A logical unit is an abstraction of a disk array that presents a virtual disk to the operating system, while physical and logical volumes are abstractions used by the operating system to divide these virtual disks into smaller, independent file systems.

Having covered some of the terms for collections of blocks, the question arises as to where the file illusion should be maintained: in the server or at the other end of the storage area network?

The traditional answer is the server. It accesses storage as disk blocks and maintains the metadata. Most file systems use a file cache, so it is the job of the server to maintain consistency of file accesses. The disks may be *direct attached*—located inside the server box connected to an I/O bus—or attached over a storage area network, but the server transmits data blocks to the storage subsystem.

The alternative answer is that the disk subsystem itself maintains the file abstraction, and the server uses a file system protocol to communicate with storage. Example protocols are Network File System (NFS) for UNIX systems and Common Internet File System (CIFS) for Windows systems. Such devices are called *network attached storage* (NAS) devices since it makes no sense for storage to be directly attached to the server. The name is something of a misnomer because a storage area network like FC-AL can also be used to connect to block servers. The term *filer* is often used for NAS devices that only provide file service and file storage. Network Appliances is one of the first companies to make filers.

Recently new products have been announced that sit between the compute server and the disk array controller. They provide snapshots of storage, caching, backup, and so on. The goal is to make the storage system easier to manage.

The driving force behind placing storage on the network is to make it easier for many computers to share information and for operators to maintain it.

Caches Cause Problems for Operating Systems—Stale Data

The prevalence of caches in computer systems has added to the responsibilities of the operating system. Caches imply the possibility of two copies of the data—one each for cache and main memory—while virtual memory can result in three copies—for cache, memory, and disk. These copies bring up the possibility of *stale data:* the CPU or I/O system could modify one copy without updating the other copies (see page 480). Either the operating system or the hardware must make sure that the CPU reads the most recently input data and that I/O outputs the correct data, in the presence of caches and virtual memory.

There are two parts to the stale-data problem:

1. The I/O system sees stale data on output because memory is not up to date.

2. The CPU sees stale data in the cache on input after the I/O system has updated memory.

The first dilemma is how to output correct data if there is a cache and I/O is connected to memory. A write-through cache solves this by ensuring that memory will have the same data as the cache. A write-back cache requires the operating system to flush output addresses to make sure they are not in the cache. This flush takes time, even if the data are not in the cache, since address checks are sequential. Alternatively, the hardware can check cache tags during output to see if they are in a write-back cache, and only interact with the cache if the output tries to read data that are in the cache.

The second problem is ensuring that the cache won't have stale data after input. The operating system can guarantee that the input data area can't possibly be in the cache. If it can't guarantee this, the operating system flushes input addresses to make sure they are not in the cache. Again, this takes time, whether or not the input addresses are in the cache. As before, extra hardware can be added to check tags during an input and invalidate the data if there is a conflict.

These problems are like cache coherency in a multiprocessor, discussed in Chapter 6. I/O can be thought of as a second dedicated processor in a multiprocessor.

Switches Replacing Buses

The cost of replacing passive buses with point-to-point links and switches (Chapter 8) is dropping as Moore's Law continues to reduce the cost of components. Combined with the higher I/O bandwidth demands from faster processors, faster disks, and faster local area networks, the decreasing cost advantage of buses means the days of buses in desktop and server computers are numbered. In 2001, high-end servers have already replaced processor-memory buses with switches—see Figure 7.14 on page 698—and switches are now available for high-speed storage buses, such as fibre channel.

Not only do switched networks provide more aggregate bandwidth than do buses, the point-to-point links can be much longer. For example, the planned successor to the PCI I/O bus, called *Infiniband*, uses point-to-point links and switches. It delivers 2–24G bits/sec of bandwidth per link and stretches the maximum length of the interconnect using copper wire from 0.5 m of a PCI bus to 17 m.

We'll return to discussion of switches in the next chapter.

Replication of Processors for Dependability

In this and previous chapters, we have discussed providing extra resources to check and correct errors in main memory and in storage. As Moore's Law continues and dependability increases in importance for servers, some manufacturers are placing multiple processors on a single chip for the primary purpose of improving the reliability of the processor.

The state of the art in processor dependability is likely the IBM 390 mainframe. Naturally, all its caches and main memory are protected by ECC, but so are the register files. The G6 chips and modules include up to 14 processors, some of which are used as built-in spares. Each processor has redundant instruction fetch/decode, execution units, L1 cache, and register file to check for errors. At the completion of every instruction, the results produced by the two instruction execution units are compared and, if equal, the results of the instruction are checkpointed for recovery in case the next instruction fails. Upon detecting an inconsistency, the processor will retry instructions several times to see if the error was transient. If an error is not transient, the hardware can swap in a spare processor in less than a second without disrupting the application.

7.11   Designing an I/O System in Five Easy Pieces

The art of I/O system design is to find a design that meets goals for cost, dependability, and variety of devices while avoiding bottlenecks in I/O performance. Avoiding bottlenecks means that components must be balanced between main memory and the I/O device, because performance—and hence effective cost-performance—can only be as good as the weakest link in the I/O chain. The architect must also plan for expansion so that customers can tailor the I/O to their applications. This expansibility, both in numbers and types of I/O devices, has its costs in longer I/O buses, larger power supplies to support I/O devices, and larger cabinets. Finally, storage must be dependable, adding new constraints on proposed designs

In designing an I/O system, analyze performance, cost, capacity, and availability using varying I/O connection schemes and different numbers of I/O devices of each type. Here is one series of steps to follow in designing an I/O system. The answers for each step may be dictated by market requirements or simply by cost, performance, and availability goals.

1. List the different types of I/O devices to be connected to the machine, or list the standard buses that the machine will support.

2. List the physical requirements for each I/O device. Requirements include size, power, connectors, bus slots, expansion cabinets, and so on.

3. List the cost of each I/O device, including the portion of cost of any controller needed for this device.

4. List the reliability of each I/O device.

5. Record the CPU resource demands of each I/O device. This list should include

   ■ Clock cycles for instructions used to initiate an I/O, to support operation of an I/O device (such as handling interrupts), and to complete I/O

   ■ CPU clock stalls due to waiting for I/O to finish using the memory, bus, or cache

   ■ CPU clock cycles to recover from an I/O activity, such as a cache flush

6. List the memory and I/O bus resource demands of each I/O device. Even when the CPU is not using memory, the bandwidth of main memory and the I/O bus is limited.

7. The final step is assessing the performance and availability of the different ways to organize these I/O devices. Performance can only be properly evaluated with simulation, although it may be estimated using queuing theory. Reliability can be calculated assuming I/O devices fail independently and that the times to failure are exponentially distributed. Availability can be computed from reliability by estimating MTTF for the devices, taking into account the time from failure to repair.

You then select the best organization, given your cost, performance, and availability goals.

Cost-performance goals affect the selection of the I/O scheme and physical design. Performance can be measured either as megabytes per second or I/Os per second, depending on the needs of the application. For high performance, the only limits should be speed of I/O devices, number of I/O devices, and speed of memory and CPU. For low cost, the only expenses should be those for the I/O devices themselves and for cabling to the CPU. Cost-performance design, of course, tries for the best of both worlds. Availability goals depend in part on the cost of unavailability to an organization.

To make these ideas clearer, the next dozen pages go through five examples. Each looks at constructing a disk array with about 2 TB of capacity for user data with two sizes of disks. To offer a gentle introduction to I/O design and evaluation, the examples evolve in realism.

To try to avoid getting lost in the details, let's start with an overview of the five examples:

1. *Naive cost-performance design and evaluation*—The first example calculates cost-performance of an I/O system for the two types of disks. It ignores dependability concerns and makes the simplifying assumption of allowing 100% utilization of I/O resources. This example is also the longest.

2. *Availability of the first example*—The second example calculates the poor availability of this naive I/O design.

3. *Response times of the first example*—The third example uses queuing theory to calculate the impact on response time of trying to use 100% of an I/O resource.

4. *More realistic cost-performance design and evaluation*—Since the third example shows the folly of 100% utilization, the fourth example changes the design to obey common rules of thumb on utilization of I/O resources. It then evaluates cost-performance.

5. *More realistic design for availability and its evaluation*—Since the second example shows the poor availability when dependability is ignored, this final example uses a RAID 5 design. It then calculates availability and performance.

Figure 7.36 summarizes changes in the results in cost-performance, latency, and availability as examples become more realistic. You may want to first skim the examples, and then dive in when one catches your fancy.

	Simplistic organization (examples 1, 2, 3)	Performance-tuned organization (example 4)	Performance- and availability-tuned organization (example 5)
	Small vs. large disks	Small vs. large disks	Small vs. large disks
Cost of 1.9 TB system	$47,200 vs. $45,200	$49,200 vs. $47,200	$57,750 vs. $54,625
Performance (IOPS)	6,144 vs. 3,072 IOPS	4,896 vs. 2,448 IOPS	6,120 vs. 3,060 IOPS
Cost-performance	$8 vs. $15 per IOPS	$10 vs. $19 per IOPS	$9 vs. $18 per IOPS
Disk utilization	100%	80%	80%
Disk access latency	238 ms (@ 97%)	41 ms	41 ms
Availability: MTTF (hours)	9,524 vs. 15,385	—	2,500,000 vs. 5,200,000

Figure 7.36 Summary of cost, performance, and availability metrics of the five examples. Note that performance in the fifth example assumes all I/Os are reads.

First Example: Naive Design and Cost-Performance

Now let's take a long look at the cost-performance of two I/O organizations. This simple performance analysis assumes that resources can be used at 100% of their peak rate without degradation due to queuing. (The fourth example takes a more realistic view.)

Example   Assume the following performance and cost information:

- A 2500 MIPS CPU costing $20,000.
- A 16-byte-wide interleaved memory that can be accessed every 10 ns.
- 1000 MB/sec I/O bus with room for 20 Ultra3 SCSI buses and controllers.
- Wide Ultra3 SCSI buses that can transfer 160 MB/sec and support up to 15 disks per bus (these are also called SCSI *strings*).
- A $500 Ultra3 SCSI controller that adds 0.3 ms of overhead to perform a disk I/O.
- An operating system that uses 50,000 CPU instructions for a disk I/O.
- A choice of a large disk containing 80 GB or a small disk containing 40 GB, each costing $10 per GB.
- A $1500 enclosure supplies power and cooling to either eight 80 GB disks or twelve 40 GB disks.
- Both disks rotate at 15,000 RPM, have a 5 ms average seek time, and can transfer 40 MB/sec.
- The storage capacity must be 1920 GB.
- The average I/O size is 32 KB.

Evaluate the cost per I/O per second (IOPS) of using small or large drives. Assume that every disk I/O requires an average seek and average rotational delay. Use the optimistic assumption that all devices can be used at 100% of capacity and that the workload is evenly divided among all disks.

Answer   I/O performance is limited by the weakest link in the chain, so we evaluate the maximum performance of each link in the I/O chain for each organization to determine the maximum performance of that organization.

Let's start by calculating the maximum number of IOPS for the CPU, main memory, and I/O bus. The CPU I/O performance is determined by the speed of the CPU and the number of instructions to perform a disk I/O:

$$\text{Maximum IOPS for CPU} = \frac{2500 \text{ MIPS}}{50,000 \text{ instructions per I/O}} = 50,000 \text{ IOPS}$$

The maximum performance of the memory system is determined by the memory cycle time, the width of the memory, and the size of the I/O transfers:

$$\text{Maximum IOPS for main memory} = \frac{(1/10 \text{ ns}) \times 16}{32 \text{ KB per I/O}} \approx 50,000 \text{ IOPS}$$

The I/O bus maximum performance is limited by the bus bandwidth and the size of the I/O:

$$\text{Maximum IOPS for the I/O bus} = \frac{1000 \text{ MB/sec}}{32 \text{ KB per I/O}} \approx 31,250 \text{ IOPS}$$

Thus, no matter which disk is selected, the I/O bus limits the maximum performance to no more than 31,250 IOPS.

Now it's time to look at the performance of the next link in the I/O chain, the SCSI controllers. The time to transfer 32 KB over the SCSI bus is

$$\text{Ultra3 SCSI bus transfer time} = \frac{32 \text{ KB}}{160 \text{ MB/sec}} = 0.2 \text{ ms}$$

Adding the 0.3 ms SCSI controller overhead means 0.5 ms per I/O, making the maximum rate per controller

$$\text{Maximum IOPS per Ultra3 SCSI controller} = \frac{1}{0.5 \text{ ms}} = 2000 \text{ IOPS}$$

All organizations will use several controllers, so 2000 IOPS is not the limit for the whole system.

The final link in the chain is the disks themselves. The time for an average disk I/O is

$$\text{I/O time} = 5 \text{ ms} + \frac{0.5}{15,000 \text{ RPM}} + \frac{32 \text{ KB}}{40 \text{ MB/sec}} = 5 + 2.0 + 0.8 = 7.8 \text{ ms}$$

Therefore, disk performance is

$$\text{Maximum IOPS (using average seeks) per disk} = \frac{1}{7.8 \text{ ms}} \approx 128 \text{ IOPS}$$

The number of disks in each organization depends on the size of each disk: 1920 GB can be either 24 disks of 80 GB each or 48 disks of 40 GB each. The maximum number of I/Os for all the disks is

$$\text{Maximum IOPS for 24 80 GB disks} = 24 \times 128 = 3072 \text{ IOPS}$$
$$\text{Maximum IOPS for 48 40 GB disks} = 48 \times 128 = 6144 \text{ IOPS}$$

Thus, provided there are enough SCSI strings, the disks become the new limit to maximum performance: 3072 IOPS for the 80 GB disks and 6144 IOPS for the 40 GB disks.

Although we have determined the performance of each link of the I/O chain, we still have to determine how many SCSI buses and controllers to use and how many disks to connect to each controller, as this may further limit maximum performance. The I/O bus is limited to 20 SCSI controllers, and the limit is 15 disks per SCSI string. The minimum number of controllers for the 80 GB disks is

Minimum number of SCSI-2 strings for 24 80 GB disks = $\left\lceil \dfrac{24}{15} \right\rceil$ or 2 strings

and for 40 GB disks

Minimum number of SCSI-2 strings for 48 40 GB disks = $\left\lceil \dfrac{48}{15} \right\rceil$ or 4 strings

Although the formulas suggest the ideal number of strings, they must be matched with the requirements of the physical packaging. Three enclosures needed for 24 80 GB disks are a poor match to two strings, although four strings needed for 48 40 GB disks are a good match to the four enclosures. Thus, we increase the number of strings to three for the big disks.

We can calculate the maximum IOPS for each configuration:

$$\text{Maximum IOPS for 3 Ultra3 SCSI strings} = 3 \times 2000 = 6000 \text{ IOPS}$$
$$\text{Maximum IOPS for 4 Ultra3 SCSI strings} = 4 \times 2000 = 8000 \text{ IOPS}$$

The maximum performance of this number of controllers is higher than the disk I/O throughput, so there is no benefit of adding more strings and controllers.

Using the format

Min(CPU limit, memory limit, I/O bus limit, disk limit, string limit)

the maximum performance of each option is limited by the bottleneck (in bold-face):

80 GB disks, 2 strings = Min(50,000, 50,000, 31,250, **3072**, 6000) = 3072 IOPS

40 GB disks, 4 strings = Min(50,000, 50,000, 31,250, **6144**, 8000) = 6144 IOPS

We can now calculate the cost for each organization:

80 GB disks = $20,000 + 3 \times \$500 + 24 \times (80 \times \$10) + \$1500 \times \left\lceil \dfrac{24}{8} \right\rceil = \$45,200$

40 GB disks = $20,000 + 4 \times \$500 + 48 \times (40 \times \$10) + \$1500 \times \left\lceil \dfrac{48}{12} \right\rceil = \$47,200$

Finally, the cost per IOPS is $15 for the large disks and $8 for the small disks. Calculating the maximum number of average I/Os per second, assuming 100% utilization of the critical resources, the small disks have about 1.9 times better cost-performance than the large disks in this example.

Second Example: Calculating MTTF of First Example

We ignored dependability in the previous design, so let's look at the resulting mean time to fail.

Example   For the organizations in the last example, calculate the MTTF. Make the following assumptions, again assuming exponential lifetimes:

- CPU/memory MTTF is 1,000,000 hours.
- Disk MTTF is 1,000,000 hours.
- SCSI controller MTTF is 500,000 hours.
- Power supply MTTF is 200,000 hours.
- Fan MTTF is 200,000 hours.
- SCSI cable MTTF is 1,000,000 hours.
- Enclosure MTTF is 1,000,000 hours (not including MTTF of one fan and one power supply).

Answer   Collecting these together, we compute these failure rates:

$$\text{Failure rate}_{\text{big disks}} = \frac{1}{1,000,000} + \frac{24}{1,000,000} + \frac{3}{500,000} + \frac{3}{200,000} + \frac{3}{200,000} + \frac{3}{1,000,000} + \frac{3}{1,000,000}$$

$$= \frac{1 + 24 + 6 + 15 + 15 + 3 + 3}{1,000,000 \text{ hours}} = \frac{67}{1,000,000 \text{ hours}}$$

$$\text{Failure rate}_{\text{small disks}} = \frac{1}{1,000,000} + \frac{48}{1,000,000} + \frac{4}{500,000} + \frac{4}{200,000} + \frac{4}{200,000} + \frac{4}{1,000,000} + \frac{4}{1,000,000}$$

$$= \frac{1 + 48 + 8 + 20 + 20 + 4 + 4}{1,000,000 \text{ hours}} = \frac{105}{1,000,000 \text{ hours}}$$

The MTTF for the system is just the inverse of the failure rate:

$$\text{MTTF}_{\text{big disks}} = \frac{1}{\text{Failure rate}_{\text{big disks}}} = \frac{1,000,000 \text{ hours}}{67} = 14,925 \text{ hours}$$

$$\text{MTTF}_{\text{small disks}} = \frac{1}{\text{Failure rate}_{\text{small disks}}} = \frac{1,000,000 \text{ hours}}{105} = 9524 \text{ hours}$$

The smaller, more numerous drives have almost twice the cost-performance but about 60% of the reliability, and the collective reliability for both options is only about 1% of a single disk.

Third Example: Calculating Response Time of First Example

The first example assumed that resources can be used 100%. It is instructive to see the impact on response time as we approach 100% utilization of a resource. Let's do this for just one disk to keep the calculations simple.

Example   Recalculate performance in terms of response time. To simplify the calculation, ignore the SCSI strings and controller and just calculate for one disk. From the example above, the average disk service time is 7.8 ms. Assume Poisson arrivals with an exponential service time. Plot the mean response time for the following number of I/Os per second: 64, 72, 80, 88, 96, 104, 112, 120, and 124.

Answer   To be able to calculate the average response time, we can use the equation for an M/M/1 queue given the previous assumptions about arrival rates and services times. From page 728, the equation for time waiting in the queue is (evaluated for 64 I/O requests per second)

$$\text{Server utilization} = \text{Arrival rate} \times \text{Time}_{server} = 64 \times 0.0078 = 0.50$$

$$\text{Time}_{queue} = \text{Time}_{server} \times \frac{\text{Server utilization}}{(1 - \text{Server utilization})} = 7.8 \text{ ms} \times \frac{0.50}{1 - 0.50} = 7.8 \times \frac{0.5}{0.5} = 7.8 \text{ ms}$$

$$\text{Time}_{system} = \text{Time}_{server} + \text{Time}_{queue} = 7.8 + 7.8 = 15.6 \text{ ms}$$

Figure 7.37 shows the utilization and mean response time for other request rates, and Figure 7.38 plots the response times versus request rate.

Fourth Example: More Realistic Design and Cost-Performance

Figure 7.38 shows the severe increase in response time when trying to use 100% of a server. A number of rules of thumb have been evolved to guide I/O designers to keep response time and contention low:

Request rate	Utilization	Mean response time (ms)
64	50%	15.6
72	56%	17.8
80	62%	20.7
88	69%	24.9
96	75%	31.1
104	81%	41.3
112	87%	61.7
120	94%	121.9
124	97%	237.8

Figure 7.37 Utilization and mean response time for one disk in the prior example, ignoring the impact of SCSI buses and controllers. The nominal service time is 7.8 ms. 100% utilization of disks is unrealistic.

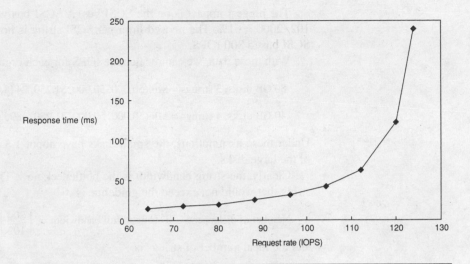

Figure 7.38 Plot of response times in Figure 7.37.

- No disk should be used more than 80% of the time.
- No disk arm should be seeking more than 60% of the time.
- No disk string should be utilized more than 40%.
- No I/O bus should be utilized more than 75%.

One reason the SCSI string bandwidth is set so low is that there is about a 20% SCSI command overhead on data transfers, further reducing available bandwidth.

Example   Recalculate performance in the previous example using these rules of thumb, and show the utilization of each component before and after these assumptions.

Answer   First let's see how much the resources are utilized using the previous assumptions. The new limit on IOPS for disks used 80% of the time is $128 \times 0.8 = 102$ IOPS. Notice that the IOPS is in the relatively flat part of the response time graph in Figure 7.38, as we would hope. The utilization of seek time per disk is

$$\frac{\text{Time of average seek}}{\text{Time between I/Os}} = \frac{5}{\dfrac{1}{102 \text{ IOPS}}} = \frac{5}{9.8} = 51\%$$

This is below the rule of thumb of 60%.

The I/O bus can support 31,250 IOPS, but the most that is used before was 6144 IOPS, which is just 6144/31,250 or a 20% utilization. Thus, the I/O bus is far below the suggested limit.

The biggest impact is on the SCSI bus. A SCSI bus with 12 disks uses $12 \times 102/2000 = 61\%$. The revised limit per SCSI string is now 40%, which limits a SCSI bus to 800 IOPS.

With these data, we can recalculate IOPS for each organization:

80 GB disks, 3 strings = Min(50,000, 50,000, 31,250, 2448, **2400**) = 2400 IOPS

40 GB disks, 4 strings = Min(50,000, 50,000, 31,250, 4896, **3200**) = 3200 IOPS

Under these assumptions, the small disks have about 1.3 times the performance of the large disks.

Clearly, the string bandwidth is the bottleneck now. The number of disks per string that would not exceed the guideline is

$$\text{Number of disks per SCSI string at full bandwidth} = \left\lfloor \frac{800}{102} \right\rfloor = \lfloor 7.8 \rfloor = 7 \text{ disks}$$

and the ideal number of strings is

$$\text{Number of SCSI strings with 80 GB disks} = \left\lceil \frac{24}{7} \right\rceil = \lceil 3.6 \rceil = 4 \text{ strings}$$

$$\text{Number of SCSI strings with 40 GB disks} = \left\lceil \frac{48}{7} \right\rceil = \lceil 6.9 \rceil = 7 \text{ strings}$$

As mentioned earlier, the number of strings must match the packaging requirements. Three enclosures needed for 24 80 GB disks are a poor match to four strings, and seven strings needed for 48 40 GB disks are a poor match to the four enclosures. Thus, we increase the number of enclosures to four for the big disks and increase the number of strings to eight for the small disks, so that each small-disk enclosure has two strings.

The IOPS for the suggested organization is

80 GB disks, 4 strings = Min(50,000, 50,000, 31,250, **2448**, 3200) = 2448 IOPS

40 GB disks, 8 strings = Min(50,000, 50,000, 31,250, **4896**, 6400) = 4896 IOPS

We can now calculate the cost for each organization:

80 GB disks, 4 strings = $20,000 + 4 \times \$500 + 24 \times (80 \times \$10) + 4 \times \$1500 = \$47,200$

40 GB disks, 8 strings = $20,000 + 8 \times \$500 + 48 \times (40 \times \$10) + 4 \times \$1500 = \$49,200$

The respective cost per IOPS is $19 versus $10, or an advantage of about 1.9 for the small disks. Compared with the naive assumption that we could use 100% of resources, the cost per IOPS increased about 1.3 times.

Figure 7.39 shows the utilization of each resource before and after following these guidelines. Exercise 7.20 explores what happens when this SCSI limit is relaxed.

Resource	Rule of thumb	100% utilization		Following the rule of thumb			
		80 GB disks, 3 strings	40 GB disks, 4 strings	80 GB disks, 3 strings	40 GB disks, 4 strings	80 GB disks, 4 strings	40 GB disks, 8 strings
CPU		6%	12%	5%	6%	5%	10%
Memory		6%	12%	5%	6%	5%	10%
I/O bus	75%	10%	20%	8%	10%	8%	16%
SCSI buses	40%	**51%**	**77%**	40%	40%	31%	31%
Disks	80%	**100%**	**100%**	78%	52%	80%	80%
Seek utilization	60%	**64%**	**64%**	50%	33%	51%	51%
IOPS		3072	6144	2400	3200	2448	4896

Figure 7.39 The percentage of utilization of each resource, before and after using the rules of thumb. Bold font shows resources in violation of the rules of thumb. Using the prior example, the utilization of three resources violated the rules of thumb: SCSI buses, disks, and seek utilization.

Fifth Example: Designing for Availability

Just as the fourth example made a more realistic design for performance, we can show a more realistic design for dependability. To tolerate faults we will add redundant hardware: extra disks, controllers, power supplies, fans, and controllers in a RAID 5 configuration.

To calculate reliability now, we need a formula to show what to expect when we can tolerate a failure and still provide service. To simplify the calculations we assume that the lifetimes of the components are exponentially distributed and that there is no dependency between the component failures. Instead of mean time to failure, we calculate *mean time until data loss* (MTDL), since a single failure will not, in general, result in lost service. For RAID, data are lost only if a second disk failure occurs in the group protected by parity before the first failed disk is repaired. Mean time until data loss is the mean time until a disk will fail divided by the chance that one of the remaining disks in the parity group will fail before the first failure is repaired. Thus, if the chance of a second failure before repair is large, then MTDL is small, and vice versa.

Assuming independent failures, since we have N disks, the mean time until one disk fails is MTTF_{disk}/N. The good approximation of the probability of the second failure is MTTR over the mean time until one of the remaining $G - 1$ disks in the parity group will fail. Similar to before, the mean time for $G - 1$ disks is $(\text{MTTF}_{disk}/(G - 1))$. Hence, a reasonable approximation for MTDL for a RAID [Chen et al. 1994] is

$$\text{MTDL}_1 = \frac{\text{MTTF}_{disk}/N}{\dfrac{\text{MTTR}_{disk}}{(\text{MTTF}_{disk}/(G-1))}} = \frac{\text{MTTF}_{disk}^2/N}{(G-1) \times \text{MTTR}_{disk}} = \frac{\text{MTTF}_{disk}^2}{N \times (G-1) \times \text{MTTR}_{disk}}$$

where N is the number of disks in the system and G is the number of disks in a group protected by parity. Thus, MTDL increases with increased disk reliability, reduced parity group size, and reduced MTTR.

The physical design of the disk array gives a strong suggestion to the parity group size. Figure 7.40 shows two ways of organizing a RAID. The problem with option 1 is that if the string or string controller fails, then all the disks in the RAID group fail, and data are lost. Option 2, called *orthogonal RAID,* in contrast loses only one disk per RAID group even if a string controller fails. Note that if the string is located in a single enclosure, then orthogonal RAID also protects against power supply and fan failures.

Example   For the organizations in the fourth example and using the MTTF ratings of the components in the second example, create orthogonal RAID arrays and calculate the MTDL for the arrays.

Answer   Both organizations use four enclosures, so we add a fifth enclosure in each to provide redundancy to tolerate faults. The redundant enclosure contains 1 controller and 6 large disks, or 2 controllers and 12 small disks. The failure rate of the enclosures can be calculated similarly to a previous example:

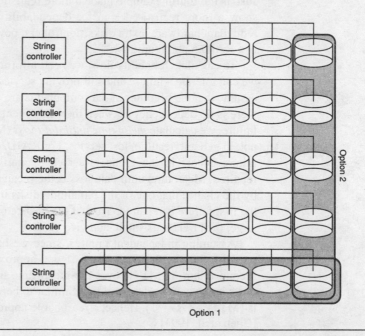

Option 1

Figure 7.40 Two RAID organizations. Orthogonal RAID (option 2) allows the RAID fault-tolerant scheme to protect against string faults as well as disk faults.

$$\text{Enclosure failure rate}_{\text{big disks}} = \frac{6}{1,000,000} + \frac{1}{500,000} + \frac{1}{200,000} + \frac{1}{200,000} + \frac{1}{1,000,000} + \frac{1}{1,000,000}$$

$$= \frac{6+2+5+5+1+1}{1,000,000 \text{ hours}} = \frac{20}{1,000,000 \text{ hours}}$$

$$\text{Enclosure failure rate}_{\text{small disks}} = \frac{12}{1,000,000} + \frac{2}{500,000} + \frac{1}{200,000} + \frac{1}{200,000} + \frac{2}{1,000,000} + \frac{1}{1,000,000}$$

$$= \frac{12+4+5+5+2+1}{1,000,000 \text{ hours}} = \frac{29}{1,000,000 \text{ hours}}$$

The MTTF for each enclosure is just the inverse of the failure rate:

$$\text{MTTF}_{\text{big disks}} = \frac{1}{\text{Failure rate}_{\text{big disks}}} = \frac{1,000,000 \text{ hours}}{20} = 50,000 \text{ hours}$$

$$\text{MTTF}_{\text{small disks}} = \frac{1}{\text{Failure rate}_{\text{small disks}}} = \frac{1,000,000 \text{ hours}}{29} \approx 34,500 \text{ hours}$$

As the array can continue to provide data despite the loss of a single component, we can modify the disk MTDL to calculate for enclosures:

$$\text{MTDL}_{\text{RAID}} = \frac{\text{MTTF}_{\text{enclosure}}^{2}}{N \times (G-1) \times \text{MTTR}_{\text{enclosure}}}$$

In this case, $N = G$ = the number of enclosures. Even if we assume it takes 24 hours to replace an enclosure ($\text{MTTR}_{\text{enclosure}}$), the MTDL for each organization is

$$\text{MTDL}_{\text{big disk RAID}} = \frac{50,000^{2}}{5 \times (5-1) \times 24} = \frac{2,500,000,000 \text{ hours}}{480} \approx 5,200,000 \text{ hours}$$

$$\text{MTDL}_{\text{small disk RAID}} = \frac{34,500^{2}}{5 \times (5-1) \times 24} = \frac{1,190,250,000 \text{ hours}}{480} \approx 2,500,000 \text{ hours}$$

We can now calculate the higher cost for RAID 5 organizations:

80 GB disks, 5 strings = $20,000 + 5 \times \$500 + 30 \times (80 \times \$10) + 5 \times \$1500 = \$54,000$

40 GB disks, 10 strings = $20,000 + 10 \times \$500 + 60 \times (40 \times \$10) + 5 \times \$1500 = \$56,500$

If we evaluated the cost-reliability, the large disk system costs $10 per thousand hours of MTDL, while the small disk system costs $23 per thousand hours of MTDL.

The IOPS for the more dependable organization now depends on the mix of reads and writes in the I/O workload, since writes in RAID 5 systems are much slower than writes for RAID 0 systems. For simplicity, let's assume 100% reads. Since RAID 5 allows reads to all disks, and there are more disks and strings in our dependable design, read performance improves as well as dependability:

80 GB disks, 5 strings = Min(50,000, 50,000, 31,250, **3060**, 4000) = 3060 IOPS

40 GB disks, 10 strings = Min(50,000, 50,000, 31,250, **6120**, 8000) = 6120 IOPS

We can now calculate the cost per IOPS for RAID 5 organizations. Compared to the results from the first example, the cost per IOPS increased slightly from $15 to $18 and from $8 to $9, respectively.

In both cases, given the previous reliability assumptions, the mean time to data loss for redundant arrays containing several dozen disks is greater than the mean time to failure of a single disk. At least for a read-only workload, the cost-performance impact of dependability is small. Thus, a weakness was turned into a strength: The larger number of components allows redundancy so that some can fail without affecting the service.

7.12 Putting It All Together: EMC Symmetrix and Celerra

The EMC Symmetrix is one of the leading disk arrays that works with most computer systems. The EMC Celerra is a relatively new filer for both UNIX NFS and Windows CIFS file systems. Both machines have significant features to improve dependability of storage. After reviewing the two architectures, we'll summarize the results of their performance and dependability benchmarks.

EMC Symmetrix 8000

The Symmetrix 8000 holds up to 384 disks, which are protected either via mirroring (RAID 1) or via a variation of RAID 5 that EMC calls RAID-S. The RAID-S group size is four or eight drives. At 73 GB per drive, the total raw capacity is about 28 TB. Figure 7.41 shows its organization.

The internal architecture is built around four buses that run at 60 MHz and transfer 64 bits of data and 16 bits of error correcting code (ECC). With this scheme, any number of incorrect bits in any two nibbles can be detected while any number of incorrect bits in one nibble can be corrected. Each component is connected to two buses so that failure of a bus does not disconnect the component from the system. The components that connect to these four buses are as follows:

- *Channel directors* connect the server host to the internal buses of the disk array and work with SCSI, FC-AL, and ESCON (IBM mainframe I/O bus). They also run the algorithms to manage the caches. Up to 16 channel directors are provided, packaged 2 directors per card.

- *Disk cache memory* acts as a speed-matching buffer between the host servers and the disks; in addition, it exploits locality to reduce accesses to the disks. There are up to four slots for cache boards, and each contains 1 GB to 8 GB.

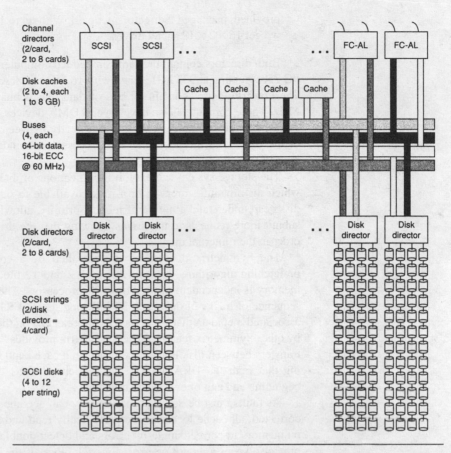

Figure 7.41 EMC Symmetrix 8000 organization. Every component is paired so that there is no single point of failure. If mirroring is used, then the disks are also paired. If RAID-S is used, there is one block of parity for every four to eight blocks.

Each system has at least two cache boards, producing systems that have from 2 GB to 32 GB of cache. EMC claims 90% to 95% read hit rates for the largest cache size. The caches will also buffer writes, allowing the system to report that the write is completed before it reaches the disk. The channel director monitors the amount of dirty data. It will not send the write complete signal if the cache is behind and the channel director needs to flush more data to disk to reduce the length of the write buffer queue. Symmetrix does not include batteries in the cache for nonvolatility, but instead provides batteries for the whole array to protect the entire system from short power failures.

■   *Disk directors* connect the internal buses to the disks. Each disk director has two Ultra1 SCSI strings, running at 40 MB/sec in 2001. Each string uses a redundant SCSI controller on a different director to watch the behavior of the primary controller and to take over in case it fails. Up to 16 disk directors are provided, packaged 2 directors per card. With up to 12 SCSI disks on a string, we get $16 \times 2 \times 12 = 384$ drives.

Both directors contain the same embedded computers. They have two Power-PC 750s running at 333 MHz, each with 16 MB of DRAM and a 1 MB L2 cache. The PowerPC buses contain 32 bits of data plus 4 bits for ECC, and run at 33 MHz. These computers also have several DMA devices, so requested data do not go through the computer memory, but directly between the disks and the cache, or the cache and the host bus. The processors act independently, sharing only boot ROMs and an Ethernet port.

The storage system can exploit modifications of disks as requested by EMC, which disk manufacturers in turn make available to others. For example, some disks can understand a notion of request priority, allowing the storage system to submit more requests to the drives knowing that the drives will maintain proper order in their internal queues.

The Symmetrix disk cache is controlled by a combination of LRU and prefetching algorithms, fetching between 2 and 12 blocks at a time. The cache memory is independent of the PowerPC processors. The cache is structured as a sequence of tracks of data each 32 KB long. Each 4 KB segment of a track has associated metadata that contains CRC checksums on the data and metadata used by other Symmetrix features. The Symmetrix provides "end-to-end" checking on transfers between disk to cache and between cache and the host server by ensuring that both the DRAM ECC and associated CRC checksums match at the beginning and end of every data transfer.

As faults must be activated before they can become effective errors and then corrected, all cache locations are periodically read and rewritten using the ECC on memory to correct single-bit errors and detect double-bit errors. Cache scrubbing also keeps a record of errors for each block. If the channel director finds an uncorrectable error, then this section of the cache is "fenced" and removed from service. The data are first copied to another block of the cache. The service processor (see below) then contacts EMC to request repair of the failed component.

During idle time, disk scrubbing is performed analogously to cache scrubbing above, with the same benefit of turning latent errors into activated errors during relatively idle times. Correctable errors are logged, and uncorrectable errors cause the bad disk sector to be replaced, with the missing data coming from the redundant information. If too many sectors in a track must be skipped, the whole track is fenced. Such repairs to the cache and to the disks are transparent to the user.

Rather than have an XOR engine only in the disk directors, RAID 5 parity calculations are done inside the drives themselves and combined by the directors as needed. As mentioned earlier, small writes in RAID 5 involve four accesses over two disks. This optimization avoids having to read the rest of the data blocks of a group to calculate parity on a "small" write. Symmetrix supplies the new data and asks the disk to calculate which bits changed, and then passes this information to the disk containing parity for it to read the old parity and modify it.

Having the disk drive perform the XOR calculations provides two benefits. First, it avoids having an XOR engine become a bottleneck by spreading the function to each disk. Second, it allows the older data to be read and rewritten without an intervening seek; the same benefit applies when updating parity.

In addition to the dynamic nature of managing the cache, the Symmetrix can change how mirroring works to get better performance from the second disk. It monitors access patterns to the data and changes policy depending on the pattern. Data are organized into logical volumes, so there is a level of indirection between the logical data accesses and the layout of data on the physical disks. Depending on whether accesses are sequential or random, the mirror policy options include

- *Interleaved*—The mirrors alternate which cylinders they serve, ranging from every other cylinder to large blocks of cylinders. This policy helps with sequential accesses by allowing one disk to seek to the next cylinder while the other disk is reading data.

- *Mixed*—One disk serves the first half of the data and one disk serves the second half. This policy helps with random accesses by allowing the two independent requests to be overlapped.

Policy options also let only a single disk serve all accesses, which helps error recovery.

The Symmetrix 8000 also has a service processor. It is just a laptop that talks to all directors over an internal Ethernet. To allow remote maintenance of the disk array, the service processor is also connected to a telephone line. All system errors are logged to the service processor, which filters the log to determine whether it should contact EMC headquarters to see if repair is warranted. That is, it is predicting potential failures. If it suspects a failure, it contacts support personnel who review the data and decide if intervention is required. They can call back into the service processor to collect more data and to probe the Symmetrix to determine the root cause of the error. A customer service engineer is then dispatched to replace the failing component.

In addition to error logging and remote support, the service processor is used for code installation and upgrades, creating and modifying system configurations, running scripts, and other maintenance activities. To allow upgrades in the field, the service processor can systematically upgrade the EEPROMs of each director and then put the director into a busy state so that it performs no storage accesses until it reboots with the new software.

EMC Celerra 500

The Celerra contains no disk storage itself, but simply connects to clients on one side and to Symmetrix disk arrays on the other. Using the NAS terminology, it is called a *filer*. Its job is to translate the file requests from clients into commands for data from Symmetrix arrays, and to transfer files as requested.

The Celerra has 14 slots for *data movers,* which are simply PC motherboards that connect to the Symmetrix array via two SCSI buses. Each data mover contains a 700 MHz Pentium III processor, PCI bus, and 512 MB of DRAM. It also supports several varieties of network cards with a varying number of networks: ATM, FDDI, two 1G bit Ethernets per card, and eight 100M bit Ethernets per card. Each data mover acts as a fully autonomous file server, running EMC's real-time operating system called DART.

In addition to the data movers, there are two *control stations,* which act analogously to the service processor in the Symmetrix array. A pair of control stations provides protection in case one fails. The hardware used in control stations is the same as the hardware used in the data movers, but with a different function. They run Linux as their operating system.

Celerra has an extensive set of features to provide dependable file service:

- The Celerra has multiple fans, multiple power supplies, multiple batteries, and two power cords to the box. In every case, a single failure of one of these components does not affect behavior of the system.

- Each data mover can contact all the disks in the Symmetrix array over either SCSI bus, allowing the Symmetrix to continue despite a bus failure.

- Each data mover has two internal Ethernet cards, allowing communication with the control station to continue even if one card or network fails.

- Each data mover has at least two interfaces for clients, allowing redundant connections so that clients have at least two paths to each data mover.

- The software allows a data mover to act as a standby spare.

- There is space for a redundant control station, to take over in case the primary control station fails.

The Celerra relies on the service processor in the Symmetrix box to call home when attention is needed.

EMC Symmetrix and Celerra Performance and Availability

Figure 7.32 on page 733 shows the performance of the Celerra 507 with the Symmetrix 8700 running SPECSFS97, as the number of data movers scales from 2 to 14. The 100,000 NFS operations per second with 14 data movers set the record at the time it was submitted. Despite their focus on dependability—with a large number of features to detect and predict failures and to reduce mean time to repair—the Celerra/Symmetrix combination had leading performance on benchmark results.

The disk cache of the EMC Symmetrix disk array was subjected to initial availability and maintainability benchmarking [Lambright 2000]. A small number of experiments were performed with the goal of learning more about how to perform availability and maintainability benchmarks.

Faults were injected via software, going from narrowly focused faults to very broad faults. These were not intended to represent typical faults; they were intended to stress the system, and many are unlikely to occur in real systems.

As mentioned earlier, the EMC array has the ability to shrink the size of the cache in response to faults by fencing off a portion of the cache. It also has error correction that can prevent a fault from causing a failure. The system under test had 8 GB of cache and 96 disks each with 18 GB of capacity, and it was connected to an IBM mainframe over 12 channels. The workload was random I/O with 75% reads and 25% writes. Performance was evaluated using EMC benchmarks.

The first fault tests the behavior of the system when the CPUs in the front and back end get confused: the data structure representing which portions of the cache were available or fenced is not identical in each CPU. Thus, some CPUs assumed that the cache was bigger than what other CPUs assumed. Figure 7.42 shows the behavior when half of the CPUs are out of sync. A fault was injected at the 5th minute and corrected at the 10th minute. The I/O rate increases in the 12th minute as the system catches up with delayed requests.

Performance dropped because some CPUs would try to access disabled memory, generating an error. As each error happened there was a short delay to report it; as the number of CPUs reporting errors increased, so did the delay.

The second fault experiment forced improper behavior of a cache software lock. The lock protects metadata related to the LRU replacement algorithm. The fault simulated a CPU in an infinite loop that repeatedly takes the cache lock without releasing it. Figure 7.43 shows the results: The flawed CPU takes the lock in the 6th, 10th, and 15th minute, each time holding it for 20 seconds. Note that the y-axis reports response time, so smaller is better. As expected, response time was impacted by this fault.

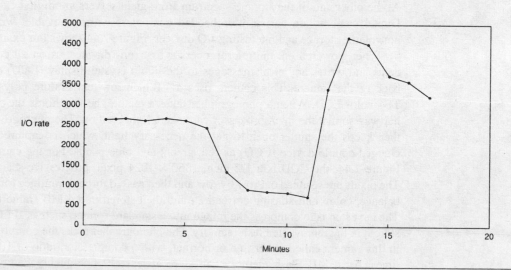

Figure 7.42 I/O rate as Symmetrix CPUs become inconsistent in their model of the size of the cache. Faults were inserted in the 5th minute and corrected in the 10th minute.

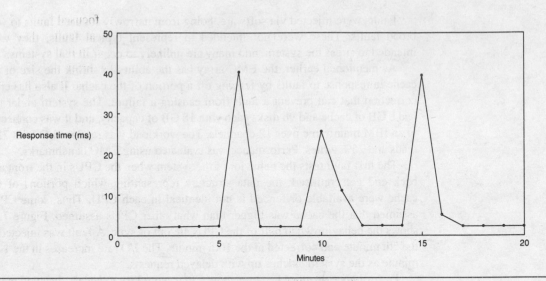

Figure 7.43 Host response time as a rogue CPU hogs a lock for metadata. The lock was held for 20 seconds at minutes 6, 10, and 15.

Standard maintenance techniques fixed the first error, but the second error was much more difficult to diagnose. The benchmark experiments led to suggestions on improving EMC management utilities.

7.13   Another View: Sanyo VPC-SX500 Digital Camera

At the other end of the storage spectrum from giant servers are digital cameras. Digital cameras are basically embedded computers with removable, writable, nonvolatile storage and interesting I/O devices. Figure 7.44 shows our example.

When powered on, the microprocessor first runs diagnostics on all components and writes any error messages to the liquid crystal display (LCD) on the back of the camera. This camera uses a 1.8-inch low-temperature polysilicon TFT color LCD. When a photographer takes a picture, he first holds the shutter halfway so that the microprocessor can take a light reading. The microprocessor then keeps the shutter open to get the necessary light, which is captured by a charged-couple device (CCD) as red, green, and blue pixels. For the camera in Figure 7.44, the CCD is a 1/2-inch, 1360 × 1024 pixel, progressive-scan chip. The pixels are scanned out row by row and then passed through routines for white balance, color, and aliasing correction, and then stored in a 4 MB frame buffer. The next step is to compress the image into a standard format, such as JPEG, and store it in the removable Flash memory. The photographer picks the compression, in this camera called either fine or normal, with a compression ratio of 10 to 20 times. An 8 MB Flash memory can store at least 19 fine-quality compressed images or 31 normal-quality compressed images. The microprocessor then updates the LCD display to show that there is room for one less picture.

Figure 7.44 The Sanyo VPC-SX500 with flash memory card and IBM Microdrive.
Although newer cameras offer more pixels per picture, the principles are the same. This
1360 x 1024 pixel digital camera stores pictures either using CompactFlash memory,
which ranges from 8 MB to 64 MB, or using a 340 MB IBM Microdrive. It is 4.3 inches
wide x 2.5 inches high x 1.6 inches deep, and it weighs 7.4 ounces. In addition to taking
a still picture and converting it to JPEG format every 0.9 seconds, it can record a Quick
Time video clip at VGA size (640 x 480). Using the IBM Microdrive, it can record up to 7.5
minutes at 15 frames per second with sound (10,000 images) or 50 minutes for 160 x
120 pixel video with sound. Without video, it can record up to 12 hours of 8-bit 8 KHz
audio. The Flash memory storage capacity is 5 to 40 times shorter, so its video and
audio capacity are also 5X to 40X smaller. One technological advantage is the use of a
custom system on a chip to reduce size and power, so the camera only needs two AA
batteries to operate versus four in other digital cameras.

Although the previous paragraph covers the basics of a digital camera, there
are many more features that are included: showing the recorded images on the
color LCD display; sleep mode to save battery life; monitoring battery energy;
buffering to allow recording a rapid sequence of uncompressed images; and, in
this camera, video recording using MPEG format and audio recording using
WAV format.

The VPC-SX500 camera allows the photographer to use a 340 MB IBM
Microdrive instead of CompactFlash memory. Figure 7.45 compares Compact-
Flash and the IBM Microdrive.

Characteristics	Sandisk Type I CompactFlash SDCFB-64-144	Sandisk Type II CompactFlash SDCF2B-300-530	IBM 340 MB Microdrive DSCM-10340
Formatted data capacity (MB)	64	300	340
Bytes per sector	512	512	512
Data transfer rate (MB/sec)	4 (burst)	4 (burst)	2.6–4.2
Link speed to buffer (MB/sec)	6	6	13
Power standby/operating (W)	0.15 / 0.66	0.15/0.66	0.07/0.83
Size: height × width × depth (inches)	1.43 × 1.68 × 0.13	1.43 × 1.68 × 0.20	1.43 × 1.68 × 0.20
Weight in grams (454 grams/pound)	11.4	13.5	16
Write cycles before sector wear-out	300,000	300,000	not applicable
Load/unload cycles (on/off)	not applicable	not applicable	300,000
Nonrecoverable read errors per bits read	< 1 per 10^{14}	< 1 per 10^{14}	< 1 per 10^{13}
Shock tolerance: operating, not operating	2000 G, 2000 G	2000 G, 2000 G	175 G, 1500 G
Mean time between failures (hours)	> 1,000,000	> 1,000,000	(see caption)
Best price (in August 2001)	$41	$595	$165

Figure 7.45 Characteristics of three storage alternatives for digital cameras. IBM matches the Type II form factor in the Microdrive, while the CompactFlash card uses that space to include many more Flash chips. IBM does not quote MTTF for the 1.0-inch drives, but the service life is five years or 8800 powered-on hours, whichever is first.

The CompactFlash standard package was proposed by Sandisk Corporation in 1994 for the PCMCIA-ATA cards of portable PCs. Because it follows the ATA interface, it simulates a disk interface including seek commands, logical tracks, and so on. It includes a built-in controller to support many types of Flash memory and to help with chip yield for Flash memories by mapping out bad blocks.

The electronic brain of this camera is an embedded computer with several special functions embedded on the chip [Okada et al. 1999]. Figure 7.46 shows the block diagram of a chip similar to the one in the camera. Such chips have been called *systems on a chip* (SOC) because they essentially integrate into a single chip all the parts that were found on a small printed circuit board of the past. SOC generally reduces size and lowers power compared to less integrated solutions. Sanyo claims SOC enables the camera to operate on half the number of batteries and to offer a smaller form factor than competitors' cameras. For higher performance, it has two buses. The 16 bit bus is for the many slower I/O devices: Smart Media interface, program and data memory, and DMA. The 32-bit bus is for the SDRAM, the signal processor (which is connected to the CCD), the Motion JPEG encoder, and the NTSC/PAL encoder (which is connected to the LCD). Unlike desktop microprocessors, note the large variety of I/O buses that this chip must integrate. The 32-bit RISC MPU is a proprietary design and runs at 28.8 MHz, the same clock rate as the buses. This 700 mW chip contains 1.8 M transistors in a 10.5 × 10.5 mm die implemented using a 0.35-micron process.

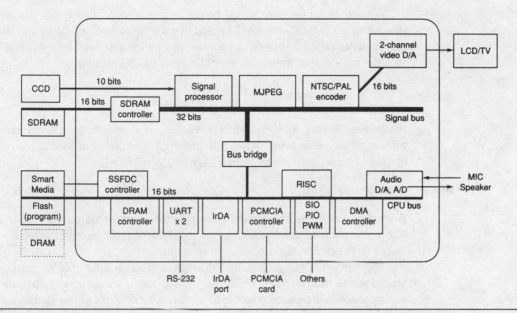

Figure 7.46 The system on a chip (SOC) found in Sanyo digital cameras. This block diagram, found in Okada et al. [1999], is for the predecessor of the SOC in the camera in Figure 7.45. The successor SOC, called Super Advanced IC, uses three buses instead of two, operates at 60 MHz, consumes 800 mW, and fits 3.1M transistors in a 10.2 x 10.2 mm die using a 0.35-micron process. Note that this embedded system has twice as many transistors as the state-of-the-art, high-performance microprocessor in 1990! The SOC in the figure is limited to processing 1024 x 768 pixels, but its successor supports 1360 x 1024 pixels.

7.14 Fallacies and Pitfalls

Fallacy *The rated mean time to failure of disks is 1,200,000 hours or almost 140 years, so disks practically never fail.*

The current marketing practices of disk manufacturers can mislead users. How is such an MTTF calculated? Early in the process manufacturers will put thousands of disks in a room, run them for a few months, and count the number that fail. They compute MTTF as the total number of hours that the disks were cumulatively up divided by the number that failed.

One problem is that this number far exceeds the lifetime of a disk, which is commonly assumed to be five years or 43,800 hours. For this large MTTF to make some sense, disk manufacturers argue that the model corresponds to a user who buys a disk, and then keeps replacing the disk every five years—the planned lifetime of the disk. The claim is that if many customers (and their great-grandchildren) did this for the next century, on average they would replace a disk 27 times before a failure, or about 140 years.

A more useful measure would be percentage of disks that fail. Assume 1000 disks with a 1,000,000-hour MTTF and that the disks are used 24 hours a day. If you replaced failed disks with a new one having the same reliability characteristics, the number that would fail over five years (43,800 hours) is

$$\text{Failed disks} = \frac{1000 \text{ drives} \times 43,800 \text{ hours/drive}}{1,000,000 \text{ hours/failure}} = 44$$

Stated alternatively, 4.4% would fail over the 5-year period. If they were powered on less per day, then fewer would fail, provided the number of load/unload cycles are not exceeded (see Figure 7.2 on page 682).

Fallacy *Components fail fast.*

A good deal of the fault-tolerant literature is based on the simplifying assumption that a component operates perfectly until a latent error becomes effective, and then a failure occurs that stops the component.

The Tertiary Disk project had the opposite experience. Many components started acting strangely long before they failed, and it was generally up to the system operator to determine whether to declare a component as failed. The component would generally be willing to continue to act in violation of the service agreement (see Section 7.4) until an operator "terminated" that component.

Figure 7.47 shows the history of four drives that were terminated, and the number of hours they started acting strangely before they were replaced.

Messages in system log for failed disk	Number of log messages	Duration (hours)
Hardware Failure (Peripheral device write fault [for] Field Replaceable Unit)	1763	186
Not Ready (Diagnostic failure: ASCQ = Component ID [of] Field Replaceable Unit)	1460	90
Recovered Error (Failure Prediction Threshold Exceeded [for] Field Replaceable Unit)	1313	5
Recovered Error (Failure Prediction Threshold Exceeded [for] Field Replaceable Unit)	431	17

Figure 7.47 Record in system log for 4 of the 368 disks in Tertiary Disk that were replaced over 18 months. See Talagala and Patterson [1999]. These messages, matching the SCSI specification, were placed into the system log by device drivers. Messages started occurring as much as a week before one drive was replaced by the operator. The third and fourth messages indicate that the drive's failure prediction mechanism detected and predicted imminent failure, yet it was still hours before the drives were replaced by the operator.

Fallacy   *Computers systems achieve 99.999% availability ("five nines"), as advertised.*

Marketing departments of companies making servers have started bragging about the availability of their computer hardware; in terms of Figure 7.48, they claim availability of 99.999%, nicknamed *five nines*. Even the marketing departments of operating system companies have tried to give this impression.

Five minutes of unavailability per year is certainly impressive, but given the failure data collected in surveys, it's hard to believe. For example, Hewlett-Packard claims that the HP-9000 server hardware and HP-UX operating system can deliver a 99.999% availability guarantee "in certain pre-defined, pre-tested customer environments" (see Hewlett-Packard [1998]). This guarantee does not include failures due to operator faults, application faults, or environmental faults, which are likely the dominant fault categories today. Nor does it include scheduled downtime. It is also unclear what the financial penalty is to a company if a system does not match its guarantee.

Microsoft has also promulgated a five nines marketing campaign. In January 2001, *www.microsoft.com* was unavailable for 22 hours. For its Web site to achieve 99.999% availability, it will require a clean slate for the next 250 years.

In contrast to marketing suggestions, well-managed servers in 2001 typically achieve 99% to 99.9% availability.

Pitfall   *Where a function is implemented affects its reliability.*

In theory, it is fine to move the RAID function into software. In practice, it is very difficult to make it work reliably.

The software culture is generally based on eventual correctness via a series of releases and patches. It is also difficult to isolate from other layers of software. For example, proper software behavior is often based on having the proper version and patch release of the operating system. Thus, many customers have lost data due to software bugs or incompatibilities in environment in software RAID systems.

Obviously, hardware systems are not immune to bugs, but the hardware culture tends to place a greater emphasis on testing correctness in the initial release.

Unavailability (minutes per year)	Availability (percent)	Availability class ("number of nines")
50,000	90%	1
5,000	99%	2
500	99.9%	3
50	99.99%	4
5	99.999%	5
0.5	99.9999%	6
0.05	99.99999%	7

Figure 7.48 Minutes unavailable per year to achieve availability class (from Gray and Siewlorek [1991]). Note that five nines means unavailable five minutes per year.

In addition, the hardware is more likely to be independent of the version of the operating system.

Fallacy *Semiconductor memory will soon replace magnetic disks in desktop and server computer systems.*

When the first edition of this book was written, disks were growing in capacity at 29% per year and DRAMs at 60% per year. One exercise even asked when DRAMs would match the cost per bit of magnetic disks.

At about the same time, these same questions were being asked inside disk manufacturing companies such as IBM. Therefore, disk manufacturers pushed the rate of technology improvement to match the rate of DRAMs—60% per year—with magnetoresistive heads being the first advance to accelerate disk technology. Figure 7.49 shows the relative areal density of DRAM to disk, with the gap closing in the late 1980s and widening ever since. In 2001, the gap is larger than it was in 1975. Instead of DRAMs wiping out disks, disks are wiping out tapes!

Fallacy *Since head-disk assemblies of disks are the same technology independent of the disk interface, the disk interface matters little in price.*

Since the high-tech portions of the disk are the heads, arms, platters, motors, and so on, it stands to reason that the I/O interface should matter little in the price of a disk. Perhaps you should pay $25 extra per drive for the more complicated SCSI interface versus the PC IDE interface. Figure 7.50 shows that this reason does not stand.

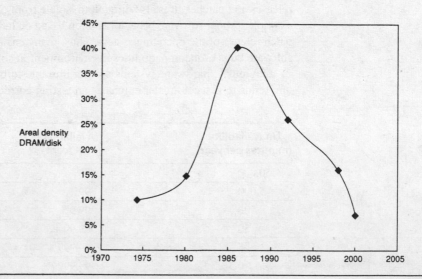

Figure 7.49 Areal density of DRAMs versus maximal areal density of magnetic disks in products, as a percentage, over time. Source: *New York Times*, 2/23/98, page C3, "Makers of disk drives crowd even more data into even smaller spaces." Year 2000 data added to the *New York Times* Information.

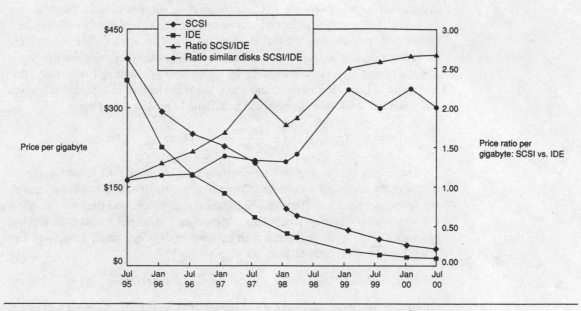

Figure 7.50 Price per gigabyte of 3.5-inch disks between 1995 and 2000 for IDE/ATA and SCSI drives. The data come from the same sources as Figure 7.3 on page 685. The downward-heading lines plot price per gigabyte, and the upward-heading lines plot ratio of SCSI price to IDE price. The first upward line is simply the ratio of the average price per gigabyte of SCSI versus IDE. The second such line is limited to comparisons of disks with the same capacity and the same RPM; it is the geometric mean of the ratios of the prices of the similar disks for each month. Note that the ratio of SCSI prices to IDE/ATA prices got larger over time, presumably because of the increasing volume of IDE versus SCSI drives and increasing competition for IDE disk suppliers.

There are two explanations for a factor of 2.5 difference in price per mega-byte between SCSI and IDE disks. First, the PC market is much more competitive than the server market; PCs normally use IDE drives, and servers normally use SCSI drives. Second, SCSI drives tend to be higher performance in rotation speed and seek times. To try to account for the performance differences, the second ratio line in Figure 7.50 is limited to comparisons of disks with similar capacity and performance but different interfaces, yet the ratio in 2000 was still about 2.0.

A third argument for the price difference is called the *manufacturing learning curve*. The rationale is that every doubling in manufacturing volume reduces costs by a significant percentage. Since about 10 times as many IDE/ATA drives are sold per year as SCSI drives, if manufacturing costs dropped 20% for every doubling in volume, the learning curve effect would explain a cost factor of 1.8.

Fallacy *The time of an average seek of a disk in a computer system is the time for a seek of one-third the number of cylinders.*

This fallacy comes from confusing the way manufacturers market disks with the expected performance, and from the false assumption that seek times are linear in distance. The one-third-distance rule of thumb comes from calculating the distance of a seek from one random location to another random location, not including the current cylinder and assuming there are a large number of cylinders. In the past, manufacturers listed the seek of this distance to offer a consistent basis for comparison. (As mentioned on page 683, today they calculate the "average" by timing all seeks and dividing by the number.) Assuming (incorrectly) that seek time is linear in distance, and using the manufacturer's reported minimum and "average" seek times, a common technique to predict seek time is

$$\text{Time}_{seek} = \text{Time}_{minimum} + \frac{\text{Distance}}{\text{Distance}_{average}} \times (\text{Time}_{average} - \text{Time}_{minimum})$$

The fallacy concerning seek time is twofold. First, seek time is *not* linear with distance; the arm must accelerate to overcome inertia, reach its maximum traveling speed, decelerate as it reaches the requested position, and then wait to allow the arm to stop vibrating (*settle time*). Moreover, sometimes the arm must pause to control vibrations. For disks with more than 200 cylinders, Chen and Lee [1995] modeled the seek distance as

$$\text{Seek time(Distance)} = a \times \sqrt{\text{Distance} - 1} + b \times (\text{Distance} - 1) + c$$

where a, b, and c are selected for a particular disk so that this formula will match the quoted times for Distance = 1, Distance = max, and Distance = 1/3 max. Figure 7.51 plots this equation versus the fallacy equation. Unlike the first equation, the square root of the distance reflects acceleration and deceleration.

The second problem is that the average in the product specification would only be true if there were no locality to disk activity. Fortunately, there is both

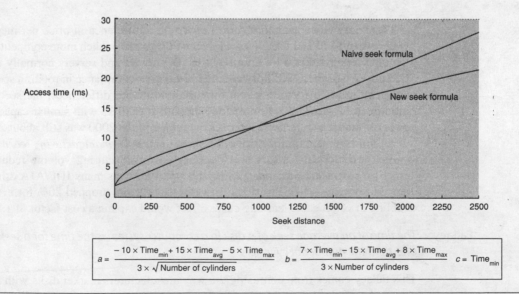

Figure 7.51 Seek time versus seek distance for sophisticated model versus naive model. Chen and Lee [1995] found that the equations shown above for parameters a, b, and c worked well for several disks.

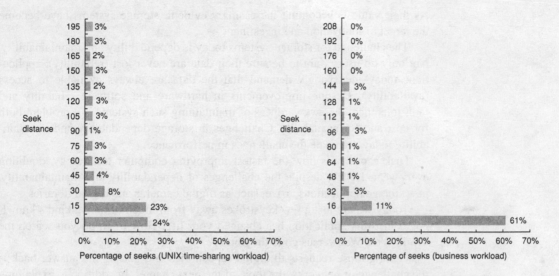

Figure 7.52 Sample measurements of seek distances for two systems. The measurements on the left were taken on a UNIX time-sharing system. The measurements on the right were taken from a business-processing application in which the disk seek activity was scheduled to improve throughput. Seek distance of 0 means the access was made to the same cylinder. The rest of the numbers show the collective percentage for distances between numbers on the y-axis. For example, 11% for the bar labeled 16 in the business graph means that the percentage of seeks between 1 and 16 cylinders was 11%. The UNIX measurements stopped at 200 of the 1000 cylinders, but this captured 85% of the accesses. The business measurements tracked all 816 cylinders of the disks. The only seek distances with 1% or greater of the seeks that are not in the graph are 224 with 4%, and 304, 336, 512, and 624, each having 1%. This total is 94%, with the difference being small but nonzero distances in other categories. Measurements courtesy of Dave Anderson of Seagate.

temporal and spatial locality (see page 393 in Chapter 5): Disk blocks get used more than once, and disk blocks near the current cylinder are more likely to be used than those farther away. For example, Figure 7.52 shows sample measurements of seek distances for two workloads: a UNIX time-sharing workload and a business-processing workload. Notice the high percentage of disk accesses to the same cylinder, labeled distance 0 in the graphs, in both workloads.

Thus, this fallacy couldn't be more misleading. (The exercises debunk this fallacy in more detail.)

7.15   Concluding Remarks

Storage is one of those technologies that we tend to take for granted. And yet, if we look at the true status of things today, storage is king. One can even argue that servers, which have become commodities, are now becoming peripheral to storage devices. Driving that point home are some estimates from IBM, which expects storage sales to surpass server sales in the next two years.

Michael Vizard
editor in chief, *Infoworld,* August 11, 2001

As their value is becoming increasingly evident, storage systems have become the target of innovation and investment.

The challenge for storage systems today is dependability and maintainability. Not only do users want to be sure their data are never lost (reliability), applications today increasingly demand that the data are always available to access (availability). Despite improvements in hardware and software reliability and fault tolerance, the awkwardness of maintaining such systems is a problem both for cost and for availability. Challenges in storage dependability and maintainability today dominate the challenges in performance.

Disk capacity is now the fastest improving computer technology, doubling every year. Hence, despite the challenges of dependability and maintainability, new storage applications arrive, such as digital cameras and digital libraries.

Today we are just a few keystrokes away from much of humankind's knowledge. Just this application has changed your life: How often do you search the World Wide Web versus go to the library?

Getting those requests to digital repositories and getting the answer back is the challenge of networks, the topic of the next chapter. In addition to explaining the Internet, the next chapter also gives the anatomy of a Web search engine, showing how a network of thousands of desktop computers can provide a valuable and reliable service.

7.16   Historical Perspective and References

Mass storage is a term used there to imply a unit capacity in excess of one million alphanumeric characters...

Hoagland [1963]

The variety of storage I/O and issues leads to a varied history for the rest of the story. (Smotherman [1989] explores the history of I/O in more depth.) This section discusses magnetic storage, RAID, and I/O buses and controllers. Jain [1991] and Lazowska et al. [1984] offer books for those interested in learning more about queuing theory.

Magnetic Storage

Magnetic recording was invented to record sound, and by 1941, magnetic tape was able to compete with other storage devices. It was the success of the ENIAC in 1947 that led to the push to use tapes to record digital information. Reels of magnetic tapes dominated removable storage through the 1970s. In the 1980s, the IBM 3480 cartridge became the de facto standard, at least for mainframes. It can transfer at 3 MB/sec by reading 18 tracks in parallel. The capacity is just 200 MB for this 1/2-inch tape. The 9840 cartridge, used by StorageTek in the Powder-Horn, transfers at 10 MB/sec and stores 20,000 MB. This device records the tracks in a zigzag fashion rather than just longitudinally, so that the head reverses direction to follow the track. This technique is called *serpentine recording*. Another 1/2-inch tape is Digital Linear Tape, with DLT7000 storing 35,000 MB and transferring at 5 MB/sec. Its competitor is helical scan, which rotates the head to get the increased recording density. In 2001, the 8 mm helical-scan tapes contain 20,000 MB and transfer at about 3 MB/sec. Whatever their density and cost, the serial nature of tapes creates an appetite for storage devices with random access.

In 1953, Reynold B. Johnson of IBM picked a staff of 15 scientists with the goal of building a radically faster random access storage system than tape. The goal was to have the storage equivalent of 50,000 standard IBM punch cards and to fetch the data in a single second. Johnson's disk drive design was simple but untried: The magnetic read/write sensors would have to float a few thousandths of an inch above the continuously rotating disk. Twenty-four months later the team emerged with the functional prototype. It weighed one ton and occupied about 300 cubic feet of space. The RAMAC-350 (Random Access Method of Accounting Control) used 50 platters that were 24 inches in diameter, rotated at 1200 RPM, with a total capacity of 5 MB and an access time of 1 second.

Starting with the RAMAC, IBM maintained its leadership in the disk industry, with its storage headquarters in San Jose, California, where Johnson's team did its work. Many of the future leaders of competing disk manufacturers started their careers at IBM, and many disk companies are located near San Jose.

Although RAMAC contained the first disk, a major breakthrough in magnetic recording was found in later disks with air-bearing read/write heads, where the head would ride on a cushion of air created by the fast-moving disk surface. This cushion meant the head could both follow imperfections in the surface and yet be very close to the surface. Subsequent advances have come largely from improved quality of components and higher precision. In 2001, heads fly 2 to 3 microinches above the surface, whereas in the RAMAC drive they were 1000 microinches away.

Moving-head disks quickly became the dominant high-speed magnetic storage, although their high cost meant that magnetic tape continued to be used extensively until the 1970s. The next important development for hard disks was the removable hard disk drive developed by IBM in 1962; this made it possible to share the expensive drive electronics and helped disks overtake tapes as the preferred storage medium. The IBM 1311 disk in 1962 had an areal density of 50,000 bits per square inch and a cost of about $800 per megabyte.

IBM also invented the floppy disk drive in 1970, originally to hold microcode for the IBM 370 series. Floppy disks became popular with the PC about 10 years later.

The second major disk breakthrough was the so-called Winchester disk design in about 1973. Winchester disks benefited from two related properties. First, integrated circuits lowered the costs of not only CPUs, but also of disk controllers and the electronics to control disk arms. Reductions in the cost of the disk electronics made it unnecessary to share the electronics, and thus made nonremovable disks economical. Since the disk was fixed and could be in a sealed enclosure, both the environmental and control problems were greatly reduced. Sealing the system allowed the heads to fly closer to the surface, which in turn enabled increases in areal density. The first sealed disk that IBM shipped had two spindles, each with a 30 MB disk; the moniker "30-30" for the disk led to the name Winchester. (America's most popular sporting rifle, the Winchester 94, was nicknamed the "30-30" after the caliber of its cartridge.) Winchester disks grew rapidly in popularity in the 1980s, completely replacing removable disks by the middle of that decade. Before this time, the cost of the electronics to control the disk meant that the media had to be removable.

In 2001, IBM sold disks with 25 billion bits per square inch at a price of about $0.01 per megabyte. (See Hospodor and Hoagland [1993] for more on magnetic storage trends.) The disk industry today is responsible for 90% of the mass storage market.

As mentioned in Section 7.14, as DRAMs started to close the areal density gap and appeared to be catching up with disk storage, internal meetings at IBM called into question the future of disk drives. Disk designers concluded that disks must improve at 60% per year to forestall the DRAM threat, in contrast to the historical 29% per year. The essential enabler was magnetoresistive heads, with giant magnetoresistive heads enabling the current densities.

Because of this competition, the gap in time between when a density record is achieved in the lab and when a disk is shipped with that density has closed considerably. In 2001, the lab record is 60G bits/square inch, but drives are shipping with a third of that density. It is also unclear to disk engineers whether evolutionary change will achieve 1000G bits/square inch.

The personal computer created a market for small form factor disk drives, since the 14-inch disk drives used in mainframes were bigger than the PC. In 2001, the 3.5-inch drive was the market leader, although the smaller 2.5-inch drive needed for laptop computers was significant in sales volume. Personal video recorders (PVRs)—which record television on disk instead of tape—may become a significant consumer of disk drives. Existing form factors and speed are sufficient, with the focus on low noise and high capacity for PVRs. Hence, a market for large, slow, quiet disks may develop. It remains to be seen whether handheld devices or video cameras, requiring even smaller disks, will become as significant in sales volume as PCs or laptops. For example, 1.8-inch drives were developed in the early 1990s for palmtop computers, but that market chose Flash instead, and hence 1.8-inch drives disappeared.

RAID

The small form factor hard disks for PCs in the 1980s led a group at Berkeley to propose redundant arrays of inexpensive disks (RAID). This group had worked on the reduced instruction set computers effort, and so expected much faster CPUs to become available. Their questions were, What could be done with the small disks that accompanied their PCs? and What could be done in the area of

I/O to keep up with much faster processors? They argued to replace one main-frame drive with 50 small drives, as you could get much greater performance with that many independent arms. The many small drives even offered savings in power consumption and floor space.

The downside of many disks was much lower MTTF. Hence, on their own they reasoned out the advantages of redundant disks and rotating parity to address how to get greater performance with many small drives yet have reliability as high as that of a single mainframe disk.

The problem they experienced when explaining their ideas was that some researchers had heard of disk arrays with some form of redundancy, and they didn't understand the Berkeley proposal. Hence, the first RAID paper [Patterson, Gibson, and Katz 1987] is not only a case for arrays of small form factor disk drives, but something of a tutorial and classification of existing work on disk arrays. Mirroring (RAID 1) had long been used in fault-tolerant computers such as those sold by Tandem; Thinking Machines had arrays with 32 data disks and 7 check disks using ECC for correction (RAID 2) in 1987, and Honeywell Bull had a RAID 2 product even earlier; and disk arrays with a single parity disk had been used in scientific computers in the same time frame (RAID 3). Their paper then described a single parity disk with support for sector accesses (RAID 4) and rotated parity (RAID 5). Chen et al. [1994] survey the original RAID ideas, com-mercial products, and more recent developments.

Unknown to the Berkeley group, engineers at IBM working on the AS/400 computer also came up with rotated parity to give greater reliability for a collec-tion of large disks. IBM filed a patent on RAID 5 before the Berkeley group wrote their paper. Patents for RAID 1, RAID 2, and RAID 3 from several compa-nies predate the IBM RAID 5 patent, which has led to plenty of courtroom action.

The Berkeley paper was written before the World Wide Web, but it captured the imagination of many engineers, as copies were faxed around the world. One engineer at what is now Seagate received seven copies of the paper from friends and customers.

EMC had been a supplier of DRAM boards for IBM computers, but around 1988 new policies from IBM made it nearly impossible for EMC to continue to sell IBM memory boards. Apparently, the Berkeley paper also crossed the desks of EMC executives, and so they decided to go after the market dominated by IBM disk storage products instead. As the paper advocated, their model was to use many small drives to compete with mainframe drives, and EMC announced a RAID product in 1990. It relied on mirroring (RAID 1) for reliability; RAID 5 products came much later for EMC. Over the next year, Micropolis offered a RAID 3 product; Compaq offered a RAID 4 product; and Data General, IBM, and NCR offered RAID 5 products.

The RAID ideas soon spread to the rest of the workstation and server indus-try. An article explaining RAID in *Byte* magazine (see Anderson [1990]) led to RAID products being offered on desktop PCs, which was something of a surprise to the Berkeley group. They had focused on performance with good availability, but higher availability was attractive to the PC market.

Another surprise was the cost of the disk arrays. With redundant power supplies and fans, the ability to "hot swap" a disk drive, the RAID hardware controller itself, the redundant disks, and so on, the first disk arrays cost many times the cost of the disks. Perhaps as a result, the "inexpensive" in RAID morphed into "independent." Many marketing departments and technical writers today know of RAID only as "redundant arrays of independent disks."

The EMC transformation was successful; in 2000 EMC was the leading supplier of storage systems. RAID was a $27 billion industry in 2000, and more than 80% of the non-PC drive sales were found in RAIDs.

In recognition of their role, in 1999 Garth Gibson, Randy Katz, and David Patterson received the IEEE Reynold B. Johnson Information Storage Award "for the development of Redundant Arrays of Inexpensive Disks (RAID)."

I/O Buses and Controllers

The ubiquitous microprocessor has inspired not only the personal computers of the 1970s, but also the trend in the late 1980s and 1990s of moving controller functions into I/O devices. I/O devices continued this trend by moving controllers into the devices themselves. These devices are called *intelligent devices,* and some bus standards (e.g., SCSI) have been created specifically for them. Intelligent devices can relax the timing constraints by handling many low-level tasks themselves and queuing the results. For example, many SCSI-compatible disk drives include a track buffer on the disk itself, supporting read ahead and connect/disconnect. Thus, on a SCSI string some disks can be seeking and others loading their track buffer while one is transferring data from its buffer over the SCSI bus. The controller in the original RAMAC, built from vacuum tubes, only needed to move the head over the desired track, wait for the data to pass under the head, and transfer data with calculated parity.

SCSI, which stands for *small computer systems interface,* is an example of one company inventing a bus and generously encouraging other companies to build devices that would plug into it. Shugart created this bus, originally called SASI. It was later standardized by the IEEE.

There have been several candidates to be the successor to SCSI, with the current leading contender being Fibre Channel Arbitrated Loop (FC-AL). The SCSI committee continues to increase the clock rate of the bus, giving this standard a new life, and SCSI is lasting much longer than some of its proposed successors.

Perhaps the first multivendor bus was the PDP-11 Unibus in 1970 from DEC. Alas, this open-door policy on buses is in contrast to companies with proprietary buses using patented interfaces, thereby preventing competition from plug-compatible vendors. Making a bus proprietary also raises costs and lowers the number of available I/O devices that plug into it, since such devices must have an interface designed just for that bus. The PCI bus pushed by Intel represented a return to open, standard I/O buses inside computers. Its immediate successor is PCI-X, with Infiniband under development in 2000. Both were standardized by multi-company trade associations.

The machines of the RAMAC era gave us I/O interrupts as well as storage devices. The first machine to extend interrupts from detecting arithmetic abnormalities to detecting asynchronous I/O events is credited as the NBS DYSEAC in 1954 [Leiner and Alexander 1954]. The following year, the first machine with DMA was operational, the IBM SAGE. Just as today's DMA has, the SAGE had address counters that performed block transfers in parallel with CPU operations.

The early IBM 360s pioneered many of the ideas that we use in I/O systems today. The 360 was the first commercial machine to make heavy use of DMA, and it introduced the notion of I/O programs that could be interpreted by the device. Chaining of I/O programs was an important feature. The concept of channels introduced in the 360 corresponds to the I/O bus of today.

Myer and Sutherland [1968] wrote a classic paper on the trade-off of complexity and performance in I/O controllers. Borrowing the religious concept of the "wheel of reincarnation," they eventually noticed they were caught in a loop of continuously increasing the power of an I/O processor until it needed its own simpler coprocessor. The quote on page 700 captures their cautionary tale.

The IBM mainframe I/O channels, with their I/O processors, can be thought of as an inspiration for Infiniband, with their processors on their Host Channel Adaptor cards. How Infiniband will compete with FC-AL as an I/O interconnect will be interesting to watch. Infiniband is one of the storage area networks discussed in the next chapter.

References

Anderson, M. H. [1990]. "Strength (and safety) in numbers (RAID, disk storage technology)," *Byte* 15:13 (December), 337–339.

Anon. et al. [1985]. "A measure of transaction processing power," Tandem Tech. Rep. TR 85.2. Also appeared in *Datamation,* April 1, 1985.

Bashe, C. J., W. Buchholz, G. V. Hawkins, J. L. Ingram, and N. Rochester [1981]. "The architecture of IBM's early computers," *IBM J. Research and Development* 25:5 (September), 363–375.

Bashe, C. J., L. R. Johnson, J. H. Palmer, and E. W. Pugh [1986]. *IBM's Early Computers,* MIT Press, Cambridge, Mass.

Blaum, M., J. Brady, J. Bruck, and J. Menon [1994]. "EVENODD: An optimal scheme for tolerating double disk failures in RAID architectures," *Proc. 21st Annual Symposium on Computer Architecture* (April), Chicago, Ill., 245–254.

Brady, J. T. [1986]. "A theory of productivity in the creative process," *IEEE CG&A* (May), 25–34.

Brown, A., and D. A. Patterson [2000]. "Towards maintainability, availability, and growth benchmarks: A case study of software RAID systems." *Proc. 2000 USENIX Annual Technical Conf.* (June), San Diego, Calif.

Bucher, I. V., and A. H. Hayes [1980]. "I/O performance measurement on Cray-1 and CDC 7000 computers," *Proc. Computer Performance Evaluation Users Group, 16th Meeting,* NBS 500-65, 245–254.

Chen, P. M., G. A. Gibson, R. H. Katz, and D. A. Patterson [1990]. "An evaluation of redundant arrays of inexpensive disks using an Amdahl 5890," *Proc. 1990 ACM SIGMETRICS Conf. on Measurement and Modeling of Computer Systems* (May), Boulder, Colo.

Chen, P. M., and E. K. Lee [1995]. "Striping in a RAID level 5 disk array," *Proc. 1995 ACM SIGMETRICS Conf. on Measurement and Modeling of Computer Systems* (May), 136–145.

Chen, P. M., E. K. Lee, G. A. Gibson, R. H. Katz, and D. A. Patterson [1994]. "RAID: High-performance, reliable secondary storage," *ACM Computing Surveys* 26:2 (June), 145–188.

Doherty, W. J., and R. P. Kelisky [1979]. "Managing VM/CMS systems for user effectiveness," *IBM Systems J.* 18:1, 143–166.

Enriquez, P. [2001]. "What happened to my dial tone? A study of FCC service disruption reports," poster, *Richard Tapia Symposium on the Celebration of Diversity in Computing,* October 18–20, Houston, Tex.

Friesenborg, S. E., and R. J. Wicks [1985]. "DASD expectations: The 3380, 3380-23, and MVS/XA," Tech. Bulletin GG22-9363-02 (July 10), Washington Systems Center.

Gibson, G. A. [1992]. *Redundant Disk Arrays: Reliable, Parallel Secondary Storage,* ACM Distinguished Dissertation Series, MIT Press, Cambridge, Mass.

Goldstein, S. [1987]. "Storage performance—an eight year outlook," Tech. Rep. TR 03.308-1 (October), Santa Teresa Laboratory, IBM, San Jose, Calif.

Gray, J. [1990]. "A census of Tandem system availability between 1985 and 1990," *IEEE Transactions on Reliability,* 39:4 (October) 409–418.

Gray, J. (ed.) [1993]. *The Benchmark Handbook for Database and Transaction Processing Systems,* 2nd ed., Morgan Kaufmann Publishers, San Francisco.

Gray, J., and A. Reuter [1993]. *Transaction Processing: Concepts and Techniques,* Morgan Kaufmann Publishers, San Francisco.

Gray, J., and D. P. Siewiorek [1991]. "High-availability computer systems." *Computer* 24:9 (September), 39–48.

Henly, M., and B. McNutt [1989]. "DASD I/O characteristics: A comparison of MVS to VM," Tech. Rep. TR 02.1550 (May), IBM, General Products Division, San Jose, Calif.

Hewlett-Packard [1998]. "HP's '5NINES:5MINUTES' vision extends leadership and redefines high availability in mission-critical environments" (February 10), *www.future.enterprisecomputing.hp.com/ia64/news/5nines_vision_pr.html.*

Hoagland, A. S. [1963]. *Digital Magnetic Recording,* Wiley, New York.

Hospodor, A. D., and A. S. Hoagland [1993]. "The changing nature of disk controllers." *Proc. IEEE* 81:4 (April), 586–594.

IBM [1982]. *The Economic Value of Rapid Response Time,* GE20-0752-0, White Plains, N.Y., 11–82.

Imprimis [1989]. *Imprimis Product Specification, 97209 Sabre Disk Drive IPI-2 Interface 1.2 GB,* Document No. 64402302 (May).

Jain, R. [1991]. *The Art of Computer Systems Performance Analysis: Techniques for Experimental Design, Measurement, Simulation, and Modeling,* Wiley, New York.

Katz, R. H., D. A. Patterson, and G. A. Gibson [1989]. "Disk system architectures for high performance computing," *Proc. IEEE* 77:12 (December), 1842–1858.

Kim, M. Y. [1986]. "Synchronized disk interleaving," *IEEE Trans. on Computers* C-35:11 (November), 978–988.

Kuhn, D. R. [1997]. "Sources of failure in the public switched telephone network," *IEEE Computer* 30:4 (April), 31–36.

Lambright, D. [2000]. "Experiences in measuring the reliability of a cache-based storage system," *Proc. of First Workshop on Industrial Experiences with Systems Software* (WIESS 2000), collocated with the 4th Symposium on Operating Systems Design and Implementation (OSDI), San Diego, Calif. (October 22).

Laprie, J.-C. [1985]. "Dependable computing and fault tolerance: Concepts and terminology," *Fifteenth Annual Int'l Symposium on Fault-Tolerant Computing FTCS 15.* Digest of Papers. Ann Arbor, Mich. (June 19–21), 2–11.

Lazowska, E. D., J. Zahorjan, G. S. Graham, and K. C. Sevcik [1984]. *Quantitative System Performance: Computer System Analysis Using Queueing Network models,* Prentice Hall, Englewood Cliffs, N.J. (Although out of print, it is available online at *www.cs.washington.edu/homes/lazowska/qsp/*).

Leiner, A. L. [1954]. "System specifications for the DYSEAC," *J. ACM* 1:2 (April), 57–81.

Leiner, A. L., and S. N. Alexander [1954]. "System organization of the DYSEAC," *IRE Trans. of Electronic Computers* EC-3:1 (March), 1–10.

Maberly, N. C. [1966]. *Mastering Speed Reading,* New American Library, New York.

Major, J. B. [1989]. "Are queuing models within the grasp of the unwashed?," *Proc. Int'l Conf. on Management and Performance Evaluation of Computer Systems,* Reno, Nev. (December 11–15), 831–839.

Mueller, M., L. C. Alves, W. Fischer, M. L. Fair, I. Modi [1999]. "RAS strategy for IBM S/390 G5 and G6," *IBM J. Research and Development,* 43:5–6 (September–November), 875–888.

Murphy, B., and T. Gent [1995]. "Measuring system and software reliability using an automated data collection process," *Quality and Reliability Engineering International,* 11:5 (September–October), 341–353.

Myer, T. H., and I. E. Sutherland [1968]. "On the design of display processors," *Communications of the ACM,* 11:6 (June), 410–414.

National Storage Industry Consortium [1998]. *Tape Roadmap* (June), *www.nsic.org.*

Nelson, V. P. [1990]. "Fault-tolerant computing: Fundamental concepts." *Computer,* 23:7 (July), 19–25.

Okada, S., S. Okada, Y. Matsuda, T. Yamada, and A. Kobayashi [1999]. "System on a chip for digital still camera," *IEEE Trans. on Consumer Electronics,* 45:3, (August), 584–590.

Patterson, D. A., G. A. Gibson, and R. H. Katz [1987]. "A case for redundant arrays of inexpensive disks (RAID)," Tech. Rep. UCB/CSD 87/391, Univ. of Calif. Also appeared in *ACM SIGMOD Conf. Proc.,* Chicago, June 1–3, 1988, 109–116.

Pavan, P., R. Bez, P. Olivo, and E. Zanoni [1997]. "Flash memory cells—an overview." *Proc. IEEE,* 85:8 (August), 1248–1271.

Robinson, B., and L. Blount [1986]. "The VM/HPO 3880-23 performance results," IBM Tech. Bulletin GG66-0247-00 (April), Washington Systems Center, Gaithersburg, Md.

Salem, K., and H. Garcia-Molina [1986]. "Disk striping," *IEEE 1986 Int'l Conf. on Data Engineering,* February 5–7, Washington, D.C., 249–259.

Scranton, R. A., D. A. Thompson, and D. W. Hunter [1983]. "The access time myth," Tech. Rep. RC 10197 (45223) (September 21), IBM, Yorktown Heights, N.Y.

Seagate [2000]. *Seagate Cheetah 73 Family: ST173404LW/LWV/LC/LCV Product Manual,* Volume 1, *www.seagate.com/support/disc/manuals/scsi/29478b.pdf.*

Smotherman, M. [1989]. "A sequencing-based taxonomy of I/O systems and review of historical machines," *Computer Architecture News* 17:5 (September), 5–15. Reprinted in *Computer Architecture Readings,* Morgan Kaufmann, 1999, 451–461.

Talagala, N. [2000]. "Characterizing large storage systems: Error behavior and performance benchmarks," Ph.D dissertation CSD-99-1066, June 13, 2000.

Talagala, N., R. Arpaci Dusseau, and D. Patterson [2000]. "Micro-benchmark based extraction of local and global disk characteristics," CSD-99-1063, June 13, 2000.

Talagala, N., S. Asami, D. Patterson, R. Futernick, and D. Hart [2000]. "The art of massive storage: A case study of a Web image archive," *Computer* (November).

Talagala, N., and D. Patterson [1999]. "An analysis of error behavior in a large storage system," Tech. Report UCB//CSD-99-1042, Computer Science Division, University of California at Berkeley (February).

Thadhani, A. J. [1981]. "Interactive user productivity," *IBM Systems J*. 20:4, 407–423.

Exercises

Solutions to the "starred" exercises appear in Appendix B.

⭐ 7.1 [15] <7.14> Using the two formulas in the fallacy starting on page 767 and the coefficient definitions given in the caption of Figure 7.51 (page 768), calculate the seek time each way for moving the arm over one-third of the cylinders of the disks in Figure 7.2 (page 682). Assume that the disk access is a read. What is the error with respect to the manufacturer's reported average seek time for the two formulas? What does this say about the suitability of the coefficient definitions in Figure 7.51 for the disks in Figure 7.2? (*Hint:* Using a spreadsheet program will be helpful to find the answers for this and several other exercises in this chapter.)

7.2 [25] <7.14> Using the two formulas in the fallacy starting on page 767 and the coefficient definitions given in Figure 7.51 (page 768), write a short program to calculate two "average" seek times by estimating the time for all possible seeks using these formulas and then dividing by the number of seeks. How close are the answers for Exercise 7.1 to these answers?

7.3 [15/12] <7.14> Average seek distance depends on the actual disk accesses generated by a workload.

    a. [15] <7.14> Using the statistics in the caption of Figure 7.52 (page 769) and in the displayed bar graphs, calculate the average seek distance for the two workloads. Use the midpoint of a range as the seek distance. For example, use 98 as the seek distance for the entry representing 91–105 in Figure 7.52. For the business workload, just ignore the missing 6% of the seeks. For the UNIX workload, assume the missing 15% of the seeks have an average distance of 300 cylinders.

    b. [12] <7.14> If the two workloads in Figure 7.52 were each measured on the three disks in Figure 7.2, what similarities and what differences could be expected in the three sets of results? Explain.

7.4 [20] <7.14> Figure 7.2 (page 682) gives the manufacturers' average seek times. Using the two formulas in the fallacy starting on page 767, the definitions of the coefficients given in Figure 7.51 (page 768), and assuming the statistics in Figure 7.52 (page 769) and read accesses only, what are the average seek times for each workload on the disks in Figure 7.2? Make the same assumptions as in part (a) of Exercise 7.3.

7.5 [10/10/10/10/10] <7.2> In this exercise, we will run a program to evaluate the behavior of a disk drive. Disk sectors are addressed sequentially within a track, tracks sequentially within cylinders, and cylinders sequentially within the disk. Determining head switch time and cylinder switch time is difficult because of rotational effects. Even determining platter count, sectors/track, rotational delay, and minimum time to media is difficult based on observation of typical disk workloads. The key is to factor out disk rotational effects by making consecutive seeks to individual sectors with addresses that differ by a linearly increasing amount starting with 0, 1, 2, and so forth.

The Skippy algorithm, from work by Nisha Talagala and colleagues of U.C. Berkeley [2000], is

```
fd = open("raw disk device");
for (i = 0; i < measurements; i++) {
        //time the following sequence, and output <i, time>
        lseek(fd, i * SINGLE_SECTOR, SEEK_CUR);
        write(fd, buffer, SINGLE_SECTOR);
}
close(fd);
```

The basic algorithm skips through the disk, increasing the distance of the seek by one sector before every write, and outputs the distance and time for each write. The raw device interface is used to avoid file system optimizations. SINGLE_SECTOR is the size of a single sector in bytes. The SEEK_CUR argument to lseek moves the file pointer an amount relative to the current pointer. A technical report describing Skippy and two other disk drive microbenchmarks (run in seconds or minutes rather than hours or days) is at *http://sunsite.berkeley.edu/Dienst/UI/2.0/Describe/ncstrl.ucb/CSD-99-1063*.

Run the Skippy algorithm on a disk drive of your choosing.

a. [10] <7.2> What is the number of heads? The number of platters?

b. [10] <7.2> What is the rotational latency?

c. [10] <7.2> What is the head switch time?

d. [10] <7.2> What is the cylinder switch time?

e. [10] <7.2> What is the minimum time to media plus transfer time? The minimum time to media is the minimum time to access the disk platter surface. A disk request completes in the sum of the minimum time to media plus the transfer time if there is no rotational or seek latency.

7.6 [10/10/10/10/10] <7.2> Figure 7.53 shows the output from running the benchmark Skippy on a disk.

a. [10] <7.2> What is the number of heads? The number of platters?

b. [10] <7.2> What is the rotational latency?

c. [10] <7.2> What is the head switch time?

d. [10] <7.2> What is the cylinder switch time?

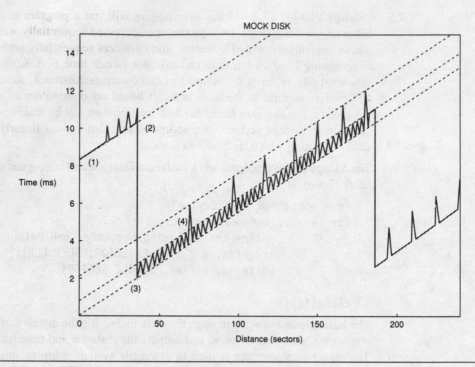

MOCK DISK

Time (ms)

Distance (sectors)

Figure 7.53 Example output of Skippy for a hypothetical disk.

e. [10] <7.2> What is the minimum time to media plus transfer time? The minimum time to media is the minimum time to access the disk platter surface. A disk request completes in the sum of the minimum time to media plus the transfer time if there is no rotational or seek latency.

7.7 [20/15/15/15/15/15] <7.7> The I/O bus and memory system of a computer are capable of sustaining 1000 MB/sec without interfering with the performance of a 2500 MIPS CPU (costing $20,000). Here are the assumptions about the software:

■ Each transaction requires 4 disk reads plus 2 disk writes.

■ The operating system uses 35,000 instructions for each disk read or write.

■ The database software executes 50,000 instructions to process a transaction.

■ The transfer size is 512 bytes.

You have a choice of two different types of disks:

■ A small disk that stores 40 GB and costs $400.

■ A big disk that stores 80 MB and costs $800.

Either disk in the system can support on average 100 disk reads or writes per second.

Answer parts (a)–(f) using the TPC-C benchmark (complex query OLTP) in Section 7.9. Assume that the requests are spread evenly to all the disks, that there is no waiting time due to busy disks or controllers, and that the account file must be large enough to handle 10,000 transactions per minute (tpm) according to the benchmark ground rules.

a. [20] <7.7> How many TPC-C transactions per second are possible with each disk choice, assuming that each uses the minimum number of disks to hold the account file?

b. [15] <7.7> What is the system cost per transaction per second of each alternative for TPC-C?

c. [15] <7.7> How fast does a CPU need to be to make the 1000 MB/sec I/O bus a bottleneck for TPS? (Assume that you can continue to add disks.)

d. [15] <7.7> As manager of MTP (Mega TP), you are deciding whether to spend your development money building a faster CPU or improving the performance of the software. The database group says they can reduce a transaction to 2 disk reads and 1 disk write and cut the database instructions per transaction to 30,000. The hardware group can build a faster CPU that sells for the same amount as the slower CPU with the same development budget. (Assume you can add as many disks as needed to get higher performance.) How much faster does the CPU have to be to match the performance gain of the software improvement?

e. [15] <7.7> The MTP I/O group was listening at the door during the software presentation. They argue that advancing technology will allow CPUs to get faster without significant investment, but that the cost of the system will be dominated by disks if they don't develop new small, faster disks. Assume the next CPU is 100% faster at the same cost and that the new disks have the same capacity as the old ones. Given the new CPU and the old software, what will be the cost of a system with enough old small disks so that they do not limit the TPS of the system?

f. [15] <7.7> Start with the same assumptions as in part (e). Now assume that you have as many new disks as you had old small disks in the original design. How fast must the new disks be (I/Os per second) to achieve the same TPS rate with the new CPU as the system in part (e)?

⭐ 7.8   [20] <7.7> Assume that we have the following two magnetic disk configurations: a single disk and an array of four disks. Each disk has 12 surfaces, 27,723 tracks per surface, and 528 sectors/track. Each sector holds 512 bytes, and it revolves at 10,000 RPM. The minimum, maximum, and average seeks times are 0.5 ms, 10.5 ms, and 4.9 ms, respectively. Use the seek time formula in the fallacy starting on page 767, including the equations in Figure 7.51 (page 768). The time to switch between surfaces is the same as to move the arm one track. In the disk array all the spindles are synchronized—sector 0 in every disk rotates under the head at the exact same time—and the arms on all four disks are always over the same track. The data is "striped" across all four disks, so four consecutive sectors on a single-disk system will be spread one sector per disk in the array. The delay of the disk controller is 0.3 ms per transaction, either for a single disk or for the array. Assume the performance of the I/O system is limited only by the disks and that there is a path to each disk in the array. Calculate the performance in both I/Os per second and megabytes per second of these two disk organizations, assuming the request pattern is random reads of 4 KB of sequential sectors. Assume the 4 KB are aligned under the same arm on each disk in the array.

7.9 [20] <7.7> Start with the same assumptions as in Exercise 7.8. Now calculate the performance in both I/Os per second and megabytes per second of these two disk organizations assuming the request pattern is reads of 4 KB of **sequential** sectors where the average seek distance is 10 tracks. Assume the 4 KB are aligned under the same arm on each disk in the array.

7.10 [20] <7.7> Start with the same assumptions as in Exercise 7.8. Now calculate the performance in both I/Os per second and megabytes per second of these two disk organizations assuming the request pattern is random reads of 1 MB of sequential sectors. (If it matters, assume the disk controller allows the sectors to arrive in any order.)

7.11 [20] <7.2> Assume that we have one disk defined as in Exercise 7.8. Assume that we read the next sector after any read and that *all* read requests are one sector in length. We store the extra sectors that were read ahead in a disk cache. Assume that the probability of receiving a request for the sector we read ahead at some time in the future (before it must be discarded because the disk cache buffer fills) is 0.1. Assume that we must still pay the controller overhead on a disk cache read hit, and the transfer time for the disk cache is 50 ns per word. Is the read-ahead strategy faster? (*Hint:* Solve the problem in the steady state by assuming that the disk cache contains the appropriate information and assuming that a request has just missed.)

7.12 [20/10/20/20] <7.7–7.10> Assume the following information about a MIPS machine:

■ Loads take 2 cycles.

■ Stores take 2 cycles.

■ All other instructions are 1 cycle.

Use the summary instruction mix information on MIPS for gcc from Figure 2.32.

Here are the cache statistics for a write-through cache:

■ Each cache block is 4 words, and the whole block is read on any miss.

■ A cache miss takes 23 cycles.

■ Write through takes 16 cycles to complete, and there is no write buffer.

Here are the cache statistics for a write-back cache:

■ Each cache block is 4 words, and the whole block is read on any miss.

■ A cache miss takes 23 cycles for a clean block and 31 cycles for a dirty block.

■ Assume that on a miss, 30% of the time the block is dirty.

Assume that the bus
- is only busy during transfers
- transfers on average 1 word/clock cycle
- must read or write a single word at a time (it is not faster to access two at once)

a. [20] <7.7–7.10> Assume that DMA I/O can take place simultaneously with CPU cache hits. Also assume that the operating system can guarantee that there will be no stale-data problem in the cache due to I/O. The sector size is 1 KB. Assume the cache miss rate is 5%. On average, what percentage of the bus is used for each cache write policy? (This measure is called the *traffic ratio* in cache studies.)

b. [10] <7.7–7.10> Start with the same assumptions as in part (a). If the bus can be loaded up to 80% of capacity without suffering severe performance penalties, how much memory bandwidth is available for I/O for each cache write policy? The cache miss rate is still 5%.

c. [20] <7.7–7.10> Start with the same assumptions as in part (a). Assume that a disk sector read takes 1000 clock cycles to initiate a read, 100,000 clock cycles to find the data on the disk, and 1000 clock cycles for the DMA to transfer the data to memory. How many disk reads can occur per million instructions executed for each write policy? How does this change if the cache miss rate is cut in half?

d. [20] <7.7–7.10> Start with the same assumptions as in part (c). Now you can have any number of disks. Assuming ideal scheduling of disk accesses, what is the maximum number of sector reads that can occur per million instructions executed?

7.13 [50] < 7.7> Take your favorite computer and write a program that achieves maximum bandwidth to and from disks. What is the percentage of the bandwidth that you achieve compared with what the I/O device manufacturer claims?

7.14 [20] <7.2, 7.4> Search the World Wide Web to find descriptions of recent magnetic disks of different diameters. Be sure to include at least the information in Figure 7.2 on page 682.

7.15 [20] <7.14> Using data collected in Exercise 7.14, plot the two projections of seek time as used in Figure 7.51 (page 768). What seek distance has the largest percentage of difference between these two predictions? If you have the real seek distance data from Exercise 7.14, add that data to the plot and see on average how close each projection is to the real seek times.

7.16 [15] <7.2, 7.4> Using the answer to Exercise 7.15, which disk would be a good building block to build a 2 TB storage subsystem using mirroring (RAID 1)? Why?

7.17 [15] <7.2, 7.4> Using the answer to Exercise 7.15, which disk would be a good building block to build a 20 TB storage subsystem using distributed parity (RAID 5)? Why?

7.18   [15] <7.8> Starting with the example on page 728, calculate the average length of the queue and the average length of the system for that example and the following two examples.

7.19   [15] <7.8> Redo the example that starts on page 728, but this time assume the distribution of disk service times has a squared coefficient of variance of 2.0 (C = 2.0), versus 1.0 in the example. How does this change affect the answers?

7.20   [20] <7.11> The I/O utilization rules of thumb on page 748 are just guidelines and are subject to debate. Redo the example starting on page 749, but increase the limit of SCSI utilization to 50%, 60%, . . . , until it is never the bottleneck. How does this change affect the answers? What is the new bottleneck? (*Hint:* Use a spreadsheet program to find answers.)

7.21   [15/15] <7.2> Tape libraries were invented as archival storage, and hence have relatively few readers per tape.

    a.   [15] <7.2> Calculate how long it would take to read all the data from a StorageTek PowderHorn 9310 assuming a single silo with 6000 tapes, 60 GB uncompressed capacity per tape, 16 tape drives that read at 11 MB/sec, and a maximum of 450 tape changes per hour per drive (includes tape load/unload time in the drive plus robot arm time to/from the tape storage slot in the silo).

    b.   [15] <7.2> Assume the 16 tape drives each have a helical scan read/write head with a 2000-hour rated lifetime. How many complete scans of the storage silo in part (a) can be done before exceeding the head lifetime?

7.22   [25] <7.2> Extend Figure 7.3 on page 685 and Figure 7.4 on page 686 to the present time, showing price per disk and price per gigabyte by collecting data from advertisements in the January and July issues of *PC* magazine. How fast are prices changing now?

7.23   [Discussion] <7.2> Recording density for disk drives has increased exponentially for decades. The superparamagnetic limit is a physical characteristic of recording media that may soon thwart density improvements. What is the superparamagnetic limit? Do people believe it is a real limit? What would be the impact if it were? Search the literature on magnetic recording for information to support your discussion. One place to start your investigation is *http://www.research.ibm.com /journal/rd/443/thompson.html*.

7.24   [Discussion] <7.2> With the cost in 2001 of a 40 GB IDE disk about the same as a 40 GB tape, the economics of magnetic tape are far different from earlier days when tape performed software distribution, mass storage, backup, and disaster insurance (an easy form in which to send data to a remote site) functions. What technologies or combinations of technologies are the competition faced by tape for each of these functions? What advantages are offered by the competing technologies? For which functions does tape face the strongest competition? What advantages can tape offer compared to the competing technologies?

7.25   [Discussion] <7.2> Figure 7.4 on page 686 shows that the price per gigabyte of personal computer disks decreased by a factor of 10,000 over the span of 18 years. Change of such magnitude is difficult to fully appreciate, especially so without a direct, personal context. Imagine your own life 18 years from today as it would be with 10,000-fold improvement in aspects of daily life that matter to you. Some examples might be your salary or the speed of long-distance travel. Can you find examples from outside the field of computing of comparable growth rates (about 60% per year) over a similar period?

7.26 [50] <7.5, 7.11> A more sophisticated analysis of RAID failures relies on Markov models of faults; see Gibson [1992]. Learn about Markov models and redo the simplified failure analysis of the disk array on page 746.

7.27 [Discussion] <7> Text, audio, photo, and video works of popular interest have significant economic value. Today, each of these formats when represented digitally can be stored cheaply, copied easily and exactly, and edited readily by inexpensive desktop computer systems. Recordable, removable media storage and high-speed networking provide distribution channels of improving cost and performance. Authoring and communicating digital works is within the means of more organizations and individuals than ever before, but at the same time the obstacles to the unauthorized copying and dissemination of the digital works of others are shrinking. One strategy to prevent or limit copyright infringement is to control storage technology.

What involvement have the recording and movie industries had in the computer storage marketplace for the digital audiotape, digital minidisk, CD-R, CD-RW, and DVD formats? How have the availability of standard computer bus interfaces for these devices and their hardware unit and recording media pricing been affected?

What are some of the existing technologies and proposed methods for storage devices to prevent unauthorized copying of intellectual property and to support data access models other than ownership, such as viewing restrictions, limited number of viewings, and pay-per-view (e.g., Copy Protection for Recordable Media (CPRM), CSS and region codes for DVD, and encoding to prevent media interoperability between consumer audio CD players and CD-ROM readers)? How are these techniques faring in the consumer marketplace and other marketplaces? What are or would be the effects of these access controls on an individual wishing to work with data files of his/her own authorship?

8

Interconnection Networks and Clusters

"The Medium is the Message" because it is the medium that shapes and controls the search and form of human associations and actions.

Marshall McLuhan
Understanding Media (1964)

The marvels—of film, radio, and television—are marvels of one-way communication, which is not communication at all.

Milton Mayer
*On the Remote Possibility of
Communication* (1967)

Introduction

Thus far we have covered the components of a single computer, which has been the traditional focus of computer architecture. In this chapter we see how to connect computers together, forming a community of computers. Figure 8.1 shows the generic components of this community: computer nodes, hardware and software interfaces, links to the interconnection network, and the interconnection network. Interconnection networks are also called *networks* or *communication subnets*, and nodes are sometimes called *end systems* or *hosts*. The connection of two or more interconnection networks is called *internetworking,* which relies on communication standards to convert information from one kind of network to another. The Internet is the most famous example of internetworking.

There are two reasons that computer architects should devote attention to networking. First, in addition to providing external connectivity, Moore's Law shrunk networks so much that they connect the components *within* a single computer. Using a network to connect autonomous systems within a computer has long been found in mainframes, but today such designs can be found in PCs too. Switches are replacing buses as the normal communication technique: between computers, between I/O devices, between boards, between chips, and even between modules inside chips. As a result, computer architects must understand networking terminology, problems, and solutions in order to design and evaluate modern computers.

The second reason architects should study networking is that today almost all computers are—or will be—networked to other devices. Thus, understanding networking is critical; any device without a network is somehow flawed. Just as a modern computer without a memory hierarchy is "broken"—hence a chapter just for it—a modern computer without a network is "broken" too. Hence this chapter.

This topic is vast—portions of Figure 8.1 are the subject of whole books and college courses. Networking is also a buzzword-rich environment, where many

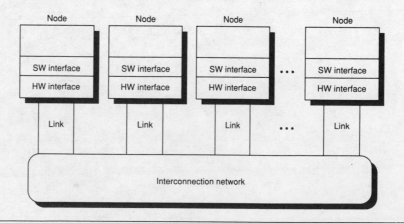

Figure 8.1 The generic interconnection network.

simple ideas are obscured behind acronyms and unusual definitions. To help you break through the buzzword barrier, Figure 8.2 is a glossary of about 80 networking terms. The goal of this chapter is to provide computer architects a gentle, qualitative introduction to networking. It defines terms, helps you understand the architectural implications of interconnection network technology, provides introductory explanations of the key ideas, and gives references to more detailed descriptions.

Most of this chapter is on networking, but the final quarter of this chapter focuses on clusters. A *cluster* is the coordinated use of interconnected computers

Term	Definition
adaptive routing	Router picks best path based upon measure of delay on outgoing links.
ΛTM	Asynchronous transfer mode is a WAN designed for real-time traffic such as digital voice.
attenuation	Loss of signal strength as signal passes through the medium over a long distance.
backpressure flow control	When the receiver cannot accept another message, separate wires between adjacent senders and receivers tell the sender to stop immediately. It causes links between two endpoints to freeze until the receiver makes room for the next message.
bandwidth	Maximum rate the network can propagate information once the message enters it.
base station	A network architecture that uses boxes connected via land lines to communicate to wireless handsets.
bisection bandwidth	Sum of the bandwidth of lines that cross that imaginary dividing line between two roughly equal parts of the network, each with half the nodes.
bit error rate	BER, the error rate of a network, typically in errors per million bits transferred.
blade	A removable computer component that fits vertically into a box in a standard VME rack.
blocking	Contention that prevents a message from making progress along a link of a switch.
bridge	OSI layer 2 networking device that connects multiple LANs, which can operate in parallel; in contrast, a router connects networks with incompatible addresses at OSI layer 3.
carrier sensing	"Listening" to the medium to be sure it is unused before trying to send a message.
category 5 wire	"Cat5" twisted-pair, copper wire used for 10, 100, and 1000M bits/sec LANs.
channel	In wireless networks, a pair of frequency bands that allow two-way communication.
checksum	A field of a message for an error detection code.
circuit switching	A circuit is established from source to destination, reserving bandwidth along a path until the circuit is broken.
cluster	Coordinated use of interconnected computers in a machine room.
coaxial cable	A single stiff copper wire is surrounded by insulating material and a shield; historically faster and longer distance than twisted-pair copper wire.
collision	Two nodes (or more) on a shared medium try to send at the same time.
collision detection	"Listening" to shared medium after sending to see if a message collided with another.
collocation site	A warehouse for remote hosting of servers with expansible networking, space, cooling, and security.
communication subnets	Another name for interconnection network *(continued)*

Figure 8.2 Networking terms in this chapter and their definitions.

Term	Definition
credit-based flow control	To reduce overhead for flow control, a sender is given a credit to send up to N packets and only checks for network delays when the credit is spent.
cut-through routing	The switch examines the header, decides where to send the message, and then starts transmitting it immediately without waiting for the rest of the message. The tail continues when the head blocks, potentially compressing the strung-out message into a single switch.
destination-based routing	The message contains a destination address, and the switch picks a path to deliver the message, often by table lookup.
deterministic routing	Router always picks the same path for the message.
end systems	Another name for interconnection network node as opposed to the intermediate switches.
end-to-end argument	Intermediate functions (error checking, performance optimization, and so on) may be incomplete as compared to performing the function end to end.
Ethernet	The most popular LAN, it has scaled from its original 3M bits/sec rate using shared media in 1975 to switched media at 1000 Mbits/second in 2001; it shows no signs of stopping.
fat tree	A network topology with extra links at each level enhancing a simple tree, so bandwidth between each level is normally constant (see Figure 8.14 on page 816).
FC-AL	Fibre Channel Arbitrated Loop; a SAN for storage devices.
frequency-division multiplexing	Divide the bandwidth of the transmission line into a fixed number of frequencies, and assign each frequency to a conversation.
full duplex	Two-way communication on a network segment.
header	The first part of a message that contains no user information, but contents help that network, such as providing the destination address.
host	Another name for interconnection network node.
hub	An OSI layer 1 networking device that connects multiple LANs to act as one.
Infiniband	An emerging standard SAN for both storage and systems in a machine room.
interference	In wireless networks, reduction of signal due to frequency reuse; frequency is reused to try to increase the number of simultaneous conversations over a large area.
internetworking	Connection of two or more interconnection networks.
IP	Internet Protocol is an OSI layer 3 protocol, at the network layer.
iSCSI	SCSI over IP networks, it is a competitor to SANs using IP and Ethernet switches.
LAN	Local area network, for machines in a building or campus, such as Ethernet.
message	The smallest piece of electronic "mail" sent over a network.
multimode fiber	An inexpensive optical fiber that reduces bandwidth and distance for cost.
multipath fading	In wireless networks, interference between multiple versions of signal that arrive at different times, determined by time between fastest signal and slowest signal relative to signal bandwidth.
multistage switch	A switch containing many smaller switches that perform a portion of routing.
OSI layer	Open System Interconnect models the network as seven layers (see Figure 8.25 on page 832).
overhead	In this chapter, networking overhead is sender overhead + receiver overhead + time of flight.
packet switching	In contrast to circuit switching, information is broken into packets (usually fixed or maximum size), each with its own destination address, and they are routed independently.

Figure 8.2 *Continued.*

Term	Definition
payload	The middle part of the message that contains user information.
peer-to-peer protocol	Communication between two nodes occurs logically at the same level of the protocol.
peer-to-peer wireless	Instead of communicating to base stations, peer-to-peer wireless networks communicate between handsets.
protocol	The sequence of steps that network software follows to communicate.
rack unit	An R.U. is 1.7 inches, the height of a single slot in a standard 19-inch VME rack; there are 44 R.U. in a standard 6-foot rack.
receiver overhead	The time for the processor to pull the message from the interconnection network.
router	OSI layer 3 networking device that connects multiples LANs with incompatible addresses.
SAN	Originally "system area network" but more recently "storage area network," it connects computers and/or storage devices in a machine room. FC-AL and Infiniband are SANs.
sender overhead	The time for the processor to inject the message into the network; the processor is busy for the entire time.
shadow fading	In wireless networks, when the received signal is blocked by objects—buildings outdoors or walls indoors.
signal-to-noise ratio	SNR, the ratio of the strength of the signal carrying information to the background noise.
simplex	One-way communication on a network segment.
single-mode fiber	"Single-wavelength" fiber is narrower and more expensive than multimode fiber, but it offers greater bandwidth and distance.
source-based routing	The message specifies the path to the destination at each switch.
store-and-forward	Each switch waits for the full message to arrive before it is sent on to the next switch.
TCP	Transmission Control Protocol, an OSI layer 4 protocol (transport layer).
throughput	In networking, measured speed of the medium or network bandwidth delivered to an application; that is, does not give credit for headers and trailers.
time of flight	The time for the first bit of the message to arrive at the receiver.
trailer	The last part of a message that has no user information but helps the network, such as error correction code.
transmission time	The time for the message to pass through the network (not including time of flight).
transport latency	Time that the message spends in the interconnection network (including time of flight).
twisted pairs	Two wires twisted together to reduce electrical interference.
virtual circuit	A logical circuit is established between source and destination for a message to follow.
WAN	Wide area network, a network across a continent, such as ATM.
wavelength division multiplexing	WDM sends different streams simultaneously on the same fiber using different wavelengths of light and then demultiplexes the different wavelengths at the receiver.
window	In TCP, the number of TCP datagrams that can be sent without waiting for approval.
wireless network	A network that communicates without physical connections, such as radio.
wormhole routing	The switch examines the header, decides where to send the message, and then starts transmitting it immediately without waiting for the rest of the message. When the head of the message blocks, the message stays strung out over the network.

Figure 8.2 *Continued.*

in a machine room. In contrast to the qualitative network introduction, these sections give a more quantitative description of clusters, including many examples. It ends with a guided tour of the Google clusters.

Let's start with the generic types of interconnections. Depending on the number of nodes and their proximity, these interconnections are given different names:

- *Wide area network* (WAN)—Also called *long-haul network,* the WAN connects computers distributed throughout the world. WANs include thousands of computers, and the maximum distance is thousands of kilometers. ATM is a current example of a WAN.

- *Local area network* (LAN)—This device connects hundreds of computers, and the distance is up to a few kilometers. Unlike a WAN, a LAN connects computers distributed throughout a building or on a campus. The most popular and enduring LAN is Ethernet.

- *Storage or system area network* (SAN)—This interconnection network is for a machine room, so the maximum distance of a link is typically less than 100 meters, and it can connect hundreds of nodes. Today SAN usually means *storage* area network as it connects computers to storage devices, such as disk arrays. Originally SAN meant a *system* area network to connect computers together, such as PCs in a cluster. A recent SAN trying to network both storage and system is Infiniband.

Figure 8.3 shows the rough relationship of these systems in terms of number of autonomous systems connected, including a bus for comparison. Note the area of overlap between buses, SANs, and LANs, which leads to product competition.

These three types of interconnection networks have been designed and sustained by several different cultures—Internet, telecommunications, workgroup/enterprise, storage, and high-performance computing—each using its own dialects and its own favorite approaches to the goal of interconnecting autonomous computers.

This chapter gives a common framework for evaluating all interconnection networks, using a single set of terms to describe the basic alternatives. Figure 8.22 in Section 8.7 gives several other examples of each of these interconnection networks. As we will see, some components are common to all types and some are quite different.

We begin the chapter in Section 8.2 by exploring the design and performance of a simple network to introduce the ideas. We then consider the following problems: which media to use as the interconnect (Section 8.3), how to connect many computers together (Sections 8.4 and 8.5), and what the practical issues are for commercial networks (Section 8.6). We follow with examples illustrating the trade-offs for each type of network (Section 8.7), and explore internetworking (Section 8.8) and crosscutting issues for networks (Section 8.9). With this gentle introduction to networks in Sections 8.2–8.9, if you are interested in more depth, you should try the suggested reading in Section 8.16. Sections 8.10–8.12 switch

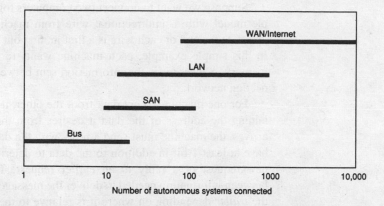

Figure 8.3 Relationship of four types of interconnects in terms of number of autonomous systems connected: bus, system or storage area network, local area network, and wide area network/Internet. Note that there are overlapping ranges where buses, SANs, and LANs compete. Some supercomputers have a switch-based custom network to interconnect up to thousands of computers; such interconnects are basically custom SANs.

to clusters, and give a more quantitative description with designs and examples. Section 8.13 gives a view of networks from the embedded perspective, using a cell phone and wireless networks as the example. We conclude in Sections 8.14–8.16 with the traditional ending of the chapters.

As we will see, networking shares more characteristics with storage than with processors and memory. Like storage, the operating system controls what features of the network are used. Again like storage, performance includes both latency and bandwidth, and queuing theory is a valuable tool. Like RAID, networking assumes failures occur, and thus dependability in the presence of errors is the norm.

A Simple Network

There is an old network saying: Bandwidth problems can be cured with money. Latency problems are harder because the speed of light is fixed—you can't bribe God.

Anonymous

To explain the complexities and concepts of networks, this section describes a simple network of two computers. We then describe the software steps for these two machines to communicate. The remainder of the section gives a detailed and then a simple performance model, including several examples to see the implications of key network parameters.

Suppose we want to connect two computers together. Figure 8.4 shows a simple model with a unidirectional wire from machine A to machine B and vice versa. At the end of each wire is a first in, first out (FIFO) queue to hold the data. In this simple example, each machine wants to read a word from the other's memory. A *message* is the information sent between machines over an interconnection network.

For one machine to get data from the other, it must first send a request containing the address of the data it desires from the other node. When a request arrives, the machine must send a reply with the data. Hence, each message must have at least 1 bit in addition to the data to determine whether the message is a new request or a reply to an earlier request. The network must distinguish between information needed to deliver the message, typically called the *header* or the *trailer* depending on where it is relative to the data, and the *payload,* which contains the data. Figure 8.5 shows the format of messages in our simple network. This example shows a single-word payload, but messages in some interconnection networks can include hundreds of words.

Interconnection networks normally involve software. Even this simple example invokes software to translate requests and replies into messages with the appropriate headers. An application program must usually cooperate with the operating system to send a message to another machine, since the network will be

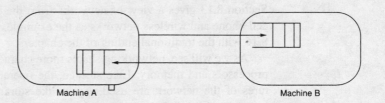

Figure 8.4 A simple network connecting two machines.

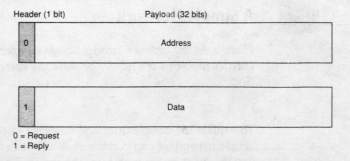

Figure 8.5 Message format for our simple network. Messages must have extra information beyond the data.

shared with all the processes running on the two machines, and the operating system cannot allow messages for one process to be received by another. Thus, the messaging software must have some way to distinguish between processes; this distinction may be included in an expanded header. Although hardware support can reduce the amount of work, most is done by software.

In addition to protection, network software is often responsible for ensuring reliable delivery of messages. The twin responsibilities are ensuring that the message is neither garbled nor lost in transit.

Adding a *checksum* field (or some other error detection code) to the message format meets the first responsibility. This redundant information is calculated when the message is first sent and checked upon receipt. The receiver then sends an acknowledgment if the message passes the test.

One way to meet the second responsibility is to have a timer record the time each message is sent and to presume the message is lost if the timer expires before an acknowledgment arrives. The message is then resent.

The software steps to send a message are as follows:

1. The application copies data to be sent into an operating system buffer.

2. The operating system calculates the checksum, includes it in the header or trailer of the message, and then starts the timer.

3. The operating system sends the data to the network interface hardware and tells the hardware to send the message.

Message reception is in just the reverse order:

3. The system copies the data from the network interface hardware into the operating system buffer.

2. The system calculates the checksum over the data. If the checksum matches the sender's checksum, the receiver sends an acknowledgment back to the sender. If not, it deletes the message, assuming that the sender will resend the message when the associated timer expires.

1. If the data pass the test, the system copies the data to the user's address space and signals the application to continue.

The sender must still react to the acknowledgment:

- When the sender gets the acknowledgment, it releases the copy of the message from the system buffer.

- If the sender gets the time-out instead of an acknowledgment, it resends the data and restarts the timer.

Here we assume that the operating system keeps the message in its buffer to support retransmission in case of failure. Figure 8.6 shows how the message format looks now.

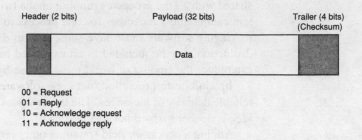

00 = Request
01 = Reply
10 = Acknowledge request
11 = Acknowledge reply

Figure 8.6 Message format for our simple network. Note that the checksum is in the trailer.

The sequence of steps that software follows to communicate is called a *protocol* and generally has the symmetric but reversed steps between sending and receiving.

Note that this example protocol above is for sending a *single* message. When an application does not require a response before sending the next message, the sender can overlap the time to send with the transmission delays and the time to receive.

A protocol must handle many more issues than reliability. For example, if two machines are from different manufacturers, they might order bytes differently within a word (see Section 2.3 of Chapter 2). The software must reverse the order of bytes in each word as part of the delivery system. It must also guard against the possibility of duplicate messages if a delayed message were to become unstuck. It is often necessary to deliver the messages to the application in the order they are sent, and so sequence numbers may be added to the header to enable assembly. Finally, it must work when the receiver's FIFO becomes full, suggesting feedback to control the flow of messages from the sender (see Section 8.4).

Now that we have covered the steps in sending and receiving a message, we can discuss performance. Figure 8.7 shows the many performance parameters of interconnection networks. This figure is critical to understanding netw
mance, so study it well! Note that the parameters in Figure 8.7 apply to the ..
connect in *many* levels of the system: inside a chip, between chips on a board, between computers in a cluster, and so on. The units change, but the principles remain the same, as does the bandwidth that results.

These terms are often used loosely, leading to confusion, so we define them here precisely:

■ *Bandwidth*—We use this most widely used term to refer to the maximum rate at which the network can propagate information once the message enters the network. Unlike disks, bandwidth includes the headers and trailers as well as the payload, and the units are traditionally bits/second rather than bytes/second. The term bandwidth is also used to mean the measured speed of the medium or network bandwidth delivered to an application. *Throughput* is sometimes used for this latter term.

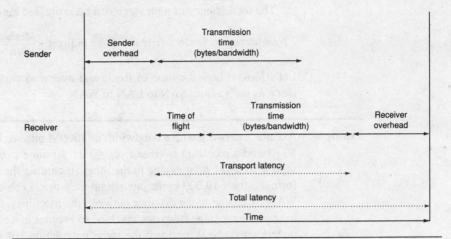

Figure 8.7 Performance parameters of interconnection networks. Depending on whether it is a SAN, LAN, or WAN, the relative lengths of the time of flight and transmission may be quite different from those shown here. (Based on a presentation by Greg Papadopolous of Sun Microsystems.)

■ *Time of flight*—The time for the first bit of the message to arrive at the receiver, including the delays due to repeaters or other hardware in the network. Time of flight can be milliseconds for a WAN or nanoseconds for a SAN.

■ *Transmission time*—The time for the message to pass through the network, not including time of flight. One way to measure it is the difference in time between when the first bit of the message arrives at the receiver and when the last bit of the message arrives at the receiver. Note that, by definition, transmission time is equal to the size of the message divided by the bandwidth. This measure assumes there are no other messages to contend for the network.

■ *Transport latency*—The sum of time of flight and transmission time. Transport latency is the time that the message spends in the interconnection network. Stated alternatively, it is the time between when the first bit of the message is injected into the network and when the last bit of the message arrives at the receiver. It does not include the overhead of injecting the message into the network or pulling it out when it arrives.

■ *Sender overhead*—The time for the processor to inject the message into the network, including both hardware and software components. Note that the processor is busy for the entire time, hence the use of the term *overhead*. Once the processor is free, any subsequent delays are considered part of the transport latency. For pedagogic reasons, we assume overhead is not dependent on message size. (Typically, only very large messages have larger overhead.)

■ *Receiver overhead*—The time for the processor to pull the message from the interconnection network, including both hardware and software components. In general, the receiver overhead is larger than the sender overhead: For example, the receiver may pay the cost of an interrupt.

The total latency of a message can be expressed algebraically:

$$\text{Total latency} = \text{Sender overhead} + \text{Time of flight} + \frac{\text{Message size}}{\text{Bandwidth}} + \text{Receiver overhead}$$

Let's look at how the time of flight and overhead parameters change in importance as we go from SAN to LAN to WAN.

Example Assume a network with a bandwidth of 1000M bits/sec has a sending overhead of 80 μs and a receiving overhead of 100 μs. Assume two machines. One wants to send a 10,000-byte message to the other (including the header), and the message format allows 10,000 bytes in a single message. Let's compare SAN, LAN, and WAN by changing the distance between the machines. Calculate the total latency to send the message from one machine to another in a SAN assuming they are 10 meters apart. Next, perform the same calculation but assume the machines are now 500 meters apart, as in a LAN. Finally, assume they are 1000 *kilometers* apart, as in a WAN.

Answer The speed of light is 299,792.5 kilometers per second in a vacuum, and signals propagate at about 63% to 66% of the speed of light in a conductor. Since this is an estimate, in this chapter we'll round the speed of light to 300,000 kilometers per second and assume we can achieve two-thirds of that in a conductor. Hence, we can estimate time of flight. Let's plug the parameters for the short distance of a SAN into the previous formula:

$$\text{Total latency} = \text{Sender overhead} + \text{Time of flight} + \frac{\text{Message size}}{\text{Bandwidth}} + \text{Receiver overhead}$$

$$= 80\ \mu s + \frac{0.01\,\text{km}}{2/3 \times 300{,}000\ \text{km/sec}} + \frac{10{,}000\ \text{bytes}}{1000\text{M bits/sec}} + 100\ \mu s$$

Converting all terms into microseconds (μs) leads to

$$\text{Total latency} = 80\ \mu s + \frac{0.01 \times 10^6}{2/3 \times 300{,}000}\ \mu s + \frac{10{,}000 \times 8}{1000}\ \mu s + 100\ \mu s$$

$$= 80\ \mu s + 0.05\ \mu s + 80\ \mu s + 100\ \mu s = 260 + 0.05\ \mu s$$

$$= 260\ \mu s$$

Substituting an example LAN distance into the third equation yields

$$\text{Total latency} = 80\ \mu s + \frac{0.5\,\text{km}}{2/3 \times 300{,}000\ \text{km/sec}} + \frac{10{,}000\ \text{bytes}}{1000\text{M bits/sec}} + 100\ \mu s$$

$$= 80\ \mu s + 2.50\ \mu s + 80\ \mu s + 100\ \mu s = 260 + 2.5\ \mu s$$

$$= 262\ \mu s$$

Substituting the WAN distance into the equation yields

$$\text{Total latency} = 80\ \mu s + \frac{1000\ \text{km}}{2/3 \times 300{,}000\ \text{km/sec}} + \frac{10{,}000\ \text{bytes}}{1000\text{M bits/sec}} + 100\ \mu s$$

$$= 80\ \mu s + 5000\ \mu s + 80\ \mu s + 100\ \mu s = 260 + 5000\ \mu s$$

$$= 5260\ \mu s$$

The increased fraction of the latency required by time of flight for long distances, as well as the greater likelihood of errors over long distances, are why wide area networks use more sophisticated and time-consuming protocols. Complexity increases from protocols used on a bus versus a LAN versus the Internet as we go from tens to hundreds to thousands of nodes.

Note that messages in LANs and WANs go through switches that add to the latency, which we neglected above. Generally, switch latency is small compared to overhead in LANs or time of flight in SANs.

As mentioned earlier, when an application does not require a response before sending the next message, the sender can overlap the sending overhead with the transport latency and receiver overhead. Increased latency affects the structure of programs that try to hide this latency, requiring quite different solutions if the latency is 1, 100, or 10,000 microseconds.

Note that the previous example shows that time of flight for SANs is so short relative to overhead that it can be ignored, yet in WANs, time of flight is so long that sender and receiver overheads can be ignored. Thus, we can simplify the performance equation by combining sender overhead, receiver overhead, and time of flight into a single term called *Overhead:*

$$\text{Total latency} \approx \text{Overhead} + \frac{\text{Message size}}{\text{Bandwidth}}$$

We can use this formula to calculate the effective bandwidth delivered by the network as message size varies:

$$\text{Effective bandwidth} = \frac{\text{Message size}}{\text{Total latency}}$$

Let's use this simpler equation to explore the impact of overhead and message size on effective bandwidth.

Example   Plot the effective bandwidth versus message size for overheads of 25 and 250 μs and for network bandwidths of 100, 1000, and 10,000M bits/sec. Vary message size from 16 bytes to 4 MB. For what message sizes is the effective bandwidth virtually the same as the raw network bandwidth? If overhead is 250 μs, for what message sizes is the effective bandwidth always less than 100M bits/sec?

Answer   Figure 8.8 plots effective bandwidth versus message size using the simplified equation above. The notation "oX,bwY" means an overhead of X microseconds and a network bandwidth of Y Mbits/sec. To amortize the cost of high overhead, message sizes must be 4 MB for effective bandwidth to be about the same as network bandwidth. Assuming the high overhead, message sizes about 3 KB or less will not break the 100M bits/sec barrier no matter what the actual network bandwidth. Thus, we must lower overhead as well as increase network bandwidth unless messages are very large.

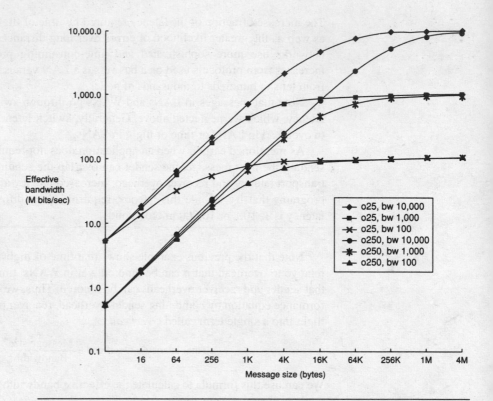

Figure 8.8 **Bandwidth delivered versus message size for overheads of 25 and 250 μs and for network bandwidths of 100, 1000, and 10,000M bits/sec.** Note that with 250 microseconds of overhead and a network bandwidth of 1000 Mbits/sec, only the 4 MB message size gets an effective bandwidth of 1000M bits/sec. In fact, message sizes must be greater than 256 bytes for the effective bandwidth to exceed 10M bits/sec. The notation "oX,bwY" means an overhead of X microseconds and a network bandwidth of Y Mbits/sec.

Hence, message size is important in getting full benefit of fast networks. What is the natural size of messages? Figure 8.9 shows the size of Network File System (NFS) messages for 239 machines at Berkeley collected over a period of one week. One plot is cumulative in messages sent, and the other is cumulative in data bytes sent. The maximum NFS message size is just over 8 KB, yet 95% of the messages are less than 192 bytes long. Figure 8.10 shows the similar results for Internet traffic, where the maximum transfer unit was 1500 bytes. Again, 60% of the messages are less than 192 bytes long, and 1500-byte messages represented 50% of the bytes transferred. Many applications send far more small messages than large messages, since requests and acknowledgments are more frequent than data.

Summarizing this section, even this simple network has brought up the issues of protection, reliability, heterogeneity, software protocols, and a more sophisticated performance model. The next four sections address other key questions:

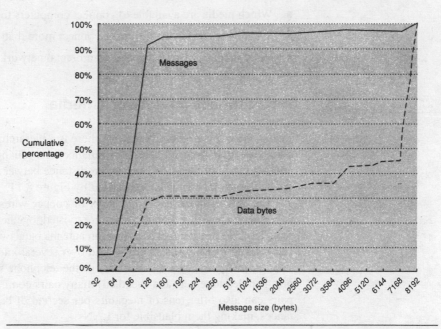

Figure 8.9 Cumulative percentage of messages and data transferred as message size varies for NFS traffic. Each *x*-axis entry includes all bytes up to the next one; for example, 32 represents 32 bytes to 63 bytes. More than half the bytes are sent in 8 KB messages, but 95% of the messages are less than 192 bytes. Figure 8.50 (page 868) shows details of this measurement. (Collected at the University of California at Berkeley.)

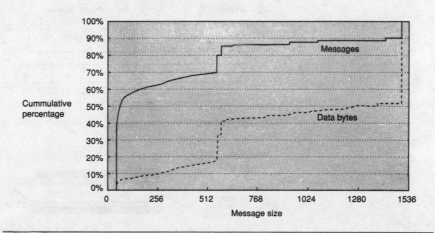

Figure 8.10 Cumulative percentage of messages and data transferred as message size varies for Internet traffic. About 40% of the messages were 40 bytes long, and 50% of the data transfer was in messages 1500 bytes long. The maximum transfer unit of most switches was 1500 bytes. (Collected by Vern Paxton on MCI Internet traffic in 1998.)

- Which media are available to connect computers together?
- What issues arise if you want to connect more than two computers?
- What practical issues arise for commercial networks?

8.3 Interconnection Network Media

Just as there is a memory hierarchy, there is a hierarchy of media to interconnect computers that varies in cost, performance, and reliability. Network media have another figure of merit, the maximum distance between nodes. This section covers three popular examples, illustrated by Figure 8.11.

The first medium is *twisted pairs* of copper wires. These are two insulated wires, each about 1 mm thick. They are twisted together to reduce electrical interference, since two parallel lines form an antenna but a twisted pair does not. As they can transfer a few megabits per second over several kilometers without amplification, twisted pairs were the mainstay of the telephone system. Telephone companies bundled together (and sheathed) many pairs coming into a building. Twisted pairs can also offer tens of megabits per second of bandwidth over shorter distances, making them plausible for LANs.

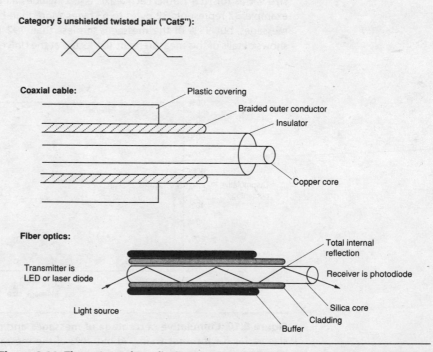

Figure 8.11 Three network media. (From a presentation by David Culler of U.C. Berkeley.)

The desire to go at higher speeds with the less expensive copper led to improvements in the quality of unshielded twisted-pair copper cabling systems. The original telephone-line quality was called level 1. Level 3 was good enough for 10M bits/sec Ethernet. The desire for even greater bandwidth lead to the level 5 or category 5, which is sufficient for 100M bits/sec Ethernet. By limiting the length to 100 meters, "Cat5" wiring can be used for 1000M bits/sec Ethernet links today. It uses the RJ-45 connector, which is similar to the connector found on telephone lines.

Coaxial cable was deployed by cable television companies to deliver a higher rate over a few kilometers. To offer high bandwidth and good noise immunity, insulating material surrounds a single stiff copper wire, and then cylindrical conductor surrounds the insulator, often woven as a braided mesh. A 50-ohm baseband coaxial cable delivers 10M bits/sec over a kilometer.

Connecting to this heavily insulated media is more challenging. The original technique was a T junction: The cable is cut in two and a connector is inserted that reconnects the cable and adds a third wire to a computer. A less invasive solution is a vampire tap: A hole of precise depth and width is first drilled into the cable, terminating in the copper core. A connector is then screwed in without having to cut the cable.

To keep up with the demands of bandwidth and distance, it became clear that the telephone company would need to find new media. The solution could be more expensive provided that it offered much higher bandwidth and that supplies were plentiful. The answer was to replace copper with glass and electrons with photons. *Fiber optics* transmits digital data as pulses of light.

A fiber optic network has three components:

■ The transmission medium, a fiber optic cable

■ The light source, an LED or laser diode

■ The light detector, a photodiode

First, cladding surrounds the glass fiber core to confine the light. A buffer then surrounds the cladding to protect the core and cladding. Note that unlike twisted pairs or coax, fibers are one-way, or *simplex,* media. A two-way, or *full duplex*, connection between two nodes requires two fibers.

Since light bends or refracts at interfaces, it can slowly spread as it travels down the cable unless the diameter of the cable is limited to one wavelength of light; then it transfers in a straight line. Thus, fiber optic cables are of two forms:

1. *Multimode fiber*—It uses inexpensive LEDs as a light source. It is typically much larger than the wavelength of light: typically 62.5 microns in diameter versus the 1.3-micron wavelength of infrared light. Since it is wider it has more dispersion problems, where some wave frequencies have different propagation velocities. The LEDs and dispersion limit it to up to a few hundred meters at 1000M bits/sec or a few kilometers at 100M bits /sec. It is older and less expensive than single-mode fiber.

2. *Single-mode fiber*—This "single-wavelength" fiber (typically 8 to 9 microns in diameter) requires more expensive laser diodes for light sources and currently transmits gigabits per second for hundreds of kilometers, making it the medium of choice for telephone companies. The loss of signal strength as it passes through a medium, called *attenuation,* limits the length of the fiber.

Although single-mode fiber is a better transmitter, it is much more difficult to attach connectors to single mode; it is less reliable and more expensive, and the cable itself has restrictions on the degree it can be bent. The cost, bandwidth, and distance of single-mode fiber are affected by the power of the light source, the sensitivity of the light detector, and the attenuation rate per kilometer of the fiber cable. Typically, glass fiber has better characteristics than the less expensive plastic fiber, and so is more widely used.

Connecting fiber optics to a computer is more challenging than connecting cable. The vampire tap solution of cable fails because it loses light. There are two forms of T-boxes:

1. Taps are fused onto the optical fiber. Each tap is passive, so a failure cuts off just a single computer.

2. In an active repeater, light is converted to electrical signals, sent to the computer, converted back to light, and then sent down the cable. If an active repeater fails, it blocks the network.

These taps and repeaters also reduce optical signal strength, reducing the useful distance of a single piece of fiber.

In both cases, fiber optics has the additional cost of optical-to-electrical and electrical-to-optical conversion as part of the computer interface. Hence, the network interface cards for fiber optics are considerably more expensive than for Cat5 copper wire. In 2001, most switches for fiber involve such a conversion to allow switching, although expensive all-optical switches are beginning to be available.

To achieve even more bandwidth from a fiber, *wavelength division multiplexing* (WDM) sends different streams simultaneously on the same fiber using different wavelengths of light, and then demultiplexes the different wavelengths at the receiver. In 2001, WDM can deliver a combined 40G bits/sec using about 8 wavelengths, with plans to go to 80 wavelengths and deliver 400G bits/sec.

The product of the bandwidth and maximum distance forms a single figure of merit: gigabit-kilometers per second. According to Desurvire [1992], since 1975 optical fibers have increased transmission capacity by tenfold every four years by this measure.

Let's compare media in an example.

Example   Suppose you have 25 magnetic tapes, each containing 40 GB. Assume that you have enough tape readers to keep any network busy. How long will it take to transmit the data over a distance of one kilometer? Assume the choices are category 5 twisted-pair wires at 100M bits/sec, multimode fiber at 1000M bits/sec, and single-mode fiber at 2500M bits/sec. How do they compare to delivering the tapes by car?

Answer   The amount of data is 1000 GB. The time for each medium is given below:

$$\text{Twisted pair} = \frac{1000 \times 1024 \times 8M \text{ bits}}{100M \text{ bits/sec}} = 81,920 \text{ sec} = 22.8 \text{ hours}$$

$$\text{Multimode fiber} = \frac{1000 \times 1024 \times 8M \text{ bits}}{1000M \text{ bits/sec}} = 8192 \text{ sec} = 2.3 \text{ hours}$$

$$\text{Single-mode fiber} = \frac{1000 \times 1024 \times 8M \text{ bits}}{2500M \text{ bits/sec}} = 3277 \text{ sec} = 0.9 \text{ hours}$$

$$\text{Car} = \text{Time to load car} + \text{Transport time} + \text{Time to unload car}$$

$$= 300 \text{ sec} + \frac{1 \text{ km}}{30 \text{ kph}} + 300 \text{ sec} = 300 \text{ sec} + 120 \text{ sec} + 300 \text{ sec}$$

$$= 720 \text{ sec} = 0.3 \text{ hours}$$

A car filled with high-density tapes is a high-bandwidth medium!

8.4   Connecting More Than Two Computers

Computer power increases by the square of the number of nodes on the network.
Robert Metcalf ("Metcalf's Law")

Thus far, we have discussed two computers communicating over private lines, but what makes interconnection networks interesting is the ability to connect hundreds of computers together. And what makes them more interesting also makes them more challenging to build.

Shared versus Switched Media

Certainly the simplest way to connect multiple computers is to have them share a single interconnection medium, just as I/O devices share a single I/O bus. The most popular LAN, Ethernet, originally was simply a bus shared by a hundred computers.

Given that the medium is shared, there must be a mechanism to coordinate and arbitrate the use of the shared medium so that only one message is sent at a time. If the network is small, it may be possible to have an additional central arbiter to give permission to send a message. (Of course, this leaves open the question of how the nodes talk to the arbiter.)

Centralized arbitration is impractical for networks with a large number of nodes spread out over a kilometer, so we must distribute arbitration. A first step toward arbitration is looking before you leap. A node first checks the network to avoid trying to send a message while another message is already on the network. If the interconnection is idle, the node tries to send. Looking first is not a guarantee of success, of course, as some other node may decide to send at the same instant. When two nodes send at the same time, it is called a *collision*. Let's assume that the network interface can detect any resulting collisions by listening to hear if the data were garbled by other data appearing on the line. Listening to avoid and detect collisions is called *carrier sensing and collision detection*. This is the second step of arbitration.

The problem is not solved. If every node on the network waited exactly the same amount of time, listened to be sure there was no traffic, and then tried to send again, we could still have synchronized nodes that would repeatedly bump heads. To avoid repeated head-on collisions, each node whose message was garbled waits (or "backs off") a *random* time before resending. Note that randomization breaks the synchronization. Subsequent collisions result in exponentially increasing time between attempts to retransmit, so as not to tax the network.

Although this approach is not guaranteed to be fair—some subsequent node may transmit while those that collided are waiting—it does control congestion on the shared medium. If the network does not have high demand from many nodes, this simple approach works well. Under high utilization, performance degrades since the medium is shared.

Another approach to arbitration is to pass a token between the nodes, with the token giving the node the right to use the network. If the shared media are connected in a ring, then the token can rotate through all the nodes on the ring.

Shared media have some of the same advantages and disadvantages as buses: They are inexpensive, but they have limited bandwidth. And like buses, they must have an arbitration scheme to solve conflicting demands.

The alternative to sharing the media is to have a dedicated line to a switch that in turn provides a dedicated line to all destinations. Figure 8.12 shows the potential bandwidth improvement of switches: *aggregate bandwidth* is many times that of a single shared medium.

Switches allow communication directly from source to destination, without intermediate nodes to interfere with these signals. Such *point-to-point* communication is faster than a line shared between many nodes because there is no arbitration and the interface is simpler electrically. Of course, it does pay the added latency of going through the switch, trading off arbitration overhead for switching overhead.

Given the obvious advantages, why weren't switches always used? Earlier computers were much slower and so could share media. In addition, applications such as the World Wide Web rely on the network much more than older applications. Finally, earlier switches would take several large boards and be as large as a computer. In 2001, a single chip contained a full 64-by-64 switch, or at least a large slice of it. Moore's Law is making switches more attractive, and so technology trends favor switches today.

Every node of a shared line will see every message, even if it is just to check to see whether or not the message is for that node, so this style of communication

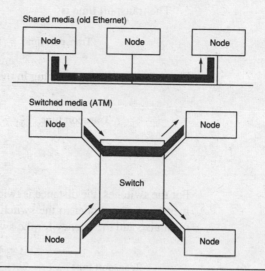

Figure 8.12 Shared medium versus switch. Ethernet was originally a shared medium, but Ethernet switches are now available. All nodes on the shared media must share the 100M bit/sec interconnection, but switches can support multiple 100M bit/sec transfers simultaneously. Low-cost Ethernet switches are sometimes implemented with an internal bus with higher bandwidth, but high-speed switches have a crossbar interconnect.

is sometimes called *broadcast* to contrast it with point-to-point. The shared medium makes it easy to broadcast a message to every node, and even to broadcast to subsets of nodes, called *multicasting*.

Switches allow multiple pairs of nodes to communicate simultaneously, giving these interconnections much higher *aggregate* bandwidth than the speed of a shared link to a node. Switches also allow the interconnection network to scale to a very large number of nodes. Switches are also called *data switching exchanges, multistage interconnection networks,* or even *interface message processors* (IMPs). Depending on the distance of the node to the switch and desired bandwidth, the network medium is either copper wire or optical fiber.

Example   Compare 16 nodes connected three ways: a single 10M bit/sec shared medium; a switch connected via Cat5, each segment running at 10M bits/sec; and a switch connected via optical fibers, each running at 1000M bits/sec. The shared medium is 500 meters long, and the average length of each segment to a switch is 50 meters. Both switches can support the full bandwidth. Assume each switch adds 5 µs to the latency. Calculate the aggregate bandwidth and transport latency. Assume the average message size is 125 bytes, and ignore the overhead of sending or receiving a message and contention for the network.

Answer   The aggregate bandwidth of each example is the simplest calculation: 100M bits/ sec for the shared medium; 16 × 100, or 1600M bits/sec for the switched twisted pairs; and 16 × 1000, or 16,000M bits/sec for the switched optical fibers.

The transport time is

$$\text{Transport time} = \text{Time of flight} + \frac{\text{Message size}}{\text{Bandwidth}}$$

For shared media we just plug in the distance, bandwidth, and message size:

$$
\begin{aligned}
\text{Transport time}_{shared} &= \frac{500/1000 \times 10^6}{2/3 \times 300,000}\ \mu s + \frac{125 \times 8}{100}\ \mu s \\
&= 2.5\ \mu s + 10\ \mu s \\
&= 12.5\ \mu s
\end{aligned}
$$

For the switches, the distance is twice the average segment, since there is one segment from the sender to the switch and one from the switch to the receiver. We must also add the latency for the switch.

$$
\begin{aligned}
\text{Transport time}_{switch} &= 2 \times \left(\frac{50/1000 \times 10^6}{2/3 \times 300,000}\right)\ \mu s + 5\ \mu s + \frac{125 \times 8}{100}\ \mu s \\
&= 0.5\ \mu s + 5\ \mu s + 10\ \mu s \\
&= 15.5\ \mu s
\end{aligned}
$$

$$
\begin{aligned}
\text{Transport time}_{fiber} &= 2 \times \left(\frac{50/1000 \times 10^6}{2/3 \times 300,000}\right)\ \mu s + 5\ \mu s + \frac{125 \times 8}{1000}\ \mu s \\
&= 0.5\ \mu s + 5\ \mu s + 1\ \mu s \\
&= 6.5\ \mu s
\end{aligned}
$$

Although the bandwidth of the switch is many times the shared media, the latency for unloaded networks is comparable.

Switches allow communication to harvest the same rapid advance from silicon as have processors and main memory. Whereas the switches from telecommunications companies were once the size of mainframe computers, today we see single-chip switches. Just as single-chip processors led to processors replacing logic in a surprising number of places, single-chip switches are increasingly replacing buses and shared media networks.

Connection-Oriented versus Connectionless Communication

Before computers arrived on the scene, the telecommunications industry allowed communication around the world. An operator set up a *connection* between a caller and a callee, and once the connection was established, a conversation could continue for hours. To share transmission lines over long distances, the telecommunications industry used switches to multiplex several conversations on the same lines. Since audio transmissions have relatively low bandwidth, the solution was to divide the bandwidth of the transmission line into a fixed number of frequencies, with each frequency assigned to a conversation. This technique is called *frequency-division multiplexing.*

Although a good match for voice, frequency-division multiplexing is inefficient for sending data. The problem is that the frequency channel is dedicated to the conversation whether or not there is anything being said. Hence, the long-distance lines are "busy" based on the *number* of conversations, and not on the *amount* of information being sent at a particular time. An alternative style of communication is called *connectionless,* where each package is routed to the destination by looking at its address. The postal system is a good example of connectionless communication.

Closely related to the idea of connection versus connectionless communication are the terms *circuit switching* and *packet switching.* Circuit switching is the traditional way to offer a connection-based service. A circuit is established from source to destination to carry the conversation, reserving bandwidth until the circuit is broken. The alternative to circuit-switched transmission is to divide the information into *packets,* or *frames,* with each packet including the destination of the packet plus a portion of the information. Queuing theory in Section 7.8 tells us that packets cannot use all of the bandwidth, but in general, this *packet-switched* approach allows more use of the bandwidth of the medium and is the traditional way to support connectionless communication.

Example Let's compare a single 1000M bit/sec packet-switched network with ten 100M bit/sec packet-switched networks. Assume that the mean size of a packet is 250 bytes, the arrival rate is 250,000 packets per second, and the interarrival times are exponentially distributed. What is the mean response time for each alternative? What is the intuitive reason behind the difference?

Answer From Section 7.8, we can use an M/M/1 queue to calculate the mean response time for the single fast network:

$$\text{Service rate} = \frac{\text{Bandwidth}}{\text{Message size}} = \frac{1000 \times 10^6}{250 \times 8} = \frac{1000 \times 10^6}{2000} = 500{,}000 \text{ packets per second}$$

$$\text{Time}_{server} = \frac{1}{500{,}000} = 2\ \mu s$$

$$\text{Utilization} = \frac{\text{Arrival rate}}{\text{Service rate}} = \frac{250{,}000}{500{,}000} = 0.5$$

$$\text{Time}_{queue} = \text{Time}_{server} \times \frac{\text{Server utilization}}{(1 - \text{Server utilization})} = 2\ \mu s \times \frac{0.5}{1 - 0.5} = 2 \times \frac{0.5}{0.5} = 2\ \mu s$$

$$\text{Mean response time} = \text{Time}_{queue} + \text{Time}_{server} = 2 + 2 = 4\ \mu s$$

The 10 slow networks can be modeled by an M/M/m queue, and the appropriate formulas are found in Section 7.8:

$$\text{Service rate} = \frac{100 \times 10^6}{250 \times 8} = \frac{100 \times 10^6}{2000} = 50{,}000 \text{ packets per second}$$

$$\text{Time}_{server} = \frac{1}{50{,}000} = 0.00002 \text{ sec} = 20 \text{ } \mu s$$

$$\text{Utilization} = \frac{\text{Arrival rate}}{m \times \text{Service rate}} = \frac{250{,}000}{10 \times 50{,}000} = \frac{250{,}000}{500{,}000} = 0.5$$

$$\text{Time}_{queue} = \text{Time}_{server} \times \frac{\text{Server utilization}}{m \times (1 - \text{Server utilization})} = 20 \text{ } \mu s \times \frac{0.5}{10 \times (1 - 0.5)} = 2 \times \frac{0.5}{0.5} = 2 \text{ } \mu s$$

$$\text{Mean response time} = \text{Time}_{queue} + \text{Time}_{server} = 2 + 20 = 22 \text{ } \mu s$$

The intuition is clear from the results: The service time is much less for the faster network even though the queuing times are the same. This intuition is the argument for "statistical multiplexing" using packets; queuing times are not worse for a single faster network, and the latency for a single packet is much less. Stated alternatively, you get better latency when you use an unloaded fast network, and data traffic is bursty so it works.

Although connections traditionally align with circuit switching, providing the user with the appearance of a logical connection on top of a packet-switched network is certainly possible. TCP/IP, as we will see in Section 8.8, is a connection-oriented service that operates over packet-switched networks.

Routing: Delivering Messages

Given that the path between nodes may be difficult to navigate depending upon the topology, the system must be able to route the message to the desired node. Shared media have a simple solution: The message is broadcast to *all* nodes that share the media, and each node looks at an address within the message to see whether the message is for that node. This routing also made it easy to broadcast one message to all nodes by reserving one address for everyone; broadcast is much harder to support in switch-based networks.

Switched media use three solutions for routing. In *source-based routing*, the message specifies the path to the destination. Since the network merely follows directions, it can be simpler. A second alternative is the *virtual circuit*, whereby a circuit is established between source and destination, and the message simply names the circuit to follow. ATM uses virtual circuits. The third approach is a *destination-based routing*, where the message merely contains a destination address, and the switch must pick a path to deliver the message. IP uses destination routing. Hence, ATM switches are simpler conceptually; once a virtual circuit is established, packet switching is very fast. On the other hand, an IP router must decide how to route every packet it receives by doing a routing table lookup on every packet.

Destination-based routing may be *deterministic* and always follow the same path, or it may be *adaptive*, allowing the network to pick different routes to avoid failures or congestion. Closely related to adaptive routing is *randomized routing*, whereby the network will randomly pick between several equally good paths to spread the traffic throughout the network, thereby avoiding hot spots.

Switches in WANs route messages using a *store-and-forward* policy; each switch waits for the full message to arrive in the switch before it is sent on to the next switch. Generally store-and-forward can retry a message within the network in case of failure. The alternative to store-and-forward, available in some SANs, is for the switch to examine the header, decide where to send the message, and then start transmitting it immediately without waiting for the rest of the message. It requires retransmission from the source on a failure within the network.

This alternative is called either *cut-through routing* or *wormhole routing*. In wormhole routing, when the head of the message is blocked, the message stays strung out over the network, potentially blocking other messages. Cut-through routing lets the tail continue when the head is blocked, compressing the strung-out message into a single switch. Clearly, cut-through routing requires a buffer large enough to hold the largest packet, while wormhole routing needs only to buffer the piece of the packet sent between switches.

The advantage of both cut-through and wormhole routing over store-and-forward is that latency reduces from a function of the number of intermediate switches *multiplied* by the size of the packet to the time for the first part of the packet to negotiate the switches *plus* the transmission time.

Example The CM-5 supercomputer used wormhole routing, with each switch buffer being just 4 bits per port. Compare efficiency of store-and-forward versus wormhole routing for a 128-node machine using a CM-5 interconnection sending a 16-byte payload. Assume each switch takes 0.25 μs and that the transfer rate is 20 MB/sec.

Answer The CM-5 interconnection for 128 nodes is hierarchical (see Figure 8.14 on page 816), and a message goes through seven intermediate switches. Each CM-5 packet has 4 bytes of header information, so the length of this packet is 20 bytes. The time to transfer 20 bytes over one CM-5 link is

$$\frac{20}{20 \text{ MB/sec}} = 1 \text{ μs}$$

Then the time for store-and-forward is

(Switches × Switch delay) + ((Switches + 1) × Transfer time) = (7 × 0.25) + (8 × 1) = 9.75 μ

while wormhole routing is

(Switches × Switch delay) + Transfer time = (7 × 0.25) + 1 = 2.75 μsecs

For this example, wormhole routing improves latency by more than a factor of 3.

A final routing issue is the order in which packets arrive. Some networks require that packets arrive in the order sent. The alternative removes this restriction, requiring software to reassemble the packets in proper order.

Congestion Control

One advantage of a circuit-switched network is that once a circuit is established, it ensures there is sufficient bandwidth to deliver all the information sent along that circuit. Moreover, switches along a path can be requested to give specific quality-of-service guarantees. Thus, interconnection bandwidth is reserved as circuits are established rather than consumed as data are sent, and if the network is full, no more circuits can be established. You may have encountered this blockage when trying to place a long-distance phone call on a popular holiday or to a television show, as the telephone system tells you that "all circuits are busy" and asks you to please call back at a later time.

Packet-switched networks generally do not reserve interconnect bandwidth in advance, so the interconnection network can become clogged with too many packets. Just as with rush-hour traffic, a traffic jam of packets increases packet latency. Packets take longer to arrive, and in extreme cases fewer packets per second are delivered by the interconnect, just as is the case for the poor rush-hour commuters. There is even the computer equivalent of gridlock: *Deadlock* is achieved when packets in the interconnect can make no forward progress no matter what sequence of events happens. Chapter 6 addresses how to avoid this ultimate congestion in the context of a multiprocessor. Higher-bandwidth and longer-distance networks exacerbate these problems, as this example illustrates.

Example   Assume a 155M bit/sec network stretching from San Francisco to New York City. How many bytes will be in flight? What is the number if the network is upgraded to 1000M bits/sec?

Answer   Use the prior assumptions and speed of light. The distance between San Francisco and New York City is 4120 km. Calculating time of flight:

$$\text{Time of flight} = \frac{4120 \text{ km}}{2/3 \times 300{,}000 \text{ km/sec}} = 0.0206 \text{ sec}$$

Let's assume the network delivers 50% of the peak bandwidth. The number of bytes in transit on a 155M bit/sec network is

$$\text{Bytes in transit} = \text{Delivered bandwidth} \times \text{Time of flight}$$
$$= \frac{0.5 \times 155\text{M bits/sec}}{8} \times 0.0206 \text{ sec} = 9.7 \text{ MB/sec} \times 0.0206 \text{ sec}$$
$$= 0.200 \text{ MB}$$

At 1000M bits/sec the number is

$$\text{Bytes in transit} = \frac{0.5 \times 1000\text{M bits/sec}}{8} \times 0.0206 \text{ sec} = 62.5 \text{ MB/sec} \times 0.0206 \text{ sec}$$

$$= 1.718 \text{ MB}$$

More than a megabyte of messages will be a challenge to control and to store in the network.

The solution to congestion is to prevent new packets from entering the network until traffic reduces, just as metering lights guarding on-ramps control the rate of cars entering a freeway. There are three basic schemes used for congestion control in computer interconnection networks, each with its own weaknesses: packet discarding, flow control, and choke packets.

The simplest, and most callous, is *packet discarding*. If a packet arrives at a switch and there is no room in the buffer, the packet is discarded. This scheme relies on higher-level software that handles errors in transmission to resend lost packets. Internetworking protocols such as UDP discard packets.

The second scheme is to rely on *flow control* between pairs of receivers and senders. The idea is to use feedback to tell the sender when it is allowed to send the next packet. One version of feedback is via separate wires between adjacent senders and receivers that tell the sender to stop immediately when the receiver cannot accept another message. This *backpressure* feedback is rapidly sent back to the original sender over dedicated lines, causing all links between the two endpoints to be frozen until the receiver can make room for the next message. Backpressure flow control is common in supercomputer networks, SANs, and even some gigabit Ethernet switches, which send fake collision signals to control flow.

A more sophisticated variation of feedback is for the ultimate destination to give the original sender a credit to send *n* packets before getting permission to send more—generically called *credit-based flow control*. A *window* is one version of credit-based flow control. The window's size determines the minimum frequency of communication from receiver to sender. The goal of the window is to send enough packets to overlap the latency of the interconnection with the overhead to send and receive a packet. The TCP protocol uses a window.

This brings us to a point of confusion on terminology in many papers and textbooks. Note that flow control describes just two nodes of the interconnection and not the total interconnection network between all end systems. *Congestion control* refers to schemes that reduce traffic when the collective traffic of all nodes is too large for the network to handle. Hence, flow control helps congestion control, but it is not a universal solution.

Choke packets are the basis of the third scheme. The observation is that you only want to limit traffic when the network is congested. The idea is for each switch to see how busy it is, entering a warning state when it passes a threshold. Each packet received by the switch in a warning state is sent back to the source via a choke packet that includes the intended destination. The source is expected to reduce traffic to that destination by a fixed percentage. Since it likely will have already sent many packets along that path, it waits for all the packets in transit to be returned before taking choke packets seriously.

8.5 Network Topology

The number of topologies described in publications would be difficult to count, but the number that have been used commercially is just a handful, with designers of parallel supercomputers being the most visible and imaginative. They have used regular topologies to simplify packaging and scalability. The topologies of SANS, LANs, and WANs are more haphazard, having more to do with the challenges of long distance or simply the connection of equipment purchased over several years. Topology matters less today than it did in the past. You don't want to rewrite your application for each new topology, but you would like the system to take advantage of locality that naturally occurs in programs.

Centralized Switch

Figure 8.13 illustrates two of the popular switch organizations, with the path from node P_0 to node P_6 shown in gray in each topology. A fully connected, or *crossbar,* interconnection allows any node to communicate with any other node in one pass through the interconnection. Routing depends on the style of addressing. In source-based routing, the message includes a sequence of outbound arcs to reach a destination. Once an outgoing arc is picked, that portion of the routing sequence may be dropped from the packet. In destination-based routing, a table decides which port to take for a given address. Some networks will run programs in the switches ("spanning tree protocols") to generate the routing table on the fly once the network is connected. The Internet does something similar for routing.

An *Omega interconnection* uses less hardware than the crossbar interconnection ($n/2 \log_2 n$ versus n^2 switches), but contention is more likely to occur between messages. The amount of contention depends on the pattern of communication. This form of contention is called *blocking*. For example, in the Omega interconnection in Figure 8.13 a message from P_1 to P_7 blocks while waiting for a message from P_0 to P_6. Of course, if two nodes try to send to the same destination—both P_0 and P_1 send to P_6—there will be contention for that link, even in the crossbar. Routing in an Omega net uses the same techniques as in a full crossbar.

A tree is the basis of another switch, with bandwidth added higher in the tree to match the requirements of common communications patterns. Figure 8.14 shows this topology, called a *fat tree*. Interconnections are normally drawn as graphs, with each arc of the graph representing a link of the communication interconnection, with nodes shown as black squares and switches shown as shaded circles.

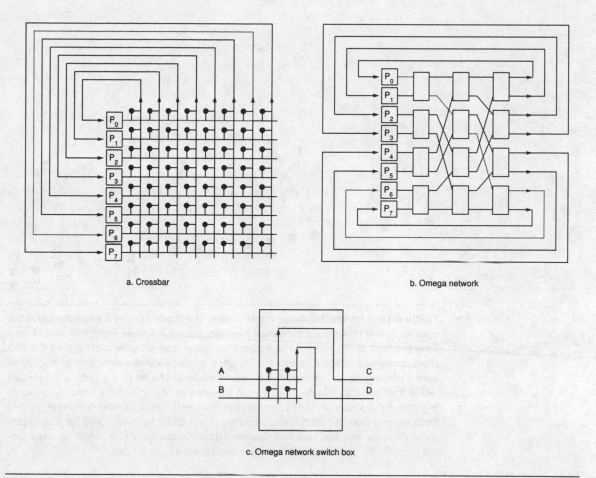

a. Crossbar

b. Omega network

c. Omega network switch box

Figure 8.13 Popular switch topologies for eight nodes. The links are unidirectional; data come in at the left and exit out the right link. The switch box in (c) can pass A to C and B to D or B to C and A to D. The crossbar uses n^2 switches, where n is the number of processors, while the Omega network uses $n/2 \log_2 n$ of the large switch boxes, each of which is logically composed of four of the smaller switches. In this case the crossbar uses 64 switches versus 12 switch boxes or 48 switches in the Omega network. The crossbar, however, can simultaneously route any permutation of traffic pattern between processors. The Omega network cannot.

To double the number of nodes in a fat tree, we just add another level to the top of the tree. Notice that this also increases the bandwidth at the top of the tree, which is an advantage of a fat tree.

Figure 8.14 shows that there are multiple paths between any two nodes in a fat tree. For example, between node 0 and node 8 there are four paths. Such redundancy can help with fault tolerance. In addition, if messages are randomly assigned to different paths, then this should spread the load throughout the switch and result in fewer congestion problems.

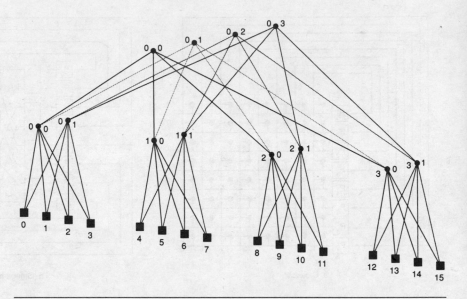

Figure 8.14 A fat-tree topology for 16 nodes. The shaded circles are switches, and the squares at the bottom are processor-memory nodes. A simple 4-ary tree would only have the links at the front of the figure; that is, the tree with the root labeled 0,0. This three-dimensional view suggests the increase in bandwidth via extra links at each level over a simple tree, so bandwidth between each level of a fat tree is normally constant rather than reduced by a factor of 4 as in a 4-ary tree. Multiple paths and random routing give it the ability to route common patterns well, which ensures no single pattern from a broad class of communication patterns will do badly. In the CM-5 fat-tree implementation, the switches have four downward connections and two or four upward connections; in this figure the switches have two upward connections.

Thus far, the switch is separate from the processor and memory, and assumed to be located in a central location. Looking inside this switch, we see many smaller switches. The term *multistage switch* is sometimes used to refer to centralized units to reflect the multiple steps that a message may travel before it reaches a computer.

Distributed Switch

Instead of centralizing these small switching elements, an alternative is to place one small switch at every computer, yielding a distributed switching function.

Given a distributed switch, the question is how to connect the switches together. Figure 8.15 shows that a low-cost alternative to full interconnection is a network that connects a sequence of nodes together. This topology is called a *ring*. Since some nodes are not directly connected, some messages will have to hop along intermediate nodes until they arrive at the final destination. Unlike shared lines, a

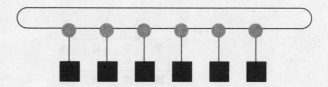

Figure 8.15 A ring network topology.

ring is capable of many simultaneous transfers: The first node can send to the second at the same time as the third node can send to the fourth, for example. Rings are not quite as good as this sounds because the average message must travel through $n/2$ switches, where n is the number of nodes. To first order, a ring is like a pipelined bus: On the plus side are point-to-point links, and on the minus side are "bus repeater" delays.

One variation of rings used in local area networks is the *token ring*. To simplify arbitration, a single slot, or *token,* goes around the ring to determine which node is allowed to send a message. A node can send only when it gets the token. (A token is simply a special bit pattern.) In this section we evaluate the ring as a topology with more bandwidth than a bus, neglecting its advantages in arbitration.

A straightforward but expensive alternative to a ring is to have a dedicated communication link between every element of a distributed switch. The tremendous improvement in performance of fully connected switches is offset by the enormous increase in cost, typically going up with the square of the number of nodes. This cost inspires designers to invent new topologies that are between the cost of rings and the performance of fully connected networks. The evaluation of success depends in large part on the nature of the communication in the interconnection network. Real machines frequently add extra links to these simple topologies to improve performance and reliability. Figure 8.16 illustrates three popular topologies for high-performance computers with distributed switches.

One popular measure for interconnections, in addition to the ones covered in Section 8.2, is the *bisection bandwidth.* This measure is calculated by dividing the interconnect into two roughly equal parts, each with half the nodes. You then sum the bandwidth of the lines that cross that imaginary dividing line. For fully connected interconnections the bisection bandwidth is proportional to $(n/2)^2$, where n is the number of nodes. For a bus, bisection bandwidth is just the speed of one link.

Since some interconnections are not symmetric, the question arises as to where to draw the imaginary line when bisecting the interconnect. Bisection bandwidth is a worst-case metric, so the answer is to choose the division that makes interconnection performance worst. Stated alternatively, calculate bisection bandwidths for all pairs of equal-sized parts, and pick the smallest. Figure 8.17 summarizes these different topologies using bisection bandwidth and the number of links for 64 nodes.

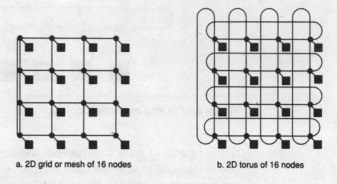

a. 2D grid or mesh of 16 nodes   b. 2D torus of 16 nodes

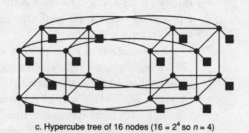

c. Hypercube tree of 16 nodes ($16 = 2^4$ so $n = 4$)

Figure 8.16 Network topologies that have appeared in commercial supercomputers. The shaded circles represent switches, and the black squares represent nodes. Even though a switch has many links, generally only one goes to the node. Frequently these basic topologies are supplemented with extra arcs to improve performance and reliability. For example, connecting the switches in the left and right columns of the 2D grid using the unused ports on each switch forms a 2D torus. The Boolean hypercube topology is an *n*-dimensional interconnect for 2^n nodes, requiring *n* ports per switch (plus one for the processor), and thus *n* nearest neighbor nodes.

Evaluation category	Bus	Ring	2D torus	6-cube	Fully connected
Performance					
Bisection bandwidth	1	2	16	32	1024
Cost					
Ports per switch	NA	3	5	7	64
Total number of lines	1	128	192	256	2080

Figure 8.17 Relative cost and performance of several interconnects for 64 nodes. The bus is the standard reference at unit cost, and of course there can be more than one data line along each link between nodes. Note that any network topology that scales the bisection bandwidth linearly must scale the number of interconnection lines faster than linearly. Figure 8.13(a) is an example of a fully connected network.

Example   A common communication pattern in scientific programs is to consider the nodes as elements of a two-dimensional array and then have communication to the nearest neighbor in a given direction. (This pattern is sometimes called *NEWS communication,* standing for north, east, west, and south, the directions on the compass.) Map an eight-by-eight array onto the 64 nodes in each topology, and assume every link of every interconnect is the same speed. How long does it take each node to send one message to its northern neighbor and one to its eastern neighbor? Ignore nodes that have no northern or eastern neighbors.

Answer   In this case, we want to send $2 \times (64 - 8)$, or 112, messages. Here are the cases, again in increasing order of difficulty of explanation:

- *Bus*—The placement of the eight-by-eight array makes no difference for the bus, since all nodes are equally distant. The 112 transfers are done sequentially, taking 112 time units.

- *Fully connected*—Again the nodes are equally distant; all transfers are done in parallel, taking one time unit.

- *Ring*—Here the nodes are differing distances. Assume the first row of the array is placed on nodes 0 to 7, the second row on nodes 8 to 15, and so on. It takes just one time unit to send to the eastern neighbor, for this is a send from node n to node $n + 1$. In this scheme the northern neighbor is exactly eight nodes away, so it takes eight time units for each node to send to its northern neighbor. The ring total is nine time units.

- *2D torus*—There are eight rows and eight columns in our grid of 64 nodes, which is a perfect match to the NEWS communication. It takes just two time units to send to the northern and eastern neighbors.

- *6-cube*—It is possible to place the array so that it will take just two time units for this communication pattern, as in the case of the torus.

This simple analysis of interconnection networks in this section ignores several important practical considerations in the construction of an interconnection network. First, these three-dimensional drawings must be mapped onto chips, boards, and cabinets that are essentially two-dimensional media, often treelike. For example, due to the fixed height of cabinets, an n-node Intel Paragon used an $n/16 \times 16$ rectangular grid rather than the ideal of $\sqrt{n} \times \sqrt{n}$. Another consideration is the internal speed of the switch: If it is fixed, then more links per switch means lower bandwidth per link, potentially affecting the desirability of different topologies. Yet another consideration is that the latency through a switch depends on the complexity of the routing pattern, which in turn depends on the topology. Finally, the bandwidth from the processor is often the limiting factor: If there is only one port in and out of the processor, then it can only send or receive one message per time unit regardless of the technology.

Topologies that appear elegant when sketched on the blackboard may look awkward when constructed from chips, cables, boards, and boxes. The bottom line is that quality of implementation matters more than topology. To put these topologies in perspective, Figure 8.18 lists those used in commercial high-performance computers.

Once again the issues discussed in this section apply at many levels, from inside a chip to a country-sized WAN. The redundancy of a topology matters so that the network can survive despite failures. This is true within a switch as well, so that a single chip failure need not lead to switch failure. It also must be true for a WAN, so that a single backhoe cannot take down the network of a country. The switch then depends on the implementation technology and the demands of the application: It is a multistage network whose topology can be anything from a bus to an Omega network.

Institution	Name	Number of nodes	Basic topology	Data bits/link	Network clock rate (MHz)	Peak BW/link (MB/sec)	Bisection (MB/sec)	Year
Thinking Machines	CM-2	1024 to 4096	12-cube	1	7	1	1,024	1987
Intel	Delta	540	2D grid	16	40	40	640	1991
Thinking Machines	CM-5	32 to 2048	multistage fat tree	4	40	20	10,240	1991
Intel	Paragon	4 to 2048	2D grid	16	100	175	6,400	1992
IBM	SP-2	2 to 512	multistage fat tree	8	40	40	20,480	1993
Cray Research	T3E	16 to 2048	3D torus	16	300?	600	122,000	1997
Intel	ASCI Red	4536 (× 2 CPUs)	2D grid			800	51,600	1996
IBM	ASCI Blue Pacific	1336 (× 4 CPUs)				150		
SGI	ASCI Blue Mountain	1464 (× 2 CPUs)	fat hypercube			800	200 × nodes	1998
IBM	ASCI Blue Horizon	144 (× 8 CPUs)	multistage Omega			115		1999
IBM	SP	1 to 512 (× 2 to 16 CPUs)	multistage Omega			500		2000
IBM	ASCI White	484 (× 16 CPUs)	multistage Omega			500		2001

Figure 8.18 Characteristics of interconnections of some commercial supercomputers. The bisection bandwidth is for the largest machine. The 2D grid of the Intel Delta is 16 rows by 35 columns and the ASCI Red is 38 rows by 32 columns. The fat-tree topology of the CM-5 is restricted in the lower two levels, hence the lower bandwidth in the bisection. Note that the Cray T3E has two processors per node, and the Intel Paragon has from two to four processors per node.

<table>
<tr><td>**8.6**</td><td></td></tr>
</table>

8.6   Practical Issues for Commercial Interconnection Networks

There are practical issues in addition to the technical issues described so far that are important considerations for some interconnection networks: connectivity, standardization, and fault tolerance.

Connectivity

The number of machines that communicate affects the complexity of the network and its protocols. The protocols must target the largest size of the network and handle the types of anomalous events that occur. Hundreds of machines communicating are much easier than millions.

Connecting the Network to the Computer

Where the network attaches to the computer affects both the network interface hardware and software. Questions include whether to use the memory bus or the I/O bus, whether to use polling or interrupts, and how to avoid invoking the operating system. The network interface is often the network bottleneck.

Computers have a hierarchy of buses with different cost-performance. For example, a personal computer in 2001 had a memory bus, a PCI bus for fast I/O devices, and a USB bus for slow I/O devices. I/O buses follow open standards and have less stringent electrical requirements. Memory buses, on the other hand, provide higher bandwidth and lower latency than I/O buses. Where to connect the network to the machine depends on the performance goals and whether you hope to buy a standard network interface card or are willing to design or buy one that only works with the memory bus on your model of computer. A few SANs plug into the memory bus, but most SANs and all LANs and WANs plug into the I/O bus.

The location of the network connection significantly affects the software interface to the network as well as the hardware. As mentioned in Section 7.10, one key is whether the interface is coherent with the processor's caches: The sender may have to flush the cache before each send, and the receiver may have to flush its cache before each receive to prevent the stale-data problem. Such flushes increase send and receive overhead. A memory bus is more likely to be cache coherent than an I/O bus and therefore more likely to avoid these extra cache flushes.

A question related to where to connect to the computer is how to connect to the software: Do you use programmed I/O or direct memory access (DMA) to send a message? (See Section 7.10.) In general, DMA is the best way to send large messages. Whether to use DMA to send small messages depends on the efficiency of the interface to the DMA. The DMA interface is usually memory mapped, and so each interaction is typically at the speed of main memory rather than of a cache access. If DMA setup takes many accesses, each running at uncached memory speeds, then the sender overhead may be so high that it is faster to simply send the data directly to the interface.

Standardization: Cross-Company Interoperability

Standards are useful in many places in computer design, but with interconnection networks they are often critical. Advantages of successful standards include low cost and stability. The customer has many vendors to choose from, which keeps price close to cost due to competition. It makes the viability of the interconnection independent of the stability of a single company. Components designed for a standard interconnection may also have a larger market, and this higher volume can lower the vendor's costs, further benefiting the customer. Finally, a standard allows many companies to build products with interfaces to the standard, so the customer does not have to wait for a single company to develop interfaces to all the products the customer might be interested in.

One drawback of standards is the time it takes for committees to agree on the definition of standards, which is a problem when technology is changing quickly. Another problem is *when* to standardize: on one hand, designers would like to have a standard before anything is built; on the other, it would be better if something is built before standardization to avoid legislating useless features or omitting important ones. When done too early, it is often done entirely by committee, which is like asking all of the chefs in France to prepare a single dish of food; masterpieces are rarely served. Standards can also suppress innovation at that level, since the standard fixes interfaces.

LANs and WANs use standards and interoperate effectively. WANs involve many types of companies and must connect to many brands of computers, so it is difficult to imagine a proprietary WAN ever being successful. The ubiquitous nature of the Ethernet shows the popularity of standards for LANs as well as WANs, and it seems unlikely that many customers would tie the viability of their LAN to the stability of a single company.

Alas, some SANs are standardized yet switches from different companies do not interoperate, and some interoperate as well as LANs and WANs.

Message Failure Tolerance

Although some hardware designers try to build fault-free networks, in practice it is only a question of the rate of faults, not whether you can prevent them. Thus, the communication system must have mechanisms for retransmission of a message in case of failure. Often it is handled in higher layers of the software protocol at the endpoints, requiring retransmission at the source. Given the long time of flight for WANs, often they can retransmit from hop to hop rather than relying only on retransmission from the source.

Node Failure Tolerance

The second practical issue refers to whether or not the interconnection relies on all the nodes being operational in order for the interconnection to work properly. Since software failures are generally much more frequent than hardware failures, the question is whether a software crash on a single node can prevent the rest of the nodes from communicating.

Clearly, WANs would be useless if they demanded that thousands of computers spread across a continent be continuously available, and so they all tolerate the failures of individual nodes. LANs connect dozens to hundreds of computers together, and again it would be impractical to require that no computer ever fail. All successful LANs normally survive node failures.

Although most SANs have the ability to work around failed nodes and switches, it is not clear that all communication layer software supports this feature. Typically, low-latency schemes sacrifice fault tolerance.

Example   Figure 8.19 shows the number of failures of 58 desktop computers on a local area network for a period of just over one year. Suppose that one local area network is based on a network that requires all machines to be operational for the interconnection network to send data; if a node crashes, it cannot accept messages, so the interconnection becomes choked with data waiting to be delivered. An alternative is the traditional local area network, which can operate in the presence of node failures; the interconnection simply discards messages for a node that decides not to accept them. Assuming that you need to have both your workstation and the connecting LAN to get your work done, how much greater are your chances of being prevented from getting your work done using the failure-intolerant LAN versus traditional LANs? Assume the downtime for a crash is less than 30 minutes. Calculate using the one-hour intervals from this figure.

Answer   Assuming the numbers for Figure 8.19, the percentage of hours that you can't get your work done using the failure-intolerant network is

$$\frac{\text{Intervals with failures}}{\text{Total intervals}} = \frac{\text{Total intervals} - \text{Intervals no failures}}{\text{Total intervals}}$$

$$= \frac{8974 - 8605}{8974} = \frac{369}{8974} = 4.1\%$$

The percentage of hours that you can't get your work done using the traditional network is just the time your workstation has crashed. If these failures are equally distributed among workstations, the percentage is

$$\frac{\text{Failures/Machines}}{\text{Total intervals}} = \frac{654/58}{8974} = \frac{11.28}{8974} = 0.13\%$$

Failed machines per time interval	One-hour intervals with number of failed machines in first column	Total failures per one-hour interval	One-day intervals with number of failed machines in first column	Total failures per one-day interval
0	8605	0	184	0
1	264	264	105	105
2	50	100	35	70
3	25	75	11	33
4	10	40	6	24
5	7	35	9	45
6	3	18	6	36
7	1	7	4	28
8	1	8	4	32
9	2	18	2	18
10	2	20		
11	1	11	2	22
12			1	12
17	1	17		
20	1	20		
21	1	21	1	21
31			1	31
38			1	38
58			1	58
Total	**8974**	**654**	**373**	**573**

Figure 8.19 Measurement of reboots of 58 DECstation 5000s running Ultrix over a 373-day period. These reboots are distributed into time intervals of one hour and one day. The first column sorts the intervals according to the number of machines that failed in that interval. The next two columns concern one-hour intervals, and the last two columns concern one-day intervals. The second and fourth columns show the number of intervals for each number of failed machines. The third and fifth columns are just the product of the number of failed machines and the number of intervals. For example, there were 50 occurrences of one-hour intervals with two failed machines, for a total of 100 failed machines, and there were 35 days with two failed machines, for a total of 70 failures. As we would expect, the number of failures per interval changes with the size of the interval. For example, the day with 31 failures might include one hour with 11 failures and one hour with 20 failures. The last row shows the total number of each column: The number of failures doesn't agree because multiple reboots of the same machine in the same interval do not result in separate entries. (Randy Wang of U.C. Berkeley collected these data.)

Hence, you are more than 30 times more likely to be prevented from getting your work done with the failure-intolerant LAN than with the traditional LAN, according to the failure statistics in Figure 8.19. Stated alternatively, the person responsible for maintaining the LAN would receive a 30-fold increase in phone calls from irate users!

One practical issue ties to node failure tolerance: If the interconnection can survive a failure, can it also continue operation while a new node is added to the interconnection? If not, each addition of a new node disables the interconnection network. Disabling is impractical for both WANs and LANs.

Finally, we have been discussing the ability of the network to operate in the presence of failed nodes. Clearly as important to the happiness of the network administrator is the reliability of the network media and switches themselves, since their failure is certain to frustrate much of the user community.

8.7   Examples of Interconnection Networks

To further understand these issues, we look at 10 design decisions on the topics we covered so far using examples from LAN, SAN, and WAN:

■   What is the target bandwidth?

■   What is the message format?

■   Which media are used?

■   Is the network shared or switched?

■   Is it connection oriented or connectionless?

■   Does it use store-and-forward or cut-through routing?

■   Is routing use source based, destination based, or virtual-circuit based?

■   What is used for congestion control?

■   What topologies are supported?

■   Does it follow a standard?

Ethernet: *The* Local Area Network

The first example is the Ethernet. It has been extraordinarily successful, with the 10M bit/sec standard proposed in 1978 used practically everywhere. In 2001, the 100M bit/sec standard proposed in 1994 was closing in popularity. Many classes of computers include Ethernet as a standard interface. This packet-switched network is connectionless, and it routes using the destination address. Figure 8.20 shows the packet formats for Ethernet, as well as the other two examples. Ethernet is codified as IEEE standard 802.3.

Designed originally for coaxial cable, today Ethernets are primarily Cat5 copper wire, with optical fiber reserved for longer distances and higher bandwidths. There is even a wireless version, which is testimony to its ubiquity.

Computers became thousands of times faster than they were in 1978, and the shared interconnection was no faster for almost 20 years. Hence, past engineers invented temporary solutions until a faster Ethernet was available. One solution was to use multiple Ethernets to connect machines, and to connect these smaller

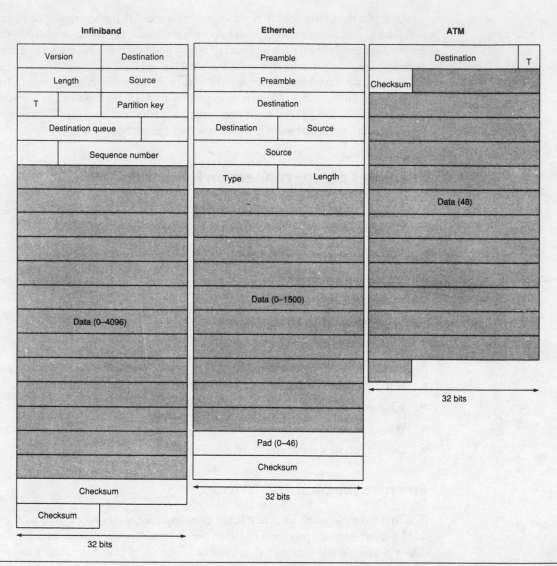

Figure 8.20 Packet format for Infiniband, Ethernet, and ATM. ATM calls their messages "cells" instead of packets, so the proper name is ATM cell format. The width of each drawing is 32 bits. All three formats have destination addressing fields, encoded differently for each situation. All three also have a checksum field to catch transmission errors, although the ATM checksum field is calculated only over the header; ATM relies on higher-level protocols to catch errors in the data. Both Infiniband and Ethernet have a length field, since the packets hold a variable amount of data, with the former counted in 32-bit words and the latter in bytes. Infiniband and ATM headers have a type field (T) that gives the type of packet. The remaining Ethernet fields are a preamble to allow the receiver to recover the clock from the self-clocking code used on the Ethernet, the source address, and a pad field to make sure the smallest packet is 64 bytes (including the header). Infiniband includes a version field for protocol version, a sequence number to allow in-order delivery, a field to select the destination queue, and a partition key field. Infiniband has many more small fields not shown and many other packet formats; above is a simplified view. ATM's short, fixed packet is a good match to real-time demand of digital voice.

Ethernets with devices that can take traffic from one Ethernet and pass it on to another as needed. These devices allow individual Ethernets to operate in parallel, thereby increasing the aggregate interconnection bandwidth of a collection of computers. In effect these devices provide similar functionality to the switches described previously for point-to-point networks.

Figure 8.21 shows the potential parallelism. Depending on how they pass traffic and what kinds of interconnections they can put together, these devices have different names:

■ *Bridges*—These devices connect LANs together, passing traffic from one side to another depending on the addresses in the packet. Bridges operate at the Ethernet protocol level and are usually simpler and cheaper than routers, discussed next. Using the notation of the OSI model described in the next section (see Figure 8.25 on page 832), bridges operate at layer 2, the data link layer.

■ *Routers* or *gateways*—These devices connect LANs to WANs, or WANs to WANs, and resolve incompatible addressing. Generally slower than bridges, they operate at OSI layer 3, the network layer. Routers divide the interconnect into separate smaller subnets, which simplifies manageability and improves security.

The final network devices are *hubs,* but they merely extend multiple segments into a single LAN. Thus, hubs do not help with performance, as only one message can transmit at a time. Hubs operate at OCI layer 1, called the physical layer. Since these devices were not planned as part of the Ethernet standard, their ad hoc nature has added to the difficulty and cost of maintaining LANs.

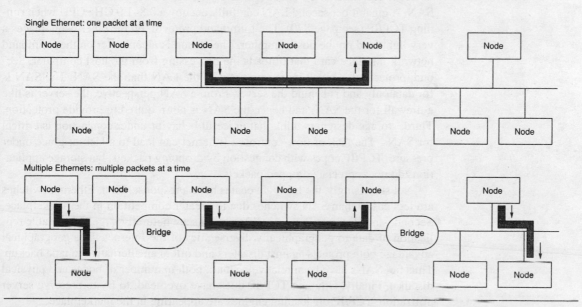

Figure 8.21 The potential increased bandwidth of using many Ethernets and bridges.

In 2001, Ethernet link speed was available at 10, 100, and 1000M bits/sec, with 10,000M bits/sec likely available in 2002–2003. Although 10 and 100M bits/sec can share the media with multiple devices, 1000M bits/sec and above relies on point-to-point links and switches. Ethernet switches normally use cut-through routing.

Due to its age, Ethernet has no real flow control. It originally used carrier sensing with exponential back-off (see page 806) to arbitrate for the shared media. Some switches try to use that interface to retrofit their version of flow control, but flow control is not part of an Ethernet standard.

Storage Area Network: Infiniband

A SAN that tries to optimize based on shorter distances is Infiniband. This new standard has clock rates of 2.5 GHz and can transmit data at a peak speed of 2000M bits/sec per link. These point-to-point links can be bundled together in groups of 4–12 to give 4–12 times the bandwidth per link. Like Ethernet, it is a packet-switched, connectionless network. It also relies only on switches, as does gigabit Ethernet, and also uses cut-through routing and destination-based addressing. The distances are much shorter than Ethernet, with category 5 wire limited to 17 meters and optical fiber limited to 100 meters. It uses backpressure for flow control (see page 813). When going to storage, it relies on the SCSI command set. Although it is not a traditional standard, a trade organization of cooperating companies is responsible for Infiniband.

Given the similarities, why do you need a separate standard for a storage area network versus a local area network? The storage community believes a SAN has different emphasis from a LAN. First, protocol overhead is much lower for a SAN. A gigabit per second LAN can fully occupy a 0.8–1.0 GHz CPU when running TCP/IP (see page 870). The Infiniband protocol, on the other hand, places a very light load on the host computer. The reason is a controller on the Infiniband network interface card that offloads the processing from the host computer. Second, protection is much more important in the LAN than the SAN. The SAN is for data only and is behind the server. From a SAN perspective, the server is like a firewall for the SAN, and hence the SAN is not required to provide protection. Third, storage designers think that graceful behavior under congestion is critical for SANs. The lack of flow control in Ethernet can lead to a lack of grace under pressure. TCP/IP copes with congestion by dropping packets, but storage applications do not appreciate dropped packets.

Not surprisingly, the LAN advocates have a response. First, Ethernet switches are less costly than SAN switches due to greater competition in the marketplace. Second, since Internet Protocol (IP) networks are naturally large, they enable replication of data to geographically diverse sites of the Internet. This geographical advantage both protects against disasters and offers an alternative to tape backup. Thus far, SANs have been relatively small, both in number of nodes and physical distance. Finally, although TCP/IP does have overhead, to try to preserve server utilization, TCP/IP off-loading engines are appearing in the marketplace.

Some LAN advocates are embracing a standard called *iSCSI,* which exports native SCSI commands over IP networks. The operating system intercepts SCSI commands, and repackages and sends them in a TCP/IP message. At the receiving end, it unpacks messages into SCSI commands and issues them locally. iSCSI allows a company to send SCSI commands and data over its internal WAN or, if transmitted over the Internet, to locations with Internet access.

Wide Area Network: ATM

Asynchronous Transfer Mode (ATM) is the latest of the ongoing standards set by the telecommunications industry. Although it flirted as competition to Ethernet as a LAN in the 1990s, today ATM has retreated to its WAN stronghold.

The telecommunications standard has scalable bandwidth built in. It starts at 155M bits/sec, and scales by factors of 4 to 620M bits/sec, 2480M bits/sec, and so on. Since it is a WAN, ATM's medium is fiber, both single mode and multimode. Although it is a switched medium, unlike the other examples, it relics on connections for communication. ATM uses virtual channels for routing to multiplex different connections on a single network segment, thereby avoiding the inefficiencies of conventional connection-based networking. The WAN focus also leads to store-and-forward routing. Unlike the other protocols, Figure 8.20 shows ATM has a small, fixed-sized packet. (For those curious about the selection of a 48-byte payload, see Section 8.16.) It uses a credit-based flow control scheme (see page 813).

The reason for connections and small packets is quality of service. Since the telecommunications industry is concerned about voice traffic, predictability matters as well as bandwidth. Establishing a connection has less variability than connectionless networking, and it simplifies store-and-forward routing. The small, fixed packet also makes it simpler to have fast routers and switches. Toward that goal, ATM even offers its own protocol stack to compete with TCP/IP. Surprisingly, even though the switches are simple, the ATM suite of protocols is large and complex. The dream was a seamless infrastructure from LAN to WAN, avoiding the hodgepodge of routers common today. That dream has faded from inspiration to nostalgia.

Summary

Figure 8.22 summarizes answers to the 10 questions from the start of this section. It covers the three example networks discussed here, plus a few others. This section shows how similar technology gets different spins for different concerns of LAN, SAN, and WAN. Nevertheless, the inherent similarity leads to marketplace competition. ATM tried (and failed) to usurp the LAN championship from Ethernet, and in 2001 Ethernet/iSCSI is trying to compete with Fibre Channel Arbitrated Loop (FC-AL) and Infiniband for the SAN markets.

	LAN			SAN			WAN
	10M bit Ethernet	100M bit Ethernet	1000M bit Ethernet	FC-AL	Infiniband	Myrinet	ATM
Length (meters)	500/2500	200	100	30/1000	17/100	10/550/ 10000	
Number of data lines	1	1	4/1	2	1, 4, or 12	?	1
Clock rate (MHz)	10	100	1000	1000	2500	1000	155/622 . . .
Switch?	optional	optional	yes	optional	yes	yes	yes
Nodes	≤254	≤254	≤254	≤127	≤≈1000	≤≈1000	≈10000
Media	copper	copper	copper/fiber	copper/ fiber	copper/fiber	copper/ multimode/ single-mode fiber	copper/fiber
Peak link BW (M bits/sec)	10	100	1000	800	2000, 8000, or 24000	1300 to 2000	155/622/ . . .
Topology	line or star	line or star	star	ring or star	star	star	star
Connectionless?	yes	yes	yes	yes	yes	yes	no
Routing	destination based	destination based	destination based	destination based	destination based	destination based	virtual circuit
Store-and-forward?	no	no	no	no	no	no	yes
Congestion control	carrier sense	carrier sense	carrier sense	credit based	back-pressure	back-pressure	credit based
Standard	IEEE 802.3	IEEE 802.3	IEEE 802.3ab-1999	ANSI Task Group X3T11	Infiniband Trade Association	ANSI/ VITA 26-1998	ATM Forum

Figure 8.22 **Several examples of LAN, SAN, and WAN interconnection networks.** FC-AL is a network for disks.

8.8   Internetworking

Undoubtedly one of the most important innovations in the communications community has been internetworking. It allows computers on independent and incompatible networks to communicate reliably and efficiently. Figure 8.23 illustrates the need to cross networks. It shows the networks and machines involved in transferring a file from Stanford University to the University of California at Berkeley, a distance of about 75 km.

The low cost of internetworking is remarkable. For example, it is vastly less expensive to send electronic mail than to make a coast-to-coast telephone call and leave a message on an answering machine. This dramatic cost improvement is achieved using the same long-haul communication lines as the telephone call, which makes the improvement even more impressive.

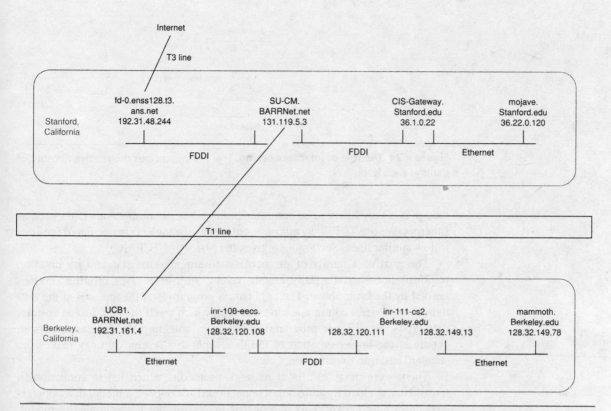

Figure 8.23 The connection established between mojave.stanford.edu and mammoth.berkeley.edu (1995). FDDI is a 100M bit/sec LAN, while a T1 line is a 1.5M bit/sec telecommunications line and a T3 is a 45M bit/sec telecommunications line. BARRNet stands for Bay Area Research Network. Note that inr-111-cs2.Berkeley.edu is a router with two Internet addresses, one for each port.

The enabling technologies for internetworking are software standards that allow reliable communication without demanding reliable networks. The underlying principle of these successful standards is that they were composed as a hierarchy of layers, each layer taking responsibility for a portion of the overall communication task. Each computer, network, and switch implements its layer of the standards, relying on the other components to faithfully fulfill their responsibilities. These layered software standards are called *protocol families* or *protocol suites*. They enable applications to work with any interconnection without extra work by the application programmer. Figure 8.24 suggests the hierarchical model of communication.

The most popular internetworking standard is TCP/IP (transmission control protocol/internet protocol). This protocol family is the basis of the humbly named Internet, which connects tens of millions of computers around the world. This popularity means TCP/IP is used even when communicating locally across compatible networks; for example, the network file system NFS uses IP even

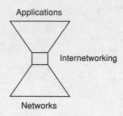

Figure 8.24 The role of internetworking. The width indicates the relative number of items at each level.

though it is very likely to be communicating across a homogenous LAN such as Ethernet. We use TCP/IP as our protocol family example; other protocol families follow similar lines. Section 8.16 gives the history of TCP/IP.

The goal of a family of protocols is to simplify the standard by dividing responsibilities hierarchically among layers, with each layer offering services needed by the layer above. The application program is at the top, and at the bottom is the physical communication medium, which sends the bits. Just as abstract data types simplify the programmer's task by shielding the programmer from details of the implementation of the data type, this layered strategy makes the standard easier to understand.

There were many efforts at network protocols, which led to confusion in terms. Hence, Open Systems Interconnect (OSI) developed a model that popularized describing networks as a series of layers. Figure 8.25 shows the model.

Layer number	Layer name	Main function	Example protocol	Network component
7	Application	Used for applications specifically written to run over the network	FTP, DNS, NFS, http	gateway, smart switch
6	Presentation	Translates from application to network format, and vice versa		gateway
5	Session	Establishes, maintains, and ends sessions across the network	Named pipes, RPC	gateway
4	Transport	Additional connection below the session layer	TCP	gateway
3	Network	Translates logical network address and names to their physical address (e.g., computer name to MAC address)	IP	router, ATM switch
2	Data Link	Turns packets into raw bits and at the receiving end turns bits into packets	Ethernet	bridge, network interface card
1	Physical	Transmits raw bit stream over physical cable	IEEE 802	hub

Figure 8.25 The OSI model layers. Based on *www.geocities.com/SiliconValley/Monitor/3131/ne/osimodel.html*.

Although all protocols do not exactly follow this layering, the nomenclature for the different layers is widely used. Thus, you can hear discussions about a simple layer 3 switch versus a layer 7 smart switch.

The key to protocol families is that communication occurs *logically at the same level* of the protocol in both sender and receiver, but *services of the lower level implement it*. This style of communication is called *peer-to-peer*. As an analogy, imagine that General A needs to send a message to General B on the battlefield. General A writes the message, puts it in an envelope addressed to General B, and gives it to a colonel with orders to deliver it. This colonel puts it in an envelope, and writes the name of the corresponding colonel who reports to General B, and gives it to a major with instructions for delivery. The major does the same thing and gives it to a captain, who gives it to a lieutenant, who gives it to a sergeant. The sergeant takes the envelope from the lieutenant, puts it into an envelope with the name of a sergeant who is in General B's division, and finds a private with orders to take the large envelope. The private borrows a motorcycle and delivers the envelope to the other sergeant. Once it arrives, it is passed up the chain of command, with each person removing an outer envelope with his name on it and passing on the inner envelope to his superior. As far as General B can tell, the note is from another general. Neither general knows who was involved in transmitting the envelope, nor how it was transported from one division to the other.

Protocol families follow this analogy more closely than you might think, as Figure 8.26 shows. The original message includes a header and possibly a trailer sent by the lower-level protocol. The next-lower protocol in turn adds its own header to the message, possibly breaking it up into smaller messages if it is too large for this layer. Reusing our analogy, a long message from the general is divided and placed in several envelopes if it could not fit in one. This division of the message and appending of headers and trailers continues until the message

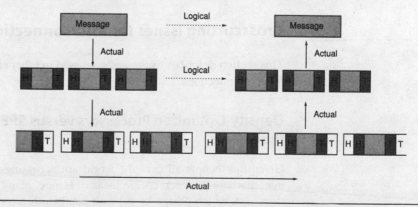

Figure 8.26 A generic protocol stack with two layers. Note that communication is peer-to peer, with headers and trailers for the peer added at each sending layer and removed by each receiving layer. Each layer offers services to the one above to shield it from unnecessary details.

descends to the physical transmission medium. The message is then sent to the destination. Each level of the protocol family on the receiving end will check the message at its level and peel off its headers and trailers, passing it on to the next higher level and putting the pieces back together. This nesting of protocol layers for a specific message is called a *protocol stack*, reflecting the last in, first out nature of the addition and removal of headers and trailers.

As in our analogy, the danger in this layered approach is the considerable latency added to message delivery. Clearly, one way to reduce latency is to reduce the number of layers. But keep in mind that protocol families *define* a standard, but do not force how to *implement* the standard. Just as there are many ways to implement an instruction set architecture, there are many ways to implement a protocol family.

Our protocol stack example is TCP/IP. Let's assume that the bottom protocol layer is Ethernet. The next level up is the Internet Protocol or IP layer; the official term for an IP packet is a *datagram*. The IP layer routes the datagram to the destination machine, which may involve many intermediate machines or switches. IP makes a best effort to deliver the packets, but does not guarantee delivery, content, or order of datagrams. The TCP layer above IP makes the guarantee of reliable, in-order delivery and prevents corruption of datagrams.

Following the example in Figure 8.26, assume an application program wants to send a message to a machine via an Ethernet. It starts with TCP. The largest number of bytes that can be sent at once is 64 KB. Since the data may be much larger than 64 KB, TCP must divide them into smaller segments and reassemble them in proper order upon arrival. TCP adds a 20-byte header (Figure 8.27) to every datagram, and passes them down to IP. The IP layer above the physical layer adds a 20-byte header, also shown in Figure 8.27. The data sent down from the IP level to the Ethernet are sent in packets with the format shown in Figure 8.20. Note that the TCP packet appears inside the data portion of the IP datagram, just as Figure 8.26 suggests.

8.9   Crosscutting Issues for Interconnection Networks

This section describes five topics discussed in other chapters that are fundamental to interconnections.

Density-Optimized Processors versus SPEC-Optimized Processors

Given that people all over the world are accessing Web sites, it doesn't really matter where your servers are located. Hence, many servers are kept at *collocation sites,* which charge by network bandwidth reserved and used, and by space occupied and power consumed.

Desktop microprocessors in the past have been designed to be as fast as possible at whatever heat could be dissipated, with little regard to the size of the package and surrounding chips. One microprocessor in 2001 burned 135 watts! Floor

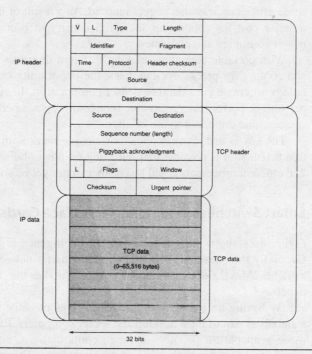

Figure 8.27 The headers for IP and TCP. This drawing is 32 bits wide. The standard headers for both are 20 bytes, but both allow the headers to optionally lengthen for rarely transmitted information. Both headers have a length of header field (L) to accommodate the optional fields, as well as source and destination fields. The length field of the whole datagram is in a separate length field in IP, while TCP combines the length of the datagram with the sequence number of the datagram by giving the sequence number in bytes. TCP uses the checksum field to be sure that the datagram is not corrupted, and the sequence number field to be sure the datagrams are assembled into the proper order when they arrive. IP provides checksum error detection only for the header, since TCP has protected the rest of the packet. One optimization is that TCP can send a sequence of datagrams before waiting for permission to send more. The number of datagrams that can be sent without waiting for approval is called the *window*, and the window field tells how many bytes may be sent beyond the byte being acknowledged by this datagram. TCP will adjust the size of the window depending on the success of the IP layer in sending datagrams; the more reliable and faster it is, the larger TCP makes the window. Since the window slides forward as the data arrive and are acknowledged, this technique is called a *sliding window protocol*. The *piggyback acknowledgment* field of TCP is another optimization. Since some applications send data back and forth over the same connection, it seems wasteful to send a datagram containing only an acknowledgment. This piggyback field allows a datagram carrying data to also carry the acknowledgment for a previous transmission, "piggybacking" on top of a data transmission. The *urgent pointer* field of TCP gives the address within the datagram of an important byte, such as a break character. This pointer allows the application software to skip over data so that the user doesn't have to wait for all prior data to be processed before seeing a character that tells the software to stop. The *identifier* field and *fragment* field of IP allow intermediary machines to break the original datagram into many smaller datagrams. A unique identifier is associated with the original datagram and placed in every fragment, with the fragment field saying which piece is which. The *time-to-live* field allows a datagram to be killed off after going through a maximum number of intermediate switches no matter where it is in the network. Knowing the maximum number of hops that it will take for a datagram to arrive—if it ever arrives—simplifies the protocol software. The *protocol* field identifies which possible upper layer protocol sent the IP datagram; in our case, it is TCP. The *V* (for *version*) and *type* fields allow different versions of the IP protocol software for the network. Explicit version numbering is included so that software can be upgraded gracefully machine by machine, without shutting down the entire network.

space efficiency was also largely ignored. As a result of these priorities, power is a major cost for collocation sites, and density of processors is limited by the power consumed and dissipated.

With portable computers making different demands on power consumption and cooling for processors and disks, the opportunity exists for using this technology to create considerably denser computation. In such a case performance per watt or performance per cubic foot could replace performance per microprocessor as the important figure of merit.

The key is that many applications already work with large clusters (see Section 8.10), so it is possible that replacing 64 power-hungry processors with, say, 256 efficient processors could be cheaper to run yet be software compatible.

Smart Switches versus Smart Interface Cards

Figure 8.28 shows a trade-off is where intelligence is located in the network. Generally the question is whether to have smarter network interfaces or smarter switches. Making one side smarter generally makes the other side easier and less expensive.

By having an inexpensive interface it was possible for Ethernet to become standard as part of most desktop and server computers. Lower-cost switches were made available for people with small configurations, not needing sophisticated routing tables and spanning tree protocols of larger Ethernet switches.

Infiniband is trying a hybrid approach by offering lower-cost interface cards for less demanding devices, such as disks, in the hope that it will be included with some I/O devices. As Infiniband is planned as the successor to PCI bus, computers may come with a Host Channel Adapter built in.

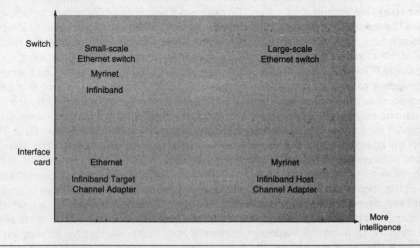

Figure 8.28 Intelligence in a network: switch versus interface card. Note that Ethernet switches come in two styles, depending on the size of the network, and that Infiniband network interfaces come in two styles, depending on whether they are attached to a computer or to a storage device. Myrinet is a proprietary system area network.

Protection and User Access to the Network

A challenge is to ensure safe communication across a network without invoking the operating system in the common case. The Cray Research T3D supercomputer offers an interesting case study. It supports a global address space, so loads and stores can access memory across the network. Protection is ensured because each access is checked by the TLB.

To support transfer of larger objects, a block transfer engine (BLT) was added to the hardware. Protection of access requires invoking the operating system before using the BLT, to check the range of accesses to be sure there will be no protection violations.

Figure 8.29 compares the bandwidth delivered as the size of the object varies for reads and writes. For very large reads, 512 KB, the BLT does achieve the highest performance: 140 MB/sec. But simple loads get higher performance for 8 KB or less. For the write case, both achieve a peak of 90 MB/sec, presumably because of the limitations of the memory bus. But for writes, BLT can only match the performance of simple stores for transfers of 2 MB; anything smaller and it's faster to send stores. Clearly, a BLT that avoided invoking the operating system in the common case would be more useful.

Efficient Interface to Memory Hierarchy versus Interconnection Network

Traditional evaluations of processor performance, such as SPECint and SPECfp, encourage integration of the memory hierarchy with the processor, as the efficiency of the memory hierarchy translates directly into processor performance. Hence,

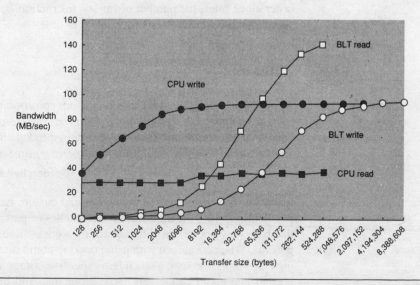

Figure 8.29 Bandwidth versus transfer size for simple memory access instructions versus a block transfer device on the Cray Research T3D. (From Arpaci et al. [1995].)

microprocessors have first-level caches on chip along with buffers for writes, and usually have second-level caches on chip or immediately next to the chip.

Benchmarks such as SPECint and SPECfp do not reward good interfaces to interconnection networks, and hence many machines make the access time to the network delayed by the full memory hierarchy. Writes must lumber their way through full write buffers, and reads must go through the cycles of first- and second-level cache misses before reaching the interconnection. This hierarchy results in newer systems having higher latencies to interconnections than older machines.

Let's compare three machines from the past: a 40 MHz SPARCstation-2, a 50 MHz SPARCstation-20 without an external cache, and a 50 MHz SPARCstation-20 with an external cache. According to SPECint95, this list is in order of increasing performance. The time to access the I/O bus (S-bus), however, increases in this sequence: 200 ns, 500 ns, and 1000 ns. The SPARCstation-2 is fastest because it has a single bus for memory and I/O, and there is only one level to the cache. The SPARCstation-20 memory access must first go over the memory bus (M-bus) and then to the I/O bus, adding 300 ns. Machines with a second-level cache pay an extra penalty of 500 ns before accessing the I/O bus.

On the other hand, recent computers have dramatically improved memory bandwidth, which is helpful to network bandwidth.

Compute-Optimized Processors versus Receiver Overhead

The overhead to receive a message likely involves an interrupt, which bears the cost of flushing and then restarting the processor pipeline. As mentioned earlier, reading network status and receiving data from the network interface likely operate at cache miss speeds. As microprocessors become more superscalar and go to faster clock rates, the number of missed instruction issue opportunities per message reception is likely to rise quickly over time.

8.10 Clusters

... do-it-yourself Beowulf clusters built from commodity hardware and software ... has mobilized a community around a standard architecture and tools. Beowulf's economics and sociology are poised to kill off the other ... architectural lines—and will likely affect traditional supercomputer centers as well.

Gordon Bell and Jim Gray [2001]

Instead of relying on custom machines and custom networks to build massively parallel machines, the introduction of switches as part of LAN technology meant that high network bandwidth and scaling were available from off-the-shelf components. When combined with using desktop computers and disks as the computing and storage devices, a much less expensive computing infrastructure could be created that could tackle very large problems. And by their component nature, *clusters* are much easier to scale and more easily isolate failures.

There are many mainframe applications—such as databases, file servers, Web servers, simulations, and multiprogramming/batch processing—amenable to running on more loosely coupled machines than the cache-coherent NUMA machines of Chapter 6. These applications often need to be highly available, requiring some form of fault tolerance and repairability. Such applications—plus the similarity of the multiprocessor nodes to desktop computers and the emergence of high-bandwidth, switch-based local area networks—lead to clusters of off-the-shelf, whole computers for large-scale processing.

Performance Challenges of Clusters

One drawback is that clusters are usually connected using the I/O bus of the computer, whereas multiprocessors are usually connected on the memory bus of the computer. The memory bus has higher bandwidth and much lower latency, allowing multiprocessors to drive the network link at higher speed and to have fewer conflicts with I/O traffic on I/O-intensive applications. This connection point also means that clusters generally use software-based communication, while multiprocessors use hardware for communication. However, it makes connections nonstandard and hence more expensive.

A second weakness is the division of memory: A cluster of N machines has N independent memories and N copies of the operating system, but a shared address multiprocessor allows a single program to use almost all the memory in the computer. Thus, a sequential program in a cluster has $1/N$th the memory available compared to a sequential program in a shared-memory multiprocessor. Interestingly, the drop in DRAM prices has made memory costs so low that this multiprocessor advantage was much less important in 2001 than it was in 1995. The primary issue in 2001 was whether the maximum memory per cluster node was sufficient for the application.

Dependability and Scalability Advantage of Clusters

The weakness of separate memories for program size turns out to be a strength in system availability and expansibility. Since a cluster consists of independent computers connected through a local area network, it is much easier to replace a machine without bringing down the system in a cluster than in a shared-memory multiprocessor. Fundamentally, the shared address means that it is difficult to isolate a processor and replace a processor without significant work by the operating system and hardware designer. Since the cluster software is a layer that runs on top of local operating systems running on each computer, it is much easier to disconnect and replace a broken machine.

Given that clusters are constructed from whole computers and independent, scalable networks, this isolation also makes it easier to expand the system without bringing down the application that runs on top of the cluster. High availability and rapid, incremental extensibility make clusters attractive to service providers for the World Wide Web.

Pros and Cons of Cost of Clusters

One drawback of clusters has been the cost of ownership. Administering a cluster of N machines is close to the cost of administering N independent machines, while the cost of administering a shared address space multiprocessor with N processors is close to the cost of administering a single, big machine.

Another difference between the two tends to be the price for equivalent computing power for large-scale machines. Since large-scale multiprocessors have small volumes, the extra development costs of large machines must be amortized over few systems, resulting in higher cost to the customer. As we will see, even prices for components common to small machines are increased, possibly to recover development. In addition, the manufacturing learning curve (see page 767) brings down the price of components used in the high-volume PC market. Since the same switches sold in high volume for small systems can be composed to construct large networks for large clusters, local area network switches have the same economy-of-scale advantages as small computers.

Originally, the partitioning of memory into separate modules in each node was a significant disadvantage to clusters, as division means memory is used less efficiently than on a shared address computer. The incredible drop in price of memory has mitigated this weakness, dramatically changing the trade-offs in favor of clusters.

Shooting for the Best of Both Worlds

As is often the case with two competing solutions, each side tries to borrow ideas from the other to become more attractive.

On one side of the battle, to combat the high-availability weakness of multiprocessors, hardware designers and operating system developers are trying to offer the ability to run multiple operating systems on portions of the full machine. The goal is that a node can fail or be upgraded without bringing down the whole machine. For example, the Sun Fire 6800 server has these features (see Section 5.15).

On the other side of the battle, since both system administration and memory size limits are approximately linear in the number of independent machines, some are reducing the cluster problems by constructing clusters from small-scale shared-memory multiprocessors.

A more radical approach is to keep storage outside of the cluster, possibly over a SAN, so that all computers inside can be treated as clones of one another. As the nodes may cost on the order of a few thousand dollars, it can be cheaper to simply discard a flaky node than spend the labor costs to try hard to repair it. The tasks of the failed node are then handed off to another clone. Clusters are also benefiting from faster SANs and from network interface cards that offer lower-overhead communication.

Popularity of Clusters

Low cost, scaling, and fault isolation proved a perfect match to the companies providing services over the Internet since the mid-1990s. Internet applications such as search engines and email servers are amenable to more loosely coupled computers, since the parallelism consists of millions of independent tasks. Hence, companies like Amazon, AOL, Google, Hotmail, Inktomi, WebTV, and Yahoo rely on clusters of PCs or workstations to provide services used by millions of people every day. We delve into Google in Section 8.12.

Clusters are growing in popularity in the scientific computing market as well. Figure 8.30 shows the mix of architecture styles between 1993 and 2000 for the top 500 fastest scientific computers. One attraction is that individual scientists can afford to construct clusters themselves, allowing them to dedicate their cluster to their problem. Shared supercomputers are placed on a monthly allocation of CPU time, so it is plausible for a scientist to get more work done from a private cluster than from a shared supercomputer. It is also relatively easy for the scientist to scale his computing over time as he gets more money for computing.

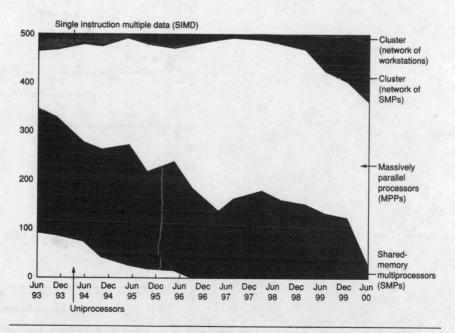

Figure 8.30 Plot of top 500 supercomputer sites between 1993 and 2000. Note that clusters of various kinds grew from 2% to almost 30% in the last three years, while uniprocessors and SMPs have almost disappeared. In fact, most of the MPPs in the list look similar to clusters. In 2001, the top 500 collectively has a performance of about 100 tera-FLOPS [Bell 2001]. Performance is measured as the speed of running Linpack, which solves a dense system of linear equations. This list at *www.top500.org* is updated twice a year.

Clusters are also growing in popularity in the database community. Figure 8.31 plots the cost-performance and the cost-performance per processor of the different architecture styles running the TPC-C benchmark. Note in the top graph that not only are clusters fastest, they achieve good cost-performance. For example, five SMPs with just 6–8 processors have worse cost-performance than the 280-processor cluster! Only small SMPs with 2–4 processors have much better cost-performance than clusters. This combination of high performance and cost-effectiveness is rare. Figure 8.32 shows similar results for TPC-H.

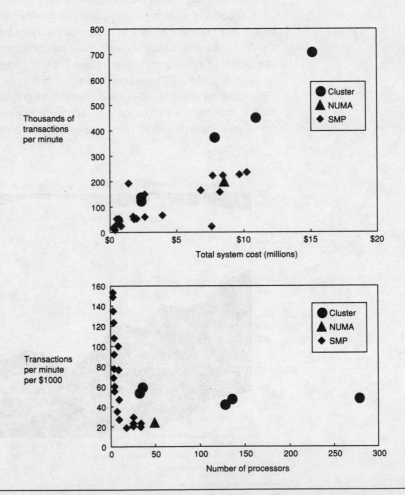

Figure 8.31 Performance, cost, and cost-performance per processor for TPC-C. Not only do clusters have the highest tpmC rating (top), they have better cost-performance ($/tpmC) for any SMP (bottom) with a total cost over $1 million. The bottom graph shows that clusters get high performance by scaling. They can sustain 40–50 transactions per minute per $1000 of cost from 32 to 280 processors. Figure 8.40 on page 853 describes the leftmost cluster, and Figure 8.41 on page 855 shows the cost model of TPC-C in more detail. These plots are for all computers that have run version 5 of the TPC-C benchmark as of August 2001.

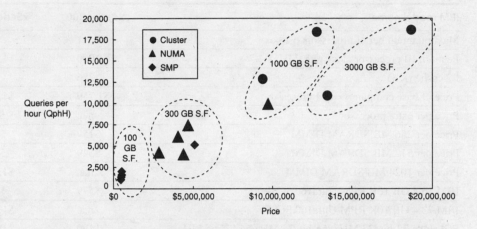

Figure 8.32 Performance versus cost for TPC-H in August 2001. Clusters are used for the largest computers, NUMA the smaller computers, and SMP the smallest. In violation of TPC-H rules, this figure plots results for different TPC-H scale factors (SF): 100 GB, 300 GB, 1000 GB, and 3000 GB. The ovals separate them.

The bottom half of Figure 8.31 shows the scalability of clusters for TPC-C. They scale by about a factor of 8 in price or processors while maintaining respectable cost-performance.

Now that we have covered the pros and cons of clusters and showed their successes in several fields, the next step is to design some clusters.

8.11   Designing a Cluster

To take the discussion of clusters from the abstract to the concrete, this section goes through four examples of cluster design. Like Section 7.11 in the previous chapter, the examples evolve in realism. The examples of the last chapter that examined performance and availability apply to clusters as well. Instead, we show cost trade-offs, a topic rarely found in computer architecture.

In each case we are designing a system with about 32 processors, 32 GB of DRAM, and 32 or 64 disks. Figure 8.33 lists the components we use to construct the cluster, including their prices.

Before starting the examples, Figure 8.33 confirms some of the philosophical points of the prior section. Note the difference in cost and speed of processors in the smaller systems versus the larger multiprocessor. In addition, the price per DRAM DIMM goes up with the size of the computers.

Regarding the processors, the server chip includes a much larger L2 cache, increasing from 0.25 MB to 1 MB. Due to its much larger die size, the price of the 1 MB cache chip is more than double the 0.25 MB cache. The purpose of the larger L2 cache is to reduce memory bandwidth to allow eight processors to share a memory system. Not only are these large cache chips much more expensive, it

IBM model name	xSeries 300	xSeries 330	xSeries 370
Maximum number of processors per box	1	2	8
Pentium III processor clock rate (MHz)	1,000	1,000	700
L2 cache (KB)	256	256	1,024
Price of base computer with 1 processor	$1,759	$1,939	$14,614
Price per extra processor	n.a.	$799	$1,779
Price per 256 MB SDRAM DIMM	$159	$269	$369
Price per 512 MB SDRAM DIMM	$549	$749	$1,069
Price per 1024 MB SDRAM DIMM	n.a.	$1,689	$2,369
IBM 36.4 GB 10K RPM Ultra160 SCSI	$579	$639	$639
IBM 73.4 GB 10K RPM Ultra160 SCSI	n.a.	$1,299	$1,299
PCI slots: 32-bit, 33 MHz /64-bit, 33 MHz/64-bit, 66 MHz	1/0/0	0/2/0	0/8/4
Rack space (VME rack units)	1	1	8
Power supply	200 W	200 W	3×750 W
Emulex cLAN-1000 host adapter (1G bit)	$795	$795	$795
Emulex cLAN5000 8-port switch	$6,280	$6,280	$6,280
Emulex cLAN5000 rack space (R.U.)	1	1	1
Emulex cLAN5300 30-port switch	$15,995	$15,995	$15,995
Emulex cLAN5300 rack space (R.U.)	2	2	2
Emulex cLAN-1000 10-meter cable	$135	$135	$135
Extra PCI Ultra160 SCSI adapter	$299	$299	$299
EXP300 storage enclosure (up to 14 disks)	$3,179	$3,179	$3,179
EXP300 rack space (VME rack units)	3	3	3
Ultra2 SCSI 4-meter cable	$105	$105	$105
Standard 19-in rack (44 VME rack units)	$1,795	$1,795	$1,795

Figure 8.33 Prices of options for three rack-mounted servers from IBM and 1G bit Ethernet switches from Emulex in August 2001. Note the higher price for processors and DRAM DIMMs with larger computers. The base price of these computers includes 256 MB of DRAM (512 MB for an eight-way server), two slots for disks, an UltraSCSI 160 adapter, two 100M bit Ethernets, a CD-ROM drive, a floppy drive, six to eight fans, and SVGA graphics. The power supply for the Emulex switches is 200 watts and 500 watts for the EXP300. In the xSeries 370 you must add an accelerator costing $1,249 to go over four CPUs.

has also been hard for Intel to achieve the clock rates similar to the small cache chips: 700 MHz versus 1000 MHz in August 2001.

The higher price of the DRAM is harder to explain. For example, all include ECC. The uniprocessor uses 133 MHz SDRAM, and the two-way and eight-way both use registered DIMM modules (RDIMM) SDRAM. There might be a slightly higher cost for the buffered DRAM between the uniprocessor and two-way boxes, but it is hard to explain increasing price 1.5 times for the eight-way SMP versus the two-way SMP. In fact, the eight-way SDRAM operates at just

100 MHz. Presumably, customers willing to pay a premium for processors for an eight-way SMP are also willing to pay more for memory.

Reasons for higher price matter little to the designer of a cluster. The task is to minimize cost for a given performance target. To motivate this section, here is an overview of the four examples:

1. *Cost of cluster hardware alternatives with local disk*—The first example compares the cost of building from a uniprocessor, a two-way SMP, and an eight-way SMP. In this example, the disks are directly attached to the computers in the cluster.

2. *Cost of cluster hardware alternatives with disks over SAN*—The second example moves the disk storage behind a RAID controller on a storage area network.

3. *Cost of cluster options that is more realistic*—The third example includes the cost of software, the cost of space, some maintenance costs, and operator costs.

4. *Cost and performance of a cluster for transaction processing*—This final example describes a similar cluster tailored by IBM to run the TPC-C benchmark. (It is one of the cluster results in Figure 8.31.) This example has more memory and many more disks to achieve a high TPC-C result, and at the time of this writing, it is the 13th fastest TPC-C system. In fact, the machine with the fastest TPC-C is just a replicated version of this cluster with a bigger LAN switch. This section highlights the differences between this database-oriented cluster and the prior examples.

First Example: Cost of Cluster Hardware Alternatives with Local Disk

This first example looks only at the hardware cost of the three alternatives using the IBM pricing information. We'll look at the cost of software and space later.

Example   Using the information in Figure 8.33, compare the cost of the hardware for three clusters built from the three options in the figure. In addition, calculate the rack space. The goal for this example is to construct a cluster with 32 processors, 32 GB of memory protected by ECC, and more than 2 TB of disk. Connect the clusters with 1G bit, switched Ethernet.

Answer   Figure 8.34 shows the logical organization of the three clusters.

Let's start with the 1-processor option (IBM xSeries model 300). First, we need 32 processors and thus 32 computers. The maximum memory for this computer is 1.5 GB, allowing 1 GB × 32 = 32 GB. Each computer can hold two disks, and the largest disk available in the model 300 is 36.4 GB, yielding 32 × 2 × 36.4 GB or 2330 GB. Using the built-in slots for storage is the least-expensive solution, so we'll take this option. Each computer needs its own G bit host adapter,

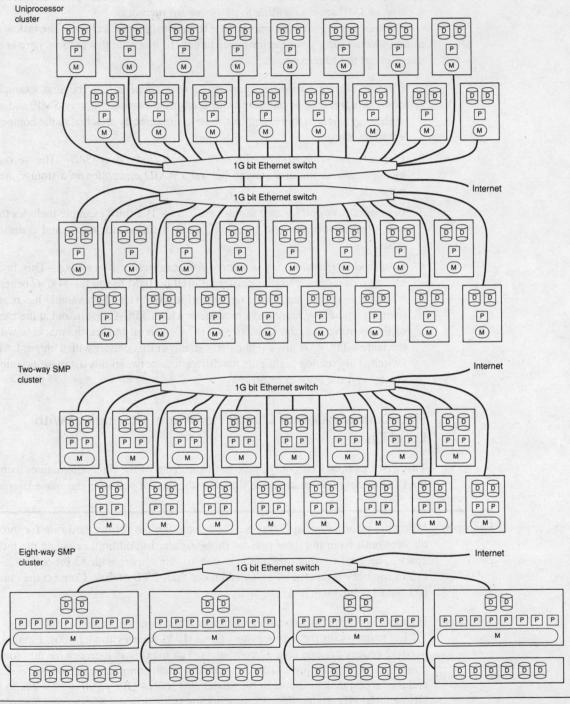

Figure 8.34 Three cluster organizations based on uniprocessors (top), two-way SMPs (middle), and eight-way SMPs (bottom). P stands for processor, M for memory (1, 2, and 8 GB), and D for disk (36.4, 73.4, 73.4 GB).

but 32 cables are more than a 30-port switch can handle. Thus, we use two Emulex cLAN5300 switches. We connect the two switches together with four cables, leaving plenty for the ports for the 32 computers.

A standard VME rack is 19 inches wide and about 6 feet tall, with a typical depth of 30 inches. This size is so popular that it has its own units: 1 VME rack unit (RU) is about 1.75 inches high, so a rack can hold objects up to 44 RU. The 32 uniprocessor computers each use 1 rack unit of space, plus 2 rack units for each switch, for a total of 36 rack units. This fits snugly in one standard rack.

For the 2-processor case (model 330), everything is halved. The 32 processors need only 16 computers. The maximum memory is 4 GB, but we need just 2 GB per computer to hit our target of 32 GB total. This model allows 73.4 GB disks, so we need only $16 \times 2 \times 73.4$ GB to reach 2.3 TB, and these disks fit in the slots in the computers. A single 30-port switch has more ports than we need. The total space demand is 18 RU ($16 \times 1 + 1 \times 2$), or less than half a standard rack.

The 8-processor case (model 370) needs only 4 computers to hold 32 processors. The maximum memory is 32 GB, but we need just 8 GB per computer to reach our target. Since there are only 4 computers, the 8-port switch is fine. The shortcoming is in disks. At 2 disks per computer, these 4 computers can hold at most 8 disks, and the maximum capacity per disk is still 73.4 GB. The solution is to add a storage expansion box (EXP300) to each computer, which can hold up to 14 disks. This solution requires adding an external UltraSCSI controller to each computer as well. The rack space is 8 RU for the computer, 3 RU for the disk enclosure, and 1 RU for the switch. Alas, the total is $4 \times (8 + 3) + 1$ or 45 rack units, which just misses the maximum of a standard rack. Hence, this option occupies two racks.

Figure 8.35 shows the total cost of each option. This example shows some issues for clusters:

- *Expansibility incurs high prices.* For example, just four of the base eight-way SMPs—each with just one processor and 0.5 GB of DRAM—cost more than 32 uniprocessor computers, each with one processor and 0.25 GB of DRAM. The only hope of cost competitiveness is to occupy all the options of a large SMP.

- *Network versus local bus trade-off.* Figure 8.35 shows how the larger SMPs need to spend less on networking, as the memory buses carry more of the communication workload.

The uniprocessor cluster costs 1.1 times the two-way SMP option, and the eight-way SMP cluster costs 1.6 times the two-way SMP. The two-way SMP wins the cost competition because the components are relatively cost-effective and it needs fewer systems and network components.

Second Example: Using a SAN for Disks

The previous example uses disks local to the computer. Although this can reduce costs and space, the problems for the operator are that (1) there is no protection

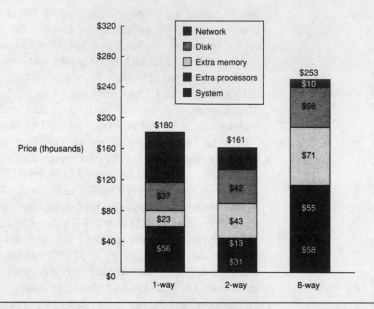

Figure 8.35 Price of three clusters with a total of 32 processors, 32 GB memory, and 2.3 TB disk. Note the reduction in network costs as the size of the SMP increases, since the memory buses supply more of the interprocessor communication. Rack prices are included in the total price, but are too small to show in the bars. They account for $1725 in the first two cases and $3450 in the third case.

against a single disk failure, and (2) there is state in each computer that must be managed separately. Hence, the system is down on a disk failure until the operator arrives, and there is no separate visibility or access to storage.

This second example centralizes the disks behind a RAID controller in each case using FC-AL as the storage area network. To keep comparisons fair, we continue the use of IBM components. Figure 8.36 lists the costs of the components in this option. Note that this IBM RAID controller requires FC-AL disks.

IBM FC-AL high-availability RAID storage server	$15,999
IBM 73.4 GB 10K RPM FC-AL disk	$1,699
IBM EXP500 FC-AL storage enclosure (up to 10 disks)	$3,815
FC-AL 10-meter cables	$100
IBM PCI FC-AL host bus adapter	$1,485
IBM FC-AL RAID server rack space (VME rack units)	3
IBM EXP500 FC-AL rack space (VME rack units)	3

Figure 8.36 Components for storage area network cluster.

Example   Using the information in Figure 8.36, calculate the cost of the hardware for the three previous clusters but now use the SAN and RAID controller.

Answer   The change from the clusters in the first example is that we remove all internal SCSI disks and replace them with FC-AL disks behind the RAID storage server. To connect to the RAID box, we add an FC-AL host bus adapter per computer to the uniprocessor and two-way SMP clusters and replace the SCSI host bus adapter in the eight-way SMP cluster.

FC-AL can be connected in a loop with up to 127 devices, so there is no problem in connecting the computers to the RAID box. The RAID box has a separate FC-AL loop for the disks. It has room for 10 FC-AL disks, so we need three EXP500 enclosures for the remaining 22 FC-AL disks. (The FC-AL disks are half-height, which are taller than the low-profile SCSI disks, so we can fit only 10 FC-AL disks per enclosure.) We just need to add cables for each segment of the loop.

Since the RAID box needs 3 rack units as do each of the 3 enclosures, we need 12 additional rack units of space. This adds a second rack to the uniprocessor cluster, but there is sufficient space in the racks of the other clusters. If we use RAID 5 and have a parity group size of 8 disks, we still have 28 disks of data, or 28×73.4 or 2.05 TB of user data, which is sufficient for our goals.

Figure 8.37 shows the hardware costs of this solution. Since there must be one FC-AL host bus adapter per computer, they cost enough to bring the prices of the uniprocessor and eight-way SMP clusters to parity. The two-way SMP is still substantially cheaper. Notice that again the cost of both the LAN network and the SAN network decrease as the number of computers in the cluster decreases.

The SAN adds about $40,000–$100,000 to the price of the hardware for the clusters. We'll see in the next example whether we justify such costs.

Third Example: Accounting for Other Costs

The first and second examples only calculated the cost of the hardware (which is what you might expect from a book on computer architecture). There are two other obvious costs not included: software and the cost of a maintenance agreement for the hardware. Figure 8.38 lists the costs covered in this example.

Notice that Microsoft quadruples the price when the operating system runs on a computer with 5–8 processors versus a computer with 1–4 processors. Moreover, the database cost is primarily a *linear* function of the number of processors. Once again, software pricing appears to be based on value to the customer versus cost of development.

Another significant cost is the cost of the operators to keep the machine running, upgrade software, perform backup and restore, and so on. In 2001, the cost (including overhead) was about $100,000 per year for an operator.

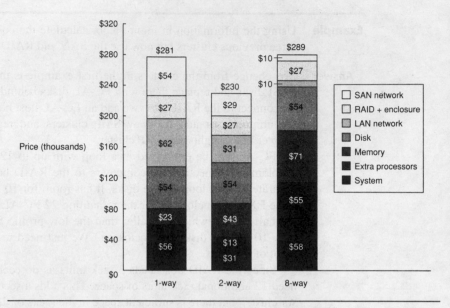

Figure 8.37 Prices for hardware for three clusters using SAN for storage. As in Figure 8.35, the cost of the SAN network also shrinks as the servers increase in number of processors per computer. They share the FC-AL host bus adapters and also have fewer cables. Rack prices are too small to see in the columns, but they account for $3450, $1725, and $3450, respectively.

Software: Windows 2000 1–4 CPUs + IBM Director	$799
Software: Windows 2000 1–8 CPUs + IBM Director	$3,295
Software: SQL Server Database (per processor!)	$16,541
3-year HW maintenance: LAN switches + HBA	$45,000
3-year HW maintenance: IBM xSeries computers	7.5%
Rack space rental (monthly per rack)	$800 to $1200
Extra 20 amp circuit per rack (monthly)	$200 to $400
Bandwidth charges per megabit (monthly)	$500 to $2000
Operator costs (yearly)	$100,000
DLT tapes (40 GB raw, 80 GB compressed)	$70

Figure 8.38 Components for storage area network cluster in 2001. Notice the higher cost of the operating system in the larger server. (Red Hat Linux 7.1, however, is $49 for all three.)

In addition to labor costs, backup uses up tapes to act as the long-term storage for system. A typical backup policy is daily incremental dumps and weekly full dumps. A common practice is to save four weekly tapes and then one full dump per month for the last six months. The total is 10 full dumps, plus a week of incremental dumps.

There are other costs, however. One is the cost of the space to house the server. Thus, collocation sites have been created to provide virtual machine rooms for companies. They provide scalable space, power, cooling, and network bandwidth plus physical security. They make money by charging rent for space, for network bandwidth, and for optional services from on-site administrators.

Collocation rates are negotiated and much cheaper per unit as space requirements increase. A rough guideline in 2001 is that rack space, which includes one 20 amp circuit, costs $800–$1200 per month. It drops by 20% if you use more than 75–100 racks. Each additional 20 amp circuit per rack costs another $200–$400 per month. Although we are not calculating these costs in this case, they also charge for network bandwidth: $1500–$2000 per M bits/sec per month if your continuous use is just 1–10M bits/sec, dropping to $500–$750 per M bits/sec per month, if your continuous use measures 1–2G bits/sec.

Pacific Gas and Electric in Silicon Valley limits a single building to having no more than 12 megawatts of power, and the typical size of a building is no more than 100,000 square feet. Thus, a guideline is that collocation sites are designed assuming no more than 100 watts per square foot. If you include the space for people to get access to a rack to repair and replace components, a rack needs about 10 square feet. Thus, collocation sites expect at most 1000 watts per rack.

Example   Using the information in Figure 8.38, calculate the total cost of ownership for three years: purchase prices, operator costs, and maintenance costs.

Answer   Figure 8.39 shows the total cost of ownership for the six clusters.

To keep things simple, we assume each system with local disks needs a full-time operator, but the clusters that access their disks over a SAN with RAID need only a half-time operator. Thus, operator cost is $3 \times \$100,000 = \$300,000$, or $3 \times \$50,000 = \$150,000$.

For backup, let's assume we need enough tapes to store 2 TB for a full dump. We need four sets for the weekly dumps plus six more sets so that we can have a six-month archive. Tape units normally compress their data to get a factor of 2 in density, so we'll assume compression successfully turns 40 GB drives into 80 GB drives. The cost of these tapes is

$$10 \times \frac{2000 \text{ GB}}{80 \text{ GB/tape}} \times \$70 = 10 \times 25 \times \$70 = \$17,500$$

The daily backups depend on the amount of data changed. If two tapes per day are sufficient (up to 8% changes per day), we need to spend another

$$7 \times 2 \times \$70 = 14 \times \$70 = \$980$$

The figure lists maintenance costs for the computers and the LAN. The disks come with a three-year warranty, so there is no extra maintenance cost for them. The cost per rack of rental space for three years is $3 \times 12 \times \$1000$ or $\$36,000$.

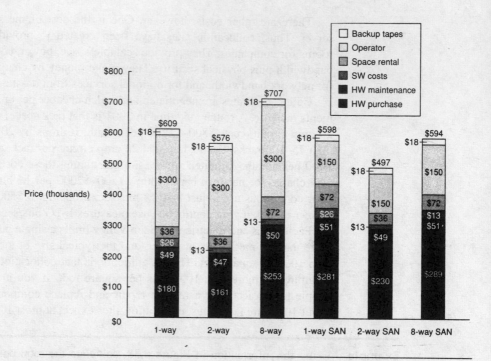

Price (thousands)

Figure 8.39 Total cost of ownership for three years for clusters in Figures 8.35 and 8.37. Operator costs are as significant as purchase price, and hence the assumption that SAN halves operator costs is very significant.

Figure 8.39 shows the two-way SMP using SAN is the winner. Note that hardware costs are only a half to a third of the cost of ownership. Over three years the operator costs can be more than the cost of purchase of the hardware, so reducing those costs significantly reduces total cost of ownership.

Our results depend on some critical assumptions, but surveys of the total cost of ownership for items with storage go up to factors of 5–10 over purchase price.

Fourth Example: Cost and Performance of a Cluster for Transaction Processing

The August 2001 TPC-C report includes a cluster built from building blocks similar to the previous examples. This cluster also has 32 processors, uses the same IBM computers as building blocks, and uses the same switch to connect computers together. Figure 8.40 shows its organization. It achieves 121,319 queries per hour for $2.2 million.

Here are the key differences:

- *Disk size*—Since TPC-C cares more about I/Os per second (IOPS) than disk capacity, this cluster uses many small, fast disks. The use of small disks gives

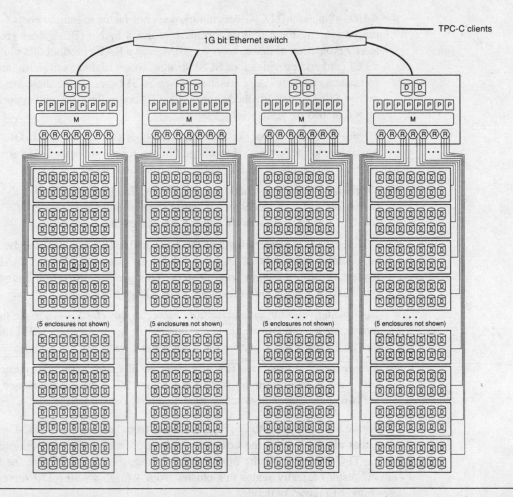

Figure 8.40 **IBM cluster for TPC-C. This cluster has 32 Pentium III processors, each running at 900 MHz with a 2 MB L2 cache.** The total of DRAM memory is 128 GB. Seven PCI slots in each computer contain RAID controllers (R for RAID), and each has four Ultra160 SCSI strings. These strings connect to 13 storage enclosures per computer, giving 52 total. Each enclosure has 14 SCSI disks, either 9.1 GB or 18.2 GB. The total is 560 9.1 GB disks and 140 18.2 GB disks. There are also two 9.1 GB disks inside each computer that are used for paging and rebooting.

many more IOPS for the same capacity. These disks also rotate at 15,000 RPM versus 10,000 RPM, delivering more IOPS per disk. The 9.1 GB disk costs $405, and the 18.2 GB disk costs $549, or an increase in dollars per GB of a factor of 1.7–2.5. The totals are 560 9.1 GB disks and 160 18.2 GB disks, yielding a total capacity of 8 TB. (Presumably the reason for the mix of sizes is to get sufficient capacity and IOPS to run the benchmark.) These 720 disks need $\lceil 720/14 \rceil$ or 52 enclosures, which is 13 enclosures per computer. In contrast, earlier eight-way clusters achieved 2 TB with 32 disks, as we cared more about cost per GB than IOPS.

- *RAID*—Since the TPC-C benchmark does not factor in human costs for running a system, there is little incentive to use a SAN. TPC-C does require a RAID protection of disks, however. IBM used a RAID product that plugs into a PCI card and provides four SCSI strings. To get higher availability and performance, each enclosure attaches to two SCSI buses. Thus, there are 52×2 or 104 SCSI cables attached to the 28 RAID controllers, which support up to 28×4 or 106 strings.

- *Memory*—Conventional wisdom for TPC-C is to pack as much DRAM as possible into the servers. Hence, each of the four eight-way SMPs is stuffed with the maximum of 32 GB, yielding a total of 128 GB.

- *Processor*—This benchmark uses the 900 MHz Pentium III with a 2 MB L2 cache. The price is $6599 as compared to prior eight-way clusters for $1799 for the 700 MHz Pentium III with a 1 MB L2 cache.

- *PCI slots*—This cluster uses 7 of the 12 available PCI bus slots for the RAID controllers compared to 1 PCI bus slot for an external SCSI or FC-AL controller in the prior eight-way clusters. This greater utilization follows the guideline of trying to use all resources of a large SMP.

- *Tape reader, monitor, uninterruptible power supply (UPS)*—To make the system easier to come up and to keep running for the benchmark, IBM includes one DLT tape reader, four monitors, and four UPSs.

- *Maintenance and spares*—TPC-C allows use of spares to reduce maintenance costs, which is a minimum of two spares or 10% of the items. Hence, there are two spare Ethernet switches, host adapters, and cables for TPC-C.

Figure 8.41 compares the eight-way cluster from before to this TPC-C cluster. Note that almost half of the cost is in software, installation, and maintenance for the TPC-C cluster. At the time of this writing, the computer with the fastest TPC-C result basically scales this cluster from 4 to 35 xSeries 370 servers and uses bigger Ethernet switches.

Summary of Examples

With completion of the cluster tour, you've seen a variety of cluster designs, including one representative of the state-of-the-art cost-performance cluster in 2001. Note that we concentrated on cost in constructing these clusters, but only book length prevents us from evaluating the performance and availability bottlenecks in these designs. Given the similarity to performance analysis of storage systems in the last chapter, we leave that to you in the exercises.

Having completed the tour of cluster examples, a few things stand out. First, the cost of purchase is less than half the cost of ownership. Thus, inventions that only help with hardware costs can solve only a part of the problem. For example, despite the higher costs of SAN, they may lower cost of ownership sufficiently to justify the investment. Second, the smaller computers are generally cheaper and faster for a given function compared to the larger computers. In this case, the

	Eight-way SAN cluster		TPC-C cluster	
4 systems (700 MHz/1 MB vs. 900 MHz/2 MB)	$58	17%	$76	3%
28 extra processors (700 MHz/1 MB vs. 900 MHz/2 MB)	$55	16%	$190	8%
Extra memory (8 GB vs. 32 GB)	$71	20%	$306	14%
Disk drives (2 TB/73.4 GB vs. 8 TB/9.1, 18.2 GB)	$54	15%	$316	14%
Disk enclosures (3 vs. 52)	$11	3%	$165	7%
RAID controller (1 vs. 28)	$16	4%	$69	3%
LAN network (1 switch/4 HBAs vs. 3 switches/6 HBAs)	$10	3%	$24	1%
SAN network (4 NICs, cables vs. 0)	$10	3%	n.a.	0%
Software (Windows vs. Windows + SQL server + installation)	$13	4%	$951	42%
Maintenance + hardware setup costs	$51	14%	$115	5%
Racks, UPS, backup (2 racks vs. 7 racks + 4 UPSs + 1 tape unit)	$3	1%	$40	2%
Total	$352	100%	$2,252	100%

Figure 8.41   Comparing eight-way SAN cluster and TPC-C cluster in price (in $1000s) and percentage. The higher cost of the system and extra processors is due to using the faster chips with the larger caches. Memory costs are higher due to more total memory and using the more expensive 1 GB DIMMs. The increased disk costs and disk enclosure costs are due to higher capacity and using smaller drives. Software costs increase due to adding an SQL server database plus IBM charges for software installation of this cluster. Similarly, although hardware maintenance costs are close, IBM charged to set up seven racks of hardware, whereas we assumed the customer assembled two racks of hardware "for free." Finally, SAN costs are higher due to the TPC-C policy of buying spares to lower maintenance costs.

larger cache required to allow several processors to share a bus means a much larger die, which increases cost and limits clock rate. Third, space and power matter for both ends of the computing spectrum: clusters at the high end and embedded computers at the low end.

8.12   Putting It All Together: The Google Cluster of PCs

Figure 8.42 shows the rapid growth of the World Wide Web and the corresponding demand for searching it. The number of pages indexed grew by a factor of 1000 between 1994 and 1997, but people were still only interested in the top 10 answers, which was a problem for search engines. In 1997, only one-quarter of the search engines would find themselves in their top 10 queries.

Google was designed first to be a search engine that could scale at that growth rate. In addition to keeping up with the demand, Google improved the relevance of the top queries produced so that users would likely get the desired result. For example, Figure 8.43 shows the first Google result for the query "Hennessy Patterson," which from your authors' perspective is the right answer. Techniques to improve search relevance include ranking pages by popularity, examining the text at the anchor sites of the URLs, and proximity of keyword text within a page.

Date	Web pages indexed (millions)	Queries per day (millions)	Search engine
April 1994	0.11	0.0015	World Wide Web Worm
November 1997	100	20	AltaVista
December 2000	1327	70	Google

Figure 8.42 Growth in pages indexed and search queries performed by several search engines [Brin and Page 1998]. Searches have been growing about 20% per month at Google, or about 8.9 times per year. Most of the 1.3 billion pages are fully indexed and cached at Google. Google indexes pages but does not necessarily cache all pages of URLs it finds, so about 40% of the 1.3 billion are just URLs without cached copies of the page at Google.

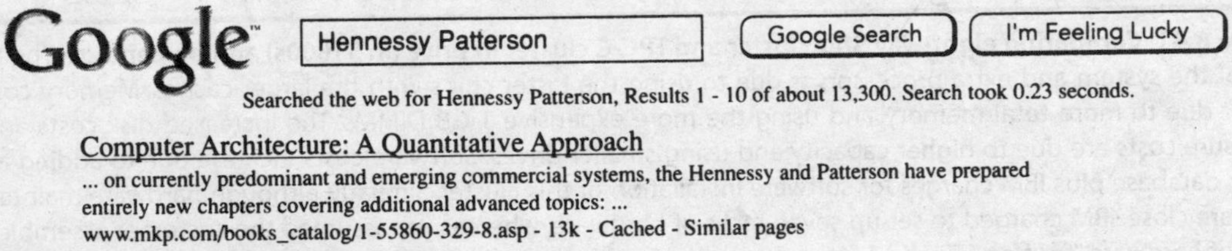

Google™ Hennessy Patterson   (Google Search) (I'm Feeling Lucky)

Searched the web for Hennessy Patterson, Results 1 - 10 of about 13,300. Search took 0.23 seconds.

Computer Architecture: A Quantitative Approach

... on currently predominant and emerging commercial systems, the Hennessy and Patterson have prepared entirely new chapters covering additional advanced topics: ...
www.mkp.com/books_catalog/1-55860-329-8.asp - 13k - Cached - Similar pages

Figure 8.43 First entry in result of a search for "Hennessy Patterson." Note that the search took less than 1/4 second, that it includes a capsule summary of the contents from the Web page at Morgan Kaufmann, and that it offers you to either follow the actual URL (*www.mkp ...*) or just read the cached copy of the page (Cached) stored in the Google cluster.

Search engines also have a major reliability requirement, since people are using them at all times of the day and from all over the world. Google must essentially be continuously available.

Since a search engine is normally interacting with a person, its latency must not exceed its users' patience. Google's goal is that no search takes more than 0.5 seconds, including network delays.

As the previous figures show, bandwidth is also vital. In 2000, Google served an *average* of almost 1000 queries per second as well as searched and indexed more than a billion pages.

In addition, a search engine must crawl the Web regularly to have up-to-date information to search. Google crawls the entire Web and updates its index every four weeks, so that every Web page is visited once a month. Google also keeps a local copy of the text of most pages so that it can provide the snippet text as well as offer a cached copy of the page, as shown in Figure 8.43.

Description of the Google Infrastructure

To keep up with such demand, in December 2000 Google used more than 6000 processors and 12,000 disks, giving Google a total of about 1 petabyte of disk storage. At the time, the Google site was likely the single system with the largest storage capacity in the private sector.

Rather than achieving availability by using RAID storage, Google relies on redundant sites, each with thousands of disks and processors: two sites in Silicon Valley and one in Virginia. The search index, which is a small number of terabytes, plus the repository of cached pages, which is on the order of the same size, are replicated across the three sites. Thus, if a single site fails, there are still two more that can retain the service. In addition, the index and repository are replicated within a site to help share the workload as well as to continue to provide service within a site even if components fail.

Each site is connected to the Internet via OC48 (2488M bit/sec) links of the collocation site. To provide against failure of the collocation link, there is a separate OC12 link connecting the two Silicon Valley sites so that in an emergency both sites can use the Internet link at one site. The external link is unlikely to fail at both sites since different network providers supply the OC48 lines. (The Virginia site now has a sister site so as to provide the same benefits.)

Figure 8.44 shows the floor plan of a typical site. The OC48 link connects to two Foundry BigIron 8000 switches via a large Cisco 12000 switch. Note that this link is also connected to the rest of the servers in the site. These two switches are redundant so that a switch failure does not disconnect the site. There is also an OC12 link from the Foundry switches to the sister site for emergencies. Each switch can connect to 128 1G bit/sec Ethernet lines. Racks of PCs, each with 4 1G bit/sec Ethernet interfaces, are connected to the two Foundry switches. Thus, a single site can support $2 \times 128/4$ or 64 racks of PCs.

Figure 8.45 shows Google's rack of PCs. Google uses PCs that are only 1 VME rack unit. To connect these PCs to the Foundry switches, it uses an HP Ethernet switch. It is 4 RU high, leaving room in the rack for 40 PCs. This switch has modular network interfaces, which are organized as removable *blades*. Each blade can contain 8 100M bit/sec Ethernet interfaces or a single 1G bit/sec Ethernet interface. Thus, 5 blades are used to connect 100M bit/sec Cat5 cables to each of the 40 PCs in the rack, and 2 blades are used to connect 1G bit/sec copper cables to the two Foundry switches.

As Figure 8.45 shows, to pack even more PCs in a rack Google uses the same configuration in the *front and back* of the rack, yielding 80 PCs and two switches per rack. There is about a 3-inch gap in the middle between the columns of PCs for the hot air to exit, which is drawn out of the "chimney" via exhaust fans at the top of the rack.

The PC itself is fairly standard: two ATA/IDE drives, 256 MB of SDRAM, a modest Intel microprocessor, a PC motherboard, one power supply, and a few fans. Each PC runs the Linux operating system. To get the best value per dollar, every 2–3 months Google increases the capacity of the drives or the speed of the

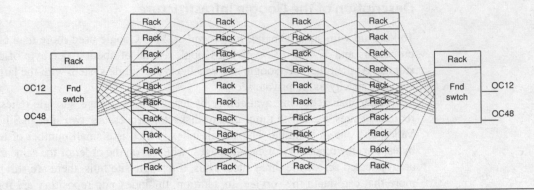

Figure 8.44 Floor plan of a Google cluster, from a God's-eye view. There are 40 racks, each connected via 4 copper G bit Ethernet links to two redundant Foundry 128 by 128 switches ("Fnd swtch"). Figure 8.45 shows a rack contains 80 PCs, so this facility has about 3200 PCs. (For clarity, the links are only shown for the top and bottom rack in each row.) These racks are on a raised floor so that the cables can be hidden and protected. Each Foundry switch in turn is connected to the collocation site network via an OC48 (2.4G bit) link to the Internet. There are two Foundry switches so that the cluster is still connected even if one switch fails. There is also a separate OC12 (622M bit) link to a separate nearby collocation site in case the OC48 network of one collocation site fails; it can still serve traffic over the OC12 to the other site's network. Each Foundry switch can handle 128 1G bit Ethernet lines, and each rack has 2 1G bit Ethernet lines per switch, so the maximum number of racks for the site is 64. The two racks near the Foundry switches contain a few PCs to act as front ends and help with tasks such as html service, load balancing, monitoring, and UPS to keep the switch and fronts up in case of a short power failure. It would seem that a facility that has redundant diesel engines to provide independent power for the whole site would make UPS redundant. A survey of data center users suggests power failures still happen yearly.

processor. Thus, the 40-rack site shown in Figure 8.44 was populated between March and November 2000 with microprocessors that varied from a 533 MHz Celeron to an 800 MHz Pentium III, disks that varied in capacity between 40 and 80 GB and in speed between 5400 and 7200 RPM, and memory bus speed that was either 100 or 133 MHz.

Performance

Each collocation site connects to the Internet via OC48 (2488M bit/sec) links, which is shared by Google and the other Internet service providers. If a typical response to a query is, say, 4000 bytes, then the average bandwidth demand is

$$\frac{70,000,000 \text{ queries/day} \times 4000 \text{ B/query} \times 8 \text{ bits/B}}{24 \times 60 \times 60 \text{ sec/day}} = \frac{2,240,000\text{M bits}}{86,400 \text{ sec}} \approx 26\text{M bits/sec}$$

which is just 1% of the link speed of each site. Even if we multiply by a factor of 4 to account for peak versus average demand and requests as well as responses, Google needs little of that bandwidth.

Crawling the Web and updating the sites needs much more bandwidth than serving the queries. Let's estimate some parameters to put things into perspective. Assume that it takes 7 days to crawl a billion pages:

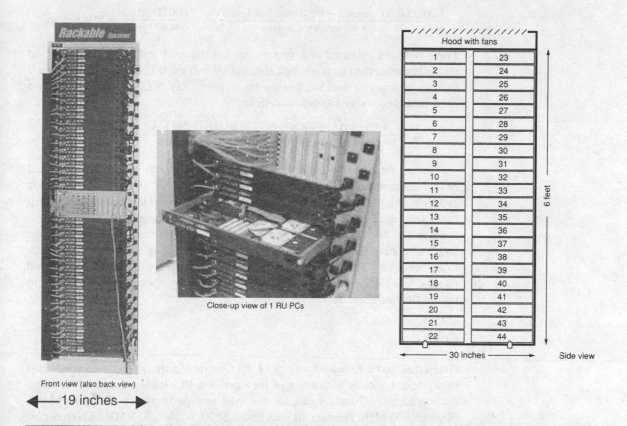

Front view (also back view)

◄——19 inches——►

Close-up view of 1 RU PCs

Hood with fans

1	23
2	24
3	25
4	26
5	27
6	28
7	29
8	30
9	31
10	32
11	33
12	34
13	35
14	36
15	37
16	38
17	39
18	40
19	41
20	42
21	43
22	44

6 feet

◄—— 30 inches ——►   Side view

Figure 8.45 Front view, side view, and close-up of a rack of PCs used by Google. The photograph on the left shows the HP Procurve 4000M Ethernet switch in the middle, with 20 PCs above and 20 PCs below. Each PC connects via a Cat5 cable on the left side to the switch in the middle, running 100M bit Ethernet. Each "blade" of the switch can hold eight 100M bit Ethernet interfaces or one 1G bit interface. There are also two 1G bit Ethernet links leaving the switch on the right. Thus, each PC has only two cables: one Ethernet and one power cord. The far right of the photo shows a power strip, with each of the 40 PCs and the switch connected to it. Each PC is 1 VME rack unit (RU) high. The switch in the middle is 4 RU high. The photo in the middle is a close-up of a rack, showing contents of a 1 RU PC. This unit contains two Maxtor DiamondMax 5400 RPM IDE drives on the right of the box, 256 MB of 100 MHz SDRAM, a PC motherboard, a single power supply, and an Intel microprocessor. Each PC runs versions 2.2.16 or 2.2.17 Linux kernels on a slightly modified Red Hat release. Between March 2000 and November 2000, over the period the Google site was populated, the microprocessor varied in performance from a 533 MHz Celeron to an 800 MHz Pentium III. The goal was selecting good cost-performance, which was often close to $200 per chip. Disk capacity varied from 40 GB to 80 GB. You can see the Ethernet cables on the left, power cords on the right, and table Ethernet cables connected to the switch at the top of the figure. In December 2000 the unassembled parts costs were about $500 for the two drives, $200 for the microprocessor, $100 for the motherboard, and $100 for the DRAM. Including the enclosure, power supply, fans, cabling, and so on, an assembled PC might cost $1300 to $1700. The drawing on the right shows that PCs are kept in two columns, front and back, so that a single rack holds 80 PCs and two switches. The typical power per PC is about 55 watts and about 70 watts per switch, so a rack uses about 4500 watts. Heat is exhausted into a 3-inch vent between the two columns, and the hot air is drawn out the top using fans. (The drawing shows 22 PCs per side, each 2 RU high, instead of the Google configuration of 40 1 RU PCs plus a switch per side.) (Photos and figure from Rackable Systems: *www.rackable.com/advantage.htm*.)

$$\frac{1,000,000,000 \text{ pages} \times 4000 \text{ B/page} \times 8 \text{ bits/B}}{24 \times 60 \times 60 \text{ sec/day} \times 7 \text{ days}} = \frac{32,000,000\text{M bits}}{604,800 \text{ sec}} \approx 53\text{M bits/sec}$$

These data are collected at a single site, but the final multiterabyte index and repository must then be replicated at the other two sites. If we assume we have 7 days to replicate the data and that we are shipping, say, 5 TB from one site to two sites, then the average bandwidth demand is

$$2 \times \frac{5,000,000 \text{ MB} \times 8 \text{ bits/B}}{24 \times 60 \times 60 \text{ sec/day} \times 7\text{days}} = \frac{80,000,000\text{M bits}}{604,800 \text{ sec}} \approx 132\text{M bits/sec}$$

Hence, the machine-to-person bandwidth is relatively trivial, with the real bandwidth demand being machine to machine. Moreover, Google's search rate is growing 20% per month, and the number of pages indexed has more than doubled every year since 1997, so bandwidth must be available for growth.

Time of flight for messages across the United States takes about 0.1 seconds, so it's important for Europe to be served from the Virginia site and for California to be served by Silicon Valley sites. To try to achieve the goal of 1/2 second latency, Google software normally guesses where the search is from in order to reduce time-of-flight delays.

Cost

Given that the basic building block of the Google cluster is a PC, the capital cost of a site is typically a function of the cost of a PC. Rather than buy the latest microprocessor, Google looks for the best cost-performance. Thus, in March 2000 an 800 MHz Pentium III cost about $800, while a 533 MHz Celeron cost under $200, and the difference in performance couldn't justify the extra $600 per machine. (When you purchase PCs by the thousands, every $100 per PC is important.) By November the price of the 800 MHz Pentium III dropped to $200, so it was a better investment. When accounting for this careful buying plus the enclosures and power supplies, we estimate the PC cost was $1300 to $1700.

The switches cost about $1500 for the HP Ethernet switch and about $100,000 each for the Foundry switches. If the racks themselves cost about $1000 to $2000 each, the total capital cost of a 40-rack site is about $4.5 million to $6.0 million. Including 3200 microprocessors and 0.8 TB of DRAM, the disk storage costs about $10,000 to $15,000 per terabyte. To put this into perspective, the leading performer for the TPC-C database benchmark in August 2001 was a scaled-up version of the cluster from the last example. The hardware alone cost about $10.8 million, which includes 280 microprocessors, 0.5 TB of DRAM, and 116 TB SCSI disks organized as RAID 1. Ignoring the RAID 1 overhead, disk storage cost about $93,000 per terabyte, about a factor of 8 higher than Google despite having 1/8 the number of processors and about 5/8 the DRAM.

The Google rack with 80 PCs, with each PC operating at about 55 W, uses 4500 W in 10 square feet. It is considerably higher than the 1000 W per rack expected by the collocation sites. Each Google rack also uses 60 amps. As mentioned above, reducing power per PC is a major opportunity for the future of such clusters, especially as the cost per kilowatt-hour is increasing and the cost per M bits/sec is decreasing.

Reliability

Not surprisingly, the biggest source of failures in the Google PC is software. On an average day, about 20 machines will be rebooted, and that normally solves the problem. To reduce the number of cables per PC as well as cost, Google has no ability to remotely reboot a machine. The software stops giving work to a machine when it observes unusual behavior, and the operator calls the collocation site and tells them the location of the machine that needs to be rebooted, and a person at the site finds the label and pushes the switch on the front panel. Occasionally the person hits the wrong switch either by mistake or due to mislabeling on the outside of the box.

The next reliability problem is the hardware, which has about 1/10th the failures of software. Typically, about 2% to 3% of the PCs have need to be replaced per year, with failures due to disks and DRAM accounting for 95% of these failures. The remaining 5% are due to problems with the motherboard, power supply, connectors, and so on. The microprocessors themselves never seem to fail.

The DRAM failures are perhaps a third of the failures. Google sees errors both from bits changing inside DRAM and when bits transfer over the 100–133 MHz bus. There was no ECC protection available on PC desktop motherboard chip sets in 2000, so it was not used. The DRAM is determined to be the problem when Linux cannot be installed with a proper checksum until the DRAM is replaced. As PC motherboard chip sets become available, Google plans to start using ECC both to correct some failures but, more importantly, to make it easier to see when DRAMs fail. The extra cost of the ECC is trivial given the wide fluctuation in DRAM prices; careful purchasing procedures are more important than whether or not the DIMM has ECC.

Disks are the remaining PC failures. In addition to the standard failures that result in a message to the error log in the console, in almost equal numbers these disks will occasionally result in a *performance failure,* with no error message to the log. Instead of delivering normal read bandwidths at 28 MB/sec, disks will suddenly drop to 4 MB/sec or even 0.8 MB/sec. As the disks are under warranty for five years, Google sends the disks back to the manufacturer for either operational or performance failures to get replacements. Thus, there has been no exploration of the reason for the disk anomalies.

When a PC has problems, it is reconfigured out of the system, and about once a week a person removes the broken PCs. They are usually repaired and then reinserted into the rack.

In regards to the switches, over a two-year period perhaps 200 of the HP Ethernet switches were deployed, and 2 or 3 have failed. None of the six Foundry switches has failed in the field, although some have had problems on delivery. These switches have a blade-based design with 16 blades per switch, and 2 or 3 of the blades have failed.

The final issue is collocation reliability. The experience of many Internet service providers is that once a year there will be a power outage that affects either the whole site or a major fraction of a site. On average, there is also a network outage so that the whole site is disconnected from the Internet. These outages can last for hours.

Note also that collocation site reliability follows a "bathtub" curve: high failures in the beginning, which quickly fall to low rates in the middle, and then rise to high rates at the end. When they are new, the sites are empty and so continuously filled with new equipment. With more people and new equipment being installed, there is a higher outage rate. Once the site is full of equipment, there are fewer people around and less change, so the site has a low failure rate. Once the equipment becomes outdated and it starts being replaced, the activity in the site increases and so does the failure rate. Thus, the failure rate of a site depends in part on its age, just as the classic bathtub reliability curves would predict. It is also a function of the people, and if there is a turnover in people, the fault rate can change.

Google accommodates collocation unreliability by having multiple sites with different network providers, plus leased lines between pairs of site for emergencies. Power failures, network outages, and so on do not affect the availability of the Google service.

8.13 Another View: Inside a Cell Phone

In 1999, there were 76 million cellular subscribers in the United States, a 25% growth rate from the year before. That growth rate is almost 35% per year worldwide, as developing countries find it much cheaper to install cellular towers than copper-wire-based infrastructure. Thus, in many countries, the number of cell phones in use exceeds the number of wired phones in use.

Not surprisingly, the cellular handset market is growing at 35% per year, with about 280 million cellular phone handsets sold in 1999. To put that in perspective, in the same year sales of personal computers were 120 million. These numbers mean that tremendous engineering resources are available to improve cell phones, and cell phones are probably leaders in engineering innovation per cubic inch [Grice and Kanellos 2000].

Before unveiling the anatomy of a cell phone, let's try a short introduction to wireless technology.

Background on Wireless Networks

Networks can be created out of thin air as well as out of copper and glass, creating *wireless networks*. Much of this section is based on a report from the National Research Council [1997].

A radio wave is an electromagnetic wave propagated by an antenna. Radio waves are modulated, which means that the sound signal is superimposed on the stronger radio wave that carries the sound signal, and hence is called the *carrier signal.* Radio waves have a particular wavelength or frequency: They are measured either as the length of the complete wave or as the number of waves per second. Long waves have low frequencies, and short waves have high frequencies. FM radio stations transmit on the band of 88 MHz–108 MHz using frequency modulations (FM) to record the sound signal.

By tuning into different frequencies, a radio receiver can pick up a specific signal. In addition to AM and FM radio, other frequencies are reserved for citizen band radio, television, pagers, air traffic control radar, Global Positioning System, and so on. In the United States, the Federal Communications Commission decides who gets to use which frequencies and for what purpose.

The *bit error rate* (BER) of a wireless link is determined by the received signal power, noise due to interference caused by the receiver hardware, interference from other sources, and characteristics of the channel. Noise is typically proportional to the radio frequency bandwidth, and a key measure is the *signal-to-noise ratio* (SNR) required to achieve a given BER. Figure 8.46 lists more challenges for wireless communication.

Typically, wireless communication is selected because the communicating devices are mobile or because wiring is inconvenient, which means the wireless network must rearrange itself dynamically. Such rearrangement makes routing more challenging. A second challenge is that wireless signals are not protected and hence are subject to mutual interference, especially as devices move. Power is another challenge for wireless communication, both because the devices tend to be battery powered and because antennas radiate power to communicate and little of it reaches the receiver. As a result, raw bit error rates are typically a thousand to a million times higher than copper wire.

There are two primary architectures for wireless networks: *base station* architectures and *peer-to-peer* architectures. Base stations are connected by land lines for longer-distance communication, and the mobile units communicate only with a single local base station. Peer-to-peer architectures allow mobile units to communicate with each other, and messages hop from one unit to the next until delivered

Challenge	Description	Impact
Path loss	Received power divided by transmitted power; the radio must overcome signal-to-noise ratio (SNR) of noise from interference. Path loss is exponential in distance and depends on interference if it is above 100 meters.	1 W transmit power, 1 GHz transmit frequency, 1M bit/sec data rate at 10^{-7} BER, distance between radios can be 728 meters in free space vs. 4 meters in a dense jungle.
Shadow fading	Received signal blocked by objects, buildings outdoors, or walls indoors; increase power to improve received SNR. It depends on the number of objects and their dielectric properties.	If transmitter is moving, need to change transmit power to ensure received SNR in region.
Multipath fading	Interference between multiple versions of signal that arrive at different times, determined by time between fastest signal and slowest signal relative to signal bandwidth.	900 MHz transmit frequency signal power changes every 30 cm.
Interference	Frequency reuse, adjacent channel, narrow band interference.	Requires filters, spread spectrum.

Figure 8.46 Challenges for wireless communication.

to the desired unit. Although peer-to-peer is more reconfigurable, base stations tend to be more reliable since there is only one hop between the device and the station. *Cellular telephony,* the most popular example of wireless networks, relies on radio with base stations.

Cellular systems exploit exponential path loss to reuse the same frequency at spatially separated locations, thereby greatly increasing the number of customers served. Cellular systems will divide a city into nonoverlapping hexagonal cells that use different frequencies if nearby, reusing a frequency only when cells are far enough apart so that mutual interference is acceptable.

At the intersection of three hexagonal cells is a base station with transmitters and antennas that is connected to a switching office that coordinates handoffs when a mobile device leaves one cell and goes into another, as well as accepts and places calls over land lines. Depending on topography, population, and so on, the radius of a typical cell is 2–10 miles.

The Cell Phone

Figure 8.47 shows the components of a radio, which is the heart of a cell phone. Radio signals are first received by the antenna, amplified, passed through a mixer, then filtered, demodulated, and finally decoded. The antenna acts as the interface between the medium through which radio waves travel and the electronics of the transmitter or receiver. Antennas can be designed to work best in particular directions, giving both transmission and reception directional properties. Modulation encodes information in the amplitude, phase, or frequency of the signal to increase its robustness under impaired conditions. Radio transmitters go through the same steps, just in the opposite order.

Originally, all components were analog, but over time most were replaced by digital components, requiring the radio signal to be converted from analog to digital. The desire for flexibility in the number of radio bands led to software rou-

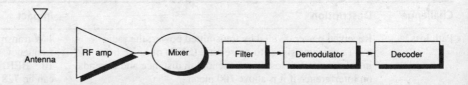

Figure 8.47 A radio receiver consists of an antenna, radio frequency amplifier, mixer, filters, demodulator, and decoder. A mixer accepts two signal inputs and forms an output signal at the sum and difference frequencies. Filters select a narrower band of frequencies to pass on to the next stage. Modulation encodes information to make it more robust. Decoding turns signals into information. Depending on the application, all electrical components can be either analog or digital. For example, a car radio is all analog components, but a PC modem is all digital except for the amplifier. Today analog silicon chips are used for the RF amplifier and first mixer in cellular phones.

tines replacing some of these functions in programmable chips, such as digital signal processors. Because such processors are typically found in mobile devices, emphasis is placed on performance per joule to extend battery life, performance per square millimeter of silicon to reduce size and cost, and bytes per task to reduce memory size.

Figure 8.48 shows the generic block diagram of the electronics of a cell phone handset, with the DSP performing the signal processing and the microcontroller handling the rest of the tasks. Cell phone handsets are basically mobile computers acting as a radio. They include standard I/O devices—keyboard and LCD display—plus a microphone, speaker, and antenna for wireless networking. Battery efficiency affects sales, both for standby power when waiting for a call and for minutes of speaking.

When a cell phone is turned on, the first task is to find a cell. It scans the full bandwidth to find the strongest signal, which it keeps doing every 7 seconds or if the signal strength drops, since it is designed to work from moving vehicles. It then picks an unused radio channel. The local switching office registers the cell phone and records its phone number and electronic serial number, and assigns it a voice channel for the phone conversation. To be sure the cell phone got the right channel, the base station sends a special tone on it, which the cell phone sends back to acknowledge it. The cell phone times out after 5 seconds if it doesn't hear the supervisory tone, and it starts the process all over again. The original base station makes a handoff request to the incoming base station as the signal strength drops offs.

To achieve a two-way conversation over radio, frequency bands are set aside for each direction, forming a frequency pair or *channel*. The original cellular base stations transmitted at 869.04–893.97 MHz (called the *forward path*), and cell phones transmitted at 824.04–848.97 MHz (called the *reverse path*), with the frequency gap to keep them from interfering with each other. Cells might have had between 4 and 80 channels. Channels were divided into setup channels for call setup, and voice channels that handle the data or voice traffic.

The communication is done digitally, just like a modem, at 9600 bits/sec. Since wireless is a lossy medium, especially from a moving vehicle, the handset

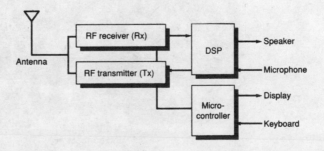

Figure 8.48   Block diagram of a cell phone. The DSP performs the signal processing steps of Figure 8.47, and the microcontroller controls the user interface, battery management, and call setup. (Based on Figure 1.3 of Groe and Larson [2000].)

sends each message five times. To preserve battery life, the original cell phones typically transmit at two signal strengths—0.6 W and 3.0 W—depending on the distance to the cell. This relatively low power not only allows smaller batteries and thus smaller cell phones, but it also aids frequency reuse, which is the key to cellular telephony.

Figure 8.49 shows a circuit board from an Nokia digital phone, with the components identified. Note that the board contains two processors. A Z-80 microcontroller is responsible for controlling the functions of the board, I/O with the keyboard and display, and coordinating with the base station. The DSP handles all signal compression and decompression. In addition there are dedicated chips for analog-to-digital and digital-to-analog conversion, amplifiers, power management, and RF interfaces.

In 2001, a cell phone had about 10 integrated circuits, including parts made in exotic technologies like gallium arsinide and silicon germanium as well as standard CMOS. The economics and desire for flexibility will likely shrink this to a few chips, but it appears that a separate microcontroller and DSP will be found inside those chips, with code implementing many of the functions.

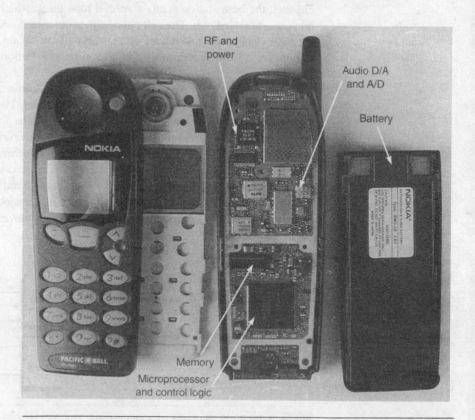

Figure 8.49 Circuit card from an Nokia cell phone. (Courtesy HowStuffWorks, Inc.)

Cell Phone Standards and Evolution

Improved communication speeds for cellular phones were developed with multiple standards. *Code division multiple access* (CDMA), as one popular example, uses a wider radio frequency band for a path than the original cellular phones, called *advanced mobile phone service* (AMPS), a mostly analog system. The wider frequency makes it more difficult to block and is called *spread spectrum*. Other standards are *time division multiple access* (TDMA) and *global system for mobile communication* (GSM). These second-generation standards—CDMA, GSM, and TDMA—are mostly digital.

The big difference for CDMA is that all callers share the same channel, which operates at a much higher rate, and then distinguishes the different calls by encoding each one uniquely. Each CDMA phone call starts at 9600 bits/sec; it is then encoded and transmitted as equal-sized messages at 1.25M bits/sec. Rather than send each signal five times as in AMPS, each bit is stretched so that it takes 11 times the minimum frequency, thereby accommodating interference and yet successful transmission. The base station receives the messages, and it separates them into the separate 9600 bit/sec streams for each call.

To enhance privacy, CDMA uses pseudorandom sequences from a set of 64 predefined codes. To synchronize the handset and base station so as to pick a common pseudorandom seed, CDMA relies on a clock from the Global Positioning System, which continuously transmits an accurate time signal. By carefully selecting the codes, the shared traffic sounds like random noise to the listener. Hence, as more users share a channel there is more noise, and the signal-to-noise ratio gradually degrades. Thus, the capacity of the CDMA system is a matter of taste, depending upon the sensitivity of the listener to background noise.

In addition, CDMA uses speech compression and varies the rate of data transferred depending upon how much activity is going on in the call. Both these techniques preserve bandwidth, which allows for more calls per cell. CDMA must regulate power carefully so that signals near the cell tower do not overwhelm those from far away, with the goal of all signals reaching the tower at about the same level. The side benefit is that CDMA handsets emit less power, which both helps battery life and increases capacity when users are close to the tower.

Thus, compared to AMPS, CDMA improves the capacity of a system by up to an order of magnitude, has better call quality, has better battery life, and enhances users' privacy. After considerable commercial turmoil, there is a new third-generation standard called International Mobile Telephony 2000 (IMT-2000), based primarily on two competing versions of CDMA and one TDMA. This standard may lead to cell phones that work anywhere in the world.

8.14   **Fallacies and Pitfalls**

Myths and hazards are widespread with interconnection networks. This section has just a few warnings, so proceed carefully.

Pitfall *Using bandwidth as the only measure of network performance.*

Many network companies apparently believe that given sophisticated protocols like TCP/IP that maximize delivered bandwidth, there is only one figure of merit for networks. This may be true for some applications, such as video, where there is little interaction between the sender and the receiver. Many applications, however, are of a request-response nature, and so for every large message there must be one or more small messages. One example is NFS.

Figure 8.50 compares a shared 10M bit/sec Ethernet LAN to a switched 155M bit/sec ATM LAN for NFS traffic. Ethernet drivers were better tuned than

Size	Number of messages	Overhead (sec) ATM	Overhead (sec) Ethernet	Number of data bytes	Transmission (sec) ATM	Transmission (sec) Ethernet	Total time (sec) ATM	Total time (sec) Ethernet
32	771,060	532	389	33,817,052	4	48	536	436
64	56,923	39	29	4,101,088	0	5	40	34
96	4,082,014	2,817	2,057	428,346,316	46	475	2,863	2,532
128	5,574,092	3,846	2,809	779,600,736	83	822	3,929	3,631
160	328,439	227	166	54,860,484	6	56	232	222
192	16,313	11	8	3,316,416	0	3	12	12
224	4,820	3	2	1,135,380	0	1	3	4
256	24,766	17	12	9,150,720	1	9	18	21
512	32,159	22	16	25,494,920	3	23	25	40
1,024	69,834	48	35	70,578,564	8	72	56	108
1,536	8,842	6	4	15,762,180	2	14	8	19
2,048	9,170	6	5	20,621,760	2	19	8	23
2,560	20,206	14	10	56,319,740	6	51	20	61
3,072	13,549	9	7	43,184,992	4	39	14	46
3,584	4,200	3	2	16,152,228	2	14	5	17
4,096	67,808	47	34	285,606,596	29	255	76	290
5,120	6,143	4	3	35,434,680	4	32	8	35
6,144	5,858	4	3	37,934,684	4	34	8	37
7,168	4,140	3	2	31,769,300	3	28	6	30
8,192	287,577	198	145	2,390,688,480	245	2,132	444	2,277
Total	11,387,913	7,858	5,740	4,352,876,316	452	4,132	8,310	9,872

Figure 8.50 Total time on a 10M bit Ethernet and a 155M bit ATM, calculating the total overhead and transmission time separately. Note that the size of the headers needs to be added to the data bytes to calculate transmission time. The higher overhead of the software driver for ATM offset the higher bandwidth of the network. These measurements were performed in 1994 using SPARCstation 10s, the Fore Systems SBA-200 ATM interface card, and the Fore Systems ASX-200 switch. (NFS measurements taken by Mike Dahlin of U.C. Berkeley.)

the ATM drivers, such that 10M bit/sec Ethernet was faster than 155M bit/sec ATM for payloads of 512 bytes or less. Figure 8.50 shows the overhead time, transmission time, and total time to send all the NFS messages over Ethernet and ATM. The peak link speed of ATM is 15 times faster, and the measured link speed for 8 KB messages is almost 9 times faster. Yet the higher overheads offset the benefits so that ATM would transmit NFS traffic only 1.2 times faster.

Pitfall   *Ignoring software overhead when determining performance.*

Low software overhead requires cooperation with the operating system as well as with the communication libraries. Figure 8.50 gives one example.

Another example comes from supercomputers. The CM-5 supercomputer had a software overhead of 20 μs to send a message and a hardware overhead of 0.5 μs. The Intel Paragon reduced the hardware overhead to just 0.2 μs, but the initial release of software has a software overhead of 250 μs. Later releases reduced this overhead to 25 μs, which still dominates the hardware overhead.

This pitfall is simply Amdahl's Law applied to networks: faster network hardware is superfluous if there is not a corresponding decrease in software overhead.

Pitfall   *Trying to provide features only within the network versus end to end.*

The concern is providing at a lower level features that can only be accomplished at the highest level, thus only partially satisfying the communication demand. Saltzer, Reed, and Clark [1984] give the *end-to-end argument* as

> The function in question can completely and correctly be specified only with the knowledge and help of the application standing at the endpoints of the communication system. Therefore, providing that questioned function as a feature of the communication system itself is not possible. [page 278]

Their example of the pitfall was a network at MIT that used several gateways, each of which added a checksum from one gateway to the next. The programmers of the application assumed the checksum guaranteed accuracy, incorrectly believing that the message was protected while stored in the memory of each gateway. One gateway developed a transient failure that swapped one pair of bytes per million bytes transferred. Over time the source code of one operating system was repeatedly passed through the gateway, thereby corrupting the code. The only solution was to correct the infected source files by comparing to paper listings and repairing the code by hand! Had the checksums been calculated and checked by the application running on the end systems, safety would have been assured.

There is a useful role for intermediate checks, however, provided that end-to-end checking is available. End-to-end checking may show that something is broken between two nodes, but it doesn't point to where the problem is. Intermediate checks can discover the broken component.

A second issue regards performance using intermediate checks. Although it is sufficient to retransmit the whole in case of failures from the endpoint, it can be much faster to retransmit a portion of the message at an intermediate point rather than wait for a time-out and a full message retransmit at the endpoint. Balakrishnan et al. [1997] found that, for wireless networks, such an intermediate retransmission for TCP/IP communication results in 10% to 30% higher throughput.

Pitfall *Relying on TCP/IP for all networks, regardless of latency, bandwidth, or software requirements.*

The network designers on the first workstations decided it would be elegant to use a single protocol stack no matter where the destination of the message: Across a room or across an ocean, the TCP/IP overhead must be paid. This might have been a wise decision, especially given the unreliability of early Ethernet hardware, but it sets a high software overhead barrier for commercial systems. Such an obstacle lowers the enthusiasm for low-latency network interface hardware and low-latency interconnection networks if the software is just going to waste hundreds of microseconds when the message must travel only dozens of meters. It also can use significant processor resources. One rough rule of thumb is that each M bit/sec of TCP/IP bandwidth needs about 1 MHz of processor speed, and so a 1000M bit/sec link could saturate a processor with an 800–1000 MHz clock.

The flip side is that, from a software perspective, TCP/IP is the most desirable target since it is the most connected and hence provides the largest number of opportunities. The downside of using software optimized to a particular LAN or SAN is that it is limited. For example, communication from a Java program depends on TCP/IP, so optimization for another protocol would require creation of glue software to interface Java to it.

TCP/IP advocates point out that the protocol itself is theoretically not as burdensome as the current implementations, but progress has been modest in commercial systems. There are also TCP/IP off-loading engines entering the market, with the hope of preserving the universal software model while reducing processor utilization and message latency. If processors continue to improve much faster than network speeds, or if multiple processors become ubiquitous, software TCP/IP may become less significant for processor utilization and message latency.

8.15 | Concluding Remarks

Networking is one of the most exciting fields in computer science and engineering today. The purpose of this chapter is to lower the cost of entry into this field by providing definitions and the basic issues so that readers can more easily go into more depth.

The Internet and World Wide Web pervade our society and will likely revolutionize how we access information. Although we couldn't have the Internet without the telecommunication media, it is protocol suites such as TCP/IP that make electronic communication practical. More than most areas of computer science and engineering, these protocols embrace failures as the norm; the network must operate reliably in the presence of failures. Interconnection network hardware and software blend telecommunications with data communications, calling into question whether they should remain as separate academic disciplines or be combined into a single field.

The silicon revolution has made its way to the switch: just as the "killer micro" changed computing, whatever turns out to be the "killer network" will transform communication. We are seeing the same dramatic change in cost-performance in switches as the mainframe-minicomputer-microprocessor change did to processors. In 2001, companies that make switches are acquiring companies that make embedded microprocessors, just to have better microprocessors for their switches.

Inexpensive switches mean that network bandwidth can scale with the number of nodes, even to the level of the traditional I/O bus. Both I/O designers and memory system designers must consider how to best select and deploy switches. Thus, networking issues apply to all levels of computer systems today: communication within chips, between chips on a board, between boards, and between computers in a machine room, on a campus, or in a country.

The availability and scalability of networks are transforming the machine room. Disks are being connected over SAN to servers versus being directly attached, and clusters of smaller computers connected by a LAN are replacing large servers. The cost-performance, scalability, and fault isolation of clusters have made them attractive to diverse communities: database, scientific computing, and Internet service providers. It's hard to think what else these communities have in common. The challenge for clusters today is the cost of administration.

After decades of low network performance on shared media, networking is in "catch-up" mode and should improve faster than microprocessors. We are not near any performance plateaus, so we expect rapid advance in SANs, LANs, and WANs. This greater network performance is key to the information- and communication-centric vision of the future of our field. The dramatic improvement in cost-performance of communications has enabled millions of people around the world to find others with common interests. As the quotes at the beginning of this chapter suggest, we believe this revolution in two-way communication will change the form of human associations and actions.

8.16   Historical Perspective and References

This chapter has taken the unusual perspective that computers inside the machine room on a LAN or SAN and computers on an intercontinental WAN share many of the same concerns. Although this observation may be true, their histories are very different. We highlight readings on each topic, but good general texts on networking have been written by Davie, Peterson, and Clark [1999] and by Kurose and Ross [2001].

Wide Area Networks

The earliest of the data interconnection networks are WANs. The forerunner of the Internet is the ARPANET, which in 1969 connected computer science departments across the United States that had research grants funded by the Advanced Research Project Agency (ARPA), a U.S. government agency. It was originally envisioned as using reliable communications at lower levels. It was the practical experience with failures of underlying technology that led to the failure-tolerant TCP/IP, which is the basis for the Internet today. Vint Cerf and Robert Kahn are credited with developing the TCP/IP protocols in the mid-1970s, winning the ACM Software Award in recognition of that achievement. Kahn [1972] is an early reference on the ideas of ARPANET. For those interested in learning more about TPC/IP, Stevens [1994–1996] has written classic books on the topic.

In 1975, there were roughly 100 networks in the ARPANET; in 1983, only 200. In 1995, the Internet encompassed 50,000 networks worldwide, about half of which were in the United States. That number is hard to calculate for 2000, but the number of IP hosts grew by a factor of 20 in five years. The key networks that made the Internet possible, such as ARPANET and NSFNET, have been replaced by fully commercial systems, and yet the Internet still thrives.

The exciting application of the Internet is the World Wide Web, developed by Tim Berners-Lee, a programmer at the European Center for Particle Research (CERN) in 1989 for information access. In 1992, a young programmer at the University of Illinois, Marc Andreessen, developed a graphical interface for the Web called Mosaic. It became immensely popular. He later became a founder of Netscape, which popularized commercial browsers. In May 1995, at the time of the second edition of this book, there were over 30,000 Web pages, and the number was doubling every two months. During the writing of the third edition of this book, there were almost 100 million Internet hosts and more than 1.3 billion Web pages.

Alles [1995] offers a good survey on ATM. ATM is just the latest of the ongoing standards set by the telecommunications industry, and it is undoubtedly the future for this community. Communication forces standardization by competitive companies, sometimes leading to anomalies. For example, the telecommunication companies in North America wanted to use 64-byte packets to match their existing equipment, while the Europeans wanted 32-byte packets to match their existing equipment. The new standard compromise was 48 bytes to ensure that neither group had an advantage in the marketplace!

Finally, WANs today rely on fiber. Fiber has made such advances that its original assumption of packet switching is no longer true: WAN bandwidth is not precious. Today WAN fibers are often underutilized. Goralski [1997] discusses advances in fiber optics.

Local Area Networks

ARPA's success with wide area networks led directly to the most popular local area networks. Many researchers at Xerox Palo Alto Research Center had been funded by ARPA while working at universities, and so they all knew the value of networking. In 1974, this group invented the Alto, the forerunner of today's desktop computers [Thacker et al. 1982], *and* the Ethernet [Metcalfe and Boggs 1976], today's LAN. This group—David Boggs, Butler Lampson, Ed McCreight, Bob Sprowl, and Chuck Thacker—became luminaries in computer science and engineering, collecting a treasure chest of awards among them.

This first Ethernet provided a 3M bit/sec interconnection, which seemed like an unlimited amount of communication bandwidth with computers of that era. It relied on the interconnect technology developed for the cable television industry. Special microcode support gave a round-trip time of 50 μs for the Alto over Ethernet, which is still a respectable latency. It was Boggs' experience as a ham radio operator that led to a design that did not need a central arbiter, but instead listened before use and then varied back-off times in case of conflicts.

The announcement by Digital Equipment Corporation, Intel, and Xerox of a standard for 10M bit/sec Ethernet was critical to the commercial success of Ethernet. This announcement short-circuited a lengthy IEEE standards effort, which eventually did publish IEEE 802.3 as a standard for Ethernet.

There have been several unsuccessful candidates in trying to replace the Ethernet. The FDDI committee, unfortunately, took a very long time to agree on the standard, and the resulting interfaces were expensive. It was also a shared medium when switches were becoming affordable. ATM also missed the opportunity due in part to the long time to standardize the LAN version of ATM.

Because of failures of the past, LAN modernization efforts have been centered on extending Ethernet to lower-cost media, to switched interconnect, to higher link speeds, and to new domains such as wireless communication. Spurgeon [2001] has a nice online summary of Ethernet technology, including some of its history.

Massively Parallel Processors

One of the places of innovation in interconnect networks was in massively parallel processors (MPPs). An early MPP was the Cosmic Cube [Seitz 1985], which used Ethernet interface chips to connect 8086 computers in a hypercube. SAN interconnections have improved considerably since then, with messages routed automatically through intermediate switches to their final destinations at high bandwidths and with low latency. Considerable research has gone into the benefits of different topologies in both construction and program behavior. Whether due to faddishness or changes in technology is hard to say, but topologies certainly become very popular and then disappear. The hypercube, widely popular in the 1980s, almost disappeared from MPPs of the 1990s. Cut-through routing, however, has been preserved and is covered by Dally and Seitz [1986].

Chapter 6 records the poor current state of such machines. Government programs such as the Accelerated Strategic Computing Initiative (ASCI) still result in a handful of one-of-a-kind MPPs costing $50 to $100 million, yet these are basically clusters of SMPs.

Clusters

Clusters were probably "invented" in the 1960s by customers who could not fit all their work on one computer, or who needed a backup machine in case of failure of the primary machine [Pfister 1998]. Tandem introduced a 16-node cluster in 1975. Digital followed with VAX clusters, introduced in 1984. They were originally independent computers that shared I/O devices, requiring a distributed operating system to coordinate activity. Soon they had communication links between computers, in part so that the computers could be geographically distributed to increase availability in case of a disaster at a single site. Users log onto the cluster and are unaware of which machine they are running on. DEC (now Compaq) sold more than 25,000 clusters by 1993. Other early companies were Tandem (now Compaq) and IBM (still IBM), and today virtually every company has cluster products. Most of these products are aimed at availability, with performance scaling as a secondary benefit. Yet in 2001 clusters generally dominated the list of top performers of the TPC-C database benchmark.

Scientific computing on clusters emerged as a competitor to MPPs. In 1993, the Beowulf project started with the goal of fulfilling NASA's desire for a 1 GFLOPS computer for under $50,000. In 1994, a 16-node cluster built from off-the-shelf PCs using 80486s achieved that goal [Bell 2001]. This emphasis led to a variety of software interfaces to make it easier to submit, coordinate, and debug large programs or a large number of independent programs. In 2001, the fastest (and largest) supercomputers were typically clusters, at least by some popular measures.

Efforts were made to reduce latency of communication in clusters as well as to increase bandwidth, and several research projects worked on that problem. (One commercial result of the low-latency research was the VI interface standard, which has been embraced by Infiniband, discussed below.) Low latency then proved useful in other applications. For example, in 1997 a cluster of 100 Ultra-SPARC desktop computers at UC Berkeley, connected by 160 MB/sec per link Myrinet switches, was used to set world records in database sort—sorting 8.6 GB of data originally on disk in 1 minute—and in cracking an encrypted message—taking just 3.5 hours to decipher a 40-bit DES key. This research project, called Network of Workstations [Anderson, Culler, and Patterson 1995], also developed the Inktomi search engine, which led to a start-up company with the same name.

For those interested in learning more, Pfister [1998] has written an entertaining book on clusters. In even greater detail, Sterling [2001] has written a do-it-yourself book on how to build a Beowulf cluster.

System or Storage Area Networks (SANs)

At the second edition of this book, a new class of networks was emerging: system area networks. These networks were designed for a single room or single floor (thus the length is tens to hundreds of meters) and were for use in clusters. Close distance means the wires can be wider and faster at lower cost, network hardware can ensure in-order delivery, and cascading switches consume less handshaking time. There is also less reason to go to the cost of optical fiber, since the distance advantage of fiber is less important for SANs. The limited size of the networks also makes source-based routing plausible, further simplifying the network. Both Tandem Computers and Myricom sold SANs.

In the intervening years the acronym SAN has been co-opted to also mean *storage* area networks, whereby networking technology is used to connect storage devices to compute servers. Today most people mean "storage" when they say SAN. The most widely used example in 2001 was Fibre Channel Arbitrated Loop (FC-AL). Not only are disk arrays attached to servers via FC-AL links, there are even some disks with FC-AL links. There are also companies selling FC-AL switches so that storage area networks can enjoy the benefits of greater bandwidth and interconnectivity of switching.

In October 2000 the Infiniband Trade Association announced the version 1.0 specification of Infiniband. Led by Intel, HP, IBM, Sun, and other companies, it was proposed as a successor to the PCI bus that brings point-to-point links and switches with its own set of protocols. Its characteristics are desirable potentially both for system area networks to connect clusters and for storage area networks to connect disk arrays to servers. To learn more, see the Infiniband standard on the Web [Infiniband Trade Association 2001].

The chief competition for Infiniband is the rapidly improving Ethernet technology. The Internet Engineering Task Force is proposing a standard called iSCSI to send SCSI commands over IP networks [Satran et al. 2001]. Given the likely cost advantages of the higher-volume Ethernet switches and interface cards, in 2001, it was unclear who would win.

Will Infiniband take over the machine room, leaving the WAN as the only link that is not Infiniband? Or will Ethernet dominate the machine room, even taking over some of the role of storage area networks, leaving Infiniband to simply be an I/O bus replacement? Or will there be a three-level solution: Infiniband in the machine room, Ethernet in the building and on the campus, and WAN for the country? Will TCP/IP off-loading engines become available that can reduce processor utilization and provide low latency yet still provide the software interfaces and generality of TCP/IP? Or will software TCP/IP and faster multiprocessors be sufficient?

In 2001, it was very hard to tell which would win. A wonderful characteristic of computer architecture is that such issues will not remain endless academic debates, unresolved as people rehash the same arguments repeatedly. Instead, the battle is fought in the marketplace, with well-funded and talented groups giving their best efforts at shaping the future. Moreover, constant changes to technology reward those who are either astute or lucky. The best combination of technology and follow-through has often determined commercial success.

Let the games begin! Time will tell us who wins and who loses, and we will likely know the score by the next edition of this text.

References

Alles, A. [1995]. "ATM internetworking" (May), *www.cisco.com/warp/public/614/12.html*.

Anderson, T. E., D. E. Culler, and D. Patterson [1995]. "A case for NOW (networks of workstations)," *IEEE Micro 15:1* (February), 54–64.

Arpaci, R. H., D. E. Culler, A. Krishnamurthy, S. G. Steinberg, and K. Yelick [1995]. "Empirical evaluation of the CRAY-T3D: A compiler perspective," *Proc. 23rd Int'l Symposium on Computer Architecture* (June), Italy.

Balakrishnan, H. V. N. Padmanabhan, S. Seshan, and R. H. Katz [1997]. "A comparison of mechanisms for improving TCP performance over wireless links," *IEEE/ACM Trans. on Networking,* 5:6 (December), 756–769.

Bell, G., and J. Gray [2001]. "Crays, clusters and centers," Microsoft Research Technical Report, MSR-TR-2001-76.

Brain, M. [2000]. "Inside a digital cell phone," *www.howstuffworks.com/inside-cell-phone.htm*.

Brewer, E. A., and B. C. Kuszmaul [1994]. "How to get good performance from the CM-5 data network." *Proc. Eighth Int'l Parallel Processing Symposium* (April), Cancun, Mexico.

Brin, S., and L. Page [1998]. "The anatomy of a large-scale hypertextual Web search engine," *Proc. 7th Int'l World Wide Web Conf.,* Brisbane, Qld., Australia (April 14–18), 107–117.

Comer, D. [1993]. *Internetworking with TCP/IP,* 2nd ed., Prentice Hall, Englewood Cliffs, N.J.

Dally, W. J., and C. I. Seitz [1986]. "The torus routing chip," *Distributed Computing* 1:4, 187–196.

Davie, B. S., L. L. Peterson, and D. Clark [1999]. *Computer Networks: A Systems Approach,* 2nd ed., Morgan Kaufmann Publishers, San Francisco.

Desurvire, E. [1992]. "Lightwave communications: The fifth generation," *Scientific American* (International Edition) 266:1 (January), 96–103.

Goralski, W. [1997]. *SONET: A Guide to Synchronous Optical Network,* McGraw-Hill, New York.

Grice, C., and M. Kanellos [2000]. "Cell phone industry at crossroads: Go high or low?," *CNET News* (August 31), *technews.netscape.com/news/0-1004-201-2518386-0.html?tag=st.ne.1002.tgif.sf*.

Groe, J. B., and L. E. Larson [2000]. *CDMA Mobile Radio Design,* Artech House, Boston.

Infiniband Trade Association [2001]. *InfiniBand Architecture Specifications Release 1.0.a, www.infinibandta.org*.

Kahn, R. E. [1972]. "Resource-sharing computer communication networks," *Proc. IEEE* 60:11 (November), 1397–1407.

Kurose, J. F., and K. W. Ross [2001]. *Computer Networking: A Top-Down Approach Featuring the Internet,* Addison-Wesley, Boston.

Metcalfe, R. M. [1993]. "Computer/network interface design: Lessons from Arpanet and Ethernet." *IEEE J. on Selected Areas in Communications* 11:2 (February), 173–180.

Metcalfe, R. M., and D. R. Boggs [1976]. "Ethernet: Distributed packet switching for local computer networks," *Comm. ACM* 19:7 (July), 395–404.

National Research Council [1997]. *The Evolution of Untethered Communications,* Computer Science and Telecommunications Board, National Academy Press, Washington, D.C.

Partridge, C. [1994]. *Gigabit Networking.* Addison-Wesley, Reading, Mass.

Pfister, Gregory F. [1998]. *In Search of Clusters,* 2nd ed., Prentice Hall, Upper Saddle River, N.J.

Saltzer, J. H., D. P. Reed, and D. D. Clark [1984]. "End-to-end arguments in system design," *ACM Trans. on Computer Systems* 2:4 (November), 277–288.

Satran, J., D. Smith, K. Meth, C. Sapuntzakis, M. Wakeley, P. Von Stamwitz, R. Haagens, E. Zeidner, L. Dalle Ore, and Y. Klein [2001]. "iSCSI," IPS working group of IETF, Internet draft *www.ietf.org/internet-drafts/draft-ietf-ips-iscsi-07.txt.*

Seitz, C. L. [1985]. "The Cosmic Cube (concurrent computing), "*Communications of the ACM* 28:1 (January), 22–33.

Spurgeon, C. [2001]. "Charles Spurgeon's Ethernet Web site," *wwwhost.ots.utexas.edu /ethernet/ethernet-home.html.*

Sterling, T. [2001]. *Beowulf PC Cluster Computing with Windows and Beowulf PC Cluster Computing with Linux,* MIT Press, Cambridge, Mass.

Stevens, W. R. [1994–1996]. *TCP/IP Illustrated* (three volumes), Addison-Wesley, Reading, Mass.

Tanenbaum, A. S. [1988]. *Computer Networks,* 2nd ed., Prentice Hall, Englewood Cliffs, N.J.

Thacker, C. P., E. M. McCreight, B. W. Lampson, R. F. Sproull, and D. R. Boggs [1982]. Alto: A personal computer," in *Computer Structures: Principles and Examples*, D. P. Siewiorek, C. G. Bell, and A. Newell, eds., McGraw-Hill, New York, 549–572.

Walrand, J. [1991]. *Communication Networks: A First Course*, Aksen Associates: Irwin, Homewood, Ill.

Exercises

Solutions to "starred" exercises appear in Appendix B.

✪ 8.1 [15] <8.2> Assume the total overhead to send a zero-length data packet on an Ethernet is 100 microseconds and that an unloaded network can transmit at 90% of the peak 1000M bit/sec rating. For the purposes of this question, assume the size of the Ethernet header and trailer is 56 bytes. Assume a continuous stream of packets of the same size. Plot the delivered bandwidth of user data in M bits/sec as the payload data size varies from 32 bytes to the maximum size of 1500 bytes in 32-byte increments.

8.2 [10] <8.2> Exercise 8.1 suggests that the delivered Ethernet bandwidth to a single user may be disappointing. Making the same assumptions as in that exercise, by how much would the maximum payload size have to be increased to deliver half of the peak bandwidth?

8.3 [10] <8.2> One reason that ATM has a fixed transfer size is that when a short message is behind a long message, a node may need to wait for an entire transfer to complete. For applications that are time-sensitive, such as when transmitting voice or video, the large transfer size may result in transmission delays that are too long for the application. On an unloaded interconnection, what is the worst-case delay in microseconds if a node must wait for one full-size Ethernet packet versus an ATM transfer? See Figure 8.20 (page 826) to find the packet sizes. For this question assume you can transmit at 100% of the 622M bits/sec of the ATM network and 100% of the 1000M bit/sec Ethernet.

8.4 [10] <8.2> Exercise 8.2 suggests the need for expanding the maximum payload to increase the delivered bandwidth, but Exercise 8.3 suggests the impact on worst-case latency of making it longer. What would be the impact on latency of increasing the maximum payload size by the answer to Exercise 8.2?

✪ 8.5 [10/10] <8.2, 8.14> Figure 8.50 on page 868 compares latencies for a high-bandwidth network with high overhead and a low-bandwidth network with low overhead for different TCP/IP message sizes.

    a. [10] <8.2, 8.14> For what message sizes is the delivered bandwidth higher for the high-bandwidth network?

    b. [10] <8.2, 8.14> For your answer to part (a), what is the delivered bandwidth for each network?

8.6 [15] <8.2, 8.14> Using the statistics in Figure 8.50 on page 868, estimate the per-message overhead for each network.

8.7 [15] <8.2, 8.14> Exercise 8.5 calculates which message sizes are faster for two networks with different overhead and peak bandwidth. Using the statistics in Figure 8.50 on page 868, what is the percentage of messages that are transmitted more quickly on the network with low overhead and bandwidth? What is the percentage of data transmitted more quickly on the network with high overhead and bandwidth?

8.8 [15] <8.2, 8.14> One interesting measure of the latency and bandwidth of an interconnection is to calculate the size of a message needed to achieve one-half of the peak bandwidth. This halfway point is sometimes referred to as $n_{1/2}$, taken from the terminology of vector processing. Using Figure 8.50 on page 868, estimate $n_{1/2}$ for TCP/IP message using 155M bit/sec ATM and 10M bit/sec Ethernet.

✪ 8.9 [15] <8.3> Is electronic communication always fastest for longer distances than the example on page 804? Calculate the time to send 1000 GB using 25 8-mm tapes and an overnight delivery service versus sending 1000 GB by FTP over the Internet. Make the following four assumptions:

    ■ The tapes are picked up at 4 P.M. Pacific time and delivered 4200 km away at 10 A.M. Eastern time (7 A.M. Pacific time).

    ■ On one route the slowest link is a T3 line, which transfers at 45M bits/sec.

    ■ On another route the slowest link is a 100M bit/sec Ethernet.

    ■ You can use 50% of the slowest link between the two sites.

Will all the bytes sent by either Internet route arrive before the overnight delivery person arrives?

8.10 [10] <8.3> For the same assumptions as Exercise 8.9, what is the bandwidth of overnight delivery for a 1000 GB package?

8.11 [10] <8.3> For the same assumptions as Exercise 8.9, what is the minimum bandwidth of the slowest link to beat overnight delivery? What standard network options match that speed?

8.12   [15] <8.4> The original Ethernet standard was for 10M bits/sec and a maximum distance of 2.5 km. How many bytes could be in flight in the original Ethernet? Assume you can use 90% of the peak bandwidth. (*Hint:* See the example on page 812.)

8.13   [15] <8.4> Flow control is a problem for WAN due to long time of flight, as the example on page 812 illustrates. Ethernet did not include flow control when it was first standardized at 10M bits/sec. Calculate the number of bytes in flight for a 10G bit/sec Ethernet over a 100 meter link, assuming you can use 90% of peak bandwidth. What does your answer mean for network designers?

✪ 8.14   [15] <8.4, 8.11> The example on page 811 shows the value of wormhole routing for a custom network. Ethernet switches used to build clusters often do not support wormhole routing. Compare the time to transfer 1500 bytes over a 1000M bit/sec Ethernet with and without wormhole routing for a 64-node cluster. Assume each Ethernet switch takes 1.0 microseconds and that a message goes through seven intermediate switches.

8.15   [15] <8.4, 8.11> Making the same assumptions as in Exercise 8.14, what is the difference between wormhole and store and forward for 32 bytes?

8.16   [15] <8.4> One way to reduce latency is to use larger switches. Unlike Exercise 8.14 above, let's assume we need only three intermediate switches to connect any two nodes in the cluster. Make the same assumptions as in Exercise 8.14 for the remaining parameters. What is the difference between wormhole and store and forward for 1500 bytes? For 32 bytes?

8.17   [15] <8.4> Draw the topology of a 6-cube similar to the drawing of the 4-cube in Figure 8.16 on page 818.

8.18   [12/12/20] <8.5> The Omega network shown in Figure 8.13 on page 815 consists of three columns of four switches, each with two inputs and two outputs. Each switch can be set to *straight,* which connects the upper switch input to the upper switch output and the lower input to the lower output, and to *exchange,* which connects the upper input to the lower output and vice versa for the lower input. For each column of switches, label the inputs and outputs 0, 1, . . . , 7 from top to bottom, to correspond with the numbering of the processors.

   a.   [12] <8.5> When a switch is set to exchange and a message passes through, what is the relationship between the label values for the switch input and output used by the message? (*Hint:* Think in terms of operations on the digits of the binary representation of the label number.)

   b.   [12] <8.5> Between any two switches in adjacent columns that are connected by a link, what is the relationship between the label of the output connected to the input?

   c.   [20] <8.5> Based on your results in parts (a) and (b), design and describe a simple routing scheme for distributed control of the Omega network. A message will carry a *routing tag* computed by the sending processor. Describe how the processor computes the tag and how each switch can set itself by examining a bit of the routing tag.

⭐ 8.19 [12] <8.5> Design a network topology using 18-port crossbar switches that has the minimum number of switches to connect 64 nodes. Each switch port supports communication to and from one device.

8.20 [15] <8.5> Design a network topology that has the minimum latency through the switches for 64 nodes using 18-port crossbar switches. Assume unit delay in the switches and zero delay for wires.

8.21 [15] <8.5> Design a switch topology that balances the bandwidth required for all links for 64 nodes using 18-port crossbar switches. Assume a uniform traffic pattern.

8.22 [15] <8.5> Compare the interconnection latency of a crossbar, Omega network, and fat tree with eight nodes. Use Figure 8.13 on page 815 and add a fat tree similar to Figure 8.14 on page 816 as a third option. Assume that the fat tree is built entirely from two-input, two-output switches so that its hardware is more comparable to that of the Omega network. Assume that each switch costs a unit time delay. Assume the fat tree randomly picks a path, so give the best case and worst case for each example. How long will it take to send a message from node P0 to P6? How long will it take P1 and P7 to also communicate?

8.23 [12/12/12/15/15/18] <8.7> Use the M/M/1 queuing model to answer this exercise. Measurements of a network bridge show that packets arrive at 200 packets per second and that the gateway forwards them in about 2 ms.

a. [12] <8.7> What is the utilization of the gateway?

b. [12] <8.7> What is the mean number of packets in the gateway?

c. [12] <8.7> What is the mean time spent in the gateway?

d. [15] <8.7> Plot the response time versus utilization as you vary the arrival rate.

e. [15] <8.7> For an M/M/1 queue, the probability of finding n or more tasks in the system is Utilization^n. What is the chance of an overflow of the FIFO if it can hold 10 messages?

f. [18] <8.7> How big must the gateway be to have packet loss due to FIFO overflow less than one packet per million?

8.24 [20] <8.7> The imbalance between the time of sending and receiving can cause problems in network performance. Sending too fast can cause the network to back up and increase the latency of messages, since the receivers will not be able to pull out the message fast enough. A technique called *bandwidth matching* proposes a simple solution: Slow down the sender so that it matches the performance of the receiver [Brewer and Kuszmaul 1994]. If two machines exchange an equal number of messages using a protocol like UDP, one will get ahead of the other, causing it to send all its messages first. After the receiver puts all these messages away, it will then send its messages. Estimate the performance for this case versus a bandwidth-matched case. Assume the send overhead is 200 microseconds, the receive overhead is 300 microseconds, time of flight is 5 microseconds, latency is 10 microseconds, and that the two machines want to exchange 100 messages.

8.25   [40] <8.7> Compare the performance of UDP with and without bandwidth matching by slowing down the UDP send code to match the receive code as advised by bandwidth matching [Brewer 1994]. Devise an experiment to see how much performance changes as a result. How should you change the send rate when two nodes send to the same destination? What if one sender sends to two destinations?

8.26   [20/20/20] <8.8> If you have access to a UNIX system, use ping to explore the Internet. First read the manual page. Then use ping without option flags to be sure you can reach the following sites. It should say that X is alive. Depending on your system, you may be able to see the path by setting the flags to verbose mode (-v) and trace route mode (-R) to see the path between your machine and the example machine. Alternatively, you may need to use the program traceroute to see the path. If so, try its manual page. You may want to use the UNIX command script to make a record of your session.

    a.   [20] <8.8> Trace the route to another machine on the same local area network. What is the latency?

    b.   [20] <8.8> Trace the route to another machine on your campus that is *not* on the same local area network. What is the latency?

    c.   [20] <8.8> Trace the route to another machine *off campus*. For example, if you have a friend you send email to, try tracing that route. See if you can discover what types of networks are used along that route. What is the latency?

8.27   [15] <8.8> Use FTP to transfer a file from a remote site and then between local sites on the same LAN. What is the difference in bandwidth for each transfer? Try the transfer at different times of day or days of the week. Is the WAN or LAN the bottleneck?

8.28   [20] <8.10> Figure 8.31 on page 842 shows the mix of types of computers in the top 10 of performance and price-performance for TPC-C. The top 10 of TPC-C has changed since these data were collected. Create your own version of Figure 8.31 using the most recent TPC-C results. How has the mix changed since the data in the original figure? Is there a trend?

8.29   [20] <8.10> This exercise is the same as Exercise 8.28, but this time use Figure 8.32 on page 843 for TPC-H.

8.30   [20] <8.10> Figure 8.30 on page 841 shows the top 500 supercomputers by machine type as of the publication of the third edition. Continue that graph to the most recent results. How has it changed since the data in the original figure? Have the trends continued, or not?

✪ 8.31   [20/15/15] <7.11, 8.11> Section 7.11 showed how to calculate the reliability of a system. This exercise applies those same techniques to the first cluster example of Section 8.11. Use the same assumptions for components as Section 7.11, and assume that the MTTF of a switch is 1,000,000 hours.

    a. [20] <7.11, 8.11> What is the MTTF of the one-way, two-way, and eight-way clusters for the first example in Section 8.11?

    b. [15] <7.11, 8.11> Where are the single points of failure?

    c. [15] <7.11, 8.11> How could the designs be changed to improve MTTF?

8.32 [20/15/15] <7.11, 8.11> Perform the same analysis as in Exercise 8.31, but this time use the second cluster example of Section 8.11. What would have to change in the design of the system to make an FC-AL switch valuable?

8.33 [20/15/15] <7.11, 8.11> Perform the same analysis as in Exercise 8.31, but this time use the fourth cluster example of Section 8.11. Assume the MTTF of a RAID controller is 1,000,000 hours.

8.34 [20/20/15/15/15] <7.11, 8.11> Section 7.11 showed how to estimate cost-performance of I/Os per second (IOPS) for a system. This exercise applies those same techniques to the first cluster example of Section 8.11. Use the same assumptions for components as Section 7.11. The average seek time for both disks is 5 ms, and the data transfer rate is 30 MB/sec for the smaller disk and 45 MB/sec for the larger disk. To simplify the calculations, assume the MIPS rating of the CPU is equal to the clock rate and that the switch is not a bottleneck.

    a. [20] <7.11, 8.11> Assuming you can use 100% of the resources, what is the IOPS performance of the one-way, two-way, and eight-way clusters for the first example in Section 8.11? What is the cost per IOPS?

    b. [20] <7.11, 8.11> This time assume the more realistic limits on resources as in the fourth example in Section 7.11. What is the IOPS performance of the one-way, two-way, and eight-way clusters for the first example in Section 8.11? What is the cost per IOPS?

    c. [15] <7.11, 8.11> Where are the performance bottlenecks?

    d. [15] <7.11, 8.11> How could the designs be changed to improve performance?

    e. [15] <7.11, 8.11> What must be the bandwidth of each switch to avoid a switch becoming a bottleneck?

8.35 [20/20/15/15/15] <8.11> Perform the same analysis as in Exercise 8.34, but this time use the second cluster example of Section 8.11.

8.36 [20/20/15/15/15] <7.11, 8.11> Perform the same analysis as in Exercise 8.34, but this time use the fourth cluster example of Section 8.11. Assume the RAID controller is not a bottleneck.

8.37 [20] <8.11> Find a cluster from Compaq or Dell with results reported in one of the TPC benchmarks. Note that the executive overview lists all the components and their prices at the time of the benchmark. They can serve as good placeholders until or unless you can find the current real prices online. They also supply maintenance costs. Go to the Dell or Compaq Web sites to determine the most recent prices of the varying cluster strategies as we did in the examples. What changes would you make to the first cluster example in Section 8.11? How would the costs change today for that first example?

8.38 [40] <6, 8.11> If you have access to an SMP and a cluster, write a program to measure latency of communication and bandwidth of communication between processors.

8.39 [20] <8.9, 8.12> The Google cluster was constructed from 1 rack unit PCs, each with one processor and two disks. Today there are considerably denser options. How much less floor space would it take if we replace the 1 RU PCs with modern alternatives? Go to the Compaq or Dell Web sites to find the densest alternative. What would be the estimated impact on cost of the equipment? What would be the estimated impact on rental cost of floor space?

8.40 [Discussion] <8.16> At the time of the writing of the third edition it was unclear what would happen with Ethernet versus Infiniband in the machine room. What are the technical advantages of each? What are the economic advantages of each? Why would people maintaining the system prefer one to the other? How popular is each network today?

A

Pipelining: Basic and Intermediate Concepts

It is quite a three-pipe problem.

Sir Arthur Conan Doyle
The Adventures of Sherlock Holmes

A.1   Introduction

Many readers of this text will have covered the basics of pipelining in another text (such as our more basic text *Computer Organization and Design*) or in another course. Because Chapters 3 and 4 build heavily on this material, readers should ensure that they are familiar with the concepts discussed in this appendix before proceeding. As you read Chapter 3, you may find it helpful to turn to this material for a quick review.

We begin the appendix with the basics of pipelining, including discussing the data path implications, introducing hazards, and examining the performance of pipelines. This section describes the basic five-stage RISC pipeline that is the basis for the rest of the appendix. Section A.2 describes the issue of hazards, why they cause performance problems and how they can be dealt with. Section A.3 discusses how the simple five-stage pipeline is actually implemented, focusing on control and how hazards are dealt with.

Section A.4 discusses the interaction between pipelining and various aspects of instruction set design, including discussing the important topic of exceptions and their interaction with pipelining. Readers unfamiliar with the concepts of precise and imprecise interrupts and resumption after exceptions will find this material useful, since they are key to understanding the more advanced approaches in Chapter 3.

Section A.5 discusses how the five-stage pipeline can be extended to handle longer-running floating-point instructions. Section A.6 puts these concepts together in a case study of a deeply pipelined processor, the MIPS R4000/4400, including both the eight-stage integer pipeline and the floating-point pipeline. In contrast, Section A.7 discusses the MIPS R4300 series, a popular embedded processor, which uses the simple five-stage pipeline structure.

Section A.8 introduces the concept of dynamic scheduling and the use of scoreboards to implement dynamic scheduling. It is introduced as a crosscutting issue, since it can be used to serve as an introduction to the core concepts in Chapter 3, which focused on dynamically scheduled approaches. Section A.8 is also a gentle introduction to the more complex Tomasulo's algorithm covered in Chapter 3. Although Tomasulo's algorithm can be covered and understood without introducing scoreboarding, the scoreboarding approach is simpler and easier to comprehend.

The last three sections of this appendix (A.9–A.11) provide fallacies and pitfalls, summarize the key ideas of this appendix, and provide a brief history of the concepts described in this appendix.

What Is Pipelining?

Pipelining is an implementation technique whereby multiple instructions are overlapped in execution; it takes advantage of parallelism that exists among the actions needed to execute an instruction. Today, pipelining is the key implementation technique used to make fast CPUs.

A pipeline is like an assembly line. In an automobile assembly line, there are many steps, each contributing something to the construction of the car. Each step operates in parallel with the other steps, although on a different car. In a computer pipeline, each step in the pipeline completes a part of an instruction. Like the assembly line, different steps are completing different parts of different instructions in parallel. Each of these steps is called a *pipe stage* or a *pipe segment*. The stages are connected one to the next to form a pipe—instructions enter at one end, progress through the stages, and exit at the other end, just as cars would in an assembly line.

In an automobile assembly line, *throughput* is defined as the number of cars per hour and is determined by how often a completed car exits the assembly line. Likewise, the throughput of an instruction pipeline is determined by how often an instruction exits the pipeline. Because the pipe stages are hooked together, all the stages must be ready to proceed at the same time, just as we would require in an assembly line. The time required between moving an instruction one step down the pipeline is a *processor cycle*. Because all stages proceed at the same time, the length of a processor cycle is determined by the time required for the slowest pipe stage, just as in an auto assembly line, the longest step would determine the time between advancing the line. In a computer, this processor cycle is usually 1 clock cycle (sometimes it is 2, rarely more).

The pipeline designer's goal is to balance the length of each pipeline stage, just as the designer of the assembly line tries to balance the time for each step in the process. If the stages are perfectly balanced, then the time per instruction on the pipelined processor—assuming ideal conditions—is equal to

$$\frac{\text{Time per instruction on unpipelined machine}}{\text{Number of pipe stages}}$$

Under these conditions, the speedup from pipelining equals the number of pipe stages, just as an assembly line with n stages can ideally produce cars n times as fast. Usually, however, the stages will not be perfectly balanced; furthermore, pipelining does involve some overhead. Thus, the time per instruction on the pipelined processor will not have its minimum possible value, yet it can be close.

Pipelining yields a reduction in the average execution time per instruction. Depending on what you consider as the baseline, the reduction can be viewed as decreasing the number of clock cycles per instruction (CPI), as decreasing the clock cycle time, or as a combination. If the starting point is a processor that takes multiple clock cycles per instruction, then pipelining is usually viewed as reducing the CPI. This is the primary view we will take. If the starting point is a processor that takes 1 (long) clock cycle per instruction, then pipelining decreases the clock cycle time.

Pipelining is an implementation technique that exploits parallelism among the instructions in a sequential instruction stream. It has the substantial advantage that, unlike some speedup techniques (see Chapter 6), it is not visible to the programmer. In this appendix we will first cover the concept of pipelining using a classic five-stage pipeline; other chapters investigate the more sophisticated pipelining techniques in use in modern processors. Before we say more about pipelining and its use in a processor, we need a simple instruction set, which we introduce next.

The Basics of a RISC Instruction Set

Throughout this book we use a RISC (reduced instruction set computer) architecture or load-store architecture to illustrate the basic concepts, although nearly all the ideas we introduce in this book are applicable to other processors. In this section we introduce the core of a typical RISC architecture. In this appendix, and throughout the book, our default RISC architecture is MIPS. In many places, the concepts are significantly similar that we will not need to distinguish the exact architecture. RISC architectures are characterized by a few key properties, which dramatically simplify their implementation:

- All operations on data apply to data in registers and typically change the entire register (32 or 64 bits per register).

- The only operations that affect memory are load and store operations that move data from memory to a register or to memory from a register, respectively. Load and store operations that load or store less than a full register (e.g., a byte, 16 bits, or 32 bits) are often available.

- The instruction formats are few in number with all instructions typically being one size.

These simple properties lead to dramatic simplifications in the implementation of pipelining, which is why these instruction sets were designed this way.

For consistency with the rest of the text, we use MIPS64, the 64-bit version of the MIPS instruction set. The extended 64-bit instructions are generally designated by having a D on the start or end of the mnemonic. For example DADD is the 64-bit version of an add instruction, while LD is the 64-bit version of a load instruction.

Like other RISC architectures, the MIPS instruction set provides 32 registers, although register 0 always has the value 0. Most RISC architectures, like MIPS, have three classes of instructions (see Chapter 2 for more detail):

1. *ALU instructions*—These instructions take either two registers or a register and a sign-extended immediate (called ALU immediate instructions, they have a 16-bit offset in MIPS), operate on them, and store the result into a third register. Typical operations include add (DADD), subtract (DSUB), and logical operations (such as AND or OR), which do not differentiate between 32-bit and 64-bit versions. Immediate versions of these instructions use the same mnemonics with a suffix of I. In MIPS, there are both signed and unsigned forms of the arithmetic instructions; the unsigned forms, which do not generate overflow exceptions—and thus are the same in 32-bit and 64-bit mode—have a U at the end (e.g., DADDU, DSUBU, DADDUI).

2. *Load and store instructions*—These instructions take a register source, called the *base register,* and an immediate field (16-bit in MIPS), called the *offset,* as operands. The sum—called the *effective address*—of the contents of the base register and the sign-extended offset is used as a memory address. In the case of a load instruction, a second register operand acts as the destination for the data loaded from memory. In the case of a store, the second register operand is the source of the data that is stored into memory. The instructions load word (LD) and store word (SD) load or store the entire 64-bit register contents.

3. *Branches and jumps*—Branches are conditional transfers of control. There are usually two ways of specifying the branch condition in RISC architectures: with a set of condition bits (sometimes called a condition code) or by a limited set of comparisons between a pair of registers or between a register and zero. MIPS uses the latter. For this appendix, we consider only comparisons for equality between two registers. In all RISC architectures, the branch destination is obtained by adding a sign-extended offset (16 bits in MIPS) to the current PC. Unconditional jumps are provided in many RISC architectures, but we will not cover jumps in this appendix.

A Simple Implementation of a RISC Instruction Set

To understand how a RISC instruction set can be implemented in a pipelined fashion, we need to understand how it is implemented *without* pipelining. This section shows a simple implementation where every instruction takes at most 5 clock cycles. We will extend this basic implementation to a pipelined version, resulting in a much lower CPI. Our unpipelined implementation is not the most economical or the highest-performance implementation without pipelining. Instead, it is designed to lead naturally to a pipelined implementation. Implementing the instruction set requires the introduction of several temporary registers that are not part of the architecture; these are introduced in this section to simplify pipelining. Our implementation will focus only on a pipeline for an integer subset of a RISC architecture that consists of load-store word, branch, and integer ALU operations.

Every instruction in this RISC subset can be implemented in at most 5 clock cycles. The 5 clock cycles are as follows.

1. *Instruction fetch cycle* (IF):

Send the program counter (PC) to memory and fetch the current instruction from memory. Update the PC to the next sequential PC by adding 4 (since each instruction is 4 bytes) to the PC.

2. *Instruction decode/register fetch cycle* (ID):

Decode the instruction and read the registers corresponding to register source specifiers from the register file. Do the equality test on the registers as they are read, for a possible branch. Sign-extend the offset field of the instruction in case it is needed. Compute the possible branch target address by adding the sign-extended offset to the incremented PC. In an aggressive implementation, which we assume, the branch can be completed at the end of this stage, by storing the branch-target address into the PC, if the condition test yielded true.

Decoding is done in parallel with reading registers, which is possible because the register specifiers are at a fixed location in a RISC architecture. This technique is known as *fixed-field decoding*. Note that we may read a register we don't use, which doesn't help but also doesn't hurt performance. (It does waste energy to read an unneeded register, and power-sensitive designs might avoid this.) Because the immediate portion of an instruction is also located in an identical place, the sign-extended immediate is also calculated during this cycle in case it is needed.

3. *Execution/effective address cycle* (EX):

The ALU operates on the operands prepared in the prior cycle, performing one of three functions depending on the instruction type.

- Memory reference: The ALU adds the base register and the offset to form the effective address.

- Register-Register ALU instruction: The ALU performs the operation specified by the ALU opcode on the values read from the register file.

- Register-Immediate ALU instruction: The ALU performs the operation specified by the ALU opcode on the first value read from the register file and the sign-extended immediate.

In a load-store architecture the effective address and execution cycles can be combined into a single clock cycle, since no instruction needs to simultaneously calculate a data address and perform an operation on the data.

4. *Memory access* (MEM):

If the instruction is a load, memory does a read using the effective address computed in the previous cycle. If it is a store, then the memory writes the data from the second register read from the register file using the effective address.

5. *Write-back cycle* (WB):

- Register-Register ALU instruction or Load instruction:

Write the result into the register file, whether it comes from the memory system (for a load) or from the ALU (for an ALU instruction).

In this implementation, branch instructions require 2 cycles, store instructions require 4 cycles, and all other instructions require 5 cycles. Assuming a branch frequency of 12% and a store frequency of 10%, a typical instruction distribution leads to an overall CPI of 4.54. This implementation, however, is not optimal either in achieving the best performance or in using the minimal amount of hardware given the performance level; we leave the improvement of this design as an exercise for you and instead focus on pipelining this version.

The Classic Five-Stage Pipeline for a RISC Processor

We can pipeline the execution described above with almost no changes by simply starting a new instruction on each clock cycle. (See why we chose this design!) Each of the clock cycles from the previous section becomes a *pipe stage*—a cycle in the pipeline. This results in the execution pattern shown in Figure A.1, which is the typical way a pipeline structure is drawn. Although each instruction takes 5 clock cycles to complete, during each clock cycle the hardware will initiate a new instruction and will be executing some part of the five different instructions.

You may find it hard to believe that pipelining is as simple as this; it's not. In this and the following sections, we will make our RISC pipeline "real" by dealing with problems that pipelining introduces.

To start with, we have to determine what happens on every clock cycle of the processor and make sure we don't try to perform two different operations with the same data path resource on the same clock cycle. For example, a single ALU cannot be asked to compute an effective address and perform a subtract operation at the same time. Thus, we must ensure that the overlap of instructions in the pipeline cannot cause such a conflict. Fortunately, the simplicity of a RISC instruction set makes resource evaluation relatively easy. Figure A.2 shows a simplified version of a RISC data path drawn in pipeline fashion. As you can see, the major functional units are used in different cycles, and hence overlapping the execution of multiple instructions introduces relatively few conflicts. There are three observations on which this fact rests.

First, we use separate instruction and data memories, which we would typically implement with separate instruction and data caches (discussed in Chapter 5). The use of separate caches eliminates a conflict for a single memory that would arise between instruction fetch and data memory access. Notice that if our pipelined processor has a clock cycle that is equal to that of the unpipelined version, the memory system must deliver five times the bandwidth. This increased demand is one cost of higher performance.

	Clock number								
Instruction number	1	2	3	4	5	6	7	8	9
Instruction i	IF	ID	EX	MEM	WB				
Instruction $i + 1$		IF	ID	EX	MEM	WB			
Instruction $i + 2$			IF	ID	EX	MEM	WB		
Instruction $i + 3$				IF	ID	EX	MEM	WB	
Instruction $i + 4$					IF	ID	EX	MEM	WB

Figure A.1 Simple RISC pipeline. On each clock cycle, another instruction is fetched and begins its 5-cycle execution. If an instruction is started every clock cycle, the performance will be up to five times that of a processor that is not pipelined. The names for the stages in the pipeline are the same as those used for the cycles in the unpipelined implementation: IF = instruction fetch, ID = instruction decode, EX = execution, MEM = memory access, and WB = write back.

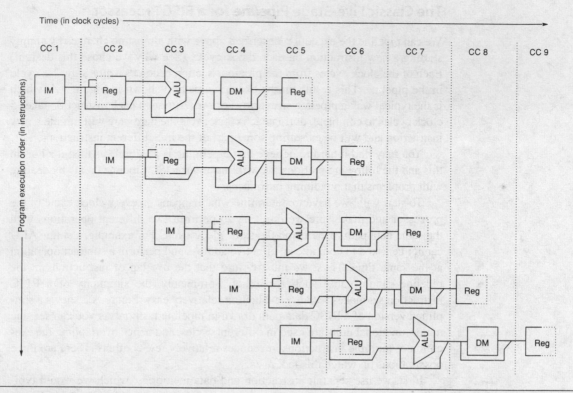

Figure A.2 The pipeline can be thought of as a series of data paths shifted in time. This shows the overlap among the parts of the data path, with clock cycle 5 (CC 5) showing the steady-state situation. Because the register file is used as a source in the ID stage and as a destination in the WB stage, it appears twice. We show that it is read in one part of the stage and written in another by using a solid line, on the right or left, respectively, and a dashed line on the other side. The abbreviation IM is used for instruction memory, DM for data memory, and CC for clock cycle.

Second, the register file is used in the two stages: one for reading in ID and one for writing in WB. These uses are distinct, so we simply show the register file in two places. Hence, we need to perform two reads and one write every clock cycle. To handle reads and a write to the same register (and for another reason, which will become obvious shortly), we perform the register write in the first half of the clock cycle and the read in the second half.

Third, Figure A.2 does not deal with the PC. To start a new instruction every clock, we must increment and store the PC every clock, and this must be done during the IF stage in preparation for the next instruction. Furthermore, we must also have an adder to compute the potential branch target during ID. One further problem is that a branch does not change the PC until the ID stage. This causes a problem, which we ignore for now, but will handle shortly.

Although it is critical to ensure that instructions in the pipeline do not attempt to use the hardware resources at the same time, we must also ensure that instructions in different stages of the pipeline do not interfere with one another. This separation is done by introducing *pipeline registers* between successive stages of the pipeline, so that at the end of a clock cycle all the results from a given stage are stored into a register that is used as the input to the next stage on the next clock cycle. Figure A.3 shows the pipeline drawn with these pipeline registers.

Although many figures will omit such registers for simplicity, they are required to make the pipeline operate properly and must be present. Of course, similar registers would be needed even in a multicycle data path that had no pipelining (since only values in registers are preserved across clock boundaries). In the case of a pipelined processor, the pipeline registers also play the key role of carrying intermediate results from one stage to another where the source and destination may be directly adjacent. For example, the register value to be stored during a store instruction is read during RF, but not actually used until MEM; it is

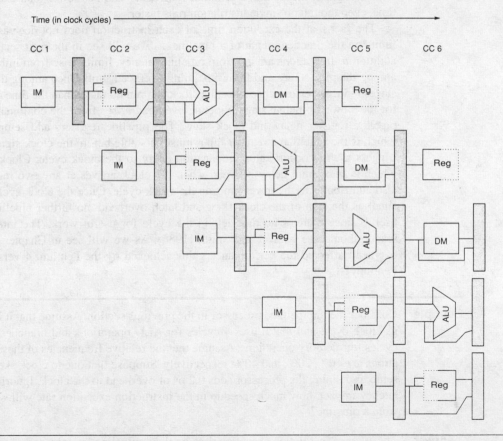

Figure A.3 A pipeline showing the pipeline registers between successive pipeline stages. Notice that the registers prevent interference between two different instructions in adjacent stages in the pipeline. The registers also play the critical role of carrying data for a given instruction from one stage to the other. The edge-triggered property of registers—that is, that the values change instantaneously on a clock edge—is critical. Otherwise, the data from one instruction could interfere with the execution of another!

passed through two pipeline registers to reach the data memory during the MEM stage. Likewise, the result of an ALU instruction is computed during EX, but not actually stored until WB; it arrives there by passing through two pipeline registers. It is sometimes useful to name the pipeline registers, and we follow the convention of naming them by the pipeline stages they connect, so that the registers are called ID/IF, IF/RF, RF/EX, EX/MEM, MEM/WB.

Basic Performance Issues in Pipelining

Pipelining increases the CPU instruction throughput—the number of instructions completed per unit of time—but it does not reduce the execution time of an individual instruction. In fact, it usually slightly increases the execution time of each instruction due to overhead in the control of the pipeline. The increase in instruction throughput means that a program runs faster and has lower total execution time, even though no single instruction runs faster!

The fact that the execution time of each instruction does not decrease puts limits on the practical depth of a pipeline, as we will see in the next section. In addition to limitations arising from pipeline latency, limits arise from imbalance among the pipe stages and from pipelining overhead. Imbalance among the pipe stages reduces performance since the clock can run no faster than the time needed for the slowest pipeline stage. Pipeline overhead arises from the combination of pipeline register delay and clock skew. The pipeline registers add setup time, which is the time that a register input must be stable before the clock signal that triggers a write occurs, plus propagation delay to the clock cycle. Clock skew, which is maximum delay between when the clock arrives at any two registers, also contributes to the lower limit on the clock cycle. Once the clock cycle is as small as the sum of the clock skew and latch overhead, no further pipelining is useful, since there is no time left in the cycle for useful work. The interested reader should see Kunkel and Smith [1986]. As we will see in Chapter 3, this overhead affected the performance gains achieved by the Pentium 4 versus the Pentium III.

Example Consider the unpipelined processor in the previous section. Assume that it has a 1 ns clock cycle and that it uses 4 cycles for ALU operations and branches and 5 cycles for memory operations. Assume that the relative frequencies of these operations are 40%, 20%, and 40%, respectively. Suppose that due to clock skew and setup, pipelining the processor adds 0.2 ns of overhead to the clock. Ignoring any latency impact, how much speedup in the instruction execution rate will we gain from a pipeline?

Answer The average instruction execution time on the unpipelined processor is

$$\text{Average instruction execution time} = \text{Clock cycle} \times \text{Average CPI}$$
$$= 1 \text{ ns} \times ((40\% + 20\%) \times 4 + 40\% \times 5)$$
$$= 1 \text{ ns} \times 4.4$$
$$= 4.4 \text{ ns}$$

In the pipelined implementation, the clock must run at the speed of the slowest stage plus overhead, which will be $1 + 0.2$ or 1.2 ns; this is the average instruction execution time. Thus, the speedup from pipelining is

$$\text{Speedup from pipelining} = \frac{\text{Average instruction time unpipelined}}{\text{Average instruction time pipelined}}$$

$$= \frac{4.4 \text{ ns}}{1.2 \text{ ns}} = 3.7 \text{ times}$$

The 0.2 ns overhead essentially establishes a limit on the effectiveness of pipelining. If the overhead is not affected by changes in the clock cycle, Amdahl's Law tells us that the overhead limits the speedup.

This simple RISC pipeline would function just fine for integer instructions if every instruction were independent of every other instruction in the pipeline. In reality, instructions in the pipeline can depend on one another; this is the topic of the next section.

A.2   The Major Hurdle of Pipelining—Pipeline Hazards

There are situations, called *hazards,* that prevent the next instruction in the instruction stream from executing during its designated clock cycle. Hazards reduce the performance from the ideal speedup gained by pipelining. There are three classes of hazards:

1. *Structural hazards* arise from resource conflicts when the hardware cannot support all possible combinations of instructions simultaneously in overlapped execution.

2. *Data hazards* arise when an instruction depends on the results of a previous instruction in a way that is exposed by the overlapping of instructions in the pipeline.

3. *Control hazards* arise from the pipelining of branches and other instructions that change the PC.

Hazards in pipelines can make it necessary to *stall* the pipeline. Avoiding a hazard often requires that some instructions in the pipeline be allowed to proceed while others are delayed. For the pipelines we discuss in this appendix, when an instruction is stalled, all instructions issued *later* than the stalled instruction—and hence not as far along in the pipeline—are also stalled. Instructions issued *earlier* than the stalled instruction—and hence farther along in the pipeline—must continue, since otherwise the hazard will never clear. As a result, no new instructions are fetched during the stall. We will see several examples of how pipeline stalls operate in this section—don't worry, they aren't as complex as they might sound!

Performance of Pipelines with Stalls

A stall causes the pipeline performance to degrade from the ideal performance. Let's look at a simple equation for finding the actual speedup from pipelining, starting with the formula from the previous section.

$$\text{Speedup from pipelining} = \frac{\text{Average instruction time unpipelined}}{\text{Average instruction time pipelined}}$$

$$= \frac{\text{CPI unpipelined} \times \text{Clock cycle unpipelined}}{\text{CPI pipelined} \times \text{Clock cycle pipelined}}$$

$$= \frac{\text{CPI unpipelined}}{\text{CPI pipelined}} \times \frac{\text{Clock cycle unpipelined}}{\text{Clock cycle pipelined}}$$

Pipelining can be thought of as decreasing the CPI or the clock cycle time. Since it is traditional to use the CPI to compare pipelines, let's start with that assumption. The ideal CPI on a pipelined processor is almost always 1. Hence, we can compute the pipelined CPI:

$$\text{CPI pipelined} = \text{Ideal CPI} + \text{Pipeline stall clock cycles per instruction}$$

$$= 1 + \text{Pipeline stall clock cycles per instruction}$$

If we ignore the cycle time overhead of pipelining and assume the stages are perfectly balanced, then the cycle time of the two processors can be equal, leading to

$$\text{Speedup} = \frac{\text{CPI unpipelined}}{1 + \text{Pipeline stall cycles per instruction}}$$

One important simple case is where all instructions take the same number of cycles, which must also equal the number of pipeline stages (also called the *depth of the pipeline*). In this case, the unpipelined CPI is equal to the depth of the pipeline, leading to

$$\text{Speedup} = \frac{\text{Pipeline depth}}{1 + \text{Pipeline stall cycles per instruction}}$$

If there are no pipeline stalls, this leads to the intuitive result that pipelining can improve performance by the depth of the pipeline.

Alternatively, if we think of pipelining as improving the clock cycle time, then we can assume that the CPI of the unpipelined processor, as well as that of the pipelined processor, is 1. This leads to

$$\text{Speedup from pipelining} = \frac{\text{CPI unpipelined}}{\text{CPI pipelined}} \times \frac{\text{Clock cycle unpipelined}}{\text{Clock cycle pipelined}}$$

$$= \frac{1}{1 + \text{Pipeline stall cycles per instruction}} \times \frac{\text{Clock cycle unpipelined}}{\text{Clock cycle pipelined}}$$

In cases where the pipe stages are perfectly balanced and there is no overhead, the clock cycle on the pipelined processor is smaller than the clock cycle of the unpipelined processor by a factor equal to the pipelined depth:

$$\text{Clock cycle pipelined} = \frac{\text{Clock cycle unpipelined}}{\text{Pipeline depth}}$$

$$\text{Pipeline depth} = \frac{\text{Clock cycle unpipelined}}{\text{Clock cycle pipelined}}$$

This leads to the following:

$$\text{Speedup from pipelining} = \frac{1}{1 + \text{Pipeline stall cycles per instruction}} \times \frac{\text{Clock cycle unpipelined}}{\text{Clock cycle pipelined}}$$

$$= \frac{1}{1 + \text{Pipeline stall cycles per instruction}} \times \text{Pipeline depth}$$

Thus, if there are no stalls, the speedup is equal to the number of pipeline stages, matching our intuition for the ideal case.

Structural Hazards

When a processor is pipelined, the overlapped execution of instructions requires pipelining of functional units and duplication of resources to allow all possible combinations of instructions in the pipeline. If some combination of instructions cannot be accommodated because of resource conflicts, the processor is said to have a *structural hazard*.

The most common instances of structural hazards arise when some functional unit is not fully pipelined. Then a sequence of instructions using that unpipelined unit cannot proceed at the rate of one per clock cycle. Another common way that structural hazards appear is when some resource has not been duplicated enough to allow all combinations of instructions in the pipeline to execute. For example, a processor may have only one register-file write port, but under certain circumstances, the pipeline might want to perform two writes in a clock cycle. This will generate a structural hazard.

When a sequence of instructions encounters this hazard, the pipeline will stall one of the instructions until the required unit is available. Such stalls will increase the CPI from its usual ideal value of 1.

Some pipelined processors have shared a single-memory pipeline for data and instructions. As a result, when an instruction contains a data memory reference, it will conflict with the instruction reference for a later instruction, as shown in Figure A.4. To resolve this hazard, we stall the pipeline for 1 clock cycle when the data memory access occurs. A stall is commonly called a *pipeline bubble* or just *bubble,* since it floats through the pipeline taking space but carrying no useful work. We will see another type of stall when we talk about data hazards.

Designers often indicate stall behavior using a simple diagram with only the pipe stage names, as in Figure A.5. The form of Figure A.5 shows the stall by indicating the cycle when no action occurs and simply shifting instruction 3 to the right (which delays its execution start and finish by 1 cycle). The effect of the

Time (in clock cycles)

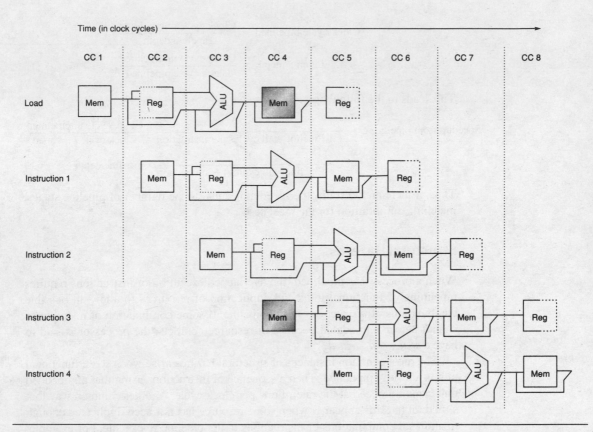

Figure A.4 A processor with only one memory port will generate a conflict whenever a memory reference occurs. In this example the load instruction uses the memory for a data access at the same time instruction 3 wants to fetch an instruction from memory.

pipeline bubble is actually to occupy the resources for that instruction slot as it travels through the pipeline.

Example   Let's see how much the load structural hazard might cost. Suppose that data references constitute 40% of the mix, and that the ideal CPI of the pipelined processor, ignoring the structural hazard, is 1. Assume that the processor with the structural hazard has a clock rate that is 1.05 times higher than the clock rate of the processor without the hazard. Disregarding any other performance losses, is the pipeline with or without the structural hazard faster, and by how much?

Answer   There are several ways we could solve this problem. Perhaps the simplest is to compute the average instruction time on the two processors:

$$\text{Average instruction time} = \text{CPI} \times \text{Clock cycle time}$$

Instruction	Clock cycle number									
	1	2	3	4	5	6	7	8	9	10
Load instruction	IF	ID	EX	MEM	WB					
Instruction $i + 1$		IF	ID	EX	MEM	WB				
Instruction $i + 2$			IF	ID	EX	MEM	WB			
Instruction $i + 3$				stall	IF	ID	EX	MEM	WB	
Instruction $i + 4$						IF	ID	EX	MEM	WB
Instruction $i + 5$							IF	ID	EX	MEM
Instruction $i + 6$								IF	ID	EX

Figure A.5   A pipeline stalled for a structural hazard—a load with one memory port. As shown here, the load instruction effectively steals an instruction-fetch cycle, causing the pipeline to stall—no instruction is initiated on clock cycle 4 (which normally would initiate instruction $i + 3$). Because the instruction being fetched is stalled, all other instructions in the pipeline before the stalled instruction can proceed normally. The stall cycle will continue to pass through the pipeline, so that no instruction completes on clock cycle 8. Sometimes these pipeline diagrams are drawn with the stall occupying an entire horizontal row and instruction 3 being moved to the next row; in either case, the effect is the same, since instruction $i + 3$ does not begin execution until cycle 5. We use the form above, since it takes less space in the figure.

Since it has no stalls, the average instruction time for the ideal processor is simply the Clock cycle time$_{ideal}$. The average instruction time for the processor with the structural hazard is

$$
\begin{aligned}
\text{Average instruction time} &= \text{CPI} \times \text{Clock cycle time} \\
&= (1 + 0.4 \times 1) \times \frac{\text{Clock cycle time}_{ideal}}{1.05} \\
&= 1.3 \times \text{Clock cycle time}_{ideal}
\end{aligned}
$$

Clearly, the processor without the structural hazard is faster; we can use the ratio of the average instruction times to conclude that the processor without the hazard is 1.3 times faster.

As an alternative to this structural hazard, the designer could provide a separate memory access for instructions, either by splitting the cache into separate instruction and data caches, or by using a set of buffers, usually called *instruction buffers*, to hold instructions. Chapter 5 discusses both the split cache and instruction buffer ideas.

If all other factors are equal, a processor without structural hazards will always have a lower CPI. Why, then, would a designer allow structural hazards? The primary reason is to reduce cost of the unit, since pipelining all the functional units, or duplicating them, may be too costly. For example, processors that support both an instruction and a data cache access every cycle (to prevent the structural hazard of the above example) require twice as much total memory bandwidth and often have higher bandwidth at the pins. Likewise, fully pipelining a floating-point multiplier consumes lots of gates. If the structural hazard is rare, it may not be worth the cost to avoid it.

Data Hazards

A major effect of pipelining is to change the relative timing of instructions by overlapping their execution. This overlap introduces data and control hazards. Data hazards occur when the pipeline changes the order of read/write accesses to operands so that the order differs from the order seen by sequentially executing instructions on an unpipelined processor. Consider the pipelined execution of these instructions:

```
DADD    R1,R2,R3
DSUB    R4,R1,R5
AND     R6,R1,R7
OR      R8,R1,R9
XOR     R10,R11,R11
```

All the instructions after the DADD use the result of the DADD instruction. As shown in Figure A.6, the ADD instruction writes the value of R1 in the WB pipe stage, but the DSUB instruction reads the value during its ID stage. This problem is called a *data hazard*. Unless precautions are taken to prevent it, the SUB instruction will read the wrong value and try to use it. In fact, the value used by the DSUB instruction is not even deterministic: Though we might think it logical to assume that SUB would always use the value of R1 that was assigned by an instruction prior to ADD, this is not always the case. If an interrupt should occur between the DADD and DSUB instructions, the WB stage of the DADD will complete, and the value of R1 at that point will be the result of the DADD. This unpredictable behavior is obviously unacceptable.

The AND instruction is also affected by this hazard. As we can see from Figure A.6, the write of R1 does not complete until the end of clock cycle 5. Thus, the AND instruction that reads the registers during clock cycle 4 will receive the wrong results.

The XOR instruction operates properly because its register read occurs in clock cycle 6, after the register write. The OR instruction also operates without incurring a hazard because we perform the register file reads in the second half of the cycle and the writes in the first half.

The next subsection discusses a technique to eliminate the stalls for the hazard involving the SUB and AND instructions.

Minimizing Data Hazard Stalls by Forwarding

The problem posed in Figure A.6 can be solved with a simple hardware technique called *forwarding* (also called *bypassing* and sometimes *short-circuiting*). The

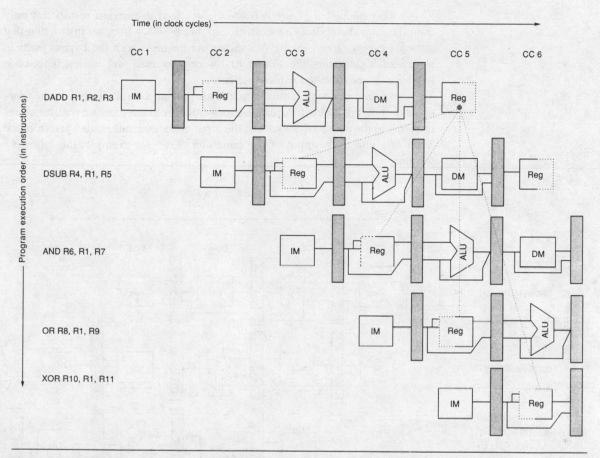

Figure A.6 The use of the result of the DADD instruction in the next three instructions causes a hazard, since the register is not written until after those instructions read it.

key insight in forwarding is that the result is not really needed by the DSUB until after the DADD actually produces it. If the result can be moved from the pipeline register where the DADD stores it to where the DSUB needs it, then the need for a stall can be avoided. Using this observation, forwarding works as follows:

1. The ALU result from both the EX/MEM and MEM/WB pipeline registers is always fed back to the ALU inputs.

2. If the forwarding hardware detects that the previous ALU operation has written the register corresponding to a source for the current ALU operation, control logic selects the forwarded result as the ALU input rather than the value read from the register file.

Notice that with forwarding, if the DSUB is stalled, the DADD will be completed and the bypass will not be activated. This relationship is also true for the case of an interrupt between the two instructions.

As the example in Figure A.6 shows, we need to forward results not only from the immediately previous instruction, but possibly from an instruction that started 2 cycles earlier. Figure A.7 shows our example with the bypass paths in place and highlighting the timing of the register read and writes. This code sequence can be executed without stalls.

Forwarding can be generalized to include passing a result directly to the functional unit that requires it: A result is forwarded from the pipeline register corresponding to the output of one unit to the input of another, rather than just from the result of a unit to the input of the same unit. Take, for example, the following sequence:

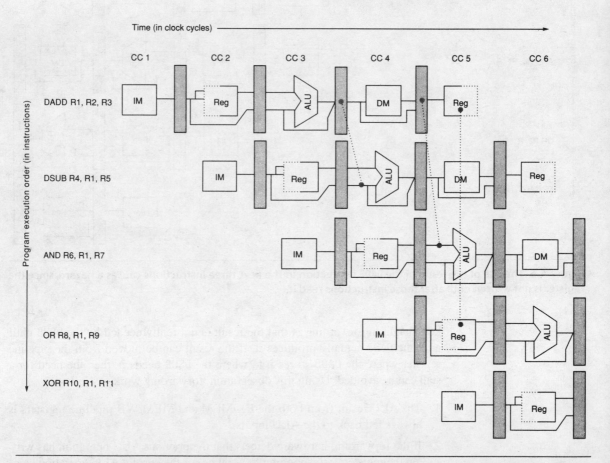

Figure A.7 A set of instructions that depends on the DADD result uses forwarding paths to avoid the data hazard. The inputs for the DSUB and AND instructions forward from the pipeline registers to the first ALU input. The OR receives its result by forwarding through the register file, which is easily accomplished by reading the registers in the second half of the cycle and writing in the first half, as the dashed lines on the registers indicate. Notice that the forwarded result can go to either ALU input; in fact, both ALU inputs could use forwarded inputs from either the same pipeline register or from different pipeline registers. This would occur, for example, if the AND instruction was AND R6, R1, R4.

```
DADD    R1,R2,R3
LD      R4,0(R1)
SD      R4,12(R1)
```

To prevent a stall in this sequence, we would need to forward the values of the ALU output and memory unit output from the pipeline registers to the ALU and data memory inputs. Figure A.8 shows all the forwarding paths for this example.

Data Hazards Requiring Stalls

Unfortunately, not all potential data hazards can be handled by bypassing. Consider the following sequence of instructions:

```
LD      R1,0(R2)
DSUB    R4,R1,R5
AND     R6,R1,R7
OR      R8,R1,R9
```

The pipelined data path with the bypass paths for this example is shown in Figure A.9. This case is different from the situation with back-to-back ALU

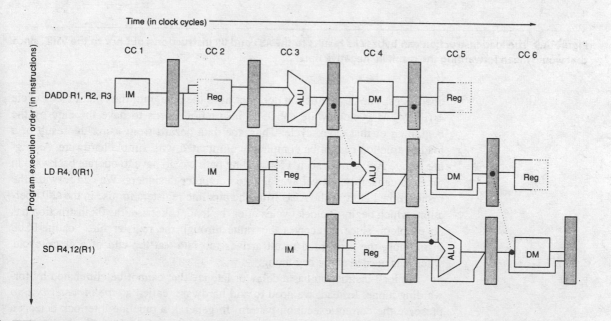

Figure A.8   Forwarding of operand required by stores during MEM. The result of the load is forwarded from the memory output to the memory input to be stored. In addition, the ALU output is forwarded to the ALU input for the address calculation of both the load and the store (this is no different than forwarding to another ALU operation). If the store depended on an immediately preceding ALU operation (not shown above), the result would need to be forwarded to prevent a stall.

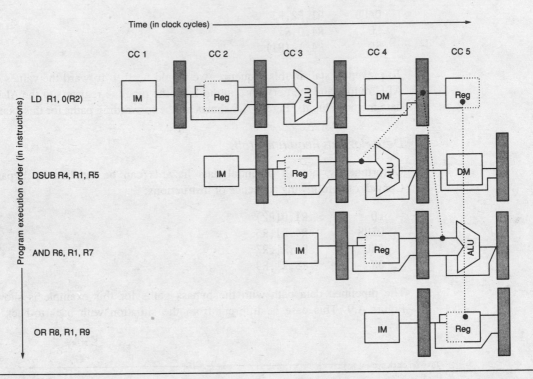

Figure A.9 The load instruction can bypass its results to the AND and OR instructions, but not to the DSUB, since that would mean forwarding the result in "negative time."

operations. The LD instruction does not have the data until the end of clock cycle 4 (its MEM cycle), while the DSUB instruction needs to have the data by the beginning of that clock cycle. Thus, the data hazard from using the result of a load instruction cannot be completely eliminated with simple hardware. As Figure Figure A.9 shows, such a forwarding path would have to operate backward in time—a capability not yet available to computer designers! We *can* forward the result immediately to the ALU from the pipeline registers for use in the AND operation, which begins 2 clock cycles after the load. Likewise, the OR instruction has no problem, since it receives the value through the register file. For the DSUB instruction, the forwarded result arrives too late—at the end of a clock cycle, when it is needed at the beginning.

The load instruction has a delay or latency that cannot be eliminated by forwarding alone. Instead, we need to add hardware, called a *pipeline interlock,* to preserve the correct execution pattern. In general, a pipeline interlock detects a hazard and stalls the pipeline until the hazard is cleared. In this case, the interlock stalls the pipeline, beginning with the instruction that wants to use the data until the source instruction produces it. This pipeline interlock introduces a stall or bubble, just as it did for the structural hazard. The CPI for the stalled instruction increases by the length of the stall (1 clock cycle in this case).

LD R1,0(R2)	IF	ID	EX	MEM	WB				
DSUB R4,R1,R5		IF	ID	EX	MEM	WB			
AND R6,R1,R7			IF	ID	EX	MEM	WB		
OR R8,R1,R9				IF	ID	EX	MEM	WB	

LD R1,0(R2)	IF	ID	EX	MEM	WB				
DSUB R4,R1,R5		IF	ID	stall	EX	MEM	WB		
AND R6,R1,R7			IF	stall	ID	EX	MEM	WB	
OR R8,R1,R9				stall	IF	ID	EX	MEM	WB

Figure A.10 In the top half, we can see why a stall is needed: The MEM cycle of the load produces a value that is needed in the EX cycle of the DSUB, which occurs at the same time. This problem is solved by inserting a stall, as shown in the bottom half.

Figure A.10 shows the pipeline before and after the stall using the names of the pipeline stages. Because the stall causes the instructions starting with the DSUB to move 1 cycle later in time, the forwarding to the AND instruction now goes through the register file, and no forwarding at all is needed for the OR instruction. The insertion of the bubble causes the number of cycles to complete this sequence to grow by one. No instruction is started during clock cycle 4 (and none finishes during cycle 6).

Branch Hazards

Control hazards can cause a greater performance loss for our MIPS pipeline than do data hazards. When a branch is executed, it may or may not change the PC to something other than its current value plus 4. Recall that if a branch changes the PC to its target address, it is a *taken* branch; if it falls through, it is *not taken,* or *untaken.* If instruction *i* is a taken branch, then the PC is normally not changed until the end of ID, after the completion of the address calculation and comparison.

Figure A.11 shows that the simplest method of dealing with branches is to redo the fetch of the instruction following a branch, once we detect the branch during ID (when instructions are decoded). The first IF cycle is essentially a stall,

Branch instruction	IF	ID	EX	MEM	WB		
Branch successor		IF	IF	ID	EX	MEM	WB
Branch successor + 1				IF	ID	EX	MEM
Branch successor + 2					IF	ID	EX

Figure A.11 A branch causes a 1-cycle stall in the five-stage pipeline. The instruction after the branch is fetched, but the instruction is ignored, and the fetch is restarted once the branch target is known. It is probably obvious that if the branch is not taken, the second IF for branch successor is redundant. This will be addressed shortly.

because it never performs useful work. You may have noticed that if the branch is untaken, then the repetition of the IF stage is unnecessary since the correct instruction was indeed fetched. We will develop several schemes to take advantage of this fact shortly.

One stall cycle for every branch will yield a performance loss of 10% to 30% depending on the branch frequency, so we will examine some techniques to deal with this loss.

Reducing Pipeline Branch Penalties

There are many methods for dealing with the pipeline stalls caused by branch delay; we discuss four simple compile time schemes in this subsection. In these four schemes the actions for a branch are static—they are fixed for each branch during the entire execution. The software can try to minimize the branch penalty using knowledge of the hardware scheme and of branch behavior. Chapters 3 and 4 look at more powerful hardware and software techniques for both static and dynamic branch prediction.

The simplest scheme to handle branches is to *freeze* or *flush* the pipeline, holding or deleting any instructions after the branch until the branch destination is known. The attractiveness of this solution lies primarily in its simplicity both for hardware and software. It is the solution used earlier in the pipeline shown in Figure A.11. In this case the branch penalty is fixed and cannot be reduced by software.

A higher-performance, and only slightly more complex, scheme is to treat every branch as not taken, simply allowing the hardware to continue as if the branch were not executed. Here, care must be taken not to change the processor state until the branch outcome is definitely known. The complexity of this scheme arises from having to know when the state might be changed by an instruction and how to "back out" such a change.

In the simple five-stage pipeline, this *predicted-not-taken* or *predicted-untaken* scheme is implemented by continuing to fetch instructions as if the branch were a normal instruction. The pipeline looks as if nothing out of the ordinary is happening. If the branch is taken, however, we need to turn the fetched instruction into a no-op and restart the fetch at the target address. Figure A.12 shows both situations.

An alternative scheme is to treat every branch as taken. As soon as the branch is decoded and the target address is computed, we assume the branch to be taken and begin fetching and executing at the target. Because in our five-stage pipeline we don't know the target address any earlier than we know the branch outcome, there is no advantage in this approach for this pipeline. In some processors—especially those with implicitly set condition codes or more powerful (and hence slower) branch conditions—the branch target is known before the branch outcome, and a predicted-taken scheme might make sense. In either a predicted-taken or predicted-not-taken scheme, the compiler can improve performance by organizing the code so that the most frequent path matches the hardware's choice. Our fourth scheme provides more opportunities for the compiler to improve performance.

Untaken branch instruction	IF	ID	EX	MEM	WB			
Instruction $i + 1$		IF	ID	EX	MEM	WB		
Instruction $i + 2$			IF	ID	EX	MEM	WB	
Instruction $i + 3$				IF	ID	EX	MEM	WB
Instruction $i + 4$					IF	ID	EX	MEM	WB

Taken branch instruction	IF	ID	EX	MEM	WB			
Instruction $i + 1$		IF	**idle**	**idle**	**idle**	**idle**		
Branch target			IF	ID	EX	MEM	WB	
Branch target + 1				IF	ID	EX	MEM	WB
Branch target + 2					IF	ID	EX	MEM	WB

Figure A.12   The predicted-not-taken scheme and the pipeline sequence when the branch is untaken (top) and taken (bottom). When the branch is untaken, determined during ID, we have fetched the fall-through and just continue. If the branch is taken during ID, we restart the fetch at the branch target. This causes all instructions following the branch to stall 1 clock cycle.

A fourth scheme in use in some processors is called *delayed branch*. This technique was heavily used in early RISC processors and works reasonably well in the five-stage pipeline. In a delayed branch, the execution cycle with a branch delay of one is

```
branch instruction
sequential successor₁
branch target if taken
```

The sequential successor is in the *branch delay slot*. This instruction is executed whether or not the branch is taken. The pipeline behavior of the five-stage pipeline with a branch delay is shown in Figure A.13. Although it is possible to have a branch delay longer than one, in practice, almost all processors with delayed branch have a single instruction delay; other techniques are used if the pipeline has a longer potential branch penalty.

The job of the compiler is to make the successor instructions valid and useful. A number of optimizations are used. Figure A.14 shows the three ways in which the branch delay can be scheduled.

The limitations on delayed-branch scheduling arise from (1) the restrictions on the instructions that are scheduled into the delay slots and (2) our ability to predict at compile time whether a branch is likely to be taken or not. To improve the ability of the compiler to fill branch delay slots, most processors with conditional branches have introduced a *canceling* or *nullifying* branch. In a canceling branch, the instruction includes the direction that the branch was predicted. When the branch behaves as predicted, the instruction in the branch delay slot is simply executed as it would normally be with a delayed branch. When the branch is incorrectly predicted, the instruction in the branch delay slot is simply

Untaken branch instruction	IF	ID	EX	MEM	WB			
Branch delay instruction ($i + 1$)		IF	ID	EX	MEM	WB		
Instruction $i + 2$			IF	ID	EX	MEM	WB	
Instruction $i + 3$				IF	ID	EX	MEM	WB
Instruction $i + 4$					IF	ID	EX	MEM	WB
Taken branch instruction	IF	ID	EX	MEM	WB			
Branch delay instruction ($i + 1$)		IF	ID	EX	MEM	WB		
Branch target			IF	ID	EX	MEM	WB	
Branch target + 1				IF	ID	EX	MEM	WB
Branch target + 2					IF	ID	EX	MEM	WB

Figure A.13 The behavior of a delayed branch is the same whether or not the branch is taken. The instructions in the delay slot (there is only one delay slot for MIPS) are executed. If the branch is untaken, execution continues with the instruction after the branch delay instruction; if the branch is taken, execution continues at the branch target. When the instruction in the branch delay slot is also a branch, the meaning is unclear: If the branch is not taken, what should happen to the branch in the branch delay slot? Because of this confusion, architectures with delay branches often disallow putting a branch in the delay slot.

turned into a no-op. We explore the performance of canceling delayed branches in Exercise A.7.

Performance of Branch Schemes

What is the effective performance of each of these schemes? The effective pipeline speedup with branch penalties, assuming an ideal CPI of 1, is

$$\text{Pipeline speedup} = \frac{\text{Pipeline depth}}{1 + \text{Pipeline stall cycles from branches}}$$

Because of the following:

$$\text{Pipeline stall cycles from branches} = \text{Branch frequency} \times \text{Branch penalty}$$

we obtain

$$\text{Pipeline speedup} = \frac{\text{Pipeline depth}}{1 + \text{Branch frequency} \times \text{Branch penalty}}$$

The branch frequency and branch penalty can have a component from both unconditional and conditional branches. However, the latter dominate since they are more frequent.

Example For a deeper pipeline, such as that in a MIPS R4000, it takes at least three pipeline stages before the branch-target address is known and an additional cycle before the branch condition is evaluated, assuming no stalls on the registers in the

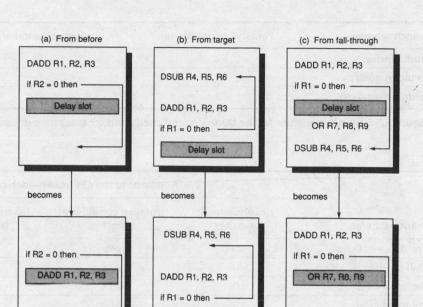

Figure A.14   Scheduling the branch delay slot. The top box in each pair shows the code before scheduling; the bottom box shows the scheduled code. In (a) the delay slot is scheduled with an independent instruction from before the branch. This is the best choice. Strategies (b) and (c) are used when (a) is not possible. In the code sequences for (b) and (c), the use of R1 in the branch condition prevents the DADD instruction (whose destination is R1) from being moved after the branch. In (b) the branch delay slot is scheduled from the target of the branch; usually the target instruction will need to be copied because it can be reached by another path. Strategy (b) is preferred when the branch is taken with high probability, such as a loop branch. Finally, the branch may be scheduled from the not-taken fall-through as in (c). To make this optimization legal for (b) or (c), it must be OK to execute the moved instruction when the branch goes in the unexpected direction. By OK we mean that the work is wasted, but the program will still execute correctly. This is the case, for example, in (c) if R7 were an unused temporary register when the branch goes in the unexpected direction.

conditional comparison. A three-stage delay leads to the branch penalties for the three simplest prediction schemes listed in Figure A.15.

   Find the effective addition to the CPI arising from branches for this pipeline, assuming the following frequencies:

Unconditional branch	4%
Conditional branch, untaken	6%
Conditional branch, taken	10%

Branch scheme	Penalty unconditional	Penalty untaken	Penalty taken
Flush pipeline	2	3	3
Predicted taken	2	3	2
Predicted untaken	2	0	3

Figure A.15 Branch penalties for the three simplest prediction schemes for a deeper pipeline.

Branch scheme	Additions to the CPI from branch costs			
	Unconditional branches	Untaken conditional branches	Taken conditional branches	All branches
Frequency of event	4%	6%	10%	20%
Stall pipeline	0.08	0.18	0.30	0.56
Predicted taken	0.08	0.18	0.20	0.46
Predicted untaken	0.08	0.00	0.30	0.38

Figure A.16 CPI penalties for three branch-prediction schemes and a deeper pipeline.

Answer We find the CPIs by multiplying the relative frequency of unconditional, conditional untaken, and conditional taken branches by the respective penalties. The results are shown in Figure A.16.

The differences among the schemes are substantially increased with this longer delay. If the base CPI was 1 and branches were the only source of stalls, the ideal pipeline would be 1.56 times faster than a pipeline that used the stall-pipeline scheme. The predicted-untaken scheme would be 1.13 times better than the stall-pipeline scheme under the same assumptions.

A.3 How Is Pipelining Implemented?

Before we proceed to basic pipelining, we need to review a simple implementation of an unpipelined version of MIPS.

A Simple Implementation of MIPS

In this section we follow the style of Section A.1, showing first a simple unpipelined implementation and then the pipelined implementation. This time, however, our example is specific to the MIPS architecture.

In this subsection we focus on a pipeline for an integer subset of MIPS that consists of load-store word, branch equal zero, and integer ALU operations. Later in this appendix, we will incorporate the basic floating-point operations. Although we discuss only a subset of MIPS, the basic principles can be extended to handle all the instructions.

Every MIPS instruction can be implemented in at most 5 clock cycles. The 5 clock cycles are as follows.

1. *Instruction fetch cycle* (IF):

   ```
   IR ← Mem[PC];
   NPC ← PC + 4;
   ```

   Operation: Send out the PC and fetch the instruction from memory into the instruction register (IR); increment the PC by 4 to address the next sequential instruction. The IR is used to hold the instruction that will be needed on subsequent clock cycles; likewise the register NPC is used to hold the next sequential PC.

2. *Instruction decode/register fetch cycle* (ID):

   ```
   A ← Regs[rs];
   B ← Regs[rt];
   Imm ← sign-extended immediate field of IR;
   ```

   Operation: Decode the instruction and access the register file to read the registers (rs and rt are the register specifiers). The outputs of the general-purpose registers are read into two temporary registers (A and B) for use in later clock cycles. The lower 16 bits of the IR are also sign extended and stored into the temporary register Imm, for use in the next cycle.

   Decoding is done in parallel with reading registers, which is possible because these fields are at a fixed location in the MIPS instruction format (see Figure 2.27 on page 132). Because the immediate portion of an instruction is located in an identical place in every MIPS format, the sign extended immediate is also calculated during this cycle in case it is needed in the next cycle.

3. *Execution/effective address cycle* (EX):

   The ALU operates on the operands prepared in the prior cycle, performing one of four functions depending on the MIPS instruction type.

   ▪ Memory reference:

   ```
   ALUOutput ← A + Imm;
   ```

   Operation: The ALU adds the operands to form the effective address and places the result into the register ALUOutput.

   ▪ Register-Register ALU instruction:

   ```
   ALUOutput ← A func B;
   ```

   Operation: The ALU performs the operation specified by the function code on the value in register A and on the value in register B. The result is placed in the temporary register ALUOutput.

   ▪ Register-Immediate ALU instruction:

   ```
   ALUOutput ← A op Imm;
   ```

Operation: The ALU performs the operation specified by the opcode on the value in register A and on the value in register Imm. The result is placed in the temporary register ALUOutput.

■ Branch:

```
ALUOutput ← NPC + (Imm << 2);
Cond ← (A == 0)
```

Operation: The ALU adds the NPC to the sign-extended immediate value in Imm, which is shifted left by 2 bits to create a word offset, to compute the address of the branch target. Register A, which has been read in the prior cycle, is checked to determine whether the branch is taken. Since we are considering only one form of branch (BEQZ), the comparison is against 0. Note that BEQZ is actually a pseudoinstruction that translates to a BEQ with RO as an operand. For simplicity, this is the only form of branch we consider.)

The load-store architecture of MIPS means that effective address and execution cycles can be combined into a single clock cycle, since no instruction needs to simultaneously calculate a data address, calculate an instruction target address, and perform an operation on the data. The other integer instructions not included above are jumps of various forms, which are similar to branches.

4. *Memory access/branch completion cycle* (MEM):

The PC is updated for all instructions: PC ← NPC;

■ Memory reference:

```
LMD ← Mem[ALUOutput] or
Mem[ALUOutput] ← B;
```

Operation: Access memory if needed. If instruction is a load, data returns from memory and is placed in the LMD (load memory data) register; if it is a store, then the data from the B register is written into memory. In either case the address used is the one computed during the prior cycle and stored in the register ALUOutput.

■ Branch:

```
if (cond) PC ← ALUOutput
```

Operation: If the instruction branches, the PC is replaced with the branch destination address in the register ALUOutput.

5. *Write-back cycle* (WB):

■ Register-Register ALU instruction:

```
Regs[rd] ← ALUOutput;
```

■ Register-Immediate ALU instruction:

```
Regs[rt] ← ALUOutput;
```

■ Load instruction:

```
Regs[rt] ← LMD;
```

Operation: Write the result into the register file, whether it comes from the memory system (which is in LMD) or from the ALU (which is in ALUOutput); the register destination field is also in one of two positions (rd or rt) depending on the effective opcode.

Figure A.17 shows how an instruction flows through the data path. At the end of each clock cycle, every value computed during that clock cycle and required on a later clock cycle (whether for this instruction or the next) is written into a storage device, which may be memory, a general-purpose register, the PC, or a temporary register (i.e., LMD, Imm, A, B, IR, NPC, ALUOutput, or Cond). The temporary registers hold values between clock cycles for one instruction, while the other storage elements are visible parts of the state and hold values between successive instructions.

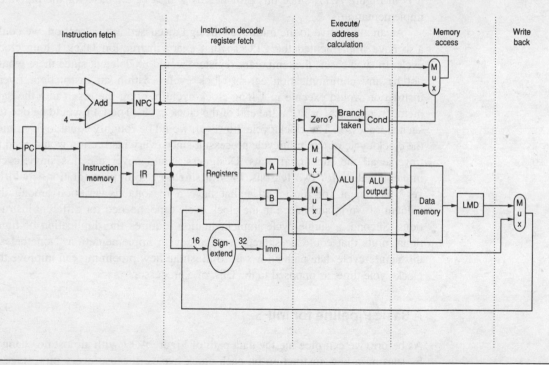

Figure A.17 The implementation of the MIPS data path allows every instruction to be executed in 4 or 5 clock cycles. Although the PC is shown in the portion of the data path that is used in instruction fetch and the registers are shown in the portion of the data path that is used in instruction decode/register fetch, both of these functional units are read as well as written by an instruction. Although we show these functional units in the cycle corresponding to where they are read, the PC is written during the memory access clock cycle and the registers are written during the write-back clock cycle. In both cases, the writes in later pipe stages are indicated by the multiplexer output (in memory access or write back) that carries a value back to the PC or registers. These backward-flowing signals introduce much of the complexity of pipelining, since they indicate the possibility of hazards.

Although all processors today are pipelined, this multicycle implementation is a reasonable approximation of how most processors would have been implemented in earlier times. A simple finite-state machine could be used to implement the control following the 5-cycle structure shown above. For a much more complex processor, microcode control could be used. In either event, an instruction sequence like that above would determine the structure of the control.

There are some hardware redundancies that could be eliminated in this multicycle implementation. For example, there are two ALUs: one to increment the PC and one used for effective address and ALU computation. Since they are not needed on the same clock cycle, we could merge them by adding additional multiplexers and sharing the same ALU. Likewise, instructions and data could be stored in the same memory, since the data and instruction accesses happen on different clock cycles.

Rather than optimize this simple implementation, we will leave the design as it is in Figure A.17, since this provides us with a better base for the pipelined implementation.

As an alternative to the multicycle design discussed in this section, we could also have implemented the CPU so that every instruction takes 1 long clock cycle. In such cases, the temporary registers would be deleted, since there would not be any communication across clock cycles within an instruction. Every instruction would execute in 1 long clock cycle, writing the result into the data memory, registers, or PC at the end of the clock cycle. The CPI would be one for such a processor. The clock cycle, however, would be roughly equal to five times the clock cycle of the multicycle processor, since every instruction would need to traverse all the functional units. Designers would never use this single-cycle implementation for two reasons. First, a single-cycle implementation would be very inefficient for most CPUs that have a reasonable variation among the amount of work, and hence in the clock cycle time, needed for different instructions. Second, a single-cycle implementation requires the duplication of functional units that could be shared in a multicycle implementation. Nonetheless, this single-cycle data path allows us to illustrate how pipelining can improve the clock cycle time, as opposed to the CPI, of a processor.

A Basic Pipeline for MIPS

As before, we can pipeline the data path of Figure A.17 with almost no changes by starting a new instruction on each clock cycle. Because every pipe stage is active on every clock cycle, all operations in a pipe stage must complete in 1 clock cycle and any combination of operations must be able to occur at once. Furthermore, pipelining the data path requires that values passed from one pipe stage to the next must be placed in registers. Figure A.18 shows the MIPS pipeline with the appropriate registers, called *pipeline registers* or *pipeline latches,* between each pipeline stage. The registers are labeled with the names of the stages they connect. Figure A.18 is drawn so that connections through the pipeline registers from one stage to another are clear.

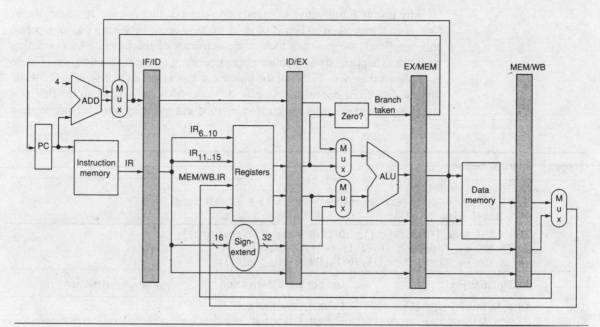

Figure A.18   The data path is pipelined by adding a set of registers, one between each pair of pipe stages. The registers serve to convey values and control information from one stage to the next. We can also think of the PC as a pipeline register, which sits before the IF stage of the pipeline, leading to one pipeline register for each pipe stage. Recall that the PC is an edge-triggered register written at the end of the clock cycle; hence there is no race condition in writing the PC. The selection multiplexer for the PC has been moved so that the PC is written in exactly one stage (IF). If we didn't move it, there would be a conflict when a branch occurred, since two instructions would try to write different values into the PC. Most of the data paths flow from left to right, which is from earlier in time to later. The paths flowing from right to left (which carry the register write-back information and PC information on a branch) introduce complications into our pipeline.

All of the registers needed to hold values temporarily between clock cycles within one instruction are subsumed into these pipeline registers. The fields of the instruction register (IR), which is part of the IF/ID register, are labeled when they are used to supply register names. The pipeline registers carry both data and control from one pipeline stage to the next. Any value needed on a later pipeline stage must be placed in such a register and copied from one pipeline register to the next, until it is no longer needed. If we tried to just use the temporary registers we had in our earlier unpipelined data path, values could be overwritten before all uses were completed. For example, the field of a register operand used for a write on a load or ALU operation is supplied from the MEM/WB pipeline register rather than from the IF/ID register. This is because we want a load or ALU operation to write the register designated by that operation, not the register field of the instruction currently transitioning from IF to ID! This destination register field is simply copied from one pipeline register to the next, until it is needed during the WB stage.

Any instruction is active in exactly one stage of the pipeline at a time; therefore, any actions taken on behalf of an instruction occur between a pair of pipeline registers. Thus, we can also look at the activities of the pipeline by examining what has to happen on any pipeline stage depending on the instruction type. Figure A.19 shows this view. Fields of the pipeline registers are named so as to show the flow of data from one stage to the next. Notice that the actions in the first two stages are independent of the current instruction type; they must be independent

Stage	Any instruction		

IF	`IF/ID.IR ← Mem[PC];`
	`IF/ID.NPC,PC ← (if ((EX/MEM.opcode == branch) & EX/MEM.cond){EX/MEM.`
	`ALUOutput} else {PC+4});`		

ID	`ID/EX.A ← Regs[IF/ID.IR[rs]]; ID/EX.B ← Regs[IF/ID.IR[rt]];`
	`ID/EX.NPC ← IF/ID.NPC; ID/EX.IR ← IF/ID.IR;`
	`ID/EX.Imm ← sign-extend(IF/ID.IR[immediate field]);`		

	ALU instruction	**Load or store instruction**	**Branch instruction**

EX	`EX/MEM.IR ← ID/EX.IR;`
	`EX/MEM.ALUOutput ←`
	`ID/EX.A func ID/EX.B;`
	`or`
	`EX/MEM.ALUOutput ←`
	`ID/EX.A op ID/EX.Imm;`
		`EX/MEM.IR← ID/EX.IR`
		`EX/MEM.ALUOutput ←`
		`ID/EX.A + ID/EX.Imm;`
		
		`EX/MEM.B ← ID/EX.B;`
			`EX/MEM.ALUOutput ←`
			`ID/EX.NPC +`
			`(ID/EX.Imm << 2);`
			
			`EX/MEM.cond ←`
			`(ID/EX.A == 0);`

MEM	`MEM/WB.IR ← EX/MEM.IR;`
	`MEM/WB.ALUOutput ←`
	`EX/MEM.ALUOutput;`
		`MEM/WB.IR ← EX/MEM.IR;`
		`MEM/WB.LMD ←`
		`Mem[EX/MEM.ALUOutput];`
		`or`
		`Mem[EX/MEM.ALUOutput] ←`
		`EX/MEM.B;`	

WB	`Regs[MEM/WB.IR[rd]] ←`
	`MEM/WB.ALUOutput;`
	`or`
	`Regs[MEM/WB.IR[rt]] ←`
	`MEM/WB.ALUOutput;`
		`For load only:`
		`Regs[MEM/WB.IR[rt]] ←`
		`MEM/WB.LMD;`	

Figure A.19 Events on every pipe stage of the MIPS pipeline. Let's review the actions in the stages that are specific to the pipeline organization. In IF, in addition to fetching the instruction and computing the new PC, we store the incremented PC both into the PC and into a pipeline register (NPC) for later use in computing the branch-target address. This structure is the same as the organization in Figure A.18, where the PC is updated in IF from one or two sources. In ID, we fetch the registers, extend the sign of the lower 16 bits of the IR (the immediate field), and pass along the IR and NPC. During EX, we perform an ALU operation or an address calculation; we pass along the IR and the B register (if the instruction is a store). We also set the value of cond to 1 if the instruction is a taken branch. During the MEM phase, we cycle the memory, write the PC if needed, and pass along values needed in the final pipe stage. Finally, during WB, we update the register field from either the ALU output or the loaded value. For simplicity we always pass the entire IR from one stage to the next, although as an instruction proceeds down the pipeline, less and less of the IR is needed.

because the instruction is not decoded until the end of the ID stage. The IF activity depends on whether the instruction in EX/MEM is a taken branch. If so, then the branch-target address of the branch instruction in EX/MEM is written into the PC at the end of IF; otherwise the incremented PC will be written back. (As we said earlier, this effect of branches leads to complications in the pipeline that we deal with in the next few sections.) The fixed-position encoding of the register source operands is critical to allowing the registers to be fetched during ID.

To control this simple pipeline we need only determine how to set the control for the four multiplexers in the data path of Figure A.18. The two multiplexers in the ALU stage are set depending on the instruction type, which is dictated by the IR field of the ID/EX register. The top ALU input multiplexer is set by whether the instruction is a branch or not, and the bottom multiplexer is set by whether the instruction is a register-register ALU operation or any other type of operation. The multiplexer in the IF stage chooses whether to use the value of the incremented PC or the value of the EX/MEM.ALUOutput (the branch target) to write into the PC. This multiplexer is controlled by the field EX/MEM.cond. The fourth multiplexer is controlled by whether the instruction in the WB stage is a load or an ALU operation. In addition to these four multiplexers, there is one additional multiplexer needed that is not drawn in Figure A.18, but whose existence is clear from looking at the WB stage of an ALU operation. The destination register field is in one of two different places depending on the instruction type (register-register ALU versus either ALU immediate or load). Thus, we will need a multiplexer to choose the correct portion of the IR in the MEM/WB register to specify the register destination field, assuming the instruction writes a register.

Implementing the Control for the MIPS Pipeline

The process of letting an instruction move from the instruction decode stage (ID) into the execution stage (EX) of this pipeline is usually called *instruction issue;* an instruction that has made this step is said to have *issued*. For the MIPS integer pipeline, all the data hazards can be checked during the ID phase of the pipeline. If a data hazard exists, the instruction is stalled before it is issued. Likewise, we can determine what forwarding will be needed during ID and set the appropriate controls then. Detecting interlocks early in the pipeline reduces the hardware complexity because the hardware never has to suspend an instruction that has updated the state of the processor, unless the entire processor is stalled. Alternatively, we can detect the hazard or forwarding at the beginning of a clock cycle that uses an operand (EX and MEM for this pipeline). To show the differences in these two approaches, we will show how the interlock for a RAW hazard with the source coming from a load instruction (called a *load interlock*) can be implemented by a check in ID, while the implementation of forwarding paths to the ALU inputs can be done during EX. Figure A.20 lists the variety of circumstances that we must handle.

Let's start with implementing the load interlock. If there is a RAW hazard with the source instruction being a load, the load instruction will be in the EX

Situation	Example code sequence	Action
No dependence	LD **R1**,45(R2) DADD R5,R6,R7 DSUB R8,R6,R7 OR R9,R6,R7	No hazard possible because no dependence exists on R1 in the immediately following three instructions.
Dependence requiring stall	LD **R1**,45(R2) DADD R5,**R1**,R7 DSUB R8,R6,R7 OR R9,R6,R7	Comparators detect the use of R1 in the DADD and stall the DADD (and DSUB and OR) before the DADD begins EX.
Dependence overcome by forwarding	LD **R1**,45(R2) DADD R5,R6,R7 DSUB R8,**R1**,R7 OR R9,R6,R7	Comparators detect use of R1 in DSUB and forward result of load to ALU in time for DSUB to begin EX.
Dependence with accesses in order	LD **R1**,45(R2) DADD R5,R6,R7 DSUB R8,R6,R7 OR R9,**R1**,R7	No action required because the read of R1 by OR occurs in the second half of the ID phase, while the write of the loaded data occurred in the first half.

Figure A.20 Situations that the pipeline hazard detection hardware can see by comparing the destination and sources of adjacent instructions. This table indicates that the only comparison needed is between the destination and the sources on the two instructions following the instruction that wrote the destination. In the case of a stall, the pipeline dependences will look like the third case once execution continues. Of course hazards that involve R0 can be ignored since the register always contains 0, and the test above could be extended to do this.

Opcode field of ID/EX (ID/EX.IR$_{0..5}$)	Opcode field of IF/ID (IF/ID.IR$_{0..5}$)	Matching operand fields
Load	Register-register ALU	ID/EX.IR[rt] == IF/ID.IR[rs]
Load	Register-register ALU	ID/EX.IR[rt] == IF/ID.IR[rt]
Load	Load, store, ALU immediate, or branch	ID/EX.IR[rt] == IF/ID.IR[rs]

Figure A.21 The logic to detect the need for load interlocks during the ID stage of an instruction requires three comparisons. Lines 1 and 2 of the table test whether the load destination register is one of the source registers for a register-register operation in ID. Line 3 of the table determines if the load destination register is a source for a load or store effective address, an ALU immediate, or a branch test. Remember that the IF/ID register holds the state of the instruction in ID, which potentially uses the load result, while ID/EX holds the state of the instruction in EX, which is the load instruction.

stage when an instruction that needs the load data will be in the ID stage. Thus, we can describe all the possible hazard situations with a small table, which can be directly translated to an implementation. Figure A.21 shows a table that detects all load interlocks when the instruction using the load result is in the ID stage.

Once a hazard has been detected, the control unit must insert the pipeline stall and prevent the instructions in the IF and ID stages from advancing. As we said earlier, all the control information is carried in the pipeline registers. (Carrying the instruction along is enough, since all control is derived from it.) Thus, when we detect a hazard we need only change the control portion of the ID/EX pipeline register to all 0s, which happens to be a no-op (an instruction that does nothing, such as DADD R0,R0,R0). In addition, we simply recirculate the contents of the IF/ID registers to hold the stalled instruction. In a pipeline with more complex hazards, the same ideas would apply: We can detect the hazard by comparing some set of pipeline registers and shift in no-ops to prevent erroneous execution.

Implementing the forwarding logic is similar, although there are more cases to consider. The key observation needed to implement the forwarding logic is that the pipeline registers contain both the data to be forwarded as well as the source and destination register fields. All forwarding logically happens from the ALU or data memory output to the ALU input, the data memory input, or the zero detection unit. Thus, we can implement the forwarding by a comparison of the destination registers of the IR contained in the EX/MEM and MEM/WB stages against the source registers of the IR contained in the ID/EX and EX/MEM registers. Figure A.22 shows the comparisons and possible forwarding operations where the destination of the forwarded result is an ALU input for the instruction currently in EX.

In addition to the comparators and combinational logic that we need to determine when a forwarding path needs to be enabled, we also need to enlarge the multiplexers at the ALU inputs and add the connections from the pipeline registers that are used to forward the results. Figure A.23 shows the relevant segments of the pipelined data path with the additional multiplexers and connections in place.

For MIPS, the hazard detection and forwarding hardware is reasonably simple; we will see that things become somewhat more complicated when we extend this pipeline to deal with floating point. Before we do that, we need to handle branches.

Dealing with Branches in the Pipeline

In MIPS, the branches (BEQ and BNE) require testing a register for equality to another register, which may be R0. If we consider only the cases of BEQZ and BNEZ, which require a zero test, it is possible to complete this decision by the end of the ID cycle by moving the zero test into that cycle. To take advantage of an early decision on whether the branch is taken, both PCs (taken and untaken) must be computed early. Computing the branch-target address during ID requires an additional adder because the main ALU, which has been used for this function so far, is not usable until EX. Figure A.24 shows the revised pipelined data path. With the separate adder and a branch decision made during ID, there is only a 1-clock-cycle stall on branches. Although this reduces the branch delay to 1 cycle,

Pipeline register containing source instruction	Opcode of source instruction	Pipeline register containing destination instruction	Opcode of destination instruction	Destination of the forwarded result	Comparison (if equal then forward)
EX/MEM	Register-register ALU	ID/EX	Register-register ALU, ALU immediate, load, store, branch	Top ALU input	EX/MEM.IR[rd] == ID/EX.IR[rs]
EX/MEM	Register-register ALU	ID/EX	Register-register ALU	Bottom ALU input	EX/MEM.IR[rd] == ID/EX.IR[rt]
MEM/WB	Register-register ALU	ID/EX	Register-register ALU, ALU immediate, load, store, branch	Top ALU input	MEM/WB.IR[rd] == ID/EX.IR[rs]
MEM/WB	Register-register ALU	ID/EX	Register-register ALU	Bottom ALU input	MEM/WB.IR[rd] == ID/EX.IR[rt]
EX/MEM	ALU immediate	ID/EX	Register-register ALU, ALU immediate, load, store, branch	Top ALU input	EX/MEM.IR[rt] == ID/EX.IR[rs]
EX/MEM	ALU immediate	ID/EX	Register-register ALU	Bottom ALU input	EX/MEM.IR[rt] == ID/EX.IR[rt]
MEM/WB	ALU immediate	ID/EX	Register-register ALU, ALU immediate, load, store, branch	Top ALU input	MEM/WB.IR[rt] == ID/EX.IR[rs]
MEM/WB	ALU immediate	ID/EX	Register-register ALU	Bottom ALU input	MEM/WB.IR[rt] == ID/EX.IR[rt]
MEM/WB	Load	ID/EX	Register-register ALU, ALU immediate, load, store, branch	Top ALU input	MEM/WB.IR[rt] == ID/EX.IR[rs]
MEM/WB	Load	ID/EX	Register-register ALU	Bottom ALU input	MEM/WB.IR[rt] == ID/EX.IR[rt]

Figure A.22 Forwarding of data to the two ALU inputs (for the instruction in EX) can occur from the ALU result (in EX/MEM or in MEM/WB) or from the load result in MEM/WB. There are 10 separate comparisons needed to tell whether a forwarding operation should occur. The top and bottom ALU inputs refer to the inputs corresponding to the first and second ALU source operands, respectively, and are shown explicitly in Figure A.17 on page A-29 and in Figure A.23 on page A-37. Remember that the pipeline latch for destination instruction in EX is ID/EX, while the source values come from the ALUOutput portion of EX/MEM or MEM/WB or the LMD portion of MEM/WB. There is one complication not addressed by this logic: dealing with multiple instructions that write the same register. For example, during the code sequence DADD R1, R2, R3; DADDI R1, R1, #2; DSUB R4, R3, R1, the logic must ensure that the DSUB instruction uses the result of the DADDI instruction rather than the result of the DADD instruction. The logic shown above can be extended to handle this case by simply testing that forwarding from MEM/WB is enabled only when forwarding from EX/MEM is not enabled for the same input. Because the DADDI result will be in EX/MEM, it will be forwarded, rather than the DADD result in MEM/WB.

it means that an ALU instruction followed by a branch on the result of the instruction will incur a data hazard stall. Figure A.25 shows the branch portion of the revised pipeline table from Figure A.19.

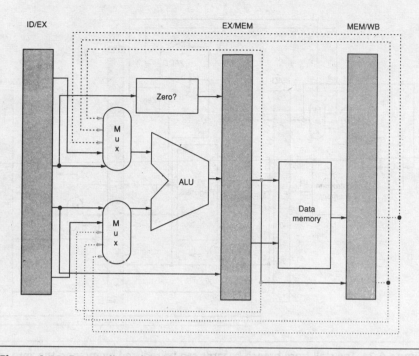

Figure A.23 Forwarding of results to the ALU requires the addition of three extra inputs on each ALU multiplexer and the addition of three paths to the new inputs. The paths correspond to a bypass of (1) the ALU output at the end of the EX, (2) the ALU output at the end of the MEM stage, and (3) the memory output at the end of the MEM stage.

In some processors, branch hazards are even more expensive in clock cycles than in our example, since the time to evaluate the branch condition and compute the destination can be even longer. For example, a processor with separate decode and register fetch stages will probably have a *branch delay*—the length of the control hazard—that is at least 1 clock cycle longer. The branch delay, unless it is dealt with, turns into a branch penalty. Many older CPUs that implement more complex instruction sets have branch delays of 4 clock cycles or more, and large, deeply pipelined processors often have branch penalties of 6 or 7. In general, the deeper the pipeline, the worse the branch penalty in clock cycles. Of course, the relative performance effect of a longer branch penalty depends on the overall CPI of the processor. A high CPI processor can afford to have more expensive branches because the percentage of the processor's performance that will be lost from branches is less.

A.4   What Makes Pipelining Hard to Implement?

Now that we understand how to detect and resolve hazards, we can deal with some complications that we have avoided so far. The first part of this section

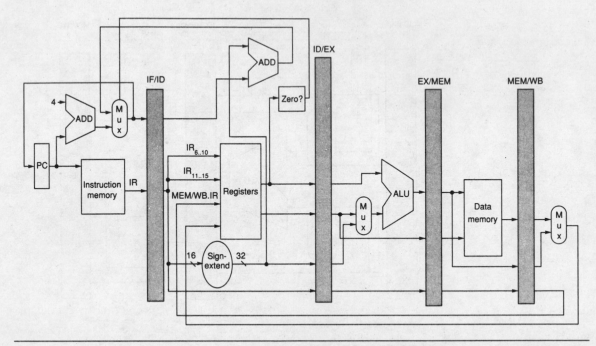

Figure A.24 The stall from branch hazards can be reduced by moving the zero test and branch-target calcula-tion into the ID phase of the pipeline. Notice that we have made two important changes, each of which removes 1 cycle from the 3-cycle stall for branches. The first change is to move both the branch-target address calculation and the branch condition decision to the ID cycle. The second change is to write the PC of the instruction in the IF phase, using either the branch-target address computed during ID or the incremented PC computed during IF. In compari-son, Figure A.18 obtained the branch-target address from the EX/MEM register and wrote the result during the MEM clock cycle. As mentioned in Figure A.18, the PC can be thought of as a pipeline register (e.g., as part of ID/IF), which is written with the address of the next instruction at the end of each IF cycle.

considers the challenges of exceptional situations where the instruction execution order is changed in unexpected ways. In the second part of this section, we dis-cuss some of the challenges raised by different instruction sets.

Dealing with Exceptions

Exceptional situations are harder to handle in a pipelined CPU because the over-lapping of instructions makes it more difficult to know whether an instruction can safely change the state of the CPU. In a pipelined CPU, an instruction is executed piece by piece and is not completed for several clock cycles. Unfortunately, other instructions in the pipeline can raise exceptions that may force the CPU to abort the instructions in the pipeline before they complete. Before we discuss these problems and their solutions in detail, we need to understand what types of situa-tions can arise and what architectural requirements exist for supporting them.

Pipe stage	Branch instruction
IF	IF/ID.IR $\leftarrow$ Mem[PC]; **IF/ID.NPC,PC $\leftarrow$ (if ((IF/ID.opcode == branch) & (Regs[IF/ID.IR$_{6..10}$] op 0)) {IF/ID.NPC + (IF/ID.IR$_{16}$)^{16}##IF/ID.IR$_{16..31}$##00} else {PC+4});**
ID	ID/EX.A $\leftarrow$ Regs[IF/ID.IR$_{6..10}$]; ID/EX.B $\leftarrow$ Regs[IF/ID.IR$_{11..15}$]; ID/EX.IR $\leftarrow$ IF/ID.IR; ID/EX.Imm $\leftarrow$ (IF/ID.IR$_{16}$)^{16}##IF/ID.IR$_{16..31}$
EX	
MEM	
WB	

Figure A.25 This revised pipeline structure is based on the original in Figure A.19. It uses a separate adder, as in Figure A.24, to compute the branch-target address during ID. The operations that are new or have changed are in bold. Because the branch-target address addition happens during ID, it will happen for all instructions; the branch condition (Regs[IF/ID.IR$_{6..10}$] *op* 0) will also be done for all instructions. The selection of the sequential PC or the branch-target PC still occurs during IF, but it now uses values from the ID/EX register, which correspond to the values set by the previous instruction. This change reduces the branch penalty by 2 cycles: one from evaluating the branch target and condition earlier and one from controlling the PC selection on the same clock rather than on the next clock. Since the value of cond is set to 0, unless the instruction in ID is a taken branch, the processor must decode the instruction before the end of ID. Because the branch is done by the end of ID, the EX, MEM, and WB stages are unused for branches. An additional complication arises for jumps that have a longer offset than branches. We can resolve this by using an additional adder that sums the PC and lower 26 bits of the IR after shifting left by 2 bits.

Types of Exceptions and Requirements

The terminology used to describe exceptional situations where the normal execution order of instruction is changed varies among CPUs. The terms *interrupt*, *fault*, and *exception* are used, although not in a consistent fashion. We use the term *exception* to cover all these mechanisms, including the following:

- I/O device request
- Invoking an operating system service from a user program
- Tracing instruction execution
- Breakpoint (programmer-requested interrupt)
- Integer arithmetic overflow
- FP arithmetic anomaly
- Page fault (not in main memory)
- Misaligned memory accesses (if alignment is required)
- Memory protection violation
- Using an undefined or unimplemented instruction
- Hardware malfunctions
- Power failure

When we wish to refer to some particular class of such exceptions, we will use a longer name, such as I/O interrupt, floating-point exception, or page fault. Figure A.26 shows the variety of different names for the common exception events above.

Although we use the term *exception* to cover all of these events, individual events have important characteristics that determine what action is needed in the hardware. The requirements on exceptions can be characterized on five semi-independent axes:

Exception event	IBM 360	VAX	Motorola 680x0	Intel 80x86
I/O device request	Input/output interruption	Device interrupt	Exception (level 0...7 autovector)	Vectored interrupt
Invoking the operating system service from a user program	Supervisor call interruption	Exception (change mode supervisor trap)	Exception (unimplemented instruction)— on Macintosh	Interrupt (INT instruction)
Tracing instruction execution	Not applicable	Exception (trace fault)	Exception (trace)	Interrupt (single-step trap)
Breakpoint	Not applicable	Exception (breakpoint fault)	Exception (illegal instruction or breakpoint)	Interrupt (breakpoint trap)
Integer arithmetic overflow or underflow; FP trap	Program interruption (overflow or underflow exception)	Exception (integer overflow trap or floating underflow fault)	Exception (floating-point coprocessor errors)	Interrupt (overflow trap or math unit exception)
Page fault (not in main memory)	Not applicable (only in 370)	Exception (translation not valid fault)	Exception (memory-management unit errors)	Interrupt (page fault)
Misaligned memory accesses	Program interruption (specification exception)	Not applicable	Exception (address error)	Not applicable
Memory protection violations	Program interruption (protection exception)	Exception (access control violation fault)	Exception (bus error)	Interrupt (protection exception)
Using undefined instructions	Program interruption (operation exception)	Exception (opcode privileged/ reserved fault)	Exception (illegal instruction or break-point/unimplemented instruction)	Interrupt (invalid opcode)
Hardware malfunctions	Machine-check interruption	Exception (machine-check abort)	Exception (bus error)	Not applicable
Power failure	Machine-check interruption	Urgent interrupt	Not applicable	Nonmaskable interrupt

Figure A.26 The names of common exceptions vary across four different architectures. Every event on the IBM 360 and 80x86 is called an *interrupt,* while every event on the 680x0 is called an *exception.* VAX divides events into *interrupts* or *exceptions.* Adjectives *device, software,* and *urgent* are used with VAX interrupts, while VAX exceptions are subdivided into *faults, traps,* and *aborts.*

1. *Synchronous versus asynchronous*—If the event occurs at the same place every time the program is executed with the same data and memory allocation, the event is *synchronous*. With the exception of hardware malfunctions, asynchronous events are caused by devices external to the CPU and memory. Asynchronous events usually can be handled after the completion of the current instruction, which makes them easier to handle.

2. *User requested versus coerced*—If the user task directly asks for it, it is a *user-requested* event. In some sense, user-requested exceptions are not really exceptions, since they are predictable. They are treated as exceptions, however, because the same mechanisms that are used to save and restore the state are used for these user-requested events. Because the only function of an instruction that triggers this exception is to cause the exception, user-requested exceptions can always be handled after the instruction has completed. *Coerced* exceptions are caused by some hardware event that is not under the control of the user program. Coerced exceptions are harder to implement because they are not predictable.

3. *User maskable versus user nonmaskable*—If an event can be masked or disabled by a user task, it is *user maskable*. This mask simply controls whether the hardware responds to the exception or not.

4. *Within versus between instructions*—This classification depends on whether the event prevents instruction completion by occurring in the middle of execution—no matter how short—or whether it is recognized *between* instructions. Exceptions that occur *within* instructions are usually synchronous, since the instruction triggers the exception. It's harder to implement exceptions that occur within instructions than those between instructions, since the instruction must be stopped and restarted. Asynchronous exceptions that occur within instructions arise from catastrophic situations (e.g., hardware malfunction) and always cause program termination.

5. *Resume versus terminate*—If the program's execution always stops after the interrupt, it is a *terminating* event. If the program's execution continues after the interrupt, it is a *resuming* event. It is easier to implement exceptions that terminate execution, since the CPU need not be able to restart execution of the same program after handling the exception.

Figure A.27 classifies the examples from Figure A.26 according to these five categories. The difficult task is implementing interrupts occurring within instructions where the instruction must be resumed. Implementing such exceptions requires that another program must be invoked to save the state of the executing program, correct the cause of the exception, and then restore the state of the program before the instruction that caused the exception can be tried again. This process must be effectively invisible to the executing program. If a pipeline provides the ability for the processor to handle the exception, save the state, and restart without affecting the execution of the program, the pipeline or processor is said to be *restartable*. While early supercomputers and microprocessors often lacked this

Exception type	Synchronous vs. asynchronous	User request vs. coerced	User maskable vs. nonmaskable	Within vs. between instructions	Resume vs. terminate
I/O device request	Asynchronous	Coerced	Nonmaskable	Between	Resume
Invoke operating system	Synchronous	User request	Nonmaskable	Between	Resume
Tracing instruction execution	Synchronous	User request	User maskable	Between	Resume
Breakpoint	Synchronous	User request	User maskable	Between	Resume
Integer arithmetic overflow	Synchronous	Coerced	User maskable	Within	Resume
Floating-point arithmetic overflow or underflow	Synchronous	Coerced	User maskable	Within	Resume
Page fault	Synchronous	Coerced	Nonmaskable	Within	Resume
Misaligned memory accesses	Synchronous	Coerced	User maskable	Within	Resume
Memory protection violations	Synchronous	Coerced	Nonmaskable	Within	Resume
Using undefined instructions	Synchronous	Coerced	Nonmaskable	Within	Terminate
Hardware malfunctions	Asynchronous	Coerced	Nonmaskable	Within	Terminate
Power failure	Asynchronous	Coerced	Nonmaskable	Within	Terminate

Figure A.27 Five categories are used to define what actions are needed for the different exception types shown in Figure A.26. Exceptions that must allow resumption are marked as resume, although the software may often choose to terminate the program. Synchronous, coerced exceptions occurring within instructions that can be resumed are the most difficult to implement. We might expect that memory protection access violations would always result in termination; however, modern operating systems use memory protection to detect events such as the first attempt to use a page or the first write to a page. Thus, CPUs should be able to resume after such exceptions.

property, almost all processors today support it, at least for the integer pipeline, because it is needed to implement virtual memory (see Chapter 5).

Stopping and Restarting Execution

As in unpipelined implementations, the most difficult exceptions have two properties: (1) they occur within instructions (that is, in the middle of the instruction execution corresponding to EX or MEM pipe stages), and (2) they must be restartable. In our MIPS pipeline, for example, a virtual memory page fault resulting from a data fetch cannot occur until sometime in the MEM stage of the instruction. By the time that fault is seen, several other instructions will be in execution. A page fault must be restartable and requires the intervention of another process, such as the operating system. Thus, the pipeline must be safely shut down and the state saved so that the instruction can be restarted in the correct state. Restarting is usually implemented by saving the PC of the instruction at which to restart. If the restarted instruction is not a branch, then we will continue to fetch the sequential successors and begin their execution in the normal fashion. If the restarted instruction is a branch, then we will reevaluate the branch condition and begin fetching from either the target or the fall-through. When an exception occurs, the pipeline control can take the following steps to save the pipeline state safely:

1. Force a trap instruction into the pipeline on the next IF.

2. Until the trap is taken, turn off all writes for the faulting instruction and for all instructions that follow in the pipeline; this can be done by placing zeros into the pipeline latches of all instructions in the pipeline, starting with the instruction that generates the exception, but not those that precede that instruction. This prevents any state changes for instructions that will not be completed before the exception is handled.

3. After the exception-handling routine in the operating system receives control, it immediately saves the PC of the faulting instruction. This value will be used to return from the exception later.

When we use delayed branches, as mentioned in the last section, it is no longer possible to re-create the state of the processor with a single PC because the instructions in the pipeline may not be sequentially related. So we need to save and restore as many PCs as the length of the branch delay plus one. This is done in the third step above.

After the exception has been handled, special instructions return the processor from the exception by reloading the PCs and restarting the instruction stream (using the instruction RFE in MIPS). If the pipeline can be stopped so that the instructions just before the faulting instruction are completed and those after it can be restarted from scratch, the pipeline is said to have *precise exceptions*. Ideally, the faulting instruction would not have changed the state, and correctly handling some exceptions requires that the faulting instruction have no effects. For other exceptions, such as floating-point exceptions, the faulting instruction on some processors writes its result before the exception can be handled. In such cases, the hardware must be prepared to retrieve the source operands, even if the destination is identical to one of the source operands. Because floating-point operations may run for many cycles, it is highly likely that some other instruction may have written the source operands (as we will see in the next section, floating-point operations often complete out of order). To overcome this, many recent high-performance CPUs have introduced two modes of operation. One mode has precise exceptions and the other (fast or performance mode) does not. Of course, the precise exception mode is slower, since it allows less overlap among floating-point instructions. In some high-performance CPUs, including Alpha 21064, Power2, and MIPS R8000, the precise mode is often much slower (> 10 times) and thus useful only for debugging of codes.

Supporting precise exceptions is a requirement in many systems, while in others it is "just" valuable because it simplifies the operating system interface. At a minimum, any processor with demand paging or IEEE arithmetic trap handlers must make its exceptions precise, either in the hardware or with some software support. For integer pipelines, the task of creating precise exceptions is easier, and accommodating virtual memory strongly motivates the support of precise exceptions for memory references. In practice, these reasons have led designers and architects to always provide precise exceptions for the integer pipeline. In this section we describe how to implement precise exceptions for the MIPS integer pipeline. We will describe techniques for handling the more complex challenges arising in the FP pipeline in Section A.5.

Exceptions in MIPS

Figure A.28 shows the MIPS pipeline stages and which "problem" exceptions might occur in each stage. With pipelining, multiple exceptions may occur in the same clock cycle because there are multiple instructions in execution. For example, consider this instruction sequence:

LD	IF	ID	EX	MEM	WB	
DADD		IF	ID	EX	MEM	WB

This pair of instructions can cause a data page fault and an arithmetic exception at the same time, since the LD is in the MEM stage while the DADD is in the EX stage. This case can be handled by dealing with only the data page fault and then restarting the execution. The second exception will reoccur (but not the first, if the software is correct), and when the second exception occurs, it can be handled independently.

In reality, the situation is not as straightforward as this simple example. Exceptions may occur out of order; that is, an instruction may cause an exception before an earlier instruction causes one. Consider again the above sequence of instructions, LD followed by DADD. The LD can get a data page fault, seen when the instruction is in MEM, and the DADD can get an instruction page fault, seen when the DADD instruction is in IF. The instruction page fault will actually occur first, even though it is caused by a later instruction!

Since we are implementing precise exceptions, the pipeline is required to handle the exception caused by the LD instruction first. To explain how this works, let's call the instruction in the position of the LD instruction *i,* and the

Pipeline stage	Problem exceptions occurring
IF	Page fault on instruction fetch; misaligned memory access; memory protection violation
ID	Undefined or illegal opcode
EX	Arithmetic exception
MEM	Page fault on data fetch; misaligned memory access; memory protection violation
WB	None

Figure A.28 Exceptions that may occur in the MIPS pipeline. Exceptions raised from instruction or data memory access account for six out of eight cases.

instruction in the position of the DADD instruction $i + 1$. The pipeline cannot simply handle an exception when it occurs in time, since that will lead to exceptions occurring out of the unpipelined order. Instead, the hardware posts all exceptions caused by a given instruction in a status vector associated with that instruction. The exception status vector is carried along as the instruction goes down the pipeline. Once an exception indication is set in the exception status vector, any control signal that may cause a data value to be written is turned off (this includes both register writes and memory writes). Because a store can cause an exception during MEM, the hardware must be prepared to prevent the store from completing if it raises an exception.

When an instruction enters WB (or is about to leave MEM), the exception status vector is checked. If any exceptions are posted, they are handled in the order in which they would occur in time on an unpipelined processor—the exception corresponding to the earliest instruction (and usually the earliest pipe stage for that instruction) is handled first. This guarantees that all exceptions will be seen on instruction i before any are seen on $i + 1$. Of course, any action taken in earlier pipe stages on behalf of instruction i may be invalid, but since writes to the register file and memory were disabled, no state could have been changed. As we will see in Section A.5, maintaining this precise model for FP operations is much harder.

In the next subsection we describe problems that arise in implementing exceptions in the pipelines of processors with more powerful, longer-running instructions.

Instruction Set Complications

No MIPS instruction has more than one result, and our MIPS pipeline writes that result only at the end of an instruction's execution. When an instruction is guaranteed to complete, it is called *committed*. In the MIPS integer pipeline, all instructions are committed when they reach the end of the MEM stage (or beginning of WB) and no instruction updates the state before that stage. Thus, precise exceptions are straightforward. Some processors have instructions that change the state in the middle of the instruction execution, before the instruction and its predecessors are guaranteed to complete. For example, autoincrement addressing modes in the IA-32 architecture cause the update of registers in the middle of an instruction execution. In such a case, if the instruction is aborted because of an exception, it will leave the processor state altered. Although we know which instruction caused the exception, without additional hardware support the exception will be imprecise because the instruction will be half finished. Restarting the instruction stream after such an imprecise exception is difficult. Alternatively, we could avoid updating the state before the instruction commits, but this may be difficult or costly, since there may be dependences on the updated state: Consider a VAX instruction that autoincrements the same register multiple times. Thus, to maintain a precise exception model, most processors with such instructions have the ability to back out any state changes made before the instruction is committed. If an exception occurs, the processor uses this ability to reset the state of the processor to its value before the interrupted instruction started. In the next section, we will see that a more powerful MIPS floating-point pipeline can introduce similar problems, and Section A.8 introduces techniques that substantially complicate exception handling.

A related source of difficulties arises from instructions that update memory state during execution, such as the string copy operations on the VAX or IBM 360 (see Appendices E and F online). To make it possible to interrupt and restart these instructions, the instructions are defined to use the general-purpose registers as working registers. Thus the state of the partially completed instruction is always in the registers, which are saved on an exception and restored after the exception, allowing the instruction to continue. In the VAX an additional bit of state records when an instruction has started updating the memory state, so that when the pipeline is restarted, the CPU knows whether to restart the instruction from the beginning or from the middle of the instruction. The IA-32 string instructions also use the registers as working storage, so that saving and restoring the registers saves and restores the state of such instructions.

A different set of difficulties arises from odd bits of state that may create additional pipeline hazards or may require extra hardware to save and restore. Condition codes are a good example of this. Many processors set the condition codes implicitly as part of the instruction. This approach has advantages, since condition codes decouple the evaluation of the condition from the actual branch. However, implicitly set condition codes can cause difficulties in scheduling any pipeline delays between setting the condition code and the branch, since most instructions set the condition code and cannot be used in the delay slots between the condition evaluation and the branch.

Additionally, in processors with condition codes, the processor must decide when the branch condition is fixed. This involves finding out when the condition code has been set for the last time before the branch. In most processors with implicitly set condition codes, this is done by delaying the branch condition evaluation until all previous instructions have had a chance to set the condition code.

Of course, architectures with explicitly set condition codes allow the delay between condition test and the branch to be scheduled; however, pipeline control must still track the last instruction that sets the condition code to know when the branch condition is decided. In effect, the condition code must be treated as an operand that requires hazard detection for RAW hazards with branches, just as MIPS must do on the registers.

A final thorny area in pipelining is multicycle operations. Imagine trying to pipeline a sequence of VAX instructions such as this:

```
MOVL    R1,R2                       ;moves between registers
ADDL3   42(R1),56(R1)+,@(R1)       ;adds memory locations
SUBL2   R2,R3                       ;subtracts registers
MOVC3   @(R1)[R2],74(R2),R3        ;moves a character string
```

These instructions differ radically in the number of clock cycles they will require, from as low as one up to hundreds of clock cycles. They also require different numbers of data memory accesses, from zero to possibly hundreds. The data hazards are very complex and occur both between and within instructions. The simple solution of making all instructions execute for the same number of clock cycles is unacceptable because it introduces an enormous number of hazards and bypass conditions and makes an immensely long pipeline. Pipelining the VAX at the instruction level is difficult, but a clever solution was found by the VAX 8800 designers. They pipeline the *microinstruction* execution: a microinstruction is a simple instruction used in sequences to implement a more complex instruction set. Because the microinstructions are simple (they look a lot like MIPS), the pipeline control is much easier. Since 1995, all Intel IA-32 microprocessors have used this strategy of converting the IA-32 instructions into microoperations, and then pipelining the microoperations.

In comparison, load-store processors have simple operations with similar amounts of work and pipeline more easily. If architects realize the relationship between instruction set design and pipelining, they can design architectures for more efficient pipelining. In the next section we will see how the MIPS pipeline deals with long-running instructions, specifically floating-point operations.

For many years the interaction between instruction sets and implementations was believed to be small, and implementation issues were not a major focus in designing instruction sets. In the 1980s it became clear that the difficulty and inefficiency of pipelining could both be increased by instruction set complications. In the 1990s, all companies moved to simpler instructions sets with the goal of reducing the complexity of aggressive implementations.

A.5   Extending the MIPS Pipeline to Handle Multicycle Operations

We now want to explore how our MIPS pipeline can be extended to handle floating-point operations. This section concentrates on the basic approach and the design alternatives, closing with some performance measurements of a MIPS floating-point pipeline.

It is impractical to require that all MIPS floating-point operations complete in 1 clock cycle, or even in 2. Doing so would mean accepting a slow clock, or using enormous amounts of logic in the floating-point units, or both. Instead, the floating-point pipeline will allow for a longer latency for operations. This is easier to grasp if we imagine the floating-point instructions as having the same pipeline as the integer instructions, with two important changes. First, the EX cycle may be repeated as many times as needed to complete the operation—the number of repetitions can vary for different operations. Second, there may be multiple floating-point functional units. A stall will occur if the instruction to be issued will either cause a structural hazard for the functional unit it uses or cause a data hazard.

For this section, let's assume that there are four separate functional units in our MIPS implementation:

1. The main integer unit that handles loads and stores, integer ALU operations, and branches

2. FP and integer multiplier

3. FP adder that handles FP add, subtract, and conversion

4. FP and integer divider

If we also assume that the execution stages of these functional units are not pipe-lined, then Figure A.29 shows the resulting pipeline structure. Because EX is not pipelined, no other instruction using that functional unit may issue until the previous instruction leaves EX. Moreover, if an instruction cannot proceed to the EX stage, the entire pipeline behind that instruction will be stalled.

In reality, the intermediate results are probably not cycled around the EX unit as Figure A.29 suggests; instead, the EX pipeline stage has some number of clock delays larger than 1. We can generalize the structure of the FP pipeline shown in Figure A.29 to allow pipelining of some stages and multiple ongoing operations. To describe such a pipeline, we must define both the latency of the functional units and also the *initiation interval* or *repeat interval*. We define latency the same way we defined it earlier: the number of intervening cycles between an instruction that produces a result and an instruction that uses the result. The initiation or repeat interval is the number of cycles that must elapse between issuing two operations of a given type. For example, we will use the latencies and initiation intervals shown in Figure A.30.

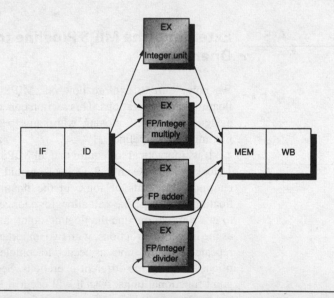

Figure A.29 The MIPS pipeline with three additional unpipelined, floating-point, functional units. Because only one instruction issues on every clock cycle, all instructions go through the standard pipeline for integer operations. The floating-point operations simply loop when they reach the EX stage. After they have finished the EX stage, they proceed to MEM and WB to complete execution.

Functional unit	Latency	Initiation interval
Integer ALU	0	1
Data memory (integer and FP loads)	1	1
FP add	3	1
FP multiply (also integer multiply)	6	1
FP divide (also integer divide)	24	25

Figure A.30 Latencies and initiation intervals for functional units.

With this definition of latency, integer ALU operations have a latency of 0, since the results can be used on the next clock cycle, and loads have a latency of 1, since their results can be used after one intervening cycle. Since most operations consume their operands at the beginning of EX, the latency is usually the number of stages after EX that an instruction produces a result—for example, zero stages for ALU operations and one stage for loads. The primary exception is stores, which consume the value being stored 1 cycle later. Hence the latency to a store for the value being stored, but not for the base address register, will be 1 cycle less. Pipeline latency is essentially equal to 1 cycle less than the depth of the execution pipeline, which is the number of stages from the EX stage to the stage that produces the result. Thus, for the example pipeline just above, the number of stages in an FP add is four, while the number of stages in an FP multiply is seven. To achieve a higher clock rate, designers need to put fewer logic levels in each pipe stage, which makes the number of pipe stages required for more complex operations larger. The penalty for the faster clock rate is thus longer latency for operations.

The example pipeline structure in Figure A.30 allows up to four outstanding FP adds, seven outstanding FP/integer multiplies, and one FP divide. Figure A.31 shows how this pipeline can be drawn by extending Figure A.29. The repeat interval is implemented in Figure A.31 by adding additional pipeline stages, which will be separated by additional pipeline registers. Because the units are independent, we name the stages differently. The pipeline stages that take multiple clock cycles, such as the divide unit, are further subdivided to show the latency of those stages. Because they are not complete stages, only one operation may be active. The pipeline structure can also be shown using the familiar diagrams from earlier in the appendix, as Figure A.32 shows for a set of independent FP operations and FP loads and stores. Naturally, the longer latency of the FP operations increases the frequency of RAW hazards and resultant stalls, as we will see later in this section.

The structure of the pipeline in Figure A.31 requires the introduction of the additional pipeline registers (e.g., A1/A2, A2/A3, A3/A4) and the modification of the connections to those registers. The ID/EX register must be expanded to connect ID to EX, DIV, M1, and A1; we can refer to the portion of the register associated with one of the next stages with the notation ID/EX, ID/DIV, ID/M1, or ID/A1. The pipeline register between ID and all the other stages may be thought

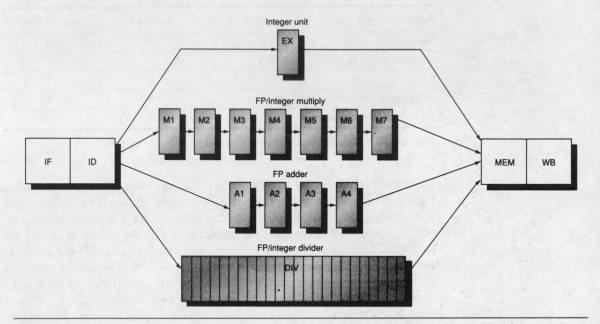

Figure A.31 A pipeline that supports multiple outstanding FP operations. The FP multiplier and adder are fully pipelined and have a depth of seven and four stages, respectively. The FP divider is not pipelined, but requires 24 clock cycles to complete. The latency in instructions between the issue of an FP operation and the use of the result of that operation without incurring a RAW stall is determined by the number of cycles spent in the execution stages. For example, the fourth instruction after an FP add can use the result of the FP add. For integer ALU operations, the depth of the execution pipeline is always one and the next instruction can use the results.

MUL.D	IF	ID	*M1*	M2	M3	M4	M5	M6	**M7**	MEM	WB
ADD.D		IF	ID	*A1*	A2	A3	**A4**	MEM	WB		
L.D			IF	ID	*EX*	**MEM**	WB				
S.D				IF	ID	*EX*	*MEM*	WB			

Figure A.32 The pipeline timing of a set of independent FP operations. The stages in italics show where data are needed, while the stages in bold show where a result is available. The ".D" extension on the instruction mnemonic indicates double-precision (64-bit) floating-point operations. FP loads and stores use a 64-bit path to memory so that the pipelining timing is just like an integer load or store.

of as logically separate registers and may, in fact, be implemented as separate registers. Because only one operation can be in a pipe stage at a time, the control information can be associated with the register at the head of the stage.

Hazards and Forwarding in Longer Latency Pipelines

There are a number of different aspects to the hazard detection and forwarding for a pipeline like that in Figure A.31:

1. Because the divide unit is not fully pipelined, structural hazards can occur. These will need to be detected and issuing instructions will need to be stalled.

2. Because the instructions have varying running times, the number of register writes required in a cycle can be larger than 1.

3. WAW hazards are possible, since instructions no longer reach WB in order. Note that WAR hazards are not possible, since the register reads always occur in ID.

4. Instructions can complete in a different order than they were issued, causing problems with exceptions; we deal with this in the next subsection.

5. Because of longer latency of operations, stalls for RAW hazards will be more frequent.

The increase in stalls arising from longer operation latencies is fundamentally the same as that for the integer pipeline. Before describing the new problems that arise in this FP pipeline and looking at solutions, let's examine the potential impact of RAW hazards. Figure A.33 shows a typical FP code sequence and the resultant stalls. At the end of this section, we'll examine the performance of this FP pipeline for our SPEC subset.

Now look at the problems arising from writes, described as (2) and (3) in the earlier list. If we assume the FP register file has one write port, sequences of FP operations, as well as an FP load together with FP operations, can cause conflicts for the register write port. Consider the pipeline sequence shown in Figure A.34. In clock cycle 11, all three instructions will reach WB and want to write the register file. With only a single register file write port, the processor must serialize the instruction completion. This single register port represents a structural hazard. We could increase the number of write ports to solve this, but that solution may be unattractive since the additional write ports would be used only rarely. This is because the maximum steady-state number of write ports needed is 1. Instead, we choose to detect and enforce access to the write port as a structural hazard.

										Clock cycle number							
Instruction	1	2	3	4	5	6	7	8	9	10	11	12	13	14	15	16	17
L.D F4,0(R2)	IF	ID	EX	MEM	WB												
MUL.D F0,F4,F6		IF	ID	stall	M1	M2	M3	M4	M5	M6	M7	MEM	WB				
ADD.D F2,F0,F8			IF	stall	ID	stall	stall	stall	stall	stall	stall	A1	A2	A3	A4	MEM	
S.D F2,0(R2)				IF	stall	stall	stall	stall	stall	stall	stall	ID	EX	stall	stall	stall	MEM

Figure A.33 A typical FP code sequence showing the stalls arising from RAW hazards. The longer pipeline substantially raises the frequency of stalls versus the shallower integer pipeline. Each instruction in this sequence is dependent on the previous and proceeds as soon as data are available, which assumes the pipeline has full bypassing and forwarding. The SD must be stalled an extra cycle so that its MEM does not conflict with the ADD.D. Extra hardware could easily handle this case.

Instruction	Clock cycle number										
	1	2	3	4	5	6	7	8	9	10	11
MUL.D F0,F4,F6	IF	ID	M1	M2	M3	M4	M5	M6	M7	MEM	WB
...		IF	ID	EX	MEM	WB					
...			IF	ID	EX	MEM	WB				
ADD.D F2,F4,F6				IF	ID	A1	A2	A3	A4	MEM	WB
...					IF	ID	EX	MEM	WB		
...						IF	ID	EX	MEM	WB	
L.D F2,0(R2)							IF	ID	EX	MEM	WB

Figure A.34 Three instructions want to perform a write back to the FP register file simultaneously, as shown in clock cycle 11. This is *not* the worst case, since an earlier divide in the FP unit could also finish on the same clock. Note that although the MUL.D, ADD.D, and L.D all are in the MEM stage in clock cycle 10, only the L.D actually uses the memory, so no structural hazard exists for MEM.

There are two different ways to implement this interlock. The first is to track the use of the write port in the ID stage and to stall an instruction before it issues, just as we would for any other structural hazard. Tracking the use of the write port can be done with a shift register that indicates when already-issued instructions will use the register file. If the instruction in ID needs to use the register file at the same time as an instruction already issued, the instruction in ID is stalled for a cycle. On each clock the reservation register is shifted 1 bit. This implementation has an advantage: It maintains the property that all interlock detection and stall insertion occurs in the ID stage. The cost is the addition of the shift register and write conflict logic. We will assume this scheme throughout this section.

An alternative scheme is to stall a conflicting instruction when it tries to enter either the MEM or WB stage. If we wait to stall the conflicting instructions until they want to enter the MEM or WB stage, we can choose to stall either instruction. A simple, though sometimes suboptimal, heuristic is to give priority to the unit with the longest latency, since that is the one most likely to have caused another instruction to be stalled for a RAW hazard. The advantage of this scheme is that it does not require us to detect the conflict until the entrance of the MEM or WB stage, where it is easy to see. The disadvantage is that it complicates pipeline control, as stalls can now arise from two places. Notice that stalling before entering MEM will cause the EX, A4, or M7 stage to be occupied, possibly forcing the stall to trickle back in the pipeline. Likewise, stalling before WB would cause MEM to back up.

Our other problem is the possibility of WAW hazards. To see that these exist, consider the example in Figure A.34. If the L.D instruction were issued one cycle earlier and had a destination of F2, then it would create a WAW hazard, because it would write F2 one cycle earlier than the ADD.D. Note that this hazard only occurs when the result of the ADD.D is overwritten *without* any instruction ever using it! If there were a use of F2 between the ADD.D and the L.D, the pipeline would need to be stalled for a RAW hazard, and the LD would not issue until the ADD.D was completed. We could argue that, for our pipeline, WAW hazards only occur when a useless instruction is executed, but we must still detect them and make sure that the result of the LD appears in F2 when we are done. (As we will see in Section A.9, such sequences sometimes *do* occur in reasonable code.)

There are two possible ways to handle this WAW hazard. The first approach is to delay the issue of the load instruction until the ADD.D enters MEM. The second approach is to stamp out the result of the ADD.D by detecting the hazard and changing the control so that the ADD.D does not write its result. Then the L.D can issue right away. Because this hazard is rare, either scheme will work fine—you can pick whatever is simpler to implement. In either case, the hazard can be detected during ID when the L.D is issuing. Then stalling the L.D or making the ADD.D a no-op is easy. The difficult situation is to detect that the L.D might finish before the ADD.D, because that requires knowing the length of the pipeline and the current position of the ADD.D. Luckily, this code sequence (two writes with no intervening read) will be very rare, so we can use a simple solution: If an instruction in ID wants to write the same register as an instruction already issued, do not issue the instruction to EX. In Section A.8, we will see how additional hardware can eliminate stalls for such hazards. First, let's put together the pieces for implementing the hazard and issue logic in our FP pipeline.

In detecting the possible hazards, we must consider hazards among FP instructions, as well as hazards between an FP instruction and an integer instruction. Except for FP loads-stores and FP-integer register moves, the FP and integer registers are distinct. All integer instructions operate on the integer registers, while the floating-point operations operate only on their own registers. Thus, we need only consider FP loads-stores and FP register moves in detecting hazards between FP and integer instructions. This simplification of pipeline control is an additional advantage of having separate register files for integer and floating-point data. (The main advantages are a doubling of the number of registers, without making either set larger, and an increase in bandwidth without adding more ports to either set. The main disadvantage, beyond the need for an extra register file, is the small cost of occasional moves needed between the two register sets.) Assuming that the pipeline does all hazard detection in ID, there are three checks that must be performed before an instruction can issue:

1. *Check for structural hazards*—Wait until the required functional unit is not busy (this is only needed for divides in this pipeline) and make sure the register write port is available when it will be needed.

2. *Check for a RAW data hazard*—Wait until the source registers are not listed as pending destinations in a pipeline register that will not be available when this instruction needs the result. A number of checks must be made here, depending on both the source instruction, which determines when the result will be available, and the destination instruction, which determines when the value is needed. For example, if the instruction in ID is an FP operation with source register F2, then F2 cannot be listed as a destination in ID/A1, A1/A2,

or A2/A3, which correspond to FP add instructions that will not be finished when the instruction in ID needs a result. (ID/A1 is the portion of the output register of ID that is sent to A1.) Divide is somewhat more tricky, if we want to allow the last few cycles of a divide to be overlapped, since we need to handle the case when a divide is close to finishing as special. In practice, designers might ignore this optimization in favor of a simpler issue test.

3. *Check for a WAW data hazard*—Determine if any instruction in A1, . . . , A4, D, M1, . . . , M7 has the same register destination as this instruction. If so, stall the issue of the instruction in ID.

Although the hazard detection is more complex with the multicycle FP operations, the concepts are the same as for the MIPS integer pipeline. The same is true for the forwarding logic. The forwarding can be implemented by checking if the destination register in any of EX/MEM, A4/MEM, M7/MEM, D/MEM, or MEM/WB registers is one of the source registers of a floating-point instruction. If so, the appropriate input multiplexer will have to be enabled so as to choose the forwarded data. In the exercises, you will have the opportunity to specify the logic for the RAW and WAW hazard detection as well as for forwarding.

Multicycle FP operations also introduce problems for our exception mechanisms, which we deal with next.

Maintaining Precise Exceptions

Another problem caused by these long-running instructions can be illustrated with the following sequence of code:

```
DIV.D    F0,F2,F4
ADD.D    F10,F10,F8
SUB.D    F12,F12,F14
```

This code sequence looks straightforward; there are no dependences. A problem arises, however, because an instruction issued early may complete after an instruction issued later. In this example, we can expect ADD.D and SUB.D to complete *before* the DIV.D completes. This is called *out-of-order completion* and is common in pipelines with long-running operations (see Section A.8). Because hazard detection will prevent any dependence among instructions from being violated, why is out-of-order completion a problem? Suppose that the SUB.D causes a floating-point arithmetic exception at a point where the ADD.D has completed but the DIV.D has not. The result will be an imprecise exception, something we are trying to avoid. It may appear that this could be handled by letting the floating-point pipeline drain, as we do for the integer pipeline. But the exception may be in a position where this is not possible. For example, if the DIV.D decided to take a floating-point-arithmetic exception after the add completed, we could not have a precise exception at the hardware level. In fact, because the ADD.D destroys one of its operands, we could not restore the state to what it was before the DIV.D, even with software help.

This problem arises because instructions are completing in a different order than they were issued. There are four possible approaches to dealing with out-of-order completion. The first is to ignore the problem and settle for imprecise exceptions. This approach was used in the 1960s and early 1970s. It is still used in some supercomputers, where certain classes of exceptions are not allowed or are handled by the hardware without stopping the pipeline. It is difficult to use this approach in most processors built today because of features such as virtual memory and the IEEE floating-point standard, which essentially require precise exceptions through a combination of hardware and software. As mentioned earlier, some recent processors have solved this problem by introducing two modes of execution: a fast, but possibly imprecise mode and a slower, precise mode. The slower precise mode is implemented either with a mode switch or by insertion of explicit instructions that test for FP exceptions. In either case the amount of overlap and reordering permitted in the FP pipeline is significantly restricted so that effectively only one FP instruction is active at a time. This solution is used in the DEC Alpha 21064 and 21164, in the IBM Power1 and Power2, and in the MIPS R8000.

A second approach is to buffer the results of an operation until all the operations that were issued earlier are complete. Some CPUs actually use this solution, but it becomes expensive when the difference in running times among operations is large, since the number of results to buffer can become large. Furthermore, results from the queue must be bypassed to continue issuing instructions while waiting for the longer instruction. This requires a large number of comparators and a very large multiplexer.

There are two viable variations on this basic approach. The first is a *history file,* used in the CYBER 180/990. The history file keeps track of the original values of registers. When an exception occurs and the state must be rolled back earlier than some instruction that completed out of order, the original value of the register can be restored from the history file. A similar technique is used for autoincrement and autodecrement addressing on processors like VAXes. Another approach, the *future file,* proposed by Smith and Pleszkun [1988], keeps the newer value of a register; when all earlier instructions have completed, the main register file is updated from the future file. On an exception, the main register file has the precise values for the interrupted state. In Chapter 3, we will see extensions of this idea, which are used in processors such as the PowerPC 620 and the MIPS R10000 to allow overlap and reordering while preserving precise exceptions.

A third technique in use is to allow the exceptions to become somewhat imprecise, but to keep enough information so that the trap-handling routines can create a precise sequence for the exception. This means knowing what operations were in the pipeline and their PCs. Then, after handling the exception, the software finishes any instructions that precede the latest instruction completed, and the sequence can restart. Consider the following worst-case code sequence:

Instruction$_1$—A long-running instruction that eventually interrupts execution.

Instruction$_2$, . . . , Instruction$_{n-1}$—A series of instructions that are not completed.

Instruction$_n$—An instruction that is finished.

Given the PCs of all the instructions in the pipeline and the exception return PC, the software can find the state of instruction$_1$ and instruction$_n$. Because instruction$_n$ has completed, we will want to restart execution at instruction$_{n+1}$. After handling the exception, the software must simulate the execution of instruction$_1$, . . . , instruction$_{n-1}$. Then we can return from the exception and restart at instruction$_{n+1}$. The complexity of executing these instructions properly by the handler is the major difficulty of this scheme.

There is an important simplification for simple MIPS-like pipelines: If instruction$_2$, . . . , instruction$_n$ are all integer instructions, then we know that if instruction$_n$ has completed, all of instruction$_2$, . . . , instruction$_{n-1}$ have also completed. Thus, only floating-point operations need to be handled. To make this scheme tractable, the number of floating-point instructions that can be overlapped in execution can be limited. For example, if we only overlap two instructions, then only the interrupting instruction need be completed by software. This restriction may reduce the potential throughput if the FP pipelines are deep or if there are a significant number of FP functional units. This approach is used in the SPARC architecture to allow overlap of floating-point and integer operations.

The final technique is a hybrid scheme that allows the instruction issue to continue only if it is certain that all the instructions before the issuing instruction will complete without causing an exception. This guarantees that when an exception occurs, no instructions after the interrupting one will be completed and all of the instructions before the interrupting one can be completed. This sometimes means stalling the CPU to maintain precise exceptions. To make this scheme work, the floating-point functional units must determine if an exception is possible early in the EX stage (in the first 3 clock cycles in the MIPS pipeline), so as to prevent further instructions from completing. This scheme is used in the MIPS R2000/3000, the R4000, and the Intel Pentium. It is discussed further in Appendix H.

Performance of a MIPS FP Pipeline

The MIPS FP pipeline of Figure A.31 on page A-50 can generate both structural stalls for the divide unit and stalls for RAW hazards (it also can have WAW hazards, but this rarely occurs in practice). Figure A.35 shows the number of stall cycles for each type of floating-point operation on a per-instance basis (i.e., the first bar for each FP benchmark shows the number of FP result stalls for each FP add, subtract, or compare). As we might expect, the stall cycles per operation track the latency of the FP operations, varying from 46% to 59% of the latency of the functional unit.

Figure A.36 gives the complete breakdown of integer and floating-point stalls for five SPECfp benchmarks. There are four classes of stalls shown: FP result stalls, FP compare stalls, load and branch delays, and floating-point structural

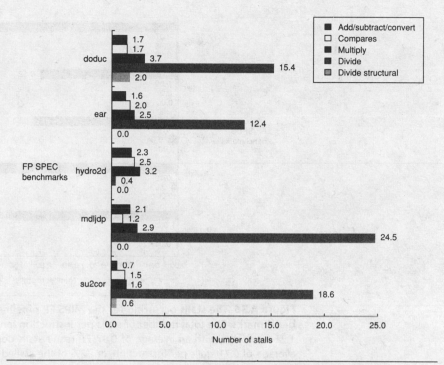

Figure A.35 Stalls per FP operation for each major type of FP operation for the SPEC89 FP benchmarks. Except for the divide structural hazards, these data do not depend on the frequency of an operation, only on its latency and the number of cycles before the result is used. The number of stalls from RAW hazards roughly tracks the latency of the FP unit. For example, the average number of stalls per FP add, subtract, or convert is 1.7 cycles, or 56% of the latency (3 cycles). Likewise, the average number of stalls for multiplies and divides are 2.8 and 14.2, respectively, or 46% and 59% of the corresponding latency. Structural·hazards for divides are rare, since the divide frequency is low.

delays. The compiler tries to schedule both load and FP delays before it schedules branch delays. The total number of stalls per instruction varies from 0.65 to 1.21.

A.6   Putting It All Together: The MIPS R4000 Pipeline

In this section we look at the pipeline structure and performance of the MIPS R4000 processor family, which includes the 4400. The R4000 implements MIPS64 but uses a deeper pipeline than that of our five-stage design both for integer and FP programs. This deeper pipeline allows it to achieve higher clock rates by decomposing the five-stage integer pipeline into eight stages. Because cache access is particularly time critical, the extra pipeline stages come from decomposing the memory access. This type of deeper pipelining is sometimes called *superpipelining*.

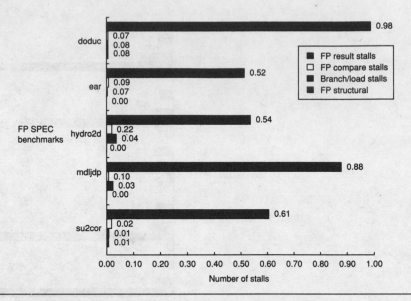

Figure A.36 The stalls occurring for the MIPS FP pipeline for five of the SPEC89 FP benchmarks. The total number of stalls per instruction ranges from 0.65 for su2cor to 1.21 for doduc, with an average of 0.87. FP result stalls dominate in all cases, with an average of 0.71 stalls per instruction, or 82% of the stalled cycles. Compares generate an average of 0.1 stalls per instruction and are the second largest source. The divide structural hazard is only significant for doduc.

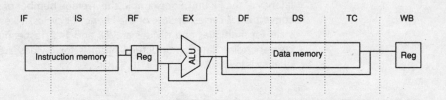

Figure A.37 The eight-stage pipeline structure of the R4000 uses pipelined instruction and data caches. The pipe stages are labeled and their detailed function is described in the text. The vertical dashed lines represent the stage boundaries as well as the location of pipeline latches. The instruction is actually available at the end of IS, but the tag check is done in RF, while the registers are fetched. Thus, we show the instruction memory as operating through RF. The TC stage is needed for data memory access, since we cannot write the data into the register until we know whether the cache access was a hit or not.

Figure A.37 shows the eight-stage pipeline structure using an abstracted version of the data path. Figure A.38 shows the overlap of successive instructions in the pipeline. Notice that although the instruction and data memory occupy multiple cycles, they are fully pipelined, so that a new instruction can start on every

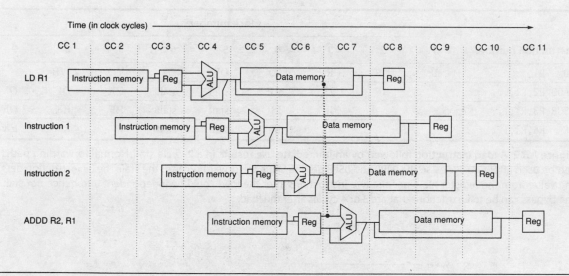

Figure A.38 The structure of the R4000 integer pipeline leads to a 2-cycle load delay. A 2-cycle delay is possible because the data value is available at the end of DS and can be bypassed. If the tag check in TC indicates a miss, the pipeline is backed up a cycle, when the correct data are available.

clock. In fact, the pipeline uses the data before the cache hit detection is complete; Chapter 5 discusses how this can be done in more detail.

The function of each stage is as follows:

- IF—First half of instruction fetch; PC selection actually happens here, together with initiation of instruction cache access.

- IS—Second half of instruction fetch, complete instruction cache access.

- RF—Instruction decode and register fetch, hazard checking, and also instruction cache hit detection.

- EX—Execution, which includes effective address calculation, ALU operation, and branch-target computation and condition evaluation.

- DF—Data fetch, first half of data cache access.

- DS—Second half of data fetch, completion of data cache access.

- TC—Tag check, determine whether the data cache access hit.

- WB—Write back for loads and register-register operations.

In addition to substantially increasing the amount of forwarding required, this longer-latency pipeline increases both the load and branch delays. Figure A.38 shows that load delays are 2 cycles, since the data value is available at the end of DS. Figure A.39 shows the shorthand pipeline schedule when a use immediately follows a load. It shows that forwarding is required for the result of a load instruction to a destination that is 3 or 4 cycles later.

Instruction number	Clock number								
	1	2	3	4	5	6	7	8	9
LD R1,...	IF	IS	RF	EX	DF	DS	TC	WB	
DADD R2,R1,...		IF	IS	RF	stall	stall	EX	DF	DS
DSUB R3,R1,...			IF	IS	stall	stall	RF	EX	DF
OR R4,R1,...				IF	stall	stall	IS	RF	EX

Figure A.39 A load instruction followed by an immediate use results in a 2-cycle stall. Normal forwarding paths can be used after two cycles, so the DADD and DSUB get the value by forwarding after the stall. The OR instruction gets the value from the register file. Since the two instructions after the load could be independent and hence not stall, the bypass can be to instructions that are 3 or 4 cycles after the load.

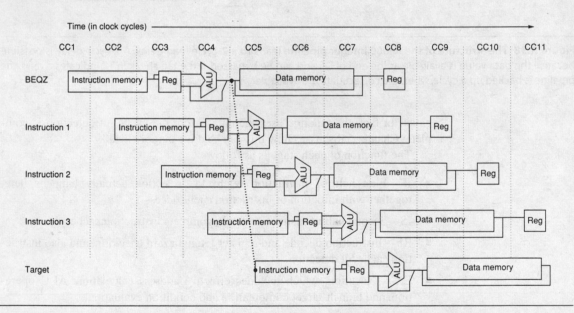

Figure A.40 The basic branch delay is 3 cycles, since the condition evaluation is performed during EX.

Figure A.40 shows that the basic branch delay is 3 cycles, since the branch condition is computed during EX. The MIPS architecture has a single-cycle delayed branch. The R4000 uses a predicted-not-taken strategy for the remaining 2 cycles of the branch delay. As Figure A.41 shows untaken branches are simply 1-cycle delayed branches, while taken branches have a 1-cycle delay slot followed by 2 idle cycles. The instruction set provides a branch-likely instruction, which we described earlier and which helps in filling the branch delay slot. Pipeline interlocks enforce both the 2-cycle branch stall penalty on a taken branch and any data hazard stall that arises from use of a load result.

Instruction number	Clock number								
	1	2	3	4	5	6	7	8	9
Branch instruction	IF	IS	RF	EX	DF	DS	TC	WB	
Delay slot		IF	IS	RF	EX	DF	DS	TC	WB
Stall			stall	stall	stall	stall	stall	stall	stall
Stall			stall	stall	stall	stall	stall	stall	stall
Branch target					IF	IS	RF	EX	DF

Instruction number	Clock number								
	1	2	3	4	5	6	7	8	9
Branch instruction	IF	IS	RF	EX	DF	DS	TC	WB	
Delay slot		IF	IS	RF	EX	DF	DS	TC	WB
Branch instruction + 2			IF	IS	RF	EX	DF	DS	TC
Branch instruction + 3				IF	IS	RF	EX	DF	DS

Figure A.41 A taken branch, shown in the top portion of the figure, has a 1-cycle delay slot followed by a 2-cycle stall, while an untaken branch, shown in the bottom portion, has simply a 1-cycle delay slot. The branch instruction can be an ordinary delayed branch or a branch-likely, which cancels the effect of the instruction in the delay slot if the branch is untaken.

In addition to the increase in stalls for loads and branches, the deeper pipeline increases the number of levels of forwarding for ALU operations. In our MIPS five-stage pipeline, forwarding between two register-register ALU instructions could happen from the ALU/MEM or the MEM/WB registers. In the R4000 pipeline, there are four possible sources for an ALU bypass: EX/DF, DF/DS, DS/TC, and TC/WB. Exercise 4.8 asks you to explore all the possible forwarding conditions for the MIPS instruction set using an R4000-style pipeline.

The Floating-Point Pipeline

The R4000 floating-point unit consists of three functional units: a floating-point divider, a floating-point multiplier, and a floating-point adder. The adder logic is used on the final step of a multiply or divide. Double-precision FP operations can take from 2 cycles (for a negate) up to 112 cycles for a square root. In addition, the various units have different initiation rates. The floating-point functional unit can be thought of as having eight different stages, listed in Figure A.42; these stages are combined in different orders to execute various FP operations.

There is a single copy of each of these stages, and various instructions may use a stage zero or more times and in different orders. Figure A.43 shows the latency, initiation rate, and pipeline stages used by the most common double-precision FP operations.

Stage	Functional unit	Description
A	FP adder	Mantissa ADD stage
D	FP divider	Divide pipeline stage
E	FP multiplier	Exception test stage
M	FP multiplier	First stage of multiplier
N	FP multiplier	Second stage of multiplier
R	FP adder	Rounding stage
S	FP adder	Operand shift stage
U		Unpack FP numbers

Figure A.42 The eight stages used in the R4000 floating-point pipelines.

FP instruction	Latency	Initiation interval	Pipe stages
Add, subtract	4	3	U, S + A, A + R, R + S
Multiply	8	4	U, E + M, M, M, M, N, N + A, R
Divide	36	35	U, A, R, D^{27}, D + A, D + R, D + A, D + R, A, R
Square root	112	111	U, E, $(A+R)^{108}$, A, R
Negate	2	1	U, S
Absolute value	2	1	U, S
FP compare	3	2	U, A, R

Figure A.43 The latencies and initiation intervals for the FP operations both depend on the FP unit stages that a given operation must use. The latency values assume that the destination instruction is an FP operation; the latencies are 1 cycle less when the destination is a store. The pipe stages are shown in the order in which they are used for any operation. The notation S+A indicates a clock cycle in which both the S and A stages are used. The notation D^{28} indicates that the D stage is used 28 times in a row.

From the information in Figure A.43, we can determine whether a sequence of different, independent FP operations can issue without stalling. If the timing of the sequence is such that a conflict occurs for a shared pipeline stage, then a stall will be needed. Figures A.44, A.45, A.46, and A.47 show four common possible two-instruction sequences: a multiply followed by an add, an add followed by a multiply, a divide followed by an add, and an add followed by a divide. The figures show all the interesting starting positions for the second instruction and whether that second instruction will issue or stall for each position. Of course, there could be three instructions active, in which case the possibilities for stalls are much higher and the figures more complex.

Operation	Issue/stall	Clock cycle												
		0	1	2	3	4	5	6	7	8	9	10	11	12
Multiply	Issue	U	E + M	M	M	M	N	N + A	R					
Add	Issue		U	S + A	A + S	R + S								
	Issue			U	S + A	A + R	R + S							
	Issue				U	S + A	A + R	R + S						
	Stall					U	S + A	**A + R**	**R + S**					
	Stall						U	**S + A**	**A + R**	R + S				
	Issue							U	S + A	A + R	R + S			
	Issue								U	S + A	A + R	R + S		

Figure A.44 An FP multiply issued at clock 0 is followed by a single FP add issued between clocks 1 and 7. The second column indicates whether an instruction of the specified type stalls when it is issued *n* cycles later, where *n* is the clock cycle number in which the U stage of the second instruction occurs. The stage or stages that cause a stall are highlighted. Note that this table deals with only the interaction between the multiply and *one* add issued between clocks 1 and 7. In this case, the add will stall if it is issued 4 or 5 cycles after the multiply; otherwise, it issues without stalling. Notice that the add will be stalled for 2 cycles if it issues in cycle 4 since on the next clock cycle it will still conflict with the multiply; if, however, the add issues in cycle 5, it will stall for only 1 clock cycle, since that will eliminate the conflicts.

Operation	Issue/stall	Clock cycle												
		0	1	2	3	4	5	6	7	8	9	10	11	12
Add	Issue	U	S + A	A + R	R + S									
Multiply	Issue		U	E + M	M	M	M	N	N + A	R				
	Issue			U	M	M	M	M	N	N + A	R			

Figure A.45 A multiply issuing after an add can always proceed without stalling, since the shorter instruction clears the shared pipeline stages before the longer instruction reaches them.

Performance of the R4000 Pipeline

In this section we examine the stalls that occur for the SPEC92 benchmarks when running on the R4000 pipeline structure. There are four major causes of pipeline stalls or losses:

1. *Load stalls*—Delays arising from the use of a load result 1 or 2 cycles after the load

2. *Branch stalls*—2-cycle stall on every taken branch plus unfilled or canceled branch delay slots

3. *FP result stalls*—Stalls because of RAW hazards for an FP operand

Operation	Issue/stall	Clock cycle											
		25	26	27	28	29	30	31	32	33	34	35	36
Divide	Issued in cycle 0...	D	D	D	D	D	D+A	D+R	D+A	D+R	A	R	
Add	Issue		U	S+A	A+R	R+S							
	Issue			U	S+A	A+R	R+S						
	Stall				U	S+A	A+R	R+S					
	Stall					U	S+A	A+R	R+S				
	Stall						U	S+A	A+R	R+S			
	Stall							U	S+A	A+R	R+S		
	Stall								U	S+A	A+R	R+S	
	Stall									U	S+A	A+R	R+S
	Issue										U	S+A	A+R
	Issue											U	S+A
	Issue												U

Figure A.46 **An FP divide can cause a stall for an add that starts near the end of the divide.** The divide starts at cycle 0 and completes at cycle 35; the last 10 cycles of the divide are shown. Since the divide makes heavy use of the rounding hardware needed by the add, it stalls an add that starts in any of cycles 28–33. Notice the add starting in cycle 28 will be stalled until cycle 34. If the add started right after the divide, it would not conflict, since the add could complete before the divide needed the shared stages, just as we saw in Figure A.45 for a multiply and add. As in the earlier figure, this example assumes *exactly* one add that reaches the U stage between clock cycles 26 and 35.

Operation	Issue/stall	Clock cycle											
		0	1	2	3	4	5	6	7	8	9	10	11	12
Add	Issue	U	S+A	A+R	R+S									
Divide	Stall		U	A	R	D	D	D	D	D	D	D	D	D
	Issue			U	A	R	D	D	D	D	D	D	D	D
	Issue				U	A	R	D	D	D	D	D	D	D

Figure A.47 **A double-precision add is followed by a double-precision divide.** If the divide starts 1 cycle after the add, the divide stalls, but after that there is no conflict.

4. *FP structural stalls*—Delays because of issue restrictions arising from conflicts for functional units in the FP pipeline

Figure A.48 shows the pipeline CPI breakdown for the R4000 pipeline for the 10 SPEC92 benchmarks. Figure A.49 shows the same data but in tabular form.

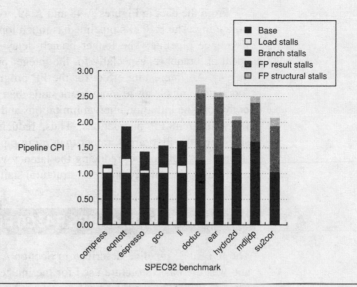

Figure A.48 The pipeline CPI for 10 of the SPEC92 benchmarks, assuming a perfect cache. The pipeline CPI varies from 1.2 to 2.8. The leftmost five programs are integer programs, and branch delays are the major CPI contributor for these. The rightmost five programs are FP, and FP result stalls are the major contributor for these. Figure A.49 shows the numbers used to construct this plot.

Benchmark	Pipeline CPI	Load stalls	Branch stalls	FP result stalls	FP structural stalls
compress	1.20	0.14	0.06	0.00	0.00
eqntott	1.88	0.27	0.61	0.00	0.00
espresso	1.42	0.07	0.35	0.00	0.00
gcc	1.56	0.13	0.43	0.00	0.00
li	1.64	0.18	0.46	0.00	0.00
Integer average	1.54	0.16	0.38	0.00	0.00
doduc	2.84	0.01	0.22	1.39	0.22
mdljdp2	2.66	0.01	0.31	1.20	0.15
ear	2.17	0.00	0.46	0.59	0.12
hydro2d	2.53	0.00	0.62	0.75	0.17
su2cor	2.18	0.02	0.07	0.84	0.26
FP average	2.48	0.01	0.33	0.95	0.18
Overall average	2.00	0.10	0.36	0.46	0.09

Figure A.49 The total pipeline CPI and the contributions of the four major sources of stalls are shown. The major contributors are FP result stalls (both for branches and for FP inputs) and branch stalls, with loads and FP structural stalls adding less.

From the data in Figures A.48 and A.49, we can see the penalty of the deeper pipelining. The R4000's pipeline has much longer branch delays than the classic five-stage pipeline. The longer branch delay substantially increases the cycles spent on branches, especially for the integer programs with a higher branch frequency. An interesting effect for the FP programs is that the latency of the FP functional units leads to more result stalls than the structural hazards, which arise both from the initiation interval limitations and from conflicts for functional units from different FP instructions. Thus, reducing the latency of FP operations should be the first target, rather than more pipelining or replication of the functional units. Of course, reducing the latency would probably increase the structural stalls, since many potential structural stalls are hidden behind data hazards.

A.7   Another View: The MIPS R4300 Pipeline

The five-stage pipeline described in Section A.1 is considered a classic pipeline and was the basic structure used for the integer pipeline on the early RISC processors. Today, it is still heavily used as the pipeline structure for low-end to midrange embedded microprocessors. The MIPS R4300 series, manufactured by NEC, is a 64-bit processor implementing the MIPS64 instruction set intended for the embedded space. Versions of this processor have been used in a wide variety of embedded applications: as the CPU in the Nintendo-64 game processor, in a range of high-end color laser printers, and as the CPU in a network router. The NEC VR 4122, which we mentioned in Chapter 1, is a version of this design incorporating only the integer data path and using software for floating-point operations.

The R4300 pipeline implements floating point by extending the pipeline length through the addition of multiple EX stages for floating-point operations. This introduces one complexity that we have not seen in the simple integer pipeline: the possibility of instructions completing out of order. The extra length of the floating-point pipeline means that unless we add unused stages to the integer pipeline (and thereby increase the number of bypass checks that must be done), an integer instruction can complete and write its results before an earlier floating-point instruction completes. Normally this will not be a problem, but if the floating-point instruction generates an exception, this exception could be raised after the integer instruction has completed, thereby leading to an *imprecise interrupt* (i.e., some instructions after the instruction causing an exception have completed, while the interrupting instruction has not yet completed). The MIPS R4300 uses the scheme discussed in Section A.5 to prevent imprecise interrupts from the FP unit. We will return to the topics of out-of-order instruction completion and precise interrupts in Chapter 3.

Figure A.50 summarizes four versions of the MIPS R4300 processor.

Clock frequency (MHz)	Performance SPECInt 92	Performance SPECFP 92	Power consumption (W)
80	48	36	1.5
100	60	45	1.8
133	80	60	1.9
167	100	75	2.4

Figure A.50 Four versions of the MIPS R4300. Like many other processors in the embedded space, the manufacturers of the R4300 typically publish "Dhrystone MIPS." In addition, they do not ship a full system, so it is impossible to generate true SPEC measurements. The SPEC92 numbers are manufacturer's estimates.

A.8   Crosscutting Issues

RISC Instruction Sets and Efficiency of Pipelining

We have already discussed the advantages of instruction set simplicity in building pipelines. Simple instruction sets offer another advantage: They make it easier to schedule code to achieve efficiency of execution in a pipeline. To see this, consider a simple example: Suppose we need to add two values in memory and store the result back to memory. In some sophisticated instruction sets this will take only a single instruction; in others it will take two or three. A typical RISC architecture would require four instructions (two loads, an add, and a store). These instructions cannot be scheduled sequentially in most pipelines without intervening stalls.

With a RISC instruction set, the individual operations are separate instructions and may be individually scheduled either by the compiler (using the techniques we discussed earlier and more powerful techniques discussed in Chapter 4) or using dynamic hardware scheduling techniques (which we discuss next and in further detail in Chapter 3). These efficiency advantages, coupled with the greater ease of implementation, appear to be so significant that almost all recent pipelined implementations of complex instruction sets actually translate their complex instructions into simple RISC-like operations, and then schedule and pipeline those operations. Chapter 3 shows that both the Pentium III and Pentium 4 use this approach.

Dynamically Scheduled Pipelines

Simple pipelines fetch an instruction and issue it, unless there is a data dependence between an instruction already in the pipeline and the fetched instruction that cannot be hidden with bypassing or forwarding. Forwarding logic reduces the effective pipeline latency so that certain dependences do not result in hazards. If there is an unavoidable hazard, then the hazard detection hardware stalls the pipeline (starting with the instruction that uses the result). No new instructions are fetched or issued until the dependence is cleared. To overcome these performance losses, the compiler can attempt to schedule instructions to avoid the hazard; this approach is called *compiler* or *static scheduling*.

Several early processors used another approach, called *dynamic scheduling*, whereby the hardware rearranges the instruction execution to reduce the stalls. This section offers a simpler introduction to dynamic scheduling by explaining the scoreboarding technique of the CDC 6600. Some readers will find it easier to read this material before plunging into the more complicated Tomasulo scheme, which is covered in Chapter 3. Before proceeding, you may find it useful to read the first few pages (up to the section labeled "Dynamic Scheduling Using Tomasulo's Approach") to understand the core idea and its motivation better.

All the techniques discussed in this appendix so far use in-order instruction issue, which means that if an instruction is stalled in the pipeline, no later instructions can proceed. With in-order issue, if two instructions have a hazard between them, the pipeline will stall, even if there are later instructions that are independent and would not stall.

In the MIPS pipeline developed earlier, both structural and data hazards were checked during instruction decode (ID): When an instruction could execute properly, it was issued from ID. To allow us to begin executing the SUB.D in the above example, we must separate the issue process into two parts: checking the structural hazards and waiting for the absence of a data hazard. We can still check for structural hazards when we issue the instruction; thus, we still use in-order instruction issue. However, we want the instructions to begin execution as soon as their data operands are available. Thus, the pipeline will do *out-of-order execution*, which implies *out-of-order completion*. To implement out-of-order execution, we must split the ID pipe stage into two stages:

1. *Issue*—Decode instructions, check for structural hazards.

2. *Read operands*—Wait until no data hazards, then read operands.

The IF stage proceeds the issue stage, and the EX stage follows the read operands stage, just as in the MIPS pipeline. As in the MIPS floating-point pipeline, execution may take multiple cycles, depending on the operation. Thus, we may need to distinguish when an instruction *begins execution* and when it *completes execution;* between the two times, the instruction is *in execution*. This allows multiple instructions to be in execution at the same time. In addition to these changes to the pipeline structure, we will also change the functional unit design by varying the number of units, the latency of operations, and the functional unit pipelining, so as to better explore these more advanced pipelining techniques.

Dynamic Scheduling with a Scoreboard

In a dynamically scheduled pipeline, all instructions pass through the issue stage in order (in-order issue); however, they can be stalled or bypass each other in the second stage (read operands) and thus enter execution out of order. *Scoreboard-ing* is a technique for allowing instructions to execute out of order when there are sufficient resources and no data dependences; it is named after the CDC 6600 scoreboard, which developed this capability.

Before we see how scoreboarding could be used in the MIPS pipeline, it is important to observe that WAR hazards, which did not exist in the MIPS floating-point or integer pipelines, may arise when instructions execute out of order. For example, consider the following code sequence:

```
DIV.D    F0,F2,F4
ADD.D    F10,F0,F8
SUB.D    F8,F8,F14
```

There is an antidependence between the ADD.D and the SUB.D: If the pipeline exe-cutes the SUB.D before the ADD.D, it will violate the antidependence, yielding incorrect execution. Likewise, to avoid violating output dependences, WAW haz-ards (e.g., as would occur if the destination of the SUB.D were F10) must also be detected. As we will see, both these hazards are avoided in a scoreboard by stall-ing the later instruction involved in the antidependence.

The goal of a scoreboard is to maintain an execution rate of one instruction per clock cycle (when there are no structural hazards) by executing an instruc-tion as early as possible. Thus, when the next instruction to execute is stalled, other instructions can be issued and executed if they do not depend on any active or stalled instruction. The scoreboard takes full responsibility for instruction issue and execution, including all hazard detection. Taking advantage of out-of-order execution requires multiple instructions to be in their EX stage simulta-neously. This can be achieved with multiple functional units, with pipelined functional units, or with both. Since these two capabilities—pipelined functional units and multiple functional units—are essentially equivalent for the purposes of pipeline control, we will assume the processor has multiple functional units.

The CDC 6600 had 16 separate functional units, including 4 floating-point units, 5 units for memory references, and 7 units for integer operations. On a pro-cessor for the MIPS architecture, scoreboards make sense primarily on the floating-point unit since the latency of the other functional units is very small. Let's assume that there are two multipliers, one adder, one divide unit, and a sin-gle integer unit for all memory references, branches, and integer operations. Although this example is simpler than the CDC 6600, it is sufficiently powerful to demonstrate the principles without having a mass of detail or needing very long examples. Because both MIPS and the CDC 6600 are load-store architec-tures, the techniques are nearly identical for the two processors. Figure A.51 shows what the processor looks like.

Every instruction goes through the scoreboard, where a record of the data dependences is constructed; this step corresponds to instruction issue and replaces part of the ID step in the MIPS pipeline. The scoreboard then determines when the instruction can read its operands and begin execution. If the scoreboard decides the instruction cannot execute immediately, it monitors every change in

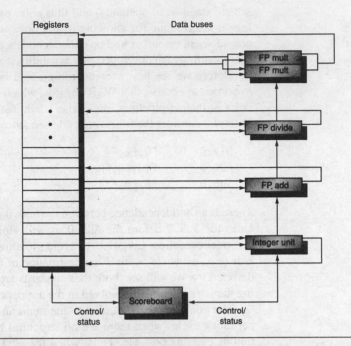

Registers   Data buses

Figure A.51 The basic structure of a MIPS processor with a scoreboard. The scoreboard's function is to control instruction execution (vertical control lines). All data flows between the register file and the functional units over the buses (the horizontal lines, called trunks in the CDC 6600). There are two FP multipliers, an FP divider, an FP adder, and an integer unit. One set of buses (two inputs and one output) serves a group of functional units. The details of the scoreboard are shown in Figures A.52–A.55.

the hardware and decides when the instruction *can* execute. The scoreboard also controls when an instruction can write its result into the destination register. Thus, all hazard detection and resolution is centralized in the scoreboard. We will see a picture of the scoreboard later (Figure A.52 on page A-73), but first we need to understand the steps in the issue and execution segment of the pipeline.

Each instruction undergoes four steps in executing. (Since we are concentrating on the FP operations, we will not consider a step for memory access.) Let's first examine the steps informally and then look in detail at how the scoreboard keeps the necessary information that determines when to progress from one step to the next. The four steps, which replace the ID, EX, and WB steps in the standard MIPS pipeline, are as follows:

1. *Issue*—If a functional unit for the instruction is free and no other active instruction has the same destination register, the scoreboard issues the instruction to the functional unit and updates its internal data structure. This step replaces a portion of the ID step in the MIPS pipeline. By ensuring that no other active functional unit wants to write its result into the destination

register, we guarantee that WAW hazards cannot be present. If a structural or WAW hazard exists, then the instruction issue stalls, and no further instructions will issue until these hazards are cleared. When the issue stage stalls, it causes the buffer between instruction fetch and issue to fill; if the buffer is a single entry, instruction fetch stalls immediately. If the buffer is a queue with multiple instructions, it stalls when the queue fills.

2. *Read operands*—The scoreboard monitors the availability of the source operands. A source operand is available if no earlier issued active instruction is going to write it. When the source operands are available, the scoreboard tells the functional unit to proceed to read the operands from the registers and begin execution. The scoreboard resolves RAW hazards dynamically in this step, and instructions may be sent into execution out of order. This step, together with issue, completes the function of the ID step in the simple MIPS pipeline.

3. *Execution*—The functional unit begins execution upon receiving operands. When the result is ready, it notifies the scoreboard that it has completed execution. This step replaces the EX step in the MIPS pipeline and takes multiple cycles in the MIPS FP pipeline.

4. *Write result*—Once the scoreboard is aware that the functional unit has completed execution, the scoreboard checks for WAR hazards and stalls the completing instruction, if necessary.

A WAR hazard exists if there is a code sequence like our earlier example with ADD.D and SUB.D that both use F8. In that example we had the code

```
DIV.D    F0,F2,F4
ADD.D    F10,F0,F8
SUB.D    F8,F8,F14
```

ADD.D has a source operand F8, which is the same register as the destination of SUB.D. But ADD.D actually depends on an earlier instruction. The scoreboard will still stall the SUB.D in its Write Result stage until ADD.D reads its operands. In general, then, a completing instruction cannot be allowed to write its results when

▪ there is an instruction that has not read its operands that precedes (i.e., in order of issue) the completing instruction, and

▪ one of the operands is the same register as the result of the completing instruction.

If this WAR hazard does not exist, or when it clears, the scoreboard tells the functional unit to store its result to the destination register. This step replaces the WB step in the simple MIPS pipeline.

At first glance, it might appear that the scoreboard will have difficulty separating RAW and WAR hazards. Exercise A.13 will help you understand how the scoreboard distinguishes these two cases and thus knows when to prevent a WAR hazard by stalling an instruction that is ready to write its results.

Because the operands for an instruction are read only when both operands are available in the register file, this scoreboard does not take advantage of forwarding. Instead registers are only read when they are both available. This is not as large a penalty as you might initially think. Unlike our simple pipeline of earlier, instructions will write their result into the register file as soon as they complete execution (assuming no WAR hazards), rather than wait for a statically assigned write slot that may be several cycles away. The effect is reduced pipeline latency and benefits of forwarding. There is still one additional cycle of latency that arises since the write result and read operand stages cannot overlap. We would need additional buffering to eliminate this overhead.

Based on its own data structure, the scoreboard controls the instruction progression from one step to the next by communicating with the functional units. There is a small complication, however. There are only a limited number of source operand buses and result buses to the register file, which represents a structural hazard. The scoreboard must guarantee that the number of functional units allowed to proceed into steps 2 and 4 do not exceed the number of buses available. We will not go into further detail on this, other than to mention that the CDC 6600 solved this problem by grouping the 16 functional units together into four groups and supplying a set of buses, called *data trunks,* for each group. Only one unit in a group could read its operands or write its result during a clock.

Now let's look at the detailed data structure maintained by a MIPS scoreboard with five functional units. Figure A.52 shows what the scoreboard's information looks like partway through the execution of this simple sequence of instructions:

```
L.D     F6,34(R2)
L.D     F2,45(R3)
MUL.D   F0,F2,F4
SUB.D   F8,F6,F2
DIV.D   F10,F0,F6
ADD.D   F6,F8,F2
```

There are three parts to the scoreboard:

1. *Instruction status*—Indicates which of the four steps the instruction is in.

2. *Functional unit status*—Indicates the state of the functional unit (FU). There are nine fields for each functional unit:

   ▪ Busy—Indicates whether the unit is busy or not.

   ▪ Op—Operation to perform in the unit (e.g., add or subtract).

   ▪ Fi—Destination register.

   ▪ Fj, Fk—Source-register numbers.

   ▪ Qj, Qk—Functional units producing source registers Fj, Fk.

   ▪ Rj, Rk—Flags indicating when Fj, Fk are ready and not yet read. Set to No after operands are read.

Instruction		Instruction status			
		Issue	Read operands	Execution complete	Write result
L.D	F6,34(R2)	√	√	√	√
L.D	F2,45(R3)	√	√	√	
MUL.D	F0,F2,F4	√			
SUB.D	F8,F6,F2	√			
DIV.D	F10,F0,F6	√			
ADD.D	F6,F8,F2				

Name	Functional unit status								
	Busy	Op	Fi	Fj	Fk	Qj	Qk	Rj	Rk
Integer	Yes	Load	F2	R3				No	
Mult1	Yes	Mult	F0	F2	F4	Integer		No	Yes
Mult2	No								
Add	Yes	Sub	F8	F6	F2		Integer	Yes	No
Divide	Yes	Div	F10	F0	F6	Mult1		No	Yes

	Register result status								
	F0	F2	F4	F6	F8	F10	F12	...	F30
FU	Mult1	Integer			Add	Divide			

Figure A.52   Components of the scoreboard. Each instruction that has issued or is pending issue has an entry in the instruction status table. There is one entry in the functional unit status table for each functional unit. Once an instruction issues, the record of its operands is kept in the functional unit status table. Finally, the register result table indicates which unit will produce each pending result; the number of entries is equal to the number of registers. The instruction status table says that (1) the first L.D has completed and written its result, and (2) the second L.D has completed execution but has not yet written its result. The MUL.D, SUB.D, and DIV.D have all issued but are stalled, waiting for their operands. The functional unit status says that the first multiply unit is waiting for the integer unit, the add unit is waiting for the integer unit, and the divide unit is waiting for the first multiply unit. The ADD.D instruction is stalled because of a structural hazard; it will clear when the SUB.D completes. If an entry in one of these scoreboard tables is not being used, it is left blank. For example, the Rk field is not used on a load and the Mult2 unit is unused, hence their fields have no meaning. Also, once an operand has been read, the Rj and Rk fields are set to No. Figure A.55 shows why this last step is crucial.

3. *Register result status*—Indicates which functional unit will write each register, if an active instruction has the register as its destination. This field is set to blank whenever there are no pending instructions that will write that register.

Now let's look at how the code sequence begun in Figure A.52 continues execution. After that, we will be able to examine in detail the conditions that the scoreboard uses to control execution.

Example   Assume the following EX cycle latencies (chosen to illustrate the behavior and not representative) for the floating-point functional units: Add is 2 clock cycles, multiply is 10 clock cycles, and divide is 40 clock cycles. Using the code segment in Figure A.52 and beginning with the point indicated by the instruction status in Figure A.52, show what the status tables look like when MUL.D and DIV.D are each ready to go to the Write Result state.

Answer   There are RAW data hazards from the second L.D to MUL.D, ADD.D, and SUB.D, from MUL.D to DIV.D, and from SUB.D to ADD.D. There is a WAR data hazard between DIV.D and ADD.D and SUB.D. Finally, there is a structural hazard on the add functional unit for ADD.D and SUB.D. What the tables look like when MUL.D and DIV.D are ready to write their results is shown in Figures A.53 and A.54, respectively.

		Instruction status			
Instruction		**Issue**	**Read operands**	**Execution complete**	**Write result**
L.D	F6,34(R2)	√	√	√	√
L.D	F2,45(R3)	√	√	√	√
MUL.D	F0,F2,F4	√	√	√	
SUB.D	F8,F6,F2	√	√	√	√
DIV.D	F10,F0,F6	√			
ADD.D	F6,F8,F2	√	√	√	

				Functional unit status					
Name	**Busy**	**Op**	**Fi**	**Fj**	**Fk**	**Qj**	**Qk**	**Rj**	**Rk**
Integer	No								
Mult1	Yes	Mult	F0	F2	F4			No	No
Mult2	No								
Add	Yes	Add	F6	F8	F2			No	No
Divide	Yes	Div	F10	F0	F6	Mult1		No	Yes

			Register result status					
	F0	**F2**	**F4**	**F6**	**F8**	**F10**	**F12**	**...**	**F30**
FU	Mult 1			Add		Divide			

Figure A.53 Scoreboard tables just before the MUL.D goes to write result. The DIV.D has not yet read either of its operands, since it has a dependence on the result of the multiply. The ADD.D has read its operands and is in execution, although it was forced to wait until the SUB.D finished to get the functional unit. ADD.D cannot proceed to write result because of the WAR hazard on F6, which is used by the DIV.D. The Q fields are only relevant when a functional unit is waiting for another unit.

Instruction		Instruction status			
		Issue	Read operands	Execution complete	Write result
L.D	F6,34(R2)	√	√	√	√
L.D	F2,45(R3)	√	√	√	√
MUL.D	F0,F2,F4	√	√	√	√
SUB.D	F8,F6,F2	√	√	√	√
DIV.D	F10,F0,F6	√	√	√	
ADD.D	F6,F8,F2	√	√	√	√

Name	Functional unit status								
	Busy	Op	Fi	Fj	Fk	Qj	Qk	Rj	Rk
Integer	No								
Mult1	No								
Mult2	No								
Add	No								
Divide	Yes	Div	F10	F0	F6			No	No

	Register result status							
	F0	F2	F4	F6	F8	F10	F12	...	F30
FU						Divide		

Figure A.54 Scoreboard tables just before the DIV.D goes to write result. ADD.D was able to complete as soon as DIV.D passed through read operands and got a copy of F6. Only the DIV.D remains to finish.

Now we can see how the scoreboard works in detail by looking at what has to happen for the scoreboard to allow each instruction to proceed. Figure A.55 shows what the scoreboard requires for each instruction to advance and the book-keeping action necessary when the instruction does advance. The scoreboard records operand specifier information, such as register numbers. For example, we must record the source registers when an instruction is issued. Because we refer to the contents of a register as Regs[D], where D is a register name, there is no ambiguity. For example, Fj[FU] ← S1 causes the register *name* S1 to be placed in Fj[FU], rather than the *contents* of register S1.

The costs and benefits of scoreboarding are interesting considerations. The CDC 6600 designers measured a performance improvement of 1.7 for FOR-TRAN programs and 2.5 for hand-coded assembly language. However, this was

Instruction status	Wait until	Bookkeeping
Issue	Not Busy [FU] and not Result [D]	Busy[FU]←yes; Op[FU]←op; Fi[FU]←D; Fj[FU]←S1; Fk[FU]←S2; Qj←Result[S1]; Qk← Result[S2]; Rj← not Qj; Rk← not Qk; Result[D]←FU;
Read operands	Rj and Rk	Rj← No; Rk← No; Qj←0; Qk←0
Execution complete	Functional unit done	
Write result	$\forall f((Fj[f] \neq Fi[FU]$ or $Rj[f] = No)$ & $(Fk[f] \neq Fi[FU]$ or $Rk[f] = No))$	$\forall f($if Qj$[f]$=FU then Rj$[f]$←Yes); $\forall f($if Qk$[f]$=FU then Rk$[f]$←Yes); Result[Fi[FU]]← 0; Busy[FU]← No

Figure A.55 Required checks and bookkeeping actions for each step in instruction execution. FU stands for the functional unit used by the instruction, D is the destination register name, S1 and S2 are the source register names, and op is the operation to be done. To access the scoreboard entry named Fj for functional unit FU we use the notation Fj[FU]. Result[D] is the name of the functional unit that will write register D. The test on the write result case prevents the write when there is a WAR hazard, which exists if another instruction has this instruction's destination (Fi[FU]) as a source (Fj[f] or Fk[f]) and if some other instruction has written the register (Rj = Yes or Rk = Yes). The variable f is used for any functional unit.

measured in the days before software pipeline scheduling, semiconductor main memory, and caches (which lower memory access time). The scoreboard on the CDC 6600 had about as much logic as one of the functional units, which is surprisingly low. The main cost was in the large number of buses—about four times as many as would be required if the CPU only executed instructions in order (or if it only initiated one instruction per execute cycle). The recently increasing interest in dynamic scheduling is motivated by attempts to issue more instructions per clock (so the cost of more buses must be paid anyway) and by ideas like speculation (explored in Section 4.6) that naturally build on dynamic scheduling.

A scoreboard uses the available ILP to minimize the number of stalls arising from the program's true data dependences. In eliminating stalls, a scoreboard is limited by several factors:

1. *The amount of parallelism available among the instructions*—This determines whether independent instructions can be found to execute. If each instruction depends on its predecessor, no dynamic scheduling scheme can reduce stalls. If the instructions in the pipeline simultaneously must be chosen from the same basic block (as was true in the 6600), this limit is likely to be quite severe.

2. *The number of scoreboard entries*—This determines how far ahead the pipeline can look for independent instructions. The set of instructions examined as candidates for potential execution is called the *window*. The size of the scoreboard determines the size of the window. In this section, we assume a window does not extend beyond a branch, so the window (and the scoreboard) always contains straight-line code from a single basic block. Chapter 4 shows how the window can be extended beyond a branch.

3. *The number and types of functional units*—This determines the importance of structural hazards, which can increase when dynamic scheduling is used.

4. *The presence of antidependences and output dependences*—These lead to WAR and WAW stalls.

Chapters 3 and 4 focus on techniques that attack the problem of exposing and better utilizing available ILP. The second and third factors can be attacked by increasing the size of the scoreboard and the number of functional units; however, these changes have cost implications and may also affect cycle time. WAW and WAR hazards become more important in dynamically scheduled processors because the pipeline exposes more name dependences. WAW hazards also become more important if we use dynamic scheduling with a branch-prediction scheme that allows multiple iterations of a loop to overlap.

A.9 Fallacies and Pitfalls

Pitfall *Unexpected execution sequences may cause unexpected hazards.*

At first glance, WAW hazards look like they should never occur in a code sequence because no compiler would ever generate two writes to the same register without an intervening read. But they can occur when the sequence is unexpected. For example, the first write might be in the delay slot of a taken branch when the scheduler thought the branch would not be taken. Here is the code sequence that could cause this:

```
        BNEZ    R1,foo
        DIV.D   F0,F2,F4; moved into delay slot
                ;from fall through
        .....
        .....
foo:    L.D     F0,qrs
```

If the branch is taken, then before the DIV.D can complete, the LD will reach WB, causing a WAW hazard. The hardware must detect this and may stall the issue of the LD. Another way this can happen is if the second write is in a trap routine. This occurs when an instruction that traps and is writing results continues and completes after an instruction that writes the same register in the trap handler. The hardware must detect and prevent this as well.

Pitfall *Extensive pipelining can impact other aspects of a design, leading to overall worse cost-performance.*

The best example of this phenomenon comes from two implementations of the VAX, the 8600 and the 8700. When the 8600 was initially delivered, it had a cycle time of 80 ns. Subsequently, a redesigned version, called the 8650, with a 55 ns clock was introduced. The 8700 has a much simpler pipeline that operates at the microinstruction level, yielding a smaller CPU with a faster clock cycle of 45 ns. The overall outcome is that the 8650 has a CPI advantage of about 20%, but the 8700 has a clock rate that is about 20% faster. Thus, the 8700 achieves the same performance with much less hardware.

Pitfall *Evaluating a compile time scheduler on the basis of unoptimized code.*

Unoptimized code—containing redundant loads, stores, and other operations that might be eliminated by an optimizer—is much easier to schedule than "tight" optimized code. This holds for scheduling both control delays (with delayed branches) and delays arising from RAW hazards. In gcc running on an R3000, which has a pipeline almost identical to that of Section A.1, the frequency of idle clock cycles increases by 18% from the unoptimized and scheduled code to the optimized and scheduled code. Of course, the optimized program is much faster, since it has fewer instructions. To fairly evaluate a scheduler, you must use optimized code, since in the real system you will derive good performance from other optimizations in addition to scheduling.

A.10 Concluding Remarks

At the beginning of the 1980s, pipelining was a technique reserved primarily for supercomputer and large multimillion dollar mainframes. By the mid-1980s, the first pipelined microprocessors appeared and helped transform the world of computing, allowing microprocessors to bypass minicomputers in performance and eventually to take on and outperform mainframes. By the early 1990s, high-end embedded microprocessors embraced pipelining, and desktops were headed toward the use of the sophisticated dynamically scheduled, multiple-issue approaches discussed in Chapter 3. The material in this appendix, which was considered reasonably advanced for graduate students when this text first appeared in 1990, is now considered basic undergraduate material and can be found in processors costing less than $10!

A.11 Historical Perspective and References

This section describes some of the major advances in pipelining through the CDC 6600. Chapters 3 and 4 expand on this basic history.

Early Pipelined CPUs

The first general-purpose pipelined processor is considered to be Stretch, the IBM 7030. Stretch followed the IBM 704 and had a goal of being 100 times faster than the 704. The goal was a stretch from the state of the art at that time—hence the nickname. The plan was to obtain a factor of 1.6 from overlapping fetch, decode, and execute, using a four-stage pipeline. Bloch [1959] and

Bucholtz [1962] describe the design and engineering trade-offs, including the use of ALU bypasses.

A series of general pipelining descriptions that appeared in the late 1970s and early 1980s provided most of the terminology and described most of the basic techniques used in simple pipelines. These surveys include Keller [1975], Ramamoorthy and Li [1977], Chen [1980], and Kogge's book [1981], devoted entirely to pipelining. Davidson and his colleagues [1971, 1975] developed the concept of pipeline reservation tables as a design methodology for multicycle pipelines with feedback (also described in Kogge [1981]). Many designers use a variation of these concepts, in either designing pipelines or in creating software to schedule them.

The RISC processors were originally designed with ease of implementation and pipelining in mind. Several of the early RISC papers, published in the early 1980s, attempt to quantify the performance advantages of the simplification in instruction set. The best analysis, however, is a comparison of a VAX and a MIPS implementation published by Bhandarkar and Clark in 1991, 10 years after the first published RISC papers (see Figure 2.41 on page 154). After 10 years of arguments about the implementation benefits of RISC, this paper convinced even the most skeptical designers of the advantages of a RISC instruction set architecture.

J. E. Smith and his colleagues have written a number of papers examining instruction issue, exception handling, and pipeline depth for high-speed scalar CPUs. Kunkel and Smith [1986] evaluate the impact of pipeline overhead and dependences on the choice of optimal pipeline depth; they also have an excellent discussion of latch design and its impact on pipelining. Smith and Pleszkun [1988] evaluate a variety of techniques for preserving precise exceptions. Weiss and Smith [1984] evaluate a variety of hardware pipeline scheduling and instruction issue techniques.

The MIPS R4000 was one of the first deeply pipelined microprocessors and is described by Killian [1991] and by Heinrich [1993]. The initial Alpha implementation (the 21064) has a similar instruction set and similar integer pipeline structure, with more pipelining in the floating-point unit.

The Introduction of Dynamic Scheduling

In 1964 CDC delivered the first CDC 6600. The CDC 6600 was unique in many ways. In addition to introducing scoreboarding, the CDC 6600 was the first processor to make extensive use of multiple functional units. It also had peripheral processors that used multithreading. The interaction between pipelining and instruction set design was understood, and a simple, load-store instruction set was used to promote pipelining. The CDC 6600 also used an advanced packaging technology. Thornton [1964] describes the pipeline and I/O processor architecture, including the concept of out-of-order instruction execution. Thornton's book [1970] provides an excellent description of the entire processor, from technology to architecture, and includes a foreword by Cray. (Unfortunately, this book is currently out of print.) The CDC 6600 also has an instruction scheduler for the FORTRAN compilers, described by Thorlin [1967].

References

Bhandarkar, D., and D. W. Clark [1991]. "Performance from architecture: Comparing a RISC and a CISC with similar hardware organizations," *Proc. Fourth Conf. on Architectural Support for Programming Languages and Operating Systems*, IEEE/ACM (April), Palo Alto, Calif., 310–319.

Bloch, E. [1959]. "The engineering design of the Stretch computer," *Proc. Fall Joint Computer Conf.*, 48–59.

Bucholtz, W. [1962]. *Planning a Computer System: Project Stretch*, McGraw-Hill, New York.

Chen, T. C. [1980]. "Overlap and parallel processing," in *Introduction to Computer Architecture*, H. Stone, ed., Science Research Associates, Chicago, 427–486.

Clark, D. W. [1987]. "Pipelining and performance in the VAX 8800 processor," *Proc. Second Conf. on Architectural Support for Programming Languages and Operating Systems*, IEEE/ACM (March), Palo Alto, Calif., 173–177.

Davidson, E. S. [1971]. "The design and control of pipelined function generators," *Proc. Conf. on Systems, Networks, and Computers*, IEEE (January), Oaxtepec, Mexico, 19–21.

Davidson, E. S., A. T. Thomas, L. E. Shar, and J. H. Patel [1975]. "Effective control for pipelined processors," *COMPCON, IEEE* (March), San Francisco, 181–184.

Ditzel, D. R., and H. R. McLellan [1987]. "Branch folding in the CRISP microprocessor: Reducing the branch delay to zero," *Proc. 14th Symposium on Computer Architecture* (June), Pittsburgh, 2–7.

Emer, J. S., and D. W. Clark [1984]. "A characterization of processor performance in the VAX-11/780," *Proc. 11th Symposium on Computer Architecture* (June), Ann Arbor, Mich., 301–310.

Heinrich, J. [1993]. *MIPS R4000 User's Manual*, Prentice Hall, Englewood Cliffs, N.J.

Keller, R. M. [1975]. "Look-ahead processors," *ACM Computing Surveys* 7:4 (December), 177–195.

Killian, E. [1991]. "MIPS R4000 technical overview–64 bits/100 MHz or bust," *Hot Chips III Symposium Record* (August), Stanford University, 1.6–1.19.

Kogge, P. M. [1981]. *The Architecture of Pipelined Computers*, McGraw-Hill, New York.

Kunkel, S. R., and J. E. Smith [1986]. "Optimal pipelining in supercomputers," *Proc. 13th Symposium on Computer Architecture* (June), Tokyo, 404–414.

Ramamoorthy, C. V., and H. F. Li [1977]. "Pipeline architecture," *ACM Computing Surveys* 9:1 (March), 61–102.

Rymarczyk, J. [1982]. "Coding guidelines for pipelined processors," *Proc. Symposium on Architectural Support for Programming Languages and Operating Systems*, IEEE/ACM (March), Palo Alto, Calif., 12–19.

Sites, R. [1979]. *Instruction Ordering for the CRAY-1 Computer*, Tech. Rep. 78-CS-023 (July), Dept. of Computer Science, Univ. of Calif., San Diego.

Smith, J. E., and A. R. Pleszkun [1988]. "Implementing precise interrupts in pipelined processors," *IEEE Trans. on Computers* 37:5 (May), 562–573. (This paper is based on an earlier paper that appeared in *Proc. 12th Symposium on Computer Architecture*, June 1988.)

Thorlin, J. F. [1967]. "Code generation for PIE (parallel instruction execution) computers," *Proc. Spring Joint Computer Conf.*, 27.

Thornton, J. E. [1964]. "Parallel operation in the Control Data 6600," *Proc. AFIPS Fall Joint Computer Conf., Part II*, 26, 33–40.

Thornton, J. E. [1970]. *Design of a Computer, the Control Data 6600*, Scott, Foresman, Glenview, Ill.

Weiss, S., and J. E. Smith [1984]. "Instruction issue logic for pipelined supercomputers," *Proc. 11th Symposium on Computer Architecture* (June), Ann Arbor, Mich., 110–118.

Exercises

Solutions to the "starred" exercises appear in Appendix B.

A.1 [15/15/15] <A.2> Use the following code fragment:

```
Loop:   LD      R1,0(R2)     ;load R1 from address 0+R2
        DADDI   R1,R1,#1     ;R1=R1+1
        SD      0(R2),R1     ;store R1 at address 0+R2
        DADDI   R2,R2,#4     ;R2=R2+4
        DSUB    R4,R3,R2     ;R4=R3-R2
        BNEZ    R4,Loop      ;branch to Loop if R4!=0
```

Assume that the initial value of R3 is R2 + 396.

Throughout this exercise use the classic RISC five-stage integer pipeline (see Figure A.1) and assume all memory accesses take 1 clock cycle.

a. [15] <A.2> Show the timing of this instruction sequence for the RISC pipeline *without* any forwarding or bypassing hardware but assuming a register read and a write in the same clock cycle "forwards" through the register file, as in Figure A.6. Use a pipeline timing chart like Figure A.6. Assume that the branch is handled by flushing the pipeline. If all memory references take 1 cycle, how many cycles does this loop take to execute?

b. [15] <A.2> Show the timing of this instruction sequence for the RISC pipeline with normal forwarding and bypassing hardware. Use a pipeline timing chart like Figure A.6. Assume that the branch is handled by predicting it as not taken. If all memory references take 1 cycle, how many cycles does this loop take to execute?

c. [15] <A.2> Assume the RISC pipeline with a single-cycle delayed branch and normal forwarding and bypassing hardware. Schedule the instructions in the loop including the branch delay slot. You may reorder instructions and modify the individual instruction operands, but do not undertake other loop transformations that change the number or opcode of the instructions in the loop (that's for Chapter 4!). Show a pipeline timing diagram and compute the number of cycles needed to execute the entire loop.

⭐ A.2 [15/15] <A.2, A.4, A.5> Use the following code fragment:

```
Loop:   L.D     F0,0(R2)
        L.D     F4,0(R3)
        MUL.D   F0,F0,F4
        ADD.D   F2,F0,F2
        DADDUI  R2,R2,#8
        DADDUI  R3,R3,#8
        DSUBU   R5,R4,R2
        BNEZ    R5,Loop
```

Assume that the initial value of R4 is R2 + 792.

For this exercise assume the standard five-stage integer pipeline and the MIPS FP pipeline as described in Section A.5. If structural hazards are due to write-back contention, assume the earliest instruction gets priority and other instructions are stalled.

a. [15] <A.2, A.4, A.5> Show the timing of this instruction sequence for the MIPS FP pipeline *without* any forwarding or bypassing hardware but assuming a register read and a write in the same clock cycle "forwards" through the register file. Assume that the branch is handled by flushing the pipeline. If all memory references hit in the cache, how many cycles does this loop take to execute?

b. [15] <A.2, A.4, A.5> Show the timing of this instruction sequence for the MIPS FP pipeline with normal forwarding and bypassing hardware. Assume that the branch is handled by predicting it as not taken. If all memory references hit in the cache, how many cycles does this loop take to execute?

✪ A.3 [15] <A.2> Suppose the branch frequencies (as percentages of all instructions) are as follows:

Conditional branches	15%
Jumps and calls	1%
Conditional branches	60% are taken

We are examining a four-deep pipeline where the branch is resolved at the end of the second cycle for unconditional branches and at the end of the third cycle for conditional branches. Assuming that only the first pipe stage can always be done independent of whether the branch goes and ignoring other pipeline stalls, how much faster would the machine be without any branch hazards?

✪ A.4 [15] <A.1, A.2> A reduced hardware implementation of the classic five-stage RISC pipeline might use the EX stage hardware to perform a branch instruction comparison and then not actually deliver the branch target PC to the IF stage until the clock cycle in which the branch instruction reaches the MEM stage. Control hazard stalls can be reduced by resolving branch instructions in ID, but improving performance in one respect may reduce performance in other circumstances. How does determining branch outcome in the ID stage have the potential to increase data hazard stall cycles?

A.5 [12/13/20/20/15/15] <A.2, A.3> For these problems, we will explore a pipeline for a register-memory architecture. The architecture has two instruction formats: a register-register format and a register-memory format. There is a single-memory addressing mode (offset + base register).

There is a set of ALU operations with format

    ALUop Rdest, Rsrc$_1$, Rsrc$_2$

or

    ALUop Rdest, Rsrc$_1$, MEM

where the ALUop is one of the following: Add, Subtract, And, Or, Load (Rsrc$_1$ ignored), Store. Rsrc or Rdest are registers. MEM is a base register and offset pair.

Branches use a full compare of two registers and are PC-relative. Assume that this machine is pipelined so that a new instruction is started every clock cycle. The following pipeline structure—similar to that used in the VAX 8700 micropipeline [Clark 1987]—is

IF	RF	ALU1	MEM	ALU2	WB			
	IF	RF	ALU1	MEM	ALU2	WB		
		IF	RF	ALU1	MEM	ALU2	WB	
			IF	RF	ALU1	MEM	ALU2	WB
				IF	RF	ALU1	MEM	ALU2	WB
					IF	RF	ALU1	MEM	ALU2	WB

The first ALU stage is used for effective address calculation for memory references and branches. The second ALU cycle is used for operations and branch comparison. RF is both a decode and register-fetch cycle. Assume that when a register read and a register write of the same register occur in the same clock the write data is forwarded.

a. [12] <A.2> Find the number of adders needed, counting any adder or incrementer; show a combination of instructions and pipe stages that justify this answer. You need only give one combination that maximizes the adder count.

b. [13] <A.2> Find the number of register read and write ports and memory read and write ports required. Show that your answer is correct by showing a combination of instructions and pipeline stage indicating the instruction and the number of read ports and write ports required for that instruction.

c. [20] <A.4> Determine any *data forwarding* for any ALUs that will be needed. Assume that there are separate ALUs for the ALU1 and ALU2 pipe stages. Put in all forwarding among ALUs needed to avoid or reduce stalls. Show the relationship between the two instructions involved in forwarding using the format of the table in Figure A.22 but ignoring the last two columns. Be careful to consider forwarding across an intervening instruction, for example,

```
ADD      R1, ...
any instruction
ADD      ..., R1, ...
```

d. [20] <A.3> Show all data forwarding requirements needed to avoid or reduce stalls when either the source or destination unit is not an ALU. Use the same format as Figure A.22, again ignoring the last two columns. Remember to forward to and from memory references.

e. [15] <A.3> Show all the remaining hazards that involve at least one unit other than an ALU as the source or destination unit. Use a table like that in Figure A.21, but listing the length of hazard in place of the last column.

f. [15] <A.2> Show all control hazard types by example and state the length of the stall. Use a format like Figure A.11, labeling each example.

A.6 [12/13/13/15/15] <A.1, A.2, A.3> We will now add support for register-memory ALU operations to the classic five-stage RISC pipeline. To offset this increase in complexity, *all* memory addressing will be restricted to register indirect (i.e., all addresses are simply a value held in a register: no offset or displacement may be added to the register value). For example, the register-memory instruction ADD R4, R5, (R1) means add the contents of register R5 to the contents of the memory location with address equal to the value in register R1 and put the sum in register R4. Register-register ALU operations are unchanged. Answer the following for the integer RISC pipeline.

a. [12] <A.1> List a rearranged order of the five traditional stages of the RISC pipeline that will support register-memory operations implemented exclusively by register indirect addressing.

b. [13] <A.2, A.3> Describe what new forwarding paths are needed for the rearranged pipeline by stating the source, destination, and information transferred on each needed new path.

c. [13] <A.2, A.3> For the reordered stages of the RISC pipeline, what new data hazards are created by this addressing mode? Give an instruction sequence illustrating each new hazard.

d. [15] <A.3> List all ways that the RISC pipeline with register-memory ALU operations can have a different instruction count for a given program than the original RISC pipeline. Give a pair of specific instruction sequences, one for the original pipeline and one for the rearranged pipeline, to illustrate each way.

e. [15] <A.3> Assume all instructions take 1 clock cycle per stage. List all ways that the register-memory RISC can have a different CPI for a given program as compared to the original RISC pipeline.

A.7 [10/15/15] <A.2> Scheduling branch delay slots (see the three ways in Figure A.14) can improve performance. Assume a single branch delay slot and an instruction execution pipeline that determines branch outcome in the second stage.

a. [10] <A.2> For a delayed branch instruction, what is the penalty for each branch delay slot scheduling scheme if the branch is taken and if it is not taken, and what condition, if any, must be satisfied to ensure correct execution?

b. [15] <A.2> A cancel-if-not-taken branch instruction (also called *branch likely* and implemented in MIPS) does not execute the instruction in the delay slot if the branch is not taken. Thus, a compiler need not be as conservative when filling the delay slot. For each branch delay slot scheduling scheme, what is the penalty if the branch is taken and if it is not taken, and what condition, if any, must be satisfied to ensure correct execution?

c. [15] <A.2> Assume that an instruction set has a delayed branch and a cancel-if-not-taken branch. When should a compiler use each branch instruction and from where should the slot be filled?

A.8 [15] <A.5> Create a table showing the forwarding logic for the R4000 integer pipeline using the same format as that in Figure A.22. Include only the MIPS instructions we considered in Figure A.22.

★ A.9 [15] <A.5> Create a table showing the R4000 integer hazard detection using the same format as that in Figure A.21. Include only the MIPS instructions we considered in Figure A.22.

A.10 [25] <A.5> Suppose MIPS had only one register set. Construct the forwarding table for the FP and integer instructions using the format of Figure A.22. Ignore FP and integer divides.

A.11 [15] <A.5> Construct a table like Figure A.21 to check for WAW stalls in the MIPS FP pipeline of Figure A.31. Do not consider FP divides.

A.12 [20/22/22] <A.4, A.6> In this exercise, we will look at how a common vector loop runs on statically and dynamically scheduled versions of the MIPS pipeline. The loop is the so-called DAXPY loop (discussed extensively in Appendix G) and the central operation in Gaussian elimination. The loop implements the vector operation $Y = a \times X + Y$ for a vector of length 100. Here is the MIPS code for the loop:

```
foo:    L.D      F2,0(R1)      ;load X(i)
        MULT.D   F4,F2,F0      ;multiply a*X(i)
        L.D      F6,0(R2)      ;load Y(i)
        ADD.D    F6,F4,F6      ;add a*X(i) + Y(i)
        S.D      0(R2),F6      ;store Y(i)
        DADDUI   R1,R1,#8      ;increment X index
        DADDUI   R2,R2,#8      ;increment Y index
        DSGTUI   R3,R1,done    ;test if done
        BEQZ     R3,foo        ;loop if not done
```

For (a)–(c), assume that the integer operations issue and complete in 1 clock cycle (including loads) and that their results are fully bypassed. Ignore the branch delay. You will use the FP latencies (only) shown in Figure A.30 (page A-49), *but* assume that the FP unit is fully pipelined. For scoreboards below, assume an instruction waiting for a result from another function unit can pass through read operands at the same time the result is written. Also assume that an instruction in WR completing will allow a currently active instruction that is waiting on the same functional unit to issue in the same clock cycle in which the first instruction completes WR.

a. [20] <A.4> For this problem use the MIPS pipeline of Section A.5 with the pipeline latencies from Figure A.30, but a fully pipelined FP unit, so the initiation interval is 1. Show the number of stall cycles for each instruction and what clock cycle each instruction begins execution (i.e., enters its first EX cycle) on the first iteration of the loop. How many clock cycles does each loop iteration take?

b. [22] <A.6> Using the MIPS code for SAXPY above, show the state of the scoreboard tables (as in Figure A.53) when the SGTI instruction reaches Write Result. Assume that issue and read operands each take a cycle. Assume that there is one integer functional unit that takes only a single execution cycle (the latency to use is 0 cycles, including loads and stores). Assume the FP unit configuration of Figure A.51 with the FP latencies of Figure A.30. The branch should not be included in the scoreboard.

c. [22] <A.6> Using the MIPS code for SAXPY above, assume a scoreboard with the FP functional units described in Figure A.51, plus one integer functional unit (also used for load-store). Assume the latencies shown in Figure A.56. Show the state of the scoreboard (as in Figure A.53) when the branch issues for the second time. Assume the branch was correctly predicted taken and took 1 cycle. How many clock cycles does each loop iteration take? You may ignore any register port/bus conflicts.

A.13 [25] <A.8> It is critical that the scoreboard be able to distinguish RAW and WAR hazards, because a WAR hazard requires stalling the instruction doing the writing until the instruction reading an operand initiates execution, but a RAW hazard requires delaying the reading instruction until the writing instruction finishes— just the opposite. For example, consider the sequence

```
MUL.D    F0,F6,F4
DSUB.D   F8,F0,F2
ADD.D    F2,F10,F2
```

The DSUB.D depends on the MUL.D (a RAW hazard) and thus the MUL.D must be allowed to complete before the DSUB.D; if the MUL.D were stalled for the DSUB.D due to the inability to distinguish between RAW and WAR hazards, the processor will deadlock. This sequence contains a WAR hazard between the ADD.D and the DSUB.D, and the ADD.D cannot be allowed to complete until the DSUB.D begins execution. The difficulty lies in distinguishing the RAW hazard between MUL.D and DSUB.D, and the WAR hazard between the DSUB.D and ADD.D.

To see just why the three-instruction scenario is important, trace the handling of each instruction stage by stage through Issue, Read Operands, Execute, and Write

Instruction producing result	Instruction using result	Latency in clock cycles
FP multiply	FP ALU op	6
FP add	FP ALU op	4
FP multiply	FP store	5
FP add	FP store	3
Integer operation (including load)	Any	0

Figure A.56 Pipeline latencies where latency is number of cycles between producing and consuming instruction.

Result. Assume that each scoreboard stage other than Execute takes 1 clock cycle. Assume that the MUL.D instruction requires 3 clock cycles to execute and that the DSUB.D and ADD.D instructions each take 1 cycle to execute. Finally, assume the processor has two multiply function units and two add function units. Present the trace as follows.

Step 1. Make a table with the column headings Instruction, Issue, Read Operands, Execute, Write Result, and Comment. In the first column, list the instructions in program order (be generous with space between instructions; larger table cells will better hold the results of your analysis). Start the table by writing a 1 in the Issue column of the MUL.D instruction row to show that MUL.D completes the Issue stage in clock cycle 1. Now, fill in the stage columns of the table through the cycle at which the scoreboard first stalls an instruction.

Step 2. For a stalled instruction write the words "waiting at clock cycle X," where X is the number of the current clock cycle, in the appropriate table column to show that the scoreboard is resolving an RAW or WAR hazard by stalling that stage. In the Comment column, state what type of hazard and what dependent instruction is causing the wait.

Step 3. Adding the words "completes with clock cycle Y" to a "waiting" table entry, fill in the rest of the table through the time when all instructions are complete. For an instruction that stalled, add a description in the Comments column telling why the wait ended when it did and how deadlock was avoided. (*Hint:* Think about how WAW hazards are prevented and what this implies about active instruction sequences.) Note the completion order of the three instructions as compared to their program order.

Solutions to Selected Exercises

Captain Kirk
You ought to sell an instruction and maintenance manual with this thing.

Cyrano Jones
If I did, what would happen to man's search for knowledge?

Star Trek
"The Trouble with Tribbles" (Dec. 29, 1967)

Introduction

Captain Kirk and Cyrano Jones were both right. With respect to exercises, a solution can confirm your understanding, provide new insight into the material, and speed attainment of deeper understanding. On the other hand, turning immediately to a provided solution robs you of the opportunity to discover the intellectual territory firsthand.

In the spirit of personal exploration, this appendix provides solutions to a representative subset of the exercises. Generally, the solutions present a way of approaching the exercise as well as the required solution. We encourage you to use the solutions provided here as an aid to your own search for knowledge.

B.1 Chapter 1 Solutions

1.4 a. Speedup $= \dfrac{\text{Number of floating-point instructions DFT}}{\text{Number of floating-point instructions FFT}}$

$= \dfrac{n^2}{n \log_2 n}$

Thus,

n	8	16	32	64	128	256	512	1024
Speedup	2.7	4.0	6.4	10.7	18.2	32.0	56.9	102.4

Also,

$$\lim_{n \to \infty} \text{Speedup} = \lim_{n \to \infty} \frac{n^2}{n \log_2 n} = \infty$$

b. Percent reduction $= 1 - \dfrac{\text{Number of floating-point instructions FFT}}{\text{Number of floating-point instructions DFT}}$

$= 1 - \dfrac{1024 \times \log_2 1024}{1024^2}$

$= 99\%$

c. Choosing to include a branch-target buffer in a processor means adding circuitry to the unenhanced design. This increases die size, testing time, and power consumption, making the enhanced processor more costly. Choosing to use an equivalent, asymptotically faster algorithm, such as the FFT, incurs no cost. Thus, the better algorithm will be universally adopted.

1.6 The proposed formulation for $MIPS_B$ can be rewritten as

$$\frac{MIPS_A}{D_A} = \frac{MIPS_B}{D_B}$$

Examining the units of each factor, we have

$$\frac{\text{Computer } A \text{ instructions/second}}{\text{Dhrystone/second}} = \frac{\text{Computer } B \text{ instructions/second}}{\text{Dhrystone/second}}$$

The time units factor out, revealing that the formulation is founded upon the assumption that

$$\text{Computer } A \text{ instructions/Dhrystone} = \text{Computer } B \text{ instructions/Dhrystone}$$

Unless Computer A and Computer B have the same instruction set architecture and execute identically compiled Dhrystone executables, this assumption is likely false. If so, the formulation for $MIPS_B$ is also incorrect.

1.10 a. $\text{MFLOPS} = \dfrac{\text{Number of floating-point operations in a program}}{\text{Execution time in seconds} \times 10^6}$

The exercise statement gives 100×10^6 as the number of floating-point operations, and Figure 1.15 gives the execution times. Figure B.1 shows the times and MFLOPS rates for each computer and program.

b. From the computed MFLOPS and the formulas for arithmetic, geometric, and harmonic means, we find the results in Figure B.2.

c. The arithmetic mean of MFLOPS rates trends inversely with total execution time. The geometric means, regardless of which normalization is used, do not show each difference in total execution time. Harmonic mean tracks total execution time best.

Program	Computer A		Computer B		Computer C	
	Time	MFLOPS	Time	MFLOPS	Time	MFLOPS
P1	1	100	10	10	20	5
P2	1000	0.1	100	1	20	5

Figure B.1 MFLOPS achieved by three computers for two programs.

Mean	Computer		
	A	B	C
Arithmetic	50.1	5.5	5.0
Harmonic	0.2	1.8	5.0
Geometric (normalize to A)	1.0	1.0	1.6
Geometric (normalize to B)	1.0	1.0	1.6
Geometric (normalize to C)	0.6	0.6	1.0

Figure B.2 Means of the MFLOPS ratings.

1.13   a.   Let the data value sets be

$$A = \{10^7, 10^7, 10^7, 10^7, 10^7, 10^7, 10^7, 10^7, 10^7, 1\}$$

and

$$B = \{1, 1, 1, 1, 1, 1, 1, 1, 1, 10^7\}$$

Arithmetic mean $(A) = 9 \times 10^6$

Median $(A) = 10 \times 10^6$

Arithmetic mean $(B) = 1 \times 10^6$

Median $(B) = 1$

Set A mean and median are within 10% in value, but set B mean and median are far apart. A large outlying value seriously distorts the arithmetic mean, while a small outlying value has a lesser effect.

     b.   Harmonic mean $(A) = 10.0$

Harmonic mean $(B) = 1.1$

In this case the set B harmonic mean is very close to the median, but set A harmonic mean is much smaller than the set A median. The harmonic mean is more affected by a small outlying value than a large one.

     c.   Which is closest depends on the nature of the outlying data point. Neither mean produces a statistic that is representative of the data values under all circumstances.

     d.   Let the new data sets be

$$C = \{1, 1, 1, 1, 1, 1, 1, 1, 1, 2\}$$

and

$$D = \{10^7, 10^7, 10^7, 10^7, 10^7, 10^7, 10^7, 10^7, 10^7, 5 \times 10^6\}$$

Then

Arithmetic mean $(C) = 9.5 \times 10^6$

Harmonic mean $(C) = 9.1 \times 10^6$

Median $(C) = 10 \times 10^6$

and

Arithmetic mean $(D) = 1.1$

Harmonic mean $(D) = 1.05$

Median $(D) = 1$

In both cases, the means and medians are close. Summarizing a set of data values that has less disparity among the values by stating a statistic, such as mean or median, is intrinsically more meaningful.

1.16   Amdahl's Law can be generalized to handle multiple enhancements. If only one enhancement can be used at a time during program execution, then

$$\text{Speedup} = \left[1 - \sum_i \text{FE}_i + \sum_i \frac{\text{FE}_i}{\text{SE}_i}\right]^{-1}$$

where FE_i is the fraction of time that enhancement i can be used and SE_i is the speedup of enhancement i. For a single enhancement the equation reduces to the familiar form of Amdahl's Law.

a. With three enhancements we have

$$\text{Speedup} = \left[1 - (\text{FE}_1 + \text{FE}_2 + \text{FE}_3) + \frac{\text{FE}_1}{\text{SE}_1} + \frac{\text{FE}_2}{\text{SE}_2} + \frac{\text{FE}_3}{\text{SE}_3}\right]^{-1}$$

Substituting in the known quantities gives

$$10 = \left[1 - (0.25 + 0.25 + \text{FE}_3) + \frac{0.25}{30} + \frac{0.25}{20} + \frac{\text{FE}_3}{15}\right]^{-1}$$

Solving yields

$$\text{FE}_3 = 0.45$$

Thus, the third enhancement must be usable 45% of the time.

b. Let T_e and TNE_e denote execution time with enhancements and the time during enhanced execution in which no enhancements are in use, respectively. Let T_{original} and $\text{FNE}_{\text{original}}$ stand for execution time without enhancements and the fraction of that time that cannot be enhanced. Finally, let FNE_e represent the fraction of the reduced (enhanced) execution time for which no enhancement is in use. By definition,

$$\text{FNE}_e = \frac{\text{TNE}_e}{T_e}$$

Because the time spent executing code that cannot be enhanced is the same whether enhancements are in use or not, and by Amdahl's Law, we have

$$\frac{\text{TNE}_e}{T_e} = \frac{\text{FNE}_{\text{original}} \times T_{\text{original}}}{T_{\text{original}}/\text{Speedup}}$$

Cancelling factors and substituting equivalent expressions for $\text{FNE}_{\text{original}}$ and Speedup yields

$$\frac{\text{FNE}_{\text{original}} \times T_{\text{original}}}{T_{\text{original}}/\text{Speedup}} = \frac{1 - \sum_i \text{FE}_i}{1 - \sum_i \text{FE}_i + \sum_i \frac{\text{FE}_i}{\text{SE}_i}}$$

Substituting with known quantities,

$$\text{FNE}_e = \frac{1 - (0.25 + 0.35 + 0.10)}{1 - (0.25 + 0.35 + 0.10) + \left(\frac{0.25}{30} + \frac{0.35}{20} + \frac{0.10}{15}\right)} = \frac{0.3}{0.3325} = 90\%$$

c. Let the speedup when implementing only enhancement i be $Speedup_i$, and let $Speedup_{ij}$ denote the speedup when employing enhancements i and j.

$$Speedup_1 = \left(1 - 0.15 + \frac{0.15}{30}\right)^{-1} = 1.17$$

$$Speedup_2 = \left(1 - 0.15 + \frac{0.15}{20}\right)^{-1} = 1.17$$

$$Speedup_3 = \left(1 - 0.7 + \frac{0.7}{15}\right)^{-1} = 2.88$$

Thus, if only one enhancement can be implemented, enhancement 3 offers much greater speedup.

$$Speedup_{12} = \left[1 - (0.15 + 0.15) + \frac{0.15}{30} + \frac{0.15}{20}\right]^{-1} = 1.40$$

$$Speedup_{13} = \left[1 - (0.15 + 0.7) + \frac{0.15}{30} + \frac{0.7}{15}\right]^{-1} = 4.96$$

$$Speedup_{23} = \left[1 - (0.15 + 0.7) + \frac{0.15}{20} + \frac{0.7}{15}\right]^{-1} = 4.90$$

Thus, if only a pair of enhancements can be implemented, enhancements 1 and 3 offer the greatest speedup.

Selecting the fastest enhancement(s) may not yield the highest speedup. As Amdahl's Law states, an enhancement contributes to speedup only for the fraction of time that it can be used.

1.18   a. $$MFLOPS_{native} = \frac{Number\ of\ floating\text{-}point\ operations}{Execution\ time\ in\ seconds \times 10^6}$$

$$= \frac{199827008653}{287 \times 10^6}$$

$$= 696$$

Because one of the two measured values (time) is reported with only three significant digits, the answer should be stated to three significant digits precision.

b. There are four 171.swim operations that are not explicitly given normalized values: load, store, copy, and convert. Let's think through what normalized values to use for these instructions.

First, convert comprises only 0.006% of the FP operations. Thus, convert would have to correspond to about 1000 normalized FP operations to have any effect on MFLOPS reported with three significant digits. It seems unlikely that convert would be this much more time-consuming than exponentiation or a trig function. Any less and there is no effect. So let's apply an important principle—keep models simple—and model convert as one normalized FP operation.

Next, copy replicates a value, making it available at a second location. This same behavior can be produced by adding zero to a value and saving the result in a new location. So, reasonably, copy should have the same normalized FP count as add.

Finally, load and store interact with computer memory. They can be quick to the extent that the memory responds quickly to an access request, unlike divide, square root, exponentiation, and sin, which are computed using a series of approximation steps to reach an answer. Because load and store are very common, Amdahl's Law suggests making them fast. So assume a normalized FP value of 1 for load and store. Note that any increase would significantly affect the result.

With the above normalized FP operations model, we have

$$\text{MFLOPS}_{normalized} = \frac{\text{Normalized number of floating-point operations}}{\text{Execution time in seconds} \times 10^6}$$

$$= \frac{204111836401}{287}$$

$$= 711$$

B.2 Chapter 2 Solutions

2.2 **Stack advantage.** Stack instructions have the smallest encoding because no operand or result locations are named.

Stack disadvantages. Operands must be in the correct order on the stack or else it must be possible to "convert" the initial result. The order of subtraction can be changed by negating the result because $A - B = -(B - A)$. However, there is no simple way to transform the result of "shift left A by B bit positions" to "shift left B by A bit positions." So, in general, operands must be in the correct order. An instruction to exchange the top two stack elements would be handy.

Accumulator advantage. Smaller instruction encoding because only one operand location is named.

Accumulator disadvantages. Operands must be in the correct order; that is, the correct operand must be in the accumulator. A swap instruction to exchange the accumulator contents with an operand location would be useful.

Load-store advantage. Because operands are in registers, operand order can always be as needed without any exchanges.

Load-store disadvantage. Larger instruction encoding size.

2.4   a.   Accumulator architecture code:

```
Load B          ;Acc ← B
Add C           ;Acc ← Acc + C
Store A         ;Mem[A] ← Acc
Add C           ;Acc ← "A" + C
Store B         ;Mem[B] ← Acc
Negate          ;Acc ← − Acc
Add A           ;Acc ← "− B" + A
Store D         ;Mem[D] ← Acc
```

Memory-memory architecture code:

```
Add A, B, C     ;Mem[A] ← Mem[B] + Mem[C]
Add B, A, C     ;Mem[B] ← Mem[A] + Mem[C]
Sub D, A, B     ;Mem[D] ← Mem[A] − Mem[B]
```

Stack architecture code: (TOS is top of stack, NTTOS is the next to the top of stack, and * is the initial contents of TOS)

```
Push B          ;TOS ← Mem[B], NTTOS ← *
Push C          ;TOS ← Mem[C], NTTOS ← TOS
Add             ;TOS ← TOS + NTTOS, NTTOS ← *
Pop A           ;Mem[A] ← TOS, TOS ← *
Push A          ;TOS ← Mem[A], NTTOS ← *
Push C          ;TOS ← Mem[C], NTTOS ← TOS
Add             ;TOS ← TOS + NTTOS, NTTOS ← *
Pop B           ;Mem[B] ← TOS, TOS ← *
Push B          ;TOS ← Mem[B], NTTOS ← *
Push A          ;TOS ← Mem[A], NTTOS ← TOS
Sub             ;TOS ← TOS − NTTOS, NTTOS ← *
Pop D           ;Mem[D] ← TOS, TOS ← *
```

Load-store architecture code:

```
Load    R1,B        ;R1 ← Mem[B]
Load    R2,C        ;R2 ← Mem[C]
Add     R3,R1,R2    ;R3 ← R1 + R2 = B + C
Add     R1,R3,R2    ;R1 ← R3 + R2 = A + C
Sub     R4,R3,R1    ;R4 ← R3 − R1 = A − B
Store   A,R3        ;Mem[A] ← R3
Store   B,R1        ;Mem[B] ← R1
Store   D,R4        ;Mem[D] ← R4
```

2.8   The point of this exercise is to highlight the value of compiler optimizations (see Exercise 2.9). In this exercise registers are not used to hold updated values; values are stored to memory when updated and subsequently reloaded. Because all the addresses of all the variables (including all array elements) can fit in 16 bits, we can use immediate instructions to load addresses. Figure B.3 shows one possible translation of the given C code fragment.

```
ex2_8:    DADD    R1,R0,R0        ;R0 = 0, initialize i = 0
          SW      2000(R0),R1     ;store i

loop:     LD      R1,2000(R0)     ;get value of i
          DSLL    R2,R1,#3        ;R2 = word offset of B[i]
          DADDI   R3,R2,#5000     ;add base address of B to R2

          LD      R4,0(R3)        ;load B[i]
          LD      R5,1500(R0)     ;load C

          DADD    R6,R4,R5        ;B[i] + C

          LD      R1,2000(R0)     ;get value of i
          DSLL    R2,R1,#3        ;R2 = word offset of A[i]
          DADDI   R7,R2,#0        ;add base address of A to R2
          SD      0(R7),R6        ;A[i] ← B[i] + C

          LD      R1,2000(R0)     ;get value of i
          DADDI   R1,R1,#1        ;increment i
          SD      2000(R0),R1     ;store i

          LD      R1,2000(R0)     ;get value of i
          DADDI   R8,R1,#-101     ;is counter at 101?
          BNEZ    R8,loop         ;if not 101, repeat
```

Figure B.3 MIPS code to implement the C loop without using registers to hold updated values for future use or to pass values to a subsequent loop iteration.

The number of instructions executed dynamically is the number of initialization instructions plus the number of instructions in the loop times the number of iterations:

$$\text{Instructions executed} = 2 + (16 \times 101) = 1618$$

The number of memory-data references is a count of the load and store instructions executed:

$$\text{Memory-data references executed} = 0 + (8 \times 101) = 808$$

Since MIPS instructions are 4 bytes in size, code size is the number of instructions times 4:

$$\text{Instruction bytes} = 4 \times 18 = 72$$

2.14   a.

	Pixel 1			Pixel 2	
R	G	B	R	G	B
E5	F1	D7	AA	C4	DE
+ 20	+ 20	+ 20	+ 20	+ 20	+ 20
05	11	F7	CA	E4	FE

0511F7 is not brighter and has a significant color shift because the red and green brightness are much less now than the blue brightness. CAE4FE is brighter.

b.

	Pixel 1			Pixel 2	
R	G	B	R	G	B
E5	F1	D7	AA	C4	DE
$+_s$ 20	$+_s$ 20	$+_s$ 20	$+_s$ 20	$+_s$ 20	$+_s$ 20
FF	FF	F7	CA	E4	FE

Both results are now brighter.

2.18   Take the code sequence one line at a time.

1. A = B + C   ;The operands here are given, not computed by the code, so copy propagation will not transform this statement.

2. B = A + C   ;Here A is a computed value, so transform the code by substituting A = B + C to get
   = B + C + C   ;Now no operand is computed

3. D = A - B   ;Both operands are computed so substitute for both to get
   = (B + C) - (B + C + C) ;Simplify algebraically to get
   = - C   ;This is a given, not computed, operand

Copy propagation has increased the work in statement 2 from one addition to two. It has changed the work in statement 3 from subtraction to negation, possibly a savings. The above suggests that writing optimizing compilers means incorporating sophisticated trade-off analysis capability to control any optimizing steps, if the best results are to be achieved.

B.3   Chapter 3 Solutions

3.2

Code fragment	Data dependence?	Dynamic scheduling sufficient for out-of-order execution?
DADDI R1,R1,#4 LD R2,7(R1)	True dependence on R1	No. Changing instruction order will break program semantics.
DADD R3,R1,R2 S.D R2,7(R1)	None	Yes
S.D R2,7(R1) S.D F2,200(R7)	Output dependence may exist	Maybe. If the hardware computes the effective addresses early enough, then the store order may be exchanged.
BEZ R1,place S.D R1,7(R1)	None	No. Changing instruction order is speculative until the branch resolves.

3.5   a.   In the following table, the column headings (1), (2), (3), and (4) correspond to the four items of information named in the exercise statement. N/A means "not applicable."

Row	(1)	(2)	(3)	(4)
Issue FP Operation	yes	no	single issue	N/A
Issue Load or Store	yes	no	single issue	N/A
Issue Load only	yes	no	single issue	N/A
Issue Store only	yes	no	single issue	N/A
Execute FP Operation	yes	yes	N/A	structural hazard, not enough functional units
Execute Load-Store step 1	no	no	only 1 load queue only 1 store queue FIFO queues	N/A
Execute Load step 2	no	no	only 1 load queue FIFO queue	N/A
Write result FP Operation or Load	no	no	only 1 CDB	N/A
Write result Store	no	yes	N/A	number of memory ports and the protocol for computing effective addresses

b.   The base register address name is held in rs.

Proof: In the Issue step rs is stored in reservation station field Vj. In the Execute Load-Store step 1 phase field A holds the immediate value operand and is added to Vj to compute the effective address, which is stored back in field A.

c. The Address Unit performs: Execute Load-Store step 1, wait until RS[r].Qj = 0 & r is head of load-store queue, compute RS[r].A ← RS[r].Vj + RS[r].A. It may also manage the load-store buffer.

d. The entries for integer ALU operation instructions are identical to those for FP Operation in Issue, Execute, and Write result, with the caveat that Regs[] and RegisterStat[] refer to the integer register file, not the floating-point register file.

e. Change the Issue phase "Wait until" conditions to be

Station r empty & no pending (unresolved) branch

for instructions other than Load and Store, and to

Buffer r empty & no pending (unresolved) branch

for Load and Store instructions.

3.9 Consider two branches, B1 and B2, that are executed alternately. In the following tables columns labeled P show the value of a 1-bit predictor shared by B1 and B2. Columns labeled B1 and B2 show the actions of the branches. Time increases to the right. T stands for taken, NT for not taken. The predictor is initialized to NT.

a.

	P	B1	P	B2	P	B1	P	B2	P	B1	P	B2	P	B1	P	B2
	NT	T	T	NT	NT	NT	NT	T	T	T	T	NT	NT	NT	NT	T
Correct prediction?		—	no	—	no	—	yes	—	no	—	yes	—	no	—	yes	—	no

Here, B1 and B2 each alternate taken/not taken. If they each had a 1-bit predictor, each would always be mispredicted. Because a single predictor is shared here, prediction accuracy improves from 0% to 50%.

b.

	P	B1	P	B2	P	B1	P	B2	P	B1	P	B2	P	B1	P	B2
	NT	T	T	NT	NT	T	T	NT	NT	T	T	NT	NT	T	T	NT
Correct prediction?		—	no	—	no	—	no	—	no	—	no	—	no	—	no	—	no

Here, B1 is always taken, B2 is always not taken, and they are interleaved as in part (a). If each had a 1-bit predictor, each would be correctly predicted after an initial transient. Because of predictor sharing here, accuracy is 0%.

c. If a predictor is being shared by a set of branch instructions, then over the course of program execution set membership will likely change. When a new branch enters the set or an old one leaves the set, the branch action history represented by the state of the predictor is unlikely to predict new set behavior as well as it did old set behavior, which had some time to affect predictor state. The transient intervals following set changes likely will reduce long-term prediction accuracy.

3.14   To compare the performance of systems with and without a branch-target buffer (BTB) for conditional branches, we determine the speedup of the CPIs for the two designs, CPI_{BTB} and $CPI_{no\ BTB}$. (We might also approach this exercise by figuring out the speedup of the pipeline speedups with and without the BTB—the resulting speedup equation, when simplified, is identical to the equation for the speedup of the CPIs.) The speedup is given by

$$Speedup = \frac{CPI_{no\ BTB}}{CPI_{BTB}} = \frac{CPI_{base} + Stalls_{no\ BTB}}{CPI_{base} + Stalls_{BTB}} \tag{B.1}$$

From the exercise statement CPI_{base} is 1.0, which, by definition, accounts for everything *except* conditional branches. To complete the solution, we must find the number of stall cycles that are caused by unconditional branches in the machines with and without BTBs. To find the stall terms, $Stalls_{BTB}$ and $Stalls_{no\ BTB}$, we begin with the following expression:

$$Stalls = \sum_{s\in Stall} Frequency_s \times Penalty_s \tag{B.2}$$

which sums over all stall cases related to branch folding the product of the frequency of the stall case and the penalty.

The value for $Stalls_{no\ BTB}$ follows simply from the exercise statement and Equation B.2:

$$Stalls_{no\ BTB} = 15\% \times 2 = 0.30 \tag{B.3}$$

As the system without a BTB has a fixed two-cycle branch penalty, the stall contribution from branches is simply the product of the frequency of branches and the number of penalty cycles. Computing $Stalls_{BTB}$ is a bit more involved.

To find $Stalls_{BTB}$ we must consider each possible BTB outcome from a conditional branch. There are three cases: first, the branch can miss the BTB; second, the branch can hit the BTB and be correctly predicted; and finally, the branch can hit the BTB and be incorrectly predicted. Figure B.4 summarizes these observations. The frequencies and penalties can be found from the exercise statement and the discussion of BTBs in Section 3.4 of the text. For example, if the BTB hits and correctly predicts a branch, there is no penalty (because the BTB returns the next PC in time to be used for the fetch of the instruction following the branch). This case occurs with a frequency per instruction given by the frequency of branches (15%) multiplied by the frequency of branches that are in the BTB (90%) multiplied by the frequency of branches that are in the BTB and are predicted correctly (90%).

BTB result	BTB prediction	Frequency (per instruction)	Penalty (cycles)
Miss	—	$15\% \times 10\% = 1.5\%$	3
Hit	Correct	$15\% \times 90\% \times 90\% = 12.1\%$	0
Hit	Incorrect	$15\% \times 90\% \times 10\% = 1.3\%$	4

Figure B.4 A summary of the behavior of a BTB for conditional branches.

From Equation B.2 and Figure B.4, we can compute $Stalls_{BTB}$:

$$Stalls_{BTB} = (1.5\% \times 3) + (12.1\% \times 0) + (1.3\% \times 4) = 0.097$$

This result along with Equation B.3 can be plugged into Equation B.1 to arrive at

$$Speedup = \frac{CPI_{base} + Stalls_{no\ BTB}}{CPI_{base} + Stalls_{BTB}} = \frac{1.0 + 0.30}{1.0 + 0.097} = 1.2$$

Therefore, adding a BTB for conditional branches makes the DLX pipeline about 20% faster.

3.17 a. The same data dependences—true, anti-, and output—must be checked for, but without the issue restriction we would expect dependences to be much more common within a fetched pair of instructions.

   b. Remember that the given pipeline is a very simple five-stage design with no structural hazards and with instructions taking one clock cycle in each stage. Register names are 5 bits. Checking only for data hazards means just checking instructions i and $i + 1$ in ID for dependence on instructions in EX (cannot forward ALU results in time) and Load instructions in MEM (also cannot forward memory read data in time). ID must check each operand of each instruction in ID with the destination registers of both instructions in EX and any load instructions in MEM. ID must also check the operands of instruction $i + 1$ against the result of instruction i because forwarding cannot prevent a data hazard if there is a dependence. Figure B.5 shows the comparisons needed.

   The column and row labels in Figure B.5 are the names that must be brought to comparators in ID. There are nine 5-bit names for a total of 45 bits. The X symbols in Figure B.5 denote the comparisons that must be performed. The count is 18.

   If issue width is doubled, then there are up to four instructions at each stage. Figure B.6 shows the required comparisons.

   Doubling the issue width requires comparison with 19 5-bit names for 95 bits, as shown in Figure B.6. The total comparisons to be performed are 76.

	Results				
Operands	ID_i	EX_1	EX_2	MEM_1	MEM_2
ID_{i+1} Op 1	X	X	X	X	X
ID_{i+1} Op 2	X	X	X	X	X
ID_i Op 1		X	X	X	X
ID_i Op 2		X	X	X	X

Figure B.5 Comparisons required to check for data hazards in two-issue pipeline. ID_x is an instruction in the ID stage; ID_x Op 1 and ID_x Op 2 denote the first and second operands of ID_x. EX_i and MEM_i stand for instructions in the EX and MEM stages. An X means that a comparison is performed.

| | | | | | Results | | | | | | |
Operands	ID_{i+2}	ID_{i+1}	ID_i	EX_1	EX_2	EX_3	EX_4	MEM_1	MEM_2	MEM_3	MEM_4
ID_{i+3} Op 1	X	X	X	X	X	X	X	X	X	X	X
ID_{i+3} Op 2	X	X	X	X	X	X	X	X	X	X	X
ID_{i+2} Op 1		X	X	X	X	X	X	X	X	X	X
ID_{i+2} Op 2		X	X	X	X	X	X	X	X	X	X
ID_{i+1} Op 1			X	X	X	X	X	X	X	X	X
ID_{i+1} Op 2			X	X	X	X	X	X	X	X	X
ID_i Op 1				X	X	X	X	X	X	X	X
ID_i Op 2				X	X	X	X	X	X	X	X

Figure B.6 Comparisons required to check for data hazards in four-issue pipeline. The notation used is the same as in Figure B.5.

The growth in data hazard checking work in ID is more than linear in issue width.

c. Number of compares $= 2n * n + 2(n - 1) + 2(n - 2) + \ldots + 2(1)$

$$= 4n^2 + 2 \sum_{i=1}^{n-1} i$$

$$= 4n^2 + 2\left[\frac{n(n-1)}{2}\right]$$

$$= 5n^2 - n$$

3.20   When speculation is correct, it allows an instruction that should execute to execute earlier by reducing or eliminating stalls that would occur if execution were delayed until the instruction was no longer speculative. Early execution of a required instruction has no effect on instruction count or clock cycle. The reduction in stall cycles improves CPI.

When speculation is incorrect, instructions that are not on the path of execution are executed and their results ignored. There is no effect on clock cycle time, but the dynamic instruction count increases. The mix of instructions executed may change and lead to a minor effect on CPI, but the majority of the increase in CPU time will be due to the cycles spent on incorrectly speculated instructions, which is best modeled as an increase in IC.

3.21

	ROB Fields			Committed?
Entry	Instruction	Destination	Value	Yes/no
0	ADD.D	F0	F8 + F8	Yes
1	MUL.D	F2	–	No
2	SUB.D	F4	–	No
0	DADDI	R10	R12 + R12	No
1				
2				

There is no value entry for MUL.D because its 10-cycle latency means it has not yet completed execution. There is no value entry for SUB.D because it is dependent on MUL.D. ROB entry 0 initially held ADD.D but has been overwritten by ADDI; entries 1 and 2 hold their initial data.

B.4   Chapter 4 Solutions

4.1   a. Figure B.7 shows pipeline structure.

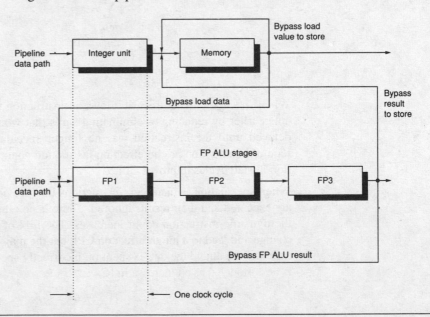

Figure B.7 Pipeline structure implied by Figure 4.1 and full forwarding. An equally valid structure would show the FP ALU as a single stage taking three clock cycles to perform its work.

b. Figure B.8 shows the latency of each unit.

Functional unit	Row of Figure 4.1 that determines the clock cycles needed for this functional unit		
Integer Unit	FP ALU op	Store double	2
	or		
	Load double	FP ALU op	1
Memory	Load double	FP ALU op	1
	or		
	Load double	Store double	0
FP ALU	FP ALU op	Another FP ALU op	3

Figure B.8 Information determining latency of each functional unit.

To derive the answer to part (a) from Figure 4.1 and an assumption that all results can be forwarded, start with the FP ALU to Another FP ALU latency. Given forwarding, a latency of i between instructions using the same FU implies that there are i stages in the FU, if fully pipelined.

Next, if a load can supply a data value to a store with zero latency, then the Memory stage must take only one cycle. Bypassing a load result (a data value read from memory) to the FP ALU with a latency of one means the output of the Memory stage must fall at the end of the clock cycle following the first FP ALU clock cycle. This positions the Memory stage in time with respect to the FP ALU.

Finally, the Integer Unit precedes the Memory stage and computes effective addresses for it. If a load (an integer operation) can supply an FP ALU op with only one cycle of latency, then the EA calculation must start and finish in one cycle. By similar reasoning, if an FP ALU op can supply a store with a two-cycle latency, then the store EA must have been computed in one cycle in the Integer Unit.

4.5   There are six dependences in the C loop presented in the exercise:

1. Anti dependence from S1 to S1 on a.

2. True dependence from S1 to S2 on a.

3. Loop-carried true dependence from S4 to S1 on b.

4. Loop-carried true dependence from S4 to S3 on b.

5. Loop-carried true dependence from S3 to S3 on b.

6. Loop-carried output dependence from S3 to S3 on a.

For a loop to be parallel, each iteration must be independent of all others, which is not the case in the code used for this exercise.

Because dependences 3, 4, and 5 are "true" dependences, they can not be removed through renaming or other such techniques. In addition, as these dependences are loop-carried, they imply that iterations of the loop are not independent. These factors together imply the loop can not be made parallel as the loop is written. By "rewriting" the loop it may be possible to find a loop that is functionally equivalent to the original loop that can be made parallel.

4.7   a.   The given code has a loop-carried dependence from iteration i to $i + 1$ and high latency dependences within and between loop bodies. Simply unrolling twice yields

```
foo:    L.D      F0,0(R1)
        L.D      F4,0(R2)
        L.D      F6,#-8(R1)
        MUL.D    F0,F0,F4        ;1 from L.D F4,0(R2)
        L.D      F8,#-8(R2)
        DADDUI   R1,R1,#-16
        MUL.D    F6,F6,F8        ;1 from L.D F8,-8(R2)
        ADD.D    F2,F0,F2        ;3 from MUL.D F0,F0,F4
        DADDUI   R2,R2,#-16
        stall
        BNEZ     R1,foo
        ADD.D    F2,F6,F2        ;in slot, 3 from ADD.D F2,F0,F2
```

The dependence chain from one ADD.D to the next ADD.D forces the stall. Unrolling further will only aggravate the problem. We must break the dependence chain to schedule without stalls.

A solution takes advantage of the commutativity and associativity of dot product to compute two running sums in the loop, one for even elements and one for odd elements, and combines the two partial sums outside the loop body to get the final result. The code for this solution is

```
foo:    L.D      F0,0(R1)
        L.D      F6,-8(R1)
        L.D      F4,0(R2)
        L.D      F8,-8(R2)
        MUL.D    F0,F0,F4        ;1 from L.D F4,0(R2)
        MUL.D    F6,F6,F8        ;1 from L.D F8,-8(R2)
        DADDIU   R1,R1,-16
        DADDIU   R2,R2,-16
        ADD.D    F2,F0,F2        ;3 from MUL.D F0,F0,F4
        BNEZ     R1,foo
        ADD.D    F10,F6,F10      ;3 from MUL.D F6,F6,F8
                                 ;and fill branch delay slot
bar:    ADD.D    F2,F2,F10       ;combine even and odd
                                 ;elements
```

The code shown assumes the loop executes a nonzero, even number of times. The loop itself is stall free, but there are three stalls when the loop exits. The loop body takes 11 clock cycles.

b. Figure B.9 shows the schedule of execution for the transferred code.

	Integer instruction		FP instruction	Clock cycle
foo:	L.D	F0,0(R1)		1
	L.D	F6,-8(R1)		2
	L.D	F4,0(R2)		3
	L.D	F8,-8(R2)		4
	DADDUI	R1,R1,#-16	MUL.D F0,F0,F4	5
	DADDUI	R2,R1,#-16	MUL.D F6,F6,F8	6
	stall			7
	stall			8
	BNEZ	R1,foo	ADD.D F2,F0,F2	9
			ADD.D F10,F6,F10	10
				...
bar:			ADD.D F2,F2,F10	14

Figure B.9 The unrolled and scheduled code as it would look on a superscalar MIPS.

The loop body now takes 10 cycles instead of 11, a very limited return from the superscalar hardware.

4.12 Normalizing the loop leads to the modified C code, shown in Figure B.10. The greatest common divisor (GCD) test indicates the potential for dependence within an array indexed by the functions $ai + b$ and $cj + d$ if the following condition holds:

$$(d - b) \bmod \gcd (c, a) = 0$$

Applying the GCD test with, in this case, $a = 2$, $b = 0$, $c = 100$, and $d = 1$ allows us to determine if there is a dependence in the loop. Thus, $\gcd (2, 100) = 2$ and $d - b = 1$. Because one is a factor of two, the GCD test indicates that there is a dependence in the code. In reality, there is not a dependence in the code since the loop loads its values from a[101], a[201], ..., a[5001] and assigns these values to a[2], a[4], ..., a[100].

```
for(i = 1; i <= 50; i++) {
    a[2*i] = a[(100*i)+1];
}
```

Figure B.10 Normalized loop.

4.17   The branch is written to skip the LW instructions if R10 = 0, so let's assume the branch guards against a memory access violation. A violation would terminate the program, so if LW R8,0(R10) is moved before the branch, the effective address must not be zero. The load can be guarded by conditional move instructions if there are two unused registers available. One of the registers must contain a safe address for the load. The code is

```
DADDI    R29,R0,#1000    ;initialize R29 to a safe address
LW       R1,40(R2)
MOV      R30,R8          ;save R8 in unused R30
CMOVNZ   R29,R10,R10     ;R29 is unused and contains a safe
                         ;address. R29 ← R10 if R10
                         ;contains a safe address ≠ 0
LW       R8,0(R29)       ;speculative load
CMOVZ    R8,R30,R10      ;if R10 = 0 load is incorrectly
                         ;speculated so restore R8
BEQZ     R10,L
LW       R9,0(R8)
```

Both loads after the branch can be speculated using only conditional moves. One more unused register is needed. The code is

```
ADDI     R29,R0,#1000
LW       R1,40(R2)
MOV      R30,R8
MOV      R31,R9          ;save R9 in unused R31
CMOVNZ   R29,R10,R10
LW       R8,0(R29)
LW       R9,0(R8)        ;now this load is speculated
CMOVZ    R8,R30,R10
CMOVZ    R9,R31,R10      ;restore R9 if needed
```

There is no branch instruction at all, but there is a significant conditional instruction overhead.

4.20   Predicated instructions maintain a straight-line program execution path. They are useful for collapsing relatively balanced, parallel, rejoining execution paths by removing the conditional branch and transforming its function into new data dependence.

In general a fork with nonrejoining execution paths, established by a branch, will be too unbalanced for predicated instructions to offer any performance improvement. There is no point in using predication if performance will be worse than retaining the branch.

4.24   For the processor of Figure 4.1 the integer load latency is 1, and the floating-point load latency is either 1 or 0 depending on the destination. The processor of Figure 4.15 has the same integer load latency, but has a much greater floating-point load latency of 9.

The value of an ALAT is to allow loads to easily be moved earlier than preceding stores. This is essential if loads are to be scheduled much earlier. However, to avoid causing data hazard stalls, a load need only be scheduled earlier than its dependent instructions by an amount equal to the load latency.

Thus, an ALAT is more beneficial to the processor of Figure 4.15 because it will be needed more often to hide the long floating-point latency of that processor.

<table>
<tr><td>B.5</td><td></td></tr>
</table>

Chapter 5 Solutions

5.1   This exercise uses differences in cache organizations to illustrate how benchmarks can present a skewed perspective of system performance. Because system performance is heavily influenced by the memory hierarchy (if you do not believe this, take a look at Figure 5.2 in the text again!), it is possible to develop code that runs poorly on a particular cache organization. This exercise should drive home not only an appreciation for the influence of cache organization on performance, but also an appreciation of how difficult it is for a single program to provide a reasonable summary of *general* system performance.

a. Consider the MIPS code blurb shown in Figure B.11. We make two assumptions in this code: First, the value of r0 is zero; second, locations f00 and bar both map onto the same set in both caches. For example, foo and bar could be 0x00000000 and 0x80000000 (these addresses are in hexadecimal), respectively, since both addresses reside in set zero of either cache.

On Cache A, this code only causes two compulsory misses to load the two instructions into the cache. After that, all accesses generated by the code hit the cache. For Cache B, all the accesses miss the cache because a direct-mapped cache can only store one block in each set, yet the program has two active blocks that map to the same set. The cache will "thrash" because when it generates an access to foo, the block containing bar is resident in the cache, and when it generates an access to bar, the block containing foo is resident in the cache.

This is a good example of where a victim cache [Jouppi 1990] could eliminate the performance benefit of the associative cache. Keep in mind that in this example the information that Cache B misses on is always recently resident.

```
foo:    beqz    r0,bar    ;branch iff r0 == 0
          .
          .
          .
bar:    beqz    r0,foo    ;branch iff r0 == 0
```

Figure B.11 MIPS code that performs better on Cache A.

```
baz:    sw      0(r1),r0    ;store r0 to memory
qux:    beqz    r0,baz      ;branch iff r0 == 0
```

Figure B.12 MIPS code that performs better on Cache B.

b. Consider the MIPS code blurb shown in Figure B.12. We make two assumptions: first, locations baz and qux and the location pointed to by 0(r1) map to different sets within the caches and are all initially resident; second, r0 is zero (as it always is for MIPS).

This code illustrates the main thrust of a program that makes a system with Cache B outperform a system with Cache A, that is, one that repeatedly writes to a location that is resident in both caches. Each time the sw executes on Cache A, the data stored are written to memory because Cache A is write through. For Cache B, the sw always finds the appropriate block in the cache (as we assume the data at location 0(r1) are resident in the cache) and updates only the cache block, as the cache is write back; the block is not written to main memory until it is replaced.

c. With all accesses hits, Cache A allows the processor to maintain CPI = 1. Cache B misses each access at a cost of 100 ns, or 200 clock cycles. Thus Cache B allows its processor to achieve CPI = 200. Cache A offers a speedup of 200 over Cache B.

d. In the steady state, Cache B hits on every write and, so, maintains CPI = 1. Cache A writes to memory on each store, consuming an extra 100 ns each time. Cache B allows the processor to complete one iteration in 2 clocks. With Cache A the processor needs 202 clocks per iteration. Cache B offers a speedup of 101 over Cache A.

5.6 The merging write buffer links the CPU to the write-back L2 cache. Two CPU writes cannot merge if they are to different sets in L2. So, for each new entry into the buffer a quick check on only those address bits that determine the L2 set number need be performed at first. If there is no match in this "screening" test, then the new entry is not merged. If there is a set number match, then all address bits can be checked for a definitive result.

As the associativity of L2 increases, the rate of false positive matches from the simplified check will increase, reducing performance.

5.16 a. Program basic blocks are often short (less than 10 instructions). Even program run blocks, sequences of instructions executed between branches, are not very long. Prefetching obtains the next sequential block, but program execution does not continue to follow locations PC, PC + 4, PC + 8, . . . , for very long. So as blocks get larger the probability that a program will not execute all instructions in the block, but rather take a branch to another instruction address, increases. Prefetching instructions benefit performance when the program continues straight-line execution into the next block. So as instruction cache blocks increase in size, prefetching becomes less attractive.

b. Data structures often comprise lengthy sequences of memory addresses. Program access of a data structure often takes the form of a sequential sweep. Large data blocks work well with such access patterns, and prefetching is likely still of value due to the highly sequential access patterns.

5.19   a. We can expect software to be slower due to the overhead of a context switch to the handler code, but the sophistication of the replacement algorithm can be higher for software and a wider variety of virtual memory organizations can be readily accommodated.

Hardware should be faster, but less flexible.

b. Factors other than whether miss handling is done in software or hardware can quickly dominate handling time. Is the page table itself paged? Can software implement a more efficient page table search algorithm than hardware? What about hardware TLB entry prefetching?

c. Page table structures that change dynamically would be difficult to handle in hardware but possible in software.

d.

Program	Weight	TLB misses/1000 instructions
gcc	50%	0.30
perl	25%	0.26
ijpeg	25%	0.10

$$\text{Workload miss rate} = \sum_i \text{Weight}_i \times (\text{TLB misses}/1000)_i$$

$$= 0.5 \times 0.30 + 0.25 \times 0.26 + 0.25 \times 0.10$$

$$= 0.22/1000 \text{ instructions}$$

Cost of a hardware handler is given as 10 cycles/miss, so penalty is 2.175 cycles/1000 instructions and the effect on CPI is an increase of 0.0022 clocks/instruction.

Similarly, for a software handler costing 30 cycles/miss, the effect on CPI is 0.0066 clocks/instruction.

The second workload is

Program	Weight	TLB misses/1000 instructions
swim	30%	0.10
wave5	30%	0.89
hydro2d	20%	0.19
gcc	10%	0.30

$$\text{Workload miss rate} = \sum_i \text{Weight}_i \times (\text{TLB misses}/1000)_i = 0.37$$

The hardware penalty is 0.0037 clocks/instruction. The software penalty is 0.011 clocks/instruction.

e. The TLB miss times are too small. Handling a TLB miss requires finding and transferring a page table entry in main memory to the TLB. A main memory access typically takes on the order of 100 clocks, already much greater than the miss times in part (d).

f. Floating-point programs often traverse large data structures and thus more often reference a large number of pages. It is thus more likely that the TLB will experience a higher rate of capacity misses.

5.25 Out-of-order (OOO) execution will change both the timing of and sequence of cache accesses with respect to that of in-order execution. Some specific differences and their effect on what cache design is most desirable are explored in the following.

Because OOO reduces data hazard stalls, the pace of cache access, both to instructions and data, will be higher than if execution were in order. Thus, the pipeline demand for available cache bandwidth is higher with OOO. This affects cache design in areas such as block size, write policy, and prefetching.

Block size has a strong effect on the delivered bandwidth between the cache and the next lower level in the memory hierarchy. A write-through write policy requires more bandwidth to the next lower memory level than does write back, generally, and use of a dirty bit further reduces the bandwidth demand of a write-back policy. Prefetching increases the bandwidth demand. Each of these cache design parameters—block size, write policy, and prefetching—is in competition with the pipeline for cache bandwidth, and OOO increases the competition. Cache design should adapt for this shift in bandwidth demand toward the pipeline.

Cache accesses for data and, because of exceptions, instructions occur during execution. OOO execution will change the sequence of these accesses and may also change their pacing.

A change in sequence will interact with the cache replacement policy. Thus, a particular cache and replacement policy that performs well on a chosen application when execution of the superscalar pipeline is in order may perform differently—even quite differently—when execution is OOO.

If there are multiple functional units for memory access, then OOO execution may allow bunching multiple accesses into the same clock cycle. Thus, the instantaneous or peak memory access bandwidth from the execution portion of the superscalar can be higher with OOO.

Imprecise exceptions are another cause of change in the sequence of memory accesses from that of in-order execution. With OOO some instructions from earlier in the program order may not have made their memory accesses, if any, at the time of the exception. Such accesses may become interleaved with instruction and data accesses of the exception-handling code. This increases the opportunity for capacity and conflict misses. So a cache design with size and/or associativity to deliver lower numbers of capacity and conflict misses may be needed to meet the demands of OOO.

Chapter 6 Solutions

6.4   To keep the figures from becoming cluttered, the coherence protocol is split into two parts as was done in Figure 6.11 in the text. Figure B.13 presents the CPU portion of the coherence protocol, and Figure B.14 presents the bus portion of the protocol. In both of these figures, the arcs indicate transitions and the text along each arc indicates the stimulus (in normal text) and bus action (in bold text) that occurs during the transition between states. Finally, like the text, we assume a write hit is handled as a write miss.

Figure B.13 presents the behavior of state transitions caused by the CPU itself. In this case, a write to a block in either the invalid or shared state causes us to broadcast a "write invalidate" to flush the block from any other caches that hold the block and move to the exclusive state. We can leave the exclusive state through either an invalidate from another processor (which occurs on the bus side of the coherence protocol state diagram), or a read miss generated by the CPU (which occurs when an exclusive block of data is displaced from the cache by a second block). In the shared state only a write by the CPU or an invalidate from another processor can move us out of this state. In the case of transitions caused by events external to the CPU, the state diagram is fairly simple, as shown in Figure B.14.

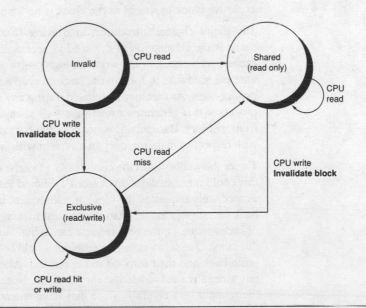

Figure B.13 CPU portion of the simple cache coherency protocol for write-through caches.

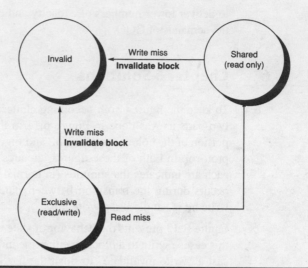

Figure B.14 Bus portion of the simple cache coherency protocol for write-through caches.

When another processor writes a block that is resident in our cache, we unconditionally invalidate the corresponding block in our cache. This ensures that the next time we read the data, we will load the updated value of the block from memory. Also, whenever the bus sees a read miss, it must change the state of an exclusive block to shared as the block is no longer exclusive to a single cache.

The major change introduced in moving from a write-back to write-through cache is the elimination of the need to access dirty blocks in another processor's caches. As a result, in the write-through protocol it is no longer necessary to provide the hardware to force write back on read accesses or to abort pending memory accesses. As memory is updated during any write on a write-through cache, a processor that generates a read miss will always retrieve the correct information from memory. Basically, it is not possible for valid cache blocks to be incoherent with respect to main memory in a system with write-through caches.

6.10   The problem illustrates the complexity of cache coherence protocols. In this case, this could mean that the processor P1 evicted that cache block from its cache and immediately requested the block in subsequent instructions. Given that the write-back message is longer than the request message, with networks that allow out-of-order requests, the new request can arrive before the write back arrives at the directory. One solution to this problem would be to have the directory wait for the write back and then respond to the request. Alternatively, the directory can send out a negative acknowledgment (NACK). Note that these solutions need to be thought out very carefully since they have potential to lead to deadlocks based on the particular implementation details of the system. Formal methods are often used to check for races and deadlocks.

6.13   a.   Figure 6.50 presents two cases for average remote access time where the accessed remote block is in its home node: (1) shared or invalid in the home caches (called unowned) and (2) dirty. The less likely situation of a remote access to a clean block in the exclusive state within its home node is ignored.

An important assumption in this exercise is to use the average remote memory latency data in the second section of Figure 6.50. A more realistic situation would have some nonzero fraction of remote accesses of the three-hop variety.

With only unowned and dirty blocks, average remote access time is a function of the fractions of accesses that are unowned and dirty.

$$\text{Wildfire}_{avg} = (1 - 0.8) \times 1774 \text{ ns} + (0.8) \times 2162 \text{ ns} = 2056 \text{ ns}$$
$$\text{Origin}_{avg} = (1 - 0.8) \times 973 \text{ ns} + (0.8) \times 1531 \text{ ns} = 1419 \text{ ns}$$

b.   For unowned blocks, the difference in average remote access time between Wildfire and Origin is 1774 ns – 973 ns = 801 ns. For dirty blocks, the difference is 2162 ns – 1531 = 631 ns. Thus, to minimize the difference in average remote access time all remote accesses should be to dirty blocks. Any fraction of accesses to unowned blocks will only increase the difference.

c.   If all accesses are either unowned or dirty, then

$$1 - \text{Fraction dirty} = \text{Fraction unowned}$$

Using the data from the first section of Figure 6.51, the average bandwidth measurements for mixtures of local accesses on the two machines will be

$$\text{Wildfire}_{avg \; local \; BW} = \text{Fraction unowned} \times 312 \text{ MB/sec} + \text{Fraction dirty} \times 246 \text{ MB/sec}$$

$$\text{Origin}_{avg \; local \; BW} = \text{Fraction unowned} \times 554 \text{ MB/sec} + \text{Fraction dirty} \times 182 \text{ MB/sec}$$

Setting the two machine bandwidths equal, substituting 1 – Fraction dirty for Fraction unowned and solving yields 79% dirty accesses.

6.18   With a broadcast protocol for lock variables, every time a lock is released, the new value of the lock variable is broadcast to all processors. This means processors will never miss when reading the lock variable.

Assume that every cache has the block containing the lock variable initially. The table shows that the average will be 550 clocks over the course of all 10 lock/unlock pairs. The total time will be 5500 cycles.

Event	Duration
Read (hit) of lock by all processors	0
Write (miss) broadcast by releasing processor	100
Read (hit) of lock (processors see lock is free)	0
Write/swap broadcast by one processor plus nine extra write broadcasts	1000
Total time for one processor to acquire and release	1100

6.20
```
fetch_and_increment (count);  /* atomic update */
if (count == total) {          /* all processes arrived */
    count = 0;                 /* reset counter */
    release = 1;               /* release processes */
}
else {                         /* more to arrive at barrier */
    spin (release == 1);       /* wait for signal to proceed */
```

For n processes, this code executes n fetch-and-increment operations, n cache misses to access release, and $n - 1$ more cache misses when release is finally set to 1 by the last processor to reach the barrier. (The last processor to reach the barrier will hit in its cache when it reads release the first time when spinning.) This is a total of $3n - 1$ bus transactions. For 10 processors this is 29 bus transactions or 2900 clock cycles.

6.23   As with similar examples and exercises in the text, we ignore the time to actually read or write a lock. Each of the n processes requires c cycles to lock the counter associated with the barrier, update its value, and release the lock. In the worst case, all n processors simultaneously attempt to lock the counter and update the value. Because the lock serializes access to the counter, the processors update the counter one at a time. Thus, it takes nc cycles for all processors to arrive at the barrier.

6.30   Constructive cache interference is likely to happen when near-identical threads comprise the workload. Each thread will execute nearly identical code, so cache blocks become shared among the threads. Also, sharing of data among the threads leads to cache block reuse. Overall, the cache miss rates can be similar to that for a single thread with appropriate software-mapping policies for the threads.

6.34   a. Four cores, each 64 KB, means 256 KB of data. If that is duplicated in the 1 MB L2 cache, then that is a 25% upper bound on wasted capacity.

b. Effectively the L2 now behaves as a large victim cache for the four core L1 caches. Clean blocks that are replaced in an L1 cache cause a write back to the L2 cache.

With a multiprocessor system there are more issues related to coherence and allocation/replacement policies. We may need to keep a duplicate copy of the L1 tags and state at the L2 controllers. Additionally, we may also need to extend the state information in the L1 cache to include, for example, a notion of ownership.

Chapter 7 Solutions

7.1

Figure 7.2 data	Seagate	Travelstar	Microdrive
Number of cylinders	14100	21664	7167
Average read access seek (ms)	5.6	12	12
Minimum read access seek (ms)	0.6	2.5	1.0
Maximum read access seek (ms)	14	23	19
One-third cylinders seek distance	4700	7221	2389
Linear seek time model formula for seek time (ms)	15.6	31.0	34.0
Difference from manufacturer's reported average seek time (ms)	10.0	19.0	22.0
Chen and Lee (1995) model:			
Coefficients, to two significant digits			
$a =$	0.022	0.091	0.30
$b =$	0.00076	0.00033	−0.00098
$c =$	0.60	2.5	1.0
Chen and Lee model formula for seek time (distance)	5.7	12.5	12.8
Difference from manufacturer's reported average seek time (ms)	0.09	0.50	0.81

The Chen and Lee coefficients, in combination with their nonlinear model, predict the seek times of the three disk drives of Figure 7.2 well, certainly much better than does the model that seek time is linear with seek distance.

7.6   a.   Number of heads = 15; number of platters = 8

   b.   Rotational latency = 8.33 ms

   c.   Head switch time = 1.4 ms

   d.   Cylinder switch time = 2.1 ms

   e.   Minimum time to media plus transfer time = 2.0 ms

7.8   From the seek-time formula, seek time = 5.13 ms. Reading 1 MB requires accessing 2048 512-byte sectors (if 1 MB = 2^{20} bytes; if 1 MB is taken as 10^6 bytes, then adjust accordingly). Disk rotation allow access to

$$\frac{528 \times 10,000}{60} = 88,000 \text{ sectors/sec}$$

Thus, 23.3 ms are needed to read 1 MB.

The read time for the single disk is

$$\text{Time}_{\text{single}} = 1 + 3 + 5.13 + 23.3 = 32.4 \text{ ms}$$

The read time for the four-disk array is

$$\text{Time}_{\text{array}} = 1 + 3 + 5.13 + \frac{23.3}{4} = 15.0 \text{ ms}$$

These times imply transfer rates as follows:

$$\text{I/O}_{\text{single}} = \frac{1}{32.4 \text{ ms}} = 30.9 \text{ I/O/sec or } 30.9 \text{ MB/sec}$$

$$\text{I/O}_{\text{array}} = \frac{1}{15.0 \text{ ms}} = 66.7 \text{ I/O/sec or } 66.7 \text{ MB/sec}$$

B.8   Chapter 8 Solutions

8.1   Delivered bandwidth = Megabits per second including overhead, so the formula is

$$\frac{\text{Packet size} \times 8}{\text{Overhead} + (\text{Ethernet header/trailer size} + \text{Packet size}) \times 8/(0.9 \times 1000\text{M bits/sec})}$$

$$= \frac{\text{Packet size} \times 8}{100 \text{ μs} + (56 + \text{Packet size}) \times 8/(900 \text{ bits/μs})}$$

Thus a stream of 32-byte payloads delivers a user data bandwidth of 2.5M bits per second, and a stream of 1500-byte payloads delivers a user data bandwidth of 105.4M bits per second. The graph is in Figure B.15.

8.5   a. All message sizes of 224 bytes or more have a total time for ATM that is less than for Ethernet; therefore, ATM delivers higher bandwidth.

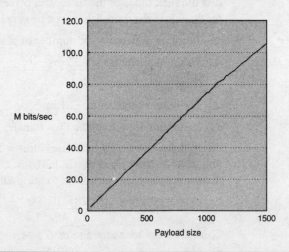

Figure B.15 M bits per second of user data as payload size varies.

b. The 155M bit/sec ATM takes 3 seconds to transmit 4820 messages of size 224, while the 10M bit/sec Ethernet takes 4 seconds. The effective bandwidths are 2.9 and 2.2M bits/sec, respectively. For the largest message size the effective bandwidths are 42.4 and 8.3M bits/sec, respectively. Figure B.16 shows the effective bandwidths for all the message sizes.

8.9   The two Internet alternatives take 99 hours or 45 hours, respectively, for the whole 1000 GB to arrive. At 15 hours door to door, the overnight delivery service is faster.

8.14   The length of a full Ethernet packet is 1500 + 56 bytes. The time to transfer 1556 bytes over a 1G bit/sec Ethernet link (assuming 90% of peak bandwidth) is

$$\frac{1556 \text{ bytes}}{0.9 \times 1000M \text{ bits/sec}} = \frac{1556 \text{ bytes}}{112.5 \text{ MB/sec}} = 13.8 \text{ μs}$$

Then the time for store and forward is

$$(\text{Switches} \times \text{Switch delay}) + ((\text{Switches} + 1) \times \text{Transfer time})$$
$$= (7 \times 1.0) + (8 \times 13.8) = 117.6 \text{ μs}$$

while wormhole routing is

$$(\text{Switches} \times \text{Switch delay}) + \text{Transfer time} = (7 \times 1.0) + 13.8 = 20.8 \text{ μs}$$

For this example, wormhole routing improves latency by more than a factor of 5.

8.19   Use 16 ports from each of four 18-port switches to connect to the 64 nodes. Then use the two remaining ports on each switch to join the switches in a ring.

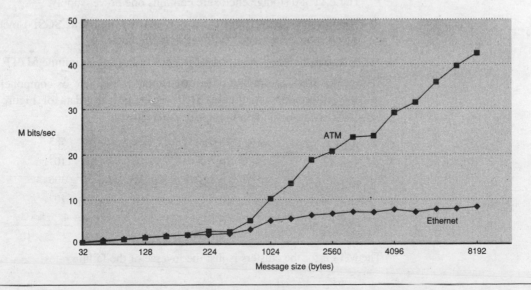

Figure B.16   Effective delivered bandwidth for ATM and Ethernet.

8.31   a. This exercise says to use the same assumptions for components as in the second example in Section 7.11 except for a 1G bit Ethernet switch. The first step, then, in solving this exercise is to relate the example of Section 7.11 to the components of the three cluster computers so that each can be assigned an MTTF. The set of components in the example is CPU/memory, disk, SCSI controller, power supply, fan, SCSI cable, and enclosure for disks external to the CPU/memory housing. The external disk enclosure contains one fan and one power supply.

A number of additional assumptions are necessary or helpful in mapping all the cluster components to those in the example and in taking care of all the details. These assumptions are

■ Each processor and 1 GB of memory has the MTTF of a CPU/memory unit.

■ CPU/memory unit MTTF is unaffected by clock rate or L2 size.

■ Disk MTTF is independent of disk capacity.

■ Each server has one Emulex cLAN-1000 host adapter (1G bit) card with MTTF equal to that of a SCSI controller.

■ Ethernet switch MTTF is independent of the number of switch ports.

■ The two disks that each computer can hold have a SCSI controller.

■ Each power supply has the same MTTF, regardless of the rating in watts.

■ There is one fan in each power supply.

■ The EXP300 storage enclosure contains one power supply.

■ The Emulex cLAN-1000 10-meter cable and the Ultra2 SCSI 4-meter cable each have the same MTTF as a SCSI cable.

■ A standard 19-inch rack (44 VME rack units) has an infinite MTTF.

Using the above assumptions we can generate the table of component and quantity information in Figure B.17. Collecting the data of Figure B.17 together, we compute failure rates for each cluster:

$$\text{Failure rate}_{\text{1-way}} = \frac{32 + 64 + 2 + 37}{10^6} + \frac{32 + 32}{2 \times 10^5} + \frac{32 + 32}{5 \times 10^6} = \frac{583}{10^6}$$

$$\text{Failure rate}_{\text{2-way}} = \frac{32 + 32 + 1 + 17}{10^6} + \frac{16 + 16}{2 \times 10^5} + \frac{16 + 16}{5 \times 10^6} = \frac{306}{10^6}$$

$$\text{Failure rate}_{\text{8-way}} = \frac{32 + 32 + 4 + 4 + 1 + 5}{10^6} + \frac{12 + 12 + 4 + 4}{2 \times 10^5} + \frac{8 + 4}{5 \times 10^6} = \frac{262}{10^6}$$

The MTTF for the clusters is just the inverse of the failure rates.

Component	MTTF (hours)	How many?		
		1-way	2-way	8-way
CPU/memory	1,000,000	32	32	32
Disk	1,000,000	64	32	32
CPU power supply	200,000	32	16	12
CPU/memory power supply fan	200,000	32	16	12
SCSI controller	500,000	32	16	8
EXP300 storage enclosure	1,000,000	0	0	4
EXP300 power supply	200,000	0	0	4
EXP300 fan	200,000	0	0	4
SCSI cable	1,000,000	0	0	4
cLAN host adapter	500,000	32	16	4
1G bit Ethernet switch	1,000,000	2	1	1
cLAN-1000 10-meter cable (between servers and switch and between switches)	1,000,000	37	17	5
Standard 19-inch rack	N/A	1	1	2
Total component count		264	147	120

Figure B.17 Quantities of components for each cluster configuration.

$$MTTF_{1\text{-way}} = \frac{1}{Failure\ rate_{1\text{-way}}} = \frac{1,000,000\ hours}{583} = 1715\ hours$$

$$MTTF_{2\text{-way}} = \frac{1}{Failure\ rate_{2\text{-way}}} = \frac{1,000,000\ hours}{306} = 3268\ hours$$

$$MTTF_{8\text{-way}} = \frac{1}{Failure\ rate_{8\text{-way}}} = \frac{1,000,000\ hours}{262} = 3817\ hours$$

To put the MTTF times in some perspective, a year lasts about 8766 hours. The 8-way cluster design achieves its better MTTF by having fewer total components, but in particular by having fewer of the low-MTTF power supply and fan components.

b. To name the single point of failure there must first be a definition of failure. For these clusters the goal is to have a system with 32 processors, 32 GB of memory, and more than 2 TB of disk. The organizations shown in Figure 8.34 also show an Internet connection. The definition of failure then is falling below the required numbers and amounts of processors, memory, and storage plus losing Internet access.

For the uniprocessor-based cluster in Figure 8.34 the single points of failure are

- Any processor (cluster falls below required number of processors and amount of memory)
- Any CPU power supply (processor cannot operate)
- Any CPU power supply fan (power supply will go offline)
- Any cLAN-1000 host adapter (isolates a processor, its memory, and two disks)
- An Ethernet switch failure (isolates half of the processors, memory, and disk and may cut Internet access)
- An Ethernet cable failure other than that of the four cables connecting the two switches (cuts off one processor module or cuts Internet access)

Failure of one disk or one SCSI controller will not cause the uniprocessor-based cluster to fail to meet its goals.

For the two-way SMP cluster the single points of failure are

- Any processor (cluster falls below required number of processors and amount of memory)
- Any CPU power supply (two processors cannot operate)
- Any CPU power supply fan (power supply will go offline)
- Any cLAN-1000 host adapter (isolates two processors, their memory, and two disks)
- An Ethernet switch failure (isolates all the processors, memory, and disk and cuts Internet access)
- Any Ethernet cable failure (cuts off two processors or cuts Internet access)

Failure of one disk or one SCSI controller will not cause the two-way SMP cluster to fail to meet its goals.

For the eight-way SMP cluster the single points of failure are

- Any processor (cluster falls below required number of processors and amount of memory)
- Any CPU power supply (assumes that the other two power supplies will be insufficient or not configured to carry the total power load of the server)
- Any CPU power supply fan (power supply will go offline)
- Any cLAN-1000 host adapter (isolates eight processors, their memory, and eight disks)
- An Ethernet switch failure (isolates all the processors, memory, and disk and cuts Internet access)
- Any Ethernet cable failure (cuts off eight processors or cuts Internet access)
- Any SCSI controller for the disks in an EXP300 storage enclosure (cluster loses six disks and falls below the required amount of storage)

c. Generally, the strategy to improve MTTF is some combination of reduced component count, substitution of higher-MTTF components for lower-MTTF components, and design with redundancy so that there are fewer or no single points of failure.

For each of the cluster designs loss of one processor is a failure, so adding a spare CPU/memory component would go a long way to improving cluster MTTF. All of the cluster designs have unused ports on the Ethernet switch, so adding another server requires only the additional server and another Ethernet cable. Interestingly, the uniprocessor-based cluster, which has the lowest MTTF because of its high component count, is the cheapest of the clusters to incrementally grow the number of processors. Assuming the cluster software could automatically handle single-processor failure, adding one spare server to the uniprocessor design should improve cluster MTTF significantly. Adding a spare processor is more expensive with the two-way and eight-way servers, but also offers cluster MTTF improvement.

Replicating other aspects of the clusters may be more difficult. For components such as the power supplies, building servers with two power supplies operating in parallel and each supplying half the server power while running at just 40% of rated capacity of the power supply and with just one fan per power supply might have sufficient cost-performance to be a good choice. Such a configuration can fail over to one power supply for all the server's power needs in the event of a single fan or supply failure without overstressing and quickly failing the supply that picks up the full load. Replicating the Ethernet switches would double the number of needed host adapters and cables and would require a dual Internet connection. Perhaps a better solution would be to mount the switch in the coolest part of the standard 19-inch rack (likely at the bottom) and hope that cooler operating temperatures will lead to above-average MTTF for that component.

B.9   Appendix A Solutions

A.2   The pipeline of Sections A.4 and A.5 resolves branches in ID and has multiple execution function units. More than one instruction may be in execution at the same time, but the exercise statement says write-back contention is possible and is handled by processing one instruction at a time in that stage.

Figure A.30 lists the latencies for the functional units; however, it is important to note that these data are for functional unit results forwarded to the EX stage. In particular, despite a latency of 1 for data memory access, it is still the case that for a cache hit the MEM stage completes memory access in one clock cycle.

Finally, examining the code reveals that the loop iterates 99 times. With this and analysis of iteration timing on the pipeline, we can determine loop execution time.

a. Figure B.18 shows the timing of instructions from the loop for the first version of pipeline hardware.

Instruction		Clock cycle																										
		1	2	3	4	5	6	7	8	...	13	14	15	16	17	18	19	20	21	22	23	24	25	26	27
L.D	F0,0(R2)	F	D	E	M	W																				
L.D	F4,0(R3)		F	D	E	M	W																			
MUL.D	F0,F0,F4			F	D	s	s	E	E	...	E	M	W													
ADD.D	F2,F0,F2				F	s	s	D	s	...	s	s	s	E	E	E	E	M	W							
DADDUI	R2,R2,#8					F	s	...			s	s	s	D	E	M	W									
DADDUI	R3,R3,#8													F	D	E	M	W								
DSUBU	R5,R4,R2														F	D	s	E	M	W						
BNEZ	R5,Loop															F	s	D	s	r						
L.D	F0,0(R2)																F	s	s	F	D	E	M	W		

Figure B.18 Pipeline timing diagram for the pipeline without forwarding, branches that flush the pipeline, memory references that hit in cache, and FP latencies from Figure A.30. The abbreviations F, D, E, M, and W denote the fetch, decode, execute, memory access, and write-back stages, respectively. Pipeline stalls are indicated by s, branch resolution by r. One complete loop iteration plus the first instruction of the subsequent iteration is shown to make clear how the branch is handled. Because branch instructions complete (resolve) in the decode stage, use of the following stages by the BNEZ instruction is not depicted.

There are several stall cycles shown in the timing diagram:

- Cycles 5–6: MUL.D stalls in ID to wait for F0 and F4 to be written back by the L.D instructions.

- Cycles 8–15: ADD.D stalls in ID to wait for MUL.D to write back F0.

- Cycle 19: DSUBU stalls in ID to wait for DADDUI to write back R2.

- Cycles 21–22: BNEZ stalls in ID to wait for DSUBU to write back R5. Because the register file can read and write in the same cycle, the BNEZ can read the DSUBU result and resolve in the same cycle in which DSUBU writes that result.

- Cycle 20: While not labeled a stall, because initially it does not appear to be a stall, the fetch made in this cycle will be discarded because this pipeline design handles the uncertainty of where to fetch after a branch by flushing the stages with instructions fetched after the branch. The pipeline begins processing after the branch with the correct fetch in cycle 23.

There are no structural hazard stalls due to write-back contention because processing instructions as soon as otherwise possible happens to use WB at most once in any clock cycle.

Figure B.18 shows two instructions simultaneously in execution in clock cycles 17 and 18, but because different functional units are handling each instruction there is no structural hazard.

The first iteration ends with cycle 22, and the next iteration starts with cycle 23. Thus, each of the 99 loop iterations will take 22 cycles, so the total loop execution time is $99 \times 22 = 2178$ clock cycles.

b. Figure B.19 shows the timing of instructions from the loop for the second version of pipeline hardware.

There are several stall cycles shown in the timing diagram:

- Cycle 5: MUL.D stalls at ID waiting for L.D to forward F4 to EX from MEM. F0 reaches the register file by the first half of cycle 5 and thus is read by ID during this stall cycle.

- Cycles 7–12: ADD.D stalls at ID waiting for MUL.D to produce and forward the new value for F0.

- Cycle 16: DSUBU is stalled at ID to avoid contention with ADD.D for the WB stage. Note the complexity of pipeline state analysis that the ID stage must perform to ensure correct pipeline operation.

- Cycle 18: BNEZ stalls in ID to wait for DSUBU to produce and forward the new value for R5. While forwarding may deliver the needed value earlier in the clock cycle than can reading from the register file, and so in principle the branch could resolve earlier in the cycle, the next PC value cannot be used until the IF stage is ready, which will be with cycle 19.

- Cycle 17: Initially this cycle does not appear to be a stall because branches are predicted not taken and this fetch is from the fall-through location. However, for all but the last loop iteration this branch is mispredicted. Thus, the fetch in cycle 17 must be redone at the branch target, as shown in cycle 19.

										Clock cycle											
Instruction		1	2	3	4	5	6	7	...	12	13	14	15	16	17	18	19	20	21	22	23
L.D	F0,0(R2)	F	D	E	M	W															
L.D	F4,0(R3)		F	D	E	M	W														
MUL.D	F0,F0,F4			F	D	s	E	E	...	E	M	W									
ADD.D	F2,F0,F2				F	s	D	s	...	s	E	E	E	E	M	W					
DADDUI	R2,R2,#8					F	s	...		s	D	E	M	W							
DADDUI	R3,R3,#8										F	D	E	M	W						
DSUBU	R5,R4,R2											F	D	s	E	M	W				
BNEZ	R5,Loop												F	s	D	r					
L.D	F0,0(R2)																F	s	F	D	E	M	W

Figure B.19 Pipeline timing diagram for the pipeline with forwarding, branches handled by predicted-not-taken, memory references that hit in cache, and FP latencies from Figure A.30. The notation used is the same as in Figure B.18.

Again, there are instances of two instructions in the execute stage simultaneously, but using different functional units.

The first iteration ends in cycle 19 when DSUBU writes back R5. The second iteration begins with the fetch of L.D F0, 0(R2) in cycle 19. Thus, all iterations, except the last, take 18 cycles. The last iteration completes in a total of 19 cycles. However, if there were code following the instructions of the loop, they would start after only 16 cycles of the last iteration because the branch is predicted correctly for the last iteration.

The total loop execution time is $98 \times 18 + 19 = 1783$ clock cycles.

A.3   This exercise asks, "How much faster would the machine be . . . ," which should make you immediately think speedup. In this case, we are interested in how the presence or absence of control hazards changes the pipeline speedup. Recall one of the expressions for the speedup from pipelining presented on page A-13

$$\text{Pipeline speedup} = \frac{1}{1 + \text{Pipeline stalls}} \times \text{Pipeline depth} \qquad \text{(B.4)}$$

where the only contributions to Pipeline stalls arise from control hazards because the exercise is only focused on such hazards. To solve this exercise, we will compute the speedup due to pipelining both with and without control hazards and then compare these two numbers.

For the "ideal" case where there are no control hazards, and thus stalls, Equation B.4 yields

$$\text{Pipeline speedup}_{\text{ideal}} = \frac{1}{1 + 0} \, (4) = 4 \qquad \text{(B.5)}$$

where, from the exercise statement the pipeline depth is 4 and the number of stalls is 0 as there are no control hazards.

For the "real" case where there are control hazards, the pipeline depth is still 4, but the number of stalls is no longer 0 as it was in Equation B.5. To determine the value of Pipeline stalls, which includes the effects of control hazards, we need three pieces of information. First, we must establish the "types" of control flow instructions we can encounter in a program. From the exercise statement, there are three types of control flow instructions: taken conditional branches, not-taken conditional branches, and jumps and calls. Second, we must evaluate the number of stall cycles caused by each type of control flow instruction. And third, we must find the frequency at which each type of control flow instruction occurs in code. Such values are given in the exercise statement.

To determine the second piece of information, the number of stall cycles created by each of the three types of control flow instructions, we examine how the pipeline behaves under the appropriate conditions. For the purposes of discussion, we will assume the four stages of the pipeline are Instruction Fetch, Instruction Decode, Execute, and Write Back (abbreviated IF, ID, EX, and WB, respectively). A specific structure is not necessary to solve the exercise; this structure was chosen simply to ease the following discussion.

First, let us consider how the pipeline handles a jump or call. Figure B.20 illustrates the behavior of the pipeline during the execution of a jump or call. Because the first pipe stage can always be done independently of whether the control flow instruction goes or not, in cycle 2 the pipeline fetches the instruction following the jump or call (note that this is all we can do—IF must update the PC, and the next sequential address is the only address known at this point; however, this behavior will prove to be beneficial for conditional branches as we will see shortly). By the end of cycle 2, the jump or call resolves (recall that the exercise specifies that calls and jumps resolve at the end of the second stage), and the pipeline realizes that the fetch it issued in cycle 2 was to the wrong address (remember, the fetch in cycle 2 retrieves the instruction immediately following the control flow instruction rather than the target instruction), so the pipeline reissues the fetch of instruction $i + 1$ in cycle 3. This causes a one-cycle stall in the pipeline since the fetches of instructions after $i + 1$ occur one cycle later than they ideally could have.

Figure B.21 illustrates how the pipeline stalls for two cycles when it encounters a taken conditional branch. As was the case for unconditional branches, the fetch issued in cycle 2 fetches the instruction after the branch rather than the instruction at the target of the branch. Therefore, when the branch finally resolves in cycle 3 (recall that the exercise specifies that conditional branches resolve at the end of the third stage), the pipeline realizes it must reissue the fetch for instruction $i + 1$ in cycle 4, which creates the two-cycle penalty.

Figure B.22 illustrates how the pipeline stalls for a single cycle when it encounters a not-taken conditional branch. For not-taken conditional branches, the fetch of instruction $i + 1$ issued in cycle 2 actually obtains the correct instruction. This occurs because the pipeline fetches the next sequential instruction from the program by default—which happens to be the instruction that follows a not-taken branch. Once the conditional branch resolves in cycle 3, the pipeline determines it does not need to reissue the fetch of instruction $i + 1$ and therefore can resume executing the instruction it fetched in cycle 2. Instruction $i + 1$ cannot leave the IF stage until *after* the branch resolves because the exercise specifies the pipeline is only capable of using the IF stage while a branch is being resolved.

Instruction	Clock cycle					
	1	2	3	4	5	6
Jump or call	IF	ID	EX	WB		
$i + 1$		IF	IF	ID	EX	...
$i + 2$			*stall*	IF	ID	...
$i + 3$				*stall*	IF	...

Figure B.20 Effects of a jump or call Instruction on the pipeline.

	Clock cycle					
Instruction	**1**	**2**	**3**	**4**	**5**	**6**
Taken branch	IF	ID	EX	WB		
$i + 1$		IF	*stall*	IF	ID	...
$i + 2$			*stall*	*stall*	IF	...
$i + 3$				*stall*	*stall*	...

Figure B.21 **Effects of a taken conditional branch on the pipeline.**

	Clock cycle					
Instruction	**1**	**2**	**3**	**4**	**5**	**6**
Not-taken branch	IF	ID	EX	WB		
$i + 1$		IF	*stall*	ID	EX	...
$i + 2$			*stall*	IF	ID	...
$i + 3$				*stall*	IF	...

Figure B.22 **Effects of a not-taken conditional branch on the pipeline.**

Combining all of our information on control flow instruction type, stall cycles, and frequency leads us to Figure B.23. Note that this figure accounts for the taken/not-taken nature of conditional branches. With this information we can compute the stall cycles caused by control flow instructions:

$$\text{Pipeline stalls}_{\text{real}} = (1 \times 1\%) + (2 \times 9\%) + (1 \times 6\%) = 0.24$$

where each term is the product of a frequency and a penalty. We can now plug the appropriate value for Pipeline stalls$_{\text{real}}$ into Equation B.4 to arrive at the pipeline speedup in the "real" case:

$$\text{Pipeline speedup}_{\text{real}} = \frac{1}{1 + 0.24} \; (4.0) = 3.23 \tag{B.6}$$

Finding the speedup of the ideal over the real pipelining speedups from Equations B.5 and B.6 leads us to the final answer:

$$\text{Pipeline speedup}_{\text{without control hazards}} = \frac{4}{3.23} = 1.24$$

Control flow type	Frequency (per instruction)	Stalls (cycles)
Jumps and calls	1%	1
Conditional (taken)	15% × 60% = 9%	2
Conditional (not taken)	15% × 40% = 6%	1

Figure B.23 **A summary of the behavior of control flow instructions.**

Thus, the presence of control hazards in the pipeline loses approximately 24% of the speedup you achieve without such hazards.

A.4   If a branch outcome is to be determined earlier, then the branch must be able to read its operand equally early. Branch direction is controlled by a register value that may either be loaded or computed. If the branch register value comparison is performed in the EX stage, then forwarding can deliver a computed value produced by the immediately preceding instruction if that instruction needs only one cycle in EX. There is no data hazard stall for this case. Forwarding can deliver a loaded value without a data hazard stall if the load can perform memory access in a single cycle and if at least one instruction separates it from the branch.

If now the branch compare is done in the ID stage, the two forwarding cases just discussed will each result in one data hazard stall cycle because the branch will need its operand one cycle before it exists in the pipeline. Often, instructions can be scheduled so that there are more instructions between the one producing the value and the dependent branch. With enough separation there is no data hazard stall.

So, resolving branches early reduces the control hazard stalls in a pipeline. However, without a sufficient combination of forwarding and scheduling, the savings in control hazard stalls will be offset by an increase in data hazard stalls.

A.9   Detecting MIPS R4000 integer hazards requires examining the pipeline for all stages where integer results are produced and for all stages where integer results are used. Integer results can be written either to the register file or to memory. A result written to memory cannot be used by the pipeline until a load instruction reads it, so we need only consider integer instructions that read from and write to the register file to detect pipeline integer hazards.

Integer ALU and load instructions are the MIPS R4000 instructions that produce integer results written to the register file. ALU results are produced at the end of EX; load results are produced at the end of DS. (Although we must wait for the tag check in TC before knowing if the cache access was a hit, we ignore this issue here, as it is outside the functional scope of the integer hazard detection circuitry.) ALU, load, store, and branch instructions all have integer operands. ALU instructions use their operands in EX. Load instructions use their operand in EX. Store instructions use their integer operands in both EX and DF. MIPS R4000 evaluates branch conditions in EX, thus branch instruction integer register operands are used in EX. With this information about result creation and use locations, we can now determine the integer hazards in the MIPS R4000.

An ALU instruction may produce a result that is used by another ALU instruction or by a load, store, or branch instruction. All of these result uses are in either the EX or DF stages. ALU instructions take only one cycle to execute in the MIPS R4000 pipeline, so forwarding from the output of the EX stage or later in the pipeline can prevent a stall for these uses even if the using instruction immediately follows the producing ALU instruction.

The other integer instruction that produces a result for the register file is the load. Because R4000 uses a deeper pipeline with three memory access stages, the opportunity for forwarding to prevent data dependences from causing data hazards is less than for the classic five-stage RISC pipeline. The fact that the R4000 pipeline can forward the value of a data cache hit from the DS stage reduces, but does not eliminate, data hazard stalls. For loads there can be hazards.

The answer given in the table assumes that the pipeline interlock stops instruction progress at the RF stage (see Figure A.37).

Note that if a value was forwarded from the DS stage and then there is a cache miss, then when the pipeline is "backed up a cycle" (see Figure A.38 caption) to recover from the data cache miss, the effect of the forwarding of incorrect data must also be undone.

Location of load instruction	Opcode field of IS/RF	Matching operand fields	Interlock for how long? (cycles)
RF/EX	Reg-reg ALU, ALU immediate, load, store, or branch	Any register operand	2
EX/DF	Same as above	Same as above	1
DF/DS	N/A	N/A	Forwarding handles this case

Figure B.24 The logic to detect integer interlocks during the RF stage of the MIPS R4000. Of the integer instructions, only a load may require a pipeline stall. In all cases the load destination register is compared to all of the register operands of the instruction in the RF stage. Remember that the IS/RF register holds the state of the instruction in RF. The duration of the interlock is the time necessary for the load instruction to reach the output of the DS stage, at which point the value can be forwarded.

A Survey of RISC Architectures for Desktop, Server, and Embedded Computers

RISC: any computer announced after 1985.

Steven Przybylski
A Designer of the Stanford MIPS

This appendix is available online at *www.mkp.com/CA3/*.

An Alternative to RISC:
The Intel 80x86

The x86 isn't all that complex—it just doesn't make a lot of sense.

Mike Johnson
Leader of 80x86 Design at AMD,
Microprocessor Report (1994)

This appendix is available online at *www.mkp.com/CA3/*.

Another Alternative to RISC: The VAX Architecture

In principle, there is no great challenge in designing a large virtual address minicomputer system. . . . The real challenge lies in two areas: compatibility—very tangible and important; and simplicity —intangible but nonetheless important.

William Strecker
"VAX-11/780—A Virtual Address Extension
to the PDP-11 Family," AFIPS Proc.,
National Computer Conference, 1978.

Entities should not be multiplied unnecessarily.

William of Occam
Quodlibeta Septem, 1320
(This quote is known as "Occam's Razor.")

This appendix is available online at *www.mkp.com/CA3/*.

F

The IBM 360/370 Architecture for Mainframe Computers

We are not at all humble in this announcement. This is the most important product announcement that this corporation has ever made in its history. It's not a computer in any previous sense. It's not a product, but a line of products . . . that spans in performance from the very low part of the computer line to the very high.

IBM spokesman
at announcement of System/360 (1964)

This appendix is available online at *www.mkp.com/CA3/*.

G

Vector Processors

Revised by Krste Asanovic
Department of Electrical Engineering and Computer Science, MIT

I'm certainly not inventing vector processors. There are three kinds
that I know of existing today. They are represented by the Illiac-IV, the
(CDC) Star processor, and the TI (ASC) processor. Those three were all
pioneering processors. . . . One of the problems of being a pioneer is
you always make mistakes and I never, never want to be a pioneer. It's
always best to come second when you can look at the mistakes the
pioneers made.

Seymour Cray
Public lecture at Lawrence Livermore Laboratories
on the introduction of the Cray-1 (1976)

This appendix is available online at *www.mkp.com/CA3/*.

Computer Arithmetic

by David Goldberg
Xerox Palo Alto Research Center

The Fast drives out the Slow even if the Fast is wrong.

W. Kahan

This appendix is available online at *www.mkp.com/CA3/*.

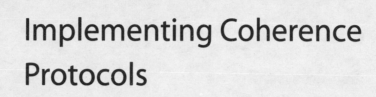

Implementing Coherence Protocols

The devil is in the details.

Classic Proverb

This appendix is available online at *www.mkp.com/CA3/*.

References

Adve, S. V., and K. Gharachorloo [1996]. "Shared memory consistency models: A tutorial," *IEEE Computer* 29:12 (December), 66–76.

Adve, S. V., and M. D. Hill [1990]. "Weak ordering—a new definition," *Proc. 17th Int'l Symposium on Computer Architecture* (June), Seattle, Wash., 2–14.

Agarwal, A. [1987]. *Analysis of Cache Performance for Operating Systems and Multiprogramming*, Ph.D. thesis, Stanford Univ., Tech. Rep. No. CSL-TR-87-332 (May).

Agarwal, A., R. Bianchini, D. Chaiken, K. Johnson, and D. Kranz [1995]. "The MIT Alewife machine: Architecture and performance," *Int'l Symposium on Computer Architecture* (Denver, Colo.), June, 2–13.

Agarwal, A., J. L. Hennessy, R. Simoni, and M. A. Horowitz [1988]. "An evaluation of directory schemes for cache coherence," *Proc. 15th Int'l Symposium on Computer Architecture* (June), 280–289.

Agarwal, A., J. Kubiatowicz, D. Kranz, B.-H. Lim, D. Yeung, G. D'Souza, and M. Parkin [1993]. "Sparcle: An evolutionary processor design for large-scale multiprocessors," *IEEE Micro* 13 (June), 48–61.

Agarwal, A., and S. D. Pudar [1993]. "Column-associative caches: A technique for reducing the miss rate of direct-mapped caches," 20th Annual Int'l Symposium on Computer Architecture ISCA '20, San Diego, Calif., May 16–19. *Computer Architecture News* 21:2 (May), 179–190.

Agerwala, T., and J. Cocke [1987]. "High performance reduced instruction set processors," IBM Tech. Rep. (March).

Alles, A. [1995]. "ATM internetworking" (May), *www.cisco.com/warp/public/614/12.html*.

Almasi, G. S., and A. Gottlieb [1989]. *Highly Parallel Computing,* Benjamin/Cummings, Redwood City, Calif.

Alverson, G., R. Alverson, D. Callahan, B. Koblenz, A. Porterfield, and B. Smith [1992]. "Exploiting heterogeneous parallelism on a multithreaded multiprocessor," *Proc. 1992 Int'l Conf. on Supercomputing* (November), 188–197.

Amdahl, G. M. [1967]. "Validity of the single processor approach to achieving large scale computing capabilities," *Proc. AFIPS Spring Joint Computer Conf.* 30, Atlantic City, N.J. (April), 483–485.

Amdahl, G. M., G. A. Blaauw, and F. P. Brooks, Jr. [1964]. "Architecture of the IBM System 360," *IBM J. Research and Development* 8:2 (April), 87–101.

Amza C., A. L. Cox, S. Dwarkadas, P. Keleher, H. Lu, R. Rajamony, W. Yu, and W. Zwaenepoel [1996]. "Treadmarks: Shared memory computing on networks of workstations," *IEEE Computer* 29(2) (February), 18–28.

Anderson, D. W., F. J. Sparacio, and R. M. Tomasulo [1967]. "The IBM 360 Model 91: Processor philosophy and instruction handling," *IBM J. Research and Development* 11:1 (January), 8–24.

Anderson, M. H. [1990]. "Strength (and safety) in numbers (RAID, disk storage technology)," *Byte* 15:13 (December), 337–339.

Anderson, T. E., D. E. Culler, and D. Patterson [1995]. "A case for NOW (networks of workstations)," *IEEE Micro* 15:1 (February), 54–64.

Ang, B., D. Chiou, D. Rosenband, M. Ehrlich, L. Rudolph, and Arvind [1998]. "StarT-Voyager: A flexible platform for exploring scalable SMP issues," *Proc. of SC'98,* Orlando, Fla., November.

Anon. et al. [1985]. "A measure of transaction processing power," Tandem Tech. Rep. TR 85.2. Also appeared in *Datamation,* April 1, 1985.

Archibald, J., and J.-L. Baer [1986]. "Cache coherence protocols: Evaluation using a multiprocessor simulation model," *ACM Trans. on Computer Systems* 4:4 (November), 273–298.

Arpaci, R. H., D. E. Culler, A. Krishnamurthy, S. G. Steinberg, and K. Yelick [1995]. "Empirical evaluation of the CRAY-T3D: A compiler perspective," *Proc. 23rd Int'l Symposium on Computer Architecture* (June), Italy.

Atanasoff, J. V. [1940]. "Computing machine for the solution of large systems of linear equations," Internal Report, Iowa State University, Ames.

Austin, T. M., and G. Sohi [1992]. "Dynamic dependency analysis of ordinary programs," *Proc. 19th Symposium on Computer Architecture* (May), Gold Coast, Australia, 342–351.

Babbay, F., and A. Mendelson [1998]. "Using value prediction to increase the power of speculative execution hardware," *ACM Trans. on Computer Systems* 16:3 (August), 234–270.

Baer, J.-L., and W.-H. Wang [1988]. "On the inclusion property for multi-level cache hierarchies," *Proc. 15th Annual Symposium on Computer Architecture* (May–June), Honolulu, 73–80.

Bakoglu, H. B., G. F. Grohoski, L. E. Thatcher, J. A. Kaeli, C. R. Moore, D. P. Tattle, W. E. Male, W. R. Hardell, D. A. Hicks, M. Nguyen Phu, R. K. Montoye, W. T. Glover, and S. Dhawan [1989]. "IBM second-generation RISC processor organization," *Proc. Int'l Conf. on Computer Design,* IEEE (October), Rye, N.Y., 138–142.

Balakrishnan, H. V. N. Padmanabhan, S. Seshan, and R. H. Katz [1997]. "A comparison of mechanisms for improving TCP performance over wireless links," *IEEE/ACM Trans. on Networking,* 5:6 (December), 756–769.

Ball, T., and J. R. Larus [1993]. "Branch prediction for free," *Proc. SIGPLAN 1993 Conf. on Programming Language Design and Implementation,* June, 300–313.

Barroso, L. A., K. Gharachorloo, and E. Bugnion [1998]. "Memory system characterization of commercial workloads," *Proc. 25th Int'l Symposium on Computer Architecture,* Barcelona (July), 3–14.

Barton, R. S. [1961]. "A new approach to the functional design of a computer," *Proc. Western Joint Computer Conf.,* 393–396.

Bashe, C. J., W. Buchholz, G. V. Hawkins, J. L. Ingram, and N. Rochester [1981]. "The architecture of IBM's early computers," *IBM J. Research and Development* 25:5 (September), 363–375.

Bashe, C. J., L. R. Johnson, J. H. Palmer, and E. W. Pugh [1986]. *IBM's Early Computers,* MIT Press, Cambridge, Mass.

Baskett, F., T. Jermoluk, and D. Solomon [1988]. "The 4D-MP graphics superworkstation: Computing + graphics = 40 MIPS + 40 MFLOPS and 10,000 lighted polygons per second," *Proc. COMPCON Spring,* San Francisco, 468–471.

BBN Laboratories [1986]. "Butterfly parallel processor overview," Tech. Rep. 6148, BBN Laboratories, Cambridge, Mass.

Bell, C. G. [1984]. "The mini and micro industries," *IEEE Computer* 17:10 (October), 14–30.

Bell, C. G. [1985]. "Multis: A new class of multiprocessor computers," *Science* 228 (April 26), 462–467.

Bell, C. G. [1989]. "The future of high performance computers in science and engineering," *Comm.* ACM 32:9 (September), 1091–1101.

Bell, C. G., J. C. Mudge, and J. E. McNamara [1978]. *A DEC View of Computer Engineering,* Digital Press, Bedford, Mass.

Bell, C. G,. and W. D. Strecker [1976]. "Computer structures: What have we learned from the PDP-11?," *Proc. Third Annual Symposium on Computer Architecture* (January), Pittsburgh, 1–14.

Bell, G., R. Cady, H. McFarland, B. DeLagi, J. O'Laughlin, R. Noonan, and W. Wulf [1970]. "A new architecture for mini-computers: The DEC PDP-11," *Proc. AFIPS SJCC,* 657–675.

Bell, G., and J. Gray [2001]. "Crays, clusters and centers," Microsoft Research Technical Report, MSR-TR-2001-76.

Bell, G., and W. D. Strecker [1998]. "Computer structures: What have we learned from the PDP-11?" *25 Years of the International Symposia on Computer Architecture (Selected Papers),* ACM, 138–151.

Bhandarkar, D. P. [1995]. *Alpha Architecture Implementations,* Digital Press, Newton, Mass.

Bhandarkar, D., and D. W. Clark [1991]. "Performance from architecture: Comparing a RISC and a CISC with similar hardware organizations," *Proc. Fourth Conf. on Architectural Support for Programming Languages and Operating Systems,* IEEE/ACM (April), Palo Alto, Calif., 310–319.

Bhandarkar, D., and J. Ding [1997]. "Performance characterization of the Pentium Pro processor," *Proc. Third Int'l Symposium on High Performance Computer Architecture,* IEEE (February), San Antonio, 288–297.

Bier, J. [1997]. "The evolution of DSP processors," presentation at U.C. Berkeley, November 14.

Blaum, M., J. Brady, J. Bruck, and J. Menon [1994]. "EVENODD: An optimal scheme for tolerating double disk failures in RAID architectures," *Proc. 21st Annual Symposium on Computer Architecture* (April), Chicago, Ill., 245–254.

Bloch, E. [1959]. "The engineering design of the Stretch computer," *Proc. Fall Joint Computer Conf.,* 48–59.

Boddie, J. R. [2000]. "History of DSPs," *www.lucent.com/micro/dsp/dsphist.html.*

Borg, A., R. E. Kessler, and D. W. Wall [1990]. "Generation and analysis of very long address traces," *Proc. 17th Annual Int'l Symposium on Computer Architecture,* Seattle, Wash., May 28–31, 270–279.

Bouknight, W. J, S. A. Deneberg, D. E. McIntyre, J. M. Randall, A. H. Sameh, and D. L. Slotnick [1972]. "The Illiac IV system," *Proc. IEEE* 60:4, 369–379. Also appears in D. P. Siewiorek, C. G. Bell, and A. Newell, *Computer Structures: Principles and Examples,* McGraw-Hill, New York (1982), 306–316.

Brady, J. T. [1986]. "A theory of productivity in the creative process," *IEEE CG&A* (May), 25–34.

Brain, M. [2000]. "Inside a digital cell phone," *www.howstuffworks.com/inside-cell-phone.htm.*

Brewer, E. A., and B. C. Kuszmaul [1994]. "How to get good performance from the CM-5 data network." *Proc. Eighth Int'l Parallel Processing Symposium* (April), Cancun, Mexico.

Brin, S., and L. Page [1998]. "The anatomy of a large-scale hypertextual Web search engine," *Proc. 7th Int'l World Wide Web Conf.*, Brisbane, Qld., Australia (April 14–18), 107–117.

Brown, A., and D. A. Patterson [2000]. "Towards maintainability, availability, and growth benchmarks: A case study of software RAID systems." *Proc. 2000 USENIX Annual Technical Conf.* (June), San Diego, Calif.

Bucher, I. V., and A. H. Hayes [1980]. "I/O performance measurement on Cray-1 and CDC 7000 computers," *Proc. Computer Performance Evaluation Users Group, 16th Meeting*, NBS 500-65, 245–254.

Bucholtz, W. [1962]. *Planning a Computer System: Project Stretch*, McGraw-Hill, New York.

Burkhardt, H., III, S. Frank, B. Knobe, and J. Rothnie [1992]. "Overview of the KSR1 computer system," Tech. Rep. KSR-TR-9202001, Kendall Square Research, Boston (February).

Burks, A. W., H. H. Goldstine, and J. von Neumann [1946]. "Preliminary discussion of the logical design of an electronic computing instrument," Report to the U.S. Army Ordnance Department, p. 1; also appears in *Papers of John von Neumann,* W. Aspray and A. Burks, eds., MIT Press, Cambridge, Mass., and Tomash Publishers, Los Angeles, Calif., 1987, 97–146.

Calder, B., G. Reinman, and D. Tullsen [1999]. "Selective value prediction". *Proc. 26th Int'l Symposium on Computer Architecture (ISCA)*, Atlanta, June.

Cantin, J. F., and M. D. Hill [2001]. *Cache Performance for Selected SPEC CPU2000 Benchmarks, www.jfred.org/cache-data.html* (June).

Case, R. P., and A. Padegs [1978]. "The architecture of the IBM System/370," *Communications of the ACM* 21:1, 73–96. Also appears in D. P. Siewiorek, C. G. Bell, and A. Newell, *Computer Structures: Principles and Examples,* McGraw-Hill, New York (1982), 830–855.

Censier, L., and P. Feautrier [1978]. "A new solution to coherence problems in multicache systems," *IEEE Trans. on Computers* C-27:12 (December), 1112–1118.

Chandra, R., S. Devine, B. Verghese, A. Gupta, and M. Rosenblum [1994]. "Scheduling and page migration for multiprocessor compute servers," Sixth Int'l Conf. on Architectural Support for Programming Languages and Operating Systems (ASPLOS-VI), ACM, Santa Clara, Calif., October, 12–24.

Chang, P. P., S. A. Mahlke, W. Y. Chen, N. J. Warter, and W. W. Hwu [1991]. "IMPACT: An architectural framework for multiple-instruction-issue processors," *Proc. 18th Int'l Symposium on Computer Architecture* (May), 266–275.

Charlesworth, A. E. [1981]. "An approach to scientific array processing: The architecture design of the AP-120B/FPS-164 family," *Computer* 14:9 (September), 18–27.

Charlesworth, A. [1998]. "Starfire: Extending the SMP envelope," *IEEE Micro* 18:1 (January/February), 39–49.

Chen, P. M., and E. K. Lee [1995]. "Striping in a RAID level 5 disk array," *Proc. 1995 ACM SIGMETRICS Conf. on Measurement and Modeling of Computer Systems* (May), 136–145.

Chen, P. M., G. A. Gibson, R. H. Katz, and D. A. Patterson [1990]. "An evaluation of redundant arrays of inexpensive disks using an Amdahl 5890," *Proc. 1990 ACM SIG-*

METRICS Conf. on Measurement and Modeling of Computer Systems (May), Boulder, Colo.

Chen, P. M., E. K. Lee, G. A. Gibson, R. H. Katz, and D. A. Patterson [1994]. "RAID: High-performance, reliable secondary storage," *ACM Computing Surveys* 26:2 (June), 145–188.

Chen, T. C. [1980]. "Overlap and parallel processing," in *Introduction to Computer Architecture,* H. Stone, ed., Science Research Associates, Chicago, 427–486.

Chow, F. C. [1983]. *A Portable Machine-Independent Global Optimizer—Design and Measurements,* Ph.D. thesis, Stanford Univ. (December).

Chrysos, G. Z., and J. S. Emer [1998]. "Memory dependence prediction using store sets," *Proc. 25th Int'l Symposium on Computer Architecture (ISCA),* June, Barcelona, 142–153.

Clark, D. W. [1983]. "Cache performance of the VAX-11/780," *ACM Trans. on Computer Systems* 1:1, 24–37.

Clark, D. W. [1987]. "Pipelining and performance in the VAX 8800 processor," *Proc. Second Conf. on Architectural Support for Programming Languages and Operating Systems,* IEEE/ACM (March), Palo Alto, Calif., 173–177.

Clark, D. W., and J. S. Emer [1985]. "Performance of the VAX-11/780 translation buffer: Simulation and measurement," *ACM Trans. on Computer Systems* 3:1 (February), 31–62.

Clark, D., and H. Levy [1982]. "Measurement and analysis of instruction set use in the VAX-11/780," *Proc. Ninth Symposium on Computer Architecture* (April), Austin, Tex., 9–17.

Clark, D., and W. D. Strecker [1980]. "Comments on 'the case for the reduced instruction set computer'," *Computer Architecture News* 8:6 (October), 34–38.

Clark, W. A. [1957]. "The Lincoln TX-2 computer development," *Proc. Western Joint Computer Conference* (February), Institute of Radio Engineers, Los Angeles, 143–145.

Colwell, R. P., R. P. Nix, J. J. O'Donnell, D. B. Papworth, and P. K. Rodman [1987]. "A VLIW architecture for a trace scheduling compiler," *Proc. Second Conf. on Architectural Support for Programming Languages and Operating Systems,* IEEE/ACM (March), Palo Alto, Calif., 180–192.

Colwell, R. P., and R. Steck [1995]. "A 0.6um BiCMOS processor with dynamic execution." *Proc. of Int'l Symposium on Solid State Circuits,* 176–177.

Comer, D. [1993]. *Internetworking with TCP/IP,* 2nd ed., Prentice Hall, Englewood Cliffs, N.J.

Compaq Computer Corporation [1999]. *Compiler Writer's Guide for the Alpha 21264,* Order Number EC-RJ66A-TE, June, *www1.support.compaq.com/alpha-tools/documentation/current/21264_EV67/ec-rj66a-te_comp_writ_gde_for_alpha21264.pdf.*

Conti, C., D. H. Gibson, and S. H. Pitkowsky [1968]. "Structural aspects of the System/360 Model 85, Part I: General organization," *IBM Systems J.* 7:1, 2–14.

Crawford, J., and P. Gelsinger [1988]. *Programming the 80386,* Sybex Books, Alameda, Calif.

Culler, D. E., J. P. Singh, and A. Gupta [1999]. *Parallel Computer Architecture: A Hardware/Software Approach,* Morgan Kaufmann, San Francisco.

Curnow, H. J., and B. A. Wichmann [1976]. "A synthetic benchmark," *The Computer J.,* 19:1, 43–49.

Cvetanovic, Z., and R. E. Kessler [2000]. "Performance analysis of the Alpha 21264-based Compaq ES40 system," *Proc. 27th Annual Int'l Symposium on Computer*

Architecture, Vancouver, Canada, June 10–14, IEEE Computer Society Press, 192–202.

Dally, W. J., and C. I. Seitz [1986]. "The torus routing chip," *Distributed Computing* 1:4, 187–196.

Davidson, E. S. [1971]. "The design and control of pipelined function generators," *Proc. Conf. on Systems, Networks, and Computers,* IEEE (January), Oaxtepec, Mexico, 19–21.

Davidson, E. S., A. T. Thomas, L. E. Shar, and J. H. Patel [1975]. "Effective control for pipelined processors," *COMPCON, IEEE* (March), San Francisco, 181–184.

Davie, B. S., L. L. Peterson, and D. Clark [1999]. *Computer Networks: A Systems Approach,* 2nd ed., Morgan Kaufmann Publishers, San Francisco.

Dehnert, J. C., P. Y.-T. Hsu, and J. P. Bratt [1989]. "Overlapped loop support on the Cydra 5," *Proc. Third Conf. on Architectural Support for Programming Languages and Operating Systems* (April), IEEE/ACM, Boston, 26–39.

Desurvire, E. [1992]. "Lightwave communications: The fifth generation," *Scientific American* (International Edition) 266:1 (January), 96–103.

Diep, T. A., C. Nelson, and J. P. Shen [1995]. "Performance evaluation of the PowerPC 620 microarchitecture," *Proc. 22nd Symposium on Computer Architecture* (June), Santa Margherita, Italy.

Ditzel, D. R., and H. R. McLellan [1987]. "Branch folding in the CRISP microprocessor: Reducing the branch delay to zero," *Proc. 14th Symposium on Computer Architecture* (June), Pittsburgh, 2–7.

Ditzel, D. R., and D. A. Patterson [1980]. "Retrospective on high-level language computer architecture," *Proc. Seventh Annual Symposium on Computer Architecture,* La Baule, France (June), 97–104.

Doherty, W. J., and R. P. Kelisky [1979]. "Managing VM/CMS systems for user effectiveness," *IBM Systems J.* 18:1, 143–166.

Dubois, M., C. Scheurich, and F. Briggs [1988]. "Synchronization, coherence, and event ordering," *IEEE Computer* 9-21 (February).

Edmondson, J. H., P. I. Rubinfield, R. Preston, and V. Rajagopalan [1995]. "Superscalar instruction execution in the 21164 Alpha microprocessor," *IEEE Micro* 15:2, 33–43.

Eggers, S. [1989]. *Simulation Analysis of Data Sharing in Shared Memory Multiprocessors,* Ph.D. thesis, Univ. of California, Berkeley. Computer Science Division Tech. Rep. UCB/CSD 89/501 (April).

Elder, J., A. Gottlieb, C. K. Kruskal, K. P. McAuliffe, L. Randolph, M. Snir, P. Teller, and J. Wilson [1985]. "Issues related to MIMD shared-memory computers: The NYU Ultracomputer approach," *Proc. 12th Int'l Symposium on Computer Architecture* (June), Boston, 126–135.

Ellis, J. R. [1986]. *Bulldog: A compiler for VLIW architectures,* MIT Press, Cambridge, Mass.

Emer, J. S., and D. W. Clark [1984]. "A characterization of processor performance in the VAX-11/780," *Proc. 11th Symposium on Computer Architecture* (June), Ann Arbor, Mich., 301–310.

Enriquez, P. [2001]. "What happened to my dial tone? A study of FCC service disruption reports," poster, *Richard Tapia Symposium on the Celebration of Diversity in Computing,* October 18–20, Houston, Tex.

Erlichson, A., N. Nuckolls, G. Chesson, and J. L. Hennessy [1996]. "SoftFLASH: Analyzing the performance of clustered distributed virtual shared memory," *Proc. 7th Sym-*

posium on Architectural Support for Programming Languages and Operating Systems (ASPLOS-VII), October, 210–220.

Fabry, R. S. [1974]. "Capability based addressing," Comm. ACM 17:7 (July), 403–412.

Falsafi, B., and D. A. Wood [1997]. "Reactive NUMA: A design for unifying S-COMA and CC-NUMA," Proc. 24th Int'l Symposium on Computer Architecture, June, Denver, Colo., 229–240.

Farkas, K. I., P. Chow, N. P. Jouppi, and Z. Vranesic [1997]. "Memory-system design considerations for dynamically-scheduled processors," Proc. 24th Annual Int'l Symposium on Computer Architecture, Denver, Col., June 2–4, 133–143.

Farkas, K. I., and N. P. Jouppi [1994]. "Complexity/performance trade-offs with nonblocking loads," Proc. 21st Annual Int'l Symposium on Computer Architecture, Chicago (April).

Farkas, K. I., N. P. Jouppi, and P. Chow [1995]. "How useful are non-blocking loads, stream buffers and speculative execution in multiple issue processors?," Proc. First IEEE Symposium on High-Performance Computer Architecture, Raleigh, N.C., January 22–25, 78–89.

Fisher, J. A. [1981]. "Trace scheduling: A technique for global microcode compaction," IEEE Trans. on Computers 30:7 (July), 478–490.

Fisher, J. A. [1983]. "Very long instruction word architectures and ELI-512," Proc. Tenth Symposium on Computer Architecture (June), Stockholm, 140–150.

Fisher, J. A., J. R. Ellis, J. C. Ruttenberg, and A. Nicolau [1984]. "Parallel processing: A smart compiler and a dumb processor," Proc. SIGPLAN Conf. on Compiler Construction (June), Palo Alto, Calif., 11–16.

Fisher, J. A., and S. M. Freudenberger [1992]. "Predicting conditional branches from previous runs of a program," Proc. Fifth Conf. on Architectural Support for Programming Languages and Operating Systems, IEEE/ACM (October), Boston, 85–95.

Fisher, J. A., and B. R. Rau [1993]. Journal of Supercomputing (January), Kluwer.

Flemming, P. J., and J. J. Wallace [1986]. "How not to lie with statistics: The correct way to summarize benchmarks results," Comm. ACM 29:3 (March), 218–221.

Flynn, M. J. [1966]. "Very high-speed computing systems," Proc. IEEE 54:12 (December), 1901–1909.

Forgie, J. W. [1957]. "The Lincoln TX-2 input-output system," Proc. Western Joint Computer Conference (February), Institute of Radio Engineers, Los Angeles, 156–160.

Foster, C. C., and E. M. Riseman [1972]. "Percolation of code to enhance parallel dispatching and execution," IEEE Trans. on Computers C-21:12 (December), 1411–1415.

Frank, S. J. [1984]. "Tightly coupled multiprocessor systems speed memory access time," Electronics 57:1 (January), 164–169.

Friesenborg, S. E., and R. J. Wicks [1985]. "DASD expectations: The 3380, 3380-23, and MVS/XA," Tech. Bulletin GG22-9363-02 (July 10), Washington Systems Center.

Fuller, S. H., and W. E. Burr [1977]. "Measurement and evaluation of alternative computer architectures," Computer 10:10 (October), 24–35.

Gagliardi, U. O. [1973]. "Report of workshop 4—software-related advances in computer hardware," Proc. Symposium on the High Cost of Software, Menlo Park, Calif., 99–120.

Gajski, D., D. Kuck, D. Lawrie, and A. Sameh [1983]. "CEDAR—a large scale multiprocessor," Proc. Int'l Conf. on Parallel Processing (August), 524–529.

Gallagher, D. M., W. Y. Chen, S. A. Mahlke, J. C. Gyllenhaal, and W.W. Hwu [1994]. "Dynamic memory disambiguation using the memory conflict buffer," Proc. Sixth

Int'l Conf. on Architectural Support for Programming Languages and Operating Systems (October), Santa Clara, Calif., 183–193.

Galles, M. [1996]. "Scalable pipelined interconnect for distributed endpoint routing: The SGI SPIDER chip," *Proc. Hot Interconnects '96,* Stanford University, August.

Game, M., and A. Booker [1999]. "CodePack code compression for PowerPC processors," *MicroNews,* 5:1, *www.chips.ibm.com/micronews/vol5_no1/codepack.html.*

Gao, Q. S. [1993]. "The Chinese remainder theorem and the prime memory system," 20th Annual Int'l Symposium on Computer Architecture ISCA '20, San Diego, Calif., May 16–19, *Computer Architecture News* 21:2 (May), 337–340.

Garner, R., A. Agarwal, F. Briggs, E. Brown, D. Hough, B. Joy, S. Kleiman, S. Munchnik, M. Namjoo, D. Patterson, J. Pendleton, and R. Tuck [1988]. "Scalable processor architecture (SPARC)," *COMPCON, IEEE* (March), San Francisco, 278–283.

Gee, J. D., M. D. Hill, D. N. Pnevmatikatos, and A. J. Smith [1993]. "Cache performance of the SPEC92 benchmark suite," *IEEE Micro* 13:4 (August), 17–27.

Gehringer, E. F., D. P. Siewiorek, and Z. Segall [1987]. *Parallel Processing: The Cm* Experience,* Digital Press, Bedford, Mass.

Gharachorloo, K., A. Gupta, and J. L. Hennessy [1992]. "Hiding memory latency using dynamic scheduling in shared-memory multiprocessors," *Proc. 19th Annual Int'l Symposium on Computer Architecture,* Gold Coast, Australia, June.

Gharachorloo, K., D. Lenoski, J. Laudon, P. Gibbons, A. Gupta, and J. L. Hennessy [1990]. "Memory consistency and event ordering in scalable shared-memory multiprocessors," *Proc. 17th Int'l Symposium on Computer Architecture* (June), Seattle, Wash., 15–26.

Gibson, D. H. [1967]. "Considerations in block-oriented systems design," *AFIPS Conf. Proc.* 30, SJCC, 75–80.

Gibson, G. A. [1992]. *Redundant Disk Arrays: Reliable, Parallel Secondary Storage,* ACM Distinguished Dissertation Series, MIT Press, Cambridge, Mass.

Gibson, J. C. [1970]. "The Gibson mix," Rep. TR. 00.2043, IBM Systems Development Division, Poughkeepsie, N.Y. (Research done in 1959.)

Gibson, J., R. Kunz, D. Ofelt, M. Horowitz, J. Hennessy, and M. Heinrich [2000]. "FLASH vs. (simulated) FLASH: Closing the simulation loop," *Proc. 9th Conf. on Architectural Support for Programming Languages and Operating Systems* (November), San Jose, Calif., 49–58.

Goldstein, S. [1987]. "Storage performance—an eight year outlook," Tech. Rep. TR 03.308-1 (October), Santa Teresa Laboratory, IBM, San Jose, Calif.

Goldstine, H. H. [1972]. *The Computer: From Pascal to von Neumann,* Princeton University Press, Princeton, N.J.

González, J., and A. González [1998]. "Limits of instruction level parallelism with data speculation," *Proc. of the VECPAR Conf.,* 585–598.

Goodman, J. R. [1983]. "Using cache memory to reduce processor memory traffic," *Proc. 10th Int'l Symposium on Computer Architecture* (June), Stockholm, Sweden, 124–131.

Goralski, W. [1997]. *SONET: A Guide to Synchronous Optical Network,* McGraw-Hill, New York.

Gray, J. [1990]. "A census of Tandem system availability between 1985 and 1990," *IEEE Transactions on Reliability,* 39:4 (October) 409–418.

Gray, J. (ed.) [1993]. *The Benchmark Handbook for Database and Transaction Processing Systems,* 2nd ed., Morgan Kaufmann Publishers, San Francisco.

Gray, J., and A. Reuter [1993]. *Transaction Processing: Concepts and Techniques,* Morgan Kaufmann Publishers, San Francisco.

Gray, J., and D. P. Siewiorek [1991]. "High-availability computer systems." *Computer* 24:9 (September), 39–48.

Grice, C., and M. Kanellos [2000]. "Cell phone industry at crossroads: Go high or low?," *CNET News* (August 31), *technews.netscape.com/news/0-1004-201-2518386-0.html? tag=st.ne.1002.tgif.sf.*

Groe, J. B., and L. E. Larson [2000]. *CDMA Mobile Radio Design,* Artech House, Boston.

Hagersten E., and M. Koster [1998]. "WildFire: A scalable path for SMPs," *Proc. Fifth Int'l Symposium on High Performance Computer Architecture.*

Hagersten, E., A. Landin, and S. Haridi [1992]. "DDM—a cache-only memory architecture," *IEEE Computer* 25:9 (September), 44–54.

Handy, J. [1993]. *The Cache Memory Book*, Academic Press, Boston.

Hauck, E. A., and B. A. Dent [1968]. "Burroughs' B6500/B7500 stack mechanism," *Proc. AFIPS SJCC*, 245–251.

Heald, R., K. Aingaran, C. Amir, M. Ang, M. Boland, A. Das, P. Dixit, G. Gouldsberry, J. Hart, T. Horel, W.-J. Hsu, J. Kaku, C. Kim, S. Kim, F. Klass, H. Kwan, R. Lo, H. McIntyre, A. Mehta, D. Murata, S. Nguyen, Y.-P. Pai, S. Patel, K. Shin, K. Tam, S. Vishwanthaiah, J. Wu, G. Yee, and H. You [2000]. "Implementation of third-generation SPARC V9 64-b microprocessor," *ISSCC Digest of Technical Papers,* 412–413 and slide supplement.

Heinrich, J. [1993]. *MIPS R4000 User's Manual,* Prentice Hall, Englewood Cliffs, N.J.

Henly, M., and B. McNutt [1989]. "DASD I/O characteristics: A comparison of MVS to VM," Tech. Rep. TR 02.1550 (May), IBM, General Products Division, San Jose, Calif.

Hennessy, J. [1984]. "VLSI processor architecture," *IEEE Trans. on Computers* C-33:11 (December), 1221–1246.

Hennessy, J. [1985]. "VLSI RISC processors," *VLSI Systems Design* VI:10 (October), 22–32.

Hennessy, J., N. Jouppi, F. Baskett, and J. Gill [1981]. "MIPS: A VLSI processor architecture," *Proc. CMU Conf. on VLSI Systems and Computations* (October), Computer Science Press, Rockville, Md.

Hewlett-Packard [1998]. "HP's '5NINES:5MINUTES' vision extends leadership and redefines high availability in mission-critical environments" (February 10), *www.future .enterprisecomputing.hp.com/ia64/news/5nines_vision_pr.html.*

Hill, M. D. [1987]. *Aspects of Cache Memory and Instruction Buffer Performance*, Ph.D. thesis, University of Calif. at Berkeley, Computer Science Division, Tech. Rep. UCB/ CSD 87/381 (November).

Hill, M. D. [1988]. "A case for direct mapped caches," *Computer* 21:12 (December), 25–40.

Hill, M. D. [1998]. "Multiprocessors should support simple memory consistency models," *IEEE Computer* 31:8 (August), 28–34.

Hillis, W. D. [1985]. *The Connection Multiprocessor*, MIT Press, Cambridge, Mass.

Hirata, H., K. Kimura, S. Nagamine, Y. Mochizuki, A. Nishimura, Y. Nakase, and T. Nishizawa [1992]. "An elementary processor architecture with simultaneous instruction issuing from multiple threads," *Proc. 19th Annual Int'l Symposium on Computer Architecture* (May), 136–145.

Hoagland, A. S. [1963]. *Digital Magnetic Recording,* Wiley, New York.

Hockney, R. W., and C. R. Jesshope [1988]. *Parallel Computers-2, Architectures, Programming and Algorithms,* Adam Hilger Ltd., Bristol, England.

Holland, J. H. [1959]. "A universal computer capable of executing an arbitrary number of subprograms simultaneously," *Proc. East Joint Computer Conf.* 16, 108–113.

Hopkins, M. [2000]. "A critical look at IA-64: Massive resources, massive ILP, but can it deliver?" *Microprocessor Report* (February).

Hord, R. M. [1982]. *The Illiac-IV, The First Supercomputer,* Computer Science Press, Rockville, Md.

Horel, T., and G. Lauterbach [1999]. "UltraSPARC-III: Designing third-generation 64-bit performance," *IEEE Micro* 19:3 (May–June), 73–85.

Hospodor, A. D., and A. S. Hoagland [1993]. "The changing nature of disk controllers." *Proc. IEEE* 81:4 (April), 586–594.

Hristea, C., D. Lenoski, and J. Keen [1997]. "Measuring memory hierarchy performance of cache-coherent multiprocessors using micro benchmarks," *Proc. Supercomputing 97,* San Jose, Calif., November.

Hsu, P. [1994]. "Designing the TFP microprocessor," *IEEE Micro* 18:2 (April), 2333.

Hughes, C. J., P. Kaul, S. V. Adve, R. Jain, C. Park, and J. Srinivasan [2001]. "Variability in the execution of multimedia applications and implications for architecture, "*Proc. 28th Annual Int'l Symposium on Computer Architecture,* Goteborg, Sweden, June 30–July 4, 254–265.

Hwang, K. [1993]. *Advanced Computer Architecture and Parallel Programming,* McGraw-Hill, New York.

Hwu, W.-M., and Y. Patt [1986]. "HPSm, a high performance restricted data flow architecture having minimum functionality," *Proc. 13th Symposium on Computer Architecture* (June), Tokyo, 297–307.

Hwu, W. W., S. A. Mahlke, W. Y. Chen, P. P. Chang, N. J. Warter, R. A. Bringmann, R. O. Ouellette, R. E. Hank, T. Kiyohara, G. E. Haab, J. G. Holm, and D. M. Lavery [1993]. "The superblock: An effective technique for VLIW and superscalar compilation," *J. Supercomputing* 7:1, 2 (March), 229–248.

IBM [1982]. *The Economic Value of Rapid Response Time,* GE20-0752-0, White Plains, N.Y., 11–82.

IBM [1990]. "The IBM RISC System/6000 processor" (collection of papers), *IBM J. Research and Development* 34:1 (January).

Imprimis [1989]. *Imprimis Product Specification, 97209 Sabre Disk Drive IPI-2 Interface 1.2 GB,* Document No. 64402302 (May).

Infiniband Trade Association [2001]. *InfiniBand Architecture Specifications Release 1.0.a, www.infinibandta.org.*

Intel [2001]. "Using MMX instructions to convert RGB to YUV color conversion," *cedar.intel.com/cgi-bin/ids.dll/content/content.jsp?cntKey=Legacy::irtm_AP548_9996&cntType=IDS_EDITORIAL.*

Jain, R. [1991]. *The Art of Computer Systems Performance Analysis: Techniques for Experimental Design, Measurement, Simulation, and Modeling,* Wiley, New York.

Johnson, M. [1990]. *Superscalar Microprocessor Design,* Prentice Hall, Englewood Cliffs, N.J.

Jordan, H. F. [1983]. "Performance measurements on HEP: A pipelined MIMD computer," *Proc. 10th Symposium on Computer Architecture* (June), 207–212.

Jouppi, N. P. [1990]. "Improving direct-mapped cache performance by the addition of a small fully-associative cache and prefetch buffers," *Proc. 17th Annual Int'l Symposium on Computer Architecture,* 364–73.

Jouppi, N. P. [1998]. "Retrospective: Improving direct-mapped cache performance by the addition of a small fully-associative cache and prefetch buffers," *25 Years of the Int'l Symposia on Computer Architecture (Selected Papers)*, ACM, 71–73.

Jouppi, N. P., and D. W. Wall [1989]. "Available instruction-level parallelism for super-scalar and superpipelined processors," *Proc. Third Conf. on Architectural Support for Programming Languages and Operating Systems*, IEEE/ACM (April), Boston, 272–282.

Jouppi, N. P., and S. J. E. Wilton [1994]. "Trade-offs in two-level on-chip caching," *Proc. 21st Annual Int'l Symposium on Computer Architecture*, Chicago, April 18–21, 34–45.

Kaeli, D. R., and P. G. Emma [1991]. "Branch history table prediction of moving target branches due to subroutine returns," *Proc. 18th Int'l Symposium on Computer Architecture (ISCA)*, Toronto, May, 34–42.

Kahn, R. E. [1972]. "Resource-sharing computer communication networks," *Proc. IEEE* 60:11 (November), 1397–1407.

Kane, G. [1986]. *MIPS R2000 RISC Architecture*, Prentice Hall, Englewood Cliffs, N.J.

Katz, R. H., D. A. Patterson, and G. A. Gibson [1989]. "Disk system architectures for high performance computing," *Proc. IEEE* 77:12 (December), 1842–1858.

Keckler, S. W., and W. J. Dally [1992]. "Processor coupling: Integrating compile time and runtime scheduling for parallelism," *Proc. 19th Annual Int'l Symposium on Computer Architecture* (May), 202–213.

Keller, R. M. [1975]. "Look-ahead processors," *ACM Computing Surveys* 7:4 (December), 177–195.

Kessler, R. E. [1999]. "The Alpha 21264 microprocessor," *IEEE Micro* 19:2 (March/April), 24–36.

Kilburn, T., D. B. G. Edwards, M. J. Lanigan, and F. H. Sumner [1962]. "One-level storage system," *IRE Trans. on Electronic Computers* EC-11 (April) 223–235. Also appears in D. P. Siewiorek, C. G. Bell, and A. Newell, *Computer Structures: Principles and Examples* (1982), McGraw-Hill, New York, 135–148.

Killian, E. [1991]. "MIPS R4000 technical overview—64 bits/100 MHz or bust," *Hot Chips III Symposium Record* (August), Stanford University, 1.6–1.19.

Kim, M. Y. [1986]. "Synchronized disk interleaving," *IEEE Trans. on Computers* C-35:11 (November), 978–988.

Kogge, P. M. [1981]. *The Architecture of Pipelined Computers*, McGraw-Hill, New York.

Kontothanassis, L., G. Hunt, R. Stets, N. Hardavellas, M. Cierniak, S. Parthasarathy, W. Meira, S. Dwarkadas, and M. Scott [1997]. "VM-based shared memory on low-latency, remote-memory-access networks," *Proc. 24th Annual Int'l. Symposium on Computer Architecture* (June), Denver, Colo.

Kozyrakis, C. [2000]. "Vector IRAM: A media-oriented vector processor with embedded DRAM," presentation at Hot Chips 12 Conf., Palo Alto, Calif, 13–15.

Kroft, D. [1981]. "Lockup-free instruction fetch/prefetch cache organization," *Proc. Eighth Annual Symposium on Computer Architecture* (May 12–14), Minneapolis, 81–87.

Kroft, D. [1998]. "Retrospective: Lockup-free instruction fetch/prefetch cache organization," *25 Years of the Int'l Symposia on Computer Architecture (Selected Papers)*, ACM, 20–21.

Kuhn, D. R. [1997]. "Sources of failure in the public switched telephone network," *IEEE Computer* 30:4 (April), 31–36.

Kumar, A. [1997]. "The HP PA-8000 RISC CPU," *IEEE Micro* 17:2 (March/April).

Kunimatsu, A., N. Ide, T. Sato, Y. Endo, H. Murakami, T. Kamei, M. Hirano, F. Ishihara, H. Tago, M. Oka, A. Ohba, T. Yutaka, T. Okada, and M. Suzuoki [2000]. "Vector unit architecture for emotion synthesis," *IEEE Micro* 20:2 (March–April), 40–47.

Kunkel, S. R., and J. E. Smith [1986]. "Optimal pipelining in supercomputers," *Proc. 13th Symposium on Computer Architecture* (June), Tokyo, 404–414.

Kurose, J. F., and K. W. Ross [2001]. *Computer Networking: A Top-Down Approach Featuring the Internet,* Addison-Wesley, Boston.

Kuskin, J., D. Ofelt, M. Heinrich, J. Heinlein, R. Simoni, K. Gharachorloo, J. Chapin, D. Nakahira, J. Baxter, M. Horowitz, A. Gupta, M. Rosenblum, and J. L. Hennessy [1994]. "The Stanford FLASH multiprocessor," *Proc. 21st Int'l Symposium on Computer Architecture,* Chicago, April.

Lam, M. [1988]. "Software pipelining: An effective scheduling technique for VLIW processors," *SIGPLAN Conf. on Programming Language Design and Implementation,* ACM (June), Atlanta, Ga., 318–328.

Lam, M. S., E. E. Rothberg, and M. E. Wolf [1991]. "The cache performance and optimizations of blocked algorithms," Fourth Int'l Conf. on Architectural Support for Programming Languages and Operating Systems, Santa Clara, Calif., April 8–11. *SIGPLAN Notices* 26:4 (April), 63–74.

Lam, M. S., and R. P. Wilson [1992]. "Limits of control flow on parallelism," *Proc. 19th Symposium on Computer Architecture* (May), Gold Coast, Australia, 46–57.

Lambright, D. [2000]. "Experiences in measuring the reliability of a cache-based storage system," *Proc. of First Workshop on Industrial Experiences with Systems Software* (WIESS 2000), collocated with the 4th Symposium on Operating Systems Design and Implementation (OSDI), San Diego, Calif. (October 22).

Lamport, L. [1979]. "How to make a multiprocessor computer that correctly executes multiprocess programs," *IEEE Trans. on Computers* C-28:9 (September), 241–248.

Laprie, J.-C. [1985]. "Dependable computing and fault tolerance: Concepts and terminology," *Fifteenth Annual Int'l Symposium on Fault-Tolerant Computing FTCS 15.* Digest of Papers. Ann Arbor, Mich. (June 19–21), 2–11.

Larson, E. R. [1973]. "Findings of fact, conclusions of law, and order for judgment," File No. 4-67, Civ. 138, *Honeywell v. Sperry-Rand and Illinois Scientific Development,* U.S. District Court for the State of Minnesota, Fourth Division (October 19).

Laudon, J., A. Gupta, and M. Horowitz [1994]. "Interleaving: A multithreading technique targeting multiprocessors and workstations," *Proc. Sixth Int'l Conf. on Architectural Support for Programming Languages and Operating Systems* (October), Boston, 308–318.

Laudon, J., and D. Lenoski [1997]. "The SGI Origin: A ccNUMA highly scalable server," *Proc. 24th Int'l Symposium on Computer Architecture* (June), Denver, Colo., 241–251.

Lauterbach G., and T. Horel [1999]. "UltraSPARC-III: Designing third generation 64-bit performance," *IEEE Micro* 19:3 (May/June).

Lazowska, E. D., J. Zahorjan, G. S. Graham, and K. C. Sevcik [1984]. *Quantitative System Performance: Computer System Analysis Using Queueing Network models,* Prentice Hall, Englewood Cliffs, N.J. (Although out of print, it is available online at *www.cs.washington.edu/homes/lazowska/qsp/*).

Lebeck, A. R., and D. A. Wood [1994]. "Cache profiling and the SPEC benchmarks: A case study," *Computer* 27:10 (October), 15–26.

Lee, R. [1989]. "Precision architecture," *Computer* 22:1 (January), 78–91.

Leiner, A. L. [1954]. "System specifications for the DYSEAC," *J. ACM* 1:2 (April), 57–81.

Leiner, A. L., and S. N. Alexander [1954]. "System organization of the DYSEAC," *IRE Trans. of Electronic Computers* EC-3:1 (March), 1–10.

Lenoski, D., J. Laudon, K. Gharachorloo, A. Gupta, and J. L. Hennessy [1990]. "The Stanford DASH multiprocessor," *Proc. 17th Int'l Symposium on Computer Architecture* (June), Seattle, Wash., 148–159.

Lenoski, D., J. Laudon, K. Gharachorloo, W.-D. Weber, A. Gupta, J. L. Hennessy, M. A. Horowitz, and M. Lam [1992]. "The Stanford DASH multiprocessor," *IEEE Computer* 25:3 (March).

Levy, H., and R. Eckhouse [1989]. *Computer Programming and Architecture: The VAX*, Digital Press, Boston.

Li, K. [1988]. "IVY: A shared virtual memory system for parallel computing," *Proc. 1988 Int'l Conf. on Parallel Processing*, Pennsylvania State University Press.

Lindholm, T., and F. Yellin [1999]. *The Java Virtual Machine Specification*, second edition, Addison-Wesley, Reading, Mass. Also available online at *java.sun.com/docs /books/vmspec/*.

Lipasti, M. II., and J. P. Shcn [1996]. "Exceeding the dataflow limit via value prediction," *Proc. 29th Annual ACM/IEEE Int'l Symposium on Microarchitecture* (December).

Lipasti, M. H., C. B. Wilkerson, and J. P. Shen [1996]. "Value locality and load value prediction," *Proc. Seventh Symposium on Architectural Support for Programming Languages and Operating Systems* (October), 138–147.

Liptay, J. S. [1968]. "Structural aspects of the System/360 Model 85, Part II: The cache," *IBM Systems J.* 7:1, 15–21.

Lo, J., L. Barroso, S. Eggers, K. Gharachorloo, H. Levy, and S. Parekh [1998]. "An analysis of database workload performance on simultaneous multithreaded processors," *Proc. 25th Int'l Symposium on Computer Architecture* (June), 39–50.

Lo, J., S. Eggers, J. Emer, H. Levy, R. Stamm, and D. Tullsen [1997]. "Converting thread-level parallclism into instruction-level parallelism via simultaneous multithreading," *ACM Transactions on Computer Systems* 15:2 (August), 322–354.

Lovett, T., and S. Thakkar [1988]. "The Symmetry multiprocessor system," *Proc. 1988 Int'l Conf. of Parallel Processing*, University Park, Penn., 303–310.

Lubeck, O., J. Moore, and R. Mendez [1985]. "A benchmark comparison of three supercomputers: Fujitsu VP-200, Hitachi S810/20, and Cray X-MP/2," *Computer* 18:12 (December), 10–24.

Luk, C.-K., and T. C Mowry [1999]. "Automatic compiler-inserted prefetching for pointer-based applications," *IEEE Trans. on Computers*, 48:2 (February), 134–141.

Lunde, A. [1977]. "Empirical evaluation of some features of instruction set processor architecture," *Comm. ACM* 20:3 (March), 143–152.

Maberly, N. C. [1966]. *Mastering Speed Reading*, New American Library, New York.

Mahlke, S. A., W. Y. Chen, W.-M. Hwu, B. R. Rau, and M. S. Schlansker [1992]. "Sentinel scheduling for VLIW and superscalar processors," *Proc. Fifth Conf. on Architectural Support for Programming Languages and Operating Systems* (October), Boston, IEEE/ACM, 238–247.

Mahlke, S. A., R. E. Hank, J. E. McCormick, D. I. August, and W. W. Hwu [1995]. "A comparison of full and partial predicated execution support for ILP processors," *Proc. 22nd Annual Int'l Symposium on Computer Architecture* (June), Santa Margherita Ligure, Italy, 138–149.

Major, J. B. [1989]. "Are queuing models within the grasp of the unwashed?," *Proc. Int'l Conf. on Management and Performance Evaluation of Computer Systems*, Reno, Nev. (December 11–15), 831–839.

McCalpin, J. D. [2001]. *STREAM: Sustainable Memory Bandwidth in High Performance Computers, www.cs.virginia.edu/stream/.*

McFarling, S. [1989]. "Program optimization for instruction caches," *Proc. Third Int'l Conf. on Architectural Support for Programming Languages and Operating Systems* (April 3–6), Boston, 183–191.

McFarling, S. [1993]. "Combining branch predictors," WRL Technical Note TN-36 (June), Digital Western Research Laboratory, Palo Alto, Calif.

McFarling, S., and J. Hennessy [1986]. "Reducing the cost of branches," *Proc. 13th Symposium on Computer Architecture* (June), Tokyo, 396–403.

McGhan, H., and M. O'Connor [1998]. "PicoJava: A direct execution engine for Java bytecode," *Computer* 31:10 (October), 22–30.

McKeeman, W. M. [1967]. "Language directed computer design," *Proc. 1967 Fall Joint Computer Conf.,* Washington, D.C., 413–417.

McMahon, F. M. [1986]. "The Livermore FORTRAN kernels: A computer test of numerical performance range," Tech. Rep. UCRL-55745, Lawrence Livermore National Laboratory, Univ. of California, Livermore (December).

Mellor-Crummey, J. M., and M. L. Scott [1991]. "Algorithms for scalable synchronization on shared-memory multiprocessors," *ACM Trans. on Computer Systems* 9:1 (February), 21–65.

Menabrea, L. F. [1842]. "Sketch of the analytical engine invented by Charles Babbage," *Bibiothèque Universelle de Genève* (October).

Metcalfe, R. M. [1993]. "Computer/network interface design: Lessons from Arpanet and Ethernet." *IEEE J. on Selected Areas in Communications* 11:2 (February), 173–180.

Metcalfe, R. M., and D. R. Boggs [1976]. "Ethernet: Distributed packet switching for local computer networks," *Comm. ACM* 19:7 (July), 395–404.

Metropolis, N., J. Howlett, and G-C Rota, eds. [1980]. *A History of Computing in the Twentieth Century,* Academic Press, New York.

Meyers, G. J. [1978]. "The evaluation of expressions in a storage-to-storage architecture," *Computer Architecture News* 7:3 (October), 20–23.

Meyers, G. J. [1982]. *Advances in Computer Architecture*, second edition, Wiley, New York.

Mitchell, D. [1989]. "The Transputer: The time is now," *Computer Design* (RISC supplement), 40–41.

Miya, E. N. [1985]. "Multiprocessor/distributed processing bibliography," *Computer Architecture News* (ACM SIGARCH) 13:1, 27–29.

Moshovos, A., S. Breach, T. N. Vijaykumar, and G. S. Sohi [1997]. "Dynamic speculation and synchronization of data dependences," *Proc. 24th Int'l Symposium on Computer Architecture (ISCA),* June, Boulder, Colo.

Moshovos, A., and G. S. Sohi [1997]. "Streamlining inter-operation memory communication via data dependence prediction," *Proc. 30th Annual Int'l Symposium on Microarchitecture (MICRO-30),* December, 235–245.

Moussouris, J., L. Crudele, D. Freitas, C. Hansen, E. Hudson, S. Przybylski, T. Riordan, and C. Rowen [1986]. "A CMOS RISC processor with integrated system functions," *Proc. COMPCON, IEEE* (March), San Francisco, 191.

Mowry, T. C., S. Lam, and A. Gupta [1992]. "Design and evaluation of a compiler algorithm for prefetching," Fifth Int'l Conf. on Architectural Support for Programming

Languages and Operating Systems (ASPLOS-V), Boston, October 12–15, *SIGPLAN Notices* 27:9 (September), 62–73.

Mueller, M., L. C. Alves, W. Fischer, M. L. Fair, I. Modi [1999]. "RAS strategy for IBM S/390 G5 and G6," *IBM J. Research and Development,* 43:5–6 (September–November), 875–888.

Murphy, B., and T. Gent [1995]. "Measuring system and software reliability using an automated data collection process," *Quality and Reliability Engineering International,* 11:5 (September–October), 341–353.

Myer, T. H., and I. E. Sutherland [1968]. "On the design of display processors," *Communications of the ACM,* 11:6 (June), 410–414.

National Research Council [1997]. *The Evolution of Untethered Communications,* Computer Science and Telecommunications Board, National Academy Press, Washington, D.C.

National Storage Industry Consortium [1998]. *Tape Roadmap* (June), *www.nsic.org.*

Nelson, V. P. [1990]. "Fault-tolerant computing: Fundamental concepts." *Computer,* 23:7 (July), 19–25.

Nicolau, A., and J. A. Fisher [1984]. "Measuring the parallelism available for very long instruction word architectures," *IEEE Trans. on Computers* C-33:11 (November), 968–976.

Nikhil, R. S., G. M. Papadopoulos, and Arvind [1992]. "*T: A multithreaded massively parallel architecture," *Proc. 19th Int'l Symposium on Computer Architecture,* Gold Coast, Australia, May, 156–167.

Noordergraaf, L., and R. van der Pas [1999]. "Performance experiences on Sun's WildFire prototype," *Proc. Supercomputing 99,* Portland, Ore., November.

Oka, M., and M. Suzuoki [1999]. "Designing and programming the emotion engine," *IEEE Micro* 19:6 (November–December), 20–28.

Okada, S., S. Okada, Y. Matsuda, T. Yamada, and A. Kobayashi [1999]. "System on a chip for digital still camera," *IEEE Trans. on Consumer Electronics,* 45:3, (August), 584–590.

Pabst, T. [2000]. "Performance showdown at 133 MHz FSB—the best platform for coppermine," *www6.tomshardware.com/mainboard/00q1/000302/.*

Palacharla, S., and R. E. Kessler [1994]. "Evaluating stream buffers as a secondary cache replacement," *Proc. 21st Annual Int'l Symposium on Computer Architecture,* Chicago, April 18–21, 24–33.

Pan, S.-T., K. So, and J. T. Rameh [1992]. "Improving the accuracy of dynamic branch prediction using branch correlation," *Proc. Fifth Conf. on Architectural Support for Programming Languages and Operating Systems,* IEEE/ACM (October), Boston, 76–84.

Partridge, C. [1994]. *Gigabit Networking.* Addison-Wesley, Reading, Mass.

Patterson, D. [1985]. "Reduced instruction set computers," *Comm. ACM* 28:1 (January), 8–21.

Patterson, D. A., and D. R. Ditzel [1980]. "The case for the reduced instruction set computer," *Computer Architecture News* 8:6 (October), 25–33.

Patterson, D. A., P. Garrison, M. Hill, D. Lioupis, C. Nyberg, T. Sippel, and K. Van Dyke [1983]. "Architecture of a VLSI instruction cache for a RISC," *10th Annual Int'l Conf. on Computer Architecture Conf. Proc.,* Stockholm, Sweden, June 13–16, 108–116.

Patterson, D. A., G. A. Gibson, and R. H. Katz [1987]. "A case for redundant arrays of inexpensive disks (RAID)," Tech. Rep. UCB/CSD 87/391, Univ. of Calif. Also appeared in *ACM SIGMOD Conf. Proc.*, Chicago, June 1–3, 1988, 109–116.

Pavan, P., R. Bez, P. Olivo, and E. Zanoni [1997]. "Flash memory cells—an overview." *Proc. IEEE*, 85:8 (August), 1248–1271.

Pfister, Gregory F. [1998]. *In Search of Clusters,* 2nd ed., Prentice Hall, Upper Saddle River, N.J.

Pfister, G. F., W. C. Brantley, D. A. George, S. L. Harvey, W. J. Kleinfekder, K. P. McAuliffe, E. A. Melton, V. A. Norton, and J. Weiss [1985]. "The IBM research parallel processor prototype (RP3): Introduction and architecture," *Proc. 12th Int'l Symposium on Computer Architecture* (June), Boston, 764–771.

Postiff, M.A., D. A. Greene, G. S. Tyson, and T. N. Mudge [1992]. "The limits of instruction level parallelism in SPEC95 applications," *Computer Architecture News* 27:1 (March), 31–40.

Przybylski, S. A. [1990]. *Cache Design: A Performance-Directed Approach,* Morgan Kaufmann, San Francisco.

Przybylski, S. A., M. Horowitz, and J. L. Hennessy [1988]. "Performance trade-offs in cache design," *Proc. 15th Annual Symposium on Computer Architecture* (May–June), Honolulu, 290–298.

Radin, G. [1982]. "The 801 minicomputer," *Proc. Symposium Architectural Support for Programming Languages and Operating Systems* (March), Palo Alto, Calif., 39–47.

Ramamoorthy, C. V., and H. F. Li [1977]. "Pipeline architecture," *ACM Computing Surveys* 9:1 (March), 61–102.

Rau, B. R. [1994]. "Iterative modulo scheduling: An algorithm for software pipelining loops," *Proc. 27th Annual Int'l Symposium on Microarchitecture* (November), San Jose, Calif., 63–74.

Rau, B. R., C. D. Glaeser, and R. L. Picard [1982]. "Efficient code generation for horizontal architectures: Compiler techniques and architectural support," *Proc. Ninth Symposium on Computer Architecture* (April), 131–139.

Rau, B. R., D. W. L. Yen, W. Yen, and R. A. Towle [1989]. "The Cydra 5 departmental supercomputer: Design philosophies, decisions, and trade-offs," *IEEE Computers* 22:1 (January), 12–34.

Redmond, K. C., and T. M. Smith [1980]. *Project Whirlwind—The History of a Pioneer Computer,* Digital Press, Boston.

Reinhardt, S. K., J. R. Larus, and D. A. Wood [1994]. "Tempest and Typhoon: User-level shared memory," *Proc. 21st Annual Int'l Symposium on Computer Architecture,* Chicago, April, 325–336.

Reinman, G., and N. P. Jouppi. [1999]. "Extensions to CACTI," *research.compaq.com /wrl/people/jouppi/CACTI.html.*

Rettberg, R. D., W. R. Crowther, P. P. Carvey, and R. S. Towlinson [1990]. "The Monarch parallel processor hardware design," *IEEE Computer* 23:4 (April).

Riemens, A., K. A. Vissers, R. J. Schutten, F. W. Sijstermans, G. J. Hekstra, and G. D. La Hei [1999]."Trimedia CPU64 application domain and benchmark suite," *Proc. 1999 IEEE Int'l Conf. on Computer Design: VLSI in Computers and Processors, ICCD'99,* Austin, Tex., October 10–13, 580–585.

Riseman, E. M., and C. C. Foster [1972]. "Percolation of code to enhance parallel dispatching and execution," *IEEE Trans. on Computers* C-21:12 (December), 1411–1415.

Robinson, B., and L. Blount [1986]. "The VM/HPO 3880-23 performance results," IBM Tech. Bulletin GG66-0247-00 (April), Washington Systems Center, Gaithersburg, Md.

Ropers, A., H. W. Lollman, and J. Wellhausen [1999]. "DSPstone: Texas Instruments TMS320C54x," Technical Report Nr. IB 315 1999/9-ISS-Version 0.9, Aachen University of Technology, *www.ert.rwth-aachen.de/Projekte/Tools/coal/dspstone_c54x/index.html*.

Rosenblum, M., S. A. Herrod, E. Witchel, and A. Gupta [1995]. "Complete computer simulation: The SimOS approach," in *IEEE Parallel and Distributed Technology* (now called *Concurrency*) 4:3, 34–43.

Rymarczyk, J. [1982]. "Coding guidelines for pipelined processors," *Proc. Symposium on Architectural Support for Programming Languages and Operating Systems,* IEEE/ACM (March), Palo Alto, Calif., 12–19.

Saavedra-Barrera, R. H. [1992]. *CPU Performance Evaluation and Execution Time Prediction Using Narrow Spectrum Benchmarking,* Ph.D. dissertation, University of Calif., Berkeley (May).

Salem, K., and H. Garcia-Molina [1986]. "Disk striping," *IEEE 1986 Int'l Conf. on Data Engineering,* February 5–7, Washington, D.C., 249–259.

Saltzer, J. H., D. P. Reed, and D. D. Clark [1984]. "End-to-end arguments in system design," *ACM Trans. on Computer Systems* 2:4 (November), 277–288.

Samples, A. D., and P. N. Hilfinger [1988]. "Code reorganization for instruction caches," Tech. Rep. UCB/CSD 88/447 (October), University of Calif., Berkeley.

Satran, J., D. Smith, K. Meth, C. Sapuntzakis, M. Wakeley, P. Von Stamwitz, R. Haagens, E. Zeidner, L. Dalle Ore, and Y. Klein [2001]. "iSCSI," IPS working group of IETF, Internet draft *www.ietf.org/internet-drafts/draft-ietf-ips-iscsi-07.txt*.

Saulsbury, A., T. Wilkinson, J. Carter, and A. Landin [1995]. "An argument for Simple COMA," *Proc. First Conf. on High Performance Computer Architectures* (January), Raleigh, N. C., 276–285.

Schwartz, J. T. [1980]. "Ultracomputers," *ACM Trans. on Programming Languages and Systems* 4:2, 484–521.

Scott, S. L. [1996]. "Synchronization and communication in the T3E multiprocessor," *Proc. Architectural Support for Programming Languages and Operating Systems (ASPLOS-VII),* Cambridge, Mass., October, 26–36.

Scott, S. L., and G. M. Thorson [1996]. "The Cray T3E network: Adaptive routing in a high performance 3D torus," *Proc. Symposium on High Performance Interconnects (Hot Interconnects 4),* Stanford University, August, 14–156.

Scranton, R. A., D. A. Thompson, and D. W. Hunter [1983]. "The access time myth," Tech. Rep. RC 10197 (45223) (September 21), IBM, Yorktown Heights, N.Y.

Seagate [2000]. *Seagate Cheetah 73 Family: ST173404LW/LWV/LC/LCV Product Manual,* Volume 1, *www.seagate.com/support/disc/manuals/scsi/29478b.pdf*.

Seitz, C. L. [1985]. "The Cosmic Cube (concurrent computing)," *Communications of the ACM* 28:1 (January), 22–33.

Shurkin, J. [1984]. *Engines of the Mind: A History of the Computer,* W. W. Norton, New York.

Singh, J. P., J. L. Hennessy, and A. Gupta [1993]. "Scaling parallel programs for multiprocessors: Methodology and examples," *Computer* 26:7 (July), 22–33.

Sites, R. [1979]. *Instruction Ordering for the CRAY-1 Computer,* Tech. Rep. 78-CS-023 (July), Dept. of Computer Science, Univ. of Calif., San Diego.

Sites, R. L. (ed.) [1992]. *Alpha Architecture Reference Manual,* Digital Press, Burlington, Mass.

Slater, R. [1987]. *Portraits in Silicon,* MIT Press, Cambridge, Mass.

Slotnick, D. L., W. C. Borck, and R. C. McReynolds [1962]. "The Solomon computer," *Proc. Fall Joint Computer Conf.* (December), Philadelphia, 97–107.

Smith, A. J. [1982]. "Cache memories," *Computing Surveys* 14:3 (September), 473–530.

Smith, A., and J. Lee [1984]. "Branch prediction strategies and branch-target buffer design," *Computer* 17:1 (January), 6–22.

Smith, B. J. [1978]. "A pipelined, shared resource MIMD computer," *Proc. 1978 ICPP* (August), 6–8.

Smith, J. E. [1981]. "A study of branch prediction strategies," *Proc. Eighth Symposium on Computer Architecture* (May), Minneapolis, 135–148.

Smith, J. E. [1984]. "Decoupled access/execute computer architectures," *ACM Trans. on Computer Systems* 2:4 (November), 289–308.

Smith, J. E. [1988]. "Characterizing computer performance with a single number," *Comm. ACM* 31:10 (October), 1202–1206.

Smith, J. E. [1989]. "Dynamic instruction scheduling and the Astronautics ZS-1," *Computer* 22:7 (July), 21–35.

Smith, J. E., G. E. Dermer, B. D. Vanderwarn, S. D. Klinger, C. M. Rozewski, D. L. Fowler, K. R. Scidmore, and J. P. Laudon [1987]. "The ZS-1 central processor," *Proc. Second Conf. on Architectural Support for Programming Languages and Operating Systems,* IEEE/ACM (March), Palo Alto, Calif., 199–204.

Smith, J. E., and J. R. Goodman [1983]. "A study of instruction cache organizations and replacement policies," *Proc. 10th Annual Symposium on Computer Architecture* (June 5–7), Stockholm, 132–137.

Smith, J. E., and A. R. Pleszkun [1988]. "Implementing precise interrupts in pipelined processors," *IEEE Trans. on Computers* 37:5 (May), 562–573. (This paper is based on an earlier paper that appeared in *Proc. 12th Symposium on Computer Architecture,* June 1988.)

Smith, M. D., M. Horowitz, and M. S. Lam [1992]. "Efficient superscalar performance through boosting," *Proc. Fifth Conf. on Architectural Support for Programming Languages and Operating Systems* (October), Boston, IEEE/ACM, 248–259.

Smith, M. D., M. Johnson, and M. A. Horowitz [1989]. "Limits on multiple instruction issue," *Proc. Third Conf. on Architectural Support for Programming Languages and Operating Systems,* IEEE/ACM (April), Boston, 290–302.

Smotherman, M. [1989]. "A sequencing-based taxonomy of I/O systems and review of historical machines," *Computer Architecture News* 17:5 (September), 5–15. Reprinted in *Computer Architecture Readings,* Morgan Kaufmann, 1999, 451–461.

Sodani, A., and G. Sohi [1997]. "Dynamic Instruction Reuse," *Proc. 24th Int'l Symposium on Computer Architecture* (June).

Sohi, G. S. [1990]. "Instruction issue logic for high-performance, interruptible, multiple functional unit, pipelined computers," *IEEE Trans. on Computers* 39:3 (March), 349–359.

Sohi, G. S., and S. Vajapeyam [1989]. "Tradeoffs in instruction format design for horizontal architectures," *Proc. Third Conf. on Architectural Support for Programming Languages and Operating Systems,* IEEE/ACM (April), Boston, 15–25.

Soundararajan, V., M. Heinrich, B. Verghese, K. Gharachorloo, A. Gupta, and J. L. Hennessy [1998]. "Flexible use of memory for replication/migration in cache-coherent

DSM multiprocessors," *Proc. 25th Int'l Symposium on Computer Architecture* (June), Barcelona, 342–355.

SPEC [1989]. *SPEC Benchmark Suite Release 1.0* (October 2).

SPEC [1994]. *SPEC Newsletter* (June).

Spurgeon, C. [2001]. "Charles Spurgeon's Ethernet Web site," *wwwhost.ots.utexas.edu /ethernet/ethernet-home.html.*

Stenström, P., T. Joe, and A. Gupta [1992]. "Comparative performance evaluation of cache-coherent NUMA and COMA architectures," *Proc. 19th Annual Int'l Symposium on Computer Architecture,* May, Queensland, Australia, 80–91.

Sterling, T. [2001]. *Beowulf PC Cluster Computing with Windows and Beowulf PC Cluster Computing with Linux,* MIT Press, Cambridge, Mass.

Stern, N. [1980]. "Who invented the first electronic digital computer?" *Annals of the History of Computing* 2:4 (October), 375–376.

Stevens, W. R. [1994–1996]. *TCP/IP Illustrated* (three volumes), Addison-Wesley, Reading, Mass.

Stokes, J. [2000]. "Sound and Vision: A Technical Overview of the Emotion Engine," *arstechnica.com/reviews/1q00/playstation2/ee-1.html.*

Stone, H. [1991]. *High Performance Computers,* Addison-Wesley, New York.

Strauss, W. [1998]. "DSP strategies 2002," *Forward Concepts, www.usadata.com/market_ research/spr_05/spr_r127-005.htm.*

Strecker, W. D. [1976]. "Cache memories for the PDP-11?," *Proc. Third Annual Symposium on Computer Architecture* (January), Pittsburgh, 155–158.

Strecker, W. D. [1978]. "VAX-11/780: A virtual address extension of the PDP-11 family," *Proc. AFIPS National Computer Conf.* 47, 967–980.

Sugumar, R. A, and S. G. Abraham [1993]. "Efficient simulation of caches under optimal replacement with applications to miss characterization," *1993 ACM Sigmetrics Conf. on Measurement and Modeling of Computer Systems,* Santa Clara, Calif., May 17–21, 24–35.

Sussenguth, E. [1999]. "IBM's ACS-1 Machine," *IEEE Computer* 22:11 (November).

Swan, R. J., A. Bechtolsheim, K. W. Lai, and J. K. Ousterhout [1977]. "The implementation of the Cm* multi-microprocessor," *Proc. AFIPS National Computing Conf.,* 645–654.

Swan, R. J., S. H. Fuller, and D. P. Siewiorek [1977]. "Cm*—a modular, multi- microprocessor," *Proc. AFIPS National Computer Conf.* 46, 637–644.

Talagala, N. [2000]. "Characterizing large storage systems: Error behavior and performance benchmarks," Ph.D dissertation CSD-99-1066, June 13, 2000.

Talagala, N., R. Arpaci-Dusseau, and D. Patterson [2000]. "Micro-benchmark based extraction of local and global disk characteristics," CSD-99-1063, June 13, 2000.

Talagala, N., S. Asami, D. Patterson, R. Futernick, and D. Hart [2000]. "The art of massive storage: A case study of a Web image archive," *Computer* (November).

Talagala, N., and D. Patterson [1999]. "An analysis of error behavior in a large storage system," Tech. Report UCB//CSD-99-1042, Computer Science Division, University of California at Berkeley (February).

Tanenbaum, A. S. [1978]. "Implications of structured programming for machine architecture," *Comm. ACM* 21:3 (March), 237–246.

Tanenbaum, A. S. [1988]. *Computer Networks,* 2nd ed., Prentice Hall, Englewood Cliffs, N.J.

Tang, C. K. [1976]. "Cache design in the tightly coupled multiprocessor system," *Proc. AFIPS National Computer Conf.,* New York (June), 749–753.

Taylor, G., P. Hilfinger, J. Larus, D. Patterson, and B. Zorn [1986]. "Evaluation of the SPUR LISP architecture," *Proc. 13th Symposium on Computer Architecture* (June), Tokyo.

Texas Instruments [2000]. "History of innovation: 1980s," *www.ti.com/corp/docs/company/history/1980s.shtml.*

Thacker, C. P., E. M. McCreight, B. W. Lampson, R. F. Sproull, and D. R. Boggs [1982]. Alto: A personal computer," in *Computer Structures: Principles and Examples*, D. P. Siewiorek, C. G. Bell, and A. Newell, eds., McGraw-Hill, New York, 549–572.

Thadhani, A. J. [1981]. "Interactive user productivity," *IBM Systems J.* 20:4, 407–423.

Thekkath, R., A. P. Singh, J. P. Singh, S. John, and J. L. Hennessy [1997]. "An evaluation of a commercial CC-NUMA architecture—the CONVEX Exemplar SPP1200," *Proc. 11th Int'l Parallel Processing Symposium (IPPS '97)*, Geneva, Switzerland, April.

Thorlin, J. F. [1967]. "Code generation for PIE (parallel instruction execution) computers," *Proc. Spring Joint Computer Conf.*, 27.

Thornton, J. E. [1964]. "Parallel operation in the Control Data 6600," *Proc. AFIPS Fall Joint Computer Conf., Part II*, 26, 33–40.

Thornton, J. E. [1970]. *Design of a Computer, the Control Data 6600*, Scott, Foresman, Glenview, Ill.

Tjaden, G. S., and M. J. Flynn [1970]. "Detection and parallel execution of independent instructions," *IEEE Trans. on Computers* C-19:10 (October), 889–895.

Tomasulo, R. M. [1967]. "An efficient algorithm for exploiting multiple arithmetic units," *IBM J. Research and Development* 11:1 (January), 25–33.

Torrellas, J., A. Gupta, and J. Hennessy [1992]. "Characterizing the caching and synchronization performance of a multiprocessor operating system," Fifth Int'l Conf. on Architectural Support for Programming Languages and Operating Systems (ASPLOS-V), Boston, October 12–15, *SIGPLAN Notices* 27:9 (September), 162–174.

Touma, W. R. [1993]. *The Dynamics of the Computer Industry: Modeling the Supply of Workstations and Their Components*, Kluwer Academic, Boston.

Tullsen, D. M., S. J. Eggers, J. S. Emer, H. M. Levy, J. L. Lo, and R. L. Stamm [1996]. "Exploiting choice: Instruction fetch and issue on an implementable simultaneous multithreading processor," *Proc. 23rd Annual Int'l Symposium on Computer Architecture* (May), 191–202.

Tullsen, D. M., S. J. Eggers, and H. M. Levy [1995]. "Simultaneous multithreading: Maximizing on-chip parallelism," *Proc. 22nd Int'l Symposium on Computer Architecture* (June), 392–403.

Ungar, D., R. Blau, P. Foley, D. Samples, and D. Patterson [1984]. "Architecture of SOAR: Smalltalk on a RISC," *Proc. 11th Symposium on Computer Architecture* (June), Ann Arbor, Mich., 188–197.

Unger, S. H. [1958]. "A computer oriented towards spatial problems," *Proc. Institute of Radio Engineers* 46:10 (October), 1744–1750.

van Eijndhoven, J. T. J., F. W. Sijstermans, K. A. Vissers, E. J. D. Pol, M. I. A. Tromp, P. Struik, R. H. J. Bloks, P. van der Wolf, A. D. Pimentel, H. P. E. Vranken [1999]. "Trimedia CPU64 architecture," *Proc. 1999 IEEE Int'l Conf. on Computer Design: VLSI in Computers and Processors, ICCD'99*, Austin, Tex., October 10–13, 586–592.

Wakerly, J. [1989]. *Microcomputer Architecture and Programming*, Wiley, New York.

Wall, D. W. [1991]. "Limits of instruction-level parallelism," *Proc. Fourth Conf. on Architectural Support for Programming Languages and Operating Systems* (April), Santa Clara, Calif., IEEE/ACM, 248–259.

Wall, D. W. [1993]. *Limits of Instruction-Level Parallelism,* Research Rep. 93/6, Western Research Laboratory, Digital Equipment Corp. (November).

Walrand, J. [1991]. *Communication Networks: A First Course*, Aksen Associates: Irwin, Homewood, Ill.

Wang, W.-H., J.-L. Baer, and H. M. Levy [1989]. "Organization and performance of a two-level virtual-real cache hierarchy," *Proc. 16th Annual Symposium on Computer Architecture* (May 28–June 1), Jerusalem, 140–148.

Waters, F., ed. [1986]. *IBM RT Personal Computer Technology,* IBM, Austin, Tex., SA 23-1057.

Weicker, R. P. [1984]. "Dhrystone: A synthetic systems programming benchmark," *Comm. ACM* 27:10 (October), 1013–1030.

Weiss, S., and J. E. Smith [1984]. "Instruction issue logic for pipelined supercomputers," *Proc. 11th Symposium on Computer Architecture* (June), Ann Arbor, Mich., 110–118.

Weiss, S., and J. E. Smith [1987]. "A study of scalar compilation techniques for pipelined supercomputers," *Proc. Second Conf. on Architectural Support for Programming Languages and Operating Systems* (March), IEEE/ACM, Palo Alto, Calif., 105–109.

Weiss, S., and J. E. Smith [1994]. *Power and PowerPC*, Morgan Kaufmann, San Francisco.

Wiecek, C. [1982]. "A case study of the VAX 11 instruction set usage for compiler execution," *Proc. Symposium on Architectural Support for Programming Languages and Operating Systems* (March), IEEE/ACM, Palo Alto, Calif., 177–184.

Wilkes, M. [1965]. "Slave memories and dynamic storage allocation," *IEEE Trans. Electronic Computers* EC-14:2 (April), 270–271.

Wilkes, M. V. [1982]. "Hardware support for memory protection: Capability implementations," *Proc. Symposium on Architectural Support for Programming Languages and Operating Systems* (March 1–3), Palo Alto, Calif., 107–116.

Wilkes, M. V. [1985]. *Memoirs of a Computer Pioneer,* MIT Press, Cambridge, Mass.

Wilkes, M. V. [1995]. *Computing Perspectives,* Morgan Kaufmann, San Francisco.

Wilkes, M. V., D. J. Wheeler, and S. Gill [1951]. *The Preparation of Programs for an Electronic Digital Computer*, Addison-Wesley, Cambridge, Mass.

Wilson, A. W., Jr. [1987]. "Hierarchical cache/bus architecture for shared-memory multiprocessors," *Proc. 14th Int'l Symposium on Computer Architecture* (June), Pittsburgh, 244–252.

Wilson, R. P., and M. S. Lam [1995]. "Efficient context-sensitive pointer analysis for C programs," *Proc. ACM SIGPLAN'95 Conf. on Programming Language Design and Implementation,* La Jolla, Calif., June, 1–12.

Wolfe, A., and J. P. Shen [1991]. "A variable instruction stream extension to the VLIW architecture." *Proc. Fourth Conference on Architectural Support for Programming Languages and Operating Systems* (April), Santa Clara, Calif., 2–14.

Wood, D. A., and M. D. Hill [1995]. "Cost-effective parallel computing," *IEEE Computer* 28:2 (February).

Wulf, W. [1981]. "Compilers and computer architecture," *Computer* 14:7 (July), 41–47.

Wulf, W., and C. G. Bell [1972]. "C.mmp—A multi-mini-processor," *Proc. AFIPS Fall Joint Computing Conf.* 41, part 2, 765–777.

Wulf, W., and S. P. Harbison [1978]. "Reflections in a pool of processors—an experience report on C.mmp/Hydra," *Proc. AFIPS 1978 National Computing Conf.* 48 (June), Anaheim, Calif., 939–951.

Wulf, W. A., R. Levin, and S. P. Harbison [1981]. *Hydra/C.mmp: An Experimental Computer System,* McGraw-Hill, New York.

Yamamoto, W., M. J. Serrano, A. R. Talcott, R. C. Wood, and M. Nemirosky [1994]. "Performance estimation of multistreamed, superscalar processors," *Proc. 27th Hawaii Int'l Conf. on System Sciences* (January), I:195–204.

Yeager, K. [1996]. "The MIPS R10000 superscalar microprocessor," *IEEE Micro* 16:2 (April), 28–40.

Yeh, T., and Y. N. Patt [1992]. "Alternative implementations of two-level adaptive branch prediction," *Proc. 19th Int'l Symposium on Computer Architecture* (May), Gold Coast, Australia, 124–134.

Yeh, T., and Y. N. Patt [1993]. "A comparison of dynamic branch predictors that use two levels of branch history," *Proc. 20th Symposium on Computer Architecture* (May), San Diego, 257–266.

Index

7503

Subset of the Instructions in MIPS64

Instruction type/opcode	Instruction meaning
Data transfers	*Move data between registers and memory, or between the integer and FP or special registers; only memory address mode is 16-bit displacement + contents of a GPR*
LB,LBU,SB	Load byte, load byte unsigned, store byte (to/from integer registers)
LH,LHU,SH	Load half word, load half word unsigned, store half word (to/from integer registers)
LW,LWU,SW	Load word, load word unsigned, store word (to/from integer registers)
LD,SD	Load double word, store double word (to/from integer registers)
L.S,L.D,S.S,S.D	Load SP float, load DP float, store SP float, store DP float
MFC0,MTC0	Copy from/to GPR to/from a special register
MOV.S,MOV.D	Copy one SP or DP FP register to another FP register
MFC1,MTC1	Copy 32 bits from/to FP registers to/from integer registers
Arithmetic/logical	*Operations on integer or logical data in GPRs; signed arithmetic trap on overflow*
DADD,DADDI,DADDU, DADDIU	Add, add immediate (all immediates are 16 bits); signed and unsigned
DSUB,DSUBU	Subtract; signed and unsigned
DMUL,DMULU,DDIV, DDIVU,MADD	Multiply and divide, signed and unsigned; multiply-add; all operations take and yield 64-bit values
AND,ANDI	And, and immediate
OR,ORI,XOR,XORI	Or, or immediate, exclusive or, exclusive or immediate
LUI	Load upper immediate; loads bits 32 to 47 of register with immediate, then sign-extends
DSLL,DSRL,DSRA,DSLLV, DSRLV,DSRAV	Shifts: both immediate (DS__) and variable form (DS__V); shifts are shift left logical, right logical, right arithmetic
SLT,SLTI,SLTU,SLTIU	Set less than, set less than immediate; signed and unsigned
Control	*Conditional branches and jumps; PC-relative or through register*
BEQZ,BNEZ	Branch GPR equal/not equal to zero; 16-bit offset from PC + 4
BEQ,BNE	Branch GPR equal/not equal; 16-bit offset from PC + 4
BC1T,BC1F	Test comparison bit in the FP status register and branch; 16-bit offset from PC + 4
MOVN,MOVZ	Copy GPR to another GPR if third GPR is negative, zero
J,JR	Jumps: 26-bit offset from PC + 4 (J) or target in register (JR)
JAL,JALR	Jump and link: save PC + 4 in R31, target is PC-relative (JAL) or a register (JALR)
TRAP	Transfer to operating system at a vectored address
ERET	Return to user code from an exception; restore user mode
Floating point	*FP operations on DP and SP formats*
ADD.D,ADD.S,ADD.PS	Add DP, SP numbers, and pairs of SP numbers
SUB.D,SUB.S,ADD.PS	Subtract DP, SP numbers, and pairs of SP numbers
MUL.D,MUL.S,MUL.PS	Multiply DP, SP floating point, and pairs of SP numbers
MADD.D,MADD.S,MADD.PS	Multiply-add DP, SP numbers and pairs of SP numbers
DIV.D,DIV.S,DIV.PS	Divide DP, SP floating point, and pairs of SP numbers
CVT._._	Convert instructions: CVT.x.y converts from type x to type y, where x and y are L (64-bit integer), W (32-bit integer), D (DP), or S (SP). Both operands are FPRs.
C.__.D,C.__.S	DP and SP compares: "__" = LT,GT,LE,GE,EQ,NE; sets bit in FP status register